Financial Aid for the Disabled and Their Families 2010-2012

RSP FINANCIAL AID DIRECTORIES
OF INTEREST TO THE DISABLED
AND THEIR FAMILIES

College Student's Guide to Merit and Other No-Need Funding, 2010-2012
More than 1,200 merit and other no-need funding opportunities for currently-enrolled or returning college students are described in this highly-praised directory. Named by *Choice* as one of the "Outstanding Titles of the Year." 470 pages. ISBN 1-58841-212-1. $32.50, plus $7 shipping.

Directory of Financial Aids for Women, 2009-2011
Called "the cream of the crop" by *School Library Journal,* this award-winning directory describes more than 1,400 scholarships, fellowships, grants, awards, and internships set aside specifically for women. 552 pages. ISBN 1-58841-194-X. $45, plus $7 shipping.

Financial Aid for African Americans, 2009-2011
Selected as *Reference Books Bulletin's* "Editor's Choice," this directory describes in detail more than 1,250 scholarships, fellowships, grants, and internships open to African Americans at all levels (high school seniors through professionals and postdoctorates). 500 pages. ISBN 1-58841-177-X. $42.50, plus $7 shipping.

Financial Aid for Asian Americans, 2009-2011
This is the source to use if you are looking for financial aid for Asian Americans; more than 1,000 sources of free money are described and thoroughly indexed. 406 pages. ISBN 1-58841-178-8. $40, plus $7 shipping.

Financial Aid for Hispanic Americans, 2009-2011
Nearly 1,200 funding programs open to Americans of Mexican, Puerto Rican, Central American, or other Latin American heritage are described here. 474 pages. ISBN 1-58841-179-6. $42.50, plus $7 shipping.

Financial Aid for Native Americans, 2009-2011
Detailed information is provided on 1,200 funding opportunities open to American Indians, Native Alaskans, and Native Pacific Islanders. 526 pages. ISBN 1-58841-180-X. $45, plus $7 shipping.

Financial Aid for Research and Creative Activities Abroad, 2010-2012
Described here are more than 1,000 scholarships, fellowships, grants, etc. available to support research, professional, or creative activities abroad. 422 pages. ISBN 1-58841-206-7. $45, plus $7 shipping.

Financial Aid for Study and Training Abroad, 2010-2012
This directory, which the reviewers call "invaluable," describes nearly 1,000 financial aid opportunities available to support study abroad. 362 pages. ISBN 1-58841-205-9. $40, plus $7 shipping.

Financial Aid for the Disabled and Their Families, 2010-2012
Named one of the "Best Reference Books of the Year" by *Library Journal,* this directory describes in detail more than 1,250 funding opportunities. 480 pages. ISBN 1-58841-204-0. $40, plus $7 shipping.

Financial Aid for Veterans, Military Personnel, and Their Families, 2010-2012
According to *Reference Book Review,* this directory (with its 1,100 entries) is "the most comprehensive guide available on the subject." 436 pages. ISBN 1-58841-209-1. $40, plus $7 shipping.

High School Senior's Guide to Merit and Other No-Need Funding, 2010-2012
Here's your guide to 1,100 funding programs that *never* look at income level when making awards to college-bound high school seniors. 416 pages. ISBN 1-58841-212-1. $29.95, plus $7 shipping.

How to Pay for Your Degree in Nursing, 2010-2012
You'll find 900 scholarships, fellowships, loans, grants, and awards here that can be used for study, research, professional, or other nursing activities. 250 pages. ISBN 1-58841-207-5. $30, plus $7 shipping.

Kaplan Scholarships, 2010
Given 5 stars (highest rating) on Amazon.com, this directory identifies 3,000 of the best scholarships and other sources of "free" money for beginning and continuing undergraduate students. 576 pages. ISBN 1-4195-5308-9. $22.50, plus $7 shipping.

Money for Christian College Students, 2010-2012
This is the only directory to describe nearly 800 funding opportunities available to support Christian students working on an undergraduate or graduate degree. 275 pages. ISBN 1-58841-196-6. $30, plus $7 shipping.

Money for Graduate Students in the Social & Behavioral Sciences, 2010-2012
If you are looking for money for a graduate degree in the social/behavioral sciences, this is the source to use. Described in this award-winning directory are the 1,000 biggest and best fellowships, grants, and awards available. 316 pages. ISBN 1-58841-201-6. $42.50, plus $7 shipping.

Financial Aid for the Disabled and Their Families 2010-2012

Twelfth Edition

Gail Ann Schlachter
R. David Weber

A List of Scholarships, Fellowships/Grants, Grants-in-Aid, and Awards Established Primarily or Exclusively for Persons with Disabilities or Members of Their Families, Plus a Set of Six Indexes: Sponsor, Program Title, Residency, Tenability, Subject, and Deadline Date

Reference Service Press
El Dorado Hills, California

© 2010 by Gail Ann Schlachter

Library of Congress Cataloging in Publication No.
87-063263

ISBN 10: 1588412040
ISBN 13: 9781588412041
ISSN: 0898-9222

10 9 8 7 6 5 4 3 2 1

Reference Service Press (RSP) began in 1977 with a single financial aid publication *(Directory of Financial Aids for Women)* and now specializes in the development of financial aid resources in multiple formats, including books, large print books, disks, CD-ROMs, print-on-demand reports, eBooks, and online sources. Long recognized as a leader in the field, RSP has been called, by the *Simba Report on Directory Publishing,* "a true success in the world of independent directory publishers." Both Kaplan Educational Centers and Military.com have hailed RSP as "the leading authority on scholarships."

Reference Service Press
El Dorado Hills Business Park
5000 Windplay Drive, Suite 4
El Dorado Hills, CA 95762
(916) 939-9620
Fax: (916) 939-9626
E-mail: info@rspfunding.com
Visit our web site: www.rspfunding.com

Manufactured in the United States of America
Price: $40.00, plus $7 shipping.

ACADEMIC INSTITUTIONS, LIBRARIES, ORGANIZATIONS, AND OTHER QUANTITY BUYERS:
Discounts on this book are available for bulk purchases. Write or call for information on our discount programs.

Contents

Indexes **411**

Introduction

WHY THIS DIRECTORY IS NEEDED

With a total population of 49 million, the disabled constitute America's largest "minority" group. Each year, billions of dollars in financial aid are set aside to assist persons with disabilities and members of their families. But, how can these individuals find out about the available funding?

Traditional financial aid directories don't offer much assistance. Instead, those resources have tended to focus either on a small portion of the total funding or on only one type of funding. For example, the latest edition of *Career Resource Guide for People with Disabilities* (last published by Ferguson in 2006) contains thousands of entries, but only a small number identify funding—and many of those programs are for researchers and organizations working to help the disabled, not for the disabled themselves. Similarly, general financial aid directories have never included more than a few of the programs designed primarily or exclusively for persons with disabilities or their families. The *Scholarship Book* (published by Prentice Hall) is representative; it describes thousands of diverse funding opportunities, but less than 150 of those are aimed specifically at either disabled persons or members of their family.

As a result, many individuals with disabilities and members of their family (along with the counselors and librarians there to serve them) have been unaware of the vast array of funding programs available to them. Now, with the ongoing publication of the award-winning *Financial Aid for the Disabled and Their Families,* all that has changed. Here, in one place, you can now find comprehensive information on the biggest and best financial aid opportunities set aside specifically for persons with disabilities or members of their family.

WHAT MAKES THIS DIRECTORY UNIQUE

Financial Aid for the Disabled and Their Families is the first and only publication to identify and provide comprehensive information on the more than 1,250 programs specifically set aside to provide funding to those with physical, sensory, or other disabilities, as well as to their family members. The listings in this book cover every major field of study, are sponsored by more than 600 different private and public agencies and organizations, and are open to all levels of applicants—from high school and college students to professionals, postdoctorates, and others.

In addition to its comprehensive coverage, the 2010-2012 edition of the directory offers several other unique features. First, all funding described here is substantial; every program offers at least $1,000, and many award $20,000 or more. Even better, all of this is "free" money; not one dollar will ever need to be repaid (provided, of course, recipients meet the program requirements). Another plus: you can take the money awarded by these funding programs to any number of locations. Unlike other financial aid directories, which often list large numbers of scholarships available only to students enrolled at one specific school, all of the entries in this book are "portable." And, many of the programs listed here have never been covered in other financial aid directories. So, even if you have searched elsewhere, you will want to look here for new leads.

Here's another advantage: unlike other funding directories, which generally follow a straight alphabetical arrangement, this one groups entries by both type of disability (e.g., hearing impairments, orthopedic impairments) and type of program (e.g., scholarships, grants-in-aid)—making it easy for a user to search for appropriate programs. The same convenience is offered in the indexes, where the entries are also subdivided by disability and program type. With this unique arrangement, users with one set of characteristics (e.g., persons with hearing impairments) will be able to find all programs set aside spe-

5

cifically for them—and not be distracted or have to waste time sorting through descriptions of programs intended for individuals with other types of disabilities.

In fact, everything about the directory has been designed to make your search for funding as easy as possible. You can identify programs not only by recipient group and type of funding, but also by program title, sponsoring organizations, where you live, where you want to spend the money, individual subject areas, and even deadline date (so fundseekers working within specific time constraints can locate programs that are still open). Plus, you'll find all the information you need to decide if a program is a match for you: purpose, eligibility requirements, financial data, duration, special features, limitations, number awarded, and application date. You even get fax numbers, toll-free numbers, e-mail addresses, and web site locations (when available), along with complete contact information, to make your requests for applications proceed smoothly.

Reviewers have consistently praised the unique value of *Financial Aid for the Disabled and Their Families.* For example, *Disability Resources Monthly* called the directory a "must-have." *College Financial Aid* agreed and, because of its "wealth of information," gave the directory its "four-star" (highest) rating. *American Reference Books Annual* predicted that "this directory will assuredly be a major reference tool in most libraries" and labeled it "an essential purchase." The directory has been chosen as one of the "best reference books of the year" by *Library Journal* and as one of the "outstanding reference books of the year" by the New York Public Library, which commended Reference Service Press for its "excellent contribution in an area of publishing where quality is at a premium."

THE EXTENT OF UPDATING IN THE 2010-2012 EDITION

The preparation of each new edition of *Financial Aid for the Disabled and Their Families* involves extensive updating and revision. To insure that the information included in the directory is both reliable and current, the editors at Reference Service Press 1) review and update all programs open to persons with disabilities or members of their families currently in our funding database and 2) search exhaustively for new program leads in a variety of sources, including printed directories, news reports, journals, newsletters, house organs, annual reports, and sites on the Internet. Our policy is to write program descriptions only from information supplied in print or online by the sponsoring organization (no information is ever taken from secondary sources). When that information could not be found, we sent up to four letters or e-mails (followed by up to three telephone inquiries, if necessary) to those sponsors. Despite our best efforts, however, some sponsoring organizations still failed to respond and, as a result, their programs are not included in this edition of the directory.

The 2010-2012 edition of the directory completely revises and updates the earlier biennial edition. Programs that have ceased operations have been dropped. Profiles of continuing programs have been rewritten to reflect operations in 2010-2012; more than 80 percent of these programs reported substantive changes in their locations, requirements (particularly application deadline), or benefits since 2008. In addition, more than 450 new entries have been added to the program section of the directory. The resulting listing identifies more than 1,250 available funding opportunities: scholarships, fellowships, grants, grants-in-aid, and awards.

HOW THE DIRECTORY IS ORGANIZED

Financial Aid for the Disabled and Their Families is divided into two separate parts: 1) a descriptive list of financial aid programs designed primarily or exclusively for persons with disabilities and their families and 2) a set of six indexes.

Financial Aid Available to the Disabled and Their Families. The first part of the directory describes 1,257 funding opportunities aimed primarily or exclusively at persons with disabilities and members of their families. The programs described are sponsored by federal and state government agencies, professional organizations, foundations, educational associations, and military/veterans organizations. They are open to applicants at any level (high school through postdoctoral) to support a whole host of activities, including education, research, travel, training, equipment acquisition, career development, and innovative effort. All areas of the sciences, social sciences, and humanities are covered.

Entries in this part are grouped into the following six chapters, to make it easy to search for funding intended for members of specific disability groups (the list is based on a condensation of the disability categories established in Public Law 94-142, the Education for All Handicapped Children Act):

Visual Disabilities: Programs open to individuals who have visual impairments (are partially sighted or blind), with or without correction.

Hearing Disabilities: Programs open to individuals who have difficulty in receiving linguistic information, with or without amplification.

Orthopedic and Developmental Disabilities: Programs open to individuals with 1) a severe orthopedic impairment caused by birth defects (e.g., absence of an extremity), diseases, or other causes (e.g., accidents, amputations), or 2) a severe, chronic disability that was manifested before the age of 22 (e.g., spina bifida).

Communication and Other Disabilities: Programs open to individuals who have a communication disorder (such as stuttering or voice impairment), have a learning disability (including such conditions as brain injury and dyslexia), are emotionally disturbed, or have other chronic or acute health problems, such as cancer, tuberculosis, or hemophilia.

Disabilities in General: Programs open to persons with any disability (programs that do not specify or restrict the type of eligible disabilities).

Families of the Disabled: Programs open to the children, stepchildren, adopted children, grandchildren, parents, siblings, and other dependents or family members of persons with disabilities.

To make it easy to target available funding, each of these six chapters is then further divided (when appropriate) into four type-of-funding sections.

Scholarships: "Free" money available to support study or research at the undergraduate level in the United States. Usually no return of service or repayment is required.

Fellowships/Grants: "Free" money available to support graduate, postgraduate, or postdoctoral study, research, or creative activities in the United States. Usually no return of service or repayment is required.

Grants-in-Aid: Funding intended to assist with personal needs, including emergency situations, property and income tax liabilities, assistive technology, and the adaptation of housing and vehicles.

Awards: Competitions, prizes, and honoraria granted in recognition or support of creative work and public service.

Within each of these sections, entries are arranged alphabetically by program title. Some programs supply assistance to more than one specific group or supply more than one type of assistance, so those are listed in all relevant subsections. For example, since the Georgia Council of the Blind Scholarships are open to either legally blind Georgia residents or their children, the program is described in both the Visual Disabilities *and* Families of the Disabled chapters. Similarly, the Allie Raney Hunt Scholarship is open to oral deaf undergraduate *and* graduate students, so the program entry is included in both the Scholarships *and* Fellowships sections of the Hearing Disabilities chapter.

We have designed each program profile to include information, when available, on program title, organization address, telephone number, fax and toll-free numbers, e-mail address, web site, purpose, eligibility, money awarded, duration, special features, limitations, number of awards, and application deadline. (Refer to the sample on page 9).

Each of the entries in the directory has been written using information provided by the sponsoring organizations (in print or online) through the first half of 2010. While the listing is intended to cover available funding as comprehensively as possible, some sponsoring organizations did not respond to our research inquiries and, consequently, are not included in this edition of the directory.

Indexes. The directory's six indexes make it easy to target appropriate financial aid opportunities. Program Title, Sponsoring Organization, Residency, Tenability, Subject, and Calendar Indexes all follow a word-by-word alphabetical arrangement and refer the user to the appropriate entry by number.

Program Title Index. This index lists alphabetically all program titles and variant names (former names, popular names, abbreviations, etc.) of the scholarships, fellowships/grants, grants-in-aid, and awards covered in the first part of the directory. Since one program can be listed in more than one section (e.g., a program providing assistance to the disabled *and* to members of the disabled's family for either undergraduate *or* graduate study would be listed in four sections), each entry number in the index has been coded to indicate both availability groups (e.g., families of the disabled) and program type (e.g., scholarship, award). By using this coding system, readers can easily identify the programs that match their financial needs and eligibility characteristics.

Sponsoring Organization Index. This index provides an alphabetical listing of the more than 600 organizations sponsoring financial aid programs represented in the first part of the directory. As in the Program Title Index, entry numbers have been coded to indicate both recipient gruop and program type.

Residency Index. This index identifies the residency requirements of the programs listed in the directory. Index entries (state, region, country) are arranged alphabetically (word by word). To facilitate access, the geographic terms in the index are subdivided by recipient group and program type. Use this index when you are looking for money set aside for persons with disabilities and members of their families residing in a particular geographic area.

Tenability Index. This index identifies the geographic locations where the funding described in the directory may be used. Index entries (city, county, state, region, country) are arranged alphabetically (word by word) and subdivided by both availability group and program type. Use this index when you or your family members are looking for money to support research, study, or other activities in a particular geographic area.

Subject Index. This index allows the reader to use more than 150 subject terms to access the financial aid programs designed primarily or exclusively for persons with disabilities and members of their families listed in the first part of the directory. Extensive "see" and "see also" references facilitate the search for appropriate financial aid programs.

Calendar Index. To assist fundseekers who often must work within specific time constraints, the Calendar Index identifies financial aid programs by filing date. The Calendar Index is arranged by type of program (scholarships, grants-in-aid, etc.) and divided according to recipient group (hearing impaired, families of the disabled, etc.) and month during which the deadline falls. Filing dates can and quite often do vary from year to year; consequently, this index should be used only as a guide for deadlines beyond 2012.

WHAT'S EXCLUDED?

The focus of this directory is on substantive ($1,000 or more) "portable" (noninstitution-specific) programs available primarily or exclusively to persons with disabilities and their families or descendants. Excluded from this list are:

Awards open equally to all segments of the population. Only funding opportunities open primarily or exclusively to persons with disabilities, or members of their families, are covered here. For information on unrestricted programs, see a general directory like *Kaplan Scholarships.*

Financial aid programs administered by academic institutions solely for the benefit of their currently-enrolled students. Financial aid seekers should write directly to individual schools for this information.

Services, such as training and counseling, that do not involve actual financial assistance to the disabled person. To obtain information on these benefits, check with the appropriate federal, state, local, or private social service agency in your area.

Nonmonetary benefits, such as special license plates for persons with disabilities. To obtain information, check with the appropriate agency in your area.

SAMPLE ENTRY

(1) **[470]**

(2) **INA BRUDNICK SCHOLARSHIP AWARD**

(3) Great Comebacks Award Program
c/o ConvaTec Customer Interaction Center
100 Headquarters Park Drive
Skillman, NJ 08558
Toll-free: (800) 422-8811
E-mail: info@greatcomebacks.com
Web: www.greatcomebacks.com

(4) **Summary** To provide financial assistance to college students with an inflammatory bowel disease (IBD) or other related physical conditions.

(5) **Eligibility** This program is open to people between 17 and 24 years of age who have undergone an ostomy and/or have an IBD (Crohn's disease or ulcerative colitis). Applicants must be able to demonstrate financial need. Along with their application, they must submit statements on how their life has been changed or affected by their medical condition and their ostomy, how their comeback has positively affected their life and those around them, and what advice they would give to others struggling with similar medical conditions or facing ostomy surgery.

(6) **Financial data** The stipend is $1,000.

(7) **Duration** 1 year.

(8) **Additional data** This scholarship is provided by ConvaTec, a Bristol-Myers Squibb Company, and the Crohn's and Colitis Foundation of America.

(9) **Number awarded** 4 each year: 1 from each region of the country.

(10) **Deadline** July of each year.

DEFINITION

(1) **Entry number:** Consecutive number assigned to the references and used to index the entry.

(2) **Program title:** Title of scholarship, fellowship, grant-in-aid, or award.

(3) **Sponsoring organization:** Name, address, telephone numbers, toll-free number, fax number, e-mail address, and web site (when information was supplied) for organization sponsoring the program.

(4) **Summary:** Identifies the major program requirements; read the rest of the entry for additional detail.

(5) **Eligibility:** Qualifications required of applicants, plus information on application procedures and selection process.

(6) **Financial data:** Financial details of the program, including fixed sum, average amount, or range of funds offered, expenses for which funds may and may not be applied, and cash-related benefits supplied (e.g., room and board).

(7) **Duration:** Period for which support is provided; renewal prospects.

(8) **Additional data:** Any unusual (generally non-monetary) benefits, features, restrictions, or limitations associated with the program.

(9) **Number awarded:** Total number of recipients each year or other specified period.

(10) **Deadline:** The month by which applications must be submitted.

Indirect aid programs, where funds go to agencies, organizations, researchers, and educational institutions that provide services to persons with disabilities or that study disabilities (rather than directly to the disabled or their families). For information on these programs, consult the various grants directories (such as the *Annual Register of Grant Support* or the *Directory of Research Grants)* or conduct a computerized search, using GrantSelect or another database.

Money for study or research outside the United States. Since there are comprehensive and up-to-date directories that describe all available funding for study and research abroad (see Reference Service Press's publications list opposite the title page in this directory), only programs that support study, research, or other activities in the United States are covered here.

Money that must be repaid. Only "free money" is identified here. If a program requires repayment or charges interest, it's not listed. Now you can find out about billions of dollars in aid and know that you will never have to repay any of this money.

Restrictive programs, where the funds are generally available only to a limited geographic area (specific cities or counties only), to a very limited membership group (e.g., a local union), or in limited amounts (under $1,000). To get information on these more restrictive programs, contact Reference Service Press directly or access RSP FundingFinder, Reference Service Press's subscription-based online funding database.

TIPS TO HELP YOU USE THE DIRECTORY

To Locate Funding Available to Individuals with Various Types of Disabilities. To bring programs with similar eligibility requirements together, the directory is organized into six availability chapters: Visual Disabilities; Hearing Disabilities; Orthopedic and Developmental Disabilities; Communication and Other Disabilities; Disabilities in General; and Families of the Disabled. If you have a disability, be sure to check not only the chapter that covers your specific disability (e.g., Hearing Disabilities chapter) but also the Disabilities in General chapter, where programs that do not specify or restrict the type of eligible disabilities are listed.

To Locate Programs Offering a Particular Type of Assistance. If you are looking for programs offering a particular type of financial aid (e.g., a scholarship for undergraduate courses, an award for outstanding literary achievement), turn to the appropriate chapter in the first part (e.g., Disabilities in General, Families of the Disabled) and read through all the entries in the section that applies (e.g., scholarships, awards). Since programs with multiple purposes are listed in every appropriate location, each of the four type-of-funding sections functions as a self-contained entity. Because of that, you can browse through any of the sections in the directory without first consulting an index.

To Locate a Particular Financial Aid Program. If you know the name of a particular financial aid program *and* the type of assistance offered by the program (e.g., scholarship) *and* the availability (e.g., visual disabilities, hearing disabilities), then go directly to the appropriate category in the first part of the directory, where you will find the program profiles arranged alphabetically by title. But be careful: program titles can be misleading! The George H. Nofer Scholarship is available only to graduate students and therefore is listed under Fellowships/Grants not Scholarships. The Harry G. Starr Award isn't a competition; rather, it's a scholarship. Consequently, if you are looking for a specific program and do not find it in the section you have checked, be sure to refer to the Program Title Index to see if it is covered elsewhere in the directory. To save time, always check the Program Title Index first if you know the name of a specific award but are not sure under which section it has been listed.

To Browse Quickly Through the Listings. Turn to the type of funding and recipient categories that interest you and read the "Summary" field in each entry. In seconds, you'll know if this is an opportunity that might apply to you. If it is, read the rest of the information in the entry to make sure you meet all of the program requirements before writing or going online for an application form. Remember: don't apply if you don't qualify!

To Locate Programs Sponsored by a Particular Organization. The Sponsoring Organization Index makes it easy to determine groups that provide financial assistance to persons with disabilities and their families, or to identify specific financial aid programs offered by a particular organization. Each entry number in the index is coded to identify recipient group and program type, enabling users to target appropriate entries.

To Locate Programs Open to Residents of or Tenable in a Particular Area. The Residency Index identifies financial aid programs open to residents of a particular state, region, or country. The Tenability Index shows where the money can be spent. In both indexes, "see" and "see also" references are used liberally, and index entries for a particular geographic area are divided by both type of disability and type of funding.

To Locate Financial Aid Programs for Persons with Disabilities and Their Families in a Particular Subject Area. Turn to the Subject Index first if you are interested in identifying financial aid programs for the disabled and their families in a particular field. To help you target your search, the type of funding indexed (scholarships, fellowships/grants, grants-in-aid, awards) and the availability group (e.g., hearing disabilities) are clearly identified. Extensive cross-references are provided.

To Locate Financial Aid Programs for Persons with Disabilities and Their Families by Deadline Date. If you are working with specific time constraints and want to weed out the financial aid programs whose filing dates you won't be able to meet, turn first to the Calendar Index and check the program references listed under the program type, appropriate group, and month of interest to you. If, instead, you want to identify every relevant funding program, regardless of filing dates, then go to the first part of the directory and read through all the entries in each of the program categories (scholarships, grants-in-aid, etc.) that apply.

To Locate Information on Geographically Restricted or Financially Limited Funding Programs. Only programs aimed at large segments of the population (at least a state) or offering significant awards (nothing under $1,000) are covered in this directory. To get information on the other, more limited programs, contact Reference Service Press to learn how to search its comprehensive database directly.

To Locate Financial Aid Programs Open to All Segments of the Population. Only programs designed with the disabled and their families in mind are listed in this publication. However, there are thousands of other programs that are open equally to all segments of the population. To identify these programs, talk to your local librarian, check with your vocational rehabilitation or campus financial aid counselor, use a general financial aid directory (like *Kaplan Scholarships*), or use an online scholarship or grant database (like RSP FundingFinder).

PLANS TO UPDATE THE DIRECTORY

This volume, covering 2010-2012, is the twelfth biennial edition of *Financial Aid for the Disabled and Their Families*. The next edition will cover the years 2012-2014 and will be released in early 2012.

OTHER RELATED PUBLICATIONS

In addition to *Financial Aid for the Disabled and Their Families,* Reference Service Press publishes several other titles dealing with fundseeking, including the biennially-issued *Money for Graduate Students in the Social & Behavioral Sciences, Directory of Financial Aids for Women,* and *Financial Aid for Veterans, Military Personnel, and Their Families.* Since each of these titles focuses on a separate population group, there is little duplication in the listings. In fact, fewer than five percent of the programs described in *Financial Aid for the Disabled and Their Families* can be found in any of RSP's financial aid titles, with one exception. Because veterans constitute such a large portion of the disabled population, there is somewhat more overlap (approximately 15 percent) in the entries included in *Financial Aid for Veterans, Military Personnel and Their Families* and *Financial Aid for the Disabled and Their Families.* For more information on these and other related publications, you can 1) write to Reference Service Press' Marketing Department at 5000 Windplay Drive, Suite 4, El Dorado Hills, CA 95762; 2) call us at (916) 939-9620; 3) send us an e-mail message at info@rspfunding.com; 4) fax us at (916) 939-9626; or 5) visit our web site: www.rspfunding.com.

ACKNOWLEDGEMENTS

A debt of gratitude is owed all the organizations that contributed information to this edition of *Financial Aid for the Disabled and Their Families*. Their generous cooperation has helped to make the twelfth edition of this award-winning publication a current and comprehensive survey of funding programs.

ABOUT THE AUTHORS

Dr. Gail Schlachter has worked for more than three decades as a library manager, a library educator, and an administrator of library-related publishing companies. Among the reference books to her credit are the biennially-issued *Money for Graduate Students in the Arts & Humanities* and two award-winning bibliographic guides: *Minorities and Women: A Guide to Reference Literature in the Social Sciences* (which was chosen as an "Outstanding Reference Title of the Year" by *Choice)* and *Reference Sources in Library and Information Services* (which won the first Knowledge Industry Publications "Award for Library Literature"). She was the reference book review editor for *RQ* (now *Reference and User Services Quarterly)* for 10 years, is a past president of the American Library Association's Reference and User Services Association (RUSA, formerly RASD), is serving her fifth term on the American Library Association's governing council, and is a former editor-in-chief of *Reference and User Services Quarterly.* In recognition of her outstanding contributions to reference service, Dr. Schlachter was named the "Outstanding Alumna" by the University of Wisconsin School of Library and Information Studies and has been awarded both the Isadore Gilbert Mudge Citation and the Louis Shores/Oryx Press Award.

Dr. R. David Weber taught history and economics at Los Angeles Harbor College (in Wilmington, California) for many years and continues to teach history as an emeritus professor. During his years of full-time teaching there, and at East Los Angeles College, he directed the Honors Program and was frequently selected as the "Teacher of the Year." Dr. Weber is the author of several critically-acclaimed reference works, including *Dissertations in Urban History* and the three-volume *Energy Information Guide.* With Gail Schlachter, he is the author of Reference Service Press' *College Student's Guide to Merit and Other No-Need Funding,* which was selected by *Choice* as one of the "Outstanding Academic Titles of the Year," and a number of other financial aid titles, including *Financial Aid for African Americans,* which was named the "Editor's Choice" by *Reference Books Bulletin.*

Visual Disabilities

Scholarships ●

Fellowships/Grants ●

Grants-in-Aid ●

Awards ●

Described here are 266 programs open to individuals who have visual impairments (are partially sighted or blind), with or without correction. Of these, 119 entries cover scholarships (to pursue studies or research on the undergraduate level in the United States); 67 cover fellowships or grants (to pursue graduate or postdoctoral study or research in the United States); 74 cover grants-in-aid (to support emergency situations, travel, income/property tax liabilities, or the acquisition of assistive technology); and 6 cover awards, competitions, prizes, and honoraria (to recognize or support creative work and public service). If you are looking for a particular program and don't find it in this chapter, be sure to check the Program Title Index to see if it is covered elsewhere in the directory.

Scholarships

[1]
ABC SCHOLARSHIPS

Association of Blind Citizens
P.O. Box 246
Holbrook, MA 02343
(781) 961-1023   Fax: (781) 961-0004
E-mail: scholarship@blindcitizens.org
Web: www.blindcitizens.org/abc_scholarship.htm

Summary To provide financial assistance for college to individuals who are blind or visually impaired.

Eligibility This program is open to high school seniors, high school graduates, and currently-enrolled college students who are blind or visually impaired. Applicants must be interested in working on a college degree. Along with their application, they must submit an autobiography, indicating how the scholarship award would help them achieve their goal of attending college or a recognized vocational program; a high school or college transcript; a certificate of legal blindness or a letter from their ophthalmologist; and 2 letters of reference. The highest ranked applicant receives the Reggie Johnson Memorial Scholarship.

Financial data Stipends are $2,000 or $1,000. Funds may be used to pay for tuition, living expenses, or related expenses resulting from vision impairment.

Duration 1 year.

Number awarded 8 each year: 1 at $2,000 (the Reggie Johnson Memorial Scholarship) and 7 at $1,000.

Deadline April of each year.

[2]
ACADEMIC EXCELLENCE SCHOLARSHIPS OF THE FLORIDA COUNCIL FOR THE BLIND

Florida Council for the Blind
c/o Barbara Grill, Education and Leadership
  Committee
2030 Preymore Street
Osprey, FL 34229
(941) 966-7056   E-mail: grillbh@comcast.net
Web: www.fcb.org/ScholApInfo.htm

Summary To provide financial assistance to blind residents of Florida who plan to attend college in any state and can demonstrate academic and leadership excellence.

Eligibility This program is open to blind residents of Florida who are attending or planning to attend a college or university in any state. Applicants must have a GPA of 3.0 or higher and be able to demonstrate academic and leadership excellence. Along with their application, they must submit a narrative statement on their vocational objectives and outlook for employment in their chosen field. Financial need is not considered in the selection process.

Financial data The stipend is $2,000.

Duration 1 year.

Number awarded 2 each year.

Deadline March of each year.

[3]
ACBCO SCHOLARSHIPS

American Council of the Blind of Colorado
Attn: Executive Director
1536 Wynkoop Street, Suite 201
Denver, CO 80202
(303) 831-0117   Toll Free: (888) 775-2221
Fax: (303) 454-3378 E-mail: barbara.boyer@acbco.org
Web: www.acbco.org

Summary To provide financial assistance for college or graduate school to blind students from Colorado.

Eligibility This program is open to legally blind students who are residents of Colorado. Applicants must be working on an undergraduate (academic, vocational, or certificate) or graduate (master's or doctoral) degree. A cumulative GPA of 3.3 or higher is generally required, but extenuating circumstances may be considered. Along with their application, they must submit a 750-word statement describing their educational, career, and personal goals. Financial need is also considered in the selection process.

Financial data The stipend is $2,500. Funds are paid directly to the recipient's college or university.

Duration 1 year.

Number awarded 4 each year.

Deadline January of each year.

[4]
ALLEN-SPRINKLE MEMORIAL GIFT

National Federation of the Blind of West Virginia
c/o Debbi Wilson, Scholarship Committee Chair
1430 Magnolia Court
Cumberland, MD 21502
(301) 777-3017
Web: www.nfbwv.org/downloadscholarship.htm

Summary To provide financial assistance to legally blind residents of West Virginia who are interested in attending college or graduate school in any state.

Eligibility This program is open to legally blind residents of Virginia who are graduating high school seniors, undergraduates, or graduate students. Applicants must be enrolled or planning to enroll full time at an accredited college, university, postsecondary vocational institute, or graduate school in any state. Along with their application, they must submit 2 letters of recommendation, transcripts, verification of blindness, and a personal letter that includes the kinds of things that interest them, their goals and aspirations, and how this scholarship would help them. Selection is based on academic excellence, community service, and financial need.

Financial data The stipend is $1,000.

Duration 1 year.

Additional data The winner is expected to attend the annual convention of the National Federation of the Blind of West Virginia.

Number awarded 1 each year.

Deadline June of each year.

[5]
AMERICAN COUNCIL OF THE BLIND OF TEXAS SCHOLARSHIPS

American Council of the Blind of Texas
c/o Ginger Kraft, Scholarship Chair
4105 Blue Flag Lane
Fort Worth, TX 76137
(817) 306-0154   E-mail: gkraft5@charter.net
Web: www.acbtexas.org/scholarshipinfo.html

Summary To provide financial assistance to blind and visually impaired residents of Texas who are interested in attending college in any state.

Eligibility This program is open to residents of Texas who can document legal or total blindness. Applicants must be enrolled or planning to enroll at a college, university, or vocational/trade school in any state. They must have a GPA of 3.0 or higher. Along with their application, they must submit documentation of financial need, transcripts, a copy of their acceptance letter (if not yet attending college), 2 to 3 letters of recommendation not more than 12 months old, and a 1- to 2-page autobiography, including information on their family, hobbies, activities, community service, and educational and career goals. Selection is based on career goals, academic achievement, and letters of recommendation.

Financial data Stipends range from $250 to $1,000 per year. Funds may be used for any educational purpose, including tuition, books, housing, and transportation.

Duration 1 year; recipients may reapply.

Additional data Recipients do not need to study in a field related to blindness; in general, they may major in any field (although 1 of the scholarships is specifically for a student interested in majoring in food service and another is specifically for a student majoring in business administration).

Number awarded Varies each year. Recently, 8 of these scholarships were awarded: 1 at $1,000; 3 at $500; and 4 at $250.

Deadline June of each year.

[6]
ARNOLD SADLER MEMORIAL SCHOLARSHIP

American Council of the Blind
Attn: Coordinator, Scholarship Program
2200 Wilson Boulevard, Suite 650
Arlington, VA 22201
(202) 467-5081   Toll Free: (800) 424-8666
Fax: (703) 465-5085   E-mail: info@acb.org
Web: www.acb.org

Summary To provide financial assistance to undergraduate or graduate students who are blind and are interested in studying in a field of service to persons with disabilities.

Eligibility This program is open to undergraduate and graduate students in rehabilitation, education, law, or other fields of service to persons with disabilities. Applicants must be legally blind in both eyes. Along with their application, they must submit verification of legal blindness in both eyes; SAT, ACT, GRE, or similar scores; information on extracurricular activities (including membership in the American Council of the Blind); employment record; and an autobiographical sketch that includes their personal goals, strengths, weaknesses, hobbies, honors, achievements, and reasons for choice of field or courses of study. A cumulative GPA of 3.3 or higher is generally required. Financial need is not considered in the selection process.

Financial data The stipend is $1,500. In addition, the winner receives a Kurzweil-1000 Reading System.

Duration 1 year.

Additional data This scholarship is funded by the Arnold Sadler Memorial Scholarship Fund. Scholarship winners are expected to be present at the council's annual conference; the council will cover all reasonable expenses connected with convention attendance.

Number awarded 1 each year.

Deadline February of each year.

[7]
BAY STATE COUNCIL OF THE BLIND SCHOLARSHIP

American Council of the Blind
Attn: Coordinator, Scholarship Program
2200 Wilson Boulevard, Suite 650
Arlington, VA 22201
(202) 467-5081   Toll Free: (800) 424-8666
Fax: (703) 465-5085   E-mail: info@acb.org
Web: www.acb.org

Summary To provide financial assistance for college to blind students from Massachusetts.

Eligibility This program is open to legally blind students who are residents of Massachusetts or attending college in the state. Applicants must submit verification of legal blindness in both eyes; SAT or ACT scores; information on extracurricular activities (including membership in the American Council of the Blind); employment record; and an autobiographical sketch that includes their personal goals, strengths, weaknesses, hobbies, honors, achievements, and reasons for choice of field or courses of study. A cumulative GPA of 3.3 or higher is generally required. Financial need is not considered in the selection process.

Financial data The stipend is $1,000. In addition, the winner receives a Kurzweil-1000 Reading System.

Duration 1 year.

Additional data This scholarship is sponsored by the Bay State Council of the Blind, an affiliate of the American Council of the Blind. Scholarship winners are expected to be present at the council's annual conference; the council will cover all reasonable expenses connected with convention attendance.

Number awarded 1 each year.

Deadline February of each year.

[8]
CAREER ENHANCEMENT SCHOLARSHIP OF THE FLORIDA COUNCIL FOR THE BLIND

Florida Council for the Blind
c/o Barbara Grill, Education and Leadership
  Committee
2030 Preymore Street
Osprey, FL 34229
(941) 966-7056   E-mail: grillbh@comcast.net
Web: www.fcb.org/ScholApInfo.htm

Summary To provide financial assistance to blind residents of Florida who plan to attend college in any state to study a field that will increase advancement potential in their chosen career.

Eligibility This program is open to blind residents of Florida who are attending or planning to attend a college or university in any state. Applicants must have a GPA of 3.0 or higher. They must intend to work on a degree that will increase advancement potential in their chosen field. Along with their application, they must submit a narrative statement on their vocational objectives and outlook for employment in their chosen field. Financial need is not considered in the selection process.

Financial data The stipend is $1,500.

Duration 1 year.

Number awarded 1 each year.

Deadline March of each year.

[9]
CCB SCHOLARSHIPS

California Council of the Blind
Attn: Executive Office
1510 J Street, Suite 125
Sacramento, CA 95814
(916) 441-2100 Toll Free: (800) 221-6359 (within CA)
Fax: (916) 441-2188   E-mail: ccotb@ccbnet.org
Web: www.ccbnet.org/scholar.htm

Summary To provide financial assistance for undergraduate or graduate study in any state to blind people in California.

Eligibility Applicants must be legally blind residents of California who are enrolled or planning to enroll full time at an accredited college or university at either the undergraduate or graduate level. The school may be in any state. Along with their application, they must submit a 200-word statement on their purpose in undertaking college work and their vocational goals. Selection is based on academic achievement and financial need.

Financial data The amount of the assistance depends on the availability of funds and the needs of the applicant.

Duration 1 year; may be renewed. For graduate students, support is limited to 2 years of work for a master's degree or 3 years for a Ph.D.

Number awarded Varies each year.

Deadline June of each year.

[10]
CCLVI FRED SCHEIGERT SCHOLARSHIPS

Council of Citizens with Low Vision International
c/o American Council of the Blind
2200 Wilson Boulevard, Suite 650
Arlington, VA 22201
(202) 467-5081   Toll Free: (800) 733-2258
Fax: (703) 465-5085   E-mail: scholarship@cclvi.org
Web: www.cclvi.org/scholars.htm

Summary To provide financial assistance to entering and continuing undergraduate and graduate students with low vision.

Eligibility This program is open to full-time undergraduate and graduate students who have been certified by an ophthalmologist as having low vision (acuity of 20/70 or worse in the better seeing eye with best correction or side vision with a maximum diameter of no greater than 30 degrees). Applicants may be part-time or full-time entering freshmen, undergraduates, or graduate students. They must have a GPA of 3.2 or higher.

Financial data The stipend is $3,000.

Duration 1 year.

Number awarded 3 each year.

Deadline February of each year.

[11]
CHARLES AND MELVA T. OWEN MEMORIAL SCHOLARSHIPS

National Federation of the Blind
Attn: Scholarship Committee
1800 Johnson Street
Baltimore, MD 21230
(410) 659-9314, ext. 2415   Fax: (410) 685 5653
E-mail: scholarships@nfb.org
Web: www.nfb.org/nfb/scholarship_program.asp

Summary To provide financial assistance to entering or continuing undergraduate or graduate students who are blind.

Eligibility This program is open to legally blind students who are working on or planning to work full time on an undergraduate or graduate degree. Scholarships, however, are not awarded for the study of religion or solely to further general or cultural education; the academic program should be directed towards attaining financial independence. Along with their application, they must submit transcripts, standardized test scores, proof of legal blindness, 2 letters of recommendation, and a letter of endorsement from their National Federation of the Blind state president or designee. Selection is based on academic excellence, service to the community, and financial need.

Financial data Stipends are $10,000 or $3,000.

Duration 1 year; recipients may resubmit applications up to 2 additional years.

Additional data Scholarships are awarded at the federation convention in July. Recipients must attend the convention at federation expense; that funding is in addition to the scholarship grant.

Number awarded   2 each year: 1 at $10,000 and 1 at $3,000.

Deadline   March of each year.

[12]
CHICAGO LIGHTHOUSE SCHOLARSHIPS

Chicago Lighthouse for People who are Blind or
  Visually Impaired
Attn: Scholarship Program Coordinator
1850 West Roosevelt Road
Chicago, IL 60608-1298
(312) 666-1331   Fax: (312) 243-8539
TDD: (312) 666-8874
E-mail: scholarships@chicagolighthouse.org
Web: www.thechicagolighthouse.org

Summary   To provide financial assistance to blind or visually impaired college and graduate students from any state.

Eligibility   This program is open to residents of any state who are blind or visually impaired. Applicants must be attending or planning to attend an accredited college, university, or community college as an undergraduate or graduate student. Along with their application, they must submit an essay about their visual impairment, background, educational and career goals, and how this scholarship will help achieve those goals.

Financial data   Stipends range up to $5,000.

Duration   1 year.

Additional data   This program includes the Mary Kathryn and Michael Panitch Scholarships. This program was established in 2004 and limited to students from the Chicago area. Recently, it has began to accept applications from students living in any state.

Number awarded   Varies each year; recently, 14 of these scholarships were awarded.

Deadline   April of each year.

[13]
CIB/BONNIE AND ERICH OHLENDORF AWARD

Connecticut Institute for the Blind
Attn: Vice President for Development
120 Holcomb Street
Hartford, CT 06112-1589
(860) 242-2274, ext. 3834   Fax: (860) 242-3103
E-mail: hi-c@ciboakhill.org
Web: www.ciboakhill.org/ways_to_give/donor.asp

Summary   To provide financial assistance for college to Connecticut high school seniors who are legally blind.

Eligibility   This program is open to seniors graduating from high schools in Connecticut who are legally blind. Applicants must be planning to enroll in a postsecondary educational institution. They must be able to demonstrate financial need. Along with their application, they must submit answers to questions about their major accomplishments, who or what has helped them in their accomplishments, the extracurricular activities (including sports) in which they were involved in high school, their involvement in their community, their goals for the next 5 years, how an

award would help them achieve their goals, how they will be financing their college education, and why they feel they should be considered for an award.

Financial data   A stipend is awarded (amount not specified).

Duration   1 year.

Additional data   This program was established in 2000. The Connecticut Institute for the Blind, doing business as Oak Hill, also operates independent living facilities in West Hartford and Wethersfield for blind, visually impaired, and disabled individuals.

Number awarded   1 each year.

Deadline   December of each year.

[14]
COMPUTER SCIENCE SCHOLARSHIP

National Federation of the Blind
Attn: Scholarship Committee
1800 Johnson Street
Baltimore, MD 21230
(410) 659-9314, ext. 2415   Fax: (410) 685-5653
E-mail: scholarships@nfb.org
Web: www.nfb.org/nfb/scholarship_program.asp

Summary   To provide financial assistance to entering and continuing undergraduate and graduate students who are legally blind and working on a degree in computer science.

Eligibility   This program is open to legally blind students who are working on or planning to work full time on an undergraduate or graduate degree in computer science. Along with their application, they must submit transcripts, standardized test scores, proof of legal blindness, 2 letters of recommendation, and a letter of endorsement from their National Federation of the Blind state president or designee. Selection is based on academic excellence, service to the community, and financial need.

Financial data   The stipend is $3,000.

Duration   1 year; recipients may resubmit applications up to 2 additional years.

Additional data   Scholarships are awarded at the federation convention in July. Recipients must attend the convention at federation expense; that funding is in addition to the scholarship grant.

Number awarded   1 each year.

Deadline   March of each year.

[15]
DALE M. SCHOETTLER SCHOLARSHIP FOR VISUALLY IMPAIRED STUDENTS

California State University
CSU Foundation
Attn: Director, Foundation Programs and Services
401 Golden Shore, Sixth Floor
Long Beach, CA 90802-4210
(562) 951-4768   E-mail: abrown@calstate.edu
Web: www.calstate.edu/foundation/scholarship.shtml

Summary   To provide financial assistance to undergraduate and graduate students with visual impairments at campuses of the California State University (CSU) system.

Eligibility This program is open to undergraduate and graduate students enrolled at CSU campuses who have been declared visually impaired or legally blind. Applicants must have a cumulative GPA of 2.8 or higher.

Financial data The stipend is $6,500.

Duration 1 year.

Number awarded 15 each year.

Deadline Deadline not specified.

[16]
DAVID NEWMEYER SCHOLARSHIP

American Council of the Blind of Ohio
Attn: Executive Director
P.O. Box 307128
Gahanna, OH 43230-7128
(614) 221-6688 Toll Free: (800) 835-2226 (within OH)
E-mail: mary.hiland@sbcglobal.net
Web: www.acbohio.org/application_cur.php

Summary To provide financial assistance to entering or continuing Ohio undergraduate students who are blind.

Eligibility This program is open to 1) residents of Ohio who are high school seniors or current college students, and 2) students at colleges and universities in Ohio. Applicants must be legally blind and working on or planning to work on an undergraduate degree in any field. Along with their application, they must submit transcripts (must have a GPA of 3.0 or higher), a certificate of legal blindness, and an essay of 250 to 500 words on their career objectives, future plans, personal goals, other academic or personal qualities, and why they believe they are qualified to receive this scholarship. Financial need is not the sole factor considered in the selection process.

Financial data The stipend is $2,000 per year.

Duration 1 year; recipients may reapply.

Additional data Winners are required to attend the Saturday morning business meeting and Sunday breakfast of the sponsor's annual convention; a stipend for meals and workshops is provided.

Number awarded 1 each year.

Deadline July of each year.

[17]
DELTA GAMMA FOUNDATION RUTH BILLOW MEMORIAL EDUCATION FUND

Delta Gamma Foundation
Attn: Director, Service for Sight
3250 Riverside Drive
P.O. Box 21397
Columbus, OH 43221-0397
(614) 481-8169   Fax: (614) 481-0133
E-mail: dgfoundation@deltagamma.org
Web: www.deltagamma.org

Summary To provide financial assistance to undergraduate or graduate members of Delta Gamma sorority who are visually impaired or preparing for a career in working with the visually impaired.

Eligibility This program is open to undergraduate and graduate members of the sorority who are either 1) blind or visually impaired or 2) pursuing professional training in areas related to working with persons who are blind or visually impaired or in sight preservation. Applicants must be pursuing a program of postsecondary education in the United States or Canada.

Financial data The stipend is $1,000 for undergraduates or $2,500 for graduate students.

Duration 1 year or more.

Number awarded 2 each year: 1 to an undergraduate and 1 to a graduate student.

Deadline Applications may be submitted at any time.

[18]
DORTHEA AND ROLAND BOHDE SCHOLASTIC ACHIEVEMENT SCHOLARSHIP

American Council of the Blind
Attn: Coordinator, Scholarship Program
2200 Wilson Boulevard, Suite 650
Arlington, VA 22201
(202) 467-5081   Toll Free: (800) 424-8666
Fax: (703) 465-5085   E-mail: info@acb.org
Web: www.acb.org

Summary To provide financial assistance to outstanding blind students.

Eligibility This program is open to legally blind students enrolling or continuing in an undergraduate program. Applicants must submit verification of legal blindness in both eyes; SAT or ACT scores; information on extracurricular activities (including membership in the American Council of the Blind); employment record; and an autobiographical sketch that includes their personal goals, strengths, weaknesses, hobbies, honors, achievements, and reasons for choice of field or courses of study. A cumulative GPA of 3.0 or higher is generally required. Financial need is not considered in the selection process.

Financial data A stipend is awarded (amount not specified). In addition, the winner receives a Kurzweil-1000 Reading System.

Duration 1 year.

Additional data This program is supported by Guide Dogs for the Blind. The scholarship winner is expected to be present at the council's annual national convention; the council will cover all reasonable costs connected with convention attendance.

Number awarded 1 each year.

Deadline February of each year.

[19]
DR. MAE DAVIDOW MEMORIAL SCHOLARSHIP

American Council of the Blind
Attn: Coordinator, Scholarship Program
2200 Wilson Boulevard, Suite 650
Arlington, VA 22201
(202) 467-5081   Toll Free: (800) 424-8666
Fax: (703) 465-5085   E-mail: info@acb.org
Web: www.acb.org

Summary To provide financial assistance for college to blind students from Pennsylvania.

Eligibility This program is open to legally blind students who are residents of Pennsylvania or attending college in the state. Applicants must submit verification of legal blindness in both eyes; SAT or ACT scores; information on extracurricular activities (including membership in the American Council of the Blind); employment record; and an autobiographical sketch that includes their personal goals, strengths, weaknesses, hobbies, honors, achievements, and reasons for choice of field or courses of study. A cumulative GPA of 3.3 or higher is generally required. Financial need is not considered in the selection process.

Financial data The stipend is $1,500. In addition, the winner receives a Kurzweil-1000 Reading System.

Duration 1 year.

Additional data This scholarship is sponsored by the Pennsylvania Council of the Blind, an affiliate of the American Council of the Blind. Scholarship winners are expected to be present at the council's annual conference; the council will cover all reasonable expenses connected with convention attendance.

Number awarded 1 each year.

Deadline February of each year.

[20]
DR. NICHOLAS S. DICAPRIO SCHOLARSHIP

American Council of the Blind
Attn: Coordinator, Scholarship Program
2200 Wilson Boulevard, Suite 650
Arlington, VA 22201
(202) 467-5081   Toll Free: (800) 424-8666
Fax: (703) 465-5085   E-mail: info@acb.org
Web: www.acb.org

Summary To provide financial assistance to outstanding blind undergraduates.

Eligibility This program is open to legally blind undergraduate students. Applicants must submit verification of legal blindness in both eyes; SAT or ACT scores; information on extracurricular activities (including membership in the American Council of the Blind); employment record; and an autobiographical sketch that includes their personal goals, strengths, weaknesses, hobbies, honors, achievements, and reasons for choice of field or courses of study. A cumulative GPA of 3.3 or higher is generally required. Financial need is not considered in the selection process.

Financial data The stipend is $2,500. In addition, the winner receives a Kurzweil-1000 Reading System.

Duration 1 year.

Additional data The scholarship winner is expected to be present at the council's annual national convention; the council will cover all reasonable costs connected with convention attendance.

Number awarded 1 each year.

Deadline February of each year.

[21]
DR. S. BRADLEY BURSON MEMORIAL SCHOLARSHIP

American Council of the Blind
Attn: Coordinator, Scholarship Program
2200 Wilson Boulevard, Suite 650
Arlington, VA 22201
(202) 467-5081   Toll Free: (800) 424-8666
Fax: (703) 465-5085   E-mail: info@acb.org
Web: www.acb.org

Summary To provide financial assistance to blind students who are working on an undergraduate or graduate degree in designated fields of science.

Eligibility This program is open to undergraduate or graduate students working on a degree in the "hard" sciences (i.e., biology, chemistry, physics, and engineering, but not computer science). Applicants must be legally blind in both eyes. Along with their application, they must submit verification of legal blindness in both eyes; SAT, ACT, GRE, or similar scores; information on extracurricular activities (including membership in the American Council of the Blind); employment record; and an autobiographical sketch that includes their personal goals, strengths, weaknesses, hobbies, honors, achievements, and reasons for choice of field or courses of study. A cumulative GPA of 3.3 or higher is generally required. Financial need is not considered in the selection process.

Financial data The stipend is $1,000. In addition, the winner receives a Kurzweil-1000 Reading System.

Duration 1 year.

Additional data Scholarship winners are expected to be present at the council's annual conference; the council will cover all reasonable expenses connected with convention attendance.

Number awarded 1 each year.

Deadline February of each year.

[22]
DUANE BUCKLEY MEMORIAL SCHOLARSHIP

American Council of the Blind
Attn: Coordinator, Scholarship Program
2200 Wilson Boulevard, Suite 650
Arlington, VA 22201
(202) 467-5081   Toll Free: (800) 424-8666
Fax: (703) 465-5085   E-mail: info@acb.org
Web: www.acb.org

Summary To provide financial assistance for college to blind high school seniors.

Eligibility This program is open to graduating high school seniors who are legally blind in both eyes. Applicants must submit verification of legal blindness in both eyes; SAT or ACT scores; information on extracurricular activities (including membership in the American Council of the Blind); employment record; and an autobiographical sketch that includes their personal goals, strengths, weaknesses, hobbies, honors, achievements, and reasons for choice of field or courses of study. A cumulative GPA of 3.3 or higher is generally required. Financial need is not considered in the selection process.

Financial data The stipend is $1,000. In addition, the winner receives a Kurzweil-1000 Reading System.

Duration 1 year.

Additional data The scholarship winner is expected to be present at the council's annual national convention; the council will cover all reasonable costs connected with convention attendance.

Number awarded 1 each year.

Deadline February of each year.

[23]
ELLEN BEACH MACK SCHOLARSHIP

American Council of the Blind of South Carolina
c/o Betty Jones, President
101 Sherard Avenue
Ninety Six, SC 29666
(864) 543-2993 E-mail: mrsbettyjno1@hotmail.com
Web: www.acbsc.org

Summary To provide financial assistance to entering and continuing undergraduate and graduate students with visual impairments in South Carolina.

Eligibility This program is open to residents of South Carolina who are legally blind in both eyes. Applicants must be currently enrolled or accepted at a technical school, college, university, or graduate school. Along with their application, they must submit a letter of recommendation, transcript, and a 2-page autobiographical sketch that describes their goals, strengths, weaknesses, and other pertinent information.

Financial data The stipend is $1,000.

Duration 1 year.

Number awarded 1 or more each year.

Deadline September of each year.

[24]
ESTHER V. TAYLOR SCHOLARSHIPS

Kansas Association for the Blind and Visually Impaired
603 S.W. Topeka Boulevard, Suite 304B
Topeka, KS 66603
(785) 235-8990 Toll Free: (800) 749-1499 (within KS)
E-mail: kabvi@att.net
Web: www.kabvi.com/Scholarship%20Opportunity.html

Summary To provide financial assistance to residents of Kansas who are blind or visually impaired and interested in attending college in any state.

Eligibility This program is open to blind and visually impaired residents of Kansas who are attending or planning to attend a college, university, or technical school in any state. Applicants must submit an autobiographical sketch that includes their goals, strengths, weaknesses, hobbies, honors, extracurricular activities, and achievements. Financial need is considered in the selection process.

Financial data The stipend is $1,000.

Duration 1 year.

Number awarded 2 each year.

Deadline April of each year.

[25]
E.U. PARKER SCHOLARSHIP

National Federation of the Blind
Attn: Scholarship Committee
1800 Johnson Street
Baltimore, MD 21230
(410) 659-9314, ext. 2415 Fax: (410) 685-5653
E-mail: scholarships@nfb.org
Web: www.nfb.org/nfb/scholarship_program.asp

Summary To provide financial assistance to entering and continuing undergraduate and graduate students who are blind.

Eligibility This program is open to legally blind students who are working on or planning to work full time on an undergraduate or graduate degree. Along with their application, they must submit transcripts, standardized test scores, proof of legal blindness, 2 letters of recommendation, and a letter of endorsement from their letter of endorsement from their National Federation of the Blind state president or designee. Selection is based on academic excellence, service to the community, and financial need.

Financial data The stipend is $3,000.

Duration 1 year; recipients may resubmit applications up to 2 additional years.

Additional data Scholarships are awarded at the federation convention in July. Recipients must attend the convention at federation expense; that funding is in addition to the scholarship grant.

Number awarded 1 each year.

Deadline March of each year.

[26]
EUNICE FIORITO MEMORIAL SCHOLARSHIP

American Council of the Blind
Attn: Coordinator, Scholarship Program
2200 Wilson Boulevard, Suite 650
Arlington, VA 22201
(202) 467-5081 Toll Free: (800) 424-8666
Fax: (703) 465-5085 E-mail: info@acb.org
Web: www.acb.org

Summary To provide financial assistance to undergraduate or graduate students who are blind and are interested in studying in a field of advocacy or service for persons with disabilities.

Eligibility This program is open to undergraduate and graduate students in rehabilitation, education, law, or other fields of service or advocacy for persons with disabilities. Applicants must be legally blind in both eyes. Along with their application, they must submit verification of legal blindness in both eyes; SAT, ACT, GRE, or similar scores; information on extracurricular activities (including membership in the American Council of the Blind); employment record; and an autobiographical sketch that includes their personal goals, strengths, weaknesses, hobbies, honors, achievements, and reasons for choice of field or courses of study. A cumulative GPA of 3.3 or higher is generally required. Financial need is not considered in the selection process. Preference is given to students with little or no vision.

Financial data The stipend is $2,000. In addition, the winner receives a Kurzweil-1000 Reading System.

Duration 1 year.

Additional data The scholarship winner is expected to be present at the council's annual national convention; the council will cover all reasonable costs connected with convention attendance.

Number awarded 1 each year.

Deadline February of each year.

[27]
FERDINAND TORRES SCHOLARSHIP

American Foundation for the Blind
Attn: Scholarship Committee
11 Penn Plaza, Suite 300
New York, NY 10001
(212) 502-7661   Toll Free: (800) AFB-LINE
Fax: (212) 502-7771   TDD: (212) 502-7662
E-mail: afbinfo@afb.net
Web: www.afb.org/Section.asp?Documentid=2962

Summary To provide financial assistance for college or graduate school to blind students, especially immigrants and those from New York City.

Eligibility Applicants must be legally blind and reside in the United States, although U.S. citizenship is not necessary. They must present evidence of economic need, legal blindness, and acceptance into a full-time undergraduate or graduate program. Preference is given to new immigrants and residents of New York City. Along with their application, they must submit a 200-word essay that includes their past and recent achievements and accomplishments; their intended field of study and why they have chosen it; the role their visual impairment has played in shaping their life; their financial need and how they would use the scholarship; and (for immigrants) their country of origin and their reasons for coming to the United States.

Financial data The stipend is $2,500.

Duration 1 year.

Number awarded 1 each year.

Deadline April of each year.

[28]
FLORENCE MARGARET HARVEY MEMORIAL SCHOLARSHIP

American Foundation for the Blind
Attn: Scholarship Committee
11 Penn Plaza, Suite 300
New York, NY 10001
(212) 502-7661   Toll Free: (800) AFB-LINE
Fax: (212) 502-7771   TDD: (212) 502-7662
E-mail: afbinfo@afb.net
Web: www.afb.org/Section.asp?Documentid=2962

Summary To provide financial assistance to blind undergraduate and graduate students who wish to study in the field of rehabilitation and/or education of the blind.

Eligibility This program is open to legally blind juniors, seniors, or graduate students. U.S. citizenship is required.

Applicants must be studying in the field of rehabilitation and/or education of visually impaired and blind persons. Along with their application, they must submit a 200-word essay that includes their past and recent achievements and accomplishments; their intended field of study and why they have chosen it; and the role their visual impairment has played in shaping their life. Financial need is considered in the selection process.

Financial data The stipend is $1,000.

Duration 1 year.

Additional data This scholarship is supported by the Delta Gamma Foundation and administered by the American Foundation for the Blind.

Number awarded 1 each year.

Deadline April of each year.

[29]
FLOYD CALLWARD MEMORIAL SCHOLARSHIP

National Federation of the Blind of New Hampshire
c/o Marie Johnson, President
11 Springfield Street
Concord, NH 03301
(603) 225-7917   E-mail: jomar2000@comcast.net

Summary To provide financial assistance to blind students in New Hampshire who are interested in working on an undergraduate or graduate degree at a school in any state.

Eligibility This program is open to legally blind and totally blind residents of New Hampshire who are attending or planning to attend college or graduate school in any state. Applicants may be attending college immediately after high school, returning to college at a later age, attending graduate or professional school, or enrolled in postsecondary vocational training. Along with their application, they must submit 1) a letter describing what they have done to deal with situations involving their blindness, their personal goals and aspirations, and how the scholarship will help them; 2) 2 letters of recommendation; 3) high school or college transcripts; 4) a list of honors and awards; and 5) information on community service and volunteer work. There are no restrictions on level, gender, or field of study. Financial need is not considered.

Financial data The stipend is $1,000. The funds may be used to purchase education-related equipment or services or to defray the costs of tuition, board, and other school fees.

Duration 1 year.

Additional data This program was established in 1990.

Number awarded 1 or more each year.

Deadline October of each year.

[30]
FLOYD QUALLS MEMORIAL SCHOLARSHIPS

American Council of the Blind
Attn: Coordinator, Scholarship Program
2200 Wilson Boulevard, Suite 650
Arlington, VA 22201
(202) 467-5081   Toll Free: (800) 424-8666
Fax: (703) 465-5085   E-mail: info@acb.org
Web: www.acb.org

Summary To provide financial assistance to entering and continuing undergraduate and graduate students who are blind.

Eligibility This program is open to legally blind students in 4 categories: entering freshmen in academic programs, undergraduates (sophomores, juniors, and seniors) in academic programs, graduate students in academic programs, and vocational school students or students working on an associate's degree from a community college. Applicants must submit verification of legal blindness in both eyes; SAT, ACT, GRE, or similar scores; information on extracurricular activities (including membership in the American Council of the Blind); employment record; and an autobiographical sketch that includes their personal goals, strengths, weaknesses, hobbies, honors, achievements, and reasons for choice of field or courses of study. A cumulative GPA of 3.3 or higher is generally required. Financial need is not considered in the selection process.

Financial data The stipend is $2,500. In addition, the winners receive a Kurzweil-1000 Reading System.

Duration 1 year.

Additional data Scholarship winners are expected to be present at the council's annual conference; the council will cover all reasonable expenses connected with convention attendance.

Number awarded 4 each year: 1 in each of the 4 categories.

Deadline February of each year.

[31]
FRIENDS-IN-ART SCHOLARSHIP

Friends-in-Art
c/o Nancy Pendegraph, President
2331 Poincianna Street
Huntsville, AL 35801
E-mail: nansong@knology.net
Web: www.friendsinart.com/scholarship.htm

Summary To provide financial assistance to blind students who are majoring or planning to major in fields related to the arts.

Eligibility This program is open to blind and visually impaired high school seniors and college students who are majoring or planning to major in music, art, drama, or creative writing. Applicants must be residents of North America. Music students must submit a tape with their performance of a fast piece and a slow piece; art students must submit 10 slides of their work; drama students must submit a tape with a dramatic presentation and a comic presentation; creative writing students must submit examples of their work. Selection is based on achievement, talent, and excellence in the arts.

Financial data The stipend is $1,500.

Duration 1 year.

Additional data This program began in 1999.

Number awarded 1 each year.

Deadline May of each year.

[32]
GAYLE M. KRAUSE-EDWARDS SCHOLARSHIP

Florida Council for the Blind
c/o Barbara Grill, Education and Leadership
  Committee
2030 Preymore Street
Osprey, FL 34229
(941) 966-7056   E-mail: grillbh@comcast.net
Web: www.fcb.org/ScholApInfo.htm

Summary To provide financial assistance to blind residents of Florida who plan to attend college in any state and can demonstrate outstanding academic and leadership achievements.

Eligibility This program is open to blind residents of Florida who are attending or planning to attend a college or university in any state. Applicants must have a GPA of 3.5 or higher and be able to demonstrate outstanding academic and leadership achievements. Along with their application, they must submit a narrative statement on their vocational objectives and outlook for employment in their chosen field. Financial need is not considered in the selection process.

Financial data The stipend is $2,000.

Duration 1 year.

Number awarded 1 each year.

Deadline March of each year.

[33]
GEORGIA COUNCIL OF THE BLIND SCHOLARSHIPS

Georgia Council of the Blind
850 Gaines School Road
Athens, GA 30605
Toll Free: (877) 667-6815
E-mail: marshafarrow@alltel.net
Web: www.georgiacounciloftheblind.org

Summary To provide financial assistance students in Georgia who plan to attend college or graduate school in any state and are either legally blind or have legally blind parents.

Eligibility This program is open to residents of Georgia who are either 1) legally blind students, or 2) sighted students financially dependent on legally blind parents. Applicants must be enrolled or accepted for enrollment at a vocational/technical school, a 2-year or 4-year college, or a master's or doctoral program in any state. All fields of study are eligible. Selection is based on academic transcripts, 2 letters of recommendation, a 1-page typed statement of the applicant's educational goals, an audio cassette recording of the applicant reading the goals statement, extracurricular activities, and financial need.

Financial data Stipends up to $1,000 per year are available.

Duration 1 year; recipients may reapply.

Additional data This program began in 1988.

Number awarded 1 or more each year.

Deadline June of each year.

[34]
GLADYS C. ANDERSON MEMORIAL SCHOLARSHIP

American Foundation for the Blind
Attn: Scholarship Committee
11 Penn Plaza, Suite 300
New York, NY 10001
(212) 502-7661   Toll Free: (800) AFB-LINE
Fax: (212) 502-7771   TDD: (212) 502-7662
E-mail: afbinfo@afb.net
Web: www.afb.org/Section.asp?Documentid=2962

Summary To provide financial assistance to legally blind women who are studying classical or religious music at the undergraduate or graduate school level.

Eligibility This program is open to women who are legally blind, U.S. citizens, and enrolled in an undergraduate or graduate degree program in classical or religious music. Along with their application, they must submit a 200-word essay that includes their past and recent achievements and accomplishments; their intended field of study and why they have chosen it; and the role their visual impairment has played in shaping their life. They must also submit a sample performance tape or CD of up to 30 minutes. Financial need is considered in the selection process.

Financial data The stipend is $1,000.

Duration 1 academic year.

Number awarded 1 each year.

Deadline April of each year.

[35]
GUIDE DOGS FOR THE BLIND DOROTHEA AND ROLAND BOHDE LEADERSHIP SCHOLARSHIP

National Federation of the Blind
Attn: Scholarship Committee
1800 Johnson Street
Baltimore, MD 21230
(410) 659-9314, ext. 2415   Fax: (410) 685-5653
E-mail: scholarships@nfb.org
Web: www.nfb.org/nfb/scholarship_program.asp

Summary To provide financial assistance to blind undergraduate and graduate students, especially those who use a guide dog.

Eligibility This program is open to legally blind students who are working on or planning to work full time on an undergraduate or graduate degree. Preference is given to applicants who have chosen to use a guide dog as their primary travel aid. Along with their application, they must submit transcripts, standardized test scores, proof of legal blindness, 2 letters of recommendation, and a letter of endorsement from their National Federation of the Blind

state president or designee. Selection is based on academic excellence, service to the community, and financial need.

Financial data The stipend is $3,000.

Duration 1 year; recipients may resubmit applications up to 2 additional years.

Additional data Scholarships are awarded at the federation convention in July. Recipients must attend the convention at federation expense; that funding is in addition to the scholarship grant.

Number awarded 1 each year.

Deadline March of each year.

[36]
GUILDSCHOLAR PROGRAM

Jewish Guild for the Blind
Attn: GuildScholar Program
15 West 65th Street
New York, NY 10023
(212) 769-7801   Toll Free: (800) 284-4422
Fax: (212) 769-6266   E-mail: guildscholar@jgb.org
Web: www.jgb.org/guildscholar.asp?GS=TRue

Summary To provide financial assistance for college to blind high school seniors.

Eligibility This program is open to college-bound high school seniors who can document legal blindness. Applicants must submit copies of school transcripts and SAT or ACT scores, proof of U.S. citizenship, 3 letters of recommendation, proof of legal blindness, a 500-word personal statement describing their educational and personal goals, a 500-word essay describing the influence of an outstanding teacher on their education, and documentation of financial need (if they wish that to be considered in the selection process).

Financial data The stipend ranges up to $15,000.

Duration 1 year.

Additional data This program was established in 2004.

Number awarded 12 to 15 each year.

Deadline June of each year (the end of the junior year of high school).

[37]
HANK HOFSTETTER OPPORTUNITY GRANTS

American Council of the Blind of Indiana
c/o James R. Durst
Indiana School for the Blind
7725 North College Avenue
Indianapolis, IN 46240
Web: indianaacb.tripod.com/hofstetter.htm

Summary To provide financial assistance to Indiana residents who are blind and desire materials or equipment to continue their education or meet other needs.

Eligibility This fund is open to certified legally blind Indiana residents who are unable to obtain funding through other means. Applicants must need funding for an activity, materials, and/or equipment that will enhance their educational, entrepreneurial, or vocational aims. Along with their application, they must submit a 1-page statement on why they should be considered for a grant, a list of other options or sources that have already been tried, and a reference letter.

Financial data The amount awarded varies, depending upon the needs of the recipient. A total of $1,000 is available annually.

Number awarded 1 or more each year.

Deadline Requests may be submitted at any time but should be received at least 90 days prior to the need.

[38]
HANK LEBONNE SCHOLARSHIP

National Federation of the Blind
Attn: Scholarship Committee
1800 Johnson Street
Baltimore, MD 21230
(410) 659-9314, ext. 2415   Fax: (410) 685-5653
E-mail: scholarships@nfb.org
Web: www.nfb.org/nfb/scholarship_program.asp

Summary To provide financial assistance to legally blind students working on or planning to work on an undergraduate or graduate degree.

Eligibility This program is open to legally blind students who are working on or planning to work full time on an undergraduate or graduate degree. Along with their application, they must submit transcripts, standardized test scores, proof of legal blindness, 2 letters of recommendation, and a letter of endorsement from their National Federation of the Blind state president or designee. Selection is based on academic excellence, service to the community, and financial need.

Financial data The stipend is $5,000.

Duration 1 year; recipients may resubmit applications up to 2 additional years.

Additional data Scholarships are awarded at the federation convention in July. Recipients must attend the convention at federation expense; that funding is in addition to the scholarship grant.

Number awarded 1 each year.

Deadline March of each year.

[39]
HARRY G. STARR AWARD

Lighthouse International
Attn: Scholarship and Career Awards
111 East 59th Street
New York, NY 10022-1202
(212) 821-9428   Toll Free: (800) 829-0500
Fax: (212) 821-9703   TDD: (212) 821-9713
E-mail: sca@lighthouse.org
Web: www.lighthouse.org

Summary To provide financial assistance to legally blind undergraduate students residing and attending school in designated eastern states.

Eligibility This program is open to legally blind U.S. citizens who are residents of Connecticut, Delaware, Florida, Georgia, Maine, Maryland, Massachusetts, New Hampshire, New Jersey, New York, North Carolina, Pennsylvania, Rhode Island, South Carolina, Vermont, Virginia, Washington, D.C., or West Virginia. Applicants must be

working on an undergraduate degree at a school in those states. Along with their application, they must submit a 500-word essay describing their academic achievements and career goals. Financial need is not considered in the selection process.

Financial data The stipend is $5,000.

Duration 1 year.

Additional data This award was first presented in 2008.

Number awarded 1 each year.

Deadline February of each year.

[40]
HARRY LUDWIG MEMORIAL SCHOLARSHIP

Oregon Student Assistance Commission
Attn: Grants and Scholarships Division
1500 Valley River Drive, Suite 100
Eugene, OR 97401-2146
(541) 687-7395   Toll Free: (800) 452-8807, ext. 7395
Fax: (541) 687-7414   TDD: (800) 735-2900
E-mail: awardinfo@osac.state.or.us
Web: www.osac.state.or.us/osac_programs.html

Summary To provide financial assistance to residents of Oregon who are visually impaired and are interested in attending college or graduate school in the state.

Eligibility This program is open to residents of Oregon who are visually impaired (have residual acuity of 20/70 or less in the better eye with correction, or their visual field is restricted to 20 degrees or less in the better eye). Applicants must be enrolled or planning to enroll as full-time undergraduate or graduate students at a college or university in Oregon.

Financial data Stipend amounts vary; recently, they were at least $1,643.

Duration 1 year.

Additional data This program is administered by the Oregon Student Assistance Commission (OSAC) with funds provided by the Oregon Community Foundation, 1221 S.W. Yamhill, Suite 100, Portland, OR 97205, (503) 227-6846, Fax: (503) 274-7771.

Number awarded Varies each year; recently, 7 of these scholarships were awarded.

Deadline February of each year.

[41]
HAWAII ASSOCIATION OF THE BLIND SCHOLARSHIP

Hawaii Association of the Blind
Attn: Scholarship Committee
1255 Nuuanu Avenue, Number 1102
Honolulu, HI 96817
(808) 521-6213   E-mail: toyamaj005@hawaii.rr.com
Web: www.acb.org/hawaii/scholarship.htm

Summary To provide financial assistance to blind residents of Hawaii who plan to attend college in any state.

Eligibility This program is open to Hawaii residents who meet the legal definition of blindness or visual impairment. Applicants must be members of the American Council of the Blind but may not be members of any other national organization for the blind. They must submit high school and/or college transcripts, 2 letters of reference, and a 2-page letter describing their educational goals.

Financial data Stipends are at least $500 per semester ($1,000 per year).

Duration 1 year.

Number awarded 1 or more each year.

Deadline May of each year for fall semester; November of each year for spring semester.

[42]
HAZEL TEN BROEK MEMORIAL SCHOLARSHIP

National Federation of the Blind of Washington
c/o Rita Szantay, Scholarship Chair
1420 Fifth Avenue, Suite 2200
Seattle, WA 98101
(206) 224-7242   E-mail: rszantay@speakeasy.net
Web: www.nfbw.org

Summary To provide financial assistance for undergraduate or graduate study in any state to blind students in Washington.

Eligibility This program is open to legally blind residents of Washington state who are working on or planning to work on a full-time college or graduate degree at a school in any state. Applicants must submit a list of honors and awards they have received, information on their community service involvement, high school and/or college transcripts, and 3 letters of reference.

Financial data The stipend is $2,000.

Duration 1 year.

Additional data This scholarship was first awarded in 1996. Winners must attend the state convention of the National Federation of the Blind of Washington to accept the award; convention expenses are covered.

Number awarded 1 each year.

Deadline August of each year.

[43]
HERMIONE GRANT CALHOUN SCHOLARSHIP

National Federation of the Blind
Attn: Scholarship Committee
1800 Johnson Street
Baltimore, MD 21230
(410) 659-9314, ext. 2415   Fax: (410) 685-5653
E-mail: scholarships@nfb.org
Web: www.nfb.org/nfb/scholarship_program.asp

Summary To provide financial assistance to female blind students interested in working on an undergraduate or graduate degree.

Eligibility This program is open to legally blind women who are working on or planning to work full time on an undergraduate or graduate degree. Along with their application, they must submit transcripts, standardized test scores, proof of legal blindness, 2 letters of recommendation, and a letter of endorsement from their National Federation of the Blind state president or designee. Selection is based on academic excellence, service to the community, and financial need.

Financial data The stipend is $3,000.

Duration 1 year; recipients may resubmit applications up to 2 additional years.

Additional data Scholarships are awarded at the federation convention in July. Recipients attend the convention at federation expense; that funding is in addition to the scholarship grant.

Number awarded 1 each year.

Deadline March of each year.

[44]
HOWARD BROWN RICKARD SCHOLARSHIP

National Federation of the Blind
Attn: Scholarship Committee
1800 Johnson Street
Baltimore, MD 21230
(410) 659-9314, ext. 2415   Fax: (410) 685-5653
E-mail: scholarships@nfb.org
Web: www.nfb.org/nfb/scholarship_program.asp

Summary To provide financial assistance for college or graduate school to blind students studying or planning to study law, medicine, engineering, architecture, or the natural sciences.

Eligibility This program is open to legally blind students who are enrolled in or planning to enroll in a full-time undergraduate or graduate course of study. Applicants must be studying or planning to study law, medicine, engineering, architecture, or the natural sciences. Along with their application, they must submit transcripts, standardized test scores, proof of legal blindness, 2 letters of recommendation, and a letter of endorsement from their National Federation of the Blind state president or designee. Selection is based on academic excellence, service to the community, and financial need.

Financial data The stipend is $3,000.

Duration 1 year; recipients may resubmit applications up to 2 additional years.

Additional data Scholarships are awarded at the federation convention in July. Recipients must attend the convention at federation expense; that funding is in addition to the scholarship grant.

Number awarded 1 each year.

Deadline March of each year.

[45]
JAMES DOYLE CASE MEMORIAL SCHOLARSHIPS

Mississippi Council of the Blind
P.O. Box 31112
Jackson, MS 39286-1112
(601) 371-0616   Toll Free: (888) 346-5622 (within MS)
Web: www.acb.org/mcb

Summary To provide financial assistance to legally blind residents of Mississippi and their children who plan to attend college or graduate school in any state.

Eligibility This program is open to residents of Mississippi who are legally blind or the children of at least 1 legally blind parent. Applicants must be enrolled or accepted for enrollment in an undergraduate or graduate program in any state and carrying or planning to carry at least 12 academic hours. Along with their application, they must submit a 2-page autobiographical sketch, transcripts, standardized test scores (ACT or SAT for undergraduates; GRE, MCAT, LSAT, etc. for graduate students), 2 letters of recommendation, proof of acceptance from a postsecondary school, and verification of blindness of the qualifying person (applicant or parent).

Financial data The stipend is $1,500 per year.

Duration 4 years.

Number awarded 2 each year.

Deadline February of each year.

[46]
JAMES R. OLSEN MEMORIAL SCHOLARSHIP

American Council of the Blind
Attn: Coordinator, Scholarship Program
2200 Wilson Boulevard, Suite 650
Arlington, VA 22201
(202) 467-5081   Toll Free: (800) 424-8666
Fax: (703) 465-5085   E-mail: info@acb.org
Web: www.acb.org

Summary To provide financial assistance to outstanding blind students.

Eligibility This program is open to legally blind students enrolling or continuing in an undergraduate program. Applicants must submit verification of legal blindness in both eyes; SAT or ACT scores; information on extracurricular activities (including membership in the American Council of the Blind); employment record; and an autobiographical sketch that includes their personal goals, strengths, weaknesses, hobbies, honors, achievements, and reasons for choice of field or courses of study. A cumulative GPA of 3.3 or higher is generally required. Financial need is not considered in the selection process.

Financial data A stipend is awarded (amount not specified). In addition, the winner receives a Kurzweil-1000 Reading System.

Duration 1 year.

Additional data The scholarship winner is expected to be present at the council's annual national convention; the council will cover all reasonable costs connected with convention attendance.

Number awarded 1 each year.

Deadline February of each year.

[47]
JEANNETTE C. EYERLY MEMORIAL SCHOLARSHIP

National Federation of the Blind
Attn: Scholarship Committee
1800 Johnson Street
Baltimore, MD 21230
(410) 659-9314, ext. 2415   Fax: (410) 685-5653
E-mail: scholarships@nfb.org
Web: www.nfb.org/nfb/scholarship_program.asp

Summary To provide financial assistance to legally blind students working on or planning to work on an undergraduate or graduate degree.

Eligibility This program is open to legally blind students who are working on or planning to work full time on an undergraduate or graduate degree. Along with their application, they must submit transcripts, standardized test scores, proof of legal blindness, 2 letters of recommendation, and a letter of endorsement from their National Federation of the Blind state president or designee. Selection is based on academic excellence, service to the community, and financial need.

Financial data The stipend is $3,000.

Duration 1 year; recipients may resubmit applications up to 2 additional years.

Additional data Scholarships are awarded at the federation convention in July. Recipients must attend the convention at federation expense; that funding is in addition to the scholarship grant.

Number awarded 1 each year.

Deadline March of each year.

[48]
JENNICA FERGUSON MEMORIAL SCHOLARSHIP OF OHIO

National Federation of the Blind of Ohio
c/o Barbara Pierce, Scholarship Committee Chair
237 Oak Street
Oberlin, OH 44074-1517
(440) 775-2216   E-mail: bpierce@nfb.org
Web: www.nfbohio.org

Summary To provide financial assistance to blind residents of Ohio who are interested in working on an undergraduate or graduate degree at a school in any state.

Eligibility This program is open to residents of Ohio who are legally blind. Applicants must be attending or planning to attend an accredited institution of higher education as a full-time undergraduate or graduate student. Along with their application, they must submit 2 letters of recommendation, current transcripts, a letter about themselves that includes how they have dealt with their blindness and their hopes and dreams, and a letter from an officer of the National Federation of the Blind of Ohio indicating that they have discussed their scholarship application with that officer. Selection is based on academic excellence, community service, and financial need.

Financial data The stipend is $1,500.

Duration 1 year.

Number awarded 1 each year.

Deadline April of each year.

[49]
JOHN A. COCCOMO, SR. AWARDS

Connecticut Institute for the Blind
Attn: Vice President for Development
120 Holcomb Street
Hartford, CT 06112-1589
(860) 242-2274, ext. 3834   Fax: (860) 242-3103
E-mail: hi-c@ciboakhill.org
Web: www.ciboakhill.org/ways_to_give/donor.asp

Summary To provide financial assistance for college to Connecticut high school seniors who are legally blind.

Eligibility This program is open to seniors graduating from high schools in Connecticut who are legally blind. Applicants must be planning to enroll in a postsecondary educational institution. They must be able to demonstrate financial need. Along with their application, they must submit answers to questions about their major accomplishments, who or what has helped them in their accomplishments, the extracurricular activities (including sports) in which they were involved in high school, their involvement in their community, their goals for the next 5 years, how an award would help them achieve their goals, how they will be financing their college education, and why they feel they should be considered for an award.

Financial data A stipend is awarded (amount not specified).

Duration 1 year.

Additional data This program was established in 1993. The Connecticut Institute for the Blind, doing business as Oak Hill, also operates independent living facilities in West Hartford and Wethersfield for blind, visually impaired, and disabled individuals.

Number awarded 1 or more each year.

Deadline December of each year.

[50]
JOHN FREEBAIRN SCHOLARSHIP

Utah Council of the Blind
c/o Leslie Gertsch, Executive Director
1301 West 500 South
Woods Cross, UT 84087-2224
(801) 292-1156   Fax: (801) 292-6046
E-mail: lgertsch@comcast.net
Web: www.acb.org/utah

Summary To provide financial assistance to members of the Utah Council of the Blind (UCB) who plan to attend college or graduate school in the state.

Eligibility This program is open to UCB members who are entering or enrolled as an undergraduate or graduate student at a college or university in Utah. Applicants must be blind or visually impaired, defined as having a visual acuity of less than 20/70, a visual field not exceeding 30 degrees, or a functional visual impairment of similar degree in the best eye with best correction. Along with their application, they must submit an autobiographical sketch that includes their personal goals, strengths, weaknesses, hobbies, honors, achievements, the course of study they are pursuing, and why they have chosen it. Financial need is not considered in the selection process. Interviews may be held.

Financial data The stipend is $1,500.

Duration 1 year; may be renewed.

Number awarded 1 each year.

Deadline April of each year.

[51]
JOHN T. MCCRAW SCHOLARSHIPS

National Federation of the Blind of Maryland
c/o Melissa Riccobono, President
1026 East 36th Street
Baltimore, MD 21218
(410) 235-3073   E-mail: president@nfbmd.org
Web: www.nfbmd.org/students.html

Summary To provide financial assistance for college to blind students from Maryland.

Eligibility This program is open to legally blind students who are residents of Maryland or enrolled full time at a university, 2- or 4-year college, or vocational/technical school in the state. Applicants must be able to demonstrate potential for sustained superior academic performance and promise of exceptional career development. Along with their application, they must submit 2 letters of recommendation, a current transcript, and a statement that describes the honors they have received, what they have done to deal with situations involving their blindness, what they are like as a person, their goals and aspirations, and how this scholarship will help them.

Financial data The stipend is either $2,000 or $1,500.

Duration 1 year; recipients may reapply.

Additional data A special scholarship may be awarded to former McCraw Scholarship recipients. To apply for this special scholarship, former recipients must still meet all of the requirements for the scholarship program and submit a new application. Recipients must attend the sponsor's annual convention; financial assistance to attend the convention may be provided if the recipient needs and requests it (this is in addition to the scholarship grant).

Number awarded 2 each year: 1 at $2,000 and 1 at $1,500.

Deadline April of each year.

[52]
JUDY VAN NOSTRAND ARTS AWARD

Lighthouse International
Attn: Scholarship and Career Awards
111 East 59th Street
New York, NY 10022-1202
(212) 821-9428   Toll Free: (800) 829-0500
Fax: (212) 821-9703   TDD: (212) 821-9713
E-mail: sca@lighthouse.org
Web: www.lighthouse.org

Summary To provide financial assistance to legally blind high school seniors in selected eastern states who plan to attend college in those states and major in the arts.

Eligibility This program is open to high school seniors or recent high school graduates now planning to begin college who are legally blind and U.S. citizens. Applicants must be residents of Connecticut, Delaware, Florida, Georgia, Maine, Maryland, Massachusetts, New Hampshire, New Jersey, New York, North Carolina, Pennsylvania, Rhode Island, South Carolina, Vermont, Virginia, Washington, D.C., or West Virginia and planning to attend school in those states. They must be planning to major in a field related to the arts. Along with their application, they must submit a 500-word essay, describing their academic achievements and career goals. Financial need is not considered in the selection process.

Financial data   The stipend is $5,000.

Duration   1 year.

Number awarded   1 each year.

Deadline   February of each year.

[53]
KELLIE CANNON MEMORIAL SCHOLARSHIP

American Council of the Blind
Attn: Coordinator, Scholarship Program
2200 Wilson Boulevard, Suite 650
Arlington, VA 22201
(202) 467-5081   Toll Free: (800) 424-8666
Fax: (703) 465-5085   E-mail: info@acb.org
Web: www.acb.org

Summary   To provide financial assistance to students who are blind and interested in preparing for a career in the computer field.

Eligibility   This program is open to high school seniors, high school graduates, and college students who are blind and interested in majoring in computer information systems or data processing. Applicants must submit verification of legal blindness in both eyes; SAT or ACT scores; information on extracurricular activities (including membership in the American Council of the Blind); employment record; and an autobiographical sketch that includes their personal goals, strengths, weaknesses, hobbies, honors, achievements, and reasons for choice of field or courses of study. A cumulative GPA of 3.3 or higher is generally required. Financial need is not considered in the selection process, but the severity of the applicant's visual impairment and his/her study methods are taken into account.

Financial data   The stipend is $1,000. In addition, the winner receives a Kurzweil-1000 Reading System.

Duration   1 year.

Additional data   This program is sponsored by Blind Information Technology Specialist (BITS), Inc, a special interest affiliate of the American Council of the Blind. The scholarship winner is expected to be present at the council's annual national convention; the council will cover all reasonable costs connected with convention attendance.

Number awarded   1 each year.

Deadline   February of each year.

[54]
KENNETH JERNIGAN SCHOLARSHIP

National Federation of the Blind
Attn: Scholarship Committee
1800 Johnson Street
Baltimore, MD 21230
(410) 659-9314, ext. 2415   Fax: (410) 685-5653
E-mail: scholarships@nfb.org
Web: www.nfb.org/nfb/scholarship_program.asp

Summary   To provide financial assistance to entering or continuing undergraduate and graduate blind students.

Eligibility   This program is open to legally blind students who are working on or planning to work full time on an undergraduate or graduate degree. Along with their application, they must submit transcripts, standardized test scores, proof of legal blindness, 2 letters of recommendation, and a letter of endorsement from their National Federation of the Blind state president or designee. Selection is based on academic excellence, service to the community, and financial need.

Financial data   The stipend is $12,000.

Duration   1 year; recipients may resubmit applications up to 2 additional years.

Additional data   Scholarships are awarded at the federation convention in July. Recipients must attend the convention at federation expense; that funding is in addition to the scholarship grant. This scholarship is given by the American Action Fund for Blind Children and Adults, a nonprofit organization that assists blind people.

Number awarded   1 each year.

Deadline   March of each year.

[55]
KUCHLER-KILLIAN MEMORIAL SCHOLARSHIP

National Federation of the Blind
Attn: Scholarship Committee
1800 Johnson Street
Baltimore, MD 21230
(410) 659-9314, ext. 2415   Fax: (410) 685-5653
E-mail: scholarships@nfb.org
Web: www.nfb.org/nfb/scholarship_program.asp

Summary   To provide financial assistance to blind students working on an undergraduate or graduate degree in any field.

Eligibility   This program is open to legally blind students who are working on or planning to work full time on an undergraduate or graduate degree in any field. Along with their application, they must submit transcripts, standardized test scores, proof of legal blindness, 2 letters of recommendation, and a letter of endorsement from their National Federation of the Blind state president or designee. Selection is based on academic excellence, service to the community, and financial need.

Financial data   The stipend is $3,000.

Duration   1 year; recipients may resubmit applications up to 2 additional years.

Additional data   Scholarships are awarded at the federation convention in July. Recipients must attend the convention at federation expense; that funding is in addition to the scholarship grant.

Number awarded   1 each year.

Deadline   March of each year.

[56]
LANCASTER SCHOLARSHIP

Susquehanna Foundation for the Blind
244 North Queen Street, Suite 301
Lancaster, PA 17603
(717) 393-5894   Fax: (717) 435-8367
E-mail: Info@sfblind.org
Web: sfblind.com/Content/scholarships.asp

Summary To provide financial assistance to Pennsylvania residents who are legally blind veterans and interested in working on a degree at any level at a college in any state.
Eligibility This program is open to veterans who are residents of Pennsylvania and legally blind. Applicants must be attending or planning to attend an institution of higher education at any level in any state. Along with their application, they must submit a brief description of their career goal. Financial need is considered in the selection process.
Financial data The stipend is $1,000 per year.
Duration 1 year; may be renewed up to 3 additional years.
Number awarded 1 or more each year.
Deadline Deadline not specified.

[57]
LIGHTHOUSE INTERNATIONAL COLLEGE-BOUND AWARD

Lighthouse International
Attn: Scholarship and Career Awards
111 East 59th Street
New York, NY 10022-1202
(212) 821-9428   Toll Free: (800) 829-0500
Fax: (212) 821-9703   TDD: (212) 821-9713
E-mail: sca@lighthouse.org
Web: www.lighthouse.org

Summary To provide financial assistance to legally blind high school seniors in selected eastern states who plan to attend college in those states.
Eligibility This program is open to high school seniors or recent high school graduates now planning to begin college who are legally blind and U.S. citizens. Applicants must be residents of Connecticut, Delaware, Florida, Georgia, Maine, Maryland, Massachusetts, New Hampshire, New Jersey, New York, North Carolina, Pennsylvania, Rhode Island, South Carolina, Vermont, Virginia, Washington, D.C., or West Virginia and planning to attend school in those states. Along with their application, they must submit a 500-word essay describing their academic achievements and career goals. Financial need is not considered in the selection process.
Financial data The stipend is $5,000.
Duration 1 year.
Number awarded 1 each year.
Deadline February of each year.

[58]
LIGHTHOUSE INTERNATIONAL UNDERGRADUATE AWARD

Lighthouse International
Attn: Scholarship and Career Awards
111 East 59th Street
New York, NY 10022-1202
(212) 821-9428   Toll Free: (800) 829-0500
Fax: (212) 821-9703   TDD: (212) 821-9713
E-mail: sca@lighthouse.org
Web: www.lighthouse.org

Summary To provide financial assistance to legally blind undergraduate students residing and attending school in designated eastern states.
Eligibility This program is open to legally blind U.S. citizens who are residents of Connecticut, Delaware, Florida, Georgia, Maine, Maryland, Massachusetts, New Hampshire, New Jersey, New York, North Carolina, Pennsylvania, Rhode Island, South Carolina, Vermont, Virginia, Washington, D.C., or West Virginia. Applicants must be working on an undergraduate degree at a school in those states. Along with their application, they must submit a 500-word essay describing their academic achievements and career goals. Financial need is not considered in the selection process.
Financial data The stipend is $5,000.
Duration 1 year.
Number awarded 1 each year.
Deadline February of each year.

[59]
MARY ZOE ALLEE SCHOLARSHIP

Wyoming Council of the Blind
c/o Betty Matthews
374 West Alger, Apartment A
Sheridan, WY 82801
E-mail: abbietaylor501@msn.com
Web: www.wycb.info

Summary To provide financial assistance to blind residents of Wyoming who are interested in attending college or graduate school in any state.
Eligibility This program is open to residents of Wyoming who are legally blind or visually impaired. Applicants must be entering or enrolled at a vocational training program, college, university, community college, or graduate school in any state. Along with their application, they must submit a 2-page autobiographical sketch that includes their goals, strengths, weaknesses, hobbies, honors, achievements, the field of study they have chosen, and the reason why they have chosen it. Financial need is not considered in the selection process. Leading candidates are interviewed.
Financial data The stipend is $1,000.
Duration 1 year.
Number awarded 1 each year.
Deadline April of each year.

[60]
MASSACHUSETTS REHABILITATION COMMISSION OR COMMISSION FOR THE BLIND TUITION WAIVER PROGRAM

Massachusetts Office of Student Financial Assistance
454 Broadway, Suite 200
Revere, MA 02151
(617) 727-9420   Fax: (617) 727-0667
E-mail: osfa@osfa.mass.edu
Web: www.osfa.mass.edu

Summary To provide financial assistance for college to Massachusetts residents who are clients of specified state disability agencies.

Eligibility Applicants for this assistance must be certified as clients by the Massachusetts Rehabilitation Commission or Commission for the Blind. They must have been permanent residents of Massachusetts for at least 1 year, must be U.S. citizens or permanent residents, and may not be in default on any federal student loan.

Financial data Eligible clients are exempt from any tuition payments for an undergraduate degree or certificate program at public colleges or universities in Massachusetts.

Duration Up to 4 academic years, for a total of 130 semester hours.

Additional data Recipients may enroll either part or full time in a Massachusetts publicly-supported institution.

Number awarded Varies each year.

Deadline Deadline not specified.

[61]
MAX EDELMAN SCHOLARSHIP

American Council of the Blind of Ohio
Attn: Executive Director
P.O. Box 307128
Gahanna, OH 43230-7128
(614) 221-6688 Toll Free: (800) 835-2226 (within OH)
E-mail: mary.hiland@sbcglobal.net
Web: www.acbohio.org/application_cur.php

Summary To provide financial assistance to entering or continuing undergraduate students in Ohio who are blind.

Eligibility This program is open to 1) residents of Ohio who are high school seniors or current college students, and 2) students at colleges and universities in Ohio. Applicants must be legally blind and working on or planning to work on an undergraduate degree in any field. Along with their application, they must submit transcripts (must have a GPA of 3.0 or higher), a certificate of legal blindness, and an essay of 250 to 500 words on their career objectives, future plans, personal goals, other academic or personal qualities, and why they believe they are qualified to receive this scholarship. Financial need is not the only factor considered in the selection process.

Financial data The stipend is $2,000 per year.

Duration 1 year; recipients may reapply.

Additional data Winners are required to attend the Saturday morning business meeting and Sunday breakfast of the sponsor's annual convention; a stipend for meals and workshops is provided.

Number awarded 1 each year.

Deadline July of each year.

[62]
MCGREGOR SCHOLARSHIP PROGRAM

Iowa Braille School
Attn: Scholarship Committee
1002 G Avenue
Vinton, IA 52349
(319) 472-5221, ext. 1105 Fax: (319) 472-4371
E-mail: mcgregorscholar@iowa-braille.k12.ia.us
Web: www.iowa-braille.k12.ia.us

Summary To provide financial assistance for college to Iowa residents who are blind.

Eligibility This program is open to residents of Iowa who became blind or visually impaired prior to reaching the age of 21. Applicants must be graduating high school seniors, high school graduates, or GED recipients who are within 8 years of high school graduation or receipt of the GED. They must be attending or planning to attend an accredited college, university, or vocational school within the United States as a full-time student. Along with their application, they must submit an autobiographical sketch (from 300 to 500 words) that includes a statement of their goals and how this scholarship will help them achieve those goals.

Financial data The stipend is $2,500 per year.

Duration 1 year; may be renewed if the recipient maintains a GPA of 2.5 or higher.

Additional data Information on this program is available from the Teachers of the Visually Impaired throughout Iowa, the Iowa Department for the Blind, and the Iowa Braille School.

Number awarded Varies each year; recently, 7 of these scholarships were awarded.

Deadline April of each year.

[63]
MICHAEL J. MCGOWAN LEADERSHIP SCHOLARSHIP AWARD

National Organization for Albinism and
Hypopigmentation
Attn: Scholarship Committee
P.O. Box 959
East Hampstead, NH 03826-0959
(603) 887-2310 Toll Free: (800) 473-2310
Fax: (800) 648-2310
E-mail: scholarship@albinism.org
Web: www.albinism.org/noahprojects.html

Summary To provide financial assistance to undergraduate students with albinism.

Eligibility This program is open to students with albinism who are enrolled or planning to enroll in an undergraduate program at an institution of higher education. Applicants must submit a 500-word essay on their leadership potential, extracurricular involvement, academic achievement, educational background, and vocational goals; an eye report documenting a diagnosis of albinism; at least 2 letters of recommendation; an academic transcript (including SAT/ACT scores, if applicable); and a letter of acceptance of proof of enrollment from an institution of higher learning.

Financial data The stipend is $5,000.

Duration 1 year.

Additional data This program was established in 2008. Albinism is a condition that frequently leads to vision difficulties.

Number awarded 1 each year.

Deadline April of each year.

[64]
MID-TENNESSEE COUNCIL OF THE BLIND SCHOLARSHIPS

Mid-Tennessee Council of the Blind
3201 Aspen Grove Drive, M10
Franklin, TN 37067
(615) 227-1941
Web: www.acb.org/Tennessee/index.html

Summary   To provide financial assistance to blind students in Tennessee who are interested in attending college in the state.

Eligibility   This program is open to residents of Tennessee who are legally blind in both eyes. Applicants must have completed at least 1 semester of college or vocational instruction at a state-approved school in Tennessee. They must have a GPA of 2.5 or higher. Most scholarships require full-time enrollment, although 1 is reserved for a student who is working full time and attending school part time.

Financial data   The stipend is $1,000.

Duration   1 year.

Number awarded   1 or more each year.

Deadline   June of each year.

[65]
MISSOURI COUNCIL OF THE BLIND SCHOLARSHIPS

Missouri Council of the Blind
5453 Chippewa Street
St. Louis, MO 63109-1635
(314) 832-7172   Toll Free: (800) 342-5632 (within MO)
Fax: (314) 832-7796
E-mail: executivedirector@missouricounciloftheblind.
  org
Web: www.missouricounciloftheblind.org

Summary   To provide financial assistance for college or graduate school to blind students in Missouri.

Eligibility   This program is open to Missouri residents who are high school or college graduates, legally blind, and in good academic standing. Applicants must be working on or planning to work on an undergraduate or graduate degree. They should have a specific goal in mind and that goal should be realistically within reach.

Financial data   The stipend is $1,200.

Duration   1 year; may be renewed if the recipient maintains a GPA of 2.0 or higher.

Number awarded   Varies each year; recently, 14 of these scholarships were awarded.

Deadline   May of each year.

[66]
MISSOURI REHABILITATION SERVICES FOR THE BLIND

Missouri Department of Social Services
Attn: Family Support Division
615 Howerton Court
P.O. Box 2320
Jefferson City, MO 65102-2320
(573) 751-4249   Fax: (573) 751-4984
TDD: (800) 735-2966
Web: www.dss.mo.gov/fsd/rsb/index.htm

Summary   To provide support to blind and visually impaired residents of Missouri who are engaged in rehabilitation training, including enrollment at a college or university.

Eligibility   This program is open to residents of Missouri who qualify as visually impaired, ranging from those who cannot read regular print to those who are totally blind. Applicants must be engaged in a program of vocational rehabilitation, including full-time enrollment at a college or university in Missouri or another state.

Financial data   A range of support services are available. For college and university students, that includes transportation; housing and maintenance (up to the cost of double occupancy dormitory charges at the University of Missouri at Columbia); books, equipment, tools, and supplies; reader service; and interpreter service for deaf-blind persons.

Duration   Qualified blind people are eligible for this assistance as long as they are attending college.

Number awarded   Varies each year.

Deadline   Deadline not specified.

[67]
MOUSE HOLE SCHOLARSHIPS

Blind Mice Mart
16810 Pinemoor Way
Houston, TX 77058
(713) 883-7277   E-mail: blindmicemart@att.net
Web: www.blindmicemart.com

Summary   To provide financial assistance for college to blind students and the children of blind parents.

Eligibility   This program is open to visually impaired students and to sighted students who have visually impaired parents. Applicants must be high school seniors or graduates who have never been enrolled in college. Along with their application, they must submit an essay, between 3 and 15 pages in length, on a topic that changes annually; recently, students were asked to speculate on what will be happening to them in the following 10 years. Essays are judged on originality, creativity, grammar, spelling, and the judge's overall impression of the applicant.

Financial data   The maximum stipend is $1,250.

Duration   1 year.

Additional data   These scholarships were first awarded in 2003.

Number awarded   Varies each year; the program attempts to award 2 scholarships at $1,250 and others depending on the availability of funds. Recently, a total of $4,250 in scholarships were awarded.

Deadline May of each year.

[68]
NATIONAL FEDERATION OF THE BLIND OF CALIFORNIA SCHOLARSHIPS

National Federation of the Blind of California
c/o Mary Willows, President
39481 Gallaudet Drive, Apartment 127
Fremont, CA 94538
(510) 248-0100   Toll Free: (877) 558-6524
E-mail: mwillows@sbcglobal.net
Web: www.nfbcal.org/nfbc/scholarships.html

Summary To provide financial assistance to blind residents of California interested in attending college or graduate school in any state.

Eligibility This program is open to residents of California who are legally blind. Applicants must be enrolled or planning to enroll as a full time student in an undergraduate or graduate degree program in any state. They must have a GPA of 3.0 or higher. Along with their application, they must submit a 500-word statement on the educational and career goals they wish to achieve with the assistance of this scholarship, their involvement in the blindness community, the alternative techniques they use to do their school work (e.g., Braille, large print, recording, adapted computer), and any rehabilitation services they are receiving. Financial need is not considered in the selection process.

Financial data Stipends range from $2,000 to $5,000.

Duration 1 year.

Additional data This program includes the following named awards: the Gerald Drake Memorial Scholarship, the LaVyrl "Pinky" Johnson Memorial Scholarship, the Julie Landucci Scholarship, and the Lawrence "Muzzy" Marcelino Memorial Scholarship.

Number awarded Several each year.

Deadline August of each year.

[69]
NATIONAL FEDERATION OF THE BLIND OF COLORADO SCHOLARSHIP

National Federation of the Blind of Colorado
c/o Colorado Center for the Blind
2233 West Shepperd Avenue
Littleton, CO 80120-2038
(303) 778-1130   Toll Free: (800) 401-4NFB
Fax: (303) 778-1598   E-mail: nfbco@nfbco.org
Web: www.nfbco.org/nfbcoscholarships.html

Summary To provide financial assistance for college to visually impaired students in Colorado.

Eligibility This program is open to legally blind residents of Colorado who are enrolled or planning to enroll as a full-time student at a college or university in the state (except for 1 scholarship reserved for an applicant who is employed full time and studying part time). Applicants must submit 2 letters of recommendation, current transcripts, a personal letter that describes their best qualities,

and a letter from a state officer of the National Federation of the Blind of Colorado indicating that they have discussed their scholarship application with that officer. Selection is based on academic excellence, service to the community, and financial need.

Financial data The stipend ranges from $800 to $6,000.

Duration 1 year; recipients may reapply.

Number awarded Varies each year; a total of $15,000 is available for this program annually.

Deadline April of each year.

[70]
NATIONAL FEDERATION OF THE BLIND OF CONNECTICUT SCHOLARSHIPS

National Federation of the Blind of Connecticut
477 Connecticut Boulevard, Suite 217
East Hartford, CT 06108
(860) 289-1971   E-mail: info@nfbct.org
Web: www.nfbct.org/html/schform.htm

Summary To provide financial assistance for college or graduate school to blind students from Connecticut.

Eligibility This program is open to full-time undergraduate and graduate students who are legally blind. Applicants must be residents of Connecticut or attending school in the state. Along with their application, they must submit 2 letters of recommendation, academic transcripts, a description of their career goals and how this scholarship might help them achieve those, and a letter from a state officer of the National Federation of the Blind of Connecticut confirming that they have discussed their application with him or her. Selection is based on academic excellence, service to the community, and financial need.

Financial data Stipends are $8,000, $4,000, or $3,000.

Duration 1 year.

Additional data This program consists of the following named awards: the C. Rodney Demarest Memorial Scholarship ($3,000), the Howard E. May Memorial Scholarship ($6,000), the Jonathan May Memorial Scholarship ($5,000), and the Mary Main Memorial Scholarship ($4,000). The latter 3 programs are supported by the John A. Coccomo, Sr. Foundation. Recipients are expected to attend the annual convention of the National Federation of the Blind of Connecticut.

Number awarded 4 each year.

Deadline September of each year.

[71]
NATIONAL FEDERATION OF THE BLIND OF FLORIDA SCHOLARSHIPS

National Federation of the Blind of Florida
c/o Richard Brown, Scholarship Chair
4617 Casswell Drive
New Port Richey, FL 34653
(386) 481-4418   E-mail: nfbfscholarships@gmail.com
Web: www.nfbflorida.org

Summary To provide financial assistance to legally blind residents of Florida who are attending college in any state.

Eligibility This program is open to legally blind residents of Florida who are high school seniors or college students. Applicants must be attending or planning to attend college in any state. They must have a GPA of 2.7 or higher. Along with their application, they must submit an essay on why they believe they should be selected as a winner of this scholarship, including accomplishments and aspects of their personality that the committee should consider. Financial need is not considered in the selection process.

Financial data Stipends range from $1,250 to $2,000.

Duration 1 year.

Additional data Winners are provided with ground transportation, registration, banquet fees, room, and board at the state federation's annual conference.

Number awarded 4 each year: 1 at $2,000, 1 at $1,500, and 2 at $1,250.

Deadline April of each year.

[72]
NATIONAL FEDERATION OF THE BLIND OF IDAHO SCHOLARSHIPS

National Federation of the Blind of Idaho
c/o Elsie Lamp, President
300 Willard Avenue
Pocatello, ID 83201
(208) 233-5833   Fax: (208) 232-5416
E-mail: ElsieLamp@yahoo.com
Web: www.nfbidaho.org/education/old/scholorship.htm

Summary To provide financial assistance for college to blind residents of Idaho.

Eligibility This program is open to blind residents of Idaho who are enrolled or planning to enroll in college. Selection is based on academic achievement, community service, and financial need.

Financial data Stipends are either $1,000 or $500.

Duration 1 year.

Additional data The $1,000 scholarship is sponsored by Weyerhaeuser Foundation.

Number awarded 2 each year: 1 at $1,000 and 1 at $500.

Deadline March of each year.

[73]
NATIONAL FEDERATION OF THE BLIND OF ILLINOIS SCHOLARSHIPS

National Federation of the Blind of Illinois
c/o Deborah Kent Stein, Scholarship Committee Chair
5817 North Nina Avenue
Chicago, IL 60631
(773) 631-1093   E-mail: dkent5817@worldnet.att.net
Web: www.nfbofillinois.org/NFBIscholarship.htm

Summary To provide financial assistance for college or graduate school to blind students in Illinois.

Eligibility This program is open to legally blind full-time undergraduate and graduate students. Applicants must be residents of Illinois or attending a college or university in the state. Along with their application, they must submit a personal essay that includes their strengths, achievements, and aspirations; what is important to them; who

they hope to become; if a particular person or experience has changed their life; how their blindness has affected them; and how they handle blindness at school, on the job, and in interpersonal relationships. Selection is based on academic excellence, service to the community, and financial need.

Financial data Stipends range from $1,250 to $2,000 per year.

Duration 1 year; recipients may reapply.

Additional data This program consists of the following named awards: the Peter Grunwald Scholarship (1 awarded at $2,000), the Mary MacDill Napheide Scholarships (2 awarded at $1,500 each), and the Kenneth Jernigan Scholarships (2 awarded at $1,250 each).

Number awarded 5 each year.

Deadline March of each year.

[74]
NATIONAL FEDERATION OF THE BLIND OF MINNESOTA SCHOLARSHIP

National Federation of the Blind of Minnesota
c/o Jennifer Dunnam, President
100 East 22nd Street
Minneapolis, MN 55404
(612) 929-2353 E-mail: jennifer.dunnam@earthlink.net
Web: members.tcq.net/nfbmn/students/scholarship.htm

Summary To provide financial assistance to blind residents of Minnesota who are interested in attending college in the state.

Eligibility This program is open to residents of Minnesota who are blind or visually impaired. Applicants must be attending or planning to attend a college, university, or technical school in the state. Along with their application, they must submit a personal letter on their goals and academic and community activities, official transcripts, and 2 letters of recommendation. Selection is based on scholastic excellence and community and campus service.

Financial data The stipend is $1,500.

Duration 1 year.

Additional data The recipient must attend the annual convention of the National Federation of the Blind of Minnesota; all expenses are paid.

Number awarded 1 each year.

Deadline June of each year.

[75]
NATIONAL FEDERATION OF THE BLIND OF NEBRASKA SCHOLARSHIP

National Federation of the Blind of Nebraska
c/o Shane Buresh, Scholarship Committee Chair
6210 Walker Avenue
Lincoln, NE 68507-2468
(402) 465-5468   E-mail: scholarship@ne.nfb.org
Web: www.ne.nfb.org/node/1849

Summary To provide financial assistance to blind residents of Nebraska who plan to attend college in any state.

Eligibility This program is open to residents of Nebraska who are blind and attending or planning to attend a postsecondary institution in any state. Applicants must submit a letter that describes their educational plans, vocational goals, and awards. Their letter should also explain how they deal with situations involving their blindness and how the scholarship will help them.

Financial data The maximum stipend is $1,000.

Duration 1 year.

Number awarded 5 each year: the National Federation of the Blind of Nebraska awards 1 scholarship at $1,000 and other scholarships are presented by its Lincoln and Omaha chapters and by the Nebraska Association of Blind Students.

Deadline September of each year.

[76]
NATIONAL FEDERATION OF THE BLIND OF OHIO SCHOLARSHIP

National Federation of the Blind of Ohio
c/o Barbara Pierce, Scholarship Committee Chair
237 Oak Street
Oberlin, OH 44074-1517
(440) 775-2216   E-mail: bpierce@nfb.org
Web: www.nfbohio.org

Summary To provide financial assistance to blind residents of Ohio who are interested in working on an undergraduate or graduate degree at a school in any state.

Eligibility This program is open to residents of Ohio who are legally blind. Applicants must be attending or planning to attend an accredited institution of higher education as a full-time undergraduate or graduate student. Along with their application, they must submit 2 letters of recommendation, current transcripts, a letter about themselves that includes how they have dealt with their blindness and their hopes and dreams, and a letter from an officer of the National Federation of the Blind of Ohio indicating that they have discussed their scholarship application with that officer. Selection is based on academic excellence, community service, and financial need.

Financial data The stipend is $1,000.

Duration 1 year.

Number awarded 1 each year.

Deadline April of each year.

[77]
NATIONAL FEDERATION OF THE BLIND OF OREGON SCHOLARSHIPS

National Federation of the Blind of Oregon
c/o Art Stevenson, President
1616 Fifth Street N.E.
Salem, OR 97303
(503) 585-4318   Toll Free: (800) 422-7093 (within OR)
E-mail: artds55@comcast.net
Web: www.nfb-oregon.org/scholarship.html

Summary To provide financial assistance for college or graduate school to blind residents of Oregon.

Eligibility This program is open to blind residents of Oregon who are working on or planning to work on an undergraduate or graduate degree at a college or university in the state. Applicants must be enrolled full time or enrolled part time and working full time. Along with the

application, they must submit a personal letter that includes what they consider their best qualities and the techniques and approaches they practice concerning their blindness. Selection is based on academic excellence, community service, and financial need.

Financial data Stipends are either $1,500 or $1,000.

Duration 1 year.

Number awarded 3 each year: 1 at $1,500 and 2 at $1,000.

Deadline September of each year.

[78]
NATIONAL FEDERATION OF THE BLIND OF PENNSYLVANIA SCHOLARSHIPS

National Federation of the Blind of Pennsylvania
Attn: Scholarship Committee
42 South 15th Street, Suite 222
Philadelphia, PA 19102
(215) 988-0888   E-mail: avb5073@psu.edu
Web: www.nfbp.org/students

Summary To provide financial assistance to blind residents of Pennsylvania who are interested in attending college in any state.

Eligibility This program is open to residents of Pennsylvania who are legally blind. Applicants must be enrolled or planning to enroll full time at a college or university in any state. Along with their application, they must submit a personal letter about themselves, especially the techniques and approaches they use to complete their education. Selection is based on academic excellence, community service, and financial need.

Financial data The stipend is $1,000.

Duration 1 year.

Number awarded 2 each year.

Deadline August of each year.

[79]
NATIONAL FEDERATION OF THE BLIND OF TEXAS MERIT SCHOLARSHIPS

National Federation of the Blind of Texas
Attn: Scholarship Committee
314 East Highland Mall Boulevard, Suite 253
Austin, TX 78752
(512) 323-5444   Toll Free: (866) 636-3289
Fax: (512) 420-8160
E-mail: scholarship@nfb-texas.org.
Web: www.nfb-texas.org

Summary To provide financial assistance to blind residents of Texas who are interested in attending college in any state.

Eligibility This program is open to blind residents of Texas who are enrolled or planning to enroll full time at a college or university in any state. Applicants must submit proof of legal blindness, a current transcript, a 2-page personal letter, and 2 letters of recommendation. Selection is based on academic excellence, community service, and financial need.

Financial data Stipends are $1,500 or $1,000 per year.

Duration 1 year; recipients may reapply.

Additional data This program includes 1 scholarship sponsored by the Houston chapter of the National Federation of the Blind of Texas.

Number awarded 3 each year: 1 at $1,500 and 2 at $1,000.

Deadline August of each year.

[80]
NATIONAL FEDERATION OF THE BLIND OF UTAH SCHOLARSHIPS

National Federation of the Blind of Utah
Attn: Scholarship Committee
132 Penman Lane
Bountiful, UT 84010-7634
(801) 292-3000   Toll Free: (888) 292-3007
E-mail: president@nfbutah.org
Web: nfbutah.org/scholarships

Summary To provide financial assistance to blind residents of Utah who plan to attend college or graduate school in any state.

Eligibility This program is open to legally blind residents of Utah who are working on or planning to work full time on an undergraduate or graduate degree at a school in any state. Along with their application, they must submit transcripts, standardized test scores, proof of legal blindness, 2 letters of recommendation, and a letter of endorsement from an officer of the National Federation of the Blind of Utah. Selection is based on academic excellence, service to the community, and financial need.

Financial data A stipend is awarded (amount not specified).

Duration 1 year.

Number awarded Varies each year.

Deadline March of each year.

[81]
NATIONAL FEDERATION OF THE BLIND OF VIRGINIA SCHOLARSHIPS

National Federation of the Blind of Virginia
c/o Mark Roane, Scholarship Committee Chair
702-5 Prince Edward Street
Fredericksburg, VA 22401
(540) 373-3045   E-mail: mwroane@mindspring.com
Web: www.nfbv.org

Summary To provide financial assistance to blind residents of Virginia who are interested in attending college in any state.

Eligibility This program is open to blind residents of Virginia who are graduating high school students or current college students. Applicants must be attending or planning to attend a college or university in any state. Along with their application, they must submit a 100-word essay on their most notable quality, their attitude about blindness, how they have demonstrated leadership ability, and what the selection committee needs to know about them as a blind person. Selection is based on academic excellence and community service.

Financial data A stipend is awarded (amount not specified).

Duration 1 year.

Number awarded Varies each year.

Deadline September of each year.

[82]
NATIONAL FEDERATION OF THE BLIND OF WISCONSIN SCHOLARSHIP

National Federation of the Blind of Wisconsin
c/o Cheryl Orgas, Scholarship Coordinator
4222 North Maryland Avenue
Shorewood, WI 53211
(414) 964-7995   E-mail: meekerorgas@ameritech.net.
Web: www.nfbwis.org

Summary To provide financial assistance to blind residents of Wisconsin who are interested in attending college in any state.

Eligibility This program is open to blind residents of Wisconsin who are attending or planning to attend a college or university in any state. Applicants must submit a statement detailing their strengths, personal challenges, goals, and ways of working with their blindness. They must also describe their financial need. Selection is based on academic excellence, personal achievement, and community service.

Financial data The stipend is $1,500.

Duration 1 year.

Additional data The recipient must attend both state and national conventions of the National Federation of the Blind in their entirety. Transportation, hotel accommodations, and meals are provided for the 3-day state convention and the 1-week national convention.

Number awarded 1 each year.

Deadline February of each year.

[83]
NAVY SUPPLY CORPS FOUNDATION NIB/NISH SCHOLARSHIPS

Navy Supply Corps Foundation
c/o CDR Jack Evans (ret), Chief Staff Officer
1425 Prince Avenue
Athens, GA 30606-2205
(706) 354-4111   Fax: (706) 354-0334
E-mail: foundation@usnscf.com
Web: www.usnscf.com/programs/scholarships.aspx

Summary To provide financial assistance for college to blind or disabled relatives of current or former Navy Supply Corps personnel.

Eligibility This program is open to dependents (child, grandchild, or spouse) of a living or deceased regular, retired, reserve, or prior Navy Supply Corps officer, warrant officer, or enlister personnel. Enlisted ratings that apply are AK (Aviation Storekeeper), SK (Storekeeper), MS (Mess Specialist), DK (Disbursing Clerk), SH (Ship Serviceman), LI (Lithographer), and PC (Postal Clerk). Applicants must be attending or planning to attend a 2-year or 4-year accredited college on a full-time basis and have a GPA of 2.5 or higher in high school and/or college.

They must be able to document blindness or severe disability. Selection is based on character, leadership, academic achievement, extracurricular activities, and financial need.

Financial data Stipends range from $1,000 to $5,000.

Duration 1 year.

Additional data This program was established in 2005 with support from National Industries for the Blind (NIB) and NISH (formerly the National Industries for the Severely Handicapped).

Number awarded 1 or more each year.

Deadline March of each year.

[84]
NDABF EMMA SKOGEN SCHOLARSHIP

North Dakota Association of the Blind
c/o Tammy Winn, Scholarship Committee Chair
103 Lilac Lane, Number 2
Minot AFB, ND 58704
(701) 727-9211   E-mail: roytammy@srt.com
Web: www.ndab.org/Skogen.htm

Summary To provide financial assistance for vocational school to blind students in North Dakota.

Eligibility This program is open to North Dakota residents who are blind or visually impaired and attending a vocational or trade school. Applicants must provide information on what they plan to study, where, and when; their long-term career goals; and their financial need. Selection is based on clarity of study plan, long-term career goals, GPA, letter of recommendation, extracurricular involvements, and financial need.

Financial data The stipend is $1,000.

Duration 1 year.

Additional data This program was established in 2004.

Number awarded 1 each year.

Deadline March of each year.

[85]
NFB EDUCATOR OF TOMORROW AWARD

National Federation of the Blind
Attn: Scholarship Committee
1800 Johnson Street
Baltimore, MD 21230
(410) 659-9314, ext. 2415   Fax: (410) 685-5653
E-mail: scholarships@nfb.org
Web: www.nfb.org/nfb/scholarship_program.asp

Summary To provide financial assistance to entering or continuing blind undergraduate or graduate students who wish to prepare for a career as a teacher.

Eligibility This program is open to legally blind students who are working on or planning to work full time on an undergraduate or graduate degree. Applicants must be preparing for a career in elementary, secondary, or post-secondary teaching. Along with their application, they must submit transcripts, standardized test scores, proof of legal blindness, 2 letters of recommendation, and a letter of endorsement from their National Federation of the Blind state president or designee. Selection is based on aca-

demic excellence, service to the community, and financial need.

Financial data The stipend is $3,000.

Duration 1 year; recipients may resubmit applications up to 2 additional years.

Additional data Scholarships are awarded at the federation convention in July. Recipients must attend the convention at federation expense; that funding is in addition to the scholarship grant.

Number awarded 1 each year.

Deadline March of each year.

[86]
NFB SCHOLARSHIPS

National Federation of the Blind
Attn: Scholarship Committee
1800 Johnson Street
Baltimore, MD 21230
(410) 659-9314, ext. 2415   Fax: (410) 685-5653
E-mail: scholarships@nfb.org
Web: www.nfb.org/nfb/scholarship_program.asp

Summary To provide financial assistance for college or graduate school to blind students.

Eligibility This program is open to legally blind students who are working on or planning to work on an undergraduate or graduate degree. In general, full-time enrollment is required, although 1 scholarship may be awarded to a part-time student who is working full time. Along with their application, they must submit transcripts, standardized test scores, proof of legal blindness, 2 letters of recommendation, and a letter of endorsement from their National Federation of the Blind state president or designee. Selection is based on academic excellence, service to the community, and financial need.

Financial data Stipends are $7,000, $5,000, or $3,000.

Duration 1 year; recipients may resubmit applications up to 2 additional years.

Additional data Scholarships are awarded at the federation convention in July. Recipients must attend the convention at federation expense; that funding is in addition to the scholarship grant.

Number awarded 18 each year: 2 at $7,000. 3 at $5,000, and 13 at $3,000.

Deadline March of each year.

[87]
NFBCT-COCCOMO QUARTERLY GRANTS

National Federation of the Blind of Connecticut
Attn: Quarterly Grant Committee
477 Connecticut Boulevard, Suite 217
East Hartford, CT 06108
(860) 289-1971   E-mail: info@nfbct.org
Web: www.nfbct.org/html/coccomo.htm

Summary To provide financial assistance to blind people in Connecticut interested in a program of training, employment, independent living, or technological advancement.

Eligibility This assistance is available to residents of Connecticut who meet the state's definition of legal blindness. Applicants must be seeking support for activities in the areas of training, employment, independent living, or technological advancement. A wide range of requests are considered, including a talking watch, a computer system, a note taker (such as a Braille Note or Braille Lite), payment assistance for postsecondary part-time course work, or even a new suit for the sake of maximizing impressions on job interviews. Along with their application, they must submit a statement about themselves, their goals, and how the requested product or service will enhance their daily life and/or career aspirations.

Financial data Grants depend on the nature of the request.

Duration These are 1-time grants. Recipients are eligible for a second grant 2 years after receiving the first grant.

Additional data This program is supported by the John A. Coccomo, Sr. Foundation and administered by the National Federation of the Blind of Connecticut (NFBCT).

Number awarded Varies each year.

Deadline February, May, August, or November of each year.

[88]
NFBKS/KENNETH TIEDE MEMORIAL SCHOLARSHIPS

National Federation of the Blind of Kansas
c/o Donna J. Wood, President
11405 West Grant Street
Wichita, KS 67209-4209
(316) 721-3887   E-mail: donnajwood@cox.net
Web: www.nfbks.org/state/nfb-sklr.shtml

Summary To provide financial assistance to blind residents of Kansas who are interested in attending college in any state.

Eligibility This program is open to residents of Kansas who are legally blind. Applicants must be attending or planning to attend a technical school or a college or university in any state. They must be able to attend the state convention of the National Federation of the Blind of Kansas. Selection is based on academic excellence, community service, and financial need.

Financial data A stipend is awarded (amount not specified).

Duration 1 year.

Number awarded Up to 3 each year.

Deadline March of each year.

[89]
NFBKY SCHOLARSHIPS

National Federation of the Blind of Kentucky
c/o Lora J. Felty, Scholarship Committee Chair
1127 Sharon Court
Ashland, KY 41101
(606) 324-3394   E-mail: lorafelty@windstream.net
Web: www.nfbky.org/scholarship.php

Summary To provide financial assistance for college to blind students from Kentucky.

Eligibility This program is open to legally blind and visually impaired students attending or planning to attend a postsecondary institution. Applicants must be residents of Kentucky or attending a college or university in the state. They must be eligible for services from the Kentucky Office for the Blind. Along with their application, they must submit a 2-page letter describing how the scholarship will help them achieve their career goals; how they are involved in their community, organizations, and other activities; any honors, awards, or special recognition they have received; and how they would like to be involved in the National Federation of the Blind of Kentucky.

Financial data The stipend is $1,000.

Duration 1 year.

Additional data This program includes the following named awards: the Betty Niceley Memorial Scholarship and the Emerson Foulke Memorial Scholarship. Finalists are required to attend and participate in the annual convention of the National Federation of the Blind of Kentucky; travel, hotel accommodations, registration fees, and banquet tickets are provided.

Number awarded 1 or more each year.

Deadline July of each year.

[90]
NFBLA SCHOLARSHIPS

National Federation of the Blind of Louisiana
c/o Josh Boudreaux, Scholarship Committee Chair
Louisiana Center for the Blind
101 South Trenton Street
Ruston, LA 71270
(318) 251-2891   Toll Free: (800) 234-4166
Fax: (318) 251-0109
E-mail: jboudreau@lcb-ruston.com
Web: www.nfbla.org

Summary To provide financial assistance for college to blind residents of Louisiana.

Eligibility This program is open to residents of Louisiana who are legally blind. Applicants must be enrolled or planning to enroll in a full-time postsecondary program of study or training. Selection is based on academic excellence, leadership ability, service to the community, and financial need.

Financial data Stipends range from $500 to $1,500.

Duration 1 year; recipients may reapply.

Additional data Recipients must attend the annual convention of the National Federation of the Blind of Louisiana. Convention expenses are provided.

Number awarded Varies each year. Recently, 5 of these scholarships were awarded: 1 at $1,500, 2 at $750, and 2 at $500.

Deadline Deadline not specified.

[91]
NFBNJ SCHOLARSHIPS

National Federation of the Blind of New Jersey
c/o Jerilyn L. Higgins, Scholarship Chair
2 Old Farm Road
Verona, NJ 07044-1726
(973) 239-8874   Toll Free: (866) 632-1940
E-mail: nfbnj@yahoo.com
Web: www.nfbnj.org/scholarships.php

Summary To provide financial assistance to entering and continuing undergraduate and graduate students from New Jersey who are blind.

Eligibility This program is open to legally blind students who are working on or planning to work full time on an undergraduate or graduate degree. Applicants must be residents of New Jersey or attending school in the state. Along with their application, they must submit a personal letter, 2 letters of recommendation, transcripts, and a letter of endorsement from an officer of the National Federation of the Blind of New Jersey. Selection is based on academic excellence, service to the community, and financial need.

Financial data A stipend is awarded (amount not specified).

Duration 1 year.

Number awarded 1 or more each year.

Deadline March of each year.

[92]
NFBNM SCHOLARSHIP PROGRAM

National Federation of the Blind of New Mexico
c/o Christine Hall, President
10315 Propps Drive, N.WE.
Albuquerque, NM 87112
(505) 268-3895   E-mail: c.crick@msn.com
Web: www.nfbnm.org

Summary To provide financial assistance to blind students in New Mexico who are interested in attending college in any state.

Eligibility This program is open to blind students in New Mexico who are high school seniors or currently enrolled full time in college. Applicants must submit a copy of their transcript, a 250-word essay on how this scholarship will benefit them (including comments on their philosophy of blindness), and 3 letters of recommendation (including at least 1 from a member of the National Federation of the Blind). Priority is given to applicants attending school in New Mexico, but consideration is given to individuals who plan to go outside the state.

Financial data Stipends are $1,000 or $500.

Duration 1 year.

Number awarded Varies each year. Recently, 4 of these scholarships were awarded: 1 at $1,000 and 3 at $500.

Deadline April of each year.

[93]
NFBNO SCHOLARSHIPS

National Federation of the Blind of Missouri
c/o Carol Coulter
1613 Blue Ridge Road
Columbia, MO 65202
(573) 474-3226   Toll Free: (888) 604-1774
E-mail: info@nfbmo.org
Web: www.nfbmo.org/conventions/scholarships.shtml

Summary To provide financial assistance to blind residents of Missouri who are interested in attending college in the state.

Eligibility This program is open to legally blind residents of Missouri who are attending or planning to attend a college, university, or other postsecondary institution in the state. Applicants must submit a 1,000-word letter that covers how they have prepared themselves for college, the alternative skills they will use to complete college assignments, the contributions they have made to better the cause of people who are blind, and why they have chosen the school they plan to attend during the coming year. Selection is based on that essay, 2 letters of recommendation, transcripts, and an interview with the president of their local chapter or a member of the scholarship committee.

Financial data A stipend is awarded (amount not specified).

Duration 1 year.

Additional data Recipients are invited to attend, at the sponsor's expense, the state convention where the awards are presented.

Number awarded 1 or more each year.

Deadline January of each year.

[94]
NFBNY SCHOLARSHIPS

National Federation of the Blind of New York State, Inc.
P.O. Box 205666 Sunset Station
Brooklyn, NY 11220
(718) 567-7821   Fax: (718) 765-1843
E-mail: office@nfbny.org
Web: www.nfbny.org/Scholsrships.htm

Summary To provide financial assistance to blind residents of New York who are interested in attending college or graduate school in any state.

Eligibility This program is open to residents of New York who are legally blind. Applicants must be entering or enrolled in a degree program at the undergraduate, graduate, or postgraduate level at a school in any state. Along with their application, they must submit a 500-word essay explaining their goals, attitudes, and approach to living with blindness.

Financial data A stipend is awarded (amount not specified).

Duration 1 year.

Additional data This program includes the following named awards: the Gisela Distal Memorial Scholarship and the Maryanne Swaton Memorial Scholarship. Information is also available from Raymond Wayno, Scholarship Committee Chair, (718) 491-0053.

Number awarded At least 3 each year.
Deadline October of each year.

[95]
NFBSC SCHOLARSHIPS

National Federation of the Blind of South Carolina
Attn: Scholarship Committee
119 South Kilbourne Road
Columbia, SC 29205
(803) 254-3777   E-mail: nfbsc@sc.rr.com
Web: www.nfbsc.net/scholarship.html

Summary To provide financial assistance for college to legally blind students from South Carolina.

Eligibility This program is open to legally blind undergraduates who are residents of South Carolina or attending a college or university in the state. Applicants must submit 2 letters of recommendation, a current transcript, ACT and/or SAT test scores (high school seniors only), and a 250-word personal letter explaining their reasons for applying for a scholarship and how it will assist them to achieve a professional goal. Selection is based on academic excellence community service, and financial need.

Financial data A stipend is awarded (amount not specified).

Duration 1 year.

Additional data Winners are required to attend the annual convention of the National Federation of the Blind of South Carolina at the federation's expenses.

Number awarded 1 or more each year.

Deadline May of each year.

[96]
NFBW/BEVERLY PROWS MEMORIAL SCHOLARSHIP

National Federation of the Blind of Washington
c/o Rita Szantay, Scholarship Chair
1420 Fifth Avenue, Suite 2200
Seattle, WA 98101
(206) 224-7242   E-mail: rszantay@speakeasy.net
Web: www.nfbw.org

Summary To provide financial assistance for undergraduate or graduate study in any state to blind students in Washington.

Eligibility This program is open to legally blind residents of Washington state who are working on or planning to work on a full-time college or graduate degree at a school in any state. Applicants must submit a list of honors and awards they have received, information on their community service involvement, high school and/or college transcripts, and 3 letters of reference.

Financial data The stipend is $3,000.

Duration 1 year; recipients may reapply.

Additional data This scholarship was first awarded in 1991. Winners must attend the state convention of the National Federation of the Blind of Washington to accept the award; convention expenses are covered.

Number awarded 1 each year.

Deadline August of each year.

[97]
NIB GRANT M. MACK MEMORIAL SCHOLARSHIP

American Council of the Blind
Attn: Coordinator, Scholarship Program
2200 Wilson Boulevard, Suite 650
Arlington, VA 22201
(202) 467-5081   Toll Free: (800) 424-8666
Fax: (703) 465-5085   E-mail: info@acb.org
Web: www.acb.org

Summary To provide financial assistance to blind students who are working on an undergraduate or graduate degree in business or management.

Eligibility This program is open to undergraduate and graduate students working on a degree in business or management. Applicants must submit verification of legal blindness in both eyes; SAT, ACT, GMAT, or similar scores; information on extracurricular activities (including membership in the American Council of the Blind); employment record; and an autobiographical sketch that includes their personal goals, strengths, weaknesses, hobbies, honors, achievements, and reasons for choice of field or courses of study. A cumulative GPA of 3.3 or higher is generally required. Financial need is not considered in the selection process. U.S. citizenship or permanent resident status is required.

Financial data The stipend is $2,000. In addition, the winner receives a Kurzweil-1000 Reading System.

Duration 1 year.

Additional data This scholarship is sponsored by National Industries for the Blind (NIB) in honor of a dedicated leader of the American Council of the Blind. Scholarship winners are expected to be present at the council's annual conference; the council will cover all reasonable expenses connected with convention attendance.

Number awarded 1 each year.

Deadline February of each year.

[98]
NORA WEBB-MCKINNEY SCHOLARSHIP

American Council of the Blind of Ohio
Attn: Executive Director
P.O. Box 307128
Gahanna, OH 43230-7128
(614) 221-6688   Toll Free: (800) 835-2226 (within OH)
E-mail: mary.hiland@sbcglobal.net
Web: www.acbohio.org/application_cur.php

Summary To provide financial assistance to blind and other Ohio students who are interested in working on an undergraduate or graduate degree involving service to blind people.

Eligibility This program is open to 1) residents of Ohio who are high school seniors or current undergraduate or graduate students, and 2) undergraduate and graduate students at colleges and universities in Ohio. Applicants must be interested in working on or planning to work on a degree in a field related to blindness (e.g., special education, rehabilitation teaching or counseling, orientation and mobility, or a concentration on programs serving people who are blind). They may be blind or sighted. Along with their application, they must submit transcripts (must have a GPA of 3.0 or higher) and an essay of 250 to 500 words on their career objectives, future plans, personal goals, other academic or personal qualities, and why they believe they are qualified to receive this scholarship. Financial need is not the sole factor considered in the selection process.

Financial data   The stipend is $2,000 per year.

Duration   1 year; recipients may reapply.

Additional data   Winners are required to attend the Saturday morning business meeting and Sunday breakfast of the sponsor's annual convention; a stipend for meals and workshops is provided.

Number awarded   1 each year.

Deadline   July of each year.

[99]
NORTH DAKOTA ASSOCIATION OF THE BLIND SCHOLARSHIPS

North Dakota Association of the Blind
c/o Tammy Winn, Scholarship Committee Chair
103 Lilac Lane, Number 2
Minot AFB Base, ND 58704
(701) 727-9211   E-mail: roytammy@srt.com
Web: www.ndab.org/Scholarship.html

Summary   To provide financial assistance for college or graduate school to blind students in North Dakota.

Eligibility   This program is open to North Dakota residents who are legally blind and attending an institution of higher education in the state. Applicants must be full-time students with a class standing of a sophomore through a graduate student and a GPA of 2.5 or higher. They must submit 2 letters of recommendation, transcripts, a family financial aid statement, and an essay that describes their vocational interests, how the scholarship will help them, their goals and aspirations, and what they have done to deal with situations involving their visual impairment. Selection is based on academic excellence, financial need, and service to the community.

Financial data   Stipends are $1,000 or $500.

Duration   1 year.

Additional data   This program was established in 1990.

Number awarded   3 each year: 1 at $1,000 and 2 at $500.

Deadline   March of each year.

[100]
OREGON COUNCIL OF THE BLIND SCHOLARSHIPS

American Council of the Blind
Attn: Coordinator, Scholarship Program
2200 Wilson Boulevard, Suite 650
Arlington, VA 22201
(202) 467-5081   Toll Free: (800) 424-8666
Fax: (703) 465-5085   E-mail: info@acb.org
Web: www.acb.org

Summary   To provide financial assistance for college to blind students, especially those from Oregon.

Eligibility   This program is open to legally blind students who are entering or attending college. Preference is given to residents of Oregon, but if no students from that state apply, residents of other states are considered. Applicants must submit verification of legal blindness in both eyes; SAT or ACT scores; information on extracurricular activities (including membership in the American Council of the Blind); employment record; and an autobiographical sketch that includes their personal goals, strengths, weaknesses, hobbies, honors, achievements, and reasons for choice of field or courses of study. A cumulative GPA of 3.3 or higher is generally required. Financial need is not considered in the selection process.

Financial data   The stipend is $2,500. In addition, the winners receive a Kurzweil-1000 Reading System.

Duration   1 year.

Additional data   Funding for this scholarship is provided by the Oregon Council of the Blind, an affiliate of the American Council of the Blind. Scholarship winners are expected to be present at the council's annual conference; the council will cover all reasonable expenses connected with convention attendance.

Number awarded   2 each year.

Deadline   February of each year.

[101]
PAUL AND ELLEN RUCKES SCHOLARSHIP

American Foundation for the Blind
Attn: Scholarship Committee
11 Penn Plaza, Suite 300
New York, NY 10001
(212) 502-7661   Toll Free: (800) AFB-LINE
Fax: (212) 502-7771   TDD: (212) 502-7662
E-mail: afbinfo@afb.net
Web: www.afb.org/Section.asp?Documentid=2962

Summary   To provide financial assistance to legally blind students who wish to work on a graduate or undergraduate degree in engineering or computer, physical, or life sciences.

Eligibility   This program is open to legally blind undergraduate or graduate students who are U.S. citizens working full time on a degree in engineering or the computer, physical, or life sciences. Along with their application, they must submit a 200-word essay that includes their past and recent achievements and accomplishments; their intended field of study and why they have chosen it; and the role their visual impairment has played in shaping their life. Financial need is considered in the selection process.

Financial data   The stipend is $1,000.

Duration   1 year.

Number awarded   1 each year.

Deadline   April of each year.

[102]
RED ROSE SCHOLARSHIP

Susquehanna Foundation for the Blind
244 North Queen Street, Suite 301
Lancaster, PA 17603
(717) 393-5894   Fax: (717) 435-8367
E-mail: info@sfblind.org
Web: sfblind.com/Content/scholarships.asp

Summary   To provide financial assistance to legally blind Pennsylvania residents who are interested in working on an undergraduate degree at a college in any state.

Eligibility   This program is open to residents of Pennsylvania who are legally blind. Applicants must be high school seniors or graduates planning to attend a 2- or 4-year college or university in any state. Along with their application, they must submit a brief description of their career goal. Financial need is considered in the selection process.

Financial data   The stipend is $1,500 per year.

Duration   2 years; may be renewed another 2 years by students at 4-year institutions.

Number awarded   1 or more each year.

Deadline   Deadline not specified.

[103]
R.L. GILLETTE SCHOLARSHIPS

American Foundation for the Blind
Attn: Scholarship Committee
11 Penn Plaza, Suite 300
New York, NY 10001
(212) 502-7661   Toll Free: (800) AFB-LINE
Fax: (212) 502-7771   TDD: (212) 502-7662
E-mail: afbinfo@afb.net
Web: www.afb.org/Section.asp?Documentid=2962

Summary   To provide financial assistance to legally blind undergraduate women who are studying literature or music.

Eligibility   This program is open to women who are legally blind, U.S. citizens, and enrolled full time in a 4-year baccalaureate degree program in literature or music. Along with their application, they must submit a 200-word essay that includes their past and recent achievements and accomplishments; their intended field of study and why they have chosen it; and the role their visual impairment has played in shaping their life. They must also submit a sample performance tape/CD (not to exceed 30 minutes) or a creative writing sample. Financial need is considered in the selection process.

Financial data   The stipend is $1,000.

Duration   1 academic year.

Number awarded   2 each year.

Deadline   April of each year.

[104]
ROBERT AND HAZEL STALEY MEMORIAL SCHOLARSHIP

National Federation of the Blind of North Carolina
c/o Ann Sumner
3000 Octavia Drive
Rocky Mount, NC 27804
(252) 904-0961
Web: www.nfbofnc.org

Summary   To provide financial assistance to undergraduate and graduate students from North Carolina who are blind.

Eligibility   This program is open to legally blind students who are residents of North Carolina or attending a college or university in the state. Applicants must be working on or planning to work on an undergraduate or graduate degree. Along with their application, they must submit 2 letters of recommendation, a current transcript, and a letter of introduction about themselves that includes their likes and dislikes, how their blindness has affected them, the honors and awards they have received, and their school and extracurricular activities. Selection is based on academic excellence, service to the community, and financial need.

Financial data   The stipend is $1,500. Funds may be used for the purchase of equipment, reader services, transportation, or other services or materials necessary to accomplish the recipient's educational objectives. They are not intended to offset support provided by state or federal agencies.

Duration   1 year.

Additional data   Recipients must attend the annual convention of the National Federation of the Blind of North Carolina, at federation expense, where they receive their awards.

Number awarded   Up to 2 each year.

Deadline   June of each year.

[105]
ROSS N. AND PATRICIA PANGERE FOUNDATION SCHOLARSHIPS

American Council of the Blind
Attn: Coordinator, Scholarship Program
2200 Wilson Boulevard, Suite 650
Arlington, VA 22201
(202) 467-5081   Toll Free: (800) 424-8666
Fax: (703) 465-5085   E-mail: info@acb.org
Web: www.acb.org

Summary   To provide financial assistance to blind students working on an undergraduate or graduate degree in business.

Eligibility   This program is open to undergraduate and graduate students working on a degree in business. Applicants must submit verification of legal blindness in both eyes; SAT, ACT, GMAT, or similar scores; information on extracurricular activities (including membership in the American Council of the Blind); employment record; and an autobiographical sketch that includes their personal goals, strengths, weaknesses, hobbies, honors, achievements, and reasons for choice of field or courses of study.

A cumulative GPA of 3.3 or higher is generally required. Financial need is not considered in the selection process.

Financial data The stipend is $2,500. In addition, the winner receives a Kurzweil-1000 Reading System.

Duration 1 year.

Additional data The scholarship winner is expected to be present at the council's annual national convention; the council will cover all reasonable costs connected with convention attendance.

Number awarded 2 each year.

Deadline February of each year.

[106]
RUDOLPH DILLMAN MEMORIAL SCHOLARSHIP

American Foundation for the Blind
Attn: Scholarship Committee
11 Penn Plaza, Suite 300
New York, NY 10001
(212) 502-7661   Toll Free: (800) AFB-LINE
Fax: (212) 502-7771   TDD: (212) 502-7662
E-mail: afbinfo@afb.net
Web: www.afb.org/Section.asp?Documentid=2962

Summary To provide financial assistance to legally blind undergraduate or graduate students studying in the field of rehabilitation and/or education of visually impaired and blind persons.

Eligibility This program is open to legally-blind U.S. citizens who have been accepted to an accredited undergraduate or graduate training program within the broad field of rehabilitation and/or education of blind and visually impaired persons. Along with their application, they must submit a 200-word essay that includes their past and recent achievements and accomplishments; their intended field of study and why they have chosen it; and the role their visual impairment has played in shaping their life. Financial need is considered for 1 of the scholarships.

Financial data The stipend is $2,500 per year.

Duration 1 academic year; previous recipients may not reapply.

Number awarded 4 each year: 3 without consideration of financial need and 1 based on financial need.

Deadline April of each year.

[107]
SOUTH DAKOTA FREE TUITION FOR VISUALLY IMPAIRED PERSONS

South Dakota Board of Regents
Attn: Scholarship Committee
306 East Capitol Avenue, Suite 200
Pierre, SD 57501-2545
(605) 773-3455   Fax: (605) 773-2422
E-mail: info@sdbor.edu
Web: www.sdbor.edu

Summary To provide financial assistance for college or graduate school to visually impaired residents of South Dakota.

Eligibility Eligible for this program is any visually impaired resident of South Dakota who can meet the entrance requirements for admission to a postsecondary educational institution (including graduate school and medical school) under the supervision of the state board of regents. For purposes of the program, "visual impairment" means that the person cannot, with use of correcting glasses, see sufficiently well to perform ordinary activities for which eyesight is essential. This program does not extend to visually impaired persons who are entitled to receive tuition and fee support from the state's department of vocational rehabilitation.

Financial data Qualified applicants may attend any institution under the supervision of the South Dakota Board of Regents without payment of tuition, library fees, registration fees, or any other fees.

Duration Benefits are provided until the recipient has earned 225 semester hours of credit or the equivalent.

Additional data Applicants should contact the financial aid director at the South Dakota college or university they plan to attend, not the sponsor. The exemption from charges does not apply if a course is repeated because of unsatisfactory work, unless the problem was caused by illness or some other circumstance for which the student had no responsibility.

Number awarded Varies each year.

Deadline Deadline not specified.

[108]
SUPPORT SERVICES FOR THE BLIND AND VISUALLY IMPAIRED

Lions Clubs International
Attn: Program Development Department
300 West 22nd Street
Oak Brook, IL 60523-8842
(630) 571-5466, ext. 316   Fax: (630) 571-1692
E-mail: programs@lionsclubs.org
Web: www.lionsclubs.org

Summary To provide college scholarships and other assistance to blind people.

Eligibility These programs are open to blind people and others involved in service to the blind. Applicants may be seeking support for the following activities: scholarships for the blind and visually impaired, medical research, assistive technology grants, independent mobility, transportation, reading materials and aids, audio products, Braille products, and other aids.

Financial data The amount of this assistance varies.

Additional data Support is provided by local clubs of Lions Clubs International. Requests sent to the international office are referred to the appropriate district governor. If any of the clubs within the district conduct programs for which the applicant might be considered, the governor will advise the particular club to contact the applicant. No funds are available from the office of Lions Clubs International.

Deadline Deadline not specified.

[109]
SUSQUEHANNA FOUNDATION FOR THE BLIND TRUSTEES' SCHOLARSHIP

Susquehanna Foundation for the Blind
244 North Queen Street, Suite 301
Lancaster, PA 17603
(717) 393-5894   Fax: (717) 435-8367
E-mail: info@sfblind.org
Web: sfblind.com/Content/scholarships.asp

Summary   To provide financial assistance to legally blind Pennsylvania residents who are interested in working on an undergraduate or graduate degree or other academic program at a school in any state.

Eligibility   This program is open to residents of Pennsylvania who are legally blind. Applicants must be working on an undergraduate or graduate degree or other specialized program intended to generate upward mobility in employment. Along with their application, they must submit a brief description of their career goal. Financial need is considered in the selection process.

Financial data   A stipend is awarded (amount not specified).

Duration   1 year.

Number awarded   1 or more each year.

Deadline   Deadline not specified.

[110]
TAER STUDENT WITH A VISUAL IMPAIRMENT SCHOLARSHIP

Texas Association for Education and Rehabilitation of
   the Blind and Visually Impaired
c/o Olivia Chavez
Education Service Center-Region 19
6611 Boeing Drive
El Paso, TX 79925
(915) 780-5344   Fax: (915) 780-6537
E-mail: ochavez@esc19.net
Web: www.txaer.org

Summary   To provide financial assistance to residents of Texas who have a visual impairment and are interested in attending college in any state.

Eligibility   This program is open to residents of Texas who are attending or planning to attend a college or university in any state. Applicants must be able to document a visual impairment and financial need. Along with their application, they must submit a letter regarding the goal of their education.

Financial data   The stipend is $1,000.

Duration   1 year.

Number awarded   1 or more each year.

Deadline   February of each year.

[111]
TEXAS BLIND/DEAF STUDENT EXEMPTION PROGRAM

Texas Higher Education Coordinating Board
Attn: Grants and Special Programs
1200 East Anderson Lane
P.O. Box 12788, Capitol Station
Austin, TX 78711-2788
(512) 427-6340   Toll Free: (800) 242-3062
Fax: (512) 427-6127
E-mail: grantinfo@thecb.state.tx.us
Web: www.collegeforalltexans.com

Summary   To provide a tuition exemption to blind and/or deaf residents of Texas.

Eligibility   This program is open to Texas residents who can present certification from the Department of Assistive and Rehabilitative Services of their deafness or blindness. Applicants must present to the registrar of a public college or university in Texas a copy of their high school transcript, a letter of recommendation, proof that they have met all admission requirements, and a statement of purpose that indicates the certificate, degree program, or professional enhancement that they intend to pursue.

Financial data   Eligible students are exempted from the payment of all dues, fees, and tuition charges at publicly-supported colleges and universities in Texas.

Duration   Up to 8 semesters.

Number awarded   Varies each year; recently, nearly 3,500 students received support through this program.

Deadline   Deadline not specified.

[112]
UCB POULSON FAMILY SCHOLARSHIPS

Utah Council of the Blind
c/o Leslie Gertsch, Executive Director
1301 West 500 South
Woods Cross, UT 84087-2224
(801) 292-1156   Fax: (801) 292-6046
E-mail: lgertsch@comcast.net
Web: www.acb.org/utah/ucbschol1.htm

Summary   To provide financial assistance to members of the Utah Council of the Blind (UCB) who plan to attend college or graduate school in the state.

Eligibility   This program is open to UCB members who are entering or enrolled as an undergraduate or graduate student at a college or university in Utah. Applicants must be blind or visually impaired, defined as having a visual acuity of less than 20/70, a visual field not exceeding 30 degrees, or a functional visual impairment of similar degree in the best eye with best correction. Along with their application, they must submit an autobiographical sketch that includes their personal goals, strengths, weaknesses, hobbies, honors, achievements, the course of study they are pursuing, and why they have chosen it. Financial need is not considered in the selection process. Interviews may be held.

Financial data   The stipend is $1,500.

Duration   1 year; may be renewed.

Number awarded Varies each year; recently, 5 of these scholarships were awarded.
Deadline April of each year.

[113]
WALTER YOUNG MEMORIAL SCHOLARSHIP

California Association for Postsecondary Education
  and Disability
Attn: Executive Assistant
71423 Biskra Road
Rancho Mirage, CA 92270
(760) 346-8206   Fax: (760) 340-5275
TDD: (760) 341-4084   E-mail: caped2000@aol.com
Web: www.caped.net/scholarships.html

Summary To provide financial assistance to blind and visually impaired undergraduate and graduate students in California.

Eligibility This program is open to blind and visually impaired students at public and private colleges and universities in California. Undergraduates must have completed at least 6 semester credits and have a GPA of 2.5 or higher. Graduate students must have completed at least 3 semester units and have a GPA of 3.0 or higher. Along with their application, they must submit a 1-page personal letter that demonstrates their writing skills, progress towards meeting their educational and vocational goals, management of their disability, and involvement in community activities. They must also submit a letter of recommendation from a faculty member, verification of disability, official transcripts, proof of current enrollment, and documentation of financial need.

Financial data The stipend is $1,000.
Duration 1 year.
Number awarded 1 each year.
Deadline September of each year.

[114]
WASHINGTON COUNCIL OF THE BLIND SCHOLARSHIPS

Washington Council of the Blind
c/o Julie Brannon, Scholarship Committee Chair
6801 Greenwood Avenue North, Unit 209
Seattle, WA 98103
Toll Free: (206) 547-7444
E-mail: jbrannon0612@comcast.net
Web: www.wcbinfo.org

Summary To provide financial aid to blind students in Washington who plan to attend college or graduate school in any state.

Eligibility This program is open to blind residents of Washington state who are enrolled or planning to enroll at an accredited college, university, vocational school, or graduate school in any state. Applicants must submit a 1,000-word statement of their reasons for applying for this scholarship and how it will assist them to achieve their goals. The statement should include a brief description of their background, education, work experience, economic status, strengths, weaknesses, and personal goals for the next 5 to 10 years. Interviews are required.

Financial data The stipend ranges up to $4,000.
Duration 1 year.
Number awarded 1 or more each year.
Deadline July of each year.

[115]
W.B. TAYLOR MEMORIAL SCHOLARSHIP

National Federation of the Blind of Texas
Attn: Scholarship Committee
314 East Highland Mall Boulevard, Suite 253
Austin, TX 78752
(512) 323-5444   Toll Free: (866) 636-3289
Fax: (512) 420-8160
E-mail: scholarship@nfb-texas.org.
Web: www.nfb-texas.org

Summary To provide financial assistance to blind residents of Texas who are interested in attending college in any state.

Eligibility This program is open to blind residents of Texas who are enrolled or planning to enroll full time at a college or university in any state. Applicants must submit proof of legal blindness, a current transcript, a 2-page personal letter, and 2 letters of recommendation. Selection is based on academic excellence, community service, and financial need.

Financial data The stipend is $2,000 per year.
Duration 1 year; recipients may reapply.
Number awarded 1 each year.
Deadline August of each year.

[116]
WILLIAM G. COREY MEMORIAL SCHOLARSHIP

American Council of the Blind
Attn: Coordinator, Scholarship Program
2200 Wilson Boulevard, Suite 650
Arlington, VA 22201
(202) 467-5081   Toll Free: (800) 424-8666
Fax: (703) 465-5085   E-mail: info@acb.org
Web: www.acb.org

Summary To provide financial assistance for college to blind undergraduate and graduate students from Pennsylvania.

Eligibility This program is open to legally blind undergraduate and graduate students who are residents of Pennsylvania or attending college in the state. Applicants must submit verification of legal blindness in both eyes; SAT, ACT, GRE, or similar scores; information on extracurricular activities (including membership in the American Council of the Blind); employment record; and an autobiographical sketch that includes their personal goals, strengths, weaknesses, hobbies, honors, achievements, and reasons for choice of field or courses of study. A cumulative GPA of 3.3 or higher is generally required. Financial need is not considered in the selection process.

Financial data The stipend is $1,500. In addition, the winner receives a Kurzweil-1000 Reading System.
Duration 1 year.

Additional data   Scholarship winners are expected to be present at the council's annual conference; the council will cover all reasonable expenses connected with convention attendance.

Number awarded   1 each year.

Deadline   February of each year.

[117]
WILMA H. WRIGHT MEMORIAL SCHOLARSHIP

Delta Gamma Foundation
Attn: Director of Scholarships, Fellowships and Loans
3250 Riverside Drive
P.O. Box 21397
Columbus, OH 43221-0397
(614) 481-8169   Fax: (614) 481-0133
E-mail: FNScholarFellow@deltagamma.org
Web: www.deltagamma.org

Summary   To provide financial assistance to undergraduate members of Delta Gamma sorority who are visually impaired or preparing for a career working with the visually impaired.

Eligibility   This program is open to initiated members of a collegiate chapter of Delta Gamma in the United States or Canada who have completed 3 semesters or 5 quarters of their college course and have maintained a GPA of 3.0 or higher. Applicants must submit a 1- to 2-page essay in which they introduce themselves, including their career goals, their reasons for applying for this scholarship, and the impact Delta Gamma has had on their life. Selection is based on scholastic excellence and participation in chapter, campus, and community leadership activities. Preference is given to candidates who are either 1) blind or visually impaired or 2) pursuing professional training in areas related to working with persons who are blind or visually impaired.

Financial data   The stipend is $1,000. Funds are sent directly to the recipient's university or college to be used for tuition, books, laboratory fees, room, and board. They may not be used for sorority dues, house fees, or other chapter expenses.

Duration   1 year.

Number awarded   1 each year.

Deadline   February of each year.

[118]
WISCONSIN COUNCIL OF THE BLIND AND VISUALLY IMPAIRED SCHOLARSHIPS

Wisconsin Council of the Blind and Visually Impaired
Attn: Scholarship Committee
754 Williamson Street
Madison, WI 53703
(608) 255-1166   Toll Free: (800) 783-5213
Fax: (608) 255-3301   E-mail: info@wcblind.org
Web: www.wcblind.org/services_scholarships.html

Summary   To provide financial assistance to blind students from Wisconsin who are planning to attend college in any state.

Eligibility   This program is open to legally blind residents of Wisconsin who are enrolled or entering college or voca-

tional school in any state. Applicants must have a GPA of 2.5 or higher. They must be able to identify goals for the future, including eventual employment.

Financial data   Stipends are $1,500 for full-time students or $1,000 for part-time students.

Duration   1 year.

Number awarded   9 each year: 7 for full-time students and 2 for part-time students.

Deadline   September of each year.

[119]
WISCONSIN HEARING AND VISUALLY HANDICAPPED STUDENT GRANT PROGRAM

Wisconsin Higher Educational Aids Board
131 West Wilson Street, Suite 902
P.O. Box 7885
Madison, WI 53707-7885
(608) 266-0888   Fax: (608) 267-2808
E-mail: Sandy.Thomas@wisconsin.gov
Web: heab.state.wi.us/programs.html

Summary   To provide financial support for undergraduate study to Wisconsin residents who are legally deaf or blind.

Eligibility   This program is open to Wisconsin residents who can submit evidence of a severe or profound hearing or visual impairment certified by a medical examiner. Applicants must be enrolled at a branch of the University of Wisconsin, a technical college in the state, a Wisconsin independent college or university, a tribal college in the state, or an institution out of state that specializes in the training of deaf, hard of hearing, or visually handicapped students or that offers a program of study not offered by a Wisconsin institution. Financial need is considered in the selection process.

Financial data   Grants range from $250 to $1,800 per academic year.

Duration   1 year; may be renewed up to 4 additional years.

Number awarded   Varies each year.

Deadline   Deadline not specified.

Fellowship/Grants

[120]
ACBCO SCHOLARSHIPS

American Council of the Blind of Colorado
Attn: Executive Director
1536 Wynkoop Street, Suite 201
Denver, CO 80202
(303) 831-0117   Toll Free: (888) 775-2221
Fax: (303) 454-3378 E-mail: barbara.boyer@acbco.org
Web: www.acbco.org

Summary   To provide financial assistance for college or graduate school to blind students from Colorado.

Eligibility This program is open to legally blind students who are residents of Colorado. Applicants must be working on an undergraduate (academic, vocational, or certificate) or graduate (master's or doctoral) degree. A cumulative GPA of 3.3 or higher is generally required, but extenuating circumstances may be considered. Along with their application, they must submit a 750-word statement describing their educational, career, and personal goals. Financial need is also considered in the selection process.

Financial data The stipend is $2,500. Funds are paid directly to the recipient's college or university.

Duration 1 year.

Number awarded 4 each year.

Deadline January of each year.

[121]
ALLEN-SPRINKLE MEMORIAL GIFT

National Federation of the Blind of West Virginia
c/o Debbi Wilson, Scholarship Committee Chair
1430 Magnolia Court
Cumberland, MD 21502
(301) 777-3017
Web: www.nfbwv.org/downloadscholarship.htm

Summary To provide financial assistance to legally blind residents of West Virginia who are interested in attending college or graduate school in any state.

Eligibility This program is open to legally blind residents of Virginia who are graduating high school seniors, undergraduates, or graduate students. Applicants must be enrolled or planning to enroll full time at an accredited college, university, postsecondary vocational institute, or graduate school in any state. Along with their application, they must submit 2 letters of recommendation, transcripts, verification of blindness, and a personal letter that includes the kinds of things that interest them, their goals and aspirations, and how this scholarship would help them. Selection is based on academic excellence, community service, and financial need.

Financial data The stipend is $1,000.

Duration 1 year.

Additional data The winner is expected to attend the annual convention of the National Federation of the Blind of West Virginia.

Number awarded 1 each year.

Deadline June of each year.

[122]
ARNOLD SADLER MEMORIAL SCHOLARSHIP

American Council of the Blind
Attn: Coordinator, Scholarship Program
2200 Wilson Boulevard, Suite 650
Arlington, VA 22201
(202) 467-5081   Toll Free: (800) 424-8666
Fax: (703) 465-5085   E-mail: info@acb.org
Web: www.acb.org

Summary To provide financial assistance to undergraduate or graduate students who are blind and are interested in studying in a field of service to persons with disabilities.

Eligibility This program is open to undergraduate and graduate students in rehabilitation, education, law, or other fields of service to persons with disabilities. Applicants must be legally blind in both eyes. Along with their application, they must submit verification of legal blindness in both eyes; SAT, ACT, GRE, or similar scores; information on extracurricular activities (including membership in the American Council of the Blind); employment record; and an autobiographical sketch that includes their personal goals, strengths, weaknesses, hobbies, honors, achievements, and reasons for choice of field or courses of study. A cumulative GPA of 3.3 or higher is generally required. Financial need is not considered in the selection process.

Financial data The stipend is $1,500. In addition, the winner receives a Kurzweil-1000 Reading System.

Duration 1 year.

Additional data This scholarship is funded by the Arnold Sadler Memorial Scholarship Fund. Scholarship winners are expected to be present at the council's annual conference; the council will cover all reasonable expenses connected with convention attendance.

Number awarded 1 each year.

Deadline February of each year.

[123]
BERNA SPECHT BRAILLE LITERACY AWARD

Alabama Council of the Blind
c/o David Trott, President
1018 East Street South
Talladega, AL 35160
Fax: (256) 362-5649   E-mail: dart1018@charter.net
Web: www.acbalabama.org/index_files/Page333.htm

Summary To provide funding to blind residents of Alabama interested in improving their Braille literacy.

Eligibility This program is open to Alabama residents who are legally blind. Awards are presented in 3 categories: 1) a student at the Alabama School for the Blind; 2) a student from a public school; and 3) an adult. Applicants must be interested in improving their Braille literacy through use of a Braille Writer. They must submit a 1-page essay on how they will use the Braille Writer.

Financial data A grant is awarded (amount not specified).

Duration This is a 1-time grant.

Number awarded 3 each year.

Deadline September of each year.

[124]
CCB SCHOLARSHIPS

California Council of the Blind
Attn: Executive Office
1510 J Street, Suite 125
Sacramento, CA 95814
(916) 441-2100   Toll Free: (800) 221-6359 (within CA)
Fax: (916) 441-2188   E-mail: ccotb@ccbnet.org
Web: www.ccbnet.org/scholar.htm

Summary To provide financial assistance for undergraduate or graduate study in any state to blind people in California.

Eligibility Applicants must be legally blind residents of California who are enrolled or planning to enroll full time at an accredited college or university at either the undergraduate or graduate level. The school may be in any state. Along with their application, they must submit a 200-word statement on their purpose in undertaking college work and their vocational goals. Selection is based on academic achievement and financial need.

Financial data The amount of the assistance depends on the availability of funds and the needs of the applicant.

Duration 1 year; may be renewed. For graduate students, support is limited to 2 years of work for a master's degree or 3 years for a Ph.D.

Number awarded Varies each year.

Deadline June of each year.

[125]
CCLVI FRED SCHEIGERT SCHOLARSHIPS

Council of Citizens with Low Vision International
c/o American Council of the Blind
2200 Wilson Boulevard, Suite 650
Arlington, VA 22201
(202) 467-5081   Toll Free: (800) 733-2258
Fax: (703) 465-5085   E-mail: scholarship@cclvi.org
Web: www.cclvi.org/scholars.htm

Summary To provide financial assistance to entering and continuing undergraduate and graduate students with low vision.

Eligibility This program is open to full-time undergraduate and graduate students who have been certified by an ophthalmologist as having low vision (acuity of 20/70 or worse in the better seeing eye with best correction or side vision with a maximum diameter of no greater than 30 degrees). Applicants may be part-time or full-time entering freshmen, undergraduates, or graduate students. They must have a GPA of 3.2 or higher.

Financial data The stipend is $3,000.

Duration 1 year.

Number awarded 3 each year.

Deadline February of each year.

[126]
CHARLES AND MELVA T. OWEN MEMORIAL SCHOLARSHIPS

National Federation of the Blind
Attn: Scholarship Committee
1800 Johnson Street
Baltimore, MD 21230
(410) 659-9314, ext. 2415   Fax: (410) 685-5653
E-mail: scholarships@nfb.org
Web: www.nfb.org/nfb/scholarship_program.asp

Summary To provide financial assistance to entering or continuing undergraduate or graduate students who are blind.

Eligibility This program is open to legally blind students who are working on or planning to work full time on an undergraduate or graduate degree. Scholarships, however, are not awarded for the study of religion or solely to further general or cultural education; the academic program should be directed towards attaining financial independence. Along with their application, they must submit transcripts, standardized test scores, proof of legal blindness, 2 letters of recommendation, and a letter of endorsement from their National Federation of the Blind state president or designee. Selection is based on academic excellence, service to the community, and financial need.

Financial data Stipends are $10,000 or $3,000.

Duration 1 year; recipients may resubmit applications up to 2 additional years.

Additional data Scholarships are awarded at the federation convention in July. Recipients must attend the convention at federation expense; that funding is in addition to the scholarship grant.

Number awarded 2 each year: 1 at $10,000 and 1 at $3,000.

Deadline March of each year.

[127]
CHICAGO LIGHTHOUSE SCHOLARSHIPS

Chicago Lighthouse for People who are Blind or
  Visually Impaired
Attn: Scholarship Program Coordinator
1850 West Roosevelt Road
Chicago, IL 60608-1298
(312) 666-1331   Fax: (312) 243-8539
TDD: (312) 666-8874
E-mail: scholarships@chicagolighthouse.org
Web: www.thechicagolighthouse.org

Summary To provide financial assistance to blind or visually impaired college and graduate students from any state.

Eligibility This program is open to residents of any state who are blind or visually impaired. Applicants must be attending or planning to attend an accredited college, university, or community college as an undergraduate or graduate student. Along with their application, they must submit an essay about their visual impairment, background, educational and career goals, and how this scholarship will help achieve those goals.

Financial data Stipends range up to $5,000.

Duration 1 year.

Additional data This program includes the Mary Kathryn and Michael Panitch Scholarships. This program was established in 2004 and limited to students from the Chicago area. Recently, it has began to accept applications from students living in any state.

Number awarded Varies each year; recently, 14 of these scholarships were awarded.

Deadline April of each year.

[128]
COMPUTER SCIENCE SCHOLARSHIP

National Federation of the Blind
Attn: Scholarship Committee
1800 Johnson Street
Baltimore, MD 21230
(410) 659-9314, ext. 2415   Fax: (410) 685-5653
E-mail: scholarships@nfb.org
Web: www.nfb.org/nfb/scholarship_program.asp

Summary To provide financial assistance to entering and continuing undergraduate and graduate students who are legally blind and working on a degree in computer science.

Eligibility This program is open to legally blind students who are working on or planning to work full time on an undergraduate or graduate degree in computer science. Along with their application, they must submit transcripts, standardized test scores, proof of legal blindness, 2 letters of recommendation, and a letter of endorsement from their National Federation of the Blind state president or designee. Selection is based on academic excellence, service to the community, and financial need.

Financial data The stipend is $3,000.

Duration 1 year; recipients may resubmit applications up to 2 additional years.

Additional data Scholarships are awarded at the federation convention in July. Recipients must attend the convention at federation expense; that funding is in addition to the scholarship grant.

Number awarded 1 each year.

Deadline March of each year.

[129]
DALE M. SCHOETTLER SCHOLARSHIP FOR VISUALLY IMPAIRED STUDENTS

California State University
CSU Foundation
Attn: Director, Foundation Programs and Services
401 Golden Shore, Sixth Floor
Long Beach, CA 90802-4210
(562) 951-4768   E-mail: abrown@calstate.edu
Web: www.calstate.edu/foundation/scholarship.shtml

Summary To provide financial assistance to undergraduate and graduate students with visual impairments at campuses of the California State University (CSU) system.

Eligibility This program is open to undergraduate and graduate students enrolled at CSU campuses who have been declared visually impaired or legally blind. Applicants must have a cumulative GPA of 2.8 or higher.

Financial data The stipend is $6,500.

Duration 1 year.

Number awarded 15 each year.

Deadline Deadline not specified.

[130]
DELTA GAMMA FOUNDATION RUTH BILLOW MEMORIAL EDUCATION FUND

Delta Gamma Foundation
Attn: Director, Service for Sight
3250 Riverside Drive
P.O. Box 21397
Columbus, OH 43221-0397
(614) 481-8169   Fax: (614) 481-0133
E-mail: dgfoundation@deltagamma.org
Web: www.deltagamma.org

Summary To provide financial assistance to undergraduate or graduate members of Delta Gamma sorority who are visually impaired or preparing for a career in working with the visually impaired.

Eligibility This program is open to undergraduate and graduate members of the sorority who are either 1) blind or visually impaired or 2) pursuing professional training in areas related to working with persons who are blind or visually impaired or in sight preservation. Applicants must be pursuing a program of postsecondary education in the United States or Canada.

Financial data The stipend is $1,000 for undergraduates or $2,500 for graduate students.

Duration 1 year or more.

Number awarded 2 each year: 1 to an undergraduate and 1 to a graduate student.

Deadline Applications may be submitted at any time.

[131]
DR. S. BRADLEY BURSON MEMORIAL SCHOLARSHIP

American Council of the Blind
Attn: Coordinator, Scholarship Program
2200 Wilson Boulevard, Suite 650
Arlington, VA 22201
(202) 467-5081   Toll Free: (800) 424-8666
Fax: (703) 465-5085   E-mail: info@acb.org
Web: www.acb.org

Summary To provide financial assistance to blind students who are working on an undergraduate or graduate degree in designated fields of science.

Eligibility This program is open to undergraduate or graduate students working on a degree in the "hard" sciences (i.e., biology, chemistry, physics, and engineering, but not computer science). Applicants must be legally blind in both eyes. Along with their application, they must submit verification of legal blindness in both eyes; SAT, ACT, GRE, or similar scores; information on extracurricular activities (including membership in the American Council of the Blind); employment record; and an autobiographical sketch that includes their personal goals, strengths, weaknesses, hobbies, honors, achievements, and reasons for choice of field or courses of study. A cumulative GPA of 3.3 or higher is generally required. Financial need is not considered in the selection process.

Financial data The stipend is $1,000. In addition, the winner receives a Kurzweil-1000 Reading System.

Duration 1 year.

Additional data Scholarship winners are expected to be present at the council's annual conference; the council will cover all reasonable expenses connected with convention attendance.

Number awarded 1 each year.

Deadline February of each year.

[132]
ELLEN BEACH MACK SCHOLARSHIP

American Council of the Blind of South Carolina
c/o Betty Jones, President
101 Sherard Avenue
Ninety Six, SC 29666
(864) 543-2993   E-mail: mrsbettyjno1@hotmail.com
Web: www.acbsc.org

Summary To provide financial assistance to entering and continuing undergraduate and graduate students with visual impairments in South Carolina.

Eligibility This program is open to residents of South Carolina who are legally blind in both eyes. Applicants must be currently enrolled or accepted at a technical school, college, university, or graduate school. Along with their application, they must submit a letter of recommendation, transcript, and a 2-page autobiographical sketch that describes their goals, strengths, weaknesses, and other pertinent information.

Financial data The stipend is $1,000.

Duration 1 year.

Number awarded 1 or more each year.

Deadline September of each year.

[133]
E.U. PARKER SCHOLARSHIP

National Federation of the Blind
Attn: Scholarship Committee
1800 Johnson Street
Baltimore, MD 21230
(410) 659-9314, ext. 2415   Fax: (410) 685-5653
E-mail: scholarships@nfb.org
Web: www.nfb.org/nfb/scholarship_program.asp

Summary To provide financial assistance to entering and continuing undergraduate and graduate students who are blind.

Eligibility This program is open to legally blind students who are working on or planning to work full time on an undergraduate or graduate degree. Along with their application, they must submit transcripts, standardized test scores, proof of legal blindness, 2 letters of recommendation, and a letter of endorsement from their letter of endorsement from their National Federation of the Blind state president or designee. Selection is based on academic excellence, service to the community, and financial need.

Financial data The stipend is $3,000.

Duration 1 year; recipients may resubmit applications up to 2 additional years.

Additional data Scholarships are awarded at the federation convention in July. Recipients must attend the con-

vention at federation expense; that funding is in addition to the scholarship grant.

Number awarded 1 each year.

Deadline March of each year.

[134]
EUNICE FIORITO MEMORIAL SCHOLARSHIP

American Council of the Blind
Attn: Coordinator, Scholarship Program
2200 Wilson Boulevard, Suite 650
Arlington, VA 22201
(202) 467-5081   Toll Free: (800) 424-8666
Fax: (703) 465-5085   E-mail: info@acb.org
Web: www.acb.org

Summary To provide financial assistance to undergraduate or graduate students who are blind and are interested in studying in a field of advocacy or service for persons with disabilities.

Eligibility This program is open to undergraduate and graduate students in rehabilitation, education, law, or other fields of service or advocacy for persons with disabilities. Applicants must be legally blind in both eyes. Along with their application, they must submit verification of legal blindness in both eyes; SAT, ACT, GRE, or similar scores; information on extracurricular activities (including membership in the American Council of the Blind); employment record; and an autobiographical sketch that includes their personal goals, strengths, weaknesses, hobbies, honors, achievements, and reasons for choice of field or courses of study. A cumulative GPA of 3.3 or higher is generally required. Financial need is not considered in the selection process. Preference is given to students with little or no vision.

Financial data The stipend is $2,000. In addition, the winner receives a Kurzweil-1000 Reading System.

Duration 1 year.

Additional data The scholarship winner is expected to be present at the council's annual national convention; the council will cover all reasonable costs connected with convention attendance.

Number awarded 1 each year.

Deadline February of each year.

[135]
FELLOWSHIP FOR LEADERSHIP DEVELOPMENT

National Industries for the Blind
Attn: Business Leaders Program Manager
1310 Braddock Place
Alexandria, VA 22314-1691
(703) 310-0515   E-mail: kpal@nib.org
Web: www.nib.org

Summary To provide an opportunity for blind people to gain experience and management training while working at the National Industries for the Blind (NIB).

Eligibility This program is open to blind people who have an undergraduate degree, work experience, desire to travel, and "a passion to become a business leader." Applicants must be interested in working at NIB and its associated agencies to gain experience and training in business management and leadership. They should have well-developed proficiency in Microsoft Office Suite and web experience that includes Internet research and online forms. Training workshops focus on such topics as budgeting and financial management, human resources, marketing, business law, quality assurance, business technology, operations management, planning, communications, and risk management.

Financial data Fellows receive a competitive salary with insurance and benefits.

Duration 2 years. Fellows are given 3 consecutive job assignments, each lasting 8 months and each at a different location.

Additional data Upon successful completion of the fellowship, participants are offered a responsible position within NIB or an NIB associated agency.

Number awarded 3 fellows are selected in each cycle.

Deadline August of the year before the start of a cycle.

[136]
FERDINAND TORRES SCHOLARSHIP

American Foundation for the Blind
Attn: Scholarship Committee
11 Penn Plaza, Suite 300
New York, NY 10001
(212) 502-7661   Toll Free: (800) AFB-LINE
Fax: (212) 502-7771   TDD: (212) 502-7662
E-mail: afbinfo@afb.net
Web: www.afb.org/Section.asp?Documentid=2962

Summary To provide financial assistance for college or graduate school to blind students, especially immigrants and those from New York City.

Eligibility Applicants must be legally blind and reside in the United States, although U.S. citizenship is not necessary. They must present evidence of economic need, legal blindness, and acceptance into a full-time undergraduate or graduate program. Preference is given to new immigrants and residents of New York City. Along with their application, they must submit a 200-word essay that includes their past and recent achievements and accomplishments; their intended field of study and why they have chosen it; the role their visual impairment has played in shaping their life; their financial need and how they would use the scholarship; and (for immigrants) their country of origin and their reasons for coming to the United States.

Financial data The stipend is $2,500.

Duration 1 year.

Number awarded 1 each year.

Deadline April of each year.

[137]
FLORENCE MARGARET HARVEY MEMORIAL SCHOLARSHIP

American Foundation for the Blind
Attn: Scholarship Committee
11 Penn Plaza, Suite 300
New York, NY 10001
(212) 502-7661   Toll Free: (800) AFB-LINE
Fax: (212) 502-7771   TDD: (212) 502-7662
E-mail: afbinfo@afb.net
Web: www.afb.org/Section.asp?Documentid=2962

Summary To provide financial assistance to blind undergraduate and graduate students who wish to study in the field of rehabilitation and/or education of the blind.

Eligibility This program is open to legally blind juniors, seniors, or graduate students. U.S. citizenship is required. Applicants must be studying in the field of rehabilitation and/or education of visually impaired and blind persons. Along with their application, they must submit a 200-word essay that includes their past and recent achievements and accomplishments; their intended field of study and why they have chosen it; and the role their visual impairment has played in shaping their life. Financial need is considered in the selection process.

Financial data The stipend is $1,000.

Duration 1 year.

Additional data This scholarship is supported by the Delta Gamma Foundation and administered by the American Foundation for the Blind.

Number awarded 1 each year.

Deadline April of each year.

[138]
FLOYD CALLWARD MEMORIAL SCHOLARSHIP

National Federation of the Blind of New Hampshire
c/o Marie Johnson, President
11 Springfield Street
Concord, NH 03301
(603) 225-7917   E-mail: jomar2000@comcast.net

Summary To provide financial assistance to blind students in New Hampshire who are interested in working on an undergraduate or graduate degree at a school in any state.

Eligibility This program is open to legally blind and totally blind residents of New Hampshire who are attending or planning to attend college or graduate school in any state. Applicants may be attending college immediately after high school, returning to college at a later age, attending graduate or professional school, or enrolled in postsecondary vocational training. Along with their application, they must submit 1) a letter describing what they have done to deal with situations involving their blindness, their personal goals and aspirations, and how the scholarship will help them; 2) 2 letters of recommendation; 3) high school or college transcripts; 4) a list of honors and awards; and 5) information on community service and volunteer work. There are no restrictions on level, gender, or field of study. Financial need is not considered.

Financial data   The stipend is $1,000. The funds may be used to purchase education-related equipment or services or to defray the costs of tuition, board, and other school fees.

Duration   1 year.

Additional data   This program was established in 1990.

Number awarded   1 or more each year.

Deadline   October of each year.

[139]
FLOYD QUALLS MEMORIAL SCHOLARSHIPS

American Council of the Blind
Attn: Coordinator, Scholarship Program
2200 Wilson Boulevard, Suite 650
Arlington, VA 22201
(202) 467-5081   Toll Free: (800) 424-8666
Fax: (703) 465-5085   E-mail: info@acb.org
Web: www.acb.org

Summary   To provide financial assistance to entering and continuing undergraduate and graduate students who are blind.

Eligibility   This program is open to legally blind students in 4 categories: entering freshmen in academic programs, undergraduates (sophomores, juniors, and seniors) in academic programs, graduate students in academic programs, and vocational school students or students working on an associate's degree from a community college. Applicants must submit verification of legal blindness in both eyes; SAT, ACT, GRE, or similar scores; information on extracurricular activities (including membership in the American Council of the Blind); employment record; and an autobiographical sketch that includes their personal goals, strengths, weaknesses, hobbies, honors, achievements, and reasons for choice of field or courses of study. A cumulative GPA of 3.3 or higher is generally required. Financial need is not considered in the selection process.

Financial data   The stipend is $2,500. In addition, the winners receive a Kurzweil-1000 Reading System.

Duration   1 year.

Additional data   Scholarship winners are expected to be present at the council's annual conference; the council will cover all reasonable expenses connected with convention attendance.

Number awarded   4 each year: 1 in each of the 4 categories.

Deadline   February of each year.

[140]
GEORGIA COUNCIL OF THE BLIND SCHOLARSHIPS

Georgia Council of the Blind
850 Gaines School Road
Athens, GA 30605
Toll Free: (877) 667-6815
E-mail: marshafarrow@alltel.net
Web: www.georgiacounciloftheblind.org

Summary   To provide financial assistance students in Georgia who plan to attend college or graduate school in any state and are either legally blind or have legally blind parents.

Eligibility   This program is open to residents of Georgia who are either 1) legally blind students, or 2) sighted students financially dependent on legally blind parents. Applicants must be enrolled or accepted for enrollment at a vocational/technical school, a 2-year or 4-year college, or a master's or doctoral program in any state. All fields of study are eligible. Selection is based on academic transcripts, 2 letters of recommendation, a 1-page typed statement of the applicant's educational goals, an audio cassette recording of the applicant reading the goals statement, extracurricular activities, and financial need.

Financial data   Stipends up to $1,000 per year are available.

Duration   1 year; recipients may reapply.

Additional data   This program began in 1988.

Number awarded   1 or more each year.

Deadline   June of each year.

[141]
GLADYS C. ANDERSON MEMORIAL SCHOLARSHIP

American Foundation for the Blind
Attn: Scholarship Committee
11 Penn Plaza, Suite 300
New York, NY 10001
(212) 502-7661   Toll Free: (800) AFB-LINE
Fax: (212) 502-7771   TDD: (212) 502-7662
E-mail: afbinfo@afb.net
Web: www.afb.org/Section.asp?Documentid=2962

Summary   To provide financial assistance to legally blind women who are studying classical or religious music at the undergraduate or graduate school level.

Eligibility   This program is open to women who are legally blind, U.S. citizens, and enrolled in an undergraduate or graduate degree program in classical or religious music. Along with their application, they must submit a 200-word essay that includes their past and recent achievements and accomplishments; their intended field of study and why they have chosen it; and the role their visual impairment has played in shaping their life. They must also submit a sample performance tape or CD of up to 30 minutes. Financial need is considered in the selection process.

Financial data   The stipend is $1,000.

Duration   1 academic year.

Number awarded   1 each year.

Deadline   April of each year.

[142]
GUIDE DOGS FOR THE BLIND DOROTHEA AND ROLAND BOHDE LEADERSHIP SCHOLARSHIP

National Federation of the Blind
Attn: Scholarship Committee
1800 Johnson Street
Baltimore, MD 21230
(410) 659-9314, ext. 2415   Fax: (410) 685-5653
E-mail: scholarships@nfb.org
Web: www.nfb.org/nfb/scholarship_program.asp

Summary   To provide financial assistance to blind undergraduate and graduate students, especially those who use a guide dog.

Eligibility   This program is open to legally blind students who are working on or planning to work full time on an undergraduate or graduate degree. Preference is given to applicants who have chosen to use a guide dog as their primary travel aid. Along with their application, they must submit transcripts, standardized test scores, proof of legal blindness, 2 letters of recommendation, and a letter of endorsement from their National Federation of the Blind state president or designee. Selection is based on academic excellence, service to the community, and financial need.

Financial data   The stipend is $3,000.

Duration   1 year; recipients may resubmit applications up to 2 additional years.

Additional data   Scholarships are awarded at the federation convention in July. Recipients must attend the convention at federation expense; that funding is in addition to the scholarship grant.

Number awarded   1 each year.

Deadline   March of each year.

[143]
HANK HOFSTETTER OPPORTUNITY GRANTS

American Council of the Blind of Indiana
c/o James R. Durst
Indiana School for the Blind
7725 North College Avenue
Indianapolis, IN 46240
Web: indianaacb.tripod.com/hofstetter.htm

Summary   To provide financial assistance to Indiana residents who are blind and desire materials or equipment to continue their education or meet other needs.

Eligibility   This fund is open to certified legally blind Indiana residents who are unable to obtain funding through other means. Applicants must need funding for an activity, materials, and/or equipment that will enhance their educational, entrepreneurial, or vocational aims. Along with their application, they must submit a 1-page statement on why they should be considered for a grant, a list of other options or sources that have already been tried, and a reference letter.

Financial data   The amount awarded varies, depending upon the needs of the recipient. A total of $1,000 is available annually.

Number awarded   1 or more each year.

Deadline   Requests may be submitted at any time but should be received at least 90 days prior to the need.

[144]
HANK LEBONNE SCHOLARSHIP

National Federation of the Blind
Attn: Scholarship Committee
1800 Johnson Street
Baltimore, MD 21230
(410) 659-9314, ext. 2415   Fax: (410) 685-5653
E-mail: scholarships@nfb.org
Web: www.nfb.org/nfb/scholarship_program.asp

Summary   To provide financial assistance to legally blind students working on or planning to work on an undergraduate or graduate degree.

Eligibility   This program is open to legally blind students who are working on or planning to work full time on an undergraduate or graduate degree. Along with their application, they must submit transcripts, standardized test scores, proof of legal blindness, 2 letters of recommendation, and a letter of endorsement from their National Federation of the Blind state president or designee. Selection is based on academic excellence, service to the community, and financial need.

Financial data   The stipend is $5,000.

Duration   1 year; recipients may resubmit applications up to 2 additional years.

Additional data   Scholarships are awarded at the federation convention in July. Recipients must attend the convention at federation expense; that funding is in addition to the scholarship grant.

Number awarded   1 each year.

Deadline   March of each year.

[145]
HARRY LUDWIG MEMORIAL SCHOLARSHIP

Oregon Student Assistance Commission
Attn: Grants and Scholarships Division
1500 Valley River Drive, Suite 100
Eugene, OR 97401-2146
(541) 687-7395   Toll Free: (800) 452-8807, ext. 7395
Fax: (541) 687-7414   TDD: (800) 735-2900
E-mail: awardinfo@osac.state.or.us
Web: www.osac.state.or.us/osac_programs.html

Summary   To provide financial assistance to residents of Oregon who are visually impaired and are interested in attending college or graduate school in the state.

Eligibility   This program is open to residents of Oregon who are visually impaired (have residual acuity of 20/70 or less in the better eye with correction, or their visual field is restricted to 20 degrees or less in the better eye). Applicants must be enrolled or planning to enroll as full-time undergraduate or graduate students at a college or university in Oregon.

Financial data   Stipend amounts vary; recently, they were at least $1,643.

Duration   1 year.

Additional data This program is administered by the Oregon Student Assistance Commission (OSAC) with funds provided by the Oregon Community Foundation, 1221 S.W. Yamhill, Suite 100, Portland, OR 97205, (503) 227-6846, Fax: (503) 274-7771.

Number awarded Varies each year; recently, 7 of these scholarships were awarded.

Deadline February of each year.

[146]
HAZEL TEN BROEK MEMORIAL SCHOLARSHIP

National Federation of the Blind of Washington
c/o Rita Szantay, Scholarship Chair
1420 Fifth Avenue, Suite 2200
Seattle, WA 98101
(206) 224-7242   E-mail: rszantay@speakeasy.net
Web: www.nfbw.org

Summary To provide financial assistance for undergraduate or graduate study in any state to blind students in Washington.

Eligibility This program is open to legally blind residents of Washington state who are working on or planning to work on a full-time college or graduate degree at a school in any state. Applicants must submit a list of honors and awards they have received, information on their community service involvement, high school and/or college transcripts, and 3 letters of reference.

Financial data The stipend is $2,000.

Duration 1 year.

Additional data This scholarship was first awarded in 1996. Winners must attend the state convention of the National Federation of the Blind of Washington to accept the award; convention expenses are covered.

Number awarded 1 each year.

Deadline August of each year.

[147]
HERMIONE GRANT CALHOUN SCHOLARSHIP

National Federation of the Blind
Attn: Scholarship Committee
1800 Johnson Street
Baltimore, MD 21230
(410) 659-9314, ext. 2415   Fax: (410) 685-5653
E-mail: scholarships@nfb.org
Web: www.nfb.org/nfb/scholarship_program.asp

Summary To provide financial assistance to female blind students interested in working on an undergraduate or graduate degree.

Eligibility This program is open to legally blind women who are working on or planning to work full time on an undergraduate or graduate degree. Along with their application, they must submit transcripts, standardized test scores, proof of legal blindness, 2 letters of recommendation, and a letter of endorsement from their National Federation of the Blind state president or designee. Selection is based on academic excellence, service to the community, and financial need.

Financial data The stipend is $3,000.

Duration 1 year; recipients may resubmit applications up to 2 additional years.

Additional data Scholarships are awarded at the federation convention in July. Recipients attend the convention at federation expense; that funding is in addition to the scholarship grant.

Number awarded 1 each year.

Deadline March of each year.

[148]
HOLLY ELLIOTT AND LAUREL GLASS SCHOLARSHIP ENDOWMENT

United Methodist Higher Education Foundation
Attn: Scholarships Administrator
1001 19th Avenue South
P.O. Box 340005
Nashville, TN 37203-0005
(615) 340-7385   Toll Free: (800) 811-8110
Fax: (615) 340-7330
E-mail: umhefscholarships@gbhem.org
Web: www.umhef.org/receive.php?id=endowed_funds

Summary To provide financial assistance to students at United Methodist seminaries who are deaf or deaf-blind.

Eligibility This program is open to students enrolled full time at United Methodist theological schools who are culturally deaf, orally deaf, deafened, late deafened, deaf-blind, or hard of hearing. Applicants must be preparing for specialized ministries in the church, including (but not limited to) those wishing to become ordained. They must have been active, full members of a United Methodist Church for at least 1 year prior to applying. Financial need and U.S. citizenship or permanent resident status are required.

Financial data The stipend is at least $1,000 per year.

Duration 1 year; nonrenewable.

Additional data This program was established in 2004.

Number awarded 1 each year.

Deadline May of each year.

[149]
HOWARD BROWN RICKARD SCHOLARSHIP

National Federation of the Blind
Attn: Scholarship Committee
1800 Johnson Street
Baltimore, MD 21230
(410) 659-9314, ext. 2415   Fax: (410) 685-5653
E-mail: scholarships@nfb.org
Web: www.nfb.org/nfb/scholarship_program.asp

Summary To provide financial assistance for college or graduate school to blind students studying or planning to study law, medicine, engineering, architecture, or the natural sciences.

Eligibility This program is open to legally blind students who are enrolled in or planning to enroll in a full-time undergraduate or graduate course of study. Applicants must be studying or planning to study law, medicine, engineering, architecture, or the natural sciences. Along with their application, they must submit transcripts, standardized test scores, proof of legal blindness, 2 letters of recommendation, and a letter of endorsement from their National Federation of the Blind state president or designee. Selection is based on academic excellence, service to the community, and financial need.

Financial data The stipend is $3,000.

Duration 1 year; recipients may resubmit applications up to 2 additional years.

Additional data Scholarships are awarded at the federation convention in July. Recipients must attend the convention at federation expense; that funding is in addition to the scholarship grant.

Number awarded 1 each year.

Deadline March of each year.

[150]
JAMES DOYLE CASE MEMORIAL SCHOLARSHIPS

Mississippi Council of the Blind
P.O. Box 31112
Jackson, MS 39286-1112
(601) 371-0616   Toll Free: (888) 346-5622 (within MS)
Web: www.acb.org/mcb

Summary To provide financial assistance to legally blind residents of Mississippi and their children who plan to attend college or graduate school in any state.

Eligibility This program is open to residents of Mississippi who are legally blind or the children of at least 1 legally blind parent. Applicants must be enrolled or accepted for enrollment in an undergraduate or graduate program in any state and carrying or planning to carry at least 12 academic hours. Along with their application, they must submit a 2-page autobiographical sketch, transcripts, standardized test scores (ACT or SAT for undergraduates; GRE, MCAT, LSAT, etc. for graduate students), 2 letters of recommendation, proof of acceptance from a postsecondary school, and verification of blindness of the qualifying person (applicant or parent).

Financial data The stipend is $1,500 per year.

Duration 4 years.

Number awarded 2 each year.

Deadline February of each year.

[151]
JEANNETTE C. EYERLY MEMORIAL SCHOLARSHIP

National Federation of the Blind
Attn: Scholarship Committee
1800 Johnson Street
Baltimore, MD 21230
(410) 659-9314, ext. 2415   Fax: (410) 685-5653
E-mail: scholarships@nfb.org
Web: www.nfb.org/nfb/scholarship_program.asp

Summary To provide financial assistance to legally blind students working on or planning to work on an undergraduate or graduate degree.

Eligibility This program is open to legally blind students who are working on or planning to work full time on an undergraduate or graduate degree. Along with their application, they must submit transcripts, standardized test

scores, proof of legal blindness, 2 letters of recommendation, and a letter of endorsement from their National Federation of the Blind state president or designee. Selection is based on academic excellence, service to the community, and financial need.

Financial data The stipend is $3,000.

Duration 1 year; recipients may resubmit applications up to 2 additional years.

Additional data Scholarships are awarded at the federation convention in July. Recipients must attend the convention at federation expense; that funding is in addition to the scholarship grant.

Number awarded 1 each year.

Deadline March of each year.

[152]
JENNICA FERGUSON MEMORIAL SCHOLARSHIP OF OHIO

National Federation of the Blind of Ohio
c/o Barbara Pierce, Scholarship Committee Chair
237 Oak Street
Oberlin, OH 44074-1517
(440) 775-2216   E-mail: bpierce@nfb.org
Web: www.nfbohio.org

Summary To provide financial assistance to blind residents of Ohio who are interested in working on an undergraduate or graduate degree at a school in any state.

Eligibility This program is open to residents of Ohio who are legally blind. Applicants must be attending or planning to attend an accredited institution of higher education as a full-time undergraduate or graduate student. Along with their application, they must submit 2 letters of recommendation, current transcripts, a letter about themselves that includes how they have dealt with their blindness and their hopes and dreams, and a letter from an officer of the National Federation of the Blind of Ohio indicating that they have discussed their scholarship application with that officer. Selection is based on academic excellence, community service, and financial need.

Financial data The stipend is $1,500.

Duration 1 year.

Number awarded 1 each year.

Deadline April of each year.

[153]
JOANN FISCHER SCHOLARSHIP

American Council of the Blind of Ohio
Attn: Executive Director
P.O. Box 307128
Gahanna, OH 43230-7128
(614) 221-6688   Toll Free: (800) 835-2226 (within OH)
E-mail: mary.hiland@sbcglobal.net
Web: www.acbohio.org/application_cur.php

Summary To provide financial assistance to Ohio graduate students who are blind.

Eligibility This program is open to 1) residents of Ohio who are currently enrolled as graduate students, and 2) graduate students at colleges and universities in Ohio. Applicants must be legally blind and working on or planning to work on a degree in any field. Along with their application, they must submit transcripts (must have a GPA of 3.0 or higher), a certificate of legal blindness, and an essay of 250 to 500 words on their career objectives, future plans, personal goals, other academic or personal qualities, and why they believe they are qualified to receive this scholarship. Financial need is not the sole factor considered in the selection process.

Financial data The stipend is $2,500 per year.

Duration 1 year; recipients may reapply.

Additional data Winners are required to attend the Saturday morning business meeting and Sunday breakfast of the sponsor's annual convention; a stipend for meals and workshops is provided.

Number awarded 1 each year.

Deadline July of each year.

[154]
JOHN FREEBAIRN SCHOLARSHIP

Utah Council of the Blind
c/o Leslie Gertsch, Executive Director
1301 West 500 South
Woods Cross, UT 84087-2224
(801) 292-1156   Fax: (801) 292-6046
E-mail: lgertsch@comcast.net
Web: www.acb.org/utah

Summary To provide financial assistance to members of the Utah Council of the Blind (UCB) who plan to attend college or graduate school in the state.

Eligibility This program is open to UCB members who are entering or enrolled as an undergraduate or graduate student at a college or university in Utah. Applicants must be blind or visually impaired, defined as having a visual acuity of less than 20/70, a visual field not exceeding 30 degrees, or a functional visual impairment of similar degree in the best eye with best correction. Along with their application, they must submit an autobiographical sketch that includes their personal goals, strengths, weaknesses, hobbies, honors, achievements, the course of study they are pursuing, and why they have chosen it. Financial need is not considered in the selection process. Interviews may be held.

Financial data The stipend is $1,500.

Duration 1 year; may be renewed.

Number awarded 1 each year.

Deadline April of each year.

[155]
KENNETH JERNIGAN SCHOLARSHIP

National Federation of the Blind
Attn: Scholarship Committee
1800 Johnson Street
Baltimore, MD 21230
(410) 659-9314, ext. 2415   Fax: (410) 685-5653
E-mail: scholarships@nfb.org
Web: www.nfb.org/nfb/scholarship_program.asp

Summary To provide financial assistance to entering or continuing undergraduate and graduate blind students.

Eligibility This program is open to legally blind students who are working on or planning to work full time on an undergraduate or graduate degree. Along with their application, they must submit transcripts, standardized test scores, proof of legal blindness, 2 letters of recommendation, and a letter of endorsement from their National Federation of the Blind state president or designee. Selection is based on academic excellence, service to the community, and financial need.

Financial data The stipend is $12,000.

Duration 1 year; recipients may resubmit applications up to 2 additional years.

Additional data Scholarships are awarded at the federation convention in July. Recipients must attend the convention at federation expense; that funding is in addition to the scholarship grant. This scholarship is given by the American Action Fund for Blind Children and Adults, a nonprofit organization that assists blind people.

Number awarded 1 each year.

Deadline March of each year.

[156]
KUCHLER-KILLIAN MEMORIAL SCHOLARSHIP

National Federation of the Blind
Attn: Scholarship Committee
1800 Johnson Street
Baltimore, MD 21230
(410) 659-9314, ext. 2415   Fax: (410) 685-5653
E-mail: scholarships@nfb.org
Web: www.nfb.org/nfb/scholarship_program.asp

Summary To provide financial assistance to blind students working on an undergraduate or graduate degree in any field.

Eligibility This program is open to legally blind students who are working on or planning to work full time on an undergraduate or graduate degree in any field. Along with their application, they must submit transcripts, standardized test scores, proof of legal blindness, 2 letters of recommendation, and a letter of endorsement from their National Federation of the Blind state president or designee. Selection is based on academic excellence, service to the community, and financial need.

Financial data The stipend is $3,000.

Duration 1 year; recipients may resubmit applications up to 2 additional years.

Additional data Scholarships are awarded at the federation convention in July. Recipients must attend the convention at federation expense; that funding is in addition to the scholarship grant.

Number awarded 1 each year.

Deadline March of each year.

[157]
LANCASTER SCHOLARSHIP

Susquehanna Foundation for the Blind
244 North Queen Street, Suite 301
Lancaster, PA 17603
(717) 393-5894   Fax: (717) 435-8367
E-mail: info@sfblind.org
Web: sfblind.com/Content/scholarships.asp

Summary To provide financial assistance to Pennsylvania residents who are legally blind veterans and interested in working on a degree at any level at a college in any state.

Eligibility This program is open to veterans who are residents of Pennsylvania and legally blind. Applicants must be attending or planning to attend an institution of higher education at any level in any state. Along with their application, they must submit a brief description of their career goal. Financial need is considered in the selection process.

Financial data The stipend is $1,000 per year.

Duration 1 year; may be renewed up to 3 additional years

Number awarded 1 or more each year.

Deadline Deadline not specified.

[158]
LINWOOD WALKER SCHOLARSHIP

American Council of the Blind of Ohio
Attn: Executive Director
P.O. Box 307128
Gahanna, OH 43230-7128
(614) 221-6688 Toll Free: (800) 835-2226 (within OH)
E-mail: mary.hiland@sbcglobal.net
Web: www.acbohio.org/application_cur.php

Summary To provide financial assistance to blind Ohio graduate students in service-related fields.

Eligibility This program is open to 1) residents of Ohio who are currently enrolled as graduate students, and 2) graduate students at colleges and universities in Ohio. Applicants must be legally blind and working on or planning to work on a degree in a service-related field (e.g., teaching, health care, public administration). Along with their application, they must submit transcripts (must have a GPA of 3.0 or higher), a certificate of legal blindness, and an essay of 250 to 500 words on their career objectives, future plans, personal goals, other academic or personal qualities, and why they believe they are qualified to receive this scholarship. Financial need is not the sole factor considered in the selection process.

Financial data The stipend is $2,500 per year.

Duration 1 year; recipients may reapply.

Additional data Winners are required to attend the Saturday morning business meeting and Sunday breakfast of the sponsor's annual convention; a stipend for meals and workshops is provided.

Number awarded 1 each year.

Deadline July of each year.

[159]
MISSOURI COUNCIL OF THE BLIND SCHOLARSHIPS

Missouri Council of the Blind
5453 Chippewa Street
St. Louis, MO 63109-1635
(314) 832-7172 Toll Free: (800) 342-5632 (within MO)
Fax: (314) 832-7796
E-mail: executivedirector@missouricounciloftheblind.org
Web: www.missouricounciloftheblind.org

Summary To provide financial assistance for college or graduate school to blind students in Missouri.

Eligibility This program is open to Missouri residents who are high school or college graduates, legally blind, and in good academic standing. Applicants must be working on or planning to work on an undergraduate or graduate degree. They should have a specific goal in mind and that goal should be realistically within reach.

Financial data The stipend is $1,200.

Duration 1 year; may be renewed if the recipient maintains a GPA of 2.0 or higher.

Number awarded Varies each year; recently, 14 of these scholarships were awarded.

Deadline May of each year.

[160]
NATIONAL FEDERATION OF THE BLIND OF CALIFORNIA SCHOLARSHIPS

National Federation of the Blind of California
c/o Mary Willows, President
39481 Gallaudet Drive, Apartment 127
Fremont, CA 94538
(510) 248-0100   Toll Free: (877) 558-6524
E-mail: mwillows@sbcglobal.net
Web: www.nfbcal.org/nfbc/scholarships.html

Summary To provide financial assistance to blind residents of California interested in attending college or graduate school in any state.

Eligibility This program is open to residents of California who are legally blind. Applicants must be enrolled or planning to enroll as a full time student in an undergraduate or graduate degree program in any state. They must have a GPA of 3.0 or higher. Along with their application, they must submit a 500-word statement on the educational and career goals they wish to achieve with the assistance of this scholarship, their involvement in the blindness community, the alternative techniques they use to do their school work (e.g., Braille, large print, recording, adapted computer), and any rehabilitation services they are receiving. Financial need is not considered in the selection process.

Financial data Stipends range from $2,000 to $5,000.

Duration 1 year.

Additional data This program includes the following named awards: the Gerald Drake Memorial Scholarship, the LaVyrl "Pinky" Johnson Memorial Scholarship, the Julie Landucci Scholarship, and the Lawrence "Muzzy" Marcelino Memorial Scholarship.

Number awarded Several each year.
Deadline August of each year.

[161]
NATIONAL FEDERATION OF THE BLIND OF CONNECTICUT SCHOLARSHIPS

National Federation of the Blind of Connecticut
477 Connecticut Boulevard, Suite 217
East Hartford, CT 06108
(860) 289-1971 E-mail: info@nfbct.org
Web: www.nfbct.org/html/schform.htm

Summary To provide financial assistance for college or graduate school to blind students from Connecticut.

Eligibility This program is open to full-time undergraduate and graduate students who are legally blind. Applicants must be residents of Connecticut or attending school in the state. Along with their application, they must submit 2 letters of recommendation, academic transcripts, a description of their career goals and how this scholarship might help them achieve those, and a letter from a state officer of the National Federation of the Blind of Connecticut confirming that they have discussed their application with him or her. Selection is based on academic excellence, service to the community, and financial need.

Financial data Stipends are $8,000, $4,000, or $3,000.

Duration 1 year.

Additional data This program consists of the following named awards: the C. Rodney Demarest Memorial Scholarship ($3,000), the Howard E. May Memorial Scholarship ($6,000), the Jonathan May Memorial Scholarship ($5,000), and the Mary Main Memorial Scholarship ($4,000). The latter 3 programs are supported by the John A. Coccomo, Sr. Foundation. Recipients are expected to attend the annual convention of the National Federation of the Blind of Connecticut.

Number awarded 4 each year.

Deadline September of each year.

[162]
NATIONAL FEDERATION OF THE BLIND OF ILLINOIS SCHOLARSHIPS

National Federation of the Blind of Illinois
c/o Deborah Kent Stein, Scholarship Committee Chair
5817 North Nina Avenue
Chicago, IL 60631
(773) 631-1093 E-mail: dkent5817@worldnet.att.net
Web: www.nfbofillinois.org/NFBIscholarship.htm

Summary To provide financial assistance for college or graduate school to blind students in Illinois.

Eligibility This program is open to legally blind full-time undergraduate and graduate students. Applicants must be residents of Illinois or attending a college or university in the state. Along with their application, they must submit a personal essay that includes their strengths, achievements, and aspirations; what is important to them; who they hope to become; if a particular person or experience has changed their life; how their blindness has affected them; and how they handle blindness at school, on the job, and in interpersonal relationships. Selection is based on

academic excellence, service to the community, and financial need.

Financial data Stipends range from $1,250 to $2,000 per year.

Duration 1 year; recipients may reapply.

Additional data This program consists of the following named awards: the Peter Grunwald Scholarship (1 awarded at $2,000), the Mary MacDill Napheide Scholarships (2 awarded at $1,500 each), and the Kenneth Jernigan Scholarships (2 awarded at $1,250 each).

Number awarded 5 each year.

Deadline March of each year.

[163]
NATIONAL FEDERATION OF THE BLIND OF OHIO SCHOLARSHIP

National Federation of the Blind of Ohio
c/o Barbara Pierce, Scholarship Committee Chair
237 Oak Street
Oberlin, OH 44074-1517
(440) 775-2216 E-mail: bpierce@nfb.org
Web: www.nfbohio.org

Summary To provide financial assistance to blind residents of Ohio who are interested in working on an undergraduate or graduate degree at a school in any state.

Eligibility This program is open to residents of Ohio who are legally blind. Applicants must be attending or planning to attend an accredited institution of higher education as a full-time undergraduate or graduate student. Along with their application, they must submit 2 letters of recommendation, current transcripts, a letter about themselves that includes how they have dealt with their blindness and their hopes and dreams, and a letter from an officer of the National Federation of the Blind of Ohio indicating that they have discussed their scholarship application with that officer. Selection is based on academic excellence, community service, and financial need.

Financial data The stipend is $1,000.

Duration 1 year.

Number awarded 1 each year.

Deadline April of each year.

[164]
NATIONAL FEDERATION OF THE BLIND OF OREGON SCHOLARSHIPS

National Federation of the Blind of Oregon
c/o Art Stevenson, President
1616 Fifth Street N.E.
Salem, OR 97303
(503) 585-4318 Toll Free: (800) 422-7093 (within OR)
E-mail: artds55@comcast.net
Web: www.nfb-oregon.org/scholarship.html

Summary To provide financial assistance for college or graduate school to blind residents of Oregon.

Eligibility This program is open to blind residents of Oregon who are working on or planning to work on an undergraduate or graduate degree at a college or university in the state. Applicants must be enrolled full time or enrolled part time and working full time. Along with the application, they must submit a personal letter that includes what they consider their best qualities and the techniques and approaches they practice concerning their blindness. Selection is based on academic excellence, community service, and financial need.

Financial data Stipends are either $1,500 or $1,000.

Duration 1 year.

Number awarded 3 each year: 1 at $1,500 and 2 at $1,000.

Deadline September of each year.

[165]
NATIONAL FEDERATION OF THE BLIND OF UTAH SCHOLARSHIPS

National Federation of the Blind of Utah
Attn: Scholarship Committee
132 Penman Lane
Bountiful, UT 84010-7634
(801) 292-3000　　　　　Toll Free: (888) 292-3007
E-mail: president@nfbutah.org
Web: nfbutah.org/scholarships

Summary To provide financial assistance to blind residents of Utah who plan to attend college or graduate school in any state.

Eligibility This program is open to legally blind residents of Utah who are working on or planning to work full time on an undergraduate or graduate degree at a school in any state. Along with their application, they must submit transcripts, standardized test scores, proof of legal blindness, 2 letters of recommendation, and a letter of endorsement from an officer of the National Federation of the Blind of Utah. Selection is based on academic excellence, service to the community, and financial need.

Financial data A stipend is awarded (amount not specified).

Duration 1 year.

Number awarded Varies each year.

Deadline March of each year.

[166]
NFB EDUCATOR OF TOMORROW AWARD

National Federation of the Blind
Attn: Scholarship Committee
1800 Johnson Street
Baltimore, MD 21230
(410) 659-9314, ext. 2415　　　Fax: (410) 685-5653
E-mail: scholarships@nfb.org
Web: www.nfb.org/nfb/scholarship_program.asp

Summary To provide financial assistance to entering or continuing blind undergraduate or graduate students who wish to prepare for a career as a teacher.

Eligibility This program is open to legally blind students who are working on or planning to work full time on an undergraduate or graduate degree. Applicants must be preparing for a career in elementary, secondary, or post-secondary teaching. Along with their application, they must submit transcripts, standardized test scores, proof of legal blindness, 2 letters of recommendation, and a letter of endorsement from their National Federation of the Blind

state president or designee. Selection is based on academic excellence, service to the community, and financial need.

Financial data The stipend is $3,000.

Duration 1 year; recipients may resubmit applications up to 2 additional years.

Additional data Scholarships are awarded at the federation convention in July. Recipients must attend the convention at federation expense; that funding is in addition to the scholarship grant.

Number awarded 1 each year.

Deadline March of each year.

[167]
NFB SCHOLARSHIPS

National Federation of the Blind
Attn: Scholarship Committee
1800 Johnson Street
Baltimore, MD 21230
(410) 659-9314, ext. 2415　　　Fax: (410) 685-5653
E-mail: scholarships@nfb.org
Web: www.nfb.org/nfb/scholarship_program.asp

Summary To provide financial assistance for college or graduate school to blind students.

Eligibility This program is open to legally blind students who are working on or planning to work on an undergraduate or graduate degree. In general, full-time enrollment is required, although 1 scholarship may be awarded to a part-time student who is working full time. Along with their application, they must submit transcripts, standardized test scores, proof of legal blindness, 2 letters of recommendation, and a letter of endorsement from their National Federation of the Blind state president or designee. Selection is based on academic excellence, service to the community, and financial need.

Financial data Stipends are $7,000, $5,000, or $3,000.

Duration 1 year; recipients may resubmit applications up to 2 additional years.

Additional data Scholarships are awarded at the federation convention in July. Recipients must attend the convention at federation expense; that funding is in addition to the scholarship grant.

Number awarded 18 each year: 2 at $7,000. 3 at $5,000, and 13 at $3,000.

Deadline March of each year.

[168]
NFBNJ SCHOLARSHIPS

National Federation of the Blind of New Jersey
c/o Jerilyn L. Higgins, Scholarship Chair
2 Old Farm Road
Verona, NJ 07044-1726
(973) 239-8874　　　　　Toll Free: (866) 632-1940
E-mail: nfbnj@yahoo.com
Web: www.nfbnj.org/scholarships.php

Summary To provide financial assistance to entering and continuing undergraduate and graduate students from New Jersey who are blind.

Eligibility This program is open to legally blind students who are working on or planning to work full time on an undergraduate or graduate degree. Applicants must be residents of New Jersey or attending school in the state. Along with their application, they must submit a personal letter, 2 letters of recommendation, transcripts, and a letter of endorsement from an officer of the National Federation of the Blind of New Jersey. Selection is based on academic excellence, service to the community, and financial need.

Financial data A stipend is awarded (amount not specified).

Duration 1 year.

Number awarded 1 or more each year.

Deadline March of each year.

[169]
NFBNY SCHOLARSHIPS

National Federation of the Blind of New York State, Inc.
P.O. Box 205666 Sunset Station
Brooklyn, NY 11220
(718) 567-7821   Fax: (718) 765-1843
E-mail: office@nfbny.org
Web: www.nfbny.org/Scholsrships.htm

Summary To provide financial assistance to blind residents of New York who are interested in attending college or graduate school in any state.

Eligibility This program is open to residents of New York who are legally blind. Applicants must be entering or enrolled in a degree program at the undergraduate, graduate, or postgraduate level at a school in any state. Along with their application, they must submit a 500-word essay explaining their goals, attitudes, and approach to living with blindness.

Financial data A stipend is awarded (amount not specified).

Duration 1 year.

Additional data This program includes the following named awards: the Gisela Distal Memorial Scholarship and the Maryanne Swaton Memorial Scholarship. Information is also available from Raymond Wayne, Scholarship Committee Chair, (718) 491-0053.

Number awarded At least 3 each year.

Deadline October of each year.

[170]
NFBW/BEVERLY PROWS MEMORIAL SCHOLARSHIP

National Federation of the Blind of Washington
c/o Rita Szantay, Scholarship Chair
1420 Fifth Avenue, Suite 2200
Seattle, WA 98101
(206) 224-7242   E-mail: rszantay@speakeasy.net
Web: www.nfbw.org

Summary To provide financial assistance for undergraduate or graduate study in any state to blind students in Washington.

Eligibility This program is open to legally blind residents of Washington state who are working on or planning to work on a full-time college or graduate degree at a school in any state. Applicants must submit a list of honors and awards they have received, information on their community service involvement, high school and/or college transcripts, and 3 letters of reference.

Financial data The stipend is $3,000.

Duration 1 year; recipients may reapply.

Additional data This scholarship was first awarded in 1991. Winners must attend the state convention of the National Federation of the Blind of Washington to accept the award; convention expenses are covered.

Number awarded 1 each year.

Deadline August of each year.

[171]
NIB GRANT M. MACK MEMORIAL SCHOLARSHIP

American Council of the Blind
Attn: Coordinator, Scholarship Program
2200 Wilson Boulevard, Suite 650
Arlington, VA 22201
(202) 467-5081   Toll Free: (800) 424-8666
Fax: (703) 465-5085   E-mail: info@acb.org
Web: www.acb.org

Summary To provide financial assistance to blind students who are working on an undergraduate or graduate degree in business or management.

Eligibility This program is open to undergraduate and graduate students working on a degree in business or management. Applicants must submit verification of legal blindness in both eyes; SAT, ACT, GMAT, or similar scores; information on extracurricular activities (including membership in the American Council of the Blind); employment record; and an autobiographical sketch that includes their personal goals, strengths, weaknesses, hobbies, honors, achievements, and reasons for choice of field or courses of study. A cumulative GPA of 3.3 or higher is generally required. Financial need is not considered in the selection process. U.S. citizenship or permanent resident status is required.

Financial data The stipend is $2,000. In addition, the winner receives a Kurzweil-1000 Reading System.

Duration 1 year.

Additional data This scholarship is sponsored by National Industries for the Blind (NIB) in honor of a dedicated leader of the American Council of the Blind. Scholarship winners are expected to be present at the council's annual conference; the council will cover all reasonable expenses connected with convention attendance.

Number awarded 1 each year.

Deadline February of each year.

[172]
NORA WEBB-MCKINNEY SCHOLARSHIP

American Council of the Blind of Ohio
Attn: Executive Director
P.O. Box 307128
Gahanna, OH 43230-7128
(614) 221-6688   Toll Free: (800) 835-2226 (within OH)
E-mail: mary.hiland@sbcglobal.net
Web: www.acbohio.org/application_cur.php

Summary   To provide financial assistance to blind and other Ohio students who are interested in working on an undergraduate or graduate degree involving service to blind people.

Eligibility   This program is open to 1) residents of Ohio who are high school seniors or current undergraduate or graduate students, and 2) undergraduate and graduate students at colleges and universities in Ohio. Applicants must be interested in working on or planning to work on a degree in a field related to blindness (e.g., special education, rehabilitation teaching or counseling, orientation and mobility, or a concentration on programs serving people who are blind). They may be blind or sighted. Along with their application, they must submit transcripts (must have a GPA of 3.0 or higher) and an essay of 250 to 500 words on their career objectives, future plans, personal goals, other academic or personal qualities, and why they believe they are qualified to receive this scholarship. Financial need is not the sole factor considered in the selection process.

Financial data   The stipend is $2,000 per year.

Duration   1 year; recipients may reapply.

Additional data   Winners are required to attend the Saturday morning business meeting and Sunday breakfast of the sponsor's annual convention; a stipend for meals and workshops is provided.

Number awarded   1 each year.

Deadline   July of each year.

[173]
NORTH DAKOTA ASSOCIATION OF THE BLIND SCHOLARSHIPS

North Dakota Association of the Blind
c/o Tammy Winn, Scholarship Committee Chair
103 Lilac Lane, Number 2
Minot AFB Base, ND 58704
(701) 727-9211   E-mail: roytammy@srt.com
Web: www.ndab.org/Scholarship.html

Summary   To provide financial assistance for college or graduate school to blind students in North Dakota.

Eligibility   This program is open to North Dakota residents who are legally blind and attending an institution of higher education in the state. Applicants must be full-time students with a class standing of a sophomore through a graduate student and a GPA of 2.5 or higher. They must submit 2 letters of recommendation, transcripts, a family financial aid statement, and an essay that describes their vocational interests, how the scholarship will help them, their goals and aspirations, and what they have done to deal with situations involving their visual impairment.

Selection is based on academic excellence, financial need, and service to the community.

Financial data   Stipends are $1,000 or $500.

Duration   1 year.

Additional data   This program was established in 1990.

Number awarded   3 each year: 1 at $1,000 and 2 at $500.

Deadline   March of each year.

[174]
PAUL AND ELLEN RUCKES SCHOLARSHIP

American Foundation for the Blind
Attn: Scholarship Committee
11 Penn Plaza, Suite 300
New York, NY 10001
(212) 502-7661   Toll Free: (800) AFB-LINE
Fax: (212) 502-7771   TDD: (212) 502-7662
E-mail: afbinfo@afb.net
Web: www.afb.org/Section.asp?Documentid=2962

Summary   To provide financial assistance to legally blind students who wish to work on a graduate or undergraduate degree in engineering or computer, physical, or life sciences.

Eligibility   This program is open to legally blind undergraduate or graduate students who are U.S. citizens working full time on a degree in engineering or the computer, physical, or life sciences. Along with their application, they must submit a 200-word essay that includes their past and recent achievements and accomplishments; their intended field of study and why they have chosen it; and the role their visual impairment has played in shaping their life. Financial need is considered in the selection process.

Financial data   The stipend is $1,000.

Duration   1 year.

Number awarded   1 each year.

Deadline   April of each year.

[175]
ROSS N. AND PATRICIA PANGERE FOUNDATION SCHOLARSHIPS

American Council of the Blind
Attn: Coordinator, Scholarship Program
2200 Wilson Boulevard, Suite 650
Arlington, VA 22201
(202) 467-5081   Toll Free: (800) 424-8666
Fax: (703) 465-5085   E-mail: info@acb.org
Web: www.acb.org

Summary   To provide financial assistance to blind students working on an undergraduate or graduate degree in business.

Eligibility   This program is open to undergraduate and graduate students working on a degree in business. Applicants must submit verification of legal blindness in both eyes; SAT, ACT, GMAT, or similar scores; information on extracurricular activities (including membership in the American Council of the Blind); employment record; and an autobiographical sketch that includes their personal goals, strengths, weaknesses, hobbies, honors, achievements, and reasons for choice of field or courses of study.

A cumulative GPA of 3.3 or higher is generally required. Financial need is not considered in the selection process.

Financial data The stipend is $2,500. In addition, the winner receives a Kurzweil-1000 Reading System.

Duration 1 year.

Additional data The scholarship winner is expected to be present at the council's annual national convention; the council will cover all reasonable costs connected with convention attendance.

Number awarded 2 each year.

Deadline February of each year.

[176]
ROY JOHNSON SCHOLARSHIPS

Roy Johnson Scholarship Trust Fund
Attn: James S. Buscetta, Trustee
Michigan Commission for the Blind
201 North Washington Square, Second Floor
P.O. Box 30652
Lansing, MI 48909
(517) 373-2062   Toll Free: (800) 292-4200
Fax: (517) 335-5140   TDD: (517) 373-4025

Summary To provide tuition assistance to residents of any state who are blind and interested in working on a graduate degree at a college in Michigan.

Eligibility This program is open to blind people (regardless of sex, race, color, religion, or age) who have received a bachelor's degree from an accredited college or university in the United States. Applicants must be working on or planning to work on a graduate degree at an institution in Michigan. Both college seniors and currently-enrolled graduate students are eligible. For the purposes of this award, a "blind person" means an individual who has a visual acuity of 20/200 or less in the better eye with correction, or has a limitation of vision such that the widest diameter of the visual field subtends an angular distance of not greater than 20 degrees. Factors considered in the selection process include financial need, scholastic record, college recommendations, and applicant's plans for graduate education.

Financial data Stipends range from $250 to $1,000. Funds may be used to cover tuition, room and board, or reader services.

Duration 1 year.

Additional data Funds must be used to pursue graduate studies at an accredited college in Michigan.

Number awarded Varies each year; recently, 13 of these scholarships were awarded.

Deadline May of each year.

[177]
RUDOLPH DILLMAN MEMORIAL SCHOLARSHIP

American Foundation for the Blind
Attn: Scholarship Committee
11 Penn Plaza, Suite 300
New York, NY 10001
(212) 502-7661   Toll Free: (800) AFB-LINE
Fax: (212) 502-7771   TDD: (212) 502-7662
E-mail: afbinfo@afb.net
Web: www.afb.org/Section.asp?Documentid=2962

Summary To provide financial assistance to legally blind undergraduate or graduate students studying in the field of rehabilitation and/or education of visually impaired and blind persons.

Eligibility This program is open to legally-blind U.S. citizens who have been accepted to an accredited undergraduate or graduate training program within the broad field of rehabilitation and/or education of blind and visually impaired persons. Along with their application, they must submit a 200-word essay that includes their past and recent achievements and accomplishments; their intended field of study and why they have chosen it; and the role their visual impairment has played in shaping their life. Financial need is considered for 1 of the scholarships.

Financial data The stipend is $2,500 per year.

Duration 1 academic year; previous recipients may not reapply.

Number awarded 4 each year: 3 without consideration of financial need and 1 based on financial need.

Deadline April of each year.

[178]
SOUTH DAKOTA FREE TUITION FOR VISUALLY IMPAIRED PERSONS

South Dakota Board of Regents
Attn: Scholarship Committee
306 East Capitol Avenue, Suite 200
Pierre, SD 57501-2545
(605) 773-3455   Fax: (605) 773-2422
E-mail: info@sdbor.edu
Web: www.sdbor.edu

Summary To provide financial assistance for college or graduate school to visually impaired residents of South Dakota.

Eligibility Eligible for this program is any visually impaired resident of South Dakota who can meet the entrance requirements for admission to a postsecondary educational institution (including graduate school and medical school) under the supervision of the state board of regents. For purposes of the program, "visual impairment" means that the person cannot, with use of correcting glasses, see sufficiently well to perform ordinary activities for which eyesight is essential. This program does not extend to visually impaired persons who are entitled to receive tuition and fee support from the state's department of vocational rehabilitation.

Financial data Qualified applicants may attend any institution under the supervision of the South Dakota

Board of Regents without payment of tuition, library fees, registration fees, or any other fees.

Duration Benefits are provided until the recipient has earned 225 semester hours of credit or the equivalent.

Additional data Applicants should contact the financial aid director at the South Dakota college or university they plan to attend, not the sponsor. The exemption from charges does not apply if a course is repeated because of unsatisfactory work, unless the problem was caused by illness or some other circumstance for which the student had no responsibility.

Number awarded Varies each year.

Deadline Deadline not specified.

[179]
SUPPORT SERVICES FOR THE BLIND AND VISUALLY IMPAIRED

Lions Clubs International
Attn: Program Development Department
300 West 22nd Street
Oak Brook, IL 60523-8842
(630) 571-5466, ext. 316   Fax: (630) 571-1692
E-mail: programs@lionsclubs.org
Web: www.lionsclubs.org

Summary To provide college scholarships and other assistance to blind people.

Eligibility These programs are open to blind people and others involved in service to the blind. Applicants may be seeking support for the following activities: scholarships for the blind and visually impaired, medical research, assistive technology grants, independent mobility, transportation, reading materials and aids, audio products, Braille products, and other aids.

Financial data The amount of this assistance varies.

Additional data Support is provided by local clubs of Lions Clubs International. Requests sent to the international office are referred to the appropriate district governor. If any of the clubs within the district conduct programs for which the applicant might be considered, the governor will advise the particular club to contact the applicant. No funds are available from the office of Lions Clubs International.

Deadline Deadline not specified.

[180]
SUSQUEHANNA FOUNDATION FOR THE BLIND TRUSTEES' SCHOLARSHIP

Susquehanna Foundation for the Blind
244 North Queen Street, Suite 301
Lancaster, PA 17603
(717) 393-5894   Fax: (717) 435-8367
E-mail: info@sfblind.org
Web: sfblind.com/Content/scholarships.asp

Summary To provide financial assistance to legally blind Pennsylvania residents who are interested in working on an undergraduate or graduate degree or other academic program at a school in any state.

Eligibility This program is open to residents of Pennsylvania who are legally blind. Applicants must be working on an undergraduate or graduate degree or other specialized program intended to generate upward mobility in employment. Along with their application, they must submit a brief description of their career goal. Financial need is considered in the selection process.

Financial data A stipend is awarded (amount not specified).

Duration 1 year.

Number awarded 1 or more each year.

Deadline Deadline not specified.

[181]
SUSQUEHANNA POST-GRADUATE SCHOLARSHIP

Susquehanna Foundation for the Blind
244 North Queen Street, Suite 301
Lancaster, PA 17603
(717) 393-5894   Fax: (717) 435-8367
E-mail: info@sfblind.org
Web: sfblind.com/Content/scholarships.asp

Summary To provide financial assistance to legally blind Pennsylvania residents who are interested in working on a graduate degree at a school in any state to prepare for a career in rehabilitation services for people who are blind.

Eligibility This program is open to residents of Pennsylvania who are legally blind. Applicants must be interested in working on a graduate degree in a professional field serving people who are blind (e.g., rehabilitation teaching, orientation and mobility instruction, teacher of the visually impaired). Along with their application, they must submit a brief description of their career goal. Financial need is considered in the selection process.

Financial data The stipend is $3,000 per year.

Duration 2 years.

Number awarded 1 or more each year.

Deadline Deadline not specified.

[182]
TRINKA DAVIS GRADUATE AWARD

Lighthouse International
Attn: Scholarship and Career Awards
111 East 59th Street
New York, NY 10022-1202
(212) 821-9428   Toll Free: (800) 829-0500
Fax: (212) 821-9703   TDD: (212) 821-9713
E-mail: sca@lighthouse.org
Web: www.lighthouse.org

Summary To provide financial assistance to legally blind graduate students residing and attending school in selected eastern states.

Eligibility This program is open to graduate students who are legally blind and U.S. citizens. Applicants must be residing in and working on or planning to work on a graduate degree in Connecticut, Delaware, Florida, Georgia, Maine, Maryland, Massachusetts, New Hampshire, New Jersey, New York, North Carolina, Pennsylvania, Rhode Island, South Carolina, Vermont, Virginia, Washington, D.C., or West Virginia. They must submit a 500-word essay describing their academic achievements and career goals. Financial need is not considered in the selection process.

Financial data The stipend is $5,000.

Duration 1 year.

Number awarded 1 each year.

Deadline February of each year.

[183]
UCB POULSON FAMILY SCHOLARSHIPS

Utah Council of the Blind
c/o Leslie Gertsch, Executive Director
1301 West 500 South
Woods Cross, UT 84087-2224
(801) 292-1156　　　　　　　Fax: (801) 292-6046
E-mail: lgertsch@comcast.net
Web: www.acb.org/utah/ucbschol1.htm

Summary To provide financial assistance to members of the Utah Council of the Blind (UCB) who plan to attend college or graduate school in the state.

Eligibility This program is open to UCB members who are entering or enrolled as an undergraduate or graduate student at a college or university in Utah. Applicants must be blind or visually impaired, defined as having a visual acuity of less than 20/70, a visual field not exceeding 30 degrees, or a functional visual impairment of similar degree in the best eye with best correction. Along with their application, they must submit an autobiographical sketch that includes their personal goals, strengths, weaknesses, hobbies, honors, achievements, the course of study they are pursuing, and why they have chosen it. Financial need is not considered in the selection process. Interviews may be held.

Financial data The stipend is $1,500.

Duration 1 year; may be renewed.

Number awarded Varies each year; recently, 5 of these scholarships were awarded.

Deadline April of each year.

[184]
WALTER YOUNG MEMORIAL SCHOLARSHIP

California Association for Postsecondary Education
  and Disability
Attn: Executive Assistant
71423 Biskra Road
Rancho Mirage, CA 92270
(760) 346-8206　　　　　　　Fax: (760) 340-5275
TDD: (760) 341-4084　　　E-mail: caped2000@aol.com
Web: www.caped.net/scholarships.html

Summary To provide financial assistance to blind and visually impaired undergraduate and graduate students in California.

Eligibility This program is open to blind and visually impaired students at public and private colleges and universities in California. Undergraduates must have completed at least 6 semester credits and have a GPA of 2.5 or higher. Graduate students must have completed at least 3 semester units and have a GPA of 3.0 or higher. Along with their application, they must submit a 1-page personal letter that demonstrates their writing skills, progress towards

meeting their educational and vocational goals, management of their disability, and involvement in community activities. They must also submit a letter of recommendation from a faculty member, verification of disability, official transcripts, proof of current enrollment, and documentation of financial need.

Financial data The stipend is $1,000.

Duration 1 year.

Number awarded 1 each year.

Deadline September of each year.

[185]
WASHINGTON COUNCIL OF THE BLIND SCHOLARSHIPS

Washington Council of the Blind
c/o Julie Brannon, Scholarship Committee Chair
6801 Greenwood Avenue North, Unit 209
Seattle, WA 98103
Toll Free: (206) 547-7444
E-mail: jbrannon0612@comcast.net
Web: www.wcbinfo.org

Summary To provide financial aid to blind students in Washington who plan to attend college or graduate school in any state.

Eligibility This program is open to blind residents of Washington state who are enrolled or planning to enroll at an accredited college, university, vocational school, or graduate school in any state. Applicants must submit a 1,000-word statement of their reasons for applying for this scholarship and how it will assist them to achieve their goals. The statement should include a brief description of their background, education, work experience, economic status, strengths, weaknesses, and personal goals for the next 5 to 10 years. Interviews are required.

Financial data The stipend ranges up to $4,000.

Duration 1 year.

Number awarded 1 or more each year.

Deadline July of each year.

[186]
WILLIAM G. COREY MEMORIAL SCHOLARSHIP

American Council of the Blind
Attn: Coordinator, Scholarship Program
2200 Wilson Boulevard, Suite 650
Arlington, VA 22201
(202) 467-5081　　　　　　　Toll Free: (800) 424-8666
Fax: (703) 465-5085　　　　　E-mail: info@acb.org
Web: www.acb.org

Summary To provide financial assistance for college to blind undergraduate and graduate students from Pennsylvania.

Eligibility This program is open to legally blind undergraduate and graduate students who are residents of Pennsylvania or attending college in the state. Applicants must submit verification of legal blindness in both eyes; SAT, ACT, GRE, or similar scores; information on extracurricular activities (including membership in the American Council of the Blind); employment record; and an autobiographical sketch that includes their personal goals, strengths, weaknesses, hobbies, honors, achievements, and reasons for choice of field or courses of study. A cumulative GPA of 3.3 or higher is generally required. Financial need is not considered in the selection process.

Financial data The stipend is $1,500. In addition, the winner receives a Kurzweil-1000 Reading System.

Duration 1 year.

Additional data Scholarship winners are expected to be present at the council's annual conference; the council will cover all reasonable expenses connected with convention attendance.

Number awarded 1 each year.

Deadline February of each year.

Grants-in-Aid

[187]
ALABAMA COUNTY HOMESTEAD EXEMPTIONS

Alabama Department of Revenue
Attn: Property Tax Division
Gordon Persons Building
50 North Ripley Street, Room 4126
P.O. Box 327210
Montgomery, AL 36132-7210
(334) 242-1525
Web: www.ador.state.al.us

Summary To exempt disabled, blind, and elderly residents of Alabama from ad valorem property taxes imposed by counties.

Eligibility Residents of Alabama are eligible to apply if they are over the age of 65 and have a net annual income of $12,000 or less for income tax purposes for the preceding year; or are retired due to permanent and total disability, regardless of age; or are blind, regardless of age or retirement status.

Financial data Qualifying residents are exempt from ad valorem property taxes levied by counties, including taxes levied for school districts, to a maximum of $5,000 in assessed value, or 160 acres in area.

Duration 1 year; this exemption will be granted as long as the resident continues to meet the eligibility requirements.

Number awarded Varies each year.

Deadline Deadline not specified.

[188]
ALABAMA PERSONAL PROPERTY TAX EXEMPTION FOR THE BLIND

Alabama Department of Revenue
Attn: Property Tax Division
Gordon Persons Building
50 North Ripley Street, Room 4126
P.O. Box 327210
Montgomery, AL 36132-7210
(334) 242-1525
Web: www.ador.state.al.us

Summary To exempt blind residents of Alabama from taxation on a portion of their personal property.

Eligibility Residents of Alabama are eligible for this personal property tax exemption if they are legally defined as blind.

Financial data Up to $12,000 of personal property is exempt from taxation.

Duration 1 year; this exemption will be granted as long as the resident continues to meet the eligibility requirements.

Number awarded Varies each year.

Deadline Deadline not specified.

[189]
ALABAMA STATE HOMESTEAD EXEMPTIONS

Alabama Department of Revenue
Attn: Property Tax Division
Gordon Persons Building
50 North Ripley Street, Room 4126
P.O. Box 327210
Montgomery, AL 36132-7210
(334) 242-1525
Web: www.ador.state.al.us

Summary To exempt disabled, blind, and elderly residents of Alabama from ad valorem property taxes imposed by the state.

Eligibility Residents of Alabama are eligible to apply if they are 1) over the age of 65; 2) retired due to permanent and total disability, regardless of age; or 3) blind, regardless of age or retirement status.

Financial data Qualifying residents are exempt from all ad valorem property taxes levied by the state, up to 160 acres in area.

Duration 1 year; this exemption will be granted as long as the resident continues to meet the eligibility requirements.

Number awarded Varies each year.

Deadline Deadline not specified.

[190]
AMERICAN COUNCIL OF THE BLIND OF OREGON GRANT-IN-AID

American Council of the Blind of Oregon
c/o James Edwards, President
P.O. Box 83
Lakeside, OR 97449
(541) 404-8214   E-mail: jamese.acbo@yahoo.com
Web: www.acboforegon.org/grants.html

Summary To provide funding for special purposes or purchase of equipment to blind residents of Oregon.

Eligibility This program is open to blind residents of Oregon who are either registered with the Oregon Commission for the Blind or can provide proof of legal blindness. Applicants must submit an statement of 25 to 50 words on the purpose of the proposed grant. If the application is for an equipment grant, they must provide an indication of the item's cost and name of the company from which the equipment is to be purchased. They must also include a 50- to 75-word narrative about themselves.

Financial data The amount of the grant depends on the nature of the application.

Duration 1 year.

Additional data The American Council of the Blind of Oregon is legally incorporated as the Oregon Council of the Blind.

Number awarded Varies each year.

Deadline Applications may be submitted at any time; decisions are made quarterly.

[191]
ARIZONA INCOME TAX EXEMPTION FOR THE BLIND

Arizona Department of Revenue
1600 West Monroe Street
Phoenix, AZ 85007-2650
(602) 542-3572   Toll Free: (800) 352-4090 (within AZ)
TDD: (602) 542-4021
Web: www.revenue.state.az.us

Summary To exempt a portion of the income of blind people from state income taxes in Arizona.

Eligibility This exemption is available to blind residents of Arizona who meet a legal definition of blindness.

Financial data Exempt from state income taxation is $1,500 of the income of blind people.

Duration The exemption continues as long as the recipient resides in Arizona.

Deadline Deadline not specified.

[192]
ARKANSAS DISABLED VETERANS PROPERTY TAX EXEMPTION

Arkansas Assessment Coordination Department
1614 West Third Street
Little Rock, AR 72201-1815
(501) 324-9100   Fax: (501) 324-9242
E-mail: dasbury@acd.state.ar.us
Web: www.arkansas.gov/acd

Summary To exempt from taxation the property owned by blind or disabled veterans, surviving spouses, and minor dependent children in Arkansas.

Eligibility This program is open to disabled veterans in Arkansas who have been awarded special monthly compensation by the U.S. Department of Veterans Affairs and who have 1) the loss of or the loss of use of 1 or more limbs, 2) total blindness in 1 or both eyes, or 3) total and permanent disability. The benefit also extends to veterans' unremarried surviving spouses and their minor children.

Financial data Qualifying veterans (or their unremarried widows or dependent children) are exempt from payment of all state taxes on their homestead and personal property.

Duration This exemption continues as long as the qualifying veteran (or dependent) resides in Arkansas.

Number awarded Varies each year.

Deadline Applications may be submitted at any time.

[193]
ASSOCIATION OF BLIND CITIZENS ASSISTIVE TECHNOLOGY FUND

Association of Blind Citizens
P.O. Box 246
Holbrook, MA 02343
(781) 961-1023   Fax: (781) 961-0004
E-mail: atf@blindcitizens.org
Web: www.blindcitizens.org/assistive_tech.htm

Summary To provide funding to blind people interested in purchasing adaptive devices or software.

Eligibility This program is open to legally blind residents of the United States. Applicants must be interested in purchasing a technology product that will improve their employment opportunities, increase their level of independence, and enhance their overall quality of life. They must have a family income of less than $50,000 per year and cash assets of less than $20,000. The products covered by this program must retail for at least $200 but no more than $6,000. Applicants must include a 500-word description of the device and how it will help them achieve employment or increase their independence.

Financial data Grants cover 50% of the retail price of adaptive devices or software.

Duration These are 1-time grants.

Number awarded Varies each year.

Deadline June or December of each year.

[194]
AUTOMOBILE ALLOWANCE FOR DISABLED VETERANS

Department of Veterans Affairs
Attn: Veterans Benefits Administration
810 Vermont Avenue, N.W.
Washington, DC 20420
(202) 418-4343   Toll Free: (800) 827-1000
Web: www.vba.va.gov/bin/21/Benefits

Summary To provide funding to certain disabled veterans and current service personnel who require specially adapted automobiles.

Eligibility To be eligible for a grant for an automobile, a veteran or current servicemember must have a service-connected loss or permanent loss of use of 1 or both hands or feet or permanent impairment of vision of both eyes to a prescribed degree. For adaptive equipment eligibility only, veterans entitled to compensation for ankylosis of 1 or both knees, or 1 or both hips, also qualify.

Financial data The grant consists of a payment by the Department of Veterans Affairs (VA) of up to $11,000 toward the purchase of an automobile or other conveyance. The VA will also pay for the adaptive equipment, its repair, and the replacement or reinstallation required for the safe operation of the vehicle purchased with VA assistance or for a previously or subsequently acquired vehicle.

Duration This is a 1-time grant.

Number awarded Varies each year.

Deadline Applications may be submitted at any time.

[195]
CALIFORNIA DISABLED VETERAN EXEMPTION FROM THE IN LIEU TAX FEE FOR A MANUFACTURED HOME OR MOBILEHOME

Department of Housing and Community Development
Attn: Registration and Titling
1800 Third Street
P.O. Box 2111
Sacramento, CA 95812-2111
(916) 323-9224   Toll Free: (800) 952-8356
Web: www.hcd.ca.gov

Summary To provide a special property tax exemption to blind or disabled California veterans and/or their spouses who own and occupy a mobile home.

Eligibility This program is open to disabled veterans and/or their spouses in California who have a manufactured home or mobile home as their principal place of residence. Veterans must be disabled as a result of injury or disease incurred in military service and have been a resident of California 1) at the time of entry into the service and be blind, or have lost the use of 1 or more limbs, or be totally disabled; 2) on November 7, 1972 and be blind in both eyes, or have lost the use of 2 or more limbs; or 3) on January 1, 1975 and be totally disabled. The spouses and unremarried surviving spouses of those disabled veterans are also eligible.

Financial data The exemption applies to the first $20,000 of the assessed market value of the manufactured home or mobile home. Veterans and/or spouses whose income falls below a specified level are entitled to an additional $10,000 exemption. The amount of the exemption is 100% if the home is owned by a veteran only, a veteran and spouse, or a spouse only; 50% if owned by a veteran and another person other than a spouse or by a spouse and another person other than the veteran; 67% if owned by a veteran, the spouse, and another person; 34% if owned by a veteran and 2 other people other than a spouse or by a spouse and 2 other people; 50% if owned by a veteran, the spouse, and 2 other people; or 25% if owned by a veteran and 3 other people or by a spouse and 3 other people.

Duration The exemption is available annually as long as the applicant meets all requirements.

Number awarded Varies each year.

Deadline Deadline not specified.

[196]
CALIFORNIA PROPERTY TAX EXEMPTIONS FOR VETERANS

California Department of Veterans Affairs
Attn: Division of Veterans Services
1227 O Street, Room 101
Sacramento, CA 95814
(916) 503-8397
Toll Free: (800) 952-LOAN (within CA)
Fax: (916) 653-2563   TDD: (800) 324-5966
E-mail: ruckergl@cdva.ca.gov
Web: www.cdva.ca.gov/VetService/Overview.aspx

Summary To exempt a portion of the property of blind or disabled veterans in California and their spouses from taxation.

Eligibility This exemption is available to homeowners in California who are wartime veterans in receipt of service-connected disability compensation that is 1) at the totally disabled rate, 2) for loss or loss of use of 2 or more limbs, or 3) for blindness. Unremarried surviving spouses, including registered domestic partners, of veterans who are in receipt of service-connected death benefits are also eligible.

Financial data For veterans and spouses whose total household income from all sources is greater than $49,979 per year, up to $111,296 of the assessed value of a home is exempt from taxation. For veterans and spouses whose total household income from all sources is less than $49,979 per year, up to $166,944 of the assessed value of a home is exempt from taxation.

Duration The exemption is available as long as the veteran or spouse owns a home in California.

Additional data Information is available from the local county assessors office in each California county.

Number awarded Varies each year.

Deadline Applications may be submitted at any time.

[197]
CONNECTICUT REAL ESTATE TAX EXEMPTION FOR DISABLED VETERANS

Office of Policy and Management
Attn: Intergovernmental Policy Division
450 Capitol Avenue
Hartford, CT 06106-1308
(860) 418-6278   Toll Free: (800) 286-2214 (within CT)
Fax: (860) 418-6493   TDD: (860) 418-6456
E-mail: leeann.graham@ct.gov
Web: www.ct.gov

Summary To exempt Connecticut veterans with disabilities and their surviving spouses from the payment of a portion of their local property taxes.

Eligibility There are 2 categories of Connecticut veterans who qualify for exemptions from their dwelling house and the lot on which it is located: 1) those with major service-connected disabilities (paraplegia or osteochondritis resulting in permanent loss of the use of both legs or permanent paralysis of both legs and lower parts of the body; hemiplegia with permanent paralysis of 1 leg and 1 arm or either side of the body resulting from injury to the spinal cord, skeletal structure, or brain, or from disease of the spinal cord not resulting from syphilis; total blindness; amputation of both arms, both legs, both hands or both feet, or the combination of a hand and a foot; sustained through enemy action or resulting from an accident occurring or disease contracted in such active service) and 2) those with less severe disabilities (loss of use of 1 arm or 1 leg because of service-connected injuries). Surviving unremarried spouses of eligible deceased veterans are entitled to the same exemption as would have been granted to the veteran, as long as they continue to be the legal owner/occupier of the exempted residence. An additional exemption is available to veterans and spouses whose total adjusted gross income is less than $30,500 if unmarried or $37,300 if married. If the veteran is rated as 100% disabled by the U.S. Department of Veterans Affairs (VA), the maximum income levels are $18,000 if unmarried or $21,000 if married.

Financial data Veterans in the first category receive an exemption from local property taxation of $10,000 of assessed valuation. Veterans in the second category receive exemptions of $5,000 of assessed valuation. For veterans whose income is less than the specified levels, additional exemptions of $20,000 for the first category or $10,000 for the second category are available from municipalities that choose to participate. For veterans whose income exceeds the specified levels, the additional exemption from participating municipalities is $5,000 for the first category or $2,500 for the second category. Connecticut municipalities may also elect to exempt from taxation specially adapted housing acquired or modified by a veteran under the provisions of Section 801 of Title 38 of the United States Code.

Duration 1 year; exemptions continue as long as the eligible resident (or surviving spouse) owns/occupies the primary residence and lives in Connecticut.

Number awarded Varies each year; recently, a total of 22,944 veterans received property tax exemptions through this and other programs in Connecticut.

Deadline Applications for the additional municipality exemption must be submitted to the assessor's office of the town or residence by September of every other year.

[198]
CONNECTICUT TAX RELIEF PROGRAM FOR BLIND PEOPLE

Office of Policy and Management
Attn: Intergovernmental Policy Division
450 Capitol Avenue
Hartford, CT 06106-1308
(860) 418-6322   Toll Free: (800) 286-2214 (within CT)
Fax: (860) 418-6493   TDD: (860) 418-6456
E-mail: ronald.madrid@ct.gov
Web: www.ct.gov/opm/site/default.asp

Summary To exempt blind residents of Connecticut from a portion of their personal property taxes.

Eligibility Eligible to apply for this exemption are Connecticut residents who are blind. An additional exemption may be available to blind residents whose total adjusted gross income is less than $30,500 if unmarried or $37,300 if married.

Financial data The basic state exemption is $3,000 of assessed valuation. Municipalities may elect to provide an additional exemption of $2,000 to blind residents whose income is less than the qualifying level.

Duration 1 year; exemptions continue as long as the eligible resident lives in Connecticut.

Number awarded Varies each year.

Deadline Applications for the additional municipality exemption must be submitted to the assessor's office of the town or residence by September of every other year.

[199]
DELAWARE INCOME TAX DEDUCTION FOR BLIND AND ELDERLY PERSONS

Division of Revenue
Carvel State Office Building
820 North French Street
P.O. Box 8763
Wilmington, DE 19899-8763
(302) 577-3300
Web: revenue.delaware.gov

Summary To provide a deduction from state income taxation to blind people and those over the age of 65 in Delaware.

Eligibility This deduction is available to residents of Delaware who are 1) 65 years of age or older or 2) blind.

Financial data Taxpayers are entitled to an additional standard deduction of $2,500 if they are blind or older than 65. For blind people older than 65, the additional standard deduction is $5,000.

Duration The deduction continues as long as the recipient remains a resident of Delaware for state income tax purposes.

Number awarded Varies each year.

Deadline Deadline not specified.

[200]
DISTRICT OF COLUMBIA INCOME TAX EXEMPTION FOR THE BLIND

Office of Tax and Revenue
Attn: Customer Service Center
941 North Capitol Street, N.E., First Floor
Washington, DC 20002
(202) 727-4TAX   Fax: (202) 442-6477
E-mail: otr.ocfo@dc.gov
Web: otr.cfo.dc.gov/otr/site/default.asp

Summary To exempt a portion of the income of blind people from local income taxation in the District of Columbia.

Eligibility This exemption is available to residents of the District of Columbia who are blind.

Financial data Blind residents are entitled to an exemption of $1,675 from their income for local tax purposes in the District of Columbia.

Duration The exemption continues as long as the recipient resides in the District of Columbia.

Number awarded Varies each year.

Deadline The exemption is claimed as part of the local income return, due in April of each year.

[201]
FLORIDA PROPERTY TAX EXEMPTION FOR TOTALLY AND PERMANENTLY DISABLED PERSONS

Florida Department of Revenue
Attn: Taxpayer Services
1379 Blountstown Highway
Tallahassee, FL 32304-2716
(850) 488-6800   Toll Free: (800) 352-3671
TDD: (800) 367-8331
Web: www.myflorida.com/dor/property/exemptions.html

Summary To exempt from property taxation real estate owned by blind or disabled people in Florida.

Eligibility This exemption is available to Florida residents who have real estate that they own and use as a homestead. Applicants must have 1) quadriplegia; or 2) paraplegia, hemiplegia, or other total and permanent disability, must use a wheelchair for mobility, or must be legally blind, and must have an income below a specified limit that changes annually; recently, the maximum allowable income was $25,221 per year.

Financial data All real estate used and owned as a homestead, less any portion used for commercial purposes, is exempt from taxation.

Duration The exemption applies as long as the taxpayer owns the property in Florida.

Additional data Initial applications should be made in person at the appropriate county property appraiser's office.

Number awarded Varies each year.

Deadline Applications must be submitted by February of the year for which the exemption is sought.

[202]
FRANCES S. MILLER EQUIPMENT SCHOLARSHIP FUND

LightHouse for the Blind and Visually Impaired
Attn: Development Manager
213 Van Ness Avenue
San Francisco, CA 94102
(415) 694-7359   Fax: (415) 863-7568
TDD: (415) 431-4572 E-mail: elord@lighthouse-sf.org
Web: lighthouse-sf.org

Summary To provide funding to blind students in California who need assistance for the purchase of access technology equipment.

Eligibility This program is open to blind, visually impaired, and deaf-blind students who live in California. Applicants must be able to demonstrate a need for assistance to purchase access technology equipment.

Financial data The grant is $2,500.

Duration This is a 1-time award.

Additional data This grant was first awarded in 2006.

Number awarded 1 each year.

Deadline September of each year.

[203]
GEORGIA INCOME TAX DEDUCTION FOR THE BLIND

Georgia Department of Revenue
Attn: Taxpayer Services Division
1800 Century Boulevard, Room 8300
Atlanta, GA 30345-3205
(404) 417-4477   Toll Free: (877) 602-8477
Fax: (404) 417-6628
E-mail: taxpayer.services@dor.ga.gov
Web: etax.dor.ga.gov/inctax/IndGeneralInfo.aspx

Summary To provide a deduction from state income taxation to blind people in Georgia.

Eligibility Eligible are persons classified as residents of Georgia for the purpose of state income taxation who are blind.

Financial data Qualified blind residents are entitled to a deduction of $1,300 from their state income taxation.

Duration The deduction continues as long as the recipient resides in Georgia.

Deadline Deadline not specified.

[204]
HANK HOFSTETTER OPPORTUNITY GRANTS

American Council of the Blind of Indiana
c/o James R. Durst
Indiana School for the Blind
7725 North College Avenue
Indianapolis, IN 46240
Web: indianaacb.tripod.com/hofstetter.htm

Summary To provide financial assistance to Indiana residents who are blind and desire materials or equipment to continue their education or meet other needs.

Eligibility This fund is open to certified legally blind Indiana residents who are unable to obtain funding through other means. Applicants must need funding for an activity, materials, and/or equipment that will enhance their educational, entrepreneurial, or vocational aims. Along with their application, they must submit a 1-page statement on why they should be considered for a grant, a list of other options or sources that have already been tried, and a reference letter.

Financial data The amount awarded varies, depending upon the needs of the recipient. A total of $1,000 is available annually.

Number awarded 1 or more each year.

Deadline Requests may be submitted at any time but should be received at least 90 days prior to the need.

[205]
HAWAII INCOME TAX EXEMPTION FOR DISABLED RESIDENTS
Department of Taxation
Attn: Taxpayer Services Branch
425 Queen Street
P.O. Box 259
Honolulu, HI 96809-0259
(808) 587-4242   Toll Free: (800) 222-3229
Fax: (808) 587-1488   TDD: (808) 587-1418
Web: hawaii.gov/tax

Summary   To exempt a portion of the income of blind, deaf, and other disabled residents from state income tax in Hawaii.

Eligibility   Eligible for this exemption are 1) blind residents whose central visual acuity does not exceed 20/200 in the better eye with corrective lenses or whose visual acuity is greater than 20/200 but is accompanied by a limitation in the field of vision such that the widest diameter of the visual field subtends an angle no greater than 20 degrees; 2) deaf residents whose average loss in the speech frequencies in the better ear is 82 decibels A.S.A. or worse; or 3) totally disabled residents (physically or mentally) who are unable to engage in any substantial gainful business or occupation (a person whose gross income exceeds $30,000 per year is assumed to be engaged in a substantial gainful business or occupation).

Financial data   The maximum exemptions from state income tax are as follows: single disabled resident, $7,000; disabled husband and wife, $14,000; disabled husband or wife, with non-disabled spouse under 65, $8,040; disabled husband or wife, with non-disabled spouse 65 years of age or older, $9,080.

Duration   The exemption continues as long as the recipient resides in Hawaii.

Additional data   Residents who claim this special exemption are not eligible to claim additional exemptions for their children or other dependents.

Deadline   Deadline not specified.

[206]
IDAHO CIRCUIT BREAKER PROPERTY TAX REDUCTION
Idaho State Tax Commission
Attn: Public Information Office
800 Park Boulevard, Plaza IV
P.O. Box 36
Boise, ID 83722-0410
(208) 334-7736   Toll Free: (800) 972-7660
TDD: (800) 377-3529
Web: tax.idaho.gov/propertytax/pt_homeowners.htm

Summary   To reduce a portion of the property tax of disabled and other veterans and other disabled or elderly residents of Idaho.

Eligibility   Eligible for this property tax reduction are residents of Idaho who own and live in a primary residence in the state and have an annual income of $28,000 or less (after deducting designated forms of income, including compensation received by a veteran from the U.S. Depart-

ment of Veterans Affairs for a 40% to 100% service-connected disability). Applicants must be in 1 or more of the following categories: disabled (as recognized by an appropriate federal agency), blind, former prisoner of war or hostage, veteran with at least 10% service-connected disability or receiving a VA pension for a nonservice-connected disability, 65 years of age or older, widow(er) of any age, or fatherless or motherless child under 18 years of age.

Financial data   The maximum amount of reduction is the lesser of $1,320 or the actual taxes on the recipient's qualifying home. The minimum reduction is the lesser of $100 or the actual taxes on the home.

Duration   Applications for this reduction must be submitted each year.

Additional data   All recipients of this reduction automatically receive Idaho's Homeowner's Exemption, which reduces the taxable value of the home (excluding land) by 50% or $75,000, whichever is less. Solid waste, irrigation, or other fees charged by some counties are not taxes and cannot be reduced by this program.

Number awarded   Varies each year.

Deadline   April of each year.

[207]
IDAHO INCOME TAX DEDUCTION FOR THE BLIND AND THEIR WIDOW(ER)S
Idaho State Tax Commission
Attn: Public Information Office
800 Park Boulevard, Plaza IV
P.O. Box 36
Boise, ID 83722-0410
(208) 334-7660   Toll Free: (800) 972-7660
TDD: (800) 377-3529
Web: tax.idaho.gov

Summary   To exempt a portion of the income of blind or elderly residents from state income tax in Idaho.

Eligibility   Eligible for this deduction are blind residents of Idaho and residents over the age of 65.

Financial data   Single individuals and heads of households who are blind or elderly receive an additional $1,250 standard deduction; married individuals who are blind or elderly receive an additional $1,000 standard deduction.

Duration   1 year; must reapply each year.

Number awarded   Varies each year.

Deadline   April of each year.

[208]
ILLINOIS INCOME TAX EXEMPTION FOR THE BLIND
Illinois Department of Revenue
101 West Jefferson Street
P.O. Box 19044
Springfield, IL 62794-9044
(217) 782-9337   Toll Free: (800) 732-8866
TDD: (800) 544-5304
Web: www.revenue.state.il.us

Summary   To provide an income tax deduction to blind people in Illinois.

Eligibility Legally blind residents of Illinois are entitled to take this deduction from their state income tax.

Financial data The deduction is $1,000.

Duration The deduction continues as long as the recipient resides in Illinois.

Deadline Deadline not specified.

[209]
INDIANA INCOME TAX EXEMPTION FOR THE BLIND

Indiana Department of Revenue
Attn: Taxpayer Services Division
Indiana Government Center North
100 North Senate Avenue
Indianapolis, IN 46204-2253
(317) 232-2240   TDD: (317) 232-4952
E-mail: pfrequest@dor.state.in.us
Web: www.in.gov/dor

Summary To exempt a portion of the income of blind people from state taxation in Indiana.

Eligibility Eligible are residents of Indiana who are legally blind.

Financial data An additional exemption of $1,000 from the income for state income taxation in Indiana is allowed.

Duration The exemption continues as long as the recipient resides in Indiana.

Deadline Deadline not specified.

[210]
INDIANA PROPERTY TAX DEDUCTION FOR BLIND OR DISABLED PERSONS

Department of Local Government Finance
Indiana Government Center North, Room 1058
100 North Senate Avenue
Indianapolis, IN 46201
(317) 232-3777   Fax: (317) 232-8779
E-mail: PropertyTaxInfo@dlgf.in.gov
Web: www.in.gov/dlgf

Summary To exempt Indiana residents who are blind or disabled from a portion of their property tax.

Eligibility Eligible for this program are Indiana residents who are blind or disabled and receive less than $17,000 in annual taxable income. A blind person is defined as an individual who has vision in the better eye with correcting glasses of 20/200 or less, or a disqualifying visual field defect as determined upon examination by a designated ophthalmologist or optometrist. A disabled person is defined as an individual unable to engage in any substantial gainful activity by reason of a medically determinable physical or mental impairment that can be expected to result in death or has lasted and can be expected to last for at least 12 continuous months.

Financial data The maximum property tax deduction is $12,480.

Duration This deduction may be taken annually, as long as the Indiana resident meets the requirements of the program.

Additional data Property taxes are administered by individual counties in Indiana. Further information is available from county tax assessors.

Number awarded Varies each year.

Deadline Applications must be filed during the 12 months before May of each year for which the individual wishes to obtain the deduction.

[211]
KANSAS INTANGIBLES TAX SENIOR CITIZEN OR DISABILITY EXEMPTION

Kansas Department of Revenue
Attn: Taxpayer Assistance Center
Robert B. Docking State Office Building
915 S.W. Harrison Street
Topeka, KS 66612-1712
(785) 368-8222   Toll Free: (877) 526-7738
Fax: (785) 291-3614   TDD: (785) 296-6461
Web: www.ksrevenue.org/perstaxtypeint.htm

Summary To exempt a portion of the income received by elderly, blind, or disabled residents in Kansas from the intangibles tax.

Eligibility This exemption applies to residents of local areas in Kansas that levy an intangibles tax on gross earnings received from such property as savings accounts, stocks, bonds, accounts receivable, and mortgages. Applicants must 1) be disabled, blind, or 60 years of age or older and 2) have a household income of $20,000 or less.

Financial data Qualified residents are entitled to exempt from their intangibles income an amount that depends on their income. If total household income is $15,000 or less, the exemption is $5,000. For incomes between $15,000 and $20,000, the exemption is calculated as the difference between $5,000 and the amount of the income over $15,000.

Duration This benefit continues as long as the recipient remains a resident of the Kansas locality that imposes an intangibles tax.

Number awarded Varies each year.

Deadline Deadline not specified.

[212]
KANSAS STATE DEAF-BLIND FUND

Kansas State Department of Education
Student Support Services
Attn: Kansas State Deaf-Blind Fund
120 S.E. 10th Avenue
Topeka, KS 66612-1182
(785) 296-2515   Toll Free: (800) 203-9462
Fax: (785) 296-6715   TDD: (785) 296-2515
E-mail: jhoughton@ksde.org
Web: www.kansped.org/ksde/kstars/projects.html

Summary To provide supplementary financial assistance to deaf-blind or severely disabled students in Kansas.

Eligibility Applications may be submitted by school personnel for students in Kansas (up to the age of 21) who are deaf-blind and/or have severe multiple disabilities. Approval for funding is granted on a first-come, first-served basis for the following areas: 1) assistive technology that enables a student with dual sensory impairments and with severe disabilities to participate more fully in an educational program (e.g., computers, adaptive equipment, eyeglasses, hearing aids, computer peripherals, augmentative communication devices, microswitches, software); 2) consultation; 3) evaluation for the cost of vision and/or hearing evaluations for students who are suspected of being deaf-blind, or a vision, hearing, or educational evaluation for recertification purposes; or 4) other costs associated with additional items or expenses that reflect best educational or effective practices, such as expenses involved in providing community activities. Applicants must provide documentation that other funding sources have been approached and that costs do not exceed the amount local education agencies are able to provide out of federal, state, or local funds. Priority candidates are students who have current deaf-blind certification, deaf-blind children from birth through 2 years of age, students who are exiting state hospital schools and returning to their home district, students who have a suspected vision loss and documented hearing loss and are in need of an evaluation, and students who have a suspected hearing loss and documented vision loss who are in need of an evaluation.

Financial data   Eligible students are awarded up to $3,000 per year.

Duration   1 year; may be renewed.

Number awarded   Varies each year.

Deadline   May of each year.

[213]
MAINE INCOME TAX DEDUCTION FOR THE BLIND

Maine Revenue Services
Attn: Income/Estate Tax Division
24 State House Station
Augusta, ME 04333-0024
(207) 626-8475   Fax: (207) 626-9694
E-mail: income.tax@maine.gov
Web: www.maine.gov

Summary   To deduct a portion of the income of blind and elderly Maine residents from income taxation.

Eligibility   Eligible for this deduction are inhabitants of Maine who are legally blind as determined by the Department of Human Services.

Financial data   For single and head of household taxpayers, the deduction is $1,350 if the individual is 65 or over or blind, or $2,700 if the individual is both 65 or over and blind. For married taxpayers, the deduction is $1,050 for each spouse who is 65 or over or blind.

Duration   Eligible blind residents qualify for this deduction as long as they reside in Maine.

Number awarded   Varies each year.

Deadline   The deduction is included along with the state income tax forms, filed in April of each year.

[214]
MAINE PROPERTY TAX EXEMPTION FOR THE BLIND

Maine Revenue Services
Attn: Property Tax Division
P.O. Box 9106
Augusta, ME 04332-9106
(207) 287-2011   Fax: (207) 287-6396
E-mail: prop.tax@maine.gov
Web: www.maine.gov

Summary   To exempt the estates of blind Maine residents from property taxation.

Eligibility   Eligible for this program are inhabitants of Maine who are legally blind as determined by the Department of Human Services.

Financial data   The exemption is equal to $4,000 times the certified ratio.

Duration   Eligible blind residents qualify for this exemption as long as they own residential property in Maine.

Number awarded   Varies each year.

Deadline   When an eligible person first submits an application, the proof of entitlement must reach the assessors of the local municipality prior to the end of March. Once eligibility has been established, notification need not be repeated in subsequent years.

[215]
MARYLAND INCOME TAX EXEMPTION FOR BLIND AND ELDERLY RESIDENTS

Comptroller of Maryland
Attn: Revenue Administration Division
80 Calvert Street
Annapolis, MD 21411
(410) 260-7980
Toll Free: (800) MD-TAXES (within MD)
Fax: (410) 974-3456   TDD: (410) 260-7157
E-mail: taxhelp@comp.state.md.us
Web: individuals.marylandtaxes.com

Summary   To provide a supplemental income tax exemption to blind and senior residents of Maryland.

Eligibility   Eligible are Maryland residents who are either blind or 65 years of age or older.

Financial data   Eligible Maryland residents are entitled to an additional exemption of $1,000 (in addition to the regular $3,200 personal exemption) from their income for state income tax purposes.

Duration   The exemption continues as long as the recipient resides in Maryland.

Deadline   Deadline not specified.

[216]
MARYLAND INCOME TAX EXEMPTION FOR READERS FOR BLIND RESIDENTS

Comptroller of Maryland
Attn: Revenue Administration Division
80 Calvert Street
Annapolis, MD 21411
(410) 260-7980
Toll Free: (800) MD-TAXES (within MD)
Fax: (410) 974-3456   TDD: (410) 260-7157
E-mail: taxhelp@comp.state.md.us
Web: individuals.marylandtaxes.com

Summary To exempt from state income taxation in Maryland a portion of the expenses incurred by blind people for a reader.

Eligibility Eligible are Maryland residents who 1) are blind and who pay for the use of a reader, or 2) are employers and pay for a reader for a blind employee.

Financial data Blind people may exclude up to $5,000 of expenses incurred for a reader from state income taxation. Employers may exclude up to $1,000 of expenses incurred for a reader for a blind employee.

Duration The exclusion continues as long as the recipient resides in Maryland and utilizes the services of a reader.

Deadline Deadline not specified.

[217]
MARYLAND PROPERTY TAX EXEMPTION FOR BLIND PERSONS

Maryland Department of Assessments and Taxation
Attn: Property Taxes
301 West Preston Street
Baltimore, MD 21201-2395
(410) 767-1184   Toll Free: (888) 246-5941
TDD: (800) 735-2258
Web: www.dat.state.md.us/sdatweb/exempt.html

Summary To exempt the homes of blind people and their surviving spouses from property taxation in Maryland.

Eligibility This exemption is available to residents of Maryland who have a central visual acuity of 20/200 or less in the better eye. Applicants must own a dwelling house in Maryland. Surviving spouses of deceased blind people are also eligible for the exemption.

Financial data The dwelling houses of eligible blind people and their surviving spouses is exempt from $15,000 of assessment on their dwelling house for purposes of real property taxes.

Duration The exemption is available as long as the blind person or surviving spouse owns the dwelling house in Maryland.

Number awarded Varies each year.

Deadline Applications may be submitted at any time.

[218]
MASSACHUSETTS INCOME TAX EXEMPTION FOR BLIND PEOPLE

Massachusetts Department of Revenue
Attn: Personal Income Tax
P.O. Box 7010
Boston, MA 02204
(617) 887-MDOR
Toll Free: (800) 392-6089 (within MA)
Fax: (617) 887-1900
Web: www.mass.gov

Summary To exempt a portion of the income received by blind people from state income taxation in Massachusetts.

Eligibility Eligible for this exemption are residents of Massachusetts who are classified as legally blind.

Financial data Blind persons in Massachusetts are entitled to exempt $2,200 from their income for purposes of state income taxation.

Duration The benefit continues as long as the recipient remains a resident of Massachusetts for state income tax purposes.

Number awarded Varies each year.

Deadline Deadline not specified.

[219]
MASSACHUSETTS PROPERTY TAX EXEMPTION FOR BLIND PEOPLE

Massachusetts Department of Revenue
Attn: Division of Local Services
100 Cambridge Street
Boston, MA 02114
(617) 626-2386   Fax: (617) 626-2330
E-mail: juszkiewicz@dor.state.ma.us
Web: www.mass.gov

Summary To provide a property tax exemption to homeowners in Massachusetts who are blind.

Eligibility This program is open to residents of Massachusetts who own an interest in their domicile that is worth at least $5,000. Applicants must qualify as legally blind according to specifications established by the Massachusetts Commission for the Blind.

Financial data Qualified blind people are entitled to an exemption of $437.50 from their property taxes. If their town meeting or city council has accepted certain provisions of the law, the exemption is $500.

Duration The exemptions are provided each year that the blind person lives in Massachusetts and owns the property as a domicile.

Additional data Applications are available from local assessor's offices.

Number awarded Varies each year.

Deadline Applications must be filed with the local assessor by December of each year.

[220]
MASSACHUSETTS PROPERTY TAX EXEMPTION FOR VETERANS AND THEIR FAMILIES

Massachusetts Department of Revenue
Attn: Division of Local Services
100 Cambridge Street
Boston, MA 02114
(617) 626-2386   Fax: (617) 626-2330
E-mail: juszkiewicz@dor.state.ma.us
Web: www.mass.gov

Summary To provide a property tax exemption to blind, disabled, and other veterans (and their families) in Massachusetts.

Eligibility This program is open to veterans who are residents of Massachusetts, were residents for at least 6 months prior to entering the service, have been residents for at least 5 consecutive years, and are occupying property as their domicile. Applicants must have an ownership interest in the domicile that ranges from $2,000 to $10,000, depending on the category of exemption. Veterans must have been discharged under conditions other than dishonorable. Several categories of veterans and their families qualify: 1) veterans who have a service-connected disability rating of 10% or more; veterans who have been awarded the Purple Heart; Gold Star mothers and fathers; and surviving spouses of eligible veterans who do not remarry; 2) veterans who suffered, in the line of duty, the loss or permanent lose of use of 1 foot, 1 hand, or 1 eye; veterans who received the Congressional Medal of Honor, Distinguished Service Cross, Navy Cross, or Air Force Cross; and their spouses or surviving spouses; 3) veterans who suffered, in the line of duty, the loss or permanent loss of use of both feet, both hands, or both eyes; and their spouses or surviving spouses; 4) veterans who suffered total disability in the line of duty and received assistance in acquiring specially adapted housing, which they own and occupy as their domicile; and their spouses or surviving spouses; 5) unremarried surviving spouses of military personnel who died due to injury or disease from being in a combat zone, or are missing and presumed dead due to combat; 6) veterans who suffered total disability in the line of duty and are incapable of working; and their spouses or surviving spouses; and 7) veterans who are certified by the Veterans Administration as paraplegic and their surviving spouses.

Financial data Qualified veterans and family members are entitled to an annual exemption from their taxes for the different categories: 1, $400; 2, $750; 3, $1,250; 4, $1,500; 5, full, but with a cap of $2,500 after 5 years; 6, $1,000; or 7, total.

Duration The exemptions are provided each year that the veteran or unremarried surviving spouse lives in Massachusetts and owns the property as a domicile.

Additional data Applications are available from local assessor's offices.

Number awarded Varies each year.

Deadline Applications must be filed with the local assessor by December of each year.

[221]
MASSACHUSETTS VETERANS ANNUITY PROGRAM

Department of Veterans' Services
Attn: Annuities
600 Washington Street, Suite 1100
Boston, MA 02111
(617) 210-5480   Fax: (617) 210-5755
E-mail: mdvs@vet.state.ma.us
Web: www.mass.gov/veterans

Summary To provide an annuity to blind or disabled veterans from Massachusetts and to the parents and spouses of deceased military personnel.

Eligibility This program is open to 1) veterans who are blind, double amputee, paraplegic, or have a 100% service-connected disability; 2) the parents of military personnel who died of service-connected causes; and 3) the unremarried spouses of military personnel who died of service-connected causes. Veterans must have been residents of Massachusetts at the time of entry into military service who served during specified wartime periods and received other than a dishonorable discharge. All applicants must currently be residents of Massachusetts.

Financial data Recipients are entitled to an annuity of $2,000 per year.

Duration The annuity is paid as long as the recipient continues to reside in Massachusetts.

Deadline Deadline not specified.

[222]
MICHIGAN HOMESTEAD PROPERTY TAX CREDIT FOR VETERANS AND BLIND PEOPLE

Michigan Department of Treasury
Attn: Homestead Exemption
Treasury Building
430 West Allegan Street
Lansing, MI 48922
(517) 373-3200   Toll Free: (800) 827-4000
TDD: (517) 636-4999
E-mail: treasPtd2@michigan.gov
Web: www.michigan.gov/treasury

Summary To provide a property tax credit to veterans, military personnel, their spouses, blind people, and their surviving spouses in Michigan.

Eligibility Eligible to apply are residents of Michigan who are 1) blind and own their homestead; 2) a veteran with a service-connected disability or his/her surviving spouse; 3) a surviving spouse of a veteran deceased in service; 4) a pensioned veteran, a surviving spouse of those veterans, or an active military member, all of whose household income is less than $7,500; or 5) a surviving spouse of a non-disabled or non-pensioned veteran of the Korean War, World War II, or World War I whose household income is less than $7,500. All applicants must own or rent a home in Michigan, have been a Michigan resident for at least 6 months during the year in which application is made, and fall within qualifying income levels (up to $82,650 in household income).

Financial data The maximum credit is $1,200. The exact amount varies. For homeowners, the credit depends on the state equalized value of the homestead and on an allowance for filing category. For renters, 20% of the rent is considered property tax eligible for credit.

Duration 1 year; eligibility must be established each year.

Number awarded Varies each year.

Deadline December of each year.

[223]
MICHIGAN INCOME TAX EXEMPTION FOR PEOPLE WITH DISABILITIES

Michigan Department of Treasury
Attn: Income Tax
Treasury Building
430 West Allegan Street
Lansing, MI 48922
(517) 373-3200   Toll Free: (800) 827-4000
TDD: (517) 636-4999
E-mail: treasIndTax@michigan.gov
Web: www.michigan.gov/treasury

Summary To exempt a portion of the income of deaf, blind, and disabled residents of Michigan from state income taxation.

Eligibility Eligible for this exemption are residents of Michigan who 1) receive messages through a sense other than hearing, such as lip reading or sign language; 2) have vision in their better eye of 20/200 or less with corrective lenses or peripheral field of vision of 20 degrees or less; or 3) are hemiplegic, paraplegic, quadriplegic, or totally and permanently disabled.

Financial data Qualifying people with disabilities receive an exemption of $2,200 from their adjusted gross income for purposes of state taxation.

Duration The exemption continues as long as the recipient resides in Michigan.

Deadline Deadline not specified.

[224]
MINNESOTA SPECIAL HOMESTEAD CLASSIFICATIONS

Minnesota Department of Revenue
Attn: Property Tax Division
600 North Robert Street
Mail Station 3340
St. Paul, MN 55146-3340
(651) 556-6087
Web: www.taxes.state.mn.us

Summary To provide a property tax benefit to owners of homesteads in Minnesota who are disabled, blind, or paraplegic veterans.

Eligibility This benefit is available to owners of residential real estate that is occupied and used as a homestead in Minnesota. Applicants must be certified as totally and permanently disabled, legally blind, or a paraplegic veteran living in specially adapted housing with a grant from the Veterans Administration.

Financial data Qualified property is taxed at a rate of 0.45% for the first $50,000 of market value of residential homesteads. That compares to the standard rate of 1.0% on the first $500,000 in valuation and 1.25% on valuation over $500,000.

Duration This benefit is available as long as the property is owned by a qualified person.

Number awarded Varies each year.

Deadline Applications must be submitted by September of each year.

[225]
MISSISSIPPI HOMESTEAD TAX EXEMPTION FOR THE DISABLED

Mississippi State Tax Commission
Attn: Property Tax Division
P.O. Box 1033
Jackson, MS 39215-1033
(601) 923-7631   Fax: (601) 923-7637
E-mail: property@mstc.state.ms.us
Web: www.mstc.state.ms.us/taxareas/property/main.htm

Summary To exempt from property taxes a portion of the value of homesteads owned by people with disabilities and blind people in Mississippi.

Eligibility Eligible for this exemption are residents of Mississippi who are totally disabled or legally blind and own a homestead that they occupy as a home. Disability and blindness are defined according to federal Social Security regulations.

Financial data The exemption covers the first $7,500 of assessed value of the property (or $75,000 true value).

Duration The exemption continues as long as the disabled person resides in Mississippi.

Number awarded Varies each year.

Deadline The first time an exemption is requested, it must be submitted before the end of March of that year. Subsequently, most Mississippi counties do not require renewal filing unless the disable person's homestead status changes.

[226]
MISSISSIPPI INCOME TAX EXEMPTION FOR THE BLIND

Mississippi State Tax Commission
Attn: Individual Income Tax Division
P.O. Box 1033
Jackson, MS 39215-1033
(601) 923-7089   Fax: (601) 923-7039
Web: www.mstc.state.ms.us/taxareas/individ/main.htm

Summary To exempt a portion of the income of blind people and their spouses from state income tax liability in Mississippi.

Eligibility Eligible for this exemption are residents of Mississippi who have been declared legally blind and their spouses.

Financial data The exemption is $1,500.

Duration The exemption continues as long as the blind person resides in Mississippi.

Number awarded Varies each year.

Deadline The exemption must be requested on the resident's state income tax return, which is due in April.

[227]
MISSOURI BLIND PENSION

Missouri Department of Social Services
Attn: Family Support Division
615 Howerton Court
P.O. Box 2320
Jefferson City, MO 65102-2320
(573) 751-4249   Fax: (573) 751-4984
TDD: (800) 735-2966
Web: www.dss.mo.gov/fsd/blindp.htm

Summary To provide assistance to blind residents of Missouri who are not eligible for other support.

Eligibility This program is open to blind (vision less than 5/200) residents of Missouri who are 18 years of age or older; do not own real or personal property worth more than $20,000 (excluding the value of the home used as a residence); have not given away, sold, or transferred real or personal property in order to be eligible; are of good moral character; have no sighted spouse living in Missouri who can provide support; do not publicly solicit alms; are not residents of a public, private, or endowed institution except a public medical institution; are willing to have medical treatment or an operation to cure blindness (unless 75 years of age or older); and are ineligible for federal Supplemental Security Income and Missouri Supplemental Aid to the Blind.

Financial data Eligible individuals receive a monthly cash grant of up to $651 and state-funding HealthNet coverage.

Duration Qualified blind people are eligible for this assistance as long as they reside in Missouri.

Number awarded Varies each year.

Deadline Deadline not specified.

[228]
MISSOURI INCOME TAX DEDUCTION FOR THE BLIND

Missouri Department of Revenue
Attn: Taxation Division
301 West High Street, Room 330
P.O. Box 2200
Jefferson City, MO 65105-2200
(573) 751-3505   Toll Free: (800) 877-6881
TDD: (800) 735-2966   E-mail: income@dor.mo.gov
Web: www.dor.mo.gov/tax/personal

Summary To provide an additional income tax deduction to blind people in Missouri.

Eligibility This deduction is available to all residents of Missouri who are legally classified as blind.

Financial data Blind residents are entitled to deduct an additional $1,200 from their income for taxation purposes.

Duration This deduction is available as long as the recipient remains a resident of Missouri for state income tax purposes.

Number awarded Varies each year.

Deadline Deadline not specified.

[229]
MISSOURI SUPPLEMENTAL AID TO THE BLIND

Missouri Department of Social Services
Attn: Family Support Division
615 Howerton Court
P.O. Box 2320
Jefferson City, MO 65102-2320
(573) 751-4249   Fax: (573) 751-4984
TDD: (800) 735-2966
Web: www.dss.mo.gov/fsd/sblind.htm

Summary To provide supplemental income to blind residents of Missouri.

Eligibility This program is open to blind (vision less than 5/200) residents of Missouri who are 18 years of age or older; are single and do not own real and personal property worth more than $2,000, or, if married and living with a spouse, do not own real and personal property worth more than $4,000 (the residence, clothing, furniture, household equipment, personal jewelry, or any property used directly by the blind person in earning a living are not included in that valuation); do not have parents living in Missouri or a sighted spouse who can provide support; do not publicly solicit alms; are not residents of a public, private, or endowed institution except a public medical institution; are in need of assistance because of insufficient income to meet basic needs; are U.S. citizens or eligible qualified non-citizens; and are required to apply for federal Supplemental Security Income.

Financial data Eligible individuals receive a monthly cash grant of up to $651 and state-funded HealthNet coverage.

Duration Qualified blind people are eligible for this assistance as long as they reside in Missouri.

Number awarded Varies each year.

Deadline Deadline not specified.

[230]
MONTANA INCOME TAX EXEMPTION FOR THE BLIND

Montana Department of Revenue
Attn: Individual Income Tax
125 North Roberts, Third Floor
P.O. Box 5805
Helena, MT 59604-5805
(406) 444-6900   Toll Free: (866) 859-2254
Fax: (406) 444-6642   TDD: (406) 444-2830
Web: mt.gov/revenue

Summary To provide a state income tax exemption to blind residents of Montana and their spouses.

Eligibility Eligible are all persons considered Montana residents for purposes of state income taxation who are blind or whose spouse is blind.

Financial data Blind people and their spouses may claim an additional exemption of $2,140 from their income for state taxation purposes.

Duration The exemption continues as long as the recipient resides in Montana.

Deadline Deadline not specified.

[231]
NEBRASKA INCOME TAX EXEMPTION FOR THE BLIND

Nebraska Department of Revenue
301 Centennial Mall South
P.O. Box 94818
Lincoln, NE 68509-4818
(402) 471-5729
Toll Free: (800) 742-7474 (within NE and IA)
Web: www.revenue.ne.gov

Summary To exempt a portion of the income of blind people from state taxation in Nebraska.

Eligibility This exemption is available to residents of Nebraska who are blind. Applicants must be claiming the state standard deduction on their annual state income tax return.

Financial data Blind taxpayers may add $1,050 to their standard deduction if they are married or $1,350 if they are single or head of household.

Duration The exemption is available annually.

Number awarded Varies each year.

Deadline Exemption claims are included with the state income tax return, due in April of each year.

[232]
NEW HAMPSHIRE BLIND PROPERTY TAX EXEMPTION

New Hampshire Department of Revenue
 Administration
109 Pleasant Street
Concord, NH 03301
(603) 271-2191   Fax: (603) 271-6121
TDD: (800) 735-2964
Web: revenue.nh.gov

Summary To provide blind residents of New Hampshire with a partial exemption from real estate taxes.

Eligibility Residents of New Hampshire are covered by this program if they are blind, own and occupy their primary residence in New Hampshire, and live in a municipality that has chosen through a referendum vote to grant an exemption to the legally blind.

Financial data $15,000 of the value of the residential real estate is exempted from taxation for qualifying residents. Towns may exempt any amount they determine is appropriate to address significant increases in property values.

Duration 1 year; this exemption will be continued as long as the recipient meets the eligibility requirements.

Number awarded Varies each year.

Deadline The original application for a permanent tax credit must be submitted by April.

[233]
NEW HAMPSHIRE INTEREST AND DIVIDEND TAX EXEMPTION FOR BLIND PEOPLE

New Hampshire Department of Revenue
 Administration
109 Pleasant Street
Concord, NH 03301
(603) 271-2191   Fax: (603) 271-6121
TDD: (800) 735-2964
Web: revenue.nh.gov

Summary To provide blind residents of New Hampshire with a partial exemption from taxes on interest and dividend income.

Eligibility This exemption is available to residents of New Hampshire who are blind, regardless of age, and pay taxes on income from interest and dividends.

Financial data Qualifying residents receive an exemption of $1,200 from interest and dividend income.

Duration 1 year; this exemption will be continued as long as the recipient meets the eligibility requirements.

Number awarded Varies each year.

Deadline The application for this exemption is included with the interest and dividend income tax form, due in April of each year.

[234]
NEW HAMPSHIRE PROPERTY TAX EXEMPTION FOR CERTAIN DISABLED VETERANS

New Hampshire Department of Revenue
 Administration
109 Pleasant Street
Concord, NH 03301
(603) 271-2191   Fax: (603) 271-6121
TDD: (800) 735-2964
Web: revenue.nh.gov

Summary To exempt from taxation certain property owned by New Hampshire disabled veterans or their surviving spouses.

Eligibility Eligible for this exemption are New Hampshire residents who are honorably discharged veterans with a total and permanent service-connected disability that involves double amputation of the upper or lower extremities or any combination thereof, paraplegia, or blindness of both eyes with visual acuity of 5/200 or less. Applicants or their surviving spouses must own a specially adapted homestead that has been acquired with the assistance of the U.S. Department of Veterans Affairs.

Financial data Qualifying disabled veterans and surviving spouses are exempt from all taxation on their specially adapted homestead.

Duration 1 year; once the credit has been approved, it is automatically renewed as long as the qualifying person owns the same residence in New Hampshire.

Number awarded Varies each year.

Deadline The original application for a permanent tax credit must be submitted by April.

[235]
NEW JERSEY INCOME TAX EXEMPTIONS FOR THE BLIND AND DISABLED

New Jersey Division of Taxation
Attn: Information and Publications Branch
50 Barrack Street
P.O. Box 281
Trenton, NJ 08695-0281
(609) 292-6400
Toll Free: (800) 323-4400 (within NJ, NY, PA, DE, and MD)
TDD: (800) 286-6613 (within NJ, NY, PA, DE, and MD)   E-mail: taxation@tax.state.nj.us
Web: www.state.nj.us/treasury/taxation

Summary   To provide an income tax exemption in New Jersey to blind and disabled people.

Eligibility   Residents of New Jersey who are blind or disabled are entitled to this exemption.

Financial data   Each blind or disabled person is entitled to an exemption of $1,000 from income for taxation purposes.

Duration   The exemption continues as long as the qualifying condition persists and the person remains a New Jersey resident.

Number awarded   Varies each year.

Deadline   Deadline not specified.

[236]
NEW JERSEY PARTIAL EXEMPTION FROM REALTY TRANSFER FEE FOR SENIOR CITIZENS OR DISABLED PERSONS

New Jersey Division of Taxation
Attn: Information and Publications Branch
50 Barrack Street
P.O. Box 281
Trenton, NJ 08695-0281
(609) 292-6400
Toll Free: (800) 323-4400 (within NJ, NY, PA, DE, and MD)
TDD: (800) 286-6613 (within NJ, NY, PA, DE, and MD)   E-mail: taxation@tax.state.nj.us
Web: www.state.nj.us/treasury/taxation/lpt/rtttaqs.shtml

Summary   To provide an exemption from realty transfer fees paid by senior citizens, persons with disabilities, and blind people in New Jersey.

Eligibility   Eligible for these exemptions are persons 62 years of age and older, permanently and totally disabled individuals, and blind people who are residents of New Jersey for 1 year immediately preceding October 1 of the year before the year for which the exemption is requested, and purchasers of certain residential property during the year.

Financial data   The standard realty transfer fees range from $2.90 per $500 for the first $150,000 of the sales price to $6.05 per $500 for sales prices in excess of $1,000,000. For persons who qualify for this reduction, the comparable fees range from $0.50 per $500 for the first $150,000 of the sales price to $3.40 per $500 for sales prices in excess of $1,000,000.

Duration   The exemption applies whenever a qualified purchaser buys a new residence.

Number awarded   Varies each year.

Deadline   Deadline not specified.

[237]
NEW JERSEY PROPERTY TAX DEDUCTION

New Jersey Division of Taxation
Attn: Information and Publications Branch
50 Barrack Street
P.O. Box 281
Trenton, NJ 08695-0281
(609) 292-6400
Toll Free: (800) 323-4400 (within NJ, NY, PA, DE, and MD)
TDD: (800) 286-6613 (within NJ, NY, PA, DE, and MD)   E-mail: taxation@tax.state.nj.us
Web: www.state.nj.us/treasury/taxation/njit35.shtml

Summary   To exclude from income taxation a portion of the property taxes paid by blind, disabled, and other residents of New Jersey.

Eligibility   This deduction is available to residents of New Jersey whose income is greater than $20,000 (or $10,000 if single or married filing separately). It is also available to residents, regardless of income, who are 1) blind, 2) permanently and totally disabled, or 3) 65 years of age or older. Applicants must either own the home in which they reside or rent a dwelling with its own separate kitchen and bath facilities.

Financial data   Qualified residents are entitled to deduct from their income (for state taxation purposes) 100% of their property taxes, to a maximum of $10,000. For renters, 18% of their rent is considered the equivalent of property taxes and may be deducted, to a maximum of $10,000.

Duration   The deduction continues as long as the person remains a New Jersey resident.

Additional data   This program began in 1996. Taxpayers may not claim both the property tax deduction and the property tax credit; they may claim whichever is most beneficial, but only the deduction or the credit.

Number awarded   Varies each year.

Deadline   The deduction is claimed as part of the annual income tax return, due in April of each year.

[238]
NEW MEXICO TAX EXEMPTION FOR THE BLIND AND ELDERLY

New Mexico Taxation and Revenue Department
Attn: Tax Information and Policy Office
1100 South St. Francis Drive
P.O. Box 630
Santa Fe, NM 87504-0630
(505) 827-2523
Web: www.state.nm.us/tax

Summary   To exempt a portion of the income of New Mexico residents who are blind or over the age of 65, and their surviving spouses, from state income tax liability.

Eligibility This exemption is available to residents of New Mexico who are 65 years of age or older or who are blind.

Financial data The income exemption ranges from $1,000 to $8,000, depending on filing status and income. The maximum income that still qualifies for an exemption is $25,500 for married individuals filing separate returns, $51,000 for heads of household, surviving spouses, and married individuals filing joint returns, or $28,500 for single individuals.

Duration The exemption continues as long as the qualifying resident remains in the state.

Number awarded Varies each year.

Deadline The qualifying resident claims the exemption on the New Mexico state income tax return, which is due in April.

[239]
NEW YORK STATE BLIND ANNUITY

New York State Division of Veterans' Affairs
5 Empire State Plaza, Suite 2836
Albany, NY 12223-1551
(518) 474-6114
Toll Free: (888) VETS-NYS (within NY)
Fax: (518) 473-0379   E-mail: dvainfo@ogs.state.ny.us
Web: veterans.ny.gov/blind_annuity.html

Summary To provide an annuity to blind wartime veterans and their surviving spouses in New York.

Eligibility This benefit is available to veterans who served on active duty during specified periods of war. Applicants must 1) meet the New York State standards of blindness; 2) have received an honorable or general discharge, or a discharge other than for dishonorable service; and 3) be now, and continue to be, residents of and continuously domiciled in New York State. The annuity is also payable to unremarried spouses of deceased veterans who were receiving annuity payments (or were eligible to do so) at the time of their death, and are residents of and continuously domiciled in New York State.

Financial data The annuity is currently $1,173.84 per year.

Number awarded Varies each year.

Deadline Deadline not specified.

[240]
NFBCT-COCCOMO QUARTERLY GRANTS

National Federation of the Blind of Connecticut
Attn: Quarterly Grant Committee
477 Connecticut Boulevard, Suite 217
East Hartford, CT 06108
(860) 289-1971   E-mail: info@nfbct.org
Web: www.nfbct.org/html/coccomo.htm

Summary To provide financial assistance to blind people in Connecticut interested in a program of training, employment, independent living, or technological advancement.

Eligibility This assistance is available to residents of Connecticut who meet the state's definition of legal blindness. Applicants must be seeking support for activities in the areas of training, employment, independent living, or technological advancement. A wide range of requests are considered, including a talking watch, a computer system, a note taker (such as a Braille Note or Braille Lite), payment assistance for postsecondary part-time course work, or even a new suit for the sake of maximizing impressions on job interviews. Along with their application, they must submit a statement about themselves, their goals, and how the requested product or service will enhance their daily life and/or career aspirations.

Financial data Grants depend on the nature of the request.

Duration These are 1-time grants. Recipients are eligible for a second grant 2 years after receiving the first grant.

Additional data This program is supported by the John A. Coccomo, Sr. Foundation and administered by the National Federation of the Blind of Connecticut (NFBCT).

Number awarded Varies each year.

Deadline February, May, August, or November of each year.

[241]
NORTH DAKOTA PROPERTY TAX EXEMPTION FOR THE BLIND

Office of State Tax Commissioner
State Capitol Building
600 East Boulevard Avenue, Department 127
Bismarck, ND 58505-0599
(701) 328-2770   Toll Free: (800) 638-2901
Fax: (701) 328-3700   TDD: (800) 366-6888
E-mail: taxinfo@state.nd.us
Web: www.nd.gov/tax

Summary To provide partial tax exemption in North Dakota to blind persons and their spouses.

Eligibility Blind persons are defined as those who are totally blind, who have visual acuity of not more than 20/200 in the better eye with correction, or whose vision is limited in field so that the widest diameter subtends an angle no greater than 20 degrees. Eligible for this exemption is property that is owned by a blind person, by the spouse of a blind person, or jointly by a blind person and a spouse. The property that is exempt includes the entire building classified as residential, and owned and occupied as a residence by a person who qualifies, as long as the building contains no more than 2 apartments or rental units that are leased.

Financial data The exemption applies to all or any part of fixtures, building, and improvements upon any nonfarmland up to a taxable valuation of $7,200.

Duration The exemption continues as long as the blind person resides in the home in North Dakota.

Number awarded Varies each year.

Deadline Deadline not specified.

[242]
OAK HILL LEGACY FUND GRANTS

Connecticut Institute for the Blind
Attn: Legacy Fund
120 Holcomb Street
Hartford, CT 06112-1589
(860) 286-3105   Fax: (860) 242-3103
E-mail: agritellyk@ciboakhill.org
Web: www.ciboakhill.org/ways_to_give/donor.asp

Summary To provide funding to blind Connecticut residents for projects that increase their options for independence.

Eligibility This program is open to residents of Connecticut whose vision is no more than 20/200 after correction. Preference is given to Oak Hill School graduates and former students and to others who demonstrate financial need. Applicants must be seeking funding for activities or equipment that will increase employment opportunities, enhance work productivity, or assist them in becoming more independent and for which other funding is not available. They must have applied to the state Board of Education and Services for the Blind (BESB) for funding and been denied. Along with their application, they must submit a brief description of their past and current activities and accomplishments, their need for this item or activity, what the item or activity will enable them to accomplish, a certificate of blindness or other documentation from a physician confirming legal blindness, information on financial need, and a copy of a letter from the BESB indicating why they have denied the applicant's request.

Financial data Grants range from $50 to $2,500.

Duration These are 1-time awards. They may be renewed upon reapplication but only 1 grant will be awarded in any 12-month period.

Additional data The Connecticut Institute for the Blind, doing business as Oak Hill, also operates independent living facilities in West Hartford and Wethersfield for blind, visually impaired, and disabled individuals. Grants are not intended to provide ongoing support.

Number awarded Varies each year.

Deadline January, April, July, or October of each year.

[243]
OKLAHOMA INCOME TAX EXEMPTION FOR THE BLIND

Oklahoma Tax Commission
Attn: Income Tax
2501 North Lincoln Boulevard
Oklahoma City, OK 73194-0009
(405) 521-3160   Toll Free: (800) 522-8165 (within OK)
Fax: (405) 522-0063   E-mail: otcmaster@tax.ok.gov
Web: www.tax.ok.gov/incometax.html

Summary To exempt a portion of the income of blind people and their spouses in Oklahoma from state taxation.

Eligibility This exemption is available to residents of Oklahoma and their spouses who are legally blind.

Financial data Each qualifying resident is entitled to claim an additional exemption of $1,000.

Duration The exemption is available as long as the recipient resides in Oklahoma.

Deadline Deadline not specified.

[244]
OREGON INCOME TAX DEDUCTION FOR THE BLIND

Oregon Department of Revenue
Revenue Building
955 Center Street, N.E.
Salem, OR 97310-2551
(503) 378-4988   Toll Free: (800) 356-4222 (within OR)
TDD: (800) 886-7204 (within OR)
Web: www.oregon.gov/DOR/PERTAX

Summary To enable blind residents of Oregon to deduct a portion of their income from state taxation.

Eligibility This deduction is available to blind taxpayers in Oregon who utilize the standard deduction for their income taxes.

Financial data The additional deduction is $1,200 for single people and heads of households. It is $1,000 for married people filing jointly or separately and for qualifying widow(er)s.

Duration The deduction continues as long as the recipient resides in Oregon.

Deadline Deductions are filed with state income tax returns in April of each year.

[245]
OREGON PROPERTY TAX DEFERRAL FOR DISABLED AND SENIOR CITIZENS

Oregon Department of Revenue
Attn: Property Tax Division
Revenue Building
955 Center Street, N.E.
Salem, OR 97310-2551
(503) 378-4988   Toll Free: (800) 356-4222 (within OR)
TDD: (800) 886-7204 (within OR)
Web: www.oregon.gov/DOR/SCD/disableddef.shtml

Summary To permit blind, disabled, and elderly Oregon residents to defer payment of their property taxes.

Eligibility This program is open to residents of Oregon who are determined to be eligible to receive or are receiving federal Social Security benefits due to disability or blindness. Applicants must own a residence and have a total household income less than $39,000.

Financial data The state pays all taxes on the property to the county but places a lien on the property and charges 6% per year on the deferred taxes. The lien and interest become due and payable when the disabled person or senior citizen sells the property or changes its ownership, moves permanently from the property (unless for medical reasons), or dies.

Duration 1 year; the deferment is automatically renewed as long as the property owner lives in the residence.

Number awarded Varies each year; recently, 712 disabled residents of Oregon were participating in this program.

Deadline Applications for new deferrals must be filed in the appropriate county assessor's office by April of each year.

[246]
PENNSYLVANIA BLIND VETERANS PENSION

Office of the Deputy Adjutant General for Veterans
    Affairs
Building S-0-47, FTIG
Annville, PA 17003-5002
(717) 865-8911
Toll Free: (800) 54 PA VET (within PA)
Fax: (717) 861-8589   E-mail: jamebutler@state.pa.us
Web: www.milvet.state.pa.us/DMVA/196.htm

Summary To provide financial assistance to blind residents of Pennsylvania who lost their sight while serving in the U.S. armed forces.

Eligibility Persons who have 3/60 or 10/200 or less normal vision are eligible if they are honorably-discharged veterans and were residents of Pennsylvania when they joined the U.S. armed forces. Their blindness must have resulted from a service-connected injury or disease.

Financial data The pension is $150 per month.

Duration The pension is awarded for the life of the veteran.

Number awarded Varies each year.

Deadline Applications may be submitted at any time.

[247]
PENNSYLVANIA DISABLED VETERANS REAL ESTATE TAX EXEMPTION

Office of the Deputy Adjutant General for Veterans
    Affairs
Building S-0-47, FTIG
Annville, PA 17003-5002
(717) 865-8907
Toll Free: (800) 54 PA VET (within PA)
Fax: (717) 861-8589   E-mail: jamebutler@state.pa.us
Web: www.milvet.state.pa.us/DMVA/592.htm

Summary To exempt blind and disabled Pennsylvania veterans and their unremarried surviving spouses from all state real estate taxes.

Eligibility Eligible to apply for this exemption are honorably-discharged veterans who are residents of Pennsylvania and who are blind, paraplegic, or 100% disabled from a service-connected disability sustained during wartime military service. The dwelling must be owned by the veteran solely or jointly with a spouse, and financial need for the exemption must be determined by the State Veterans' Commission. Veterans whose income is less than $79,050 per year are presumed to have financial need; veterans with income greater than $79,050 must document need. Upon the death of the veteran, the tax exemption passes on to the veteran's unremarried surviving spouse.

Financial data This program exempts the principal residence (and the land on which it stands) from all real estate taxes.

Duration The exemption continues as long as the eligible veteran or unremarried widow resides in Pennsylvania.

Number awarded Varies each year.

Deadline Deadline not specified.

[248]
RHODE ISLAND INCOME TAX DEDUCTION FOR THE BLIND

Rhode Island Division of Taxation
One Capitol Hill
Providence, RI 02908-5806
(401) 574-8829   TDD: (401) 574-8934
E-mail: txassist@tax.state.ri.gov
Web: www.tax.ri.gov

Summary To increase the standard state income tax deduction for blind people from Rhode Island.

Eligibility This additional deduction is available to residents of Rhode Island who are blind. Applicants must utilize the standard deduction schedule.

Financial data Blind taxpayers who are single or heads of households are entitled to deduct an additional $1,350 from their income for purposes of state taxation in Rhode Island; those who are married or qualifying widow(er)s may deduct an additional $1,050.

Duration The deduction is available annually.

Number awarded Varies each year.

Deadline Deduction claims are included with the state income tax return, due in April of each year.

[249]
RUTH BILLOW MEMORIAL PERSONAL AID

Delta Gamma Foundation
Attn: Director, Service for Sight
3250 Riverside Drive
P.O. Box 21397
Columbus, OH 43221-0397
(614) 481-8169   Fax: (614) 481-0133
E-mail: dgfoundation@deltagamma.org
Web: www.deltagamma.org

Summary To provide financial assistance to members of Delta Gamma sorority who are in need because of their visual impairment or that of a family member.

Eligibility This program is open to members of the sorority who require assistance 1) in order to restore or retain their sight; or 2) because of their responsibilities directly related to dependents who are blind or visually impaired. Applicants must be residents of the United States or Canada.

Financial data The amount awarded varies, depending upon individual circumstances.

Duration 1 year or more.

Number awarded Varies each year.

Deadline Applications may be submitted at any time.

[250]
SOCIAL SECURITY DISABILITY INSURANCE (SSDI) BENEFITS

Social Security Administration
6401 Security Boulevard
Baltimore, MD 21235-0001
(410) 594-1234   Toll Free: (800) 772-1213
TDD: (800) 325-0778
Web: www.ssa.gov

Summary To provide monthly benefits to workers and their families if the worker becomes disabled or blind.

Eligibility This program defines disabled people as those who are unable to do any kind of work for which they are suited and whose disability has lasted or is expected to last for at least a year or to result in death. Blind people qualify if their vision cannot be corrected to better than 20/200 in their better eye or if their visual field is 20 degrees or less, even with corrective lenses. Family members who are eligible include 1) unmarried children, including adopted children and, in some cases, stepchildren and grandchildren who are under 18 years of age (19 if still in high school full time); 2) unmarried children, over 18 years of age, if they have a disability that started before age 22; and 3) spouses who are 62 years of age or older, or of any age if caring for a child of the disabled worker who is under 16 years of age or disabled. For deceased workers, disabled widow(er)s 50 years of age or older are also eligible. Applicants must also have worked long enough and recently enough under Social Security in order to qualify. Workers who become disabled before the age of 24 need 6 credits in the 3-year period ending when the disability begins; workers who become disabled between the ages of 24 and 31 must have credit for having worked half the time between the age of 21 and the date of disability; workers 31 years of age or older at the time of disability must have earned as many total credits as needed for retirement (from 20 credits if disabled at age 31 through 42 to 40 credits if disabled at age 62 or older) and must have earned at least 20 of the credits in the 10 years immediately before becoming disabled. An exception applies to blind workers who need no recent credit but may have earned the required credit any time after 1936.

Financial data The amount of the monthly benefit depends on several factors, including the worker's age at the time of disability, the number of dependents, and the amount of earnings on which Social Security taxes have been paid. Recently, the average monthly benefit was $1,062.10 for disabled workers, $286.90 for spouses of disabled workers, and $316.40 for children of disabled workers.

Duration For a disabled or blind person, whether a worker, widow, widower, surviving divorced spouse, or person over the age of 18 who became disabled before the age of 22, monthly benefits continue until the person is no longer disabled or dies. For a dependent spouse, benefits are paid until the worker is no longer disabled or dies. For a dependent child, the benefits continue until the child marries or reaches the age of 18 (19 if still enrolled as a full-time high school student).

Additional data Disabled workers may test their ability to return to work for a trial work period of up to 9 months, during which time they receive full SSDI benefits. At the end of that period, a decision is made as to whether or not they are able to engage in substantial gainful activity. Persons who find that they cannot continue substantial gainful employment continue to receive SSDI benefits without interruption. Persons who can engage in substantial gainful activity receive benefits for an additional 3 months, after which payments cease. Several factors are considered to determine if the person can engage in substantial gainful employment, but the most important is income; for disabled people the amount is $980 a month gross wages and for blind people the income is $1,640 monthly.

Number awarded Varies; recently, approximately 7,623,000 disabled workers were receiving SSDI monthly benefits, along with 158,000 spouses and 1,681,000 children.

Deadline Deadline not specified.

[251]
SOUTH CAROLINA HOMESTEAD EXEMPTION PROGRAM

South Carolina Department of Revenue
301 Gervais Street
P.O. Box 125
Columbia, SC 29214
(803) 898-5680   Toll Free: (800) 763-1295
Fax: (803) 898-5822   E-mail: MillerC@sctax.org
Web: www.sctax.org

Summary To provide a homestead exemption to South Carolina residents who are elderly, disabled, or blind, and their widow(er)s.

Eligibility Legal residents of South Carolina who own a house or mobile home are eligible for this exemption if they are 65 years of age or older, totally and permanently disabled, or legally blind. Spouses of deceased persons who were eligible also qualify to receive the exemption if they were at least 50 years of age when their spouse died.

Financial data The first $50,000 of the fair market value of the qualified applicant's home is exempted from property taxes. The exemption is from county, municipal, school, and special assessment real estate property taxes.

Duration The exemption continues as long as the homeowners live in their primary residence in South Carolina.

Additional data This program, established in 1972, is administered by county auditors.

Number awarded Varies each year.

Deadline Persons applying for this exemption for the first time must do so prior to July of each year; subsequently, no re-application is necessary unless the title or use of the property changes.

[252]
SPECIAL HOUSING ADAPTATIONS GRANTS

Department of Veterans Affairs
Attn: Specially Adapted Housing
810 Vermont Avenue, N.W.
Washington, DC 20420
(202) 461-9546   Toll Free: (800) 827-1000
Web: www.homeloans.va.gov/sah.htm

Summary To provide grants to certain disabled veterans or servicemembers who wish to make adaptations to their home to meet their needs.

Eligibility These grants are available to veterans and servicemembers who are entitled to compensation for permanent and total service-connected disability due to: 1) blindness in both eyes with 5/200 visual acuity or less; 2) the anatomical loss or loss of use of both hands; or 3) a severe burn injury. Applicants must be planning to 1) adapt a house which they plan to purchase and in which they intend to reside; 2) adapt a house which a member of their family plans to purchase and in which they intend to reside; 3) adapt a house which they already own and in which they intend to reside; 4) adapt a house which is already owned by a member of their family in which they intend to reside; or 5) purchase a house that has already been adapted with special features that are reasonably necessary because of their disability and in which they intend to reside.

Financial data Eligible veterans and servicemembers are entitled to grants up to $12,756 to adapt a house.

Duration Eligible veterans and servicemembers are entitled to up to 3 usages of these grants.

Number awarded Varies each year.

Deadline Applications are accepted at any time.

[253]
SPECIALLY ADAPTED HOUSING GRANTS

Department of Veterans Affairs
Attn: Specially Adapted Housing
810 Vermont Avenue, N.W.
Washington, DC 20420
(202) 461-9546   Toll Free: (800) 827-1000
Web: www.homeloans.va.gov/sah.htm

Summary To provide loans, grants, and loan guaranties to certain disabled veterans and servicemembers for a home specially adapted to their needs.

Eligibility These grants are available to veterans and servicemembers who are entitled to compensation for permanent and total service-connected disability due to: 1) the loss or loss of use of both lower extremities, such as to preclude locomotion without the aid of braces, crutches, canes, or a wheelchair; or 2) blindness in both eyes, having only light perception, plus loss or loss of use of 1 lower extremity; or 3) a loss or loss of use of 1 lower extremity together with residuals of organic disease or injury or the loss or loss of use of 1 upper extremity, such as to preclude locomotion without resort to braces, canes, crutches, or a wheelchair. Applicants must be planning to 1) construct a home on land to be acquired for that purpose; 2) build a home on land already owned if it is suitable for specially adapted housing; 3) remodel an existing home if it can be

made suitable for specially adapted housing, or 4) apply funds against the unpaid principle mortgage balance of a specially adapted home that has already been acquired.

Financial data The U.S. Department of Veterans Affairs (VA) may approve a grant of not more than 50% of the cost of building, buying, or remodeling homes for eligible veterans, or paying indebtedness of such homes already acquired, up to a maximum grant of $63,780. Eligible veterans with available loan guarantee entitlements may also obtain a guaranteed loan from the VA to supplement the grant to acquire a specially adapted home. If private financing is not available, the VA may make a direct loan up to $33,000 to cover the difference between the total cost of the home and the grant.

Duration This is a 1-time grant, guaranteed loan, or direct loan.

Additional data Veterans who receive a specially adapted housing grant may be eligible for Veterans Mortgage Life Insurance.

Number awarded Varies each year.

Deadline Applications are accepted at any time.

[254]
SUPPLEMENTAL SECURITY INCOME (SSI)

Social Security Administration
6401 Security Boulevard
Baltimore, MD 21235-0001
(410) 594-1234   Toll Free: (800) 772-1213
TDD: (800) 325-0778
Web: www.socialsecurity.gov/ssi/index.htm

Summary To provide monthly payments to disabled, blind, deaf, and elderly people who have limited income and resources.

Eligibility This assistance is available to U.S. citizens and certain categories of aliens who are 65 years of age or older, blind, or disabled. A person 18 years of age or older is considered disabled if a physical or mental impairment prevents him or her from doing any substantial gainful work and is expected to last for at least 12 months or to result in death. Children under the age of 18 are considered disabled if they have a physical or mental impairment that is comparable in severity to a disability that would prevent an adult from working and is expected to last at least 12 months or result in death. Children with certain conditions are automatically disabled and eligible for these benefits; the conditions include HIV infection, blindness, deafness, cerebral palsy, Down syndrome, muscular dystrophy, significant mental deficiency, diabetes (with amputation of 1 foot), amputation of 2 limbs, or amputation of leg at the hip. Regardless of age, a person whose vision is no better than 20/200 or who has a limited visual field of 20 degrees or less with the best corrective eyeglasses is considered blind; individuals with visual impairments not severe enough to meet the definition of blindness still may qualify as disabled persons. Applicants must have limited income and limited resources (less than $2,000 for an individual or $3,000 for a couple); items excluded from resources include the home used as a principal place of residence, personal and household goods, life insurance with face value of $1,500 or less, a car, burial plots for individuals and immediate family members, and burial funds up to $1,500.

Financial data The basic monthly payment is $674 for an eligible individual or $1,011 for an eligible individual with an eligible spouse. Many states add money to that basic payment. SSI recipients may also be eligible for food stamps and other nutrition programs.

Duration Assistance is provided as long as the recipient remains blind or disabled and in financial need.

Additional data Although SSI is administered through the Social Security Administration, it is not financed by Social Security taxes. Financing of SSI is provided through general funds of the U.S. Treasury. Recipients of SSI need not have been employed or paid Social Security taxes, but they may be eligible for both SSI and Social Security. Disabled and blind applicants for SSI are referred to their state vocational rehabilitation agency to determine their eligibility for a program of vocational rehabilitation. Disabled drug addicts or alcoholics are referred for appropriate treatment if it is available at an approved facility or institution.

Number awarded Recently, approximately 7,599,000 people (including 6,395,000 who were blind and disabled) were receiving SSI benefits, including 1,172,000 under 18 years of age, 4,389,000 who were 18 to 64 years of age, and 2,038,000 who were 65 or older.

Deadline Deadline not specified.

[255]
SUPPORT SERVICES FOR THE BLIND AND VISUALLY IMPAIRED

Lions Clubs International
Attn: Program Development Department
300 West 22nd Street
Oak Brook, IL 60523-8842
(630) 571-5466, ext. 316   Fax: (630) 571-1692
E-mail: programs@lionsclubs.org
Web: www.lionsclubs.org

Summary To provide college scholarships and other assistance to blind people.

Eligibility These programs are open to blind people and others involved in service to the blind. Applicants may be seeking support for the following activities: scholarships for the blind and visually impaired, medical research, assistive technology grants, independent mobility, transportation, reading materials and aids, audio products, Braille products, and other aids.

Financial data The amount of this assistance varies.

Additional data Support is provided by local clubs of Lions Clubs International. Requests sent to the international office are referred to the appropriate district governor. If any of the clubs within the district conduct programs for which the applicant might be considered, the governor will advise the particular club to contact the applicant. No funds are available from the office of Lions Clubs International.

Deadline Deadline not specified.

[256]
TENNESSEE INCOME TAX EXEMPTION FOR BLIND RESIDENTS

Tennessee Department of Revenue
Andrew Jackson State Office Building
500 Deaderick Street
Nashville, TN 37242-1099
(615) 253-0600   Toll Free: (800) 342-1003 (within TN)
Fax: (615) 253-3580   E-mail: tn.revenue@state.tn.us
Web: www.tennessee.gov/revenue

Summary To exempt from state taxation the dividend and interest income of blind residents of Tennessee.

Eligibility This exemption applies to income received by blind residents of Tennessee as 1) dividends from stock, investment trusts, and mutual funds; and 2) interest from bonds, notes, and mortgages. As defined by this program, blindness means that vision does not exceed 20/200 in the better eye with correcting lenses or that the widest diameter of the visual field subtends an angle no greater than 20 degrees.

Financial data All dividend and interest income is exempt from taxation if the recipient meets the definition of blindness. However, when taxable interest/dividend income is received jointly by a blind person and a sighted spouse, only one half of the jointly received income is exempted from taxation. The sighted spouse is entitled only to a $1,250 exemption.

Duration The exemption continues as long as the recipient meets the definition of blindness and resides in Tennessee.

Deadline Deadline not specified.

[257]
TENNESSEE PROPERTY TAX RELIEF FOR DISABLED VETERANS AND THEIR SPOUSES

Tennessee Comptroller of the Treasury
Attn: Property Tax Relief Program
James K. Polk State Office Building
505 Deaderick Street, Room 1600
Nashville, TN 37243-1402
(615) 747-8871   Fax: (615) 532-3866
E-mail: Kim.Darden@state.tn.us
Web: www.comptroller.state.tn.us/pa/patxr.htm

Summary To provide property tax relief to blind and disabled veterans and their spouses in Tennessee.

Eligibility This exemption is offered to veterans or their surviving unremarried spouses who are residents of Tennessee and own and live in their home in the state. The veteran must have served in the U.S. armed forces and 1) have acquired, as a result of such service, a disability from paraplegia, permanent paralysis of both legs and lower part of the body resulting from traumatic injury, disease to the spinal cord or brain, legal blindness, or loss or loss of use of both legs or arms from any service-connected cause; 2) have been rated by the U.S. Department of Veterans Affairs (VA) as 100% permanently disabled as a result of service as a prisoner of war for at least 5 months; or 3) have been rated by the VA as 100% permanently and totally disabled from any other service-connected cause.

The relief does not extend to any person who was dishonorably discharged from any of the armed services.

Financial data The amount of the relief depends on the property assessment and the tax rate in the city or county where the beneficiary lives. The maximum market value on which tax relief is calculated is $175,000.

Duration 1 year; may be renewed as long as the eligible veteran or surviving unremarried spouse owns and occupies the primary residence.

Number awarded Varies each year.

Deadline Deadline not specified.

[258]
TEXAS PROPERTY TAX EXEMPTION FOR DISABLED VETERANS AND THEIR FAMILIES

Texas Veterans Commission
P.O. Box 12277
Austin, TX 78711-2277
(512) 463-5538
Toll Free: (800) 252-VETS (within TX)
Fax: (512) 475-2395   E-mail: info@tvc.state.tx.us
Web: www.tvc.state.tx.us/StateBenefits.html

Summary To extend property tax exemptions on the appraised value of their property to blind, disabled, and other Texas veterans and their surviving family members.

Eligibility Eligible veterans must be Texas residents rated at least 10% service-connected disabled. Surviving spouses and children of eligible veterans are also covered by this program.

Financial data For veterans in Texas whose disability is rated as 10% through 29%, the first $5,000 of the appraised property value is exempt from taxation; veterans rated as 30% through 49% disabled are exempt from the first $7,500 of appraised value; those with a 50% through 69% disability are exempt from the first $10,000 of appraised value; the exemption applies to the first $12,000 of appraised value for veterans with disabilities rated as 70% to 99%; veterans rated as 100% disabled are exempt from 100% of the appraised value of their property. A veteran whose disability is 10% or more and who is 65 years or older is entitled to exemption of the first $12,000 of appraised property value. A veteran whose disability consists of the loss of use of 1 or more limbs, total blindness in 1 or both eyes, or paraplegia is exempt from the first $12,000 of the appraised value. The unremarried surviving spouse of a deceased veteran who died on active duty and who, at the time of death had a compensable disability and was entitled to an exemption, is entitled to the same exemption. The surviving spouse of a person who died on active duty is entitled to exemption of the first $5,000 of appraised value of the spouse's property. Surviving spouses, however, are not eligible for the 100% exemption. A surviving child of a person who dies on active duty is entitled to exemption of the first $5,000 of appraised value of the child's property, as long as the child is unmarried and under 21 years of age.

Duration 1 year; may be renewed as long as the eligible veteran (or unremarried surviving spouse or child) owns and occupies the primary residence in Texas.

Additional data This program is administered at the local level by the various taxing authorities.

Number awarded Varies each year.

Deadline April of each year.

[259]
UTAH BLIND PROPERTY TAX EXEMPTION

Utah State Tax Commission
Attn: Property Tax Division
210 North 1950 West
Salt Lake City, UT 84134
(801) 297-3600   Toll Free: (800) 662-4335, ext. 3600
Fax: (801) 297-7699   TDD: (801) 297-2020
Web: www.tax.utah.gov

Summary To exempt from taxation a portion of the real and tangible property of blind people and their families in Utah.

Eligibility This exemption is available to legally blind property owners in Utah, along with their unremarried surviving spouses or minor orphans. First-year applications must be accompanied by a signed statement from an ophthalmologist and, if appropriate, a death certificate.

Financial data The first $11,500 of the taxable value of real and tangible personal property is exempt from taxation.

Duration The exemption is available each year the beneficiary owns property in Utah.

Number awarded Varies each year.

Deadline Applications must be submitted by August of each year.

[260]
VIRGINIA TAX EXEMPTION FOR BLIND PEOPLE

Virginia Department of Taxation
Attn: Office of Customer Services
3600 West Broad Street
P.O. Box 1115
Richmond, VA 23218-1115
(804) 367-8031   Fax: (804) 367-2537
Web: www.tax.virginia.gov

Summary To exempt a portion of the income of blind people from state income taxation in Virginia.

Eligibility This exemption is available to residents of Virginia who are considered blind for federal income tax purposes.

Financial data Qualified taxpayers are entitled to exempt $800 from their income for purposes of state taxation in Virginia.

Duration The exemption is available as long as the taxpayer lives and earns income in Virginia.

Number awarded Varies each year.

Deadline The request for an exemption is filed with the state income tax return in April of each year.

Awards

[261]
APH INSIGHTS

American Printing House for the Blind, Inc.
Attn: Public Affairs and Special Projects Manager
1839 Frankfort Avenue
P.O. Box 6085
Louisville, KY 40206-0085
(502) 895-2405   Toll Free: (800) 223-1839, ext. 357
Fax: (502) 899-2363   E-mail: rwilliams@aph.org
Web: www.aph.org/museum/enter_insights.html

Summary To recognize and reward outstanding artwork by individuals who are blind or visually impaired.

Eligibility Any person who meets the legal definition of blindness is eligible to submit artwork to be considered for the InSights exhibition. The definition of blindness is: corrected visual acuity of 20/200 or less in the better eye, or a visual field limited to 20 degrees or less. Both 2- and 3-dimensional works may be submitted. The types of work may include, but are not limited to, painting, drawing, photography, printmaking, sculpture, mixed media, collage, and crafts (e.g., pottery, weaving, woodwork). Participants may not enter more than 1 piece of artwork. Artists may not have received help in the execution of their art (although they may have received advice in selecting materials and colors). The work of students in preschool through 12th grade is judged in 6 grade placement categories; the work of adult artists is judged in categories according to medium (craft, sculpture, and 2-dimensional art). Selection is based on originality of concept, expressive use of media, and artistic excellence.

Financial data Award winners receive a cash prize and a ribbon.

Duration The competition is held annually.

Additional data Work not selected for the InSights exhibition is returned. Award winners are invited to come to Louisville to receive their awards; stipends are available to assist with travel expenses. This competition was first held in 1992.

Number awarded Varies each year; recently, 27 of these awards (first, second, and third place in each of the 9 categories) were presented.

Deadline Preschool through high school entries must be received by the end of March of each year. Adult entries must be received by mid-April.

[262]
BLIND EDUCATOR OF THE YEAR AWARD

National Federation of the Blind
Attn: Director of Community Relations
1800 Johnson Street
Baltimore, MD 21230
(410) 659-9314, ext. 272   Fax: (410) 685-5653
E-mail: CommunityRelations@nfb.org
Web: www.nfb.org

Summary To recognize and reward outstanding blind educators.

Eligibility Candidates for this award must be not only distinguished educators but individuals who have contributed to the nation. All candidates must be blind. The recipient is chosen to symbolize the best in teaching and the best in service to the blind.

Financial data The award is $1,000.

Duration The award is presented annually.

Additional data This award was established in 1986. Honorees must be present at the annual convention of the National Federation of the Blind.

Number awarded 1 each year.

Deadline Nominations must be submitted by April of each year.

[263]
CRASHING THROUGH AWARD FOR INDEPENDENT TRAVEL

Sendero Group, LLC
429 F Street, Suite 4
Davis, CA 95616
(530) 757-6800   Fax: (530) 757-6830
Web: www.senderogroup.com/ctapp.htm

Summary To recognize and reward blind people who submit essays on the independent travel they have undertaken.

Eligibility This competition is open to blind people from any country. Applicants must submit an essay about the independent travel they have undertaken; the essay should address where they went, who went with them, why the trip was significant for them and for people they met, what they learned about themselves, and how they think the adventure will affect their future. The travel may have included sighted friends, colleagues, or family, but the blind applicant must have demonstrated independent travel. Use of GPS is not required but will weigh in the applicant's favor if used. Selection of the award recipient is based on the essay (50 points); multimedia files (images, audio, video) that illustrate the travel (25 points); and 2 letters of reference (1 from a teacher) that assess the blind person and the travel experience (25 points).

Financial data The award is $2,500. Funds may be used for school, technology, travel, or any use the recipient desires.

Duration The award is presented annually.

Additional data This award was first presented in 2009.

Number awarded 1 each year.

Deadline February of each year.

[264]
INSIGHTS ART EXHIBITION

LightHouse for the Blind and Visually Impaired
Attn: Insights Coordinator
213 Van Ness Avenue
San Francisco, CA 94102
(415) 694-7335　　　　　　Fax: (415) 863-7568
TDD: (415) 431-4572
E-mail: insights@lighthouse-sf.org
Web: lighthouse-sf.org/events/insights/index.php

Summary To recognize and reward visual artists who are blind or visually impaired and submit work for an exhibition in San Francisco.

Eligibility This competition is open to all artists who are blind or visually impaired. Applicants are invited to submit up to 5 original works that were not exhibited in a previous show. Artwork can include, but is not limited to, paintings, drawings, photographs, sculpture, and mixed-media pieces; touchable art is encouraged. Works are selected on the basis of original concept, expressive use of media, and artistic excellence. The most outstanding work receives the Elva Iacono Vergari Prize.

Financial data Cash honoraria are awarded. All artists whose work is selected for exhibition receive a stipend.

Duration The competition is held annually.

Additional data This exhibition was first held in 1990.

Number awarded Varies each year; recently, 45 artists were selected to exhibit their work, of which 3 received an Elva Iacono Vergari Prize.

Deadline April of each year.

[265]
MARY P. OENSLAGER SCHOLASTIC ACHIEVEMENT AWARDS

Recording for the Blind and Dyslexic
Attn: Strategic Communications Department
Anne T. Macdonald Center
20 Roszel Road
Princeton, NJ 08540
(609) 243-7051　　　　　　Toll Free: (866) RFBD-585
E-mail: dnagy@rfbd.org
Web: www.rfbd.org/applications_awards.htm

Summary To recognize and reward the outstanding academic achievements of blind college seniors and graduate students.

Eligibility To be eligible for this award, candidates must 1) be legally blind; 2) have received, or will receive, a bachelor's, master's, or doctoral degree from a 4-year accredited college or university in the United States or its territories during the year the award is given; 3) have an overall academic average of 3.0 or higher; and 4) have been registered borrowers from Recording for the Blind and Dyslexic for at least 1 year. Selection is based on evidence of leadership, enterprise, and service to others.

Financial data Top winners receive $6,000 each, special honors winners $3,000 each, and honors winners $1,000 each.

Duration The awards are presented annually.

Additional data These awards are named for the founder of the program who established it in 1959 and endowed it with a gift of $1 million in 1990.

Number awarded 9 each year: 3 top winners, 3 special honors winners, and 3 honors winners.

Deadline April of each year.

[266]
ONKYO BRAILLE ESSAY CONTEST

National Federation of the Blind
Attn: Trisha Tatam
1800 Johnson Street
Baltimore, MD 21230
(410) 659-9314, ext. 2510　　　　　　Fax: (410) 685-5653
E-mail: ttatam@nfb.org
Web: www.nfb.org

Summary To recognize and reward outstanding essays by blind people from around the world on the impact of Braille on their lives.

Eligibility This competition is open to individuals who are blind and live in any country. Entries may be submitted in the junior group, for 25 years of age and under, or the senior group, for 26 years of age and older. Candidates must submit an essay, from 800 to 1,000 words, on 1 of the following topics: 1) how they acquire knowledge and information through Braille or audio devices; 2) how blind persons can become independent by learning Braille or music; or 3) their individual concept about world peace from the viewpoint of persons with disabilities. Essay must be written in English or their native language, in Braille, and must be completely original. Both senior and junior group participants are eligible for the Otsuki Award; the competition for Excellent Work Awards and Fine Work Awards are limited to senior group participants. Selection is based on the essay's pertinence to the selected topic, impact and credibility of the experiences described, accuracy and neatness in using Braille, and style and language skills.

Financial data The Otsuki Award is $2,000,; Excellent Work Awards are $1,000, and Fine Work Awards are $500.

Duration The competition is held annually.

Additional data This competition was established in 2003 by the Onkyo Corporation of Japan and the Braille Mainichi. In the United States, the National Federation of the Blind administers the contest on behalf of the North America-Caribbean Region of the World Blind Union.

Number awarded 7 each year: the Otsuki Award, 2 Excellent Work Awards, and 4 Fine Work Awards.

Deadline April of each year.

Hearing Disabilities

Scholarships ●

Fellowships/Grants ●

Grants-in-Aid ●

Awards ●

Described here are 64 programs open to individuals who have difficulty in receiving linguistic information, with or without amplification. Of these, 26 entries cover scholarships (to pursue studies or research on the undergraduate level in the United States); 24 cover fellowships/grants (to pursue graduate or postdoctoral study or research in the United States); 12 cover grants-in-aid (to support emergency situations, travel, income/property tax liabilities, or the acquisition of assistive technology); and 2 identify awards, competitions, or prize (to recognize or support creative work and public service). If you are looking for a particular program and don't find it in this chapter, be sure to check the Program Title Index to see if it is covered elsewhere in the directory.

Scholarships

[267]
ALLIE RANEY HUNT SCHOLARSHIP

Alexander Graham Bell Association for the Deaf and
  Hard of Hearing
Attn: Financial Aid Coordinator
3417 Volta Place, N.W.
Washington, DC 20007-2778
(202) 337-5220   Fax: (202) 337-8314
TDD: (202) 337-5221   E-mail: financialaid@agbell.org
Web: nc.agbell.org/NetCommunity/Page.aspx?pid=493

Summary To provide financial assistance to oral deaf undergraduate and graduate students with moderate to profound hearing loss.

Eligibility This program is open to oral deaf undergraduate and graduate students who have been diagnosed with a moderate to profound hearing loss prior to acquiring spoken language (hearing loss averages 60dB or greater in the better ear in the speech frequencies of 500, 1000, and 2000 Hz). Applicants must be committed to using spoken language as their primary mode of communication. They must be accepted or enrolled at a mainstream college or university as a full-time student. Along with their application, they must submit a 1-page essay discussing their career goals and how spoken communication is helping them to reach those goals as a person with a hearing loss. Financial need is considered in the selection process.

Financial data The stipend is $2,000 per year.
Duration 1 year; may be renewed 1 additional year.
Number awarded 1 each year.
Deadline February of each year.

[268]
ARTS AND SCIENCES AWARDS

Alexander Graham Bell Association for the Deaf and
  Hard of Hearing
Attn: Financial Aid Coordinator
3417 Volta Place, N.W.
Washington, DC 20007-2778
(202) 337-5220   Fax: (202) 337-8314
TDD: (202) 337-5221   E-mail: financialaid@agbell.org
Web: nc.agbell.org/NetCommunity/Page.aspx?pid=496

Summary To provide financial aid to hearing impaired students who are participating in extracurricular activities in arts and sciences.

Eligibility This program is open to residents of the United States or Canada who have been diagnosed as having a moderate to profound hearing loss (55 dB or greater loss in the better ear in the speech frequencies of 500, 1000, and 2000 Hz) and who use spoken language as their primary form of communication. They must be between 6 and 19 years of age and enrolled in an art or science program as an extracurricular activity during after-school time, summer, or weekends. Programs can be offered through museums, nature centers, art or music

centers, zoological parks, space and science camps, dance and theater studios, martial arts studios, or any other program with a focus on the arts or sciences. Recreational summer camps, sports camps or sports, and travel and study abroad programs that do not have an explicit arts or science focus are not eligible. Membership in the Alexander Graham Bell Association is not required, but preference is given to members.

Financial data The amount of the award varies, depending upon the cost of the program in which the recipient is enrolled.
Duration 1 year; may be renewed upon reapplication.
Number awarded Varies each year.
Deadline April of each year.

[269]
BENNION FAMILY SCHOLARSHIP

Alexander Graham Bell Association for the Deaf and
  Hard of Hearing
Attn: Financial Aid Coordinator
3417 Volta Place, N.W.
Washington, DC 20007-2778
(202) 337-5220   Fax: (202) 337-8314
TDD: (202) 337-5221   E-mail: financialaid@agbell.org
Web: nc.agbell.org/NetCommunity/Page.aspx?pid=493

Summary To provide financial assistance to undergraduate students with moderate to profound hearing loss.

Eligibility This program is open to undergraduate students who have been diagnosed with a moderate to profound hearing loss prior to acquiring spoken language (hearing loss averages 60dB or greater in the better ear in the speech frequencies of 500, 1000, and 2000 Hz). Applicants must be committed to using spoken language as their primary mode of communication. They must be accepted or enrolled at a mainstream college or university as a full-time student. Along with their application, they must submit a 1-page essay discussing their career goals and how spoken communication is helping them to reach those goals as a person with a hearing loss. Financial need is considered in the selection process.

Financial data The stipend is $2,000 per year.
Duration 1 year; may be renewed 1 additional year.
Number awarded 1 each year.
Deadline February of each year.

[270]
CAROLINE KARK AWARD FOR DEAF STUDENTS

New York State Grange
100 Grange Place
Cortland, NY 13045
(607) 756-7553   Fax: (607) 756-7757
E-mail: nysgrange@nysgrange.com
Web: www.nysgrange.com/educationalassistance.html

Summary To provide financial assistance to members of the Grange in New York who are deaf and attending college in any state.

Eligibility This program is open to members of the New York State Grange who are currently enrolled at a college in any state. Applicants must be deaf.

Financial data A stipend is awarded (amount not specified).

Duration 1 year; nonrenewable.

Number awarded 1 or more each year.

Deadline April of each year.

[271]
CURTIS PRIDE SCHOLARSHIP FOR THE HEARING IMPAIRED

National Head Start Association
Attn: Scholarships and Awards
1651 Prince Street
Alexandria, VA 22314
(703) 739-0875   Fax: (703) 739-0878
E-mail: yvinci@nhsa.org
Web: www.nhsa.org

Summary To provide financial assistance for college to hearing impaired students who are members of the National Head Start Association (NHSA).

Eligibility This program is open to NHSA members who have a hearing impairment. Applicants must be enrolled or planning to enroll at a 4-year college or university, 2-year community college, or vocational/technical school. They must submit a 200-word statement on their goals and aspirations for furthering their education and the role Head Start has played in their education. Selection is based on that statement (40 points), a statement of financial need (30 points), and 3 letters of reference (30 points). Students submit their applications to their local program, which forwards 1 to the state association. Each state association forwards 1 application to the regional association, which submits 1 nomination to the national headquarters.

Financial data The stipend is $1,000.

Duration 1 year.

Number awarded 1 each year.

Deadline January of each year.

[272]
DEAF AND HARD OF HEARING SECTION SCHOLARSHIP FUND

Alexander Graham Bell Association for the Deaf and
  Hard of Hearing
Attn: Financial Aid Coordinator
3417 Volta Place, N.W.
Washington, DC 20007-2778
(202) 337-5220   Fax: (202) 337-8314
TDD: (202) 337-5221   E-mail: financialaid@agbell.org
Web: nc.agbell.org/NetCommunity/Page.aspx?pid=493

Summary To provide financial assistance to undergraduate and graduate students who are members of the Alexander Graham Bell Association for the Deaf (AG Bell).

Eligibility This program is open to undergraduate and graduate students who have been diagnosed with a moderate to profound hearing loss prior to acquiring spoken language (hearing loss averages 60dB or greater in the better ear in the speech frequencies of 500, 1000, and 2000 Hz). Applicants must be committed to using spoken language as their primary mode of communication. They must be accepted or enrolled at a mainstream college or university as a full-time student. Along with their application, they must submit a 1-page essay discussing their career goals and how spoken communication is helping them to reach those goals as a person with a hearing loss. Financial need is considered in the selection process. This scholarship is reserved for students who are members of AG Bell and its Deaf and Hard of Hearing Section (DHHS).

Financial data The stipend is $1,000 per year.

Duration 1 year; may be renewed 1 additional year.

Number awarded 2 each year.

Deadline February of each year.

[273]
ELSIE M. BELL GROSVENOR SCHOLARSHIP AWARDS

Alexander Graham Bell Association for the Deaf and
  Hard of Hearing
Attn: Financial Aid Coordinator
3417 Volta Place, N.W.
Washington, DC 20007-2778
(202) 337-5220   Fax: (202) 337-8314
TDD: (202) 337-5221   E-mail: financialaid@agbell.org
Web: nc.agbell.org/NetCommunity/Page.aspx?pid=493

Summary To provide financial assistance to undergraduate and graduate students who have moderate to profound hearing loss and attend school in the Washington, D.C. area.

Eligibility This program is open to undergraduate and graduate students who have been diagnosed with a moderate to profound hearing loss prior to acquiring spoken language (hearing loss averages 60dB or greater in the better ear in the speech frequencies of 500, 1000, and 2000 Hz). Applicants must be committed to using spoken language as their primary mode of communication. They must be accepted or enrolled at a mainstream college or university in the Washington, D.C. area as a full-time student. Along with their application, they must submit a 1-page essay discussing their career goals and how spoken communication is helping them to reach those goals as a person with a hearing loss. Financial need is considered in the selection process.

Financial data The stipend is $2,000 per year.

Duration 1 year; may be renewed 1 additional year.

Number awarded 1 each year.

Deadline February of each year.

[274]
FEDERATION OF JEWISH WOMEN'S ORGANIZATION SCHOLARSHIP

Alexander Graham Bell Association for the Deaf and
  Hard of Hearing
Attn: Financial Aid Coordinator
3417 Volta Place, N.W.
Washington, DC 20007-2778
(202) 337-5220   Fax: (202) 337-8314
TDD: (202) 337-5221   E-mail: financialaid@agbell.org
Web: nc.agbell.org/NetCommunity/Page.aspx?pid=493

Summary   To provide financial assistance to undergraduate and graduate students who are hearing impaired.

Eligibility   This program is open to undergraduate and graduate students who are hearing impaired. Applicants must be accepted or enrolled at a mainstream college or university as a full-time student. Along with their application, they must submit a 1-page essay discussing their career goals and how spoken communication is helping them to reach those goals as a person with a hearing loss. Financial need is considered in the selection process.

Financial data   The stipend is $2,000 per year.

Duration   1 year; may be renewed 1 additional year.

Number awarded   1 each year.

Deadline   February of each year.

[275]
GEOFFREY FOUNDATION SCHOLARSHIPS

Geoffrey Foundation
Ocean Avenue
P.O. Box 1112
Kennebunkport, ME 04046
(207) 967-5798

Summary   To provide financial assistance to deaf students who attend school with hearing students and communicate using spoken language.

Eligibility   This program is open to U.S. citizens who are hearing impaired (severe to profound hearing loss greater than 80 dB) and are utilizing an auditory-verbal approach to communication. Applicant must be currently enrolled or planning to attend a preschool, elementary school, junior high or high school, or college for hearing students on a full-time basis in the forthcoming year. They must submit a current audiogram plus 3 letters of recommendation.

Financial data   The amount awarded varies, depending upon the needs of the recipient.

Duration   1 year or longer.

Additional data   The foundation is closely aligned with Auditory-Verbal International, Inc. and the Alexander Graham Bell Association for the Deaf. Funds are also available to support hearing research as well as programs, initiatives, or organizations of interest to the foundation. Applications may be requested only by mail.

Number awarded   Varies each year. The foundation awards grants in excess of $30,000 each year to children and college students.

Deadline   March of each year.

[276]
GRAEME CLARK SCHOLARSHIPS

Cochlear Americas
Attn: Scholarships
13059 East Peakview Avenue
Centennial, CO 80111
(303) 790-9010   Toll Free: (800) 523-5798
Fax: (303) 790-1157
E-mail: Recipients@Cochlear.com
Web: www.cochlearamericas.com/support/168.asp

Summary   To provide financial assistance for college to students who have received a cochlear nucleus implant.

Eligibility   This program is open to graduating high school seniors, current university students, and mature aged students who have been accepted into a university course. Applicants must have received a cochlear nucleus implant. Along with their application, they must submit a 1,000-word personal statement on their academic aspirations and other interests, including why they chose their proposed area of study, their post-graduate aspirations, their definition of success, and why they wish to receive this scholarship. Selection is based on academic achievement and demonstrated commitment to the ideals of leadership and humanity.

Financial data   The stipend is $2,000 per year.

Duration   1 year; may be renewed up to 3 additional years.

Additional data   This program was established in 2002.

Number awarded   Varies each year; recently, 5 of these scholarships were awarded.

Deadline   July of each year.

[277]
HENRY C. HECKER HIGH SCHOOL SCHOLARSHIP

Communication Disorders Foundation of Virginia
c/o Janet W. Stack
385 Claymont Drive
Earlysville, VA 22936
(434) 975-0611   Fax: (434) 975-4267
E-mail: jws8n@virginia.edu
Web: www.cdf-virginia.org/Student_Scholarships.html

Summary   To provide financial assistance to high school seniors in Virginia who have a hearing impairment and are interested in attending college in any state.

Eligibility   This program is open to seniors graduating from high schools in Virginia who have a hearing impairment. Applicants must have at least a "B" average and be planning to attend a college, university, vocational school, or other postsecondary institution in any state. They must submit brief statements on why they are interested in studying their proposed program; what kind of work they want to do when they complete the program; the type and severity of hearing loss they have; the kind of hearing aid, prosthetic device, or assistive learning device they use; their primary means of communication; how their hearing loss has influenced their life, educational choices, or career choices; and what they would like to teach others about hearing loss. Financial need is not considered in the selection process.

Financial data   The stipend is $1,000.

Duration   1 year.

Number awarded   1 each year.

Deadline   April of each year.

[278]
HERBERT P. FEIBELMAN, JR. SCHOLARSHIP

Alexander Graham Bell Association for the Deaf and
   Hard of Hearing
Attn: Financial Aid Coordinator
3417 Volta Place, N.W.
Washington, DC 20007-2778
(202) 337-5220   Fax: (202) 337-8314
TDD: (202) 337-5221   E-mail: financialaid@agbell.org
Web: nc.agbell.org/NetCommunity/Page.aspx?pid=493

Summary   To provide financial assistance to undergraduate and graduate students who are members of the Alexander Graham Bell Association for the Deaf (AG Bell) and their children.

Eligibility   This program is open to undergraduate and graduate students who have been diagnosed with a moderate to profound hearing loss prior to acquiring spoken language (hearing loss averages 60dB or greater in the better ear in the speech frequencies of 500, 1000, and 2000 Hz). Applicants must be committed to using spoken language as their primary mode of communication. They must be accepted or enrolled at a mainstream college or university as a full-time student. Along with their application, they must submit a 1-page essay discussing their career goals and how spoken communication is helping them to reach those goals as a person with a hearing loss. Financial need is considered in the selection process. This scholarship is reserved for students who are members of AG Bell or whose parents are members.

Financial data   The stipend is $2,500 per year.

Duration   1 year; may be renewed 1 additional year.

Number awarded   1 each year.

Deadline   February of each year.

[279]
LADIES' AUXILIARY NATIONAL RURAL LETTER CARRIERS SCHOLARSHIP

Alexander Graham Bell Association for the Deaf and
   Hard of Hearing
Attn: Financial Aid Coordinator
3417 Volta Place, N.W.
Washington, DC 20007-2778
(202) 337-5220   Fax: (202) 337-8314
TDD: (202) 337-5221   E-mail: financialaid@agbell.org
Web: nc.agbell.org/NetCommunity/Page.aspx?pid=493

Summary   To provide financial assistance to undergraduate and graduate students with moderate to profound hearing loss.

Eligibility   This program is open to undergraduate and graduate students who have been diagnosed with a moderate to profound hearing loss prior to acquiring spoken language (hearing loss averages 60dB or greater in the

better ear in the speech frequencies of 500, 1000, and 2000 Hz). Applicants must be committed to using spoken language as their primary mode of communication. They must be accepted or enrolled at a mainstream college or university as a full-time student. Along with their application, they must submit a 1-page essay discussing their career goals and how spoken communication is helping them to reach those goals as a person with a hearing loss. Financial need is considered in the selection process.

Financial data   The stipend is $2,000 per year.

Duration   1 year; may be renewed 1 additional year.

Number awarded   1 each year.

Deadline   February of each year.

[280]
LOUISE TUMARKIN ZAZOVE SCHOLARSHIPS

Louise Tumarkin Zazove Foundation
6858 North Kenneth Avenue
Chicago, IL 60712-4705
E-mail: earl@ltzfoundation.org
Web: www.ltzfoundation.org/scholarships.php

Summary   To provide financial assistance for college (and possibly for high school or graduate school) to people with hearing loss.

Eligibility   This program is open to U.S. citizens and permanent residents who have a significant bilateral hearing loss. Strong preference is given to undergraduate students, but support may be provided for graduate school or high school tuition in certain situations. Applicants must submit a transcript of high school and/or college grades, 3 letters of recommendation, documentation of the severity of the hearing loss, information on any special circumstances by or about the family, and documentation of financial need.

Financial data   A stipend is awarded (amount not specified). Funds are paid directly to schools.

Duration   1 year; may be renewed up to 3 additional years, provided the recipient continues to do well in school and demonstrate financial need.

Additional data   This program was established in 2003.

Number awarded   Varies each year; since the program was established, it has awarded 14 scholarships.

Deadline   May of each year.

[281]
LUCILLE B. ABT SCHOLARSHIPS

Alexander Graham Bell Association for the Deaf and
   Hard of Hearing
Attn: Financial Aid Coordinator
3417 Volta Place, N.W.
Washington, DC 20007-2778
(202) 337-5220   Fax: (202) 337-8314
TDD: (202) 337-5221   E-mail: financialaid@agbell.org
Web: nc.agbell.org/NetCommunity/Page.aspx?pid=493

Summary   To provide financial assistance to undergraduate and graduate students with moderate to profound hearing loss.

Eligibility   This program is open to undergraduate and graduate students who have been diagnosed with a moderate to profound hearing loss prior to acquiring spoken language (hearing loss averages 60dB or greater in the better ear in the speech frequencies of 500, 1000, and 2000 Hz). Applicants must be committed to using spoken language and lipreading as their preferred mode of communication. They must be accepted or enrolled at a mainstream college or university as a full-time student. Along with their application, they must submit a 1-page essay discussing their career goals and how spoken communication is helping them to reach those goals as a person with a hearing loss. Financial need is considered in the selection process.

Financial data The stipend is $5,000 per year.

Duration 1 year; may be renewed 1 additional year.

Number awarded 10 each year.

Deadline February of each year.

[282]
MARYLAND STATE GRANGE DEAF SCHOLARSHIP

Maryland State Grange
Attn: Master
8743 Old Kiln Road
Thurmont, MD 21788-1219
(301) 447-2075   Fax: (301) 447-2019
E-mail: rlt-rox@juno.com

Summary To provide financial assistance for college or graduate school to Maryland residents who are either deaf or preparing to work with hearing impaired people.

Eligibility This program is open to seniors graduating from high schools in Maryland and to graduates of those high schools who are attending or planning to attend college or graduate school in the state. Applicants must be 1) deaf or hearing impaired, or 2) preparing for a career working with deaf or hearing impaired people.

Financial data A stipend is awarded (amount not specified).

Duration 1 year; may be renewed if the recipient maintains a GPA of 3.0 or higher.

Number awarded 1 or more each year.

Deadline May of each year.

[283]
MINNIE PEARL SCHOLARSHIP PROGRAM

Hearing Bridges
Attn: Scholarship Program
415 Fourth Avenue South, Suite A
Nashville, TN 37201
(615) 248-8828   Toll Free: (866) 385-6524
TDD: (615) 248-8828 E-mail: info@hearingbridges.org
Web: www.hearingbridges.org/scholarships

Summary To provide financial assistance to hearing impaired high school seniors who want to attend college.

Eligibility This program is open to high school seniors who have severe to profound bilateral hearing loss and a GPA of 3.0 or higher. Applicants must be planning to enroll full time at a college, university, junior college or technical school. Along with their application, they must submit brief essays on what a college education means to them, their

goals after graduating from college, why they are a good candidate for this scholarship, and a difficult situation in their life and how they handled it. Selection is based on those essays, academic performance, extracurricular activities, an audiology report, and letters of recommendation. U.S. citizenship is required.

Financial data The stipend is $2,500 per year. Payment is made directly to the college, university, or school at the rate of $1,000 per semester; a bonus of $500 is paid directly to students who achieve a GPA of 3.5 or higher.

Duration 1 year; may be renewed up to 3 additional years if the recipient maintains a GPA of 3.0 or higher.

Additional data This program was established in 1986 when the sponsor was named EAR Foundation.

Number awarded 1 each year.

Deadline March of each year.

[284]
NATIONAL FRATERNAL SOCIETY OF THE DEAF SCHOLARSHIPS

National Fraternal Society of the Deaf
1118 South Sixth Street
Springfield, IL 62703
(217) 789-7429   Fax: (217) 789-7489
TDD: (217) 789-7438

Summary To provide financial assistance for college to members of the National Fraternal Society of the Deaf.

Eligibility This program is open to deaf, hard of hearing, or hearing persons who are enrolled in or accepted as a full-time student at a postsecondary educational institution. Applicants must have been members of the society for at least 1 year prior to application.

Financial data The stipend is $1,000.

Duration 1 year; may be renewed 1 additional year.

Additional data These scholarships have been awarded since 1973.

Number awarded 10 each year.

Deadline June of each year.

[285]
ROBERT H. WEITBRECHT SCHOLARSHIP

Alexander Graham Bell Association for the Deaf and
  Hard of Hearing
Attn: Financial Aid Coordinator
3417 Volta Place, N.W.
Washington, DC 20007-2778
(202) 337-5220   Fax: (202) 337-8314
TDD: (202) 337-5221   E-mail: financialaid@agbell.org
Web: nc.agbell.org/NetCommunity/Page.aspx?pid=493

Summary To provide financial assistance to undergraduate and graduate students with moderate to profound hearing loss, especially those working on a degree in engineering or science.

Eligibility This program is open to undergraduate and graduate students who have been diagnosed with a moderate to profound hearing loss prior to acquiring spoken language (hearing loss averages 60dB or greater in the better ear in the speech frequencies of 500, 1000, and 2000 Hz). Applicants must be able to demonstrate leadership potential and be committed to using spoken language as their primary mode of communication. They must be accepted or enrolled at a mainstream college or university as a full-time student. Along with their application, they must submit a 1-page essay discussing their career goals and how spoken communication is helping them to reach those goals as a person with a hearing loss. Financial need is considered in the selection process. Priority for this scholarship is given to applicants studying engineering or science.

Financial data The stipend is $2,500 per year.

Duration 1 year; may be renewed 1 additional year.

Number awarded 1 each year.

Deadline February of each year.

[286]
SAMUEL M. AND GERTRUDE G. LEVY SCHOLARSHIP FUND

Alexander Graham Bell Association for the Deaf and
  Hard of Hearing
Attn: Financial Aid Coordinator
3417 Volta Place, N.W.
Washington, DC 20007-2778
(202) 337-5220   Fax: (202) 337-8314
TDD: (202) 337-5221   E-mail: financialaid@agbell.org
Web: nc.agbell.org/NetCommunity/Page.aspx?pid=493

Summary To provide financial assistance to oral deaf undergraduate students with moderate to profound hearing loss.

Eligibility This program is open to oral deaf undergraduate students who have been diagnosed with a moderate to profound hearing loss prior to acquiring spoken language (hearing loss averages 60dB or greater in the better ear in the speech frequencies of 500, 1000, and 2000 Hz). Applicants must be committed to using spoken language as their primary mode of communication. They must be accepted or enrolled at a mainstream college or university as a full-time student. Along with their application, they must submit a 1-page essay discussing their career goals and how spoken communication is helping them to reach those goals as a person with a hearing loss. Financial need is considered in the selection process.

Financial data The stipend is $2,000 per year.

Duration 1 year; may be renewed 1 additional year.

Number awarded 1 each year.

Deadline February of each year.

[287]
SCHOLARSHIP TRUST FOR THE HEARING IMPAIRED

Travelers Protective Association of America
Attn: TPA Scholarship Trust for the Hearing Impaired
3755 Lindell Boulevard
St. Louis, MO 63108-3476
(314) 371-0533   Fax: (314) 371-0537
E-mail: support@tpahq.org
Web: www.tpahq.org/scholarshiptrust.html

Summary To provide assistance to deaf and hearing impaired persons interested in obtaining additional educa-

tion, mechanical devices, specialized medical treatment, or other treatments.

Eligibility This assistance is available to U.S. residents who are deaf or hearing impaired. Applicants must be able to demonstrate that they will benefit from special programs, services, or other activities for the deaf, but that they are unable to provide the necessary funds.

Financial data The grant depends on the need of the recipient.

Duration 1 year; recipients may reapply.

Additional data This fund was established in 1975. Support has been provided to children as young as 2 months and to adults as old as 82 years. Funds have been used for mechanical devices, tuition at schools that specialize in educating the deaf (e.g., Gallaudet University, Rochester Institute of Technology, Central Institute for the Deaf), note takers and interpreters in classes in regular schools that do not provide those services to the deaf, speech and language therapy (especially for those who have had the cochlear implant), medical or other specialized treatments, and computer programs that assist the deaf and their families learn and apply skills presented in the classroom.

Number awarded Varies each year; since the trust was established, it has distributed more than $1.5 million to more than 3,700 recipients.

Deadline February of each year.

[288]
SCHOLARSHIPS FOR HARD OF HEARING OR DEAF STUDENTS

Sertoma International
Attn: Director of Finance and Administration
1912 East Meyer Boulevard
Kansas City, MO 64132-1174
(816) 333-8300, ext. 214   Fax: (816) 333-4320
TDD: (816) 333-8300
E-mail: infosertoma@sertomahq.org
Web: www.sertoma.org/Scholarships

Summary To provide financial assistance for college to hearing impaired students.

Eligibility This program is open to students who have a minimum 40dB bilateral hearing loss and are interested in working full time on a bachelor's degree at a 4-year college or university in the United States. Students working on a graduate degree, community college degree, associate degree, or vocational program degree are ineligible. Applicants must have a GPA of 3.2 or higher. Along with their application, they must submit a statement on how this scholarship will help them achieve their goals. U.S. citizenship is required. Selection is based on academic achievement, honors and awards received, community volunteer activities, interscholastic activities, extracurricular activities, and 2 letters of recommendation.

Financial data The stipend is $1,000 per year.

Duration 1 year; may be renewed up to 4 times.

Additional data Sertoma, which stands for SERvice TO MAnkind, is a volunteer service organization with 25,000 members in 800 clubs across North America. Funding for this program is provided by Oticon, Inc. and the Sertoma Foundation. To request an application, students must send a self-addressed, stamped envelope.

Number awarded 20 each year.

Deadline April of each year.

[289]
TEXAS BLIND/DEAF STUDENT EXEMPTION PROGRAM

Texas Higher Education Coordinating Board
Attn: Grants and Special Programs
1200 East Anderson Lane
P.O. Box 12788, Capitol Station
Austin, TX 78711-2788
(512) 427-6340   Toll Free: (800) 242-3062
Fax: (512) 427-6127
E-mail: grantinfo@thecb.state.tx.us
Web: www.collegeforalltexans.com

Summary To provide a tuition exemption to blind and/or deaf residents of Texas.

Eligibility This program is open to Texas residents who can present certification from the Department of Assistive and Rehabilitative Services of their deafness or blindness. Applicants must present to the registrar of a public college or university in Texas a copy of their high school transcript, a letter of recommendation, proof that they have met all admission requirements, and a statement of purpose that indicates the certificate, degree program, or professional enhancement that they intend to pursue.

Financial data Eligible students are exempted from the payment of all dues, fees, and tuition charges at publicly-supported colleges and universities in Texas.

Duration Up to 8 semesters.

Number awarded Varies each year; recently, nearly 3,500 students received support through this program.

Deadline Deadline not specified.

[290]
VOLTA SCHOLARSHIP FUND

Alexander Graham Bell Association for the Deaf and
  Hard of Hearing
Attn: Financial Aid Coordinator
3417 Volta Place, N.W.
Washington, DC 20007-2778
(202) 337-5220   Fax: (202) 337-8314
TDD: (202) 337-5221   E-mail: financialaid@agbell.org
Web: nc.agbell.org/NetCommunity/Page.aspx?pid=493

Summary To provide financial assistance to oral deaf undergraduate and graduate students with moderate to profound hearing loss.

Eligibility This program is open to oral deaf undergraduate and graduate students who have been diagnosed with a moderate to profound hearing loss prior to acquiring spoken language (hearing loss averages 60dB or greater in the better ear in the speech frequencies of 500, 1000, and 2000 Hz). Applicants must be committed to using spoken language as their primary mode of communication. They must be accepted or enrolled at a mainstream college or university as a full-time student. Along with their

application, they must submit a 1-page essay discussing their career goals and how spoken communication is helping them to reach those goals as a person with a hearing loss. Financial need is considered in the selection process.

Financial data The stipend is $2,000 per year.

Duration 1 year; may be renewed 1 additional year.

Number awarded 1 each year.

Deadline February of each year.

[291]
WALTER W. AND THELMA C. HISSEY COLLEGE SCHOLARSHIPS

Alexander Graham Bell Association for the Deaf and
  Hard of Hearing
Attn: Financial Aid Coordinator
3417 Volta Place, N.W.
Washington, DC 20007-2778
(202) 337-5220   Fax: (202) 337-8314
TDD: (202) 337-5221   E-mail: financialaid@agbell.org
Web: nc.agbell.org/NetCommunity/Page.aspx?pid=493

Summary To provide financial assistance to undergraduate and graduate students with moderate to profound hearing loss.

Eligibility This program is open to undergraduate and graduate students who have been diagnosed with a moderate to profound hearing loss prior to acquiring spoken language (hearing loss averages 60dB or greater in the better ear in the speech frequencies of 500, 1000, and 2000 Hz). Applicants must be committed to using spoken language as their primary mode of communication. They must be accepted or enrolled at a mainstream college or university as a full-time student. Along with their application, they must submit a 1-page essay discussing their career goals and how spoken communication is helping them to reach those goals as a person with a hearing loss. Financial need is considered in the selection process.

Financial data The stipend is $5,000 per year.

Duration 1 year; may be renewed 1 additional year.

Number awarded 2 each year.

Deadline February of each year.

[292]
WISCONSIN HEARING AND VISUALLY HANDICAPPED STUDENT GRANT PROGRAM

Wisconsin Higher Educational Aids Board
131 West Wilson Street, Suite 902
P.O. Box 7885
Madison, WI 53707-7885
(608) 266-0888   Fax: (608) 267-2808
E-mail: Sandy.Thomas@wisconsin.gov
Web: heab.state.wi.us/programs.html

Summary To provide financial support for undergraduate study to Wisconsin residents who are legally deaf or blind.

Eligibility This program is open to Wisconsin residents who can submit evidence of a severe or profound hearing or visual impairment certified by a medical examiner. Applicants must be enrolled at a branch of the University of Wisconsin, a technical college in the state, a Wisconsin independent college or university, a tribal college in the state, or an institution out of state that specializes in the training of deaf, hard of hearing, or visually handicapped students or that offers a program of study not offered by a Wisconsin institution. Financial need is considered in the selection process.

Financial data   Grants range from $250 to $1,800 per academic year.

Duration   1 year; may be renewed up to 4 additional years.

Number awarded   Varies each year.

Deadline   Deadline not specified.

Fellowship/Grants

[293]
ALAN B., '32, AND FLORENCE B., '35, CRAMMATTE FELLOWSHIP

Gallaudet University Alumni Association
Attn: Graduate Fellowship Fund Committee
Peikoff Alumni House
Gallaudet University
800 Florida Avenue, N.E.
Washington, DC 20002-3695
(202) 651-5060   Fax: (202) 651-5062
TDD: (202) 651-5060
E-mail: alumni.relations@gallaudet.edu
Web: alumni.gallaudet.edu/GFF_Info.xml

Summary   To provide financial assistance to deaf students who wish to work on a graduate degree in a field related to business at universities for people who hear normally.

Eligibility   This program is open to deaf and hard of hearing graduates of Gallaudet University or other accredited academic institutions who have been accepted for graduate study in a business-related field at colleges or universities for people who hear normally. Applicants must be working on a doctorate or other terminal degree. Financial need is considered in the selection process.

Financial data   The amount awarded varies, depending upon the needs of the recipient and the availability of funds.

Duration   1 year; may be renewed.

Additional data   This fund is 1 of 12 designated funds included in the Graduate Fellowship Fund of the Gallaudet University Alumni Association. Recipients must carry a full-time semester load.

Number awarded   Up to 1 each year.

Deadline   April of each year.

[294]
ALLIE RANEY HUNT SCHOLARSHIP

Alexander Graham Bell Association for the Deaf and Hard of Hearing
Attn: Financial Aid Coordinator
3417 Volta Place, N.W.
Washington, DC 20007-2778
(202) 337-5220   Fax: (202) 337-8314
TDD: (202) 337-5221   E-mail: financialaid@agbell.org
Web: nc.agbell.org/NetCommunity/Page.aspx?pid=493

Summary   To provide financial assistance to oral deaf undergraduate and graduate students with moderate to profound hearing loss.

Eligibility   This program is open to oral deaf undergraduate and graduate students who have been diagnosed with a moderate to profound hearing loss prior to acquiring spoken language (hearing loss averages 60dB or greater in the better ear in the speech frequencies of 500, 1000, and 2000 Hz). Applicants must be committed to using spoken language as their primary mode of communication. They must be accepted or enrolled at a mainstream college or university as a full-time student. Along with their application, they must submit a 1-page essay discussing their career goals and how spoken communication is helping them to reach those goals as a person with a hearing loss. Financial need is considered in the selection process.

Financial data   The stipend is $2,000 per year.

Duration   1 year; may be renewed 1 additional year.

Number awarded   1 each year.

Deadline   February of each year.

[295]
ALPHA SIGMA PI FRATERNITY FELLOWSHIP

Gallaudet University Alumni Association
Attn: Graduate Fellowship Fund Committee
Peikoff Alumni House
Gallaudet University
800 Florida Avenue, N.E.
Washington, DC 20002-3695
(202) 651-5060   Fax: (202) 651-5062
TDD: (202) 651-5060
E-mail: alumni.relations@gallaudet.edu
Web: alumni.gallaudet.edu/GFF_Info.xml

Summary   To provide financial assistance to deaf students who wish to work on a doctoral degree at universities for people who hear normally.

Eligibility   This program is open to deaf and hard of hearing graduates of Gallaudet University or other accredited colleges or universities who have been accepted for graduate study at academic institutions for people who hear normally. Applicants must be working on a doctorate or other terminal degree. Preference is given to alumni members of Alpha Sigma Pi Fraternity. Financial need is considered in the selection process.

Financial data   The amount awarded varies, depending upon the needs of the recipient and the availability of funds.

Duration   1 year; may be renewed.

Additional data This program was established in 1999 as 1 of 12 designated funds within the Graduate Fellowship Fund of the Gallaudet University Alumni Association. Recipients must carry a full-time load.
Number awarded Up to 1 each year.
Deadline April of each year.

[296]
DEAF AND HARD OF HEARING SECTION SCHOLARSHIP FUND

Alexander Graham Bell Association for the Deaf and
  Hard of Hearing
Attn: Financial Aid Coordinator
3417 Volta Place, N.W.
Washington, DC 20007-2778
(202) 337-5220   Fax· (202) 337-8314
TDD: (202) 337-5221   E-mail: financialaid@agbell.org
Web: nc.agbell.org/NetCommunity/Page.aspx?pid=493

Summary To provide financial assistance to undergraduate and graduate students who are members of the Alexander Graham Bell Association for the Deaf (AG Bell).
Eligibility This program is open to undergraduate and graduate students who have been diagnosed with a moderate to profound hearing loss prior to acquiring spoken language (hearing loss averages 60dB or greater in the better ear in the speech frequencies of 500, 1000, and 2000 Hz). Applicants must be committed to using spoken language as their primary mode of communication. They must be accepted or enrolled at a mainstream college or university as a full-time student. Along with their application, they must submit a 1-page essay discussing their career goals and how spoken communication is helping them to reach those goals as a person with a hearing loss. Financial need is considered in the selection process. This scholarship is reserved for students who are members of AG Bell and its Deaf and Hard of Hearing Section (DHHS).
Financial data The stipend is $1,000 per year.
Duration 1 year; may be renewed 1 additional year.
Number awarded 2 each year.
Deadline February of each year.

[297]
DORIS BALLANCE ORMAN, '25, FELLOWSHIP

Gallaudet University Alumni Association
Attn: Graduate Fellowship Fund Committee
Peikoff Alumni House
Gallaudet University
800 Florida Avenue, N.E.
Washington, DC 20002-3695
(202) 651-5060   Fax: (202) 651-5062
TDD: (202) 651-5060
E-mail: alumni.relations@gallaudet.edu
Web: alumni.gallaudet.edu/GFF_Info.xml

Summary To provide financial assistance to deaf women who wish to work on a graduate degree at universities for people who hear normally.
Eligibility This program is open to deaf or hard of hearing women graduates of Gallaudet University or other accredited academic institutions who have been accepted for graduate study at colleges or universities for people who hear normally. Applicants must be working on a doctorate or other terminal degree. They must have a particular interest in the arts, the humanities, and community leadership. Financial need is considered in the selection process.
Financial data The amount awarded varies, depending upon the needs of the recipient and the availability of funds.
Duration 1 year; may be renewed.
Additional data This program is 1 of 12 designated funds within the Graduate Fellowship Fund of the Gallaudet University Alumni Association. Recipients must carry a full-time semester load.
Number awarded Up to 1 each year.
Deadline April of each year.

[298]
ELSIE M. BELL GROSVENOR SCHOLARSHIP AWARDS

Alexander Graham Bell Association for the Deaf and
  Hard of Hearing
Attn: Financial Aid Coordinator
3417 Volta Place, N.W.
Washington, DC 20007-2778
(202) 337-5220   Fax: (202) 337-8314
TDD: (202) 337-5221   E-mail: financialaid@agbell.org
Web: nc.agbell.org/NetCommunity/Page.aspx?pid=493

Summary To provide financial assistance to undergraduate and graduate students who have moderate to profound hearing loss and attend school in the Washington, D.C. area.
Eligibility This program is open to undergraduate and graduate students who have been diagnosed with a moderate to profound hearing loss prior to acquiring spoken language (hearing loss averages 60dB or greater in the better ear in the speech frequencies of 500, 1000, and 2000 Hz). Applicants must be committed to using spoken language as their primary mode of communication. They must be accepted or enrolled at a mainstream college or university in the Washington, D.C. area as a full-time student. Along with their application, they must submit a 1-page essay discussing their career goals and how spoken communication is helping them to reach those goals as a person with a hearing loss. Financial need is considered in the selection process.
Financial data The stipend is $2,000 per year.
Duration 1 year; may be renewed 1 additional year.
Number awarded 1 each year.
Deadline February of each year.

[299]
FEDERATION OF JEWISH WOMEN'S ORGANIZATION SCHOLARSHIP

Alexander Graham Bell Association for the Deaf and
   Hard of Hearing
Attn: Financial Aid Coordinator
3417 Volta Place, N.W.
Washington, DC 20007-2778
(202) 337-5220   Fax: (202) 337-8314
TDD: (202) 337-5221   E-mail: financialaid@agbell.org
Web: nc.agbell.org/NetCommunity/Page.aspx?pid=493

Summary   To provide financial assistance to undergraduate and graduate students who are hearing impaired.

Eligibility   This program is open to undergraduate and graduate students who are hearing impaired. Applicants must be accepted or enrolled at a mainstream college or university as a full-time student. Along with their application, they must submit a 1-page essay discussing their career goals and how spoken communication is helping them to reach those goals as a person with a hearing loss. Financial need is considered in the selection process.

Financial data   The stipend is $2,000 per year.

Duration   1 year; may be renewed 1 additional year.

Number awarded   1 each year.

Deadline   February of each year.

[300]
GALLAUDET UNIVERSITY ALUMNI ASSOCIATION GRADUATE FELLOWSHIP FUND

Gallaudet University Alumni Association
Attn: Graduate Fellowship Fund Committee
Peikoff Alumni House
Gallaudet University
800 Florida Avenue, N.E.
Washington, DC 20002-3695
(202) 651-5060   Fax: (202) 651-5062
TDD: (202) 651-5060
E-mail: alumni.relations@gallaudet.edu
Web: alumni.gallaudet.edu/GFF_Info.xml

Summary   To provide financial assistance to deaf students who wish to work on a graduate degree at universities for people who hear normally.

Eligibility   This program is open to deaf and hard of hearing graduates of Gallaudet University or other accredited academic institutions who have been accepted for graduate study at colleges or universities for people who hear normally. Applicants must be working on a doctoral or other terminal degree. Financial need is considered in the selection process.

Financial data   The amount awarded varies, depending upon the number of qualified candidates applying for assistance, the availability of funds, and the needs of individual applicants.

Duration   1 year; may be renewed.

Additional data   This program includes the following named fellowships: the Boyce R. Williams, '32; Fellowship; the David Peikoff, '29 Fellowship; the James N. Orman, '23, Fellowship; the John A. Trundle, 1885, Fellowship; the

Old Dominion Foundation Fellowship; the Waldo T., '49 and Jean Kelsch, '51, Cordano Fellowship; and the I. King Jordan, '70 Fellowship. Recipients must carry a full-time semester load.

Number awarded   7 each year.

Deadline   April of each year.

[301]
GALLAUDET UNIVERSITY PRESIDENT'S FELLOWSHIP PROGRAM

Gallaudet University
Attn: Dean of the College of Liberal Arts, Sciences,
   and Technologies
HMB S242
800 Florida Avenue, N.E.
Washington, DC 20002
(202) 651-5224   Fax: (202) 448-6949
E-mail: Rebecca.Hogan@gallaudet.edu
Web: pf.gallaudet.edu

Summary   To provide support to hearing impaired doctoral students interested in a teaching assistantship at Gallaudet University while they complete work on their degree.

Eligibility   This program is open to deaf and hard of hearing full-time graduate students working on a Ph.D. or other terminal degree at a university in the United States other than Gallaudet. Applicants must be able and willing to serve as a teaching assistant at Gallaudet while they complete work on their degree. They must already possess sign skills at an appropriate level and aspire to a teaching and research career. Fields of study vary each year; recently, they were chemistry, communication studies, counseling, and international development.

Financial data   Grants provide up to $18,000 per year for tuition; an annual stipend (amount not specified) in return for teaching duties; academic privileges, such as library, WLRC, and e-mail access; and some travel support for professional conferences.

Duration   1 year; may be renewed up to 4 additional years.

Additional data   This program was established in 2003. The program does not guarantee future employment at Gallaudet, but does require a 2-year commitment to teaching at the university if a faculty vacancy occurs. During their tenure at Gallaudet, fellows are expected to 1) serve as teaching assistants in appropriate departments and teach up to 2 courses per semester; 2) attend faculty development mentoring activities; 3) maintain good standing in their graduate program; and 4) make timely progress toward their degree.

Number awarded   Up to 5 each year.

Deadline   May of each year.

[302]
GEORGE H. NOFER SCHOLARSHIP

Alexander Graham Bell Association for the Deaf and
  Hard of Hearing
Attn: Financial Aid Coordinator
3417 Volta Place, N.W.
Washington, DC 20007-2778
(202) 337-5220   Fax: (202) 337-8314
TDD: (202) 337-5221   E-mail: financialaid@agbell.org
Web: nc.agbell.org/NetCommunity/Page.aspx?pid=492

Summary   To provide financial assistance to graduate
students in public policy or law who have moderate to profound hearing loss.

Eligibility   This program is open to 1) graduate students
working on a master's or doctoral degree in public policy;
and 2) students accepted at an accredited law school.
Applicants must have been diagnosed with a moderate to
profound hearing loss prior to acquiring spoken language
(hearing loss averages 60dB or greater in the better ear in
the speech frequencies of 500, 1000, and 2000 Hz) and be
committed to using spoken language as their primary
mode of communication. They must be accepted or
enrolled at a mainstream college or university as a full-time
student and have an undergraduate GPA of 3.0 or higher.
Along with their application, they must submit a 1-page
essay discussing their career goals and how spoken communication is helping them to reach those goals as a person with a hearing loss. Financial need is considered in the
selection process.

Financial data   The stipend is $5,000 per year.

Duration   1 year; may be renewed 2 additional years if
the recipient maintains a GPA of 3.0 or higher.

Number awarded   1 each year.

Deadline   February of each year.

[303]
HENRY SYLE MEMORIAL FELLOWSHIP FOR SEMINARY STUDIES

Gallaudet University Alumni Association
Attn: Graduate Fellowship Fund Committee
Peikoff Alumni House
Gallaudet University
800 Florida Avenue, N.E.
Washington, DC 20002-3695
(202) 651-5060   Fax: (202) 651-5062
TDD: (202) 651-5060
E-mail: alumni.relations@gallaudet.edu
Web: alumni.gallaudet.edu/GFF_Info.xml

Summary   To provide financial assistance to deaf students who wish to pursue seminary studies at universities
for people who hear normally.

Eligibility   This program is open to deaf and hard of
hearing graduates of Gallaudet University or other accredited academic institutions who have been accepted for
graduate seminary study at colleges or universities for
people who hear normally. Applicants must be working on
a doctoral or other terminal degree. Financial need is considered in the selection process.

Financial data   The amount awarded varies, depending
upon the needs of the recipient and the availability of
funds.

Duration   1 year; may be renewed.

Additional data   This fund was established in 1990 as 1
of 12 designated funds within the Graduate Fellowship
Fund of the Gallaudet University Alumni Association.
Recipients must carry a full-time semester load.

Number awarded   1 each year.

Deadline   April of each year.

[304]
HERBERT P. FEIBELMAN, JR. SCHOLARSHIP

Alexander Graham Bell Association for the Deaf and
  Hard of Hearing
Attn: Financial Aid Coordinator
3417 Volta Place, N.W.
Washington, DC 20007-2778
(202) 337-5220   Fax: (202) 337-8314
TDD: (202) 337-5221   E-mail: financialaid@agbell.org
Web: nc.agbell.org/NetCommunity/Page.aspx?pid=493

Summary   To provide financial assistance to undergraduate and graduate students who are members of the Alexander Graham Bell Association for the Deaf (AG Bell) and
their children.

Eligibility   This program is open to undergraduate and
graduate students who have been diagnosed with a moderate to profound hearing loss prior to acquiring spoken
language (hearing loss averages 60dB or greater in the
better ear in the speech frequencies of 500, 1000, and
2000 Hz). Applicants must be committed to using spoken
language as their primary mode of communication. They
must be accepted or enrolled at a mainstream college or
university as a full-time student. Along with their application, they must submit a 1-page essay discussing their
career goals and how spoken communication is helping
them to reach those goals as a person with a hearing loss.
Financial need is considered in the selection process. This
scholarship is reserved for students who are members of
AG Bell or whose parents are members.

Financial data   The stipend is $2,500 per year.

Duration   1 year; may be renewed 1 additional year.

Number awarded   1 each year.

Deadline   February of each year.

[305]
HOLLY ELLIOTT AND LAUREL GLASS SCHOLARSHIP ENDOWMENT

United Methodist Higher Education Foundation
Attn: Scholarships Administrator
1001 19th Avenue South
P.O. Box 340005
Nashville, TN 37203-0005
(615) 340-7385   Toll Free: (800) 811-8110
Fax: (615) 340-7330
E-mail: umhefscholarships@gbhem.org
Web: www.umhef.org/receive.php?id=endowed_funds

Summary   To provide financial assistance to students at
United Methodist seminaries who are deaf or deaf-blind.

Eligibility This program is open to students enrolled full time at United Methodist theological schools who are culturally deaf, orally deaf, deafened, late deafened, deaf-blind, or hard of hearing. Applicants must be preparing for specialized ministries in the church, including (but not limited to) those wishing to become ordained. They must have been active, full members of a United Methodist Church for at least 1 year prior to applying. Financial need and U.S. citizenship or permanent resident status are required.

Financial data The stipend is at least $1,000 per year.

Duration 1 year; nonrenewable.

Additional data This program was established in 2004.

Number awarded 1 each year.

Deadline May of each year.

[306]
INTERNATIONAL ALUMNAE OF DELTA EPSILON SORORITY FELLOWSHIP AWARD

International Alumnae of Delta Epsilon Sorority
c/o Virginia Borggaard
2453 Bear Den Road
Frederick, MD 21701-9321
Fax: (301) 663-3231   TDD: (301) 663-9235
E-mail: vborggaard@juno.com

Summary To provide financial assistance to deaf women who are working on a doctoral degree.

Eligibility Eligible to apply are deaf women who have completed 12 or more units in a doctoral-level program with a GPA of 3.0 or more. They need not be members of Delta Epsilon. Along with their application, they must submit official transcripts, a recent copy of their audiogram, and 2 letters of recommendation.

Financial data The stipend is $1,000.

Duration 1 year.

Number awarded 1 or more each year.

Deadline April of each year.

[307]
LADIES' AUXILIARY NATIONAL RURAL LETTER CARRIERS SCHOLARSHIP

Alexander Graham Bell Association for the Deaf and
  Hard of Hearing
Attn: Financial Aid Coordinator
3417 Volta Place, N.W.
Washington, DC 20007-2778
(202) 337-5220   Fax: (202) 337-8314
TDD: (202) 337-5221 E-mail: financialaid@agbell.org
Web: nc.agbell.org/NetCommunity/Page.aspx?pid=493

Summary To provide financial assistance to undergraduate and graduate students with moderate to profound hearing loss.

Eligibility This program is open to undergraduate and graduate students who have been diagnosed with a moderate to profound hearing loss prior to acquiring spoken language (hearing loss averages 60dB or greater in the better ear in the speech frequencies of 500, 1000, and 2000 Hz). Applicants must be committed to using spoken language as their primary mode of communication. They

must be accepted or enrolled at a mainstream college or university as a full-time student. Along with their application, they must submit a 1-page essay discussing their career goals and how spoken communication is helping them to reach those goals as a person with a hearing loss. Financial need is considered in the selection process.

Financial data The stipend is $2,000 per year.

Duration 1 year; may be renewed 1 additional year.

Number awarded 1 each year.

Deadline February of each year.

[308]
LOUIS DICARLO SCHOLARSHIP

Alexander Graham Bell Association for the Deaf and
  Hard of Hearing
Attn: Financial Aid Coordinator
3417 Volta Place, N.W.
Washington, DC 20007-2778
(202) 337-5220   Fax: (202) 337-8314
TDD: (202) 337-5221 E-mail: financialaid@agbell.org
Web: nc.agbell.org/NetCommunity/Page.aspx?pid=493

Summary To provide financial assistance to graduate students with moderate to profound hearing loss.

Eligibility This program is open to graduate students who have been diagnosed with a moderate to profound hearing loss prior to acquiring spoken language (hearing loss averages 60dB or greater in the better ear in the speech frequencies of 500, 1000, and 2000 Hz). Applicants must be committed to using spoken language as their primary mode of communication. They must be accepted or enrolled at a mainstream college or university as a full-time student. Along with their application, they must submit a 1-page essay discussing their career goals and how spoken communication is helping them to reach those goals as a person with a hearing loss. Financial need is considered in the selection process.

Financial data The stipend is $2,000 per year.

Duration 1 year; may be renewed 1 additional year.

Number awarded 1 each year.

Deadline February of each year.

[309]
LOUISE TUMARKIN ZAZOVE SCHOLARSHIPS

Louise Tumarkin Zazove Foundation
6858 North Kenneth Avenue
Chicago, IL 60712-4705
E-mail: earl@ltzfoundation.org
Web: www.ltzfoundation.org/scholarships.php

Summary To provide financial assistance for college (and possibly for high school or graduate school) to people with hearing loss.

Eligibility This program is open to U.S. citizens and permanent residents who have a significant bilateral hearing loss. Strong preference is given to undergraduate students, but support may be provided for graduate school or high school tuition in certain situations. Applicants must submit a transcript of high school and/or college grades, 3 letters of recommendation, documentation of the severity of the hearing loss, information on any special circumstances by or about the family, and documentation of financial need.

Financial data A stipend is awarded (amount not specified). Funds are paid directly to schools.

Duration 1 year; may be renewed up to 3 additional years, provided the recipient continues to do well in school and demonstrate financial need.

Additional data This program was established in 2003.

Number awarded Varies each year; since the program was established, it has awarded 14 scholarships.

Deadline May of each year.

[310]
LUCILLE B. ABT SCHOLARSHIPS

Alexander Graham Bell Association for the Deaf and
 Hard of Hearing
Attn: Financial Aid Coordinator
3417 Volta Place, N.W.
Washington, DC 20007-2778
(202) 337-5220   Fax: (202) 337-8314
TDD: (202) 337-5221   E-mail: financialaid@agbell.org
Web: nc.agbell.org/NetCommunity/Page.aspx?pid=493

Summary To provide financial assistance to undergraduate and graduate students with moderate to profound hearing loss.

Eligibility This program is open to undergraduate and graduate students who have been diagnosed with a moderate to profound hearing loss prior to acquiring spoken language (hearing loss averages 60dB or greater in the better ear in the speech frequencies of 500, 1000, and 2000 Hz). Applicants must be committed to using spoken language and lipreading as their preferred mode of communication. They must be accepted or enrolled at a mainstream college or university as a full-time student. Along with their application, they must submit a 1-page essay discussing their career goals and how spoken communication is helping them to reach those goals as a person with a hearing loss. Financial need is considered in the selection process.

Financial data The stipend is $5,000 per year.

Duration 1 year; may be renewed 1 additional year.

Number awarded 10 each year.

Deadline February of each year.

[311]
MARYLAND STATE GRANGE DEAF SCHOLARSHIP

Maryland State Grange
Attn: Master
8743 Old Kiln Road
Thurmont, MD 21788-1219
(301) 447-2075   Fax: (301) 447-2019
E-mail: rlt-rox@juno.com

Summary To provide financial assistance for college or graduate school to Maryland residents who are either deaf or preparing to work with hearing impaired people.

Eligibility This program is open to seniors graduating from high schools in Maryland and to graduates of those high schools who are attending or planning to attend col-

lege or graduate school in the state. Applicants must be 1) deaf or hearing impaired, or 2) preparing for a career working with deaf or hearing impaired people.

Financial data A stipend is awarded (amount not specified).

Duration 1 year; may be renewed if the recipient maintains a GPA of 3.0 or higher.

Number awarded 1 or more each year.

Deadline May of each year.

[312]
REGINA OLSON HUGHES, '18, FELLOWSHIP

Gallaudet University Alumni Association
Attn: Graduate Fellowship Fund Committee
Peikoff Alumni House
Gallaudet University
800 Florida Avenue, N.E.
Washington, DC 20002-3695
(202) 651-5060   Fax: (202) 651-5062
TDD: (202) 651-5060
E-mail: alumni.relations@gallaudet.edu
Web: alumni.gallaudet.edu/GFF_Info.xml

Summary To provide financial assistance to deaf students who wish to work on a graduate degree in fine arts at universities for people who hear normally.

Eligibility This program is open to deaf and hard of hearing graduates of Gallaudet University or other accredited academic institutions who have been accepted for graduate study in fine arts at colleges or universities for people who hear normally. Applicants must be working on a doctoral or other terminal degree. Financial need is considered in the selection process.

Financial data The amount awarded varies, depending upon the needs of the recipient and the availability of funds.

Duration 1 year; may be renewed.

Additional data This program, established in 1995, is 1 of 12 designated funds within the Graduate Fellowship Fund of the Gallaudet University Alumni Association. Recipients must carry a full-time semester load.

Number awarded Up to 1 each year.

Deadline April of each year.

[313]
ROBERT H. WEITBRECHT SCHOLARSHIP

Alexander Graham Bell Association for the Deaf and
 Hard of Hearing
Attn: Financial Aid Coordinator
3417 Volta Place, N.W.
Washington, DC 20007-2778
(202) 337-5220   Fax: (202) 337-8314
TDD: (202) 337-5221   E-mail: financialaid@agbell.org
Web: nc.agbell.org/NetCommunity/Page.aspx?pid=493

Summary To provide financial assistance to undergraduate and graduate students with moderate to profound hearing loss, especially those working on a degree in engineering or science.

Eligibility This program is open to undergraduate and graduate students who have been diagnosed with a moderate to profound hearing loss prior to acquiring spoken language (hearing loss averages 60dB or greater in the better ear in the speech frequencies of 500, 1000, and 2000 Hz). Applicants must be able to demonstrate leadership potential and be committed to using spoken language as their primary mode of communication. They must be accepted or enrolled at a mainstream college or university as a full-time student. Along with their application, they must submit a 1-page essay discussing their career goals and how spoken communication is helping them to reach those goals as a person with a hearing loss. Financial need is considered in the selection process. Priority for this scholarship is given to applicants studying engineering or science.

Financial data   The stipend is $2,500 per year.

Duration   1 year; may be renewed 1 additional year.

Number awarded   1 each year.

Deadline   February of each year.

[314]
VOLTA SCHOLARSHIP FUND

Alexander Graham Bell Association for the Deaf and
  Hard of Hearing
Attn: Financial Aid Coordinator
3417 Volta Place, N.W.
Washington, DC 20007-2778
(202) 337-5220   Fax: (202) 337-8314
TDD: (202) 337-5221   E-mail: financialaid@agbell.org
Web: nc.agbell.org/NetCommunity/Page.aspx?pid=493

Summary   To provide financial assistance to oral deaf undergraduate and graduate students with moderate to profound hearing loss.

Eligibility   This program is open to oral deaf undergraduate and graduate students who have been diagnosed with a moderate to profound hearing loss prior to acquiring spoken language (hearing loss averages 60dB or greater in the better ear in the speech frequencies of 500, 1000, and 2000 Hz). Applicants must be committed to using spoken language as their primary mode of communication. They must be accepted or enrolled at a mainstream college or university as a full-time student. Along with their application, they must submit a 1-page essay discussing their career goals and how spoken communication is helping them to reach those goals as a person with a hearing loss. Financial need is considered in the selection process.

Financial data   The stipend is $2,000 per year.

Duration   1 year; may be renewed 1 additional year.

Number awarded   1 each year.

Deadline   February of each year.

[315]
WALTER W. AND THELMA C. HISSEY COLLEGE SCHOLARSHIPS

Alexander Graham Bell Association for the Deaf and
  Hard of Hearing
Attn: Financial Aid Coordinator
3417 Volta Place, N.W.
Washington, DC 20007-2778
(202) 337-5220   Fax: (202) 337-8314
TDD: (202) 337-5221   E-mail: financialaid@agbell.org
Web: nc.agbell.org/NetCommunity/Page.aspx?pid=493

Summary   To provide financial assistance to undergraduate and graduate students with moderate to profound hearing loss.

Eligibility   This program is open to undergraduate and graduate students who have been diagnosed with a moderate to profound hearing loss prior to acquiring spoken language (hearing loss averages 60dB or greater in the better ear in the speech frequencies of 500, 1000, and 2000 Hz). Applicants must be committed to using spoken language as their primary mode of communication. They must be accepted or enrolled at a mainstream college or university as a full-time student. Along with their application, they must submit a 1-page essay discussing their career goals and how spoken communication is helping them to reach those goals as a person with a hearing loss. Financial need is considered in the selection process.

Financial data   The stipend is $5,000 per year.

Duration   1 year; may be renewed 1 additional year.

Number awarded   2 each year.

Deadline   February of each year.

[316]
WILLIAM C. STOKOE SCHOLARSHIP

National Association of the Deaf
8630 Fenton Street, Suite 820
Silver Spring, MD 20910-3819
(301) 587-1788   Fax: (301) 587-1791
TDD: (301) 587-1789   E-mail: nadinfo@nad.org
Web: www.nad.org

Summary   To provide financial assistance to deaf graduate students who are studying or conducting research in a field related to sign language.

Eligibility   This program is open to deaf students who have graduated from a 4-year college program and are currently enrolled in a master's or doctoral degree program in a field related to sign language or the deaf community. Applicants may also be developing a special project on 1 of those topics.

Financial data   The stipend is $2,000.

Duration   1 year.

Additional data   Most of the money for the scholarship comes from the sales of a book, *Sign Language and the Deaf Community: Essays in Honor of William C. Stokoe.* The editors and authors of the book, published in 1980 by the National Association of the Deaf, donated all their royalties to the scholarship fund. The holder of the scholarship must create and finish, within a year, a project that relates to sign language or the deaf community. The recipient must prepare a brief report (either written or videotaped) at the end of the project, which normally but not always relates to the student's work in school.

Number awarded 1 each year.

Deadline March of each year.

Grants-in-Aid

[317]
ALABAMA PERSONAL PROPERTY TAX EXEMPTION FOR THE DEAF

Alabama Department of Revenue
Attn: Property Tax Division
Gordon Persons Building
50 North Ripley Street, Room 4126
P.O. Box 327210
Montgomery, AL 36132-7210
(334) 242-1525
Web: www.ador.state.al.us

Summary To exempt deaf residents of Alabama from taxation on a portion of their personal property.

Eligibility Residents of Alabama are eligible for this personal property tax exemption if they are legally defined as "deaf mutes and insane persons."

Financial data Up to $3,000 of personal property is exempt from taxation.

Duration 1 year; this exemption will be granted as long as the resident continues to meet the eligibility requirements.

Number awarded Varies each year.

Deadline Deadline not specified.

[318]
FORD MOBILITY MOTORING PROGRAM

Ford Motor Company
Attn: Mobility Program
500 Hulet Drive
P.O. Box 529
Bloomfield Hills, MI 48303
Toll Free: (800) 952-2248, ext. 111
Fax: (248) 333-0300
TDD: (800) 833-0312
E-mail: Mobilitymotoring@Fordprogramhq.com
Web: www.mobilitymotoringprogram.com

Summary To provide a cash reimbursement for the cost of installing adaptive driving aids on new vehicles from Ford or Lincoln-Mercury.

Eligibility Eligible for this rebate are people who purchase or lease new Ford, Lincoln, or Mercury vehicles that require adaptive driving aids or conversion equipment for users with disabilities.

Financial data Up to $1,200 is reimbursed for adaptive equipment or up to $200 for alert hearing devices, lumbar support, or running boards.

Additional data The program also provides 24-hour roadside assistance.

Number awarded Varies each year.

Deadline Applicants have 12 months from the date or purchase or lease to initiate the adaptive work and 1 year from that date to process their claim.

[319]
HAWAII INCOME TAX EXEMPTION FOR DISABLED RESIDENTS

Department of Taxation
Attn: Taxpayer Services Branch
425 Queen Street
P.O. Box 259
Honolulu, HI 96809-0259
(808) 587-4242   Toll Free: (800) 222-3229
Fax: (808) 587-1488   TDD: (808) 587-1418
Web: hawaii.gov/tax

Summary To exempt a portion of the income of blind, deaf, and other disabled residents from state income tax in Hawaii.

Eligibility Eligible for this exemption are 1) blind residents whose central visual acuity does not exceed 20/200 in the better eye with corrective lenses or whose visual acuity is greater than 20/200 but is accompanied by a limitation in the field of vision such that the widest diameter of the visual field subtends an angle no greater than 20 degrees; 2) deaf residents whose average loss in the speech frequencies in the better ear is 82 decibels A.S.A. or worse; or 3) totally disabled residents (physically or mentally) who are unable to engage in any substantial gainful business or occupation (a person whose gross income exceeds $30,000 per year is assumed to be engaged in a substantial gainful business or occupation).

Financial data The maximum exemptions from state income tax are as follows: single disabled resident, $7,000; disabled husband and wife, $14,000; disabled husband or wife, with non-disabled spouse under 65, $8,040; disabled husband or wife, with non-disabled spouse 65 years of age or older, $9,080.

Duration The exemption continues as long as the recipient resides in Hawaii.

Additional data Residents who claim this special exemption are not eligible to claim additional exemptions for their children or other dependents.

Deadline Deadline not specified.

[320]
HIKE FUND GRANTS

The HIKE Fund, Inc.
c/o Shirley Terrill, Board Secretary
10115 Cherryhill Place
Spring Hill, FL 34608-7116
(352) 688-2579   Fax: (352) 688-2579
E-mail: ceterrill1@aol.com
Web: www.thehikefund.org

Summary To provide funding to children with a hearing loss who need assistance to purchase a hearing aid or other device.

Eligibility This assistance is available to children under 20 years of age. Applicants must have been identified as 1) having a need for a hearing aid or other assistive listening device, and 2) having financial need. Selection is based on family income, size of household, other medical expenses for the applicant, and the cost of the hearing technology requested.

Financial data Grants depend on the need of the family and the price indicated in the prescription accompanying the application.

Duration These are 1-time grants.

Additional data The HIKE Fund, which stands for Hearing Impaired Kids Endowment, was established by Job's Daughters International in 1986. Girls who are members of that organization continue to support the program with fund-raising activities.

Number awarded Varies each year; recently 90 of these grants, totaling $226,185.44, were awarded.

Deadline Applications may be submitted at any time.

[321]
KANSAS STATE DEAF-BLIND FUND

Kansas State Department of Education
Student Support Services
Attn: Kansas State Deaf-Blind Fund
120 S.E. 10th Avenue
Topeka, KS 66612-1182
(785) 296-2515   Toll Free: (800) 203-9462
Fax: (785) 296-6715   TDD: (785) 296-2515
E-mail: jhoughton@ksde.org
Web: www.kansped.org/ksde/kstars/projects.html

Summary To provide supplementary financial assistance to deaf-blind or severely disabled students in Kansas.

Eligibility Applications may be submitted by school personnel for students in Kansas (up to the age of 21) who are deaf-blind and/or have severe multiple disabilities. Approval for funding is granted on a first-come, first-served basis for the following areas: 1) assistive technology that enables a student with dual sensory impairments and with severe disabilities to participate more fully in an educational program (e.g., computers, adaptive equipment, eyeglasses, hearing aids, computer peripherals, augmentative communication devices, microswitches, software); 2) consultation; 3) evaluation for the cost of vision and/or hearing evaluations for students who are suspected of being deaf-blind, or a vision, hearing, or educational evaluation for recertification purposes; or 4) other costs associated with additional items or expenses that reflect best educational or effective practices, such as expenses involved in providing community activities. Applicants must provide documentation that other funding sources have been approached and that costs do not exceed the amount local education agencies are able to provide out of federal, state, or local funds. Priority candidates are students who have current deaf-blind certification, deaf-blind children from birth through 2 years of age, students who are exiting state hospital schools and returning to their home district, students who have a suspected vision loss and docu-

mented hearing loss and are in need of an evaluation, and students who have a suspected hearing loss and documented vision loss who are in need of an evaluation.

Financial data Eligible students are awarded up to $3,000 per year.

Duration 1 year; may be renewed.

Number awarded Varies each year.

Deadline May of each year.

[322]
MICHIGAN INCOME TAX EXEMPTION FOR PEOPLE WITH DISABILITIES

Michigan Department of Treasury
Attn: Income Tax
Treasury Building
430 West Allegan Street
Lansing, MI 48922
(517) 373-3200   Toll Free: (800) 827-4000
TDD: (517) 636-4999
E-mail: treasIndTax@michigan.gov
Web: www.michigan.gov/treasury

Summary To exempt a portion of the income of deaf, blind, and disabled residents of Michigan from state income taxation.

Eligibility Eligible for this exemption are residents of Michigan who 1) receive messages through a sense other than hearing, such as lip reading or sign language; 2) have vision in their better eye of 20/200 or less with corrective lenses or peripheral field of vision of 20 degrees or less; or 3) are hemiplegic, paraplegic, quadriplegic, or totally and permanently disabled.

Financial data Qualifying people with disabilities receive an exemption of $2,200 from their adjusted gross income for purposes of state taxation.

Duration The exemption continues as long as the recipient resides in Michigan.

Deadline Deadline not specified.

[323]
MOBILITY BY VOLVO

Volvo Cars of North America, LLC
Attn: Mobility by Volvo
1 Volvo Drive
Rockleigh, NJ 07647
Toll Free: (800) 803-5222   TDD: (800) 833-0312
E-mail: MobilitybyVolvo@Volvoprogramhq.com
Web: www.volvocars.us/mobility

Summary To provide a cash reimbursement for the cost of installing adaptive driving aids or alert hearing devices on new purchases of Volvo vehicles.

Eligibility This rebate is available to purchasers of new Volvo vehicles that require adaptive driving aids or alert hearing devices for users with disabilities. Applicants must obtain the equipment, have it installed, and submit a copy of their paid invoice and a copy of their medical prescription.

Financial data Up to $1,000 is provided for the cost of adding adaptive equipment or $200 for an alert hearing device.

Deadline Eligible vehicles must be upfitted with approved adaptive equipment or alert hearing devices, and requests must be submitted within 180 days of vehicle purchase.

[324]
NEW HAMPSHIRE DEAF PROPERTY TAX EXEMPTION

New Hampshire Department of Revenue
  Administration
109 Pleasant Street
Concord, NH 03301
(603) 271-2191   Fax: (603) 271-6121
TDD: (800) 735-2964
Web: revenue.nh.gov

Summary To provide deaf residents of New Hampshire with a partial exemption from real estate taxes.

Eligibility Residents of New Hampshire are covered by this program if they have lived in the state for at least 5 consecutive years, have suffered an average hearing loss of 71 Db in the better ear, own and occupy their primary residence in New Hampshire, and live in a municipality that has chosen through a referendum vote to grant an exemption to the legally deaf. Their income and assets may not exceed specified limits; the current income limit is $13,400 for single applicants or $20,400 for married applicants, and the current asset limit is $35,000, excluding the residence. Towns may set higher limits.

Financial data $15,000 of the value of the residential real estate is exempted from taxation for qualifying residents. Towns may exempt any amount they determine is appropriate to address significant increases in property values.

Duration 1 year; this exemption will be continued as long as the recipient meets the eligibility requirements.

Number awarded Varies each year.

Deadline The original application for a permanent tax credit must be submitted by April.

[325]
PARENT-INFANT FINANCIAL AID PROGRAM

Alexander Graham Bell Association for the Deaf and
  Hard of Hearing
Attn: Financial Aid Coordinator
3417 Volta Place, N.W.
Washington, DC 20007-2778
(202) 337-5220   Fax: (202) 337-8314
TDD: (202) 337-5221   E-mail: financialaid@agbell.org
Web: nc.agbell.org/NetCommunity/Page.aspx?pid=499

Summary To provide financial aid to the parents of young children with moderate to profound hearing loss who need assistance to cover expenses associated with early intervention services.

Eligibility Applicants must be parents or guardians of children less than 3 years of age who have been diagnosed as having a moderate to profound hearing loss (the

child must have an unaided Pure-Tone Average (PTA) of 55dB or more in the better hearing ear in the speech frequencies of 500, 1000, and 2000 Hz). Children with cochlear implants are eligible, but those with unilateral hearing loss are not. Spoken communication must be the child's primary mode of communication. The family must be able to demonstrate financial need. Residents of Canada, the United States, and its territories are eligible.

Financial data The amount awarded depends on the needs of the child; most awards range from $300 to $1,000 per year.

Duration 1 year.

Number awarded Varies each year.

Deadline September of each year.

[326]
PRESCHOOL FINANCIAL AID PROGRAM

Alexander Graham Bell Association for the Deaf and
  Hard of Hearing
Attn: Financial Aid Coordinator
3417 Volta Place, N.W.
Washington, DC 20007-2778
(202) 337-5220   Fax: (202) 337-8314
TDD: (202) 337-5221   E-mail: financialaid@agbell.org
Web: nc.agbell.org/NetCommunity/Page.aspx?pid=497

Summary To provide financial aid to the parents of preschool children with moderate to profound hearing loss who need assistance to cover expenses associated with early intervention services.

Eligibility Applicants must be parents or guardians of children between 4 and 6 years of age who have been diagnosed as having a moderate to profound hearing loss (the child must have an unaided Pure-Tone Average (PTA) of 55dB or more in the better hearing ear in the speech frequencies of 500, 1000, and 2000 Hz). Children with cochlear implants are eligible, but those with unilateral hearing loss are not. Spoken communication must be the child's primary mode of communication. The family must be able to demonstrate financial need. Residents of Canada, the United States, and its territories are eligible.

Financial data The amount awarded depends on the needs of the child; most grants range from $300 to $1,000 per year.

Duration 1 year; may be renewed upon reapplication, but preference is given to new applicants who are just enrolling their child in preschool.

Number awarded Varies each year.

Deadline July of each year.

[327]
SCHOLARSHIP TRUST FOR THE HEARING IMPAIRED

Travelers Protective Association of America
Attn: TPA Scholarship Trust for the Hearing Impaired
3755 Lindell Boulevard
St. Louis, MO 63108-3476
(314) 371-0533   Fax: (314) 371-0537
E-mail: support@tpahq.org
Web: www.tpahq.org/scholarshiptrust.html

Summary To provide assistance to deaf and hearing impaired persons interested in obtaining additional education, mechanical devices, specialized medical treatment, or other treatments.

Eligibility This assistance is available to U.S. residents who are deaf or hearing impaired. Applicants must be able to demonstrate that they will benefit from special programs, services, or other activities for the deaf, but that they are unable to provide the necessary funds.

Financial data The grant depends on the need of the recipient.

Duration 1 year; recipients may reapply.

Additional data This fund was established in 1975. Support has been provided to children as young as 2 months and to adults as old as 82 years. Funds have been used for mechanical devices, tuition at schools that specialize in educating the deaf (e.g., Gallaudet University, Rochester Institute of Technology, Central Institute for the Deaf), note takers and interpreters in classes in regular schools that do not provide those services to the deaf, speech and language therapy (especially for those who have had the cochlear implant), medical or other specialized treatments, and computer programs that assist the deaf and their families learn and apply skills presented in the classroom.

Number awarded Varies each year; since the trust was established, it has distributed more than $1.5 million to more than 3,700 recipients.

Deadline February of each year.

[328]
SUPPLEMENTAL SECURITY INCOME (SSI)

Social Security Administration
6401 Security Boulevard
Baltimore, MD 21235-0001
(410) 594-1234   Toll Free: (800) 772-1213
TDD: (800) 325-0778
Web: www.socialsecurity.gov/ssi/index.htm

Summary To provide monthly payments to disabled, blind, deaf, and elderly people who have limited income and resources.

Eligibility This assistance is available to U.S. citizens and certain categories of aliens who are 65 years of age or older, blind, or disabled. A person 18 years of age or older is considered disabled if a physical or mental impairment prevents him or her from doing any substantial gainful work and is expected to last for at least 12 months or to result in death. Children under the age of 18 are considered disabled if they have a physical or mental impairment that is comparable in severity to a disability that would prevent an adult from working and is expected to last at least 12 months or result in death. Children with certain conditions are automatically disabled and eligible for these benefits; the conditions include HIV infection, blindness, deafness, cerebral palsy, Down syndrome, muscular dystrophy, significant mental deficiency, diabetes (with amputation of 1 foot), amputation of 2 limbs, or amputation of leg at the hip. Regardless of age, a person whose vision is no better than 20/200 or who has a limited visual field of 20 degrees or less with the best corrective eyeglasses is considered blind; individuals with visual impairments not severe enough to meet the definition of blindness still may qualify as disabled persons. Applicants must have limited income and limited resources (less than $2,000 for an individual or $3,000 for a couple); items excluded from resources include the home used as a principal place of residence, personal and household goods, life insurance with face value of $1,500 or less, a car, burial plots for individuals and immediate family members, and burial funds up to $1,500.

Financial data The basic monthly payment is $674 for an eligible individual or $1,011 for an eligible individual with an eligible spouse. Many states add money to that basic payment. SSI recipients may also be eligible for food stamps and other nutrition programs.

Duration Assistance is provided as long as the recipient remains blind or disabled and in financial need.

Additional data Although SSI is administered through the Social Security Administration, it is not financed by Social Security taxes. Financing of SSI is provided through general funds of the U.S. Treasury. Recipients of SSI need not have been employed or paid Social Security taxes, but they may be eligible for both SSI and Social Security. Disabled and blind applicants for SSI are referred to their state vocational rehabilitation agency to determine their eligibility for a program of vocational rehabilitation. Disabled drug addicts or alcoholics are referred for appropriate treatment if it is available at an approved facility or institution.

Number awarded Recently, approximately 7,599,000 people (including 6,395,000 who were blind and disabled) were receiving SSI benefits, including 1,172,000 under 18 years of age, 4,389,000 who were 18 to 64 years of age, and 2,038,000 who were 65 or older.

Deadline Deadline not specified.

Awards

[329]
MISS DEAF AMERICA AMBASSADOR PROGRAM

National Association of the Deaf
8630 Fenton Street, Suite 820
Silver Spring, MD 20910-3819
(301) 587-1788   Fax: (301) 587-1791
TDD: (301) 587-1789   E-mail: nadinfo@nad.org
Web: www.nad.org/youth-leadership-programs

Summary To recognize and reward outstanding young deaf women.

Eligibility This is a 2-tiered competition. Young deaf women between the ages of 18 and 30 compete first on the state level; winners take part in the national pageant. Winners are selected on the basis of artistic expression, community service, academics, current events, deaf culture, and more.

Financial data The national winner receives an educational scholarship (amount not specified).

Duration The competition is held biennially during the summer of even-numbered years, in conjunction with the National Association of the Deaf conventions.

Deadline The deadline dates of the state competitions vary; check with the sponsor in your area.

[330]
OPTIMIST INTERNATIONAL COMMUNICATION CONTEST FOR THE DEAF AND HARD OF HEARING

Optimist International
Attn: Programs Department
4494 Lindell Boulevard
St. Louis, MO 63108
(314) 371-6000   Toll Free: (800) 500-8130, ext. 235
Fax: (314) 371-6006   E-mail: programs@optimist.org
Web: www.optimist.org/e/member/scholarships2.cfm

Summary To recognize and reward, with college scholarships, outstanding presentations made by hearing impaired high school students.

Eligibility This program is open to young people up to and including grade 12 in the United States and Canada, to CEGEP in Québec, and to grade 13 in the Caribbean. Applicants must be identified by a qualified audiologist as deaf or hard of hearing with a hearing loss of 40 decibels or more. They are invited to make a presentation (using oral communication, sign language, or a combination of both) from 4 to 5 minutes on a topic that changes annually; a recent topic was "Cyber Communication: Progress or Problem?" Competition is first conducted at the level of individual clubs, with winners advancing to zone and then district competitions. Selection is based on material organization (40 points), delivery and presentation (30 points), and overall effectiveness (30 points).

Financial data Each district winner receives a $2,500 college scholarship, payable to an educational institution of the recipient's choice, subject to the approval of Optimist International.

Duration The competition is held annually.

Additional data Entry information is available only from local Optimist Clubs.

Number awarded Nearly 300 Optimist International clubs participate in this program each year. Each participating district offers 1 scholarship; some districts may offer a second award with separate competitions for signing and oral competitors, or for male and female entrants.

Deadline Each club sets its own deadline. Districts must submit materials to the national office by June of each year.

Orthopedic/Developmental Disabilities

Scholarships ●

Fellowships/Grants ●

Grants-in-Aid ●

Awards ●

Described here are 77 programs open to individuals with 1) a severe orthopedic impairment caused by birth defects (e.g., absence of an extremity), diseases, or other causes (e.g., accidents, amputations), or 2) a severe, chronic disability that was manifested before age 22 (for example, spina bifida). In all, 32 entries cover scholarships (to pursue studies or research on the undergraduate level in the United States); 8 cover fellowships/grants (to pursue graduate or postdoctoral education or research in the United States); 36 cover grants-in-aid (to support emergency situations, travel, income/property tax liabilities, or the acquisition of assistive technology); and 1 describes an award, competition, or prize (to recognize or support creative work and public service). If you are looking for a particular program and don't find it in this chapter, be sure to check the Program Title Index to see if it is covered elsewhere in the directory.

Scholarships

[331]
BRYON RIESCH SCHOLARSHIPS

Bryon Riesch Paralysis Foundation
P.O. Box 1388
Waukesha, WI 53187-1388
(262) 547-2083   E-mail: info@brpf.org
Web: www.brpf.org/scholarships.htm

Summary To provide financial assistance to 1) undergraduate and graduate students who have a neurological disability or 2) the children of people with such a disability.

Eligibility This program is open to students entering or enrolled at a 2- or 4-year college or university as an undergraduate or graduate student. Applicants must have a neurological disability or be the child of a person with such a disability. They must have a GPA of 2.5 or higher in high school or college. Along with their application, they must submit a 200-word essay on why they deserve the scholarship, a statement of their 5- and 10-year goals, and a list of work experience. Financial need is not considered in the selection process.

Financial data Stipends range from $1,000 to $2,000.

Duration 1 year; may be renewed.

Number awarded 2 to 3 each semester.

Deadline June of each year for fall semester; December of each year for spring semester.

[332]
CENTRAL INDIANA COLLEGE SCHOLARSHIP

Spina Bifida Association of Central Indiana
P.O. Box 19814
Indianapolis, IN 46219-0814
(317) 592-1630
Web: www.sbaci.org

Summary To provide financial assistance to residents of Indiana who have spina bifida and are interested in attending college in any state.

Eligibility This program is open to residents of Indiana who have spina bifida. Applicants must be enrolled or planning to enroll at a college, junior college, or approved trade, vocational, or business school. They are not required to be members of the Spina Bifida Association of Central Indiana (SBACI), but they must join if granted a scholarship. Along with their application, they must submit a letter explaining their career plans and how education will contribute to their future plans. Financial need is not considered in the selection process.

Financial data The stipend is $500 per semester ($1,000 per year). Membership dues for SBACI are deducted from the disbursements.

Duration 1 semester; recipients may reapply.

Additional data The sponsoring organization has expanded its operations to serve all of Indiana.

Number awarded Up to 3 each year.

Deadline May of each year for fall semester; October of each year for spring semester.

[333]
CHAIRSCHOLARS FOUNDATION NATIONAL SCHOLARSHIPS

ChairScholars Foundation, Inc.
16101 Carencia Lane
Odessa, FL 33556-3278
(813) 926-0544   Toll Free: (888) 926-0544
Fax: (813) 920-7661
E-mail: chairscholars@tampabay.rr.com
Web: www.chairscholars.org/national.html

Summary To provide financial assistance for college to physically challenged students.

Eligibility This program is open to high school seniors and college freshmen who have a significant physical challenge, although they are not required to be in a wheelchair. Applicants should be able to demonstrate financial need, have a GPA of 3.0 or higher, and show some form of community service or social contribution in the past. Along with their application, they must submit an essay of 300 to 500 words on how they became physically challenged, how their situation has affected them and their family, and their goals and aspirations for the future. Graduate students and all students over 21 years of age are not eligible.

Financial data Stipends range from $1,000 to $5,000 per year. Funds are to be used for tuition and school expenses.

Duration Up to 4 years for high school seniors; up to 3 years for college freshmen. The maximum total award is $20,000.

Additional data This program includes the Paul John "P.J." Zuker, Jr. Memorial Scholarship and the Pablo Aguilar, Jr. Memorial Scholarship.

Number awarded 15 to 20 each year.

Deadline February of each year.

[334]
CYNTHIA RUTH RUSSELL MEMORIAL GRANTS

Kansas Masonic Foundation, Inc.
320 S.W. Eighth Avenue
P.O. Box 1217
Topeka, KS 66601-1217
(785) 357-7646   Fax: (785) 357-7406
E-mail: kmf@kmfonline.org
Web: www.kmfonline.org/content/view/15/36

Summary To provide financial assistance to physically challenged Kansas residents attending a college or university in the state.

Eligibility This program is open to residents of Kansas who are physically challenged. Applicants must be attending or planning to attend an institution of higher education in the state as a full-time undergraduate or graduate student. Along with their application, they must submit a 300-word statement on their educational goals, a short autobiography that includes a discussion of their physical challenge, a list of extracurricular activities, their latest grade transcript, letters of reference, ACT and/or SAT scores, and documentation of financial need.

Financial data A stipend is awarded (amount not specified).

Duration 1 year; recipients may reapply.

Number awarded 1 or more each year.

Deadline April of each year.

[335]
DELAWARE CHAPTER MS SOCIETY SCHOLARSHIP PROGRAM

National Multiple Sclerosis Society-Delaware Chapter
Two Mill Road, Suite 106
Wilmington, DE 19806
(302) 655-5610   Fax: (302) 655-0993
E-mail: kate.cowperthwait@msdelaware.org
Web: was.nationalmssociety.org

Summary To provide financial assistance to high school seniors and graduates from Delaware who have multiple sclerosis (MS) or have a parent with MS and are planning to attend college in any state.

Eligibility This program is open to graduating high school seniors, recent graduates, and GED recipients from Delaware who have MS or a parent who has MS. Applicants must be planning to enroll as a first-time student at a 2- or 4-year college, university, or vocational/technical school in the United States on at least a half-time basis. Along with their application, they must submit an essay on the impact MS has had on their lives. Selection is based on that essay, academic record, leadership and participation in school or community activities, work experience, goals and aspirations, an outside appraisal, special circumstances, and financial need. U.S. citizenship or permanent resident status is required.

Financial data A stipend is awarded (amount not specified).

Duration 1 year.

Number awarded Varies each year; recently, 4 of these scholarships were awarded.

Deadline January of each year.

[336]
DR. GEORGE E. HURT EDUCATIONAL SCHOLARSHIP FUND

Spina Bifida Association of North Texas
Attn: Scholarship Chair
705 West Avenue B, Suite 409
Garland, TX 75040
(972) 238-8755   Fax: (214) 703-1981
E-mail: eparham@belo.com
Web: spinabifidant.org

Summary To provide financial assistance to residents of Texas who were born with spina bifida and are interested in attending college in any state.

Eligibility This program is open to residents of Texas who were born with spina bifida. Applicants must be enrolled in or accepted into a college, junior college, or approved trade school in any state. Along with their appli-

cation, they must submit a personal statement describing their goals in life, future educational pursuits, and anything else they wish to selection committee to know about them. Selection is based on that statement, academic record, community service, work history, leadership, and financial need.

Financial data A stipend is awarded (amount not specified); funds are paid directly to the recipient to be used for payment of tuition, books, room and board, and specialized equipment needs.

Duration 1 year; may be renewed.

Number awarded 1 or more each year.

Deadline April of each year.

[337]
EAGA SCHOLARSHIP AWARD

Eastern Amputee Golf Association
Attn: Bob Buck, Executive Director
2015 Amherst Drive
Bethlehem, PA 18015-5606
Toll Free: (888) 868-0992   Fax: (610) 867-9295
E-mail: info@eaga.org
Web: www.eaga.org

Summary To provide financial assistance for college to members of the Eastern Amputee Golf Association (EAGA) and their families.

Eligibility This program is open to students who are residents of and/or currently enrolled or accepted for enrollment at a college or university in designated eastern states (Connecticut, Delaware, District of Columbia, Maine, Maryland, Massachusetts, New Hampshire, New Jersey, New York, Pennsylvania, Rhode Island, Vermont, Virginia, or West Virginia). Applicants must be amputee members of the association (those who have experienced the loss of 1 or more extremities at a major joint due to amputation or birth defect) or members of their families. Financial need is considered in the selection process.

Financial data The stipend is $1,000.

Duration 1 year; may be renewed if the recipient maintains a GPA of 2.0 or higher and continues to demonstrate financial need.

Additional data The EAGA was incorporated in 1987. It welcomes 2 types of members: amputee members and associate members (non-amputees who are interested in the organization and support its work but are not eligible for these scholarships). This program includes the following named scholarships: the Paul DesChamps Scholarship Award, the Tom Reed Scholarship, the Ray Froncillo Scholarship, the Howard Taylor Scholarship, and the Sgt. Major William Wade Memorial Scholarship.

Number awarded Varies each year; recently, 16 of these scholarships were awarded.

Deadline June of each year.

[338]
EDUCATIONAL SCHOLARSHIP IN MEMORY OF MARY ANN POTTS

Spina Bifida Association of Wisconsin
Attn: Scholarship Fund
830 North 109th Street, Suite 6
Wauwatosa, WI 53226
(414) 607-9061   Fax: (414) 607-9602
E-mail: sbawi@sbawi.org
Web: www.sbawi.org/Funding.htm

Summary   To provide financial assistance to residents of Wisconsin who have spina bifida and are interested in attending college or graduate school in any state.

Eligibility   This program is open to residents of Wisconsin of any age who are constituents of the Spina Bifida Association of Wisconsin (SBAWI). Applicants must be enrolled or planning to enroll at a college, graduate school, trade school, or specialized educational training program in any state. Along with their application, they must submit a personal statement explaining their goals and what they want to accomplish with the education or training they will receive. Selection is based on that statement, academic record, community service, work history, leadership, and financial need. Priority is given to applicants who are active in SBAWI.

Financial data   A stipend is awarded (amount not specified); funds are paid directly to the recipient's institution to be used for payment of tuition, books, room and board, and specialized equipment needs.

Duration   1 year; recipients may reapply.

Additional data   This program was established in 1996.

Number awarded   1 each year.

Deadline   March of each year.

[339]
FORWARD FACE SCHOLARSHIPS

Forward Face
Attn: Scholarship Committee
317 East 34th Street, Suite 901A
New York, NY 10016
(212) 684-5860   Fax: (212) 684-5864
E-mail: info@forwardface.org
Web: www.forwardface.org/services/scholarships.html

Summary   To provide financial assistance for educational purposes to students with craniofacial conditions.

Eligibility   This program is open to students who are 13 years of age or older and have a craniofacial condition. Applicants must write essays on how a particular teacher or faculty member has made a positive impact on them, the impact of their craniofacial condition on their educational experiences, the personal qualities and abilities that make them the best candidate for the scholarship, a description of themselves that enables the readers to get to know them as persons, and where they see themselves in 10 years. Selection is based on personal qualities, goals, and recommendations. Financial need is not a consideration.

Financial data   The scholarship is $1,000. Funds must be used for educational purposes.

Duration   1 year; nonrenewable.

Number awarded   Up to 3 each year.

Deadline   January of each year.

[340]
GREATER NEW ENGLAND CHAPTER MS SOCIETY SCHOLARSHIP PROGRAM

National Multiple Sclerosis Society-Greater New
  England Chapter
101A First Avenue, Suite 6
Waltham, MA 02451
(781) 890-4990   Fax: (781) 890-2089
E-mail: communications@mam.nmss.org
Web: was.nationalmssociety.org

Summary   To provide financial assistance to high school seniors and graduates from designated New England states who have multiple sclerosis (MS) or have a parent with MS and are planning to attend college in any state.

Eligibility   This program is open to graduating high school seniors, recent graduates, and GED recipients from Maine, Massachusetts, New Hampshire, or Vermont who have MS or a parent who has MS. Applicants must be planning to enroll as a first-time student at a 2- or 4-year college, university, or vocational/technical school in the United States on at least a half-time basis. Along with their application, they must submit an essay on the impact MS has had on their lives. Selection is based on that essay, academic record, leadership and participation in school or community activities, work experience, goals and aspirations, an outside appraisal, special circumstances, and financial need. U.S. citizenship or permanent resident status is required.

Financial data   The highest-ranked applicant receives a stipend of $3,000 per year. Other stipends range from $1,000 to $3,000.

Duration   The award for the highest-ranked applicant is for 2 years. Other awards are for 1 year and are nonrenewable.

Additional data   This program was established by the Massachusetts Chapter in 2003. In 2010, that chapter merged with the chapters in Maine, New Hampshire, and Vermont to form the Greater New England Chapter, so the program became available to residents of those states.

Number awarded   Varies each year; recently, 23 of these scholarships, with a total value of $47,600, were awarded.

Deadline   January of each year.

[341]
GREATER NORTHWEST CHAPTER MS SOCIETY SCHOLARSHIP PROGRAM

National Multiple Sclerosis Society-Greater Northwest
  Chapter
192 Nickerson Street, Suite 100
Seattle, WA 98109
(206) 284-4254   Toll Free: (800) 344-4867
Fax: (206) 284-4972
E-mail: MSnorthwest@nmsswas.org
Web: was.nationalmssociety.org

Summary To provide financial assistance to high school seniors and graduates from Alaska and Washington who have multiple sclerosis (MS) or have a parent with MS and are planning to attend college in any state.

Eligibility This program is open to graduating high school seniors, recent graduates, and GED recipients from Alaska or Washington who have MS or a parent who has MS. Applicants must be planning to enroll as a first-time student at a 2- or 4-year college, university, or vocational/technical school in the United States on at least a half-time basis. Along with their application, they must submit an essay on the impact MS has had on their lives. Selection is based on that essay, academic record, leadership and participation in school or community activities, work experience, goals and aspirations, an outside appraisal, special circumstances, and financial need. U.S. citizenship or permanent resident status is required.

Financial data Stipends range from $1,500 to $3,000.

Duration 1 year.

Number awarded Varies each year; recently, 88 students received $252,000 in scholarships from this program.

Deadline January of each year.

[342]
HAYLEY'S HOPE AND MICHAELA'S MIRACLE MS MEMORIAL FUND

National Multiple Sclerosis Society-Connecticut
  Chapter
659 Tower Avenue, First Floor
Hartford, CT 06112
(860) 913-2550   Toll Free: (800) 344-4867
Fax: (860) 714-2301
E-mail: programs@ctfightsMS.org
Web: was.nationalmssociety.org

Summary To provide financial assistance to high school seniors and graduates from Connecticut who have multiple sclerosis (MS) or have a parent with MS and are planning to attend college in any state.

Eligibility This program is open to graduating high school seniors, recent graduates, and GED recipients from Washington who have MS or a parent who has MS. Applicants must be planning to enroll as an undergraduate student at a 2- or 4-year college, university, or vocational/technical school in the United States on at least a half-time basis. Along with their application, they must submit an essay on the impact MS has had on their lives. Selection is based on that essay, academic record, leadership and participation in school or community activities, work experience, goals and aspirations, an outside appraisal, special circumstances, and financial need. U.S. citizenship or permanent resident status is required.

Financial data The stipend is $1,500.

Duration 1 year.

Number awarded Varies each year; recently, 4 of these scholarships were awarded.

Deadline January of each year.

[343]
HIGHER EDUCATION SCHOLARSHIP PROGRAM OF THE SPINA BIFIDA ASSOCIATION OF ALABAMA

Spina Bifida Association of Alabama
Attn: Scholarship Committee
P.O. Box 13254
Birmingham, AL 35202
E-mail: info@sbaofal.org
Web: www.sbaofal.org/Programs/Programs.html

Summary To provide financial assistance to Alabama residents who have spina bifida and are interested in working on an undergraduate or graduate degree at a school in any state.

Eligibility This program is open to entering or continuing undergraduate and graduate students at colleges and universities in any state who have spina bifida. Applicants must reside in Alabama and have been residents of that state for at least 2 consecutive years. Along with their application, they must submit 1) an essay on their educational and career goals, aspects of their background and character relevant to their likelihood of academic success, and other factors they wish to have considered, all in relationship to spina bifida; 2) verification of disability, signed by a physician; and 3) transcripts of grades for high school and other educational levels.

Financial data A stipend is awarded (amount not specified); funds are sent directly to the recipient's institution of higher education.

Duration 1 year; may be renewed up to 3 additional years for undergraduates, up to 1 additional years for graduate students, or up to 2 additional years for students in postgraduate school, law school, or medical school. Renewal depends on the recipient's maintaining a GPA of 2.25 or higher each semester.

Number awarded Varies each year.

Deadline May of each year.

[344]
L. MARIE HEARD EDUCATION SCHOLARSHIP PROGRAM

National Foundation for Ectodermal Dysplasias
410 East Main Street
P.O. Box 114
Mascoutah, IL 62258-0114
(618) 566-2020   Fax: (618) 566-4718
E-mail: info@nfed.org
Web: nfed.org/support_education_scholarship.asp

Summary To provide financial assistance for college to students who have ectodermal dysplasia.

Eligibility This program is open to individuals who are affected by ectodermal dysplasia syndromes and are attending or planning to attend a college, university, trade school, or junior college. Applicants must submit a 500-word essay on their choice of assigned topics that change annually. Selection is based on the essay, demonstrated academic ability, extracurricular activities, community involvement, volunteer activities for the sponsoring organization, employment, and financial need.

Financial data   Stipends are approximately $1,500.

Duration   1 year.

Additional data   This program, established in 1995, includes the following named scholarships: the Ethelyn Draser Boyd Scholarship, the Louis J. and June E. Kay Scholarship (both established in 2005), and the Clarence and Marion Bales Scholarship (established in 2008).

Number awarded   Varies each year; recently, 7 of these scholarships, with a total value of $11,000, were awarded.

Deadline   March of each year.

[345]
LAWRENCE MADEIROS SCHOLARSHIP

Adirondack Spintacular
Attn: Scholarship Panel
P.O. Box 11
Mayfield, NY 12117
(518) 863-8998   Fax: (518) 863-8998
E-mail: carol@adirondackspintacular.com
Web: www.adirondackspintacular.com

Summary   To provide financial assistance for college to high school seniors who have a chronic disorder.

Eligibility   This program is open to seniors graduating from high school who have been accepted at an accredited college or university. Applicants must be diagnosed with a chronic disorder. Along with their application, they must submit brief essays on 1) how living with or around a chronic disorder has impacted their life; 2) their goals and aspirations in life; and 3) their passion. Financial need may also be considered.

Financial data   The stipend is $1,000.

Duration   1 year.

Additional data   This program, established in 2001, is supported by the Adirondack Spintacular, a charity event in which volunteers cycle, walk, or run to raise money. Chronic disorders have included muscular dystrophy, diabetes, hemophilia, cystic fibrosis, autism, and Asperger's Syndrome.

Number awarded   Varies each year; recently, 6 of these scholarships were awarded.

Deadline   May of each year.

[346]
LITTLE PEOPLE OF AMERICA SCHOLARSHIPS

Little People of America, Inc.
Attn: Vice President of Programs
250 El Camino Real, Suite 201
Tustin, CA 92780
(714) 368-3689   Toll Free: (888) LPA-2001
Fax: (714) 368-3367   E-mail: info@lpaonline.org
Web: www.lpaonline.org

Summary   To provide financial assistance for college to members of the Little People of America (LPA), to their families, and (in limited cases) to others.

Eligibility   This program is open to members of LPA (limited to people who, for medical reasons, are 4 feet 10 inches or under in height). Applicants must be high school seniors or students attending college or trade school.

Along with their application, they must submit a 500-word personal statement that explains their reasons for applying for a scholarship, their plans for the future, how they intend to be of service to LPA after graduation, and any other relevant information about themselves, their family, their background, and their educational achievements. Financial need is also considered in the selection process. If sufficient funds are available after all LPA members have been served, scholarships may also be given, first, to immediate family members of dwarfs who are also paid members of LPA, and, second, to people with dwarfism who are not members of LPA.

Financial data   Stipends range from $250 to $1,000.

Duration   1 year; may be renewed.

Number awarded   Varies; generally between 5 and 10 each year.

Deadline   April of each year.

[347]
LOUISIANA CHAPTER MS SOCIETY SCHOLARSHIP PROGRAM

National Multiple Sclerosis Society-Louisiana Chapter
4613 Fairfield Street
Metairie, LA 70006
(504) 832-4013   Fax: (504) 831-7188
E-mail: louisianachapter@nmss.org
Web: was.nationalmssociety.org

Summary   To provide financial assistance to high school seniors and graduates from Louisiana who have multiple sclerosis (MS) or have a parent with MS and are planning to attend college in any state.

Eligibility   This program is open to graduating high school seniors, recent graduates, and GED recipients from Louisiana who have MS or a parent who has MS. Applicants must be planning to enroll as a first-time student at a 2- or 4-year college, university, or vocational/technical school in the United States on at least a half-time basis. Along with their application, they must submit an essay on the impact MS has had on their lives. Selection is based on that essay, academic record, leadership and participation in school or community activities, work experience, goals and aspirations, an outside appraisal, special circumstances, and financial need. U.S. citizenship or permanent resident status is required.

Financial data   The stipend is $2,000.

Duration   1 year; nonrenewable.

Number awarded   Varies each year; recently, 2 of these scholarships were awarded.

Deadline   January of each year.

[348]
MID-ATLANTIC CHAPTER MS SOCIETY SCHOLARSHIP PROGRAM

National Multiple Sclerosis Society-Mid-Atlantic
  Chapter
9801-I Southern Pine Boulevard
Charlotte, NC 28273
(704) 525-2955   Fax: (704) 986-7981
E-mail: ncp@nmss.org
Web: was.nationalmssociety.org

Summary To provide financial assistance to high school seniors and graduates from South Carolina and western North Carolina who have multiple sclerosis (MS) or have a parent with MS and who are planning to attend college in any state.

Eligibility This program is open to graduating high school seniors, recent graduates, and GED recipients from South Carolina and western North Carolina who have MS or a parent who has MS. Applicants must be planning to enroll as a first-time student at a 2- or 4-year college, university, or vocational/technical school in the United States on at least a half-time basis. Along with their application, they must submit an essay on the impact MS has had on their lives. Selection is based on that essay, academic record, leadership and participation in school or community activities, work experience, goals and aspirations, an outside appraisal, special circumstances, and financial need. U.S. citizenship or permanent resident status is required.

Financial data The stipend is $2,000.

Duration 1 year.

Number awarded Varies each year; recently, 4 of these scholarships were awarded.

Deadline January of each year.

[349]
MINNESOTA CHAPTER MS SOCIETY SCHOLARSHIP PROGRAM

National Multiple Sclerosis Society-Minnesota Chapter
Attn: Scholarship Program
200 12th Avenue South
Minneapolis, MN 55415
(612) 335-7955   Toll Free: (800) 582-5296
Fax: (612) 335-7997 E-mail: msparks@mssociety.org
Web: was.nationalmssociety.org

Summary To provide financial assistance to high school seniors and graduates from Minnesota who have multiple sclerosis (MS) or have a parent with MS and are planning to attend college in any state.

Eligibility This program is open to graduating high school seniors, recent graduates, and GED recipients from Minnesota who have MS or a parent who has MS. Applicants must be planning to enroll as a first-time student at a 2- or 4-year college, university, or vocational/technical school in the United States on at least a half-time basis. Along with their application, they must submit an essay on the impact MS has had on their lives. Selection is based on that essay, academic record, leadership and participation in school or community activities, work experience, goals

and aspirations, an outside appraisal, special circumstances, and financial need. U.S. citizenship or permanent resident status is required.

Financial data Stipends average approximately $2,000.

Duration 1 year.

Number awarded Varies each year; recently, 52 of these scholarships were awarded.

Deadline January of each year.

[350]
NATIONAL AMPUTEE GOLF ASSOCIATION SCHOLARSHIP

National Amputee Golf Association
Attn: Scholarship Grant Program
11 Walnut Hill Road
Amherst, NH 03031
(603) 672-6444   Toll Free: (800) 633-NAGA
Fax: (603) 672-2987   E-mail: info@nagagolf.org
Web: www.nagagolf.org/scholarship1.shtml

Summary To provide financial assistance for college to members of the National Amputee Golf Association and their dependents.

Eligibility This program is open to amputee members in good standing in the association and their dependents. Applicants must submit information on their scholastic background (GPA in high school and college, courses of study); type of amputation and cause (if applicable), a cover letter describing their plans for the future; and documentation of financial need. They need not be competitive golfers. Selection is based on academic record, financial need, involvement in extracurricular or community activities, and area of study.

Financial data The stipend for a 4-year bachelor's degree program is $2,000 per year. The stipend for a 2-year technical or associate degree is $1,000 per year.

Duration Up to 4 years, provided the recipient maintains at least half-time enrollment and a GPA of 2.0 or higher and continues to demonstrate financial need.

Number awarded 1 or more each year.

Deadline August of each year.

[351]
NATIONAL MS SOCIETY SCHOLARSHIP PROGRAM

National Multiple Sclerosis Society
Attn: Scholarship Fund
900 South Broadway, Suite 200
Denver, CO 80209
(303) 698-6100, ext. 15102
E-mail: susan.goldsmith@nmss.org
Web: www.nationalMSsociety.org/scholarship

Summary To provide financial assistance for college to students who have Multiple Sclerosis (MS) or are the children of people with MS.

Eligibility This program is open to 1) high school seniors who have MS and will be attending an accredited postsecondary school for the first time; 2) high school seniors who are the children of people with MS and will be attending an accredited postsecondary school for the first time; 3) high school (or GED) graduates of any age who have MS and will be attending an accredited postsecondary school for the first time; and 4) high school (or GED) graduates of any age who have a parent with MS and will be attending an accredited postgraduate school for the first time. Applicants must be U.S. citizens or permanent residents who plan to enroll in an undergraduate course of study at an accredited 2- or 4-year college, university, or vocational/technical school in the United States to work on a degree, license, or certificate. Along with their application, they must submit a 1-page personal statement on the impact MS has had on their life. Selection is based on that statement, academic record, leadership and participation in school or community activities, work experience, goals and aspirations, an outside appraisal, special circumstances, and financial need. The 2 highest-ranked applicants are designated as the National MS Society Presidential Scholar and the National MS Society Mike Dugan Scholar.

Financial data Stipends range from $1,000 to $3,000 per year.

Duration 1 year; may be renewed.

Additional data This program, which began in 2003, is managed by ACT Scholarship and Recognition Services, 301 ACT Drive, P.O. Box 4030, Iowa City, IA 52243-4030, (877) 789-4228.

Number awarded Varies each year; recently, 510 of these scholarships (332 new awards and 178 renewals) with a value of $1,021,600 were awarded.

Deadline January of each year.

[352]
NORTH CENTRAL CHAPTER MS SOCIETY SCHOLARSHIP PROGRAM

National Multiple Sclerosis Society-North Central
  Chapter
2508 South Carolyn Avenue
Sioux Falls, SD 57106
(605) 336-7017   Fax: (605) 336-8088
E-mail: nth@nmss.org
Web: was.nationalmssociety.org

Summary To provide financial assistance to high school seniors and graduates from Iowa, North Dakota, or South Dakota who have multiple sclerosis (MS) or have a parent with MS and are planning to attend college in any state.

Eligibility This program is open to graduating high school seniors, recent graduates, and GED recipients from Iowa, North Dakota, or South Dakota who have MS or a parent who has MS. Applicants must be planning to enroll as a first-time student at a 2- or 4-year college, university, or vocational/technical school in the United States on at least a half-time basis. Along with their application, they must submit an essay on the impact MS has had on their lives. Selection is based on that essay, academic record, leadership and participation in school or community activities, work experience, goals and aspirations, an outside appraisal, special circumstances, and financial need. U.S. citizenship or permanent resident status is required.

Financial data A stipend is awarded (amount not specified).

Duration 1 year.

Number awarded Varies each year; recently, 3 of these scholarships were awarded.

Deadline January of each year.

[353]
OKLAHOMA CHAPTER MS SOCIETY SCHOLARSHIP PROGRAM

National Multiple Sclerosis Society-Oklahoma Chapter
4606 East 67th Street, Building 7, Suite 103
Tulsa, OK 74136
(918) 488-0882   Fax: (918) 488-0913
E-mail: lisa.gray@oke.nmss.org
Web: was.nationalmssociety.org

Summary To provide financial assistance to high school seniors and graduates from Oklahoma who have multiple sclerosis (MS) or have a parent with MS and who are planning to attend college in any state.

Eligibility This program is open to graduating high school seniors, recent graduates, and GED recipients from Oklahoma who have MS or a parent who has MS. Applicants must be planning to enroll as a first-time student at a 2- or 4-year college, university, or vocational/technical school in the United States on at least a half-time basis. Along with their application, they must submit an essay on the impact MS has had on their lives. Selection is based on that essay, academic record, leadership and participation in school or community activities, work experience, goals and aspirations, an outside appraisal, special circumstances, and financial need. U.S. citizenship or permanent resident status is required.

Financial data Stipends range from $1,000 to $3,000.

Duration 1 year.

Additional data This program includes the Linda Chance Memorial Scholarship.

Number awarded Varies each year; recently, 14 of these scholarships were awarded.

Deadline January of each year.

[354]
OMAHA VOLUNTEERS FOR HANDICAPPED CHILDREN SCHOLARSHIPS

Omaha Volunteers for Handicapped Children
c/o Lois Carlson
2010 Country Club Avenue
Omaha, NE 68104
(402) 553-0378

Summary To provide financial assistance to Nebraska residents interested in attending college in any state who have a physical disability or are preparing for a career related to people with orthopedic impairments or physical disabilities.

Eligibility This program is open to residents of Nebraska who are U.S. citizens. First priority applicants must have an orthopedic impairment or physical disability and be 1) high school seniors with a GPA of 2.25 or higher and accepted into the school of their choice or 2) college students making satisfactory progress toward graduation. Second priority applicants must be enrolled in the college of their choice and preparing for a teaching or health-related career of service to people with orthopedic impairments or physical disabilities. All applicants must submit a 250-word essay on their future goals in relation to the orthopedically impaired and/or physically disabled and their need for the scholarship.

Financial data The stipend is $1,000 per year.

Duration 1 year; may be renewed.

Number awarded 5 to 10 each year.

Deadline July of each year.

[355]
OREGON CHAPTER MS SOCIETY SCHOLARSHIP PROGRAM

National Multiple Sclerosis Society-Oregon Chapter
104 S.W. Clay Street
Portland, OR 97201
(503) 223-9511   Fax: (503) 223-2911
E-mail: info@defeatms.com
Web: was.nationalmssociety.org

Summary To provide financial assistance to high school seniors and graduates from Oregon who have multiple sclerosis (MS) or have a parent with MS and who are planning to attend college in any state.

Eligibility This program is open to graduating high school seniors, recent graduates, and GED recipients from Oregon who have MS or a parent who has MS. Applicants must be planning to enroll as a first-time student at a 2- or 4-year college, university, or vocational/technical school in the United States on at least a half-time basis. Along with their application, they must submit an essay on the impact MS has had on their lives. Selection is based on that essay, academic record, leadership and participation in school or community activities, work experience, goals and aspirations, an outside appraisal, special circumstances, and financial need. U.S. citizenship or permanent resident status is required.

Financial data Stipends range from $1,500 to $3,000.

Duration 1 year.

Number awarded Varies each year; recently, 4 of these scholarships were awarded.

Deadline January of each year.

[356]
PARALYZED VETERANS OF AMERICA EDUCATIONAL SCHOLARSHIP PROGRAM

Paralyzed Veterans of America
Attn: Education and Training Foundation
801 18th Street, N.W.
Washington, DC 20006-3517
(202) 416-7651   Fax: (202) 416-7641
TDD: (202) 416-7622   E-mail: foundations@pva.org
Web: www.pva.org

Summary To provide financial assistance for college to members of the Paralyzed Veterans of America (PVA) and their families.

Eligibility This program is open to PVA members, spouses of members, and unmarried dependent children of members under 24 years of age. Applicants must be attending or planning to attend an accredited U.S. college or university. They must be U.S. citizens. Along with their application, they must submit a personal statement explaining why they wish to further their education, short- and long-term academic goals, how this will meet their career objectives, and how it will affect the PVA membership. Selection is based on that statement, academic records, letters of recommendation, and extracurricular and community activities.

Financial data Stipends are $1,000 for full-time students or $500 for part-time students.

Duration 1 year.

Additional data This program was established in 1986.

Number awarded Varies each year; recently 14 full-time and 3 part-time students received these scholarships. Since this program was established, it has awarded more than $300,000 in scholarships.

Deadline May of each year.

[357]
SBAA ONE-YEAR SCHOLARSHIP

Spina Bifida Association of America
Attn: Scholarship Committee
4590 MacArthur Boulevard, N.W., Suite 250
Washington, DC 20007-4226
(202) 944-3285, ext. 23   Toll Free: (800) 621-3141
Fax: (202) 944-3295   E-mail: sbaa@sbaa.org
Web: www.spinabifidaassociation.org

Summary To provide financial assistance to undergraduate and graduate students who have spina bifida.

Eligibility This program is open to persons of any age who were born with spina bifida and are enrolled in or accepted by a junior college, 4-year college, graduate school, or approved trade, vocational, or business school. Applicants must submit a 3-page personal statement explaining their educational goals; transcripts; standardized test scores (ACT, SAT, GRE, or equivalent; adult students may submit a recent transcript); verification of acceptance by a college; information related to financial need; letters of recommendation; and a physician's statement verifying disability.

Financial data The stipend is $2,000.

Duration 1 year.

Additional data This program was established in 1988.

Number awarded Up to 6 each year.

Deadline February of each year.

[358]
SBAC SCHOLARSHIP FUND

Spina Bifida Association of Connecticut, Inc.
Attn: Scholarship Committee
P.O. Box 2545
Hartford, CT 06146-2545
(860) 832-8905   Toll Free: (800) 574-6274
Fax: (860) 832-6260   E-mail: sbac@sbac.org
Web: www.sbac.org

Summary To provide financial assistance to residents of Connecticut who have spina bifida and are interested in attending college in any state.

Eligibility This program is open to residents of Connecticut who have spina bifida and are attending or planning to attend a college, university, trade school, vocational institution, or business school in any state. Applicants must submit an essay (2 to 3 pages) on their educational goals; reasons for selecting those goals; outstanding accomplishments or contributions made through school, extracurricular, religious group, or Spina Bifida Association of Connecticut (SBAC) member activities; and community and volunteer work. Selection is based on academic record, other efforts shown in school, involvement in the community, leadership qualities, commitment to personal goals, and work history.

Financial data The stipend is $1,000. Funds are paid directly to the recipient's school.

Duration 1 year.

Number awarded 1 or more each year.

Deadline April of each year.

[359]
SBAIL SCHOLARSHIPS

Spina Bifida Association of Illinois
8765 West Higgins Road, Suite 403
Chicago, IL 60631
(773) 444-0305   Fax: (773) 444-0327
E-mail: sbail@sbail.org
Web: www.sbail.org

Summary To provide financial assistance to residents of Illinois who have spina bifida and are interested in attending college or graduate school in any state.

Eligibility This program is open to residents of Illinois who have spina bifida. Applicants must be enrolled or planning to enroll at a 2- or 4-year college or university, technical or trade school, or business college in any state as an undergraduate or graduate student. Along with their application, they must submit essays of 250 to 500 words on 1) the accomplishments or contributions (school, extracurricular, church, community, or Spina Bifida Association of Illinois) they have made of which they are most proud; and 2) the reasons for selecting their vocational goals. Selection is based on those essays, GPA, test scores (ACT, SAT, GRE, GMAT), extracurricular activities, and financial need.

Financial data Stipends range up to $2,500.

Duration 1 year.

Additional data This program includes the Valiant Scholarship, awarded to an applicant who displays outstanding leadership, good will toward those less fortunate, and dedication to making a difference. Recipients are expected to volunteer with the Spina Bifida Association of Illinois at least once during the following year.

Number awarded Varies each year.

Deadline April of each year.

[360]
SCHOLARSHIP PROGRAM OF THE COLORADO CHAPTER MS SOCIETY

National Multiple Sclerosis Society-Colorado Chapter
900 South Broadway, Second Floor
Denver, CO 80209
(303) 698-7400   Toll Free: (800) 344-4867
Fax: (303) 698-7421
E-mail: COCreceptionist@nmss.org
Web: was.nationalmssociety.org

Summary To provide financial assistance to high school seniors and graduates from Colorado who have multiple sclerosis (MS) or have a parent with MS and are planning to attend college in any state.

Eligibility This program is open to graduating high school seniors, recent graduates, and GED recipients from Colorado who have MS or a parent who has MS. Applicants must be planning to enroll as an undergraduate student at a 2- or 4-year college, university, or vocational/technical school in the United States on at least a half-time basis. Along with their application, they must submit an essay on the impact MS has had on their lives. Selection is based on that essay, academic record, leadership and participation in school or community activities, work experience, goals and aspirations, an outside appraisal, special circumstances, and financial need. U.S. citizenship or permanent resident status is required.

Financial data A stipend is awarded (amount not specified).

Duration 1 year.

Number awarded Varies each year; recently, 3 of these scholarships were awarded.

Deadline January of each year.

[361]
TUITION WAIVER FOR DISABLED CHILDREN OF KENTUCKY VETERANS

Kentucky Department of Veterans Affairs
Attn: Division of Field Operations
321 West Main Street, Room 390
Louisville, KY 40202
(502) 595-4447   Toll Free: (800) 928-4012 (within KY)
Fax: (502) 595-4448   E-mail: Pamela.Cypert@ky.gov
Web: www.veterans.ky.gov/benefits/tuitionwaiver.htm

Summary To provide financial assistance for college to the children of Kentucky veterans who have a disability related to their parent's military service.

Eligibility This program is open to the children of veterans who have acquired a disability as a direct result of their parent's military service. The disability must have been designated by the U.S. Department of Veterans Affairs as compensable (currently defined as spina bifida). The veteran parent must 1) have served on active duty with the U.S. armed forces or in the National Guard or Reserve component on state active duty, active duty for training, or inactive duty training; and 2) be (or if deceased have been) a resident of Kentucky. Applicants must have been admitted to a state-supported university, college, or vocational training institute in Kentucky.

Financial data Eligible children are exempt from payment of tuition at state-supported institutions of higher education in Kentucky.

Duration There are no age or time limits on the waiver.

Number awarded Varies each year.

Deadline Deadline not specified.

[362]
WISCONSIN CHAPTER MS SOCIETY SCHOLARSHIP PROGRAM

National Multiple Sclerosis Society-Wisconsin Chapter
Attn: Scholarship Program
1120 James Drive, Suite A
Hartland, WI 53029
(262) 369-4420   Toll Free: (800) 242-3358 (within WI)
Fax: (262) 369-4410
E-mail: Meghan.schnabl@wisMS.org
Web: was.nationalmssociety.org

Summary To provide financial assistance to high school seniors and graduates from Wisconsin who have multiple sclerosis (MS) or have a parent with MS and are planning to attend college in any state.

Eligibility This program is open to graduating high school seniors, recent graduates, and GED recipients from Wisconsin who have MS or a parent who has MS. Applicants must be planning to enroll as a first-time student at a 2- or 4-year college, university, or vocational/technical school in the United States on at least a half-time basis. Along with their application, they must submit an essay on the impact MS has had on their lives. Selection is based on that essay, academic record, leadership and participation in school or community activities, work experience, goals and aspirations, an outside appraisal, special circumstances, and financial need. U.S. citizenship or permanent resident status is required.

Financial data Stipends average approximately $1,500.

Duration 1 year.

Number awarded Varies each year; recently, 30 of these scholarships were awarded.

Deadline January of each year.

Fellowship/Grants

[363]
BRYON RIESCH SCHOLARSHIPS

Bryon Riesch Paralysis Foundation
P.O. Box 1388
Waukesha, WI 53187-1388
(262) 547-2083   E-mail: info@brpf.org
Web: www.brpf.org/scholarships.htm

Summary To provide financial assistance to 1) undergraduate and graduate students who have a neurological disability or 2) the children of people with such a disability.

Eligibility This program is open to students entering or enrolled at a 2- or 4-year college or university as an undergraduate or graduate student. Applicants must have a neurological disability or be the child of a person with such a disability. They must have a GPA of 2.5 or higher in high school or college. Along with their application, they must submit a 200-word essay on why they deserve the scholarship, a statement of their 5- and 10-year goals, and a list of work experience. Financial need is not considered in the selection process.

Financial data Stipends range from $1,000 to $2,000.

Duration 1 year; may be renewed.

Number awarded 2 to 3 each semester.

Deadline June of each year for fall semester; December of each year for spring semester.

[364]
CRAIG H. NEILSEN FOUNDATION AWARD

Vermont Studio Center
80 Pearl Street
P.O. Box 613
Johnson, VT 05656
(802) 635-2727   Fax: (802) 635-2730
E-mail: info@vermontstudiocenter.org
Web: www.vermontstudiocenter.org

Summary To provide funding to artists and writers who have a spinal cord injury and are interested in a residency at the Vermont Studio Center in Johnson, Vermont.

Eligibility Eligible to apply for this support are painters, sculptors, printmakers, new and mixed-media artists, photographers, poets, and other writers of fiction and creative nonfiction who live with a spinal cord injury. Applicants must be interested in a residency at the center in Johnson, Vermont. Visual artists must submit up to 20 slides or visual images of their work, poets must submit up to 10 pages, and other writers must submit 10 to 15 pages. Selection is based on artistic merit.

Financial data $3750, which covers all residency fees.

Duration 4 weeks.

Additional data This award is sponsored by the Craig H. Neilsen Foundation. The application fee is $25.

Number awarded 1 each year.

Deadline February of each year.

[365]
CYNTHIA RUTH RUSSELL MEMORIAL GRANTS

Kansas Masonic Foundation, Inc.
320 S.W. Eighth Avenue
P.O. Box 1217
Topeka, KS 66601-1217
(785) 357-7646   Fax: (785) 357-7406
E-mail: kmf@kmfonline.org
Web: www.kmfonline.org/content/view/15/36

Summary To provide financial assistance to physically challenged Kansas residents attending a college or university in the state.

Eligibility This program is open to residents of Kansas who are physically challenged. Applicants must be attending or planning to attend an institution of higher education in the state as a full-time undergraduate or graduate student. Along with their application, they must submit a 300-word statement on their educational goals, a short autobiography that includes a discussion of their physical challenge, a list of extracurricular activities, their latest grade transcript, letters of reference, ACT and/or SAT scores, and documentation of financial need.

Financial data A stipend is awarded (amount not specified).

Duration 1 year; recipients may reapply.

Number awarded 1 or more each year.

Deadline April of each year.

[366]
EDUCATIONAL SCHOLARSHIP IN MEMORY OF MARY ANN POTTS

Spina Bifida Association of Wisconsin
Attn: Scholarship Fund
830 North 109th Street, Suite 6
Wauwatosa, WI 53226
(414) 607-9061   Fax: (414) 607-9602
E-mail: sbawi@sbawi.org
Web: www.sbawi.org/Funding.htm

Summary To provide financial assistance to residents of Wisconsin who have spina bifida and are interested in attending college or graduate school in any state.

Eligibility This program is open to residents of Wisconsin of any age who are constituents of the Spina Bifida Association of Wisconsin (SBAWI). Applicants must be enrolled or planning to enroll at a college, graduate school, trade school, or specialized educational training program in any state. Along with their application, they must submit a personal statement explaining their goals and what they want to accomplish with the education or training they will receive. Selection is based on that statement, academic record, community service, work history, leadership, and financial need. Priority is given to applicants who are active in SBAWI.

Financial data A stipend is awarded (amount not specified); funds are paid directly to the recipient's institution to be used for payment of tuition, books, room and board, and specialized equipment needs.

Duration 1 year; recipients may reapply.

Additional data This program was established in 1996.

Number awarded 1 each year.

Deadline March of each year.

[367]
HIGHER EDUCATION SCHOLARSHIP PROGRAM OF THE SPINA BIFIDA ASSOCIATION OF ALABAMA

Spina Bifida Association of Alabama
Attn: Scholarship Committee
P.O. Box 13254
Birmingham, AL 35202
E-mail: info@sbaofal.org
Web: www.sbaofal.org/Programs/Programs.html

Summary To provide financial assistance to Alabama residents who have spina bifida and are interested in working on an undergraduate or graduate degree at a school in any state.

Eligibility This program is open to entering or continuing undergraduate and graduate students at colleges and universities in any state who have spina bifida. Applicants must reside in Alabama and have been residents of that state for at least 2 consecutive years. Along with their application, they must submit 1) an essay on their educational and career goals, aspects of their background and character relevant to their likelihood of academic success, and other factors they wish to have considered, all in relationship to spina bifida; 2) verification of disability, signed by a physician; and 3) transcripts of grades for high school and other educational levels.

Financial data A stipend is awarded (amount not specified); funds are sent directly to the recipient's institution of higher education.

Duration 1 year; may be renewed up to 3 additional years for undergraduates, up to 1 additional years for graduate students, or up to 2 additional years for students in postgraduate school, law school, or medical school. Renewal depends on the recipient's maintaining a GPA of 2.25 or higher each semester.

Number awarded Varies each year.

Deadline May of each year.

[368]
SBAA ONE-YEAR SCHOLARSHIP

Spina Bifida Association of America
Attn: Scholarship Committee
4590 MacArthur Boulevard, N.W., Suite 250
Washington, DC 20007-4226
(202) 944-3285, ext. 23   Toll Free: (800) 621-3141
Fax: (202) 944-3295   E-mail: sbaa@sbaa.org
Web: www.spinabifidaassociation.org

Summary To provide financial assistance to undergraduate and graduate students who have spina bifida.

Eligibility This program is open to persons of any age who were born with spina bifida and are enrolled in or accepted by a junior college, 4-year college, graduate school, or approved trade, vocational, or business school. Applicants must submit a 3-page personal statement explaining their educational goals; transcripts; standardized test scores (ACT, SAT, GRE, or equivalent; adult students may submit a recent transcript); verification of acceptance by a college; information related to financial need; letters of recommendation; and a physician's statement verifying disability.

Financial data The stipend is $2,000.

Duration 1 year.

Additional data This program was established in 1988.

Number awarded Up to 6 each year.

Deadline February of each year.

[369]
SBAIL SCHOLARSHIPS

Spina Bifida Association of Illinois
8765 West Higgins Road, Suite 403
Chicago, IL 60631
(773) 444-0305   Fax: (773) 444-0327
E-mail: sbail@sbail.org
Web: www.sbail.org

Summary   To provide financial assistance to residents of Illinois who have spina bifida and are interested in attending college or graduate school in any state.

Eligibility   This program is open to residents of Illinois who have spina bifida. Applicants must be enrolled or planning to enroll at a 2- or 4-year college or university, technical or trade school, or business college in any state as an undergraduate or graduate student. Along with their application, they must submit essays of 250 to 500 words on 1) the accomplishments or contributions (school, extracurricular, church, community, or Spina Bifida Association of Illinois) they have made of which they are most proud; and 2) the reasons for selecting their vocational goals. Selection is based on those essays, GPA, test scores (ACT, SAT, GRE, GMAT), extracurricular activities, and financial need.

Financial data   Stipends range up to $2,500.

Duration   1 year.

Additional data   This program includes the Valiant Scholarship, awarded to an applicant who displays outstanding leadership, good will toward those less fortunate, and dedication to making a difference. Recipients are expected to volunteer with the Spina Bifida Association of Illinois at least once during the following year.

Number awarded   Varies each year.

Deadline   April of each year.

[370]
WHEELS FOR WHEELS AWARD

Vermont Studio Center
80 Pearl Street
P.O. Box 613
Johnson, VT 05656
(802) 635-2727   Fax: (802) 635-2730
E-mail: info@vermontstudiocenter.org
Web: www.vermontstudiocenter.org

Summary   To provide funding to artists and writers who use wheelchairs and are interested in a residency at the Vermont Studio Center in Johnson, Vermont.

Eligibility   Eligible to apply for this support are painters, sculptors, printmakers, new and mixed-media artists, photographers, poets, and other writers of fiction and creative nonfiction who use wheelchairs and/or live with a spinal cord injury. Applicants must be interested in a residency at the center in Johnson, Vermont. Visual artists must submit up to 20 slides or visual images of their work, poets must submit up to 10 pages, and other writers must submit 10 to 15 pages. Selection is based on artistic merit.

Financial data   The residency fee of $3,750 covers studio space, room, board, lectures, and studio visits. The award pays all residency fees.

Duration   4 weeks.

Additional data   This award is sponsored by the Christopher & Dana Reeve Foundation. The application fee is $25.

Number awarded   1 each year.

Deadline   February of each year.

Grants-in-Aid

[371]
ALTERNATIVES IN MOTION GRANTS

Alternatives in Motion
201 Matilda, N.E.
Grand Rapids, MI 49503
(616) 493-2620   Toll Free: (877) 468-9335
Fax: (616) 493-2621
E-mail: info@ alternativesinmotion.org
Web: www.alternativesinmotion.org

Summary   To provide funding to people who need assistance to purchase a wheelchair.

Eligibility   This program is open to people who can demonstrate a medical necessity for a wheelchair but do not have financial resources to purchase it. Interested parties must visit a local wheelchair vendor and determine their exact mobility needs in consultation with rehabilitation and seating specialists. They must submit that information (including estimates of the cost of the wheelchair), a letter of medical necessity from their physician, documentation of ineligibility for private insurance or Medicare/Medicaid, and a copy of their most recent federal tax return.

Financial data   Grants cover the full cost of wheelchairs as verified by the vendor and medical experts.

Duration   These are 1-time grants.

Additional data   This foundation was established in 1995.

Number awarded   Varies each year; recently, the foundation provided 87 wheelchairs at a cost of $171,683 in cash and $106,181 worth of in-kind donations.

Deadline   Applications may be submitted at any time.

[372]
ARKANSAS DISABLED VETERANS PROPERTY TAX EXEMPTION

Arkansas Assessment Coordination Department
1614 West Third Street
Little Rock, AR 72201-1815
(501) 324-9100   Fax: (501) 324-9242
E-mail: dasbury@acd.state.ar.us
Web: www.arkansas.gov/acd

Summary   To exempt from taxation the property owned by blind or disabled veterans, surviving spouses, and minor dependent children in Arkansas.

Eligibility   This program is open to disabled veterans in Arkansas who have been awarded special monthly compensation by the U.S. Department of Veterans Affairs and who have 1) the loss of or the loss of use of 1 or more limbs, 2) total blindness in 1 or both eyes, or 3) total and permanent disability. The benefit also extends to veterans' unremarried surviving spouses and their minor children.

Financial data Qualifying veterans (or their unremarried widows or dependent children) are exempt from payment of all state taxes on their homestead and personal property.

Duration This exemption continues as long as the qualifying veteran (or dependent) resides in Arkansas.

Number awarded Varies each year.

Deadline Applications may be submitted at any time.

[373]
AUTOMOBILE ALLOWANCE FOR DISABLED VETERANS

Department of Veterans Affairs
Attn: Veterans Benefits Administration
810 Vermont Avenue, N.W.
Washington, DC 20420
(202) 418-4343   Toll Free: (800) 827-1000
Web: www.vba.va.gov/bin/21/Benefits

Summary To provide funding to certain disabled veterans and current service personnel who require specially adapted automobiles.

Eligibility To be eligible for a grant for an automobile, a veteran or current servicemember must have a service-connected loss or permanent loss of use of 1 or both hands or feet or permanent impairment of vision of both eyes to a prescribed degree. For adaptive equipment eligibility only, veterans entitled to compensation for ankylosis of 1 or both knees, or 1 or both hips, also qualify.

Financial data The grant consists of a payment by the Department of Veterans Affairs (VA) of up to $11,000 toward the purchase of an automobile or other conveyance. The VA will also pay for the adaptive equipment, its repair, and the replacement or reinstallation required for the safe operation of the vehicle purchased with VA assistance or for a previously or subsequently acquired vehicle.

Duration This is a 1-time grant.

Number awarded Varies each year.

Deadline Applications may be submitted at any time.

[374]
CALIFORNIA DISABLED VETERAN EXEMPTION FROM THE IN LIEU TAX FEE FOR A MANUFACTURED HOME OR MOBILEHOME

Department of Housing and Community Development
Attn: Registration and Titling
1800 Third Street
P.O. Box 2111
Sacramento, CA 95812-2111
(916) 323-9224   Toll Free: (800) 952-8356
Web: www.hcd.ca.gov

Summary To provide a special property tax exemption to blind or disabled California veterans and/or their spouses who own and occupy a mobile home.

Eligibility This program is open to disabled veterans and/or their spouses in California who have a manufac-

tured home or mobile home as their principal place of residence. Veterans must be disabled as a result of injury or disease incurred in military service and have been a resident of California 1) at the time of entry into the service and be blind, or have lost the use of 1 or more limbs, or be totally disabled; 2) on November 7, 1972 and be blind in both eyes, or have lost the use of 2 or more limbs; or 3) on January 1, 1975 and be totally disabled. The spouses and unremarried surviving spouses of those disabled veterans are also eligible.

Financial data The exemption applies to the first $20,000 of the assessed market value of the manufactured home or mobile home. Veterans and/or spouses whose income falls below a specified level are entitled to an additional $10,000 exemption. The amount of the exemption is 100% if the home is owned by a veteran only, a veteran and spouse, or a spouse only; 50% if owned by a veteran and another person other than a spouse or by a spouse and another person other than the veteran; 67% if owned by a veteran, the spouse, and another person; 34% if owned by a veteran and 2 other people other than a spouse or by a spouse and 2 other people; 50% if owned by a veteran, the spouse, and 2 other people; or 25% if owned by a veteran and 3 other people or by a spouse and 3 other people.

Duration The exemption is available annually as long as the applicant meets all requirements.

Number awarded Varies each year.

Deadline Deadline not specified.

[375]
CONNECTICUT REAL ESTATE TAX EXEMPTION FOR DISABLED VETERANS

Office of Policy and Management
Attn: Intergovernmental Policy Division
450 Capitol Avenue
Hartford, CT 06106-1308
(860) 418-6278   Toll Free: (800) 286-2214 (within CT)
Fax: (860) 418-6493   TDD: (860) 418-6456
E-mail: leeann.graham@ct.gov
Web: www.ct.gov

Summary To exempt Connecticut veterans with disabilities and their surviving spouses from the payment of a portion of their local property taxes.

Eligibility There are 2 categories of Connecticut veterans who qualify for exemptions from their dwelling house and the lot on which it is located: 1) those with major service-connected disabilities (paraplegia or osteochondritis resulting in permanent loss of the use of both legs or permanent paralysis of both legs and lower parts of the body; hemiplegia with permanent paralysis of 1 leg and 1 arm or either side of the body resulting from injury to the spinal cord, skeletal structure, or brain, or from disease of the spinal cord not resulting from syphilis; total blindness; amputation of both arms, both legs, both hands or both feet, or the combination of a hand and a foot; sustained through enemy action or resulting from an accident occurring or disease contracted in such active service) and 2) those with less severe disabilities (loss of use of 1 arm or 1 leg because of service-connected injuries). Surviving unremarried spouses of eligible deceased veterans are entitled to the same exemption as would have been granted to the veteran, as long as they continue to be the legal owner/occupier of the exempted residence. An additional exemption is available to veterans and spouses whose total adjusted gross income is less than $30,500 if unmarried or $37,300 if married. If the veteran is rated as 100% disabled by the U.S. Department of Veterans Affairs (VA), the maximum income levels are $18,000 if unmarried or $21,000 if married.

Financial data   Veterans in the first category receive an exemption from local property taxation of $10,000 of assessed valuation. Veterans in the second category receive exemptions of $5,000 of assessed valuation. For veterans whose income is less than the specified levels, additional exemptions of $20,000 for the first category or $10,000 for the second category are available from municipalities that choose to participate. For veterans whose income exceeds the specified levels, the additional exemption from participating municipalities is $5,000 for the first category or $2,500 for the second category. Connecticut municipalities may also elect to exempt from taxation specially adapted housing acquired or modified by a veteran under the provisions of Section 801 of Title 38 of the United States Code.

Duration   1 year; exemptions continue as long as the eligible resident (or surviving spouse) owns/occupies the primary residence and lives in Connecticut.

Number awarded   Varies each year; recently, a total of 22,944 veterans received property tax exemptions through this and other programs in Connecticut.

Deadline   Applications for the additional municipality exemption must be submitted to the assessor's office of the town or residence by September of every other year.

[376]
DELAWARE PENSION BENEFITS FOR PARAPLEGIC VETERANS

Delaware Commission of Veterans Affairs
Robbins Building
802 Silver Lake Boulevard, Suite 100
Dover, DE 19904
(302) 739-2792   Toll Free: (800) 344-9900 (within DE)
Fax: (302) 739-2794
E-mail: antonio.davila@state.de.us
Web: veteransaffairs.delaware.gov

Summary   To provide a monthly pension to paraplegic veterans in Delaware.

Eligibility   Eligible for this benefit are Delaware residents who are paraplegic as a result of service in the U.S. armed forces of the United States while it was officially at war or during a period when the United States was engaged in hostilities with another nation as a member of the United Nations. Applicants must be listed on the rolls of the U.S. Department of Veterans Affairs as totally disabled.

Financial data   The pension is $3,000 per year.

Duration   Recipients remain eligible for this pension as long as they reside in Delaware.

Deadline   Deadline not specified.

[377]
FLORIDA PROPERTY TAX EXEMPTION FOR TOTALLY AND PERMANENTLY DISABLED PERSONS

Florida Department of Revenue
Attn: Taxpayer Services
1379 Blountstown Highway
Tallahassee, FL 32304-2716
(850) 488-6800   Toll Free: (800) 352-3671
TDD: (800) 367-8331
Web: www.myflorida.com/dor/property/exemptions.html

Summary   To exempt from property taxation real estate owned by blind or disabled people in Florida.

Eligibility   This exemption is available to Florida residents who have real estate that they own and use as a homestead. Applicants must have 1) quadriplegia; or 2) paraplegia, hemiplegia, or other total and permanent disability, must use a wheelchair for mobility, or must be legally blind, and must have an income below a specified limit that changes annually; recently, the maximum allowable income was $25,221 per year.

Financial data   All real estate used and owned as a homestead, less any portion used for commercial purposes, is exempt from taxation.

Duration   The exemption applies as long as the taxpayer owns the property in Florida.

Additional data   Initial applications should be made in person at the appropriate county property appraiser's office.

Number awarded   Varies each year.

Deadline   Applications must be submitted by February of the year for which the exemption is sought.

[378]
FORD MOBILITY MOTORING PROGRAM

Ford Motor Company
Attn: Mobility Program
500 Hulet Drive
P.O. Box 529
Bloomfield Hills, MI 48303
Toll Free: (800) 952-2248, ext. 111
Fax: (248) 333-0300
TDD: (800) 833-0312
E-mail: Mobilitymotoring@Fordprogramhq.com
Web: www.mobilitymotoringprogram.com

Summary   To provide a cash reimbursement for the cost of installing adaptive driving aids on new vehicles from Ford or Lincoln-Mercury.

Eligibility   Eligible for this rebate are people who purchase or lease new Ford, Lincoln, or Mercury vehicles that require adaptive driving aids or conversion equipment for users with disabilities.

Financial data   Up to $1,200 is reimbursed for adaptive equipment or up to $200 for alert hearing devices, lumbar support, or running boards.

Additional data   The program also provides 24-hour roadside assistance.

Number awarded   Varies each year.

Deadline   Applicants have 12 months from the date or purchase or lease to initiate the adaptive work and 1 year from that date to process their claim.

[379]
GM MOBILITY PROGRAM

General Motors Corporation
Attn: GM Mobility Assistance Center
P.O. Box 5053
Troy, MI 48007
Toll Free: (800) 323-9935   TDD: (800) TDD-9935
Web: www.gm.com/vehicles/services/gm_mobility

Summary   To provide a cash reimbursement for the cost of installing adaptive driving aids on new purchases from General Motors.

Eligibility   Eligible for this rebate are purchasers or lessees of new General Motors cars, trucks, or vans that require adaptive driving aids or conversion equipment for users with disabilities.

Financial data   Up to $1,000 is reimbursed ($1,200 for Chevy Express and GMC Savana vans).

Additional data   Applications for reimbursement are submitted through the dealer from whom the vehicle was originally purchased. Only retail purchases or leases of new General Motors vehicles qualify for this program. The reimbursement applies only to equipment installed by converters in the after market, not to factory installed equipment of any kind.

Deadline   The conversion process must be completed within 12 months from the date of purchase or lease and the claim form must be submitted within 90 days after the completion of the conversion.

[380]
MAINE TAX EXEMPTION FOR SPECIALLY ADAPTED HOUSING UNITS

Maine Revenue Services
Attn: Property Tax Division
P.O. Box 9106
Augusta, ME 04332-9106
(207) 287-2011   Fax: (207) 287-6396
E-mail: prop.tax@maine.gov
Web: www.maine.gov

Summary   To exempt the specially adapted housing units of paraplegic veterans or their surviving spouses from taxation in Maine.

Eligibility   Veterans who served in the U.S. armed forces during any federally-recognized war period, are legal residents of Maine, are paraplegic veterans within the meaning of U.S. statutes, and have received a grant from the U.S. government for specially adapted housing are eligible. The exemption also applies to property held in joint tenancy with the veteran's spouse and to the specially adapted housing of unremarried widow(er)s of eligible veterans.

Financial data   Estates of paraplegic veterans are exempt up to $50,000 of just valuation for a specially adapted housing unit.

Duration   The exemption is valid for the lifetime of the paraplegic veteran or unremarried widow(er).

Number awarded   Varies each year.

Deadline   When an eligible person first submits an application, the proof of entitlement must reach the assessors of the local municipality prior to the end of March. Once eligibility has been established, notification need not be repeated in subsequent years.

[381]
MASSACHUSETTS VETERANS ANNUITY PROGRAM

Department of Veterans' Services
Attn: Annuities
600 Washington Street, Suite 1100
Boston, MA 02111
(617) 210-5480   Fax: (617) 210-5755
E-mail: mdvs@vet.state.ma.us
Web: www.mass.gov/veterans

Summary   To provide an annuity to blind or disabled veterans from Massachusetts and to the parents and spouses of deceased military personnel.

Eligibility   This program is open to 1) veterans who are blind, double amputee, paraplegic, or have a 100% service-connected disability; 2) the parents of military personnel who died of service-connected causes; and 3) the unremarried spouses of military personnel who died of service-connected causes. Veterans must have been residents of Massachusetts at the time of entry into military service who served during specified wartime periods and received other than a dishonorable discharge. All applicants must currently be residents of Massachusetts.

Financial data   Recipients are entitled to an annuity of $2,000 per year.

Duration   The annuity is paid as long as the recipient continues to reside in Massachusetts.

Deadline   Deadline not specified.

[382]
MICHIGAN INCOME TAX EXEMPTION FOR PEOPLE WITH DISABILITIES

Michigan Department of Treasury
Attn: Income Tax
Treasury Building
430 West Allegan Street
Lansing, MI 48922
(517) 373-3200   Toll Free: (800) 827-4000
TDD: (517) 636-4999
E-mail: treasIndTax@michigan.gov
Web: www.michigan.gov/treasury

Summary   To exempt a portion of the income of deaf, blind, and disabled residents of Michigan from state income taxation.

Eligibility   Eligible for this exemption are residents of Michigan who 1) receive messages through a sense other than hearing, such as lip reading or sign language; 2) have vision in their better eye of 20/200 or less with corrective lenses or peripheral field of vision of 20 degrees or less; or

3) are hemiplegic, paraplegic, quadriplegic, or totally and permanently disabled.
Financial data Qualifying people with disabilities receive an exemption of $2,200 from their adjusted gross income for purposes of state taxation.
Duration The exemption continues as long as the recipient resides in Michigan.
Deadline Deadline not specified.

[383]
MINNESOTA SPECIAL HOMESTEAD CLASSIFICATIONS
Minnesota Department of Revenue
Attn: Property Tax Division
600 North Robert Street
Mail Station 3340
St. Paul, MN 55146-3340
(651) 556-6087
Web: www.taxes.state.mn.us
Summary To provide a property tax benefit to owners of homesteads in Minnesota who are disabled, blind, or paraplegic veterans.
Eligibility This benefit is available to owners of residential real estate that is occupied and used as a homestead in Minnesota. Applicants must be certified as totally and permanently disabled, legally blind, or a paraplegic veteran living in specially adapted housing with a grant from the Veterans Administration.
Financial data Qualified property is taxed at a rate of 0.45% for the first $50,000 of market value of residential homesteads. That compares to the standard rate of 1.0% on the first $500,000 in valuation and 1.25% on valuation over $500,000.
Duration This benefit is available as long as the property is owned by a qualified person.
Number awarded Varies each year.
Deadline Applications must be submitted by September of each year.

[384]
MOBILITY BY VOLVO
Volvo Cars of North America, LLC
Attn: Mobility by Volvo
1 Volvo Drive
Rockleigh, NJ 07647
Toll Free: (800) 803-5222   TDD: (800) 833-0312
E-mail: MobilitybyVolvo@Volvoprogramhq.com
Web: www.volvocars.us/mobility
Summary To provide a cash reimbursement for the cost of installing adaptive driving aids or alert hearing devices on new purchases of Volvo vehicles.
Eligibility This rebate is available to purchasers of new Volvo vehicles that require adaptive driving aids or alert hearing devices for users with disabilities. Applicants must obtain the equipment, have it installed, and submit a copy of their paid invoice and a copy of their medical prescription.

Financial data Up to $1,000 is provided for the cost of adding adaptive equipment or $200 for an alert hearing device.
Deadline Eligible vehicles must be upfitted with approved adaptive equipment or alert hearing devices, and requests must be submitted within 180 days of vehicle purchase.

[385]
NATIONAL CRANIOFACIAL ASSOCIATION CLIENT TRAVEL GRANTS-IN-AID
FACES: The National Craniofacial Association
P.O. Box 11082
Chattanooga, TN 37401
(423) 266-1632   Toll Free: (800) 3-FACES-3
Fax: (423) 267-3124   E-mail: faces@faces-cranio.org
Web: www.faces-cranio.org
Summary To provide funding for travel expenses for persons with severe facial deformities who travel to comprehensive medical centers for reconstructive facial surgery.
Eligibility Persons with craniofacial deformities resulting from birth defects, injury, or disease are eligible to apply for these grants-in-aid if they need to travel to comprehensive medical centers to undergo reconstructive facial surgery and/or evaluation.
Financial data Funds are available for transportation, food, lodging, parking, and tolls related to securing or undergoing treatment. No medical costs are covered. Grants also provide for 1 accompanying person for each trip.
Additional data FACES: The National Craniofacial Association was founded in 1969 as the Debbie Fox Foundation. It changed its name because it no longer serves only Debbie.
Number awarded Varies each year.
Deadline Applications may be submitted at any time.

[386]
NEBRASKA HOMESTEAD EXEMPTION
Nebraska Department of Revenue
301 Centennial Mall South
P.O. Box 94818
Lincoln, NE 68509-4818
(402) 471-5729
Toll Free: (800) 742-7474 (within NE and IA)
Web: www.revenue.state.ne.us/homestead.htm
Summary To exempt the property of Nebraska residents who are elderly, disabled, or veterans and their widow(er)s from a portion of taxation.
Eligibility This exemption is available to 3 categories of Nebraska residents: the elderly, certain people with disabilities, and certain disabled veterans and their widow(er)s. Elderly people are those 65 years of age or older who own a homestead with a value less than $95,000 or 200% of their county's average assessed value of single family residential property, whichever is greater. Disabled people are those who 1) have a permanent physical disability and have lost all mobility such as to preclude locomotion without the regular use of a mechanical aid or pros-

thesis; 2) have undergone amputation of both arms above the elbow, or 3) have a permanent partial disability of both arms in excess of 75%. They must own a homestead with a value less than $110,000 or 225% of their county's average assessed value of single family residential property, whichever is greater. Veterans are those who served on active duty in the armed forces of the United States (or a government allied with the United States) during specified periods of war and received an honorable discharge. They must 1) be drawing compensation from the U.S. Department of Veterans Affairs (VA) because of a 100% service-connected disability; 2) be totally disabled by a nonservice-connected illness or accident; or 3) own a home that is substantially contributed to by VA. Also eligible are unremarried widow(er)s of veterans who died because of a service-connected disability, whose death while on active duty was service-connected, who died while on active duty during wartime, or who drew compensation from VA because of a 100% service-connected disability The homestead maximum value is $110,000 or 225% of the county's average assessed value of single family residential property, whichever is greater. Elderly people must have a household income less than $31,301 if single or $36,801 if married. Disabled persons, veterans, and widow(er)s (except veterans and widow(er)s who own a home that is substantially contributed to by the VA) must have a household income less than $34,401 if single or $39,701 if married.

Financial data Exemptions depend on the income of the applicant, ranging from 25% to 100% of the value of the homestead. For the elderly, the maximum exemption is the taxable value of the homestead up to $40,000 or 100% of the county's average assessed value of single family residential property, whichever is greater. For disabled people and veterans, the maximum exemption is the taxable value of the homestead up to $50,000 or 120% of the county's average assessed value of single family residential property, whichever is greater. For veterans and widow(er)s whose home was substantially contributed to by the VA, the homestead is 100% exempt regardless of the value of the homestead or the income of the owner.

Duration The exemption is provided as long as the qualifying homestead owner resides in Nebraska.

Number awarded Varies each year.

Deadline Applications must be filed by June of each year.

[387]
NEW HAMPSHIRE PROPERTY TAX EXEMPTION FOR CERTAIN DISABLED VETERANS

New Hampshire Department of Revenue
  Administration
109 Pleasant Street
Concord, NH 03301
(603) 271-2191   Fax: (603) 271-6121
TDD: (800) 735-2964
Web: revenue.nh.gov

Summary To exempt from taxation certain property owned by New Hampshire disabled veterans or their surviving spouses.

Eligibility Eligible for this exemption are New Hampshire residents who are honorably discharged veterans with a total and permanent service-connected disability that involves double amputation of the upper or lower extremities or any combination thereof, paraplegia, or blindness of both eyes with visual acuity of 5/200 or less. Applicants or their surviving spouses must own a specially adapted homestead that has been acquired with the assistance of the U.S. Department of Veterans Affairs.

Financial data Qualifying disabled veterans and surviving spouses are exempt from all taxation on their specially adapted homestead.

Duration 1 year; once the credit has been approved, it is automatically renewed as long as the qualifying person owns the same residence in New Hampshire.

Number awarded Varies each year.

Deadline The original application for a permanent tax credit must be submitted by April.

[388]
NEW HAMPSHIRE SERVICE-CONNECTED TOTAL AND PERMANENT DISABILITY TAX CREDIT

New Hampshire Department of Revenue
  Administration
109 Pleasant Street
Concord, NH 03301
(603) 271-2191   Fax: (603) 271-6121
TDD: (800) 735-2964
Web: revenue.nh.gov

Summary To provide property tax credits in New Hampshire to disabled veterans or their surviving spouses.

Eligibility Eligible for this tax credit are honorably discharged veterans residing in New Hampshire who 1) have a total and permanent service-connected disability, or 2) are a double amputee or paraplegic because of a service-connected disability. Unremarried surviving spouses of qualified veterans are also eligible.

Financial data Qualifying disabled veterans and surviving spouses receive an annual credit of $700 for property taxes on residential property. In addition, individual towns in New Hampshire may adopt a local option to increase the dollar amount credited to disabled veterans, to a maximum of $2,000.

Duration 1 year; once the credit has been approved, it is automatically renewed for as long as the qualifying person owns the same residence in New Hampshire.

Number awarded Varies each year.

Deadline The original application for a permanent tax credit must be submitted by April.

[389]
NEW YORK "ELIGIBLE FUNDS" PROPERTY TAX EXEMPTIONS FOR VETERANS

New York State Division of Veterans' Affairs
5 Empire State Plaza, Suite 2836
Albany, NY 12223-1551
(518) 474-6114
Toll Free: (888) VETS-NYS (within NY)
Fax: (518) 473-0379   E-mail: dvainfo@ogs.state.ny.us
Web: veterans.ny.gov

Summary   To provide a partial exemption from property taxes to veterans and their surviving spouses who are residents of New York.

Eligibility   This program is open to veterans who have purchased properties in New York with pension, bonus, or insurance money (referred to as "eligible funds"). Specially adapted homes of paraplegics, or the homes of their widowed spouses, are also covered.

Financial data   This exemption reduces the property's assessed value to the extent that "eligible funds" were used in the purchase, generally to a maximum of $5,000. It is applicable to general municipal taxes but not to school taxes or special district levies.

Duration   This exemption is available annually.

Number awarded   Varies each year.

Deadline   Applications must be filed with the local assessor by "taxable status date;" in most towns, that is the end of February.

[390]
NORTH DAKOTA PROPERTY TAX CREDIT FOR DISABLED VETERANS

Office of State Tax Commissioner
State Capitol Building
600 East Boulevard Avenue, Department 127
Bismarck, ND 58505-0599
(701) 328-2770   Toll Free: (800) 638-2901
Fax: (701) 328-3700   TDD: (800) 366-6888
E-mail: taxinfo@state.nd.us
Web: www.nd.gov/tax

Summary   To provide property tax credits to disabled North Dakota veterans and their surviving spouses.

Eligibility   This property tax credit is available to honorably-discharged veterans who have more than a 50% service-connected disability as certified by the U.S. Department of Veterans Affairs. Applicants must own and occupy a homestead according to state law. Unremarried surviving spouses are also eligible. If a disabled veteran co-owns the property with someone other than a spouse, the credit is limited to the disabled veteran's interest in the fixtures, buildings, and improvements of the homestead.

Financial data   The credit is applied against the first $120,000 of true and full valuation of the fixtures, buildings, and improvements of the homestead, to a maximum amount calculated by multiplying $120,000 by the percentage of the disabled veteran's disability compensation rating for service-connected disabilities.

Duration   1 year; renewable as long as qualified individuals continue to reside in North Dakota and live in their homes.

Number awarded   Varies each year.

Deadline   Applications may be submitted to the county auditor at any time.

[391]
NORTH DAKOTA PROPERTY TAX EXEMPTION FOR DISABLED PERSONS CONFINED TO A WHEELCHAIR

Office of State Tax Commissioner
State Capitol Building
600 East Boulevard Avenue, Department 127
Bismarck, ND 58505-0599
(701) 328-2770   Toll Free: (800) 638-2901
Fax: (701) 328-3700   TDD: (800) 366-6888
E-mail: taxinfo@state.nd.us
Web: www.nd.gov/tax

Summary   To provide partial tax exemption in North Dakota to persons permanently confined to the use of a wheelchair and their spouses.

Eligibility   Persons permanently confined to the use of a wheelchair are those who cannot walk with the assistance of crutches or any other device and will never be able to do so; this must be certified by a physician selected by a local governing board. The property must be owned and occupied as a homestead according to state law. The homestead may be owned by the spouse or jointly owned by the disabled person and spouse provided both reside on the homestead. Qualified residents and, if deceased, their unremarried surviving spouses are entitled to this exemption. Income and assets are not considered in determining eligibility for the exemption.

Financial data   The maximum benefit may not exceed $3,600 taxable value, because a homestead is limited to $80,000 market value.

Duration   The exemption continues as long as the homestead in North Dakota is owned by the disabled person and/or the spouse.

Additional data   The exemption does not apply to special assessments levied upon the homestead.

Number awarded   Varies each year.

Deadline   Deadline not specified.

[392]
NORTH DAKOTA PROPERTY TAX EXEMPTION FOR VETERANS WHO LIVE IN SPECIALLY ADAPTED HOUSING

Office of State Tax Commissioner
State Capitol Building
600 East Boulevard Avenue, Department 127
Bismarck, ND 58505-0599
(701) 328-2770   Toll Free: (800) 638-2901
Fax: (701) 328-3700   TDD: (800) 366-6888
E-mail: taxinfo@state.nd.us
Web: www.nd.gov/tax

Summary To provide property tax exemptions to North Dakota veterans and their surviving spouses who have been awarded specially adapted housing.

Eligibility This exemption is available to paraplegic disabled veterans of the U.S. armed forces or any veteran who has been awarded specially adapted housing by the U.S. Department of Veterans Affairs. The paraplegic disability does not have to be service connected. The unremarried surviving spouses of such deceased veterans are also eligible. Income and assets are not considered in determining eligibility for the exemption.

Financial data The maximum benefit may not exceed $5,400 taxable value, because the exemption is limited to the first $120,000 of true and full value of fixtures, buildings, and improvements.

Duration 1 year; renewable as long as qualified individuals continue to reside in North Dakota and live in their homes.

Number awarded Varies each year.

Deadline Applications may be submitted to the county auditor at any time.

[393]
PENNSYLVANIA DISABLED VETERANS REAL ESTATE TAX EXEMPTION

Office of the Deputy Adjutant General for Veterans
 Affairs
Building S-0-47, FTIG
Annville, PA 17003-5002
(717) 865-8907
Toll Free: (800) 54 PA VET (within PA)
Fax: (717) 861-8589   E-mail: jamebutler@state.pa.us
Web: www.milvet.state.pa.us/DMVA/592.htm

Summary To exempt blind and disabled Pennsylvania veterans and their unremarried surviving spouses from all state real estate taxes.

Eligibility Eligible to apply for this exemption are honorably-discharged veterans who are residents of Pennsylvania and who are blind, paraplegic, or 100% disabled from a service-connected disability sustained during wartime military service. The dwelling must be owned by the veteran solely or jointly with a spouse, and financial need for the exemption must be determined by the State Veterans' Commission. Veterans whose income is less than $79,050 per year are presumed to have financial need; veterans with income greater than $79,050 must document need. Upon the death of the veteran, the tax exemption passes on to the veteran's unremarried surviving spouse.

Financial data This program exempts the principal residence (and the land on which it stands) from all real estate taxes.

Duration The exemption continues as long as the eligible veteran or unremarried widow resides in Pennsylvania.

Number awarded Varies each year.

Deadline Deadline not specified.

[394]
PENNSYLVANIA PARALYZED VETERANS PENSION

Office of the Deputy Adjutant General for Veterans
 Affairs
Building S-0-47, FTIG
Annville, PA 17003-5002
(717) 865-8911
Toll Free: (800) 54 PA VET (within PA)
Fax: (717) 861-8589   E-mail: jamebutler@state.pa.us
Web: www.milvet.state.pa.us/DMVA/197.htm

Summary To provide financial assistance to Pennsylvania veterans who became disabled while serving in the U.S. armed forces.

Eligibility Applicants must be current residents of Pennsylvania who suffered an injury or disease resulting in loss or loss of use of 2 or more extremities while serving in the U.S. armed forces during an established period of war or armed conflict or as a result of hostilities during combat-related activities in peacetime. They must be rated by the U.S. Department of Veterans Affairs as 100% permanent and service-connected disabled. At the time of entry into military service, applicants must have been residents of Pennsylvania.

Financial data The pension is $150 per month.

Duration The pension is awarded for the life of the veteran.

Number awarded Varies each year.

Deadline Applications may be submitted at any time.

[395]
PVA DISASTER RELIEF FUND

Paralyzed Veterans of America
Attn: Disaster Relief Fund
801 18th Street, N.W.
Washington, DC 20006-3517
Toll Free: (800) 555-9140   E-mail: info@pva.org
Web: www.pva.org

Summary To provide emergency assistance to members of Paralyzed Veterans of America (PVA) who have been victimized by natural disasters.

Eligibility This assistance is available to PVA members whose property has been severely damaged by natural disasters. Applicants may be seeking funding for transportation, temporary shelter, food, home repairs, or modifications that are needed for wheelchair accessibility, medical supplies, or prosthetic appliances.

Financial data Grants range up to $2,500; more than $100,000 is available for relief each year.

Additional data Membership in PVA is open to veterans with spinal cord injury or disease.

Number awarded 2 each year.

Deadline Applications may be submitted at any time.

[396]
SOUTH CAROLINA DISABLED PERSON PROPERTY TAX EXEMPTION

South Carolina Department of Revenue
Attn: Property Division
301 Gervais Street
P.O. Box 125
Columbia, SC 29214
(803) 898-5480   Fax: (803) 898-5822
Web: www.sctax.org

Summary   To exempt the home of disabled residents of South Carolina and their surviving spouses from property taxation.

Eligibility   Eligible for this exemption are residents of South Carolina who are defined as paraplegic or hemiplegic and own a dwelling house that is their domicile. The exemption is allowed to the surviving spouse of the person as long as the spouse does not remarry, resides in the dwelling, and obtains the fee or a life estate in the dwelling. Paraplegic or hemiplegic includes a person with Parkinson's Disease, multiple sclerosis, or amyotrophic lateral sclerosis that has caused the same ambulatory difficulties as a person with paraperesis or hemiparesis. Surviving spouses of those persons are not eligible for this exemption.

Financial data   The exemption applies to all taxes on 1 house and a lot (not to exceed 1 acre).

Duration   The exemption extends as long as the person with a disability resides in the house.

Number awarded   Varies each year.

Deadline   Applications may be submitted at any time.

[397]
SOUTH DAKOTA PROPERTY TAX EXEMPTION FOR PARAPLEGIC VETERANS

South Dakota Department of Revenue and Regulation
Attn: Property Tax Division
445 East Capitol Avenue
Pierre, SD 57501-3185
(605) 773-3311   Toll Free: (800) TAX-9188
Fax: (605) 773-6729   E-mail: PropTaxIn@state.sd.us
Web: www.state.sd.us

Summary   To exempt from property taxation the homes of disabled veterans in South Dakota and their widow(er)s.

Eligibility   This benefit is available to residents of South Dakota who are 1) paraplegic veterans, 2) veterans with loss or loss of use of both lower extremities, or 3) unremarried widows or widowers of such veterans. Applicants must own and occupy a dwelling (including the house, garage, and up to 1 acre on which the building is located) that is specifically designed for wheelchair use within the structure. The veteran's injury does not have to be service-connected.

Financial data   Qualified dwellings are exempt from property taxation in South Dakota.

Duration   The exemption applies as long as the dwelling is owned and occupied by the disabled veteran or widow(er).

Number awarded   Varies each year.

Deadline   Deadline not specified.

[398]
SOUTH DAKOTA PROPERTY TAX REDUCTION FOR PARAPLEGICS

South Dakota Department of Revenue and Regulation
Attn: Property Tax Division
445 East Capitol Avenue
Pierre, SD 57501-3185
(605) 773-3311   Toll Free: (800) TAX-9188
Fax: (605) 773-6729   E-mail: PropTaxIn@state.sd.us
Web: www.state.sd.us

Summary   To provide a reduction in property taxes on the homes of people with disabilities in South Dakota and their widow(er)s.

Eligibility   This benefit is available to residents of South Dakota who are 1) paraplegic individuals, 2) individuals with loss or loss of use of both lower extremities, or 3) unremarried widows or widowers of such individuals. Applicants must own and occupy a dwelling (including the house, garage, and up to 1 acre on which the building is located) that is specifically designed for wheelchair use within the structure. They must have a federal adjusted income of less than $8,000 if they live in a single-member household or less than $12,000 if they live in a multiple-member household.

Financial data   The reduction depends on the federal adjusted gross income of the applicant. For single-member households, the reduction is 100% if the income is less than $5,000, 75% if the income is between $5,000 and $6,000, 50% if the income is between $6,000 and $7,000, or 25% if the income is between $7,000 and $8,000. For multiple-member household, the reduction is 100% if the income is less than $9,000, 75% if the income is between $9,000 and $10,000, 50% if the income is between $10,000 and $11,000, or 25% if the income is between $11,000 and $12,000.

Duration   The reduction applies as long as the dwelling is owned and occupied by the disabled person or widow(er).

Number awarded   Varies each year.

Deadline   Deadline not specified.

[399]
SPECIAL HOUSING ADAPTATIONS GRANTS

Department of Veterans Affairs
Attn: Specially Adapted Housing
810 Vermont Avenue, N.W.
Washington, DC 20420
(202) 461-9546   Toll Free: (800) 827-1000
Web: www.homeloans.va.gov/sah.htm

Summary   To provide grants to certain disabled veterans or servicemembers who wish to make adaptations to their home to meet their needs.

Eligibility   These grants are available to veterans and servicemembers who are entitled to compensation for permanent and total service-connected disability due to: 1) blindness in both eyes with 5/200 visual acuity or less; 2) the anatomical loss or loss of use of both hands; or 3) a severe burn injury. Applicants must be planning to 1) adapt a house which they plan to purchase and in which they intend to reside; 2) adapt a house which a member of their family plans to purchase and in which they intend to reside; 3) adapt a house which they already own and in which they intend to reside; 4) adapt a house which is already owned by a member of their family in which they intend to reside; or 5) purchase a house that has already been adapted with special features that are reasonably necessary because of their disability and in which they intend to reside.

Financial data Eligible veterans and servicemembers are entitled to grants up to $12,756 to adapt a house.

Duration Eligible veterans and servicemembers are entitled to up to 3 usages of these grants.

Number awarded Varies each year.

Deadline Applications are accepted at any time.

[400]
SPECIALLY ADAPTED HOUSING GRANTS

Department of Veterans Affairs
Attn: Specially Adapted Housing
810 Vermont Avenue, N.W.
Washington, DC 20420
(202) 461-9546   Toll Free: (800) 827-1000
Web: www.homeloans.va.gov/sah.htm

Summary To provide loans, grants, and loan guaranties to certain disabled veterans and servicemembers for a home specially adapted to their needs.

Eligibility These grants are available to veterans and servicemembers who are entitled to compensation for permanent and total service-connected disability due to: 1) the loss or loss of use of both lower extremities, such as to preclude locomotion without the aid of braces, crutches, canes, or a wheelchair; or 2) blindness in both eyes, having only light perception, plus loss or loss of use of 1 lower extremity; or 3) a loss or loss of use of 1 lower extremity together with residuals of organic disease or injury or the loss or loss of use of 1 upper extremity, such as to preclude locomotion without resort to braces, canes, crutches, or a wheelchair. Applicants must be planning to 1) construct a home on land to be acquired for that purpose; 2) build a home on land already owned if it is suitable for specially adapted housing; 3) remodel an existing home if it can be made suitable for specially adapted housing, or 4) apply funds against the unpaid principle mortgage balance of a specially adapted home that has already been acquired.

Financial data The U.S. Department of Veterans Affairs (VA) may approve a grant of not more than 50% of the cost of building, buying, or remodeling homes for eligible veterans, or paying indebtedness of such homes already acquired, up to a maximum grant of $63,780. Eligible veterans with available loan guarantee entitlements may also obtain a guaranteed loan from the VA to supplement the grant to acquire a specially adapted home. If private financing is not available, the VA may make a direct loan up to $33,000 to cover the difference between the total cost of the home and the grant.

Duration This is a 1-time grant, guaranteed loan, or direct loan.

Additional data Veterans who receive a specially adapted housing grant may be eligible for Veterans Mortgage Life Insurance.

Number awarded Varies each year.

Deadline Applications are accepted at any time.

[401]
SPINA BIFIDA PROGRAM FOR CHILDREN OF VETERANS

Department of Veterans Affairs
Attn: Veterans Benefits Administration
810 Vermont Avenue, N.W.
Washington, DC 20420
(202) 418-4343   Toll Free: (800) 827-1000
Web: www1.va.gov/opa/ls1/11.asp

Summary To provide support to children of certain veterans who have spina bifida.

Eligibility This program is open to spina bifida patients whose veteran parent performed active military, naval, or air service 1) in the Republic of Vietnam during the period from January 9, 1962 through May 7, 1975; or 2) in or near the Korean demilitarized zone during the period from September 1, 1967 through August 31, 1971. Children may be of any age or marital status, but they must have been conceived after the date on which the veteran first served in Vietnam or Korea. The monthly allowance is set at 3 levels, depending upon the degree of disability suffered by the child. The levels are based on neurological manifestations that define the severity of disability: impairment of the functioning of the extremities, impairment of bowel or bladder function, and impairment of intellectual functioning.

Financial data Support depends on the degree of disability. The monthly rate for children at the first level is $286, the second level $984, or at the third level $1,678.

Additional data Applications are available from the nearest VA medical center. Recipients are also entitled to vocational training and medical treatment.

Number awarded Varies each year.

Deadline Applications are accepted at any time.

[402]
SUPPLEMENTAL SECURITY INCOME (SSI)

Social Security Administration
6401 Security Boulevard
Baltimore, MD 21235-0001
(410) 594-1234   Toll Free: (800) 772-1213
TDD: (800) 325-0778
Web: www.socialsecurity.gov/ssi/index.htm

Summary To provide monthly payments to disabled, blind, deaf, and elderly people who have limited income and resources.

Eligibility This assistance is available to U.S. citizens and certain categories of aliens who are 65 years of age or older, blind, or disabled. A person 18 years of age or older is considered disabled if a physical or mental impairment prevents him or her from doing any substantial gainful work and is expected to last for at least 12 months or to result in death. Children under the age of 18 are considered disabled if they have a physical or mental impairment that is comparable in severity to a disability that would prevent an adult from working and is expected to last at least 12 months or result in death. Children with certain conditions are automatically disabled and eligible for these benefits; the conditions include HIV infection, blindness, deafness, cerebral palsy, Down syndrome, muscular dystrophy, significant mental deficiency, diabetes (with amputation of 1 foot), amputation of 2 limbs, or amputation of leg at the hip. Regardless of age, a person whose vision is no better than 20/200 or who has a limited visual field of 20 degrees or less with the best corrective eyeglasses is considered blind; individuals with visual impairments not severe enough to meet the definition of blindness still may qualify as disabled persons. Applicants must have limited income and limited resources (less than $2,000 for an individual or $3,000 for a couple); items excluded from resources include the home used as a principal place of residence, personal and household goods, life insurance with face value of $1,500 or less, a car, burial plots for individuals and immediate family members, and burial funds up to $1,500.

Financial data   The basic monthly payment is $674 for an eligible individual or $1,011 for an eligible individual with an eligible spouse. Many states add money to that basic payment. SSI recipients may also be eligible for food stamps and other nutrition programs.

Duration   Assistance is provided as long as the recipient remains blind or disabled and in financial need.

Additional data   Although SSI is administered through the Social Security Administration, it is not financed by Social Security taxes. Financing of SSI is provided through general funds of the U.S. Treasury. Recipients of SSI need not have been employed or paid Social Security taxes, but they may be eligible for both SSI and Social Security. Disabled and blind applicants for SSI are referred to their state vocational rehabilitation agency to determine their eligibility for a program of vocational rehabilitation. Disabled drug addicts or alcoholics are referred for appropriate treatment if it is available at an approved facility or institution.

Number awarded   Recently, approximately 7,599,000 people (including 6,395,000 who were blind and disabled) were receiving SSI benefits, including 1,172,000 under 18 years of age, 4,389,000 who were 18 to 64 years of age, and 2,038,000 who were 65 or older.

Deadline   Deadline not specified.

[403]
TENNESSEE INCOME TAX EXEMPTION FOR QUADRIPLEGICS

Tennessee Department of Revenue
Andrew Jackson State Office Building
500 Deaderick Street
Nashville, TN 37242-1099
(615) 253-0600   Toll Free: (800) 342-1003 (within TN)
Fax: (615) 253-3580   E-mail: tn.revenue@state.tn.us
Web: www.tennessee.gov/revenue

Summary   To exempt from state taxation the dividend and interest income of quadriplegic residents of Tennessee.

Eligibility   This exemption is provided to residents of Tennessee who are certified by a medical doctor to be quadriplegic and who have taxable income that is from 1) dividends from stock, investment trusts, and mutual funds; and 2) interest from bonds, notes, and mortgages. The income must be derived from circumstances resulting in the individual's becoming a quadriplegic.

Financial data   All income is exempt from taxation if the income is derived from circumstances resulting in the applicant's becoming a quadriplegic. However, when taxable interest/dividend income is received jointly by a quadriplegic and a spouse who is not a quadriplegic or who is quadriplegic but the taxable income was not derived from circumstances resulting in the spouse's becoming quadriplegic, only one half of the jointly received income is exempted from taxation. The spouse who is not quadriplegic or whose quadriplegic condition did not result in the income is entitled only to a $1,250 exemption.

Duration   The exemption continues as long as the recipient resides in Tennessee.

Deadline   Deadline not specified.

[404]
TENNESSEE PROPERTY TAX RELIEF FOR DISABLED VETERANS AND THEIR SPOUSES

Tennessee Comptroller of the Treasury
Attn: Property Tax Relief Program
James K. Polk State Office Building
505 Deaderick Street, Room 1600
Nashville, TN 37243-1402
(615) 747-8871   Fax: (615) 532-3866
E-mail: Kim.Darden@state.tn.us
Web: www.comptroller.state.tn.us/pa/patxr.htm

Summary   To provide property tax relief to blind and disabled veterans and their spouses in Tennessee.

Eligibility   This exemption is offered to veterans or their surviving unremarried spouses who are residents of Tennessee and own and live in their home in the state. The veteran must have served in the U.S. armed forces and 1) have acquired, as a result of such service, a disability from paraplegia, permanent paralysis of both legs and lower part of the body resulting from traumatic injury, disease to the spinal cord or brain, legal blindness, or loss or loss of use of both legs or arms from any service-connected cause; 2) have been rated by the U.S. Department of Veterans Affairs (VA) as 100% permanently disabled as a result of service as a prisoner of war for at least 5 months; or 3) have been rated by the VA as 100% permanently and totally disabled from any other service-connected cause. The relief does not extend to any person who was dishonorably discharged from any of the armed services.

Financial data   The amount of the relief depends on the property assessment and the tax rate in the city or county where the beneficiary lives. The maximum market value on which tax relief is calculated is $175,000.

Duration 1 year; may be renewed as long as the eligible veteran or surviving unremarried spouse owns and occupies the primary residence.
Number awarded Varies each year.
Deadline Deadline not specified.

[405]
TEXAS PROPERTY TAX EXEMPTION FOR DISABLED VETERANS AND THEIR FAMILIES

Texas Veterans Commission
P.O. Box 12277
Austin, TX 78711-2277
(512) 463-5538
Toll Free: (800) 252-VETS (within TX)
Fax: (512) 475-2395　　　E-mail: info@tvc.state.tx.us
Web: www.tvc.state.tx.us/StateBenefits.html

Summary To extend property tax exemptions on the appraised value of their property to blind, disabled, and other Texas veterans and their surviving family members.
Eligibility Eligible veterans must be Texas residents rated at least 10% service-connected disabled. Surviving spouses and children of eligible veterans are also covered by this program.
Financial data For veterans in Texas whose disability is rated as 10% through 29%, the first $5,000 of the appraised property value is exempt from taxation; veterans rated as 30% through 49% disabled are exempt from the first $7,500 of appraised value; those with a 50% through 69% disability are exempt from the first $10,000 of appraised value; the exemption applies to the first $12,000 of appraised value for veterans with disabilities rated as 70% to 99%; veterans rated as 100% disabled are exempt from 100% of the appraised value of their property. A veteran whose disability is 10% or more and who is 65 years or older is entitled to exemption of the first $12,000 of appraised property value. A veteran whose disability consists of the loss of use of 1 or more limbs, total blindness in 1 or both eyes, or paraplegia is exempt from the first $12,000 of the appraised value. The unremarried surviving spouse of a deceased veteran who died on active duty and who, at the time of death had a compensable disability and was entitled to an exemption, is entitled to the same exemption. The surviving spouse of a person who died on active duty is entitled to exemption of the first $5,000 of appraised value of the spouse's property. Surviving spouses, however, are not eligible for the 100% exemption. A surviving child of a person who dies on active duty is entitled to exemption of the first $5,000 of appraised value of the child's property, as long as the child is unmarried and under 21 years of age.
Duration 1 year; may be renewed as long as the eligible veteran (or unremarried surviving spouse or child) owns and occupies the primary residence in Texas.
Additional data This program is administered at the local level by the various taxing authorities.
Number awarded Varies each year.
Deadline April of each year.

[406]
TOYOTA MOBILITY PROGRAM

Toyota Motor Sales, U.S.A., Inc.
Attn: Toyota Customer Experience Center
19001 South Western Avenue
Mail Drop WC10
Torrance, CA 90509-2714
Toll Free: (800) 331-4331　　　TDD: (800) 443-4999
Web: www.toyota.com/mobility

Summary To provide a cash reimbursement for the cost of installing adaptive driving aids on new purchases of Toyota vehicles.
Eligibility This rebate is available to purchasers or lessors of new Toyota vehicles that require an aftermarket alteration or equipment installation to provide a disabled user convenient access and/or the ability to drive the vehicle. Examples include adaptations that involve vehicle entry and exit, driver position, steering system, or brake and accelerator system.
Financial data Up to $1,000 is provided for the cost of adding adaptive equipment.
Deadline The adaptive equipment must be purchased and installed within 12 months of vehicle purchase or lease. A reimbursement application must be submitted within 90 days of complete installation of adaptive equipment.

Awards

[407]
JAY AND ROSE PHILLIPS AWARD

Courage Center
Attn: Vocational Services Department
3915 Golden Valley Road
Minneapolis, MN 55422
(763) 520-0263　　　Toll Free: (888) 8-INTAKE
Fax: (763) 520-0562　　　TDD: (763) 520-0245
E-mail: information@couragecenter.org
Web: www.couragecenter.org

Summary To recognize and reward residents of designated states who have a physical disability and have been employed successfully.
Eligibility This award is available to residents of Iowa, Minnesota, North Dakota, South Dakota, and Wisconsin who have a physical disability. Nominees must have been vocationally and financially independent for at least 3 years. Self-employed individuals are also eligible. Employers are encouraged to nominate their employees who meet the criteria. In the selection process, attitude, leadership, character, and community involvement are also considered.
Financial data The award is $2,000.
Duration The awards are presented annually.
Additional data This program was established in 1964.

Number awarded   Varies each year; recently, 3 of these awards were presented.
Deadline   May of each year.

Communication/Other Disabilities

Scholarships ●

Fellowships/Grants ●

Grants-in-Aid ●

Awards ●

Described here are 238 programs open to individuals who have a communication disorder (such as stuttering or voice impairment), have a learning disability (including such conditions as brain injury and dyslexia), are emotionally disturbed, or have other chronic or acute health problems, such as cancer, tuberculosis, or hemophilia. Of these, 158 entries cover scholarships (to pursue studies or research on the undergraduate level in the United States); 36 cover fellowships/grants (to pursue graduate or postdoctoral study or research in the United States); 39 cover grants-in-aid (to support emergency situations, travel, income/property tax liabilities, or the acquisition of assistive technology); and 5 cover awards, competitions, prizes, and honoraria (to recognize or support creative work and public service). If you are looking for a particular program and don't find it in this chapter, be sure to check the Program Title Index to see if it is covered elsewhere in the directory.

Scholarships

[408]
ALEX LIEBER MEMORIAL SCHOLARSHIPS

LA Kelley Communications, Inc.
65 Central Street
Georgetown, MA 01833
(978) 352-7657   Toll Free: (800) 249-7977
Fax: (978) 352-6254   E-mail: info@kelleycom.com
Web: www.kelleycom.com/AlexLieber/index.html

Summary   To provide financial assistance for college to students who have hemophilia or von Willebrand Disease.

Eligibility   This program is open to people who have hemophilia or von Willebrand Disease and who are entering or enrolled at an accredited college, university, or vocational/technical school. Applicants must submit information on 1) extracurricular activities, hobbies, and interests; 2) community service and volunteer activities; 3) work experience; 4) an historical person they admire the most and why; and 5) a current person they admire the most and why. Selection is based primarily on volunteer service; financial need is not considered.

Financial data   The stipend is $1,000. Funds are provided in the form of a credit card which the recipient may use to purchase text books, gasoline, airline tickets, computer hardware or software, or other expenses related to higher education approved by the sponsor.

Duration   1 year.

Number awarded   2 each year.

Deadline   May of each year.

[409]
ANDREW CRAIG MEMORIAL SCHOLARSHIP

PKU Organization of Illinois
P.O. Box 102
Palatine, IL 60078-0102
(630) 415-2219   Fax: (208) 978-8963
E-mail: info@pkuil.org
Web: www.pkuil.org

Summary   To provide financial assistance to Illinois residents who have been diagnosed with phenylketonuria (PKU) and are interested in attending college in any state.

Eligibility   This program is open to residents of Illinois who have been diagnosed with PKU or an allied disorder. Applicants must be enrolled or planning to enroll at an accredited college, university, or vocational school in any state. Along with their application, they must submit a short essay about themselves, their experiences with PKU or allied disorder, and their future aspirations.

Financial data   The stipend is $2,000 per year.

Duration   1 year; recipients may reapply but not in successive years.

Additional data   This program was established in 1997.

Number awarded   5 each year.

Deadline   August of each year.

[410]
ANGEL ON MY SHOULDER SCHOLARSHIPS

Angel on My Shoulder
P.O. Box 747
St. Germain, WI 54558
Toll Free: (800) 860-3431
E-mail: info@angelonmyshoulder.org
Web: www.angelonmyshoulder.org

Summary   To provide financial assistance to high school seniors in Wisconsin who plan to attend college in any state and are cancer survivors or relatives affected by cancer.

Eligibility   This program is open to seniors who are graduating from high schools in Wisconsin and planning to attend a 4-year college, technical school, or specialty school in any state. Applicants must be survivors of cancer or have an immediate family member (father, mother, sibling) affected by cancer. Along with their application, they must submit a 250-word essay on why they wish to further their formal education, including their goals and values and how the cancer experience or affiliation with the sponsoring organization has affected their life. Financial need is considered in the selection process.

Financial data   Stipends are $1,500 or $1,000.

Duration   1 year.

Additional data   This program was established in 2008.

Number awarded   Varies each year. Recently, 23 of these scholarships were awarded: 4 at $1,500 and 19 at $1,000.

Deadline   March of each year.

[411]
ANNE AND MATT HARBISON SCHOLARSHIP

P. Buckley Moss Society
20 Stoneridge Drive, Suite 102
Waynesboro, VA 22980
(540) 943-5678   Fax: (540) 949-8408
E-mail: society@mosssociety.org
Web: www.mosssociety.org/page.php?id=30

Summary   To provide financial assistance for college to high school seniors with language-related learning disabilities.

Eligibility   Eligible to be nominated for this scholarship are high school seniors with language-related learning disabilities. Nominations must be submitted by a member of the P. Buckley Moss Society. The nomination packet must include verification of a language-related learning disability from a counselor or case manager, a high school transcript, 2 letters of recommendation, and 4 essays by the nominees (on themselves; their learning disability and its effect on their lives; their extracurricular, community, work, and church accomplishments; and their plans for next year).

Financial data   The stipend is $1,500. Funds are paid to the recipient's college or university.

Duration   1 year; may be renewed for up to 3 additional years.

Additional data   This scholarship was first awarded in 1998.

Number awarded 1 each year.

Deadline March of each year.

[412]
ANNE FORD AND ALLEGRA FORD SCHOLARSHIPS

National Center for Learning Disabilities
Attn: Scholarship
381 Park Avenue South, Suite 1401
New York, NY 10016-8806
(212) 545-7510　　　　　　Toll Free: (888) 575-7373
Fax: (212) 545-9665　E-mail: AFScholarship@ncld.org
Web: www.ncld.org

Summary To provide financial assistance for college to high school seniors with learning disabilities.

Eligibility This program is open to high school seniors with learning disabilities who plan to work on a 4-year university degree. Applicants must have a GPA of 3.0 or higher and be able to demonstrate financial need. Along with their application, they must submit an essay (750 to 1,000 words in length) describing their frustrations and triumphs in dealing with their specific learning disability; their essay should also include the characteristics they possess that make them an ideal candidate for this scholarship and should make specific mention of how they believe a college education will enhance their lives. If they prefer, they may submit a video or audio tape (up to 15 minutes in length) with accompanying script or outline that presents the same information as the essay. Other required submissions include high school transcripts, 3 letters of recommendation, a financial statement, standardized test (SAT, ACT) scores, and current documentation of a learning disability that includes evaluation reports, I.E.P., and/or 504 plan. U.S. citizenship is required.

Financial data The stipend is $2,500 per year for winners. Runners-up receive a 1-time cash award (amount not specified). Winners and runners-up also receive Kurzweil 3000 Scan/Read software.

Duration 4 years for winners, provided the recipients submit annual reports (written or in video format) detailing their progress in school and describing their insights about their personal growth.

Additional data This program was established in 2002 and expanded in 2009 with support from Allegra Ford (Anne's daughter).

Number awarded 2 winners and 2 runners-up are selected each year.

Deadline December of each year.

[413]
AWOWC OF WASHINGTON, D.C. HIGH SCHOOL SCHOLARSHIPS FOR AIR FORCE DEPENDENTS

Air Force Officers' Wives' Club of Washington, D.C.
Attn: Scholarship Committee
P.O. Box 8490
Washington, DC 20032
E-mail: scholarship@afowc.com
Web: www.afowc.com/making-difference.html

Summary To provide financial assistance for college to learning disabled and other high school seniors who are dependents of Air Force members in the Washington, D.C. area.

Eligibility This program is open to high school seniors residing in the Washington, D.C. metropolitan area who are dependents of Air Force members in the following categories: active duty, retired, MIA/POW, or deceased. Also eligible are dependents whose Air Force sponsor is assigned remote from the area or reassigned during the current school year and they have remained behind to graduate. Applicants must be 1) high school seniors planning to work full time on an accredited undergraduate degree at a college or university in any state; or 2) high school seniors with a learning disability who plan to work full time on an undergraduate degree at a college or university in any state. Along with their application, they must submit a 500-word essay on a topic that changes annually; recently, applicants were asked to write on which book is required reading for all students and why. Selection is based on academic and citizenship achievements; financial need is not considered. Applicants who receive an appointment to a service academy are not eligible.

Financial data A stipend is awarded (amount not specified). Funds may be used only for payment of tuition or academic fees.

Duration 1 year.

Number awarded Varies each year.

Deadline February of each year.

[414]
BECKY COHN SCHOLARSHIP

Accredo's Hemophilia Health Services
Attn: Scholarship Committee
201 Great Circle Road
Nashville, TN 37228
(615) 850-5212　　　　　　Toll Free: (800) 800-6606
Fax: (615) 261-6730
E-mail: Shayne.harris@accredo.com
Web: www.hemophiliahealth.com/Scholarships.html

Summary To provide financial assistance for college or graduate school to people who have hemophilia or other bleeding disorders and have provided service to the bleeding disorders community.

Eligibility This program is open to individuals with hemophilia (factor VIII or IX), von Willebrand Disease (type 1, 2, 2A, 2B, 2M, 2N, or 3), factor I (fibrinogen), factor II (prothrombin), factor V (proaccelerin), factor VII (proconvertin), factor X, factor XI, factor XIII, or Glanzmann's thrombasthenia. Applicants must be 1) high school seniors; 2) college freshmen, sophomores, or juniors; or 3) college seniors planning to attend graduate school or students already enrolled in graduate school. Applicants must be enrolled or planning to enroll full time at an accredited nonprofit college, university, or vocational/technical school in the United States or Puerto Rico. Along with their application, they must submit an essay, up to 250 words, on the following topic: "What has been your involvement with and service to the bleeding disorders community?" U.S. citizenship is required. Selection is based on the essay, academic achievements and records, community involvement, and financial need.

Financial data The stipend is at least $1,500. Funds are issued payable to the recipient's school.

Duration 1 year; recipients may reapply.

Additional data This program, which started in 2009, is administered by International Scholarship and Tuition Services, Inc., P.O. Box 23737, Nashville, TN 37202-3737, (615) 320-3149, Fax: (615) 320-3151, E-mail: info@apply-ists.net.

Number awarded 1 each year.

Deadline April of each year.

[415]
BETH CAREW MEMORIAL SCHOLARSHIPS

Colburn-Keenan Foundation, Inc.
31 Moody Road
P.O. Box 811
Enfield, CT 06083-0811
(860) 749-7522   Toll Free: (800) 966-2431
Fax: (860) 763-6494
E-mail: admin@colburn-keenanfoundation.org
Web: www.colburn-keenanfoundation.org

Summary To provide financial assistance for college to students who have a bleeding disorder.

Eligibility This program is open to high school seniors and college freshmen, sophomores, and juniors who have hemophilia, von Willebrand Disease, or another related inherited bleeding disorder. Applicants must be attending or planning to attend an accredited college or university in the United States as a full-time student. Along with their application, they must submit essays on their academic goals, why they would be a good choice for this scholarship, their participation in volunteer community activities, their greatest challenge as a person living with a bleeding disorder, examples of choices they have made that demonstrate good and bad judgment on their part, and other financial assistance they are or may be receiving.

Financial data The stipend is $4,000.

Duration 1 year.

Additional data This program was established by AHF, Inc. in 2002 to honor Beth Carew, who died in 1994 as 1 of the very few women to have hemophilia A. Following the deaths of Donald Colburn and Kathy Ann Keenan, founders of AHF, the Colburn-Keenan Foundation was established; in 2007, it assumed responsibility for administering this program.

Number awarded 10 each year.

Deadline April of each year.

[416]
BEYOND THE CURE SCHOLARSHIPS

National Children's Cancer Society
Attn: Scholarships
One South Memorial Drive, Suite 800
St. Louis, MO 63102
(314) 241-1600   Toll Free: (800) 532-6459
Fax: (314) 241-1996
E-mail: pgabris@children-cancer.org
Web: www.children-cancer.org

Summary To provide financial assistance for college to childhood cancer survivors.

Eligibility This program is open to childhood cancer survivors currently younger than 25 years of age who were diagnosed before the age of 18. Applicants must be enrolled or planning to enroll full time at an accredited college, university, or vocational/technical school. Along with their application, they must submit a 1,000-word essay on how being diagnosed with cancer at a young age has impacted their life and future goals. Selection is based on that essay, GPA, medical history, commitment to community service, and financial need. U.S. citizenship is required.

Financial data Stipends range up to $5,000. Funds are disbursed directly to the recipient's institution.

Duration 1 year; may be renewed up to 3 additional years, provided the recipient remains enrolled full time, maintains an overall GPA of 2.5 or higher, and completes 15 hours of volunteer work with the sponsoring organization.

Additional data This program was established in 2008.

Number awarded Varies each year; recently, 8 new and 5 renewal scholarships were awarded.

Deadline March of each year.

[417]
BILL MCADAM SCHOLARSHIP FUND

Hemophilia Foundation of Michigan
c/o Cathy McAdam
22226 Doxtator
Dearborn, MI 48128
(313) 563-1412   E-mail: mcmcadam@comcast.net

Summary To provide financial assistance for college to students with a bleeding disorder or members of their families.

Eligibility This program is open to 1) students with a hereditary bleeding disorder (hemophilia, von Willebrand, etc.) or 2) members of their families (spouse, partner, child, sibling). Applicants must be U.S. citizens and enrolled or planning to enroll at an accredited 2- or 4-year college, trade or technical school, or other certification program. Along with their application, they must submit 2 letters of recommendation and 3 essays: 1) what they would like the scholarship committee to know about their dream career and the passion that moves them toward furthering their education; 2) a challenge they faced and how they addressed it; and 3) a thank-you note to a fictional character who gave them a gift. Financial need is not considered in the selection process.

Financial data The stipend is $2,000. Funds are paid directly to the recipient's institution.
Duration 1 year; nonrenewable.
Number awarded 1 each year.
Deadline May of each year.

[418]
BIORX/HEMOPHILIA OF NORTH CAROLINA EDUCATIONAL SCHOLARSHIPS

BioRx
200 West Lexington Avenue, Suite 203
High Point, NC 27262
(919) 749-3196   Toll Free: (866) 44-BIORX
E-mail: cbarnes@biorx.net
Web: www.biorx.net/hemo_scholarships.php

Summary To provide financial assistance for college to people with hemophilia, their caregivers, and their siblings, especially those who are interested in studying health care.
Eligibility This program is open to caregivers of children affected with bleeding disorders, people who have been diagnosed with hemophilia, and siblings of people diagnosed with hemophilia. Applicants must submit an essay of 1 to 2 page detailing their occupational goals and objectives in life and how the educational program they have chosen will meet those goals. Preference is given to applicants who are studying or planning to study a health care-related field at an accredited college, university, or certified training program. Residents of all states are eligible.
Financial data The stipend is $2,000.
Duration 1 year.
Additional data This program was established in 2004. Applications must be submitted to Hemophilia of North Carolina, P.O. Box 70, Cary, NC 27512-0070.
Number awarded 3 each year.
Deadline April of each year.

[419]
BMW SCHOLARSHIP OF HOPE

Epsilon Sigma Alpha International
Attn: ESA Foundation
P.O. Box 270517
Fort Collins, CO 80527
(970) 223-2824   Fax: (970) 223-4456
E-mail: esainfo@esaintl.com
Web: www.esaintl.com/esaf

Summary To provide financial assistance for college to students who have epilepsy.
Eligibility This program is open to students who have epilepsy. Applicants must be 1) graduating high school seniors with a GPA of 3.0 or higher or with minimum scores of 22 on the ACT or 1030 on the combined critical reading and mathematics SAT; 2) enrolled in college with a GPA of 3.0 or higher; 3) enrolled at a technical school or returning to school after an absence for retraining of job skills or obtaining a degree; or 4) engaged in online study through an accredited college, university, or vocational school. They may be attending or planning to attend an accredited school anywhere in the United States and major in any

field. Selection is based on character (10%), leadership (10%), service (35%), financial need (35%), and scholastic ability (10%).
Financial data The stipend is $1,000.
Duration 1 year; may be renewed.
Additional data Epsilon Sigma Alpha (ESA) is a women's service organization, but scholarships are available to both men and women. Completed applications must be submitted to the ESA state counselor who verifies the information before forwarding them to the scholarship director. A $5 processing fee is required.
Number awarded 1 each year.
Deadline January of each year.

[420]
BOB HERSH MEMORIAL SCHOLARSHIP

Mary M. Gooley Hemophilia Center
Attn: Scholarship Selection Committee
1415 Portland Avenue, Suite 500
Rochester, NY 14621
(585) 922-5700   Fax: (585) 922-5775
E-mail: Tricia.oppelt@rochestergeneral.org
Web: www.hemocenter.org/Scholarship%20Info.asp

Summary To provide financial assistance to people with a bleeding disorder and their families who plan to attend college to prepare for a career in a teaching or helping profession.
Eligibility This program is open to people who are affected directly or indirectly by hemophilia, von Willebrand Disease, hereditary bleeding disorder, or hemochromatosis. Applicants must be enrolled or planning to enroll at an accredited 2- or 4-year college or university, vocational/technical school, or certified training program. They must be preparing for a career in a teaching or helping profession. Along with their application, they must submit 1) a 1,000-word essay on their goals and aspirations, their biggest challenge and how they met it, and anything else they want the selection committee to know about them; and 2) a 250-word essay on any unusual family or personal circumstances have affected their achievement in school, work, or participation in school and community activities, including how the bleeding disorder of themselves or their family member has affected their life. Selection is based on the essays, academic performance, participation in school and community activities, work or volunteer experience, personal or family circumstances, recommendations, and financial need.
Financial data The stipend is $1,000.
Duration 1 year.
Additional data This program was established in 2009.
Number awarded 1 each year.
Deadline April of each year.

[421]
BONNIE STRANGIO EDUCATION SCHOLARSHIP

Boomer Esiason Foundation
c/o Jerry Cahill
483 Tenth Avenue, Suite 300
New York, NY 10018
(646) 292-7930   Fax: (646) 292-7945
E-mail: jcahillbef@aol.com
Web: www.cfscholarships.com

Summary To provide financial assistance to undergraduate and graduate students who have cystic fibrosis (CF).

Eligibility This program is open to CF patients who are working on an undergraduate or graduate degree. Applicants must be able to demonstrate exemplary service and commitment to the prevention and cure of CF. Along with their application, they must submit a letter from their doctor confirming the diagnosis of CF and a list of daily medications, information on financial need, a detailed breakdown of tuition costs from their academic institution, transcripts, and a 2-page essay on 1) their post-graduation goals and 2) the importance of compliance with CF therapies and what they practice on a daily basis to stay healthy. Selection is based on academic ability, character, leadership potential, service to the community, and financial need. Finalists are interviewed by telephone.

Financial data The stipend is $2,500. Funds are paid directly to the academic institution to assist in covering the cost of tuition and fees.

Duration 1 year; nonrenewable.

Number awarded 1 each year.

Deadline June of each year.

[422]
BOOMER ESIASON FOUNDATION SCHOLARSHIP PROGRAM

Boomer Esiason Foundation
c/o Jerry Cahill
483 Tenth Avenue, Suite 300
New York, NY 10018
(646) 292-7930   Fax: (646) 292-7945
E-mail: jcahillbef@aol.com
Web: www.cfscholarships.com

Summary To provide financial assistance to undergraduate and graduate students who have cystic fibrosis (CF).

Eligibility This program is open to CF patients who are working on an undergraduate or graduate degree. Applicants must submit a letter from their doctor confirming the diagnosis of CF and a list of daily medications, information on financial need, a detailed breakdown of tuition costs from their academic institution, transcripts, and a 2-page essay on 1) their post-graduation goals and 2) the importance of compliance with CF therapies and what they practice on a daily basis to stay healthy. Selection is based on academic ability, character, leadership potential, service to the community, and financial need. Finalists are interviewed by telephone.

Financial data Stipends range from $500 to $2,000. Funds are paid directly to the academic institution to assist in covering the cost of tuition and fees.

Duration 1 year; nonrenewable.

Additional data This program includes 1) the Sacks for CF Scholarships, funded by Novartis, which donates $1,000 for scholarships every time an NFL quarterback is sacked during the regular season; and 2) the Bonnie Strangio Education Scholarship. Recipients must be willing to participate in the sponsor's CF Ambassador Program by speaking once a year at a designated CF event to help educate the general public about CF.

Number awarded 10 to 15 each year.

Deadline March, June, September, or December of each year.

[423]
BRADLEY KRUEGER SCHOLARSHIP

Hemophilia Foundation of Illinois
Attn: Program Director
332 South Michigan Avenue, Suite 1135
Chicago, IL 60604
(312) 427-1495   E-mail: ekraemer@hfi-il.org
Web: www.hemophiliaillinois.org

Summary To provide financial assistance for attendance at a college in any state to residents of Illinois who have a bleeding disorder and their families.

Eligibility This program is open to residents of Illinois who have a bleeding disorder and their parents, siblings, and children; people who are carriers of the disease are also eligible. Applicants must be attending or planning to attend a postsecondary institution, including a trade school, in any state. Along with their application, they must submit essays on their goals for furthering their education, the steps they have taken to meet those goals, how this scholarship will help them achieve those goals, what it means to them to live with hemophilia, and what they consider their responsibility to the bleeding disorders community. Financial need is not considered in the selection process.

Financial data Stipends range up to $5,000. Funds are paid directly to the educational institution to be used for payment of tuition, room and board, books, and supplies (including computer equipment).

Duration 1 year.

Number awarded 1 or more each year.

Deadline June of each year.

[424]
CALIFORNIA YOUNG CANCER SURVIVOR SCHOLARSHIP PROGRAM

American Cancer Society-California Division
1710 Webster Street
Oakland, CA 94612
(510) 832-7012   Toll Free: (800) 877-1710, ext. 146
Fax: (510) 763-8826
E-mail: david.saunders@cancer.org
Web: www.oanoor.org

Summary To provide financial assistance for college to residents of California who have been diagnosed as having cancer.

Eligibility This program is open to residents of California who were diagnosed with cancer before the age of 18. Applicants must be currently younger than 25 years of age and attending or planning to attend an accredited 2-year or 4-year institution of higher education in California. Along with their application, they must submit 3 essays (250 words each) on their goals, life experiences, and community service. Selection is based on financial need; determination, motivation, and educational goals; GPA (2.5 or higher); and community service.

Financial data Stipends range up to $7,500 per year, depending on the need of the recipient. Funds are paid directly to the recipient's institution.

Duration 1 year.

Additional data Recipients are expected to serve a minimum of 25 volunteer hours with the American Cancer Society.

Number awarded Varies each year; recently, 45 of these scholarships were awarded.

Deadline April of each year.

[425]
CALVIN DAWSON MEMORIAL SCHOLARSHIP

Hemophilia Foundation of Greater Florida
1350 North Orange Avenue, Suite 227
Winter Park, FL 32789
Toll Free: (800) 293-6527
E-mail: info@hemophiliaflorida.org
Web: www.hemophiliaflorida.org

Summary To provide financial assistance to residents of Florida who have a bleeding disorder and are interested in attending college in any state.

Eligibility This program is open to residents of Florida who have hemophilia or other related hereditary bleeding disorder. Applicants may be graduating high school seniors or students already enrolled at a college, technical or trade school, or other certification program in any state. Along with their application, they must submit a brief essay on their occupational objectives and goals in life. Selection is based on that essay, merit, community service, and financial need.

Financial data Stipends range up to $1,000. Funds are paid directly to the recipient's college.

Duration 1 year.

Number awarded Varies each year; recently, 4 of these scholarships were awarded.

Deadline April of each year.

[426]
CANCER SURVIVORS' SCHOLARSHIP

Cancer Survivors' Fund
P.O. Box 792
Missouri City, TX 77459
(281) 437-7142   Fax: (281) 437-9568
E-mail: csf@cancersurvivorsfund.org
Web: www.cancersurvivorsfund.org

Summary To provide financial assistance for college to students who have had cancer.

Eligibility This program is open to students who are enrolled in or accepted for enrollment in an accredited undergraduate school. Applicants must be a cancer survivor or currently diagnosed with cancer; they do not have to be receiving treatment to qualify. They must submit an essay, from 500 to 1,200 words in length, on how their experience with cancer has impacted their life values and career goals. Selection is based on the applicant's personal hardship and financial need.

Financial data A stipend is awarded (amount not specified).

Duration 1 year.

Additional data Recipients must agree to do volunteer work to use their cancer experience to help other young cancer patients and survivors cope with a life-threatening or life-altering event.

Number awarded Varies each year; recently, 41 of these scholarships were awarded.

Deadline March of each year for fall semester; October of each year for spring semester.

[427]
CAROLYN'S COMPASSIONATE CHILDREN SCHOLARSHIPS

Carolyn's Compassionate Children
7163 Ayrshire Lane
Boca Raton, FL 33496
Fax: (561) 487-6162
E-mail: cccscholarship@gmail.com
Web: www.change.org/ccc

Summary To provide financial assistance for college or graduate school to childhood cancer survivors.

Eligibility This program is open to childhood cancer survivors who are attending or planning to attend college or graduate school full time. Selection is based on personal character, community service, and financial need. U.S. citizenship or permanent resident status is required.

Financial data The stipend is $1,000.

Duration 1 year.

Additional data Carolyn Rubenstein founded Carolyn's Compassionate Children in 1999 when she was 13 years of age. The organization began offering scholarships in 2003.

Number awarded Varies each year; recently, 18 of these scholarships were awarded.

Deadline May of each year.

[428]
CHILDHOOD CANCER SURVIVOR COLLEGE SCHOLARSHIP PROGRAM

American Cancer Society-Great West Division
Attn: Randi Cress
920 North Washington, Suite 200
Spokane, WA 99201
(509) 455-3440   Fax: (509) 455-3990
Web: www.cancer.org

Summary To provide financial assistance for college to high school seniors in selected western states who have been diagnosed as having cancer.

Eligibility This program is open to U.S. citizens younger than 25 years of age who are residents of Alaska, Arizona, Colorado, Idaho, Montana, North Dakota, New Mexico, Nevada, Oregon, Utah, Washington, or Wyoming. Applicants must have had a diagnosis of cancer before the age of 21 and have been accepted as a continuing or entering full-time student at an accredited community college, university, college, or vocational/technical school in any state. They must have a GPA of 2.5 or higher. Along with their application, they must submit a 500-word essay on how this scholarship will help further their academic career, including their educational, occupational, and personal goals. Selection is based on that essay (20%), financial need (50%), community service and involvement with the American Cancer Society (20%), and letters of recommendation (10%).

Financial data The stipend is $2,500 per year.

Duration 1 year; may be renewed up to 3 additional years, provided the recipient remains enrolled full time with a GPA of 2.5 or higher and volunteers with the American Cancer Society for at least 25 hours per calendar year.

Number awarded Varies each year.

Deadline February of each year.

[429]
COAGULIFE EDUCATION SCHOLARSHIPS

CoaguLife
Attn: Scholarship Selection Committee
8690 Eagle Creek Parkway
Savage, MN 55378
(952) 886-9200   Toll Free: (866) 858-9200, ext. 102
Fax: (952) 487-2829   E-mail: info@coagulife.com
Web: www.coagulife.com

Summary To provide financial assistance for college to students who have an inherited bleeding disorder.

Eligibility This program is open to college-bound graduating high school seniors or students already enrolled full time at an accredited college, university, or trade school. Applicants must have hemophilia, von Willebrand Disease, or a similar inherited bleeding disorder. Along with their application, they must submit an essay on 1 of 3 assigned topics. Selection is based on the essay, GPA, difficulty of course work, letters of recommendation, community service, and a statement regarding personal, academic, and career goals.

Financial data The maximum stipend is $5,000 per year. Awards may not exceed the total yearly cost of tuition, books, fees, room, and board. Funds are paid directly to the institution.

Duration 1 year; may be renewed as long as the recipient maintains a GPA of 3.0 or higher.

Additional data Recipients must perform at least 10 hours of community service per year for a hemophilia advocacy organization such as the National Hemophilia Foundation (NHF), the Homophilia Federation of America (HFA), local chapters of NHF or HFA, or hemophilia summer camp programs.

Number awarded 1 or more each year.

Deadline May of each year.

[430]
COMPREHENSIVE BLEEDING DISORDERS CENTER SCHOLARSHIP FUND

Community Foundation of Central Illinois
331 Fulton Street, Suite 310
Peoria, IL 61602
(309) 674-8730   Fax: (309) 674-8754
E-mail: kristan@communityfoundationci.org
Web: www.communityfoundationci.org

Summary To provide financial assistance to students with a bleeding disorder who live in the service area of the Comprehensive Bleeding Disorders Center (CBDC) in Illinois and are interested in attending college in any state.

Eligibility This program is open to residents of the CBDC service area (all of Illinois outside of Chicago) who are diagnosed with a congenital or acquired chronic bleeding disorder and have attended any hemophilia treatment center's comprehensive clinic during the past year. Applicants must be enrolled or planning to enroll at an accredited vocational/trade school, junior college, or 4-year college or university in any state. They must have a GPA of 2.0 or higher. Selection is based on their motivation to accomplish their educational and career goals, potential for scholarship, citizenship, and leadership; financial need is considered only if other factors are equal.

Financial data The stipend is $1,500. Funds are disbursed directly to the recipient's school to be used to cover the cost of tuition, books, and required fees.

Duration 1 year.

Additional data This program is supported by the CBDC, 4727 North Sheridan Road, Peoria, IL 61614, (309) 688-1345, ext. 104, E-mail: cbdc@hemophilia-ctr-peoria.com.

Number awarded 1 or more each year.

Deadline March of each year.

[431]
CRISTIN ANN BAMBINO MEMORIAL SCHOLARSHIP

New York Schools Insurance Reciprocal
Attn: Executive Director
333 Earle Ovington Boulevard, Suite 505
Uniondale, NY 11553-3624
(516) 227-3355   Toll Free: (800) 476-9747
Fax: (516) 227-2352
Web: nysir.org

Summary To provide financial assistance to special education seniors graduating from high schools that subscribe to the New York Schools Insurance Reciprocal (NYSIR) who plan to attend college in any state.

Eligibility This program is open to seniors graduating from NYSIR-subscriber high schools who have been enrolled in special education and have worked through special challenges to complete high school. Applicants must be planning to attend a college or university in any state. Along with their application, they must submit a 650-word essay on their accomplishments, how they overcame their challenges, how they can serve as a role model for other young people with special challenges, and what they plan to study in college. Financial need is not considered in the selection process.

Financial data The stipend is $3,000.

Duration 1 year.

Number awarded 1 each year.

Deadline March of each year.

[432]
CULPEPPER EXUM SCHOLARSHIP FOR PEOPLE WITH KIDNEY DISEASE

National Kidney Foundation Serving Kansas and
 Western Missouri
Attn: Scholarship Program
6405 Metcalf Avenue, Suite 204
Overland Park, KS 66202
(913) 262-1551   Toll Free: (800) 444-8113
Fax: (913) 722-4841   E-mail: nkfkswmo@kidney.org
Web: www.kidney.org/site/index.cfm?ch=305

Summary To provide financial assistance to residents of Kansas and western Missouri who are dialysis or transplant patients and interested in attending college in any state.

Eligibility This program is open to residents of Kansas and western Missouri who are attending or planning to attend a college or university in any state. Applicants must be dialysis or transplant patients. Along with their application, they must submit brief essays on their educational plans and goals and why the sponsor should choose them for this scholarship. Financial need is considered in the selection process.

Financial data The stipend is $1,000. Funds are paid directly to the recipient's institution.

Duration 1 year.

Number awarded 2 each year: 1 to a resident of Kansas and 1 to a resident of western Missouri.

Deadline May of each year.

[433]
CVS/ALL KIDS CAN SCHOLARS PROGRAM

Autism Society of America
Attn: Awards and Scholarships
4340 East-West Highway, Suite 350
Bethesda, MD 20814-4579
(301) 657-0881   Toll Free: (800) 3-AUTISM
Fax: (301) 657-0869   E-mail: info@autism-society.org
Web: www.autism-society.org

Summary To provide financial assistance for college to students with autism.

Eligibility This program is open to persons with autism who have successfully met all the requirements for admission to a college, university, trade school, or other postsecondary institution. Applicants must submit a personal statement of less than 500 words describing their qualifications and proposed plan of study, secondary school

transcripts, documentation of status as an individual with autism, and 2 letters of recommendation.

Financial data The stipend is $1,000.

Duration 1 year.

Additional data This program was established in 2006 with support from CVS/Pharmacy Charitable Trust.

Number awarded 5 each year.

Deadline March of each year.

[434]
CYSTIC FIBROSIS SCHOLARSHIPS

Cystic Fibrosis Scholarship Foundation
1555 Sherman Avenue, Suite 116
Evanston, IL 60201
(847) 328-0127   Fax: (847) 328-0127
E-mail: MKBCFSF@aol.com
Web: www.cfscholarship.org

Summary To provide financial assistance to undergraduate students who have cystic fibrosis (CF).

Eligibility This program is open to students enrolled or planning to enroll in college (either a 2-year or a 4-year program) or vocational school. Applicants must have CF. Along with their application, they must submit a 500-word essay about their favorite book from the 20th century and why. Selection is based on academic achievement, leadership, and financial need.

Financial data The stipend is $1,000 per year. Funds are sent directly to the student's institution to be used for tuition, books, room, and board.

Duration 1 year; recipients may reapply.

Additional data These scholarships were first awarded for 2002.

Number awarded Varies each year; recently, 63 of these scholarships were awarded.

Deadline March of each year.

[435]
DAKOTA PEQUENO MEMORIAL SCHOLARSHIP

Epilepsy Foundation of Michigan
Attn: Development Director
20300 Civic Center Drive, Suite 250
Southfield, MI 48076-4154
(248) 351-7979   Toll Free: (800) 377-6226
Fax: (248) 351-2101
E-mail: bromines@epilepsymichigan.org
Web: www.epilepsymichigan.org/template.php?pid=223

Summary To provide financial assistance to high school seniors and graduate in Michigan who have epilepsy and are planning to attend college in any state.

Eligibility This program is open to high school seniors and graduates between 17 and 21 years of age in Michigan who have a diagnosis of epilepsy or a seizure disorder. Applicants must be planning to enroll at a postsecondary academic or vocational program in any state. Along with their application, they must submit a brief essay about their experience dealing with epilepsy. Selection is based on that essay, how the applicant has faced challenges due to epilepsy, career goals, recommendations, and community involvement; financial need is not considered.

Financial data The stipend is $1,000.

Duration 1 year.

Additional data This scholarship was first awarded in 2009.

Number awarded 1 each year.

Deadline March of each year.

[436]
DANA WALTERS SCHOLARSHIPS

Dana Walters Scholarship Foundation
P.O. Box 723243
Atlanta, GA 31139
(770) 436-0190   E-mail: sonickaren@aol.com
Web: www.dwscholarship.com

Summary To provide financial assistance for college to residents of Georgia who have cystic fibrosis (CF) and members of their immediate families.

Eligibility This program is open to residents of Georgia who have CF or are a member of a family (including parents) of a person who has CF. Applicants must be graduating high school seniors or already have a high school diploma. They must have a combined SAT score of at least 900 or an ACT score of at least 21 and either a GPA of 2.7 or higher or a rank in the top 30% of their class. Financial need is not considered in the selection process.

Financial data The stipend is $1,000. Funds are paid directly to the recipient's college.

Duration 1 year; may be renewed.

Number awarded 1 or more each year.

Deadline March of each year.

[437]
DAVE MADEIROS CONTINUED EDUCATION SCHOLARSHIPS

Factor Foundation of America
Attn: Scholarship Committee
Peninsula Corporate Center
950 Peninsula Corporate Center, Suite 3017
Boca Raton, FL 33487
(561) 981-8814   Toll Free: (866) 843-3362
Fax: (561) 981-8622
E-mail: contactFFOA@factorfoundation.org
Web: www.factorfoundation.org/programs.htm

Summary To provide financial assistance for college to people with a bleeding disorder and their families.

Eligibility This program is open to people with a bleeding disorder and their siblings, parents, and children. Applicants must be attending or planning to attend an accredited 2- or 4-year college or university or technical school. They must be recommended by a local hemophilia chapter, physician, and/or hemophilia treatment center. Along with their application, they must submit a 500-word letter describing their goals and aspirations and how the bleeding disorders community has played a part in their life. Financial need is also considered in the selection process.

Financial data The stipend is $2,000 per year.

Duration 1 year; may be renewed if the recipient remains in good academic standing.

Additional data This program began in 2006.

Number awarded Varies each year; recently, 12 of these scholarships were awarded.

Deadline April of each year.

[438]
DAVE MADEIROS CREATIVE ARTS SCHOLARSHIP

Factor Foundation of America
Attn: Scholarship Committee
Peninsula Corporate Center
950 Peninsula Corporate Center, Suite 3017
Boca Raton, FL 33487
(561) 981-8814   Toll Free: (866) 843-3362
Fax: (561) 981-8622
E-mail: info@factorfoundation.org
Web: www.factorfoundation.org/programs.htm

Summary To provide financial assistance for artistic or sports activities to young people with a bleeding disorder and their siblings.

Eligibility This program is open to children between 5 and 17 years of age who have a bleeding disorder or are the sibling of such a person. Applicants must be interested in participating in such activities as taking musical lessons, joining a sports team, taking drawing lessons, taking a drama class, or taking a private sports class. They must be recommended by a local hemophilia chapter, physician, and/or hemophilia treatment center. Parents must submit an application that includes a 500-word essay on their desire for their child to take part in a creative art and how that experience will benefit him or her, 2 letters of reference, and documentation of financial need.

Financial data The stipend is $1,000.

Duration 1 year; recipients may reapply.

Additional data This program began in 2006.

Number awarded At least 1 each year.

Deadline April of each year.

[439]
DICK GRIFFITHS MEMORIAL SCHOLARSHIP

California Association for Postsecondary Education
  and Disability
Attn: Executive Assistant
71423 Biskra Road
Rancho Mirage, CA 92270
(760) 346-8206   Fax: (760) 340-5275
TDD: (760) 341-4084   E-mail: caped2000@aol.com
Web: www.caped.net/scholarships.html

Summary To provide financial assistance to undergraduate and graduate students in California who have a learning disability, especially involving mathematics.

Eligibility This program is open to students at public and private colleges and universities in California who have a learning disability and are especially challenged in mathematics. Undergraduates must have completed at least 6 semester credits and have a GPA of 2.5 or higher. Graduate students must have completed at least 3 semester units and have a GPA of 3.0 or higher. Along with their application, they must submit a 1-page personal letter that demonstrates their writing skills, progress towards meeting their educational and vocational goals, management of their disability, and involvement in community activities. They must also submit a letter of recommendation from a faculty member, verification of disability, official transcripts, proof of current enrollment, an essay on strategies they use to overcome their mathematics challenges, and documentation of financial need.

Financial data The stipend is $1,000.

Duration 1 year.

Number awarded 1 each year.

Deadline September of each year.

[440]
DOTTIE LOURIE MEMORIAL SCHOLARSHIP

National Kidney Foundation Serving New England
Attn: Academic Awards Committee
85 Astor Avenue, Suite 2
Norwood, MA 02062-5040
(781) 278-0222   Toll Free: (800) 542-4001
Fax: (781) 278-0333   E-mail: nkfmarinhvt@kidney.org
Web: www.kidney.org/site/index.cfm?ch=105

Summary To provide financial assistance to residents of New England who have kidney disease, are related to a person with kidney disease, or have received a kidney transplant and are interested in attending college in any state.

Eligibility This program is open to residents of Massachusetts, Rhode Island, New Hampshire, and Vermont who are enrolled or planning to enroll at a college or university in any state. Applicants must be a patient with Chronic Kidney Disease (CKD), have an immediate family member (parent, sibling) with CKD, or have had a life-saving organ transplant. Along with their application, they must submit a 2-page essay on how kidney disease or organ transplantation has impacted their life. Selection is based on academic achievement and financial need.

Financial data The stipend is $1,000. Funds are paid directly to the student.

Duration 1 year.

Number awarded 1 each year.

Deadline March of each year.

[441]
DOUG HITESHEW MEMORIAL SCHOLARSHIPS

Hemophilia Foundation of Maryland
Attn: Executive Director
13 Class Court, Suite 200
Parkville, MD 21234
(410) 661-2307   Toll Free: (800) 964-3131
Fax: (410) 661-2308   E-mail: miller8043@comcast.net
Web: www.hfmonline.org

Summary To provide financial assistance to students who have hemophilia or von Willebrand Disease and are residents of Maryland or attending college in the state.

Eligibility This program is open to students who have hemophilia or von Willebrand Disease and are entering or attending a junior college, 4-year college, university, or vocational school. Applicants must be Maryland residents or a student who has attended a Maryland school for at least 1 year. Along with their application, they must submit 1-page essays on 1) their career goals, and 2) their previous participation with the Hemophilia Foundation of Maryland and how they plan to contribute to the chapter in the future. Selection is based on those essays, academic goals, transcripts of current academic work, volunteer work, and letters of recommendation.

Financial data The stipend is $1,500.

Duration 1 year.

Additional data This program was established in 2010.

Number awarded 3 each year.

Deadline April of each year.

[442]
DR. JOHN Z. JACOBY, III SCHOLARSHIP

Cystic Fibrosis Association of Greater New York
38 West 21st Street, Room 1106
New York, NY 10010-6906

Summary To provide financial assistance to young adults with cystic fibrosis (CF) who wish to obtain additional education.

Eligibility This program is open to young adults who have CF. Applicants must be interested in obtaining additional postsecondary education leading to a career or career advancement. They must be able to demonstrate financial need.

Financial data Stipends range from $1,000 to $3,000, depending on the need of the recipient.

Duration 1 year.

Additional data This program was established in 1986 and given its current name in 1999.

Number awarded 1 or more each year.

Deadline March of each year.

[443]
DUGDALE/VAN EYS SCHOLARSHIP AWARD

Tennessee Hemophilia and Bleeding Disorders
  Foundation
Attn: Scholarship Committee
203 Jefferson Street
Smyrna, TN 37167
(615) 220-4868   Toll Free: (888) 703-3269
Fax: (615) 220-4889   E-mail: mail@thbdf.org
Web: www.thbdf.org/programs.html

Summary To provide financial assistance for college to students with hemophilia or their family members in Tennessee.

Eligibility This program is open to college-bound high school seniors, college students, and technical school students who have a bleeding disorder and are receiving treatment in Tennessee. Their children, spouses, and guardians are also eligible. Applicants must have a GPA of 2.5 or higher and be enrolled or planning to enroll full time. They must submit a 500-word essay on their life goals, a resume, 3 letters of recommendation, proof of enrollment, and documentation of community service of at least 10 hours per semester. Financial need is considered in the selection process.

Financial data   Stipends range from $500 to $2,000.

Duration   1 year; recipients may reapply.

Number awarded   6 each year: 1 at $2,000, 1 at $1,500, 1 at $1,000, and 3 at $500.

Deadline   April of each year.

[444]
EDUCATION ADVANTAGE COMMUNITY COLLEGE OR TECHNICAL SCHOLARSHIP

Baxter Healthcare Corporation
Attn: Education Advantage Program
One Baxter Parkway
Deerfield, IL 60015-4625
(847) 948-2000   Toll Free: (800) 423-2090
Fax: (800) 568-5020
E-mail: baxter@scholarshipamerica.org
Web: www.myeducationadvantage.com

Summary   To provide financial assistance to people who have hemophilia A and are interested in working on an associate degree or technical certificate.

Eligibility   This program is open to people who have hemophilia A or hemophilia with inhibitors and are enrolled or planning to enroll at a community college, junior college, trade or vocational school, or other eligible program. Applicants must submit a personal statement that focuses on their unique experiences that make them stand out from other students (e.g., their experiences of living with hemophilia, how it impacts their education or career goals, noteworthy volunteer activities within the hemophilia community). Both merit-based and need-based scholarships are available. U.S. citizenship or permanent resident status is required.

Financial data   The stipend is $2,500 per year.

Duration   1 year; may be renewed 1 additional year, provided the recipient remains enrolled full time, maintains a GPA of 2.0 or higher, provides evidence of participation in annual comprehensive clinic and routine dental care, performs 20 hours of community service, and submits a 250-word essay on their academic progress, their career goals and developments, and the value of funding assistance.

Additional data   This program is administered by Scholarship Management Services, a division of Scholarship America, One Scholarship Way, P.O. Box 297, St. Peter, MN 56082, (877) 544-3018.

Number awarded   1 or more each year.

Deadline   April of each year.

[445]
EDUCATION ADVANTAGE UNIVERSITY SCHOLARSHIP

Baxter Healthcare Corporation
Attn: Education Advantage Program
One Baxter Parkway
Deerfield, IL 60015-4625
(847) 948-2000   Toll Free: (800) 423-2090
Fax: (800) 568-5020
E-mail: baxter@scholarshipamerica.org
Web: www.myeducationadvantage.com

Summary   To provide financial assistance to people who have hemophilia A and are interested in working on a bachelor's degree.

Eligibility   This program is open to people who have hemophilia A or hemophilia with inhibitors and are enrolled or planning to enroll full time at a 4-year college or university. Applicants must submit a personal statement that focuses on their unique experiences that make them stand out from other students (e.g., their experiences of living with hemophilia, how it impacts their education or career goals, noteworthy volunteer activities within the hemophilia community). Both merit-based and need-based scholarships are available. U.S. citizenship or permanent resident status is required.

Financial data   The stipend is $15,000 per year.

Duration   1 year; may be renewed up to 3 additional years, provided the recipient remains enrolled full time, maintains a GPA of 2.0 or higher, provides evidence of participation in annual comprehensive clinic and routine dental care, performs 20 hours of community service, and submits a 250-word essay on their academic progress, their career goals and developments, and the value of funding assistance.

Additional data   This program is administered by Scholarship Management Services, a division of Scholarship America, One Scholarship Way, P.O. Box 297, St. Peter, MN 56082, (877) 544-3018.

Number awarded   1 or more each year.

Deadline   April of each year.

[446]
EDUCATION IS POWER SCHOLARSHIPS

MedProRx, Inc.
Attn: Scholarship Coordinator
140 Northway Court
Raleigh, NC 27615-4916
Toll Free: (888) KATHY-MD
E-mail: educationispower@medprorx.com
Web: www.medprorx.com/scholarship.html

Summary   To provide financial assistance for college to people with a bleeding disorder.

Eligibility   This program is open to residents of the United States who are living with hemophilia or von Willebrand Disease. Applicants must be entering or attending a community college, junior college, 4-year college, university, or vocational school. They must be able to demonstrate a record of community involvement and/or volunteer work. Along with their application, they must submit a 250-

word essay on their dreams and aspirations, what they are most passionate about, how living with a bleeding disorder has affected their life, and what they would change if they had the power to change something in the world.

Financial data Stipends range from $500 to $2,500.

Duration 1 year.

Additional data This program began in 2006.

Number awarded Varies each year; recently 79 of these scholarships were awarded.

Deadline April of each year.

[447]
EJE MEMORIAL SCHOLARSHIP

Working Against Cancer
246 Claremont Avenue
Long Beach, CA 90803
E-mail: contactus@workingagainstcancer.org
Web: www.workingagainstcancer.org

Summary To provide financial assistance to residents of California who have had cancer and are interested in attending college in any state.

Eligibility This program is open to residents of California enrolled in an academic or vocational educational program in any state. Applicants must be a cancer survivor or recently diagnosed with cancer, but they do not need to be currently receiving treatment. They must be younger than 30 years of age. Along with their application, they must submit a 500-word personal statement on how cancer has affected their life and their educational, personal, and occupational goals for the future. Financial need is also considered in the selection process.

Financial data The stipend is $1,000.

Duration 1 year.

Number awarded 1 each year.

Deadline August of each year.

[448]
ELAM BAER AND JANIS CLAY EDUCATIONAL SCHOLARSHIP

Epilepsy Foundation of Minnesota
Attn: Scholarships
1600 University Avenue West, Suite 300
St. Paul, MN 55104
(651) 287-2312   Toll Free: (800) 779-0777, ext. 2312
Fax: (651) 287-2325   E-mail: skolari@efmn.org
Web: www.epilepsyfoundationmn.org/scholarships.aspx

Summary To provide financial assistance to residents of Minnesota and eastern North Dakota who have epilepsy and are interested in attending college in any state.

Eligibility This program is open to graduating high school seniors and high school graduates who live in Minnesota or eastern North Dakota. Applicants must have a diagnosis of epilepsy or other seizure disorder. They must have been accepted at a postsecondary academic or vocational program. Along with their application, they must submit a 250-word essay on something of direct personal importance to them as a person with epilepsy. Selection is based on how the applicant has faced challenges due to epilepsy, career goals, achievements, community involve-

ment, and letters of recommendation; financial need is not considered.

Financial data The stipend is $1,000.

Duration 1 year.

Additional data These scholarships were first awarded in 2006.

Number awarded 10 each year.

Deadline March of each year.

[449]
ELIZABETH NASH FOUNDATION SCHOLARSHIP PROGRAM

Elizabeth Nash Foundation
P.O. Box 1260
Los Gatos, CA 95031-1260
E-mail: scholarships@elizabethnashfoundation.org
Web: www.elizabethnashfoundation.org

Summary To provide financial assistance for college or graduate school to individuals with cystic fibrosis (CF).

Eligibility This program is open to undergraduate and graduate students who have CF. Applicants must be able to demonstrate clear academic goals and a commitment to participate in activities outside the classroom. U.S. citizenship is required. Selection is based on academic record, character, demonstrated leadership, service to CF-related causes and the broader community, and financial need.

Financial data Stipends range from $1,000 to $2,500. Funds are paid directly to the academic institution to be applied to tuition and fees.

Duration 1 year; recipients may reapply.

Additional data This program was established in 2005. Recipients must agree to support the program by speaking at a local event or writing an article for publication by the foundation.

Number awarded Varies each year; recently, 12 of these scholarships were awarded.

Deadline April of each year.

[450]
EPILEPSY FOUNDATION OF NEW JERSEY SCHOLARSHIP PROGRAM

Epilepsy Foundation of New Jersey
1 AAA Drive, Suite 203
Trenton, NJ 08691
(609) 392-4900   Toll Free: (800) EFNJ-TIE
Fax: (609) 392-5621   E-mail: efnj@efnj.com
Web: www.efnj.com/content/info/scholarship.html

Summary To provide financial assistance to high school seniors in New Jersey who have epilepsy and are planning to attend college in any state.

Eligibility This program is open to seniors graduating from high schools in New Jersey who have epilepsy. Applicants must be planning to attend a college or university in any state. Along with their application, they must submit a brief personal statement explaining their academic and career goals. Selection is based on academic achievement, participation in activities, and financial need.

Financial data The stipend is $1,000 per year. Funds are paid directly to the recipient.
Duration 1 year.
Number awarded At least 2 each year.
Deadline May of each year.

[451]
ERIC C. MARDER SCHOLARSHIP PROGRAM

Immune Deficiency Foundation
Attn: Scholarship/Medical Programs
40 West Chesapeake Avenue, Suite 308
Towson, MD 21204-4803
(410) 321-6647   Toll Free: (800) 296-4433
Fax: (410) 321-9165   E-mail: idf@primaryimmune.org
Web: www.primaryimmune.org

Summary To provide financial assistance to undergraduates with a primary immune deficiency disease.
Eligibility This program is open to undergraduates entering or attending college or technical training school who have a primary immune deficiency disease. Applicants must submit an autobiographical essay, 2 letters of recommendation, a family financial statement, and a letter of verification from their immunologist. Financial need is the main factor considered in selecting the recipients and the size of the award.
Financial data Stipends range from $750 to $2,000, depending on the recipient's financial need.
Duration 1 year; may be renewed.
Additional data This program, established in 1986, is administered by the Immune Deficiency Foundation (IDF) with funding from CSL Behring, Baxter Healthcare Corporation, Talecris Biotherapeutics, Grifols, and Octapharma.
Number awarded Varies each year.
Deadline Deadline not specified.

[452]
ERIC DELSON MEMORIAL SCHOLARSHIP

CVS Caremark
Attn: Research Team
P.O. Box 832407
Richardson, TX 75083
Toll Free: (866) 792-2731
Web: www.caremark.com

Summary To provide financial assistance for high school, college, or graduate school to students with a bleeding disorder.
Eligibility This program is open to students diagnosed with a bleeding disorder who are 1) high school seniors, high school graduates or equivalent (GED), college students, or graduate students currently enrolled or planning to enroll full time at an accredited 2-year or 4-year college, university, or vocational/technical school; or 2) students entering grades 7-12 at a private secondary school in the United States. Selection is based on academic record, demonstrated leadership and participation in school and community activities, work experience, a statement of educational and career goals, unusual personal or family circumstances, and an outside appraisal.

Financial data The stipend is $2,500 for college students or $1,500 for high school students. Funds are paid in 2 equal installments directly to the recipient.
Duration 1 year; may be renewed for up to 3 additional years, provided the recipient maintains a GPA of 2.5 or higher for the freshman year and 3.0 or higher for subsequent years.
Additional data This program is administered by Scholarship Management Services, a division of Scholarship America, One Scholarship Way, P.O. Box 297, St. Peter, MN 56082, (507) 931-1682.
Number awarded 4 each year: 3 for college students and 1 for a high school student.
Deadline June of each year.

[453]
ERIC DOSTIE MEMORIAL COLLEGE SCHOLARSHIP

NuFACTOR Specialty Pharmacy
Attn: Scholarship Administrator
41093 Country Center Drive, Suite B
Temecula, CA 92591
(951) 296-2516   Toll Free: (800) 323-6832, ext. 1300
Fax: (877) 432-6258   E-mail: info@kelleycom.com
Web: www.nufactor.com/pages/eric_dostie.html

Summary To provide financial assistance for college to students with hemophilia or members of their families.
Eligibility This program is open to 1) students with hemophilia or a related bleeding disorder or 2) members of their families. Applicants must be U.S. citizens and enrolled or planning to enroll full time at an accredited 2- or 4-year college program. They must have a GPA of 2.5 or higher. Along with their application, they must submit a 400-word essay that explains what motivates them to pursue a higher education, what subjects they plan to study, what major forces or obstacles in their life has led to that path of study, what they plan to do with their education after school, and how that may be of benefit to humankind. Financial need is also considered in the selection process.
Financial data The stipend is $1,000.
Duration 1 year.
Number awarded 10 each year.
Deadline February of each year.

[454]
EXERCISE FOR LIFE SCHOLARSHIPS

Boomer Esiason Foundation
c/o Jerry Cahill
483 Tenth Avenue, Suite 300
New York, NY 10018
(646) 292-7930   Fax: (646) 292-7945
E-mail: jcahillbef@aol.com
Web: www.cfscholarships.com

Summary To provide financial assistance for college to high school seniors who have been involved in athletics and who have cystic fibrosis (CF).
Eligibility This program is open to CF patients who are college-bound high school seniors. Applicants must have been involved in athletics. They should be jogging on a

regular basis and training for a 1.5 mile run. Along with their application, they must submit a letter from their doctor confirming the diagnosis of CF and a list of daily medications, information on financial need, a detailed breakdown of tuition costs from their academic institution, transcripts, and a 2-page essay on 1) their post-graduation goals and 2) the importance of compliance with CF therapies and what they practice on a daily basis to stay healthy. Selection is based on academic ability, athletic ability, character, leadership potential, service to the community, financial need, and daily compliance with CF therapy. Male and female students compete separately.

Financial data   The stipend is $10,000. Funds are paid directly to the academic institution to assist in covering the cost of tuition and fees.

Duration   1 year; nonrenewable.

Number awarded   2 each year: 1 to a male and 1 to a female.

Deadline   June of each year.

[455]
FLICKER OF HOPE SCHOLARSHIPS

Flicker of Hope Foundation
Attn: Scholarship Committee
8624 Janet Lane
Vienna, VA 22180
(703) 698-1626   Fax: (703) 698-6225
E-mail: info@flickerofhope.org
Web: www.flickerofhope.org/whatwedo.htm

Summary   To provide financial assistance for college to burn survivors.

Eligibility   This program is open to high school seniors and graduates who are burn survivors and enrolled or planning to enroll in college. Applicants must submit a 500-word essay describing the circumstances of how they were burned, how that injury has affected their life, and the benefits to be derived from their planned course of study. Selection is based on severity of burn injury, academic performance, community service, and financial need.

Financial data   A stipend is awarded (amount not specified). Funds are paid directly to the postsecondary institution.

Duration   1 year.

Number awarded   Varies each year; recently, 14 of these scholarships were awarded.

Deadline   May of each year.

[456]
FRANK SELENY SCHOLARSHIPS

Hawaii Children's Cancer Foundation
1814 Liliha Street
Honolulu, HI 96817
(808) 528-5161   Toll Free: (866) 443-HCCF (within HI)
Fax: (808) 521-4689   E-mail: hccf@lava.net
Web: www.hccf.org

Summary   To provide financial assistance to residents of Hawaii who have had cancer and are interested in attending college in any state.

Eligibility   This program is open to residents of Hawaii who were diagnosed with cancer before 18 years of age. Applicants must have been accepted into a college or vocational training program in any state.

Financial data   The stipend is $1,000.

Duration   1 year.

Additional data   This foundation was established in 1991.

Number awarded   2 each year.

Deadline   Deadline not specified.

[457]
GEORGE AND LINDA PRICE SCHOLARSHIP

Hemophilia Association of the Capital Area
10560 Main Street, Suite PH-4
Fairfax, VA 22030-7182
(703) 352-7641   Fax: (703) 352-2145
E-mail: info@hacacares.org
Web: www.hacacares.org

Summary   To provide financial assistance to individuals with bleeding disorders and their families who are members of the Hemophilia Association of the Capital Area (HACA) and interested in attending college or graduate school in any state.

Eligibility   This program is open to residents of northern Virginia, Montgomery and Prince George's County in Maryland, and Washington, D.C. who have a bleeding disorder and their siblings and parents. Applicants must be members of HACA. They must be 1) high school seniors or graduates who have not yet attended college; 2) full-time freshmen, sophomores, or juniors at a college, university, or vocational/technical school in any state; or 3) college seniors planning to attend graduate school and students already enrolled at a graduate school in any state. Along with their application, they must submit a 500-word essay on what they have done to contribute to the bleeding disorders community and how they plan to contribute to that community in the future. Financial need is not considered in the selection process.

Financial data   The stipend is $2,500.

Duration   1 year; recipients may reapply.

Number awarded   2 each year.

Deadline   April of each year.

[458]
GEORGIA CHAPTER OF THE INTERNATIONAL TRANSPLANT NURSES SOCIETY SCHOLARSHIP

Georgia Transplant Foundation
Attn: Scholarship Program
600 Embassy Row, Suite 250
6600 Peachtree Dunwoody Road N.E.
Atlanta, GA 30328-6773
(770) 457-3796   Toll Free: (866) 428-9411
Fax: (770) 457-7916
Web: www.gatransplant.org/AcademicScholarships.aspx

Summary   To provide financial assistance to residents of Georgia who are transplant recipients or their siblings or dependents and interested in attending college in any state to work on a degree in health care.

Eligibility This program is open to residents of Georgia who are entering or continuing at an accredited institution of higher learning in any state to work on a degree in health care. Applicants must be an organ transplant recipient, a dependent of a recipient, or the sibling of a recipient (both the sibling and the recipient must be under 22 years of age). Along with their application, they must submit a 3-page personal statement in which they describe themselves as individuals, relate an event that changed their life or beliefs, describe an issue about which they have strong feelings, present their life goals as they relate to their field of study, explain any situation or financial concern that could impact their educational goals, answer why they feel they are eligible for this scholarship, and address their plans as those relate to their education, career, and long-term goals.

Financial data The stipend is $1,000.

Duration 1 year; nonrenewable.

Additional data This program is sponsored by the Georgia Chapter of the International Transplant Nurses Society.

Number awarded 1 each year.

Deadline May of each year.

[459]
GREAT LAKES HEMOPHILIA FOUNDATION EDUCATION SCHOLARSHIPS

Great Lakes Hemophilia Foundation
Attn: Program Services Committee
638 North 18th Street, Suite 108
Milwaukee, WI 53233
(414) 257-0200　　　　Toll Free: (888) 797-GLHF
Fax: (414) 257-1225　　　　E-mail: info@glhf.org
Web: www.glhf.org/scholar.htm

Summary To provide financial assistance to Wisconsin residents who have a bleeding disorder (and their families) and are interested in attending college in any state.

Eligibility This program is open to members of the bleeding disorder community in Wisconsin. Applicants must be attending or planning to attend college, vocational school, technical school, or a certification program in any state. Along with their application, they must submit an essay of 500 to 750 words on their educational and career goals, what they have done to work toward achieving those goals, how the education or training program in which they are enrolled will help them meet their goals, what they consider the most significant challenges associated with living with a bleeding disorder, the opportunities or benefits those challenges provided them, and how they plan on contributing back to the bleeding disorders community. First priority is given to people affected by bleeding disorders, then to parents of young children with bleeding disorders, and then to spouses of individuals with bleeding disorders. If sufficient funds are available, consideration may be given to siblings and other family members of individuals with a bleeding disorder. Financial need is considered in the selection process.

Financial data Stipends range from $500 to $2,000.

Duration 1 year.

Number awarded Several each year.

Deadline April of each year.

[460]
GREGORY W. GILE MEMORIAL SCHOLARSHIP

Epilepsy Foundation of Idaho
310 West Idaho Street
Boise, ID 83702
(208) 344-4340　　Toll Free: (800) 237-6676 (within ID)
Fax: (208) 344-0093　　E-mail: efid@epilepsyidaho.org
Web: www.epilepsyidaho.org

Summary To provide financial assistance for college to Idaho residents who have epilepsy.

Eligibility This program is open to residents of Idaho who have a medical diagnosis of epilepsy. Applicants must be enrolled or planning to enroll full time at a college or university in any state to work on an academic or vocational undergraduate degree or certificate; preference is given to applicants planning to attend an Idaho institution. Selection is based on career goals, recommendations, how the applicant has faced the challenges due to epilepsy, and financial need. U.S. citizenship or permanent resident status is required.

Financial data The stipend is approximately $1,500.

Duration 1 year.

Additional data This program was established in 1988.

Number awarded 1 each year.

Deadline March of each year.

[461]
HEMOPHILIA ASSOCIATION OF NEW JERSEY AWARDS

Hemophilia Association of New Jersey
Attn: Scholarship Committee
197 Route 18 South, Suite 206 North
East Brunswick, NJ 08816
(732) 249-6000　　　　Fax: (732) 249-7999
E-mail: mailbox@hanj.org
Web: www.hanj.org

Summary To provide financial assistance to New Jersey residents who have a bleeding disorder and are interested in attending college in any state.

Eligibility This program is open to New Jersey residents who have a bleeding disorder (Hemophilia A or B, von Willebrand Disease, or a similar blood coagulation disorder). Applicants must be attending or planning to attend an accredited college or university in any state. They must have at least a 2.5 GPA, have been actively involved in extracurricular activities, and be able to demonstrate financial need. Along with their application, they must submit a family financial profile, official transcripts, and a brief essay (up to 2 pages) on how they meet the eligibility criteria. Membership in the Hemophilia Association of New Jersey is required.

Financial data The stipend is $1,000 per year.

Duration 1 year; may be renewed for up to 3 additional years, provided the recipient maintains at least a 2.25 GPA and funding is available.
Number awarded 2 new awards each year.
Deadline April of each year.

[462]
HEMOPHILIA FEDERATION OF AMERICA EDUCATIONAL SCHOLARSHIPS

Hemophilia Federation of America
Attn: Scholarship Committee
210 Seventh Street, S.E., Suite 200B
Washington, DC 20003
(202) 675-6984   Toll Free: (800) 230-9797
Fax: (202) 675-6983   E-mail: info@hemophiliafed.org
Web: hemophiliafed.org

Summary To provide financial assistance for college to students who have a blood clotting disorder.
Eligibility This program is open to high school seniors and current college students who have a blood clotting disorder. Applicants must be attending or planning to attend an accredited 2-year or 4-year college, university, or trade school in the United States. Along with their application, they must submit a 1-page essay on their goals and aspirations and how the blood clotting community has played a part in their lives. Financial need is also considered in the selection process.
Financial data The stipend is $1,500 per year.
Duration 1 year; may be renewed.
Number awarded 6 each year.
Deadline April of each year.

[463]
HEMOPHILIA FOUNDATION OF MICHIGAN ACADEMIC SCHOLARSHIPS

Hemophilia Foundation of Michigan
Attn: Client Services Coordinator
1921 West Michigan Avenue
Ypsilanti, MI 48197
(734) 544-0015   Toll Free: (800) 482-3041
Fax: (734) 544-0095   E-mail: hfm@hfmich.org
Web: www.hfmich.org/programs/scholarships.html

Summary To provide financial assistance to Michigan residents with hemophilia and their families who are interested in attending college in any state.
Eligibility This program is open to high school seniors, high school graduates, and currently-enrolled college students who are Michigan residents and have hemophilia or another bleeding disorder. Family members of people with bleeding disorders and family members of people who have died from the complications of a bleeding disorder are also eligible. Applicants must submit a 300-word statement on their educational and career goals, the role that the bleeding disorder has played in influencing those goals, and how receiving the scholarship will help them to meet those goals. Selection is based on that statement, academic merit, employment status, reference letters, financial need, and the impact of bleeding disorder on educational activities.

Financial data Stipends range from $1,000 to $2,000.
Duration 1 year; recipients may reapply.
Number awarded 2 each year.
Deadline April of each year.

[464]
HEMOPHILIA FOUNDATION OF MINNESOTA/ DAKOTAS SCHOLARSHIPS

Hemophilia Foundation of Minnesota/Dakotas
Attn: Scholarship Program
750 South Plaza Drive, Suite 207
Mendota Heights, MN 55120
(651) 406-8655   Toll Free: (800) 994-HFMD
Fax: (651) 406-8656
E-mail: hemophiliafound@visi.com
Web: www.hfmd.org/Scholarships/Scholarships.html

Summary To provide financial assistance to residents of Minnesota, North Dakota, and South Dakota who have a bleeding disorder and are interested in attending college in any state.
Eligibility This program is open to residents of Minnesota, North Dakota, and South Dakota who have an inherited bleeding disorder and/or are patients at a hemophilia treatment center in those states. Applicants must be participating in programs and services of the Hemophilia Foundation of Minnesota/Dakotas. They must be attending or planning to attend a college or university in any state. Financial need is considered in the selection process.
Financial data The stipend is $1,000.
Duration 1 year.
Number awarded 10 each year.
Deadline May of each year.

[465]
HEMOPHILIA HEALTH SERVICES MEMORIAL SCHOLARSHIPS

Accredo's Hemophilia Health Services
Attn: Scholarship Committee
201 Great Circle Road
Nashville, TN 37228
(615) 850-5212   Toll Free: (800) 800-6606
Fax: (615) 261-6730
E-mail: Shayne.harris@accredo.com
Web: www.hemophiliahealth.com/Scholarships.html

Summary To provide financial assistance for college or graduate school to people who have hemophilia or other bleeding disorders.
Eligibility This program is open to individuals with hemophilia (factor VIII or IX), von Willebrand Disease (type 1, 2, 2A, 2B, 2M, 2N, or 3), factor I (fibrinogen), factor II (prothrombin), factor V (proaccelerin), factor VII (proconvertin), factor X, factor XI, factor XIII, or Glanzmann's thrombasthenia. Applicants must be 1) high school seniors; 2) college freshmen, sophomores, or juniors; or 3) college seniors planning to attend graduate school or students already enrolled in graduate school. Applicants must be enrolled or planning to enroll full time at an accredited nonprofit college, university, or vocational/technical school in the United States or Puerto Rico. Along with their appli-

cation, they must submit an essay, up to 250 words, on the following topic: "What has been your own personal challenge in living with a bleeding disorder?" U.S. citizenship is required. Selection is based on the essay, academic achievements and records, community involvement, and financial need.

Financial data The stipend is at least $1,500. Funds are issued payable to the recipient's school.

Duration 1 year; recipients may reapply.

Additional data This program, which started in 1995, includes the following named scholarships: the Cindy Beck Scholarship, the Osborne DeWitt Scholarship, the Tim Haas Scholarship, the Ricky Hobson Scholarship, the Michael Moses Scholarship, and the Jim Stineback Scholarship. It is administered by International Scholarship and Tuition Services, Inc., P.O. Box 23737, Nashville, TN 37202-3737, (615) 320-3149, Fax: (615) 320-3151, E-mail: info@applyists.net.

Number awarded Several each year.

Deadline April of each year.

[466]
HEMOPHILIA OF IOWA SCHOLARSHIPS

Hemophilia of Iowa, Inc.
c/o Shane Kelley, Scholarship Committee Chair
22930 20th Street
Fairbank, IA 50629
Toll Free: (319) 635-2839
E-mail: ssckelley@yahoo.com
Web: www.hemophiliaofiowa.com

Summary To provide financial assistance to members of Hemophilia of Iowa who are interested in attending college in any state.

Eligibility This program is open to members of the sponsoring organization who either have hemophilia (or a related bleeding disorder) or are the immediate family member (caregiver, sibling, child) of someone who has hemophilia or a related bleeding disorder. Applicants may be graduating high school seniors or students currently enrolled at an accredited college, university, or trade school in any state. Along with their application, they must submit brief statements on 1) their short- and long-range career plans; 2) their personal background related to the bleeding disorder community and any specific contributions they have made to the Hemophilia of Iowa community; and 3) their key reasons for selecting the profession they are pursuing. Selection is based on personal qualities and community service. Applicants who have a record of outstanding support for the mission of Hemophilia of Iowa are considered for supplemental funding provided by the John Heisner Scholarship and the Dude Cremer Scholarship.

Financial data The stipend is $1,500 for students with a bleeding disorder or $1,000 for family members. Applicants selected for the supplemental funding provided by the named scholarships receive an additional $1,000.

Duration 1 semester; recipients may reapply.

Number awarded Varies each year. Recently, 20 of these scholarships were awarded.

Deadline March of each year.

[467]
HIGH PLAINS DIVISION CANCER SURVIVOR SCHOLARSHIPS

American Cancer Society-High Plains Division
2433 Ridgepoint Drive, Suite B
Austin, TX 78754
(512) 919-1910   Toll Free: (877) 227-1618
Fax: (512) 919-1846
Web: www.cancer.org

Summary To provide financial assistance for college or graduate school to cancer patients and survivors in Hawaii, Kansas, Missouri, Nebraska, Oklahoma, and Texas.

Eligibility This program is open to residents of Hawaii, Kansas, Missouri, Nebraska, Oklahoma, and Texas who have had a cancer diagnosis before age 21. Applicants must be accepted at or attending an accredited university, graduate school, community college, or vocational/technical school in any state. They must be 25 years of age or younger at the time of applying and have a GPA of 2.0 or higher. Along with their application, they must submit 2 recommendations (including 1 from a physician verifying diagnosis), an acceptance letter from an academic institution, documentation of financial need, academic transcripts, and a 2-page essay describing their life experiences, future goals, community involvement, and cancer-related involvement.

Financial data The stipend is $1,000 per year. Funds are paid directly to the academic institution.

Duration 1 year; may be renewed.

Number awarded Varies each year; recently, 201 of these scholarships were awarded.

Deadline March of each year.

[468]
HUEY AND ANGELINA WILSON SCHOLARSHIPS

Louisiana Hemophilia Foundation
Attn: Scholarship Committee
3636 South Sherwood Forest Boulevard, Suite 450
Baton Rouge, LA 70816
(225) 291-1675   Toll Free: (800) 749-1680
Fax: (225) 291-1679 E-mail: lahemophilia@hipoint.net
Web: louisianahemophilia.org

Summary To provide financial assistance for college to Louisiana residents who have hemophilia or von Willebrand Disease.

Eligibility This program is open to residents of Louisiana who have hemophilia or von Willebrand Disease. Applicants must be enrolled or planning to enroll at a 4-year Louisiana college or university as a full-time undergraduate student. Along with their application, they must submit a 250-word essay on why they should receive this scholarship.

Financial data The stipend is $1,000 per semester.

Duration 1 semester. Recipients may reapply if they remain enrolled full time, have a GPA of 2.5 or higher, and provide 8 hours of community service to the sponsoring organization.
Number awarded Up to 15 each semester.
Deadline June of each year for fall semester; December of each year for spring semester.

[469]
I.H. MCLENDON MEMORIAL SCHOLARSHIP

Sickle Cell Disease Association of America-
  Connecticut Chapter
140 Woodland Street, Suite 102
Hartford, CT 06105
(860) 527-0147   Fax: (860) 548-0220
E-mail: scdaan1@iconn.net

Summary To provide financial assistance to high school seniors in Connecticut who have sickle cell disease and are interested in attending college in any state.
Eligibility This program is open to Connecticut residents who have sickle cell disease. Applicants must be graduating high school seniors, have a GPA of 3.0 or higher, be in the top third of their class, and be interested in attending a 2- or 4-year college or university in any state. Along with their application, they must submit a statement outlining their personal and career goals and how the scholarship will help them achieve those goals, 3 letters of recommendation, and a letter from their physician attesting to existence of sickle cell disease. Finalists are interviewed.
Financial data The stipend is $1,000.
Duration 1 year; nonrenewable.
Additional data This program is offered in collaboration with the Hartford Foundation for Public Giving.
Number awarded 1 each year.
Deadline April of each year.

[470]
INA BRUDNICK SCHOLARSHIP AWARD

Great Comebacks Award Program
c/o ConvaTec Customer Interaction Center
100 Headquarters Park Drive
Skillman, NJ 08558
Toll Free: (800) 422-8811
E-mail: info@greatcomebacks.com
Web: www.greatcomebacks.com

Summary To provide financial assistance to college students with an inflammatory bowel disease (IBD) or other related physical conditions.
Eligibility This program is open to people between 17 and 24 years of age who have undergone an ostomy and/or have an IBD (Crohn's disease or ulcerative colitis). Applicants must be able to demonstrate financial need. Along with their application, they must submit statements on how their life has been changed or affected by their medical condition and their ostomy, how their comeback has positively affected their life and those around them, and what advice they would give to others struggling with similar medical conditions or facing ostomy surgery.

Financial data The stipend is $1,000.
Duration 1 year.
Additional data This scholarship is provided by Conva-Tec, a Bristol-Myers Squibb Company, and the Crohn's and Colitis Foundation of America.
Number awarded 4 each year: 1 from each region of the country.
Deadline July of each year.

[471]
IOPO FOUNDATION SCHOLARSHIPS

Indiana Organ Procurement Organization, Inc.
Attn: IOPO Foundation Inc.
3760 Guion Road
P.O. Box 6069, Department 172
Indianapolis, IN 46202-6069
Toll Free: (888) ASK-IOPO   Fax: (317) 685-1687
E-mail: info@iopo.org
Web: www.iopo.org/about/foundation/scholarships.html

Summary To provide financial assistance for college attendance in any state to Indiana residents who are organ, tissue, or eye transplant donors, recipients, candidates, or their families.
Eligibility This program is open to Indiana residents who are organ, tissue, or eye transplant donors, recipients, candidates, or relatives (including spouses, parents, children, grandchildren, siblings, aunts, uncles, nieces, nephews, and cousins). Applicants must be high school seniors or students already attending a college or technical school in any state. They must have a GPA of 2.0 or higher; high school seniors must be in the top 50% of their class. Along with their application, they must submit a 1,500-word essay describing their career goals, experience with organ or tissue donation and/or transplantation, and personal goals. Financial need is considered in the selection process.
Financial data Recently, stipends were $3,500, $2,100, and $1,400.
Duration 1 year; nonrenewable.
Number awarded 3 each year: 1 each at $3,500, $2,100, and $1,400.
Deadline February of each year.

[472]
JAMES A. GIRARD SCHOLARSHIP

Epilepsy Foundation of Vermont
P.O. Box 6292
Rutland, VT 05702
(802) 775-1686   Toll Free: (800) 565-0972
E-mail: epilepsy@sover.net
Web: www.epilepsyvt.org/scholarships.html

Summary To provide financial assistance for college to high school seniors in Vermont who have epilepsy.
Eligibility This program is open to high school seniors in Vermont who have epilepsy. Applicants must be planning to go on to higher education after graduation.
Financial data The stipend is $1,000.
Duration 1 year.

Number awarded 1 each year.
Deadline Deadline not specified.

[473]
JAMES AND COLIN LEE WOZUMI SCHOLARSHIP

Pride Foundation
Attn: Scholarship Program Director
1122 East Pike Street
PMB 1001
Seattle, WA 98122-3934
(206) 323-3318   Toll Free: (800) 735-7287
Fax: (206) 323-1017
E-mail: scholarships@pridefoundation.org
Web: www.pridefoundation.org

Summary To provide financial assistance for college to residents of the Northwest who are HIV positive and/or focusing on the treatment and/or eradication of the HIV virus.
Eligibility This program is open to residents of Alaska, Idaho, Montana, Oregon, or Washington who attending or planning to attend a college, university, or vocational school in any state. Applicants must be goal-oriented, HIV positive, and/or focusing on the treatment and/or eradication of the HIV virus. Preference is given to students who are self-identified as gay, lesbian, bisexual, or transgender (GLBT), members of GLBT families, or allies who have been strongly supportive of the GLBT community. Selection is based on financial need, community involvement, and commitment to civil rights for all people.
Financial data Stipends average more than $2,100. Funds are paid directly to the recipient's school.
Duration 1 year; recipients may reapply.
Additional data The Pride Foundation was established in 1987 to strengthen the GLBT community.
Number awarded 1 or more each year. Since it began offering scholarships in 1993, the foundation has awarded $1.4 million to nearly 800 recipients.
Deadline January of each year.

[474]
JAY'S WORLD COLLEGE SCHOLARSHIP PROGRAM

Jay's World Childhood Cancer Foundation
P.O. Box 351
Medford, NY 11763
(631) 846-1937   E-mail: info@jaysworld.org
Web: www.jaysworld.org/html/scholarship.cfm

Summary To provide financial assistance to high school seniors in New York who have had childhood cancer and are interested in attending college in any state.
Eligibility This program is open to seniors graduating from high schools in New York who have been cured of cancer, are in remission, or are able to attend college while undergoing treatment for cancer. Applicants must submit a brief paper describing what it was like to be a child with cancer; how it affected their family, friends, and school life; what the experience has taught them; and how they think

having cancer might benefit their life in the future. Financial need is considered in the selection process.
Financial data Stipend amounts vary; recently, they averaged $5,000.
Duration 1 year.
Additional data The sponsoring foundation was founded in 1997.
Number awarded Varies each year; recently, 7 of these scholarships were awarded.
Deadline April of each year.

[475]
JEFF APODACA CELEBRATION OF LIFE SCHOLARSHIP

Jeff Apodaca Celebration of Life Foundation
c/o UNM Children's Hospital Development Office
Two Woodward Center, Suite 100
700 Lomas Boulevard, N.E.
Albuquerque, NM 87102
(505) 277-5685   Fax: (505) 277-5687
E-mail: placencia@salud.unm.edu
Web: www.jeffapodaca.com/scholorship.html

Summary To provide financial assistance to residents of New Mexico who have survived cancer and are interested in attending college in the state.
Eligibility This program is open to New Mexico residents who are attending or planning to attend a 4-year college or university in the state. Applicants must have survived cancer.
Financial data The stipend is $5,000.
Duration 1 year.
Additional data This scholarship was first awarded in 2001.
Number awarded Varies each year; recently, 3 of these scholarships were awarded.
Deadline September of each year.

[476]
JESSICA BETH SCHWARTZ MEMORIAL SCHOLARSHIP

Gift of Life Donor Program
Attn: Transplant Foundation
401 North Third Street
Philadelphia, PA 19123-4101
Toll Free: (800) DONORS-1
Web: www.donors1.org/patients/resources/jessiesday

Summary To provide financial assistance to transplant recipients who live in the service area of the Gift of Life Donor Program and are interested in attending college in any state.
Eligibility This program is open to transplant recipients who live in the eastern half of Pennsylvania, southern New Jersey, or Delaware. Applicants must be younger than 25 years of age and either graduating high school seniors or students currently enrolled at a 2- or 4-year college, university, or trade/technical school in any state. Along with their application, they must submit 1) a 200-word essay describing an educational initiative to promote organ and

tissue donation and transplantation awareness in high school or college students; 2) a 500-word personal statement describing their transplant story and extracurricular and/or volunteer activities; 3) letters of reference; and 4) a current transcript. Financial need is not considered in the selection process.

Financial data The stipend is $2,500.

Duration 1 year.

Number awarded 1 or more each year.

Deadline February of each year.

[477]
JOHN BULLER SCHOLARSHIP

Greater Houston Community Foundation
Attn: Director of Operations
4550 Post Oak Place, Suite 100
Houston, TX 77027
(713) 333-2205   Fax: (713) 333-2220
E-mail: lgardner@ghcf.org
Web: www.ghcf.org/john-buller-scholarship.php

Summary To provide financial assistance to residents of Texas who have cystic fibrosis and are interested in attending college or graduate school in any state.

Eligibility This program is open to Texas residents who have cystic fibrosis. Applicants must be enrolled or planning to enroll as an undergraduate or graduate student at an accredited 2-year or 4-year college or university in the United States. Along with their application, they must submit transcripts and information on their extracurricular activities, work experience, community service, and other activities. Financial need is considered in the selection process. U.S. citizenship is required.

Financial data The stipend is $1,000 per year.

Duration 1 year; may be renewed up to 3 additional years.

Additional data This program was established in 1997.

Number awarded 1 or more each year.

Deadline April of each year.

[478]
JOHN YOUTSEY MEMORIAL SCHOLARSHIP FUND

Hemophilia of Georgia
8800 Roswell Road, Suite 170
Atlanta, GA 30350-1844
(770) 518-8272   Fax: (770) 518-3310
E-mail: mail@hog.org
Web: www.hog.org/programs/page/scholarship

Summary To provide financial assistance to residents of Georgia who have a bleeding disorder or have lost a parent because of the disorder and are interested in attending college in any state.

Eligibility This program is open to residents of Georgia who 1) have hemophilia, von Willebrand Disease, or other inherited bleeding disorder; and 2) are children whose parent died as a result of complications from a bleeding disorder. They may be graduating high school seniors or students currently enrolled at an accredited college, university, vocational/technical school, or professional degree

program in any state. Selection is based on academic record, financial need, and personal goals.

Financial data A stipend is awarded (amount not specified).

Duration 1 year.

Number awarded Varies each year. Since this program was established, it has awarded more than 275 scholarship with a value greater than $800,000.

Deadline April of each year.

[479]
JOSHUA GOMES MEMORIAL SCHOLARSHIP

Joshua Gomes Memorial Scholarship Fund
2700 South Emerson Street
Englewood, CO 80113-1737
(303) 761-3055   E-mail: Info@joshuagomes.org
Web: www.joshuagomes.org

Summary To provide financial assistance for college or graduate school to students who have AIDS or are HIV positive.

Eligibility This program is open to full-time undergraduate and graduate students accepted or enrolled at a college or university in the United States. Applicants must have AIDS or be HIV positive. Along with their application, they must submit a 500-word essay that explains their hopes, plans, and goals for the future; how their schooling will help lay a path to fulfilling those; what motivates them to pursue higher education; what subjects they plan to study; and what led them to that path of study. Selection is based on merit and financial need.

Financial data The stipend is $1,000.

Duration 1 year; recipients may reapply.

Additional data This program was established in 2005.

Number awarded 1 or more each year.

Deadline July of each year.

[480]
KERMIT B. NASH ACADEMIC SCHOLARSHIP

Sickle Cell Disease Association of America
Attn: Scholarship Committee
231 East Baltimore Street, Suite 900
Baltimore, MD 21202
(410) 528-1555   Toll Free: (800) 421-8453
Fax: (410) 528-1495
E-mail: scdaa@sicklecelldisease.org
Web: www.sicklecelldisease.org

Summary To provide financial assistance for college to graduating high school seniors who have sickle cell disease.

Eligibility This program is open to graduating high school seniors who have sickle cell disease (not the trait). Applicants must have a GPA of 3.0 or higher and be U.S. citizens or permanent residents planning to attend an accredited 4-year college or university as a full-time student. They must submit a personal essay, up to 1,000 words, on an aspect of the impact of the disease on their lives or on society. Selection is based on GPA, general academic achievement and promise, SAT scores, leadership and community service, severity of academic challenges and obstacles posed by sickle cell disease, and the quality of their essay.

Financial data The stipend is $5,000 per year.

Duration Up to 4 years.

Additional data The Sickle Cell Disease Association of America (SCDAA) was formerly the National Association for Sickle Cell Disease. It established this program in 1999. Requests for applications must be submitted in writing; telephone requests are not honored.

Number awarded 1 each year.

Deadline May of each year.

[481]
KEVIN CHILD SCHOLARSHIP

National Hemophilia Foundation
Attn: Information Resource Center
116 West 32nd Street, 11th Floor
New York, NY 10001-3212
(212) 328-3750   Toll Free: (800) 42-HANDI, ext. 3750
Fax: (212) 328-3777   E-mail: handi@hemophilia.org
Web: www.hemophilia.org

Summary To provide financial assistance for college to students with hemophilia.

Eligibility This program is open to high school seniors entering their first year of undergraduate study as well as those currently enrolled in college. Applicants must have hemophilia A or B. Along with their application, they must submit a 1-page essay on their occupational objectives and goals in life and how the educational program they have planned will meet those objectives. Selection is based on that essay, academic performance, and participation in school and community activities.

Financial data The stipend is $1,000.

Duration 1 year.

Additional data The program was established by the Child family after the death of 21-year old Kevin in 1989.

Number awarded 1 each year.

Deadline May of each year.

[482]
KIDNEY & UROLOGY FOUNDATION OF AMERICA SCHOLARSHIP AWARDS

Kidney & Urology Foundation of America
Attn: Program Associate
152 Madison Avenue, Suite 201
New York, NY 10016
(212) 629-9770   Toll Free: (800) 633-6628
Fax: (212) 629-5652
E-mail: HReel@kidneyurology.org
Web: www.kidneyurology.org

Summary To provide financial assistance for college to patients who have been diagnosed with kidney or urologic disease.

Eligibility This program is open to young adults between 17 and 25 years of age who are attending to planning to attend college. Applicants must have been diagnosed with kidney or urologic disease. Along with their application, they must submit an essay of 1-2 pages on questions related to their disease, their educational back-

ground and goals, and their contributions to the renal, urologic, or transplant community. Selection is based on achievements, commitment to working on a college degree, and financial need. Priority is given to applicants from the sponsoring organization's participating partner centers.

Financial data The stipend is $2,000 per year. Funds are paid directly to the recipient's institution.

Duration 1 year; may be renewed up to 3 additional years.

Number awarded Varies each year; recently, 7 new and 20 renewal scholarships were awarded.

Deadline May of each year.

[483]
KYLE LEE FOUNDATION SCHOLARSHIP

Kyle Lee Foundation, Inc.
3843 South Bristol Street, Number 293
Santa Ana, CA 92704
(714) 433-3204   E-mail: foundation@kylelee28.com
Web: www.kylelee28.com

Summary To provide financial assistance for college to cancer survivors.

Eligibility This program is open to high school seniors and current college students who have had cancer, especially Ewing's sarcoma. Applicants must submit a letter from their doctor confirming their cancer diagnosis, copies of academic transcripts, 2 letters of recommendation, and a 700-word essay outlining their goals in college and how their fight with cancer has affected their life and goals.

Financial data Stipends are $1,000 or $500.

Duration 1 year.

Additional data This program was founded following the death of Kyle Lee in 2003.

Number awarded Varies each year. Recently, 5 of these scholarships were awarded.

Deadline May of each year.

[484]
LARRY DEAN DAVIS SCHOLARSHIP FUND

Brain Tumor Foundation for Children, Inc.
Attn: Scholarship Committee
6065 Roswell Road, N.E., Suite 505
Atlanta, GA 30328-4015
(404) 252-4107   Fax: (404) 252-4108
E-mail: info@braintumorkids.org
Web: www.braintumorkids.org

Summary To provide financial assistance to residents of Georgia who have had a brain or spinal cord tumor and are interested in attending college in any state.

Eligibility This program is open to Georgia residents who are survivors of a pediatric brain or spinal cord tumor. Applicants must be entering or continuing in an advanced educational setting (college, university, vocational school, or other setting) in any state. They must be able to demonstrate financial need. Along with their application, they must submit 1) an essay about their brain or spinal cord tumor experience, including surgery and/or treatment; and

2) a brief biographical sketch about themselves and their future aspirations.

Financial data   The stipend is $2,500.

Duration   1 year; nonrenewable.

Number awarded   Up to 2 each year.

Deadline   April of each year.

[485]
LARRY SMOCK SCHOLARSHIP

National Kidney Foundation of Indiana, Inc.
Attn: Program Coordinator
911 East 86th Street, Suite 100
Indianapolis, IN 46204-1848
(317) 722-5640   Toll Free: (800) 382-9971
Fax: (317) 722-5650   E-mail: nkfi@kidneyindiana.org
Web: www.kidney.org/site/303/patientAid.cfm?ch=303

Summary   To provide financial assistance to kidney patients in Indiana who are interested in pursuing higher education in an academic or monitored occupational setting in any state.

Eligibility   This program is open to Indiana residents who have at least a high school diploma or its equivalent and who have received a kidney transplant or are on dialysis. Applicants must be interested in attending college, trade school, or vocational school in any state to work on an academic or occupational degree. Finalists are interviewed. Financial need is considered in the selection process.

Financial data   A stipend is awarded (amount not specified). Funds are paid directly to the recipient's school.

Duration   1 year; may be renewed.

Additional data   This fund was established in 1992.

Number awarded   Several each year.

Deadline   February of each year.

[486]
LATREESE NICOLE FAGAN MEMORIAL SCHOLARSHIP

Latreese Nicole Fagan Memorial Scholarship Fund, Inc.
Attn: Board of Directors
P.O. Box 19370
Detroit, MI 48219-0370
(313) 531-9922   Fax: (313) 531-9926
E-mail: info@latreesefagan.org
Web: www.latreesefagan.org

Summary   To provide financial assistance for college to residents of Michigan who have lupus.

Eligibility   This program is open to residents of Michigan who are lupus patients with a board-certified physician approving the diagnosis. Applicants must be attending or planning to attend an accredited 2-year or 4-year college, university, or vocational school in Michigan. They must be between 17 and 25 years of age. Along with their application, they must submit an essay on their reasons for desiring a higher education. Selection is based on high school or college transcripts, participation in outside activities, and 3 letters of recommendation. U.S. citizenship is required.

Financial data   The stipend is $1,000. Funds are paid directly to the recipient's institution to help cover tuition, books, fees, room, and board.

Duration   1 year; nonrenewable.

Number awarded   2 each year.

Deadline   March of each year.

[487]
LAWRENCE MADEIROS SCHOLARSHIP

Adirondack Spintacular
Attn: Scholarship Panel
P.O. Box 11
Mayfield, NY 12117
(518) 863-8998   Fax: (518) 863-8998
E-mail: carol@adirondackspintacular.com
Web: www.adirondackspintacular.com

Summary   To provide financial assistance for college to high school seniors who have a chronic disorder.

Eligibility   This program is open to seniors graduating from high school who have been accepted at an accredited college or university. Applicants must be diagnosed with a chronic disorder. Along with their application, they must submit brief essays on 1) how living with or around a chronic disorder has impacted their life; 2) their goals and aspirations in life; and 3) their passion. Financial need may also be considered.

Financial data   The stipend is $1,000.

Duration   1 year.

Additional data   This program, established in 2001, is supported by the Adirondack Spintacular, a charity event in which volunteers cycle, walk, or run to raise money. Chronic disorders have included muscular dystrophy, diabetes, hemophilia, cystic fibrosis, autism, and Asperger's Syndrome.

Number awarded   Varies each year; recently, 6 of these scholarships were awarded.

Deadline   May of each year.

[488]
LEAD FOUNDATION COMMUNITY SCHOLARSHIP

Learning & Education About Disabilities
Attn: LEAD Foundation
c/o Pikes Peak Community Foundation
730 North Nevada Avenue
Colorado Springs, CO 80903
(719) 389-1251   Fax: (719) 389-1252
E-mail: LEADourkids@yahoo.com
Web: www.leadcolorado.org/scholarships.aspx

Summary   To provide financial assistance to residents of Colorado who have a learning disability and are interested in attending college in any state.

Eligibility   This program is open to Colorado residents who have a documented, specific learning disability or AD/HD (e.g., dyslexia, perceptual, or communicative disabilities). Applicants must be working on or planning to work on a postsecondary degree at a college or university in any state. Preference is given to applicants who have faced the challenges of having a learning disability and understand the importance of advocacy and self-knowledge in overcoming those challenges.

Financial data   The stipend is $1,000.

Duration   1 year.

Number awarded   1 each year.

Deadline   February of each year.

[489]
LEAD FOUNDATION SCHOLARSHIP

Pikes Peak Community Foundation
Attn: Scholarship Selection Committee
730 North Nevada Avenue
Colorado Springs, CO 80903
(719) 389-1251   Fax: (719) 389-1252
E-mail: info@ppcf.org
Web: www.ppcf.org/scholarships_and_fellowships.php

Summary   To provide financial assistance to residents of Colorado who have a learning disability and are attending college in any state.

Eligibility   This program is open to residents of Colorado who are attending a college or university in any state and have a documented learning disability and AD/HD. Applicants should be able to demonstrate that they have faced the challenges of having a learning disability, understand the importance of self-advocacy and self-knowledge in overcoming those challenges, believes in contributing to society in a way that will increase awareness of learning disabilities, and will serve as a role model for other students with learning disabilities. Along with their application, they must submit a brief statement in which they describe their disability, how it impacts their life, the date of initial diagnosis, and the date of most recent testing.

Financial data   The stipend is $1,000.

Duration   1 year.

Additional data   This program is sponsored by the LEAD (Learning and Educating About Disabilities) Foundation.

Number awarded   1 each year.

Deadline   February of each year.

[490]
LEARNING DISABILITIES ASSOCIATION OF IOWA SCHOLARSHIPS

Learning Disabilities Association of Iowa
c/o Lorna Leavitt, Scholarship Chair
209 Crestview Drive
Marcus, IA 51035
(712) 274-5136   Toll Free: (888) 690-LDAI
E-mail: levitt@morningside.edu
Web: www.lda-ia.org

Summary   To provide financial assistance to high school seniors in Iowa who have a learning disability and are interested in attending college in any state.

Eligibility   This program is open to students with learning disabilities who are graduating from high schools in Iowa. Applicants must be planning to enroll in a 2-year or 4-year college or in vocational training at a school in any state. Along with their application, they must submit an essay about themselves, including their extracurricular

and community achievements, most significant accomplishments, volunteer and paid jobs, methods of financing their education, and any accommodations they feel they will need in their postsecondary program.

Financial data   The stipend is $1,000.

Duration   1 year.

Number awarded   3 each year.

Deadline   March of each year.

[491]
LILLY REINTEGRATION SCHOLARSHIPS

The Center for Reintegration, Inc.
Attn: Lilly Secretariat
310 Busse Highway
PMB 327
Park Ridge, IL 60068-3251
Toll Free: (800) 809-8202
E-mail: lillyscholarships@reintegration.com
Web: www.reintegration.com/resources/scholarships

Summary   To provide financial assistance to undergraduate and graduate students diagnosed with schizophrenia.

Eligibility   This program is open to U.S. citizens diagnosed with bipolar disorder, schizophrenia, schizophreniform disorder, or schizoaffective disorder. Applicants must be receiving medical treatment for the disease and be actively involved in rehabilitative or reintegrative efforts. They must be interested in pursuing postsecondary education, including trade or vocational school programs, high school equivalency programs, associate degrees, bachelor's degrees, and graduate programs. Along with their application, they must submit an essay on their career goal and their rationale for choosing that goal, how this course of study will help them achieve their career goal, obstacles they have faced in life and how they have overcome them, steps they have taken to prepare for pursuit of this education, rationale for the specific school chosen, and their plans to continue treatment while pursuing an education. Selection is based on the quality of the essay, academic success, 3 references, thoughtfulness and appropriateness of academic and vocational/career goals, rehabilitation involvement, success in dealing with the disease, recent volunteer and/or vocational experience, and completion of application requirements.

Financial data   The amount awarded varies, depending upon the specific needs of the recipient. Funds may be used to pay for tuition and related expenses, such as textbooks and laboratory fees.

Duration   1 year; may be renewed.

Additional data   This program, established in 1998, is funded by Eli Lilly and Company.

Number awarded   Varies each year; generally, 70 to 120 of these scholarships (including renewals) are awarded annually.

Deadline   January of each year.

[492]
LOUISIANA HEMOPHILIA FOUNDATION SCHOLARSHIPS

Louisiana Hemophilia Foundation
Attn: Scholarship Committee
3636 South Sherwood Forest Boulevard, Suite 450
Baton Rouge, LA 70816
(225) 291-1675   Toll Free: (800) 749-1680
Fax: (225) 291-1679 E-mail: lahemophilia@hipoint.net
Web: louisianahemophilia.org

Summary To provide financial assistance for college to Louisiana residents who have hemophilia or von Willebrand Disease.

Eligibility This program is open to residents of Louisiana who have hemophilia or von Willebrand Disease. Applicants must be enrolled or planning to enroll at a 2- or 4-year Louisiana college, university, or trade school. Along with their application, they must submit a 250-word essay on why they should receive this scholarship.

Financial data The stipend is $500 per semester.

Duration 1 semester. Recipients may reapply if they remain enrolled full time, have a GPA of 2.5 or higher, and provide 8 hours of community service to the sponsoring organization.

Number awarded 3 each semester.

Deadline June of each year for fall semester; December of each year for spring semester.

[493]
LYMAN FISHER SCHOLARSHIPS

Virginia Hemophilia Foundation
P.O. Box 188
Midlothian, VA 23113-0188
Toll Free: (800) 266-8438   Fax: (804) 740-8643
E-mail: vahemophiliaed@verizon.net
Web: www.vahemophilia.org

Summary To provide financial assistance to people from Virginia who have participated in activities of the Virginia Hemophilia Foundation (VHF) and are interested in attending college.

Eligibility This program is open members of the bleeding disorder community and their families who are attending or planning to attend college. Applicants must have a record of prior participation with VHF and be a resident of Virginia or planning to attend college in Virginia. Along with their application, they must submit a brief biographical sketch of themselves that includes their interests, hobbies, vocational and educational goals, volunteer and community involvement, and work or internship experience; a description of their previous participation with VHF and how they plan to contribute to the organization and support other persons with inherited bleeding disorders; a detailed statement of financial need; a 1-page essay on their career goals; another 1-page essay on a topic of their choice; and 3 letters of recommendation.

Financial data The stipend is $2,000.

Duration 1 year.

Number awarded 2 each year.

Deadline May of each year.

[494]
MARCENA LOZANO DONATE LIFE SCHOLARSHIP FUND

Marcena Lozano Donate Life Scholarship Fund
  Committee
15 Winston Road
Buffalo, NY 14216
(716) 836-7045   E-mail: theelephantrun@aol.com
Web: www.theelephantrun.com/

Summary To provide financial assistance to organ transplant recipients who are interested in attending college in any state.

Eligibility This program is open to organ transplant recipients who are graduating high school seniors or students currently enrolled at an accredited college, university, or trade/technical certificate program in any state. Preference is given to residents of western New York. Applicants must submit a statement of their educational objectives and future life goals. Selection is based primarily on financial need.

Financial data Stipends range from $1,000 to $3,000 per year, depending on the availability of funds. Payment is made directly to the recipient's institution.

Duration 1 year; may be renewed.

Number awarded 1 or more each year.

Deadline July of each year for fall admission; November of each year for spring admission.

[495]
MARCO CAMASTRA SCHOLARSHIP AWARD

Learning Disabilities Association of North Carolina
1854A Hendersonville Road, Suite 239
Asheville, NC 28803
E-mail: ldanc@mindspring.com
Web: www.ldanc.org/services

Summary To provide financial assistance to high school seniors in North Carolina who have a learning disability and are interested in attending college in any state.

Eligibility This program is open to seniors graduating from high schools in North Carolina who have been diagnosed as having a learning disability or attention disorder. Applicants must be planning to attend a college, university, community college, or technical school in any state. They must be able to demonstrate that they have participated in school activities (e.g., sports, music, art, drama), persisted in academics, participated in community or church activities, and shown sensitivity to the needs or feelings of others. Along with their application, they must submit a short essay about their learning disability and how they feel they have adapted in order to succeed in school and/or life in general. Financial need is not considered in the selection process.

Financial data The stipend is $1,000.

Duration 1 year.

Number awarded 1 each year.

Deadline March of each year.

[496]
MARION HUBER LEARNING THROUGH LISTENING AWARDS

Recording for the Blind and Dyslexic
Attn: Strategic Communications Department
Anne T. Macdonald Center
20 Roszel Road
Princeton, NJ 08540
(609) 243-7051   Toll Free: (866) RFBD-585
E-mail: dnagy@rfbd.org
Web: www.rfbd.org/applications_awards.htm

Summary   To provide financial assistance to outstanding high school students with learning disabilities who plan to continue their education.

Eligibility   This program is open to seniors graduating from public or private high schools in the United States or its territories who have a specific learning disability (visual impairment alone does not satisfy this requirement). Applicants must be planning to continue their education at a 2-year or 4-year college or vocational school. They must be registered Recording for the Blind and Dyslexic borrowers and have earned a GPA of 3.0 or higher in grades 10-12. Selection is based on outstanding scholastic achievement, leadership, enterprise, and service to others.

Financial data   Stipends are $6,000 or $2,000.

Duration   1 year.

Additional data   This program was established in 1991.

Number awarded   6 each year: 3 at $6,000 and 3 at $2,000.

Deadline   April of each year.

[497]
MARK REAMES MEMORIAL SCHOLARSHIPS

Hemophilia Society of Colorado
Attn: Scholarship Committee
P.O. Box 4943
Englewood, CO 80155
(303) 629-6990   Toll Free: (888) 687-CLOT
Fax: (303) 629-7035   E-mail: hsc@cohemo.org
Web: www.cohemo.org

Summary   To provide financial assistance for higher education to members of the Hemophilia Society of Colorado (HSC) and to members of their families.

Eligibility   This program is open to HSC members who have hemophilia or a related inherited bleeding disorder and their immediate family members. Applicants must be enrolled or planning to enroll at a 2-year or 4-year college or university, vocational/technical school, or graduate school. Along with their application, they must submit an essay on why they think they should receive this scholarship and how it might affect their future goals. Selection is based on the essay, demonstrated scholastic ability and intellectual promise, letters of recommendation, community involvement (especially involvement with the hemophilia community), and financial need.

Financial data   The stipend is $1,000. Funds must be used for tuition, room, board, and related educational expenses.

Duration   1 year.

Number awarded   2 each year.

Deadline   April of each year.

[498]
MARY M. GOOLEY HEMOPHILIA SCHOLARSHIP

Mary M. Gooley Hemophilia Center
Attn: Scholarship Selection Committee
1415 Portland Avenue, Suite 500
Rochester, NY 14621
(585) 922-5700   Fax: (585) 922-5775
E-mail: Tricia.oppelt@rochestergeneral.org
Web: www.hemocenter.org/Scholarship%20Info.asp

Summary   To provide financial assistance to people with a bleeding disorder and their families who plan to attend college.

Eligibility   This program is open to people who are affected directly or indirectly by hemophilia, von Willebrand Disease, hereditary bleeding disorder, or hemochromatosis. Applicants must be enrolled or planning to enroll at an accredited 2- or 4-year college or university, vocational/technical school, or certified training program. Along with their application, they must submit 1) a 1,000-word essay on their goals and aspirations, their biggest challenge and how they met it, and anything else they want the selection committee to know about them; and 2) a 250-word essay on any unusual family or personal circumstances have affected their achievement in school, work, or participation in school and community activities, including how the bleeding disorder of themselves or their family member has affected their life. Selection is based on the essays, academic performance, participation in school and community activities, work or volunteer experience, personal or family circumstances, recommendations, and financial need.

Financial data   The maximum stipend is $2,000.

Duration   1 year.

Additional data   This program was established in 1996.

Number awarded   1 or 2 each year.

Deadline   April of each year.

[499]
MARYLAND COMMUNITY CANCER SCHOLARSHIP

Ulman Cancer Fund for Young Adults
Attn: Scholarship Program Coordinator
10440 Little Patuxent Parkway, Suite 1G
Columbia, MD 21044
(410) 964-0202, ext. 106   Toll Free: (888) 393-FUND
E-mail: scholarship@ulmanfund.org
Web: www.ulmanfund.org

Summary   To provide financial assistance to residents of Maryland who are cancer survivors or patients and are interested in working on an undergraduate or graduate degree at a school in the state.

Eligibility   This program is open to residents of Maryland who are younger than 35 years of age, are cancer survivors or patients, and were diagnosed after the age of 15 (including initial or secondary diagnosis, relapse, or active treatment). Applicants must be attending or planning to attend a public 2- or 4-year college, university, or vocational program in Maryland to work on an undergraduate, graduate, or professional degree. Along with their application, they must submit an essay of at least 1,000 words on a topic that changes annually but relates to young adults with cancer. Selection is based on demonstrated dedication to community service, commitment to educational and professional goals, use of their cancer experience to impact the lives of other young adults affected by cancer, medical hardship, and financial need.

Financial data The stipend is $2,500. Funds are paid directly to the educational institution.

Duration 1 year; nonrenewable.

Additional data Recipients must agree to complete 80 hours of community service.

Number awarded Varies each year; recently, 2 of these scholarships were awarded.

Deadline April of each year.

[500]
MASON E. LIFTIG ENDOWED SCHOLARSHIP

Florida Roofing, Sheet Metal and Air Conditioning
  Contractors Association
Attn: FRSA Educational and Research Foundation
P.O. Box 4850
Winter Park, FL 32793
(407) 671-3772, ext. 123   Fax: (407) 679-0010
E-mail: barbr@floridaroof.com
Web: www.floridaroof.com

Summary To provide financial assistance to residents of Florida, particularly those with learning disabilities, who are interested in attending vocational or technical school in any state to prepare for construction-related careers.

Eligibility This program is open to residents of Florida who are attending or planning to attend a vocational or technical school in any state to work on a building trade certificate. Selection is based on academic and personal achievement, with priority given to applicants preparing for construction-related careers. Special consideration is given to students with scholastic or learning disabilities.

Financial data The stipend is $1,000.

Duration 1 year.

Additional data This program was established in 2007.

Number awarded 1 or more each year.

Deadline March of each year.

[501]
MATT STAUFFER MEMORIAL SCHOLARSHIPS

Ulman Cancer Fund for Young Adults
Attn: Scholarship Program Coordinator
10440 Little Patuxent Parkway, Suite 1G
Columbia, MD 21044
(410) 964-0202, ext. 106   Toll Free: (888) 393-FUND
E-mail: scholarship@ulmanfund.org
Web: www.ulmanfund.org

Summary To provide financial assistance for college or graduate school to young adults from Washington, D.C., Maryland, or Virginia who have had cancer.

Eligibility This program is open to students who are younger than 35 years of age and have or had cancer that was diagnosed after they were 15 years of age (including initial or secondary diagnosis, relapse, or active treatment). Applicants must be residents of or attending school in Washington, D.C., Maryland, or Virginia. They must be attending or planning to attend a 2-or 4-year college, university, or vocational program to work on an undergraduate or graduate degree. Along with their application, they must submit an essay of at least 1,000 words on a topic that changes annually but relates to young adults with cancer. Selection is based on demonstrated dedication to community service, commitment to educational and professional goals, use of their cancer experience to impact the lives of other young adults affected by cancer, medical hardship, and financial need.

Financial data The stipend is $2,500. Funds are paid directly to the educational institution.

Duration 1 year.

Additional data These scholarships were first awarded in 1998. Recipients must agree to complete 80 hours of community service.

Number awarded Varies each year; recently, 2 of these scholarships were awarded.

Deadline April of each year.

[502]
MICHAEL A. COREA MEMORIAL SCHOLARSHIP

Transplant Recipients International Organization-
  Greater Cleveland Chapter
Attn: Scholarship Committee
P.O. Box 93163
Cleveland, OH 44101-5163
(440) 473-8979   E-mail: triocleveland@hotmail.com
Web: www.triocleveland.org

Summary To provide financial assistance to residents of Ohio who are transplant candidates, recipients, or donors and interested in attending college in any state.

Eligibility This program is open to Ohio residents who are incoming college freshmen, continuing college students, or adults returning to college and attending or planning to attend a college, university, or trade/technical institution in any state. Applicants must be organ or tissue transplant candidates, recipients, or living donors. They must have a cumulative GPA of 2.5 or higher and be able to demonstrate financial need. Along with their application, they must submit a 300-word statement of educational goals and objectives, a statement (250 to 300 words in length) describing how transplantation influences their life, and 3 letters of recommendation.

Financial data The stipend is $1,000. Funds are disbursed directly to the recipient's institution.

Duration 1 year; nonrenewable.

Additional data This program was established in 2009.

Number awarded At least 1 each year.

Deadline June of each year.

[503]
MICHAEL A. HUNTER MEMORIAL SCHOLARSHIP

Orange County Community Foundation
Attn: Program Associate, Donor Relations and
Scholarships
30 Corporate Park, Suite 410
Irvine, CA 92606
(949) 553-4202, ext. 46   Fax: (949) 553-4211
E-mail: cmontesano@oc-cf.org
Web: www.oc-cf.org/default.asp?contentID=89

Summary To provide financial assistance for college to leukemia and lymphoma patients and the children of non-surviving leukemia and lymphoma patients.

Eligibility This program is open to graduating high school seniors, community college students, and 4-year university students nationwide. Applicants must be leukemia or lymphoma patients and/or the children of non-surviving leukemia or lymphoma patients who are enrolled or planning to enroll full time. They must have a GPA of 3.0 or higher and be able to document financial need. Along with their application, they must submit an essay (up to 600 words) on how leukemia or lymphoma has affected their life, including the type of leukemia or lymphoma, date of diagnosis, and current status.

Financial data The stipend is $5,000.

Duration 1 year.

Number awarded 2 each year.

Deadline February of each year.

[504]
MICHAEL BENDIX SUTTON SCHOLARSHIPS

Michael Bendix Sutton Foundation
c/o Marion B. Sutton
300 Martine Avenue
White Plains, NY 10601

Summary To provide financial assistance to people with hemophilia who are pre-law students.

Eligibility This program is open to pre-law students who have hemophilia.

Financial data The stipend is $2,000.

Duration 1 year.

Number awarded 2 each year.

Deadline March of each year.

[505]
MID-SOUTH DIVISION COLLEGE SCHOLARSHIPS

American Cancer Society-Mid-South Division
1100 Ireland Way, Suite 201
Birmingham, AL 35205-7014
(205) 879-2242   Fax: (205) 930-8895
Web: www.cancer.org

Summary To provide financial assistance for college to residents of designated southern states who have been diagnosed as having cancer.

Eligibility This program is open to residents of Alabama, Arkansas, Kentucky, Louisiana, Mississippi, and Tennessee. Applicants must be younger than 25 years of age, have had a cancer diagnosis before age 21, have a GPA of 2.5 or higher, and have been accepted at an accredited school. Selection is based on academic achievement, leadership, community service, and financial need.

Financial data The stipend is $1,000.

Duration 1 year.

Additional data This program began in 2001.

Number awarded Varies each year; recently, 223 of these scholarships were awarded.

Deadline January of each year.

[506]
MIDWEST DIVISION YOUTH SCHOLARSHIP PROGRAM

American Cancer Society-Midwest Division
Attn: Youth Scholarship Program
8317 Elderberry Road
Madison, WI 53717
(608) 662-7581   Toll Free: (877) 423-9123, ext. 7581
Fax: (262) 523-5533
E-mail: tiffany.carlson@cancer.org
Web: www.cancer.org

Summary To provide financial assistance for college to residents of selected midwestern states who have been diagnosed as having cancer.

Eligibility This program is open to residents (for at least 1 year) of Iowa, Minnesota, South Dakota, or Wisconsin who were diagnosed with cancer before the age of 21 and are currently younger than 25 years of age. Applicants must have maintained a GPA above the average level and be attending or planning to attend an accredited 2- or 4-year college, university or vocational/technical school in any state. Along with their application, they must submit an essay on how cancer has impacted their life and what they want to accomplish over the next 10 to 15 years. Selection is based on their commitment to academic or vocational goals, leadership, community service, and financial need.

Financial data The stipend is $1,000. Funds are paid directly to the recipient's institution.

Duration 1 year.

Number awarded Varies each year; recently, 40 of these scholarships were awarded.

Deadline March of each year.

[507]
MIKE CONLEY MEMORIAL SCHOLARSHIPS

Hemophilia Society of Colorado
Attn: Scholarship Committee
P.O. Box 4943
Englewood, CO 80155
(303) 629-6990   Toll Free: (888) 687-CLOT
Fax: (303) 629-7035   E-mail: hsc@cohemo.org
Web: www.cohemo.org

Summary To provide financial assistance for college or graduate school to students from Colorado who have a bleeding disorder.

Eligibility   This program is open to residents of Colorado who have hemophilia or a related inherited bleeding disorder. Applicants must be enrolled or planning to enroll at a 2-year or 4-year college or university, vocational/technical school, or graduate school. Along with their application, they must submit an essay on why they think they should receive this scholarship and how it might affect their future goals. Selection is based on the essay, demonstrated scholastic ability and intellectual promise, letters of recommendation, community involvement (especially involvement with the hemophilia community), and financial need. Preference is given to students at Metropolitan State College or the University of Colorado at Denver.

Financial data   The stipend is $1,000. Funds must be used for tuition, room, board, and related educational expenses.

Duration   1 year.

Number awarded   2 each year.

Deadline   April of each year.

[508]
MIKE HYLTON AND RON NIEDERMAN SCHOLARSHIPS

Factor Support Network Pharmacy
Attn: Scholarship Committee
900 Avenida Acaso, Suite A
Camarillo, CA 93012-8749
(805) 388-9336   Toll Free: (877) FSN-4-YOU
Fax: (805) 482-6324
E-mail: Scholarships@FactorSupport.com
Web: www.factorsupport.com/scholarships.htm

Summary   To provide financial assistance for college to men with hemophilia and their immediate families.

Eligibility   This program is open to men with bleeding disorders and their immediate family members. Applicants must be entering or attending a college, university, juniors college, or vocational school. They must submit 3 short essays: 1) their career goals; 2) how hemophilia or von Willebrand Disease has affected their life; and 3) their efforts to be involved in the bleeding disorder community and what they can do to education their peers and others outside their family about bleeding disorders. Selection is based on academic goals, volunteer work, school activities, other pertinent experience and achievements, and financial need.

Financial data   The stipend is $1,000. Funds are paid directly to the recipient.

Duration   1 year.

Additional data   This program was established in 1999.

Number awarded   10 each year.

Deadline   April of each year.

[509]
MILLIE GONZALEZ MEMORIAL SCHOLARSHIPS

Factor Support Network Pharmacy
Attn: Scholarship Committee
900 Avenida Acaso, Suite A
Camarillo, CA 93012-8749
(805) 388-9336   Toll Free: (877) FSN-4-YOU
Fax: (805) 482-6324
E-mail: Scholarships@FactorSupport.com
Web: www.factorsupport.com/scholarships.htm

Summary   To provide financial assistance to women with a bleeding disorder.

Eligibility   This program is open to women with hemophilia or von Willebrand Disease who are entering or attending a college, university, juniors college, or vocational school. Applicants must submit 3 short essays: 1) their career goals; 2) how hemophilia or von Willebrand Disease has affected their life; and 3) their efforts to be involved in the bleeding disorder community and what they can do to education their peers and others outside their family about bleeding disorders. Selection is based on academic goals, volunteer work, school activities, other pertinent experience and achievements, and financial need.

Financial data   The stipend is $1,000. Funds are paid directly to the recipient.

Duration   1 year.

Number awarded   5 each year.

Deadline   April of each year.

[510]
NATIONAL COLLEGIATE CANCER FOUNDATION SCHOLARSHIP

National Collegiate Cancer Foundation
Attn: Scholarship Committee
P.O. Box 5950
Bethesda, MD 20824
(240) 515-6262   E-mail: info@collegiatecancer.org
Web: www.collegiatecancer.org/scholarships.html

Summary   To provide financial assistance for college or graduate school to cancer survivors.

Eligibility   This program is open to students between 18 and 35 years of age who are cancer survivors or currently undergoing treatment for cancer. Applicants must be enrolled or planning to enroll at a college or university to work on a certificate or an associate, bachelor's, master's, or doctoral degree. Along with their application, they must submit a 1,000-word essay on 1 of 4 assigned topics related to their experiences with cancer and college. Selection is based on the essay, letters of recommendation, displaying a "Will Win" attitude, overall story of cancer survivorship, commitment to education, and financial need.

Financial data   The stipend is $1,000.

Duration   1 year.

Number awarded   1 or more each year.

Deadline   May of each year.

[511]
NATIONAL CORNERSTONE HEALTHCARE SERVICES SCHOLARSHIPS

National Cornerstone Healthcare Services Inc
24747 Redlands Boulevard, Suite B
Loma Linda, CA 92354
Toll Free: (877) 616-6247   Fax: (877) 777-5717
E-mail: customerservice@nc-hs.com
Web: www.nc-hs.com

Summary   To provide financial assistance for college to people who have a bleeding disorder and members of their family.

Eligibility   This program is open to graduating high school seniors who are planning to attend an accredited technical school, college, or university. Applicants must have been diagnosed with a bleeding disorder or be the parent, spouse, partner, child, or sibling of a person with such a disorder. They must have a GPA of 2.5 or higher during their entire senior year of high school. Along with their application, they must submit a brief description of their dreams, goals, and objectives for attending postsecondary education. Financial need is not considered in the selection process.

Financial data   Stipends range from $500 to $1,000.

Duration   1 year.

Number awarded   1 or more each year.

Deadline   March of each year.

[512]
NATIONAL KIDNEY FOUNDATION OF UTAH AND IDAHO EDUCATIONAL SCHOLARSHIP PROGRAM

National Kidney Foundation of Utah and Idaho
3707 North Canyon Road, Suite 1D
Provo, UT 84604-4585
(801) 226-5111   Toll Free: (800) 869-5277
Fax: (801) 226-8278   E-mail: nkfu@kidneyut.org
Web: www.kidneyut.org/ps-educational-scholarship.php

Summary   To provide financial assistance for college to kidney patients in Utah and Idaho.

Eligibility   This program is open to residents of Utah and Idaho who are kidney transplant recipients or dialysis patients. Applicants must be attending or planning to attend a college or university in Utah, Wyoming, or Idaho.

Financial data   A stipend is awarded (amount not specified).

Duration   1 year.

Number awarded   Varies each year; recently, 23 of these scholarships were awarded.

Deadline   Deadline not specified.

[513]
NATIONAL KIDNEY FOUNDATION SERVING CONNECTICUT SCHOLARSHIPS

National Kidney Foundation Serving Connecticut
2139 Silas Deane Highway, Suite 208
Rocky Hill, CT 06067-2337
(860) 257-3770   Toll Free: (800) 441-1280
Fax: (860) 257-3429   E-mail: nkfct@kidney.org
Web: www.kidneyct.org/site/index.cfm?ch=102

Summary   To provide financial assistance to residents of Connecticut who are dialysis patients, kidney recipients or donors, or dependents of patients and interested in attending college in any state.

Eligibility   This program is open to residents of Connecticut who are dialysis patients, transplant recipients, dependents of a dialysis or transplant patient, or living kidney donors. Applicants must be attending or planning to attend a 2- or 4-year college, university, or trade/technical school in any state. Along with their application, they must submit a 2-page essay on 1) establishing and working toward their goals; 2) how they stay motivated despite chronic illness; or 3) the transplant experience or the kidney donation experience. Selection is based on the essay, academic merit, extracurricular activities or community service, and financial need. For applicants who have been out of school for many years, work or life experience may also be considered. U.S. citizenship is required.

Financial data   The stipend is $1,000.

Duration   1 year.

Number awarded   3 each year.

Deadline   May of each year.

[514]
NATIONAL KIDNEY FOUNDATION SERVING MAINE SCHOLARSHIPS

National Kidney Foundation Serving Maine
c/o National Kidney Foundation Serving New England
85 Astor Avenue, Suite 2
Norwood, MA 02062-5040
(781) 278-0222   Toll Free: (800) 542-4001
Fax: (781) 278-0333   E-mail: nkfmarinhvt@kidney.org
Web: www.kidney.org/site/patients/index.cfm?ch=103

Summary   To provide financial assistance to residents of Maine who are kidney patients or their family members and interested in attending college in any state.

Eligibility   This program is open to residents of Maine who are kidney patients (dialysis patients, kidney transplant recipients, or newly diagnosed patients who are in early intervention programs) or immediate family members of patients. Applicants must be attending or planning to attend an accredited college or university in any state. Along with their application, they must submit documentation of financial need and brief essays on their educational goals and how kidney disease has impacted their life. Financial need is considered in the selection process.

Financial data   A stipend is awarded (amount not specified).

Duration   1 year.

Number awarded   Varies each year; recently, 7 of these scholarships were awarded.

Deadline   July of each year.

[515]
NATIONAL KIDNEY FOUNDATION SERVING NEW ENGLAND ACADEMIC AWARD

National Kidney Foundation Serving New England
Attn: Academic Awards Committee
85 Astor Avenue, Suite 2
Norwood, MA 02062-5040
(781) 278-0222   Toll Free: (800) 542-4001
Fax: (781) 278-0333   E-mail: nkfmarinhvt@kidney.org
Web: www.kidney.org/site/index.cfm?ch=105

Summary   To provide financial assistance to high school seniors and graduates from New England who have kidney disease or are related to a person with kidney disease and are interested in attending college in any state.

Eligibility   This program is open to high school seniors and graduates from Massachusetts, Rhode Island, New Hampshire, and Vermont who are planning to enroll at a college or university in any state. Applicants must have active and current kidney disease or be immediate relatives (parents, siblings, children, legal guardians) of a person with active and current kidney disease; the disease must have a significant impact on the applicant's life. Along with their application, they must submit a 1-page essay describing how the presence of kidney disease in their family has affected their life and education goals. Selection is based on academic achievement and financial need.

Financial data   The stipend is $1,000. Funds are paid directly to the student.

Duration   1 year.

Number awarded   1 each year.

Deadline   March of each year.

[516]
NEBRASKA CHAPTER NHF SCHOLARSHIPS

National Hemophilia Foundation-Nebraska Chapter
Attn: Scholarship Selection Committee
215 Centennial Mall South, Suite 512
Lincoln, NE 68508
(402) 742-5663   Fax: (402) 742-5677
E-mail: office@nebraskanhf.org
Web: www.nebraskanhf.org

Summary   To provide financial assistance for attendance at a college in any state to high school seniors in Nebraska who have a bleeding disorder, are relatives of a person with a bleeding disorder, or are a carrier of a defective gene related to a bleeding disorder.

Eligibility   This program is open to seniors graduating from high schools in Nebraska who plan to attend a college or university in any state. Applicants must have a bleeding disorder, be an immediately family member of a person with a bleeding disorder, or be the carrier of a defective gene related to a bleeding disorder. Along with their application, they must submit a brief statement on how a bleeding disorder influences their family life and a 250-word essay on their purpose and motivation for pursuing a post-secondary educational degree. Selection is based on that statement and essay, academic promise, and financial need. Preference is given to members of the Nebraska Chapter of the National Hemophilia Foundation (NHF).

Financial data   The stipend ranges from $500 to $1,000.

Duration   1 year.

Number awarded   1 or more each year.

Deadline   June of each year.

[517]
NEW DAY EDUCATION AND REHABILITATION AWARDS

Kidney & Urology Foundation of America
Attn: Program Associate
152 Madison Avenue, Suite 201
New York, NY 10016
(212) 629-9770   Toll Free: (800) 633-6628
Fax: (212) 629-5652
E-mail: HReel@kidneyurology.org
Web: www.kidneyurology.org

Summary   To provide financial assistance to adults who have been diagnosed with kidney or urologic disease and are interested in returning to college.

Eligibility   This program is open to adults older than 25 years of age who have been diagnosed with kidney or urologic disease. Applicants must be interested in completing a degree, learning a new job skill, changing careers, or engaging in physical rehabilitation. Along with their application, they must submit an essay of 1-2 pages on questions related to their disease, their educational background and goals, and their contributions to the renal, urologic, or transplant community. Selection is based on evidence of prior achievements, motivation to accomplish stated goals, and financial need. Priority is given to applicants from the sponsoring organization's participating partner centers.

Financial data   The stipend is $1,500 per year. Funds are paid directly to the recipient's institution.

Duration   1 year; may be renewed up to 3 additional years.

Number awarded   Varies each year; recently, 4 of these awards were presented.

Deadline   May of each year.

[518]
NEW ENGLAND CHAPTER SCHOLARSHIPS

Asthma and Allergy Foundation of America-New
  England Chapter
109 Highland Avenue
Needham, MA 02494
(781) 444-7778   Toll Free: (877) 2-ASTHMA
Fax: (781) 444-7718   E-mail: aafane@aafane.org
Web: www.asthmaandallergies.org/Scholarship.html

Summary   To provide financial assistance to high school students from New England who suffer from asthma or significant allergies and plan to attend college in any state.

Eligibility   This program is open to juniors and seniors at high schools in New England who plan to begin higher education at a school in any state after graduating from high school. Applicants must suffer from asthma or significant allergies and must submit a 1-page essay on a topic that changes annually but relates to asthma. Recently, students were invited to write on "Overcoming obstacles to managing asthma or severe allergies as a teen." Selection is based on the essay, academic record, extracurricular activities, community service, work experience, and academic honors and achievements.

Financial data The stipend is $1,000.

Duration 1 year.

Additional data Recipients are expected to serve as a role model to other teens who suffer from asthma or significant allergies by appearing at 2 events and speaking to the press.

Number awarded 1 each year.

Deadline February of each year.

[519]
NEW JERSEY CENTER FOR TOURETTE SYNDROME SCHOLARSHIP

New Jersey Center for Tourette Syndrome, Inc.
50 Division Street, Suite 205
Somerville, NJ 08876
(908) 575-7350   Fax: (908) 575-8699
E-mail: info@njcts.org
Web: www.njcts.org/scholarships.php

Summary To provide financial assistance to high school seniors in New Jersey who have Tourette Syndrome and plan to attend college in any state.

Eligibility This program is open to seniors graduating from high schools in New Jersey who plan to attend a college or trade school in any state. Applicants must have been diagnosed with Tourette Syndrome. Selection is based on academic record, recommendations, and an essay or talents as demonstrated by an audiotape, compact disc, digital video disc, or videotape. Financial need is not considered in the selection process.

Financial data A stipend is awarded (amount not specified).

Duration 1 year.

Number awarded 1 each year.

Deadline March of each year.

[520]
NJCFSA COLLEGE SCHOLARSHIP

New Jersey Chronic Fatigue Syndrome Association, Inc.
P.O. Box 477
Florham Park, NJ 07932
(609) 219-0662   Toll Free: (888) 835-3677
Fax: (973) 765-0653
Web: njcfsa.org

Summary To provide financial assistance to high school seniors in New Jersey who have Chronic Fatigue Syndrome (CFS) are plan to attend college in any state.

Eligibility This program is open to seniors graduating from high schools in New Jersey and planning to attend a college, university, or technical school in any state. Applicants must have been diagnosed with CFS. They must

have a GPA of 2.0 or higher. Recent high school graduates who had to delay continuing their education because of CFS are also eligible. Along with their application, they must submit a 350-word essay on what they see as their goal for higher education or career direction and how having CFS has influenced their choice. Selection is based on that essay, merit, and financial need.

Financial data The stipend is $1,000.

Duration 1 year.

Number awarded 1 each year.

Deadline April of each year.

[521]
NORTHERN AND SOUTHERN NEW ENGLAND CHAPTER JUVENILE ARTHRITIS COLLEGE SCHOLARSHIPS

Arthritis Foundation-Northern and Southern New England Chapter
Attn: Scholarship Chair
35 Cold Spring Road, Suite 411
Rocky Hill, CT 06067
(860) 563-1177   Toll Free: (800) 541-8350
Fax: (860) 563-6018   E-mail: info.sne@arthritis.org
Web: www.arthritis.org

Summary To provide financial assistance for college to high school seniors from New England and northern New York who have arthritis or rheumatic disease.

Eligibility This program is open to 1) college-bound seniors graduating from high schools in Connecticut, Maine, New Hampshire, Rhode Island, Vermont, and northern New York (Clinton, Essex, and Franklin counties) and 2) residents of those areas currently attending college. Applicants must have been diagnosed with arthritis or rheumatic disease. Along with their application, they must submit a personal essay discussing who they are, describing their reasons for wanting to continue their education, their career objectives and goals, and how their juvenile arthritis has affected their education and career goals. Selection is based on academic achievement, impact of arthritis, and volunteer and community service; financial need is not considered.

Financial data The stipend is $1,000.

Duration 1 year.

Additional data Residents of Connecticut should contact the Arthritis Foundation office in Rocky Hill. Residents of Maine, New Hampshire, Vermont, and northern New York should contact the Arthritis Foundation, 6 Chenell Drive, Suite 260, Concord, NH 03301, (603) 224-9322, (800) 639-2113, Fax: (603) 224-3778, E-mail: info.nne@arthritis.org. Residents of Rhode Island should contact the Arthritis Foundation, Airport Office Park, 2348 Post Road, Suite 104, Warwick, RI 02886, (401) 739-3773, Fax: (401) 739-8990, E-mail: info.sne@arthritis.org.

Number awarded 3 each year.

Deadline April of each year.

[522]
OHIO YOUTH CANCER SURVIVOR COLLEGE SCHOLARSHIP

American Cancer Society-Ohio Division
Attn: Youth Survivor Scholarship Review Committee
5555 Frantz Road
Dublin, OH 43017
(614) 889-9565   Toll Free: (888) ACS-OHIO, ext. 8405
Fax: (614) 889-6578   E-mail: OhioACS@cancer.org
Web: www.cancer.org

Summary To provide financial assistance for college to residents of Ohio who have been diagnosed as having cancer.

Eligibility This program is open to residents of Ohio who were diagnosed with cancer before the age of 21. Applicants must be U.S. citizens, currently younger than 25 years of age, who plan to attend or are attending an accredited university or community college in the United States. Along with their application, they must submit an essay on their reasons for applying for this scholarship. Selection is based on academic performance, community service, and leadership.

Financial data The stipend is $1,000 per year.

Duration 1 year; recipients are encouraged to reapply.

Additional data This program was established in 2000.

Number awarded Approximately 100 each year.

Deadline January of each year.

[523]
P. BUCKLEY MOSS ENDOWED SCHOLARSHIP

P. Buckley Moss Society
20 Stoneridge Drive, Suite 102
Waynesboro, VA 22980
(540) 943-5678   Fax: (540) 949-8408
E-mail: society@mosssociety.org
Web: www.mosssociety.org/page.php?id=69

Summary To provide financial assistance to high school seniors with language-related learning disabilities who plan to study visual arts in college.

Eligibility Eligible to be nominated for this scholarship are high school seniors with language-related learning disabilities and visual arts talent. Nominations must be submitted by a member of the P. Buckley Moss Society. Nominees must be planning to attend a 4-year college or university or a 2-year community college and prepare for a career in a visual art field. The nomination packets must include evidence of financial need, verification of a language-related learning disability from a counselor or case manager, a high school transcript, 2 letters of recommendation, and 3 essays by the nominees: 1) themselves; 2) their learning disability, how it has challenged them, specific strategies they have used to cope, and its effect on their lives; and 3) where they intend to go to school and why, how they plan to use their artistic talent, and what they see themselves doing with their art in 10 years.

Financial data The stipend is $1,500. Funds are paid to the recipient's college or university.

Duration 1 year; may be renewed for up to 3 additional years.

Additional data This scholarship was first awarded in 2007.

Number awarded 1 each year.

Deadline February of each year.

[524]
PATIENT ADVOCATE FOUNDATION SCHOLARSHIPS FOR SURVIVORS

Patient Advocate Foundation
Attn: Scholarship Coordinator
421 Butler Farm Road
Hampton, VA 23669
Toll Free: (800) 532-5274   Fax: (757) 873-8999
E-mail: help@patientadvocate.org
Web: www.patientadvocate.org/events.php?p=69

Summary To provide financial assistance for college or graduate school to students seeking to initiate or complete a course of study that has been interrupted or delayed by a diagnosis of cancer or other life threatening disease.

Eligibility This program is open to students under 25 years of age who are working full time on a 2-year, 4-year, or advanced degree. The college or graduate education of applicants must have been interrupted or delayed by a diagnosis of cancer or other life threatening, chronic, or debilitating disease. They must be willing to commit to completing 20 hours of community service for the year if they are awarded a scholarship. Along with their application, they must submit a 1,000-word essay on how their diagnosis has impacted their life and future goals. Financial need is also considered in the selection process.

Financial data The stipend is $3,000. Funds are paid directly to the college or university to help cover tuition and other fee costs. The cost of books is not included.

Duration 1 year; may be renewed up to 3 additional years, provided the recipient remains enrolled full time, maintains a GPA of 3.0 or higher, and performs 20 hours of community service.

Additional data This program includes the Cheryl Grimmel Award, the Jo Ann Davis Award, the Monica Bailes Award, the Robin L. Prachel Award, the Mary T. Christian Award, the Karen Condon Reeder Award, and the Jim Meade and Luke Barlow Award. Support for 1 of the scholarships is provided by the United Health Foundation.

Number awarded Varies each year; recently, 12 of these scholarships were awarded.

Deadline April of each year.

[525]
PEDIATRIC BRAIN TUMOR FOUNDATION SCHOLARSHIP PROGRAM

Pediatric Brain Tumor Foundation of the United States
Attn: Family Support Program Manager
302 Ridgefield Court
Asheville, NC 28806
(828) 665-6891, ext. 306   Toll Free: (800) 253-6530
Fax: (828) 665-6894   E-mail: pbtfus@pbtfus.org
Web: www.pbtfus.org/survivors/education/scholarships

Summary To provide financial assistance for college to survivors of a brain or spinal cord tumor.

Eligibility This program is open to high school seniors and current college students who have been diagnosed with a childhood brain or spinal cord tumor. Applicants must be enrolled or planning to enroll at a technical school, vocational school, junior college, or 4-year college or university. They must submit an essay, proof of tumor diagnosis, GPA, intent to register for college, high school transcripts, and recommendations.

Financial data The stipend is $2,500 per year.

Duration 2 years.

Additional data This program receives funding from the Tim and Tom Gullikson Family Support Fund.

Number awarded Varies each year; recently, 236 of these scholarships were awarded.

Deadline February of each year.

[526]
PETER AND BRUCE BIDSTRUP SCHOLARSHIP FUND

Arizona Kidney Foundation
Attn: Patient Services Director
4203 East Indian School Road, Suite 140
Phoenix, AZ 85018
(602) 840-1644   Fax: (602) 840-2360
E-mail: glennas@azkidney.org
Web: www.azkidney.org

Summary To provide financial assistance for college to kidney patients in Arizona.

Eligibility This program is open to students in Arizona who are undergoing dialysis treatment or have received kidney transplants. Applicants must be attending or planning to attend a college, community college, or technical school in Arizona. Financial need is considered in the selection process.

Financial data This scholarship pays the tuition fees at schools in Arizona.

Additional data This scholarship fund was established in 1985 to honor Peter and Bruce Bidstrup, who did not survive kidney disease. Its selection committee is chaired by their mother, Carol Bidstrup. Recipients must attend school in Arizona.

Number awarded Varies each year.

Deadline Deadline not specified.

[527]
PETER HERCHENBACH MEMORIAL SCHOLARSHIPS

Peter Herchenbach Memorial Fund
19377 Peterson Road
Libertyville, IL 60048
(847) 612-7958
Web: petspals.org

Summary To provide financial assistance to residents of Illinois who have been diagnosed with cancer or other life-threatening disease and are interested in attending college in any state.

Eligibility This program is open to Illinois residents under 24 years of age who are high school seniors or freshmen, sophomores, or juniors at an institution of higher education in any state. Applicants must have been diagnosed with cancer or other life-threatening disease. In the selection process, no consideration is given to gender, race, academic record, or socioeconomic status. Special consideration is given to applicants known for their outgoing "will win" attitude despite being physically compromised by their disease.

Financial data The stipend is $5,000.

Duration 1 year.

Number awarded 1 or more each year.

Deadline March of each year.

[528]
PFIZER EPILEPSY SCHOLARSHIP AWARD

Pfizer Inc.
c/o Adelphi Eden Health Communications
30 Irving Place, 10th Floor
New York, NY 10003
Toll Free: (800) AWARD-PF
E-mail: info@epilepsy-scholarship.com
Web: www.epilepsy-scholarship.com

Summary To provide financial assistance for college or graduate school to individuals with epilepsy.

Eligibility Applicants must be under a physician's care for epilepsy (taking prescribed medication) and must submit an application with 2 letters of recommendation (1 from the physician) and verification of academic status. They must be high school seniors entering college in the fall; college freshmen, sophomores, or juniors continuing in the fall; or college seniors planning to enter graduate school in the fall. Along with their application, they must submit a 250-word essay on something they have dealt with as a person with epilepsy; they may choose to write on 1) how they have overcome the challenges of epilepsy; 2) what living with epilepsy means to them; 3) someone who has been helpful to them in their success; or 4) an achievement of which they are proud. Selection is based on success in overcoming the challenges of epilepsy, success in school, participation in extracurricular or community activities, and desire to make the most out of college or graduate school; financial need is not considered.

Financial data The stipend is $2,000.

Duration 1 year; nonrenewable.

Number awarded 40 each year.

Deadline June of each year.

[529]
PROFESSOR ULLA HEDNER SCHOLARSHIPS

Novo Nordisk Inc.
Attn: Customer Care
100 College Road West
Princeton, NJ 08540
(609) 987-5800   Toll Free: (877) NOVO-777
Fax: (800) 826-6993
Web: www.changingpossibilities-us.com

Summary To provide financial assistance to high school seniors and current college students who have a bleeding disorder.

Eligibility This program is open to high school seniors and students under 23 years of age currently enrolled in college or vocational school. Applicants must have hemophilia with an inhibitor or factor VII deficiency. Along with their application, they must submit a 500-word essay on 1 of the following topics: 1) how has having hemophilia with inhibitors, congenital factor VII deficiency, or acquired hemophilia affected their life; 2) how has having hemophilia with inhibitors, congenital factor VII deficiency, or acquired hemophilia affected their educational goals; or 3) how will they use their education to achieve their life goals.

Financial data Stipends range from $2,000 to $7,000 per year.

Duration 1 year; recipients may reapply.

Additional data This program is offered as part of SevenSECURE, P.O. Box 18648, Louisville, KY 40261.

Number awarded Varies each year.

Deadline April of each year.

[530]
PROJECT RED FLAG ACADEMIC SCHOLARSHIP FOR WOMEN WITH BLEEDING DISORDERS

National Hemophilia Foundation
Attn: Manager of Education
P.O. Box 971483
Ypsilanti, MI 48197
(734) 890-2504   E-mail: pflax@hemophilia.org
Web: www.projectredflag.org/scholarship.htm

Summary To provide financial assistance for college or graduate school to women who have a bleeding disorder.

Eligibility This program is open to women who are entering or already enrolled in an undergraduate or graduate program at a university, college, or accredited vocational school. Applicants must have von Willebrand Disease, hemophilia or other clotting factor deficiency, or carrier status. Along with their application, they must submit a 250-word essay that describes how their education and future career plans will benefit others in the bleeding disorders community. Financial need is not considered in the selection process.

Financial data The stipend is $2,500.

Duration 1 year.

Additional data The program was established in 2005 in partnership with the Centers for Disease Control and Prevention (CDC) and with support from CSL Behring.

Number awarded 2 each year.

Deadline May of each year.

[531]
RACHEL WARNER SCHOLARSHIP

Committee of Ten Thousand
236 Massachusetts Avenue, N.E., Suite 609
Washington, DC 20002-4971
(202) 543-0988   Toll Free: (800) 488-2688
Fax: (202) 543-6720   E-mail: cott-dc@earthlink.net
Web: www.cott1.org/fullstory.html?id=50

Summary To provide financial assistance for college to people with a bleeding disorder.

Eligibility This program is open to people who have a bleeding disorder. Applicants must be attending or planning to attend college. Along with their application, they must submit a 1-page essay about their past and proposed future plans.

Financial data Stipends range up to $1,000.

Duration 1 year.

Number awarded 1 or more each year.

Deadline April of each year.

[532]
RALPH G. NORMAN SCHOLARSHIPS

Learning Disabilities Association of Arkansas
P.O. Box 95255
North Little Rock, AR 72190-5255
(501) 666-8777   E-mail: ldaarkansas@yahoo.com
Web: ldaarkansas.org/Volunteers.php

Summary To provide financial assistance for college to residents of Arkansas who have a learning disability.

Eligibility This program is open to Arkansas residents who have a learning disability. Applicants must be graduating high school seniors, current college students, or GED recipients. Along with their application, they must submit documentation of their disability, transcripts of all high school and/or college courses, 2 letters of recommendation, and a 2-paragraph statement of their future educational or career goals.

Financial data The stipend is $2,000.

Duration 1 year.

Number awarded 4 each year.

Deadline March of each year.

[533]
ROBERT GUTHRIE PKU SCHOLARSHIP

National PKU News
6869 Woodlawn Avenue, N.E., Suite 116
Seattle, WA 98115-5469
(206) 525-8140   Fax: (206) 525-5023
E-mail: schuett@pkunews.org
Web: www.pkunews.org/guthrie/guthrie.htm

Summary To provide financial assistance for college to students with phenylketonuria (PKU).

Eligibility This program is open to college-age people from any country who have PKU and are on the required diet. Applicants must be accepted as an undergraduate at an accredited college or technical school before the scholarship is awarded, but they may apply before acceptance is confirmed. Along with their application, they must submit a statement that includes why they are applying for the scholarship, their educational objectives and career plans, extracurricular activities, honors and awards, current diet and how they cope with it on a daily basis, overall experience with PKU, attitudes toward the PKU diet now and in the past, and the influence PKU as had on their life. Selection is based on that statement, academic record, educational and career goals, extracurricular activities, volunteer work, and letters of recommendation. Financial need is considered but is not required; students can be awarded a scholarship without having significant financial need.

Financial data Stipends vary but recently have been $2,000.

Duration 1 year.

Additional data These scholarships were first awarded in 1998.

Number awarded Varies each year; recently, 4 of these scholarships were awarded.

Deadline October of each year.

[534]
ROBERT J. AND DENNIS R. KELLY MEMORIAL SCHOLARSHIP

Hemophilia Association of New Jersey
Attn: Scholarship Committee
197 Route 18 South, Suite 206 North
East Brunswick, NJ 08816
(732) 249-6000   Fax: (732) 249-7999
E-mail: mailbox@hanj.org
Web: www.hanj.org

Summary To provide financial assistance to New Jersey residents who have a bleeding disorder and are interested in attending college in any state.

Eligibility This program is open to New Jersey residents who have a bleeding disorder (Hemophilia A or B, von Willebrand Disease, or a similar blood coagulation disorder). Applicants must be attending or planning to attend an accredited college or university in any state. They must have at least a 2.5 GPA, have been actively involved in athletics during their high school years as a participant or in a coaching capacity, and be able to demonstrate financial need. Along with their application, they must submit a family financial profile, official transcripts, and a brief essay (up to 2 pages) on how they meet the eligibility criteria. Membership in the Hemophilia Association of New Jersey is required.

Financial data The stipend is $1,000 per year.

Duration 1 year; may be renewed for up to 3 additional years, provided the recipient maintains at least a 2.25 GPA and funding is available.

Additional data Recipients are expected to continue their involvement in school sports.

Number awarded 2 new awards each year.

Deadline April of each year.

[535]
ROBIN ROMANO MEMORIAL SCHOLARSHIP

Robin Romano Memorial Fund
c/o Ken Fratus
Boston Globe Sports
135 Morrissey Boulevard
P.O. Box 55819
Boston, MA 02105-5819
(617) 929-7949   Toll Free: (800) 628-6214

Summary To provide financial assistance to high school seniors and graduates from Massachusetts who are cancer survivors and interested in attending college in any state.

Eligibility This program is open to high school seniors, high school graduates, and currently-enrolled college students who are cancer survivors and residents of Massachusetts. Applicants must be attending or planning to attend a college or university in any state.

Financial data The stipend is $7,500.

Duration Up to 4 years.

Additional data Partial scholarships are often awarded to other students. This program was started in 2000. Since then, the fund has raised nearly $150,000 and has awarded full or partial scholarships to 10 students.

Number awarded 1 or more each year.

Deadline Deadline not specified.

[536]
R.O.C.K. COLLEGE SCHOLARSHIP PROGRAM

American Cancer Society-Florida Division
3709 West Jetton Avenue
Tampa, FL 33629-5146
(813) 349-4405
Toll Free: (800) 444-1410, ext. 4405 (within FL)
Fax: (813) 254-5857
E-mail: susan.bellomy@cancer.org
Web: www.cancer.org

Summary To provide financial assistance for college to students diagnosed with cancer in Florida.

Eligibility This program is open to Florida residents who have been diagnosed with cancer before the age of 21, are under 21 at the time of application, are high school seniors or graduates, and have been accepted to an accredited 2-year or 4-year college, university, or vocational/technical school in Florida. Applicants must submit a completed application form, 3 letters of recommendation (including 1 from a physician), their financial aid form, an official transcript, their SAT and/or ACT test scores, and a 500-word essay on their journey as a cancer survivor, goals, ambitions, and how this scholarship will help them achieve academic success. Selection is based on financial need, academic record, leadership ability, and community service.

Financial data Stipends provide up to $3,000 per year for tuition plus $300 per year for textbooks.

Duration 1 year; may be renewed to a maximum of 130 semester hours over 5 years, whichever comes first.

Additional data These scholarships were first awarded in 1992 as part of the Florida division's Reaching Out to Cancer Kids (R.O.C.K.) program. Recipients are expected to complete at least 10 hours of American Cancer Society community service annually.

Number awarded   Varies each year; recently, 154 of these scholarships were awarded.

Deadline   April of each year.

[537]
ROSEMARY QUIGLEY MEMORIAL SCHOLARSHIP

Boomer Esiason Foundation
c/o Jerry Cahill
483 Tenth Avenue, Suite 300
New York, NY 10018
(646) 292-7930   Fax: (646) 292-7945
E-mail: jcahillbef@aol.com
Web: www.cfscholarships.com

Summary   To provide financial assistance to undergraduate and graduate students who have cystic fibrosis (CF).

Eligibility   This program is open to CF patients who are working on an undergraduate or graduate degree. Applicants must be able to demonstrate a clear sense of life goals and a commitment to living life to the fullest, despite having CF. Along with their application, they must submit a letter from their doctor confirming the diagnosis of CF and a list of daily medications, information on financial need, a detailed breakdown of tuition costs from their academic institution, transcripts, and a 2-page essay on 1) their post-graduation goals and 2) the importance of compliance with CF therapies and what they practice on a daily basis to stay healthy. Selection is based on academic ability, character, leadership potential, service to the community, and financial need. Finalists are interviewed by telephone.

Financial data   A stipend is awarded (amount not specified). Funds are paid directly to the academic institution to assist in covering the cost of tuition and fees.

Duration   1 year; nonrenewable.

Number awarded   1 each year.

Deadline   June of each year.

[538]
RYAN MULLALY SECOND CHANCE SCHOLARSHIPS

Ryan Mullaly Second Chance Fund
26 Meadow Lane
Pennington, NJ 08534
(609) 737-1800   E-mail: The2dChanceFund@aol.com
Web: www.ryans2dchancefund.org

Summary   To provide financial assistance for college to students who have cancer.

Eligibility   This program is open to U.S. citizens and permanent residents who were diagnosed with cancer or a recurrence of cancer between age 13 and graduation from high school. Applicants must have a treatment history that includes chemotherapy and/or radiation and must be able to demonstrate that their high school years were substantially impacted by treatment and/or side effects of treatment. They must be 22 years of age or younger and currently 1) working on an associate or bachelor's degree at an accredited 2-year or 4-year college or university, or 2)

enrolled in an accredited postsecondary vocational or trade program that will culminate in certification. Priority is given to students still undergoing treatment, those with permanent effects from treatment, and those at the beginning of their postsecondary education.

Financial data   The stipend is $1,000.

Duration   1 year; nonrenewable.

Additional data   This program was established in 2003.

Number awarded   Up to 15 each year.

Deadline   May of each year.

[539]
SACKS FOR CF SCHOLARSHIPS

Boomer Esiason Foundation
c/o Jerry Cahill
483 Tenth Avenue, Suite 300
New York, NY 10018
(646) 292-7930   Fax: (646) 292-7945
E-mail: jcahillbef@aol.com
Web: www.sacksforcf.com

Summary   To provide financial assistance to undergraduate and graduate students who have cystic fibrosis (CF).

Eligibility   This program is open to CF patients who are working on an undergraduate or graduate degree. Applicants must submit a letter from their doctor confirming the diagnosis of CF and a list of daily medications, information on financial need, a detailed breakdown of tuition costs from their academic institution, transcripts, and a 2-page essay on 1) their post-graduation goals and 2) the importance of compliance with CF therapies and what they practice on a daily basis to stay healthy. Selection is based on academic ability, character, leadership potential, service to the community, and financial need. Finalists are interviewed by telephone.

Financial data   The stipend is $1,000. Funds are paid directly to the academic institution to assist in covering the cost of tuition and fees.

Duration   1 year; nonrenewable.

Additional data   This program is funded by Solvay Pharmaceuticals, Inc., which donates $1,000 to the foundation each time a quarterback is sacked on NFL Monday Night Football games.

Number awarded   Varies each year; recently, 10 of these scholarships were awarded.

Deadline   January of each year.

[540]
SALVATORE E. QUINCI SCHOLARSHIPS

Salvatore E. Quinci Foundation
178 Florence Street
Melrose, MA 02176-3710
(781) 760-7138
Web: www.seqfoundation.org

Summary   To provide financial assistance for college to people who have a bleeding disorder.

Eligibility   This program is open to people who have been diagnosed with hemophilia or another bleeding disorder. Applicants must be attending or accepted at an accredited college, university, or vocational/technical school. Along with their application, they must submit a 1-page statement that discusses their future educational and career goals and how they plan to use the scholarship money. Selection is based on that statement, the quality of the application, high school and/or college grades, and financial need.

Financial data The stipend is $2,000. Funds must be used for tuition, fees, books, or other education-related expenses.

Duration 1 year.

Additional data Scholarships must be used within 12 months of the award date.

Number awarded 2 each year.

Deadline March of each year.

[541]
SAMFUND GRANTS AND SCHOLARSHIPS

The SAMFund for Young Adult Survivors of Cancer
89 South Street, Suite LL02
Boston, MA 02211
E-mail: grants@thesamfund.org
Web: www.thesamfund.org/pages/grants.html

Summary To provide funding to young adult cancer survivors who need assistance for the transition to post-treatment life.

Eligibility This program is open to cancer survivors between 17 and 35 years of age who are finished with active treatment and are trying to move forward with their lives. Applicants must be able to demonstrate a need for funding for such purposes as undergraduate or graduate school tuition and expenses, car and health insurance premiums, rent, fertility-related expenses, gym memberships, transportation costs, or current and residual medical bills.

Financial data Grant amounts vary; recently, they averaged approximately $2,500.

Duration These are 1-time grants.

Additional data This program, which stands for Surviving and Moving Forward, was established in 2003.

Number awarded Varies each year; since the program was established, it has awarded nearly 200 grants with a total value of $400,000.

Deadline Deadline not specified.

[542]
SCHERING-PLOUGH "WILL TO WIN" SCHOLARSHIPS

Schering-Plough Corporation
Attn: "Will to Win" Scholarship Program
P.O. Box 6503
Carlstadt, NJ 07072
Toll Free: (800) SCHERING
E-mail: requests@schering-ploughwilltowin.com
Web: www.schering-ploughwilltowin.com

Summary To provide financial assistance for college to high school seniors who have asthma.

Eligibility This program is open to high school seniors with asthma who have achieved excellence in 1 of the following 5 categories: performing arts (dance, music, theater), visual arts (painting, drawing, sculpture, photogra-

phy, film), community service, athletics, or science. Applicants must have a GPA of 3.5 or higher and a record of achievement in their entry category, including at least 1 award. They must be U.S. citizens planning to attend an accredited college or university in the United States in the following fall.

Financial data The stipend is $5,000. Funds are paid directly to the student's college.

Duration 1 year; nonrenewable.

Additional data When this program began in 1985, it was limited to athletes. It was expanded to cover the other 4 categories in 2006. If a winner is unable to use the entire scholarship for any reason, all remaining money will be donated to the high school the student attended to help another student with asthma.

Number awarded 10 each year: 2 in each of the 5 categories.

Deadline April of each year.

[543]
SCHOLARSHIP OF THE ARTS

Boomer Esiason Foundation
c/o Jerry Cahill
483 Tenth Avenue, Suite 300
New York, NY 10018
(646) 292-7930   Fax: (646) 292-7945
E-mail: jcahillbef@aol.com
Web: www.cfscholarships.com/Arts/index.htm

Summary To provide financial assistance to undergraduate and graduate students who have cystic fibrosis (CF) and are working on a degree in the arts.

Eligibility This program is open to CF patients who are working on an undergraduate or graduate degree in the arts. Applicants must submit a picture of their art work (painting, sketching, sculpture), a letter from their doctor confirming the diagnosis of CF and a list of daily medications, information on financial need, a detailed breakdown of tuition costs from their academic institution, transcripts, and a 2-page essay on 1) their post-graduation goals and 2) the importance of compliance with CF therapies and what they practice on a daily basis to stay healthy. Selection is based on academic ability, character, leadership potential, service to the community, and financial need.

Financial data Stipends range from $500 to $2,000. Funds are paid directly to the academic institution to assist in covering the cost of tuition and fees.

Duration 1 year; nonrenewable.

Number awarded 1 each year.

Deadline May of each year.

[544]
SCHWALLIE FAMILY SCHOLARSHIPS

Organization for Autism Research
Attn: Scholarship
2000 North 14th Street, Suite 710
Arlington, VA 22201
(703) 243-9710
Web: www.researchautism.org

Summary To provide financial assistance for college to individuals with autism or Asperger's Syndrome.

Eligibility This program is open to individuals with an established autism or Asperger's Syndrome diagnosis who are attending or planning to attend an accredited institution of higher education. Applicants must be enrolled at least part time and be working toward certification or accreditation in a particular field. Along with their application, they must submit a 1,000-word autobiographical essay that includes their reasons for applying for this scholarship. Selection is based on originality of content, previous challenges overcome, future aspirations, and financial need.

Financial data The stipend is $3,000.

Duration 1 year; nonrenewable.

Additional data This program was established in 2007.

Number awarded 7 each year: 4 to students at 4-year colleges or universities, 2 to students at 2-year colleges, and 1 to a student at a vocational/technical school.

Deadline April of each year.

[545]
SCOTT DELGADILLO SCHOLARSHIP

Friends of Scott Foundation
Attn: Scholarship Fund
6977 Navajo Road, Number 168
San Diego, CA 92119
(619) 223-7268   Fax: (619) 223-7002
E-mail: aztec.graphics@yahoo.com
Web: www.friendsofscott.org/scholarship.aspx

Summary To provide financial assistance for college or graduate school to childhood cancer survivors.

Eligibility This program is open to survivors of childhood cancer and to patients currently receiving treatment. Applicants must be attending or planning to attend a technical school, vocational school, junior college, or 4-year college or university as an undergraduate or graduate student. Along with their application, they must submit a 500-word essay on how their experience with cancer has impacted their life. Selection is based on financial need and personal hardship.

Financial data A stipend is awarded (amount not specified).

Duration 1 year.

Number awarded Varies each year; recently, 3 of these scholarships were awarded.

Deadline April of each year.

[546]
SCOTT TARBELL SCHOLARSHIP

Accredo's Hemophilia Health Services
Attn: Scholarship Committee
201 Great Circle Road
Nashville, TN 37228
(615) 850-5212   Toll Free: (800) 800-6606
Fax: (615) 261-6730
E-mail: Shayne.harris@accredo.com
Web: www.hemophiliahealth.com/Scholarships.html

Summary To provide financial assistance to high school seniors and current college students who have hemophilia

and are interested in working on a degree or certification in computer science and/or mathematics.

Eligibility This program is open to high school seniors and college freshmen, sophomores, and juniors who have hemophilia A or B severe. Applicants must be enrolled or planning to enroll full time at an accredited nonprofit college, university, or vocational/technical school in the United States or Puerto Rico. They must be interested in working on a degree or certification in computer science and/or mathematics. Along with their application, they must submit an essay, up to 250 words, on the following topic: "Upon receiving your education in math and/or computer science, how will you use the new technologies (e.g., computer, internet) to better mankind, and what ethical issues will you need to address?" U.S. citizenship is required. Selection is based on the essay, academic achievements and records, community involvement, and financial need.

Financial data The stipend is at least $1,500. Funds are issued payable to the recipient's school.

Duration 1 year; recipients may reapply.

Additional data This program, which started in 2003, is administered by International Scholarship and Tuition Services, Inc., P.O. Box 23737, Nashville, TN 37202-3737, (615) 320-3149, Fax: (615) 320-3151, E-mail: info@apply-ists.net.

Number awarded 1 or more each year, depending on the availability of funds.

Deadline April of each year.

[547]
SEAN SILVER MEMORIAL SCHOLARSHIP

Ulman Cancer Fund for Young Adults
Attn: Scholarship Program Coordinator
10440 Little Patuxent Parkway, Suite 1G
Columbia, MD 21044
(410) 964-0202, ext. 106   Toll Free: (888) 393-FUND
E-mail: scholarship@ulmanfund.org
Web: www.ulmanfund.org

Summary To provide financial assistance for college or graduate school to young adults who have cancer.

Eligibility This program is open to students who are younger than 30 years of age and currently undergoing active treatment for cancer. Applicants must be attending or planning to attend a 4-year college or university to work on an undergraduate or graduate degree. They must be U.S. citizens or permanent residents. Along with their application, they must submit an essay of at least 1,000 words on what they have discovered about themselves while attending school as a young adult receiving treatment for or living with cancer. Selection is based on demonstrated dedication to community service, commitment to educational and professional goals, use of their cancer experience to impact the lives of other young adults affected by cancer, medical hardship, and financial need.

Financial data The stipend is $2,500. Funds are paid directly to the educational institution.

Duration 1 year.

Additional data This scholarship was first awarded in 2008. Recipients must agree to complete 80 hours of community service.

Number awarded 1 each year.

Deadline April of each year.

[548]
SEVENSECURE ADULT EDUCATION GRANTS

Novo Nordisk Inc.
Attn: Customer Care
100 College Road West
Princeton, NJ 08540
(609) 987-5800   Toll Free: (877) NOVO-777
Fax: (800) 826-6993
Web: www.changingpossibilities-us.com

Summary To provide financial assistance for college to adults who have a bleeding disorder.

Eligibility This program is open to adults over 23 years of age currently enrolled in college or vocational school. Applicants must have hemophilia with an inhibitor or factor VII deficiency. They must be working on a certificate or associate or bachelor's degree to get more training to help improve their career or transition to a new field.

Financial data Stipends range up to $2,500 per year. Funds are paid directly to the university or institution.

Duration 1 year.

Additional data This program is offered as part of SevenSECURE, P.O. Box 18648, Louisville, KY 40261.

Number awarded Varies each year.

Deadline Applications may be submitted at any time.

[549]
SHANNON O'DANIEL MEMORIAL SCHOLARSHIP

Epilepsy Foundation of Kentuckiana
Attn: Director of Education
Kosair Charities Centre
982 Eastern Parkway
Louisville, KY 40217-1566
(502) 637-4440   Toll Free: (866) 275-1078
Fax: (502) 637-4442
Web: www.epilepsyfoundation.org

Summary To provide financial assistance to high school seniors in Kentucky and southern Indiana who have epilepsy and are interested in attending college in any state.

Eligibility This program is open to seniors graduating from high schools in Kentucky (except Boone, Campbell, Grant, and Kenton counties) or southern Indiana (Clark, Floyd, and Harrison counties) who have epilepsy or another seizure disorder and are under a physician's care. Applicants be planning to attend a college or university in any state. Along with their application, they must 250-word essays on 1) something of direct personal importance to them as a person with epilepsy; and 2) their plans for their future educational and professional endeavors. Financial need is also considered in the selection process.

Financial data The stipend is $1,000.

Duration 1 year.

Additional data This program was established in 2001.

Number awarded 1 each year.

Deadline April of each year.

[550]
SNOWDROP FOUNDATION SCHOLARSHIPS

Snowdrop Foundation
Attn: Kevin Kline, President
2310 Upland Park Drive
Sugar Land, TX 77479
(713) 232-9052
E-mail: kevin@snowdropfoundation.org
Web: www.snowdropfoundation.org

Summary To provide financial assistance for college or graduate school to students who have been diagnosed with cancer.

Eligibility This program is open to students entering or attending college or graduate school. Applicants must have been diagnosed with cancer. Along with their application, they must submit a 250-word description of themselves; a 250-word description of their family situation; information on financial need; a letter from their attending physician verifying their medical history and current medical situation; and an essay of 500 to 1,000 words on how their experience with cancer has impacted their life values and career goals.

Financial data A stipend is awarded (amount not specified).

Duration 1 year.

Number awarded Varies each year.

Deadline April of each year.

[551]
SOLVAYCARES SCHOLARSHIPS

Solvay Pharmaceuticals, Inc.
Attn: SolvayCARES Scholarship Program
901 Sawyer Road
Marietta, GA 30062
(770) 578-5898   Toll Free: (800) 354-0026, ext. 5898
Fax: (770) 578-5586
E-mail: SolvayCARES.Scholarship@solvay.com
Web: www.solvaycaresscholarship.com

Summary To provide financial assistance for college or graduate school to students with cystic fibrosis (CF).

Eligibility This program is open to high school seniors, vocational school students, college students, and graduate students with CF. U.S. citizenship is required. Applicants must submit 1) a 250-word essay on the topic, "My dream for the future is..."; and 2) a creative presentation (e.g., written work, a piece of art, a craft, collage, photograph) on what sets them apart from their peers, what inspires them to live life to the fullest, or anything else that they think makes them unique; and 3) a photograph. Selection is based on academic excellence, creativity, community involvement, and ability to serve as a role model to others with CF. The program designates 1 applicant as the Thriving Student Achiever.

Financial data The stipend is $2,500 per year. The Thriving Student Achiever receives an additional award (recently, $14,500 for a total award of $17,000 to honor the program's 17th year).

Duration   1 year.

Additional data   This program started in 1992. Winners also receive a 1-year supply of nutritional drinks and vitamins. The essay, creative presentations, and photograph of all recipients who agree to be considered are posted online so patients, families, friends, physicians, the CF community, and the general public can vote to select the Thriving Student Achiever.

Number awarded   40 each year, of whom 1 is designated the Thriving Student Achiever.

Deadline   April of each year.

[552]
SOOZIE COURTER SHARING A BRIGHTER TOMORROW HEMOPHILIA SCHOLARSHIP

Wyeth Pharmaceuticals
Attn: Hemophilia Scholarship Program
500 Arcola Road
Collegeville, PA 19426
Toll Free: (888) 999-2349
Web: www.hemophiliavillage.com/scholarship.html

Summary   To provide financial assistance for college or graduate school in any field to persons with hemophilia.

Eligibility   This program is open to persons with hemophilia (A or B) who are high school seniors, have a GED, or are currently attending an accredited college, university, junior college, vocational school, or graduate school. They must need financial assistance to work on a degree. Along with their application, they must submit a 2-page essay on their choice of assigned topics.

Financial data   The stipends are $2,500 for undergraduate students or $4,000 for graduate students.

Duration   1 year.

Additional data   This program was established in 1998 and given its current name in 2000.

Number awarded   17 each year: 12 to undergraduates and 5 to graduate students.

Deadline   April of each year.

[553]
STEPHEN T. MARCHELLO SCHOLARSHIPS

Stephen T. Marchello Scholarship Foundation
1170 East Long Place
Centennial, CO 80122
(303) 886-5018   E-mail: fmarchello@earthlink.net
Web: www.stmfoundation.org

Summary   To provide financial assistance to students from Colorado and Montana who have survived childhood cancer and are interested in attending college in any state.

Eligibility   This program is open to high school seniors who either live in or were treated for cancer in Colorado or Montana. Applicants must be working on or planning to work on an undergraduate degree at a school in any state. They must submit essays on 2 topics: 1) their academic and professional goals, why they have chosen to pursue those goals, and how this scholarship will help them obtain their goals; and 2) an event in world history that has made

a significant positive contribution and their reasons why they feel this was important. In addition to those 2 essays, selection is based on high school GPA; SAT or ACT scores; information provided by the doctor, clinic, or hospital where they were treated; and 2 letters of reference.

Financial data   Stipends range up to $2,000 per year.

Duration   1 year; may be renewed.

Additional data   This foundation was established by the family of Stephen T. Marchello, who died of cancer in 1999. It awarded its first scholarship in 2000.

Number awarded   Varies each year. Recently, 3 of these scholarships were awarded: 1 at $2,000, 1 at $1,500, and 1 at $1,000.

Deadline   March of each year.

[554]
STEVEN M. PEREZ FOUNDATION SCHOLARSHIPS

Steven M. Perez Foundation
P.O. Box 955
Melville, NY 11747
(631) 367-9016   Fax: (631) 367-3848
E-mail: info@smpfoundation.org
Web: www.smpfoundation.org

Summary   To provide financial assistance for college to high school seniors who have survived leukemia or lost a family member to cancer or a related disease.

Eligibility   This program is open to graduating high school seniors who have survived leukemia or who have lost a parent or sibling to cancer or a related disease. Applicants must be planning to attend a college or university in any state. Along with their application, they must submit medical certification, a recommendation from a counselor, and an essay that describes their connection to leukemia.

Financial data   Stipend amounts vary; recently, they averaged $1,450.

Duration   1 year.

Number awarded   Varies each year; recently, 10 of these scholarships were awarded.

Deadline   April of each year.

[555]
SUSAN BUNCH MEMORIAL SCHOLARSHIP

California Association for Postsecondary Education
   and Disability
Attn: Executive Assistant
71423 Biskra Road
Rancho Mirage, CA 92270
(760) 346-8206   Fax: (760) 340-5275
TDD: (760) 341-4084   E-mail: caped2000@aol.com
Web: www.caped.net/scholarships.html

Summary   To provide financial assistance to undergraduate and graduate students in California who have a learning disability.

Eligibility   This program is open to students at public and private colleges and universities in California who have a learning disability. Undergraduates must have completed at least 6 semester credits and have a GPA of 2.5 or higher. Graduate students must have completed at least 3 semester units and have a GPA of 3.0 or higher. Along with their application, they must submit a 1-page personal letter that demonstrates their writing skills, progress towards meeting their educational and vocational goals, management of their disability, and involvement in community activities. They must also submit a letter of recommendation from a faculty member, verification of disability, official transcripts, proof of current enrollment, and documentation of financial need.

Financial data The stipend is $1,000.

Duration 1 year.

Number awarded 1 each year.

Deadline September of each year.

[556]
THOMARA LATIMER CANCER FOUNDATION SCHOLARSHIPS

Thomara Latimer Cancer Foundation
Attn: Scholarship Committee
Franklin Plaza Center
29193 Northeastern Highway, Suite 528
Southfield, MI 48034-1006
(248) 557-2346   Fax: (248) 557-8063
E-mail: scholarships@thomlatimercares.org
Web: www.thomlatimercares.org

Summary To provide financial assistance to African American residents of Michigan, especially those who have had cancer, who are interested in studying a medically-related field at a college in any state.

Eligibility This program is open to African American residents of Michigan between 17 and 30 years of age. Applicants must be 1) a high school senior accepted at an accredited college or university in any state in a medically-related program (e.g., medical technician, physician assistant); 2) a student admitted to a medically-related professional program (e.g., nursing, medicine, physical or occupational therapy) at a college or university in any state. They must have a GPA of 3.0 or higher. Along with their application, they must submit a brief essay on why they should be awarded this scholarship. Financial need is not considered in the selection process. Special consideration is given to students who are cancer survivors.

Financial data The stipend is $1,000.

Duration 1 year; may be renewed 1 additional year.

Number awarded 10 each year.

Deadline December of each year.

[557]
THOMAS F. SMITH SCHOLARSHIP

Georgia Transplant Foundation
Attn: Scholarship Program
600 Embassy Row, Suite 250
6600 Peachtree Dunwoody Road N.E.
Atlanta, GA 30328-6773
(770) 457-3796   Toll Free: (866) 428-9411
Fax: (770) 457-7916
Web: www.gatransplant.org/AcademicScholarships.aspx

Summary To provide financial assistance to residents of Georgia who are transplant recipients and interested in attending college in any state.

Eligibility This program is open to residents of Georgia who are entering or continuing at an accredited institution of higher learning in any state. Applicants must be an organ transplant recipient. Along with their application, they must submit a 3-page personal statement in which they describe themselves as individuals, relate an event that changed their life or beliefs, describe an issue about which they have strong feelings, present their life goals as they relate to their field of study, explain any situation or financial concern that could impact their educational goals, answer why they feel they are eligible for this scholarship, and address their plans as those relate to their education, career, and long-term goals.

Financial data The stipend is $1,000 per year.

Duration 1 year; may be renewed up to 3 additional years.

Number awarded 1 or 2 each year.

Deadline May of each year.

[558]
TRIO SCHOLARSHIPS

Transplant Recipients International Organization, Inc.
Attn: Scholarship Committee
2100 M Street, N.W., Suite 170-353
Washington, DC 20037-1233
(202) 293-0980   Toll Free: (800) TRIO-386
E-mail: info@trioweb.org
Web: www.trioweb.org

Summary To provide financial assistance for college to members of the Transplant Recipients International Organization (TRIO) and their families.

Eligibility This program is open to TRIO members and their immediate family who are organ or tissue candidates, recipients, donors, or their immediate family members. Applicants must be attending or planning to attend an accredited college, university, or trade/technical certificate program. They must have a cumulative GPA of 2.5 or higher and be able to demonstrate financial need. Along with their application, they must submit a 500-word essay on their personal history and educational and career ambitions.

Financial data The stipend is $1,000.

Duration 1 year; nonrenewable.

Number awarded Several each year. Since the program was established 13 years ago, it has awarded 74 scholarships.

Deadline June of each year.

[559]
UCB FAMILY EPILEPSY SCHOLARSHIP PROGRAM

UCB, Inc.
Family Scholarship Program
c/o Hudson Medical Communications
200 White Plains Road, Second Floor
Tarrytown, NY 10591
Toll Free: (866) 825-1920
E-mail: questions@hudsonmc.com
Web: www.ucbepilepsyscholarship.com

Summary To provide financial assistance for college or graduate school to epilepsy patients and their family members and caregivers.

Eligibility This program is open to epilepsy patients and their family members and caregivers. Applicants must be working on or planning to work on an undergraduate or graduate degree at an institution of higher education in the United States. They must be able to demonstrate academic achievement, a record of participation in activities outside of school, and service as a role model. Along with their application, they must submit a 1-page essay explaining why they should be selected for the scholarship, how epilepsy has impacted their life either as a patient or as a family member or caregiver, and how they will benefit from the scholarship. U.S. citizenship or permanent resident status is required.

Financial data The stipend is $5,000.

Duration 1 year; nonrenewable.

Additional data This program, previously known as the Keppra Family Epilepsy Scholarship Program, was established in 2004.

Number awarded 40 each year.

Deadline April of each year.

[560]
UCB FAMILY RA SCHOLARSHIP PROGRAM

UCB, Inc.
8010 Arco Corporate Drive
Raleigh, NC 27617
(919) 567-3384   Fax: (919) 767-2570
Web: www.reachbeyondra.com/scholarship

Summary To provide financial assistance to undergraduate and graduate students who have rheumatoid arthritis (RA) and their families.

Eligibility This program is open to students who are either working on an associate, undergraduate, or graduate degree or are enrolled in a trade school educational program. Applicants must have been diagnosed with RA or be an immediate family member (parent, spouse, child, or sibling) of a person with RA. Along with their application, they must submit an essay of 1 to 2 pages describing how they are living beyond the boundaries of RA to demonstrate academic ambition and personal achievement and how the scholarship would impact their life.

Financial data Stipends range up to $10,000.

Duration 1 year; nonrenewable.

Additional data This program began on a pilot basis in 2008.

Number awarded 31 each year.

Deadline March of each year.

[561]
UTAH HEMOPHILIA FOUNDATION SCHOLARSHIPS

Utah Hemophilia Foundation
772 East 3300 South, Suite 210
Salt Lake City, UT 84106
(801) 484-0325   Toll Free: (877) INFO-VWD
Fax: (801) 484-4177 E-mail: info@hemophiliautah.org
Web: www.hemophiliautah.org

Summary To provide financial assistance for attendance at a college in any state to residents of Utah who have a bleeding disorder and their families.

Eligibility This program is open to people in Utah with bleeding disorders and to their spouses, children, and parents. Applicants must be members of the bleeding disorders community served by the Utah Hemophilia Foundation and/or the Hemophilia Treatment Center in Salt Lake City. They must be attending or planning to attend a college, university, trade school, or technical program in any state.

Financial data Stipends range from $500 to $1,500.

Duration 1 year.

Number awarded Varies each year.

Deadline May of each year.

[562]
VERA YIP MEMORIAL SCHOLARSHIP

Ulman Cancer Fund for Young Adults
Attn: Scholarship Committee Coordinator
4725 Dorsey Hall Drive, Suite A
PMB 505
Ellicott City, MD 21042
(410) 964-0202   Toll Free: (888) 393-FUND, ext. 103
E-mail: scholarship@ulmanfund.org
Web: www.ulmanfund.org/Default.aspx?tabid=329

Summary To provide financial assistance for college or graduate school to students from Washington, D.C., Maryland, or Virginia who either have or had cancer or have or have lost a parent to cancer.

Eligibility This program is open to students who either 1) have or had cancer, or 2) have or have lost a parent or guardian to cancer. Applicants must be residents of Washington, D.C., Maryland, or Virginia or attending college there. They must be 35 years of age or younger and attending, or planning to attend, a 2- or 4-year college, university, or vocational program to work on an undergraduate or graduate degree. Either they or their parent or guardian must have been diagnosed (including initial or secondary diagnosis, relapse, or active treatment) with cancer after they were 15 years of age. Along with their application, they must submit an essay of at least 1,000 words on how their cancer experience has shaped, changed, and/or reinforced the principles by which they live their life. Selection is based on demonstrated dedication to community service, commitment to educational and professional goals, use of their cancer experience to impact the lives of other young adults affected by cancer, medical hardship, and financial need.

Financial data The stipend is $2,500. Funds are paid directly to the educational institution.

Duration 1 year; nonrenewable.

Additional data Recipients must agree to complete 80 hours of community service.

Number awarded Varies each year; recently, 2 of these scholarships were awarded.

Deadline April of each year.

[563]
WINTERHOFF COLLEGIATE SCHOLARSHIP

Arthritis Foundation-Greater Southwest Chapter
1313 East Osborn Road, Suite 200
Phoenix, AZ 85014
(602) 264-7679   Toll Free: (800) 477-7679
Fax: (602) 264-0563
Web: www.arthritis.org

Summary To provide financial assistance to students at public universities in Arizona who have a rheumatic disease.

Eligibility This program is open to full-time undergraduate and graduate students at public 4-year universities in Arizona. Applicants must have some form of diagnosed rheumatic disease and provide a physician's certifying statement. They must be willing to be involved in Arthritis Foundation publicity and agree to meet with foundation officials in Phoenix.

Financial data The stipend is $7,500 per year.

Duration 1 year; may be renewed up to 3 additional years, provided the recipient remains enrolled full time and maintains a GPA of 2.5 or higher.

Number awarded 1 or more each year.

Deadline February of each year.

[564]
YOUNG HEROES SCHOLARSHIPS

Wipe Out Kids' Cancer
Attn: Young Heroes Scholarships
6350 LBJ Freeway, Suite 162
Dallas, TX 75240
(214) 987-4662   Fax: (214) 987-4668
E-mail: mail@wokc.org
Web: www.wokc.org

Summary To provide financial assistance for college to pediatric cancer survivors.

Eligibility This program is open to pediatric cancer survivors who are enrolled or planning to enroll at a college or university. Applicants must submit a 500-word essay on how their personal journey with cancer has prepared them for college. Selection is based on the content, originality, and overall impression of the essay (80%), and school and community recommendations (20%).

Financial data Stipends are $2,500 or $1,000.

Duration 1 year.

Additional data This program was established in 2006 by Michael Young, a baseball player for the Texas Rangers,

and his wife, Christina Barbosa-Young. Support is provided by the Texas Rangers Foundation.

Number awarded 10 each year.

Deadline February of each year.

[565]
YOUNG SURVIVOR SCHOLARSHIP PROGRAM

American Cancer Society-Great Lakes Division
Attn: College Scholarship Program
1755 Abbey Road
East Lansing, MI 48823-1907
(517) 664-1314   Toll Free: (800) 723-0360, ext. 1314
Web: www.cancer.org

Summary To provide financial assistance to residents of Michigan and Indiana who have a history of cancer and are interested in attending college in those states.

Eligibility This program is open to Michigan and Indiana residents who are U.S. citizens and have had a diagnosis of cancer before age 21. Applicants must be high school seniors or college undergraduates younger than 20 years of age. They must be enrolled or planning to enroll full time at an accredited college or university in either of the 2 states and have a GPA of 2.0 or higher. Along with their application, they must submit a 500-word essay on their personal, educational, and occupational goals. Selection is based on the essay, academic performance, community service, leadership qualities, and financial need.

Financial data The stipend is $2,500. Funds must be used for tuition.

Duration 1 year; nonrenewable.

Additional data This program was established in 1997.

Number awarded Varies each year; recently, 71 of these scholarships were awarded.

Deadline April of each year.

Fellowship/Grants

[566]
BECKY COHN SCHOLARSHIP

Accredo's Hemophilia Health Services
Attn: Scholarship Committee
201 Great Circle Road
Nashville, TN 37228
(615) 850-5212   Toll Free: (800) 800-6606
Fax: (615) 261-6730
E-mail: Shayne.harris@accredo.com
Web: www.hemophiliahealth.com/Scholarships.html

Summary To provide financial assistance for college or graduate school to people who have hemophilia or other bleeding disorders and have provided service to the bleeding disorders community.

Eligibility This program is open to individuals with hemophilia (factor VIII or IX), von Willebrand Disease (type 1, 2, 2A, 2B, 2M, 2N, or 3), factor I (fibrinogen), factor II (prothrombin), factor V (proaccelerin), factor VII (proconvertin), factor X, factor XI, factor XIII, or Glanzmann's thrombasthenia. Applicants must be 1) high school seniors; 2) college freshmen, sophomores, or juniors; or 3) college seniors planning to attend graduate school or students already enrolled in graduate school. Applicants must be enrolled or planning to enroll full time at an accredited nonprofit college, university, or vocational/technical school in the United States or Puerto Rico. Along with their application, they must submit an essay, up to 250 words, on the following topic: "What has been your involvement with and service to the bleeding disorders community?" U.S. citizenship is required. Selection is based on the essay, academic achievements and records, community involvement, and financial need.

Financial data The stipend is at least $1,500. Funds are issued payable to the recipient's school.

Duration 1 year; recipients may reapply.

Additional data This program, which started in 2009, is administered by International Scholarship and Tuition Services, Inc., P.O. Box 23737, Nashville, TN 37202-3737, (615) 320-3149, Fax: (615) 320-3151, E-mail: info@applyists.net.

Number awarded 1 each year.

Deadline April of each year.

[567]
BONNIE STRANGIO EDUCATION SCHOLARSHIP

Boomer Esiason Foundation
c/o Jerry Cahill
483 Tenth Avenue, Suite 300
New York, NY 10018
(646) 292-7930   Fax: (646) 292-7945
E-mail: jcahillbef@aol.com
Web: www.cfscholarships.com

Summary To provide financial assistance to undergraduate and graduate students who have cystic fibrosis (CF).

Eligibility This program is open to CF patients who are working on an undergraduate or graduate degree. Applicants must be able to demonstrate exemplary service and commitment to the prevention and cure of CF. Along with their application, they must submit a letter from their doctor confirming the diagnosis of CF and a list of daily medications, information on financial need, a detailed breakdown of tuition costs from their academic institution, transcripts, and a 2-page essay on 1) their post-graduation goals and 2) the importance of compliance with CF therapies and what they practice on a daily basis to stay healthy. Selection is based on academic ability, character, leadership potential, service to the community, and financial need. Finalists are interviewed by telephone.

Financial data The stipend is $2,500. Funds are paid directly to the academic institution to assist in covering the cost of tuition and fees.

Duration 1 year; nonrenewable.

Number awarded 1 each year.

Deadline June of each year.

[568]
BOOMER ESIASON FOUNDATION SCHOLARSHIP PROGRAM

Boomer Esiason Foundation
c/o Jerry Cahill
483 Tenth Avenue, Suite 300
New York, NY 10018
(646) 292-7930   Fax: (646) 292-7945
E-mail: jcahillbef@aol.com
Web: www.cfscholarships.com

Summary To provide financial assistance to undergraduate and graduate students who have cystic fibrosis (CF).

Eligibility This program is open to CF patients who are working on an undergraduate or graduate degree. Applicants must submit a letter from their doctor confirming the diagnosis of CF and a list of daily medications, information on financial need, a detailed breakdown of tuition costs from their academic institution, transcripts, and a 2-page essay on 1) their post-graduation goals and 2) the importance of compliance with CF therapies and what they practice on a daily basis to stay healthy. Selection is based on academic ability, character, leadership potential, service to the community, and financial need. Finalists are interviewed by telephone.

Financial data Stipends range from $500 to $2,000. Funds are paid directly to the academic institution to assist in covering the cost of tuition and fees.

Duration 1 year; nonrenewable.

Additional data This program includes 1) the Sacks for CF Scholarships, funded by Novartis, which donates $1,000 for scholarships every time an NFL quarterback is sacked during the regular season; and 2) the Bonnie Strangio Education Scholarship. Recipients must be willing to participate in the sponsor's CF Ambassador Program by speaking once a year at a designated CF event to help educate the general public about CF.

Number awarded 10 to 15 each year.

Deadline March, June, September, or December of each year.

[569]
CAROLYN'S COMPASSIONATE CHILDREN SCHOLARSHIPS

Carolyn's Compassionate Children
7163 Ayrshire Lane
Boca Raton, FL 33496
Fax: (561) 487-6162
E-mail: cccscholarship@gmail.com
Web: www.change.org/ccc

Summary To provide financial assistance for college or graduate school to childhood cancer survivors.

Eligibility This program is open to childhood cancer survivors who are attending or planning to attend college or graduate school full time. Selection is based on personal character, community service, and financial need. U.S. citizenship or permanent resident status is required.

Financial data The stipend is $1,000.

Duration 1 year.

Additional data Carolyn Rubenstein founded Carolyn's Compassionate Children in 1999 when she was 13 years of age. The organization began offering scholarships in 2003.

Number awarded Varies each year; recently, 18 of these scholarships were awarded.

Deadline May of each year.

[570]
DICK GRIFFITHS MEMORIAL SCHOLARSHIP

California Association for Postsecondary Education and Disability
Attn: Executive Assistant
71423 Biskra Road
Rancho Mirage, CA 92270
(760) 346-8206　　　　　　　Fax: (760) 340-5275
TDD: (760) 341-4084　　　E-mail: caped2000@aol.com
Web: www.caped.net/scholarships.html

Summary To provide financial assistance to undergraduate and graduate students in California who have a learning disability, especially involving mathematics.

Eligibility This program is open to students at public and private colleges and universities in California who have a learning disability and are especially challenged in mathematics. Undergraduates must have completed at least 6 semester credits and have a GPA of 2.5 or higher. Graduate students must have completed at least 3 semester units and have a GPA of 3.0 or higher. Along with their application, they must submit a 1-page personal letter that demonstrates their writing skills, progress towards meeting their educational and vocational goals, management of their disability, and involvement in community activities. They must also submit a letter of recommendation from a faculty member, verification of disability, official transcripts, proof of current enrollment, an essay on strategies they use to overcome their mathematics challenges, and documentation of financial need.

Financial data The stipend is $1,000.

Duration 1 year.

Number awarded 1 each year.

Deadline September of each year.

[571]
ELIZABETH NASH FOUNDATION SCHOLARSHIP PROGRAM

Elizabeth Nash Foundation
P.O. Box 1260
Los Gatos, CA 95031-1260
E-mail: scholarships@elizabethnashfoundation.org
Web: www.elizabethnashfoundation.org

Summary To provide financial assistance for college or graduate school to individuals with cystic fibrosis (CF).

Eligibility This program is open to undergraduate and graduate students who have CF. Applicants must be able to demonstrate clear academic goals and a commitment to participate in activities outside the classroom. U.S. citizenship is required. Selection is based on academic record, character, demonstrated leadership, service to CF-related causes and the broader community, and financial need.

Financial data Stipends range from $1,000 to $2,500. Funds are paid directly to the academic institution to be applied to tuition and fees.

Duration 1 year; recipients may reapply.

Additional data This program was established in 2005. Recipients must agree to support the program by speaking at a local event or writing an article for publication by the foundation.

Number awarded Varies each year; recently, 12 of these scholarships were awarded.

Deadline April of each year.

[572]
ERIC DELSON MEMORIAL SCHOLARSHIP

CVS Caremark
Attn: Research Team
P.O. Box 832407
Richardson, TX 75083
Toll Free: (866) 792-2731
Web: www.caremark.com

Summary To provide financial assistance for high school, college, or graduate school to students with a bleeding disorder.

Eligibility This program is open to students diagnosed with a bleeding disorder who are 1) high school seniors, high school graduates or equivalent (GED), college students, or graduate students currently enrolled or planning to enroll full time at an accredited 2-year or 4-year college, university, or vocational/technical school; or 2) students entering grades 7-12 at a private secondary school in the United States. Selection is based on academic record, demonstrated leadership and participation in school and community activities, work experience, a statement of educational and career goals, unusual personal or family circumstances, and an outside appraisal.

Financial data The stipend is $2,500 for college students or $1,500 for high school students. Funds are paid in 2 equal installments directly to the recipient.

Duration 1 year; may be renewed for up to 3 additional years, provided the recipient maintains a GPA of 2.5 or higher for the freshman year and 3.0 or higher for subsequent years.

Additional data This program is administered by Scholarship Management Services, a division of Scholarship America, One Scholarship Way, P.O. Box 297, St. Peter, MN 56082, (507) 931-1682.

Number awarded 4 each year: 3 for college students and 1 for a high school student.

Deadline June of each year.

[573]
GEORGE AND LINDA PRICE SCHOLARSHIP

Hemophilia Association of the Capital Area
10560 Main Street, Suite PH-4
Fairfax, VA 22030-7182
(703) 352-7641　　　　　　　Fax: (703) 352-2145
E-mail: info@hacacares.org
Web: www.hacacares.org

Summary To provide financial assistance to individuals with bleeding disorders and their families who are members of the Hemophilia Association of the Capital Area (HACA) and interested in attending college or graduate school in any state.

Eligibility This program is open to residents of northern Virginia, Montgomery and Prince George's County in Maryland, and Washington, D.C. who have a bleeding disorder and their siblings and parents. Applicants must be members of HACA. They must be 1) high school seniors or graduates who have not yet attended college; 2) full-time freshmen, sophomores, or juniors at a college, university, or vocational/technical school in any state; or 3) college seniors planning to attend graduate school and students already enrolled at a graduate school in any state. Along with their application, they must submit a 500-word essay on what they have done to contribute to the bleeding disorders community and how they plan to contribute to that community in the future. Financial need is not considered in the selection process.

Financial data The stipend is $2,500.

Duration 1 year; recipients may reapply.

Number awarded 2 each year.

Deadline April of each year.

[574]
HEMOPHILIA FEDERATION OF AMERICA ARTISTIC ENCOURAGEMENT GRANTS

Hemophilia Federation of America
Attn: Scholarship Committee
210 Seventh Street, S.E., Suite 200B
Washington, DC 20003
(202) 675-6984   Toll Free: (800) 230-9797
Fax: (202) 675-6983   E-mail: info@hemophiliafed.org
Web: hemophiliafed.org

Summary To provide funding to artists who have a blood clotting disorder and are interested in a creative endeavor.

Eligibility This program is open to artists who have a blood clotting disorder. Applicants must be interested in engaging in a creative endeavor, such as mounting an exhibit of their work (e.g., photography, painting, watercolor, animation), publishing a story or animation, writing a play, or having a recital. Along with their application, they must submit a 1-page essay on their goals and aspirations and how the blood clotting community has played a part in their life, 2 letters of reference, a 25-word summary of the proposed project, a timeline for its completion, a portfolio or sample of their work, and documentation of financial need.

Financial data The grant is $1,500.

Duration 1 year.

Number awarded 2 each year.

Deadline April of each year.

[575]
HEMOPHILIA HEALTH SERVICES MEMORIAL SCHOLARSHIPS

Accredo's Hemophilia Health Services
Attn: Scholarship Committee
201 Great Circle Road
Nashville, TN 37228
(615) 850-5212   Toll Free: (800) 800-6606
Fax: (615) 261-6730
E-mail: Shayne.harris@accredo.com
Web: www.hemophiliahealth.com/Scholarships.html

Summary To provide financial assistance for college or graduate school to people who have hemophilia or other bleeding disorders.

Eligibility This program is open to individuals with hemophilia (factor VIII or IX), von Willebrand Disease (type 1, 2, 2A, 2B, 2M, 2N, or 3), factor I (fibrinogen), factor II (prothrombin), factor V (proaccelerin), factor VII (proconvertin), factor X, factor XI, factor XIII, or Glanzmann's thrombasthenia. Applicants must be 1) high school seniors; 2) college freshmen, sophomores, or juniors; or 3) college seniors planning to attend graduate school or students already enrolled in graduate school. Applicants must be enrolled or planning to enroll full time at an accredited nonprofit college, university, or vocational/technical school in the United States or Puerto Rico. Along with their application, they must submit an essay, up to 250 words, on the following topic: "What has been your own personal challenge in living with a bleeding disorder?" U.S. citizenship is required. Selection is based on the essay, academic achievements and records, community involvement, and financial need.

Financial data The stipend is at least $1,500. Funds are issued payable to the recipient's school.

Duration 1 year; recipients may reapply.

Additional data This program, which started in 1995, includes the following named scholarships: the Cindy Beck Scholarship, the Osborne DeWitt Scholarship, the Tim Haas Scholarship, the Ricky Hobson Scholarship, the Michael Moses Scholarship, and the Jim Stineback Scholarship. It is administered by International Scholarship and Tuition Services, Inc., P.O. Box 23737, Nashville, TN 37202-3737, (615) 320-3149, Fax: (615) 320-3151, E-mail: info@applyists.net.

Number awarded Several each year.

Deadline April of each year.

[576]
HIGH PLAINS DIVISION CANCER SURVIVOR SCHOLARSHIPS

American Cancer Society-High Plains Division
2433 Ridgepoint Drive, Suite B
Austin, TX 78754
(512) 919-1910   Toll Free: (877) 227-1618
Fax: (512) 919-1846
Web: www.cancer.org

Summary To provide financial assistance for college or graduate school to cancer patients and survivors in

Hawaii, Kansas, Missouri, Nebraska, Oklahoma, and Texas.

Eligibility This program is open to residents of Hawaii, Kansas, Missouri, Nebraska, Oklahoma, and Texas who have had a cancer diagnosis before age 21. Applicants must be accepted at or attending an accredited university, graduate school, community college, or vocational/technical school in any state. They must be 25 years of age or younger at the time of applying and have a GPA of 2.0 or higher. Along with their application, they must submit 2 recommendations (including 1 from a physician verifying diagnosis), an acceptance letter from an academic institution, documentation of financial need, academic transcripts, and a 2-page essay describing their life experiences, future goals, community involvement, and cancer-related involvement.

Financial data The stipend is $1,000 per year. Funds are paid directly to the academic institution.

Duration 1 year; may be renewed.

Number awarded Varies each year; recently, 201 of these scholarships were awarded.

Deadline March of each year.

[577]
JOHN BULLER SCHOLARSHIP

Greater Houston Community Foundation
Attn: Director of Operations
4550 Post Oak Place, Suite 100
Houston, TX 77027
(713) 333-2205   Fax: (713) 333-2220
E-mail: lgardner@ghcf.org
Web: www.ghcf.org/john-buller-scholarship.php

Summary To provide financial assistance to residents of Texas who have cystic fibrosis and are interested in attending college or graduate school in any state.

Eligibility This program is open to Texas residents who have cystic fibrosis. Applicants must be enrolled or planning to enroll as an undergraduate or graduate student at an accredited 2-year or 4-year college or university in the United States. Along with their application, they must submit transcripts and information on their extracurricular activities, work experience, community service, and other activities. Financial need is considered in the selection process. U.S. citizenship is required.

Financial data The stipend is $1,000 per year.

Duration 1 year; may be renewed up to 3 additional years.

Additional data This program was established in 1997.

Number awarded 1 or more each year.

Deadline April of each year.

[578]
LILLY REINTEGRATION SCHOLARSHIPS

The Center for Reintegration, Inc.
Attn: Lilly Secretariat
310 Busse Highway
PMB 327
Park Ridge, IL 60068-3251
Toll Free: (800) 809-8202
E-mail: lillyscholarships@reintegration.com
Web: www.reintegration.com/resources/scholarships

Summary To provide financial assistance to undergraduate and graduate students diagnosed with schizophrenia.

Eligibility This program is open to U.S. citizens diagnosed with bipolar disorder, schizophrenia, schizophreniform disorder, or schizoaffective disorder. Applicants must be receiving medical treatment for the disease and be actively involved in rehabilitative or reintegrative efforts. They must be interested in pursuing postsecondary education, including trade or vocational school programs, high school equivalency programs, associate degrees, bachelor's degrees, and graduate programs. Along with their application, they must submit an essay on their career goal and their rationale for choosing that goal, how this course of study will help them achieve their career goal, obstacles they have faced in life and how they have overcome them, steps they have taken to prepare for pursuit of this education, rationale for the specific school chosen, and their plans to continue treatment while pursuing an education. Selection is based on the quality of the essay, academic success, 3 references, thoughtfulness and appropriateness of academic and vocational/career goals, rehabilitation involvement, success in dealing with the disease, recent volunteer and/or vocational experience, and completion of application requirements.

Financial data The amount awarded varies, depending upon the specific needs of the recipient. Funds may be used to pay for tuition and related expenses, such as textbooks and laboratory fees.

Duration 1 year; may be renewed.

Additional data This program, established in 1998, is funded by Eli Lilly and Company.

Number awarded Varies each year; generally, 70 to 120 of these scholarships (including renewals) are awarded annually.

Deadline January of each year.

[579]
MARK REAMES MEMORIAL SCHOLARSHIPS

Hemophilia Society of Colorado
Attn: Scholarship Committee
P.O. Box 4943
Englewood, CO 80155
(303) 629-6990   Toll Free: (888) 687-CLOT
Fax: (303) 629-7035   E-mail: hsc@cohemo.org
Web: www.cohemo.org

Summary To provide financial assistance for higher education to members of the Hemophilia Society of Colorado (HSC) and to members of their families.

Eligibility This program is open to HSC members who have hemophilia or a related inherited bleeding disorder and their immediate family members. Applicants must be enrolled or planning to enroll at a 2-year or 4-year college or university, vocational/technical school, or graduate school. Along with their application, they must submit an essay on why they think they should receive this scholarship and how it might affect their future goals. Selection is based on the essay, demonstrated scholastic ability and intellectual promise, letters of recommendation, community involvement (especially involvement with the hemophilia community), and financial need.

Financial data The stipend is $1,000. Funds must be used for tuition, room, board, and related educational expenses.

Duration 1 year.

Number awarded 2 each year.

Deadline April of each year.

[580]
MARYLAND COMMUNITY CANCER SCHOLARSHIP

Ulman Cancer Fund for Young Adults
Attn: Scholarship Program Coordinator
10440 Little Patuxent Parkway, Suite 1G
Columbia, MD 21044
(410) 964-0202, ext. 106   Toll Free: (888) 393-FUND
E-mail: scholarship@ulmanfund.org
Web: www.ulmanfund.org

Summary To provide financial assistance to residents of Maryland who are cancer survivors or patients and are interested in working on an undergraduate or graduate degree at a school in the state.

Eligibility This program is open to residents of Maryland who are younger than 35 years of age, are cancer survivors or patients, and were diagnosed after the age of 15 (including initial or secondary diagnosis, relapse, or active treatment). Applicants must be attending or planning to attend a public 2- or 4-year college, university, or vocational program in Maryland to work on an undergraduate, graduate, or professional degree. Along with their application, they must submit an essay of at least 1,000 words on a topic that changes annually but relates to young adults with cancer. Selection is based on demonstrated dedication to community service, commitment to educational and professional goals, use of their cancer experience to impact the lives of other young adults affected by cancer, medical hardship, and financial need.

Financial data The stipend is $2,500. Funds are paid directly to the educational institution.

Duration 1 year; nonrenewable.

Additional data Recipients must agree to complete 80 hours of community service.

Number awarded Varies each year; recently, 2 of these scholarships were awarded.

Deadline April of each year.

[581]
MATT STAUFFER MEMORIAL SCHOLARSHIPS

Ulman Cancer Fund for Young Adults
Attn: Scholarship Program Coordinator
10440 Little Patuxent Parkway, Suite 1G
Columbia, MD 21044
(410) 964-0202, ext. 106   Toll Free: (888) 393-FUND
E-mail: scholarship@ulmanfund.org
Web: www.ulmanfund.org

Summary To provide financial assistance for college or graduate school to young adults from Washington, D.C., Maryland, or Virginia who have had cancer.

Eligibility This program is open to students who are younger than 35 years of age and have or had cancer that was diagnosed after they were 15 years of age (including initial or secondary diagnosis, relapse, or active treatment). Applicants must be residents of or attending school in Washington, D.C., Maryland, or Virginia. They must be attending or planning to attend a 2-or 4-year college, university, or vocational program to work on an undergraduate or graduate degree. Along with their application, they must submit an essay of at least 1,000 words on a topic that changes annually but relates to young adults with cancer. Selection is based on demonstrated dedication to community service, commitment to educational and professional goals, use of their cancer experience to impact the lives of other young adults affected by cancer, medical hardship, and financial need.

Financial data The stipend is $2,500. Funds are paid directly to the educational institution.

Duration 1 year.

Additional data These scholarships were first awarded in 1998. Recipients must agree to complete 80 hours of community service.

Number awarded Varies each year; recently, 2 of these scholarships were awarded.

Deadline April of each year.

[582]
MIKE CONLEY MEMORIAL SCHOLARSHIPS

Hemophilia Society of Colorado
Attn: Scholarship Committee
P.O. Box 4943
Englewood, CO 80155
(303) 629-6990   Toll Free: (888) 687-CLOT
Fax: (303) 629-7035   E-mail: hsc@cohemo.org
Web: www.cohemo.org

Summary To provide financial assistance for college or graduate school to students from Colorado who have a bleeding disorder.

Eligibility This program is open to residents of Colorado who have hemophilia or a related inherited bleeding disorder. Applicants must be enrolled or planning to enroll at a 2-year or 4-year college or university, vocational/technical school, or graduate school. Along with their application, they must submit an essay on why they think they should receive this scholarship and how it might affect their future goals. Selection is based on the essay, demonstrated scholastic ability and intellectual promise, letters of recommendation, community involvement (especially involvement with the hemophilia community), and financial need. Preference is given to students at Metropolitan State College or the University of Colorado at Denver.

Financial data The stipend is $1,000. Funds must be used for tuition, room, board, and related educational expenses.

Duration 1 year.

Number awarded 2 each year.

Deadline April of each year.

[583]
NATIONAL COLLEGIATE CANCER FOUNDATION SCHOLARSHIP

National Collegiate Cancer Foundation
Attn: Scholarship Committee
P.O. Box 5950
Bethesda, MD 20824
(240) 515-6262   E-mail: info@collegiatecancer.org
Web: www.collegiatecancer.org/scholarships.html

Summary To provide financial assistance for college or graduate school to cancer survivors.

Eligibility This program is open to students between 18 and 35 years of age who are cancer survivors or currently undergoing treatment for cancer. Applicants must be enrolled or planning to enroll at a college or university to work on a certificate or an associate, bachelor's, master's, or doctoral degree. Along with their application, they must submit a 1,000-word essay on 1 of 4 assigned topics related to their experiences with cancer and college. Selection is based on the essay, letters of recommendation, displaying a "Will Win" attitude, overall story of cancer survivorship, commitment to education, and financial need.

Financial data The stipend is $1,000.

Duration 1 year.

Number awarded 1 or more each year.

Deadline May of each year.

[584]
PATIENT ADVOCATE FOUNDATION SCHOLARSHIPS FOR SURVIVORS

Patient Advocate Foundation
Attn: Scholarship Coordinator
421 Butler Farm Road
Hampton, VA 23669
Toll Free: (800) 532-5274   Fax: (757) 873-8999
E-mail: help@patientadvocate.org
Web: www.patientadvocate.org/events.php?p=69

Summary To provide financial assistance for college or graduate school to students seeking to initiate or complete a course of study that has been interrupted or delayed by a diagnosis of cancer or other life threatening disease.

Eligibility This program is open to students under 25 years of age who are working full time on a 2-year, 4-year, or advanced degree. The college or graduate education of applicants must have been interrupted or delayed by a diagnosis of cancer or other life threatening, chronic, or debilitating disease. They must be willing to commit to

completing 20 hours of community service for the year if they are awarded a scholarship. Along with their application, they must submit a 1,000-word essay on how their diagnosis has impacted their life and future goals. Financial need is also considered in the selection process.

Financial data The stipend is $3,000. Funds are paid directly to the college or university to help cover tuition and other fee costs. The cost of books is not included.

Duration 1 year; may be renewed up to 3 additional years, provided the recipient remains enrolled full time, maintains a GPA of 3.0 or higher, and performs 20 hours of community service.

Additional data This program includes the Cheryl Grimmel Award, the Jo Ann Davis Award, the Monica Bailes Award, the Robin L. Prachel Award, the Mary T. Christian Award, the Karen Condon Reeder Award, and the Jim Meade and Luke Barlow Award. Support for 1 of the scholarships is provided by the United Health Foundation.

Number awarded Varies each year; recently, 12 of these scholarships were awarded.

Deadline April of each year.

[585]
PFIZER EPILEPSY SCHOLARSHIP AWARD

Pfizer Inc.
c/o Adelphi Eden Health Communications
30 Irving Place, 10th Floor
New York, NY 10003
Toll Free: (800) AWARD-PF
E-mail: info@epilepsy-scholarship.com
Web: www.epilepsy-scholarship.com

Summary To provide financial assistance for college or graduate school to individuals with epilepsy.

Eligibility Applicants must be under a physician's care for epilepsy (taking prescribed medication) and must submit an application with 2 letters of recommendation (1 from the physician) and verification of academic status. They must be high school seniors entering college in the fall; college freshmen, sophomores, or juniors continuing in the fall; or college seniors planning to enter graduate school in the fall. Along with their application, they must submit a 250-word essay on something they have dealt with as a person with epilepsy; they may choose to write on 1) how they have overcome the challenges of epilepsy; 2) what living with epilepsy means to them; 3) someone who has been helpful to them in their success; or 4) an achievement of which they are proud. Selection is based on success in overcoming the challenges of epilepsy, success in school, participation in extracurricular or community activities, and desire to make the most out of college or graduate school; financial need is not considered.

Financial data The stipend is $2,000.

Duration 1 year; nonrenewable.

Number awarded 40 each year.

Deadline June of each year.

[586]
PROJECT RED FLAG ACADEMIC SCHOLARSHIP FOR WOMEN WITH BLEEDING DISORDERS

National Hemophilia Foundation
Attn: Manager of Education
P.O. Box 971483
Ypsilanti, MI 48197
(734) 890-2504   E-mail: pflax@hemophilia.org
Web: www.projectredflag.org/scholarship.htm

Summary To provide financial assistance for college or graduate school to women who have a bleeding disorder.

Eligibility This program is open to women who are entering or already enrolled in an undergraduate or graduate program at a university, college, or accredited vocational school. Applicants must have von Willebrand Disease, hemophilia or other clotting factor deficiency, or carrier status. Along with their application, they must submit a 250-word essay that describes how their education and future career plans will benefit others in the bleeding disorders community. Financial need is not considered in the selection process.

Financial data The stipend is $2,500.

Duration 1 year.

Additional data The program was established in 2005 in partnership with the Centers for Disease Control and Prevention (CDC) and with support from CSL Behring.

Number awarded 2 each year.

Deadline May of each year.

[587]
ROSEMARY QUIGLEY MEMORIAL SCHOLARSHIP

Boomer Esiason Foundation
c/o Jerry Cahill
483 Tenth Avenue, Suite 300
New York, NY 10018
(646) 292-7930   Fax: (646) 292-7945
E-mail: jcahillbef@aol.com
Web: www.cfscholarships.com

Summary To provide financial assistance to undergraduate and graduate students who have cystic fibrosis (CF).

Eligibility This program is open to CF patients who are working on an undergraduate or graduate degree. Applicants must be able to demonstrate a clear sense of life goals and a commitment to living life to the fullest, despite having CF. Along with their application, they must submit a letter from their doctor confirming the diagnosis of CF and a list of daily medications, information on financial need, a detailed breakdown of tuition costs from their academic institution, transcripts, and a 2-page essay on 1) their post-graduation goals and 2) the importance of compliance with CF therapies and what they practice on a daily basis to stay healthy. Selection is based on academic ability, character, leadership potential, service to the community, and financial need. Finalists are interviewed by telephone.

Financial data A stipend is awarded (amount not specified). Funds are paid directly to the academic institution to assist in covering the cost of tuition and fees.

Duration 1 year; nonrenewable.

Number awarded 1 each year.

Deadline June of each year.

[588]
SACKS FOR CF SCHOLARSHIPS

Boomer Esiason Foundation
c/o Jerry Cahill
483 Tenth Avenue, Suite 300
New York, NY 10018
(646) 292-7930   Fax: (646) 292-7945
E-mail: jcahillbef@aol.com
Web: www.sacksforcf.com

Summary To provide financial assistance to undergraduate and graduate students who have cystic fibrosis (CF).

Eligibility This program is open to CF patients who are working on an undergraduate or graduate degree. Applicants must submit a letter from their doctor confirming the diagnosis of CF and a list of daily medications, information on financial need, a detailed breakdown of tuition costs from their academic institution, transcripts, and a 2-page essay on 1) their post-graduation goals and 2) the importance of compliance with CF therapies and what they practice on a daily basis to stay healthy. Selection is based on academic ability, character, leadership potential, service to the community, and financial need. Finalists are interviewed by telephone.

Financial data The stipend is $1,000. Funds are paid directly to the academic institution to assist in covering the cost of tuition and fees.

Duration 1 year; nonrenewable.

Additional data This program is funded by Solvay Pharmaceuticals, Inc., which donates $1,000 to the foundation each time a quarterback is sacked on NFL Monday Night Football games.

Number awarded Varies each year; recently, 10 of these scholarships were awarded.

Deadline January of each year.

[589]
SAMFUND GRANTS AND SCHOLARSHIPS

The SAMFund for Young Adult Survivors of Cancer
89 South Street, Suite LL02
Boston, MA 02211
E-mail: grants@thesamfund.org
Web: www.thesamfund.org/pages/grants.html

Summary To provide funding to young adult cancer survivors who need assistance for the transition to post-treatment life.

Eligibility This program is open to cancer survivors between 17 and 35 years of age who are finished with active treatment and are trying to move forward with their lives. Applicants must be able to demonstrate a need for funding for such purposes as undergraduate or graduate school tuition and expenses, car and health insurance premiums, rent, fertility-related expenses, gym memberships, transportation costs, or current and residual medical bills.

Financial data Grant amounts vary; recently, they averaged approximately $2,500.

Duration These are 1-time grants.

Additional data This program, which stands for Surviving and Moving Forward, was established in 2003.

Number awarded Varies each year; since the program was established, it has awarded nearly 200 grants with a total value of $400,000.

Deadline Deadline not specified.

[590]
SCHOLARSHIP OF THE ARTS

Boomer Esiason Foundation
c/o Jerry Cahill
483 Tenth Avenue, Suite 300
New York, NY 10018
(646) 292-7930   Fax: (646) 292-7945
E-mail: jcahillbef@aol.com
Web: www.cfscholarships.com/Arts/index.htm

Summary To provide financial assistance to undergraduate and graduate students who have cystic fibrosis (CF) and are working on a degree in the arts.

Eligibility This program is open to CF patients who are working on an undergraduate or graduate degree in the arts. Applicants must submit a picture of their art work (painting, sketching, sculpture), a letter from their doctor confirming the diagnosis of CF and a list of daily medications, information on financial need, a detailed breakdown of tuition costs from their academic institution, transcripts, and a 2-page essay on 1) their post-graduation goals and 2) the importance of compliance with CF therapies and what they practice on a daily basis to stay healthy. Selection is based on academic ability, character, leadership potential, service to the community, and financial need.

Financial data Stipends range from $500 to $2,000. Funds are paid directly to the academic institution to assist in covering the cost of tuition and fees.

Duration 1 year; nonrenewable.

Number awarded 1 each year.

Deadline May of each year.

[591]
SCOTT DELGADILLO SCHOLARSHIP

Friends of Scott Foundation
Attn: Scholarship Fund
6977 Navajo Road, Number 168
San Diego, CA 92119
(619) 223-7268   Fax: (619) 223-7002
E-mail: aztec.graphics@yahoo.com
Web: www.friendsofscott.org/scholarship.aspx

Summary To provide financial assistance for college or graduate school to childhood cancer survivors.

Eligibility This program is open to survivors of childhood cancer and to patients currently receiving treatment. Applicants must be attending or planning to attend a technical school, vocational school, junior college, or 4-year college or university as an undergraduate or graduate student. Along with their application, they must submit a 500-word essay on how their experience with cancer has impacted their life. Selection is based on financial need and personal hardship.

Financial data A stipend is awarded (amount not specified).

Duration 1 year.

Number awarded Varies each year; recently, 3 of these scholarships were awarded.

Deadline April of each year.

[592]
SEAN SILVER MEMORIAL SCHOLARSHIP

Ulman Cancer Fund for Young Adults
Attn: Scholarship Program Coordinator
10440 Little Patuxent Parkway, Suite 1G
Columbia, MD 21044
(410) 964-0202, ext. 106   Toll Free: (888) 393-FUND
E-mail: scholarship@ulmanfund.org
Web: www.ulmanfund.org

Summary To provide financial assistance for college or graduate school to young adults who have cancer.

Eligibility This program is open to students who are younger than 30 years of age and currently undergoing active treatment for cancer. Applicants must be attending or planning to attend a 4-year college or university to work on an undergraduate or graduate degree. They must be U.S. citizens or permanent residents. Along with their application, they must submit an essay of at least 1,000 words on what they have discovered about themselves while attending school as a young adult receiving treatment for or living with cancer. Selection is based on demonstrated dedication to community service, commitment to educational and professional goals, use of their cancer experience to impact the lives of other young adults affected by cancer, medical hardship, and financial need.

Financial data The stipend is $2,500. Funds are paid directly to the educational institution.

Duration 1 year.

Additional data This scholarship was first awarded in 2008. Recipients must agree to complete 80 hours of community service.

Number awarded 1 each year.

Deadline April of each year.

[593]
SNOWDROP FOUNDATION SCHOLARSHIPS

Snowdrop Foundation
Attn: Kevin Kline, President
2310 Upland Park Drive
Sugar Land, TX 77479
(713) 232-9052
E-mail: kevin@snowdropfoundation.org
Web: www.snowdropfoundation.org

Summary To provide financial assistance for college or graduate school to students who have been diagnosed with cancer.

Eligibility This program is open to students entering or attending college or graduate school. Applicants must have been diagnosed with cancer. Along with their application, they must submit a 250-word description of themselves; a 250-word description of their family situation; information on financial need; a letter from their attending physician verifying their medical history and current medical situation; and an essay of 500 to 1,000 words on how their experience with cancer has impacted their life values and career goals.

Financial data A stipend is awarded (amount not specified).

Duration 1 year.

Number awarded Varies each year.

Deadline April of each year.

[594]
SOLVAYCARES SCHOLARSHIPS

Solvay Pharmaceuticals, Inc.
Attn: SolvayCARES Scholarship Program
901 Sawyer Road
Marietta, GA 30062
(770) 578-5898   Toll Free: (800) 354-0026, ext. 5898
Fax: (770) 578-5586
E-mail: SolvayCARES.Scholarship@solvay.com
Web: www.solvaycaresscholarship.com

Summary To provide financial assistance for college or graduate school to students with cystic fibrosis (CF).

Eligibility This program is open to high school seniors, vocational school students, college students, and graduate students with CF. U.S. citizenship is required. Applicants must submit 1) a 250-word essay on the topic, "My dream for the future is..."; and 2) a creative presentation (e.g., written work, a piece of art, a craft, collage, photograph) on what sets them apart from their peers, what inspires them to live life to the fullest, or anything else that they think makes them unique; and 3) a photograph. Selection is based on academic excellence, creativity, community involvement, and ability to serve as a role model to others with CF. The program designates 1 applicant as the Thriving Student Achiever.

Financial data The stipend is $2,500 per year. The Thriving Student Achiever receives an additional award (recently, $14,500 for a total award of $17,000 to honor the program's 17th year).

Duration 1 year.

Additional data This program started in 1992. Winners also receive a 1-year supply of nutritional drinks and vitamins. The essay, creative presentations, and photograph of all recipients who agree to be considered are posted online so patients, families, friends, physicians, the CF community, and the general public can vote to select the Thriving Student Achiever.

Number awarded 40 each year, of whom 1 is designated the Thriving Student Achiever.

Deadline April of each year.

[595]
SOOZIE COURTER SHARING A BRIGHTER TOMORROW HEMOPHILIA SCHOLARSHIP

Wyeth Pharmaceuticals
Attn: Hemophilia Scholarship Program
500 Arcola Road
Collegeville, PA 19426
Toll Free: (888) 999-2349
Web: www.hemophiliavillage.com/scholarship.html

Summary To provide financial assistance for college or graduate school in any field to persons with hemophilia.

Eligibility This program is open to persons with hemophilia (A or B) who are high school seniors, have a GED, or are currently attending an accredited college, university, junior college, vocational school, or graduate school. They must need financial assistance to work on a degree. Along with their application, they must submit a 2-page essay on their choice of assigned topics.

Financial data The stipends are $2,500 for undergraduate students or $4,000 for graduate students.

Duration 1 year.

Additional data This program was established in 1998 and given its current name in 2000.

Number awarded 17 each year: 12 to undergraduates and 5 to graduate students.

Deadline April of each year.

[596]
SUSAN BUNCH MEMORIAL SCHOLARSHIP

California Association for Postsecondary Education
  and Disability
Attn: Executive Assistant
71423 Biskra Road
Rancho Mirage, CA 92270
(760) 346-8206   Fax: (760) 340-5275
TDD: (760) 341-4084   E-mail: caped2000@aol.com
Web: www.caped.net/scholarships.html

Summary To provide financial assistance to undergraduate and graduate students in California who have a learning disability.

Eligibility This program is open to students at public and private colleges and universities in California who have a learning disability. Undergraduates must have completed at least 6 semester credits and have a GPA of 2.5 or higher. Graduate students must have completed at least 3 semester units and have a GPA of 3.0 or higher. Along with their application, they must submit a 1-page personal letter that demonstrates their writing skills, progress towards meeting their educational and vocational goals, management of their disability, and involvement in community activities. They must also submit a letter of recommendation from a faculty member, verification of disability, official transcripts, proof of current enrollment, and documentation of financial need.

Financial data The stipend is $1,000.

Duration 1 year.

Number awarded 1 each year.

Deadline September of each year.

[597]
UCB FAMILY EPILEPSY SCHOLARSHIP PROGRAM

UCB, Inc.
Family Scholarship Program
c/o Hudson Medical Communications
200 White Plains Road, Second Floor
Tarrytown, NY 10591
Toll Free: (866) 825-1920
E-mail: questions@hudsonmc.com
Web: www.ucbepilepsyscholarship.com

Summary To provide financial assistance for college or graduate school to epilepsy patients and their family members and caregivers.

Eligibility This program is open to epilepsy patients and their family members and caregivers. Applicants must be working on or planning to work on an undergraduate or graduate degree at an institution of higher education in the United States. They must be able to demonstrate academic achievement, a record of participation in activities outside of school, and service as a role model. Along with their application, they must submit a 1-page essay explaining why they should be selected for the scholarship, how epilepsy has impacted their life either as a patient or as a family member or caregiver, and how they will benefit from the scholarship. U.S. citizenship or permanent resident status is required.

Financial data The stipend is $5,000.

Duration 1 year; nonrenewable.

Additional data This program, previously known as the Keppra Family Epilepsy Scholarship Program, was established in 2004.

Number awarded 40 each year.

Deadline April of each year.

[598]
UCB FAMILY RA SCHOLARSHIP PROGRAM

UCB, Inc.
8010 Arco Corporate Drive
Raleigh, NC 27617
(919) 567-3384   Fax: (919) 767-2570
Web: www.reachbeyondra.com/scholarship

Summary To provide financial assistance to undergraduate and graduate students who have rheumatoid arthritis (RA) and their families.

Eligibility This program is open to students who are either working on an associate, undergraduate, or graduate degree or are enrolled in a trade school educational program. Applicants must have been diagnosed with RA or be an immediate family member (parent, spouse, child, or sibling) of a person with RA. Along with their application, they must submit an essay of 1 to 2 pages describing how they are living beyond the boundaries of RA to demonstrate academic ambition and personal achievement and how the scholarship would impact their life.

Financial data Stipends range up to $10,000.

Duration 1 year; nonrenewable.

Additional data This program began on a pilot basis in 2008.

Number awarded 31 each year.

Deadline March of each year.

[599]
VERA YIP MEMORIAL SCHOLARSHIP

Ulman Cancer Fund for Young Adults
Attn: Scholarship Committee Coordinator
4725 Dorsey Hall Drive, Suite A
PMB 505
Ellicott City, MD 21042
(410) 964-0202   Toll Free: (888) 393-FUND, ext. 103
E-mail: scholarship@ulmanfund.org
Web: www.ulmanfund.org/Default.aspx?tabid=329

Summary To provide financial assistance for college or graduate school to students from Washington, D.C., Maryland, or Virginia who either have or had cancer or have or have lost a parent to cancer.

Eligibility This program is open to students who either 1) have or had cancer, or 2) have or have lost a parent or guardian to cancer. Applicants must be residents of Washington, D.C., Maryland, or Virginia or attending college there. They must be 35 years of age or younger and attending, or planning to attend, a 2- or 4-year college, university, or vocational program to work on an undergraduate or graduate degree. Either they or their parent or guardian must have been diagnosed (including initial or secondary diagnosis, relapse, or active treatment) with cancer after they were 15 years of age. Along with their application, they must submit an essay of at least 1,000 words on how their cancer experience has shaped, changed, and/or reinforced the principles by which they live their life. Selection is based on demonstrated dedication to community service, commitment to educational and professional goals, use of their cancer experience to impact the lives of other young adults affected by cancer, medical hardship, and financial need.

Financial data The stipend is $2,500. Funds are paid directly to the educational institution.

Duration 1 year; nonrenewable.

Additional data Recipients must agree to complete 80 hours of community service.

Number awarded Varies each year; recently, 2 of these scholarships were awarded.

Deadline April of each year.

[600]
WILLARD BERNBAUM SCHOLARSHIP

Cystic Fibrosis Foundation
Attn: President
6931 Arlington Road, Suite 200
Bethesda, MD 20814
(301) 951-4422   Toll Free: (800) FIGHT CF
Fax: (301) 951-6378
Web: www.cysticfibrosis.com

Summary To provide financial assistance to graduate students who have cystic fibrosis (CF).

Eligibility This program is open to graduate students who have CF. Applicants must submit a 1-page letter describing their educational program and financial need.

Financial data The stipend is $1,000.
Duration 1 year.
Number awarded 1 or more each year.
Deadline Deadline not specified.

[601]
WINTERHOFF COLLEGIATE SCHOLARSHIP

Arthritis Foundation-Greater Southwest Chapter
1313 East Osborn Road, Suite 200
Phoenix, AZ 85014
(602) 264-7679   Toll Free: (800) 477-7679
Fax: (602) 264-0563
Web: www.arthritis.org

Summary To provide financial assistance to students at public universities in Arizona who have a rheumatic disease.

Eligibility This program is open to full-time undergraduate and graduate students at public 4-year universities in Arizona. Applicants must have some form of diagnosed rheumatic disease and provide a physician's certifying statement. They must be willing to be involved in Arthritis Foundation publicity and agree to meet with foundation officials in Phoenix.

Financial data The stipend is $7,500 per year.

Duration 1 year; may be renewed up to 3 additional years, provided the recipient remains enrolled full time and maintains a GPA of 2.5 or higher.

Number awarded 1 or more each year.

Deadline February of each year.

Grants-in-Aid

[602]
ARIZONA KIDNEY FOUNDATION ASSISTANCE PROGRAMS

Arizona Kidney Foundation
Attn: Patient Services Director
4203 East Indian School Road, Suite 140
Phoenix, AZ 85018
(602) 840-1644   Fax: (602) 840-2360
E-mail: glennas@azkidney.org
Web: www.azkidney.org

Summary To provide financial assistance for special needs to kidney patients in Arizona.

Eligibility This program is open to residents in Arizona who are undergoing dialysis treatment or have received kidney transplants. Applicants must have exhausted other sources of financial aid. The following forms of assistance are available: 1) dental program provides limited dental treatment delivered to eliminate dental caries and/or alleviate pain, infection, swelling, and/or injury, but not cosmetic, orthodontic, or prosthetic services; 2) food, requested through the patient's social worker; 3) medication, for anti-ulcer, antibiotics, anti-hypertensive meds, anti-rejection meds, phoslo, or renagel; 4) nutritional supplements, as requested by dietitian or nephrologist; 5) rent or mortgage payments; 6) utilities; and 7) transportation to and from dialysis or to and from pre- or post-transplant medical appointments.

Financial data The amount provided depends on the nature of the assistance: 1) for the dental program, selected dentists in Arizona have agreed to accept the fees offered by the sponsor as payment in full, minus a co-payment by the patient of $10 per visit; 2) the food program is limited to $240 per patient per year; 3) the full cost of medication from a restricted formulary is provided; 4) the full cost of designated nutritional supplements is provided; 5) rent or mortgage payments depend on the circumstances of each individual case; 6) utilities assistance is based on arrangements with the companies; and 7) transportation assistance is limited to $100 per patient per month.

Duration Most of the assistance programs are provided as long as the patient can document need. Nutritional supplements are limited to 6 months per year. Transportation assistance is limited to 3 weeks a month.

Number awarded Varies each year.

Deadline Deadline not specified.

[603]
CARE PROGRAM

National Gaucher Foundation, Inc.
Attn: Program Director, National Gaucher Care
  Foundation
267 Kentlands Boulevard, Box 1084
Gaithersburg, MD 20878
Toll Free: (866) 346-8176   Fax: (301) 963-4489
E-mail: blichtenstein@comcast.net
Web: www.gaucherdisease.org/psp.php

Summary To assist Gaucher patients who need help with paying their insurance premiums.

Eligibility To apply, a patient must be diagnosed with Type I Gaucher Disease, have a physician's prescription for enzyme replacement therapy, be eligible for insurance, be able to demonstrate extraordinary financial hardship, and need financial assistance to pay insurance premium payments.

Financial data This program provides funds to subsidize, or purchase in full, a health insurance policy that includes coverage for enzyme replacement therapy.

Duration The time period varies, depending on each individual case. Patients who receive grants are required to reapply on an annual basis or at the end of the designated grant period.

Additional data There are 6 genetic diseases that are prevalent in the Jewish population. Only 1 is treatable—Gaucher Disease, which is caused by a genetic mutation resulting in low levels of a key enzyme called glucocerebrosidase, important in breaking down a fatty substance in cells.

Number awarded Varies each year.

Deadline Applications may be submitted at any time and are considered on a quarterly basis.

[604]
CARE+PLUS PROGRAM

National Gaucher Foundation, Inc.
Attn: Program Director, National Gaucher Care
　Foundation
267 Kentlands Boulevard, Box 1084
Gaithersburg, MD 20878
Toll Free: (866) 346-8176　　　Fax: (301) 963-4489
E-mail: blichtenstein@comcast.net
Web: www.gaucherdisease.org/psp.php

Summary To provide assistance to needy Gaucher patients for a variety of Gaucher-related expenses, such as diagnostic tests, infusion charges, travel expenses, etc.

Eligibility To be eligible, a patient must be diagnosed with Type I Gaucher Disease, have a physician's prescription for enzyme replacement therapy, be eligible for insurance, and be able to demonstrate extraordinary financial hardship.

Financial data This program provides funds to pay for diagnostic tests and other ancillary medical expenses for Gaucher Disease not covered by insurance; infusion charges for enzyme replacement therapy not covered by insurance; membership fees for organizations that provide access to insurance for Gaucher patients; travel expenses to and from office/hospital for enzyme replacement therapy or a Gaucher medical evaluation; day care expenses for Gaucher patient's family members while the patient receives enzyme replacement therapy or a Gaucher medical evaluation; and over-the-counter medications that are prescribed for Gaucher patients.

Duration The time period varies, depending on each individual case. Patients who receive grants are required to reapply on an annual basis or at the end of the designated grant period.

Additional data There are 6 genetic diseases that are prevalent in the Jewish population. Only 1 is treatable— Gaucher Disease, which is caused by a genetic mutation resulting in low levels of a key enzyme called glucocerebrosidase, important in breaking down a fatty substance in cells.

Number awarded Varies each year.

Deadline Applications may be submitted at any time and are considered on a quarterly basis.

[605]
COAL MINERS BLACK LUNG BENEFITS

Department of Labor
Employment Standards Administration
Office of Workers' Compensation Programs
Attn: Division of Coal Mine Workers' Compensation
200 Constitution Avenue, N.W., Room C3520
Washington, DC 20210
(202) 693-0046　　　Toll Free: (800) 638-7072
TDD: (800) 326-2577
Web: www.dol.gov/dol/topic/workcomp/index.htm

Summary To provide monthly benefits to coal miners who are disabled because of pneumoconiosis (black lung disease) and to their surviving dependents.

Eligibility Present and former coal miners (including certain transportation and construction workers who were exposed to coal mine dust) and their surviving dependents, including surviving spouses, orphaned children, and totally dependent parents, brothers, and sisters, may file claims if they are totally disabled.

Financial data Benefit amounts vary; recently; the basic monthly benefit was $599 for a single totally disabled miner or surviving spouse, $898 per month for a claimant with 1 dependent, $1,048 per month for a claimant with 2 dependents, or $1,197 per month for a claimant with 3 or more dependents. Benefit payments are reduced by the amounts received for pneumoconiosis under state workers' compensation awards and by excess earnings.

Duration Benefits are paid as long as the miner is unable to work in the mines or until the miner dies.

Number awarded Varies; recently, 8,654 miners, 23,690 surviving spouses, 1,230 other eligible persons, 6,442 dependents of miners, 777 dependents of surviving spouses, and 132 dependents of other eligible persons received benefits from this program.

Deadline Deadline not specified.

[606]
DONATE LIFE SOUTH CAROLINA PATIENT ASSISTANCE PROGRAM

Donate Life South Carolina
Attn: Office Program Manager
22 Centre East
4200 East North Street
Greenville, SC 29615
(864) 609-5270　　　Toll Free: (877) 277-4866
Fax: (864) 609-5387
Web: www.donatelifesc.org

Summary To provide emergency funding to residents of South Carolina who have received an organ transplant.

Eligibility This assistance is available to transplant recipients in South Carolina. Applicants must be able to demonstrate a need for emergency support for rent or mortgage payments, utility bills, groceries, or direct costs associated with the transplant (e.g., prescriptions, travel costs, hotel stays). They must have an income less than $30,000 per year for a family of 4.

Financial data The amount of the assistance depends on several variables, including (but not limited to) type of organ transplant, the extent to which Medicaid or Medicare becomes available, types of medications involved, or types of extraneous expenses involved.

Duration Grants are provided as needed.

Additional data This sponsoring organization was formerly known as Gift of Life.

Number awarded Varies each year; recently, the program managed 73 active cases and provided $63,518 in emergency financial assistance.

Deadline Applications may be submitted at any time.

[607]
EPILEPSY FOUNDATION OF KANSAS AND WESTERN MISSOURI MEDICATION ASSISTANCE

Epilepsy Foundation of Kansas and Western Missouri
6700 Troost Avenue, Suite 316
Kansas City, MO 64131
(816) 444-2800   Toll Free: (800) 972-5163
Fax: (816) 444-6777   E-mail: info@efha.org
Web: www.epilepsyfoundation.org

Summary To provide funding to low-income residents of Kansas and western Missouri who need assistance for the purchase of anti-epilepsy medication.

Eligibility This program is open to residents of Kansas and western Missouri who have epilepsy. Applicants must be able to demonstrate that they have no insurance and need assistance for the purchase of anti-epilepsy medication. They may be seeking emergency assistance or ongoing assistance. Their family income must be less than 200% of the federal poverty level.

Financial data Emergency assistance provides a supply of medication that the foundation purchases for the consumer. Consumers determined eligible for ongoing assistance receive a membership card that they can use for a 50% discount on the cost of medication that they purchase at a participating pharmacy.

Duration Emergency assistance provides a 1-time, 1-month supply. Ongoing assistance cards are valid for 1 year but may be renewed.

Additional data This program began in 1960.

Number awarded Varies each year; recently, it provided 152 emergency medication prescriptions at a cost of $20,770.90 and 580 ongoing prescriptions at a cost of $51,528.74 (this figure includes the amount paid by consumers).

Deadline Applications may be submitted at any time.

[608]
EVELYN AND FREDRICK WEISSMAN EDUCATION AND CHARITABLE FOUNDATION GRANTS

Evelyn and Fredrick Weissman Education and
  Charitable Foundation
30238 Spring River Drive
Southfield, MI 48076-1047
(248) 203-9270

Summary To provide funding for therapy to individuals with mental disabilities in Michigan.

Eligibility This assistance is available to residents of Michigan who have a mental disability. Applicants must be seeking funding for speech and physical therapy.

Financial data The amount of the grant depends on the need of the recipient.

Duration These are 1-time grants.

Number awarded Varies each year.

Deadline Applications may be submitted at any time.

[609]
FLEX GRANT PROGRAM OF THE JIM "CATFISH" HUNTER CHAPTER

ALS Association-Jim "Catfish" Hunter Chapter
Attn: Patient and Family Services
120-101 Penmarc Drive
Raleigh, NC 27603
(919) 755-9001   Toll Free: (877) 568-4347
Fax: (919) 755-0910
E-mail: katie@CatfishChapter.org
Web: catfish.prolitical.com/outchapter/programs

Summary To provide funding for specified expenses to patients with Amyotrophic Lateral Sclerosis (ALS) in North Carolina.

Eligibility This assistance is available to patients who have a definitive diagnosis of ALS and reside in North Carolina. Applicants must be seeking funding for expenses that are not traditionally covered by insurance, Medicare, Medicaid, or other assistance programs. Examples include, but are not limited to, home modifications such as ramps and bathroom upgrades, environmental controls and generators for invasive or non-invasive breathing assistance, auto modifications, or wheelchair modifications and repairs. Selection depends on need, the number of applicants, and availability of funds.

Financial data Each grant is $500. Patients may obtain 2 grants per fiscal year, or funding of $1,000 annually.

Duration 1 year.

Additional data The North Carolina Chapter of the ALS Association was formed in 1987. In 2000, it expanded its services to include South Carolina and, in 2002, adopted the name of former professional baseball player Jim "Catfish" Hunter. In 2006, a separate South Carolina chapter was formed, so this chapter again limits its services to North Carolina. This program was established in 2007.

Number awarded Varies each year.

Deadline Applications must be submitted by the 25th day of each month.

[610]
FUND FOR WRITERS AND EDITORS WITH HIV/AIDS

PEN American Center
Attn: Coordinator, Writers Fund
588 Broadway, Suite 303
New York, NY 10012
(212) 334-1660, ext. 126   Fax: (212) 334-2181
E-mail: lara@pen.org
Web: www.pen.org/page.php/prmID/251

Summary To provide financial assistance to published writers, produced playwrights, and editors with Acquired Immune Deficiency Syndrome (AIDS) or HIV.

Eligibility Professional authors and editors with HIV or AIDS are eligible to apply if they are in need of emergency financial assistance. They must be U.S. residents and have had their works published or produced (applicants will be asked to submit samples of their work). Applicants need not be members of PEN, however. Funding is not provided to pay for research activities, to enable the completion of writing projects, or to cover publication or education expenses.

Financial data Grants up to $2,000 are available.

Duration These are 1-time grants.

Number awarded Varies each year.

Deadline June of each year.

[611]
HAWAII INCOME TAX EXCLUSION FOR PATIENTS WITH HANSEN'S DISEASE

Department of Taxation
Attn: Taxpayer Services Branch
425 Queen Street
P.O. Box 259
Honolulu, HI 96809-0259
(808) 587-4242   Toll Free: (800) 222-3229
Fax: (808) 587-1488   TDD: (808) 587-1418
Web: hawaii.gov/tax

Summary To exempt payments to patients with Hansen's Disease from state income taxation in Hawaii.

Eligibility Compensation paid by the state of Hawaii or the United States to a patient affected with Hansen's Disease (also known as leprosy) is subject to this exclusion.

Financial data All compensation is excluded from income for purposes of state taxation.

Duration The exclusion continues as long as the recipient resides in Hawaii.

Deadline Deadline not specified.

[612]
HEALTHWELL FOUNDATION GRANTS

HealthWell Foundation
P.O. Box 4133
Gaithersburg, MD 20878-4133
Toll Free: (800) 675-8416   Fax: (800) 282-7692
E-mail: info@healthwellfoundation.org
Web: www.healthwellfoundation.org

Summary To help pay the insurance premiums and copayments for people with designated illnesses.

Eligibility This assistance is available to people who need help in paying their insurance premiums or copayments (but not both) so they can obtain medications needed for designated diseases. They must have a household income below 300% to 400% of the federal poverty level (depending on the disease) and be receiving treatment for a specific disease or condition with medication dispensed in the United States. The diseases or conditions for which assistance is available are acute porphyrias, age-related macular degeneration, anemia associated with chronic renal insufficiency and chronic renal failure, ankylosing spondylitis, asthma, breast cancer, carcinoid tumors, chemotherapy induced anemia, chemotherapy induced neutropenia, colorectal carcinoma, cutaneous T-cell lymphoma, Dupuytren's Disease, glioblastoma multiforme and anaplastic astrocytoma, head and neck cancer, hepatitis B and C, Hodgkin's Disease, idiopathic thrombocytopenic purpura, immunosuppressive treatment for solid organ transplants, iron overload as a result of blood transfusions, multiple myeloma, myelodysplastic syndromes, non-Hodgkin's lymphoma, non-small cell lung cancer, psoriasis, psoriatic arthritis, rheumatoid arthritis, secondary hyperparathyroidism, and Wilms' Tumor. The diagnosis must be verified by a physician. Individuals covered by private insurance, employer-sponsored plans, Medicare, or Medicaid may be eligible.

Financial data Grants provide full or partial assistance.

Duration Up to 12 months; enrollment may be renewed.

Additional data This foundation was established in 2003.

Number awarded Varies each year. Grants are awarded on a first-come, first-served basis for each disease as long as funds are available. Recently, 50,500 patients received assistance worth more than $118 million.

Deadline Applications may be submitted at any time.

[613]
HEMOPHILIA ASSOCIATION OF THE CAPITAL AREA FAMILY ASSISTANCE PROGRAM

Hemophilia Association of the Capital Area
10560 Main Street, Suite PH-1
Fairfax, VA 22030-7182
(703) 352-7641   Fax: (703) 352-2145
E-mail: info@hacacares.org
Web: www.hacacares.org

Summary To provide emergency financial aid to individuals with bleeding disorders and their families in the Washington, D.C. area.

Eligibility This program is open to 1) residents of northern Virginia, Montgomery and Prince George's County in Maryland, and Washington, D.C.; and 2) people who receive treatment for bleeding disorders at Children's National Medical Center or Georgetown University Hospital in Washington, D.C. Also eligible are parents and caregivers of people living in their home who have a bleeding disorder relevant to the mission of the Hemophilia Association of the Capital Area (HACA). Applicants must be able to demonstrate need for assistance for 1) uncovered medical bills associated with the diagnosis and treatment of a bleeding disorder and any complications from that; or 2) basic living expense emergencies.

Financial data The amount of the assistance depends on the need of the grantee.

Duration Assistance is provided only once per calendar year.

Number awarded Varies each year.

Deadline Applications may be submitted at any time.

[614]
HEMOPHILIA FOUNDATION OF MICHIGAN EMERGENCY FINANCIAL ASSISTANCE PROGRAM

Hemophilia Foundation of Michigan
Attn: Client Services Coordinator
1921 West Michigan Avenue
Ypsilanti, MI 48197
(734) 544-0015   Toll Free: (800) 482-3041
Fax: (734) 544-0095   E-mail: hfm@hfmich.org
Web: www.hfmich.org/programs/financial_aid.html

Summary To provide financial assistance for emergency needs to Michigan residents with hemophilia.

Eligibility This program is open to residents of Michigan who have a bleeding disorder and have a temporary financial emergency. The need may be for food, utilities, rent, or car repair for individuals whose bleeding disorder impacts their income. Selection is based on severity of the need and the ability of applicants to change their financial standing. Requests may come directly from applicants or their hemophilia treatment center.

Financial data Grants depend on the availability of funds and the need of the recipient.

Duration Recipients may obtain these funds only once in each 12-month period.

Number awarded Varies each year.

Deadline Applications may be submitted at any time.

[615]
IDAHO INCOME TAX EXEMPTION FOR MAINTAINING A HOME FOR THE DEVELOPMENTALLY DISABLED

Idaho State Tax Commission
Attn: Public Information Office
800 Park Boulevard, Plaza IV
P.O. Box 36
Boise, ID 83722-0410
(208) 334-7660   Toll Free: (800) 972-7660
TDD: (800) 377-3529
Web: tax.idaho.gov

Summary To exempt from state taxation a portion of the income of residents of Idaho who maintain a home for a family member, including themselves and their spouses, who is developmentally disabled.

Eligibility Individuals in Idaho who maintain a household that includes a developmentally disabled person (of any age) are eligible for this program if they provide at least half of the support of the developmentally disabled family member. The taxpayer and spouse may be included as a member of the family. Developmental disability is defined as a chronic disability that 1) is attributable to an impairment such as mental retardation, cerebral palsy, epilepsy, autism, or related condition; 2) results in substantial functional limitation in 3 or more of the following areas of life activity: self-care, receptive and expressive language, learning, mobility, self-direction, capacity for independent living, or economic self-sufficiency; and 3) reflects the need for a combination and sequence of special, interdisciplinary or generic care, treatment, or other services that are of lifelong or extended duration and individually planned and coordinated.

Financial data The amount of the deduction is $1,000 for each developmentally disabled family member, up to a maximum of $3,000.

Duration Application for the deduction must be submitted each year.

Additional data This deduction also applies to taxpayers maintaining a home for a family member who is 65 years of age or older. Taxpayers who do not claim the $1,000 deduction may be able to claim a tax credit of $100

for each member of the family who is developmentally disabled or elderly, to a maximum of 3 members.

Number awarded Varies each year.

Deadline April of each year.

[616]
J. KIFFIN PENRY PATIENT TRAVEL ASSISTANCE FUND

Epilepsy Foundation
Attn: Public Relations Department
8301 Professional Place
Landover, MD 20785-2237
Toll Free: (800) 470-1655, ext. 3726
E-mail: mthornton@efa.org
Web: www.epilepsyfoundation.org/living

Summary To provide funding to individuals who must travel to receive medical services for treatment of epilepsy.

Eligibility This program is open to individuals who must travel more than 50 miles to receive medical services for treatment of epilepsy. Applicants must be able to document that they have exhausted other funding sources available in the county and state where they live and the insurance company with which they participate. If they live within an area served by an affiliate of the Epilepsy Foundation, they must apply through that affiliate. If they live in an unserved area, they may apply through the national office.

Financial data The maximum grant per family within a 2-year time period is $2,000; most grants are for less than $1,000. Funding is provided only for travel and lodging for the individual receiving treatment and an adult companion or parent if that individual is a minor and/or cognitively unable to travel without supervision and assistance. The maximum allowance for meals is $30 per day.

Additional data This program is underwritten by Novartis Pharmaceuticals Corporation.

Number awarded Varies each year.

Deadline Applications for reimbursement may be submitted at any time, but they must be received no later than 30 days following the last day of travel.

[617]
JACK NORTON FAMILY RESPITE CARE PROGRAM

ALS Association-Minnesota Chapter
Attn: Patient Services Coordinator
333 North Washington Avenue, Suite 105
Minneapolis, MN 55401
(612) 672-0484   Toll Free: (888) 672-0484
Fax: (612) 672-9110   E-mail: anne@alsmn.org
Web: webmn.alsa.org

Summary To provide funding for respite care to residents of Minnesota and North Dakota who are a Person with Amyotrophic Lateral Sclerosis (PALS) or family member.

Eligibility This assistance is available to any PALS or family member living in Minnesota or North Dakota. The family caregiver must be living with and caring for a PALS on a full-time basis.

Financial data The program provides funding to pay for a family caregiver to assist in caring for the PALS.

Duration Funding is provided for 18 hours a month.

Additional data The Minnesota Chapter of the ALS Association arranges with an appropriate licensed home care agency to provide the respite care.

Number awarded Varies each year.

Deadline Applications may be submitted at any time.

[618]
KENTUCKY PREMIUM ASSISTANCE PROGRAM

Patient Services Incorporated
P.O. Box 1602
Midlothian, VA 23113
Toll Free: (800) 366-7741   Fax: (804) 744-5407
E-mail: uneedpsi@uneedpsi.org
Web: www.uneedpsi.org

Summary To provide funding to residents of Kentucky who have specified diseases and need help in paying for insurance.

Eligibility This assistance is available to residents of Kentucky who have hemophilia, von Willebrands Disease, cystic fibrosis, asthma, or juvenile rheumatoid arthritis and have been referred by a hemophilia treatment center or related program in the state. Applicants must be uninsured or underinsured and able to demonstrate a need for assistance to pay premiums on a private insurance policy. Their family income must be below 200% of the federal poverty level.

Financial data The amount of assistance depends on the need of the recipient and the availability of funds.

Additional data This program was established in 2000 by the Kentucky Cabinet for Health and Family Services.

Number awarded Varies each year.

Deadline Applications may be submitted at any time.

[619]
LEUKEMIA & LYMPHOMA SOCIETY CO-PAY ASSISTANCE PROGRAM

Leukemia & Lymphoma Society of America
Attn: Co-Pay Assistance Program
P.O. Box 12268
Newport News, VA 23612
Toll Free: (877) 557-2672   Fax: (877) 267-2932
Web: www.leukemia-lymphoma.org

Summary To provide funding to patients with leukemia and related diseases who need assistance with their pharmacy co-payments and insurance premiums.

Eligibility This program is open to residents of the United States and Puerto Rico who have been diagnosed with Hodgkin lymphoma, non-Hodgkin lymphoma, chronic myelogenous leukemia, chronic lymphocytic leukemia, myelodysplastic syndromes (MDS), myeloma, or Waldenstrom macroglobulinemia. Applicants must have household income at or within 500% above the U.S. federal poverty guidelines (currently ranging from $54,150 for a family of 1 up to $185,050 for a family of 8). They must need assistance for prescription drugs, private health insurance

premiums, private insurance co-pay obligations, Medicare Part B, Medicare Plan D, Medicare supplementary health insurance, or Medicare Advantage premium or co-pay obligations.

Financial data For patients with Hodgkin lymphoma, non-Hodgkin lymphoma, chronic myelogenous leukemia, chronic lymphocytic leukemia, or myelodysplastic syndromes (MDS), the maximum grant is $5,000. For patients with myeloma or Waldenstrom macroglobulinemia, the maximum grant is $10,000.

Number awarded Varies each year.

Deadline Applications may be submitted at any time.

[620]
NANCY J. MARINE PATIENT EMERGENCY ASSISTANCE FUND

National Kidney Foundation Serving Connecticut
2139 Silas Deane Highway, Suite 208
Rocky Hill, CT 06067-2337
(860) 257-3770   Toll Free: (800) 441-1280
Fax: (860) 257-3429   E-mail: nkfct@kidney.org
Web: www.kidneyct.org/site/patients/index.cfm?ch=102

Summary To provide emergency financial assistance to individuals in Connecticut who have kidney or urological problems.

Eligibility This assistance is available to pre-dialysis, dialysis, pre-transplant, and post-transplant patients in Connecticut who are referred by a social worker. Applicants should be people who would be at medical risk without assistance.

Financial data The amount awarded varies, depending upon the needs of the recipient. Funds may be used to help pay utilities, pharmacy bills, transportation, groceries, rent, and related expenses.

Duration In general, these are 1-time funds.

Number awarded Varies each year.

Deadline Applications may be submitted at any time.

[621]
NATIONAL CHILDREN'S CANCER SOCIETY FINANCIAL ASSISTANCE

National Children's Cancer Society
Attn: Patient and Family Services
One South Memorial Drive, Suite 800
St. Louis, MO 63102
(314) 241-1600   Toll Free: (800) 5-FAMILY
Fax: (314) 241-1996
E-mail: SSchuetz@children-cancer.org
Web: www.nationalchildrenscancersociety.com

Summary To provide financial assistance to children with cancer and their families.

Eligibility This assistance is available to children (under 18 years of age) with cancer and their families. Applicants must be facing medical and non-medical expenses related to treatment, including meals during treatment, health insurance premiums, medical expenses not covered by insurance, lodging during treatment, long distance calling cards, and transportation during treatment. Families with liquid assets in excess of $5,000 may be asked to partially or completely "spend down" those assets prior to receiving this assistance. Children must be U.S. citizens or permanent residents.

Financial data Assistance depends on the need of the recipient.

Duration Assistance may be provided for up to 2 months; if continuing support is still required, a request for renewal may be submitted by a hospital professional.

Number awarded Varies each year.

Deadline Applications may be submitted at any time.

[622]
NATIONAL KIDNEY FOUNDATION OF COLORADO, MONTANA AND WYOMING PATIENT EMERGENCY ASSISTANCE GRANTS

National Kidney Foundation of Colorado, Montana and
  Wyoming, Inc.
Attn: Program Director
3151 South Vaughn Way, Suite 505
Aurora, CO 80014-3514
(720) 748-9991, ext. 113   Toll Free: (800) 263-4005
Fax: (720) 748-1273
E-mail: lhellickson@kidneycimw.org
Web: www.kidneycimw.org

Summary To provide financial assistance to patients with kidney or urinary tract diseases who live in Colorado, Montana, and Wyoming.

Eligibility These programs are open patients with kidney or urinary tract diseases who reside in Colorado, Montana, or Wyoming. In general, they should be referred by a social worker because they are in need of funds to supplement the cost of medications, treatment supplies, dental needs, and transportation expenses.

Financial data The amount awarded varies, depending upon the needs of the recipient.

Duration Funds are provided as needed.

Number awarded Varies each year.

Deadline Applications may be submitted at any time.

[623]
NATIONAL KIDNEY FOUNDATION OF INDIANA EMERGENCY FINANCIAL AID

National Kidney Foundation of Indiana, Inc.
Attn: Program Coordinator
911 East 86th Street, Suite 100
Indianapolis, IN 46204-1848
(317) 722-5640   Toll Free: (800) 382-9971
Fax: (317) 722-5650   E-mail: nkfi@kidneyindiana.org
Web: www.kidney.org/site/303/patientAid.cfm?ch=303

Summary To provide emergency financial assistance to individuals in Indiana who have kidney or urinary tract diseases.

Eligibility This assistance is available to patients in Indiana who have kidney or urinary tract diseases or are a kidney transplant recipient. Applicants must need assistance for groceries, utilities, telephone bills, rent, and medical supplies and equipment not covered by a health plan. They must be referred by a social worker at a dialysis unit or transplant center.

Financial data The amount awarded varies, depending upon the needs of the recipient.

Duration In general, these are 1-time funds.

Additional data This fund is not designed to pay medical bills.

Number awarded Varies each year.

Deadline Applications may be submitted at any time.

[624]
NATIONAL KIDNEY FOUNDATION OF UTAH AND IDAHO PATIENT EMERGENCY GRANTS

National Kidney Foundation of Utah and Idaho
3707 North Canyon Road, Suite 1D
Provo, UT 84604-4585
(801) 226-5111   Toll Free: (800) 869-5277
Fax: (801) 226-8278   E-mail: nkfu@kidneyut.org
Web: www.kidneyut.org/ps-grants.php

Summary To provide emergency financial assistance to kidney patients in Utah and Idaho.

Eligibility This program is open to residents of Utah and Idaho who are kidney transplant recipients or dialysis patients. Applicants must need assistance to help pay for food, rent, utilities, transportation, vehicle maintenance, medical insurance, medications, or doctors' bills.

Financial data Grants depend on the need of the recipient.

Duration These are 1-time grants.

Number awarded Varies each year.

Deadline Applications may be submitted at any time.

[625]
NATIONAL KIDNEY FOUNDATION SERVING MAINE PATIENT ASSISTANCE GRANTS

National Kidney Foundation Serving Maine
c/o National Kidney Foundation Service New England
85 Astor Avenue, Suite 2
Norwood, MA 02062-5040
(781) 278-0222   Toll Free: (800) 542-4001
Fax: (781) 278-0333   E-mail: nkfmarinhvt@kidney.org
Web: www.kidney.org/site/patients/index.cfm?ch=103

Summary To provide financial assistance for emergency needs to kidney patients in Maine.

Eligibility This program is open to residents of Maine who are kidney patients or transplant recipients. Applicants must be able to demonstrate financial need for help with heating oil, medications, transportation to and from dialysis, housing, food, and other materials needs (e.g., glasses, dentures, utilities). They must apply through their dialysis center social worker.

Financial data The amount of the grant depends on the need of the patient.

Duration These are 1-time emergency grants.

Number awarded Varies each year.

Deadline Applications may be submitted at any time.

[626]
NATIONAL KIDNEY FOUNDATION SERVING OHIO EMERGENCY FINANCIAL ASSISTANCE

National Kidney Foundation Serving Ohio
1373 Grandview Avenue, Suite 200
Columbus, OH 43212-2804
(614) 481-4030   Fax: (614) 481-4038
E-mail: mcampbell@nkfofohio.org
Web: www.kidney.org/site/patients/index.cfm?ch=130

Summary To provide emergency financial assistance to kidney patients in Ohio.

Eligibility This assistance is available to residents of Ohio who have Chronic Kidney Disease (CKD) and are facing emergency situations. Applications must be submitted by a renal social worker.

Financial data Limited funds are available.

Number awarded Varies each year.

Deadline Applications may be submitted at any time.

[627]
PATIENT ACCESS NETWORK FINANCIAL ASSISTANCE

Patient Access Network Foundation
P.O. Box 221858
Charlotte, NC 28222-1858
Toll Free: (866) 316-PANF   Fax: (866) 316-7261
E-mail: contact@patientaccessnetwork.org
Web: www.panfoundation.org

Summary To provide co-payment assistance to people who have inadequate medical insurance and are facing specific diseases.

Eligibility This assistance is available to U.S. residents who meet specified financial, insurance, and medical criteria. Applicants must be undergoing treatment for 1 of the following diseases or conditions: acromegaly, age-related macular degeneration, ankylosing spondylitis, breast cancer, colorectal cancer, Crohn's Disease, cutaneous T-cell lymphoma (CTCL), cystic fibrosis, cytomegalovirus (CMV) prevention and treatment, Gaucher's Disease, growth hormone deficiency, hepatitis B or C, kidney transplant immunosuppressant, multiple myeloma, multiple sclerosis, myelodysplastic syndrome, non-Hodgkins lymphoma, non-small cell lung cancer, oncology cytoprotection, pancreatic cancer, plaque psoriasis, prostate cancer, renal cell carcinoma, respiratory syncytial virus (RSV), rheumatoid arthritis, or solid organ transplant immunosuppressant therapy. They must be insured and their insurance must cover the medication for which they seek assistance. The medication must fight the disease directly. The fund for each disease specifies that patient's income must fall below a specified amount, ranging from 200% to 400% of the federal poverty level. Physicians must verify all information provided on the application.

Financial data Each disease fund specifies a maximum award level of co-payment assistance for that disease; those range from $1,500 to $10,000 per year.

Duration 1 year.

Additional data This program was established in 2004.

Number awarded Varies each year. Since this program was established, it has awarded nearly $100 million in co-payment assistance to more than 66,000 patients.

Deadline Applications may be submitted at any time.

[628]
PATIENT ADVOCATE FOUNDATION CO-PAY RELIEF PROGRAM

Patient Advocate Foundation
Attn: Co-Pay Relief
421 Butler Farm Road
Hampton, VA 23669
Toll Free: (866) 512-3861   Fax: (757) 952-0119
E-mail: cpr@patientadvocate.org
Web: www.copays.org

Summary To provide funding to people who are taking medication for specified diseases and need assistance to make the co-payments required by their insurance plans.

Eligibility This program is open to patients diagnosed with the following diseases or conditions: autoimmune disorders, breast cancer, CIA/CIN, colon cancer, cutaneous T-cell lymphoma (CTCL), diabetes, head and neck cancer, hepatitis C, kidney cancer, lung cancer, lymphoma, malignant brain tumors, multiple myeloma, myelodysplastic syndrome, osteoporosis, pain, pancreatic cancer, prostate cancer, rheumatoid arthritis, or sarcoma. Applicants must be able to demonstrate financial need. Medicare Part D beneficiaries are also eligible.

Financial data Assistance with prescription drug co-payments is provided.

Duration These are 1-time grants.

Number awarded Varies each year.

Deadline Applications may be submitted at any time.

[629]
PATIENT AID PROGRAM

Bone Marrow Foundation
30 East End Avenue, Suite 1F
New York, NY 10028
(212) 838-3029   Toll Free: (800) 365-1336
Fax: (212) 223-0081
E-mail: TheBMF@bonemarrow.org
Web: www.bonemarrow.org/resources/financial_aid.html

Summary To provide financial assistance to bone marrow transplant patients and their families.

Eligibility This program is open to both children and adult bone marrow transplant patients. Patients must be affiliated with a certified transplant center that is associated with the Bone Marrow Foundation (for a list, write to the foundation). They must have a social worker and physician at the transplant center verify information about diagnosis, treatment, and financial status.

Financial data Each patient is eligible for up to $1,000. Funds are to be used to cover the costs of support services (e.g., donor searches, compatibility testing, bone marrow harvesting, medications, home care services, child care services, medical equipment, transportation, sperm banking, cord blood banking, and housing expenses associated with the transplant). This funding cannot not be used to pay outstanding medical bills or any other pre-existing bills associated with the transplant.

Duration This is generally a 1-time award, although occasionally recipients can reapply.

Additional data This program was started in 1992. Currently, it operates in 70 certified transplant centers across the country.

Number awarded Varies each year.

Deadline Applications may be submitted at any time.

[630]
PATIENT SERVICES INCORPORATED ASSISTANCE

Patient Services Incorporated
P.O. Box 1602
Midlothian, VA 23113
Toll Free: (800) 366-7741　　　Fax: (804) 744-5407
E-mail: uneedpsi@uneedpsi.org
Web: www.uneedpsi.org

Summary To provide funding to people with chronic medical illnesses who need help in paying their health insurance premiums or pharmacy co-payments.

Eligibility This assistance is available to people with chronic medical illnesses who are experiencing financial difficulty in paying their health insurance premiums or pharmacy co-payments. Currently, applicants must be affected by 1 of the following illnesses: acromegaly, advanced idiopathic Parkinson's Disease, alpha1 antitrypsin deficiency, bone metastases, chronic myelogenous leukemia, cutaneous T-cell lymphoma (CTCL), cystic fibrosis (with pseudomonas), Fabry Disease, gastrointestinal stromal tumors (GIST), hemophilia, hereditary angioedema (C1 inhibitor deficiencies), insulin-like growth factor 1 deficiency (IGF-1), MPS 1, Pompe Disease, primary immune deficiency, or severe congenital protein C deficiency.

Financial data The amount of assistance depends on the need of the recipient and the availability of funds.

Duration Assistance may be granted for 1 year.

Number awarded Varies each year.

Deadline Applications may be submitted at any time.

[631]
PENNSYLVANIA BLEEDING DISORDERS PREMIUM ASSISTANCE PROGRAM

Patient Services Incorporated
P.O. Box 1602
Midlothian, VA 23113
Toll Free: (800) 366-7741　　　Fax: (804) 744-5407
E-mail: uneedpsi@uneedpsi.org
Web: www.uneedpsi.org

Summary To provide funding to residents of Pennsylvania who have a bleeding disorder and need help in paying for insurance.

Eligibility This assistance is available to residents of Pennsylvania who have hemophilia, von Willebrands Disease, or other bleeding disorder and are referred by a local chapter of the National Hemophilia Foundation, a hemophilia treatment center, state agency, patient organization,

home care company, or other organization. Applicants must be uninsured or underinsured and able to demonstrate a need for assistance to pay premiums on a private insurance policy. Their family income must be below 200% of the federal poverty level.

Financial data The amount of assistance depends on the need of the recipient and the availability of funds.

Additional data This program was established in 2009.

Number awarded Varies each year.

Deadline Applications may be submitted at any time.

[632]
SAMFUND GRANTS AND SCHOLARSHIPS

The SAMFund for Young Adult Survivors of Cancer
89 South Street, Suite LL02
Boston, MA 02211
E-mail: grants@thesamfund.org
Web: www.thesamfund.org/pages/grants.html

Summary To provide funding to young adult cancer survivors who need assistance for the transition to post-treatment life.

Eligibility This program is open to cancer survivors between 17 and 35 years of age who are finished with active treatment and are trying to move forward with their lives. Applicants must be able to demonstrate a need for funding for such purposes as undergraduate or graduate school tuition and expenses, car and health insurance premiums, rent, fertility-related expenses, gym memberships, transportation costs, or current and residual medical bills.

Financial data Grant amounts vary; recently, they averaged approximately $2,500.

Duration These are 1-time grants.

Additional data This program, which stands for Surviving and Moving Forward, was established in 2003.

Number awarded Varies each year; since the program was established, it has awarded nearly 200 grants with a total value of $400,000.

Deadline Deadline not specified.

[633]
SOUTH CAROLINA DISABLED PERSON PROPERTY TAX EXEMPTION

South Carolina Department of Revenue
Attn: Property Division
301 Gervais Street
P.O. Box 125
Columbia, SC 29214
(803) 898-5480　　　Fax: (803) 898-5822
Web: www.sctax.org

Summary To exempt the home of disabled residents of South Carolina and their surviving spouses from property taxation.

Eligibility Eligible for this exemption are residents of South Carolina who are defined as paraplegic or hemiplegic and own a dwelling house that is their domicile. The exemption is allowed to the surviving spouse of the person as long as the spouse does not remarry, resides in the dwelling, and obtains the fee or a life estate in the dwelling. Paraplegic or hemiplegic includes a person with Parkinson's Disease, multiple sclerosis, or amyotrophic lateral sclerosis that has caused the same ambulatory difficulties as a person with paraperesis or hemiparesis. Surviving spouses of those persons are not eligible for this exemption.

Financial data The exemption applies to all taxes on 1 house and a lot (not to exceed 1 acre).

Duration The exemption extends as long as the person with a disability resides in the house.

Number awarded Varies each year.

Deadline Applications may be submitted at any time.

[634]
SOUTH CAROLINA NATIONAL KIDNEY FOUNDATION EMERGENCY FINANCIAL ASSISTANCE

National Kidney Foundation Serving the Carolinas-
South Carolina Region
Attn: Patient Services
500 Taylor Street, Suite 101
Columbia, SC 29201-3000
(803) 799-3870   Toll Free: (800) 488-2277
Fax: (803) 799-3871   E-mail: sderrick@kidneysc.org
Web: www.kidney.org/site/patients/index.cfm?ch=209

Summary To provide emergency financial assistance to kidney patients in South Carolina.

Eligibility This assistance is available to South Carolina residents who are kidney patients. Applicants must be facing a crisis situation in which they need assistance with such expenses as medications, utilities, and rent. They must apply through their clinic's social worker.

Financial data The amount of the assistance depends on the need of the patient.

Duration These are 1-time grants.

Number awarded Varies each year.

Deadline Applications may be submitted at any time.

[635]
SOUTH CAROLINA PREMIUM ASSISTANCE PROGRAM

Patient Services Incorporated
P.O. Box 1602
Midlothian, VA 23113
Toll Free: (800) 366-7741   Fax: (804) 744-5407
E-mail: uneedpsi@uneedpsi.org
Web: www.uneedpsi.org

Summary To provide funding to residents of South Carolina who have a bleeding disorder and need help in paying for insurance.

Eligibility This assistance is available to residents of South Carolina who have hemophilia, von Willebrands Disease, or other bleeding disorder and are enrolled or eligible for enrollment in the South Carolina Department of Health and Environmental Control (DHEC) Clotting Factor Program. Applicants must be uninsured or underinsured and able to demonstrate a need for assistance to pay premiums on a private insurance policy. Their family income must be below 200% of the federal poverty level.

Financial data The amount of assistance depends on the need of the recipient and the availability of funds.

Additional data This program was established in 2008 by the DHEC.

Number awarded Varies each year.

Deadline Applications may be submitted at any time.

[636]
SUPPLEMENTAL SECURITY INCOME (SSI)

Social Security Administration
6401 Security Boulevard
Baltimore, MD 21235-0001
(410) 594-1234   Toll Free: (800) 772-1213
TDD: (800) 325-0778
Web: www.socialsecurity.gov/ssi/index.htm

Summary To provide monthly payments to disabled, blind, deaf, and elderly people who have limited income and resources.

Eligibility This assistance is available to U.S. citizens and certain categories of aliens who are 65 years of age or older, blind, or disabled. A person 18 years of age or older is considered disabled if a physical or mental impairment prevents him or her from doing any substantial gainful work and is expected to last for at least 12 months or to result in death. Children under the age of 18 are considered disabled if they have a physical or mental impairment that is comparable in severity to a disability that would prevent an adult from working and is expected to last at least 12 months or result in death. Children with certain conditions are automatically disabled and eligible for these benefits; the conditions include HIV infection, blindness, deafness, cerebral palsy, Down syndrome, muscular dystrophy, significant mental deficiency, diabetes (with amputation of 1 foot), amputation of 2 limbs, or amputation of leg at the hip. Regardless of age, a person whose vision is no better than 20/200 or who has a limited visual field of 20 degrees or less with the best corrective eyeglasses is considered blind; individuals with visual impairments not severe enough to meet the definition of blindness still may qualify as disabled persons. Applicants must have limited income and limited resources (less than $2,000 for an individual or $3,000 for a couple); items excluded from resources include the home used as a principal place of residence, personal and household goods, life insurance with face value of $1,500 or less, a car, burial plots for individuals and immediate family members, and burial funds up to $1,500.

Financial data The basic monthly payment is $674 for an eligible individual or $1,011 for an eligible individual with an eligible spouse. Many states add money to that basic payment. SSI recipients may also be eligible for food stamps and other nutrition programs.

Duration Assistance is provided as long as the recipient remains blind or disabled and in financial need.

Additional data Although SSI is administered through the Social Security Administration, it is not financed by Social Security taxes. Financing of SSI is provided through general funds of the U.S. Treasury. Recipients of SSI need not have been employed or paid Social Security taxes, but they may be eligible for both SSI and Social Security. Disabled and blind applicants for SSI are referred to their state vocational rehabilitation agency to determine their eligibility for a program of vocational rehabilitation. Disabled drug addicts or alcoholics are referred for appropriate treatment if it is available at an approved facility or institution.

Number awarded   Recently, approximately 7,599,000 people (including 6,395,000 who were blind and disabled) were receiving SSI benefits, including 1,172,000 under 18 years of age, 4,389,000 who were 18 to 64 years of age, and 2,038,000 who were 65 or older.

Deadline   Deadline not specified.

[637]
SUSAN BROWN TRANSPORTATION PROGRAM

ALS Association-DC/Maryland/Virginia Chapter
Attn: Director of Patient Services
7507 Standish Place
Rockville, MD 20855
(301) 978-9855   Toll Free: (866) FITE-ALS
Fax: (301) 978-9854   E-mail: info@ALSinfo.org
Web: www.ALSinfo.org

Summary   To provide funding for transportation to Amyotrophic Lateral Sclerosis (ALS) patients in Maryland, Virginia, and Washington, D.C.

Eligibility   This assistance is available to residents of Maryland, Virginia, and Washington, D.C. who have a confirmed diagnosis of ALS and their family caregivers. Applicants must be registered with the local chapter of the ALS Association and be seeking funding for wheelchair-van transportation or (if they are not wheelchair-bound) some other form of transportation. They may have no other form of transportation readily available. The program requires that they be able to exit their home or building without the assistance of the driver, either on foot or with a wheelchair ramp.

Financial data   Grants provide up to $2,500 per year for medical appointments or up to $250 per year for non-medical transportation expenses.

Duration   1 year; may be renewed.

Number awarded   Varies each year.

Deadline   Applications may be submitted at any time.

[638]
THOMARA LATIMER CANCER FOUNDATION GRANTS

Thomara Latimer Cancer Foundation
Attn: Cancer Funding Committee
Franklin Plaza Center
29193 Northeastern Highway, Suite 528
Southfield, MI 48034-1006
(248) 557-2346   Fax: (248) 557-8063
E-mail: funding@thomlatimercares.org
Web: www.thomlatimercares.org

Summary   To provide funding to cancer patients and family members who are unable to meet expenses.

Eligibility   This program is open to cancer patients and family members who, after a thorough investigation of other resources, are unable to meet expenses that are causing a financial burden. Applicants must be seeking funding for homecare assistance (including child care); medication or treatment not covered by insurance (including alternative care, family lodging for out-of-town treatment); transportation to and from treatment, physician, support facilities; special needs funds for wigs or head coverings for diagnosis or treatment related to hair loss; or assistance with final arrangements.

Financial data   Grant amounts depend on the availability of funds.

Duration   These are 1-time grants.

Number awarded   Varies each year.

Deadline   Applications may be submitted at any time.

[639]
VIRGINIA PREMIUM ASSISTANCE PROGRAM

Patient Services Incorporated
P.O. Box 1602
Midlothian, VA 23113
Toll Free: (800) 366-7741   Fax: (804) 744-5407
E-mail: uneedpsi@uneedpsi.org
Web: www.uneedpsi.org

Summary   To provide funding to residents of Virginia who have a bleeding disorder and need help in paying for insurance.

Eligibility   This assistance is available to residents of Virginia who have hemophilia, von Willebrands Disease, or other bleeding disorder and are enrolled or eligible for enrollment in the Virginia Bleeding Disorders Program. Applicants must be uninsured or underinsured and able to demonstrate a need for assistance to pay premiums on a private insurance policy. Their family income must be below 200% of the federal poverty level.

Financial data   The amount of assistance depends on the need of the recipient and the availability of funds.

Additional data   This program was established in 1996 by the Virginia Department of Health.

Number awarded   Varies each year.

Deadline   Applications may be submitted at any time.

[640]
VIRGINIA STATE PHARMACEUTICAL ASSISTANCE PROGRAM

Patient Services Incorporated
P.O. Box 1602
Midlothian, VA 23113
Toll Free: (800) 366-7741   Fax: (804) 744-5407
E-mail: uneedpsi@uneedpsi.org
Web: www.uneedpsi.org

Summary   To provide funding to residents of Virginia who have AIDS and need help in paying their Medicare Part D premiums or medication co-payments.

Eligibility   This assistance is available to people enrolled or eligible for enrollment in the Virginia AIDS Drug Assistance Program (ADAP). Applicants must be able to demonstrate a need for assistance in paying their Medicare Part D premiums or medication co-payments. Their family income must be below 300% of the federal poverty level.

Financial data The amount of assistance depends on the need of the recipient and the availability of funds.

Additional data This program, known as Virginia SPAD, was established in 2006 by the Virginia Department of Health.

Number awarded Varies each year.

Deadline Applications may be submitted at any time.

Awards

[641]
ANDRE SOBEL AWARD

André Sobel River of Life Foundation
Attn: Awards
8899 Beverly Boulevard, Suite 111
Los Angeles, CA 90048
(310) 276-7111   Fax: (310) 276-0244
E-mail: info@andreriveroflife.org
Web: www.andreriveroflife.org/participate/award

Summary To recognize and reward young cancer survivors who submit outstanding essays on their illness.

Eligibility This competition is open to cancer survivors between 12 and 21 years of age. Applicants are allowed to define themselves as a survivor; no medical definition or certain amount of time is required. They must submit an essay, up to 1,500 words in length, on a topic that changes annually but relates to their illness. Recently, applicants were invited to write on their experience facing illness and how it has changed them.

Financial data First prize is $5,000. Other cash prizes are awarded to second- and third-place winners.

Duration The competition is held annually.

Additional data These awards were first presented in 2000.

Number awarded 3 cash prizes are awarded each year.

Deadline March of each year.

[642]
AUTISM SOCIETY OF AMERICA OUTSTANDING INDIVIDUAL OF THE YEAR AWARD

Autism Society of America
Attn: Awards and Scholarships
4340 East-West Highway, Suite 350
Bethesda, MD 20814-4579
(301) 657-0881   Toll Free: (800) 3-AUTISM
Fax: (301) 657-0869   E-mail: info@autism-society.org
Web: www.autism-society.org

Summary To recognize and reward people with autism who have excelled in an area of human activity.

Eligibility This award is presented for a demonstration of exceptional dedication or effort on the part of an individual with autism who has excelled in 1 or more areas of life

experiences or contributions. Achievements may include, but are not limited to, academics, the arts, athletics, community service, employment, extracurricular activities, transitions, or independent living skills.

Financial data The awardee receives complimentary registration to the annual conference, a special commemorative plaque, and a cash award of $1,000.

Duration The award is presented annually.

Number awarded 1 each year.

Deadline March of each year.

[643]
NOVO NORDISK DONNELLY AWARDS

World Team Tennis, Inc.
Attn: Billie Jean King WTT Charities
1776 Broadway, Suite 600
New York, NY 10019
(212) 586-3444, ext. 20   Fax: (212) 586-6277
E-mail: dstone@wtt.com
Web: www.wtt.com/page.aspx?article_id=1429

Summary To recognize and reward young tennis players who have diabetes.

Eligibility This program is open to scholar/athletes between 12 and 21 years of age who play tennis competitively either on a school team or as a ranked tournament player and have type I diabetes. Applicants must submit a 500-word essay on the significance of diabetes in their lives. Selection is based on values, commitment, sportsmanship, community involvement, and financial need.

Financial data Awards are $5,000 for winners or $2,500 for regional finalists; funds may be used for education, tennis development, and/or medical care.

Duration The nonrenewable awards are presented annually.

Additional data This program was established in 1998 by the Billie Jean King Foundation in cooperation with the American Diabetes Association. It includes 2 scholarships named after sisters, Diane Donnelly Stone and Tracey Donnelly Maltby, who have had diabetes since childhood and have played tennis competitively. Novo Nordisk sponsors the program.

Number awarded 4 each year: 2 winners and 2 regional finalists.

Deadline April of each year.

[644]
SMART KIDS WITH LEARNING DISABILITIES YOUTH ACHIEVEMENT AWARD

Smart Kids with Learning Disabilities, Inc.
38 Kings Highway North
Westport, CT 06880
(203) 226-6831   Fax: (203) 226-4861
E-mail: info@smartkidswithld.org
Web: www.smartkidswithld.org

Summary To recognize and reward high school students with learning disabilities who demonstrate outstanding achievement.

Eligibility This award is available to young people with a learning disability and/or AD/HD at the high school (or younger) level. Nominees must have demonstrated initiative, talent, determination, and accomplishment in any field, including art, music, science, mathematics, athletics, or community service. They may be nominated by a parent, teacher, mentor, coach, or themselves.

Financial data   The award is $1,000.

Duration   The award is presented annually.

Additional data   This award was first presented in 2004.

Number awarded   1 each year.

Deadline   January of each year.

[645]
TRANSPLANT SCHOLARS AWARDS

Astellas Pharma US, Inc.
Attn: Transplant Scholars Award
534 Fourth Street
San Francisco, CA 94107
Toll Free: (800) 888-7704
Web: astellastransplant.com/awards_scholar.php

Summary   To recognize and reward, with scholarships for college or graduate school, transplant recipients and donors who submit outstanding essays on their transplant experience.

Eligibility   This competition is open to liver, kidney, or heart transplant recipients who are taking Prograf and to organ donors who have donated a portion of their liver or a kidney. Applicants must be beginning higher education, returning to school after their surgery, or working on an advanced degree. They must submit a 500-word essay that describes their transplant or donation experience, how the experience has changed their life, and how they would use the scholarship award to further their education and give back to the transplant community. Selection is based on the compelling nature of the story, the educational goals of the applicant and how those were affected by transplantation, and the applicant's intention to impact the transplant community positively.

Financial data   The award is a $5,000 scholarship to be used for educational expenses.

Duration   The awards are presented annually.

Number awarded   5 each year.

Deadline   June of each year.

Disabilities in General

Scholarships ●

Fellowships/Grants ●

Grants-in-Aid ●

Awards ●

Described here are 294 programs that do not specify or restrict the type of eligible disability. Of these, 76 entries cover scholarships (to pursue studies or research on the undergraduate level in the United States); 64 cover fellowships/grants (to pursue graduate or postdoctoral education or research in the United States); 68 cover loans (to provide money that eventually must be repaid, with or without interest); 145 cover grants-in-aid (to support emergency situations, travel, income/property liabilities, or the acquisition of assistive technology); and 9 cover awards, competitions, prizes, and honoraria (to recognize or support creative work and public service). If you are looking for a particular program and don't find it in this chapter, be sure to check the Program Title Index to see if it is covered elsewhere in the directory.

Scholarships

[646]
AHIMA FOUNDATION DIVERSITY SCHOLARSHIPS

American Health Information Management Association
Attn: AHIMA Foundation
233 North Michigan Avenue, 21st Floor
Chicago, IL 60601-5809
(312) 233-1175   Fax: (312) 233-1475
E-mail: info@ahimafoundation.org
Web: www.ahimafoundation.org

Summary To provide financial assistance to members of the American Health Information Management Association (AHIMA) who are interested in working on an undergraduate degree in health information administration or technology and who will contribute to diversity in the profession.

Eligibility This program is open to AHIMA members who are enrolled at least half time in a program accredited by the Commission on Accreditation of Allied Health Education Programs. Applicants must be working on an associate degree in health information technology or a bachelor's degree in health information administration. They must have a GPA of 3.0 or higher and at least 1 full semester remaining after the date of the award. To qualify for this support, applicants must demonstrate how they will contribute to diversity in the health information management profession; diversity is defined as differences in race, ethnicity, nationality, gender, sexual orientation, socioeconomic status, age, physical capabilities, and religious beliefs. Financial need is not considered in the selection process.

Financial data Stipends are $1,000 for students working on an associate degree or $1,200 for students working on a bachelor's degree.

Duration 1 year.

Number awarded Varies each year. Recently, 8 of these scholarships were awarded.

Deadline April or October of each year.

[647]
AMERICAN ASSOCIATION ON HEALTH AND DISABILITY SCHOLARSHIPS

American Association on Health and Disability
Attn: Executive Director
110 North Washington Street, Suite 328-J
Rockville, MD 20850
(301) 545-6140, ext. 206   Fax: (301) 545-6144
E-mail: contact@aahd.us
Web: www.aahd.us

Summary To provide financial assistance to undergraduate and graduate students who have a disability, especially those studying a field related to health and disability.

Eligibility This program is open to high school graduates who have a documented disability and are enrolled in or accepted by an accredited U.S. 4-year university or graduate school on a full-time basis. Preference is given to students working on a degree in public health, disability studies, health promotion, or other field related to health and disability. Along with their application, they must submit a 3-page personal statement that includes a personal history, educational and career goals, extracurricular activities, and reasons why they should be selected to receive this scholarship. U.S. citizenship or permanent resident status is required.

Financial data Stipends range up to $1,000.

Duration 1 year.

Additional data This program was established in 2009.

Number awarded 2 each year.

Deadline November of each year.

[648]
ARKANSAS GOVERNOR'S COMMISSION ON PEOPLE WITH DISABILITIES SCHOLARSHIPS

Arkansas Governor's Commission on People with
  Disabilities
Attn: Scholarship Committee
525 West Capitol Avenue
P.O. Box 3781
Little Rock, AR 72203
(501) 296-1637   Fax: (501) 296-1883
TDD: (501) 296-1637
Web: www.arsinfo.org/default.aspx?id=31

Summary To provide financial assistance to Arkansas students with disabilities who are interested in attending college or graduate school in any state.

Eligibility This program is open to high school seniors, high school graduates, undergraduates, and graduate students who have a disability and are residents of Arkansas. Applicants must be attending or planning to attend a college or university in any state. Selection is based on a description of their disability (20 points), present and past school involvement (10 points), a brief statement on their career goals (15 points), community and volunteer activities (10 points), a brief essay on the positive or negative effects their disability has had on their life thus far (20 points), 3 letters of recommendation (10 points), and financial need (10 points).

Financial data The stipend varies, up to $1,000 per year.

Duration 1 year; recipients may reapply.

Number awarded Several each year.

Deadline February of each year.

[649]
BRIGHT LIGHTS SCHOLARSHIPS

Governor's Coalition for Youth with Disabilities
P.O. Box 2485
Hartford, CT 06146-2485
(860) 263-6018   E-mail: info@gcyd.org
Web: www.gcyd.org/scholarship.html

Summary To provide financial assistance for college to Connecticut residents who have a disability.

Eligibility This program is open to seniors graduating from high schools in Connecticut who have a disability. Applicants must be planning to attend 1) a college or university in Connecticut or any other state; 2) any of the 4 campuses of the Connecticut State University System; or 3) any of the 12 Connecticut community colleges. Along with their application, they must submit an essay of 500 to 600 words describing the nature of their disability, its limitations, and how they have overcome the challenges it has presented. Selection is based on 1) the manner in which applicants have overcome the obstacles created by their disability; 2) the degree to which they have contributed to their school and community through service, leadership, and being a positive role model; and 3) their promise for a successful career.

Financial data For students at colleges and universities nationwide, the stipend ranges from $500 to $5,000. For students at Connecticut State Universities, the stipend is $500 per semester. For students at Connecticut community colleges, the award provides full payment of tuition and fees.

Duration 1 year. National scholarships are nonrenewable, Connecticut State University scholarships may be renewed for a total of 8 semesters, and Connecticut community college scholarships may be renewed for a total of 3 years.

Additional data This program was established in 1994 with support from the governor of Connecticut and many business, labor, and individual donors in the state.

Number awarded At least 5 national scholarships (1 from each U.S. Congressional district in Connecticut), 4 Connecticut State University scholarships (1 at each campus), and 12 community college scholarships (1 at each college) are awarded each year. Since the program began, it has awarded more then 200 scholarships worth more than $600,000.

Deadline February of each year.

[650]
BUILDING RURAL INITIATIVE FOR DISABLED THROUGH GROUP EFFORT (B.R.I.D.G.E.) ENDOWMENT FUND SCHOLARSHIPS

National FFA Organization
Attn: Scholarship Office
6060 FFA Drive
P.O. Box 68960
Indianapolis, IN 46268-0960
(317) 802-4419   Fax: (317) 802-5419
E-mail: scholarships@ffa.org
Web: www.ffa.org

Summary To provide financial assistance to FFA members with disabilities who are interested in studying agriculture in college.

Eligibility This program is open to members with physical disabilities who are graduating high school seniors planning to enroll full time in college. Applicants must be interested in working on a 2-year or 4-year degree in agriculture. Selection is based on academic achievement (10 points for GPA, 10 points for SAT or ACT score, 10 points

for class rank), leadership in FFA activities (30 points), leadership in community activities (10 points), and participation in the Supervised Agricultural Experience (SAE) program (30 points). U.S. citizenship is required.

Financial data The stipend is $5,000.

Duration 1 year; nonrenewable.

Additional data This program is supported by the Dr. Scholl Foundation, Outdoor Advertising Association of America, and numerous individuals.

Number awarded 1 or more each year.

Deadline February of each year.

[651]
CALIFORNIA-HAWAII ELKS MAJOR PROJECT UNDERGRADUATE SCHOLARSHIP PROGRAM FOR STUDENTS WITH DISABILITIES

California-Hawaii Elks Association
Attn: Scholarship Committee
5450 East Lamona Avenue
Fresno, CA 93727-2224
(559) 255-4531   Fax: (559) 456-2659
Web: www.chea-elks.org/scholarshipmenu.html

Summary To provide financial assistance to residents of California and Hawaii who have a disability and are interested in attending college in any state.

Eligibility This program is open to residents of California or Hawaii who have a physical impairment, neurological impairment, visual impairment, hearing impairment, and/or speech/language disorder. Applicants must be a senior in high school, be a high school graduate, or have passed the GED test. They must be planning to attend a college, university, community college, or vocational school in any state. U.S. citizenship is required. Selection is based on financial need, GPA, severity of disability, seriousness of purpose, and depth of character. Applications are available from an Elks Lodge in California or Hawaii; students must first request an interview with the lodge's scholarship chairman, secretary, or Exalted Ruler.

Financial data The stipend is $2,000 per year for 4-year colleges or universities or $1,000 for community colleges and vocational schools.

Duration 1 year; may be renewed for up to 3 additional years or until completion of an undergraduate degree, whichever occurs first.

Number awarded 20 to 30 each year.

Deadline March of each year.

[652]
CAPED GENERAL EXCELLENCE SCHOLARSHIP

California Association for Postsecondary Education
   and Disability
Attn: Executive Assistant
71423 Biskra Road
Rancho Mirage, CA 92270
(760) 346-8206   Fax: (760) 340-5275
TDD: (760) 341-4084   E-mail: caped2000@aol.com
Web: www.caped.net/scholarships.html

Summary To provide financial assistance to undergraduate and graduate students in California who have a disability and can demonstrate academic achievement and involvement in community and campus activities.

Eligibility This program is open to students at public and private colleges and universities in California who have a disability. Undergraduates must have completed at least 6 semester credits and have a GPA of 2.5 or higher. Graduate students must have completed at least 3 semester units and have a GPA of 3.0 or higher. Applicants must submit a 1-page personal letter that demonstrates their writing skills, progress towards meeting their educational and vocational goals, management of their disability, and involvement in community activities. They must also submit a letter of recommendation from a faculty member, verification of disability, official transcripts, proof of current enrollment, and documentation of financial need. This award is presented to the applicant who demonstrates the highest level of academic achievement and involvement in community and campus life.

Financial data The stipend is $1,500.

Duration 1 year.

Number awarded 1 each year.

Deadline September of each year.

[653]
CARVER SCHOLARS PROGRAM

Roy J. Carver Charitable Trust
202 Iowa Avenue
Muscatine, IA 52761-3733
(563) 263-4010   Fax: (563) 263-1547
E-mail: info@carvertrust.org
Web: www.carvertrust.org

Summary To provide financial assistance for college to students in Iowa who have overcome significant obstacles to attend college.

Eligibility This program is open to students attending the 3 public universities in Iowa, the 23 participating private 4 year colleges and universities in the state, or a community college in Iowa and planning to transfer to 1 of those 4-year institutions. Applicants must be sophomores seeking support for their junior year. They must present evidence of unusual social and/or other barriers to attending college full time; examples include, but are not limited to, students who 1) are from 1-parent families; 2) are attending college while working full time; 3) have social, mental, or physical disabilities; or 4) have families to support. They must have graduated from a high school in Iowa or have been residents of the state for at least 5 consecutive years immediately prior to applying, be full-time students, have at least a 2.8 GPA, be U.S. citizens, and submit a financial profile indicating insufficient personal, family, and institutional resources to pay full-time college tuition. A particular goal of the program is to assist students "who fall between the cracks of other financial aid programs." Applications must be submitted to the financial aid office at the Iowa college or university the applicant attends.

Financial data Stipends generally average $5,200 at public universities or $7,600 at private colleges in Iowa.

Duration 1 year; may be renewed 1 additional year.

Additional data This program was established in 1988.

Number awarded Varies each year; since the program's establishment, it has awarded more than 1,750 scholarships worth nearly $14 million.

Deadline March of each year.

[654]
CFA INSTITUTE 11 SEPTEMBER MEMORIAL SCHOLARSHIP

CFA Institute
Attn: Research Foundation
560 Ray C. Hunt Drive
P.O. Box 3668
Charlottesville, VA 22903-0668
(434) 951-5499   Toll Free: (800) 237-8132
Fax: (434) 951-5370   E-mail: rf@cfainstitute.org
Web: www.cfainstitute.org/foundation/scholarship

Summary To provide financial assistance to individuals and their families who were disabled or killed in the September 11 terrorist attacks and who wish to major in business-related fields in college.

Eligibility College scholarships are offered to those who meet the following 2 criteria: 1) they were permanently disabled in the attacks, or were the spouses, domestic partners, or children of anyone killed or permanently disabled in the attacks, and 2) they will be working on a college-level degree in finance, economics, accounting, or business ethics. Applicants may be residents of any state or country. Selection is based on demonstrated leadership and good citizenship, academic record, and financial need.

Financial data Stipends range up to $25,000 per year, depending on the need of the recipient.

Duration 1 year; renewable up to 4 additional years.

Additional data The CFA (Chartered Financial Analyst) Institute was formerly the Association for Investment Management and Research (AIMR). It lost at least 56 of its members and CFA candidates in the terrorist attacks of 11 September. This program is managed by Scholarship Management Services, a division of Scholarship America, One Scholarship Way, P.O. Box 297, St. Peter, MN 56082, (507) 931-1682, (800) 537-4180, Fax: (507) 931-9168, E-mail: smsinfo@csfa.org.

Number awarded Varies each year; recently, 12 of these scholarships were awarded.

Deadline May of each year.

[655]
CHIEF MASTER SERGEANTS OF THE AIR FORCE SCHOLARSHIPS

Air Force Sergeants Association
Attn: Scholarship Coordinator
P.O. Box 50
Temple Hills, MD 20757
(301) 899-3500, ext. 237   Toll Free: (800) 638-0594
Fax: (301) 899-8136   E-mail: staff@hqafsa.org
Web: www.hqafsa.org

Summary To provide financial assistance for college to the dependent children of Air Force personnel.

Eligibility This program is open to the unmarried children (including stepchildren and legally adopted children) of active-duty, retired, or veteran members of the U.S. Air Force, Air National Guard, or Air Force Reserves. Applicants must be attending or planning to attend an accredited academic institution. They must have an unweighted GPA of 3.5 or higher. Along with their application, they must submit 1) a paragraph on their life objectives and what they plan to do with the education they receive; and 2) an essay on the most urgent problem facing society today. High school seniors must also submit a transcript of all high school grades and a record of their SAT or ACT scores. Selection is based on academic record, character, leadership skills, writing ability, versatility, and potential for success. Financial need is not a consideration. A unique aspect of these scholarships is that applicants may supply additional information regarding circumstances that entitle them to special consideration; examples of such circumstances include student disabilities, financial hardships, parent disabled and unable to work, parent missing in action/killed in action/prisoner of war, or other unusual extenuating circumstances.

Financial data Stipends are $3,000, $2,000, or $1,000; funds may be used for tuition, room and board, fees, books, supplies, and transportation.

Duration 1 year; may be renewed if the recipient maintains full-time enrollment.

Additional data The Air Force Sergeants Association administers this program on behalf of the Airmen Memorial Foundation. It was established in 1987 and named in honor of CMSAF Richard D. Kisling, the late third Chief Master Sergeant of the Air Force. In 1997, following the deaths of CMSAF's (Retired) Andrews and Harlow, it was given its current name.

Number awarded 12 each year: 1 at $3,000, 1 at $2,000, and 10 at $1,000. Since this program began, it has awarded more than $250,000 in scholarships.

Deadline March of each year.

[656]
CHRISTIAN A. HERTER MEMORIAL SCHOLARSHIP

Massachusetts Office of Student Financial Assistance
454 Broadway, Suite 200
Revere, MA 02151
(617) 727-9420   Fax: (617) 727-0667
E-mail: osfa@osfa.mass.edu
Web: www.osfa.mass.edu

Summary To provide financial assistance to Massachusetts high school students who have overcome major adversities and plan to attend college in any state.

Eligibility This program is open to residents of Massachusetts who are attending a secondary school in the 10th or 11th grade, have a cumulative GPA of 2.5 or higher, and are planning to work full time on an undergraduate degree at an accredited institution in the United States. Applicants must be able to demonstrate 1) difficult personal circumstances in their lives (e.g., physical or mental abuse, catastrophic illness) or other personal obstacles or hardships of a societal, geographic, mental, or physical nature; 2) high financial need; and 3) strong academic promise to continue their education beyond high school at a college or university. They must be nominated by their school or a public agency.

Financial data Awards cover up to 50% of the student's unmet financial need, to a maximum of $15,000 per year.

Duration 4 years.

Additional data This program was established in 1972.

Number awarded 25 each year.

Deadline April of each year.

[657]
CIND M. TRESER MEMORIAL SCHOLARSHIP

Washington State Environmental Health Association
Attn: Executive Secretary
103 Sea Pine Lane
Bellingham, WA 98229-9363
(360) 738-8946   Fax: (360) 738-8949
E-mail: Kerri@wseha.org
Web: www.wseha.org

Summary To provide financial assistance to disabled and other undergraduate students who are majoring in environmental health or other life sciences and are interested in preparing for a career in environmental health in the state of Washington.

Eligibility This program is open to undergraduates who 1) intend to become employed in the field of environmental health in Washington following graduation and 2) are enrolled in a program either accredited by the National Accreditation Council for Environmental Health Curricula or with a curriculum comparable to the model curriculum recommended by that Council (i.e., the program must include substantial course work in biology and microbiology, organic and inorganic chemistry, epidemiology, biostatistics, and environmental health sciences). Applicants must be members of the Washington State Environmental Health Association (WSEHA). Students of color and specially challenged students are especially encouraged to apply.

Financial data The stipend is $1,000.

Duration 1 year.

Additional data This program was formerly known as the Ed Pickett Memorial Student Scholarship. The first scholarship was awarded in 1985. Recipients must attend the association's annual educational conference to accept the scholarship award.

Number awarded 1 each year.

Deadline August of each year.

[658]
CINDY KOLB MEMORIAL SCHOLARSHIP

California Association for Postsecondary Education
  and Disability
Attn: Executive Assistant
71423 Biskra Road
Rancho Mirage, CA 92270
(760) 346-8206   Fax: (760) 340-5275
TDD: (760) 341-4084   E-mail: caped2000@aol.com
Web: www.caped.net/scholarships.html

Summary To provide financial assistance to students enrolled at 4-year college and universities in California who have a disability.

Eligibility This program is open to students at 4-year colleges and universities in California who have a disability. Applicants must have completed at least 6 semester credits with a GPA of 2.5 or higher. Along with their application, they must submit a 1-page personal letter that demonstrates their writing skills, progress towards meeting their educational and vocational goals, management of their disability, and involvement in community activities. They must also submit a letter of recommendation from a faculty member, verification of disability, official transcripts, proof of current enrollment, and documentation of financial need.

Financial data The stipend is $1,000.

Duration 1 year.

Number awarded 1 each year.

Deadline September of each year.

[659]
COURAGE CENTER SCHOLARSHIP FOR PEOPLE WITH DISABILITIES

Courage Center
Attn: Vocational Services Department
3915 Golden Valley Road
Minneapolis, MN 55422
(763) 520-0553   Toll Free: (888) 8-INTAKE
Fax: (763) 520-0392   TDD: (763) 520-0245
E-mail: vocationalservices@couragecenter.org
Web: www.couragecenter.org

Summary To provide financial assistance to Minnesota residents who have a disability and are interested in attending college in any state.

Eligibility This program is open to U.S. citizens who are residents of Minnesota or have received Courage Center services. Applicants must have a sensory impairment or physical disability and a desire to gain technical expertise beyond high school. They must be attending or planning to attend a college or technical school in any state. Along with their application, they must submit a concise essay that reflects their educational aspirations, career goals, and how a scholarship will help meet their needs. Selection is based on that essay, employment history, honors and awards, leadership experience, and financial need. Graduation ranking is not considered.

Financial data The stipend is $1,000.

Duration 1 year.

Number awarded 1 or more each year.

Deadline May of each year.

[660]
DEFENSE INTELLIGENCE AGENCY UNDERGRADUATE TRAINING ASSISTANCE PROGRAM

Defense Intelligence Agency
Attn: Human Resources, HCH-4
200 MacDill Boulevard, Building 6000
Bolling AFB, DC 20340-5100
(202) 231-8228   Fax: (202) 231-4889
TDD: (202) 231-5002   E-mail: staffing@dia.mil
Web: www.dia.mil/employment/student/index.htm

Summary To provide funding and work experience to disabled and other high school seniors and lower-division students interested in majoring in specified fields and working for the U.S. Defense Intelligence Agency (DIA).

Eligibility This program is open to graduating high school seniors and college freshmen and sophomores interested in working full time on a baccalaureate degree in 1 of the following fields in college: biology, chemistry, computer science, engineering, foreign area studies, intelligence analysis, international relations, microbiology, pharmacology, physics, political science, or toxicology. High school seniors must have a GPA of 2.75 or higher and either 1) an SAT combined critical reading and mathematics score of 1000 or higher plus 500 or higher on the writing portion or 2) an ACT score of 21 or higher. College freshmen and sophomores must have a GPA of 3.0 or higher. All applicants must be able to demonstrate financial need (household income ceiling of $70,000 for a family of 4 or $80,000 for a family of 5 or more) and leadership abilities through extracurricular activities, civic involvement, volunteer work, or part-time employment. Students and all members of their immediate family must be U.S. citizens. Minorities, women, and persons with disabilities are strongly encouraged to apply.

Financial data Students accepted into this program receive tuition (up to $18,000 per year) at an accredited college or university selected by the student and endorsed by the sponsor; reimbursement for books and needed supplies; an annual salary to cover college room and board expenses and for summer employment; and a position at the sponsoring agency after graduation. Recipients must work for DIA after college graduation for at least 1 and a half times the length of study. For participants who leave DIA earlier than scheduled, the agency arranges for payments to reimburse DIA for the total cost of education (including the employee's pay and allowances).

Duration 4 years, provided the recipient maintains a GPA of 2.75 during the freshman year and 3.0 or higher in subsequent semesters.

Additional data Recipients are provided a challenging summer internship and guaranteed a job at the agency in their field of study upon graduation.

Number awarded Only a few are awarded each year.

Deadline November of each year.

[661]
DISABLED WAR VETERANS SCHOLARSHIPS

Armed Forces Communications and Electronics
   Association
Attn: AFCEA Educational Foundation
4400 Fair Lakes Court
Fairfax, VA 22033-3899
(703) 631-6149   Toll Free: (800) 336-4583, ext. 6149
Fax: (703) 631-4693   E-mail: scholarship@afcea.org
Web: www.afcea.org

Summary   To provide financial assistance to disabled military personnel and veterans who are majoring in specified scientific fields in college.

Eligibility   This program is open to active-duty service personnel and honorably discharged U.S. military veterans, Reservists, and National Guard members who are disabled because of wounds received during service in Enduring Freedom (Afghanistan) or Iraqi Freedom operations. Applicants must be enrolled full or part time at an accredited 2- or 4-year college or university or in a distance learning or online degree program. They must be working toward a degree in engineering (aerospace, computer, electrical, or systems), computer science, computer engineering technology, computer network systems, computer information systems, electronics engineering technology, mathematics, physics, science or mathematics education, information systems management, information systems security, technology management, or other field directly related to the support of U.S. intelligence or national security enterprises. Selection is based on demonstrated academic excellence, leadership, and financial need.

Financial data   The stipend is $2,500.

Duration   1 year.

Number awarded   2 each year: 1 for spring and 1 for fall.

Deadline   March of each year for fall; November of each year for spring.

[662]
EASTER SEALS SOUTH CAROLINA EDUCATIONAL SCHOLARSHIPS

Easter Seals South Carolina
Attn: Scholarship Program
3020 Farrow Road
P.O. Box 5715
Columbia, SC 29250
(803) 429-8474   Fax: (803) 738-1934
E-mail: TAdger@sc.easterseals.com
Web: sc.easterseals.com

Summary   To provide financial assistance for college or graduate school to South Carolina students who have a disability.

Eligibility   This program is open to South Carolina residents and students attending a college or university in the state who have a significant and medically certified mobility impairment. Applicants must be enrolled or planning to enroll in an undergraduate or graduate program. They must be able to demonstrate financial need. Preference is given to students carrying at least 9 credit hours and making satisfactory academic progress toward graduation.

Financial data   The maximum stipend is $1,000.

Duration   1 year; may be renewed.

Additional data   This program was established in 1985.

Number awarded   1 or more each year.

Deadline   June of each year.

[663]
ECCLESTON-CALLAHAN SCHOLARSHIPS

Community Foundation of Central Florida
Attn: Eccleston-Callahan Memorial Fund
1411 Edgewater Drive, Suite 203
Orlando, FL 32804
(407) 872-3050   Fax: (407) 425-2990
E-mail: info@cfcflorida.org
Web: www.cfcflorida.org

Summary   To provide financial assistance to students with disabilities enrolled at specified Florida colleges and universities.

Eligibility   This program is open to students at designated colleges and universities in Florida who have a mental or physical disability. Applicants must be enrolled full time, have a GPA of 3.0 or higher, be younger than 21 years of age, and be able to demonstrate financial need.

Financial data   The stipend is $1,000 per year.

Duration   1 year; may be renewed.

Additional data   The participating institutions are the University of Florida, the University of Central Florida, Florida A&M University, Florida State University, Valencia Community College, Seminole Community College, and Orlando Tech.

Number awarded   Varies each year.

Deadline   April of each year.

[664]
EDWARD T. CONROY MEMORIAL SCHOLARSHIP PROGRAM

Maryland Higher Education Commission
Attn: Office of Student Financial Assistance
839 Bestgate Road, Suite 400
Annapolis, MD 21401-3013
(410) 260-4563   Toll Free: (800) 974-1024, ext. 4563
Fax: (410) 260-3200   TDD: (800) 735-2258
E-mail: lasplin@mhec.state.md.us
Web: www.mhec.state.md.us

Summary   To provide financial assistance for college or graduate school in Maryland to children and spouses of victims of the September 11, 2001 terrorist attacks and to specified categories of veterans, public safety employees, and their children or spouses.

Eligibility   This program is open to entering and continuing undergraduate and graduate students in the following categories: 1) children and surviving spouses of victims of the September 11, 2001 terrorist attacks who died in the World Trade Center in New York City, the Pentagon in Virginia, or United Airlines Flight 93 in Pennsylvania; 2) veterans who have, as a direct result of military service, a disability of 25% or greater and have exhausted or are no longer eligible for federal veterans' educational benefits; 3) children of armed forces members whose death or 100% disability was directly caused by military service; 4) POW/ MIA veterans of the Vietnam Conflict and their children; 5) state or local public safety officers or volunteers who became 100% disabled in the line of duty; and 6) children and unremarried surviving spouses of state or local public safety employees or volunteers who died or became 100% disabled in the line of duty. The parent, spouse, veteran, POW, or public safety officer or volunteer must have been a resident of Maryland at the time of death or when declared disabled. Financial need is not considered.

Financial data The amount of the award is equal to tuition and fees at a Maryland postsecondary institution, to a maximum of $19,000 for children and spouses of the September 11 terrorist attacks or $9,000 for all other recipients.

Duration Up to 5 years of full-time study or 8 years of part-time study.

Additional data Recipients must enroll at a 2-year or 4-year Maryland college or university as a full-time or part-time degree-seeking undergraduate or graduate student or attend a private career school.

Number awarded Varies each year.

Deadline July of each year.

[665]
EXCEPTIONAL CIRCUMSTANCES SCHOLARSHIPS

Workforce Safety & Insurance
1600 East Century Avenue, Suite 1
P.O. Box 5585
Bismarck, ND 58506-5585
(701) 328-3828   Toll Free: (800) 440-3796
Fax: (701) 328-3820   TDD: (800) 366-6888
E-mail: ndwsi@nd.gov
Web: www.workforcesafety.com

Summary To provide financial assistance for college to injured workers in North Dakota.

Eligibility This program is open to injured workers in North Dakota who can demonstrate that a program of higher or technical education would be beneficial and appropriate because of exceptional circumstances. Applicants must have completed a rehabilitation process with Workforce Safety & Insurance (WSI) and have no outstanding litigation on any rehabilitation plan.

Financial data The maximum stipend is $10,000 per year.

Duration 1 year; may be renewed up to 4 additional years, provided the recipient reapplies and maintains a satisfactory GPA.

Additional data This program was established in 1997. The sponsoring company was formerly North Dakota Workers Compensation.

Number awarded Varies each year.

Deadline Deadline not specified.

[666]
FACILITATION AWARDS FOR SCIENTISTS AND ENGINEERS WITH DISABILITIES

National Science Foundation
Office of Integrative Activities
Attn: Coordinator, Facilitation Awards for Scientists and Engineers with Disabilities
4201 Wilson Boulevard, Room 815
Arlington, VA 22230
(703) 292-4684   TDD: (800) 281-8749
Web: www.nsf.gov

Summary To provide supplemental financing to individuals with disabilities who wish to prepare for a career in science and engineering and who are working on projects supported by the National Science Foundation (NSF).

Eligibility This program is open to individuals with disabilities who are principal investigators, other senior professionals, or graduate and undergraduate students participating in a specific project supported by the foundation. Requests for special equipment or assistance necessary to enable an individual with a disability to participate in a specific NSF-supported project may be included in the original proposal submitted to a NSF program or submitted as a separate request for supplemental funding for an existing NSF grant.

Financial data Funds may be requested to purchase special equipment, modify equipment, or provide services required specifically for the work to be undertaken. No maximum amount has been set for requests, but it is expected that the cost (including equipment adaptation and installation) will not be a major proportion of the total proposed budget for the project.

Additional data Examples of specific equipment for which funds may be requested include prosthetic devices to manipulate a particular apparatus; equipment to convert sound to visual signals, or vice versa, for a particular experiment; access to a special site or to a mode of transportation; a reader or interpreter with special technical competence related to the project; or other special-purpose equipment or assistance needed to conduct a particular project. Items that compensate in a general way for the disabling condition are not eligible; examples include standard wheelchairs, general prosthetics, hearing aids, TTY/TDD devices, general readers for the blind, or ramps, elevators, or other structural modifications of research facilities.

Number awarded Varies each year.

Deadline Applications may be submitted at any time.

[667]
FAMILIES OF FREEDOM SCHOLARSHIP FUND

Scholarship America
Attn: Scholarship Management Services
One Scholarship Way
P.O. Box 297
St. Peter, MN 56082
(507) 931-1682   Toll Free: (877) 862-0136
Fax: (507) 931-9168
E-mail: familiesoffreedom@scholarshipamerica.org
Web: www.familiesoffreedom.org

Summary To provide college scholarships to financially-needy individuals and the families of individuals who were victims of the terrorist attacks on September 11, 2001.

Eligibility This program is open to the individuals who were disabled as a result of the terrorist attacks on September 11, 2001 and to the relatives of those individuals who were killed or permanently disabled during the attacks. Primarily, the fund will benefit dependents (including spouses and children) of the following groups: airplane crew and passengers; World Trade Center workers and visitors; Pentagon workers and visitors; and rescue workers, including fire fighters, emergency medical personnel, and law enforcement personnel. Applicants must be enrolled or planning to enroll in an accredited 2- or 4-year college, university, or vocational/technical school in the United States. They must be able to demonstrate financial need.

Financial data Stipends range from $1,000 to $28,000 per year, depending upon the need of the recipient. Recently, awards averaged $13,100 per academic year. Funds are distributed annually, in 2 equal installments. Checks are made payable jointly to the student and the student's school.

Duration 1 year; may be renewed.

Additional data This program was established on September 17, 2001. The fundraising goal of $100 million was reached on September 4, 2002. The fund will operate until December 31, 2030.

Number awarded This is an entitlement program; all eligible students will receive funding. Recently 1,183 students had received more than $36 million in scholarship funds.

Deadline Applications may be submitted at any time.

[668]
FARM BUREAU INSURANCE-VHSL ACHIEVEMENT AWARDS

Virginia High School League
1642 State Farm Boulevard
Charlottesville, VA 22911
(434) 977-8475   Fax: (434) 977-5943
Web: www.vhsl.org

Summary To provide financial assistance for college to disabled and other high school seniors who have participated in activities of the Virginia High School League (VHSL).

Eligibility This program is open to college-bound seniors graduating from high schools that are members of the

VHSL. Applicants must have participated in 1 or more VHSL athletic activities (baseball, basketball, cheer, cross country, field hockey, football, golf, gymnastics, soccer, softball, swimming, tennis, indoor and outdoor track, volleyball, wrestling) and/or academic activities (student publications, creative writing, theater, forensics, debate, scholastic bowl). They must have a GPA of 3.0 or higher. Each school may nominate up to 4 students: 1 female athlete, 1 male athlete, 1 academic participant, and 1 courageous achievement candidate. The courageous achievement category is reserved for students who have overcome serious obstacles to make significant contributions to athletic and/or academic activities. The obstacles may include a serious illness, injury, or disability; a challenging social or home situation; or another extraordinary situation where the student has displayed tremendous courage against overwhelming odds. Along with their application, students must submit a 500-word essay describing how extracurricular activities have enhanced their educational experience. Candidates are judged separately in the 3 VHSL groups (A, AA, and AAA). Selection is based on the essay; involvement in other school-sponsored activities; involvement in activities outside of school; and 2 letters of support.

Financial data The stipend is $1,000.

Duration 1 year.

Additional data This program, which began in 1992, is supported by Farm Bureau Insurance. The courageous achievement category, designated the Andrew Mullins Courageous Achievement Award, was added in 2002.

Number awarded 10 each year. For each of the 3 groups (A, AA, and AAA), 1 female athlete, 1 male athlete, and 1 academic participant are selected. In addition, 1 courageous achievement candidate is selected statewide.

Deadline March of each year.

[669]
GEOLOGICAL SOCIETY OF AMERICA UNDERGRADUATE STUDENT RESEARCH GRANTS

Geological Society of America
Attn: Program Officer-Grants, Awards and Recognition
3300 Penrose Place
P.O. Box 9140
Boulder, CO 80301-9140
(303) 357-1028   Toll Free: (800) 472-1988, ext. 1028
Fax: (303) 357-1070   E-mail: awards@geosociety.org
Web: www.geosociety.org/grants/ugrad.htm

Summary To provide support to disabled and other undergraduate student members of the Geological Society of America (GSA) interested in conducting research at universities in designated sections of the United States.

Eligibility This program is open to undergraduate students who are interested in conducting research and are majoring in geology at universities in 3 GSA sections: north-central, northeastern, and southeastern. Applicants must be student associates of the GSA. Applications from women, minorities, and persons with disabilities are strongly encouraged.

Financial data Grant amounts vary.

Duration 1 year.

Additional data Within the 4 participating sections, information is available from each secretary. For the name and address of the 4 section secretaries, contact the sponsor.

Number awarded 1 or more each year in each of the 4 sections.

Deadline January of each year.

[670]
GOOGLE LIME SCHOLARSHIPS FOR STUDENTS WITH DISABILITIES

Lime
590 Madison Avenue, 21st Floor
New York, NY 10022
(212) 521-4469   Fax: (212) 521-4099
E-mail: info@limeconnect.com
Web: www.limeconnect.com/google.html

Summary To provide financial assistance to students with disabilities working on a bachelor's or graduate degree in a computer-related field at a college or university in Canada or the United States.

Eligibility This program is open to students at colleges and universities in the United States or Canada who have a disability and are entering their junior or senior year of undergraduate study or are enrolled as graduate students. International students with disabilities enrolled at universities in the United States or Canada are also eligible. Applicants must be working full time on a degree in computer science, computer engineering, or a closely-related technical field. Along with their application, they must submit 2 essays of 400 to 600 words each on 1) their academic accomplishments in terms of the technical projects on which they have worked; and 2) the issue about which they are passionate, what they have done to fulfill that passion, or what they dream of doing to fulfill it. Financial need is not considered in the selection process.

Financial data The stipend is $10,000 for students at U.S. universities or $C5,000 for students at Canadian universities.

Duration 1 year.

Additional data This program is jointly sponsored by Google and Lime, an organization founded in 2006 to promote employment of people with disabilities.

Number awarded Varies each year.

Deadline May of each year.

[671]
HARRY GREGG FOUNDATION GRANTS

Harry Gregg Foundation
1 Verney Drive
Greenfield, NH 03047
(603) 547-3311, ext. 1490
Toll Free: (800) 394-3311, ext. 1490 (within NH)
Fax: (603) 547-6212
E-mail: hgf@crotchedmountain.org
Web: www.crotchedmountain.org

Summary To provide financial assistance for vocational education, assistive technology, and other purposes to children and adults in New Hampshire who have physical, emotional, or intellectual disabilities.

Eligibility This program is open to New Hampshire residents of all ages who have physical, intellectual, or emotional disabilities. Funds may be requested for broad purposes but must specifically benefit the applicant. Examples of acceptable purposes include, but are not limited to: the costs of nonreimbursed medical, dental, vision, hearing, or therapy treatments; special equipment, services, or supplies; modifications to living area, workplace, or vehicle; respite services for the recipient or care givers; costs of attending a special camp; recreational activities; and vocational education or driver training tuition assistance. Selection is based on demonstrated need for a product of service, the applicant's financial circumstances, and the ability of the foundation to help improve the quality of life of a grant recipient.

Financial data Most grants range up to $1,200.

Duration Recipients may receive a maximum of 4 grants (no more than 2 in any year).

Additional data This foundation was established in 1989. If a request is not funded, applicants may reapply 6 months later for the same or a different purpose.

Number awarded Nearly 150 each year. Since this foundation was established, it has awarded more than 5,000 grants worth nearly $2 million.

Deadline March, June, September, or December of each year.

[672]
HORATIO ALGER NATIONAL SCHOLARSHIP FINALIST PROGRAM

Horatio Alger Association of Distinguished Americans, Inc.
99 Canal Center Plaza
Alexandria, VA 22314
(703) 684-9444   Fax: (703) 548-3822
E-mail: horatioaa@aol.com
Web: www.horatioalger.com

Summary To provide financial assistance for college to high school seniors from selected states who can demonstrate integrity and perseverance in overcoming adversity.

Eligibility This program is open to seniors at high schools in states that do not currently have a state scholarship program with the Horatio Alger Association of Distinguished Americans. Applicants must be planning to enroll at a college in any state to work on a bachelor's degree (they may begin at a 2-year college and then transfer to a 4-year institution). They must be U.S. citizens, be able to demonstrate critical financial need ($50,000 or less adjusted gross income per family), have a GPA of 2.0 or higher, and have a record of involvement in co-curricular and community activities. Along with their application, they must submit 1) an essay of 250 to 350 words on their career goals and the importance of a college education in attaining those goals; 2) an essay of 150 to 200 words on the life of a member of the Horatio Alger Association and how they have applied the virtues exemplified in the member's life story in their own life; and 3) information on the adversities they have encountered. Examples of adversity include: having been in foster care or a ward of the state; having been homeless; experiencing the death, incarceration, or abandonment of a parent or guardian; living in a household where alcohol or drugs are or were abused; having a physical or mental disability or serious illness; or suffering from physical or mental abuse.

Financial data   The stipend is $1,000.

Duration   1 year.

Additional data   The states in which the association currently does not have a state scholarship program are: Alaska, Alabama, Arkansas, Colorado, Connecticut, Florida, Hawaii, Kansas, Maine, Massachusetts, Michigan, Mississippi, Nevada, New Hampshire, New Jersey, New Mexico, New York, North Carolina, Ohio, Oklahoma, Oregon, Rhode Island, South Carolina, Tennessee, Vermont, Washington, West Virginia, and Wisconsin.

Number awarded   150 each year.

Deadline   October of each year.

[673]
IDAHO MINORITY AND "AT RISK" STUDENT SCHOLARSHIP

Idaho State Board of Education
Len B. Jordan Office Building
650 West State Street, Room 307
P.O. Box 83720
Boise, ID 83720-0037
(208) 332-1574   Fax: (208) 334-2632
E-mail: scholarshiphelp@osbe.idaho.gov
Web: www.boardofed.idaho.gov

Summary   To provide financial assistance to "at risk" high school seniors in Idaho who plan to attend college in the state.

Eligibility   This program is open to residents of Idaho who are graduates of high schools in the state. Applicants must meet at least 3 of the following 5 requirements: 1) have a disability; 2) be a member of an ethnic minority group historically underrepresented in higher education in Idaho; 3) have substantial financial need; 4) be a first-generation college student; 5) be a migrant farm worker or a dependent of a farm worker. U.S. citizenship is required.

Financial data   The maximum stipend is $3,000 per year.

Duration   1 year; may be renewed for up to 3 additional years.

Additional data   This program was established in 1991 by the Idaho state legislature. Recipients must plan to attend or be attending 1 of 11 participating colleges and universities in the state on a full-time basis. For a list of those schools, write to the State of Idaho Board of Education.

Number awarded   Approximately 40 each year.

Deadline   Deadline not specified.

[674]
ILLINOIS MIA/POW SCHOLARSHIP

Illinois Department of Veterans' Affairs
833 South Spring Street
P.O. Box 19432
Springfield, IL 62794-9432
(217) 782-6641   Toll Free: (800) 437-9824 (within IL)
Fax: (217) 524-0344   TDD: (217) 524-4645
E-mail: webmail@dva.state.il.us
Web: www.veterans.illinois.gov/benefits/education.htm

Summary   To provide financial assistance for 1) the undergraduate education of Illinois dependents of disabled or deceased veterans or those listed as prisoners of war or missing in action, and 2) the rehabilitation or education of disabled dependents of those veterans.

Eligibility   This program is open to the spouses, natural children, legally adopted children, or stepchildren of a veteran or servicemember who 1) has been declared by the U.S. Department of Defense or the U.S. Department of Veterans Affairs to be permanently disabled from service-connected causes with 100% disability, deceased as the result of a service-connected disability, a prisoner of war, or missing in action, and 2) at the time of entering service was an Illinois resident or was an Illinois resident within 6 months of entering such service. Special support is available for dependents who are disabled.

Financial data   An eligible dependent is entitled to full payment of tuition and certain fees at any Illinois state-supported college, university, or community college. In lieu of that benefit, an eligible dependent who has a physical, mental, or developmental disability is entitled to receive a grant to be used to cover the cost of treating the disability at 1 or more appropriate therapeutic, rehabilitative, or educational facilities. For all recipients, the total benefit cannot exceed the cost equivalent of 4 calendar years of full-time enrollment, including summer terms, at the University of Illinois.

Duration   This scholarship may be used for a period equivalent to 4 calendar years, including summer terms. Dependents have 12 years from the initial term of study to complete the equivalent of 4 calendar years. Disabled dependents who elect to use the grant for rehabilitative purposes may do so as long as the total benefit does not exceed the cost equivalent of 4 calendar years of full-time enrollment at the University of Illinois.

Additional data   An eligible child must begin using the scholarship prior to his or her 26th birthday. An eligible spouse must begin using the scholarship prior to 10 years from the effective date of eligibility (e.g., prior to August 12, 1989 or 10 years from date of disability or death).

Number awarded   Varies each year.

Deadline   Deadline not specified.

[675]
JOE CLERES MEMORIAL SCHOLARSHIPS

New Outlook Pioneers
Attn: Scholarships
930 15th Street, 12th Floor
P.O. Box 13888
Denver, CO 80201-3888
(303) 571-1200   Toll Free: (800) 872-5995
Fax: (303) 572-0520   E-mail: d.sage@worldnet.att.net
Web: www.newoutlookpioneers.org

Summary   To provide financial assistance to students at all educational levels who are physically or mentally challenged.

Eligibility   This program is open to students with physical or mental disabilities who are enrolled or planning to enroll in high school, college, trade school, or graduate school. Applicants or their representatives must submit a 1-page essay describing how the student has met the challenge of his or her disability, including the severity of the disability. They may also include up to 1 page of supporting documentation, but photographs, audio or videotapes, display materials, films, or scrapbooks are not considered.

Financial data   Stipends range from $500 to $1,500. Funds are paid directly to the school for tuition support only.

Duration   1 year.

Additional data   This program was established in 1996 by Lucent Technologies as the New Outlook Scholarships for Students with Disabilities. The current name was adopted in 2005.

Number awarded   Approximately 20 each year.

Deadline   March of each year.

[676]
JOHN J. INGALLS MEMORIAL SCHOLARSHIP

United Cerebral Palsy of MetroBoston
Director of Development, Marketing and
   Communications
71 Arsenal Street
Watertown, MA 02472
(617) 926-5480, ext. 238   Fax: (617) 926-3059
E-mail: ucpboston@ucpboston.org
Web: www.ucp.org/ucp_local.cfm/85

Summary   To provide financial assistance to residents of Massachusetts who have a physical disability and are interested in attending college or graduate school in any state.

Eligibility   This program is open to Massachusetts residents who are high school seniors, undergraduates, or graduate students and diagnosed with a physical disability. Applicants must be enrolled or planning to enroll full time at an accredited college or university in any state. Along with their application, they must submit a 250-word essay about their disability, based on such topics as how they have overcome the challenge of their disability, what having a disability means to them, someone who has been helpful in their success, or an achievement of which they are proud. They must also submit a letter from their doctor confirming that they have a disability, 2 letters of recommen-

dation, transcripts, and an acceptance letter from the college or university of their choice.

Financial data   The stipend is $5,000.

Duration   1 year.

Additional data   This program was established in 2004.

Number awarded   3 each year.

Deadline   April of each year.

[677]
JOSEPH P. LIPMAN SCHOLARSHIPS

National High School Coaches Association
Attn: Executive Director
3276 Nazareth Road
Easton, PA 18045
(610) 923-0900   Fax: (610) 923-0800
E-mail: nhsca@nhsca.com
Web: nhsca.com

Summary   To provide financial assistance for college to high school athletes who have overcome a disability or other adversity to excel in sports.

Eligibility   This program is open to graduating high school seniors who have been involved in athletics. Applicants must be planning to attend a college or university. They must submit an application in which they describe the disability or other adversity they have overcome. Judges select the recipients on the basis of the severity of the hardships they have faced.

Financial data   The stipend is $1,000.

Duration   1 year.

Additional data   This program, which began in 2005, is sponsored by Regent Sports.

Number awarded   5 each year.

Deadline   April of each year.

[678]
LYNN M. SMITH MEMORIAL SCHOLARSHIP

California Association for Postsecondary Education
   and Disability
Attn: Executive Assistant
71423 Biskra Road
Rancho Mirage, CA 92270
(760) 346-8206   Fax: (760) 340-5275
TDD: (760) 341-4084   E-mail: caped2000@aol.com
Web: www.caped.net/scholarships.html

Summary   To provide financial assistance to community college students in California who have a disability.

Eligibility   This program is open to students at community colleges in California who have a disability. Applicants must be preparing for a vocational career and have completed at least 6 semester credits with a GPA of 2.5 or higher. Along with their application, they must submit a 1-page personal letter that demonstrates their writing skills, progress towards meeting their educational and vocational goals, management of their disability, and involvement in community activities. They must also submit a letter of recommendation from a faculty member, verification of disability, official transcripts, proof of current enrollment, and documentation of financial need.

Financial data The stipend is $1,000.
Duration 1 year.
Number awarded 1 each year.
Deadline September of each year.

[679]
MARINE CORPS LEAGUE SCHOLARSHIPS

Marine Corps League
Attn: National Executive Director
P.O. Box 3070
Merrifield, VA 22116-3070
(703) 207-9588   Toll Free: (800) MCL-1775
Fax: (703) 207-0047   E-mail: mcl@mcleague.org
Web: www.mcleague.org

Summary To provide college aid to students whose parents served in the Marines and to members of the Marine Corps League or Marine Corps League Auxiliary.

Eligibility This program is open to 1) children of Marines who lost their lives in the line of duty; 2) spouses, children, grandchildren, great-grandchildren, and stepchildren of active Marine Corps League and/or Auxiliary members; and 3) members of the Marine Corps League and/or Marine Corps League Auxiliary who are honorably discharged and in need of rehabilitation training not provided by government programs. Applicants must be seeking further education and training as a full-time student and be recommended by the commandant of an active chartered detachment of the Marine Corps League or the president of an active chartered unit of the Auxiliary. They must have a GPA of 3.0 or higher. Financial need is not considered in the selection process.

Financial data A stipend is awarded (amount not specified). Funds are paid directly to the recipient.

Duration 1 year; may be renewed up to 3 additional years (all renewals must complete an application and attach a transcript from the college or university).

Number awarded Varies, depending upon the amount of funds available each year.

Deadline June of each year.

[680]
MASSACHUSETTS REHABILITATION COMMISSION OR COMMISSION FOR THE BLIND TUITION WAIVER PROGRAM

Massachusetts Office of Student Financial Assistance
454 Broadway, Suite 200
Revere, MA 02151
(617) 727-9420   Fax: (617) 727-0667
E-mail: osfa@osfa.mass.edu
Web: www.osfa.mass.edu

Summary To provide financial assistance for college to Massachusetts residents who are clients of specified state disability agencies.

Eligibility Applicants for this assistance must be certified as clients by the Massachusetts Rehabilitation Commission or Commission for the Blind. They must have been permanent residents of Massachusetts for at least 1 year, must be U.S. citizens or permanent residents, and may not be in default on any federal student loan.

Financial data Eligible clients are exempt from any tuition payments for an undergraduate degree or certificate program at public colleges or universities in Massachusetts.

Duration Up to 4 academic years, for a total of 130 semester hours.

Additional data Recipients may enroll either part or full time in a Massachusetts publicly-supported institution.

Number awarded Varies each year.

Deadline Deadline not specified.

[681]
MAYS MISSION SCHOLARSHIPS

Mays Mission for the Handicapped, Inc.
Attn: Scholarship Program
604 Colonial Drive
Heber Springs, AR 72545
(501) 362-7526   Toll Free: (888) 503-7955
Fax: (501) 362-7529   E-mail: info@maysmission.org
Web: www.maysmission.org/schol.html

Summary To provide financial assistance to college students with significant physical and/or mental disabilities.

Eligibility This program is open to U.S. residents with significant physical and/or mental disabilities. Applicants must be working full time on a baccalaureate degree at a 4-year college or university. They must have a score of 18 or higher on the ACT or 870 or higher on the SAT. Along with their application, they must submit a short biography that includes their goals, aspirations, and accomplishments along with a brief description of how they have overcome their disability.

Financial data A stipend is awarded (amount not specified).

Duration 1 year; may be renewed, provided the recipient remains enrolled full time with a GPA of 2.3 or higher.

Number awarded 7 scholars are supported at a time.

Deadline June of each year.

[682]
MG EUGENE C. RENZI, USA (RET.)/MANTECH INTERNATIONAL CORPORATION TEACHER'S SCHOLARSHIP

Armed Forces Communications and Electronics Association
Attn: AFCEA Educational Foundation
4400 Fair Lakes Court
Fairfax, VA 22033-3899
(703) 631-6149   Toll Free: (800) 336-4583, ext. 6149
Fax: (703) 631-4693   E-mail: scholarship@afcea.org
Web: www.afcea.org

Summary To provide financial assistance to undergraduate and graduate students (particularly disabled veterans) who are preparing for a career as a teacher of science and mathematics.

Eligibility This program is open to full-time juniors, seniors, and graduate students at accredited colleges and universities in the United States. Applicants must be U.S. citizens preparing for a career as a teacher of science, mathematics, or information technology at a middle or secondary school. They must have a GPA of 3.0 or higher. In the selection process, first consideration is given to wounded or disabled veterans, then to honorably discharged veterans. Financial need is not considered.

Financial data The stipend is $2,500.

Duration 1 year.

Additional data This program was established in 2008 with support from ManTech International Corporation.

Number awarded 1 each year.

Deadline May of each year.

[683]
MICROSOFT NATIONAL SCHOLARSHIPS

Microsoft Corporation
Attn: Microsoft Scholarship Program
One Microsoft Way
Redmond, WA 98052-8303
(425) 882-8080   TDD: (800) 892-9811
E-mail: scholars@microsoft.com
Web: www.microsoft.com/college/ss_overview.mspx

Summary To provide financial assistance and summer work experience to undergraduate students, especially members of underrepresented groups, interested in preparing for a career in computer science or other related technical fields.

Eligibility This program is open to students who are enrolled full time and making satisfactory progress toward an undergraduate degree in computer science, computer engineering, or a related technical discipline (such as electrical engineering, mathematics, or physics) with a demonstrated interest in computer science. Applicants must be enrolled at a 4-year college or university in the United States, Canada, or Mexico. They must have a GPA of 3.0 or higher. Although all students who meet the eligibility criteria may apply, a large majority of the scholarships are awarded to women, underrepresented minorities (African Americans, Hispanics, and Native Americans), and students with disabilities. Along with their application, students must submit an essay that describes the following 4 items: 1) how they demonstrate their passion for technology outside the classroom; 2) the toughest technical problem they have worked on, how they addressed the problem, their role in reaching the outcome if it was team-based, and the final outcome; 3) a situation that demonstrates initiative and their willingness to go above and beyond; and 4) how they are currently funding their college education.

Financial data Scholarships cover 100% of the tuition as posted by the financial aid office of the university or college the recipient designates. Scholarships are made through that school and are not transferable to other academic institutions. Funds may be used for tuition only and may not be used for other costs on the recipient's bursar bill, such as room and board.

Duration 1 year.

Additional data Selected recipients are offered a paid summer internship where they will have a chance to develop Microsoft products.

Number awarded Varies each year; a total of $540,000 is available for this program annually.

Deadline January of each year.

[684]
MISSOURI PUBLIC SERVICE OFFICER OR EMPLOYEE'S CHILD SURVIVOR GRANT PROGRAM

Missouri Department of Higher Education
Attn: Student Financial Assistance
3515 Amazonas Drive
Jefferson City, MO 65109-5717
(573) 751-2361   Toll Free: (800) 473-6757
Fax: (573) 751-6635   E-mail: info@dhe.mo.gov
Web: www.dhe.mo.gov/publicserviceofficer.shtml

Summary To provide financial assistance for college to 1) disabled and deceased Missouri public employees and public safety officers, and 2) their spouses and children.

Eligibility This program is open to residents of Missouri who are 1) public safety officers who were permanently disabled in the line of duty; 2) spouses of public safety officers who were permanently and totally disabled in the line of duty; or 3) children of Missouri public safety officers or Department of Transportation employees who were killed or permanently disabled while engaged in the construction or maintenance of highways, roads, and bridges. Applicants must be Missouri residents enrolled or accepted for enrollment as a full-time undergraduate student at a participating Missouri college or university; children must be younger than 24 years of age. Students working on a degree or certificate in theology or divinity are not eligible. U.S. citizenship or permanent resident status is required.

Financial data The maximum annual grant is the lesser of 1) the actual tuition charged at the school where the recipient is enrolled, or 2) the amount of tuition charged to a Missouri undergraduate resident enrolled full time in the same class level and in the same academic major as an applicant at the University of Missouri at Columbia.

Duration 1 year; may be renewed.

Additional data Public safety officers include fire fighters, police officers, capitol police officers, parole officers, probation officers, state correctional employees, water safety officers, conservation officers, park rangers, and highway patrolmen.

Number awarded Varies each year; recently, 11 students received $47,045 in support from this program.

Deadline There is no application deadline, but early submission of the completed application is encouraged.

[685]
MUSICIANS WITH SPECIAL NEEDS SCHOLARSHIP

Sigma Alpha Iota Philanthropies, Inc.
One Tunnel Road
Asheville, NC 28805
(828) 251-0606   Fax: (828) 251-0644
E-mail: nh@sai-national.org
Web: www.sigmaalphaiota.org

Summary To provide financial assistance for college or graduate school to members of Sigma Alpha Iota (an organization of women musicians) who have a disability and are working on a degree in music.
Eligibility This program is open to members of the organization who either 1) have a sensory or physical impairment and are enrolled in a graduate or undergraduate degree program in music, or 2) are preparing to become a music teacher or therapist for people with disabilities. Performance majors must submit a 15-minute DVD of their work; non-performance majors must submit evidence of work in their area of specialization, such as composition, musicology, or research.
Financial data The stipend is $1,500.
Duration 1 year.
Number awarded 1 each year.
Deadline March of each year.

[686]
NASA MOTIVATING UNDERGRADUATES IN SCIENCE AND TECHNOLOGY (MUST) SCHOLARSHIP PROGRAM

Hispanic College Fund
Attn: Scholarship Processing
1301 K Street, N.W., Suite 450-A West
Washington, D.C. 20005
(202) 296-5400   Toll Free: (800) 644-4223
Fax: (202) 296-3774
E-mail: hcf-info@hispanicfund.org
Web: scholarships.hispanicfund.org/applications

Summary To provide financial assistance to members of disabled and other underrepresented groups who are working on an undergraduate degree in a field of science, technology, engineering, or mathematics (STEM).
Eligibility This program is open to U.S. citizens from an underrepresented group, including women, African Americans, Hispanic Americans, Native Americans, and persons with disabilities. Applicants must be entering their freshman, sophomore, junior, or senior year at an accredited college or university in the 50 states or Puerto Rico as a full-time student. They must have a GPA of 3.0 or higher and a major in a STEM field of study.
Financial data Stipends provide payment of 50% of the tuition and fees at the recipient's institution, to a maximum of $10,000. The stipend for the summer research experience is $5,000.
Duration 1 year; recipients may reapply.
Additional data This program is sponsored by the National Aeronautics and Space Administration (NASA) with support from the United Negro College Fund Special Programs Corporation (UNCFSP) and the Society of Hispanic Engineers-Advancing Hispanic Excellence in Technology, Engineering, Math, and Science, Inc. (AHETEMS). Scholars are eligible to participate in a summer research experience at a NASA center. All applications must be submitted online; no paper applications are available.
Number awarded 100 each year.
Deadline January of each year.

[687]
NASA SPACE GRANT COLLEGE AND FELLOWSHIP PROGRAM

National Aeronautics and Space Administration
Attn: Office of Education
300 E Street, S.W.
Mail Suite 6M35
Washington, DC 20546-0001
(202) 358-1069   Fax: (202) 358-3048
E-mail: Diane.D.DeTroye@nasa.gov
Web: www.nasa.gov

Summary To provide financial assistance to disabled and other undergraduate and graduate students interested in preparing for a career in a space-related field.
Eligibility This program is open to undergraduate and graduate students at colleges and universities that participate in the National Space Grant program of the U.S. National Aeronautics and Space Administration (NASA) through their state consortium. Applicants must be interested in a program of study and/or research in a field of science, technology, engineering, or mathematics (STEM) related to space. A specific goal of the program is to increase preparation by members of underrepresented groups (minorities, women, and persons with disabilities) for STEM space-related careers. Financial need is not considered in the selection process.
Financial data Each consortium establishes the terms of the fellowship program in its state.
Additional data NASA established the Space Grant program in 1989. It operates through 52 consortia in each state, the District of Columbia, and Puerto Rico. Each consortium includes selected colleges and universities in that state as well as other affiliates from industry, museums, science centers, and state and local agencies.
Number awarded Varies each year.
Deadline Each consortium sets its own deadlines.

[688]
NAVY SUPPLY CORPS FOUNDATION NIB/NISH SCHOLARSHIPS

Navy Supply Corps Foundation
c/o CDR Jack Evans (ret), Chief Staff Officer
1425 Prince Avenue
Athens, GA 30606-2205
(706) 354-4111   Fax: (706) 354-0334
E-mail: foundation@usnscf.com
Web: www.usnscf.com/programs/scholarships.aspx

Summary To provide financial assistance for college to blind or disabled relatives of current or former Navy Supply Corps personnel.
Eligibility This program is open to dependents (child, grandchild, or spouse) of a living or deceased regular, retired, reserve, or prior Navy Supply Corps officer, warrant officer, or enlister personnel. Enlisted ratings that apply are AK (Aviation Storekeeper), SK (Storekeeper), MS (Mess Specialist), DK (Disbursing Clerk), SH (Ship Serviceman), LI (Lithographer), and PC (Postal Clerk). Applicants must be attending or planning to attend a 2-year or 4-year accredited college on a full-time basis and

have a GPA of 2.5 or higher in high school and/or college. They must be able to document blindness or severe disability. Selection is based on character, leadership, academic achievement, extracurricular activities, and financial need.

Financial data Stipends range from $1,000 to $5,000.

Duration 1 year.

Additional data This program was established in 2005 with support from National Industries for the Blind (NIB) and NISH (formerly the National Industries for the Severely Handicapped).

Number awarded 1 or more each year.

Deadline March of each year.

[689]
NEW HAMPSHIRE CHARITABLE FOUNDATION STATEWIDE STUDENT AID PROGRAM

New Hampshire Charitable Foundation
37 Pleasant Street
Concord, NH 03301-4005
(603) 225-6641   Toll Free: (800) 464-6641
Fax: (603) 225-1700   E-mail: info@nhcf.org
Web: www.nhcf.org/page16960.cfm

Summary To provide scholarships or loans for undergraduate or graduate study in any state to New Hampshire residents.

Eligibility This program is open to New Hampshire residents who are graduating high school seniors planning to enter a 4-year college or university, undergraduate students between 17 and 23 years of age working on a 4-year degree, or graduate students of any age. Applicants must be enrolled on at least a half-time basis at a school in New Hampshire or another state. Selection is based on financial need, academic merit, community service, school activities, and work experience. Priority is given to students with the fewest financial resources.

Financial data Awards range from $500 to $3,500 and average $1,800. Most are made in the form of grants (recently, 82% of all awards) or no-interest or low-interest loans.

Duration 1 year; approximately one third of the awards are renewable.

Additional data Through this program, students submit a single application for more than 50 different scholarship and loan funds. Many of the funds have additional requirements, including field of study; residency in region, county, city, or town; graduation from designated high schools; and special attributes (e.g., of Belgian descent, employee of designated firms, customer of Granite State Telephone Company, disabled, suffering from a life-threatening or serious chronic illness, of Lithuanian descent, dependent of a New Hampshire police officer, dependent of a New Hampshire Episcopal minister, of Polish descent, former Sea Cadet or Naval Junior ROTC, or employed in the tourism industry). The Citizens' Scholarship Foundation of America reviews all applications; recipients are selected by the New Hampshire Charitable Foundation. A $20 application fee is required.

Number awarded Varies each year; approximately $700,000 is awarded annually.

Deadline April of each year.

[690]
NEW JERSEY STATE ELKS SPECIAL CHILDREN'S SCHOLARSHIP

New Jersey State Elks
Attn: Special Children's Committee
665 Rahway Avenue
P.O. Box 1596
Woodbridge, NJ 07095-1596
(732) 326-1300   E-mail: info@njelks.org
Web: www.njelks.org

Summary To provide financial assistance to high school seniors in New Jersey who have a disability and plan to attend college in any state.

Eligibility This program is open to seniors graduating from high schools in New Jersey who have a disability. Applicants must be planning to attend a college or university in any state. Selection is based on academic standing, general worthiness, and financial need. Boys and girls are judged separately.

Financial data The stipend is $2,500 per year. Funds are paid directly to the recipient's college or university.

Duration 4 years.

Number awarded 2 each year: 1 to a boy and 1 to a girl.

Deadline April of each year.

[691]
NEW JERSEY UTILITIES ASSOCIATION EQUAL EMPLOYMENT OPPORTUNITY SCHOLARSHIPS

New Jersey Utilities Association
50 West State Street, Suite 1117
Trenton, NJ 08608
(609) 392-1000   Fax: (609) 396-4231
Web: www.njua.org/html/njua_eeo_scholarship.cfm

Summary To provide financial assistance to minority, female, and disabled high school seniors in New Jersey interested in attending college in any state.

Eligibility This program is open to seniors graduating from high schools in New Jersey who are women, minorities (Black or African American, Hispanic or Latino, American Indian or Alaska Native, Asian, Native Hawaiian or Pacific Islander, or 2 or more races), and persons with disabilities. Applicants must be planning to work on a bachelor's degree at a college or university in any state. They must be able to demonstrate financial need. Children of employees of any New Jersey Utilities Association-member company are ineligible. Selection is based on overall academic excellence and demonstrated financial need. U.S. citizenship or permanent resident status is required.

Financial data The stipend is $1,500 per year.

Duration 4 years.

Number awarded 2 each year.

Deadline March of each year.

[692]
NEW YORK STATE MILITARY SERVICE RECOGNITION SCHOLARSHIPS

New York State Higher Education Services
  Corporation
Attn: Student Information
99 Washington Avenue
Albany, NY 12255
(518) 473-1574   Toll Free: (888) NYS-HESC
Fax: (518) 473-3749   TDD: (800) 445-5234
E-mail: webmail@hesc.com
Web: www.hesc.com

Summary To provide financial assistance to disabled veterans and the family members of deceased or disabled veterans who are residents of New York and interested in attending college in the state.

Eligibility This program is open to New York residents who served in the armed forces of the United States or state organized militia at any time on or after August 2, 1990 and became severely and permanently disabled as a result of injury or illness suffered or incurred in a combat theater or combat zone or during military training operations in preparation for duty in a combat theater or combat zone of operations. Also eligible are the children, spouses, or financial dependents of members of the armed forces of the United States or state organized militia who at any time after August 2, 1990 1) died, became severely and permanently disabled as a result of injury or illness suffered or incurred, or are classified as missing in action in a combat theater or combat zone of operations, 2) died as a result of injuries incurred in those designated areas, or 3) died or became severely and permanently disabled as a result of injury or illness suffered or incurred during military training operations in preparation for duty in a combat theater or combat zone of operations. Applicants must be attending or accepted at an approved program of study as full-time undergraduates at a public college or university or private institution in New York.

Financial data At public colleges and universities, this program provides payment of actual tuition and mandatory educational fees; actual room and board charged to students living on campus or an allowance for room and board for commuter students; and allowances for books, supplies, and transportation. At private institutions, the award is equal to the amount charged at the State University of New York (SUNY) for 4-year tuition and average mandatory fees (or the student's actual tuition and fees, whichever is less) plus allowances for room, board, books, supplies, and transportation.

Duration This program is available for 4 years of full-time undergraduate study (or 5 years in an approved 5-year bachelor's degree program).

Number awarded Varies each year.

Deadline April of each year.

[693]
NEW YORK STATE WORLD TRADE CENTER MEMORIAL SCHOLARSHIPS

New York State Higher Education Services
  Corporation
Attn: Student Information
99 Washington Avenue
Albany, NY 12255
(518) 473-1574   Toll Free: (888) NYS-HESC
Fax: (518) 473-3749   TDD: (800) 445-5234
E-mail: webmail@hesc.com
Web: www.hesc.com

Summary To provide financial assistance to undergraduates in New York 1) who were killed or severely and permanently disabled as a result of the terrorist attacks on September 11, 2001 or 2) who are their relatives.

Eligibility This program is open to 1) the children, spouses, and financial dependents of deceased or severely and permanently disabled victims of the September 11, 2001 terrorist attacks or the subsequent rescue and recovery operations; and 2) survivors of the terrorist attacks who are severely and permanently disabled as a result of injuries sustained in the attacks or the subsequent rescue and recovery operations. Applicants must be attending or accepted at an approved program of study as full-time undergraduates at a public college or university or private institution in New York.

Financial data At public colleges and universities, this program provides payment of actual tuition and mandatory educational fees; actual room and board charged to students living on campus or an allowance for room and board for commuter students; and allowances for books, supplies, and transportation. At private institutions, the award is equal to the amount charged at the State University of New York (SUNY) for 4-year tuition and average mandatory fees (or the student's actual tuition and fees, whichever is less) plus allowances for room, board, books, supplies, and transportation.

Duration This program is available for 4 years of full-time undergraduate study (or 5 years in an approved 5-year bachelor's degree program).

Number awarded Varies each year.

Deadline April of each year.

[694]
PATRICIA SONNTAG MEMORIAL SCHOLARSHIP

California Association for Postsecondary Education
  and Disability
Attn: Executive Assistant
71423 Biskra Road
Rancho Mirage, CA 92270
(760) 346-8206   Fax: (760) 340-5275
TDD: (760) 341-4084   E-mail: caped2000@aol.com
Web: www.caped.net/scholarships.html

Summary To provide financial assistance to students enrolled at 4-year college and universities in California who have a disability and are involved in activities or classes related to providing services to people with disabilities.

Eligibility This program is open to students at 4-year colleges and universities in California who have a disability. Applicants must have completed at least 6 semester credits with a GPA of 2.5 or higher. They must be majoring in a field related to policy formulation or service delivery to students with disabilities or be actively engaged in advocacy or leadership in campus, community, or governmental organizations that benefit individuals with disabilities, regardless of their major. Along with their application, they must submit a 1-page personal letter that demonstrates their writing skills, progress towards meeting their educational and vocational goals, management of their disability, and involvement in community activities. They must also submit a letter of recommendation from a faculty member, verification of disability, official transcripts, proof of current enrollment, and documentation of financial need.

Financial data The stipend is $1,000.

Duration 1 year.

Number awarded 1 each year.

Deadline September of each year.

[695]
PENNSYLVANIA ASSOCIATION OF MEDICAL SUPPLIERS SCHOLARSHIP

Pennsylvania Association of Medical Suppliers
777 East Park Drive, Suite 300
Harrisburg, PA 17111
(717) 909-1958   Fax: (717) 236-8767
Web: www.pamsonline.org

Summary To provide financial assistance to residents of Pennsylvania and Delaware who use home medical equipment and services to overcome a physical challenge and are interested in attending college in any state.

Eligibility This program is open to residents of Pennsylvania and Delaware who are enrolled or planning to enroll in a postsecondary educational program in any state. Applicants must have been successful in their educational pursuits while overcoming physical challenges with the help of home medical equipment and services (e.g., wheelchairs, respiratory devices). Along with their application, they must submit a short essay that describes their experiences with home medical equipment and how it helps or will help them work on a college degree.

Financial data The stipend is $1,000.

Duration 1 year.

Number awarded 1 each year.

Deadline April of each year.

[696]
P.O. PISTILLI SCHOLARSHIPS

Design Automation Conference
c/o Cherrice Traver
Union College
Steinmetz Hall, Room 202
Schenectady, NY 12308
(518) 388-6326   Fax: (518) 388-6789
E-mail: traverc@union.edu
Web: doc.union.edu/acsee.html

Summary To provide financial assistance to female, minority, or disabled high school seniors who are interested in preparing for a career in computer science or electrical engineering.

Eligibility This program is open to graduating high school seniors who are members of underrepresented groups: women, African Americans, Hispanics, Native Americans, and persons with disabilities. Applicants must be interested in preparing for a career in electrical engineering, computer engineering, or computer science. They must have at least a 3.0 GPA, have demonstrated high achievements in math and science courses, have demonstrated involvement in activities associated with the underrepresented group they represent, and be able to demonstrate significant financial need. U.S. citizenship is not required, but applicants must be U.S. residents when they apply and must plan to attend an accredited U.S. college or university. Along with their application, they must submit 3 letters of recommendation, official transcripts, ACT/SAT and/or PSAT scores, a personal statement outlining future goals and why they think they should receive this scholarship, and documentation of financial need.

Financial data Stipends are $4,000 per year. Awards are paid each year in 2 equal installments.

Duration 1 year; renewable for up to 4 additional years.

Additional data This program is funded by the Design Automation Conference of the Association for Computing Machinery's Special Interest Group on Design Automation.

Number awarded 2 to 7 each year.

Deadline January of each year.

[697]
POWERING EDUCATION SCHOLARSHIPS

Alpha One
127 Main Street
South Portland, ME 04106
(207) 767-2189   Toll Free: (800) 640-7200
Fax: (207) 799-8346   TDD: (207) 767-5387
E-mail: info@mpowerloans.org
Web: www.alphaonenow.com/info.php?id=131#finance

Summary To provide financial assistance to undergraduate and graduate students in Maine who have disabilities.

Eligibility This program is open to high school seniors, undergraduates, and graduate students at schools in Maine. Applicants must have a disability. They must have a "B" average or equivalent GPA. Along with their application, they must submit a personal essay of 1 to 2 pages on a topic of their choice, a letter of recommendation, and current transcripts.

Financial data The stipend is $2,000. Funds are paid directly to the recipient's institution after completion of the first semester, provided the student earns a GPA of 2.5 or higher.

Duration 1 year.

Number awarded 3 each year.

Deadline March of each year.

[698]
REHABGYM SCHOLARSHIP

Vermont Student Assistance Corporation
Attn: Scholarship Programs
10 East Allen Street
P.O. Box 2000
Winooski, VT 05404-2601
(802) 654-3798   Toll Free: (888) 253-4819
Fax: (802) 654-3765 TDD: (800) 281-3341 (within VT)
E-mail: info@vsac.org
Web: services.vsac.org

Summary To provide financial assistance to residents of Vermont who have undergone a significant physical challenge and plan to attend college in any state.

Eligibility This scholarship is available to residents of Vermont who are attending or planning to attend a college or university in any state. Applicants must be able to demonstrate that they have undergone a significant physical challenge or illness and have met the challenge with courage and perseverance. Along with their application, they must submit 100-word essays on 1) any significant barriers that limit their access to education, and 2) what they believe distinguishes their application from others that may be submitted. Selection is based on those essays and financial need.

Financial data The stipend is $1,000.

Duration 1 year.

Additional data This scholarship was established in 2006.

Number awarded 1 or more each year.

Deadline June of each year.

[699]
RHODE ISLAND EDUCATIONAL BENEFITS FOR DISABLED AMERICAN VETERANS

Division of Veterans Affairs
480 Metacom Avenue
Bristol, RI 02809-0689
(401) 254-8350   Fax: (401) 254-2320
TDD: (401) 254-1345 E-mail: devangelista@dhs.ri.gov
Web: www.dhs.ri.gov

Summary To provide assistance to disabled veterans in Rhode Island who wish to pursue higher education at a public institution in the state.

Eligibility This program is open to permanent residents of Rhode Island who have been verified by the Department of Veterans Affairs (DVA) as having a disability of at least 10% resulting from military service.

Financial data Eligible veterans are entitled to take courses at any public institution of higher education in Rhode Island without the payment of tuition, exclusive of other fees and charges.

Number awarded Varies each year.

Deadline Deadline not specified.

[700]
SCOTTS COMPANY SCHOLARS PROGRAM

Golf Course Superintendents Association of America
Attn: Environmental Institute for Golf
1421 Research Park Drive
Lawrence, KS 66049-3859
(785) 832-4445   Toll Free: (800) 472-7878, ext. 4445
Fax: (785) 832-3643   E-mail: mwright@gcsaa.org
Web: www.gcsaa.org

Summary To provide financial assistance and summer work experience to high school seniors and college students, particularly those from diverse backgrounds, who are preparing for a career in golf management.

Eligibility This program is open to high school seniors and college students (freshmen, sophomores, and juniors) who are interested in preparing for a career in golf management (the "green industry"). Applicants should come from diverse ethnic, cultural, or socioeconomic backgrounds, defined to include women, minorities, and people with disabilities. Selection is based on cultural diversity, academic achievement, extracurricular activities, leadership, employment potential, essay responses, and letters of recommendation. Financial need is not considered. Finalists are selected for summer internships and then compete for scholarships.

Financial data The finalists receive a $500 award to supplement their summer internship income. Scholarship stipends are $2,500.

Duration 1 year.

Additional data The program is funded from a permanent endowment established by Scotts Company. Finalists are responsible for securing their own internships.

Number awarded 5 finalists, of whom 2 receive scholarships, are selected each year.

Deadline February of each year.

[701]
SOUTH DAKOTA FREE TUITION FOR VETERANS AND OTHERS WHO PERFORMED WAR SERVICE

South Dakota Board of Regents
Attn: Scholarship Committee
306 East Capitol Avenue, Suite 200
Pierre, SD 57501-2545
(605) 773-3455   Fax: (605) 773-2422
E-mail: info@sdbor.edu
Web: www.sdbor.edu/student/prospective/Military.htm

Summary To provide free tuition at South Dakota public colleges and universities to certain veterans.

Eligibility This program is open to current residents of South Dakota who have been discharged from the military forces of the United States under honorable conditions.

Applicants must meet 1 of the following criteria: 1) served on active duty at any time between August 2, 1990 and March 3, 1991; 2) received an Armed Forces Expeditionary Medal, Southwest Asia Service Medal, or other U.S. campaign or service medal for participation in combat operations against hostile forces outside the boundaries of the United States: or 3) have a service-connected disability rating of at least 10%. They may not be eligible for any other educational assistance from the U.S. government. Qualifying veterans must apply for this benefit within 20 years after the date proclaimed for the cassation of hostilities or within 6 years from and after the date of their discharge from military service, whichever is later.

Financial data Eligible veterans are entitled to attend any South Dakota state-supported institution of higher education or state-supported technical or vocational school free of tuition and mandatory fees.

Duration Eligible veterans are entitled to receive 1 month of free tuition for each month of qualifying service, from a minimum of 1 year to a maximum of 4 years.

Number awarded Varies each year.

Deadline Deadline not specified.

[702]
STAN BECK FELLOWSHIP

Entomological Society of America
Attn: Entomological Foundation
9332 Annapolis Road, Suite 210
Lanham, MD 20706-3150
(301) 459-9082   Fax: (301) 459-9084
E-mail: melodie@entfdn.org
Web: www.entsoc.org/awards/student/beck.htm

Summary To assist disabled and other "needy" students working on an undergraduate or graduate degree in entomology who are nominated by members of the Entomological Society of America (ESA).

Eligibility This program is open to students working on an undergraduate or graduate degree in entomology at a college or university in Canada, Mexico, or the United States. Candidates must be nominated by members of the society. They must be "needy" students; for the purposes of this program, need may be based on physical limitations, or economic, minority, or environmental conditions.

Financial data The stipend is $2,000 per year.

Duration 1 year; may be renewed up to 3 additional years.

Additional data This fellowship was first awarded in 1996. Recipients are expected to be present at the society's annual meeting, where the award will be presented.

Number awarded 1 each year.

Deadline June of each year.

[703]
STATE SCHOLARSHIPS OF THE HORATIO ALGER ASSOCIATION

Horatio Alger Association of Distinguished Americans, Inc.
99 Canal Center Plaza
Alexandria, VA 22314
(703) 684-9444   Fax: (703) 548-3822
E-mail: horatioaa@aol.com
Web: www.horatioalger.com

Summary To provide financial assistance to high school seniors from designated states who plan to attend college in any state and can demonstrate integrity and perseverance in overcoming adversity.

Eligibility This program is open to seniors graduating from high schools in designated states. Applicants must be planning to enroll at a college in any state to work on a bachelor's degree (they may begin at a 2-year college and then transfer to a 4-year institution). They must be U.S. citizens, be able to demonstrate critical financial need ($50,000 or less adjusted gross income per family), have a GPA of 2.0 or higher, and have a record of involvement in co-curricular and community activities. Along with their application, they must submit 1) an essay of 250 to 350 words on their career goals and the importance of a college education in attaining those goals; 2) an essay of 150 to 200 words on the life of a member of the Horatio Alger Association and how they have applied the virtues exemplified in the member's life story in their own life; and 3) information on the adversities they have encountered. Examples of adversity include: having been in foster care or a ward of the state; having been homeless; experiencing the death, incarceration, or abandonment of a parent or guardian; living in a household where alcohol or drugs are or were abused; having a physical or mental disability or serious illness; or suffering from physical or mental abuse.

Financial data Stipends vary from state to state, ranging from $2,500 to $10,500; most are $5,000.

Duration 1 year.

Additional data The states in which programs operate are: Arizona, California, Delaware, Georgia, Idaho, Illinois, Indiana, Iowa, Kentucky, Louisiana, Maryland, Minnesota, Missouri, Montana, Nebraska, North Dakota, Pennsylvania, South Dakota, Texas, Utah, Virginia, Washington, D.C., and Wyoming. In each state, individual members of the association or corporate sponsors provide funding.

Number awarded Varies each year.

Deadline October of each year.

[704]
STATE VOCATIONAL REHABILITATION SERVICES PROGRAM

Department of Education
Office of Special Education and Rehabilitative Services
Attn: Rehabilitation Services Administration
500 12th Street, S.W., Room 503
Washington, DC 20202-2800
(202) 245-7325   Fax: (202) 245-7590
E-mail: Carol.Dobak@ed.gov
Web: www.ed.gov/programs/rsabvrs/index.html

Summary To provide financial assistance to individuals with disabilities for undergraduate or graduate study pursued as part of their program of vocational rehabilitation.

Eligibility To be eligible for vocational rehabilitation services, an individual must 1) have a physical or mental impairment that is a substantial impediment to employment; 2) be able to benefit in terms of employment from vocational rehabilitation services; and 3) require vocational rehabilitation services to prepare for, enter, engage in, or retain gainful employment. Priority is given to applicants with the most significant disabilities. Persons accepted for vocational rehabilitation develop an Individualized Written Rehabilitation Program (IWRP) in consultation with a counselor for the vocational rehabilitation agency in the state in which they live. The IWRP may include a program of postsecondary education, if the disabled person and counselor agree that such a program will fulfill the goals of vocational rehabilitation. In most cases, the IWRP will provide for postsecondary education only to a level at which the disabled person will become employable, but that may include graduate education if the approved occupation requires an advanced degree as a minimum condition of entry. Students accepted to a program of postsecondary education as part of their IWRP must apply for all available federal, state, and private financial aid.

Financial data Funding for this program is provided by the federal government through grants to state vocational rehabilitation agencies. Grants under the basic support program currently total more than $3 billion per year. States must supplement federal funding with matching funds of 21.3%. Persons who are accepted for vocational rehabilitation by the appropriate state agency receive financial assistance based on the cost of their education and other funds available to them, including their own or family contribution and other sources of financial aid. Allowable costs in most states include tuition, fees, books, supplies, room, board, transportation, personal expenses, child care, and expenses related to disability (special equipment, readers, attendants, interpreters, or notetakers).

Duration Assistance is provided until the disabled person achieves an educational level necessary for employment as provided in the IWRP.

Additional data Information on this program is available only from state vocational rehabilitation agencies.

Number awarded Varies each year. Recently, more than 1.2 million people (of whom more than 80% have significant disabilities) were participating in this program.
Deadline Deadline not specified.

[705]
STEVE FASTEAU PAST PRESIDENTS' SCHOLARSHIP

California Association for Postsecondary Education and Disability
Attn: Executive Assistant
71423 Biskra Road
Rancho Mirage, CA 92270
(760) 346-8206   Fax: (760) 340-5275
TDD: (760) 341-4084   E-mail: caped2000@aol.com
Web: www.caped.net/scholarships.html

Summary To provide financial assistance to undergraduate and graduate students in California who have a disability.

Eligibility This program is open to students at public and private colleges and universities in California who have a disability. Undergraduates must have completed at least 6 semester credits and have a GPA of 2.5 or higher. Graduate students must have completed at least 3 semester units and have a GPA of 3.0 or higher. Along with their application, they must submit a 1-page personal letter that demonstrates their writing skills, progress towards meeting their educational and vocational goals, management of their disability, and involvement in community activities. They must also submit a letter of recommendation from a faculty person, verification of disability, official transcripts, proof of current enrollment, and documentation of financial need.

Financial data The stipend is $1,000.
Duration 1 year.
Number awarded 1 each year.
Deadline September of each year.

[706]
STUDENTS WITH DISABILITIES ENDOWED SCHOLARSHIPS HONORING ELIZABETH DALEY JEFFORDS

Vermont Student Assistance Corporation
Attn: Scholarship Programs
10 East Allen Street
P.O. Box 2000
Winooski, VT 05404-2601
(802) 654-3798   Toll Free: (888) 253-4819
Fax: (802) 654-3765   TDD: (800) 281-3341 (within VT)
E-mail: info@vsac.org
Web: services.vsac.org

Summary To provide financial assistance to high school seniors with disabilities in Vermont who are interested in enrolling at a college in any state.

Eligibility This program is open to graduating high school seniors in Vermont who have a documented disability. Applicants must be planning to attend a college or university in any state. Along with their application, they must submit a 100-word essay on what they believe distinguishes their application from others that may be submitted. Selection is based on that essay, a letter of recommendation, a personal interview, and financial need.

Financial data The stipend is $1,500.

Duration 1 year; nonrenewable.

Additional data Former Senator James M. Jeffords established this program in 2006 to honor his wife.

Number awarded 2 each year.

Deadline May of each year.

[707]
SURVIVORS' AND DEPENDENTS' EDUCATIONAL ASSISTANCE PROGRAM

Department of Veterans Affairs
Attn: Veterans Benefits Administration
810 Vermont Avenue, N.W.
Washington, DC 20420
(202) 418-4343   Toll Free: (888) GI-BILL1
Web: www.gibill.va.gov/GI_Bill_Info/benefits.htm

Summary To provide financial assistance for undergraduate or graduate study to children and spouses of deceased and disabled veterans, MIAs, and POWs.

Eligibility Eligible for this assistance are spouses and children of 1) veterans who died or are permanently and totally disabled as the result of active service in the armed forces; 2) veterans who died from any cause while rated permanently and totally disabled from a service-connected disability; 3) servicemembers listed as missing in action or captured in the line of duty by a hostile force; 4) servicemembers listed as forcibly detained or interned by a foreign government or power; and 5) servicemembers who are hospitalized or receiving outpatient treatment for a service-connected permanent and total disability and are likely to be discharged for that disability. Children must be between 18 and 26 years of age, although extensions may be granted. Spouses and children over 14 years of age with physical or mental disabilities are also eligible.

Financial data Monthly stipends from this program for study at an academic institution are $925 for full time, $694 for three-quarter time, or $461 for half-time. For farm cooperative work, the monthly stipends are $745 for full-time, $559 for three-quarter time, or $372 for half-time. For an apprenticeship or on-the-job training, the monthly stipend is $674 for the first 6 months, $505 for the second 6 months, $333 for the third 6 months, and $168 for the remainder of the program. For special restorative training by beneficiaries with a physical or mental disability, the monthly stipend for full-time training is $925.

Duration Up to 45 months (or the equivalent in part-time training). Spouses must complete their training within 10 years of the date they are first found eligible. For spouses of servicemembers who died on active duty, benefits end 20 years from the date of death.

Additional data Benefits may be used to work on associate, bachelor, or graduate degrees at colleges and universities, including independent study, cooperative training, and study abroad programs. Courses leading to a certificate or diploma from business, technical, or vocational schools may also be taken. Other eligible programs

include apprenticeships, on-the-job training programs, farm cooperative courses, correspondence courses (for spouses only), secondary school programs (for recipients who are not high school graduates), tutorial assistance, remedial deficiency and refresher training, or work-study (for recipients who are enrolled at least three-quarter time). Eligible children who are handicapped by a physical or mental disability that prevents pursuit of an educational program may receive special restorative training that includes language retraining, lip reading, auditory training, Braille reading and writing, and similar programs. Eligible spouses and children over 14 years of age who are handicapped by a physical or mental disability that prevents pursuit of an educational program may receive specialized vocational training that includes specialized courses, alone or in combination with other courses, leading to a vocational objective that is suitable for the person and required by reason of physical or mental handicap. Ineligible courses include bartending; audited courses; non-accredited independent study courses; any course given by radio; self-improvement courses, such as reading, speaking, woodworking, basic seamanship, and English as a second language; audited courses; any course that is avocational or recreational in character; courses not leading to an educational, professional, or vocational objective; courses taken and successfully completed previously; courses taken by a federal government employee and paid for under the Government Employees' Training Act; and courses taken while in receipt of benefits for the same program from the Office of Workers' Compensation Programs.

Number awarded Varies each year.

Deadline Applications may be submitted at any time.

[708]
TEXAS 4-H YOUTH DEVELOPMENT FOUNDATION COURAGEOUS HEART SCHOLARSHIPS

Texas 4-H Youth Development Foundation
Attn: Executive Director
Texas A&M University
7606 Eastmark Drive, Suite 101
College Station, TX 77840-4027
(979) 845-1213   Fax: (979) 845-6495
E-mail: jereeves@ag.tamu.edu
Web: texas4-h.tamu.edu/youth/scholarship.html

Summary To provide financial assistance to high school seniors who have been active in Texas 4-H activities in spite of unforeseen obstacles related to their medical/ health, family, and/or educational situation.

Eligibility This program is open to graduating seniors at high schools in Texas who have been actively participating in 4-H and plan to attend a college, university, or accredited technical school in the state. Applicants must be able to demonstrate that they have overcome extreme obstacles related to medical, family, and/or education circumstances. They must have taken and passed all necessary standardized tests for graduation and admittance to the college or university of their choice. Along with their application, they must submit a detailed narrative of the obstacles they have or are in the process of, overcoming, including how long they have been dealing with the obstacle, the person or persons who helped them through their situation, and how 4-H has played a positive role in overcoming their obstacle. Some scholarships require a major in agriculture; others are unrestricted. U.S. citizenship is required.

Financial data   Stipends range from $1,500 to $16,000, depending on the contributions from various donors.

Duration   1 year.

Additional data   Students may not apply for both Texas FFA Association and Texas 4-H scholarships.

Number awarded   The foundation awards approximately 225 scholarships for all of its programs each year.

Deadline   Students submit their applications to their county extension office, which must forward them to the district extension office by February of each year.

[709]
TEXAS EXEMPTION FOR PEACE OFFICERS DISABLED IN THE LINE OF DUTY

Texas Higher Education Coordinating Board
Attn: Grants and Special Programs
1200 East Anderson Lane
P.O. Box 12788, Capitol Station
Austin, TX 78711-2788
(512) 427-6340   Toll Free: (800) 242-3062
Fax: (512) 427-6127
E-mail: grantinfo@thecb.state.tx.us
Web: www.collegeforalltexans.com

Summary   To provide educational assistance to disabled Texas peace officers.

Eligibility   This program is open to Texas residents who are permanently disabled as a result of an injury suffered as a peace officer and unable to continue employment as a peace officer because of the disability. Applicants must be planning to attend a publicly-supported college or university in Texas as an undergraduate student.

Financial data   Eligible students are exempted from the payment of all dues, fees, and tuition charges at publicly-supported colleges and universities in Texas.

Duration   Up to 12 semesters.

Additional data   For more information, students should contact the admission office at the institution they plan to attend.

Number awarded   Varies each year; recently, 31 of these exemptions were awarded.

Deadline   Deadline not specified.

[710]
TEXAS MUTUAL SCHOLARSHIP PROGRAM

Texas Mutual Insurance Company
Attn: Office of the President
6210 East Highway 290
Austin, TX 78723-1098
(512) 224-3820   Toll Free: (800) 859-5995, ext. 3820
Fax: (512) 224-3889   TDD: (800) 853-5339
E-mail: information@texasmutual.com
Web: www.texasmutual.com/workers/scholarship.shtm

Summary   To provide financial assistance for college to workers and their families covered by workers' compensation insurance in Texas.

Eligibility   This program is open to 1) employees who qualify for lifetime income benefits as a result of injuries suffered on the job as covered by the Texas Workers' Compensation Act; 2) children and spouses of injured workers; and 3) children and unremarried spouses of employees who died as a result of a work-related injury. Workers must be covered by the Texas Mutual Insurance Company, formerly the Texas Workers' Compensation Insurance Fund. Children must be between 16 and 25 years of age. Surviving spouses must still be eligible for workers' compensation benefits. Financial need is considered in the selection process.

Financial data   Scholarships are intended to cover normal undergraduate, technical, or vocational school tuition and fees, to a maximum of $4,000 per semester. Those funds are paid directly to the college or vocational school. The cost of course-related books and fees are also reimbursed, up to a maximum of $500 per semester. Those funds are paid directly to the student.

Duration   1 year; may be renewed if the recipient maintains a GPA of 2.5 or higher.

Number awarded   Varies each year.

Deadline   Applications may be submitted at any time.

[711]
THEODORE R. AND VIVIAN M. JOHNSON SCHOLARSHIP PROGRAM

State University System of Florida
Attn: Office of Academic and Student Affairs
325 West Gaines Street, Suite 1614
Tallahassee, FL 32399-0400
(850) 245-0466   Fax: (850) 245-9685
Web: www.flbog.org

Summary   To provide financial assistance to Florida undergraduate students with disabilities.

Eligibility   This program is open to students with disabilities enrolled at a State University System of Florida institution. Applicants must submit an official transcript (with GPA of 2.0 or higher); documentation of financial need; and documentation of the nature and/or extent of their disability, which may be in 1 or more of the following classifications: hearing impairment, physical impairment, specific learning disability, speech/language impairment, visual impairment, or other impairment.

Financial data   The stipend depends on the availability of funds.

Duration   1 year; may be renewed if the recipient maintains a GPA of 2.0 or higher and enrolls in at least 18 credits each academic year.

Additional data   This program is administered by the equal opportunity program at each of the 11 State University System of Florida 4-year institutions. Contact that office for further information. Funding is provided by the Theodore R. and Vivian M. Johnson Foundation, with matching funding from the Florida Legislature.

Number awarded Several each year.
Deadline May of each year.

[712]
TROY BARBOZA EDUCATIONAL FUND

Hawai'i Community Foundation
Attn: Scholarship Department
1164 Bishop Street, Suite 800
Honolulu, HI 96813
(808) 566-5570   Toll Free: (888) 731-3863
Fax: (808) 521-6286
E-mail: scholarships@hcf-hawaii.org
Web: www.hawaiicommunityfoundation.org

Summary To provide financial assistance for college to disabled public employees in Hawaii or their dependents.
Eligibility This program is open to 1) disabled public employees in Hawaii who were injured in the line of duty; 2) dependents or other immediate family members of public employees in Hawaii who were disabled or killed in the line of duty; and 3) private citizens who have performed a heroic act for the protection and welfare of others. The public employee must work or have worked in a job where lives are risked for the protection and safety of others. The injury must have left the employee incapacitated or incapable or continuing in his or her profession and must have occurred after October 22, 1987. Applicants must submit a short statement describing their course of study, career goals, outstanding attributes, talents, community service, family circumstances, and any other relevant information. Financial need is considered in the selection process.
Financial data The amount awarded varies, depending upon the needs of the recipient and the funds available.
Duration 1 year; scholarships for employees and their dependents may be renewed; scholarships for private citizens who have performed a heroic act are nonrenewable.
Additional data This program was established in 1991.
Number awarded 1 or more each year.
Deadline February of each year.

[713]
USOC 2002 OLYMPIC WINTER GAMES LEGACY SCHOLARSHIPS

United States Olympic Committee
Attn: Athlete Support Department
One Olympic Plaza
Colorado Springs, CO 80909-5760
(719) 632-5551   Toll Free: (800) 933-4473
Fax: (719) 578-4654
Web: teamusa.org/content/index/894

Summary To provide financial assistance to athletes who are currently in training for the Olympics or Paralympics and also residing, training, or enrolled in college in Utah.
Eligibility This program is open to athletes who have demonstrated competitive excellence in important international competitions. Applicants must 1) be enrolled at an accredited college or university in Utah or 2) have participated in the 2002 Olympics or Paralympics and be enrolled

at an accredited college or university in any state. Financial need is considered in the selection process.
Financial data Stipends range up to $5,000 per year, depending on athlete performance history. Funds are available for tuition and mandatory fees only.
Duration 1 year; may be renewed.
Additional data This program was established following the 2002 Winter Olympics in Salt Lake City. It is currently funded by AT&T.
Number awarded Varies each year.
Deadline April or October of each year.

[714]
USOC TUITION GRANTS

United States Olympic Committee
Attn: Athlete Support Department
One Olympic Plaza
Colorado Springs, CO 80909-5760
(719) 632-5551   Toll Free: (800) 933-4473
Fax: (719) 578-4654
Web: teamusa.org/content/index/894

Summary To provide financial assistance to athletes who are currently in training for the Olympics or Paralympics and also enrolled in college.
Eligibility This program is open to athletes who have demonstrated competitive excellence in important international competitions. Applicants must have been accepted to receive Elite Athlete Health Insurance and/or Direct Athlete Support from the United States Olympic Committee (USOC) and be endorsed by the National Governing Body (NGB) for their particular sport. They must be enrolled at an accredited college or university. Also eligible are retired athletes who participated in the Olympics Games or Pan American Games within the past 5 years; athletes with disabilities who are members of the current U.S. Paralympics Elite or National Team; and retired Paralympians who competed in a Paralympic Games within the past 5 years. Athletes currently in training at a U.S. Olympic Training Center are not eligible for these grants; they must apply for a B.J. Stupak Olympic Scholarship. Priority is given to applicants who have a current top 8 World Championships placement or world ranking. Financial need is considered in the selection process.
Financial data Stipends range up to $5,000 per year for athletes who have an international rank of first through fourth in their sport or up to $2,500 for athletes who rank fifth through eighth. Stipends for retired athletes are limited to $2,500. Funds are available for tuition and mandatory fees only.
Duration 1 year; may be renewed. Retired athletes are only eligible for 1 grant.
Number awarded Varies each year. Approximately $70,000 is available for this program annually.
Deadline January, April, July, or October of each year.

[715]
UTAH ELKS ASSOCIATION SPECIAL NEEDS STUDENT SCHOLARSHIP AWARD

Utah Elks Association
c/o Jim Fugua, Scholarship Chair
Provo Lodge 849
1000 South University Avenue
P.O. Box 83
Provo, UT 84603
(801) 373-0849
Web: www.elksinutah.org

Summary To provide financial assistance for college to high school seniors in Utah who have a disability or other special need.

Eligibility This program is open to seniors graduating from high schools in Utah who have a special need, such as a disability. Applicants must submit 1) a supporting letter from a doctor or professional person stating the nature of the special need, and 2) a 500-word essay on their career and life goals and their plan to achieve those. Selection is based on that essay, academic achievement, community service, honors and awards, leadership, and financial need. U.S. citizenship is required.

Financial data A stipend is awarded (amount not specified).

Duration 1 year.

Number awarded Varies each year, depending upon the funds available.

Deadline January of each year.

[716]
VOCATIONAL REHABILITATION FOR DISABLED VETERANS

Department of Veterans Affairs
Attn: Veterans Benefits Administration
Vocational Rehabilitation and Employment Service
810 Vermont Avenue, N.W.
Washington, DC 20420
(202) 418-4343   Toll Free: (800) 827-1000
Web: www.vba.va.gov/bin/vre/index.htm

Summary To provide vocational rehabilitation to certain categories of veterans with disabilities.

Eligibility This program is open to veterans who have a service-connected disability of 1) at least 10% and a serious employment handicap, or 2) at least 20% and an employment handicap. They must have been discharged or released from military service under other than dishonorable conditions. The Department of Veterans Affairs (VA) must determine that they would benefit from a training program that would help them prepare for, find, and keep suitable employment. The program may be 1) institutional training at a certificate, 2-year college, 4-year college or university, or technical program; 2) unpaid on-the-job training in a federal, state, or local agency or a federally-recognized Indian tribal agency, training in a home, vocational course in a rehabilitation facility or sheltered workshop, independent instruction, or institutional non-farm cooperative; or 3) paid training through a farm cooperative, apprenticeship, on-the-job training, or on-the-job non-farm cooperative.

Financial data While in training and for 2 months after, eligible disabled veterans may receive subsistence allowances in addition to their disability compensation or retirement pay. For most training programs, the current full-time monthly rate is $547.54 with no dependents, $679.18 with 1 dependent, $800.36 with 2 dependents, and $58.34 for each additional dependent; proportional rates apply for less than full-time training. The VA also pays the costs of tuition, books, fees, supplies, and equipment; it may also pay for special supportive services, such as tutorial assistance, prosthetic devices, lipreading training, and signing for the deaf. If during training or employment services the veteran's disabilities cause transportation expenses that would not be incurred by nondisabled persons, the VA will pay for at least a portion of those expenses. If the veteran encounters financial difficulty during training, the VA may provide an advance against future benefit payments.

Duration Up to 48 months of full-time training or its equivalent in part-time training. If a veteran with a serious disability receives services under an extended evaluation to improve training potential, the total of the extended evaluation and the training phases of the rehabilitation program may exceed 48 months. Usually, the veteran must complete a rehabilitation program within 12 years from the date of notification of entitlement to compensation by the VA. Following completion of the training portion of a rehabilitation program, a veteran may receive counseling and job search and adjustment services for 18 months.

Additional data The program may also provide employment assistance, self-employment assistance, training in a rehabilitation facility, or college and other training. Veterans who are seriously disabled may receive services and assistance to improve their ability to live more independently in their community. After completion of the training phase, the VA will assist the veteran to find and have a suitable job.

Number awarded Varies each year.

Deadline Applications are accepted at any time.

[717]
WILLIAM M. EVANS SCHOLARSHIP

Bose McKinney & Evans LLP
Attn: Scholarship Award Committee
111 Monument Circle, Suite 2700
Indianapolis, IN 46204
(317) 684-5000   Fax: (317) 684-5173
Web: www.boselaw.com/groups/scholarship.shtml

Summary To provide financial assistance to high school seniors in Indiana who are classified as special education students and who plan to attend college in any state.

Eligibility This program is open to seniors graduating from high schools in Indiana who have been classified as special education students. Applicants must be planning to attend a university, college, junior college, or vocational training program in any state. Selection is based on personal achievement, future goals, and financial need.

Financial data The stipend is $2,000.

Duration 1 year.
Additional data This program began in 1992.
Number awarded 1 each year.
Deadline March of each year.

[718]
WILLIAM MAY MEMORIAL SCHOLARSHIP

California Association for Postsecondary Education
and Disability
Attn: Executive Assistant
71423 Biskra Road
Rancho Mirage, CA 92270
(760) 346-8206   Fax: (760) 340-5275
TDD: (760) 341-4084   E-mail: caped2000@aol.com
Web: www.caped.net/scholarships.html

Summary To provide financial assistance to undergraduate and graduate students in California who have a disability.

Eligibility This program is open to students at public and private colleges and universities in California who have a disability. Undergraduates must have completed at least 6 semester credits and have a GPA of 2.5 or higher. Graduate students must have completed at least 3 semester units and have a GPA of 3.0 or higher. Along with their application, they must submit a 1-page personal letter that demonstrates their writing skills, progress towards meeting their educational and vocational goals, management of their disability, and involvement in community activities. They must also submit a letter of recommendation from a faculty member, verification of disability, official transcripts, proof of current enrollment, and documentation of financial need.

Financial data The stipend is $1,000.
Duration 1 year.
Number awarded 1 each year.
Deadline September of each year.

[719]
WISCONSIN TALENT INCENTIVE PROGRAM (TIP) GRANTS

Wisconsin Higher Educational Aids Board
131 West Wilson Street, Suite 902
P.O. Box 7885
Madison, WI 53707-7885
(608) 266-1665   Fax: (608) 267-2808
E-mail: colettem1.brown@wi.gov
Web: heab.state.wi.us/programs.html

Summary To provide financial assistance for college to needy and educationally disadvantaged students in Wisconsin.

Eligibility This program is open to residents of Wisconsin entering a college or university in the state who meet the requirements of both financial need and educational disadvantage. Financial need qualifications include 1) family contribution (a dependent student whose expected parent contribution is $200 or less, an independent student with dependents whose academic year contribution is $200 or less, or an independent student with no dependents whose maximum contribution is $200 or less); 2)

Temporary Assistance to Needy Families (TANF) or Wisconsin Works (W2) benefits (a dependent student whose family is receiving TANF or W2 benefits or an independent student who is receiving TANF or W2 benefits); or 3) unemployment (a dependent student whose parents are ineligible for unemployment compensation and have no current income from employment, or an independent student and spouse, if married, who are ineligible for unemployment compensation and have no current income from employment). Educational disadvantage qualifications include students who are 1) minorities (African American, Native American, Hispanic, or southeast Asian); 2) enrolled in a special academic support program due to insufficient academic preparation; 3) a first-generation college student (neither parent graduated from a 4-year college or university); 4) disabled according to the Department of Workforce Development, the Division of Vocational Rehabilitation, or to a Wisconsin college or university that uses the Americans with Disabilities Act definition; 5) currently or formerly incarcerated in a correctional institution; or 6) from an environmental and academic background that deters the pursuit of educational plans. Students already in college are not eligible.

Financial data Stipends range up to $1,800 per year.

Duration 1 year; may be renewed up to 4 additional years, provided the recipient continues to be a Wisconsin resident enrolled at least half time in a degree or certificate program, makes satisfactory academic progress, demonstrates financial need, and remains enrolled continuously from semester to semester and from year to year. If recipients withdraw from school or cease to attend classes for any reason (other than medical necessity), they may not reapply.

Number awarded Varies each year.
Deadline Deadline not specified.

[720]
WSAJ PRESIDENTS' SCHOLARSHIP

Washington State Association for Justice
1511 State Avenue N.E.
Olympia, WA 98506-4552
(360) 786-9100   Fax: (360) 786-9103
E-mail: adrianne@wstlaoly.org
Web: www.wstla.org/AboutUs/Historical.aspx

Summary To provide financial assistance for college to Washington residents who have a disability or have been a victim of injury.

Eligibility This program is open to seniors at high schools in Washington who are planning to work on a bachelor's degree at an institution of higher education in the state. Applicants must be able to demonstrate 1) financial need: 2) a history of achievement despite having been a victim of injury or overcoming a disability, handicap, or similar challenge; 3) a record of serving others; and 4) a commitment to apply their education toward helping others.

Financial data Stipends average $2,000. Funds are paid directly to the recipient's chosen institution of higher learning to be used for tuition, room, board, and fees.

Duration 1 year.

Additional data This fund was established in 1991 when the sponsor's name was the Washington State Trial Lawyers Association.

Number awarded 1 or more each year.

Deadline March of each year.

[721]
YELLOW RIBBON SCHOLARSHIP

Tourism Cares
Attn: National Tour Association Scholarship Fund
275 Turnpike Street, Suite 307
Canton, MA 02021
(781) 821-5990   Fax: (781) 821-8949
E-mail: info@tourismcares.org
Web: www.tourismcares.org

Summary To provide financial assistance for college or graduate school to students with disabilities who are planning a career in the travel and tourism industry.

Eligibility This program is open to citizens and permanent residents of the United States and Canada who have a physical or sensory disability. Applicants must be entering or attending an accredited 2- or 4-year college or university in the United States or Canada. They must be working on or planning to work on an undergraduate or graduate degree in a field related to travel and tourism and have a GPA of 2.5 or higher. Along with their application, they must submit a 2-page essay on contributions they feel they might make in the travel, tourism, and hospitality industry. Financial need is not considered in the selection process.

Financial data The stipend is $5,000.

Duration 1 year.

Additional data This program was established in 1993.

Number awarded 1 each year.

Deadline March of each year.

Fellowship/Grants

[722]
ACADEMIC LIBRARY ASSOCIATION OF OHIO DIVERSITY SCHOLARSHIP

Academic Library Association of Ohio
c/o Ken Burhanna, Diversity Committee Chair
Kent State University, Instructional Services
P.O. Box 5190
Kent, OH 44242-0001
(330) 672-1660   E-mail: kburhann@kent.edu
Web: www.alaoweb.org

Summary To provide financial assistance to disabled and other residents of Ohio who are working on a master's degree in library science at a school in any state and will contribute to diversity in the profession.

Eligibility This program is open to residents of Ohio who are enrolled or entering an ALA-accredited program for a master's degree in library science, either on campus or via distance education. Applicants must be able to demonstrate how they will contribute to diversity in the profession, including (but not limited to) race or ethnicity, sexual orientation, life experience, physical ability, and a sense of commitment to those and other diversity issues. Along with their application, they must submit 1) a list of participation in honors society or professional organizations, awards, scholarships, prizes, honors, or class offices; 2) a description of their leadership skills as demonstrated through community, civic, organizational, or volunteer experiences; and 3) an essay on their understanding of and commitment to diversity in libraries, including how they, as a library school student and future professional, might address the issue.

Financial data The stipend is $1,500.

Duration 1 year.

Number awarded 1 each year.

Deadline March of each year.

[723]
AFRICAN AMERICAN STUDIES PROGRAM VISITING SCHOLARS

University of Houston
African American Studies Program
Attn: Visiting Scholars Program
629 Agnes Arnold Hall
Houston, TX 77204-3047
(713) 743-2811   Fax: (713) 743-2818
E-mail: jconyers@uh.edu
Web: www.class.uh.edu/aas

Summary To provide support to disabled and other junior scholars who are interested in conducting research on the African American community while affiliated with the University of Houston's African American Studies Program.

Eligibility Applications are sought from junior scholars in social sciences, humanities, or African American studies who completed their Ph.D. within the past 6 years. They must be interested in conducting research on the African American community while affiliated with the University of Houston's African American Studies Program and in assuming a tenured or tenure-track position there after their residency as a Visiting Scholar is completed. They must be available for consultation with students and professional colleagues, make at least 2 formal presentations based on their research project, and contribute generally to the intellectual discourse in the discipline of African Studies/Africology. Along with their application, they must submit a current curriculum vitae, a 2-page description of the proposed research, 3 letters of recommendation, and a syllabus of the undergraduate course to be taught. Minorities, women, veterans, and persons with disabilities are specifically encouraged to apply.

Financial data Visiting Scholars receive a salary appropriate to their rank.

Duration 1 academic year.

Additional data Visiting Scholars are assigned a research assistant, if needed, and are provided administrative support. Recipients must teach 1 class related to African American studies. They are required to be in residence at the university for the entire academic year and must make 2 presentations on their research. In addition, they must acknowledge the sponsor's support in any publication that results from their tenure at the university.

Number awarded At least 2 each year.

Deadline February of each year.

[724]
ALEXANDER GRALNICK RESEARCH INVESTIGATOR PRIZE

American Psychological Foundation
750 First Street, N.E.
Washington, DC 20002-4242
(202) 336-5843 Fax: (202) 336-5812
E-mail: foundation@apa.org
Web: www.apa.org/apf/gralnick.html

Summary To recognize and reward disabled and other psychologists conducting exceptional research on serious mental illness.

Eligibility This program is open to psychologists who have a doctoral degree and a record of significant research productivity (for at least 8 years) and are able to demonstrate evidence on continuing creativity in the area of research on serious mental illness (including, but not limited to, schizophrenia, bipolar disorder, and paranoia). Nominees must also have significant involvement in training and development of younger investigators. They must have an affiliation with an accredited college, university, or other treatment or research institution. The sponsor encourages nominations of individuals who represent diversity in race, ethnicity, gender, age, disability, and sexual orientation.

Financial data The award is $20,000.

Duration The award is presented biennially, in even-numbered years.

Additional data This award was first presented in 2002.

Number awarded 1 each even-numbered. year.

Deadline April of each even-numbered year.

[725]
AMERICAN ASSOCIATION ON HEALTH AND DISABILITY SCHOLARSHIPS

American Association on Health and Disability
Attn: Executive Director
110 North Washington Street, Suite 328-J
Rockville, MD 20850
(301) 545-6140, ext. 206 Fax: (301) 545-6144
E-mail: contact@aahd.us
Web: www.aahd.us

Summary To provide financial assistance to undergraduate and graduate students who have a disability, especially those studying a field related to health and disability.

Eligibility This program is open to high school graduates who have a documented disability and are enrolled in or accepted by an accredited U.S. 4-year university or graduate school on a full-time basis. Preference is given to students working on a degree in public health, disability

studies, health promotion, or other field related to health and disability. Along with their application, they must submit a 3-page personal statement that includes a personal history, educational and career goals, extracurricular activities, and reasons why they should be selected to receive this scholarship. U.S. citizenship or permanent resident status is required.

Financial data Stipends range up to $1,000.

Duration 1 year.

Additional data This program was established in 2009.

Number awarded 2 each year.

Deadline November of each year.

[726]
ANNETTE URSO RICKEL DISSERTATION AWARD FOR PUBLIC POLICY

American Psychological Foundation
750 First Street, N.E.
Washington, DC 20002-4242
(202) 336-5843 Fax: (202) 336-5812
E-mail: foundation@apa.org
Web: www.apa.org/apf/rickel.html

Summary To provide funding to disabled and other psychology doctoral students interested in conducting dissertation research related to public policy on services for children and families.

Eligibility This program is open to graduate students who are enrolled full time in a graduate program in psychology at an accredited college or university in the United States or Canada. Applicants must be interested in conducting dissertation research on public policy that has the potential to improve services for children and families facing psychological issues. Examples of eligible topics include, but are not limited to, issues with at-risk populations, prevention of child abuse, services for youth in the criminal justice system, effectiveness of school programs for children with psychological issues, using psychology in public policy to improve mathematics and science education, and promoting health parenting. The sponsor encourages applications from individuals who represent diversity in race, ethnicity, gender, age, disability, and sexual orientation.

Financial data The stipend is $1,000.

Duration 1 year.

Number awarded 1 each year.

Deadline October of each year.

[727]
APF/COGDOP GRADUATE RESEARCH SCHOLARSHIPS

American Psychological Foundation
750 First Street, N.E.
Washington, DC 20002-4242
(202) 336-5843 Fax: (202) 336-5812
E-mail: foundation@apa.org
Web: www.apa.org/apf-cogdop.html

Summary To provide funding for research to disabled and other graduate students in psychology.

Eligibility Each department of psychology that is a member in good standing of the Council of Graduate Departments of Psychology (COGDOP) may nominate up to 3 candidates for these scholarships. Nominations must include a completed application form, a letter of nomination from the department chair or director of graduate studies, a letter of recommendation from the nominee's graduate research adviser, a transcript of all graduate course work completed by the nominee, a curriculum vitae, and a brief outline of the nominee's thesis or dissertation research project. The sponsor encourages applications from individuals who represent diversity in race, ethnicity, gender, age, disability, and sexual orientation.

Financial data Awards range from $1,000 to $5,000 per year. A total of $20,000 is available for these scholarships each year.

Duration 1 year.

Additional data The highest rated nominee receives the Harry and Miriam Levinson Scholarship of $5,000. The second highest rated nominee receives the Ruth G. and Joseph D. Matarazzo Scholarship of $3,000. The third highest rated nominee receives the Clarence Rosecrans Scholarship of $2,000.

Number awarded 13 each year: 1 at $5,000, 1 at $3,000, 1 at $2,000, and 10 at $1,000.

Deadline June of each year.

[728]
ARCTIC RESEARCH OPPORTUNITIES

National Science Foundation
Attn: Office of Polar Programs
4201 Wilson Boulevard, Suite 755
Arlington, VA 22230
(703) 292-8029   Fax: (703) 292-9082
TDD: (800) 281-8749
Web: www.nsf.gov

Summary To provide funding for research related to the Arctic.

Eligibility This program is open to disabled and other investigators affiliated with U.S. universities, research institutions, or other organizations, including local or state governments. Applicants must be proposing to conduct research in the 4 program areas of Arctic science: 1) Arctic Natural Sciences, with areas of special interest in marine and terrestrial ecosystems, Arctic atmospheric and oceanic dynamics and climatology, Arctic geological and glaciological processes, and their connectivity to lower latitudes; 2) Arctic Social Sciences, including (but not limited to) anthropology, archaeology, economics, geography, linguistics, political science, psychology, science and technology studies, sociology, traditional knowledge, and related subjects; 3) Arctic System Science, for research focused on a system understanding of the Arctic, understanding the behavior of the Arctic system (past, present, and future), understanding the role of the Arctic as a component of the global system, and society as an integral part of the Arctic system; or 4) Arctic Observing Networks, for work related to a pan-Arctic, science-driven, observing system. The program encourages proposals from all citizens, including women and men, underrepresented minorities, and persons with disabilities.

Financial data The amounts of the awards depend on the nature of the proposal and the availability of funds.

Number awarded Approximately 40 each year. Recently, this program awarded approximately $16 million in grants.

Deadline October of each year.

[729]
ARKANSAS GOVERNOR'S COMMISSION ON PEOPLE WITH DISABILITIES SCHOLARSHIPS

Arkansas Governor's Commission on People with Disabilities
Attn: Scholarship Committee
525 West Capitol Avenue
P.O. Box 3781
Little Rock, AR 72203
(501) 296-1637   Fax: (501) 296-1883
TDD: (501) 296-1637
Web: www.arsinfo.org/default.aspx?id=31

Summary To provide financial assistance to Arkansas students with disabilities who are interested in attending college or graduate school in any state.

Eligibility This program is open to high school seniors, high school graduates, undergraduates, and graduate students who have a disability and are residents of Arkansas. Applicants must be attending or planning to attend a college or university in any state. Selection is based on a description of their disability (20 points), present and past school involvement (10 points), a brief statement on their career goals (15 points), community and volunteer activities (10 points), a brief essay on the positive or negative effects their disability has had on their life thus far (20 points), 3 letters of recommendation (10 points), and financial need (10 points).

Financial data The stipend varies, up to $1,000 per year.

Duration 1 year; recipients may reapply.

Number awarded Several each year.

Deadline February of each year.

[730]
ASHA FOUNDATION LESLIE LONDER FUND SCHOLARSHIP

American Speech-Language-Hearing Foundation
Attn: Program Assistant
2200 Research Boulevard
Rockville, MD 20850-3289
(301) 296-8703   Toll Free: (800) 498-2071, ext. 8703
Fax: (301) 571-0457   TDD: (800) 498-2071
E-mail: foundationprograms@asha.org
Web: www.ashfoundation.org

Summary To provide financial assistance to persons with disabilities who are interested in studying communication sciences or related programs in graduate school.

Eligibility This program is open to full-time graduate students who are enrolled in communication sciences and disorders programs, with preference given to students who have a disability. Applicants must submit an essay, up to 5 pages in length, on a topic that relates to the future of leadership in the discipline. They must also submit brief statements on the major classification that best describes their impairment and the limitations their disability has posed. Selection is based on academic promise and outstanding academic achievement.

Financial data The stipend ranges from $2,000 to $4,000. Funds must be used for educational support (e.g., tuition, books, school-related living expenses), not for personal or conference travel.

Duration 1 year.

Number awarded 1 each year.

Deadline June of each year.

[731]
ASTRONOMY AND ASTROPHYSICS POSTDOCTORAL FELLOWSHIPS

National Science Foundation
Directorate for Mathematical and Physical Sciences
Attn: Division of Astronomical Sciences
4201 Wilson Boulevard, Room 1045
Arlington, VA 22230
(703) 292-7456   Fax: (703) 292-9034
TDD: (800) 281-8749   E-mail: dlehr@nsf.gov
Web: www.nsf.gov

Summary To provide funding to disabled and other recent doctoral recipients in astronomy or astrophysics who are interested in pursuing a program of research and education.

Eligibility This program is open to U.S. citizens, nationals, and permanent residents who completed a Ph.D. in astronomy or astrophysics during the previous 5 years. Applicants must be interested in a program of research of an observational, instrumental, or theoretical nature, especially research that is particularly facilitated or enabled by new ground-based capability in radio, optical/IR, or solar astrophysics. Research may be conducted at a U.S. institution of higher education; a national center, facility, or institute funded by the National Science Foundation (NSF), such as the Kavli Institute for Theoretical Physics; a U.S. nonprofit organization with research and educational missions; and/or an international site operated by a U.S. organization eligible for NSF funding, such as Cerro Tololo InterAmerican Observatory. The proposal must include a coherent program of educational activities, such as teaching a course each year at the host institution or an academic institution with ties to the host institution, developing educational materials, or engaging in a significant program of outreach or general education. The program encourages applications from all citizens, including women and men, underrepresented minorities, and persons with disabilities.

Financial data Grants up to $83,000 per year are available, including stipends of $58,000 per year, a research allowance of $12,000 per year, an institutional allowance of $3,000 per year, and a benefits allowance of $10,000 per year, paid either to the fellow or the host institution in support of fringe benefits.

Duration Up to 3 years.

Number awarded 8 to 9 each year.

Deadline October of each year.

[732]
BEHAVIORAL SCIENCES POSTDOCTORAL FELLOWSHIPS IN EPILEPSY

Epilepsy Foundation
Attn: Research Department
8301 Professional Place
Landover, MD 20785-2237
(301) 459-3700   Toll Free: (800) EFA-1000
Fax: (301) 577-2684   TDD: (800) 332-2070
E-mail: grants@efa.org
Web: www.epilepsyfoundation.org/research/grants.cfm

Summary To provide funding to disabled and other postdoctorates in the behavioral sciences who wish to pursue research training in an area related to epilepsy.

Eligibility Applicants must have received their doctoral degree in a behavioral science field by the time the fellowship begins and desire additional postdoctoral research experience in epilepsy. Academic faculty holding the rank of instructor or above are not eligible, nor are graduate or medical students, medical residents, permanent government employees, or employees in private industry. Appropriate fields of study in the behavioral sciences include sociology, social work, anthropology, nursing, economics, and others relevant to epilepsy research and practice. Because these fellowships are designed as training opportunities, the quality of the training plans and environment are considered in the selection process. Other selection criteria include the scientific quality of the proposed research, a statement regarding the relevance of the research to epilepsy, the applicant's qualifications, the preceptor's qualifications, adequacy of the facility, and related epilepsy programs at the institution. Applications from women, members of minority groups, and people with disabilities are especially encouraged. U.S. citizenship is not required, but the research must be conducted in the United States.

Financial data Grants up to $40,000 per year are available.

Duration 1 year.

Number awarded Varies each year.

Deadline February of each year.

[733]
BENTON-MEIER NEUROPSYCHOLOGY SCHOLARSHIPS

American Psychological Foundation
750 First Street, N.E.
Washington, DC 20002-4242
(202) 336-5843   Fax: (202) 336-5812
E-mail: foundation@apa.org
Web: www.apa.org/apf/hecaen.html

Summary To provide financial assistance to disabled and other neuropsychology graduate students with financial need.

Eligibility This program is open to students working full time on a graduate degree in the area of neuropsychology. Applicants must submit statements documenting their scholarly or research accomplishments, their financial need for the award, and how the scholarship money will be used. The sponsor encourages applications from individuals who represent diversity in race, ethnicity, gender, age, disability, and sexual orientation.

Financial data The stipend is $2,500.

Duration 1 year.

Additional data This program replaces the Henry Hécaen Scholarship, first awarded in 1994, and the Manfred Meier Scholarship, first awarded in 1997.

Number awarded 2 each year.

Deadline May of each year.

[734]
BIUNNO SCHOLARSHIP FOR LAW STUDENTS WITH DISABILITIES

Essex County Bar Association
Attn: Committee on the Rights of Persons with
 Disabilities
Historic Courthouse, Room B-01
470 Dr. Martin Luther King, Jr. Boulevard
Newark, NJ 07102
(973) 622-6207   Fax: (973) 622-4341
E-mail: info@EssexBar.com
Web: www.EssexBar.com

Summary To provide financial assistance to students with disabilities from New Jersey who are interested in attending law school in any state.

Eligibility Applicants must be able to demonstrate a present and permanent physical or mental disability that substantially limits 1 or more of the major life activities (medical documentation is required); be residents of New Jersey, with preference given to Essex County residents; be attending or accepted at a law school in any state; and have earned a GPA of 3.0 or higher as an undergraduate student (if an incoming law student) or in law school. Priority is given to applicants who are planning a career in the field of advocacy for persons with disabilities. Intent may be demonstrated by completion of a course in disability law, work in a disability or disability-related clinic, or prior job experience in an advocacy field or with a public interest organization. Students who can demonstrate financial need receive priority.

Financial data Stipends range from $3,000 to $6,000. Funds are paid directly to the recipient's school or to a company providing equipment for the disabled student.

Duration 1 year.

Number awarded 1 or more each year.

Deadline May of each year.

[735]
BYRD FELLOWSHIP PROGRAM

Ohio State University
Byrd Polar Research Center
Attn: Fellowship Committee
Scott Hall Room 108
1090 Carmack Road
Columbus, OH 43210-1002
(614) 292-6531   Fax: (614) 292-4697
Web: bprc.osu.edu/byrdfellow

Summary To provide funding to disabled and other postdoctorates interested in conducting research on the Arctic or Antarctic areas at Ohio State University.

Eligibility This program is open to postdoctorates of superior academic background who are interested in conducting advanced research on either Arctic or Antarctic problems at the Byrd Polar Research Center at Ohio State University. Applicants must have received their doctorates within the past 5 years. Each application should include a statement of general research interest, a description of the specific research to be conducted during the fellowship, and a curriculum vitae. Women, minorities, Vietnam-era veterans, disabled veterans, and individuals with disabilities are particularly encouraged to apply.

Financial data The stipend is $40,000 per year; an allowance of $3,000 for research and travel is also provided.

Duration 18 months.

Additional data This program was established by a major gift from the Byrd Foundation in memory of Rear Admiral Richard Evelyn Byrd and Marie Ames Byrd, his wife. Except for field work or other research activities requiring absence from campus, fellows are expected to be in residence at the university for the duration of the program.

Deadline October of each year.

[736]
CAPED GENERAL EXCELLENCE SCHOLARSHIP

California Association for Postsecondary Education
 and Disability
Attn: Executive Assistant
71423 Biskra Road
Rancho Mirage, CA 92270
(760) 346-8206   Fax: (760) 340-5275
TDD: (760) 341-4084   E-mail: caped2000@aol.com
Web: www.caped.net/scholarships.html

Summary To provide financial assistance to undergraduate and graduate students in California who have a disability and can demonstrate academic achievement and involvement in community and campus activities.

Eligibility This program is open to students at public and private colleges and universities in California who have a disability. Undergraduates must have completed at least 6 semester credits and have a GPA of 2.5 or higher. Graduate students must have completed at least 3 semester units and have a GPA of 3.0 or higher. Applicants must submit a 1-page personal letter that demonstrates their writing skills, progress towards meeting their educational and vocational goals, management of their disability, and involvement in community activities. They must also submit a letter of recommendation from a faculty member, verification of disability, official transcripts, proof of current enrollment, and documentation of financial need. This award is presented to the applicant who demonstrates the highest level of academic achievement and involvement in community and campus life.

Financial data The stipend is $1,500.

Duration 1 year.

Number awarded 1 each year.

Deadline September of each year.

[737]
CENTURY SCHOLARSHIP

American Library Association
Attn: ASCLA
50 East Huron Street
Chicago, IL 60611-2795
(312) 280-4398   Toll Free: (800) 545-2433, ext. 4398
Fax: (312) 280-5273   TDD: (888) 814-7692
E-mail: ascla@ala.org
Web: www.ala.org

Summary To provide financial assistance to library science students with disabilities.

Eligibility This program is open to students with disabilities who have been admitted to an ALA-accredited library school to work on a master's or doctoral degree. Applicants must submit medical documentation of their disability or disabilities and a description of the services and/or accommodations they require for their studies. U.S. or Canadian citizenship is required. Selection is based on academic excellence, leadership, professional goals, and financial need.

Financial data The stipend is $2,500; funds are to be used for services or accommodations not provided by law or by the university.

Duration 1 year.

Additional data This scholarship was first offered in 2000.

Number awarded 1 or more each year.

Deadline February of each year.

[738]
DEPARTMENT OF HOMELAND SECURITY SMALL BUSINESS INNOVATION RESEARCH GRANTS

Department of Homeland Security
Homeland Security Advanced Research Projects
 Agency
Attn: SBIR Program Manager
Washington, DC 20528
(202) 254-6768   Toll Free: (800) 754-3043
Fax: (202) 254-7170
E-mail: elissa.sobolewski@dhs.gov
Web: www.dhs.gov

Summary To support small businesses (especially those owned by minorities, disabled veterans, and women)

that have the technological expertise to contribute to the research and development mission of the Department of Homeland Security (DHS).

Eligibility For the purposes of this program, a "small business" is defined as a firm that is organized for profit with a location in the United States; is in the legal form of an individual proprietorship, partnership, limited liability company, corporation, joint venture, association, trust, or cooperative; is at least 51% owned and controlled by 1 or more individuals who are citizens or permanent residents of the United States; and has (including its affiliates) fewer than 500 employees. The primary employment of the principal investigator must be with the firm at the time of award and during the conduct of the proposed project. Preference is given to women-owned small business concerns, service-disabled veteran small business concerns, veteran small business concerns, and socially and economically disadvantaged small business concerns. Women-owned small business concerns are those that are at least 51% owned by a woman or women who also control and operate them. Service-disabled veteran small business concerns are those that are at least 51% owned by a service-disabled veteran and controlled by such a veteran or (for veterans with permanent and severe disability) the spouse or permanent caregiver of such a veteran. Veteran small business concerns are those that are at least 51% owned by a veteran or veterans who also control and manage them. Socially and economically disadvantaged small business concerns are at least 51% owned by an Indian tribe, a Native Hawaiian organization, a Community Development Corporation, or 1 or more socially and economically disadvantaged individuals (African Americans, Hispanic Americans, Native Americans, Asian Pacific Americans, or subcontinent Asian Americans). The project must be performed in the United States. Currently, DHS has 7 research priorities: explosives; border and maritime security; command, control, and interoperability; human factors; infrastructure and geophysical; chemical and biological; and domestic nuclear detection. Selection is based on the soundness, technical merit, and innovation of the proposed approach and its incremental progress toward topic or subtopic solution; the qualifications of the proposed principal investigators, supporting staff, and consultants; and the potential for commercial application and the benefits expected to accrue from this commercialization.

Financial data Grants are offered in 2 phases. In phase 1, awards normally range up to $100,000 (or $150,000 for domestic nuclear detection); in phase 2, awards normally range up to $750,000 (or $1,000,000 for domestic nuclear detection).

Duration Phase 1 awards may extend up to 6 months; phase 2 awards may extend up to 2 years.

Number awarded Varies each year. Recently, 61 Phase 1 awards were granted.

Deadline February of each year.

[739]
DIRECTOR'S AWARD FOR DISTINGUISHED TEACHING SCHOLARS

National Science Foundation
Directorate for Education and Human Resources
Attn: Division of Undergraduate Education
4201 Wilson Boulevard, Room 835N
Arlington, VA 22230
(703) 292-4627   Fax: (703) 292-9015
TDD: (800) 281-8749   E-mail: npruitt@nsf.gov
Web: www.nsf.gov

Summary To recognize and reward, with funding for additional research, disabled and other scholars affiliated with institutions of higher education who have contributed to teaching of science, technology, engineering, and mathematics (STEM) at the K-12 and undergraduate level.

Eligibility This program is open to teaching-scholars affiliated with institutions of higher education who are nominated by their president, chief academic officer, or other independent researcher. Nominees should have integrated research and education and approached both education and research in a scholarly manner. They should have demonstrated leadership in their respective fields as well as innovativeness and effectiveness in facilitating K-12 and undergraduate student learning in STEM disciplines. Consideration is given to faculty who have a history of substantial impact on 1) research in a STEM discipline or on STEM educational research; or 2) the STEM education of K-16 students who have diverse interests and aspirations, including future K-12 teachers of science and mathematics, students who plan to pursue STEM careers, and those who need to understand science and mathematics in a society increasingly dependent on science and technology. Based on letters of nomination, selected scholars are invited to submit applications for support of their continuing efforts to integrate education and research. Nominations of all citizens, including women and men, underrepresented minorities, and persons with disabilities are especially encouraged.

Financial data The maximum grant is $300,000 for the life of the project.

Duration 4 years.

Number awarded Approximately 6 each year.

Deadline Letters of intent are due in September of each year; full applications must be submitted in October.

[740]
DIVERSITY IN PSYCHOLOGY AND LAW RESEARCH AWARD

American Psychological Association
Attn: Division 41 (American Psychology-Law Society)
c/o Kathy Gaskey, Administrative Officer
P.O. Box 11488
Southport, NC 28461-3936
(910) 933-4018   Fax: (910) 933-4018
E-mail: apls@ec.rr.com
Web: www.ap-ls.org/about/awards.html

Summary To provide funding to disabled and other student members of the American Psychology-Law Society

(AP-LS) who are interested in conducting a research project related to diversity.

Eligibility This program is open to undergraduate and graduate student members of AP-LS who are interested in conducting research on issues related to psychology, law, multiculturalism, and/or diversity (e.g., research pertaining to psycholegal issues on race, gender, culture, sexual orientation). Students from underrepresented groups are strongly encouraged to apply; underrepresented groups include, but are not limited to, racial/ethnic minorities; first-generation college students; lesbian, gay, bisexual, and transgendered students; and physically disabled students. Applicants must submit a project description that includes a statement of the research problem, significance of the project to diversity in psychology and law, specific objectives to be accomplished during the award period, an overview of relevant literature, methodology, and budget. Selection is based on the impact of the project on diversity and multiculturalism and the expected completion within the allocated time.

Financial data The grant is $1,000.

Duration The project must be completed within 1 year.

Number awarded 3 each year.

Deadline October of each year.

[741]
DIVERSITY PROGRAM IN NEUROSCIENCE PREDOCTORAL FELLOWSHIPS

American Psychological Association
Attn: Minority Fellowship Program
750 First Street, N.E.
Washington, DC 20002-4242
(202) 336-6127   Fax: (202) 336-6012
TDD: (202) 336-6123   E-mail: mfp@apa.org
Web: www.apa.org/mfp/prprogram.html

Summary To provide financial assistance to graduate students who are interested in completing a doctorate in neuroscience, especially those whose participation will increase diversity in the field.

Eligibility This program is open to all U.S. citizens and permanent residents who are working full time on a Ph.D. degree. Applicants must have career goals that are consistent with those of this program: 1) to increase ethnic and racial diversity among neuroscience researchers; 2) to increase the number of neuroscience researchers with disabilities; 3) to increased the number of neuroscience researchers from disadvantaged backgrounds; and 4) to increase the number of neuroscientists whose work is related to the federal initiative to eliminate health disparities. They may receive their training in a range of academic departments, provided their primary activity and career aspirations are research-oriented. Students identified as underrepresented in the neurosciences are especially encouraged to apply. Students working on a doctoral degree with a primarily clinical focus (e.g., M.D. or Psy.D) are not eligible. Selection is based on commitment to a research career in neuroscience, potential demonstrated through accomplishments and goals, fit between career goals and training environment selected, scholarship and grades, and letters of recommendation.

Financial data The stipend varies but is based on the amount established by the National Institutes of Health for predoctoral students; recently, that was $20,976 per year. The fellowship also provides travel funds to attend the annual meeting of the Society for Neuroscience and a program of summer training at the Marine Biological Laboratory in Woods Hole, Massachusetts.

Duration 1 year; may be renewed for up to 2 additional years.

Additional data The program was established in 1987. It is funded by 3 components of the U.S. National Institutes of Health: the National Institute of Mental Health (NIMH), the National Institute on Drug Abuse (NIDA), and the National Institute of Neurological Disorders and Stroke (NINDS). A similar program has been established to provide funding to nueroscience postdoctorates.

Number awarded Varies each year.

Deadline January of each year.

[742]
EASTER SEALS SOUTH CAROLINA EDUCATIONAL SCHOLARSHIPS

Easter Seals South Carolina
Attn: Scholarship Program
3020 Farrow Road
P.O. Box 5715
Columbia, SC 29250
(803) 429-8474   Fax: (803) 738-1934
E-mail: TAdger@sc.easterseals.com
Web: sc.easterseals.com

Summary To provide financial assistance for college or graduate school to South Carolina students who have a disability.

Eligibility This program is open to South Carolina residents and students attending a college or university in the state who have a significant and medically certified mobility impairment. Applicants must be enrolled or planning to enroll in an undergraduate or graduate program. They must be able to demonstrate financial need. Preference is given to students carrying at least 9 credit hours and making satisfactory academic progress toward graduation.

Financial data The maximum stipend is $1,000.

Duration 1 year; may be renewed.

Additional data This program was established in 1985.

Number awarded 1 or more each year.

Deadline June of each year.

[743]
EDWARD T. CONROY MEMORIAL SCHOLARSHIP PROGRAM

Maryland Higher Education Commission
Attn: Office of Student Financial Assistance
839 Bestgate Road, Suite 400
Annapolis, MD 21401-3013
(410) 260-4563   Toll Free: (800) 974-1024, ext. 4563
Fax: (410) 260-3200   TDD: (800) 735-2258
E-mail: lasplin@mhec.state.md.us
Web: www.mhec.state.md.us

Summary To provide financial assistance for college or graduate school in Maryland to children and spouses of victims of the September 11, 2001 terrorist attacks and to specified categories of veterans, public safety employees, and their children or spouses.

Eligibility This program is open to entering and continuing undergraduate and graduate students in the following categories: 1) children and surviving spouses of victims of the September 11, 2001 terrorist attacks who died in the World Trade Center in New York City, the Pentagon in Virginia, or United Airlines Flight 93 In Pennsylvania; 2) veterans who have, as a direct result of military service, a disability of 25% or greater and have exhausted or are no longer eligible for federal veterans' educational benefits; 3) children of armed forces members whose death or 100% disability was directly caused by military service; 4) POW/MIA veterans of the Vietnam Conflict and their children; 5) state or local public safety officers or volunteers who became 100% disabled in the line of duty; and 6) children and unremarried surviving spouses of state or local public safety employees or volunteers who died or became 100% disabled in the line of duty. The parent, spouse, veteran, POW, or public safety officer or volunteer must have been a resident of Maryland at the time of death or when declared disabled. Financial need is not considered.

Financial data The amount of the award is equal to tuition and fees at a Maryland postsecondary institution, to a maximum of $19,000 for children and spouses of the September 11 terrorist attacks or $9,000 for all other recipients.

Duration Up to 5 years of full-time study or 8 years of part-time study.

Additional data Recipients must enroll at a 2-year or 4-year Maryland college or university as a full-time or part-time degree-seeking undergraduate or graduate student or attend a private career school.

Number awarded Varies each year.

Deadline July of each year.

[744]
EPILEPSY FOUNDATION RESEARCH GRANTS PROGRAM

Epilepsy Foundation
Attn: Research Department
8301 Professional Place
Landover, MD 20785-2237
(301) 459-3700   Toll Free: (800) EFA-1000
Fax: (301) 577-2684   TDD: (800) 332-2070
E-mail: grants@efa.org
Web: www.epilepsyfoundation.org/research/grants.cfm

Summary To provide funding to disabled and other junior investigators interested in conducting research that will advance the understanding, treatment, and prevention of epilepsy.

Eligibility Applicants must have a doctoral degree and an academic appointment at the level of assistant professor in a university or medical school (or equivalent standing at a research institution or medical center). They must be interested in conducting basic or clinical research in the biological, behavioral, or social sciences related to the causes of epilepsy. Faculty with appointments at the level of associate professor or higher are not eligible. Applications from women, members of minority groups, and people with disabilities are especially encouraged. U.S. citizenship is not required, but the research must be conducted in the United States. Selection is based on the scientific quality of the research plan, the relevance of the proposed research to epilepsy, the applicant's qualifications, and the adequacy of the institution and facility where research will be conducted.

Financial data The maximum grant is $50,000 per year.
Duration Up to 2 years.
Additional data Support for this program is provided by many individuals, families, and corporations, especially the American Epilepsy Society, Abbott Laboratories, Ortho-McNeil Pharmaceutical, and Pfizer Inc.
Number awarded Varies each year.
Deadline August of each year.

[745]
ETHEL LOUISE ARMSTRONG FOUNDATION SCHOLARSHIPS

Ethel Louise Armstrong Foundation, Inc.
Attn: Chairman
1482 East Valley Road, Suite 504
Santa Barbara, CA 93108
Web: www.ela.org/scholarships/scholarships.html

Summary To provide financial assistance for graduate school to women with disabilities.

Eligibility This program is open to women with disabilities who are currently enrolled in or actively applying to a graduate program at an accredited college or university in the United States. Applicants must be a member of the American Association of People with Disabilities (AAPD). Along with their application, they must submit a 1,000-word essay on "How I will change the face of disability on the planet." Selection is based on academic and leadership merit.

Financial data The stipend ranges from $500 to $2,000 per year.
Duration 1 year.
Additional data The sponsoring foundation was founded in 1994 by Margaret Staton, who was disabled by a spinal cord tumor at 2 years of age. Recipients must agree to 1) network with the sponsor's board of directors and current and alumni scholarship recipients, and 2) update the sponsor on their progress in their academic and working career.
Number awarded Varies each year; recently, 14 of these scholarships were awarded.
Deadline May of each year.

[746]
FACILITATION AWARDS FOR SCIENTISTS AND ENGINEERS WITH DISABILITIES

National Science Foundation
Office of Integrative Activities
Attn: Coordinator, Facilitation Awards for Scientists and Engineers with Disabilities
4201 Wilson Boulevard, Room 815
Arlington, VA 22230
(703) 292-4684   TDD: (800) 281-8749
Web: www.nsf.gov

Summary To provide supplemental financing to individuals with disabilities who wish to prepare for a career in science and engineering and who are working on projects supported by the National Science Foundation (NSF).

Eligibility This program is open to individuals with disabilities who are principal investigators, other senior professionals, or graduate and undergraduate students participating in a specific project supported by the foundation. Requests for special equipment or assistance necessary to enable an individual with a disability to participate in a specific NSF-supported project may be included in the original proposal submitted to a NSF program or submitted as a separate request for supplemental funding for an existing NSF grant.

Financial data Funds may be requested to purchase special equipment, modify equipment, or provide services required specifically for the work to be undertaken. No maximum amount has been set for requests, but it is expected that the cost (including equipment adaptation and installation) will not be a major proportion of the total proposed budget for the project.

Additional data Examples of specific equipment for which funds may be requested include prosthetic devices to manipulate a particular apparatus; equipment to convert sound to visual signals, or vice versa, for a particular experiment; access to a special site or to a mode of transportation; a reader or interpreter with special technical competence related to the project; or other special-purpose equipment or assistance needed to conduct a particular project. Items that compensate in a general way for the disabling condition are not eligible; examples include standard wheelchairs, general prosthetics, hearing aids, TTY/TDD devices, general readers for the blind, or ramps, elevators, or other structural modifications of research facilities.

Number awarded   Varies each year.

Deadline   Applications may be submitted at any time.

[747]
FACULTY EARLY CAREER DEVELOPMENT PROGRAM

National Science Foundation
Directorate for Education and Human Resources
Senior Staff Associate for Cross Directorate Programs
4201 Wilson Boulevard, Room 805
Arlington, VA 22230
(703) 292-8600   TDD: (800) 281-8749
Web: www.nsf.gov

Summary   To provide funding to disabled and other outstanding new faculty in science and engineering fields of interest to the National Science Foundation (NSF) who intend to develop academic careers involving both research and education.

Eligibility   This program, identified as the CAREER program, is open to faculty members who meet all of the following requirements: 1) be employed in a tenure-track (or equivalent) position at an institution in the United States, its territories or possessions, or the Commonwealth of Puerto Rico that awards degrees in a field supported by NSF or that is a nonprofit, non-degree granting organization such as a museum, observatory, or research laboratory; 2) have a doctoral degree in a field of science or engineering supported by NSF: 3) not have competed more than 3 times in this program; 4) be untenured; and 5) not be a current or former recipient of a Presidential Early Career Award for Scientists and Engineers (PECASE) or CAREER award. Applicants are not required to be U.S. citizens or permanent residents. They must submit a career development plan that indicates a description of the proposed research project, including preliminary supporting data if appropriate, specific objectives, methods, and procedures to be used, and expected significance of the results; a description of the proposed educational activities, including plans to evaluate their impact; a description of how the research and educational activities are integrated with each other; and results of prior NSF support, if applicable. Proposals from women, underrepresented minorities, and persons with disabilities are especially encouraged.

Financial data   The grant is at least $80,000 per year (or $100,000 per year for the Directorate of Biological Sciences), including indirect costs or overhead.

Duration   5 years.

Additional data   This program is operated by various disciplinary divisions within the NSF; for a list of the participating divisions and their telephone numbers, contact the sponsor. Outstanding recipients of these grants are nominated for the NSF component of the PECASE awards, which are awarded to 20 recipients of these grants as an honorary award.

Number awarded   Approximately 425 each year.

Deadline   July of each year.

[748]
FOUNDATION FOR SCIENCE AND DISABILITY GRADUATE STUDENT GRANT FUND

Foundation for Science and Disability, Inc.
c/o Richard Mankin
USDA-ARS-CMAVE
1700 S.W. 23rd Drive
Gainesville, FL 32608
(352) 374-5774   Fax: (352) 374-5804
E-mail: rmankin@nersp.nerdc.ufl.edu
Web: www.stemd.org

Summary   To provide supplemental grants to students with disabilities who are interested in working on a graduate degree in a science-related field.

Eligibility   This program is open to 1) college seniors who have a disability and have been accepted to a graduate or professional school in the sciences, and 2) graduate science students who have a disability. Applicants must be U.S. citizens interested in working on a degree in an area of engineering, mathematics, medicine, science, or technology. Along with their application, they must submit an essay (about 250 words) describing professional goals and objectives, as well as the specific purpose for which the grant would be used. Selection is based on financial need, sincerity of purpose, and scholarship and/or research ability.

Financial data   The grant is $1,000. Funds may be used for an assistive device or instrument, as financial support to work with a professor on an individual research project, or for some other special need.

Duration   The award is granted annually.

Additional data   The Foundation for Science and Disability, Inc. is an affiliate society of the American Association for the Advancement of Science.

Number awarded   Varies each year.

Deadline   November of each year.

[749]
FURNISS FOUNDATION/AOS GRADUATE FELLOWSHIP

American Orchid Society
16700 AOS Lane
Delray Beach, FL 33446-4351
(561) 404-2000   Fax: (561) 404-2045
E-mail: TheAOS@aos.org
Web: www.aos.org

Summary   To provide funding to disabled and other doctoral candidates who are conducting dissertation research related to orchids.

Eligibility   This program is open to graduate students whose doctoral dissertation relates to orchids within the disciplines of physiology, molecular biology, structure, systematics, cytology, ecology, and/or evolution. Applicants must submit an outline of their project, their college transcript, a letter of recommendation from their chair, and a 1-page statement on why their project should be considered and the impact it will have on the future of orchidology. Women, minorities, and persons with disabilities are especially encouraged to apply.

Financial data The grant is $9,000 per year. Funds are paid directly to the recipient's college or university, but indirect overhead is not allowed.

Duration Up to a maximum of 3 years.

Additional data This fellowship was first awarded in 1990.

Number awarded 1 each year.

Deadline January of each year.

[750]
GEOLOGICAL SOCIETY OF AMERICA GRADUATE STUDENT RESEARCH GRANTS

Geological Society of America
Attn: Program Officer-Grants, Awards and Recognition
3300 Penrose Place
P.O. Box 9140
Boulder, CO 80301-9140
(303) 357-1028   Toll Free: (800) 472-1988, ext. 1028
Fax: (303) 357-1070   E-mail: awards@geosociety.org
Web: www.geosociety.org/grants/gradgrants.htm

Summary To provide funding to disabled and other graduate student members of the Geological Society of America (GSA) interested in conducting research at universities in the United States, Canada, Mexico, or Central America.

Eligibility This program is open to GSA members working on a master's or doctoral degree at a university in the United States, Canada, Mexico, or Central America. Applicants must be interested in conducting geological research. Minorities, women, and persons with disabilities are strongly encouraged to apply. Selection is based on the scientific merits of the proposal, the capability of the investigator, and the reasonableness of the budget.

Financial data Grants can be used for the cost of travel, room and board in the field, services of a technician or field assistant, funding of chemical and isotope analyses, or other expenses directly related to the fulfillment of the research contract. Funds cannot be used for the purchase of ordinary field equipment, for maintenance of the families of the grantees and their assistants, as reimbursement for work already accomplished, for adviser participation, or for tuition costs. Recently, grants averaged $1,879.

Duration 1 year.

Additional data In addition to general grants, GSA awards a number of specialized grants: the Gretchen L. Blechschmidt Award for women (especially in the fields of biostratigraphy and/or paleoceanography); the John T. Dillon Alaska Research Award for earth science problems particular to Alaska; the Robert K. Fahnestock Memorial Award for the field of sediment transport or related aspects of fluvial geomorphology; the Lipman Research Award for volcanology and petrology; the Bruce L. "Biff" Reed Award for studies in the tectonic and magmatic evolution of Alaska; the Alexander Sisson Award for studies in Alaska and the Caribbean; the Harold T. Stearns Fellowship Award for work on the geology of the Pacific Islands and the circum-Pacific region; the Parke D. Snavely, Jr. Cascadia Research Fund Award for studies of the Pacific Northwest convergent margin; the Alexander and Geraldine

Wanek Fund Award for studies of coal and petroleum; the Charles A. and June R.P. Ross Research Fund Award for stratigraphy; and the John Montagne Fund Award for research in the field of quaternary geology or geomorphology. Furthermore, 9 of the 14 GSA divisions (geophysics, hydrogeology, sedimentary geology, structural geology and tectonics, archaeological geology, coal geology, planetary geology, quaternary geology and geomorphology, and engineering geology) also offer divisional grants. Some of those awards are named: the Allan V. Cox Award of the Geophysics Division, the Claude C. Albritton, Jr. Scholarship of the Archaeological Geology Division, the Antoinette Lierman Medlin Scholarships of the Coal Geology Division, the J. Hoover Mackin Research Grants and the Arthur D. Howard Research Grants of the Quaternary Geology and Geomorphology Division, and the Roy J. Shlemon Scholarship Awards of the Engineering Geology Division. In addition, 4 of the 6 geographic sections (south-central, north-central, southeastern, and northeastern) offer grants to graduate students at universities within their section.

Number awarded Varies each year; recently, the society awarded 302 grants worth more than $567,000 through this and all of its specialized programs.

Deadline January of each year.

[751]
GOOGLE LIME SCHOLARSHIPS FOR STUDENTS WITH DISABILITIES

Lime
590 Madison Avenue, 21st Floor
New York, NY 10022
(212) 521-4469   Fax: (212) 521-4099
E-mail: info@limeconnect.com
Web: www.limeconnect.com/google.html

Summary To provide financial assistance to students with disabilities working on a bachelor's or graduate degree in a computer-related field at a college or university in Canada or the United States.

Eligibility This program is open to students at colleges and universities in the United States or Canada who have a disability and are entering their junior or senior year of undergraduate study or are enrolled as graduate students. International students with disabilities enrolled at universities in the United States or Canada are also eligible. Applicants must be working full time on a degree in computer science, computer engineering, or a closely-related technical field. Along with their application, they must submit 2 essays of 400 to 600 words each on 1) their academic accomplishments in terms of the technical projects on which they have worked; and 2) the issue about which they are passionate, what they have done to fulfill that passion, or what they dream of doing to fulfill it. Financial need is not considered in the selection process.

Financial data The stipend is $10,000 for students at U.S. universities or $C5,000 for students at Canadian universities.

Duration 1 year.

Additional data This program is jointly sponsored by Google and Lime, an organization founded in 2006 to promote employment of people with disabilities.

Number awarded Varies each year.

Deadline May of each year.

[752]
HARRIETT G. JENKINS PREDOCTORAL FELLOWSHIP PROGRAM

United Negro College Fund Special Programs
  Corporation
2750 Prosperity Avenue, Suite 600
Fairfax, VA 22031
(703) 677-3400   Toll Free: (800) 530-6232
Fax: (703) 205-7645   E-mail: portal@uncfsp.org
Web: www.uncfsp.org

Summary To provide financial assistance to women, minorities, and people with disabilities working on a graduate degree in a field of interest to the National Aeronautics and Space Administration (NASA).

Eligibility This program is open to members of groups underrepresented in science, technology, engineering, and mathematics (STEM), including women, minorities, and people with disabilities. Applicants must be full-time graduate students in a program leading to a master's or doctoral degree in a NASA-related discipline (aeronautics, aerospace engineering, astronomy, atmospheric science, bioengineering, biology, chemistry, computer science, earth sciences, engineering, environmental sciences, life sciences, materials sciences, mathematics, meteorology, neuroscience, physics, or robotics). They must be U.S. citizens and have a GPA of 3.0 or higher. Doctoral students who have advanced to candidacy are ineligible.

Financial data The stipend is $22,000 per year for doctoral fellows or $16,000 for master's degree students. The tuition offset is at least $8,500. Fellows who are also selected for a mini research award at a NASA Center or the Jet Propulsion Laboratory receive an additional grant of $3,000 to $7,000.

Duration 3 years.

Additional data This program, established in 2001, is funded by NASA and administered by the United Negro College Fund Special Programs Corporation. Fellows may also compete for a mini research award to engage in a NASA research experience that is closely aligned with the research conducted at the fellow's institution. The participating NASA facilities are Ames Research Center (Moffett Field, California), Jet Propulsion Laboratory (Pasadena, California), Dryden Flight Research Center (Edwards, California), Johnson Space Center (Houston, Texas), Stennis Space Center (Stennis Space Center, Mississippi), Marshall Space Flight Center (Marshall Space Flight Center, Alabama), Glenn Research Center (Cleveland, Ohio), Kennedy Space Center (Kennedy Space Center, Florida), Langley Research Center (Hampton, Virginia), and Goddard Space Flight Center (Greenbelt, Maryland).

Number awarded Approximately 20 each year.

Deadline January of each year.

[753]
HIGH RISK RESEARCH IN ANTHROPOLOGY GRANTS

National Science Foundation
Social, Behavioral, and Economic Sciences
Attn: Division of Behavioral and Cognitive Sciences
4201 Wilson Boulevard, Room 995 N
Arlington, VA 22230
(703) 292-8759   Fax: (703) 292-9068
TDD: (800) 281-8749   E-mail: jyellen@nsf.gov
Web: www.nsf.gov

Summary To provide funding to disabled and other scholars interested in conducting high-risk research in anthropology.

Eligibility This program is open to scholars interested in conducting research projects in cultural anthropology, archaeology, or physical anthropology that might be considered too risky for normal review procedures. A project is considered risky if the data may not be obtainable in spite of all reasonable preparation on the researcher's part. Proposals for extremely urgent research where access to the data may not be available in the normal review schedule, even with all reasonable preparation by the researcher, are also appropriate for this program. Graduate students are not eligible. Applications are encouraged from all citizens, including women and men, underrepresented minorities, and persons with disabilities.

Financial data Grants up to $25,000, including indirect costs, are available.

Duration 1 year.

Number awarded Generally, 5 of these grants are awarded each year.

Deadline Applications may be submitted at any time.

[754]
INDIVIDUAL PREDOCTORAL DENTAL SCIENTIST FELLOWSHIPS

National Institute of Dental and Craniofacial Research
Attn: Research Training and Career Development
  Branch
6701 Democracy Boulevard, Room 690
Bethesda, MD 20892-4878
(301) 594-2765   Fax: (301) 402-7033
TDD: (301) 451-0088 E-mail: kevin.hardwick@nih.gov
Web: www.nidcr.nih.gov

Summary To provide financial assistance to disabled and other dental students who wish to participate in an integrated dental and graduate research training program that leads to both the D.D.S./D.M.D. and Ph.D. degrees.

Eligibility This program is open to U.S. citizens, nationals, and permanent residents who are enrolled in a formal program at an approved dental school that leads to a D.D.S. or D.M.D. degree; have been accepted in a Ph.D. program in dental, oral, and craniofacial health research from the basic, behavioral, and clinical perspectives; and have a confirmed mentor in that scientific field. Applicants may be in the third year of dental school, although preference is given to those in the first or second year. Individuals currently enrolled in a joint D.D.S./D.M.D.-Ph.D. program are eligible for consideration as trainees, but persons who obtained a Ph.D. prior to entering dental school and desire to pursue another research doctorate while in dental school are not eligible. Members of underrepresented ethnic and racial groups and individuals with disabilities are especially encouraged to apply.

Financial data   Stipends generally range from $40,000 to $50,000 per year.

Duration   Up to 5 years of support for predoctoral study or up to 3 years of support at the postdoctoral level.

Number awarded   Up to 5 each year.

Deadline   April, August, or December of each year.

[755]
INSTITUTE FOR SUPPLY MANAGEMENT SENIOR RESEARCH FELLOWSHIP PROGRAM

Institute for Supply Management
Attn: Senior Vice President
2055 East Centennial Circle
P.O. Box 22160
Tempe, AZ 85285-2160
(480) 752-6276, ext. 3029
Toll Free: (800) 888-6276, ext. 3029
Fax: (480) 752-7890   E-mail: jcavinato@ism.ws
Web: www.ism.ws

Summary   To provide funding to disabled and other emerging scholars who are interested in conducting research in purchasing and materials management.

Eligibility   This program is open to full-time faculty members at institutions anywhere in the world who wish to conduct research that can be applied to the advancement of purchasing and materials management. Applicants should normally be at the assistant or associate professor level. Assistant professors should have 3 or more years of post-degree experience. The area of study for applicants may be purchasing, business, management, logistics, economics, industrial engineering, or a related field. The program encourages applications from a diverse population, regardless of gender, race, creed, age, ethnic or national origin, sexual orientation, or disability.

Financial data   The grant is $5,000.

Duration   1 year; nonrenewable.

Additional data   The sponsoring organization was previously known as the National Association of Purchasing Management.

Number awarded   2 each year.

Deadline   January of each year.

[756]
JOE CLERES MEMORIAL SCHOLARSHIPS

New Outlook Pioneers
Attn: Scholarships
930 15th Street, 12th Floor
P.O. Box 13888
Denver, CO 80201-3888
(303) 571-1200   Toll Free: (800) 872-5995
Fax: (303) 572-0520   E-mail: d.sage@worldnet.att.net
Web: www.newoutlookpioneers.org

Summary   To provide financial assistance to students at all educational levels who are physically or mentally challenged.

Eligibility   This program is open to students with physical or mental disabilities who are enrolled or planning to enroll in high school, college, trade school, or graduate school. Applicants or their representatives must submit a 1-page essay describing how the student has met the challenge of his or her disability, including the severity of the disability. They may also include up to 1 page of supporting documentation, but photographs, audio or videotapes, display materials, films, or scrapbooks are not considered.

Financial data   Stipends range from $500 to $1,500. Funds are paid directly to the school for tuition support only.

Duration   1 year.

Additional data   This program was established in 1996 by Lucent Technologies as the New Outlook Scholarships for Students with Disabilities. The current name was adopted in 2005.

Number awarded   Approximately 20 each year.

Deadline   March of each year.

[757]
JOHN J. INGALLS MEMORIAL SCHOLARSHIP

United Cerebral Palsy of MetroBoston
Director of Development, Marketing and
   Communications
71 Arsenal Street
Watertown, MA 02472
(617) 926-5480, ext. 238   Fax: (617) 926-3059
E-mail: ucpboston@ucpboston.org
Web: www.ucp.org/ucp_local.cfm/85

Summary   To provide financial assistance to residents of Massachusetts who have a physical disability and are interested in attending college or graduate school in any state.

Eligibility   This program is open to Massachusetts residents who are high school seniors, undergraduates, or graduate students and diagnosed with a physical disability. Applicants must be enrolled or planning to enroll full time at an accredited college or university in any state. Along with their application, they must submit a 250-word essay about their disability, based on such topics as how they have overcome the challenge of their disability, what having a disability means to them, someone who has been helpful in their success, or an achievement of which they are proud. They must also submit a letter from their doctor confirming that they have a disability, 2 letters of recommendation, transcripts, and an acceptance letter from the college or university of their choice.

Financial data   The stipend is $5,000.

Duration   1 year.

Additional data   This program was established in 2004.

Number awarded   3 each year.

Deadline   April of each year.

[758]
MG EUGENE C. RENZI, USA (RET.)/MANTECH INTERNATIONAL CORPORATION TEACHER'S SCHOLARSHIP

Armed Forces Communications and Electronics
  Association
Attn: AFCEA Educational Foundation
4400 Fair Lakes Court
Fairfax, VA 22033-3899
(703) 631-6149   Toll Free: (800) 336-4583, ext. 6149
Fax: (703) 631-4693   E-mail: scholarship@afcea.org
Web: www.afcea.org

Summary   To provide financial assistance to undergraduate and graduate students (particularly disabled veterans) who are preparing for a career as a teacher of science and mathematics.

Eligibility   This program is open to full-time juniors, seniors, and graduate students at accredited colleges and universities in the United States. Applicants must be U.S. citizens preparing for a career as a teacher of science, mathematics, or information technology at a middle or secondary school. They must have a GPA of 3.0 or higher. In the selection process, first consideration is given to wounded or disabled veterans, then to honorably discharged veterans. Financial need is not considered.

Financial data   The stipend is $2,500.

Duration   1 year.

Additional data   This program was established in 2008 with support from ManTech International Corporation.

Number awarded   1 each year.

Deadline   May of each year.

[759]
MUSICIANS WITH SPECIAL NEEDS SCHOLARSHIP

Sigma Alpha Iota Philanthropies, Inc.
One Tunnel Road
Asheville, NC 28805
(828) 251-0606   Fax: (828) 251-0644
E-mail: nh@sai-national.org
Web: www.sigmaalphaiota.org

Summary   To provide financial assistance for college or graduate school to members of Sigma Alpha Iota (an organization of women musicians) who have a disability and are working on a degree in music.

Eligibility   This program is open to members of the organization who either 1) have a sensory or physical impairment and are enrolled in a graduate or undergraduate degree program in music, or 2) are preparing to become a music teacher or therapist for people with disabilities. Performance majors must submit a 15-minute DVD of their work; non-performance majors must submit evidence of work in their area of specialization, such as composition, musicology, or research.

Financial data   The stipend is $1,500.

Duration   1 year.

Number awarded   1 each year.

Deadline   March of each year.

[760]
NASA SPACE GRANT COLLEGE AND FELLOWSHIP PROGRAM

National Aeronautics and Space Administration
Attn: Office of Education
300 E Street, S.W.
Mail Suite 6M35
Washington, DC 20546-0001
(202) 358-1069   Fax: (202) 358-3048
E-mail: Diane.D.DeTroye@nasa.gov
Web: www.nasa.gov

Summary   To provide financial assistance to disabled and other undergraduate and graduate students interested in preparing for a career in a space-related field.

Eligibility   This program is open to undergraduate and graduate students at colleges and universities that participate in the National Space Grant program of the U.S. National Aeronautics and Space Administration (NASA) through their state consortium. Applicants must be interested in a program of study and/or research in a field of science, technology, engineering, or mathematics (STEM) related to space. A specific goal of the program is to increase preparation by members of underrepresented groups (minorities, women, and persons with disabilities) for STEM space-related careers. Financial need is not considered in the selection process.

Financial data   Each consortium establishes the terms of the fellowship program in its state.

Additional data   NASA established the Space Grant program in 1989. It operates through 52 consortia in each state, the District of Columbia, and Puerto Rico. Each consortium includes selected colleges and universities in that state as well as other affiliates from industry, museums, science centers, and state and local agencies.

Number awarded   Varies each year.

Deadline   Each consortium sets its own deadlines.

[761]
NATIONAL DEFENSE SCIENCE AND ENGINEERING GRADUATE FELLOWSHIP PROGRAM

American Society for Engineering Education
Attn: NDSEG Fellowship Program
1818 N Street, N.W., Suite 600
Washington, DC 20036-2479
(202) 331-3516   Fax: (202) 265-8504
E-mail: ndseg@asee.org
Web: ndseg.asee.org

Summary   To provide financial assistance to disabled and other doctoral students in areas of science and engineering that are of military importance.

Eligibility   This program is open to U.S. citizens and nationals entering or enrolled in the early stages of a doctoral program in aeronautical and astronautical engineering; biosciences, including toxicology; chemical engineering; chemistry; civil engineering; cognitive, neural, and behavioral sciences; computer and computational sciences; electrical engineering, geosciences, including terrain, water, and air; materials science and engineering;

mathematics; mechanical engineering; naval architecture and ocean engineering; oceanography; or physics, including optics. Applications are particularly encouraged from women, members of ethnic minority groups (American Indians, African Americans, Hispanics or Latinos, Native Hawaiians, Alaska Natives, Asians, and Pacific Islanders), and persons with disabilities. Selection is based on all available evidence of ability, including academic records, letters of recommendation, and GRE scores.

Financial data The annual stipend is $30,500 for the first year, $31,000 for the second year; and $31,500 for the third year; the program also pays the recipient's institution full tuition and required fees (not to include room and board). Medical insurance is covered up to $1,000 per year. An additional allowance may be considered for a student with a disability.

Duration 3 years, as long as satisfactory academic progress is maintained.

Additional data This program is sponsored by the Army Research Office, the Air Force Office of Scientific Research, and the Office of Naval Research. Recipients do not incur any military or other service obligation. They must attend school on a full-time basis.

Number awarded Approximately 200 each year.

Deadline January of each year.

[762]
NAVAL RESEARCH LABORATORY BROAD AGENCY ANNOUNCEMENT

Naval Research Laboratory
Attn: Contracting Division
4555 Overlook Avenue, S.W.
Washington, DC 20375-5320
(202) 767-5227　　　　　Fax: (202) 767-0494
Web: heron.nrl.navy.mil/contracts/home.htm

Summary To provide funding to investigators interested in conducting scientific research of interest to the U.S. Navy.

Eligibility This program is open to investigators qualified to perform research in designated scientific and technical areas. Topics cover a wide range of technical and scientific areas; recent programs included radar technology, information technology, optical sciences, tactical electronic warfare, materials science and component technology, chemistry, computational physics and fluid dynamics, plasma physics, electronics science and technology, biomolecular science and engineering, ocean and atmospheric science and technology, acoustics, remote sensing, oceanography, marine geosciences, marine meteorology, and space science. Proposals may be submitted by any non-governmental entity, including commercial firms, institutions of higher education with degree-granting programs in science or engineering, or by consortia led by such concerns. The Naval Research Laboratory (NRL) encourages participation by small businesses, small disadvantaged business concerns, women-owned small businesses, veteran-owned small businesses, service-disabled veteran-owned small businesses, HUBZone small businesses, Historically Black Colleges and Universities,

and Minority Institutions. Selection is based on the degree to which new and creative solutions to technical issues important to NRL programs are proposed and the feasibility of the proposed approach and technical objectives; the offeror's ability to implement the proposed approach; the degree to which technical data and/or computer software developed under the proposed contract are to be delivered to the NRL with rights compatible with NRL research and development objectives; and proposed cost and cost realism.

Financial data The typical range of funding is from $100,000 to $2,000,000.

Duration 1 year.

Additional data The Naval Research Laboratory conducts most of its research in its own facilities in Washington, D.C., Stennis Space Center, Mississippi, and Monterey, California, but it also funds some related research.

Number awarded Varies each year.

Deadline Each program establishes its own application deadline; for a complete list of all the programs, including their deadlines, contact the NRL.

[763]
NEW HAMPSHIRE CHARITABLE FOUNDATION STATEWIDE STUDENT AID PROGRAM

New Hampshire Charitable Foundation
37 Pleasant Street
Concord, NH 03301-4005
(603) 225-6641　　　　　Toll Free: (800) 464-6641
Fax: (603) 225-1700　　　　E-mail: info@nhcf.org
Web: www.nhcf.org/page16960.cfm

Summary To provide scholarships or loans for undergraduate or graduate study in any state to New Hampshire residents.

Eligibility This program is open to New Hampshire residents who are graduating high school seniors planning to enter a 4-year college or university, undergraduate students between 17 and 23 years of age working on a 4-year degree, or graduate students of any age. Applicants must be enrolled on at least a half-time basis at a school in New Hampshire or another state. Selection is based on financial need, academic merit, community service, school activities, and work experience. Priority is given to students with the fewest financial resources.

Financial data Awards range from $500 to $3,500 and average $1,800. Most are made in the form of grants (recently, 82% of all awards) or no-interest or low-interest loans.

Duration 1 year; approximately one third of the awards are renewable.

Additional data Through this program, students submit a single application for more than 50 different scholarship and loan funds. Many of the funds have additional requirements, including field of study; residency in region, county, city, or town; graduation from designated high schools; and special attributes (e.g., of Belgian descent, employee of designated firms, customer of Granite State Telephone Company, disabled, suffering from a life-threatening or serious chronic illness, of Lithuanian descent, dependent of a New Hampshire police officer, dependent of a New Hampshire Episcopal minister, of Polish descent, former Sea Cadet or Naval Junior ROTC, or employed in the tourism industry). The Citizens' Scholarship Foundation of America reviews all applications; recipients are selected by the New Hampshire Charitable Foundation. A $20 application fee is required.

Number awarded Varies each year; approximately $700,000 is awarded annually.

Deadline April of each year.

[764]
NIA AGING RESEARCH DISSERTATION AWARDS TO INCREASE DIVERSITY

National Institute on Aging
Attn: Office of Extramural Affairs
7201 Wisconsin Avenue, Suite 2C-218
Bethesda, MD 20814
(301) 402-7713　　　　　Fax: (301) 402-2945
TDD: (301) 451-0088
E-mail: michael-david.kerns@nih.hhs.gov
Web: www.nia.nih.gov

Summary To provide financial assistance to disabled and other underrepresented doctoral candidates who wish to conduct research on aging.

Eligibility This program is open to doctoral candidates conducting research on a dissertation with an aging-related focus, including the 4 extramural programs within the National Institute on Aging (NIA): the biology of aging program, the behavioral and social research on aging program, the neuroscience and neuropsychology of aging program, and the geriatrics and clinical gerontology program. Applicants must be 1) members of an ethnic or racial group underrepresented in biomedical or behavioral research; 2) individuals with disabilities; or 3) individuals from socially, culturally, economically, or educationally disadvantaged backgrounds that have inhibited their ability to prepare for a career in health-related research. They must be U.S. citizens, nationals, or permanent residents.

Financial data Grants provide $21,180 per year for stipend and up to $15,000 for additional expenses. No funds may be used to pay tuition or fees associated with completion of doctoral studies. The institution may receive up to 8% of direct costs as facilities and administrative costs per year.

Duration Up to 2 years.

Number awarded Up to 5 each year.

Deadline Letters of intent must be submitted by February, June, or October of each year.

[765]
NORMAN'S ORCHIDS MASTERS SCHOLARSHIP

American Orchid Society
16700 AOS Lane
Delray Beach, FL 33446-4351
(561) 404-2000　　　　　Fax: (561) 404-2045
E-mail: TheAOS@aos.org
Web: www.aos.org

Summary To provide funding for research to disabled and other students working on a master's degree in a field related to orchids.

Eligibility This program is open to students working on a master's degree at an accredited institution. Applicants must have a thesis project that deals with an aspect of orchid education, applied science, or orchid biology in the disciplines of physiology, molecular biology, structure, systematics, cytology, ecology, or evolution. They must submit a current curriculum vitae, transcripts of all college course work, a synopsis of the proposed project or research, a 1-page statement of the value of their project and importance to the future of orchid education or orchidology, and a letter of recommendation from their chairperson. Women, minorities, and persons with disabilities are especially encouraged to apply.

Financial data The grant is $5,000 per year. Funds are paid through the recipient's college or university, but institutional overhead is not allowed.

Duration 2 years.

Additional data This program, established in 2005, is supported by Norman's Orchids of Montclair, California.

Number awarded 1 each year.

Deadline September each year.

[766]
PAUL B. BEESON CAREER DEVELOPMENT AWARDS IN AGING RESEARCH PROGRAM

American Federation for Aging Research
Attn: Executive Director
55 West 39th Street, 16th Floor
New York, NY 10018
(212) 703-9977　　　　　Toll Free: (888) 582-2327
Fax: (212) 997-0330　　　　　E-mail: grants@afar.org
Web: afar.org/beeson.html

Summary To provide funding for additional training to disabled and other physicians interested in conducting aging research.

Eligibility Applicants must have a clinical doctoral degree (e.g., M.D., D.O., D.D.S) or equivalent, a combined M.D. and Ph.D. degree, or a Ph.D. in a clinical field (such as clinical psychology, nursing, or physical therapy). They must be interested in a mentored program of medical, academic, and scientific training relative to caring for older people, to be conducted at a domestic public or private institution, such as a university, college, hospital, or laboratory. The sponsoring institution must have a well-established research and clinical career development program, have faculty experienced in research on aging and geriatrics to serve as mentors, and be able to demonstrate a commitment to the applicant's development and emergence as a productive, independent investigator. U.S. citizenship, national status, or permanent resident status is required. Members of underrepresented racial and ethnic groups and individuals with disabilities are especially encouraged to apply for programs of the National Institutes of Health (NIH).

Financial data The maximum grant is $200,000 per year, or $600,000 for 3 years, $700,000 for 4 years, or $800,000 for 5 years. Salaries are paid according to the established structure at the host institution. Facilities and administrative costs are reimbursed at 8% of modified total direct costs.

Duration 3 to 5 years.

Additional data The program is sponsored by the John A. Hartford Foundation, The Atlantic Philanthropies, the Starr Foundation, the National Institutes of Health (NIH) Office of Dietary Supplements, and an anonymous donor. The program is administered by the NIH's National Institute on Aging, Office of Extramural Affairs, 7201 Wisconsin Avenue, Room 2C218, Bethesda, MD 20892-9205, (301) 496-9322, Fax: (301) 402-2945, E-mail: BarrR@mail.nih.gov. Grantees must devote at least 75% of their full-time professional effort to the goals of this program.

Number awarded 8 to 12 each year.

Deadline Letters of intent must be submitted by the end of September of each year. Complete applications are due in early November.

[767]
POSTDOCTORAL FELLOWSHIPS IN POLAR REGIONS RESEARCH

National Science Foundation
Attn: Office of Polar Programs
4201 Wilson Boulevard, Suite 755
Arlington, VA 22230
(703) 292-7434   Fax: (703) 292-9079
TDD: (800) 281-8749
Web: www.nsf.gov

Summary To provide funding to disabled and other recent postdoctorates interested in a program of research training related to the polar regions.

Eligibility This program is open to U.S. citizens and permanent residents in appropriate scientific fields who either completed a doctoral degree within the previous 4 years or will complete the degree within 1 year of the proposal deadline. Applicants may be proposing a fellowship, for which they must identify a sponsoring scientist and a U.S. host organization that have agreed to provide a program of research training for fellows, or a travel grant, for travel and per diem expenses to meet prospective sponsoring scientists in their host organizations before submitting a fellowship proposal. The host organization may be a college or university, government or national laboratory or facility, nonprofit institute, museum, or for-profit organization. The proposed or prospective research training should relate to an aspect of scientific study of the Antarctic or Arctic. The program encourages proposals from all citizens, including

women and men, underrepresented minorities, and persons with disabilities.

Financial data The maximum fellowship is $75,000 per year (including $50,000 as a stipend for the fellow, an annual research allowance of up to $11,000, an annual institutional allowance of $5,000, and an annual health insurance allowance of up to $3,600 for a single fellow, up to $6,000 for a fellow with 1 dependent, or up to $9,000 for a fellow with 2 or more dependents). The maximum travel grant is $3,000 for visits to 1 or 2 prospective host organizations. Indirect costs are not allowed for either fellowships or travel grants.

Duration Fellowships are typically 1 to 2 years long; 3-year fellowships may be justified for research and training plans that include field research.

Number awarded 5 fellowships and up to 10 travel grants may be awarded each year. Recently, this program awarded approximately $1,000,000 in fellowships and travel grants.

Deadline Applications for fellowships must be submitted by January or August of each year; applications for travel grants may be submitted at any time.

[768]
POSTDOCTORAL RESEARCH FELLOWSHIPS IN EPILEPSY

Epilepsy Foundation
Attn: Research Department
8301 Professional Place
Landover, MD 20785-2237
(301) 459-3700   Toll Free: (800) EFA-1000
Fax: (301) 577-2684   TDD: (800) 332-2070
E-mail: grants@efa.org
Web: www.epilepsyfoundation.org/research/grants.cfm

Summary To provide funding for a program of postdoctoral training to disabled and other academic physicians and scientists committed to epilepsy research.

Eligibility Applicants must have a doctoral degree (M.D., Ph.D., or equivalent) and be a resident or postdoctoral fellow at a university, medical school, research institution, or medical center. They must be interested in participating in a training experience and research project that has potential significance for understanding the causes, treatment, or consequences of epilepsy. The program is geared toward applicants who will be trained in research in epilepsy rather than those who use epilepsy as a tool for research in other fields. Equal consideration is given to applicants interested in acquiring experience either in basic laboratory research or in the conduct of human clinical studies. Academic faculty holding the rank of instructor or higher are not eligible, nor are graduate or medical students, medical residents, permanent government employees, or employees of private industry. Applications from women, members of minority groups, and people with disabilities are especially encouraged. Selection is based on scientific quality of the proposed research, a statement regarding its relevance to epilepsy, the applicant's qualifications, the preceptor's qualifications, and the adequacy of facility and related epilepsy programs at the institution.

Financial data The grant is $45,000. No indirect costs are covered.

Duration 1 year.

Additional data Support for this program is provided by many individuals, families, and corporations, especially the American Epilepsy Society, Abbott Laboratories, Ortho-McNeil Pharmaceutical, and Pfizer Inc. The fellowship must be carried out at a facility in the United States where there is an ongoing epilepsy research program.

Number awarded Varies each year.

Deadline August of each year.

[769]
POWERING EDUCATION SCHOLARSHIPS

Alpha One
127 Main Street
South Portland, ME 04106
(207) 767-2189   Toll Free: (800) 640-7200
Fax: (207) 799-8346   TDD: (207) 767-5387
E-mail: info@mpowerloans.org
Web: www.alphaonenow.com/info.php?id–131#finance

Summary To provide financial assistance to undergraduate and graduate students in Maine who have disabilities.

Eligibility This program is open to high school seniors, undergraduates, and graduate students at schools in Maine. Applicants must have a disability. They must have a "B" average or equivalent GPA. Along with their application, they must submit a personal essay of 1 to 2 pages on a topic of their choice, a letter of recommendation, and current transcripts.

Financial data The stipend is $2,000. Funds are paid directly to the recipient's institution after completion of the first semester, provided the student earns a GPA of 2.5 or higher.

Duration 1 year.

Number awarded 3 each year.

Deadline March of each year.

[770]
PREDOCTORAL RESEARCH TRAINING FELLOWSHIPS IN EPILEPSY

Epilepsy Foundation
Attn: Research Department
8301 Professional Place
Landover, MD 20785-2237
(301) 459-3700   Toll Free: (800) EFA-1000
Fax: (301) 577-2684   TDD: (800) 332-2070
E-mail: grants@efa.org
Web: www.epilepsyfoundation.org/research/grants.cfm

Summary To provide funding to disabled and other doctoral candidates in designated fields for dissertation research on a topic related to epilepsy.

Eligibility This program is open to full-time graduate students working on a Ph.D. in biochemistry, genetics, neuroscience, nursing, pharmacology, pharmacy, physiology, or psychology. Applicants must be conducting dissertation research on a topic relevant to epilepsy under the guidance of a mentor with expertise in the area of epilepsy investigation. Applications from women, members of

minority groups, and people with disabilities are especially encouraged. Selection is based on the relevance of the proposed work to epilepsy, the applicant's qualifications, the mentor's qualifications, the scientific quality of the proposed dissertation research, the quality of the training environment for research related to epilepsy, and the adequacy of the facility.

Financial data The grant is $20,000, consisting of $19,000 for a stipend and $1,000 to support travel to attend the annual meeting of the American Epilepsy Society.

Duration 1 year.

Additional data Support for this program, which began in 1998, is provided by many individuals, families, and corporations, especially the American Epilepsy Society, Abbott Laboratories, Ortho-McNeil Pharmaceutical, and Pfizer Inc.

Number awarded Varies each year.

Deadline August of each year.

[771]
RESEARCH FELLOWSHIPS OF THE NATIONAL INSTITUTE ON DISABILITY AND REHABILITATION RESEARCH

Department of Education
Office of Special Education and Rehabilitative
  Services
Attn: National Institute on Disability and Rehabilitation
  Research
400 Maryland Avenue, S.W., Room 6030, PCP
Washington, DC 20202-2700
(202) 245-7462   Fax: (202) 245-7323
TDD: (202) 205-4475   E-mail: donna.nangle@ed.gov
Web: www.ed.gov/programs/resfel/index.html

Summary To provide funding to disabled and other graduate students and experienced scholars interested in conducting research related to disabilities and rehabilitation.

Eligibility This program is open to graduate students and experienced researchers, including individuals with disabilities. Distinguished fellowships are available to individuals who have a doctorate or comparable academic status and have 7 or more years of experience relevant to rehabilitation research. Merit fellowships are open to persons who have either advanced professional training or experience in independent study in an area that is directly related to disability and rehabilitation. Selection is based on the quality and level of formal education, previous work experience, and recommendations of present or former supervisors or colleagues that include an indication of the applicant's ability to work creatively in scientific research; the quality of a research proposal; the importance of the problem to be investigated to the mission of the National Institute on Disability and Rehabilitation Research; the research hypothesis or related objectives and the methodology and design to be followed; assurance of the availability of any necessary data resources, equipment, or institutional support, including technical consultation and support where appropriate, required to carry out the proposed activity.

Financial data Distinguished fellowships are $75,000 per year; merit fellowships are $65,000 per year.

Duration 1 year.

Additional data This program was formerly designated the Mary Switzer Research Fellowships.

Number awarded Varies each year; recently, 7 of these fellowships were awarded.

Deadline September of each year.

[772]
ROBERT L. FANTZ MEMORIAL AWARD

American Psychological Foundation
750 First Street, N.E.
Washington, DC 20002-4242
(202) 336-5843   Fax: (202) 336-5812
E-mail: foundation@apa.org
Web: www.apa.org/apf/fantz.html

Summary To provide funding to disabled and other promising young investigators in psychology.

Eligibility This program is open to young investigators in psychology or related disciplines. Candidates must show 1) evidence of basic scientific research or scholarly writing in perceptual-cognitive development and the development of selection attention; and 2) research and writing on the development of individuality, creativity, and free-choice of behavior. The sponsor encourages applications from individuals who represent diversity in race, ethnicity, gender, age, disability, and sexual orientation.

Financial data The award is $2,000. Funds are paid directly to the recipient's institution for equipment purchases, travel, computer resources, or other expenses related to the work recognized by the award.

Duration The award is presented annually.

Additional data This award was first presented in 1992.

Number awarded 1 each year.

Deadline Deadline not specified.

[773]
RUTH L. KIRSCHSTEIN NATIONAL RESEARCH SERVICE AWARDS FOR INDIVIDUAL PREDOCTORAL FELLOWSHIPS TO PROMOTE DIVERSITY IN HEALTH-RELATED RESEARCH

National Institutes of Health
Office of Extramural Research
Attn: Grants Information
6705 Rockledge Drive, Suite 4090
Bethesda, MD 20892-7983
(301) 435-0714   Fax: (301) 480-0525
TDD: (301) 451-5936   E-mail: GrantsInfo@nih.gov
Web: grants.nih.gov

Summary To provide financial assistance to disabled and other underrepresented students who are interested in working on a doctoral degree and preparing for a career in biomedical and behavioral research.

Eligibility This program is open to students enrolled or accepted for enrollment in a Ph.D. or equivalent research

degree program; a formally combined M.D./Ph.D. program; or other combined professional doctoral/research Ph.D. program in the biomedical, behavioral, health, or clinical sciences. Students in health professional degree programs (e.g., M.D., D.O., D.D.S., D.V.M.) are not eligible. Applicants must be 1) members of an ethnic or racial group underrepresented in biomedical or behavioral research; 2) individuals with disabilities; or 3) individuals from socially, culturally, economically, or educationally disadvantaged backgrounds that have inhibited their ability to prepare for a career in health-related research. They must be U.S. citizens, nationals, or permanent residents.

Financial data The fellowship provides an annual stipend of $21,180, a tuition and fee allowance (60% of costs up to $16,000 or 60% of costs up to $21,000 for dual degrees), and an institutional allowance of $4,200 ($3,100 at for-profit and federal institutions) for travel to scientific meetings, health insurance, and laboratory and other training expenses.

Duration Up to 5 years.

Additional data These fellowships are offered by most components of the National Institutes of Health (NIH). Write for a list of names and telephone numbers of responsible officers at each component.

Number awarded Varies each year.

Deadline April, August, or December of each year.

[774]
RUTH L. KIRSCHSTEIN NATIONAL RESEARCH SERVICE AWARDS FOR INDIVIDUAL SENIOR FELLOWS

National Institutes of Health
Office of Extramural Research
Attn: Grants Information
6705 Rockledge Drive, Suite 4090
Bethesda, MD 20892-7983
(301) 435-0714   Fax: (301) 480-0525
TDD: (301) 451-5936   E-mail: GrantsInfo@nih.gov
Web: grants.nih.gov/grants/guide/index.html

Summary To provide funding for mentored research training to disabled and other experienced scientists who wish to make major changes in the direction of their research careers.

Eligibility This program is open to U.S. citizens, nationals, and permanent residents who have a doctoral degree and at least 7 subsequent years of relevant research or professional experience. Applications may be submitted on behalf of the candidates by a sponsoring institution, which may be a domestic or foreign, for-profit or nonprofit, public or private institution (such as a university, college, hospital, laboratory, agency or laboratory of the federal government, or intramural laboratory of the National Institutes of Health). Individuals requesting foreign-site training must justify the particular suitability of the foreign site, based on the nature of the facilities and/or training opportunity, rather than a domestic institution. In cases where there are clear scientific advantages, foreign training will be supported. Candidates must have received a Ph.D., M.D., D.O., D.C., D.D.S., D.V.M., O.D., D.P.M., Sc.D.,

Eng.D., Dr.P.H., D.N.Sc., N.D., Pharm.D., D.S.W., Psy.D., or equivalent degree from an accredited domestic or foreign institution. Members of diverse racial and ethnic groups, individuals with disabilities, and individuals from disadvantaged backgrounds are especially encouraged to apply.

Financial data The award provides an annual stipend based on the number of years of postdoctoral experience, ranging from $37,368 for less than 1 year to $51,552 for 7 or more years. For fellows sponsored by domestic nonfederal institutions, the stipend is paid through the sponsoring institution; for fellows sponsored by federal or foreign institutions, the monthly stipend is paid directly to the fellow. Institutions also receive an allowance to help defray such awardee expenses as self-only health insurance, research supplies, equipment, travel to scientific meetings, and related items; the allowance is $7,850 per 12-month period for fellows at nonfederal, nonprofit, and foreign institutions and $6,750 per 12-month period at federal laboratories and for-profit institutions. In addition, tuition and fees are reimbursed at a rate of 60%, up to $4,500; if the fellow's program supports postdoctoral individuals in formal degree-granting training, tuition is supported at the rate of 60%, up to $16,000 for an additional degree. The initial 12 months of National Research Service Award postdoctoral support carries a service payback requirement, which can be fulfilled by continued training under the award or by engaging in other health-related research training, health-related research, or health-related teaching. Fellows who fail to fulfill the payback requirement of 1 month of acceptable service for each month of the initial 12 months of support received must repay all funds received with interest.

Duration Up to 2 years.

Additional data This program is offered by 16 components of the National Institutes of Health: the National Institute on Aging, the National Institute on Alcohol Abuse and Alcoholism, the National Institute of Allergy and Infectious Diseases, the National Institute of Arthritis and Musculoskeletal and Skin Diseases, the National Cancer Institute, the National Institute of Child Health and Human Development, the National Institute on Deafness and Other Communication Disorders, the National Institute of Dental and Craniofacial Research, the National Institute of Environmental Health Sciences, the National Eye Institute, the National Institute of General Medical Sciences, the National Institute of Neurological Disorders and Stroke, the National Institute of Nursing Research, and the Office of Dietary Supplements.

Number awarded Varies each year.

Deadline April, August, or December of each year.

[775]
SARASOTA COUNTY BAR ASSOCIATION DIVERSITY SCHOLARSHIP

Community Foundation of Sarasota County
Attn: Scholarship Coordinator
2635 Fruitville Road
P.O. Box 49587
Sarasota, FL 34230-6587
(941) 556-7156   Fax: (941) 556-7157
E-mail: mimi@cfsarasota.org
Web: www.cfsarasota.org/Default.aspx?tabid=363

Summary To provide financial assistance to diverse students from any state who are attending law school in any state and interested in practicing in Sarasota County, Florida after graduation.

Eligibility This program is open to students currently enrolled in the first through third year of study at a law school in any state. Applicants must come from an underrepresented background, based on race, color, religion, national origin, ethnicity, age, gender, sexual orientation, physical disability, or socioeconomic status. They must first apply for and obtain a summer associateship with a private law firm or governmental agency in Sarasota County, Florida as an indication of their interest in eventually practicing law in the county. Upon completion of their summer employment, they receive this funding. Along with their application, they must submit a 250-word essay describing how their particular background would help the Sarasota County Bar Association in achieving its goal of making the local legal community more diverse. Financial need is considered in the selection process.

Financial data The stipend is $5,000. Funds are paid directly to the student's law school.

Duration 1 year.

Additional data This program is sponsored by the Sarasota County Bar Association and administered by the Community Foundation of Sarasota County. During their summer employment, participants are assigned an attorney mentor from the bar association Diversity Committee.

Number awarded 1 or more each year.

Deadline November of each year.

[776]
SBE DOCTORAL DISSERTATION RESEARCH IMPROVEMENT GRANTS

National Science Foundation
Attn: Social, Behavioral, and Economic Sciences
4201 Wilson Boulevard, Room 905N
Arlington, VA 22230
(703) 292-8700   Fax: (703) 292-9083
TDD: (800) 281-8749
Web: www.nsf.gov

Summary To provide partial support to disabled and other doctoral candidates conducting dissertation research in areas of interest to the Directorate for Social, Behavioral, and Economic Sciences (SBE) of the National Science Foundation (NSF).

Eligibility Applications may be submitted through regular university channels by dissertation advisers on behalf of graduate students who have advanced to candidacy and have begun or are about to begin dissertation research. Students must be enrolled at U.S. institutions, but they need not be U.S. citizens. The proposed research must relate to SBE's Division of Behavioral and Cognitive Sciences (archaeology, cultural anthropology, geography and spatial sciences, linguistics, physical anthropology, or science and innovation policy), Division of Social and Economic Sciences (decision, risk, and management science; economics; law and social science; methodology, measurement, and statistics; political science; sociology; science and innovation policy; or science, technology, and society), or Division of Science Resources Statistics (research on science and technology surveys and statistics, or science and innovation policy). Women, minorities, and persons with disabilities are strongly encouraged to apply.

Financial data   Grants have the limited purpose of providing funds to enhance the quality of dissertation research. They are to be used exclusively for necessary expenses incurred in the actual conduct of the dissertation research, including (but not limited to) conducting field research in settings away from campus that would not otherwise be possible, data collection and sample survey costs, payments to subjects or informants, specialized research equipment, analysis and services not otherwise available, supplies, travel to archives, travel to specialized facilities or field research locations, and partial living expenses for conducting necessary research away from the student's U.S. academic institution. Funding is not provided for stipends, tuition, textbooks, journals, allowances for dependents, travel to scientific meetings, publication costs, dissertation preparation or reproduction, or indirect costs.

Duration   Up to 2 years.

Number awarded   200 to 300 each year. Approximately $2.5 million is available for this program annually.

Deadline   Deadline dates for the submission of dissertation improvement grant proposals differ by program within the divisions of the SBE Directorate; applicants should obtain information regarding target dates for proposals from the relevant program.

[777]
STAN BECK FELLOWSHIP

Entomological Society of America
Attn: Entomological Foundation
9332 Annapolis Road, Suite 210
Lanham, MD 20706-3150
(301) 459-9082   Fax: (301) 459-9084
E-mail: melodie@entfdn.org
Web: www.entsoc.org/awards/student/beck.htm

Summary   To assist disabled and other "needy" students working on an undergraduate or graduate degree in entomology who are nominated by members of the Entomological Society of America (ESA).

Eligibility   This program is open to students working on an undergraduate or graduate degree in entomology at a college or university in Canada, Mexico, or the United States. Candidates must be nominated by members of the

society. They must be "needy" students; for the purposes of this program, need may be based on physical limitations, or economic, minority, or environmental conditions.

Financial data   The stipend is $2,000 per year.

Duration   1 year; may be renewed up to 3 additional years.

Additional data   This fellowship was first awarded in 1996. Recipients are expected to be present at the society's annual meeting, where the award will be presented.

Number awarded   1 each year.

Deadline   June of each year.

[778]
STAR FELLOWSHIPS FOR GRADUATE ENVIRONMENTAL STUDY

Environmental Protection Agency
Attn: National Center for Environmental Research
Ariel Rios Building
1200 Pennsylvania Avenue, N.W.
Washington, DC 20460
(202) 343-9656   Toll Free: (800) 490-9194
E-mail: willett.stephanie@epa.gov
Web: es.epa.gov/ncer/rfa

Summary   To provide financial support to disabled and other graduate students planning to obtain advanced degrees and prepare for a career in environmentally-related fields.

Eligibility   Applicants must be U.S. citizens or permanent residents enrolled or accepted for enrollment at a fully-accredited U.S. college or university. They must be interested in working on a master's or doctoral degree, in the United States or abroad, in an environmentally-related field of specialization. Specific fields of interest include environmental engineering; atmospheric sciences; environmental chemistry and environmental materials science; hydrogeology; economics; geography (limited to using GIS tools to map landscape patterns adjacent to watersheds); environmental decision-making; urban and regional planning; biochemistry, molecular biology, cell biology, developmental biology, and genetics; microbiology; public health sciences; toxicology; health physics; aquatic systems ecology; oceanography and coastal processes; and terrestrial systems ecology. Students who have been enrolled for more than 2 years in a master's program or 4 years in a doctoral program are not eligible. Women, minorities, and students with disabilities are strongly encouraged to apply.

Financial data   The total award is $37,000 per year, including a student stipend of $20,000, an expense allowance of $5,000, and an allowance of up to $12,000 for tuition and fees paid directly to the institution.

Duration   Up to 2 years for master's students; up to 3 years for doctoral students.

Additional data   This program, which began in 1995, is the graduate student component of the Science to Achieve Results (STAR) program of the Environmental Protection Agency. Fellows may conduct research outside the United States, but no additional funding is provided for foreign travel or other expenses.

Number awarded Approximately 65 each year.
Deadline Pre-applications must be submitted by October of each year.

[779]
STATE VOCATIONAL REHABILITATION SERVICES PROGRAM

Department of Education
Office of Special Education and Rehabilitative
 Services
Attn: Rehabilitation Services Administration
500 12th Street, S.W., Room 503
Washington, DC 20202-2800
(202) 245-7325   Fax: (202) 245-7590
E-mail: Carol.Dobak@ed.gov
Web: www.ed.gov/programs/rsabvrs/index.html

Summary To provide financial assistance to individuals with disabilities for undergraduate or graduate study pursued as part of their program of vocational rehabilitation.

Eligibility To be eligible for vocational rehabilitation services, an individual must 1) have a physical or mental impairment that is a substantial impediment to employment; 2) be able to benefit in terms of employment from vocational rehabilitation services; and 3) require vocational rehabilitation services to prepare for, enter, engage in, or retain gainful employment. Priority is given to applicants with the most significant disabilities. Persons accepted for vocational rehabilitation develop an Individualized Written Rehabilitation Program (IWRP) in consultation with a counselor for the vocational rehabilitation agency in the state in which they live. The IWRP may include a program of postsecondary education, if the disabled person and counselor agree that such a program will fulfill the goals of vocational rehabilitation. In most cases, the IWRP will provide for postsecondary education only to a level at which the disabled person will become employable, but that may include graduate education if the approved occupation requires an advanced degree as a minimum condition of entry. Students accepted to a program of postsecondary education as part of their IWRP must apply for all available federal, state, and private financial aid.

Financial data Funding for this program is provided by the federal government through grants to state vocational rehabilitation agencies. Grants under the basic support program currently total more than $3 billion per year. States must supplement federal funding with matching funds of 21.3%. Persons who are accepted for vocational rehabilitation by the appropriate state agency receive financial assistance based on the cost of their education and other funds available to them, including their own or family contribution and other sources of financial aid. Allowable costs in most states include tuition, fees, books, supplies, room, board, transportation, personal expenses, child care, and expenses related to disability (special equipment, readers, attendants, interpreters, or notetakers).

Duration Assistance is provided until the disabled person achieves an educational level necessary for employment as provided in the IWRP.

Additional data Information on this program is available only from state vocational rehabilitation agencies.
Number awarded Varies each year. Recently, more than 1.2 million people (of whom more than 80% have significant disabilities) were participating in this program.
Deadline Deadline not specified.

[780]
STEVE FASTEAU PAST PRESIDENTS' SCHOLARSHIP

California Association for Postsecondary Education
 and Disability
Attn: Executive Assistant
71423 Biskra Road
Rancho Mirage, CA 92270
(760) 346-8206   Fax: (760) 340-5275
TDD: (760) 341-4084   E-mail: caped2000@aol.com
Web: www.caped.net/scholarships.html

Summary To provide financial assistance to undergraduate and graduate students in California who have a disability.

Eligibility This program is open to students at public and private colleges and universities in California who have a disability. Undergraduates must have completed at least 6 semester credits and have a GPA of 2.5 or higher. Graduate students must have completed at least 3 semester units and have a GPA of 3.0 or higher. Along with their application, they must submit a 1-page personal letter that demonstrates their writing skills, progress towards meeting their educational and vocational goals, management of their disability, and involvement in community activities. They must also submit a letter of recommendation from a faculty person, verification of disability, official transcripts, proof of current enrollment, and documentation of financial need.

Financial data The stipend is $1,000.
Duration 1 year.
Number awarded 1 each year.
Deadline September of each year.

[781]
SURVIVORS' AND DEPENDENTS' EDUCATIONAL ASSISTANCE PROGRAM

Department of Veterans Affairs
Attn: Veterans Benefits Administration
810 Vermont Avenue, N.W.
Washington, DC 20420
(202) 418-4343   Toll Free: (888) GI-BILL1
Web: www.gibill.va.gov/GI_Bill_Info/benefits.htm

Summary To provide financial assistance for undergraduate or graduate study to children and spouses of deceased and disabled veterans, MIAs, and POWs.

Eligibility Eligible for this assistance are spouses and children of 1) veterans who died or are permanently and totally disabled as the result of active service in the armed forces; 2) veterans who died from any cause while rated permanently and totally disabled from a service-connected disability; 3) servicemembers listed as missing in action or captured in the line of duty by a hostile force; 4) servicemembers listed as forcibly detained or interned by a foreign government or power; and 5) servicemembers who are hospitalized or receiving outpatient treatment for a service-connected permanent and total disability and are likely to be discharged for that disability. Children must be between 18 and 26 years of age, although extensions may be granted. Spouses and children over 14 years of age with physical or mental disabilities are also eligible.

Financial data Monthly stipends from this program for study at an academic institution are $925 for full time, $694 for three-quarter time, or $461 for half-time. For farm cooperative work, the monthly stipends are $745 for full-time, $559 for three-quarter time, or $372 for half-time. For an apprenticeship or on-the-job training, the monthly stipend is $674 for the first 6 months, $505 for the second 6 months, $333 for the third 6 months, and $168 for the remainder of the program. For special restorative training by beneficiaries with a physical or mental disability, the monthly stipend for full-time training is $925.

Duration Up to 45 months (or the equivalent in part-time training). Spouses must complete their training within 10 years of the date they are first found eligible. For spouses of servicemembers who died on active duty, benefits end 20 years from the date of death.

Additional data Benefits may be used to work on associate, bachelor, or graduate degrees at colleges and universities, including independent study, cooperative training, and study abroad programs. Courses leading to a certificate or diploma from business, technical, or vocational schools may also be taken. Other eligible programs include apprenticeships, on-the-job training programs, farm cooperative courses, correspondence courses (for spouses only), secondary school programs (for recipients who are not high school graduates), tutorial assistance, remedial deficiency and refresher training, or work-study (for recipients who are enrolled at least three-quarter time). Eligible children who are handicapped by a physical or mental disability that prevents pursuit of an educational program may receive special restorative training that includes language retraining, lip reading, auditory training, Braille reading and writing, and similar programs. Eligible spouses and children over 14 years of age who are handicapped by a physical or mental disability that prevents pursuit of an educational program may receive specialized vocational training that includes specialized courses, alone or in combination with other courses, leading to a vocational objective that is suitable for the person and required by reason of physical or mental handicap. Ineligible courses include bartending; audited courses; non-accredited independent study courses; any course given by radio; self-improvement courses, such as reading, speaking, woodworking, basic seamanship, and English as a second language; audited courses; any course that is avocational or recreational in character; courses not leading to an educational, professional, or vocational objective; courses taken and successfully completed previously; courses taken by a federal government employee and paid for under the Government Employees' Training Act; and courses taken while in receipt of benefits for the same program from the Office of Workers' Compensation Programs.

Number awarded Varies each year.

Deadline Applications may be submitted at any time.

[782]
VOCATIONAL REHABILITATION FOR DISABLED VETERANS

Department of Veterans Affairs
Attn: Veterans Benefits Administration
Vocational Rehabilitation and Employment Service
810 Vermont Avenue, N.W.
Washington, DC 20420
(202) 418-4343   Toll Free: (800) 827-1000
Web: www.vba.va.gov/bin/vre/index.htm

Summary To provide vocational rehabilitation to certain categories of veterans with disabilities.

Eligibility This program is open to veterans who have a service-connected disability of 1) at least 10% and a serious employment handicap, or 2) at least 20% and an employment handicap. They must have been discharged or released from military service under other than dishonorable conditions. The Department of Veterans Affairs (VA) must determine that they would benefit from a training program that would help them prepare for, find, and keep suitable employment. The program may be 1) institutional training at a certificate, 2-year college, 4-year college or university, or technical program; 2) unpaid on-the-job training in a federal, state, or local agency or a federally-recognized Indian tribal agency, training in a home, vocational course in a rehabilitation facility or sheltered workshop, independent instruction, or institutional non-farm cooperative; or 3) paid training through a farm cooperative, apprenticeship, on-the-job training, or on-the-job non-farm cooperative.

Financial data While in training and for 2 months after, eligible disabled veterans may receive subsistence allowances in addition to their disability compensation or retirement pay. For most training programs, the current full-time monthly rate is $547.54 with no dependents, $679.18 with 1 dependent, $800.36 with 2 dependents, and $58.34 for each additional dependent; proportional rates apply for less than full-time training. The VA also pays the costs of tuition, books, fees, supplies, and equipment; it may also pay for special supportive services, such as tutorial assistance, prosthetic devices, lipreading training, and signing for the deaf. If during training or employment services the veteran's disabilities cause transportation expenses that would not be incurred by nondisabled persons, the VA will pay for at least a portion of those expenses. If the veteran encounters financial difficulty during training, the VA may provide an advance against future benefit payments.

Duration Up to 48 months of full-time training or its equivalent in part-time training. If a veteran with a serious disability receives services under an extended evaluation to improve training potential, the total of the extended evaluation and the training phases of the rehabilitation program may exceed 48 months. Usually, the veteran must complete a rehabilitation program within 12 years from the date of notification of entitlement to compensation by the VA. Following completion of the training portion of a rehabilitation program, a veteran may receive counseling and job search and adjustment services for 18 months.

Additional data The program may also provide employment assistance, self-employment assistance, training in a rehabilitation facility, or college and other training. Veterans who are seriously disabled may receive services and assistance to improve their ability to live more independently in their community. After completion of the training phase, the VA will assist the veteran to find and have a suitable job.

Number awarded Varies each year.

Deadline Applications are accepted at any time.

[783]
WILLIAM E. SIMON OLYMPIC TRUST FOR SUPPORT OF ATHLETES

United States Olympic Committee
Attn: Sports Partnerships Division
One Olympic Plaza
Colorado Springs, CO 80909-5760
(719) 632-5551   Toll Free: (800) 933-4473
Fax: (719) 866-4957 E-mail: tammie.forster@usoc.org
Web: teamusa.org/content/index/894

Summary To provide disabled and other outstanding athletes with financial assistance for competition or training expenses.

Eligibility This program is open to athletes who are currently in training or competition for the Olympics. Applicants must be U.S. citizens who can demonstrate financial need. Along with their application, they must submit a 3-page essay on their background and history in the sport, financial need or circumstances affecting their ability to train and compete, how this grant would make a difference, and what it means to be able to practice and participate in their chosen sport. Preference is given to athletes not already receiving financial support from the United States Olympic Committee (USOC) or their respective National Governing Body (NGB). Athletes with disabilities who are training for the Paralympics are also eligible.

Financial data Grant amounts vary, depending on the availability of funds, the number of qualified applicants, and the meritorious circumstances of each applicant.

Duration 1 year; may be renewed.

Additional data This program was established in 1998.

Number awarded Varies each year.

Deadline September of each year.

[784]
WILLIAM MAY MEMORIAL SCHOLARSHIP

California Association for Postsecondary Education
  and Disability
Attn: Executive Assistant
71423 Biskra Road
Rancho Mirage, CA 92270
(760) 346-8206   Fax: (760) 340-5275
TDD: (760) 341-4084   E-mail: caped2000@aol.com
Web: www.caped.net/scholarships.html

Summary To provide financial assistance to undergraduate and graduate students in California who have a disability.

Eligibility This program is open to students at public and private colleges and universities in California who have a disability. Undergraduates must have completed at least 6 semester credits and have a GPA of 2.5 or higher. Graduate students must have completed at least 3 semester units and have a GPA of 3.0 or higher. Along with their application, they must submit a 1-page personal letter that demonstrates their writing skills, progress towards meeting their educational and vocational goals, management of their disability, and involvement in community activities. They must also submit a letter of recommendation from a faculty member, verification of disability, official transcripts, proof of current enrollment, and documentation of financial need.

Financial data The stipend is $1,000.

Duration 1 year.

Number awarded I each year.

Deadline September of each year.

[785]
YELLOW RIBBON SCHOLARSHIP

Tourism Cares
Attn: National Tour Association Scholarship Fund
275 Turnpike Street, Suite 307
Canton, MA 02021
(781) 821-5990   Fax: (781) 821-8949
E-mail: info@tourismcares.org
Web: www.tourismcares.org

Summary To provide financial assistance for college or graduate school to students with disabilities who are planning a career in the travel and tourism industry.

Eligibility This program is open to citizens and permanent residents of the United States and Canada who have a physical or sensory disability. Applicants must be entering or attending an accredited 2- or 4-year college or university in the United States or Canada. They must be working on or planning to work on an undergraduate or graduate degree in a field related to travel and tourism and have a GPA of 2.5 or higher. Along with their application, they must submit a 2-page essay on contributions they feel they might make in the travel, tourism, and hospitality industry. Financial need is not considered in the selection process.

Financial data The stipend is $5,000.

Duration 1 year.

Additional data This program was established in 1993.

Number awarded 1 each year.

Deadline March of each year.

Grants-in-Aid

[786]
ACCESS FOR ATHLETES GRANTS

Challenged Athletes Foundation
Attn: Program Manager
9990 Mesa Rim Road
P.O. Box 910769
San Diego, CA 92191
(858) 866-0959   Fax: (858) 866-0958
E-mail: info@challengedathletes.org
Web: www.challengedathletes.org

Summary To provide funding to disabled athletes for travel, coaching, or equipment.

Eligibility This program is open to athletes of any age with a permanent disability that is recognized by the International Paralympic Committee. Applicants must need funding for 1 of 3 categories: 1) equipment, for wheelchairs, prosthetics, or other assistive devices; 2) training, for club or gym dues or membership fees, team or association dues or membership fees, or coaching or training expense; or 3) competition, for travel, entry fees, or other costs to participate in a recognized event. They may apply for only 1 category per year. Along with their application, they must submit information on their short- and long-term goals in the sport of their choice, how this grant will help them reach their goal, their motto or words to live by, a list of their volunteer or community service work, and documentation of financial need.

Financial data Grants for 1 year are limited to $1,500; 2-year grants average between $200 and $3,500.

Duration 1 or 2 years (equipment grants are considered 2-year grants). Recipients may reapply.

Additional data This foundation was established as the result of an event held in 1994 to raise funds for triathlete Jim MacLaren, who became a quadriplegic while competing.

Number awarded Varies each year; recently, 765 of these grants, with a value of $1,363,049, were awarded.

Deadline November of each year.

[787]
ADA FOUNDATION RELIEF GRANT PROGRAM

American Dental Association
Attn: ADA Foundation
211 East Chicago Avenue
Chicago, IL 60611
(312) 440-2547   Fax: (312) 440-3526
E-mail: adaf@ada.org
Web: www.ada.org/ada/adaf/grants/relief.asp

Summary To provide relief grants to dentists and their dependents who, because of accidental injury, a medical condition, or advanced age, are not self-supporting.

Eligibility This program is open to dentists, their spouses, and their children under 18 years of age. Dependents of deceased dentists are also eligible. Membership in the American Dental Association (ADA) is not required and members receive no special consideration in awarding of grants. Applicants must be seeking assistance because an accidental injury, advanced age, physically-debilitating illness, or medically-related condition prevents them from gainful employment and results in an inability to be wholly self-sustaining. They must apply through their component or constituent dental society, which forwards the application to the trustees of this fund.

Financial data The amount of the grant depends on the particular circumstances of each applicant, including financial need, age and physical condition, opportunity for assistance from immediate family members, financial assets, and all other relevant factors.

Duration Initial grants are for 6 months. Renewal grants are for an additional 12 months. Emergency grants are 1-time awards.

Additional data The ADA has been making relief grants to needy dentists since 1906.

Number awarded Varies each year; recently, a total of $209,964 in these grants was awarded.

Deadline Applications may be submitted at any time.

[788]
ALABAMA AD VALOREM TAX EXEMPTION FOR SPECIALLY ADAPTED HOUSES

Alabama Department of Revenue
Attn: Property Tax Division
Gordon Persons Building
50 North Ripley Street, Room 4126
P.O. Box 327210
Montgomery, AL 36132-7210
(334) 242-1525
Web: www.ador.state.al.us

Summary To provide a property tax exemption to the owners of specially adapted housing (housing adapted for disabled veterans) in Alabama.

Eligibility The home of any veteran which is or was acquired pursuant to the provisions of Public Law 702, 80th Congress (specially adapted housing grants for veterans) as amended (38 USC) will be exempted from ad valorem taxation if the house is owned and occupied by the veteran or the veteran's unremarried widow(er).

Financial data Qualifying houses are exempt from all ad valorem taxation.

Duration This exemption continues as long as the qualifying veteran or the unremarried widow(er) resides in the house.

Number awarded Varies each year.

Deadline Deadline not specified.

[789]
ALABAMA COUNTY HOMESTEAD EXEMPTIONS

Alabama Department of Revenue
Attn: Property Tax Division
Gordon Persons Building
50 North Ripley Street, Room 4126
P.O. Box 327210
Montgomery, AL 36132-7210
(334) 242-1525
Web: www.ador.state.al.us

Summary To exempt disabled, blind, and elderly residents of Alabama from ad valorem property taxes imposed by counties.

Eligibility Residents of Alabama are eligible to apply if they are over the age of 65 and have a net annual income of $12,000 or less for income tax purposes for the preceding year; or are retired due to permanent and total disability, regardless of age; or are blind, regardless of age or retirement status.

Financial data Qualifying residents are exempt from ad valorem property taxes levied by counties, including taxes levied for school districts, to a maximum of $5,000 in assessed value, or 160 acres in area.

Duration 1 year; this exemption will be granted as long as the resident continues to meet the eligibility requirements.

Number awarded Varies each year.

Deadline Deadline not specified.

[790]
ALABAMA MILITARY RETIREE INCOME TAX EXEMPTION

Alabama Department of Revenue
Attn: Income Tax Division
Gordon Persons Building
50 North Ripley Street, Room 4212
P.O. Box 327410
Montgomery, AL 36132-7410
(334) 242-1105   Fax: (334) 242-0064
E-mail: erohelpdesk@revenue.state.al.us
Web: www.ador.state.al.us

Summary To exempt a portion of the income of veterans and their survivors from taxation in Alabama.

Eligibility Eligible are Alabama recipients of regular military retired pay or military survivors benefits. Recipients of benefits paid by the U.S. Department of Veterans Affairs (including disability retirement payments) are also eligible for this exemption.

Financial data All income received as military retired pay, veterans' disability payment, or military survivors benefits is exempt from state, county, or municipal income taxation.

Duration The exemption continues as long as the recipient resides in Alabama.

Deadline Deadline not specified.

[791]
ALABAMA PRINCIPAL RESIDENCE EXEMPTION

Alabama Department of Revenue
Attn: Property Tax Division
Gordon Persons Building
50 North Ripley Street, Room 4126
P.O. Box 327210
Montgomery, AL 36132-7210
(334) 242-1525
Web: www.ador.state.al.us

Summary To exempt disabled and elderly residents of Alabama from ad valorem property taxes imposed by the state.

Eligibility Residents of Alabama are eligible to apply if they are over the age of 65 and have a net annual income of $7,500 or less for income tax purposes for the preceding year; or are totally disabled. They must own and occupy as their principal residence a single-family home with up to 160 adjacent acres.

Financial data Qualifying residents are exempt from all ad valorem property taxes levied by the state on their principal residence.

Duration 1 year; this exemption will be granted as long as the resident continues to meet the eligibility requirements.

Number awarded Varies each year.

Deadline Deadline not specified.

[792]
ALABAMA STATE HOMESTEAD EXEMPTIONS

Alabama Department of Revenue
Attn: Property Tax Division
Gordon Persons Building
50 North Ripley Street, Room 4126
P.O. Box 327210
Montgomery, AL 36132-7210
(334) 242-1525
Web: www.ador.state.al.us

Summary To exempt disabled, blind, and elderly residents of Alabama from ad valorem property taxes imposed by the state.

Eligibility Residents of Alabama are eligible to apply if they are 1) over the age of 65; 2) retired due to permanent and total disability, regardless of age; or 3) blind, regardless of age or retirement status.

Financial data Qualifying residents are exempt from all ad valorem property taxes levied by the state, up to 160 acres in area.

Duration 1 year; this exemption will be granted as long as the resident continues to meet the eligibility requirements.

Number awarded Varies each year.

Deadline Deadline not specified.

[793]
ALASKA PROPERTY TAX EXEMPTION

Division of Community and Regional Affairs
Attn: Office of the State Assessor
550 West Seventh Avenue, Suite 1790
Anchorage, AK 99501-3510
(907) 269-4605   Fax: (907) 269-4539
E-mail: Steve.VanSant@alaska.gov
Web: www.commerce.state.ak.us/dcra/osa/taxfacts.htm

Summary   To exempt from taxation the property owned by veterans with disabilities in Alaska.

Eligibility   This exemption is available to veterans in Alaska who have a disability that was incurred or aggravated in the line of duty and that has been rated as 50% or more by the military service or the U.S. Department of Veterans Affairs. Applicants must own and occupy real property that is their primary residence and permanent place of abode. Senior citizens who are 65 years of age or older are also eligible for this exemption.

Financial data   Qualified veterans are exempt from taxation on the first $150,000 of assessed valuation on real property.

Duration   The exemption continues as long as the veteran with a disability resides in Alaska.

Additional data   Applications may be obtained from the local assessor's office. Since 1986, the cost of this program has exceeded the funding available for it. As a result, recipients may be granted a prorated level of payments.

Number awarded   Varies each year. Recently, more than 25,000 disabled veterans and senior citizens received an average exemption of $1,851 on their property, which had an average assessed value of $135,486.

Deadline   Applications may be submitted at any time.

[794]
ARIZONA PROPERTY TAX EXEMPTION FOR WIDOWS, WIDOWERS, AND DISABLED PERSONS

Arizona Department of Revenue
1600 West Monroe Street
Phoenix, AZ 85007-2650
(602) 542-3572   Toll Free: (800) 352-4090 (within AZ)
TDD: (602) 542-4021
Web: www.revenue.state.az.us

Summary   To exempt a portion of the property of widow(er)s and disabled people from property taxes in Arizona.

Eligibility   This exemption is available to residents of Arizona who are widows, widowers, or permanently and totally disabled. Their total income must be less than $25,000 if no children reside with them or less than $30,000 if 1 or more of their children who are younger than 18 years of age or also disabled live with them.

Financial data   The exemption is $3,000, if the person's total assessment does not exceed $20,000. No exemption is available if the person's total assessment exceeds $20,000.

Duration   The exemption continues as long as the recipient resides in Arizona.

Deadline   Deadline not specified.

[795]
ARKANSAS DISABLED VETERANS PROPERTY TAX EXEMPTION

Arkansas Assessment Coordination Department
1614 West Third Street
Little Rock, AR 72201-1815
(501) 324-9100   Fax: (501) 324-9242
E-mail: dasbury@acd.state.ar.us
Web: www.arkansas.gov/acd

Summary   To exempt from taxation the property owned by blind or disabled veterans, surviving spouses, and minor dependent children in Arkansas.

Eligibility   This program is open to disabled veterans in Arkansas who have been awarded special monthly compensation by the U.S. Department of Veterans Affairs and who have 1) the loss of or the loss of use of 1 or more limbs, 2) total blindness in 1 or both eyes, or 3) total and permanent disability. The benefit also extends to veterans' unremarried surviving spouses and their minor children.

Financial data   Qualifying veterans (or their unremarried widows or dependent children) are exempt from payment of all state taxes on their homestead and personal property.

Duration   This exemption continues as long as the qualifying veteran (or dependent) resides in Arkansas.

Number awarded   Varies each year.

Deadline   Applications may be submitted at any time.

[796]
ARKANSAS INCOME TAX EXEMPTIONS FOR MILITARY COMPENSATION AND DISABILITY PAY

Arkansas Department of Finance and Administration
Attn: Office of Income Tax Administration
Joel Ledbetter Building, Room 110
1800 Seventh Street
P.O. Box 3628
Little Rock, AR 72203-3628
(501) 682-7225   Fax: (501) 682-7692
E-mail: individual.income@rev.state.ar.us
Web: www.arkansas.gov/dfa/income_tax/tax_index.html

Summary   To exempt a portion of the income of military personnel and disabled veterans from state income taxes in Arkansas.

Eligibility   Eligible are residents of Arkansas receiving military compensation or military disability income.

Financial data   The first $9,000 of U.S. military compensation pay or military disability income is exempt from state income taxation.

Duration   The exemptions continue as long as the recipient resides in Arkansas.

Deadline   Deadline not specified.

[797]
ARKANSAS INCOME TAX EXEMPTIONS FOR RETIREMENT AND DISABILITY PAY

Arkansas Department of Finance and Administration
Attn: Office of Income Tax Administration
Joel Ledbetter Building, Room 110
1800 Seventh Street
P.O. Box 3628
Little Rock, AR 72203-3628
(501) 682-7225   Fax: (501) 682-7692
E-mail: individual.income@rev.state.ar.us
Web: www.arkansas.gov/dfa/income_tax/tax_index.html

Summary   To exempt a portion of the income from retirement or disability plans from state income taxes in Arkansas.

Eligibility   Eligible are residents of Arkansas receiving income from retirement or disability plans. Surviving spouses also qualify for the exemption.

Financial data   Exempt from state income taxation is the first $6,000 in disability pay, retired pay, or survivors benefits. Any resident who receives both military retirement or disability pay and other retirement or disability benefits is entitled to only a single $6,000 deduction. Surviving spouses are also limited to a single $6,000 exemption. Military retirees may adjust their figures if the payment includes survivor's benefit payments; the amount of adjustment must be listed on the income statement, and supporting documentation must be submitted with the return.

Duration   The exemption continues as long as the recipient resides in Arkansas.

Deadline   Deadline not specified.

[798]
ARKANSAS SALES TAX EXEMPTION FOR ADAPTIVE MEDICAL EQUIPMENT

Arkansas Department of Finance and Administration
Attn: Sales and Use Tax Section
Joel Ledbetter Building, Room 1340
1816 Seventh Street
P.O. Box 1272
Little Rock, AR 72203-1272
(501) 682-1895   Fax: (501) 682-7904
E-mail: sales.tax@rev.state.ar.us
Web: www.arkansas.gov

Summary   To exempt adaptive equipment from sales tax in Arkansas.

Eligibility   Rental, sale, or repair of adaptive and disposable medical equipment in Arkansas qualifies for this exemption. Adaptive equipment includes wheelchairs, leg braces, raised toilet seats, wheelchair batteries, grab bars and hand rails, automobile hand controls, Braille writers, hearing aids, and other equipment used by people with disabilities.

Financial data   Qualified equipment is exempt from payment of all sales tax.

Additional data   This exemption does not apply to equipment purchased by physicians, hospitals, nursing homes, or long-term care facilities for use by their patients or residents.

Deadline   Deadline not specified.

[799]
CALIFORNIA DISABLED VETERAN EXEMPTION FROM THE IN LIEU TAX FEE FOR A MANUFACTURED HOME OR MOBILEHOME

Department of Housing and Community Development
Attn: Registration and Titling
1800 Third Street
P.O. Box 2111
Sacramento, CA 95812-2111
(916) 323-9224   Toll Free: (800) 952-8356
Web: www.hcd.ca.gov

Summary   To provide a special property tax exemption to blind or disabled California veterans and/or their spouses who own and occupy a mobile home.

Eligibility   This program is open to disabled veterans and/or their spouses in California who have a manufactured home or mobile home as their principal place of residence. Veterans must be disabled as a result of injury or disease incurred in military service and have been a resident of California 1) at the time of entry into the service and be blind, or have lost the use of 1 or more limbs, or be totally disabled; 2) on November 7, 1972 and be blind in both eyes, or have lost the use of 2 or more limbs; or 3) on January 1, 1975 and be totally disabled. The spouses and unremarried surviving spouses of those disabled veterans are also eligible.

Financial data   The exemption applies to the first $20,000 of the assessed market value of the manufactured home or mobile home. Veterans and/or spouses whose income falls below a specified level are entitled to an additional $10,000 exemption. The amount of the exemption is 100% if the home is owned by a veteran only, a veteran and spouse, or a spouse only; 50% if owned by a veteran and another person other than a spouse or by a spouse and another person other than the veteran; 67% if owned by a veteran, the spouse, and another person; 34% if owned by a veteran and 2 other people other than a spouse or by a spouse and 2 other people; 50% if owned by a veteran, the spouse, and 2 other people; or 25% if owned by a veteran and 3 other people or by a spouse and 3 other people.

Duration   The exemption is available annually as long as the applicant meets all requirements.

Number awarded   Varies each year.

Deadline   Deadline not specified.

[800]
CHILDREN OF WOMEN VIETNAM VETERANS ALLOWANCE

Department of Veterans Affairs
Attn: Veterans Benefits Administration
810 Vermont Avenue, N.W.
Washington, DC 20420
(202) 418-4343   Toll Free: (800) 827-1000
Web: www1.va.gov/opa/ls1/11.asp

Summary To provide support to children of female Vietnam veterans who have birth defects.

Eligibility This program is open to biological children of female veterans who served in the Republic of Vietnam and were conceived after the date the veteran first served, which must have been between February 28, 1961 and May 7, 1975. Applicants must have certain birth defects identified as resulting in permanent physical or mental disability. Conditions that are a family disorder, a birth-related injury, or a fetal or neonatal infirmity with well-established causes are not included.

Financial data Support depends on the degree of disability. The monthly rate for children at the first level is $131, at the second level $286, at the third level $984, or at the fourth level $1,678.

Additional data Applications are available from the nearest VA medical center. Recipients are also entitled to vocational training and medical treatment.

Number awarded Varies each year.

Deadline Applications are accepted at any time.

[801]
CHILDREN WITH SPECIAL NEEDS FUND GRANTS

Michigan Department of Community Health
Attn: Children with Special Needs Fund
Lewis Cass Building, Sixth Floor
320 South Walnut
P.O. Box 30479
Lansing, MI 48909-7979
(517) 241-7420   Toll Free: (800) 359-3722
Fax: (517) 335-8055   TDD: (866) 501-5656
E-mail: csnfund@michigan.gov
Web: www.michigan.gov

Summary To provide funding to children with disabilities in Michigan who need special equipment to meet their needs.

Eligibility This program is open to children in Michigan who are younger than 21 years of age and enrolled in (or medically eligible to enroll in) Children's Special Health Care Services of the Department of Community Health. Applicants must be able to demonstrate a need for the following special equipment: van lifts and tiedowns, wheelchair ramps into homes, air conditioners, electrical service upgrades necessitated by the eligible child's equipment, adaptive recreational equipment, or therapeutic tricycles. Along with their application, they must submit a completed financial assessment, a letter of medical necessity from the child's physician, documentation that other sources (e.g., insurance companies, professional organizations, local service groups and charities, churches) have been contacted for assistance, and 3 bids or quotes for the equipment or services being requested. Only families with income below specified levels ($54,150 for a family of 1, rising to $128,950 for a family of 5) are eligible.

Financial data The amount of the grant depends on the income of the family. The lowest level is up to $27,075 for a family of 1, rising to $64,475 for a family of 5. At that income level, maximum grants are $6,000 for van lifts,

$500 to replace a wheelchair tie-down system, $3,000 for home wheelchair ramps, $500 for air conditioners, $1,000 for electrical system upgrades, and $1,500 for therapeutic specialty tricycles. Families with higher incomes (up to the specified maximum) are eligible for smaller grants.

Duration These are 1-time grants.

Additional data This program was established in 1944 by a donation of Dow Chemical Company stock from James T. Pardee, a founder of that company. Although the program is administered by the state of Michigan, all funding is provided by the return on that donation and subsequent private support.

Number awarded Varies each year.

Deadline Applications may be submitted at any time.

[802]
CHRYSLER AUTOMOBILITY PROGRAM

Chrysler Corporation
Attn: Automobility Program
P.O. Box 5080
Troy, MI 48007-5080
Toll Free: (800) 255-9877   Fax: (904) 828-6717
TDD: (800) 922-3826
Web: www.chryslergroupllc.com/community/automobility

Summary To provide a cash reimbursement for the cost of installing adaptive driving aids on new purchases from Chrysler Motors.

Eligibility Eligible for this rebate are purchasers of new Chrysler Motors cars, trucks, or vans that require adaptive driving aids or conversion equipment for users with disabilities.

Financial data Conversions to Dodge Caravan, Dodge Grand Caravan, and Chrysler Town & Country models are reimbursed up to $1,000. The maximum reimbursement on all other Chrysler vehicle models is $750. Dodge and Freightliner Sprinter models qualify for a maximum reimbursement of $500 on wheelchair lifts. Running boards qualify for maximum reimbursement of $400 and alerting devices for $200.

Additional data Applications for reimbursement are submitted through the dealer from whom the vehicle was originally purchased. Only retail purchases and leases of new Chrysler Motors vehicles qualify for this program. The reimbursement applies only to equipment installed by converters in the after market, not to factory installed equipment of any kind.

Deadline The conversion process must be completed within 6 months of vehicle purchase or lease. Reimbursement claims must be submitted within 60 days after completion of the conversion.

[803]
COLONIAL CHAPTER PARALYZED VETERANS ASSOCIATION ASSISTANCE

Paralyzed Veterans of America-Colonial Chapter
28 Peddler's Row
Christiana, DE 19702
(302) 368-4898   Toll Free: (800) 786-2039
Fax: (302) 368-4293   E-mail: office@colonialPVA.org
Web: www.colonialpva.org/programs/prosthetics.php

Summary   To provide funding for the purchase of equipment or other assistance for people with disabilities in Delaware, Maryland, New Jersey, and southeastern Pennsylvania.

Eligibility   This program is open to people with disabilities who live in Delaware, Maryland, New Jersey, or southeastern Pennsylvania. Applicants do not need to be veterans and assistance is not limited by age or type of disability. They must be interested in purchasing equipment (e.g., ramps, prostheses, wheelchairs) or other assistance (e.g., van adaptations, home modifications).

Financial data   The maximum award is generally about $1,500.

Number awarded   Varies each year.

Deadline   Applications may be submitted at any time.

[804]
COLORADO PENSION/ANNUITY SUBTRACTION

Colorado Department of Revenue
Attn: Taxpayer Service Division
1375 Sherman Street, Room 242A
Denver, CO 80261-0005
(303) 232-2446   Toll Free: (800) 811-0172
Web: www.colorado.gov

Summary   To exempt a portion of the income of disabled and other persons over the age of 55 from state income taxation in Colorado.

Eligibility   This exemption is available to taxpayers over the age of 55 who are classified as Colorado residents for purposes of state income taxation, and to beneficiaries (such as a widowed spouse or orphan child) who are receiving a pension or annuity because of the death of the person who earned the pension. To qualify, the payment must be a retirement benefit that arose from an employer/employee relationship, service in the uniformed services of the United States, or contributions to a retirement plan that are deductible for federal income tax purposes. Disability retirement payments received by persons 55 years of age or older also qualify.

Financial data   For retirees who are at least 65 years of age, up to $24,000 of qualified pension or retirement income may be excluded from income for purposes of Colorado state taxation. For persons who are at least 55 but under 65 years of age, up to $20,000 of qualified pension or retirement income may be excluded.

Duration   The exclusion continues as long as the recipient resides in Colorado.

Additional data   Disability retirement payments received by persons under 55 years of age do not qualify for the pension exclusion.

Deadline   Deadline not specified.

[805]
COLORADO PROPERTY TAX EXEMPTION FOR DISABLED VETERANS

Division of Veterans Affairs
7465 East First Avenue, Suite C
Denver, CO 80230
(303) 343-1268   Fax: (303) 343-7238
Web: www.dmva.state.co.us/page/va/prop_tax

Summary   To provide a partial exemption of taxes on property owned by disabled veterans in Colorado.

Eligibility   This exemption is open to veterans who reside in Colorado and have been rated 100% service-connected disabled by the U.S. Department of Veterans Affairs. Applicants must have been honorably discharged and must own property in Colorado which they use as their primary residence. The exemption also applies to members of the National Guard or Reserves who sustained their injury during a period in which they were called to active duty, property owned by a veteran's spouse if both occupy the property as their primary residence, and property owned by a trust or other legal entity if the veteran or spouse is a major of the trust or other legal entity, the property was transferred solely for estate planning purposes, and the veteran or spouse would otherwise be the owner of record.

Financial data   For qualifying veterans, 50% of the first $200,000 of actual value of the primary residence is exempted from taxes.

Duration   The exemption continues as long as the veteran resides in the property.

Additional data   This program was approved by Colorado voters in 2006.

Number awarded   Varies each year.

Deadline   Applications must be submitted by June of the year for which the exemption is requested.

[806]
COMBAT-RELATED SPECIAL COMPENSATION

U.S. Army
Human Resources Command
Attn: AHRC-DZB-CRSC
200 Stovall Street
Alexandria, VA 22332-0470
Toll Free: (866) 281-3254
E-mail: CRSC.info@us.army.mil
Web: www.defenselink.mil/prhome/mppcrsc.html

Summary   To provide supplemental compensation to military retirees who are receiving disability pay from the U.S. Department of Veterans Affairs (VA).

Eligibility   This program is open to retirees from the U.S. uniformed services who either 1) served at least 20 years on active duty; 2) served in the Reserves or National Guard, received a 20-year retirement letter, and are at least 60 years of age; 3) performed reserve service under the Reserve TERA program, completed at least 15 but less than 20 years of combined active and reserve service, and are at least 60 years of age; or 4) are currently entitled to military retired pay for any reason, other than early reserve retirement for physical disabilities not incurred in line of duty. Applicants must have a VA disability rating of 10% or higher, be drawing retirement pay, and be receiving VA disability pay. Their disability must be not just service connected but also combat related. Spouses and other dependents are not eligible for this program.

Financial data Qualified veterans receive compensation that depends on their combat-related disability rating (which may differ from their VA service-connected disability rating). They continue to receive their full military retirement pay (unlike VA disability compensation, which acted as an offset for an equivalent reduction in military retirement pay). The compensation is non-taxable.

Duration This compensation is payable for the life of the veteran.

Additional data The Combat-Related Special Compensation Program (CRSC I) began in June, 2003. The program was revised to offer compensation to a larger group of retirees and CRSC II began in January, 2004. Another revision in January, 2008 again expanded eligibility requirements. Military retirees must apply through the armed forces branch in which they served. Navy and Marine Corps personnel should contact the Naval Council of Review Boards, Attn: Combat-Related Special Compensation Branch, 720 Kennon Street, S.E., Suite 309, Washington Navy Yard, DC 20374-5023, (877) 366-2772. Air Force personnel should contact the Disability Division (CRSC), 550 C Street West, Suite 6, Randolph AFB, TX 78150-4708, (800), 616-3775, Fax: (210) 565-1101. The program is also available to retirees from the other uniformed services (Coast Guard, National Oceanic and Atmospheric Administration, and Public Health Service). Information is available from those services.

Number awarded Varies each year. Currently, more than 50,000 retirees are receiving payments of more than $59 million per month.

Deadline Applications may be submitted at any time.

[807]
CONNECTICUT DISABLED TAX RELIEF PROGRAM

Office of Policy and Management
Attn: Intergovernmental Policy Division
450 Capitol Avenue
Hartford, CT 06106-1308
(860) 418-6382   Toll Free: (800) 286-2214 (within CT)
Fax: (860) 418-6493   TDD: (860) 418-6456
E-mail: frank.intino@ct.gov
Web: www.ct.gov

Summary To exempt disabled residents of Connecticut from a portion of their personal property taxes.

Eligibility Eligible to apply for this exemption are Connecticut residents who are rated as totally and permanently disabled by the U.S. Social Security Administration. If they never engaged in employment covered by Social Security, they are also eligible if they have become qualified for permanent and total disability benefits under any federal, state, or local government retirement or disability plan. An additional exemption may be available to residents whose total adjusted gross income is less than $30,500 if unmarried or $37,300 if married.

Financial data The basic state exemption is $1,000 of assessed valuation. Municipalities may elect to provide an additional exemption of $1,000 to residents whose income is less than the qualifying level.

Duration 1 year; exemptions continue as long as the eligible resident lives in Connecticut.

Number awarded Varies each year; recently, a total of 12,658 residents received property tax exemptions through this program.

Deadline Applications for the additional municipality exemption must be submitted to the assessor's office of the town or residence by September of every other year.

[808]
CONNECTICUT ELDERLY AND DISABLED HOMEOWNERS TAX RELIEF PROGRAM

Office of Policy and Management
Attn: Intergovernmental Policy Division
450 Capitol Avenue
Hartford, CT 06106-1308
(860) 418-6382   Toll Free: (800) 286-2214 (within CT)
Fax: (860) 418-6493   TDD: (860) 418-6456
E-mail: frank.intino@ct.gov
Web: www.ct.gov

Summary To provide a credit to elderly and disabled residents of Connecticut for a portion of their real property taxes.

Eligibility Eligible to apply for this relief are Connecticut residents who are 1) over 65 years of age, or 2) rated as totally and permanently disabled by the U.S. Social Security Administration. If they never engaged in employment covered by Social Security, they are also eligible if they have become qualified for permanent and total disability benefits under any federal, state, or local government retirement or disability plan. Applicants must have total adjusted gross income less than $30,500 if unmarried or $37,300 if married. The credit applies to property owned by the applicant and located on a "standard building lot," including residences, mobile homes, life care facilities, modular homes, condominiums, and dwellings on leased land.

Financial data The credit depends on the income of the recipient, to a maximum of $1,250 for married homeowners or $1,000 for unmarried homeowners.

Duration 1 year; the credit is available as long as the eligible homeowner lives in Connecticut.

Number awarded Varies each year; recently, a total of 39,434 homeowners received property tax credits through this program.

Deadline Applications must be submitted to the assessor's office of the town or residence by May of every other year.

[809]
CONNECTICUT SOLDIERS', SAILORS' AND MARINES' FUND

Connecticut Department of Veterans' Affairs
Attn: Soldiers', Sailors' and Marines' Fund
864 Wethersfield Avenue
Hartford, CT 06114-3184
(860) 296-0719   Toll Free: (800) 491-4941 (within CT)
Fax: (860) 296-0820
E-mail: john.monahan@po.state.ct.us
Web: www.state.ct.us/ssmf

Summary   To provide temporary financial assistance to needy Connecticut veterans.

Eligibility   This program is open to veterans who were honorably discharged after at least 90 days of service during wartime (World War I, World War II, Korea, Vietnam, Lebanon, Grenada, Operation Ernest Will, Panama, or the Persian Gulf) and are currently residents of Connecticut. Applicants must be able to demonstrate need for the following types of assistance: medical expenses; emergent dental care; prescription medications; eye examination and purchase of eyeglasses; audiological evaluation and hearing aids; assistance with rental payments or mortgage interest payments; utilities (including gas, water, electric, and fuel oil); funeral expenses; or prosthetic devices and durable medical equipment. Support is not provided for payment of taxes; payment of insurance premiums (except medical insurance); purchase of real estate or payments of principal on mortgages; payment of telephone or cable bills; purchase of equities, bonds, or mutual funds; alimony or child support payments; payment of personal debts, credit card bills, past-due bills, loans, or other obligations; or purchase of furniture, automobiles, or other capital goods.

Financial data   The fund provides payments in the form of short-term grants.

Duration   The funds are provided for emergency situations only; the program does not assist with ongoing financial needs.

Additional data   This program is subsidized by the state of Connecticut but administered by the American Legion of Connecticut.

Number awarded   Varies each year.

Deadline   Applications may be submitted at any time.

[810]
CONNECTICUT VETERANS' ADDITIONAL EXEMPTION TAX RELIEF PROGRAM

Office of Policy and Management
Attn: Intergovernmental Policy Division
450 Capitol Avenue
Hartford, CT 06106-1308
(860) 418-6278   Toll Free: (800) 286-2214 (within CT)
Fax: (860) 418-6493   TDD: (860) 418-6456
E-mail: leeann.graham@ct.gov
Web: www.ct.gov

Summary   To exempt disabled veterans and their surviving spouses who are residents of Connecticut from a portion of their personal property taxes.

Eligibility   Eligible to apply for this exemption are Connecticut veterans who are rated as disabled by the U.S. Department of Veterans Affairs (VA). Unremarried surviving spouses of qualified veterans are also eligible. An additional exemption may be available to veterans and spouses whose total adjusted gross income is less than $30,500 if unmarried or $37,300 if married. If the veteran is rated as 100% disabled by the U.S. Department of Veterans Affairs (VA), the maximum income levels are $18,000 if unmarried or $21,000 if married.

Financial data   The amount of the exemption depends on the level of the VA disability rating: for 10% to 25%, it is $1,500; for more than 25% to 50%, $2,000; for more than 50% to 75%, $2,500; for more than 75% and for veterans older than 65 years of age with any level of disability, $3,000. Municipalities may elect to provide an additional exemption, equal to twice the amount provided, to veterans and spouses whose income is less than the qualifying level. For veterans and spouses who do not meet the income requirement, the additional exemption from participating municipalities is equal to 50% of the basic state exemption.

Duration   1 year; exemptions continue as long as the eligible resident lives in Connecticut.

Number awarded   Varies each year; recently, a total of 20,117 veterans received property tax exemptions through this and other programs in Connecticut.

Deadline   Applications for the additional municipality exemption must be submitted to the assessor's office of the town of residence by September of every other year.

[811]
DAV DISASTER RELIEF FUND

Disabled American Veterans
P.O. Box 14301
Cincinnati, OH 45250-0301
(859) 441-7300   Toll Free: (877) 426-2838
Fax: (859) 441-1416   E-mail: ahdav@one.net
Web: www.dav.org/veterans/DisasterRelief.aspx

Summary   To identify and assist needy disabled veterans who have survived a natural calamity.

Eligibility   At times of natural disaster (e.g., flood, earthquake, tornado, or other calamity) representatives of the Disabled American Veterans (DAV) will search out disabled veterans who need assistance.

Financial data   The amount of assistance depends on the nature of the disasters and the needs of veterans; recently, an annual total of $191,000 was dispersed to help disabled veterans secure temporary lodging, food, and other necessities.

Duration   These funds are granted to relieve emergency situations only; they are not available on an ongoing basis.

Additional data   Disabled veterans need not be DAV members to receive aid through this program. Since this program began in 1968, it has dispersed more than $7.1 million. DAV formerly operated a separate Emergency Relief Fund but incorporated that into this program.

Number awarded Varies each year. Recently, more than 200 grants totaling $148,860 were awarded.

Deadline Funds are made available as soon as the need arises.

[812]
DEATH PENSION FOR SURVIVORS OF VETERANS

Department of Veterans Affairs
Attn: Veterans Benefits Administration
810 Vermont Avenue, N.W.
Washington, DC 20420
(202) 418-4343   Toll Free: (800) 827-1000
Web: www.vba.va.gov/bin/21/pension/spousepen.htm

Summary To provide pensions to disabled and other spouses and children of deceased veterans with wartime service.

Eligibility This program is open to surviving spouses and unmarried children of deceased veterans who were discharged under conditions other than dishonorable and who had at least 90 days of active military service, at least 1 day of which was during a period of war. Veterans who enlisted after September 7, 1980 generally had to have served at least 24 months or the full period for which they were called to active duty. The countable income of spouses and children must be below specified limits.

Financial data The pension program pays the difference, in 12 monthly installments, between countable income and the specified income level. Currently, those limits are the following: surviving spouse without dependent children, $7,933; surviving spouse with 1 dependent child, $10,385; surviving spouse in need of regular aid and attendance without dependent children, $12,681; surviving spouse in need of regular aid and attendance with 1 dependent child, $15,128; surviving spouse permanently housebound without dependent children, $9,696; surviving spouse permanently housebound with 1 dependent child, $12,144; increase for each additional dependent child, $2,020; surviving children who are living alone, $2,020.

Duration For surviving spouse: until remarriage. For surviving unmarried child: until the age of 18, or 23 if attending a VA-approved school. For surviving child with disability: as long as the condition exists or until marriage.

Number awarded Varies each year.

Deadline Applications may be submitted at any time.

[813]
DELAWARE INCOME TAX EXCLUSION FOR DISABLED AND ELDERLY PERSONS

Division of Revenue
Carvel State Office Building
820 North French Street
P.O. Box 8763
Wilmington, DE 19899-8763
(302) 577-3300
Web: revenue.delaware.gov

Summary To provide a partial exemption from state income taxation to people with disabilities and those over the age of 60 in Delaware.

Eligibility This exemption is available to residents of Delaware who are 60 years of age or over or totally and permanently disabled. Married applicants filing a joint return must have a combined earned income of less than $5,000 and total gross income less than $20,000; applicants who are single or married and filing a separate return must have earned income of less than $2,500 and total gross income less than $10,000.

Financial data Married residents filing a joint return are entitled to exempt $4,000 from their gross income for purposes of state income taxation; single residents and married residents filing a separate return are entitled to exclude $2,000 from their gross income.

Duration The exemption continues as long as the recipient remains a resident of Delaware for state income tax purposes.

Number awarded Varies each year.

Deadline Deadline not specified.

[814]
DISABILITY PENSION PROGRAM FOR VETERANS

Department of Veterans Affairs
Attn: Veterans Benefits Administration
810 Vermont Avenue, N.W.
Washington, DC 20420
(202) 418-4343   Toll Free: (800) 827-1000
Web: www.vba.va.gov/bin/21/pension/vetpen.htm

Summary To provide a pension for disabled or elderly veterans who served during wartime.

Eligibility This program is open to veterans who were discharged under conditions other than dishonorable and who had at least 90 days of active military service, at least 1 day of which was during a period of war. They must be permanently and totally disabled or older than 65 years of age. Veterans who enlisted after September 7, 1980 generally had to have served at least 24 months or the full period for which they were called to active duty. The countable income of veterans must be below specified limits. Veterans of the Mexican Border Period and World War I qualify for additional payment as an Early War Veteran.

Financial data The pension program pays the difference, in 12 monthly installments, between countable income and the specified income level. Currently, those limits are the following: veteran with no dependents, $11,830; veteran with a spouse or child, $15,493; veteran in need of regular aid and attendance with no dependents, $19,736; veteran in need of regular aid and attendance with 1 dependent, $23,396; veteran permanently housebound without dependents, $14,457; veteran permanently housebound with 1 dependent, $18,120; 2 veterans married to each other, $14,493; increase for each additional dependent child, $2,020; additional payment for Early War Veterans, $2,686 for each of the preceding categories.

Duration The pension is paid for the life of the recipient.

Number awarded Varies each year.

Deadline Applications are accepted at any time.

[815]
DISTRICT OF COLUMBIA DISABILITY INCOME TAX EXCLUSION

Office of Tax and Revenue
Attn: Customer Service Center
941 North Capitol Street, N.E., First Floor
Washington, DC 20002
(202) 727-4TAX   Fax: (202) 442-6477
E-mail: otr.ocfo@dc.gov
Web: otr.cfo.dc.gov/otr/site/default.asp

Summary To exclude a portion of the disability pay received by residents of the District of Columbia from local income taxation.

Eligibility This exclusion is available to residents of the District of Columbia who retired on disability and were permanently and totally disabled when they retired. Applicants must have received disability pay and did not elect to treat that income as a pension for federal purposes. They must be younger than 65 years of age.

Financial data Up to $5,200 per year of disability pay may be excluded from income for purposes of District taxation. The amount of the exclusion is reduced by the excess of the person's federal adjusted gross income over $15,000.

Duration The exclusion continues as long as the recipient resides in the District of Columbia.

Number awarded Varies each year.

Deadline The exclusion is claimed as part of the local income return, due in April of each year.

[816]
DISTRICT OF COLUMBIA INCOME TAX EXCLUSION FOR THE DISABLED

Office of Tax and Revenue
Attn: Customer Service Center
941 North Capitol Street, N.E., First Floor
Washington, DC 20002
(202) 727-4TAX   Fax: (202) 442-6477
E-mail: otr.ocfo@dc.gov
Web: otr.cfo.dc.gov/otr/site/default.asp

Summary To exclude a portion of the income of people with disabilities from local income taxation in the District of Columbia.

Eligibility This exclusion is available to residents of the District of Columbia who have been determined by the Social Security Administration to be totally and permanently disabled. Applicants must be receiving Supplemental Security Income or Social Security Disability Income and have total household adjusted gross income less than $100,000.

Financial data Residents with disabilities are entitled to exclude $10,000 from their income for local tax purposes in the District of Columbia.

Duration The exclusion continues as long as the recipient resides in the District of Columbia.

Number awarded Varies each year.

Deadline The exemption is claimed as part of the local income return, due in April of each year.

[817]
ELSIE S. BELLOWS FUND GRANTS

United Cerebral Palsy
Attn: Bellows Fund
1660 L Street, N.W., Suite 700
Washington, DC 20036-5602
(202) 776-0406   Toll Free: (800) USA-5UCP
Fax: (202) 776-0414   TDD: (202) 973-7197
E-mail: info@ucp.org
Web: www.ucp.org/ucp_channelsub.cfm/1/14/11830

Summary To provide funding to individuals with disabilities interested in purchasing assistive technology equipment.

Eligibility This program is open to individuals with disabilities who are represented by a local affiliate of United Cerebral Palsy (UCP). Applicants must be interested in purchasing assistive technology devices, such as wheelchairs (manual or electric), augmentative communication devices, environmental controls, computer equipment, lifts, or hearing aids. Funding is not available for automobiles, evaluations or other assistive technology services, or furniture and appliances that are not adapted. The individuals must have exhausted all governmental and personal financial resources available to them. Applications must be submitted on their behalf by a local UCP affiliate.

Financial data Grants depend on the availability of funds and the cost of the proposed assistive technology purchase. Each UCP chapter is allocated between $2,250 and $3,750 for its grants.

Duration These are 1-time grants.

Additional data This program was established in 1995.

Number awarded Varies each year; recently, approximately $273,000 was available for these grants.

Deadline Applications may be submitted at any time.

[818]
FACILITATION AWARDS FOR SCIENTISTS AND ENGINEERS WITH DISABILITIES

National Science Foundation
Office of Integrative Activities
Attn: Coordinator, Facilitation Awards for Scientists and
  Engineers with Disabilities
4201 Wilson Boulevard, Room 815
Arlington, VA 22230
(703) 292-4684   TDD: (800) 281-8749
Web: www.nsf.gov

Summary To provide supplemental financing to individuals with disabilities who wish to prepare for a career in science and engineering and who are working on projects supported by the National Science Foundation (NSF).

Eligibility This program is open to individuals with disabilities who are principal investigators, other senior professionals, or graduate and undergraduate students participating in a specific project supported by the foundation.

Requests for special equipment or assistance necessary to enable an individual with a disability to participate in a specific NSF-supported project may be included in the original proposal submitted to a NSF program or submitted as a separate request for supplemental funding for an existing NSF grant.

Financial data Funds may be requested to purchase special equipment, modify equipment, or provide services required specifically for the work to be undertaken. No maximum amount has been set for requests, but it is expected that the cost (including equipment adaptation and installation) will not be a major proportion of the total proposed budget for the project.

Additional data Examples of specific equipment for which funds may be requested include prosthetic devices to manipulate a particular apparatus; equipment to convert sound to visual signals, or vice versa, for a particular experiment; access to a special site or to a mode of transportation; a reader or interpreter with special technical competence related to the project; or other special-purpose equipment or assistance needed to conduct a particular project. Items that compensate in a general way for the disabling condition are not eligible; examples include standard wheelchairs, general prosthetics, hearing aids, TTY/TDD devices, general readers for the blind, or ramps, elevators, or other structural modifications of research facilities.

Number awarded Varies each year.

Deadline Applications may be submitted at any time.

[819]
FEDERAL INCOME TAX CREDIT FOR THE ELDERLY OR THE DISABLED

Internal Revenue Service
1111 Constitution Avenue, N.W.
Washington, DC 20224
Toll Free: (800) TAX-FORM
Web: www.irs.gov

Summary To provide a federal income tax credit for certain elderly and disabled citizens.

Eligibility Eligible for this credit are U.S. citizens or residents who are either 1) 65 years of age or older or 2) under 65 and retired on permanent and total disability, not yet of mandatory retirement age, and receiving taxable disability benefits. Beneficiaries of this credit must also have adjusted gross income below certain levels depending on their filing status: $17,500 for single, head of household, or qualifying widow(er) with dependent child filers; $20,000 for married taxpayers filing a joint return if only 1 spouse is elderly or disabled; $25,000 for married taxpayers filing a joint return if both spouses qualify as elderly or disabled; or $12,500 for married taxpayers filing a separate return who did not live with their spouse at any time during the year. Alternatively, taxpayers also qualify if the total of their nontaxable Social Security and other nontaxable pension(s) is less than $5,000 for single, head of household, or qualifying widow(er) with dependent child filers; $5,000 for married taxpayers filing a joint return if only 1 spouse is elderly or disabled; $7,500 for married taxpayers filing a joint return if both spouses qualify as elderly or disabled; or

$3,750 for married taxpayers filing a separate return who did not live with their spouse at any time during the year.

Financial data The amount of this credit is calculated on the basis of the filing status and income of the recipient, up to a maximum of $1,125 per year.

Duration 1 year; must reapply each year.

Number awarded Varies each year.

Deadline This credit is applied to the qualifying tax filers' federal income tax return, which is due in April of each year.

[820]
FLORIDA PROPERTY TAX DISABILITY EXEMPTION FOR EX-SERVICE MEMBERS

Florida Department of Revenue
Attn: Taxpayer Services
1379 Blountstown Highway
Tallahassee, FL 32304-2716
(850) 488-6800   Toll Free: (800) 352-3671
TDD: (800) 367-8331
Web: www.myflorida.com/dor/property/exemptions.html

Summary To exempt a portion of the value of property owned by disabled veterans in Florida.

Eligibility This exemption is available to veterans who have at least a 10% service-connected disability and are Florida residents owning taxable property.

Financial data $5,000 of the value of the property is exempt from taxation.

Duration The exemption applies as long as the taxpayer owns the property in Florida.

Additional data Initial applications should be made in person at the appropriate county property appraiser's office.

Number awarded Varies each year.

Deadline Applications must be submitted by February of the year for which the exemption is sought.

[821]
FLORIDA SERVICE-CONNECTED TOTAL AND PERMANENT DISABILITY PROPERTY TAX EXEMPTION

Florida Department of Revenue
Attn: Taxpayer Services
1379 Blountstown Highway
Tallahassee, FL 32304-2716
(850) 488-6800   Toll Free: (800) 352-3671
TDD: (800) 367-8331
Web: www.myflorida.com/dor/property/exemptions.html

Summary To exempt from property taxation real estate owned by disabled veterans and their surviving spouses.

Eligibility This exemption is available to Florida residents who have real estate that they own and use as a homestead. Applicants must be honorably-discharged veterans with a service-connected total and permanent disability. Under certain circumstances, the benefit of this exemption can carry over to a surviving spouse.

Financial data All real estate used and owned as a homestead, less any portion used for commercial purposes, is exempt from taxation.

Duration The exemption applies as long as the taxpayer owns the property in Florida.

Additional data Initial applications should be made in person at the appropriate county property appraiser's office.

Number awarded Varies each year.

Deadline Applications must be submitted by February of the year for which the exemption is sought.

[822]
FOUNDATION FOR SCIENCE AND DISABILITY GRADUATE STUDENT GRANT FUND

Foundation for Science and Disability, Inc.
c/o Richard Mankin
USDA-ARS-CMAVE
1700 S.W. 23rd Drive
Gainesville, FL 32608
(352) 374-5774   Fax: (352) 374-5804
E-mail: rmankin@nersp.nerdc.ufl.edu
Web: www.stemd.org

Summary To provide supplemental grants to students with disabilities who are interested in working on a graduate degree in a science-related field.

Eligibility This program is open to 1) college seniors who have a disability and have been accepted to a graduate or professional school in the sciences, and 2) graduate science students who have a disability. Applicants must be U.S. citizens interested in working on a degree in an area of engineering, mathematics, medicine, science, or technology. Along with their application, they must submit an essay (about 250 words) describing professional goals and objectives, as well as the specific purpose for which the grant would be used. Selection is based on financial need, sincerity of purpose, and scholarship and/or research ability.

Financial data The grant is $1,000. Funds may be used for an assistive device or instrument, as financial support to work with a professor on an individual research project, or for some other special need.

Duration The award is granted annually.

Additional data The Foundation for Science and Disability, Inc. is an affiliate society of the American Association for the Advancement of Science.

Number awarded Varies each year.

Deadline November of each year.

[823]
GEORGIA HOMESTEAD TAX EXEMPTION FOR DISABLED VETERANS

Georgia Department of Revenue
Attn: Property Tax Division
4245 International Parkway, Suite A
Hapeville, GA 30354-3918
(404) 968-0707   Fax: (404) 968-0778
E-mail: Local.Government.Services@dor.ga.gov
Web: etax.dor.ga.gov

Summary To exempt from property taxation a portion of the value of homesteads owned by disabled veterans in Georgia and their families.

Eligibility This program is open to residents of Georgia who qualify as a 100% disabled veteran under any of several provisions of state law. Surviving spouses and minor children are also eligible. Applicants must actually occupy a homestead and use it as their legal residence for all purposes.

Financial data The first $50,000 of assessed valuation of the homestead owned by disabled veterans or their family members is exempt from property taxes for state, county, municipal, and school purposes.

Duration The exemption remains in effect as long as the veteran or family member owns and resides in the homestead.

Number awarded Varies each year.

Deadline Applications must be filed with local tax officials by February of each year.

[824]
GEORGIA INCOME TAX EXEMPTION FOR DISABLED PERSONS

Georgia Department of Revenue
Attn: Taxpayer Services Division
1800 Century Boulevard, Room 8300
Atlanta, GA 30345-3205
(404) 417-4477   Toll Free: (877) 602-8477
Fax: (404) 417-6628
E-mail: taxpayer.services@dor.ga.gov
Web: etax.dor.ga.gov/inctax/IndGeneralInfo.aspx

Summary To exempt a portion of the retirement income of the elderly and persons with disabilities from state income taxation in Georgia.

Eligibility Eligible are persons classified as residents of Georgia for the purpose of state income taxation who are either 62 years of age or older or permanently and totally disabled (regardless of age).

Financial data Up to $35,000 of retirement income received by people with disabilities or the elderly is exempt from state income taxation.

Duration The exemption continues as long as the recipient resides in Georgia.

Deadline Deadline not specified.

[825]
GRANTS FOR ACCESSIBILITY

Corporation for Independent Living
157 Charter Oak Avenue, Third Floor
Hartford, CT 06106
(860) 563-6011, ext. 221   Fax: (860) 563-2562
E-mail: access@cilhomes.org
Web: www.cilhomes.org/accessolutions.html

Summary To provide grants to low- or moderate-income residents of Connecticut who have physical disabilities (as well as their parents) and need to modify their existing housing.

Eligibility Eligible to participate in this program are Connecticut residents who have a physical disability (including people in wheelchairs, the deaf or hearing impaired, the blind or visually impaired, and people who have multiple sclerosis, cerebral palsy, traumatic brain injury, or any other physical disability), own their homes, and have a total household income at or below 80% of median income. Also eligible are homeowner parents of a child who is physically disabled and tenants who have the landlord's written consent to make accessibility renovations. Applicants must have total household income that is less than 80% of the state median. Grant funds may be used to purchase and install fixtures and improvements required to improve accessibility and/or usability of a residential dwelling in Connecticut.

Financial data Grants range from $5,000 to $50,000. Initially, a full lien is placed against the recipient's home. Total lien amounts are reduced automatically by 10% every year. At the end of 10 years, the grant is forgiven in full and the lien is removed.

Additional data Funding for this program, which began in 1984, is provided by the Connecticut Department of Economic and Community Development.

Number awarded Varies each year. Since the program began, more than 1,500 individuals have received grants.

Deadline Applications may be submitted at any time.

[826]
HARRY GREGG FOUNDATION GRANTS

Harry Gregg Foundation
1 Verney Drive
Greenfield, NH 03047
(603) 547-3311, ext. 1490
Toll Free: (800) 394-3311, ext. 1490 (within NH)
Fax: (603) 547-6212
E-mail: hgf@crotchedmountain.org
Web: www.crotchedmountain.org

Summary To provide financial assistance for vocational education, assistive technology, and other purposes to children and adults in New Hampshire who have physical, emotional, or intellectual disabilities.

Eligibility This program is open to New Hampshire residents of all ages who have physical, intellectual, or emotional disabilities. Funds may be requested for broad purposes but must specifically benefit the applicant. Examples of acceptable purposes include, but are not limited to: the costs of nonreimbursed medical, dental, vision, hearing, or therapy treatments; special equipment, services, or supplies; modifications to living area, workplace, or vehicle; respite services for the recipient or care givers; costs of attending a special camp; recreational activities; and vocational education or driver training tuition assistance. Selection is based on demonstrated need for a product of service, the applicant's financial circumstances, and the ability of the foundation to help improve the quality of life of a grant recipient.

Financial data Most grants range up to $1,200.

Duration Recipients may receive a maximum of 4 grants (no more than 2 in any year).

Additional data This foundation was established in 1989. If a request is not funded, applicants may reapply 6 months later for the same or a different purpose.

Number awarded Nearly 150 each year. Since this foundation was established, it has awarded more than 5,000 grants worth nearly $2 million.

Deadline March, June, September, or December of each year.

[827]
HAWAII GRANTS FOR SPECIAL HOUSING FOR DISABLED VETERANS

Office of Veterans Services
Attn: Veterans Services Coordinator
459 Patterson Road
E-Wing, Room 1-A103
Honolulu, HI 96819-1522
(808) 433-0420   Fax: (808) 433-0385
E-mail: ovs@ovs.hawaii.gov
Web: Hawaii.gov

Summary To provide grants to disabled veterans in Hawaii for purchasing or remodeling a home.

Eligibility This program is open to totally disabled veterans in Hawaii. Applicants must be proposing to purchase or remodel a home to improve handicapped accessibility.

Financial data Grants up to $5,000 are available.

Duration These are 1-time grants.

Deadline Deadline not specified.

[828]
HAWAII INCOME TAX EXEMPTION FOR DISABLED RESIDENTS

Department of Taxation
Attn: Taxpayer Services Branch
425 Queen Street
P.O. Box 259
Honolulu, HI 96809-0259
(808) 587-4242   Toll Free: (800) 222-3229
Fax: (808) 587-1488   TDD: (808) 587-1418
Web: hawaii.gov/tax

Summary To exempt a portion of the income of blind, deaf, and other disabled residents from state income tax in Hawaii.

Eligibility Eligible for this exemption are 1) blind residents whose central visual acuity does not exceed 20/200 in the better eye with corrective lenses or whose visual acuity is greater than 20/200 but is accompanied by a limitation in the field of vision such that the widest diameter of the visual field subtends an angle no greater than 20 degrees; 2) deaf residents whose average loss in the speech frequencies in the better ear is 82 decibels A.S.A. or worse; or 3) totally disabled residents (physically or mentally) who are unable to engage in any substantial gainful business or occupation (a person whose gross income exceeds $30,000 per year is assumed to be engaged in a substantial gainful business or occupation).

Financial data The maximum exemptions from state income tax are as follows: single disabled resident, $7,000; disabled husband and wife, $14,000; disabled husband or wife, with non-disabled spouse under 65, $8,040; disabled husband or wife, with non-disabled spouse 65 years of age or older, $9,080.

Duration The exemption continues as long as the recipient resides in Hawaii.

Additional data Residents who claim this special exemption are not eligible to claim additional exemptions for their children or other dependents.

Deadline Deadline not specified.

[829]
HAWAII PROPERTY TAX EXEMPTIONS FOR DISABLED VETERANS

Office of Veterans Services
Attn: Veterans Services Coordinator
459 Patterson Road
E-Wing, Room 1-A103
Honolulu, HI 96819-1522
(808) 433-0420   Fax: (808) 433-0385
E-mail: ovs@ovs.hawaii.gov
Web: www.dod.state.hi.us/ovs/benefits.html

Summary To exempt the homes of disabled veterans and surviving spouses in Hawaii from real estate taxation.

Eligibility This program is open to totally disabled veterans in Hawaii and their surviving spouses.

Financial data The real property owned and occupied as a home is exempt from taxation.

Duration The exemption applies as long as the disabled veteran or his/her widow(er) resides in Hawaii.

Deadline Deadline not specified.

[830]
HOMECHOICE MORTGAGE LOAN PROGRAM

Fannie Mae
Attn: Resource Center
13150 Worldgate Drive
Herndon, VA 20170-4376
Toll Free: (800) 7-FANNIE
E-mail: resource_center@fanniemae.com
Web: www.fanniemae.com

Summary To provide mortgage loans to people with disabilities and their families.

Eligibility This program is open to people with low to moderate income who have a disability as defined by the Americans with Disabilities Act of 1990 or have family members with disabilities living with them. Applicants must be interested in obtaining a mortgage loan for purchase of owner-occupied single-family detached homes, townhouses, or condominiums. Non-occupant co-borrowers may be considered if they are a family member or legal guardian. Nontraditional credit histories are considered.

Financial data No loan limits are specified. The program offers flexibility in the areas of loan-to-value ratios, down payment sources, qualifying ratios, and the establishment of credit.

Duration 15- and 30-year fixed-rate mortgages are available.

Additional data Loans under this program are available through coalitions in 23 states comprised of organizations and agencies working together to create homeownership opportunities for people with disabilities. For further information on those coalitions, contact Fannie Mae.

Number awarded Varies each year.

Deadline Applications may be submitted at any time.

[831]
IDAHO CIRCUIT BREAKER PROPERTY TAX REDUCTION

Idaho State Tax Commission
Attn: Public Information Office
800 Park Boulevard, Plaza IV
P.O. Box 36
Boise, ID 83722-0410
(208) 334-7736   Toll Free: (800) 972-7660
TDD: (800) 377-3529
Web: tax.idaho.gov/propertytax/pt_homeowners.htm

Summary To reduce a portion of the property tax of disabled and other veterans and other disabled or elderly residents of Idaho.

Eligibility Eligible for this property tax reduction are residents of Idaho who own and live in a primary residence in the state and have an annual income of $28,000 or less (after deducting designated forms of income, including compensation received by a veteran from the U.S. Department of Veterans Affairs for a 40% to 100% service-connected disability). Applicants must be in 1 or more of the following categories: disabled (as recognized by an appropriate federal agency), blind, former prisoner of war or hostage, veteran with at least 10% service-connected disability or receiving a VA pension for a nonservice-connected disability, 65 years of age or older, widow(er) of any age, or fatherless or motherless child under 18 years of age.

Financial data The maximum amount of reduction is the lesser of $1,320 or the actual taxes on the recipient's qualifying home. The minimum reduction is the lesser of $100 or the actual taxes on the home.

Duration Applications for this reduction must be submitted each year.

Additional data All recipients of this reduction automatically receive Idaho's Homeowner's Exemption, which reduces the taxable value of the home (excluding land) by 50% or $75,000, whichever is less. Solid waste, irrigation, or other fees charged by some counties are not taxes and cannot be reduced by this program.

Number awarded Varies each year.

Deadline April of each year.

[832]
IDAHO RETIREMENT BENEFITS DEDUCTION

Idaho State Tax Commission
Attn: Public Information Office
800 Park Boulevard, Plaza IV
P.O. Box 36
Boise, ID 83722-0410
(208) 334-7660   Toll Free: (800) 972-7660
TDD: (800) 377-3529
Web: tax.idaho.gov

Summary To deduct the retirement and disability income of certain residents from state income tax in Idaho.

Eligibility Eligible for this deduction are full-year residents of Idaho who are age 65 or older, or disabled and age 62 and older, and who are receiving the following annuities and benefits: 1) retirement annuities paid by the United States to a retired civil service employee or the unremarried widow of the employee; 2) retirement benefits paid from the firemen's retirement fund of the state of Idaho to a retired fireman or the unremarried widow of a retired fireman; 3) retirement benefits paid from the policeman's retirement fund of a city within Idaho to a retired policeman or the unremarried widow of a retired policeman; or 4) retirement benefits paid by the United States to a retired member of the U.S. military service or the unremarried widow of those veterans.

Financial data The amount of retirement or disability benefits may be deducted from taxable state income in Idaho, to a maximum deduction of $39,330 for married couples or $26,220 for single persons.

Duration 1 year; must reapply each year.

Number awarded Varies each year.

Deadline April of each year.

[833]
IDAHO WAR VETERAN'S EMERGENCY GRANT PROGRAM

Idaho Division of Veterans Services
Attn: Office of Veterans Advocacy
444 Fort Street
Boise, ID 83702
(208) 577-2300   Fax: (208) 577-2333
E-mail: info@veterans.idaho.gov
Web: www.veterans.idaho.gov/Veterans_Advocacy.aspx

Summary To provide emergency assistance to disabled veterans, wartime veterans, and their families in Idaho.

Eligibility Eligible for these grants are veterans who had at least 90 days of honorable wartime military service while a resident of Idaho. Veterans with a service-connected disability are eligible with earlier separation. Surviving spouses and dependent children are also eligible. Applicants must be current residents of Idaho in need of assistance because of a major catastrophe (e.g., natural disaster or death of a spouse or child), loss of job because of a disability, or other extreme financial emergency (e.g., cutoff notice from a utility company, eviction notice from a landlord, arrears payment notice from the lien holder of a home).

Financial data The maximum amount available under this program is $1,000, issued in small incremental grants.

Duration The limit of $1,000 applies for the lifetime of each veteran or his/her family.

Additional data This program was established by the Idaho legislature in lieu of granting a wartime bonus to Idaho veterans.

Number awarded Varies each year.

Deadline Deadline not specified.

[834]
ILLINOIS DISABLED PERSONS' HOMESTEAD EXEMPTION

Illinois Department of Revenue
101 West Jefferson Street
P.O. Box 19044
Springfield, IL 62794-9044
(217) 782-9337   Toll Free: (800) 732-8866
TDD: (800) 544-5304
Web: www.revenue.state.il.us

Summary To reduce the value for property taxation of homesteads owned by disabled residents of Illinois.

Eligibility This exemption is available to residents of Illinois who own a homestead in the state as their primary residence. Applicants must have a verified disability.

Financial data Qualifying homeowners receive a $2,000 reduction in the equalized assessed value (EAV) of their property.

Duration Homeowners must file an annual application to continue to receive this exemption.

Additional data This program was established in 2007.

Deadline Deadline not specified.

[835]
ILLINOIS DISABLED VETERANS' STANDARD HOMESTEAD EXEMPTION

Illinois Department of Revenue
101 West Jefferson Street
P.O. Box 19044
Springfield, IL 62794-9044
(217) 782-9337   Toll Free: (800) 732-8866
TDD: (800) 544-5304
Web: www.revenue.state.il.us

Summary To reduce the value for property taxation of homesteads owned by disabled veterans in Illinois.

Eligibility This exemption is available to veterans who own or lease a homestead in Illinois as their primary residence. Applicants must have a service-connected disability verified by the U.S. Department of Veterans Affairs of at least 50%.

Financial data Veterans whose disability is rated as at least 50% but less than 75% receive a $2,500 reduction in the equalized assessed value (EAV) of their property. Veterans whose disability is rated as at least 75% receive a $5,000 reduction in the EAV of their property.

Duration Veterans must file an annual application to continue to receive this exemption.

Additional data This program was established in 2007.

Deadline Deadline not specified.

[836]
ILLINOIS INCOME TAX SUBTRACTION FOR GOVERNMENT RETIREES

Illinois Department of Revenue
101 West Jefferson Street
P.O. Box 19044
Springfield, IL 62794-9044
(217) 782-9337   Toll Free: (800) 732-8866
TDD: (800) 544-5304
Web: www.revenue.state.il.us

Summary To exempt the retirement and disability income of veterans and other government employees from state taxation in Illinois.

Eligibility This exemption applies to the income received from government retirement and disability plans, including military plans.

Financial data All government retirement and disability income of eligible residents is exempt from state income taxation.

Duration The exemption continues as long as the recipient resides in Illinois.

Deadline Deadline not specified.

[837]
ILLINOIS SPECIALLY ADAPTED HOUSING TAX EXEMPTION

Illinois Department of Veterans' Affairs
833 South Spring Street
P.O. Box 19432
Springfield, IL 62794-9432
(217) 782-6641   Toll Free: (800) 437-9824 (within IL)
Fax: (217) 524-0344   TDD: (217) 524-4645
E-mail: webmail@dva.state.il.us
Web: www.veterans.illinois.gov/benefits/realestate.htm

Summary To provide an exemption on the assessed value of specially adapted housing to Illinois veterans with disabilities and their spouses.

Eligibility Specially adapted housing units for disabled veterans that have been purchased or constructed with federal funds are eligible for this exemption. The exemption is extended to the veteran, the spouse, or the unremarried surviving spouse.

Financial data Under this program, an exemption is allowed on the assessed value of eligible real property, up to a maximum of $70,000 of assessed valuation.

Duration 1 year; renewable as long as the veteran, or spouse, or unremarried surviving spouse resides in the specially adapted housing in Illinois.

Number awarded Varies each year.

Deadline Applications for the exemption may be submitted at any time.

[838]
ILLINOIS TAX EXEMPTION FOR MOBILE HOMES

Illinois Department of Veterans' Affairs
833 South Spring Street
P.O. Box 19432
Springfield, IL 62794-9432
(217) 782-6641   Toll Free: (800) 437-9824 (within IL)
Fax: (217) 524-0344   TDD: (217) 524-4645
E-mail: webmail@dva.state.il.us
Web: www.veterans.illinois.gov/benefits/realestate.htm

Summary To provide an exemption on the assessed value of mobile homes to Illinois veterans with disabilities and their spouses.

Eligibility This exemption applies to taxes imposed on mobile homes in Illinois. The property must be owned and used exclusively by a disabled veteran, spouse, or unremarried surviving spouse as a home. The veteran must have received authorization of the Specially Adapted Housing Grant by the U.S. Department of Veterans Affairs, whether that benefit was used or not. Disabled veterans who currently live in a mobile home and never received the Specially Adapted Housing Grant are not eligible.

Financial data Qualifying veterans, spouses, and unmarried surviving spouses are exempt from property taxes imposed by the state of Illinois on mobile homes.

Duration 1 year; renewable as long as the veteran, or spouse, or unremarried surviving spouse resides in the mobile home in Illinois.

Number awarded Varies each year.

Deadline Applications for the exemption may be submitted at any time.

[839]
INDIANA DISABILITY RETIREMENT INCOME TAX DEDUCTION

Indiana Department of Revenue
Attn: Taxpayer Services Division
Indiana Government Center North
100 North Senate Avenue
Indianapolis, IN 46204-2253
(317) 232-2240   TDD: (317) 232-4952
E-mail: pfrequest@dor.state.in.us
Web: www.in.gov/dor

Summary To exempt a portion of the disability income of Indiana residents from state taxation.

Eligibility This exclusion is available to residents of Indiana who retired on disability and were permanently and totally disabled when they retired. Applicants must have received disability pay and did not elect to treat that income as a pension for federal purposes. They must be younger than 65 years of age.

Financial data Up to $5,200 per year of disability pay may be excluded from income for purposes of state taxation. The amount of the exclusion is reduced by the excess of the person's federal adjusted gross income over $15,000.

Duration The exclusion is available as long as the recipient resides in Indiana.
Deadline Deadline not specified.

[840]
INDIANA PROPERTY TAX DEDUCTION FOR BLIND OR DISABLED PERSONS

Department of Local Government Finance
Indiana Government Center North, Room 1058
100 North Senate Avenue
Indianapolis, IN 46201
(317) 232-3777   Fax: (317) 232-8779
E-mail: PropertyTaxInfo@dlgf.in.gov
Web: www.in.gov/dlgf

Summary To exempt Indiana residents who are blind or disabled from a portion of their property tax.

Eligibility Eligible for this program are Indiana residents who are blind or disabled and receive less than $17,000 in annual taxable income. A blind person is defined as an individual who has vision in the better eye with correcting glasses of 20/200 or less, or a disqualifying visual field defect as determined upon examination by a designated ophthalmologist or optometrist. A disabled person is defined as an individual unable to engage in any substantial gainful activity by reason of a medically determinable physical or mental impairment that can be expected to result in death or has lasted and can be expected to last for at least 12 continuous months.

Financial data The maximum property tax deduction is $12,480.

Duration This deduction may be taken annually, as long as the Indiana resident meets the requirements of the program.

Additional data Property taxes are administered by individual counties in Indiana. Further information is available from county tax assessors.

Number awarded Varies each year.

Deadline Applications must be filed during the 12 months before May of each year for which the individual wishes to obtain the deduction.

[841]
INDIANA PROPERTY TAX DEDUCTIONS FOR DISABLED VETERANS

Department of Local Government Finance
Indiana Government Center North, Room 1058
100 North Senate Avenue
Indianapolis, IN 46201
(317) 232-3777   Fax: (317) 232-8779
E-mail: PropertyTaxInfo@dlgf.in.gov
Web: www.in.gov/dlgf

Summary To exempt disabled Indiana veterans and their spouses from a portion of their property taxes.

Eligibility This program is open to the following categories of veterans who are residents of Indiana: 1) served honorably at least 90 days and are either totally disabled (the disability does not need to be service-connected) or are at least 62 years of age and have at least a 10% service-connected disability; 2) served honorably during war-

time and have at least a 10% service-connected disability; or 3) served honorably during wartime and either have a 100% service-connected disability or are at least 62 years of age and have at least a 10% service connected disability. A statutory disability rating for pulmonary tuberculosis does not qualify. A disability incurred during Initial Active Duty for Training (IADT) with the National Guard or Reserves is eligible only if the disability occurred from an event during the period of active duty and that duty was performed during wartime. Surviving spouses of those 3 categories of veterans are also eligible.

Financial data Property tax exemptions are $12,480 for veterans and spouses in the first category (only if the assessed value of the combined real and personal property owned by the veteran or spouse does not exceed $143,160), $24,960 in the second category, or $37,440 in the third category; there is no limit on the value of the property owned by a surviving spouse).

Duration 1 year; may be renewed as long as the eligible veteran or surviving unremarried spouse owns and occupies the primary residence in Indiana.

Number awarded Varies each year.

Deadline Applications must be submitted no later than May of each year.

[842]
INJURED MARINE SEMPER FI GRANTS

Injured Marine Semper Fi Fund
c/o Wounded Warrior Center
Building H49
P.O. Box 555193
Camp Pendleton, CA 92055-5193
(760) 725-3680   Fax: (760) 725-3685
E-mail: info@semperfifund.org
Web: www.semperfifund.org

Summary To provide supplemental assistance to Marines injured in combat and training operations and their families.

Eligibility This program is open to Marines injured in combat operations and training accidents and their families. Applicants must need financial assistance to deal with the personal and financial disruption associated with leaving their home, their family, and their job during hospitalization, rehabilitation, and recuperation. Applications are available at military hospitals.

Financial data Funds are available for such expenses as child care, travel expenses for families, and other necessities. Assistance is also available for the purchase of adaptive transportation, home modifications, and specialized equipment such as wheelchairs, audio/visual equipment for the blind, and software for traumatic brain injuries.

Duration Grants are provided as needed.

Additional data This fund was established in 2004 by a small group of Marine Corps spouses.

Number awarded Varies each year. Since this program was established, it has awarded more than 18,300 grants worth more than $37 million.

Deadline Applications may be submitted at any time.

[843]
IOWA DISABILITY INCOME TAX EXCLUSION

Iowa Department of Revenue
Attn: Taxpayer Services
Hoover State Office Building
1305 East Walnut
P.O. Box 10457
Des Moines, IA 50306-0457
(515) 281-3114   Toll Free: (800) 367-3388 (within IA)
Fax: (515) 242-6487   E-mail: idr@iowa.gov
Web: www.iowa.gov/tax

Summary To exclude a portion of the disability income of residents of Iowa from state income taxation.

Eligibility This exclusion is available to residents of Iowa who retired on disability and were permanently and totally disabled when they retired. Applicants must have received disability pay and did not elect to treat that income as a pension for federal purposes. They must be younger than 65 years of age.

Financial data Up to $5,200 per year of disability pay may be excluded from income for purposes of state taxation. The amount of the exclusion is reduced by the excess of the person's federal adjusted gross income over $15,000.

Duration The exclusion continues until the recipient reaches the age of 65 years.

Number awarded Varies each year.

Deadline Deadline not specified.

[844]
IOWA PENSION/RETIREMENT INCOME EXCLUSION

Iowa Department of Revenue
Attn: Taxpayer Services
Hoover State Office Building
1305 East Walnut
P.O. Box 10457
Des Moines, IA 50306-0457
(515) 281-3114   Toll Free: (800) 367-3388 (within IA)
Fax: (515) 242-6487   E-mail: idr@iowa.gov
Web: www.iowa.gov/tax

Summary To exempt a portion of the income received by disabled and other retirees in Iowa, as well as their surviving spouses, from state taxation.

Eligibility This exemption applies to the retirement income of residents of Iowa who are 1) 55 years of age or older, 2) disabled, or 3) a surviving spouse or a survivor having an insurable interest in an individual who would have qualified from the exclusion on the basis of age or disability.

Financial data For joint filers, the exclusion is the lesser of $12,000 or the taxable amount of the retirement income; for all other statuses of filers, each eligible taxpayer can claim as an exemption the lesser of $6,000 or the taxable amount of the retirement income.

Duration The exemption continues as long as the recipient remains a resident of Iowa for state income tax purposes.

Number awarded Varies each year.

Deadline Deadline not specified.

[845]
IOWA PROPERTY TAX CREDIT FOR DISABLED AND ELDERLY RESIDENTS

Iowa Department of Revenue
Attn: Property Tax Division
Hoover State Office Building
1305 East Walnut
P.O. Box 10457
Des Moines, IA 50306-0457
(515) 281-4040   Toll Free: (800) 367-3388 (within IA)
Fax: (515) 242-6487   E-mail: idr@iowa.gov
Web: www.iowa.gov/tax

Summary To provide a property tax credit to residents of Iowa who have a disability or are elderly.

Eligibility This credit is available to residents of Iowa who are either totally disabled and over 18 years of age or 65 years of age or older. Applicants must have household income less than $20,031 per year.

Financial data Eligible residents receive a percentage credit on their property taxes that depends on their household income: from $0.00 to $10,318.99: 100%; from 10,319 to $11,532.99: 85%; from 11,533 to 12,746.99: 70%, from $12,747 to 15,174.99: 50%; from 15,175 to $17,602.99: 35%; or from $17,603 to $20,030.99: 25%.

Duration The credit continues as long as the recipient remains a resident of Iowa and owns a homestead subject to property taxation.

Number awarded Varies each year. Recently, the total value of credits extended through this program was more than $23 million.

Deadline Claims must be filed with the county treasurer by the end of May of each year. The treasurer may extend the filing deadline to the end of September, or the Director of Revenue may extend the filing deadline to the end of December.

[846]
KANSAS DISABLED ACCESS INCOME TAX CREDIT

Kansas Department of Revenue
Attn: Taxpayer Assistance Center
Robert B. Docking State Office Building
915 S.W. Harrison Street
Topeka, KS 66612-1712
(785) 368-8222   Toll Free: (877) 526-7738
Fax: (785) 291-3614   TDD: (785) 296-6461
Web: www.ksrevenue.org/taxcredits-disabled.htm

Summary To provide an income tax credit to individual and business taxpayers in Kansas who incur certain expenditures to make their property accessible to people with disabilities.

Eligibility This credit is available to state income taxpayers in Kansas who make buildings or facilities accessible and usable by persons with disabilities in conformity with the Americans with Disabilities Act of 1990. The credit applies to the taxpayer's principal dwelling or the principal dwelling of a lineal ascendant or descendant, including construction of a small barrier-free living unit attached to the principal dwelling. The only expenditures that qualify for this credit are those that are specifically intended to 1) make an existing facility accessible to people with disabilities; 2) remove existing architectural barriers; or 3) modify or adapt an existing facility or piece of equipment in order to employ people with disabilities.

Financial data For individuals, the amount of the credit depends on adjusted gross income and the amount of the expenditure, ranging from 100% of the expenditure for incomes less than $25,000, to 50% for incomes greater than $45,000 but less than $55,000; persons with incomes greater than $55,000 do not qualify for the credit; the maximum individual credit is $9,000. For businesses, the credit is 50% of the amount of the expenditure, to a maximum of $10,000.

Duration This is a 1-time credit.

Number awarded Varies each year.

Deadline Claims are filed with the state income tax return, due in April.

[847]
KANSAS INTANGIBLES TAX SENIOR CITIZEN OR DISABILITY EXEMPTION

Kansas Department of Revenue
Attn: Taxpayer Assistance Center
Robert B. Docking State Office Building
915 S.W. Harrison Street
Topeka, KS 66612-1712
(785) 368-8222   Toll Free: (877) 526-7738
Fax: (785) 291-3614   TDD: (785) 296-6461
Web: www.ksrevenue.org/perstaxtypeint.htm

Summary To exempt a portion of the income received by elderly, blind, or disabled residents in Kansas from the intangibles tax.

Eligibility This exemption applies to residents of local areas in Kansas that levy an intangibles tax on gross earnings received from such property as savings accounts, stocks, bonds, accounts receivable, and mortgages. Applicants must 1) be disabled, blind, or 60 years of age or older and 2) have a household income of $20,000 or less.

Financial data Qualified residents are entitled to exempt from their intangibles income an amount that depends on their income. If total household income is $15,000 or less, the exemption is $5,000. For incomes between $15,000 and $20,000, the exemption is calculated as the difference between $5,000 and the amount of the income over $15,000.

Duration This benefit continues as long as the recipient remains a resident of the Kansas locality that imposes an intangibles tax.

Number awarded Varies each year.

Deadline Deadline not specified.

[848]
KANSAS STATE DEAF-BLIND FUND

Kansas State Department of Education
Student Support Services
Attn: Kansas State Deaf-Blind Fund
120 S.E. 10th Avenue
Topeka, KS 66612-1182
(785) 296-2515   Toll Free: (800) 203-9462
Fax: (785) 296-6715   TDD: (785) 296-2515
E-mail: jhoughton@ksde.org
Web: www.kansped.org/ksde/kstars/projects.html

Summary To provide supplementary financial assistance to deaf-blind or severely disabled students in Kansas.

Eligibility Applications may be submitted by school personnel for students in Kansas (up to the age of 21) who are deaf-blind and/or have severe multiple disabilities. Approval for funding is granted on a first-come, first-served basis for the following areas: 1) assistive technology that enables a student with dual sensory impairments and with severe disabilities to participate more fully in an educational program (e.g., computers, adaptive equipment, eyeglasses, hearing aids, computer peripherals, augmentative communication devices, microswitches, software); 2) consultation; 3) evaluation for the cost of vision and/or hearing evaluations for students who are suspected of being deaf-blind, or a vision, hearing, or educational evaluation for recertification purposes; or 4) other costs associated with additional items or expenses that reflect best educational or effective practices, such as expenses involved in providing community activities. Applicants must provide documentation that other funding sources have been approached and that costs do not exceed the amount local education agencies are able to provide out of federal, state, or local funds. Priority candidates are students who have current deaf-blind certification, deaf-blind children from birth through 2 years of age, students who are exiting state hospital schools and returning to their home district, students who have a suspected vision loss and documented hearing loss and are in need of an evaluation, and students who have a suspected hearing loss and documented vision loss who are in need of an evaluation.

Financial data Eligible students are awarded up to $3,000 per year.

Duration 1 year; may be renewed.

Number awarded Varies each year.

Deadline May of each year.

[849]
KENTUCKY HOMESTEAD EXEMPTION FOR THE DISABLED

Kentucky Finance and Administration Cabinet
Attn: Department of Revenue
200 Fair Oaks Lane, Fourth Floor
Frankfort, KY 40620
(502) 564-8338   Fax: (502) 564-8368
E-mail: Finance.Cabinet@ky.gov
Web: revenue.ky.gov

Summary To exempt the homestead of totally disabled and elderly Kentucky residents from property taxation.

Eligibility Applicants must be classified as 1) totally disabled under a program authorized by the U.S. government or by the Railroad Retirement System, or 2) 65 years of age or older on January 1 of the year in which application is made.

Financial data Up to $33,700 of the assessed valuation of the property is exempt from taxation.

Duration This exemption continues as long as the recipient resides in Kentucky and is certified as disabled. Until age 65, however, eligible disabled recipients must apply for the exemption on an annual basis.

Additional data Applicants for this exemption must own and reside in the property.

Number awarded Varies each year.

Deadline Deadline not specified.

[850]
LONGSHORE AND HARBOR WORKERS' COMPENSATION PROGRAM

Department of Labor
Employment Standards Administration
Office of Workers' Compensation Programs
Attn: Division of Longshore and Harbor Workers'
  Compensation
200 Constitution Avenue, N.W., Room C4315
Washington, DC 20210
(202) 693-0038   Toll Free: (800) 638-7072
Fax: (202) 693-1380   TDD: (800) 326-2577
Web: www.dol.gov/dol/topic/workcomp/index.htm

Summary To provide benefits to maritime workers disabled or killed during the course of employment and to their spouses.

Eligibility This program is open to longshoremen, harbor workers, and other maritime workers who are injured during the course of employment; by extension, various other classes of private industry workers (including workers engaged in the extraction of natural resources on the outer continental shelf, employees of defense contractors overseas, and employees at post exchanges on military bases) are also eligible if they become disabled for work-related causes. In addition, survivor benefits are provided if the work-related injury causes the employee's death.

Financial data The compensation for disability is 66 2/3% of the employee's average weekly wage, with a minimum of 50% of the national average weekly wage (NAWW) and a maximum of 200% of the NAWW. In a recent year, the Department of Labor calculated the NAWW as $612.33, so the minimum weekly disability payment was $306.17 and the maximum was $1,224.66. Death benefits are equivalent to the average weekly wage of the deceased employee, with a minimum equivalent to 100% of the NAWW and a maximum equivalent to 200% of the NAWW.

Duration Benefits are paid as long as the worker remains disabled; death benefits are paid for the life of the qualified survivor.

Additional data This program also provides medical benefits and rehabilitation services to qualifying long-shoremen, harbor workers, and other workers.

Number awarded Varies; more than 15,000 maritime workers recently received compensation and medical benefits through this program.

Deadline Deadline not specified.

[851]
LOUISIANA DISABILITY INCOME EXCLUSION

Louisiana Department of Revenue
Attn: Individual Income Tax
P.O. Box 201
Baton Rouge, LA 70821
(225) 219-0102
Web: www.revenue.louisiana.gov

Summary To exclude a portion of disability income from state taxation in Louisiana.

Eligibility This exclusion is available to residents of Louisiana who receive income for a permanent total disability.

Financial data Up to $6,000 of disability income may be excluded from income for state taxation purposes.

Duration The exclusion is available as long as the recipient remains a resident of Louisiana for state income tax purposes and receives disability income.

Number awarded Varies each year.

Deadline Deadline not specified.

[852]
LOUISIANA INCOME TAX DEDUCTION FOR ADAPTIVE HOME IMPROVEMENTS FOR DISABLED INDIVIDUALS

Louisiana Department of Revenue
Attn: Individual Income Tax
P.O. Box 201
Baton Rouge, LA 70821
(225) 219-0102
Web: www.revenue.louisiana.gov

Summary To provide a state income tax deduction to people in Louisiana who have a disability and make improvements to their home.

Eligibility This deduction is available to residents of Louisiana who have a permanent disability and incur expenses for adaptations to their primary residence. Their gross family income must be $50,000 or less. Personal living expenses, amounts paid that increase the value of the residence, amounts spent in restoring property, or life insurance premiums are not deductible.

Financial data Up to $5,000 spent on disability adaptations may be deducted from income for state taxation purposes.

Duration The deduction is available in any year the adaptations are made.

Number awarded Varies each year.

Deadline Deadline not specified.

[853]
MAINE PROPERTY TAX EXEMPTIONS FOR VETERANS

Maine Revenue Services
Attn: Property Tax Division
P.O. Box 9106
Augusta, ME 04332-9106
(207) 287-2011   Fax: (207) 287-6396
E-mail: prop.tax@maine.gov
Web: www.maine.gov

Summary To exempt the estates of disabled Maine veterans and selected family members from property taxation.

Eligibility Eligible for this program are veterans who served in wartime during World War I, World War II, the Korean campaign, the Vietnam war, the Persian Gulf war, or other recognized service periods, are legal residents of Maine, and are either older than 62 years of age or are receiving a pension or compensation from the U.S. government for total disability (whether service connected or not). Vietnam veterans must have served 180 days on active duty unless discharged earlier for a service-connected disability. The exemption also includes 1) property held in joint tenancy with the veterans' spouses, and 2) property of unremarried widow(er)s, minor children, and mothers of deceased veterans, if those dependents are receiving a pension or compensation from the U.S. government.

Financial data Estates of disabled veterans and eligible dependents, including both real and personal property, are exempt up to $6,000 of just valuation. For veterans and dependents who served in wartime prior to World War II, estates up to $7,000 are exempt.

Duration Veterans, spouses, unremarried widow(er)s, and mothers are eligible for this exemption throughout their lifetimes; minor children of veterans are eligible until they reach the age of 18.

Number awarded Varies each year.

Deadline When an eligible person first submits an application, the proof of entitlement must reach the assessors of the local municipality prior to the end of March. Once eligibility has been established, notification need not be repeated in subsequent years.

[854]
MARYLAND PENSION EXCLUSION FOR DISABLED AND ELDERLY RESIDENTS

Comptroller of Maryland
Attn: Revenue Administration Division
80 Calvert Street
Annapolis, MD 21411
(410) 260-7980
Toll Free: (800) MD-TAXES (within MD)
Fax: (410) 974-3456   TDD: (410) 260-7157
E-mail: taxhelp@comp.state.md.us
Web: individuals.marylandtaxes.com

Summary To exempt a portion of the income of disabled and elderly residents (and selected spouses) from state income taxation in Maryland.

Eligibility Eligible are Maryland residents who receive income from a pension, annuity, or endowment from an employee retirement system and who are at least 65 years of age or classified as totally disabled; spouses of disabled persons also qualify. The disability must be a mental or physical impairment that prevents the person from engaging in gainful activity and that is expected to be of long, continuing, or indefinite duration (or to result in death).

Financial data Persons with disabilities, who have a spouse who is totally disabled, or who are 65 years of age or older may exclude from state taxation up to $24,000 of income received as a pension, annuity, or endowment.

Duration The exemption continues as long as the recipient resides in Maryland.

Deadline Deadline not specified.

[855]
MARYLAND PROPERTY TAX EXEMPTION FOR DISABLED VETERANS AND SURVIVING SPOUSES

Maryland Department of Assessments and Taxation
Attn: Property Taxes
301 West Preston Street
Baltimore, MD 21201-2395
(410) 767-1184   Toll Free: (888) 246-5941
TDD: (800) 735-2258
Web: www.dat.state.md.us/sdatweb/exempt.html

Summary To exempt the homes of disabled veterans and their surviving spouses from property taxation in Maryland.

Eligibility This exemption is available to armed services veterans with a permanent service-connected disability rated 100% by the U.S. Department of Veterans Affairs who own a dwelling house in Maryland. Unremarried surviving spouses are also eligible.

Financial data The dwelling houses of eligible veterans and surviving spouses is exempt from real property taxes.

Duration The exemption is available as long as the veteran or surviving spouse owns the dwelling house in Maryland.

Number awarded Varies each year.

Deadline Applications may be submitted at any time.

[856]
MARYLAND REAL PROPERTY TAX EXEMPTION FOR DISABLED VETERANS

State Department of Assessments and Taxation
Attn: Tax Credit Program
301 West Preston Street, Room 900
Baltimore, MD 21201-2395
(410) 767-1184   Toll Free: (888) 246-5941 (within MD)
TDD: (800) 735-2258
E-mail: taxcredits@dat.state.md.us
Web: www.dat.state.md.us

Summary To exempt the homes of disabled veterans and their spouses from property taxation in Maryland.

Eligibility This program is open to Maryland residents who are veterans with a 100% service-connected permanent disability and their surviving spouses.

Financial data The dwelling houses owned by qualifying disabled veterans and their spouses are exempt from real property taxes in Maryland.

Duration This exemption continues as long as the qualifying disabled veterans or spouses reside in Maryland and own their home.

Deadline Deadline not specified.

[857]
MASSACHUSETTS PROPERTY TAX EXEMPTION FOR VETERANS AND THEIR FAMILIES

Massachusetts Department of Revenue
Attn: Division of Local Services
100 Cambridge Street
Boston, MA 02114
(617) 626-2386   Fax: (617) 626-2330
E-mail: juszkiewicz@dor.state.ma.us
Web: www.mass.gov

Summary To provide a property tax exemption to blind, disabled, and other veterans (and their families) in Massachusetts.

Eligibility This program is open to veterans who are residents of Massachusetts, were residents for at least 6 months prior to entering the service, have been residents for at least 5 consecutive years, and are occupying property as their domicile. Applicants must have an ownership interest in the domicile that ranges from $2,000 to $10,000, depending on the category of exemption. Veterans must have been discharged under conditions other than dishonorable. Several categories of veterans and their families qualify: 1) veterans who have a service-connected disability rating of 10% or more; veterans who have been awarded the Purple Heart; Gold Star mothers and fathers; and surviving spouses of eligible veterans who do not remarry; 2) veterans who suffered, in the line of duty, the loss or permanent loss of use of 1 foot, 1 hand, or 1 eye; veterans who received the Congressional Medal of Honor, Distinguished Service Cross, Navy Cross, or Air Force Cross; and their spouses or surviving spouses; 3) veterans who suffered, in the line of duty, the loss or permanent loss of use of both feet, both hands, or both eyes; and their spouses or surviving spouses; 4) veterans who suffered total disability in the line of duty and received assistance in acquiring specially adapted housing, which they own and occupy as their domicile; and their spouses or surviving spouses; 5) unremarried surviving spouses of military personnel who died due to injury or disease from being in a combat zone, or are missing and presumed dead due to combat; 6) veterans who suffered total disability in the line of duty and are incapable of working; and their spouses or surviving spouses; and 7) veterans who are certified by the Veterans Administration as paraplegic and their surviving spouses.

Financial data Qualified veterans and family members are entitled to an annual exemption from their taxes for the different categories: 1, $400; 2, $750; 3, $1,250; 4, $1,500; 5, full, but with a cap of $2,500 after 5 years; 6, $1,000; or 7, total.

Duration The exemptions are provided each year that the veteran or unremarried surviving spouse lives in Massachusetts and owns the property as a domicile.

Additional data Applications are available from local assessor's offices.

Number awarded Varies each year.

Deadline Applications must be filed with the local assessor by December of each year.

[858]
MASSACHUSETTS VETERANS ANNUITY PROGRAM

Department of Veterans' Services
Attn: Annuities
600 Washington Street, Suite 1100
Boston, MA 02111
(617) 210-5480   Fax: (617) 210-5755
E-mail: mdvs@vet.state.ma.us
Web: www.mass.gov/veterans

Summary To provide an annuity to blind or disabled veterans from Massachusetts and to the parents and spouses of deceased military personnel.

Eligibility This program is open to 1) veterans who are blind, double amputee, paraplegic, or have a 100% service-connected disability; 2) the parents of military personnel who died of service-connected causes; and 3) the unremarried spouses of military personnel who died of service-connected causes. Veterans must have been residents of Massachusetts at the time of entry into military service who served during specified wartime periods and received other than a dishonorable discharge. All applicants must currently be residents of Massachusetts.

Financial data Recipients are entitled to an annuity of $2,000 per year.

Duration The annuity is paid as long as the recipient continues to reside in Massachusetts.

Deadline Deadline not specified.

[859]
MICHIGAN HOMESTEAD PROPERTY TAX CREDIT FOR VETERANS AND BLIND PEOPLE

Michigan Department of Treasury
Attn: Homestead Exemption
Treasury Building
430 West Allegan Street
Lansing, MI 48922
(517) 373-3200   Toll Free: (800) 827-4000
TDD: (517) 636-4999
E-mail: treasPtd2@michigan.gov
Web: www.michigan.gov/treasury

Summary To provide a property tax credit to veterans, military personnel, their spouses, blind people, and their surviving spouses in Michigan.

Eligibility Eligible to apply are residents of Michigan who are 1) blind and own their homestead; 2) a veteran with a service-connected disability or his/her surviving spouse; 3) a surviving spouse of a veteran deceased in service; 4) a pensioned veteran, a surviving spouse of those veterans, or an active military member, all of whose household income is less than $7,500; or 5) a surviving spouse of a non-disabled or non-pensioned veteran of the Korean War, World War II, or World War I whose household income is less than $7,500. All applicants must own or rent a home in Michigan, have been a Michigan resident for at least 6 months during the year in which application is made, and fall within qualifying income levels (up to $82,650 in household income).

Financial data The maximum credit is $1,200. The exact amount varies. For homeowners, the credit depends on the state equalized value of the homestead and on an allowance for filing category. For renters, 20% of the rent is considered property tax eligible for credit.

Duration 1 year; eligibility must be established each year.

Number awarded Varies each year.

Deadline December of each year.

[860]
MICHIGAN INCOME TAX EXEMPTION FOR PEOPLE WITH DISABILITIES

Michigan Department of Treasury
Attn: Income Tax
Treasury Building
430 West Allegan Street
Lansing, MI 48922
(517) 373-3200   Toll Free: (800) 827-4000
TDD: (517) 636-4999
E-mail: treasIndTax@michigan.gov
Web: www.michigan.gov/treasury

Summary To exempt a portion of the income of deaf, blind, and disabled residents of Michigan from state income taxation.

Eligibility Eligible for this exemption are residents of Michigan who 1) receive messages through a sense other than hearing, such as lip reading or sign language; 2) have vision in their better eye of 20/200 or less with corrective lenses or peripheral field of vision of 20 degrees or less; or 3) are hemiplegic, paraplegic, quadriplegic, or totally and permanently disabled.

Financial data Qualifying people with disabilities receive an exemption of $2,200 from their adjusted gross income for purposes of state taxation.

Duration The exemption continues as long as the recipient resides in Michigan.

Deadline Deadline not specified.

[861]
MICHIGAN VETERANS TRUST FUND EMERGENCY GRANTS

Department of Military and Veterans Affairs
Attn: Michigan Veterans Trust Fund
2500 South Washington Avenue
Lansing, MI 48913-5101
(517) 483-5469   E-mail: paocmn@michigan.gov
Web: www.michigan.gov/dmva

Summary To provide temporary financial assistance to disabled and other Michigan veterans and their families, if they are facing personal emergencies.

Eligibility Eligible for this assistance are veterans and their families residing in Michigan who are temporarily unable to provide the basic necessities of life. Support is not provided for long-term problems or chronic financial difficulties. The qualifying veteran must have been discharged under honorable conditions with at least 180 days of active wartime service or have been separated as a result of a physical or mental disability incurred in the line of duty.

Financial data No statutory limit exists on the amount of assistance that may be provided; a local board in each Michigan county determines if the applicant is genuinely needy and the amount of assistance to be awarded.

Duration This assistance is provided to meet temporary needs only.

Number awarded Varies each year.

Deadline Applications may be submitted at any time.

[862]
MINNESOTA INCOME TAX SUBTRACTION FOR THE ELDERLY OR DISABLED

Minnesota Department of Revenue
Attn: Individual Income Tax Division
600 North Robert Street
Mail Station 5510
St. Paul, MN 55146-5510
(651) 296-3781 Toll Free: (800) 652-9094 (within MN)
E-mail: indinctax@state.mn.us
Web: www.taxes.state.mn.us

Summary To exempt from state taxation a portion of the income received by residents of Minnesota who are disabled or elderly.

Eligibility This exemption is available to residents of Minnesota who are either 65 years of age or older or permanently and totally disabled and receiving disability income from the Social Security Administration or U.S. Department of Veterans Affairs. Their adjusted gross income must be less than $42,000 if married filing a joint return and both spouses qualify, $38,500 if married filing a joint return and 1 spouse qualifies, $21,000 if married filing a separate return, or $33,700 if filing single, head of household, or qualifying widow(er).

Financial data Qualified taxpayers are entitled to subtract from their income for purposes of Minnesota state taxation $18,000 if married filing a joint return and both spouses qualify, $14,500 if married filing a joint return and 1 spouse qualifies, $9,000 if married filing a separate return, or $14,500 if filing single, head of household, or qualifying widow(er).

Duration This exemption is available as long as the taxpayer resides in Minnesota.

Number awarded Varies each year.

Deadline Income tax returns must be submitted by April of each year.

[863]
MINNESOTA SPECIAL HOMESTEAD CLASSIFICATIONS

Minnesota Department of Revenue
Attn: Property Tax Division
600 North Robert Street
Mail Station 3340
St. Paul, MN 55146-3340
(651) 556-6087
Web: www.taxes.state.mn.us

Summary To provide a property tax benefit to owners of homesteads in Minnesota who are disabled, blind, or paraplegic veterans.

Eligibility This benefit is available to owners of residential real estate that is occupied and used as a homestead in Minnesota. Applicants must be certified as totally and permanently disabled, legally blind, or a paraplegic veteran living in specially adapted housing with a grant from the Veterans Administration.

Financial data Qualified property is taxed at a rate of 0.45% for the first $50,000 of market value of residential homesteads. That compares to the standard rate of 1.0% on the first $500,000 in valuation and 1.25% on valuation over $500,000.

Duration This benefit is available as long as the property is owned by a qualified person.

Number awarded Varies each year.

Deadline Applications must be submitted by September of each year.

[864]
MINNESOTA STATE SOLDIERS ASSISTANCE PROGRAM

Minnesota Department of Veterans Affairs
Veterans Service Building
20 West 12th Street, Room 206C
St. Paul, MN 55155-2006
(651) 757-1556   Toll Free: (888) LINK-VET
Fax: (651) 296-3954
E-mail: kathy.schwartz@state.mn.us
Web: www.mdva.state.mn.us/financialassistance.htm

Summary To provide emergency financial assistance to disabled veterans and their families in Minnesota.

Eligibility This assistance is available to veterans who are unable to work because of a temporary disability (from service-connected or other causes). Their dependents and survivors are also eligible. Applicants must also meet income and asset guidelines and be residents of Minnesota.

Financial data The maximum grant is $1,500. Funds may be used to pay for food and shelter, utility bills, and emergency medical treatment (including optical and dental benefits).

Duration This is a short-term program, with benefits payable up to 6 months only. If the veteran's disability is expected to be long term in nature or permanent, the department may continue to provide assistance while application is made for long-term benefits, such as Social Security disability or retirement benefits.

Number awarded Varies each year. A total of $1.4 million is available for this program annually.

Deadline Applications may be submitted at any time.

[865]
MISSISSIPPI AD VALOREM TAX EXEMPTION FOR DISABLED VETERANS

Mississippi State Veterans Affairs Board
3460 Highway 80 East
P.O. Box 5947
Pearl, MS 39288-5947
(601) 576-4850   Fax: (601) 576-4868
E-mail: grice@vab.state.ms.us
Web: www.vab.state.ms.us/booklet.htm

Summary To exempt the property of disabled veterans from ad valorem taxation in Mississippi.

Eligibility This exemption applies to homesteads owned by American veterans in Mississippi who were honorably discharged. Applicants must have a 100% permanent service-connected disability.

Financial data All qualifying homesteads of $7,500 or less in assessed value are exempt from ad valorem taxation.

Duration This exemption applies as long as the disabled veteran owns the homestead in Mississippi.

Number awarded Varies each year.

Deadline Deadline not specified.

[866]
MISSISSIPPI HOMESTEAD TAX EXEMPTION FOR THE DISABLED

Mississippi State Tax Commission
Attn: Property Tax Division
P.O. Box 1033
Jackson, MS 39215-1033
(601) 923-7631   Fax: (601) 923-7637
E-mail: property@mstc.state.ms.us
Web: www.mstc.state.ms.us/taxareas/property/main.htm

Summary To exempt from property taxes a portion of the value of homesteads owned by people with disabilities and blind people in Mississippi.

Eligibility Eligible for this exemption are residents of Mississippi who are totally disabled or legally blind and own a homestead that they occupy as a home. Disability and blindness are defined according to federal Social Security regulations.

Financial data The exemption covers the first $7,500 of assessed value of the property (or $75,000 true value).

Duration The exemption continues as long as the disabled person resides in Mississippi.

Number awarded Varies each year.

Deadline The first time an exemption is requested, it must be submitted before the end of March of that year. Subsequently, most Mississippi counties do not require renewal filing unless the disable person's homestead status changes.

[867]
MISSOURI SENIOR CITIZEN, DISABLED VETERAN, AND DISABLED PERSON PROPERTY TAX CREDIT CLAIM

Missouri Department of Revenue
Attn: Taxation Division
301 West High Street, Room 330
P.O. Box 2800
Jefferson City, MO 65105-2800
(573) 751-3505   Toll Free: (800) 877-6881
TDD: (800) 735-2966
E-mail: PropertyTaxCredit@dor.mo.gov
Web: www.dor.mo.gov/tax/personal

Summary To provide a property tax credit to low-income disabled veterans, senior citizens, and other persons with disabilities or their spouses in Missouri.

Eligibility This program is open to residents of Missouri (or their spouses) whose net household income does not exceed certain limits ($27,500 per year if they rented or did not own and occupy their home for the entire year, $30,000 if they owned and occupied their home for the entire year) and have paid property tax or rent on their homestead during the tax year. Applicants must be 1) 65 years of age or older, 2) classified by the U.S. Department of Veterans Affairs as a 100% service-connected disabled veteran, 3) 60 years of age or older and receiving surviving spouse Society Security benefits, or 4) 100% disabled.

Financial data The tax credit depends on the claimant's income and amount paid in property taxes or rent, up to a maximum of $1,100 per year for property tax or $750 per year for rent.

Duration The tax credit is available annually.

Number awarded Varies each year.

Deadline Eligible veterans, people with disabilities, and senior citizens may claim this credit when they file their state income tax return, in April of each year.

[868]
MONTANA DISABILITY INCOME EXCLUSION

Montana Department of Revenue
Attn: Individual Income Tax
125 North Roberts, Third Floor
P.O. Box 5805
Helena, MT 59604-5805
(406) 444-6900   Toll Free: (866) 859-2254
Fax: (406) 444-6642   TDD: (406) 444-2830
Web: mt.gov/revenue

Summary To provide a state income tax exclusion to residents of Montana who receive disability payments.

Eligibility Eligible are all persons considered Montana residents for purposes of state income taxation who are receiving disability payments. They must be under 65 years of age, be retired on disability, be permanently and totally disabled, and not have chosen to treat their disability income as a pension or annuity.

Financial data Eligible residents may exclude up to $5,200 a year of disability payments.

Duration The exclusion continues as long as the recipient resides in Montana and receives disability payments.

Deadline Deadline not specified.

[869]
MONTANA DISABLED AMERICAN VETERAN PROPERTY TAX BENEFIT

Montana Department of Revenue
Attn: Property Tax
125 North Roberts, Third Floor
P.O. Box 5805
Helena, MT 59604-5805
(406) 444-6900   Toll Free: (866) 859-2254
Fax: (406) 444-1505   TDD: (406) 444-2830
Web: mt.gov/revenue

Summary To reduce the property tax rate in Montana for disabled veterans and their surviving spouses.

Eligibility This benefit is available to residents of Montana who own and occupy property in the state. Applicants must have been honorably discharged from active service in the armed forces and be currently rated 100% disabled or compensated at the 100% disabled rate because of a service-connected disability. They must have an adjusted gross income less than $52,899 if married or $45,846 if single. Also eligible are unremarried surviving spouses with an adjusted gross income less than $39,968 whose spouse was a veteran with a 100% service-connected disability or compensation at the 100% disabled rate at the time of death, died while on active duty, or died of a service-connected disability.

Financial data Qualifying veterans and surviving spouses are entitled to a reduction in local property taxes on their residence, 1 attached or detached garage, and up to 1 acre of land. The amount of the reduction depends on the status of the applicant (married, single, or surviving spouse) and adjusted gross income, but ranges from 50% to 100%.

Duration The reduction continues as long as the recipient resides in Montana and owns and occupies property used as a primary residence.

Number awarded Varies each year.

Deadline Applications must be filed with the local Department of Revenue Office by April of each year.

[870]
MONTANA TAX EXEMPTION FOR CERTAIN DISABLED OR DECEASED VETERANS' RESIDENCES

Montana Veterans' Affairs Division
1900 Williams Street
P.O. Box 5715
Helena, MT 59604
(406) 324-3740   Fax: (406) 324-3745
E-mail: lehall@mt.gov
Web: dma.mt.gov/mvad/functions/state.asp

Summary To exempt from taxation the real property of disabled or deceased veterans and their widow(er)s in Montana.

Eligibility This exemption applies to residential property in Montana that is owned and occupied by an honorably-discharged veteran who is rated as 100% disabled or is being paid at the 100% disabled rate by the U.S. Department of Veterans Affairs (DVA). Also eligible are unremarried spouses of deceased veterans who own and occupy a residence in Montana. Spouses must obtain documentation from the DVA that the veteran was rated as 100% disabled or was being paid at the 100% disabled rate at the time of death, or that the veteran died while on active duty.

Financial data Eligible veterans or spouses are entitled to real property tax relief that depends on their income. Single veterans with an income of $30,000 or less are exempt from all property taxes; if their income is $30,001 to $33,000, they pay 20% of the regular tax; those with income from $33,001 to $36,000 pay 30% of the regular tax; and those with income from $36,001 to $39,000 pay 50% of the regular tax. Married veterans with an income of $36,000 or less are exempt from all property taxes; if their income is $36,001 to $39,000, they pay 20% of the regular tax; those with income from $39,001 to $42,000 pay 30% of the regular tax; and those with income from $42,001 to $45,000 pay 50% of the regular tax. Surviving spouses with an income of $25,000 or less are exempt from all property taxes; if their income is $25,001 to $28,000, they pay 20% of the regular tax; those with income from $28,001 to $31,000 pay 30% of the regular tax; and those with income from $31,001 to $34,000 pay 50% of the regular tax.

Duration The exemption continues as long as the residence in Montana is owned and occupied by the disabled veteran or, if deceased, by the veteran's unremarried spouse.

Number awarded Varies each year.

Deadline Deadline not specified.

[871]
MUSICIANS FOUNDATION FINANCIAL ASSISTANCE

Musicians Foundation, Inc.
875 Sixth Avenue, Suite 2303
New York, NY 10001
(212) 239-9137   Fax: (212) 239-9138
E-mail: info@musiciansfoundation.org
Web: www.musiciansfoundation.org

Summary To provide emergency assistance to disabled and other professional musicians who need assistance for living, medical, or related expenses.

Eligibility Eligible to apply for this assistance are professional musicians who are working in the United States, regardless of their genre. Applicants must need financial assistance because of their age, illness, disability, or other misfortune. Their family members may also apply.

Financial data The amount awarded varies, depending upon the needs of the recipient. Funds are to be used to meet current living, medical, and related costs.

Duration These are generally 1-time awards.

Additional data This foundation was incorporated in 1914. The foundation does not award scholarships, loans, business funds, or unemployment assistance.

Number awarded Varies each year.

Deadline Applications may be submitted at any time.

[872]
NEVADA DISABLED VETERAN'S TAX EXEMPTION

Nevada Office of Veterans' Services
Attn: Executive Director
5460 Reno Corporate Drive
Reno, NV 89511
(775) 688-1653   Fax: (775) 688-1656
Web: veterans.nv.gov/NOVS/Veterans%20Benefits.html

Summary To exempt from taxation in Nevada a portion of the property owned by disabled veterans or their surviving spouses.

Eligibility This program is open to veterans who are residents of Nevada and have incurred a service-connected disability of 60% or more. Applicants must have received an honorable separation from military service. The widow(er) of a disabled veteran, who was eligible at the time of death, may also be eligible for this benefit.

Financial data Veterans and widow(er)s are entitled to exempt from taxation a portion of their property's assessed value. The amount depends on the extent of the disability and the year filed; it ranges from $6,250 to $20,000 and doubles over a 4-year period.

Duration Disabled veterans and their widow(er)s are entitled to this exemption as long as they live in Nevada.

Additional data Disabled veterans and widow(er)s are able to split their exemption between vehicle taxes and/or property taxes. Further information is available at local county assessors' offices.

Number awarded Varies each year.

Deadline Deadline not specified.

[873]
NEW HAMPSHIRE DISABLED PROPERTY TAX EXEMPTION

New Hampshire Department of Revenue
  Administration
109 Pleasant Street
Concord, NH 03301
(603) 271-2191   Fax: (603) 271-6121
TDD: (800) 735-2964
Web: revenue.nh.gov

Summary To provide disabled residents of New Hampshire with a partial exemption from real estate taxes.

Eligibility Residents of New Hampshire are covered by this program if they are eligible for benefits to the disabled from the U.S. Social Security Administration, own and occupy their primary residence in New Hampshire, and live in a municipality that has chosen through a referendum vote to grant an exemption to the disabled. Their income and assets may not exceed specified limits; the current income limit is $13,400 for single applicants or $20,400 for married applicants, and the current asset limit is $35,000, excluding the residence. Towns may set higher limits.

Financial data The amount of the exemption (and the allowable level of income and assets) is determined by a vote of the municipality.

Duration 1 year; this exemption will be continued as long as the recipient meets the eligibility requirements.

Number awarded Varies each year.

Deadline The original application for a permanent tax credit must be submitted by April.

[874]
NEW HAMPSHIRE INTEREST AND DIVIDEND TAX EXEMPTION FOR PEOPLE WITH DISABILITIES

New Hampshire Department of Revenue
 Administration
109 Pleasant Street
Concord, NH 03301
(603) 271-2191　　　　　　Fax: (603) 271-6121
TDD: (800) 735-2964
Web: revenue.nh.gov

Summary To provide disabled residents of New Hampshire with a partial exemption from taxes on interest and dividend income.

Eligibility This exemption is available to residents of New Hampshire who have a disability, are unable to work, are younger than 65 years of age, and pay taxes on income from interest and dividends.

Financial data Qualifying residents receive an exemption of $1,200 from interest and dividend income.

Duration 1 year; this exemption will be continued as long as the recipient meets the eligibility requirements.

Number awarded Varies each year.

Deadline The application for this exemption is included with the interest and dividend income tax form, due in April of each year.

[875]
NEW HAMPSHIRE SERVICE-CONNECTED TOTAL AND PERMANENT DISABILITY TAX CREDIT

New Hampshire Department of Revenue
 Administration
109 Pleasant Street
Concord, NH 03301
(603) 271-2191　　　　　　Fax: (603) 271-6121
TDD: (800) 735-2964
Web: revenue.nh.gov

Summary To provide property tax credits in New Hampshire to disabled veterans or their surviving spouses.

Eligibility Eligible for this tax credit are honorably discharged veterans residing in New Hampshire who 1) have a total and permanent service-connected disability, or 2) are a double amputee or paraplegic because of a service-connected disability. Unremarried surviving spouses of qualified veterans are also eligible.

Financial data Qualifying disabled veterans and surviving spouses receive an annual credit of $700 for property taxes on residential property. In addition, individual towns in New Hampshire may adopt a local option to increase the

dollar amount credited to disabled veterans, to a maximum of $2,000.

Duration 1 year; once the credit has been approved, it is automatically renewed for as long as the qualifying person owns the same residence in New Hampshire.

Number awarded Varies each year.

Deadline The original application for a permanent tax credit must be submitted by April.

[876]
NEW JERSEY HOMESTEAD REBATE FOR THE ELDERLY AND DISABLED

New Jersey Division of Taxation
Attn: Information and Publications Branch
50 Barrack Street
P.O. Box 281
Trenton, NJ 08695-0281
(609) 292-6400
Toll Free: (888) 238-1233 (within NJ, NY, PA, DE, and
 MD)
TDD: (800) 286-6613 (within NJ, NY, PA, DE, and
 MD)　　　　　　E-mail: taxation@tax.state.nj.us
Web: www.state.nj.us

Summary To refund a portion of property taxes paid by residents of New Jersey, especially those who are disabled elderly.

Eligibility This rebate is available to all residents of New Jersey, but separate provisions apply to those who are permanently and totally disabled or 65 years of age or older. Applicants must either 1) own and occupy a home in New Jersey that is their principal residence and have qualifying income of $150,000 or less, or 2) rented and occupied a dwelling in New Jersey that is their principal residence and have qualifying income of $100,000 or less.

Financial data The rebate depends on income. For homeowners, it ranges from $500 to $1,200. Alternatively, homeowners may elect to receive a percentage of the first $10,000 in property taxes paid; that percentage is 20% if qualifying income is less than $100,000 or 10% if qualifying income is from $100,001 to $150,000. For married couples, heads of household, and widow(er)s who rent, the rebate is $160 if qualifying income is from $70,001 to $100,000 or from $160 to $860 if qualifying income is less than $70,000. For single renters, the rebate is $160 if qualifying income is from $35,001 to $100,000 or from $160 to $860 if qualifying income is less than $35,000.

Duration The rebate is available as long as the person remains a New Jersey resident.

Additional data This program was established in 2007 as a replacement for the New Jersey FAIR Rebate Program.

Number awarded Varies each year.

Deadline Senior and disabled homeowners must file their applications by October of each year. Tenants must file their applications as part of the annual income tax return, due in April of each year.

[877]
NEW JERSEY INCOME TAX EXCLUSIONS FOR PERSONS WITH DISABILITIES

New Jersey Division of Taxation
Attn: Information and Publications Branch
50 Barrack Street
P.O. Box 281
Trenton, NJ 08695-0281
(609) 292-6400
Toll Free: (800) 323-4400 (within NJ, NY, PA, DE, and MD)
TDD: (800) 286-6613 (within NJ, NY, PA, DE, and MD)   E-mail: taxation@tax.state.nj.us
Web: www.state.nj.us/treasury/taxation

Summary   To exclude from income taxation in New Jersey certain benefits received by veterans and other persons with disabilities.

Eligibility   Residents of New Jersey with disabilities are entitled to this exclusion if they are receiving benefits from public agencies, including compensation from the U.S. Department of Veterans Affairs for permanent and total disability or from the state of New Jersey for temporary disability.

Financial data   Disability payments are excluded from income for state taxation purposes.

Duration   The exclusion applies as long as the individual receives qualifying disability payments.

Number awarded   Varies each year.

Deadline   Deadline not specified.

[878]
NEW JERSEY INCOME TAX EXEMPTIONS FOR THE BLIND AND DISABLED

New Jersey Division of Taxation
Attn: Information and Publications Branch
50 Barrack Street
P.O. Box 281
Trenton, NJ 08695-0281
(609) 292-6400
Toll Free: (800) 323-4400 (within NJ, NY, PA, DE, and MD)
TDD: (800) 286-6613 (within NJ, NY, PA, DE, and MD)   E-mail: taxation@tax.state.nj.us
Web: www.state.nj.us/treasury/taxation

Summary   To provide an income tax exemption in New Jersey to blind and disabled people.

Eligibility   Residents of New Jersey who are blind or disabled are entitled to this exemption.

Financial data   Each blind or disabled person is entitled to an exemption of $1,000 from income for taxation purposes.

Duration   The exemption continues as long as the qualifying condition persists and the person remains a New Jersey resident.

Number awarded   Varies each year.

Deadline   Deadline not specified.

[879]
NEW JERSEY PARTIAL EXEMPTION FROM REALTY TRANSFER FEE FOR SENIOR CITIZENS OR DISABLED PERSONS

New Jersey Division of Taxation
Attn: Information and Publications Branch
50 Barrack Street
P.O. Box 281
Trenton, NJ 08695-0281
(609) 292-6400
Toll Free: (800) 323-4400 (within NJ, NY, PA, DE, and MD)
TDD: (800) 286-6613 (within NJ, NY, PA, DE, and MD)   E-mail: taxation@tax.state.nj.us
Web: www.state.nj.us/treasury/taxation/lpt/rtttaqs.shtml

Summary   To provide an exemption from realty transfer fees paid by senior citizens, persons with disabilities, and blind people in New Jersey.

Eligibility   Eligible for these exemptions are persons 62 years of age and older, permanently and totally disabled individuals, and blind people who are residents of New Jersey for 1 year immediately preceding October 1 of the year before the year for which the exemption is requested, and purchasers of certain residential property during the year.

Financial data   The standard realty transfer fees range from $2.90 per $500 for the first $150,000 of the sales price to $6.05 per $500 for sales prices in excess of $1,000,000. For persons who qualify for this reduction, the comparable fees range from $0.50 per $500 for the first $150,000 of the sales price to $3.40 per $500 for sales prices in excess of $1,000,000.

Duration   The exemption applies whenever a qualified purchaser buys a new residence.

Number awarded   Varies each year.

Deadline   Deadline not specified.

[880]
NEW JERSEY PENSION EXCLUSION

New Jersey Division of Taxation
Attn: Information and Publications Branch
50 Barrack Street
P.O. Box 281
Trenton, NJ 08695-0281
(609) 292-6400
Toll Free: (800) 323-4400 (within NJ, NY, PA, DE, and MD)
TDD: (800) 286-6613 (within NJ, NY, PA, DE, and MD)   E-mail: taxation@tax.state.nj.us
Web: www.state.nj.us/treasury/taxation

Summary   To exclude from taxation a portion of the retirement income of elderly and disabled residents of New Jersey.

Eligibility   Residents of New Jersey who are permanently and totally disabled or 62 years of age or older may exclude all or a portion of pension and annuity income from taxable income. They must have gross income (before subtracting any pension exclusion) of $100,000 or less.

Financial data   The annual exclusion is $20,000 for a married couple filing jointly, $10,000 for a married person filing separately, or $15,000 for a single individual, head of household, or qualifying widow(er).

Duration　The exclusion continues as long as the person remains a New Jersey resident.

Number awarded　Varies each year.

Deadline　Deadline not specified.

[881]
NEW JERSEY PROPERTY TAX DEDUCTION

New Jersey Division of Taxation
Attn: Information and Publications Branch
50 Barrack Street
P.O. Box 281
Trenton, NJ 08695-0281
(609) 292-6400
Toll Free: (800) 323-4400 (within NJ, NY, PA, DE, and MD)
TDD: (800) 286-6613 (within NJ, NY, PA, DE, and MD)　　　　　　E-mail: taxation@tax.state.nj.us
Web: www.state.nj.us/treasury/taxation/njit35.shtml

Summary　To exclude from income taxation a portion of the property taxes paid by blind, disabled, and other residents of New Jersey.

Eligibility　This deduction is available to residents of New Jersey whose income is greater than $20,000 (or $10,000 if single or married filing separately). It is also available to residents, regardless of income, who are 1) blind, 2) permanently and totally disabled, or 3) 65 years of age or older. Applicants must either own the home in which they reside or rent a dwelling with its own separate kitchen and bath facilities.

Financial data　Qualified residents are entitled to deduct from their income (for state taxation purposes) 100% of their property taxes, to a maximum of $10,000. For renters, 18% of their rent is considered the equivalent of property taxes and may be deducted, to a maximum of $10,000.

Duration　The deduction continues as long as the person remains a New Jersey resident.

Additional data　This program began in 1996. Taxpayers may not claim both the property tax deduction and the property tax credit; they may claim whichever is most beneficial, but only the deduction or the credit.

Number awarded　Varies each year.

Deadline　The deduction is claimed as part of the annual income tax return, due in April of each year.

[882]
NEW JERSEY PROPERTY TAX EXEMPTION FOR DISABLED VETERANS OR SURVIVING SPOUSES

New Jersey Division of Taxation
Attn: Information and Publications Branch
50 Barrack Street
P.O. Box 281
Trenton, NJ 08695-0281
(609) 292-6400
Toll Free: (800) 323-4400 (within NJ, NY, PA, DE, and MD)
TDD: (800) 286-6613 (within NJ, NY, PA, DE, and MD)　　　　　　E-mail: taxation@tax.state.nj.us
Web: www.state.nj.us/treasury/taxation/otherptr.shtml

Summary　To provide a real estate tax exemption to New Jersey veterans with disabilities and certain surviving widow(er)s.

Eligibility　This exemption is available to New Jersey residents who have been honorably discharged with active wartime service in the U.S. armed forces and have been certified by the U.S. Department of Veterans Affairs as totally and permanently disabled as a result of wartime service-connected conditions. Unremarried surviving spouses of eligible disabled veterans or of certain wartime servicepersons who died on active duty are also entitled to this exemption. Applicants must be the full owner of and a permanent resident in the dwelling house for which the exemption is claimed.

Financial data　A 100% exemption from locally-levied real estate taxes is provided.

Duration　1 year; the exemption continues as long as the eligible veteran remains a resident of New Jersey.

Additional data　This program is administered by the local tax assessor or collector. Veterans who are denied exemptions have the right to appeal the decision to their county and state governments.

Number awarded　Varies each year.

Deadline　Applications may be submitted at any time.

[883]
NEW JERSEY PROPERTY TAX REIMBURSEMENT

New Jersey Division of Taxation
Attn: Information and Publications Branch
50 Barrack Street
P.O. Box 281
Trenton, NJ 08695-0281
(609) 292-6400
Toll Free: (800) 882-6597 (within NJ, NY, PA, DE, and MD)
TDD: (800) 286-6613 (within NJ, NY, PA, DE, and MD)　　　　　　E-mail: taxation@tax.state.nj.us
Web: www.state.nj.us/treasury/taxation/propfrez.shtml

Summary　To reimburse residents of New Jersey who are disabled or elderly for the increase in property taxes due on their home.

Eligibility　This reimbursement is available to residents of New Jersey who are either 1) 65 years of age or older, or 2) receiving federal Social Security disability benefits. Applicants must have lived in New Jersey continuously for at least 10 years and have owned and lived in their home (or have leased a site in a mobile home park on which they have placed a manufactured or mobile home that they own) for at least 3 years. Their annual income must be $80,000 or less. They must have paid the full amount of property taxes due on their home for the past 2 years.

Financial data Qualifying homeowners are entitled to reimbursement of all property taxes they have paid in excess of the base year (the first year in which they met all the eligibility requirements).

Duration The reimbursement is available as long as the person remains a New Jersey resident and meets eligibility requirements.

Number awarded Varies each year.

Deadline May of each year.

[884]
NEW MEXICO DISABLED VETERAN PROPERTY TAX EXEMPTION

New Mexico Department of Veterans' Services
Attn: Benefits Division
407 Galisteo Street, Room 142
Santa Fe, NM 87504
(505) 827-6374   Toll Free: (866) 433-VETS
Fax: (505) 827-6372
E-mail: alan.martinez@state.nm.us
Web: www.dvs.state.nm.us/benefits.html

Summary To exempt disabled veterans and their spouses from payment of property taxes in New Mexico.

Eligibility This exemption is available to veterans who are rated 100% service-connected disabled by the U.S. Department of Veterans Affairs, are residents of New Mexico, and own a primary residence in the state. Also eligible are qualifying veterans' unremarried surviving spouses, if they are New Mexico residents and continue to own the residence.

Financial data Veterans and surviving spouses are exempt from payment of property taxes in New Mexico.

Duration 1 year; continues until the qualifying veteran or spouse no longer live in the residence.

Number awarded Varies each year.

Deadline Deadline not specified.

[885]
NEW YORK ALTERNATIVE PROPERTY TAX EXEMPTIONS FOR VETERANS

New York State Division of Veterans' Affairs
5 Empire State Plaza, Suite 2836
Albany, NY 12223-1551
(518) 474-6114
Toll Free: (888) VETS-NYS (within NY)
Fax: (518) 473-0379   E-mail: dvainfo@ogs.state.ny.us
Web: veterans.ny.gov/property_tax_exemption.html

Summary To provide wartime veterans and their spouses who are residents of New York with a partial exemption from property taxes.

Eligibility This program is open to veterans who served during specified periods of wartime. Applicants must have been discharged under honorable conditions; additional benefits are available to those who served in a combat zone and to those who have a service-connected disability. The legal title to the property must be in the name of the veteran or the spouse of the veteran or both, or the unremarried surviving spouse of the veteran. The property must be used exclusively for residential purposes. This program is only available in counties, cities, towns, and villages in New York that have opted to participate.

Financial data This program provides an exemption of 15% of the assessed valuation of the property, to a basic maximum of $12,000 per year; local governments may opt for reduced maximums of $9,000 or $6,000, or for increased maximums of $15,000 to $36,000. For combat-zone veterans, an additional 10% of the assessed valuation is exempt, to a basic maximum of $8,000 per year; local governments may opt for a reduced maximum of $6,000 or $4,000, or for increased maximums of $10,000 to $24,000. For disabled veterans, the exemption is the percentage of assessed value equal to half of the service-connected disability rating, to a basic maximum of $40,000 per year; local governments may opt for a reduced maximum of $30,000 or $20,000, or for increased maximums of $50,000 to $120,000. At its option, New York City and other high appreciation municipalities may use the following increased maximum exemptions: war veteran, $54,000; combat-zone veteran, $36,000; disabled veteran, $180,000.

Duration This exemption is available annually.

Number awarded Varies each year.

Deadline Applications must be filed with the local assessor by "taxable status date;" in most towns, that is the end of February.

[886]
NEW YORK STATE DISABILITY INCOME EXCLUSION

New York State Department of Taxation and Finance
W.A. Harriman Campus
Tax and Finance Building
Albany, NY 12227-0001
(518) 438-8581   Toll Free: (800) 225-5829 (within NY)
Web: www.nystax.gov

Summary To exclude disability pay from state income taxation in New York.

Eligibility Eligible are persons who are considered residents of New York for state income taxation purposes and who are receiving any form of disability retirement pay. Applicants must be permanently and totally disabled and not yet 65 years of age.

Financial data Eligible residents may exclude either their actual weekly disability pay or $100 per week ($5,200 per year), whichever is less. The amount of the exclusion is reduced by the amount that the applicant's federal adjusted gross income exceeds $15,000, so no exclusion is available if that exceeds $20,200 and 1 person could take the exclusion or $25,400 if both spouses could take the exclusions.

Duration The exclusion is provided as long as the recipient remains a resident of New York.

Number awarded Varies each year.

Deadline Deadline not specified.

[887]
NORTH CAROLINA PROPERTY TAX RELIEF FOR DISABLED VETERANS

North Carolina Department of Revenue
Attn: Property Tax Division
501 North Wilmington Street
P.O. Box 871
Raleigh, NC 27602
(919) 733-7711   Fax: (919) 733-1821
Web: www.dornc.com/taxes/property/exemptions.html

Summary To provide property tax relief to disabled North Carolina veterans.

Eligibility Disabled veterans who are residents of North Carolina are eligible for these programs. They must own 1) a vehicle that is altered with special equipment to accommodate a service-connected disability; or 2) specially adapted housing purchased with the assistance of the U.S. Department of Veterans Affairs.

Financial data Qualifying vehicles are exempt from personal property taxes. Qualifying housing is eligible for an exemption on the first $45,000 in assessed value of the housing and land that is owned and used as a residence by the disabled veteran.

Duration The exemptions continue as long as the eligible veteran is a resident of North Carolina.

Number awarded Varies each year.

Deadline Deadline not specified.

[888]
NORTH CAROLINA PROPERTY TAX RELIEF FOR ELDERLY AND PERMANENTLY DISABLED PERSONS

North Carolina Department of Revenue
Attn: Property Tax Division
501 North Wilmington Street
P.O. Box 871
Raleigh, NC 27602
(919) 733-7711   Fax: (919) 733-1821
Web: www.dornc.com/taxes/property/exemptions.html

Summary To provide property tax relief to elderly and disabled North Carolina residents.

Eligibility This program is open to residents of North Carolina who 1) are permanently and totally disabled or at least 65 years of age, and 2) have an income of less than $26,500. Applicants must own and occupy real property as their permanent residence.

Financial data Qualified owners are exempt from taxation on 50% of the appraised value of their property or $25,000, whichever is greater.

Duration The exemptions continue as long as the eligible property owner is a resident of North Carolina.

Number awarded Varies each year.

Deadline Applications must be submitted by May of each year.

[889]
NORTH DAKOTA HOMESTEAD CREDIT FOR SENIOR CITIZENS OR DISABLED PERSONS

Office of State Tax Commissioner
State Capitol Building
600 East Boulevard Avenue, Department 127
Bismarck, ND 58505-0599
(701) 328-2770   Toll Free: (800) 638-2901
Fax: (701) 328-3700   TDD: (800) 366-6888
E-mail: taxinfo@state.nd.us
Web: www.nd.gov/tax

Summary To provide property tax credits for disabled or senior citizen residents of North Dakota.

Eligibility To qualify for this program, applicants must be residents of North Dakota and either totally and permanently disabled (regardless of age) or at least 65 years of age. For spouses who are living together, only 1 can apply for the credit. Applicants must reside in the property for which the credit is claimed. Their income cannot exceed $26,000 and their aggregate assets cannot exceed $75,000 (excluding the first unencumbered $100,000 of market value of their homestead).

Financial data The credit depends on the income of the taxpayer, ranging from 20% (or a maximum of $900) for people with incomes from $24,001 to $26,000, to 100% (or a maximum of $4,500) for people with incomes up to $18,000.

Duration Once approved, the deduction continues as long as the recipient meets the qualification requirements.

Additional data No person whose homestead is a farm structure exempt from taxation can qualify to receive this property tax credit.

Number awarded Varies each year.

Deadline Applications must be submitted in January of the year for which the property tax credit is requested.

[890]
NORTH DAKOTA PROPERTY TAX CREDIT FOR DISABLED VETERANS

Office of State Tax Commissioner
State Capitol Building
600 East Boulevard Avenue, Department 127
Bismarck, ND 58505-0599
(701) 328-2770   Toll Free: (800) 638-2901
Fax: (701) 328-3700   TDD: (800) 366-6888
E-mail: taxinfo@state.nd.us
Web: www.nd.gov/tax

Summary To provide property tax credits to disabled North Dakota veterans and their surviving spouses.

Eligibility This property tax credit is available to honorably-discharged veterans who have more than a 50% service-connected disability as certified by the U.S. Department of Veterans Affairs. Applicants must own and occupy a homestead according to state law. Unremarried surviving spouses are also eligible. If a disabled veteran co-owns the property with someone other than a spouse, the credit is limited to the disabled veteran's interest in the fixtures, buildings, and improvements of the homestead.

Financial data The credit is applied against the first $120,000 of true and full valuation of the fixtures, buildings, and improvements of the homestead, to a maximum amount calculated by multiplying $120,000 by the percentage of the disabled veteran's disability compensation rating for service-connected disabilities.

Duration 1 year; renewable as long as qualified individuals continue to reside in North Dakota and live in their homes.

Number awarded Varies each year.

Deadline Applications may be submitted to the county auditor at any time.

[891]
NORTH DAKOTA PROPERTY TAX EXEMPTION FOR VETERANS WHO LIVE IN SPECIALLY ADAPTED HOUSING

Office of State Tax Commissioner
State Capitol Building
600 East Boulevard Avenue, Department 127
Bismarck, ND 58505-0599
(701) 328-2770   Toll Free: (800) 638-2901
Fax: (701) 328-3700   TDD: (800) 366-6888
E-mail: taxinfo@state.nd.us
Web: www.nd.gov/tax

Summary To provide property tax exemptions to North Dakota veterans and their surviving spouses who have been awarded specially adapted housing.

Eligibility This exemption is available to paraplegic disabled veterans of the U.S. armed forces or any veteran who has been awarded specially adapted housing by the U.S. Department of Veterans Affairs. The paraplegic disability does not have to be service connected. The unremarried surviving spouses of such deceased veterans are also eligible. Income and assets are not considered in determining eligibility for the exemption.

Financial data The maximum benefit may not exceed $5,400 taxable value, because the exemption is limited to the first $120,000 of true and full value of fixtures, buildings, and improvements.

Duration 1 year; renewable as long as qualified individuals continue to reside in North Dakota and live in their homes.

Number awarded Varies each year.

Deadline Applications may be submitted to the county auditor at any time.

[892]
OHIO HOMESTEAD EXEMPTION FOR SENIOR CITIZENS, DISABLED PERSONS AND SURVIVING SPOUSES

Ohio Department of Taxation
Attn: Tax Equalization Division
P.O. Box 530
Columbus, OH 43216-0530
(614) 466-5744 Toll Free: (800) 282-1780 (within OH)
Fax: (614) 752-9822
Web: tax.ohio.gov

Summary To exempt a portion of the value of homesteads owned by senior citizens and disabled persons (along with their surviving spouses) from property taxation in Ohio.

Eligibility This exemption is available to residents of Ohio who are 65 years of age or older or who have a total and permanent disability. Applicants must own and occupy their home as their principal place of residence. Surviving spouses of persons who were receiving the exemption at the time of their death are also eligible if they were at least 59 years of age on the date of the decedent's death. There is no income limitation.

Financial data Qualifying homeowners may exempt up to $25,000 from the assessed value of their home for purposes of property taxation.

Duration The exemption is available as long as the recipient resides in Ohio and owns his or her home.

Number awarded Varies each year.

Deadline Applications must be submitted to the county auditor by May of each year.

[893]
OHIO INCOME TAX DEDUCTION FOR DISABILITY BENEFITS

Ohio Department of Taxation
Attn: Income Tax Audit Division
30 East Broad Street
P.O. Box 182847
Columbus, OH 43218-2847
(614) 433-5817 Toll Free: (800) 282-1780 (within OH)
Fax: (614) 433-7771
Web: tax.ohio.gov

Summary To deduct disability benefits from state income taxation in Ohio.

Eligibility This deduction is available to residents of Ohio who are receiving benefits from an employee's disability plan paid as the result of a permanent physical or mental disability. Payments that otherwise qualify as retirement or pension benefits, temporary wage continuation plans, and payments for temporary illnesses or injuries do not qualify.

Financial data All payments for permanent disability are excluded from income for purposes of Ohio state taxation.

Duration The exclusion is available as long as the recipient resides in Ohio and receives eligible disability payments.

Number awarded Varies each year.
Deadline Deadline not specified.

[894]
OHIO VETERANS' FINANCIAL ASSISTANCE

Ohio Department of Veterans Services
77 South High Street, 7th Floor
Columbus, OH 43215
(614) 644-0898   Toll Free: (888) DVS-OHIO
Fax: (614) 728-9498   E-mail: ohiovet@dvs.ohio.gov
Web: dvs.ohio.gov

Summary To provide emergency aid to Ohio veterans, military personnel, and their dependents who, because of disability or disaster, are in financial need.

Eligibility This assistance is available to veterans and active-duty members of the U.S. armed forces, as well as their spouses, surviving spouses, dependent parents, minor children, and wards. Applicants must have been residents of the Ohio county in which they are applying for at least 3 months. They must be able to demonstrate need for relief because of sickness, accident, or destitution.

Financial data The amount granted varies, depending on the needs of the recipient.

Duration These are emergency funds only and are not designed to be a recurring source of income.

Additional data These grants are made by the various county veterans services offices in Ohio.

Number awarded Varies each year.

Deadline Applications may be submitted at any time.

[895]
OKLAHOMA DISABILITY DEDUCTION

Oklahoma Tax Commission
Attn: Income Tax
2501 North Lincoln Boulevard
Oklahoma City, OK 73194-0009
(405) 521-3160   Toll Free: (800) 522-8165 (within OK)
Fax: (405) 522-0063   E-mail: otcmaster@tax.ok.gov
Web: www.tax.ok.gov/incometax.html

Summary To provide an income tax deduction to Oklahoma residents with disabilities who incur expenses for modifying facilities.

Eligibility This deduction is available to Oklahoma residents who have a physical disability that constitutes a substantial handicap to employment. Applicants must have incurred expenses to modify a motor vehicle, home, or work place necessary to compensate for the disability.

Financial data All expenses allowed by the Social Security Administration may be deducted from income for purposes of Oklahoma taxation.

Duration The deduction may be taken in any year when qualifying expenses are incurred.

Deadline Income tax returns must be filed by April of each year.

[896]
OKLAHOMA FINANCIAL ASSISTANCE PROGRAM

Oklahoma Department of Veterans Affairs
Veterans Memorial Building
2311 North Central Avenue
P.O. Box 53067
Oklahoma City, OK 73152
(405) 521-3684   Fax: (405) 521-6533
E-mail: scylmer@odva.state.ok.us
Web: www.ok.gov

Summary To provide emergency aid to Oklahoma veterans and their families who, because of disability or disaster, are in financial need.

Eligibility This program is open to veterans with at least 90 days of wartime service and an honorable discharge who are current residents of Oklahoma and have resided in the state for at least 1 year immediately preceding the date of application. Applicants must be seeking assistance because of an interruption or loss of job and income resulting from illness, injury, or disaster (such as loss of home due to fire, floor, or storm). Widow(er)s and minor children may also qualify for the benefit.

Financial data The amount of the grant depends on the need of the recipient.

Duration The grant is available only on a 1-time basis.

Additional data No financial assistance will be granted when regular monetary benefits are being received from other state agencies. The funds cannot be used for old debts, car payments, or medical expenses.

Number awarded Varies each year.

Deadline Applications must be submitted to the local post or chapter of a veterans services organization for initial approval or disapproval. They may be submitted at any time during the year.

[897]
OKLAHOMA PROPERTY TAX EXEMPTION FOR DISABLED VETERANS

Oklahoma Tax Commission
Attn: Property Tax
2501 North Lincoln Boulevard
Oklahoma City, OK 73194-0009
(405) 521-3178   Toll Free: (800) 522-8165 (within OK)
Fax: (405) 522-0063   E-mail: otcmaster@tax.ok.gov
Web: www.tax.ok.gov

Summary To exempt the property of disabled veterans and their surviving spouses from taxation in Oklahoma.

Eligibility This program is available to Oklahoma residents who are veterans honorably discharged from a branch of the armed forces or the Oklahoma National Guard. Applicants must have a 100% permanent disability sustained through military action or accident or resulting from a disease contracted while in active service; the disability must be certified by the U.S. Department of Veterans Affairs. They must own property that qualifies for the Oklahoma homestead exemption. Surviving spouses of qualified veterans are also eligible.

Financial data Qualified veterans and surviving spouses are eligible for exemption of the taxes on the full fair cash value of their homestead.

Duration The exemption is available as long as the veteran or surviving spouse resides in Oklahoma and owns a qualifying homestead.

Additional data This exemption was first available in 2006.

Deadline Deadline not specified.

[898]
OPERATION REBOUND GRANTS

Challenged Athletes Foundation
Attn: Program Manager
9990 Mesa Rim Road
P.O. Box 910709
San Diego, CA 92191
(858) 866-0959   Fax: (858) 866-0958
E-mail: info@challengedathletes.org
Web: www.challengedathletes.org

Summary To provide funding to veterans and September 11 first responders who became disabled as a result of service and wish to participate in athletic activities.

Eligibility This program is open to 1) veterans and service members who suffered a permanent physical disability (such as loss of a limb(s), sight, or spinal cord injury, in the Global War on Terror; and 2) law enforcement personnel, fire fighters, and others who were the first to respond to the September 11, 2001 attacks and became disabled as a result. Applicants must need funding for 1 of 3 categories: 1) equipment, for wheelchairs, prosthetics, or other assistive devices; 2) training, for club or gym dues or membership fees, team or association dues or membership fees, or coaching or training expense; or 3) competition, for travel, entry fees, or other costs to participate in a recognized event. They may apply for only 1 category per year. Along with their application, they must submit a brief autobiography with their personal and athletic goals, a brief summary of their military or law enforcement history, a statement on how they are planning to raise awareness for "Operation Rebound" and the Challenged Athletes Foundation, and documentation of financial need.

Financial data Grant amounts depend on the documented need of the applicant.

Duration These are 1-time grants, but recipients may reapply.

Additional data This program was established for veterans in 2004 and expanded to include first responders in 2008.

Number awarded Varies each year.

Deadline Applications may be submitted at any time, but they must be received at least 90 days prior to the date needed.

[899]
OREGON INCOME TAX CREDIT FOR THE ELDERLY OR DISABLED

Oregon Department of Revenue
Revenue Building
955 Center Street, N.E.
Salem, OR 97310-2551
(503) 378-4988   Toll Free: (800) 356-4222 (within OR)
TDD: (800) 886-7204 (within OR)
Web: www.oregon.gov/DOR/PERTAX

Summary To provide an income tax credit to Oregon residents who are elderly or disabled.

Eligibility This credit is available to taxpayers in Oregon who qualify for the federal elderly or disabled income tax credit. Taxpayers may claim this credit or the retirement income credit, but not both in the same year.

Financial data The credit is equal to 40% of the federal credit.

Duration The credit continues as long as the recipient resides in Oregon.

Additional data People who claim this credit may not also claim the retirement income credit.

Deadline Credits are filed with state income tax returns in April of each year.

[900]
OREGON PROPERTY TAX DEFERRAL FOR DISABLED AND SENIOR CITIZENS

Oregon Department of Revenue
Attn: Property Tax Division
Revenue Building
955 Center Street, N.E.
Salem, OR 97310-2551
(503) 378-4988   Toll Free: (800) 356-4222 (within OR)
TDD: (800) 886-7204 (within OR)
Web: www.oregon.gov/DOR/SCD/disableddef.shtml

Summary To permit blind, disabled, and elderly Oregon residents to defer payment of their property taxes.

Eligibility This program is open to residents of Oregon who are determined to be eligible to receive or are receiving federal Social Security benefits due to disability or blindness. Applicants must own a residence and have a total household income less than $39,000.

Financial data The state pays all taxes on the property to the county but places a lien on the property and charges 6% per year on the deferred taxes. The lien and interest become due and payable when the disabled person or senior citizen sells the property or changes its ownership, moves permanently from the property (unless for medical reasons), or dies.

Duration 1 year; the deferment is automatically renewed as long as the property owner lives in the residence.

Number awarded Varies each year; recently, 712 disabled residents of Oregon were participating in this program.

Deadline Applications for new deferrals must be filed in the appropriate county assessor's office by April of each year.

[901]
OREGON PROPERTY TAX EXEMPTION FOR VETERANS WITH DISABILITIES AND THEIR SPOUSES

Oregon Department of Revenue
Attn: Property Tax Division
Revenue Building
955 Center Street, N.E.
Salem, OR 97310-2551
(503) 378-4988 Toll Free: (800) 356-4222 (within OR)
TDD: (800) 886-7204 (within OR)
Web: www.oregon.gov/DOR/PTD/IC_310_676.shtml

Summary To exempt disabled Oregon veterans and their spouses from a portion of their property taxes.

Eligibility Qualifying veterans are those who received a discharge or release under honorable conditions after service of either 1) 90 consecutive days during World War I, World War II, or the Korean Conflict; or 2) 210 consecutive days after January 31, 1955. Eligible individuals must meet 1 of these conditions: 1) a war veteran who is officially certified by the U.S. Department of Veterans Affairs (VA) or any branch of the U.S. armed forces as having disabilities of 40% or more; 2) a war veteran who is certified each year by a licensed physician as being 40% or more disabled and has total gross income that is less than 185% of the federal poverty level (currently $18,130 for a family of 1, rising to $62,160 for a family of 8); or 3) a war veteran's surviving spouse who has not remarried, even if the veteran's spouse was not disabled or did not take advantage of the exemption if disabled. Recipients of this exemption must own and live on a property in Oregon.

Financial data The exemption is $15,450 of the homestead property's real market value.

Duration 1 year; may be renewed as long as the eligible veteran or surviving unremarried spouse owns and occupies the primary residence.

Number awarded Varies each year.

Deadline This exemption is not automatic. Applications must be submitted by March of each year.

[902]
OREGON PROPERTY TAX EXEMPTION FOR VETERANS WITH SERVICE-CONNECTED DISABILITIES AND THEIR SPOUSES

Oregon Department of Revenue
Attn: Property Tax Division
Revenue Building
955 Center Street, N.E.
Salem, OR 97310-2551
(503) 378-4988 Toll Free: (800) 356-4222 (within OR)
TDD: (800) 886-7204 (within OR)
Web: www.oregon.gov/DOR/PTD/IC_310_676.shtml

Summary To exempt Oregon veterans with service-connected disabilities and their spouses from a portion of their property taxes.

Eligibility Qualifying veterans are those who received a discharge or release under honorable conditions after service of either 1) 90 consecutive days during World War I, World War II, or the Korean Conflict; or 2) 210 consecutive

days after January 31, 1955. Eligible individuals must meet 1 of these conditions: 1) a war veteran who is certified by the U.S. Department of Veterans Affairs (VA) or any branch of the U.S. armed forces as having service-connected disabilities of 40% or more; or 2) a surviving spouse of a war veteran who died because of service-connected injury or illness or who received at least 1 year of this exemption. Recipients of this exemption must own and live on a property in Oregon.

Financial data The exemption is $18,540 of the homestead property's real market value.

Duration 1 year; may be renewed as long as the eligible veterans or surviving spouse owns and occupies the primary residence.

Number awarded Varies each year.

Deadline This exemption is not automatic. Applications must be submitted by March of each year.

[903]
PENNSYLVANIA DISABLED VETERANS REAL ESTATE TAX EXEMPTION

Office of the Deputy Adjutant General for Veterans Affairs
Building S-0-47, FTIG
Annville, PA 17003-5002
(717) 865-8907
Toll Free: (800) 54 PA VET (within PA)
Fax: (717) 861-8589   E-mail: jamebutler@state.pa.us
Web: www.milvet.state.pa.us/DMVA/592.htm

Summary To exempt blind and disabled Pennsylvania veterans and their unremarried surviving spouses from all state real estate taxes.

Eligibility Eligible to apply for this exemption are honorably-discharged veterans who are residents of Pennsylvania and who are blind, paraplegic, or 100% disabled from a service-connected disability sustained during wartime military service. The dwelling must be owned by the veteran solely or jointly with a spouse, and financial need for the exemption must be determined by the State Veterans' Commission. Veterans whose income is less than $79,050 per year are presumed to have financial need; veterans with income greater than $79,050 must document need. Upon the death of the veteran, the tax exemption passes on to the veteran's unremarried surviving spouse.

Financial data This program exempts the principal residence (and the land on which it stands) from all real estate taxes.

Duration The exemption continues as long as the eligible veteran or unremarried widow resides in Pennsylvania.

Number awarded Varies each year.

Deadline Deadline not specified.

[904]
PENNSYLVANIA VETERANS EMERGENCY ASSISTANCE

Office of the Deputy Adjutant General for Veterans Affairs
Building S-0-47, FTIG
Annville, PA 17003-5002
(717) 865-8905
Toll Free: (800) 54 PA VET (within PA)
Fax: (717) 861-8589   E-mail: jamebutler@state.pa.us
Web: www.milvet.state.pa.us/DMVA/185.htm

Summary   To provide financial aid on an emergency and temporary basis to Pennsylvania veterans (or their dependents) who are disabled, sick, or without means.

Eligibility   Eligible to apply for this assistance are honorably-discharged veterans who served in the U.S. armed forces during wartime and are now disabled, sick, or in financial need. Widow(er)s or orphan children of recently deceased veterans are also eligible if the veteran would have qualified prior to death. Applicants must have been residents of Pennsylvania for 1 year prior to the date of application.

Financial data   Financial aid for the necessities of life (food, shelter, fuel, and clothing) is provided. The amount depends on the number of persons in the household and the Pennsylvania county in which the veteran or dependent lives; recently, monthly grants for 1-person households ranged from $174 to $215, for 2-person households from $279 to $330, for 3-person households from $365 to $431, for 4-person households from $454 to $514, for 5-person households from $543 to $607, and for 6-person households from $614 to $687.

Duration   Aid is provided on a temporary basis only, not to exceed 3 months in a 12-month period.

Number awarded   Varies each year.

Deadline   Applications may be submitted at any time, but the factors that caused the emergency must have occurred within 180 days prior to the application.

[905]
SENTINELS OF FREEDOM SCHOLARSHIPS

Sentinels of Freedom
P.O. Box 1316
San Ramon, CA 94583
(925) 353-7100   Fax: (925) 353-3900
E-mail: info@sentinelsoffreedom.org
Web: www.sentinelsoffreedom.org

Summary   To provide funding to veterans and current military personnel who became disabled as a result of injuries sustained in the line of duty on or after September 11, 2001.

Eligibility   This program is open to members of the U.S. Air Force, Army, Coast Guard, Marines, or Navy who sustained injuries in the line of duty on or after September 11, 2001. Applicants must be rated as 60% or more disabled as a result of 1 or more of the following conditions: amputation, blindness, deafness, paraplegia, severe burns, limited traumatic brain injury (TDI), or limited post traumatic stress disorder (PTSD); other severe injuries may be considered on a case-by-case basis. They must complete an interview process and demonstrate that they have the skills, experience, and attitude that lead to employment.

Financial data   Assistance is available for the following needs: housing (adapted for physical needs if necessary), new furniture and other household supplies, career-placement assistance and training, new adaptive vehicles, educational opportunities in addition to the new GI Bill, or financial and personal mentorship.

Duration   Assistance may be provided for up to 4 years.

Additional data   The first assistance granted by this program was awarded in 2004.

Number awarded   Varies each year. Since the program was established, it has supported 32 current and former service members.

Deadline   Applications may be submitted at any time.

[906]
SINGERS' FINANCIAL AID

Society of Singers
Attn: Human Services Department
15456 Ventura Boulevard, Suite 304
Sherman Oaks, CA 91403
(818) 995-7100, ext. 104   Toll Free: (866) 767-7671
Fax: (818) 995-7466   E-mail: help@singers.org
Web: www.singers.org/programs.html

Summary   To provide assistance to professional singers who are facing medical or other crises.

Eligibility   This program is open to professional singers who have derived their primary income from singing for 5 years or more. Applicants must have financial needs resulting from medical, personal, or family crises. They must submit 5 years of career documentation, copies of bills for which help is needed, diagnosis letter and treatment plan from primary physicians or dentists with costs estimates or bills, and documentation of financial need.

Financial data   Grants are paid directly to creditors to provide for such needs as rent, utilities, medical and/or dental expenses, substance abuse rehabilitation, psychotherapy, or HIV/AIDS treatment. Support is not provided for credit card debts, tax debts, loans, voice lessons, demos, headshots, or other music projects.

Duration   These are 1-time grants.

Number awarded   Varies each year.

Deadline   Applications may be submitted at any time.

[907]
SOCIAL SECURITY DISABILITY INSURANCE (SSDI) BENEFITS

Social Security Administration
6401 Security Boulevard
Baltimore, MD 21235-0001
(410) 594-1234   Toll Free: (800) 772-1213
TDD: (800) 325-0778
Web: www.ssa.gov

Summary   To provide monthly benefits to workers and their families if the worker becomes disabled or blind.

Eligibility   This program defines disabled people as those who are unable to do any kind of work for which they are suited and whose disability has lasted or is expected to last for at least a year or to result in death. Blind people qualify if their vision cannot be corrected to better than 20/200 in their better eye or if their visual field is 20 degrees or less, even with corrective lenses. Family members who are eligible include 1) unmarried children, including adopted children and, in some cases, stepchildren and grandchildren who are under 18 years of age (19 if still in high school full time); 2) unmarried children, over 18 years of age, if they have a disability that started before age 22; and 3) spouses who are 62 years of age or older, or of any age if caring for a child of the disabled worker who is under 16 years of age or disabled. For deceased workers, disabled widow(er)s 50 years of age or older are also eligible. Applicants must also have worked long enough and recently enough under Social Security in order to qualify. Workers who become disabled before the age of 24 need 6 credits in the 3-year period ending when the disability begins; workers who become disabled between the ages of 24 and 31 must have credit for having worked half the time between the age of 21 and the date of disability; workers 31 years of age or older at the time of disability must have earned as many total credits as needed for retirement (from 20 credits if disabled at age 31 through 42 to 40 credits if disabled at age 62 or older) and must have earned at least 20 of the credits in the 10 years immediately before becoming disabled. An exception applies to blind workers who need no recent credit but may have earned the required credit any time after 1936.

Financial data The amount of the monthly benefit depends on several factors, including the worker's age at the time of disability, the number of dependents, and the amount of earnings on which Social Security taxes have been paid. Recently, the average monthly benefit was $1,062.10 for disabled workers, $286.90 for spouses of disabled workers, and $316.40 for children of disabled workers.

Duration For a disabled or blind person, whether a worker, widow, widower, surviving divorced spouse, or person over the age of 18 who became disabled before the age of 22, monthly benefits continue until the person is no longer disabled or dies. For a dependent spouse, benefits are paid until the worker is no longer disabled or dies. For a dependent child, the benefits continue until the child marries or reaches the age of 18 (19 if still enrolled as a full-time high school student).

Additional data Disabled workers may test their ability to return to work for a trial work period of up to 9 months, during which time they receive full SSDI benefits. At the end of that period, a decision is made as to whether or not they are able to engage in substantial gainful activity. Persons who find that they cannot continue substantial gainful employment continue to receive SSDI benefits without interruption. Persons who can engage in substantial gainful activity receive benefits for an additional 3 months, after which payments cease. Several factors are considered to determine if the person can engage in substantial gainful employment, but the most important is income; for disabled people the amount is $980 a month gross wages and for blind people the income is $1,640 monthly.

Number awarded Varies; recently, approximately 7,623,000 disabled workers were receiving SSDI monthly benefits, along with 158,000 spouses and 1,681,000 children.
Deadline Deadline not specified.

[908]
SOUTH CAROLINA HOMESTEAD EXEMPTION PROGRAM

South Carolina Department of Revenue
301 Gervais Street
P.O. Box 125
Columbia, SC 29214
(803) 898-5680   Toll Free: (800) 763-1295
Fax: (803) 898-5822   E-mail: MillerC@sctax.org
Web: www.sctax.org

Summary To provide a homestead exemption to South Carolina residents who are elderly, disabled, or blind, and their widow(er)s.

Eligibility Legal residents of South Carolina who own a house or mobile home are eligible for this exemption if they are 65 years of age or older, totally and permanently disabled, or legally blind. Spouses of deceased persons who were eligible also qualify to receive the exemption if they were at least 50 years of age when their spouse died.

Financial data The first $50,000 of the fair market value of the qualified applicant's home is exempted from property taxes. The exemption is from county, municipal, school, and special assessment real estate property taxes.

Duration The exemption continues as long as the homeowners live in their primary residence in South Carolina.

Additional data This program, established in 1972, is administered by county auditors.

Number awarded Varies each year.

Deadline Persons applying for this exemption for the first time must do so prior to July of each year; subsequently, no re-application is necessary unless the title or use of the property changes.

[909]
SOUTH CAROLINA PERMANENT DISABILITY RETIREMENT INCOME TAX EXCLUSION

South Carolina Department of Revenue
301 Gervais Street
P.O. Box 125
Columbia, SC 29214
(803) 898-5000   Toll Free: (800) 763-1295
Fax: (803) 898-5822
Web: www.sctax.org

Summary To exempt the retirement income received by people with total and permanent disabilities from state taxation in South Carolina.

Eligibility This exemption is available to residents of South Carolina who are permanently and totally disabled and who are also unable to be gainfully employed. People who are receiving disability income from 1 job but are able to perform another job are not eligible for this exclusion.

Financial data Qualified permanent disability retirement income is exempt from state income taxation in South Carolina.

Duration The exemption continues as long as the recipient resides in South Carolina and receives the specified disability retirement income.

Number awarded Varies each year.

Deadline Deadline not specified.

[910]
SOUTH CAROLINA PROPERTY TAX EXEMPTION FOR DISABLED VETERANS, LAW ENFORCEMENT OFFICERS, AND FIREFIGHTERS

South Carolina Department of Revenue
Attn: Property Division
301 Gervais Street
P.O. Box 125
Columbia, SC 29214
(803) 898-5480   Fax: (803) 898-5822
Web: www.sctax.org

Summary To exempt the residence of disabled South Carolina veterans, law enforcement officers, fire fighters, their unremarried widow(er)s, and others from property taxation.

Eligibility This exemption is available to owners of homes in South Carolina who are veterans of the U.S. armed forces, former law enforcement officers, or former fire fighters (including volunteer fire fighters). Applicants must be permanently and totally disabled from service-connected causes. The exemption is also available to qualified surviving spouses (defined to include unremarried spouses of disabled veterans, law enforcement officers, and fire fighters, as well as surviving spouses of servicemembers killed in the line of duty, law enforcement officers who died in the line of duty, and fire fighters who died in the line of duty).

Financial data The exemption applies to all taxes on 1 house and a lot (not to exceed 1 acre).

Duration The exemption extends as long as the veteran, law enforcement officer, or fire fighter resides in the house, or as long as the spouse of a deceased veteran, servicemember, law enforcement officer, or fire fighter remains unremarried and resides in the original house or a single new dwelling.

Number awarded Varies each year.

Deadline Applications may be submitted at any time.

[911]
SOUTH DAKOTA SALES AND PROPERTY TAX REFUND FOR SENIOR AND DISABLED CITIZENS

South Dakota Department of Revenue and Regulation
Attn: Special Tax Division
445 East Capitol Avenue
Pierre, SD 57501-3185
(605) 773-3311   Toll Free: (800) TAX-9188
Fax: (605) 773-6729   E-mail: specialt@state.sd.us
Web: www.state.sd.us

Summary To provide a partial refund of sales taxes to elderly and disabled residents (including disabled veterans) in South Dakota.

Eligibility This program is open to residents of South Dakota who either have a qualified disability or are 66 years of age or older. Applicants must live alone and have a yearly income of less than $10,250 or live in a household whose members' combined income is less than $13,250. Veterans must have a disability of 60% or greater. Other people with disabilities must have been qualified to receive Social Security disability benefits or Supplemental Security Income disability benefits.

Financial data Qualified residents are entitled to a refund of a portion of the sales or property taxes they paid during the preceding calendar year.

Duration Residents of South Dakota are entitled to this refund annually.

Additional data This program has been in effect since 1974. South Dakotans are not entitled to both a sales tax refund and a property tax refund in the same year. The state will calculate both refunds and pay the amount that is greater.

Number awarded Varies each year.

Deadline June of each year.

[912]
TENNESSEE PROPERTY TAX RELIEF FOR DISABLED AND ELDERLY HOMEOWNERS

Tennessee Comptroller of the Treasury
Attn: Property Tax Relief Program
James K. Polk State Office Building
505 Deaderick Street, Room 1600
Nashville, TN 37243-1402
(615) 747-8871   Fax: (615) 532-3866
E-mail: Kim.Darden@state.tn.us
Web: www.comptroller.state.tn.us/pa/patxr.htm

Summary To provide property tax relief for elderly and disabled home owners in Tennessee.

Eligibility This exemption is offered to residents of Tennessee who own and live in their home and are either 1) 65 years of age or older, or 2) totally and permanently disabled as rated by the Social Security Administration or other appropriate agency. To qualify, the combined income of all owners of the property cannot exceed $25,360.

Financial data The amount of the relief depends on the property assessment and the tax rate in the city or county where the beneficiary lives. The maximum market value on which tax relief is calculated is $25,000.

Duration 1 year; may be renewed as long as the qualified Tennessee resident owns and occupies the primary residence.

Number awarded Varies each year.

Deadline Deadline not specified.

[913]
TENNESSEE PROPERTY TAX RELIEF FOR DISABLED VETERANS AND THEIR SPOUSES

Tennessee Comptroller of the Treasury
Attn: Property Tax Relief Program
James K. Polk State Office Building
505 Deaderick Street, Room 1600
Nashville, TN 37243-1402
(615) 747-8871   Fax: (615) 532-3866
E-mail: Kim.Darden@state.tn.us
Web: www.comptroller.state.tn.us/pa/patxr.htm

Summary   To provide property tax relief to blind and disabled veterans and their spouses in Tennessee.

Eligibility   This exemption is offered to veterans or their surviving unremarried spouses who are residents of Tennessee and own and live in their home in the state. The veteran must have served in the U.S. armed forces and 1) have acquired, as a result of such service, a disability from paraplegia, permanent paralysis of both legs and lower part of the body resulting from traumatic injury, disease to the spinal cord or brain, legal blindness, or loss or loss of use of both legs or arms from any service-connected cause; 2) have been rated by the U.S. Department of Veterans Affairs (VA) as 100% permanently disabled as a result of service as a prisoner of war for at least 5 months; or 3) have been rated by the VA as 100% permanently and totally disabled from any other service-connected cause. The relief does not extend to any person who was dishonorably discharged from any of the armed services.

Financial data   The amount of the relief depends on the property assessment and the tax rate in the city or county where the beneficiary lives. The maximum market value on which tax relief is calculated is $175,000.

Duration   1 year; may be renewed as long as the eligible veteran or surviving unremarried spouse owns and occupies the primary residence.

Number awarded   Varies each year.

Deadline   Deadline not specified.

[914]
TEXAS HOME OF YOUR OWN START-UP ASSISTANCE

Texas Home of Your Own Coalition
900 Congress, Suite 220
Austin, TX 78701
(512) 472-9195   Toll Free: (800) 988-HOYO
Fax: (512) 472-8026   TDD: (512) 472-9195
Web: www.advocacyinc.org/txhome.cfm

Summary   To provide funding to Texas residents with disabilities who are interested in purchasing or modifying a home.

Eligibility   This program is open to residents of Texas who have a documentable disability and meet income guidelines (that vary by city and county). Applicants must be interested in obtaining funding for 1) down payment and closing costs for purchase of a home; or 2) home accessibility modifications and barrier removal related to their disability.

Financial data   Maximum grants are $15,000 for down payment or closing cost assistance or $20,000 for home accessibility modifications.

Duration   These are 1-time grants.

Additional data   Funding for this program is provided by the Texas Planning Council for Developmental Disabilities.

Number awarded   Varies each year.

Deadline   Applications may be submitted at any time.

[915]
TEXAS PROPERTY TAX EXEMPTION FOR DISABLED VETERANS AND THEIR FAMILIES

Texas Veterans Commission
P.O. Box 12277
Austin, TX 78711-2277
(512) 463-5538
Toll Free: (800) 252-VETS (within TX)
Fax: (512) 475-2395   E-mail: info@tvc.state.tx.us
Web: www.tvc.state.tx.us/StateBenefits.html

Summary   To extend property tax exemptions on the appraised value of their property to blind, disabled, and other Texas veterans and their surviving family members.

Eligibility   Eligible veterans must be Texas residents rated at least 10% service-connected disabled. Surviving spouses and children of eligible veterans are also covered by this program.

Financial data   For veterans in Texas whose disability is rated as 10% through 29%, the first $5,000 of the appraised property value is exempt from taxation; veterans rated as 30% through 49% disabled are exempt from the first $7,500 of appraised value; those with a 50% through 69% disability are exempt from the first $10,000 of appraised value; the exemption applies to the first $12,000 of appraised value for veterans with disabilities rated as 70% to 99%; veterans rated as 100% disabled are exempt from 100% of the appraised value of their property. A veteran whose disability is 10% or more and who is 65 years or older is entitled to exemption of the first $12,000 of appraised property value. A veteran whose disability consists of the loss of use of 1 or more limbs, total blindness in 1 or both eyes, or paraplegia is exempt from the first $12,000 of the appraised value. The unremarried surviving spouse of a deceased veteran who died on active duty and who, at the time of death had a compensable disability and was entitled to an exemption, is entitled to the same exemption. The surviving spouse of a person who died on active duty is entitled to exemption of the first $5,000 of appraised value of the spouse's property. Surviving spouses, however, are not eligible for the 100% exemption. A surviving child of a person who dies on active duty is entitled to exemption of the first $5,000 of appraised value of the child's property, as long as the child is unmarried and under 21 years of age.

Duration   1 year; may be renewed as long as the eligible veteran (or unremarried surviving spouse or child) owns and occupies the primary residence in Texas.

Additional data   This program is administered at the local level by the various taxing authorities.

Number awarded Varies each year.
Deadline April of each year.

[916]
TROOPS-TO-TEACHERS PROGRAM

Defense Activity for Non-Traditional Education Support
Attn: Troops to Teachers
6490 Sauffley Field Road
Pensacola, FL 32509-5243
(850) 452-1241   Toll Free: (800) 231-6242
Fax: (850) 452-1096   E-mail: ttt@navy.mil
Web: www.dantes.doded.mil

Summary To provide a bonus to disabled and other veterans and military personnel interested in a second career as a public school teacher.

Eligibility This program is open to 1) active-duty military personnel who are retired, have an approved date of retirement within 1 year, or separated on or after January 8, 2002 for physical disability; 2) members of a Reserve component who are retired, currently serving in the Selected Reserve with 10 or more years of credible service and commit to serving an additional 3 years, separated on or after January 8, 2002 due to a physical disability, or transitioned from active duty on or after January 8, 2002 after at least 6 years on active duty and commit to 3 years with a Selected Reserve unit. Applicants must have a baccalaureate or advanced degree, the equivalent of 1 year of college with 6 years of work experience in a vocational or technical field, or meet state requirements for vocational/technical teacher referral. A bonus is available to applicants who are willing to accept employment as a teacher in 1) a school district that has at least 10% of the students from families living below the poverty level, and 2) at a specific school within the district where at least 50% of the students are eligible for the free or reduced cost lunch program or where at least 13.5% of the students have disabilities. A stipend is available to applicants who are willing to accept employment as a teacher at 1) any school within a "high need" district that has at least 20% of the students from families living below the poverty level, or 2) at a specific school where at least 50% of the students are eligible for the free or reduced cost lunch program or at least 13.5% of the students have disabilities, as long as that school is in a district that has between 10% and 20% of students who come from poverty-level families. Preference is given to applicants interested in teaching mathematics, science, or special education.

Financial data A bonus of $10,000 is awarded to recipients who agree to teach for 3 years in a school that serves a high percentage of students from low-income families. A stipend of $5,000 is awarded to recipients who agree to teach for 3 years in a school located in a "high-need" district; stipend funds are intended to help pay for teacher certification costs.

Duration The bonuses are intended as 1-time grants.

Additional data This program was established in 1994 by the Department of Defense (DoD). In 2000, program oversight and funding were transferred to the U.S. Department of Education, but DoD continues to operate the program. The No Child Left Behind Act of 2001 provided for continuation of the program.

Number awarded Varies each year.
Deadline Deadline not specified.

[917]
UTAH DISABLED VETERAN PROPERTY TAX ABATEMENT

Utah Division of Veteran's Affairs
Attn: Director
550 Foothill Boulevard, Room 202
Salt Lake City, UT 84108
(801) 326-2372   Toll Free: (800) 894-9497 (within UT)
Fax: (801) 326-2369   E-mail: veterans@utah.gov
Web: veterans.utah.gov

Summary To exempt a portion of the property of disabled veterans and their families in Utah from taxation.

Eligibility This program is available to residents of Utah who are disabled veterans or their unremarried widow(er)s or minor orphans. The disability must be at least 10% and incurred as the result of injuries in the line of duty.

Financial data The exemption is based on the disability rating of the veteran, to a maximum of $219,164 for a 100% disability.

Duration This benefit is available as long as the disabled veteran or family members reside in Utah.

Deadline Tax exemption applications must be filed with the county government of residence by August of the initial year; once eligibility has been established, reapplication is not required.

[918]
UTAH VETERAN'S PROPERTY TAX EXEMPTION

Utah State Tax Commission
Attn: Property Tax Division
210 North 1950 West
Salt Lake City, UT 84134
(801) 297-3600   Toll Free: (800) 662-4335, ext. 3600
Fax: (801) 297-7699   TDD: (801) 297-2020
Web: www.tax.utah.gov

Summary To exempt from taxation a portion of the real and tangible property of disabled veterans and their families in Utah.

Eligibility This exemption is available to property owners in Utah who are veterans with a disability of at least 10% incurred in the line of duty, along with their unremarried surviving spouses or minor orphans. First year applications must be accompanied by proof of military service and proof of disability or death.

Financial data The exemption depends on the percentage of disability, up to $228,505 of taxable value of a residence.

Duration The exemption is available each year the beneficiary owns property in Utah.

Number awarded Varies each year.

Deadline Applications must be submitted by August of each year.

[919]
VERMONT PROPERTY TAX EXEMPTION FOR DISABLED VETERANS

Vermont Department of Taxes
Attn: Property Valuation and Review Division
P.O. Box 1577
Montpelier, VT 05601-1577
(802) 828-5860   Fax: (802) 828-2824
Web: www.state.vt.us/tax/pvrmilitary.shtml

Summary To exempt disabled Vermont veterans and their dependents from the payment of at least a portion of the state's property tax.

Eligibility Entitled to a property tax exemption are veterans of any war (or their spouses, widow(er)s, or children) who are receiving wartime disability compensation for at least a 50% disability, wartime death compensation, wartime dependence and indemnity compensation, or pension for disability paid through any military department or the Department of Veterans Affairs. Unremarried widow(er)s of previously qualified veterans are also entitled to the exemption whether or not they are receiving government compensation or a pension.

Financial data Up to $10,000 of the assessed value of real and personal property belonging to eligible veterans or their unremarried widow(er)s is exempt from taxation; individual towns may increase the exemption to as much as $40,000.

Duration 1 year; may be renewed as long as the eligible veteran or widow(er) continues to be the owner/occupant of the residence and lives in Vermont.

Additional data Only 1 exemption may be allowed on a property.

Number awarded Varies each year.

Deadline April of each year.

[920]
VETERANS DISABILITY COMPENSATION

Department of Veterans Affairs
Attn: Veterans Benefits Administration
810 Vermont Avenue, N.W.
Washington, DC 20420
(202) 418-4343   Toll Free: (800) 827-1000
Web: www.vba.va.gov/bin/21/compensation/index.htm

Summary To provide monthly compensation to veterans who have a disability that occurred or was made worse during military service.

Eligibility Disabled persons who are eligible for compensation under this program are those whose disability resulted from injury or disease incurred or aggravated during active service in the U.S. armed forces in the line of duty during wartime or peacetime service. They must have been discharged or separated under other than dishonorable conditions.

Financial data Disabled veterans who are found to be eligible for disability compensation are entitled to monthly payments, depending on the degree of disability as determined by the Department of Veterans Affairs. Recent monthly rates for veterans living alone with no dependents ranged from $123 for 10% disability to $2,673 for 100%

disability. Veterans whose service-connected disabilities are rated at 30% or more are entitled to additional allowances for dependent children, spouses, and/or parents. The additional amount is determined according to the number of dependents and the degree of disability. Recently, those supplements ranged from $45 to $150 for a spouse, from $30 to $100 for the first child under 18 years of age, from $22 to $75 for each additional child under 18 years of age, from $72 to $240 for each additional child over 18 years of age and enrolled in school, and from $35 to $120 for each parent. In addition, a veteran whose disability is rated at 30% or more and whose spouse is in need of the aid and attendance of another person may receive an additional amount, ranging from $40 to $136.

Duration Compensation continues as long as the veteran remains disabled.

Additional data In addition to monthly compensation under this program, disabled veterans may also be entitled to prosthetic appliances if they are receiving treatment in a facility under the direct jurisdiction of the Department of Veterans Affairs (VA), or outpatient care under certain specified conditions. Blind veterans are eligible for various aids and services, including adjustment to blindness training, home improvements and structural alterations, low vision aids and training in their use, guide dogs, and material for the blind from the Library of Congress. Former prisoners of war who were incarcerated for at least 30 days and have at least a 10% disability are entitled to a presumption of service connection. Persian Gulf veterans who suffer from chronic disabilities resulting from undiagnosed illnesses may receive disability compensation. VA rating boards determine the degree of disability of each veteran, based on an estimate of the extent to which certain disabilities reduce the typical veteran's ability to earn a living. If a veteran has 2 or more disabilities, the rating board will determine a combined rating and base compensation on that figure.

Number awarded Varies each year.

Deadline Applications are accepted at any time.

[921]
VETERANS SPECIAL MONTHLY COMPENSATION

Department of Veterans Affairs
Attn: Veterans Benefits Administration
810 Vermont Avenue, N.W.
Washington, DC 20420
(202) 418-4343   Toll Free: (800) 827-1000
Web: www.vba.va.gov/bin/21/compensation/index.htm

Summary To provide monthly compensation to veterans who have a disability that exceeds the 100% combined degree compensation or that results from special circumstances.

Eligibility This assistance is available to honorably-discharged veterans who have service-connected disabilities that have resulted in anatomical loss or loss of use of 1 hand, 1 foot, both buttocks, 1 or more creative organs, blindness of 1 eye having only light perception, deafness of both ears, having absence of air and bone conduction, complete organic aphonia with constant inability to communicate by speech, or (in the case of a female veteran) loss of 25% or more of tissue from a single breast or both breasts. Additional assistance is available to veterans who are permanently bedridden or so helpless as to be in need of regular aid and attendance. A special allowance is also available to veterans who have a spouse determined to require regular aid and attendance.

Financial data Disabled veterans who are found to be eligible for special compensation are entitled to monthly payments, depending on the nature of the disability and the type and number of dependants. Recent monthly rates ranged from $2,993 to $7,650 for veterans living alone with no dependents, from $3,143 to $7,800 for a veteran and spouse, from $3,252 to $7,909 for a veteran with spouse and 1 child, from $3,094 to $7,751 for a veteran and 1 child, $75 for each additional child under 18 years of age, and $240 for each additional child over 18 years of age and enrolled in school. Other rates are available for veterans who live with 1 or more parents. In addition, a veteran whose spouse is in need of the aid and attendance of another person may receive an additional $136.

Duration Compensation continues as long as the veteran remains disabled.

Number awarded Varies each year.

Deadline Applications are accepted at any time.

[922]
VOCATIONAL REHABILITATION FOR DISABLED VETERANS

Department of Veterans Affairs
Attn: Veterans Benefits Administration
Vocational Rehabilitation and Employment Service
810 Vermont Avenue, N.W.
Washington, DC 20420
(202) 418-4343   Toll Free: (800) 827-1000
Web: www.vba.va.gov/bin/vre/index.htm

Summary To provide vocational rehabilitation to certain categories of veterans with disabilities.

Eligibility This program is open to veterans who have a service-connected disability of 1) at least 10% and a serious employment handicap, or 2) at least 20% and an employment handicap. They must have been discharged or released from military service under other than dishonorable conditions. The Department of Veterans Affairs (VA) must determine that they would benefit from a training program that would help them prepare for, find, and keep suitable employment. The program may be 1) institutional training at a certificate, 2-year college, 4-year college or university, or technical program; 2) unpaid on-the-job training in a federal, state, or local agency or a federally-recognized Indian tribal agency, training in a home, vocational course in a rehabilitation facility or sheltered workshop, independent instruction, or institutional non-farm cooperative; or 3) paid training through a farm cooperative, apprenticeship, on-the-job training, or on-the-job non-farm cooperative.

Financial data While in training and for 2 months after, eligible disabled veterans may receive subsistence allowances in addition to their disability compensation or retire-

ment pay. For most training programs, the current full-time monthly rate is $547.54 with no dependents, $679.18 with 1 dependent, $800.36 with 2 dependents, and $58.34 for each additional dependent; proportional rates apply for less than full-time training. The VA also pays the costs of tuition, books, fees, supplies, and equipment; it may also pay for special supportive services, such as tutorial assistance, prosthetic devices, lipreading training, and signing for the deaf. If during training or employment services the veteran's disabilities cause transportation expenses that would not be incurred by nondisabled persons, the VA will pay for at least a portion of those expenses. If the veteran encounters financial difficulty during training, the VA may provide an advance against future benefit payments.

Duration Up to 48 months of full-time training or its equivalent in part-time training. If a veteran with a serious disability receives services under an extended evaluation to improve training potential, the total of the extended evaluation and the training phases of the rehabilitation program may exceed 48 months. Usually, the veteran must complete a rehabilitation program within 12 years from the date of notification of entitlement to compensation by the VA. Following completion of the training portion of a rehabilitation program, a veteran may receive counseling and job search and adjustment services for 18 months.

Additional data The program may also provide employment assistance, self-employment assistance, training in a rehabilitation facility, or college and other training. Veterans who are seriously disabled may receive services and assistance to improve their ability to live more independently in their community. After completion of the training phase, the VA will assist the veteran to find and have a suitable job.

Number awarded Varies each year.

Deadline Applications are accepted at any time.

[923]
WASHINGTON PROPERTY TAX ASSISTANCE PROGRAM FOR WIDOWS OR WIDOWERS OF VETERANS

Washington State Department of Revenue
Attn: Property Tax Division
P.O. Box 47471
Olympia, WA 98504-7471
(360) 570-5873   Toll Free: (800) 647-7706
Fax: (360) 586-7602   TDD: (800) 451-7985
Web: dor.wa.gov

Summary To exempt from taxation in Washington a portion of the assessed valuation of property owned by senior citizens and people with disabilities who are widows or widowers of veterans.

Eligibility This exemption is available to residents of Washington who are either 62 years of age or older or who have a disability that prevents them from being gainfully employed and is expected to last for at least 12 months. Applicants must be the unmarried widow or widower of a veteran who 1) died as a result of a service-connected disability; 2) was 100% disabled for 10 years prior to his or her death; 3) was a former prisoner of war and rated as 100%

disabled for at least 1 year prior to death; or 4) died in active duty or in active training status. They must own property that they use as their principal home for at least 6 months of the year; mobile homes may qualify as a residence even if its owner does not own the land where it is located. Their annual disposable income may not exceed $40,000 per year.

Financial data The exemption is $100,000 of the home's assessed value if disposable income is $30,000 or less, $75,000 if disposable income is $30,001 to $35,000, or $50,000 if disposable income is $35,001 to $40,000.

Duration The exemption is available as long as the widow or widower meets the eligibility requirements.

Additional data This program offered assistance beginning with the 2006 tax year.

Number awarded Varies each year.

Deadline Applications are due 30 days before taxes are due.

[924]
WASHINGTON PROPERTY TAX EXEMPTIONS FOR SENIOR CITIZENS AND DISABLED PERSONS

Washington State Department of Revenue
Attn: Property Tax Division
P.O. Box 47471
Olympia, WA 98504-7471
(360) 570-5867   Toll Free: (800) 647-7706
Fax: (360) 586-7602   TDD: (800) 451-7985
Web: dor.wa.gov

Summary To exempt a portion of the property owned by senior citizens and people with disabilities, including their surviving spouses, from taxation in Washington.

Eligibility This exemption is available to residents of Washington who are 1) unable to work because of a disability, 2) veterans with a 100% service-connected disability, 3) at least 61 years of age, or 4) a surviving spouse at least 57 years of age of a person who was approved for this exemption. Applicants must own property that they use as their principal home for at least 6 months of the year; mobile homes may qualify as a residence even if its owner does not own the land where it is located. Their annual disposable income may not exceed $35,000 per year.

Financial data Property owners whose annual income is $25,000 or less are exempt from regular property taxes on the first $60,000 or 60% of their home's assessed value, whichever is greater. Property owners whose annual income is between $25,001 and $30,000 are exempt from regular property taxes on $50,000 or 35% of the assessed value, whichever is greater, not to exceed $70,000 or the assessed value. Property owners whose annual income is $35,000 or less are exempt from all levies that have been approved by voters in excess of regular property taxes.

Duration The exemption is available as long as the property owner meets the eligibility requirements.

Number awarded Varies each year.

Deadline Applications for each year are due by December of the preceding year.

[925]
WEST VIRGINIA HOMESTEAD EXEMPTION

West Virginia State Tax Department
Attn: Property Tax Division
1124 Smith Street
P.O. Box 2389
Charleston, WV 25301
(304) 558-3940
Toll Free: (800) WVA-TAXS (within WV)
Fax: (304) 558-1843   TDD: (800) 282-9833
Web: www.wva.state.wv.us/wvtax/default.aspx

Summary To provide a partial exemption of property taxes on residences owned by disabled or elderly persons and retired veterans in West Virginia.

Eligibility Eligible for this exemption are single-family residences owned and occupied by any person who is permanently and totally disabled or at least 65 years old. Applicants must have been West Virginia residents for 2 consecutive calendar years prior to the tax year to which the exemption relates. Members of the U.S. military forces who maintain West Virginia as their state of residence throughout military service and return to the state to purchase a homestead upon retirement or separation from the military because of permanent and total disability are considered to meet the residency requirement and also qualify for this exemption.

Financial data The exemption applies to the first $20,000 of the total assessed value of eligible property.

Duration The exemption continues as long as the eligible property is owned and occupied by the qualifying person in West Virginia.

Additional data Applications for this program are submitted to the office of the county assessor in each West Virginia county.

Number awarded Varies each year.

Deadline Individuals with disabilities apply for this exemption during July, August, or September of any year. Once they have filed for the exemption, they do not need to refile in subsequent years if they sign a statement that they will notify the assessor within 30 days if they cease to be eligible for the exemption on the basis of disability.

[926]
WEST VIRGINIA SENIOR CITIZEN OR DISABILITY INCOME TAX EXEMPTION

West Virginia State Tax Department
Attn: Taxpayer Services Division
P.O. Box 3784
Charleston, WV 25337-3784
(304) 558-3333 Toll Free: (800) 982-8297 (within WV)
Fax: (304) 558-3269   TDD: (800) 282-9833
Web: www.wva.state.wv.us/wvtax/default.aspx

Summary To provide income tax exemptions for West Virginia residents with disabilities and their surviving spouses.

Eligibility Residents of West Virginia who are totally and permanently disabled (or 65 years of age or older) are eligible for this income tax exemption. Surviving spouses of eligible residents are also entitled to the exemption.

Financial data Qualifying taxpayers may deduct from state income taxation up to $8,000 for a single return or a maximum of $8,000 per person for a joint return.

Duration The exemption continues as long as the eligible resident (or his/her spouse) remains a resident of West Virginia.

Deadline Deadline not specified.

[927]
WISCONSIN DISABILITY INCOME EXCLUSION

Wisconsin Department of Revenue
Attn: Division of Income, Sales and Excise Tax
2135 Rimrock Road
P.O. Box 8933
Madison, WI 53708-8933
(608) 266-2772   Fax: (608) 267-0834
E-mail: income@revenue.wi.gov
Web: www.revenue.wi.gov

Summary To exclude from state income taxation a portion of the disability income received by residents of Wisconsin.

Eligibility This exclusion is available to residents of Wisconsin who are younger than 65 years of age but who are retired on permanent and total disability.

Financial data Up to $5,200 per year may be excluded from income for purposes of state taxation. The exclusion is reduced by any income over $15,000 per year. Generally, no exclusion is left if income is greater than $20,200 if 1 person could take the exclusion or $25,400 if both husband and wife could take the exclusion.

Duration The exclusion is available as long as the recipient resides in Wisconsin.

Number awarded Varies each year.

Deadline Income tax returns must be filed by April of each year.

[928]
WISCONSIN VETERANS AND SURVIVING SPOUSES PROPERTY TAX CREDIT

Wisconsin Department of Revenue
Attn: Customer Service and Education Bureau
2135 Rimrock Road
P.O. Box 8949
Madison, WI 53708-8949
(608) 266-2776   Fax: (608) 267-1030
Web: www.revenue.wi.gov

Summary To provide an income tax credit to disabled Wisconsin veterans and their surviving spouses equal to the amount of property taxes they pay.

Eligibility This credit is available to Wisconsin veterans who served on active duty under honorable conditions in the U.S. armed forces and have resided in Wisconsin for any consecutive 5-year period after entry into active duty. Applicants must have either a service-connected disability rating of 100% or a 100% disability rating based on individual unemployability. Also eligible are unremarried surviving spouses of such disabled veterans and of members of the National Guard or a Reserve component of the U.S. armed forces who were residents of Wisconsin and died in the line of duty while on active or inactive duty for training purposes.

Financial data Eligible veterans and surviving spouses are entitled to an income tax credit equal to the amount of property taxes they pay on their principal residence.

Duration The credit is available as long as the recipient resides in Wisconsin.

Number awarded Varies each year.

Deadline Income tax returns must be filed by April of each year.

[929]
WRITERS EMERGENCY ASSISTANCE FUND

American Society of Journalists and Authors
Attn: Charitable Trust
1501 Broadway, Suite 302
New York, NY 10036
(212) 997-0947   Fax: (212) 937-2315
E-mail: weaf@asja.org
Web: www.asja.org/weaf.php

Summary To assist professional freelance writers who are in financial need because of a disability or other causes.

Eligibility This program is open to established freelance nonfiction writers who, because of advancing age, illness, disability, or extraordinary professional crisis, are unable to work. Applicants need not be members of the American Society of Journalists and Authors, but they must establish a record of past professional freelance writing over a sustained period of years. They must be 60 years of age or older, be so disabled that their normal writing capacity has been severely diminished, or (regardless of age or disability) be caught up in a professional crisis (such as a lawsuit) where a grant would help. Grants are not available to beginning freelancers seeking funds for writing projects nor for works-in-progress of any kind.

Financial data Awards depend on the need of the recipient and the availability of funds.

Duration A recipient may apply for an additional grant at the end of a 12-month period.

Additional data Applications may be submitted by either the applicant or a nominator on the applicant's behalf. This program, established in 1982, was formerly known as the Llewellyn Miller Fund.

Number awarded Varies each year. Since the program began, it has issued more than 160 grants with a total value of approximately $400,000.

Deadline Applications may be submitted at any time.

[930]
WYOMING VETERANS PROPERTY TAX EXEMPTION

Wyoming Department of Revenue
Attn: Property Tax Relief Program
122 West 25th Street, Second Floor West
Cheyenne, WY 82002-0110
(307) 777-5235   Fax: (307) 777-7527
E-mail: DirectorOfRevenue@wy.gov
Web: revenue.state.wy.us

Summary To provide a partial tax exemption on the property owned by veterans and their surviving spouses in Wyoming.

Eligibility This program is open to honorably-discharged veterans who were Wyoming residents at the time they entered military service and have resided in Wyoming for 3 years prior to applying for this exemption. Applicants must have served during specified periods of wartime or have received an armed forces expeditionary medal or other authorized service or campaign medal for service in an armed conflict in a foreign country. Surviving spouses of qualified veterans are also eligible. The exemption applies to county fees only, not state fees.

Financial data Veterans and spouses may exempt $3,000 in assessed value of property from taxation per year. Disabled veterans are entitled to additional exemptions that depend on the level of their disability, to a maximum of $2,000 for a 100% disability.

Duration Veterans and spouses are entitled to use these exemptions as long as they reside in Wyoming and own the property as their principal residence.

Number awarded Varies each year.

Deadline Applicants must advise their county assessor of their intent to use the exemption by May of each year.

Awards

[931]
CHARLES L. BREWER DISTINGUISHED TEACHING OF PSYCHOLOGY AWARD

American Psychological Foundation
750 First Street, N.E.
Washington, DC 20002-4242
(202) 336-5843　　　　　　　　Fax: (202) 336-5812
E-mail: foundation@apa.org
Web: www.apa.org/apf/brewer.html

Summary To recognize and reward distinguished career contributions to the teaching of psychology.

Eligibility This award is available to psychologists who demonstrate outstanding teaching. Selection is based on evidence of influence as a teacher of students who become psychologists, research on teaching, development of effective teaching methods and/or materials, development of innovation curricula and courses, performance as a classroom teacher, demonstrated training of teachers of psychology, teaching of advanced research methods and practice in psychology, and/or administrative facilitation of teaching. Nominators must complete an application form, write a letter of support, and submit the nominee's current vitae and bibliography. The sponsor encourages nominations of individuals who represent diversity in race, ethnicity, gender, age, disability, and sexual orientation.

Financial data Awardees receive a plaque, a $2,000 honorarium, and an all-expense paid trip to the annual convention where the award is presented.

Duration The award is presented annually.

Additional data This award, originally named the Distinguished Teaching in Psychology Award, was first presented in 1970.

Number awarded 1 each year.

Deadline Nominations must be submitted by November of each year.

[932]
DIRECTOR'S AWARD FOR DISTINGUISHED TEACHING SCHOLARS

National Science Foundation
Directorate for Education and Human Resources
Attn: Division of Undergraduate Education
4201 Wilson Boulevard, Room 835N
Arlington, VA 22230
(703) 292-4627　　　　　　　Fax: (703) 292-9015
TDD: (800) 281-8749　　　　　E-mail: npruitt@nsf.gov
Web: www.nsf.gov

Summary To recognize and reward, with funding for additional research, disabled and other scholars affiliated with institutions of higher education who have contributed to teaching of science, technology, engineering, and mathematics (STEM) at the K-12 and undergraduate level.

Eligibility This program is open to teaching-scholars affiliated with institutions of higher education who are nominated by their president, chief academic officer, or other independent researcher. Nominees should have integrated research and education and approached both education and research in a scholarly manner. They should have demonstrated leadership in their respective fields as well as innovativeness and effectiveness in facilitating K-12 and undergraduate student learning in STEM disciplines. Consideration is given to faculty who have a history of substantial impact on 1) research in a STEM discipline or on STEM educational research; or 2) the STEM education of K-16 students who have diverse interests and aspirations, including future K-12 teachers of science and mathematics, students who plan to pursue STEM careers, and those who need to understand science and mathematics in a society increasingly dependent on science and technology. Based on letters of nomination, selected scholars are invited to submit applications for support of their continuing efforts to integrate education and research. Nominations of all citizens, including women and men, underrepresented minorities, and persons with disabilities are especially encouraged.

Financial data The maximum grant is $300,000 for the life of the project.

Duration 4 years.

Number awarded Approximately 6 each year.

Deadline Letters of intent are due in September of each year; full applications must be submitted in October.

[933]
INTERNATIONAL YOUNG SOLOISTS AWARD

VSA arts
Attn: Education Office
818 Connecticut Avenue, N.W., Suite 600
Washington, DC 20006
(202) 628-2800   Toll Free: (800) 933-8721
Fax: (202) 429-0868   TDD: (202) 737-0645
E-mail: soloists@vsarts.org
Web: www.vsarts.org/x22.xml

Summary To recognize and reward young musicians from any country who are physically or mentally challenged.

Eligibility Contestants must be vocalists or instrumentalists under 25 years of age (or under 30 if from outside the United States) who have a disability. Musical ensembles of 2 to 8 performers are also eligible. Applicants may be performers of any type of music, including country, classical, jazz, rap, rock, bluegrass, or ethnic. They are required to submit an audition tape and a 1-page biography that describes why they should be selected to receive this award. Tapes are evaluated on the basis of technique, tone, intonation, rhythm, and interpretation.

Financial data The award is $5,000. Funds must be used to assist the recipients' music career.

Duration The competition is held annually.

Additional data Applications must first be submitted to the respective state organization of VSA arts. This program was formerly known as the Panasonic Young Soloists Award.

Number awarded 4 each year: 2 from the United States and 2 from other countries.

Deadline November of each year.

[934]
JOSEPH B. GITTLER AWARD

American Psychological Foundation
750 First Street, N.E.
Washington, DC 20002-4242
(202) 336-5843   Fax: (202) 336-5812
E-mail: foundation@apa.org
Web: www.apa.org/apf/gittler.html

Summary To recognize and reward disabled and other psychologists who have made outstanding contributions to the philosophical foundations of the discipline.

Eligibility This award is available to scholars whose body of work or whose individual work has transformed the philosophical foundations of psychological knowledge. Self-nominations are welcome. The sponsor encourages nominations of individuals who represent diversity in race, ethnicity, gender, age, disability, and sexual orientation.

Financial data The award is $10,000.

Duration The award is presented annually.

Number awarded 1 each year.

Deadline Nominations must be submitted by May of each year.

[935]
JOYCE WALSH JUNIOR DISABILITY AWARDS

National Federation of Music Clubs
1646 Smith Valley Road
Greenwood, IN 46142
(317) 882-4003   Fax: (317) 882-4019
E-mail: info@nfmc-music.org
Web: www.nfmc-music.org

Summary To recognize and reward, with financial assistance for further study, young instrumentalists and vocalists with disabilities who are members of the National Federation of Music Clubs (NFMC).

Eligibility This program is open to musicians (instrumentalists or vocalists) who are between 12 and 18 years of age, U.S. citizens, and junior members of the federation. Applicants must submit 1) a letter from a medical doctor stating the nature and duration of a mental or physical disability; 2) a CD, up to 10 minutes in length, of their performance of 2 selections from contrasting style periods; and 3) a letter of recommendation from a teacher, tutor, or clergyman. Financial need is not considered in the selection process.

Financial data The awards are $1,500 for first place and $1,000 for second place. In addition, regional awards are $500. All awards must be used for musical study.

Duration The awards are presented annually.

Additional data These awards are funded by the T-Shirt Project Endowment. There is a $2 entry fee.

Number awarded 7 each year: 1 first-place award, 1 second-place award, and 5 regional awards (1 in each of the 5 NFMC regions).

Deadline February of each year.

[936]
JUDD JACOBSON MEMORIAL AWARD

Courage Center
Attn: Vocational Services
3915 Golden Valley Road
Minneapolis, MN 55422
(763) 520-0263   Toll Free: (888) 8-INTAKE
Fax: (763) 520-0562   TDD: (763) 520-0245
E-mail: sue.warner@courage.org
Web: www.couragecenter.org

Summary To recognize and reward residents of designated states who have a disability and have established their own business.

Eligibility This award is available to residents of Iowa, Minnesota, North Dakota, South Dakota, and Wisconsin who have a physical or sensory disability. Nominees must be at least 18 years of age and have established a successful business or entrepreneurial endeavor. They should be able to demonstrate entrepreneurial skill, financial need, and personal commitment, and they should have received little or no previous public recognition.

Financial data The award is $5,000; funds must be used to further the awardee's entrepreneurial business endeavor.

Duration The award is presented annually.

Additional data This program was established in 1992.

Number awarded 1 each year.
Deadline May of each year.

[937]
NICHOLAS AND DOROTHY CUMMINGS PSYCHE PRIZE

American Psychological Foundation
750 First Street, N.E.
Washington, DC 20002-4242
(202) 336-5843   Fax: (202) 336-5812
E-mail: foundation@apa.org
Web: www.apa.org/apf/cummings.html

Summary To recognize and reward disabled and other psychologists who have made outstanding contributions to expanding the role of psychologists as behavioral care providers.

Eligibility This award is available to licensed psychologists who have at least 10 years of experience and work in an integrated primary care setting (rather than in a collaborative practice). Nominees must be involved in a comprehensive medical setting, rather than in a specialized program dealing with a single issue or disease. They must have demonstrated past accomplishments and future plans to expand the acceptance of psychologists as behavioral care providers working alongside and colocated with physicians in the primary care settings of health care delivery. Letters of nomination must be accompanied by a description of the nominee's mentoring experience, training and development of other psychologists in the field; a 1- to 2-page statement of accomplishments to date; a letter, written by the nominee, outlining plans for the next 5 years; and a curriculum vitae. Self-nominations are accepted. The sponsor encourages nominations of individuals who represent diversity in race, ethnicity, gender, age, disability, and sexual orientation.

Financial data The awardee receives a $50,000 grant.
Duration The prize is awarded annually.
Additional data This prize was established in 2004 by the Nicholas and Dorothy Cummings Foundation.
Number awarded 1 each year.
Deadline November of each year.

[938]
PAUL G. HEARNE/AAPD LEADERSHIP AWARDS

American Association of People with Disabilities
1629 K Street, N.W., Suite 950
Washington, DC 20006
(202) 457-0046   Toll Free: (800) 840-8844
Fax: (202) 457-0473   TDD: (202) 457-0046
E-mail: awards@aapd.com
Web: www.aapd-dc.org/DMD/PaulHearneAward.html

Summary To recognize and reward people with disabilities who provide outstanding leadership in their communities.

Eligibility These awards are presented to emerging leaders with disabilities who demonstrate outstanding leadership while having a positive impact on the community of people with disabilities. Applicants must demonstrate 1) leadership achievements that show a positive impact on the broad community of people with disabilities or within their area of disability interest; 2) connections they have made between individuals with disabilities and others in their communities; 3) a positive vision for the disability community and a continuing commitment to their leadership activities; 4) the demonstrated ability to collaborate with other leaders, to follow when necessary, and to cultivate new leaders within their organizations and communities; and 5) potential to contribute at a national level.

Financial data The award is $10,000. Funds are intended to enable recipients to continue their leadership activities.

Duration The awards are presented annually.

Additional data The Milbank Foundation for Rehabilitation established this program in 1999. Sponsorship was assumed by the American Association of People with Disabilities (AAPD) in 2000. Funding is currently provided by the Mitsubishi Electric America Foundation. Recipients are paired with a nationally-recognized leader in the disability community who supports them through mentoring.

Number awarded Up to 2 each year.
Deadline September of each year.

[939]
VSA ARTS PLAYWRIGHT DISCOVERY AWARD

VSA arts
Attn: Education Office
818 Connecticut Avenue, N.W., Suite 600
Washington, DC 20006
(202) 628-2800   Toll Free: (800) 933-8721
Fax: (202) 429-0868   TDD: (202) 737-0645
E-mail: playwright@vsarts.org
Web: www.vsarts.org/x244.xml

Summary To recognize and reward young playwrights who submit scripts that deal with disabilities.

Eligibility This program is open to U.S. citizens and permanent residents in grades 6-12 who submit an original, unproduced, and unpublished script for a 1-act play (less than 40 pages in length) that addresses the issue of disability. Applicants are not required to have a disability, but their script must examine how disability affects their lives and the lives of others. They may write from their own experience or about an experience in the life of another person or fictional character. Plays are intended for an audience of middle through high school students and adults and must be appropriate in language and subject matter for that age group.

Financial data The winner receives an award of $2,000, a trip to Washington, D.C. to attend the award presentation and see a professional production or staged reading of their play at the John F. Kennedy Center for the Performing Arts, a mentoring luncheon with distinguished members of the selection committee, and press opportunities.

Duration The competition is held annually.

Additional data The sponsor, VSA arts, was formerly known as Very Special Arts.

Number awarded 1 each year.
Deadline April of each year.

Families of the Disabled

Scholarships •

Fellowships/Grants •

Grants-in-Aid •

Awards •

Described here are 318 programs open to the children, stepchildren, adopted children, grandchildren, parents, siblings, or other dependents or family members of the disabled. Of these, 174 entries cover scholarships (to pursue studies or research on the undergraduate level in the United States); 29 cover fellowships/grants (to pursue graduate or postdoctoral study or research in the United States); 113 cover grants-in-aids (to support emergency situations, travel, income/property tax liabilities, or the acquisition of assistive technology); and 2 identity awards, competitions, prizes, or honoraria (to recognize or support creative work and public service). If you are looking for a particular program and don't find it in this chapter, be sure to check the Program Title Index to see if it is covered elsewhere in the directory.

Scholarships

[940]
AIR LINE PILOTS ASSOCIATION SCHOLARSHIP PROGRAM

Air Line Pilots Association
Attn: Maggie Erzen
1625 Massachusetts Avenue, N.W.
Washington, DC 20036
(703) 689-2270　　E-mail: Maggie.Erzen@alpa.org
Web: www.alpa.org

Summary To provide financial assistance for college to the children of disabled or deceased members of the Air Line Pilots Association.

Eligibility This program is open to children of medically retired, long-term disabled, or deceased members of the Air Line Pilots Association. Although the program envisions selection of students enrolling as college freshman, eligible individuals who are already enrolled in college may also apply. Selection is based on a number of factors, including academic record and financial need.

Financial data The stipend is $3,000 per year.

Duration 1 year; may be renewed up to 3 additional years, if the student maintains a GPA of 3.0 or higher.

Number awarded Each year, the association grants 1 new 4-year award and continues 3 previously-made awards.

Deadline March of each year.

[941]
ALABAMA G.I. DEPENDENTS' SCHOLARSHIP PROGRAM

Alabama Department of Veterans Affairs
770 Washington Avenue, Suite 530
Montgomery, AL 36102-1509
(334) 242-5077　　Fax: (334) 242-5102
E-mail: willie.moore@va.state.al.us
Web: www.va.state.al.us/scholarship.htm

Summary To provide educational benefits to the dependents of disabled, deceased, and other Alabama veterans.

Eligibility Eligible are spouses, children, stepchildren, and unremarried widow(er)s of veterans who served honorably for 90 days or more and 1) are currently rated as 20% or more service-connected disabled or were so rated at time of death; 2) were a former prisoner of war; 3) have been declared missing in action; 4) died as the result of a service-connected disability; or 5) died while on active military duty in the line of duty. The veteran must have been a permanent civilian resident of Alabama for at least 1 year prior to entering active military service; veterans who were not Alabama residents at the time of entering active military service may also qualify if they have a 100% disability and were permanent residents of Alabama for at least 5 years prior to filing the application for this program or prior to death, if deceased. Children and stepchildren must be

under the age of 26, but spouses and unremarried widow(er)s may be of any age.

Financial data Eligible dependents may attend any state-supported Alabama institution of higher learning or enroll in a prescribed course of study at any Alabama state-supported trade school without payment of any tuition, book fees, or laboratory charges.

Duration This is an entitlement program for 4 years of full-time undergraduate or graduate study or part-time equivalent. Spouses and unremarried widow(er)s whose veteran spouse is rated between 20% and 90% disabled, or 100% disabled but not permanently so, may attend only 2 standard academic years.

Additional data Benefits for children, spouses, and unremarried widow(er)s are available in addition to federal government benefits. Assistance is not provided for non-credit courses, placement testing, GED preparation, continuing educational courses, pre-technical courses, or state board examinations.

Number awarded Varies each year.

Deadline Applications may be submitted at any time.

[942]
ALABAMA SCHOLARSHIPS FOR DEPENDENTS OF BLIND PARENTS

Alabama Department of Rehabilitation Services
Attn: Debra Culver
602 South Lawrence Street
Montgomery, AL 36104
(256) 293-7500　　Toll Free: (800) 441-7607
Fax: (256) 293-7383　　TDD: (800) 499-1816
E-mail: dculver@rehab.state.al.us
Web: www.rehab.state.al.us

Summary To provide financial assistance for college to students whose blind parents are residents of Alabama.

Eligibility Eligible to apply are seniors or recent graduates of Alabama high schools whose family head of household is blind and whose annual family income is limited (less than $9,000 for a family with 1 child, $12,000 with 2 children, $15,000 with 3 children, or $18,000 with 4 or more children). Applicants must 1) have been permanent residents of Alabama for at least 5 years, 2) apply within 2 years after graduation from high school, and 3) be under 23 years of age.

Financial data Eligible students receive free tuition, waiver of fees, and necessary textbooks at any Alabama state-supported postsecondary institution.

Duration Up to 36 months at an institution of higher education, or for the period required to complete a course of study at a trade school.

Additional data Recipients must complete their course of study within 5 years (unless interrupted by military service), but at least prior to the age of 30.

Number awarded Varies each year.

Deadline Deadline not specified.

[943]
ANGEL ON MY SHOULDER SCHOLARSHIPS

Angel on My Shoulder
P.O. Box 747
St. Germain, WI 54558
Toll Free: (800) 860-3431
E-mail: info@angelonmyshoulder.org
Web: www.angelonmyshoulder.org

Summary To provide financial assistance to high school seniors in Wisconsin who plan to attend college in any state and are cancer survivors or relatives affected by cancer.

Eligibility This program is open to seniors who are graduating from high schools in Wisconsin and planning to attend a 4-year college, technical school, or specialty school in any state. Applicants must be survivors of cancer or have an immediate family member (father, mother, sibling) affected by cancer. Along with their application, they must submit a 250-word essay on why they wish to further their formal education, including their goals and values and how the cancer experience or affiliation with the sponsoring organization has affected their life. Financial need is considered in the selection process.

Financial data Stipends are $1,500 or $1,000.

Duration 1 year.

Additional data This program was established in 2008.

Number awarded Varies each year. Recently, 23 of these scholarships were awarded: 4 at $1,500 and 19 at $1,000.

Deadline March of each year.

[944]
ARKANSAS LAW ENFORCEMENT OFFICERS' DEPENDENTS' SCHOLARSHIPS

Arkansas Department of Higher Education
Attn: Financial Aid Division
114 East Capitol Avenue
Little Rock, AR 72201-3818
(501) 371-2050   Toll Free: (800) 54-STUDY
Fax: (501) 371-2001   E-mail: finaid@adhe.edu
Web: www.adhe.edu

Summary To provide financial assistance for undergraduate education to the dependents of deceased or disabled Arkansas law enforcement officers, fire fighters, or other designated public employees.

Eligibility This program is open to the spouses and/or children (natural, adopted, or step) of Arkansas residents who were killed or permanently disabled in the line of duty as law enforcement officers, municipal and/or college or university police officers, sheriffs and deputy sheriffs, constables, state correction employees, game wardens, state park employees who are commissioned law enforcement officers or emergency response employees, full-time or volunteer fire fighters, state forestry employees engaged in fighting forest fires, certain Arkansas Highway and Transportation Department employees, emergency medical technicians, or Department of Community Punishment employees. Children must be less than 23 years of age.

Spouses may not have remarried. All applicants must have been Arkansas residents for at least 6 months.

Financial data The scholarship covers tuition, on-campus room charges, and fees (but not books, school supplies, food, materials, or dues for extracurricular activities) at any state-supported college or university in Arkansas.

Duration Up to 8 semesters, as long as the student is working on a baccalaureate or associate degree.

Number awarded Varies each year.

Deadline July of each year for fall term, November of each year for spring or winter term, April of each year for first summer session, or June of each year for second summer session.

[945]
ARKANSAS MILITARY DEPENDENTS' SCHOLARSHIP PROGRAM

Arkansas Department of Higher Education
Attn: Financial Aid Division
114 East Capitol Avenue
Little Rock, AR 72201-3818
(501) 371-2050   Toll Free: (800) 54-STUDY
Fax: (501) 371-2001   E-mail: finaid@adhe.edu
Web: www.adhe.edu

Summary To provide financial assistance for educational purposes to dependents of certain categories of Arkansas veterans.

Eligibility This program is open to the natural children, adopted children, stepchildren, and spouses of Arkansas residents who have been declared to be a prisoner of war, killed in action, missing in action, killed on ordnance delivery, or 100% totally and permanently disabled during, or as a result of, active military service. Applicants and their parent or spouse must be residents of Arkansas. They must be working on, or planning to work on, a bachelor's degree or certificate of completion at a public college, university, or technical school in Arkansas.

Financial data The program pays for tuition, general registration fees, special course fees, activity fees, room and board (if provided in campus facilities), and other charges associated with earning a degree or certificate.

Duration 1 year; undergraduates may obtain renewal as long as they make satisfactory progress toward a baccalaureate degree; graduate students may obtain renewal as long as they maintain a minimum GPA of 2.0 and make satisfactory progress toward a degree.

Additional data This program was established in 1973 as the Arkansas Missing in Action/Killed in Action Dependents Scholarship Program to provide assistance to the dependents of veterans killed in action, missing in action, or declared a prisoner of war. In 2005, it was amended to include dependents of disabled veterans and given its current name. Applications must be submitted to the financial aid director at an Arkansas state-supported institution of higher education or state-supported technical/vocational school.

Number awarded Varies each year; recently, 4 of these scholarships were awarded.

Deadline July of each year for fall term, November of each year for spring or winter term, April of each year for first summer session, or June of each year for second summer session.

[946]
BARBARA PALO FOSTER MEMORIAL SCHOLARSHIP

Ulman Cancer Fund for Young Adults
Attn: Scholarship Program Coordinator
10440 Little Patuxent Parkway, Suite 1G
Columbia, MD 21044
(410) 964-0202, ext. 106 Toll Free: (888) 393-FUND
E-mail: scholarship@ulmanfund.org
Web: www.ulmanfund.org

Summary To provide financial assistance to undergraduate and graduate nursing students who have a parent with cancer.

Eligibility This program is open to nursing students who have or have lost a parent to cancer. Applicants must be younger than 35 years of age and enrolled in, or planning to enroll in, an undergraduate or graduate program in nursing. They must demonstrate an interest in furthering patient education, focusing on persons from medically underserved communities and/or women's health issues. Along with their application, they must submit an essay of at least 1,000 words on the ways in which their experiences as a member of a marginalized group within the cancer community (i.e., young adults affected by cancer) have taught them lessons that inspire them to be of service to other socially, politically, and or economically marginalized people in the healthcare system. Selection is based on demonstrated dedication to community service, commitment to educational and professional goals, use of their cancer experience to impact the lives of other young adults affected by cancer, medical hardship, and financial need.

Financial data The stipend is $2,500. Funds are paid directly to the educational institution.

Duration 1 year; nonrenewable.

Additional data Recipients must agree to complete 50 hours of community service.

Number awarded 1 each year.

Deadline April of each year.

[947]
BILL MCADAM SCHOLARSHIP FUND

Hemophilia Foundation of Michigan
c/o Cathy McAdam
22226 Doxtator
Dearborn, MI 48128
(313) 563-1412 E-mail: mcmcadam@comcast.net

Summary To provide financial assistance for college to students with a bleeding disorder or members of their families.

Eligibility This program is open to 1) students with a hereditary bleeding disorder (hemophilia, von Willebrand, etc.) or 2) members of their families (spouse, partner, child,

sibling). Applicants must be U.S. citizens and enrolled or planning to enroll at an accredited 2- or 4-year college, trade or technical school, or other certification program. Along with their application, they must submit 2 letters of recommendation and 3 essays: 1) what they would like the scholarship committee to know about their dream career and the passion that moves them toward furthering their education; 2) a challenge they faced and how they addressed it; and 3) a thank-you note to a fictional character who gave them a gift. Financial need is not considered in the selection process.

Financial data The stipend is $2,000. Funds are paid directly to the recipient's institution.

Duration 1 year; nonrenewable.

Number awarded 1 each year.

Deadline May of each year.

[948]
BIORX/HEMOPHILIA OF NORTH CAROLINA EDUCATIONAL SCHOLARSHIPS

BioRx
200 West Lexington Avenue, Suite 203
High Point, NC 27262
(919) 749-3196 Toll Free: (866) 44-BIORX
E-mail: cbarnes@biorx.net
Web: www.biorx.net/hemo_scholarships.php

Summary To provide financial assistance for college to people with hemophilia, their caregivers, and their siblings, especially those who are interested in studying health care.

Eligibility This program is open to caregivers of children affected with bleeding disorders, people who have been diagnosed with hemophilia, and siblings of people diagnosed with hemophilia. Applicants must submit an essay of 1 to 2 page detailing their occupational goals and objectives in life and how the educational program they have chosen will meet those goals. Preference is given to applicants who are studying or planning to study a health care-related field at an accredited college, university, or certified training program. Residents of all states are eligible.

Financial data The stipend is $2,000.

Duration 1 year.

Additional data This program was established in 2004. Applications must be submitted to Hemophilia of North Carolina, P.O. Box 70, Cary, NC 27512-0070.

Number awarded 3 each year.

Deadline April of each year.

[949]
BLACKHORSE SCHOLARSHIP

Blackhorse Association
P.O. Box 630141
Nacogdoches, TX 75963-0141
E-mail: info@blackhorse.org
Web: www.blackhorse.org

Summary To provide financial assistance for college to children of members of the Blackhorse Association who are currently serving or have served with the 11th Armored Cavalry Regiment (ACR).

Eligibility This program is open to the natural and adopted children of current or former 11th ACR solders who are also members of the association. Applicants must be attending or planning to attend college. In the selection process, first priority is given to children who lost a parent in service of the regiment; second priority is given to children of those incapacitated by wounds or injury while serving the regiment; third priority is given based on financial need of the applicant and family.

Financial data The stipend is $3,000 per year.

Duration 1 year; may be renewed.

Additional data The Blackhorse Association was founded in 1970 by veterans of the 11th ACR who had served in Vietnam.

Number awarded Varies each year; recently, 3 of these scholarships were awarded. Since this program was established, it has awarded more than $300,000 in scholarships.

Deadline March of each year.

[950]
BOB HERSH MEMORIAL SCHOLARSHIP

Mary M. Gooley Hemophilia Center
Attn: Scholarship Selection Committee
1415 Portland Avenue, Suite 500
Rochester, NY 14621
(585) 922-5700   Fax: (585) 922-5775
E-mail: Tricia.oppelt@rochestergeneral.org
Web: www.hemocenter.org/Scholarship%20Info.asp

Summary To provide financial assistance to people with a bleeding disorder and their families who plan to attend college to prepare for a career in a teaching or helping profession.

Eligibility This program is open to people who are affected directly or indirectly by hemophilia, von Willebrand Disease, hereditary bleeding disorder, or hemochromatosis. Applicants must be enrolled or planning to enroll at an accredited 2- or 4-year college or university, vocational/technical school, or certified training program. They must be preparing for a career in a teaching or helping profession. Along with their application, they must submit 1) a 1,000-word essay on their goals and aspirations, their biggest challenge and how they met it, and anything else they want the selection committee to know about them; and 2) a 250-word essay on any unusual family or personal circumstances have affected their achievement in school, work, or participation in school and community activities, including how the bleeding disorder of themselves or their family member has affected their life. Selection is based on the essays, academic performance, participation in school and community activities, work or volunteer experience, personal or family circumstances, recommendations, and financial need.

Financial data The stipend is $1,000.

Duration 1 year.

Additional data This program was established in 2009.

Number awarded 1 each year.

Deadline April of each year.

[951]
BRADLEY KRUEGER SCHOLARSHIP

Hemophilia Foundation of Illinois
Attn: Program Director
332 South Michigan Avenue, Suite 1135
Chicago, IL 60604
(312) 427-1495   E-mail: ekraemer@hfi-il.org
Web: www.hemophiliaillinois.org

Summary To provide financial assistance for attendance at a college in any state to residents of Illinois who have a bleeding disorder and their families.

Eligibility This program is open to residents of Illinois who have a bleeding disorder and their parents, siblings, and children; people who are carriers of the disease are also eligible. Applicants must be attending or planning to attend a postsecondary institution, including a trade school, in any state. Along with their application, they must submit essays on their goals for furthering their education, the steps they have taken to meet those goals, how this scholarship will help them achieve those goals, what it means to them to live with hemophilia, and what they consider their responsibility to the bleeding disorders community. Financial need is not considered in the selection process.

Financial data Stipends range up to $5,000. Funds are paid directly to the educational institution to be used for payment of tuition, room and board, books, and supplies (including computer equipment).

Duration 1 year.

Number awarded 1 or more each year.

Deadline June of each year.

[952]
BRYON RIESCH SCHOLARSHIPS

Bryon Riesch Paralysis Foundation
P.O. Box 1388
Waukesha, WI 53187-1388
(262) 547-2083   E-mail: info@brpf.org
Web: www.brpf.org/scholarships.htm

Summary To provide financial assistance to 1) undergraduate and graduate students who have a neurological disability or 2) the children of people with such a disability.

Eligibility This program is open to students entering or enrolled at a 2- or 4-year college or university as an undergraduate or graduate student. Applicants must have a neurological disability or be the child of a person with such a disability. They must have a GPA of 2.5 or higher in high school or college. Along with their application, they must submit a 200-word essay on why they deserve the scholarship, a statement of their 5- and 10-year goals, and a list of work experience. Financial need is not considered in the selection process.

Financial data Stipends range from $1,000 to $2,000.

Duration 1 year; may be renewed.

Number awarded 2 to 3 each semester.

Deadline June of each year for fall semester; December of each year for spring semester.

[953]
CALIFORNIA FEE WAIVER PROGRAM FOR CHILDREN OF VETERANS

California Department of Veterans Affairs
Attn: Division of Veterans Services
1227 O Street, Room 105
Sacramento, CA 95814
(916) 503-8397
Toll Free: (800) 952-LOAN (within CA)
Fax: (916) 653-2563   TDD: (800) 324-5966
E-mail: ruckergl@cdva.ca.gov
Web: www.cdva.ca.gov/VetService/Waivers.aspx

Summary To provide financial assistance for college to the children of disabled or deceased veterans in California.

Eligibility Eligible for this program are the children of veterans who 1) died of a service-connected disability; 2) had a service-connected disability at the time of death; or 3) currently have a service-connected disability of any level of severity. Applicants must plan to attend a community college in California, branch of the California State University system, or campus of the University of California. Their income, including the value of support received from parents, cannot exceed $11,201. California veteran status is not required for this program. Dependents in college who are eligible to receive federal education benefits from the U.S. Department of Veterans Affairs are not eligible for these fee waivers.

Financial data This program provides for waiver of registration fees to students attending any publicly-supported community or state college or university in California.

Duration 1 year; may be renewed.

Number awarded Varies each year.

Deadline Deadline not specified.

[954]
CALIFORNIA FEE WAIVER PROGRAM FOR DEPENDENTS OF DECEASED OR DISABLED NATIONAL GUARD MEMBERS

California Department of Veterans Affairs
Attn: Division of Veterans Services
1227 O Street, Room 105
Sacramento, CA 95814
(916) 503-8397
Toll Free: (800) 952-LOAN (within CA)
Fax: (916) 653-2563   TDD: (800) 324-5966
E-mail: ruckergl@cdva.ca.gov
Web: www.cdva.ca.gov/VetService/Waivers.aspx

Summary To provide financial assistance for college to dependents of disabled and deceased members of the California National Guard.

Eligibility Eligible for this program are spouses, children, and unremarried widow(er)s of members of the California National Guard who, in the line of duty and in the active service of the state, were killed, died of a disability, or became permanently disabled. Applicants must be attending or planning to attend a community college, branch of the California State University system, or campus of the University of California.

Financial data Full-time college students receive a waiver of tuition and registration fees at any publicly-supported community or state college or university in California.

Duration 1 year; may be renewed.

Number awarded Varies each year.

Deadline Deadline not specified.

[955]
CALIFORNIA FEE WAIVER PROGRAM FOR DEPENDENTS OF TOTALLY DISABLED VETERANS

California Department of Veterans Affairs
Attn: Division of Veterans Services
1227 O Street, Room 105
Sacramento, CA 95814
(916) 503-8397
Toll Free: (800) 952-LOAN (within CA)
Fax: (916) 653-2563   TDD: (800) 324-5966
E-mail: ruckergl@cdva.ca.gov
Web: www.cdva.ca.gov/VetService/Waivers.aspx

Summary To provide financial assistance for college to dependents of disabled and other California veterans.

Eligibility Eligible for this program are spouses (including registered domestic partners), children, and unremarried widow(er)s of veterans who are currently totally service-connected disabled (or are being compensated for a service-connected disability at a rate of 100%) or who died of a service-connected cause or disability. The veteran parent must have served during a qualifying war period and must have been discharged or released from military service under honorable conditions. The child cannot be over 27 years of age (extended to 30 if the student was in the military); there are no age limitations for spouses or surviving spouses. This program does not have an income limit. Dependents in college are not eligible if they are qualified to receive educational benefits from the U.S. Department of Veterans Affairs. Applicants must be attending or planning to attend a community college, branch of the California State University system, or campus of the University of California.

Financial data Full-time college students receive a waiver of tuition and registration fees at any publicly-supported community or state college or university in California.

Duration Children of eligible veterans may receive postsecondary benefits until the needed training is completed or until the dependent reaches 27 years of age (extended to 30 if the dependent serves in the armed forces). Widow(er)s and spouses are limited to a maximum of 48 months' full-time training or the equivalent in part-time training.

Number awarded Varies each year.

Deadline Deadline not specified.

[956]
CALIFORNIA LAW ENFORCEMENT PERSONNEL DEPENDENTS GRANT PROGRAM

California Student Aid Commission
Attn: Specialized Programs
10811 International Drive
P.O. Box 419029
Rancho Cordova, CA 95741-9029
(916) 526-8276   Toll Free: (888) CA-GRANT
Fax: (916) 526-7977 E-mail: specialized@csac.ca.gov
Web: www.csac.ca.gov/doc.asp?id=109

Summary To provide financial assistance for college to the dependents of California law enforcement officers who have been totally disabled or killed in the line of duty.

Eligibility This program is open to the natural children, adopted children, and spouses of a California peace officer (Highway Patrol, marshal, sheriff, police officer), employee of the Department of Corrections or Youth Authority, or fire fighter. The parent or spouse must have died or become totally disabled as the result of an accident or injury caused by external violence or physical force incurred in the performance of duty. Applicants must be enrolled in at least 6 units at an accredited California postsecondary institution and able to demonstrate financial need.

Financial data Stipends range from $100 to $11,259 per year, depending on the need of the recipient.

Duration 1 academic year; may be renewed for up to 5 additional years at 4-year colleges and universities or up to 3 additional years at community colleges.

Additional data If the student receives other scholarships or grants, the award may be adjusted or withdrawn, depending upon financial need. Acceptance of work-study, loans, or employment will generally not affect the amount of money offered through this program.

Number awarded Varies each year; recently, 11 students received $82,000 in assistance from this program.

Deadline Applications may be submitted at any time.

[957]
CFA INSTITUTE 11 SEPTEMBER MEMORIAL SCHOLARSHIP

CFA Institute
Attn: Research Foundation
560 Ray C. Hunt Drive
P.O. Box 3668
Charlottesville, VA 22903-0668
(434) 951-5499   Toll Free: (800) 237-8132
Fax: (434) 951-5370   E-mail: rf@cfainstitute.org
Web: www.cfainstitute.org/foundation/scholarship

Summary To provide financial assistance to individuals and their families who were disabled or killed in the September 11 terrorist attacks and who wish to major in business-related fields in college.

Eligibility College scholarships are offered to those who meet the following 2 criteria: 1) they were permanently disabled in the attacks, or were the spouses, domestic partners, or children of anyone killed or permanently disabled in the attacks, and 2) they will be working on a college-level degree in finance, economics, accounting, or business ethics. Applicants may be residents of any state or country. Selection is based on demonstrated leadership and good citizenship, academic record, and financial need.

Financial data Stipends range up to $25,000 per year, depending on the need of the recipient.

Duration 1 year; renewable up to 4 additional years.

Additional data The CFA (Chartered Financial Analyst) Institute was formerly the Association for Investment Management and Research (AIMR). It lost at least 56 of its members and CFA candidates in the terrorist attacks of 11 September. This program is managed by Scholarship Management Services, a division of Scholarship America, One Scholarship Way, P.O. Box 297, St. Peter, MN 56082, (507) 931-1682, (800) 537-4180, Fax: (507) 931-9168, E-mail: smsinfo@csfa.org.

Number awarded Varies each year; recently, 12 of these scholarships were awarded.

Deadline May of each year.

[958]
CHIEF MASTER SERGEANTS OF THE AIR FORCE SCHOLARSHIPS

Air Force Sergeants Association
Attn: Scholarship Coordinator
P.O. Box 50
Temple Hills, MD 20757
(301) 899-3500, ext. 237   Toll Free: (800) 638-0594
Fax: (301) 899-8136   E-mail: staff@hqafsa.org
Web: www.hqafsa.org

Summary To provide financial assistance for college to the dependent children of Air Force personnel.

Eligibility This program is open to the unmarried children (including stepchildren and legally adopted children) of active-duty, retired, or veteran members of the U.S. Air Force, Air National Guard, or Air Force Reserves. Applicants must be attending or planning to attend an accredited academic institution. They must have an unweighted GPA of 3.5 or higher. Along with their application, they must submit 1) a paragraph on their life objectives and what they plan to do with the education they receive; and 2) an essay on the most urgent problem facing society today. High school seniors must also submit a transcript of all high school grades and a record of their SAT or ACT scores. Selection is based on academic record, character, leadership skills, writing ability, versatility, and potential for success. Financial need is not a consideration. A unique aspect of these scholarships is that applicants may supply additional information regarding circumstances that entitle them to special consideration; examples of such circumstances include student disabilities, financial hardships, parent disabled and unable to work, parent missing in action/killed in action/prisoner of war, or other unusual extenuating circumstances.

Financial data Stipends are $3,000, $2,000, or $1,000; funds may be used for tuition, room and board, fees, books, supplies, and transportation.

Duration 1 year; may be renewed if the recipient maintains full-time enrollment.

Additional data The Air Force Sergeants Association administers this program on behalf of the Airmen Memorial Foundation. It was established in 1987 and named in honor of CMSAF Richard D. Kisling, the late third Chief Master Sergeant of the Air Force. In 1997, following the deaths of CMSAF's (Retired) Andrews and Harlow, it was given its current name.

Number awarded 12 each year: 1 at $3,000, 1 at $2,000, and 10 at $1,000. Since this program began, it has awarded more than $250,000 in scholarships.

Deadline March of each year.

[959]
CHILDREN OF INJURED WORKERS SCHOLARSHIPS

Children of Injured Workers, Inc.
4983 Brittonfield Parkway
East Syracuse, NY 13057
(315) 449-1306   Fax: (315) 449-4358
E-mail: info@kidschanceny.org
Web: www.kidschanceny.org

Summary To provide financial assistance to residents of New York whose parent was seriously injured or killed in a workplace accident and who are interested in attending college in any state.

Eligibility This program is open to New York residents attending or planning to attend a college or technical school in any state. Applicants must be the child of a worker who suffered injury or death in an accident that is either established or accepted under the Workers' Compensation Law of the state of New York. The injury or death must have had a demonstrable impact on the financial ability of the child to attend college.

Financial data A stipend is awarded (amount not specified).

Duration 1 year; recipients may reapply.

Number awarded Varies each year.

Deadline Deadline not specified.

[960]
COLORADO DEPENDENTS TUITION ASSISTANCE PROGRAM

Colorado Commission on Higher Education
1560 Broadway, Suite 1600
Denver, CO 80202
(303) 866-2723   Fax: (303) 866-4266
E-mail: cche@state.co.us
Web: highered.colorado.gov

Summary To provide financial assistance for college to the dependents of disabled or deceased Colorado National Guardsmen, law enforcement officers, and fire fighters.

Eligibility Eligible for the program are dependents of Colorado law enforcement officers, fire fighters, and National Guardsmen disabled or killed in the line of duty, as well as dependents of prisoners of war or service personnel listed as missing in action. Students must be Colorado residents under 22 years of age enrolled at 1) a state-supported 2- or 4-year Colorado college or university; 2) a private college, university, or vocational school in Colorado approved by the commission; or 3) an out-of-state 4-year college. Financial need is considered in the selection process.

Financial data Eligible students receive free tuition at Colorado public institutions of higher education. If the recipient wishes to attend a private college, university, or proprietary school, the award is limited to the amount of tuition at a comparable state-supported institution. Students who have applied to live in a dormitory, but have not been accepted because there is not enough space, may be provided supplemental assistance. Students who choose to live off-campus are not eligible for room reimbursement or a meal plan. Students who attend a nonresidential Colorado institution and do not live at home are eligible for a grant of $1,000 per semester to assist with living expenses. Students who attend an out-of-state institution are eligible for the amount of tuition equivalent to that at a comparable Colorado public institution, but they are not eligible for room and board.

Duration Up to 6 years or until completion of a bachelor's degree, provided the recipient maintains a GPA of 2.5 or higher.

Additional data Recipients must attend accredited postsecondary institutions in Colorado.

Number awarded Varies each year; recently, nearly $365,000 was allocated to this program.

Deadline Deadline not specified.

[961]
DANA WALTERS SCHOLARSHIPS

Dana Walters Scholarship Foundation
P.O. Box 723243
Atlanta, GA 31139
(770) 436-0190   E-mail: sonickaren@aol.com
Web: www.dwscholarship.com

Summary To provide financial assistance for college to residents of Georgia who have cystic fibrosis (CF) and members of their immediate families.

Eligibility This program is open to residents of Georgia who have CF or are a member of a family (including parents) of a person who has CF. Applicants must be graduating high school seniors or already have a high school diploma. They must have a combined SAT score of at least 900 or an ACT score of at least 21 and either a GPA of 2.7 or higher or a rank in the top 30% of their class. Financial need is not considered in the selection process.

Financial data The stipend is $1,000. Funds are paid directly to the recipient's college.

Duration 1 year; may be renewed.

Number awarded 1 or more each year.

Deadline March of each year.

[962]
DAVE MADEIROS CONTINUED EDUCATION SCHOLARSHIPS

Factor Foundation of America
Attn: Scholarship Committee
Peninsula Corporate Center
950 Peninsula Corporate Center, Suite 3017
Boca Raton, FL 33487
(561) 981-8814   Toll Free: (866) 843-3362
Fax: (561) 981-8622
E-mail: contactFFOA@factorfoundation.org
Web: www.factorfoundation.org/programs.htm

Summary To provide financial assistance for college to people with a bleeding disorder and their families.

Eligibility This program is open to people with a bleeding disorder and their siblings, parents, and children. Applicants must be attending or planning to attend an accredited 2- or 4-year college or university or technical school. They must be recommended by a local hemophilia chapter, physician, and/or hemophilia treatment center. Along with their application, they must submit a 500-word letter describing their goals and aspirations and how the bleeding disorders community has played a part in their life. Financial need is also considered in the selection process.

Financial data The stipend is $2,000 per year.

Duration 1 year; may be renewed if the recipient remains in good academic standing.

Additional data This program began in 2006.

Number awarded Varies each year; recently, 12 of these scholarships were awarded.

Deadline April of each year.

[963]
DAVE MADEIROS CREATIVE ARTS SCHOLARSHIP

Factor Foundation of America
Attn: Scholarship Committee
Peninsula Corporate Center
950 Peninsula Corporate Center, Suite 3017
Boca Raton, FL 33487
(561) 981-8814   Toll Free: (866) 843-3362
Fax: (561) 981-8622
E-mail: info@factorfoundation.org
Web: www.factorfoundation.org/programs.htm

Summary To provide financial assistance for artistic or sports activities to young people with a bleeding disorder and their siblings.

Eligibility This program is open to children between 5 and 17 years of age who have a bleeding disorder or are the sibling of such a person. Applicants must be interested in participating in such activities as taking musical lessons, joining a sports team, taking drawing lessons, taking a drama class, or taking a private sports class. They must be recommended by a local hemophilia chapter, physician, and/or hemophilia treatment center. Parents must submit an application that includes a 500-word essay on their desire for their child to take part in a creative art and how that experience will benefit him or her, 2 letters of reference, and documentation of financial need.

Financial data The stipend is $1,000.

Duration 1 year; recipients may reapply.

Additional data This program began in 2006.

Number awarded At least 1 each year.

Deadline April of each year.

[964]
DAVID NELSON JR. MEMORIAL FUND SCHOLARSHIP

Gift of Life Donor Program
Attn: David Nelson Jr. Memorial Fund
401 North Third Street
Philadelphia, PA 19123-4101
Toll Free: (800) DONORS-1
Web: www.davidnelsonjrmemorialfund.org

Summary To provide financial assistance to the children of organ and tissue donors who live in the service area of the Gift of Life Donor Program and are interested in attending high school in the region or college in any state.

Eligibility This program is open to the children of organ and tissue donors who live in the eastern half of Pennsylvania, southern New Jersey, or Delaware. Applicants must be younger than 25 years of age and either currently enrolled at 1) a private or parochial high school in the region, or 2) a 2- or 4-year college, university, or trade/technical school in any state. Along with their application, they must submit a brief statement summarizing their academic ambitions and extracurricular and/or volunteer activities and a 500-word essay describing how organ or tissue donation has touched their life. Financial need is not considered in the selection process.

Financial data The stipend is $1,000.

Duration 1 year.

Number awarded 1 or more each year.

Deadline February of each year.

[965]
DELAWARE CHAPTER MS SOCIETY SCHOLARSHIP PROGRAM

National Multiple Sclerosis Society-Delaware Chapter
Two Mill Road, Suite 106
Wilmington, DE 19806
(302) 655-5610   Fax: (302) 655-0993
E-mail: kate.cowperthwait@msdelaware.org
Web: was.nationalmssociety.org

Summary To provide financial assistance to high school seniors and graduates from Delaware who have multiple sclerosis (MS) or have a parent with MS and are planning to attend college in any state.

Eligibility This program is open to graduating high school seniors, recent graduates, and GED recipients from Delaware who have MS or a parent who has MS. Applicants must be planning to enroll as a first-time student at a 2- or 4-year college, university, or vocational/technical school in the United States on at least a half-time basis. Along with their application, they must submit an essay on the impact MS has had on their lives. Selection is based on that essay, academic record, leadership and participation in school or community activities, work experience, goals and aspirations, an outside appraisal, special circumstances, and financial need. U.S. citizenship or permanent resident status is required.

Financial data A stipend is awarded (amount not specified).

Duration 1 year.

Number awarded Varies each year; recently, 4 of these scholarships were awarded.

Deadline January of each year.

[966]
DISABLED WORKERS COMMITTEE SCHOLARSHIP

Disabled Workers Committee
Attn: Matthew Shafner, Scholarship Committee Chair
2 Union Plaza, Suite 200
New London, CT 06320
(860) 442-4416

Summary To provide financial assistance to children of people with disabilities in Connecticut who are interested in attending college in any state.

Eligibility This program is open to seniors graduating from high schools in Connecticut whose parent is totally and permanently disabled as the result of an injury. The injury must arise out of the workplace. Applicants must be interested in attending a college or university in any state. Selection is based on academic achievement and financial need.

Financial data The stipend is $5,000.

Duration 1 year.

Number awarded 2 each year.

Deadline April of each year.

[967]
DOTTIE LOURIE MEMORIAL SCHOLARSHIP

National Kidney Foundation Serving New England
Attn: Academic Awards Committee
85 Astor Avenue, Suite 2
Norwood, MA 02062-5040
(781) 278-0222   Toll Free: (800) 542-4001
Fax: (781) 278-0333   E-mail: nkfmarinhvt@kidney.org
Web: www.kidney.org/site/index.cfm?ch=105

Summary To provide financial assistance to residents of New England who have kidney disease, are related to a person with kidney disease, or have received a kidney transplant and are interested in attending college in any state.

Eligibility This program is open to residents of Massachusetts, Rhode Island, New Hampshire, and Vermont who are enrolled or planning to enroll at a college or university in any state. Applicants must be a patient with Chronic Kidney Disease (CKD), have an immediate family member (parent, sibling) with CKD, or have had a life-saving organ transplant. Along with their application, they must submit a 2-page essay on how kidney disease or organ transplantation has impacted their life. Selection is based on academic achievement and financial need.

Financial data The stipend is $1,000. Funds are paid directly to the student.

Duration 1 year.

Number awarded 1 each year.

Deadline March of each year.

[968]
DUGDALE/VAN EYS SCHOLARSHIP AWARD

Tennessee Hemophilia and Bleeding Disorders Foundation
Attn: Scholarship Committee
203 Jefferson Street
Smyrna, TN 37167
(615) 220-4868   Toll Free: (888) 703-3269
Fax: (615) 220-4889   E-mail: mail@thbdf.org
Web: www.thbdf.org/programs.html

Summary To provide financial assistance for college to students with hemophilia or their family members in Tennessee.

Eligibility This program is open to college-bound high school seniors, college students, and technical school students who have a bleeding disorder and are receiving treatment in Tennessee. Their children, spouses, and guardians are also eligible. Applicants must have a GPA of 2.5 or higher and be enrolled or planning to enroll full time. They must submit a 500-word essay on their life goals, a resume, 3 letters of recommendation, proof of enrollment, and documentation of community service of at least 10 hours per semester. Financial need is considered in the selection process.

Financial data Stipends range from $500 to $2,000.

Duration 1 year; recipients may reapply.

Number awarded 6 each year: 1 at $2,000, 1 at $1,500, 1 at $1,000, and 3 at $500.

Deadline April of each year.

[969]
DUNKERLEY FAMILY SCHOLARSHIP

Georgia Transplant Foundation
Attn: Scholarship Program
600 Embassy Row, Suite 250
6600 Peachtree Dunwoody Road N.E.
Atlanta, GA 30328-6773
(770) 457-3796   Toll Free: (866) 428-9411
Fax: (770) 457-7916
Web: www.gatransplant.org/AcademicScholarships.aspx

Summary To provide financial assistance to residents of Georgia who are dependents of transplant recipients and interested in attending college in any state.

Eligibility This program is open to residents of Georgia who are entering or continuing at an accredited institution of higher learning in any state. Applicants must be the dependent of an organ transplant recipient. Along with their application, they must submit a 3-page personal statement in which they describe themselves as individuals, relate an event that changed their life or beliefs, describe an issue about which they have strong feelings, present their life goals as they relate to their field of study, explain any situation or financial concern that could impact their educational goals, answer why they feel they are eligible for this scholarship, and address their plans as those relate to their education, career, and long-term goals.

Financial data The stipend is $1,000 per year.

Duration 1 year; may be renewed up to 3 additional years.

Number awarded 1 or 2 each year.

Deadline May of each year.

[970]
EAGA SCHOLARSHIP AWARD

Eastern Amputee Golf Association
Attn: Bob Buck, Executive Director
2015 Amherst Drive
Bethlehem, PA 18015-5606
Toll Free: (888) 868-0992   Fax: (610) 867-9295
E-mail: info@eaga.org
Web: www.eaga.org

Summary To provide financial assistance for college to members of the Eastern Amputee Golf Association (EAGA) and their families.

Eligibility This program is open to students who are residents of and/or currently enrolled or accepted for enrollment at a college or university in designated eastern states (Connecticut, Delaware, District of Columbia, Maine, Maryland, Massachusetts, New Hampshire, New Jersey, New York, Pennsylvania, Rhode Island, Vermont, Virginia, or West Virginia). Applicants must be amputee members of the association (those who have experienced the loss of 1 or more extremities at a major joint due to amputation or birth defect) or members of their families. Financial need is considered in the selection process.

Financial data The stipend is $1,000.

Duration 1 year; may be renewed if the recipient maintains a GPA of 2.0 or higher and continues to demonstrate financial need.

Additional data The EAGA was incorporated in 1987. It welcomes 2 types of members: amputee members and associate members (non-amputees who are interested in the organization and support its work but are not eligible for these scholarships). This program includes the following named scholarships: the Paul DesChamps Scholarship Award, the Tom Reed Scholarship, the Ray Froncillo Scholarship, the Howard Taylor Scholarship, and the Sgt. Major William Wade Memorial Scholarship.

Number awarded Varies each year; recently, 16 of these scholarships were awarded.

Deadline June of each year.

[971]
EDWARD T. CONROY MEMORIAL SCHOLARSHIP PROGRAM

Maryland Higher Education Commission
Attn: Office of Student Financial Assistance
839 Bestgate Road, Suite 400
Annapolis, MD 21401-3013
(410) 260-4563   Toll Free: (800) 974-1024, ext. 4563
Fax: (410) 260-3200   TDD: (800) 735-2258
E-mail: lasplin@mhec.state.md.us
Web: www.mhec.state.md.us

Summary To provide financial assistance for college or graduate school in Maryland to children and spouses of victims of the September 11, 2001 terrorist attacks and to specified categories of veterans, public safety employees, and their children or spouses.

Eligibility This program is open to entering and continuing undergraduate and graduate students in the following categories: 1) children and surviving spouses of victims of the September 11, 2001 terrorist attacks who died in the World Trade Center in New York City, the Pentagon in Virginia, or United Airlines Flight 93 in Pennsylvania; 2) veterans who have, as a direct result of military service, a disability of 25% or greater and have exhausted or are no longer eligible for federal veterans' educational benefits; 3) children of armed forces members whose death or 100% disability was directly caused by military service; 4) POW/MIA veterans of the Vietnam Conflict and their children; 5) state or local public safety officers or volunteers who became 100% disabled in the line of duty; and 6) children and unremarried surviving spouses of state or local public safety employees or volunteers who died or became 100% disabled in the line of duty. The parent, spouse, veteran, POW, or public safety officer or volunteer must have been a resident of Maryland at the time of death or when declared disabled. Financial need is not considered.

Financial data The amount of the award is equal to tuition and fees at a Maryland postsecondary institution, to a maximum of $19,000 for children and spouses of the September 11 terrorist attacks or $9,000 for all other recipients.

Duration Up to 5 years of full-time study or 8 years of part-time study.

Additional data Recipients must enroll at a 2-year or 4-year Maryland college or university as a full-time or part-time degree-seeking undergraduate or graduate student or attend a private career school.

Number awarded Varies each year.

Deadline July of each year.

[972]
ELKS NATIONAL FOUNDATION EMERGENCY EDUCATIONAL FUND GRANTS

Elks National Foundation
Attn: Scholarship Department
2750 North Lake View Avenue
Chicago, IL 60614-2256
(773) 755-4732   Fax: (773) 755-4729
E-mail: scholarship@elks.org
Web: www.elks.org/enf/scholars/eefgrants.cfm

Summary To provide emergency financial assistance to college students who are children of deceased or disabled members of B.P.O. Elks.

Eligibility This program is open to children of Elks who have died or are totally disabled. Applicants must be unmarried, under 23 years of age, able to demonstrate financial need, and attending a college or university in the United States as a full-time undergraduate student. The student's parent must have been a member in good standing at the time of death or, if disabled, have been a member in good standing before he or she became incapacitated and must continue to be an Elk in good standing when the application for assistance is submitted. Applications must give the B.P.O. Elks Lodge affiliation of the Elk parent.

Financial data The amount of the assistance depends on the need of the applicant but normally ranges up to $4,000 per year.

Duration 1 year; may be renewed up to 3 additional years.

Number awarded Varies each year.

Deadline December of each year for new applications; October of each year for renewal applications.

[973]
ERIC DOSTIE MEMORIAL COLLEGE SCHOLARSHIP

NuFACTOR Specialty Pharmacy
Attn: Scholarship Administrator
41093 Country Center Drive, Suite B
Temecula, CA 92591
(951) 296-2516   Toll Free: (800) 323-6832, ext. 1300
Fax: (877) 432-6258   E-mail: info@kelleycom.com
Web: www.nufactor.com/pages/eric_dostie.html

Summary To provide financial assistance for college to students with hemophilia or members of their families.

Eligibility This program is open to 1) students with hemophilia or a related bleeding disorder or 2) members of their families. Applicants must be U.S. citizens and enrolled or planning to enroll full time at an accredited 2- or 4-year college program. They must have a GPA of 2.5 or higher. Along with their application, they must submit a 400-word essay that explains what motivates them to pursue a higher education, what subjects they plan to study, what major forces or obstacles in their life has led to that path of study, what they plan to do with their education after school, and how that may be of benefit to humankind. Financial need is also considered in the selection process.

Financial data The stipend is $1,000.

Duration 1 year.

Number awarded 10 each year.

Deadline February of each year.

[974]
EXEMPTION FOR DEPENDENTS OF TEXAS VETERANS

Texas Higher Education Coordinating Board
Attn: Grants and Special Programs
1200 East Anderson Lane
P.O. Box 12788, Capitol Station
Austin, TX 78711-2788
(512) 427-6340   Toll Free: (800) 242-3062
Fax: (512) 427-6127
E-mail: grantinfo@thecb.state.tx.us
Web: www.collegeforalltexans.com

Summary To exempt children of disabled or deceased veterans of the U.S. military from payment of tuition at public universities in Texas.

Eligibility This program is open to residents of Texas whose parent was a resident of the state at the time of

entry into the U.S. military and who died or became totally disabled as a result of service-related injury or illness. Applicants may not be in default on a loan made or guaranteed by the state of Texas or in default on a federal education loan if that default affects their eligibility for GI education benefits. They must be attending or planning to attend a public college or university in the state.

Financial data Eligible students are exempt from payment of tuition, dues, fees, and charges at state-supported colleges and universities in Texas.

Duration 1 year; may be renewed.

Additional data This program was established under provisions of the Hazlewood Act, and is also referred to as Hazlewood Exemption for Dependents of Texas Veterans.

Number awarded Varies each year; recently, 9 of these awards were granted.

Deadline Deadline not specified.

[975]
FAMILIES OF FREEDOM SCHOLARSHIP FUND

Scholarship America
Attn: Scholarship Management Services
One Scholarship Way
P.O. Box 297
St. Peter, MN 56082
(507) 931-1682   Toll Free: (877) 862-0136
Fax: (507) 931-9168
E-mail: familiesoffreedom@scholarshipamerica.org
Web: www.familiesoffreedom.org

Summary To provide college scholarships to financially-needy individuals and the families of individuals who were victims of the terrorist attacks on September 11, 2001.

Eligibility This program is open to the individuals who were disabled as a result of the terrorist attacks on September 11, 2001 and to the relatives of those individuals who were killed or permanently disabled during the attacks. Primarily, the fund will benefit dependents (including spouses and children) of the following groups: airplane crew and passengers; World Trade Center workers and visitors; Pentagon workers and visitors; and rescue workers, including fire fighters, emergency medical personnel, and law enforcement personnel. Applicants must be enrolled or planning to enroll in an accredited 2- or 4-year college, university, or vocational/technical school in the United States. They must be able to demonstrate financial need.

Financial data Stipends range from $1,000 to $28,000 per year, depending upon the need of the recipient. Recently, awards averaged $13,100 per academic year. Funds are distributed annually, in 2 equal installments. Checks are made payable jointly to the student and the student's school.

Duration 1 year; may be renewed.

Additional data This program was established on September 17, 2001. The fundraising goal of $100 million was reached on September 4, 2002. The fund will operate until December 31, 2030.

Number awarded This is an entitlement program; all eligible students will receive funding. Recently 1,183 students had received more than $36 million in scholarship funds.

Deadline   Applications may be submitted at any time.

[976]
FIRST CAVALRY DIVISION ASSOCIATION SCHOLARSHIPS

First Cavalry Division Association
Attn: Foundation
302 North Main Street
Copperas Cove, TX 76522-1703
(254) 547-6537   Fax: (254) 547-8853
E-mail: firstcav@1cda.org
Web: www.1cda.org

Summary   To provide financial assistance for undergraduate education to soldiers currently or formerly assigned to the First Cavalry Division and their families.

Eligibility   This program is open to children of soldiers who died or have been declared totally and permanently disabled from injuries incurred while serving with the First Cavalry Division during any armed conflict; children of soldiers who died while serving in the First Cavalry Division during peacetime; and active-duty soldiers currently assigned or attached to the First Cavalry Division and their spouses and children.

Financial data   The stipend is $1,200 per year. The checks are made out jointly to the student and the school and may be used for whatever the student needs, including tuition, books, and clothing.

Duration   1 year; may be renewed up to 3 additional years.

Additional data   Requests for applications must be accompanied by a self-addressed stamped envelope.

Number awarded   Varies each year. Since the program was established, it has awarded more than $640,500 to 444 children of disabled and deceased Cavalry members and more than $184,500 to 224 current members of the Division and their families.

Deadline   June of each year.

[977]
FIRST MARINE DIVISION ASSOCIATION SCHOLARSHIPS

First Marine Division Association
410 Pier View Way
Oceanside, CA 92054
(760) 967-8561   Toll Free: (877) 967-8561
Fax: (760) 967-8567   E-mail: oldbreed@sbcglobal.net
Web: www.1stmarinedivisionassociation.org

Summary   To provide financial assistance for college to dependents of deceased or disabled veterans of the First Marine Division.

Eligibility   This program is open to dependents of veterans who served in the First Marine Division or in a unit attached to that Division, are honorably discharged, and now are either totally and permanently disabled or deceased from any cause. Applicants must be attending or planning to attend an accredited college, university, or trade school as a full-time undergraduate student. Gradu-

ate students and students still in high school or prep school are not eligible.

Financial data   The stipend is $1,750 per year.

Duration   1 year; may be renewed up to 3 additional years.

Additional data   Award winners who marry before completing the course or who drop out for non-scholastic reasons must submit a new application before benefits can be resumed.

Number awarded   Varies each year; since the program began, more than 520 students have received more than $1.5 million in tuition assistance.

Deadline   Deadline not specified.

[978]
FLORIDA SCHOLARSHIPS FOR CHILDREN AND SPOUSES OF DECEASED OR DISABLED VETERANS

Florida Department of Education
Attn: Office of Student Financial Assistance
325 West Gaines Street
Tallahassee, FL 32399-0400
(850) 410-5160   Toll Free: (888) 827-2004
Fax: (850) 487-1809   E-mail: osfa@fldoe.org
Web: www.floridastudentfinancialaid.org

Summary   To provide financial assistance for college to the children and spouses of Florida veterans who are disabled, deceased, or officially classified as prisoners of war (POW) or missing in action (MIA).

Eligibility   This program is open to residents of Florida who are the dependent children or spouses of veterans or service members who 1) died as a result of service-connected injuries, diseases, or disabilities sustained while on active duty during a period of war; 2) have a service-connected 100% total and permanent disability; or 3) were classified as POW or MIA by the U.S. armed forces or as civilian personnel captured while serving with the consent or authorization of the U.S. government during wartime service. The veteran or service member must have been a resident of Florida for at least 1 year before death, disability, or POW/MIA status. Children must be between 16 and 22 years of age. Spouses of deceased veterans or service members must be unremarried and must apply within 5 years of their spouse's death. Spouses of disabled veterans must have been married for at least 1 year. The official military and residency status of the veteran parent or spouse must be verified by the Florida Department of Veterans' Affairs.

Financial data   Stipends are $126 per semester hour for students at 4-year institutions, $78 per semester hour for students at 2-year institutions, $87 per semester hour for students enrolled in community college baccalaureate programs, or $64 per semester hour for students at career and technical centers.

Duration   1 quarter or semester; may be renewed for up to 110% of the required credit hours of an initial baccalaureate or certificate program, provided the student maintains a GPA of 2.0 or higher.

Number awarded Varies each year; recently, 295 new and 331 renewal scholarships were awarded.

Deadline March of each year.

[979]
FOLDS OF HONOR SCHOLARSHIPS

Folds of Honor Foundation
7030 South Yale, Suite 600
Tulsa, OK 74136
(918) 591-2406　　　　　　Fax: (918) 494-9826
E-mail: lhromas@foldsofhonor.org
Web: www.foldsofhonor.com/scholarships.php

Summary To provide financial assistance for college to the spouses and children of service members killed or disabled as a result of service in the Global War on Terror.

Eligibility This program is open to the spouses and children of 1) an active-duty or Reserve component soldier, sailor, airman, Marine, or Coast Guardsman killed or disabled in the Global War on Terror; 2) an active-duty or Reserve component soldier, sailor, airman, Marine, or Coast Guardsman who is currently classified as a POW or MIA; 3) a veteran who died from any cause while such service-connected disability was in existence; 4) a service member missing in action or captured in the line of duty by a hostile force; 5) a service member forcible detained or interned in the line of duty by a foreign government or power; or 6) a service member who received a Purple Heart medal. Immediate-use scholarships are available to spouses or dependents currently attending or accepted into a 2- or 4-year college or university or a vocational, technical, or other certification program. Future-use scholarships are available to young children of service members and held for them until they are ready to attend college.

Financial data Stipends range from $2,000 to $2,500. Funds are dispersed directly to the recipient's institution.

Duration 1 year.

Additional data These scholarships were first awarded in 2008.

Number awarded Varies each year; recently, approximately 360 of these scholarships were awarded.

Deadline May of each year.

[980]
FRANCIS P. MATTHEWS AND JOHN E. SWIFT EDUCATIONAL TRUST SCHOLARSHIPS

Knights of Columbus
Attn: Department of Scholarships
P.O. Box 1670
New Haven, CT 06507-0901
(203) 752-4332　　　　　　Fax: (203) 772-2696
E-mail: info@kofc.org
Web: www.kofc.org

Summary To provide financial assistance at Catholic colleges or universities to children of disabled or deceased veterans, law enforcement officers, or firemen who are/were also Knights of Columbus members.

Eligibility This program is open to children of members of the sponsoring organization who are high school seniors planning to attend a 4-year Catholic college or university. The parent must be 1) totally and permanently disabled or deceased as a result of military service during the Korean Conflict, the Vietnam War, Cyprus, the Persian Gulf War, Iraq, Afghanistan, or Pakistan; 2) a full-time law enforcement officer who became disabled or died as a result of criminal violence; or 3) a fire fighter who became disabled or deceased in the line of duty. For the children of veterans, the death or disability must have occurred during a period of conflict or within 10 years of its official termination.

Financial data The amounts of the awards vary but are designed to cover tuition, to a maximum of $25,000 per year, at the Catholic college or university of the recipient's choice. Funds are not available for room, board, books, fees, transportation, dues, computers, or supplies.

Duration 1 year; may be renewed up to 3 additional years.

Number awarded Varies each year.

Deadline February of each year.

[981]
FREE TUITION FOR DEPENDENTS OF DISABLED OR DECEASED SOUTH DAKOTA NATIONAL GUARD MEMBERS

South Dakota Board of Regents
Attn: Scholarship Committee
306 East Capitol Avenue, Suite 200
Pierre, SD 57501-2545
(605) 773-3455　　　　　　Fax: (605) 773-2422
E-mail: info@sdbor.edu
Web: www.sdbor.edu/student/prospective/Military.htm

Summary To provide financial assistance for college to the dependents of disabled and deceased members of the South Dakota National Guard.

Eligibility This program is open to the spouses and children of members of the South Dakota Army or Air National Guard who died or sustained a total and permanent disability while on state active duty, federal active duty, or any authorized duty training. Applicants must be younger than 25 years of age and proposing to work on an undergraduate degree at a public institution of higher education in South Dakota.

Financial data Qualifying applicants are eligible to attend a state-supported postsecondary institution in South Dakota without payment of tuition.

Duration 8 semesters or 12 quarters of either full- or part-time study.

Number awarded Varies each year.

Deadline Deadline not specified.

[982]
FREEDOM ALLIANCE SCHOLARSHIPS

Freedom Alliance
Attn: Scholarship Fund
22570 Markey Court, Suite 240
Dulles, VA 20166-6915
(703) 444-7940　　　　　　Toll Free: (800) 475-6620
Fax: (703) 444-0803
Web: www.freedomalliance.org

Summary To provide financial assistance for college to the children of deceased and disabled military personnel.

Eligibility This program is open to high school seniors, high school graduates, and undergraduate students under 26 years of age who are dependent children of military personnel (soldier, sailor, airman, Marine, or Guardsman). The military parent must 1) have been killed or permanently disabled as a result of an operational mission or training accident, or 2) be currently classified as a POW or MIA. For disabled parents, the disability must be permanent, service connected, and rated at 100% by the U.S. Department of Veterans Affairs. Applicants must submit a 500-word essay on what their parent's service means to them.

Financial data A stipend is awarded (amount not specified).

Duration 1 year; may be renewed up to 3 additional years, provided the recipient remains enrolled full time with a GPA of 2.0 or higher.

Number awarded Varies each year; recently, 167 of these scholarships were awarded.

Deadline August of each year.

[983]
FRIENDS OF 440 SCHOLARSHIPS

Friends of 440 Scholarship Fund, Inc.
9350 South Dixie Highway, Tenth Floor
Miami, FL 33156-2900
(305) 671-1300
Web: www.440scholarship.org

Summary To provide financial assistance to Florida residents whose parent was killed or permanently disabled in an employment-related accident and who are interested in attending college in any state.

Eligibility This program is open to students who are dependents or descendants of workers injured or killed in the course and scope of their employment and who are eligible to receive benefits under the Florida Workers' Compensation system. Dependents and descendants of people who are primarily engaged in the administration of the Florida Workers' Compensation law are also eligible. Applicants must be attending or planning to attend a college or university in any state. High school seniors must have a GPA of 2.7 or higher; students currently enrolled in college must have a GPA of 3.0 or higher. Selection is based on merit, financial need, and connection to the worker's compensation field.

Financial data Stipends range up to $6,000 per year. Funds may be used to cover the cost of tuition, room, board, and books.

Duration 1 year; may be renewed, provided the recipient maintains a GPA of 3.0 or higher.

Additional data This program, established in 1991, takes its name from the Florida Workers' Compensation Law, which is chapter 440 of Florida Statutes.

Number awarded Varies each year; recently, 43 of these scholarships, worth more than $73,000, were awarded.

Deadline February of each year.

[984]
GALA SCHOLARSHIP

Disabled American Veterans-Department of New Jersey
135 West Hanover Street, Fourth Floor
Trenton, NJ 08618
(609) 396-2885   Fax: (609) 396-9562
Web: www.davnj.org

Summary To provide financial assistance to the children and grandchildren of members of the Disabled American Veterans in New Jersey who are interested in attending college in any state.

Eligibility This program is open to graduating high school seniors who are the child or grandchild of a member of the Disabled American Veterans in New Jersey. Applicants must be planning to attend a college or university in any state. Along with their application, they must submit 1) letters of recommendation; 2) a transcript that includes information on their GPA, SAT scores, and class rank; and 3) a 500-word article on a topic that changes regularly (recently, students were asked to present their opinion on the war in Iraq). Selection is based on character (20%), Americanism and community service (20%), leadership (20%), scholarship (20%), and need (20%).

Financial data The stipend is $1,000.

Duration 1 year; nonrenewable.

Number awarded 1 each year.

Deadline March of each year.

[985]
GENERAL HENRY H. ARNOLD EDUCATION GRANT PROGRAM

Air Force Aid Society
Attn: Education Assistance Department
241 18th Street South, Suite 202
Arlington, VA 22202-3409
(703) 607-3072, ext. 51   Toll Free: (800) 429-9475
Fax: (703) 607-3022
Web: www.afas.org/Education/ArnoldEdGrant.cfm

Summary To provide financial assistance for college to dependents of active-duty, retired, disabled, or deceased Air Force personnel.

Eligibility This program is open to 1) dependent children of Air Force personnel who are active duty, Reservists on extended active duty, retired due to length of active-duty service or disability, or deceased while on active duty or in retired status; 2) spouses of active-duty Air Force members and Reservists on extended active duty; and 3) surviving spouses of Air Force members who died while on active duty or in retired status. Applicants must be enrolled or planning to enroll as full-time undergraduate students in an accredited college, university, or vocational/trade school. Spouses must be attending school within the 48 contiguous states. Selection is based on family income and education costs.

Financial data The stipend is $2,000.

Duration 1 year; may be renewed if the recipient maintains a GPA of 2.0 or higher.

Additional data Since this program was established in the 1988-89 academic year, it has awarded more than 88,000 grants.
Number awarded Varies each year.
Deadline March of each year.

[986]
GEORGE AND LINDA PRICE SCHOLARSHIP

Hemophilia Association of the Capital Area
10560 Main Street, Suite PH-4
Fairfax, VA 22030-7182
(703) 352-7641   Fax: (703) 352-2145
E-mail: info@hacacares.org
Web: www.hacacares.org

Summary To provide financial assistance to individuals with bleeding disorders and their families who are members of the Hemophilia Association of the Capital Area (HACA) and interested in attending college or graduate school in any state.
Eligibility This program is open to residents of northern Virginia, Montgomery and Prince George's County in Maryland, and Washington, D.C. who have a bleeding disorder and their siblings and parents. Applicants must be members of HACA. They must be 1) high school seniors or graduates who have not yet attended college; 2) full-time freshmen, sophomores, or juniors at a college, university, or vocational/technical school in any state; or 3) college seniors planning to attend graduate school and students already enrolled at a graduate school in any state. Along with their application, they must submit a 500-word essay on what they have done to contribute to the bleeding disorders community and how they plan to contribute to that community in the future. Financial need is not considered in the selection process.
Financial data The stipend is $2,500.
Duration 1 year; recipients may reapply.
Number awarded 2 each year.
Deadline April of each year.

[987]
GEORGE BARTOL MEMORIAL SCHOLARSHIPS

George Bartol Memorial Scholarship Fund
c/o Kari Bartol Romano
4616 Edgewater Drive
Orlando, FL 32804
(407) 718-7601   E-mail: livebait3@aol.com
Web: www.mindsmatterusa.org/Scholarship.html

Summary To provide financial assistance for college to children of brain tumor patients.
Eligibility This program is open to students enrolled full time at an accredited 2- or 4-year college or university who have a GPA of 2.5 or higher. Applicants must have a parent battling a primary brain tumor or a parent who has passed away as a result of a primary brain tumor. They must be between 18 and 23 years of age. Along with their application, they must submit 5 essays on the following topics: 1) their parent who has lost their battle to a primary brain tumor or who is currently battling a primary brain tumor; 2)

their academic and professional goals; 3) the advice they would give to another child whose parent was just diagnosed with brain cancer; 4) their current financial status and how their parent's medical condition has increased their financial need for this scholarship; and 5) how their parent's medical condition has changed their outlook on life. Selection is based on the essays, grades, letters of recommendation, and financial need. Children of Vietnam veterans who have not been awarded VA Chapter 35 benefits are strongly encouraged to apply.
Financial data The stipend is $1,000 per semester ($3,000 per year, including summer semester). Students at schools on the quarter system may receive $750 per quarter ($3,000 per year, including summer quarter). Funds are paid directly to the financial aid office at the school the recipient is attending.
Duration 1 semester or quarter; may be renewed if the recipient maintains a GPA of 2.5 or higher.
Additional data This program was established in 2004.
Number awarded Varies each year; recently, 3 of these scholarships were awarded.
Deadline September of each year.

[988]
GEORGIA CHAPTER OF THE INTERNATIONAL TRANSPLANT NURSES SOCIETY SCHOLARSHIP

Georgia Transplant Foundation
Attn: Scholarship Program
600 Embassy Row, Suite 250
6600 Peachtree Dunwoody Road N.E.
Atlanta, GA 30328-6773
(770) 457-3796   Toll Free: (866) 428-9411
Fax: (770) 457-7916
Web: www.gatransplant.org/AcademicScholarships.aspx

Summary To provide financial assistance to residents of Georgia who are transplant recipients or their siblings or dependents and interested in attending college in any state to work on a degree in health care.
Eligibility This program is open to residents of Georgia who are entering or continuing at an accredited institution of higher learning in any state to work on a degree in health care. Applicants must be an organ transplant recipient, a dependent of a recipient, or the sibling of a recipient (both the sibling and the recipient must be under 22 years of age). Along with their application, they must submit a 3-page personal statement in which they describe themselves as individuals, relate an event that changed their life or beliefs, describe an issue about which they have strong feelings, present their life goals as they relate to their field of study, explain any situation or financial concern that could impact their educational goals, answer why they feel they are eligible for this scholarship, and address their plans as those relate to their education, career, and long-term goals.
Financial data The stipend is $1,000.
Duration 1 year; nonrenewable.

Additional data This program is sponsored by the Georgia Chapter of the International Transplant Nurses Society.

Number awarded 1 each year.

Deadline May of each year.

[989]
GEORGIA COUNCIL OF THE BLIND SCHOLARSHIPS

Georgia Council of the Blind
850 Gaines School Road
Athens, GA 30605
Toll Free: (877) 667-6815
E-mail: marshafarrow@alltel.net
Web: www.georgiacounciloftheblind.org

Summary To provide financial assistance students in Georgia who plan to attend college or graduate school in any state and are either legally blind or have legally blind parents.

Eligibility This program is open to residents of Georgia who are either 1) legally blind students, or 2) sighted students financially dependent on legally blind parents. Applicants must be enrolled or accepted for enrollment at a vocational/technical school, a 2-year or 4-year college, or a master's or doctoral program in any state. All fields of study are eligible. Selection is based on academic transcripts, 2 letters of recommendation, a 1-page typed statement of the applicant's educational goals, an audio cassette recording of the applicant reading the goals statement, extracurricular activities, and financial need.

Financial data Stipends up to $1,000 per year are available.

Duration 1 year; recipients may reapply.

Additional data This program began in 1988.

Number awarded 1 or more each year.

Deadline June of each year.

[990]
GEORGIA LAW ENFORCEMENT PERSONNEL DEPENDENTS GRANT

Georgia Student Finance Commission
Attn: Scholarships and Grants Division
2082 East Exchange Place, Suite 200
Tucker, GA 30084-5305
(770) 724-9000   Toll Free: (800) 505-GSFC
Fax: (770) 724-9089   E-mail: gsfcinfo@gsfc.org
Web: www.gacollege411.org

Summary To provide financial assistance for college to children of disabled or deceased Georgia law enforcement personnel.

Eligibility Eligible to apply are dependent children of law enforcement officers, fire fighters, and prison guards in Georgia who have been permanently disabled or killed in the line of duty. Applicants must be enrolled as full-time undergraduate students in a Georgia private or public college, university, or technical institution. U.S. citizenship or permanent resident status and compliance with the Georgia Drug-Free Postsecondary Education Act are required. Financial need is not considered in the selection process.

Financial data The grant is $2,000 per academic year, not to exceed $8,000 during an entire program of study.

Duration 1 year; may be renewed (if satisfactory progress is maintained) for up to 3 additional years.

Additional data This program was established in 1972.

Number awarded Varies each year; recently, 20 of these grants were awarded.

Deadline Applications must be submitted on or before the last day of the academic term.

[991]
GEORGIA PUBLIC SAFETY MEMORIAL GRANT

Georgia Student Finance Commission
Attn: Scholarships and Grants Division
2082 East Exchange Place, Suite 200
Tucker, GA 30084-5305
(770) 724-9000   Toll Free: (800) 505-GSFC
Fax: (770) 724-9089   E-mail: gsfcinfo@gsfc.org
Web: www.gacollege411.org

Summary To provide financial assistance for college to the children of Georgia public safety officers who have been permanently disabled or killed in the line of duty.

Eligibility This program is open to dependent children of Georgia law enforcement officers, fire fighters, EMT, correction officers, or prison guards who have been permanently disabled or killed in the line of duty. Applicants must be enrolled or accepted as full-time undergraduate students in a Georgia public college, university, or technical institution and be in compliance with the Georgia Drug-Free Postsecondary Education Act. U.S. citizenship or permanent resident status is required. Financial need is not considered in the selection process.

Financial data The award covers the cost of attendance at a public postsecondary school in Georgia, minus any other aid received.

Duration 1 year; may be renewed (if satisfactory progress is maintained) for up to 3 additional years.

Additional data This program, which began in 1994, is funded by the Georgia Lottery for Education.

Number awarded Varies each year; recently, 18 of these grants were awarded.

Deadline July of each year.

[992]
GEORGIA TRANSPLANT FOUNDATION SIBLING SCHOLARSHIP

Georgia Transplant Foundation
Attn: Scholarship Program
600 Embassy Row, Suite 250
6600 Peachtree Dunwoody Road N.E.
Atlanta, GA 30328-6773
(770) 457-3796   Toll Free: (866) 428-9411
Fax: (770) 457-7916
Web: www.gatransplant.org/AcademicScholarships.aspx

Summary To provide financial assistance to residents of Georgia who are siblings of transplant recipients and interested in attending college in any state.

Eligibility This program is open to residents of Georgia who are entering or continuing at an accredited institution of higher learning in any state. Applicants must be the sibling of an organ transplant recipient (both the sibling and the recipient must be under 22 years of age). Along with their application, they must submit a 3-page personal statement in which they describe themselves as individuals, relate an event that changed their life or beliefs, describe an issue about which they have strong feelings, present their life goals as they relate to their field of study, explain any situation or financial concern that could impact their educational goals, answer why they feel they are eligible for this scholarship, and address their plans as those relate to their education, career, and long-term goals.

Financial data The stipend is $1,000 per year.

Duration 1 year; may be renewed up to 3 additional years.

Number awarded 1 or 2 each year.

Deadline May of each year.

[993]
GEORGIA'S HERO SCHOLARSHIP PROGRAM

Georgia Student Finance Commission
Attn: Scholarships and Grants Division
2082 East Exchange Place, Suite 200
Tucker, GA 30084-5305
(770) 724-9000   Toll Free: (800) 505-GSFC
Fax: (770) 724-9089   E-mail: gsfcinfo@gsfc.org
Web: www.gacollege411.org

Summary To provide financial assistance for college to members of the National Guard or Reserves in Georgia and the children and spouses of deceased or disabled Guard or Reserve members.

Eligibility This program is open to Georgia residents who are active members of the Georgia National Guard or U.S. Military Reserves, were deployed outside the United States for active-duty service on or after February 1, 2003 to a location designated as a combat zone, and served in that combat zone for at least 181 consecutive days. Also eligible are 1) the children, younger than 25 years of age, of Guard and Reserve members who completed at least 1 term of service (of 181 days each) overseas on or after February 1, 2003; 2) the children, younger than 25 years of age, of Guard and Reserve members who were killed or totally disabled during service overseas on or after February 1, 2003, regardless of their length of service; and 3) the spouses of Guard and Reserve members who were killed in a combat zone, died as a result of injuries, or became 100% disabled as a result of injuries received in a combat zone during service overseas on or after February 1, 2003, regardless of their length of service. Applicants must be interested in attending a unit of the University System of Georgia, a unit of the Georgia Department of Technical and Adult Education, or an eligible private college or university in Georgia.

Financial data The stipend is $2,000 per academic year, not to exceed $8,000 during an entire program of study.

Duration 1 year; may be renewed (if satisfactory progress is maintained) for up to 3 additional years.

Additional data This program, which stands for Helping Educate Reservists and their Offspring, was established in 2005.

Number awarded Varies each year.

Deadline June of each year.

[994]
GOLD STAR SCHOLARSHIP PROGRAM FOR SURVIVING CHILDREN OF NAVAL PERSONNEL DECEASED AFTER RETIREMENT

Navy-Marine Corps Relief Society
Attn: Education Division
875 North Randolph Street, Suite 225
Arlington, VA 22203-1757
(703) 696-4960   Fax: (703) 696-0144
E-mail: education@nmcrs.org
Web: www.nmcrs.org/goldstar.html

Summary To provide financial assistance for college to the children of Navy or Marine Corps personnel who died as a result of disabilities or length of service.

Eligibility This program is open to the unmarried, dependent children, stepchildren, or legally adopted children under the age of 23 of members of the Navy or Marine Corps who died after retirement due to disability or length of service. Applicants must be enrolled or planning to enroll full time at a college, university, or vocational/technical school. They must have a GPA of 2.0 or higher and be able to demonstrate financial need.

Financial data Stipends range from $500 to $2,500 per year. Funds are disbursed directly to the financial institution.

Duration 1 year; may be renewed up to 3 additional years.

Number awarded Varies each year.

Deadline February of each year.

[995]
GREAT LAKES HEMOPHILIA FOUNDATION EDUCATION SCHOLARSHIPS

Great Lakes Hemophilia Foundation
Attn: Program Services Committee
638 North 18th Street, Suite 108
Milwaukee, WI 53233
(414) 257-0200   Toll Free: (888) 797-GLHF
Fax: (414) 257-1225   E-mail: info@glhf.org
Web: www.glhf.org/scholar.htm

Summary To provide financial assistance to Wisconsin residents who have a bleeding disorder (and their families) and are interested in attending college in any state.

Eligibility This program is open to members of the bleeding disorder community in Wisconsin. Applicants must be attending or planning to attend college, vocational school, technical school, or a certification program in any state. Along with their application, they must submit an essay of 500 to 750 words on their educational and career goals, what they have done to work toward achieving those goals, how the education or training program in which they are enrolled will help them meet their goals, what they consider the most significant challenges associated with living with a bleeding disorder, the opportunities or benefits those challenges provided them, and how they plan on contributing back to the bleeding disorders community. First priority is given to people affected by bleeding disorders, then to parents of young children with bleeding disorders, and then to spouses of individuals with bleeding disorders. If sufficient funds are available, consideration may be given to siblings and other family members of individuals with a bleeding disorder. Financial need is considered in the selection process.

Financial data   Stipends range from $500 to $2,000.

Duration   1 year.

Number awarded   Several each year.

Deadline   April of each year.

[996]
GREATER NEW ENGLAND CHAPTER MS SOCIETY SCHOLARSHIP PROGRAM

National Multiple Sclerosis Society-Greater New
England Chapter
101A First Avenue, Suite 6
Waltham, MA 02451
(781) 890-4990   Fax: (781) 890-2089
E-mail: communications@mam.nmss.org
Web: was.nationalmssociety.org

Summary   To provide financial assistance to high school seniors and graduates from designated New England states who have multiple sclerosis (MS) or have a parent with MS and are planning to attend college in any state.

Eligibility   This program is open to graduating high school seniors, recent graduates, and GED recipients from Maine, Massachusetts, New Hampshire, or Vermont who have MS or a parent who has MS. Applicants must be planning to enroll as a first-time student at a 2- or 4-year college, university, or vocational/technical school in the United States on at least a half-time basis. Along with their application, they must submit an essay on the impact MS has had on their lives. Selection is based on that essay, academic record, leadership and participation in school or community activities, work experience, goals and aspirations, an outside appraisal, special circumstances, and financial need. U.S. citizenship or permanent resident status is required.

Financial data   The highest-ranked applicant receives a stipend of $3,000 per year. Other stipends range from $1,000 to $3,000.

Duration   The award for the highest-ranked applicant is for 2 years. Other awards are for 1 year and are nonrenewable.

Additional data   This program was established by the Massachusetts Chapter in 2003. In 2010, that chapter merged with the chapters in Maine, New Hampshire, and Vermont to form the Greater New England Chapter, so the program became available to residents of those states.

Number awarded   Varies each year; recently, 23 of these scholarships, with a total value of $47,600, were awarded.

Deadline   January of each year.

[997]
GREATER NORTHWEST CHAPTER MS SOCIETY SCHOLARSHIP PROGRAM

National Multiple Sclerosis Society-Greater Northwest
Chapter
192 Nickerson Street, Suite 100
Seattle, WA 98109
(206) 284-4254   Toll Free: (800) 344-4867
Fax: (206) 284-4972
E-mail: MSnorthwest@nmsswas.org
Web: was.nationalmssociety.org

Summary   To provide financial assistance to high school seniors and graduates from Alaska and Washington who have multiple sclerosis (MS) or have a parent with MS and are planning to attend college in any state.

Eligibility   This program is open to graduating high school seniors, recent graduates, and GED recipients from Alaska or Washington who have MS or a parent who has MS. Applicants must be planning to enroll as a first-time student at a 2- or 4-year college, university, or vocational/technical school in the United States on at least a half-time basis. Along with their application, they must submit an essay on the impact MS has had on their lives. Selection is based on that essay, academic record, leadership and participation in school or community activities, work experience, goals and aspirations, an outside appraisal, special circumstances, and financial need. U.S. citizenship or permanent resident status is required.

Financial data   Stipends range from $1,500 to $3,000.

Duration   1 year.

Number awarded   Varies each year; recently, 88 students received $252,000 in scholarships from this program.

Deadline   January of each year.

[998]
GWOT ASSISTANCE FUND

Navy-Marine Corps Relief Society
Attn: Education Division
875 North Randolph Street, Suite 225
Arlington, VA 22203-1757
(703) 696-4960   Fax: (703) 696-0144
E-mail: education@nmcrs.org
Web: www.nmcrs.org/goldstar.html

Summary   To provide financial assistance for college to the spouses of deceased Navy and Marine Corps military personnel who became disabled or died during the Global War on Terrorism (GWOT).

Eligibility   This program is open to the spouses of disabled or deceased sailors and Marines who were injured or died while on active duty under hostile fire in a theater of combat operations during the GWOT. Applicants must be enrolled or planning to enroll full or part time at a college, university, or vocational/technical school. They must have a GPA of 2.0 or higher and be able to demonstrate financial need.

Financial data Stipends range from $500 to $2,500 per year. Funds are disbursed directly to the financial institution.

Duration 1 year; may be renewed up to 3 additional years.

Number awarded Varies each year.

Deadline February of each year.

[999]
HAYLEY'S HOPE AND MICHAELA'S MIRACLE MS MEMORIAL FUND

National Multiple Sclerosis Society-Connecticut
  Chapter
659 Tower Avenue, First Floor
Hartford, CT 06112
(860) 913-2550   Toll Free: (800) 344-4867
Fax: (860) 714-2301
E-mail: programs@ctfightsMS.org
Web: was.nationalmssociety.org

Summary To provide financial assistance to high school seniors and graduates from Connecticut who have multiple sclerosis (MS) or have a parent with MS and are planning to attend college in any state.

Eligibility This program is open to graduating high school seniors, recent graduates, and GED recipients from Washington who have MS or a parent who has MS. Applicants must be planning to enroll as an undergraduate student at a 2- or 4-year college, university, or vocational/technical school in the United States on at least a half-time basis. Along with their application, they must submit an essay on the impact MS has had on their lives. Selection is based on that essay, academic record, leadership and participation in school or community activities, work experience, goals and aspirations, an outside appraisal, special circumstances, and financial need. U.S. citizenship or permanent resident status is required.

Financial data The stipend is $1,500.

Duration 1 year.

Number awarded Varies each year; recently, 4 of these scholarships were awarded.

Deadline January of each year.

[1000]
HEMOPHILIA FEDERATION OF AMERICA PARENT CONTINUING EDUCATION SCHOLARSHIPS

Hemophilia Federation of America
Attn: Scholarship Committee
210 Seventh Street, S.E., Suite 200B
Washington, DC 20003
(202) 675-6984   Toll Free: (800) 230-9797
Fax: (202) 675-6983   E-mail: info@hemophiliafed.org
Web: hemophiliafed.org

Summary To provide financial assistance for college to parents of children with a blood clotting disorder.

Eligibility This program is open to parents of children who have a blood clotting disorder. Applicants must be

attending or planning to attend an accredited 2-year or 4-year college, university, or trade school in the United States. Along with their application, they must submit a 1-page essay on their goals and aspirations and how the blood clotting community has played a part in their lives. Financial need is considered in the selection process.

Financial data The stipend is $1,500 per year.

Duration 1 year; may be renewed.

Number awarded 1 each year.

Deadline April of each year.

[1001]
HEMOPHILIA FEDERATION OF AMERICA SIBLING CONTINUING EDUCATION SCHOLARSHIPS

Hemophilia Federation of America
Attn: Scholarship Committee
210 Seventh Street, S.E., Suite 200B
Washington, DC 20003
(202) 675-6984   Toll Free: (800) 230-9797
Fax: (202) 675-6983   E-mail: info@hemophiliafed.org
Web: hemophiliafed.org

Summary To provide financial assistance for college to siblings of people with a blood clotting disorder.

Eligibility This program is open to siblings of people who have a blood clotting disorder. Applicants must be attending or planning to attend an accredited 2-year or 4-year college, university, or trade school in the United States. Along with their application, they must submit a 1-page essay on their goals and aspirations and how the blood clotting community has played a part in their lives. Financial need is also considered in the selection process.

Financial data The stipend is $1,500 per year.

Duration 1 year; may be renewed.

Number awarded 1 each year.

Deadline April of each year.

[1002]
HEMOPHILIA FOUNDATION OF MICHIGAN ACADEMIC SCHOLARSHIPS

Hemophilia Foundation of Michigan
Attn: Client Services Coordinator
1921 West Michigan Avenue
Ypsilanti, MI 48197
(734) 544-0015   Toll Free: (800) 482-3041
Fax: (734) 544-0095   E-mail: hfm@hfmich.org
Web: www.hfmich.org/programs/scholarships.html

Summary To provide financial assistance to Michigan residents with hemophilia and their families who are interested in attending college in any state.

Eligibility This program is open to high school seniors, high school graduates, and currently-enrolled college students who are Michigan residents and have hemophilia or another bleeding disorder. Family members of people with bleeding disorders and family members of people who have died from the complications of a bleeding disorder are also eligible. Applicants must submit a 300-word statement on their educational and career goals, the role that the bleeding disorder has played in influencing those goals, and how receiving the scholarship will help them to meet those goals. Selection is based on that statement, academic merit, employment status, reference letters, financial need, and the impact of bleeding disorder on educational activities.

Financial data Stipends range from $1,000 to $2,000.

Duration 1 year; recipients may reapply.

Number awarded 2 each year.

Deadline April of each year.

[1003]
HEMOPHILIA OF IOWA SCHOLARSHIPS

Hemophilia of Iowa, Inc.
c/o Shane Kelley, Scholarship Committee Chair
22930 20th Street
Fairbank, IA 50629
Toll Free: (319) 635-2839
E-mail: ssckelley@yahoo.com
Web: www.hemophiliaofiowa.com

Summary To provide financial assistance to members of Hemophilia of Iowa who are interested in attending college in any state.

Eligibility This program is open to members of the sponsoring organization who either have hemophilia (or a related bleeding disorder) or are the immediate family member (caregiver, sibling, child) of someone who has hemophilia or a related bleeding disorder. Applicants may be graduating high school seniors or students currently enrolled at an accredited college, university, or trade school in any state. Along with their application, they must submit brief statements on 1) their short- and long-range career plans; 2) their personal background related to the bleeding disorder community and any specific contributions they have made to the Hemophilia of Iowa community; and 3) their key reasons for selecting the profession they are pursuing. Selection is based on personal qualities and community service. Applicants who have a record of outstanding support for the mission of Hemophilia of Iowa are considered for supplemental funding provided by the John Heisner Scholarship and the Dude Cremer Scholarship.

Financial data The stipend is $1,500 for students with a bleeding disorder or $1,000 for family members. Applicants selected for the supplemental funding provided by the named scholarships receive an additional $1,000.

Duration 1 semester; recipients may reapply.

Number awarded Varies each year. Recently, 20 of these scholarships were awarded.

Deadline March of each year.

[1004]
IDAHO PUBLIC SAFETY OFFICER DEPENDENT SCHOLARSHIP

Idaho State Board of Education
Len B. Jordan Office Building
650 West State Street, Room 307
P.O. Box 83720
Boise, ID 83720-0037
(208) 332-1574   Fax: (208) 334-2632
E-mail: scholarshiphelp@osbe.idaho.gov
Web: www.boardofed.idaho.gov

Summary To provide financial assistance for college to dependents of disabled or deceased Idaho public safety officers.

Eligibility Eligible for these scholarships are dependents of full-time Idaho public safety officers employed in the state who were killed or disabled in the line of duty.

Financial data Each scholarship provides a full waiver of tuition and fees at public institutions of higher education or public vocational schools within Idaho, an allowance of $500 per semester for books, on-campus housing, and a campus meal plan.

Duration Benefits are available for a maximum of 36 months.

Number awarded Varies each year; recently, 4 of these scholarships were awarded.

Deadline Deadline not specified.

[1005]
ILLINOIS CHILDREN OF VETERANS SCHOLARSHIPS

Illinois Department of Veterans' Affairs
833 South Spring Street
P.O. Box 19432
Springfield, IL 62794-9432
(217) 782-6641   Toll Free: (800) 437-9824 (within IL)
Fax: (217) 524-0344   TDD: (217) 524-4645
E-mail: webmail@dva.state.il.us
Web: www.veterans.illinois.gov/benefits/education.htm

Summary To provide financial assistance for college to the children of Illinois veterans (with preference given to the children of disabled or deceased veterans).

Eligibility Each county in the state is entitled to award an honorary scholarship to the child of a veteran of World War I, World War II, the Korean Conflict, the Vietnam Conflict, or any time after August 2, 1990. Preference is given to children of disabled or deceased veterans.

Financial data Students selected for this program receive free tuition at any branch of the University of Illinois.

Duration Up to 4 years.

Number awarded Each county in Illinois is entitled to award 1 scholarship. The Board of Trustees of the university may, from time to time, add to the number of honorary scholarships (when such additions will not create an unnecessary financial burden on the university).

Deadline Deadline not specified.

[1006]
ILLINOIS GRANT PROGRAM FOR DEPENDENTS OF CORRECTIONAL OFFICERS

Illinois Student Assistance Commission
Attn: Scholarship and Grant Services
1755 Lake Cook Road
Deerfield, IL 60015-5209
(847) 948-8550   Toll Free: (800) 899-ISAC
Fax: (847) 831-8549   TDD: (800) 526-0844
E-mail: collegezone@isac.org
Web: www.collegezone.com/studentzone/407_635.htm

Summary To provide financial assistance to the children or spouses of disabled or deceased Illinois correctional workers who plan to attend college in the state.

Eligibility This program is open to the spouses and children of Illinois correctional officers who were at least 90% disabled or killed in the line of duty. Applicants must be enrolled on at least a half-time basis as an undergraduate at an approved Illinois public or private 2-year or 4-year college or university. They need not be Illinois residents at the time of application. U.S. citizenship or eligible non-citizen status is required.

Financial data The grants provide full payment of tuition and mandatory fees at approved public colleges in Illinois or an equivalent amount at private colleges.

Duration Up to 8 academic semesters or 12 academic quarters of study.

Number awarded Varies each year.

Deadline September of each year for the academic year; February of each year for spring semester or winter or spring quarter; June of each year for summer term.

[1007]
ILLINOIS GRANT PROGRAM FOR DEPENDENTS OF POLICE OR FIRE OFFICERS

Illinois Student Assistance Commission
Attn: Scholarship and Grant Services
1755 Lake Cook Road
Deerfield, IL 60015-5209
(847) 948-8550   Toll Free: (800) 899-ISAC
Fax: (847) 831-8549   TDD: (800) 526-0844
E-mail: collegezone@isac.org
Web: www.collegezone.com/studentzone/407_633.htm

Summary To provide financial assistance to the children or spouses of disabled or deceased Illinois police or fire officers who plan to attend college or graduate school in the state.

Eligibility This program is open to the spouses and children of Illinois police and fire officers who were at least 90% disabled or killed in the line of duty. Applicants must be enrolled on at least a half-time basis in either undergraduate or graduate study at an approved Illinois public or private 2-year or 4-year college, university, or hospital school. They need not be Illinois residents at the time of application. U.S. citizenship or eligible non-citizen status is required.

Financial data The grants provide full payment of tuition and mandatory fees at approved public colleges in Illinois or an equivalent amount at private colleges.

Duration Up to 8 academic semesters or 12 academic quarters of study.

Number awarded Varies each year.

Deadline September of each year for the academic year; February of each year for spring semester or winter or spring quarter; June of each year for summer term.

[1008]
ILLINOIS MIA/POW SCHOLARSHIP

Illinois Department of Veterans' Affairs
833 South Spring Street
P.O. Box 19432
Springfield, IL 62794-9432
(217) 782-6641   Toll Free: (800) 437-9824 (within IL)
Fax: (217) 524-0344   TDD: (217) 524-4645
E-mail: webmail@dva.state.il.us
Web: www.veterans.illinois.gov/benefits/education.htm

Summary To provide financial assistance for 1) the undergraduate education of Illinois dependents of disabled or deceased veterans or those listed as prisoners of war or missing in action, and 2) the rehabilitation or education of disabled dependents of those veterans.

Eligibility This program is open to the spouses, natural children, legally adopted children, or stepchildren of a veteran or servicemember who 1) has been declared by the U.S. Department of Defense or the U.S. Department of Veterans Affairs to be permanently disabled from service-connected causes with 100% disability, deceased as the result of a service-connected disability, a prisoner of war, or missing in action, and 2) at the time of entering service was an Illinois resident or was an Illinois resident within 6 months of entering such service. Special support is available for dependents who are disabled.

Financial data An eligible dependent is entitled to full payment of tuition and certain fees at any Illinois state-supported college, university, or community college. In lieu of that benefit, an eligible dependent who has a physical, mental, or developmental disability is entitled to receive a grant to be used to cover the cost of treating the disability at 1 or more appropriate therapeutic, rehabilitative, or educational facilities. For all recipients, the total benefit cannot exceed the cost equivalent of 4 calendar years of full-time enrollment, including summer terms, at the University of Illinois.

Duration This scholarship may be used for a period equivalent to 4 calendar years, including summer terms. Dependents have 12 years from the initial term of study to complete the equivalent of 4 calendar years. Disabled dependents who elect to use the grant for rehabilitative purposes may do so as long as the total benefit does not exceed the cost equivalent of 4 calendar years of full-time enrollment at the University of Illinois.

Additional data An eligible child must begin using the scholarship prior to his or her 26th birthday. An eligible spouse must begin using the scholarship prior to 10 years from the effective date of eligibility (e.g., prior to August 12, 1989 or 10 years from date of disability or death).

Number awarded Varies each year.

Deadline Deadline not specified.

[1009]
INDIANA CHILD OF VETERAN AND PUBLIC SAFETY OFFICER SUPPLEMENTAL GRANT PROGRAM

State Student Assistance Commission of Indiana
Attn: Grant Division
150 West Market Street, Suite 500
Indianapolis, IN 46204-2811
(317) 232-2350   Toll Free: (888) 528-4719 (within IN)
Fax: (317) 232-3260   E-mail: grants@ssaci.state.in.us
Web: www.in.gov/ssaci/2338.htm

Summary To provide financial assistance to residents of Indiana who are the children or spouses of specified categories of deceased or disabled veterans or public safety officers and interested in attending college or graduate school in the state.

Eligibility This program is open to 1) children of disabled Indiana veterans; 2) children and spouses of members of the Indiana National Guard killed while serving on state active duty; and 3) children and spouses of Indiana public safety officers killed in the line of duty. The veterans portion is open to Indiana residents who are the natural or adopted children of veterans who served in the active-duty U.S. armed forces during a period of wartime. Applicants may be of any age; parents must have lived in Indiana for at least 3 years during their lifetime. The veteran parent must also 1) have a service-connected disability as determined by the U.S. Department of Veterans Affairs or the Department of Defense; 2) have received a Purple Heart Medal; or 3) have been a resident of Indiana at the time of entry into the service and declared a POW or MIA after January 1, 1960. Students at the Indiana Soldiers' and Sailors' Children's Home are also eligible. The National Guard portion of this program is open to children and spouses of members of the Indiana National Guard who suffered a service-connected death while serving on state active duty. The public safety officer portion of this program is open to 1) the children and spouses of regular law enforcement officers, regular fire fighters, volunteer fire fighters, county police reserve officers, city police reserve officers, paramedics, emergency medical technicians, and advanced emergency medical technicians killed in the line of duty, and 2) the children and spouses of Indiana state police troopers permanently and totally disabled in the line of duty. Children must be younger than 23 years of age and enrolled full time in an undergraduate or graduate degree program at a public college or university in Indiana. Spouses must be enrolled in an undergraduate program and must have been married to the covered public safety officer at the time of death or disability.

Financial data Qualified applicants receive a 100% remission of tuition and all mandatory fees for undergraduate or graduate work at state-supported postsecondary schools and universities in Indiana. Support is not provided for such fees as room and board.

Duration Up to 124 semester hours of study.

Additional data The veterans portion of this program is administered by the Indiana Department of Veterans' Affairs, 302 West Washington Street, Room E-120, Indianapolis, IN 46204-2738, (317) 232-3910, (800) 400-4520,

Fax: (317) 232-7721, E-mail: jkiser@dva.state.in.us. The National Guard portion of this program is administered by Joint Forces Headquarters, Attn: Education Services Office, 9301 East 59th Street, Lawrence, IN 46216, (317) 964-7023, Fax: (317) 964-7028.

Number awarded Varies each year.

Deadline Applications must be submitted at least 30 days before the start of the college term.

[1010]
IOPO FOUNDATION SCHOLARSHIPS

Indiana Organ Procurement Organization, Inc.
Attn: IOPO Foundation Inc.
3760 Guion Road
P.O. Box 6069, Department 172
Indianapolis, IN 46202-6069
Toll Free: (888) ASK-IOPO   Fax: (317) 685-1687
E-mail: info@iopo.org
Web: www.iopo.org/about/foundation/scholarships.html

Summary To provide financial assistance for college attendance in any state to Indiana residents who are organ, tissue, or eye transplant donors, recipients, candidates, or their families.

Eligibility This program is open to Indiana residents who are organ, tissue, or eye transplant donors, recipients, candidates, or relatives (including spouses, parents, children, grandchildren, siblings, aunts, uncles, nieces, nephews, and cousins). Applicants must be high school seniors or students already attending a college or technical school in any state. They must have a GPA of 2.0 or higher; high school seniors must be in the top 50% of their class. Along with their application, they must submit a 1,500-word essay describing their career goals, experience with organ or tissue donation and/or transplantation, and personal goals. Financial need is considered in the selection process.

Financial data Recently, stipends were $3,500, $2,100, and $1,400.

Duration 1 year; nonrenewable.

Number awarded 3 each year: 1 each at $3,500, $2,100, and $1,400.

Deadline February of each year.

[1011]
JAMES DOYLE CASE MEMORIAL SCHOLARSHIPS

Mississippi Council of the Blind
P.O. Box 31112
Jackson, MS 39286-1112
(601) 371-0616   Toll Free: (888) 346-5622 (within MS)
Web: www.acb.org/mcb

Summary To provide financial assistance to legally blind residents of Mississippi and their children who plan to attend college or graduate school in any state.

Eligibility This program is open to residents of Mississippi who are legally blind or the children of at least 1 legally blind parent. Applicants must be enrolled or accepted for enrollment in an undergraduate or graduate program in any state and carrying or planning to carry at least 12 academic hours. Along with their application, they must submit a 2-page autobiographical sketch, transcripts, standardized test scores (ACT or SAT for undergraduates; GRE, MCAT, LSAT, etc. for graduate students), 2 letters of recommendation, proof of acceptance from a postsecondary school, and verification of blindness of the qualifying person (applicant or parent).

Financial data The stipend is $1,500 per year.

Duration 4 years.

Number awarded 2 each year.

Deadline February of each year.

[1012]
JEANNE E. BRAY MEMORIAL SCHOLARSHIP

National Rifle Association of America
Attn: Law Enforcement Activities Division
11250 Waples Mill Road
Fairfax, VA 22030-7400
(703) 267-1131   E-mail: selkin@nrahq.org
Web: www.nrahq.org/law/lebenefits.asp

Summary To provide financial assistance for college to children of law enforcement officers who are members of the National Rifle Association (NRA).

Eligibility This program is open to NRA members who are the dependent children of 1) currently serving full-time commissioned peace officers who are also NRA members; 2) deceased full-time commissioned peace officers who lost their lives in the performance of assigned peace officer duties and were current members of NRA at the time of their death; 3) retired full-time commissioned peace officers who are also NRA members; and 4) full-time commissioned peace officers, disabled and retired as a result of a line of duty incident, who are also current NRA members. Applicants must be U.S. citizens who have a GPA of 3.0 or higher and scores of at least 950 on the SAT I or 25 on the ACT. Along with their application, they must submit an essay of 500 to 700 words in support of the rights secured by the second amendment to the constitution.

Financial data The stipend is $2,000 per year.

Duration Up to 4 years, provided the recipient maintains a GPA of 2.0 or higher.

Number awarded 1 or more each year.

Deadline November of each year.

[1013]
JOHN YOUTSEY MEMORIAL SCHOLARSHIP FUND

Hemophilia of Georgia
8800 Roswell Road, Suite 170
Atlanta, GA 30350-1844
(770) 518-8272   Fax: (770) 518-3310
E-mail: mail@hog.org
Web: www.hog.org/programs/page/scholarship

Summary To provide financial assistance to residents of Georgia who have a bleeding disorder or have lost a parent because of the disorder and are interested in attending college in any state.

Eligibility This program is open to residents of Georgia who 1) have hemophilia, von Willebrand Disease, or other

inherited bleeding disorder; and 2) are children whose parent died as a result of complications from a bleeding disorder. They may be graduating high school seniors or students currently enrolled at an accredited college, university, vocational/technical school, or professional degree program in any state. Selection is based on academic record, financial need, and personal goals.

Financial data A stipend is awarded (amount not specified).

Duration 1 year.

Number awarded Varies each year. Since this program was established, it has awarded more than 275 scholarship with a value greater than $800,000.

Deadline April of each year.

[1014]
JON C. LADDA MEMORIAL FOUNDATION SCHOLARSHIP

Jon C. Ladda Memorial Foundation
P.O. Box 55
Unionville, CT 06085
E-mail: info@jonladda.org
Web: www.jonladda.org

Summary To provide financial assistance for college to children of deceased and disabled U.S. Naval Academy graduates and members of the Navy submarine service.

Eligibility This program is open to children of U.S. Naval Academy graduates and members of the U.S. Navy submarine service. The parent must have died on active duty or been medically retired with a 100% disability. Applicants must be enrolled or accepted at a 4-year college or university, including any of the service academies. Along with their application, they must submit an essay on a topic that changes annually. Selection is based on academic achievement, financial need, and merit.

Financial data A stipend is awarded (amount not specified). Funds are disbursed directly to the recipient's institution.

Duration 1 year; may be renewed.

Number awarded 1 or more each year.

Deadline March of each year.

[1015]
KATHERN F. GRUBER SCHOLARSHIPS

Blinded Veterans Association
477 H Street, N.W.
Washington, DC 20001-2694
(202) 371-8880   Toll Free: (800) 669-7079
Fax: (202) 371-8258   E-mail: bva@bva.org
Web: www.bva.org/services.html

Summary To provide financial assistance for undergraduate or graduate study to spouses and children of blinded veterans.

Eligibility This program is open to dependent children and spouses of blinded veterans of the U.S. armed forces. The veteran need not be a member of the Blinded Veterans Association. The veteran's blindness may be either service connected or nonservice connected, but it must meet the following definition: central visual acuity of 20/200 or less in the better eye with corrective glasses, or central visual acuity of more than 20/200 if there is a field defect in which the peripheral field has contracted to such an extent that the widest diameter of visual field subtends an angular distance no greater than 20 degrees in the better eye. Applicants must have been accepted or be currently enrolled as a full-time student in an undergraduate or graduate program at an accredited institution of higher learning. Along with their application, they must submit a 300-word essay on their career goals and aspirations. Financial need is not considered in the selection process.

Financial data The stipend is $2,000; funds are intended to be used to cover the student's expenses, including tuition, other academic fees, books, dormitory fees, and cafeteria fees. Funds are paid directly to the recipient's school.

Duration 1 year; recipients may reapply.

Additional data Scholarships may be used for only 1 degree (vocational, bachelor's, or graduate) or nongraduate certificate (e.g., nursing, secretarial).

Number awarded 6 each year.

Deadline April of each year.

[1016]
KENTUCKY DECEASED OR DISABLED LAW ENFORCEMENT OFFICER AND FIRE FIGHTER DEPENDENT TUITION WAIVER

Kentucky Fire Commission
Attn: Executive Director
300 North Main Street
Versailles, KY 40383
(859) 256-3478   Toll Free: (800) 782-6823
Fax: (859) 256-3125   E-mail: ronnie.day@kctcs.net
Web: www.kctcs.edu/kyfirecommission

Summary To provide financial assistance for college to the children and spouses of Kentucky police officers or fire fighters deceased or disabled in the line of duty.

Eligibility This program is open to spouses, widow(er)s, and children of Kentucky residents who became a law enforcement officer, fire fighter, or volunteer fire fighter and who 1) were killed while in active service or training for active service; 2) died as a result of a service-connected disability; or 3) became permanently and totally disabled as a result of active service or training for active service. Children must be younger than 23 years of age; spouses and widow(er)s may be of any age.

Financial data Recipients are entitled to a waiver of tuition at state-supported universities, community colleges, and technical training institutions in Kentucky.

Duration 1 year; may be renewed up to a maximum total of 36 months.

Number awarded Varies each year; all qualified applicants are entitled to this aid.

Deadline Deadline not specified.

[1017]
KENTUCKY VETERANS TUITION WAIVER PROGRAM

Kentucky Department of Veterans Affairs
Attn: Division of Field Operations
321 West Main Street, Room 390
Louisville, KY 40202
(502) 595-4447   Toll Free: (800) 928-4012 (within KY)
Fax: (502) 595-4448   E-mail: Pamela.Cypert@ky.gov
Web: www.veterans.ky.gov/benefits/tuitionwaiver.htm

Summary To provide financial assistance for college to the children, spouses, or unremarried widow(er)s of disabled or deceased Kentucky veterans.

Eligibility This program is open to the children, stepchildren, spouses, and unremarried widow(er)s of veterans who are residents of Kentucky (or were residents at the time of their death). The qualifying veteran must meet 1 of the following conditions: 1) died on active duty (regardless of wartime service); 2) died as a result of a service-connected disability (regardless of wartime service); 3) has a 100% service-connected disability; 4) is totally disabled (non-service connected) with wartime service; or 5) is deceased and served during wartime. The military service may have been as a member of the U.S. armed forces, the Kentucky National Guard, or a Reserve component; service in the Guard or Reserves must have been on state active duty, active duty for training, inactive duty training, or active duty with the U.S. armed forces. Children of veterans must be under 23 years of age; no age limit applies to spouses or unremarried widow(er)s. All applicants must be attending or planning to attend a 2-year, 4-year, or vocational technical school operated and funded by the Kentucky Department of Education.

Financial data Eligible dependents and survivors are exempt from tuition and matriculation fees at any state-supported institution of higher education in Kentucky.

Duration Tuition is waived until the recipient completes 45 months of training, receives a college degree, or (in the case of children of veterans) reaches 26 years of age, whichever comes first. Spouses and unremarried widow(er)s are not subject to the age limitation.

Number awarded Varies each year.

Deadline Deadline not specified.

[1018]
KERIN KELLER MEMORIAL SCHOLARSHIP

College Planning Network
Attn: Vicki Breithaupt
43 Bentley Place
Port Townsend, WA 98368
(206) 323-0624   E-mail: seacpn@collegeplan.org
Web: www.collegeplan.org

Summary To provide financial assistance to residents of Washington who are related to a breast cancer patient and planning to study business or communications at a college in the state.

Eligibility This program is open to residents of Washington who are attending or planning to attend an accredited 2-year or 4-year college or university in the state.

Applicants must major in business or communications; a focus in marketing, advertising, and public relations is strongly encouraged. They must be related to a victim of breast cancer. Along with their application, they must submit 2 letters of recommendation, a list of significant activities and honors, an official transcript from the high school or college they are currently attending, and a 1-page essay explaining their relationship to a victim of breast cancer and how this award will help them attain their educational goals. Financial need is considered in the selection process, but it is not the determining factor.

Financial data The stipend is $1,000.

Duration 1 year.

Additional data This program is sponsored by Ad Club Seattle, formerly the Seattle Advertising Federation.

Number awarded 1 each year.

Deadline March of each year.

[1019]
KIDS' CHANCE OF ARIZONA SCHOLARSHIPS

Kids' Chance of Arizona
P.O. Box 36753
Phoenix, AZ 85067-6753
(602) 253-4360   Toll Free: (877) 253-4360
Web: www.azkidschance.org

Summary To provide financial assistance to Arizona residents whose parent was killed or permanently disabled in an employment-related accident and who are interested in attending college in any state.

Eligibility This program is open to Arizona residents between 16 and 25 years of age whose parent was killed or disabled in an employment-related accident. Applicants must be attending or planning to attend a college, university, or trade school in any state. They must submit high school transcripts, letters of recommendation, verification of school attendance, and a 1-page letter explaining their educational goals and need for financial assistance.

Financial data A stipend is awarded (amount not specified).

Duration 1 year; may be renewed.

Additional data This program was established in 1997.

Number awarded Varies each year; since the program was established, it has awarded 137 scholarships worth $260,987.57.

Deadline Deadline not specified.

[1020]
KIDS' CHANCE OF ARKANSAS SCHOLARSHIPS

Kids' Chance of Arkansas, Inc.
Attn: Scholarship Board
P.O. Box 250249
Little Rock, AR 72225-0249
Toll Free: (866) 880-8444
E-mail: KidsChance@awcc.state.ar.us
Web: www.awcc.state.ar.us/kids_chance/kchance1.html

Summary To provide financial assistance to Arkansas residents whose parent was killed or permanently disabled in an employment-related accident and who are interested in attending college in any state.

Eligibility This program is open to children of workers who have been killed or become permanently and totally disabled from a compensable Arkansas Workers' Compensation injury or accident. Applicants must be between 16 and 22 years of age; be able to demonstrate academic achievement and aptitude; and be attending or planning to attend an accredited vocational/technical school, college, or university in any state. The injury or death of their parent must have resulted in a decrease in family earnings that creates an obstacle to the continuation of their education. Along with their application, they must submit a 2-page essay that includes 1) the circumstances of the work-related injury or death of their parent or guardian; 2) their academic and career aspirations; and 3) the biggest challenge in attending college and plans to overcome it.

Financial data The stipend depends on the financial need of the recipient.

Duration 1 year.

Additional data This program was established in 2002.

Number awarded Varies each year; recently, 27 of these scholarships, with a value of $56,000, were awarded.

Deadline May of each year.

[1021]
KIDS' CHANCE OF GEORGIA SCHOLARSHIPS

Kids' Chance of Georgia, Inc.
2024 Powers Ferry Road, Suite 225
Atlanta, GA 30339
(770) 933-7767   E-mail: info@kidschancega.org
Web: www.kidschancega.org

Summary To provide financial assistance to Georgia residents whose parent was killed or permanently disabled in an employment-related accident and who are interested in attending college in any state.

Eligibility This program is open to Georgia residents between 16 and 25 years of age whose parent's on-the-job death or injury resulted in a substantial decline in family income. Applicants must be enrolled or planning to enroll full time at a college, university, or technical school in any state.

Financial data The stipend depends on the financial need of the recipient, to a maximum of $5,333. Funds may be used for tuition, books, housing, meals, transportation, and/or as a supplement to the income of the family to compensate for money the student would earn by dropping out of school.

Duration 1 year; may be renewed if the recipient maintains satisfactory academic progress.

Additional data This program was established by the Workers' Compensation Section of the Georgia Bar in 1988. It has served as a model for comparable programs that currently operate in 29 other states.

Number awarded Varies each year.

Deadline Deadline not specified.

[1022]
KIDS' CHANCE OF INDIANA SCHOLARSHIP PROGRAM

Kids' Chance of Indiana, Inc.
Attn: Scholarship Committee
721 East Broadway
Fortville, IN 46040
(317) 485-0043, ext. 123   Fax: (317) 485-4299
E-mail: office@kidschancein.org
Web: www.kidschancein.org/scholarship.html

Summary To provide financial assistance to Indiana residents whose parent was killed or permanently disabled in a work-related accident and who are interested in attending college or graduate school in any state.

Eligibility This program is open to Indiana residents between 16 and 25 years of age who are the children of workers fatally or catastrophically injured as a result of a work-related accident or occupational disease. The death or injury must be compensable by the Workers' Compensation Board of the state of Indiana and must have resulted in a substantial decline in the family's income that is likely to impede the student's pursuit of his or her educational objectives. Applicants must be attending or planning to attend a trade/vocational school, junior/community college, 4-year college or university, or graduate school in any state. Financial need is considered in the selection process.

Financial data Stipends range up to $3,000 per year. Funds may be used for tuition and fees, books, room and board, and utilities.

Duration 1 year; may be renewed.

Number awarded Varies each year.

Deadline Deadline not specified.

[1023]
KIDS' CHANCE OF KENTUCKY SCHOLARSHIPS

Kids' Chance of Kentucky
Attn: Scholarship Committee
P.O. Box 910234
Lexington, KY 40591
(859) 608-2383   Fax: (859) 219-0194
E-mail: gdavis5@alltel.net
Web: www.kidschanceky.org

Summary To provide financial assistance to Kentucky residents whose parent was killed or seriously injured in an employment-related accident and who are interested in attending college in any state.

Eligibility This program is open to residents of Kentucky between 16 and 25 years of age. Applicants must be the natural child, adopted child, stepchild, or full dependent of a worker killed or permanent injured in a compensable work-related accident during the course of employment with a Kentucky employer and entitled to receive benefits under the Kentucky Workers' Compensation Act. They must be attending or planning to attend college in any state. The parent's death or injury must have resulted in a substantial decline in the family income. Selection is based primarily on financial need, although academic achieve-

ment, aptitude, and community service are also considered.

Financial data The stipend depends on the need of the recipient. Funds may be used to cover tuition, books, housing, and meals.

Duration 1 year; may be renewed.

Additional data This program was established in 2003.

Number awarded Varies each year.

Deadline April of each year for fall and spring semester; October of each year for spring semester.

[1024]
KIDS' CHANCE OF LOUISIANA SCHOLARSHIPS

Kids' Chance of Louisiana
c/o The Louisiana Bar Foundation
909 Poydras Street, Suite 1550
New Orleans, LA 70112
(504) 561-1046   Fax: (504) 566-1926
E-mail: kidschance@raisingthebar.org
Web: www.raisingthebar.org

Summary To provide financial assistance to Louisiana residents whose parent was killed or permanently disabled in an employment-related accident and who are interested in attending college in the state.

Eligibility This program is open to Louisiana residents between 16 and 25 years of age who are the dependent of a worker killed or permanently and totally disabled in an accident that is compensable under a state or federal Workers' Compensation Act or law. Applicants must be attending or planning to attend an accredited Louisiana university; community, technical, or vocational college; or state-approved proprietary school. Financial need is considered in the selection process.

Financial data Stipends range from $500 to $3,000. Funds, paid directly to the school where the child is enrolled, may be used for tuition, books, fees, room, and general living expenses.

Duration 1 year; recipients may reapply as long as they maintain a "C" average or higher.

Additional data This program was established in 2004.

Number awarded Varies each year; recently, 19 of these scholarships were awarded. Since the program began, it has awarded 109 scholarships worth $188,500.

Deadline February of each year.

[1025]
KIDS' CHANCE OF MARYLAND SCHOLARSHIPS

Kids' Chance of Maryland, Inc.
P.O. Box 20262
Baltimore, MD 21284
(410) 832-4702   Fax: (410) 832-4726
E-mail: info@kidschance-md.org
Web: www.kidschance-md.org

Summary To provide financial assistance to Maryland residents whose parent was killed or permanently disabled in an employment-related accident and who are interested in attending college in any state.

Eligibility This program is open to Maryland residents between 16 and 25 years of age who have a parent permanently or catastrophically injured or killed in an employment-related accident compensable under the Maryland Workers' Compensation Act. The parent's death or injury must have resulted in a substantial decline in the family income. Applicants must be attending or planning to attend college or technical school in any state. Financial need is considered in the selection process.

Financial data Stipends depend on the need of the students. Recently, they ranged from $3,500 to $8,000. Funds are intended to cover tuition and books but may also including housing and meals.

Duration 1 year; recipients may reapply.

Number awarded Varies each year; recently, 14 of these scholarships were awarded.

Deadline Deadline not specified.

[1026]
KIDS' CHANCE OF MISSISSIPPI SCHOLARSHIP FUND

Mississippi Bar Foundation
Attn: Administrative Law and Workers' Compensation
  Section
643 North State Street
P.O. Box 2168
Jackson, MS 39225-2168
(601) 948-5234   Fax: (601) 355-8635
E-mail: acook@msbar.org
Web: www.msbar.org/kidchance.php

Summary To provide financial assistance to Mississippi residents whose parent was killed or disabled on the job and who are interested in attending college in any state.

Eligibility This program is open to Mississippi residents between 17 and 23 years of age who have had a parent killed or permanently and totally disabled in an accident that is compensable under the Mississippi Workers' Compensation Act. Applicants must demonstrate substantial financial need.

Financial data A stipend is awarded (amount not specified).

Duration 1 year; may be renewed.

Number awarded Varies each year.

Deadline April of each year.

[1027]
KIDS' CHANCE OF MISSOURI SCHOLARSHIPS

Kids' Chance Inc. of Missouri
Attn: Scholarship Committee
P.O. Box 410384
St. Louis, MO 63141
(314) 997-3390   Toll Free: (800) 484-5733, ext. 5437
Fax: (314) 432-5894   E-mail: susgrp@charter.net
Web: www.mokidschance.org

Summary To provide financial assistance to Missouri residents whose parent was killed or permanently disabled in a work-related accident and who are interested in attending college in any state.

Eligibility This program is open to Missouri residents whose parent sustained a serious injury or fatality in a Missouri work-related accident covered by workers' compensation. Applicants must be attending or planning to attend an accredited vocational school or college within the United States. They must be able to demonstrate financial need.

Financial data Stipends depend on the need of the recipient. Funds may be used to cover tuition, books, supplies, housing, meals, and other expenses not covered by other grants and/or scholarships.

Duration 1 year; recipients may reapply.

Additional data This program was established in 1996.

Number awarded Varies each year.

Deadline April or October of each year.

[1028]
KIDS' CHANCE OF NORTH CAROLINA SCHOLARSHIPS

Kids' Chance of North Carolina, Inc.
P.O. Box 470426
Charlotte, NC 28247-0426
(704) 264-9111   Toll Free: (800) 246-8599
Fax: (704) 553-0241   E-mail: info@kidschancenc.org
Web: www.kidschancenc.org/scholarship.php

Summary To provide financial assistance to North Carolina residents whose parent was seriously injured or killed in a workplace accident and who are interested in attending college in any state.

Eligibility This program is open to residents of North Carolina between 16 and 25 years of age who are attending or planning to attend college or vocational school in any state. Applicants must be children of employees who have been seriously injured or killed as a result of a workplace accident that is covered under the North Carolina Workers' Compensation Act. They must be able to demonstrate financial hardship caused by the death or serious injury of their parent.

Financial data Stipends range up to $5,000 per year. Funds may be used for tuition, books, meals, housing, and transportation, and/or they may be used to supplement the income of the family to compensate for money the student would earn by dropping out of school.

Duration 1 year; may be renewed if the recipient maintains an acceptable academic level.

Additional data This program was established in 2004.

Number awarded Varies each year; recently, 8 of these scholarships were awarded.

Deadline Deadline not specified.

[1029]
KIDS' CHANCE OF OHIO SCHOLARSHIPS

Kids' Chance of Ohio
Attn: Executive Director
52 East Gay Street
P.O. Box 1008
Columbus, OH 43216-1008
(614) 464-6410   E-mail: raminor@vssp.com
Web: www.kidschanceohio.org/scholarshipprogram.html

Summary   To provide financial assistance for undergraduate or graduate study in any state to children of Ohio employees who were killed or disabled as a result of a work-related injury or occupational disease.

Eligibility   This program is open to the children between 16 and 25 years of age of employees who have been declared to be permanently and totally disabled or who were fatally injured as a result of a work-related injury or occupational disease. The death, injury, or illness must have occurred as a result of work activities performed for an Ohio employer covered by the Ohio workers' compensation law, although neither the student nor the parent is required to be Ohio residents. The injury or death must have resulted in a decline in the family's income. Applicants must be attending or planning to attend a college, university, community college, trade/vocational school, industrial/commercial training, or graduate school in any state.

Financial data   The stipend depends on the need of the recipient, to a maximum of $5,000 per year. Funds may be used for payment of tuition, fees, books, room, and board.

Duration   1 year; recipients may reapply.

Number awarded   Varies each year.

Deadline   Applications must be submitted at least 1 month prior to the beginning of the semester or quarter.

[1030]
KIDS' CHANCE OF PENNSYLVANIA SCHOLARSHIPS

Kids' Chance of Pennsylvania
P.O. Box 543
Pottstown, PA 19464
(610) 970-9143   Fax: (610) 970-7520
E-mail: info@kidschanceofpa.org
Web: www.kidschanceofpa.org/scholarship.html

Summary   To provide financial assistance to Pennsylvania residents whose parent was killed or permanently disabled in a work-related accident and who are interested in attending college in any state.

Eligibility   This program is open to Pennsylvania residents between 16 and 25 years of age who have been accepted by an accredited postsecondary educational institution anywhere in the United States. At least 1 parent must have been killed or seriously injured as a result of a work-related accident covered under the Pennsylvania Workers' Compensation Act. Financial need is considered in the selection process.

Financial data   Stipends range from $500 to $5,000.

Duration   1 year; may be renewed.

Additional data   This program began in 1997. Matching funding for students with remaining unmet financial need is provided by the Pennsylvania Higher Education Assistance Agency (PHEAA) in collaboration with American Education Services. Students who demonstrate exceptional academic progress and significant financial need receive funding through a grant from the ACE INA Foundation.

Number awarded   Varies each year; recently, 37 of these scholarships were awarded. Since the program began, it has awarded 334 scholarships with a value of $532,750.

Deadline   April of each year.

[1031]
KIDS' CHANCE OF SOUTH CAROLINA SCHOLARSHIPS

Kids' Chance of South Carolina
P.O. Box 11155
Columbia, SC 29211
(803) 356-5862   Fax: (803) 356-0935
E-mail: info@kidschancesc.org
Web: www.kidschancesc.org/scholarship_program.html

Summary   To provide financial assistance to South Carolina residents whose parent was killed or permanently disabled in a work-related accident and who are interested in attending college or graduate school in any state.

Eligibility   This program is open to South Carolina residents between 16 and 25 years of age who are the children of workers fatally or catastrophically injured as a result of a work-related accident or occupational disease. Applicants must be attending or planning to attend a trade school, vocational school, community or junior college, 4-year college or university, or graduate school in any state. The work-related injury or occupational disease from which their parent suffers or died must be compensable by the Workers' Compensation Board of the state of South Carolina and must have resulted in a substantial decline in the family's income that is likely to interfere with the student's pursuit of his or her educational objectives.

Financial data   Stipends range from $500 to $6,000 per year. Funds may be used for tuition and fees, books, room and board, and utilities.

Duration   1 year; may be renewed.

Number awarded   Varies each year.

Deadline   Applications must be submitted 1 month before the beginning of the semester.

[1032]
KIDS' CHANCE OF WASHINGTON SCHOLARSHIPS

Kids' Chance of Washington
P.O. Box 185
Olympia, WA 98507-0185
Toll Free: (800) 572-5762   Fax: (360) 943-2333
E-mail: debbie@wscff.org
Web: www.kidschancewa.com

Summary   To provide financial assistance to residents of Washington whose parent or spouse was killed or seriously disabled in a workplace accident and who are interested in attending college in any state.

Eligibility   This program is open to Washington residents attending or planning to attend an accredited community college, university, college, or technical/vocational school in any state. Applicants must be the child or spouse of a Washington worker permanently or catastrophically injured or deceased while on the job. Selection is based primarily on financial need.

Financial data A stipend is awarded (amount not specified). Funds are paid directly to the student's school to be used for tuition, books, fees, room, and general living expenses.

Duration 1 year; may be renewed.

Additional data This program was established in 2001.

Number awarded Varies each year.

Deadline Deadline not specified.

[1033]
KIDS' CHANCE OF WEST VIRGINIA SCHOLARSHIPS

Greater Kanawha Valley Foundation
Attn: Scholarship Coordinator
1600 Huntington Square
900 Lee Street, East
P.O. Box 3041
Charleston, WV 25331-3041
(304) 346-3620   Toll Free: (800) 467-5909
Fax: (304) 346-3640   E-mail: shoover@tgkvf.org
Web: www.tgkvf.org/scholar.htm

Summary To provide financial assistance for college to students whose parent was injured or killed in a West Virginia work-related accident.

Eligibility This program is open to children between 16 and 25 years of age whose parent 1) was fatally injured in a West Virginia work-related accident, or 2) is currently receiving permanent total disability benefits from the West Virginia Workers' Compensation Division. Applicants may reside in any state and be pursuing any field of study at an accredited trade or vocational school, college, or university. They must have at least a 2.5 GPA and demonstrate good moral character. Preference is given to applicants who can demonstrate financial need, academic excellence, leadership abilities, and contributions to school and community.

Financial data The stipend is $1,000 per year.

Duration 1 year; may be renewed.

Additional data This program is sponsored by Kids' Chance of West Virginia, Inc.

Number awarded Varies each year; recently, 8 of these scholarships were awarded.

Deadline January of each year.

[1034]
KIDS' CHANCE SCHOLARSHIP FUND

Alabama Law Foundation
415 Dexter Avenue
P.O. Box 671
Montgomery, AL 36101
(334) 269-1515   Fax: (334) 261-6310
E-mail: info@alfinc.org
Web: www.alfinc.org/kidschance.cfm

Summary To provide financial assistance to Alabama residents whose parent was killed or disabled on the job and who are interested in attending college in any state.

Eligibility This program is open to high school seniors and college students (including students at technical colleges) in Alabama whose parent was killed or permanently

and totally disabled in an on-the-job accident. Applicants must be attending or planning to attend a college or technical school in any state. Financial need is considered in the selection process.

Financial data Stipends range from $500 to $2,500 but do not exceed the cost of tuition and books at the most expensive public university in Alabama.

Additional data This program was established in 1992 by the Workers' Compensation Section of the Alabama State Bar and is currently administered by the Alabama Law Foundation.

Number awarded Varies each year; since the program was established, it has awarded more than 100 scholarships worth more than $375,000.

Deadline April of each year.

[1035]
LITTLE PEOPLE OF AMERICA SCHOLARSHIPS

Little People of America, Inc.
Attn: Vice President of Programs
250 El Camino Real, Suite 201
Tustin, CA 92780
(714) 368-3689   Toll Free: (888) LPA-2001
Fax: (714) 368-3367   E-mail: info@lpaonline.org
Web: www.lpaonline.org

Summary To provide financial assistance for college to members of the Little People of America (LPA), to their families, and (in limited cases) to others.

Eligibility This program is open to members of LPA (limited to people who, for medical reasons, are 4 feet 10 inches or under in height). Applicants must be high school seniors or students attending college or trade school. Along with their application, they must submit a 500-word personal statement that explains their reasons for applying for a scholarship, their plans for the future, how they intend to be of service to LPA after graduation, and any other relevant information about themselves, their family, their background, and their educational achievements. Financial need is also considered in the selection process. If sufficient funds are available after all LPA members have been served, scholarships may also be given, first, to immediate family members of dwarfs who are also paid members of LPA, and, second, to people with dwarfism who are not members of LPA.

Financial data Stipends range from $250 to $1,000.

Duration 1 year; may be renewed.

Number awarded Varies; generally between 5 and 10 each year.

Deadline April of each year.

[1036]
LOUISIANA CHAPTER MS SOCIETY SCHOLARSHIP PROGRAM

National Multiple Sclerosis Society-Louisiana Chapter
4613 Fairfield Street
Metairie, LA 70006
(504) 832-4013   Fax: (504) 831-7188
E-mail: louisianachapter@nmss.org
Web: was.nationalmssociety.org

Summary To provide financial assistance to high school seniors and graduates from Louisiana who have multiple sclerosis (MS) or have a parent with MS and are planning to attend college in any state.

Eligibility This program is open to graduating high school seniors, recent graduates, and GED recipients from Louisiana who have MS or a parent who has MS. Applicants must be planning to enroll as a first-time student at a 2- or 4-year college, university, or vocational/technical school in the United States on at least a half-time basis. Along with their application, they must submit an essay on the impact MS has had on their lives. Selection is based on that essay, academic record, leadership and participation in school or community activities, work experience, goals and aspirations, an outside appraisal, special circumstances, and financial need. U.S. citizenship or permanent resident status is required.

Financial data The stipend is $2,000.

Duration 1 year; nonrenewable.

Number awarded Varies each year; recently, 2 of these scholarships were awarded.

Deadline January of each year.

[1037]
LOUISIANA EDUCATIONAL BENEFITS FOR CHILDREN, SPOUSES, AND SURVIVING SPOUSES OF VETERANS

Louisiana Department of Veterans Affairs
Attn: Education Program
1885 Wooddale Boulevard, Room 1013
P.O. Box 94095, Capitol Station
Baton Rouge, LA 70804-9095
(225) 922-0500, ext. 206   Toll Free: (877) GEAUXVA
Fax: (225) 922-0511
E-mail: Bill.Dixon@vetaffairs.la.gov
Web: vetaffairs.la.gov/education

Summary To provide financial assistance to children, spouses, and surviving spouses of certain disabled or deceased Louisiana veterans who plan to attend college in the state.

Eligibility This program is open to children (between 16 and 25 years of age), spouses, or surviving spouses of veterans who served during specified periods of war time and 1) were killed in action or died in active service; 2) died of a service-connected disability; 3) are missing in action (MIA) or a prisoner of war (POW); 4) sustained a disability rated as 90% or more by the U.S. Department of Veterans Affairs; or 5) have been determined to be unemployable as a result of a service-connected disability. Deceased, MIA, and POW veterans must have resided in Louisiana for at least 12 months prior to entry into service. Living disabled veterans must have resided in Louisiana for at least 24 months prior to the applicant's admission into the program.

Financial data Eligible persons accepted as full-time students at Louisiana state-supported colleges, universities, trade schools, or vocational/technical schools are admitted free and are exempt from payment of tuition, laboratory, athletic, medical, and other special fees. Free registration does not cover books, supplies, room and board, or fees assessed by the student body on themselves (such as yearbooks and weekly papers).

Duration Support is provided for a maximum of 4 school years, to be completed in not more than 5 years from date of original entry.

Additional data Attendance must be on a full-time basis. Surviving spouses must remain unremarried and must take advantage of the benefit within 10 years after eligibility is established.

Number awarded Varies each year.

Deadline Applications must be received no later than 3 months prior to the beginning of a semester.

[1038]
LYMAN FISHER SCHOLARSHIPS

Virginia Hemophilia Foundation
P.O. Box 188
Midlothian, VA 23113-0188
Toll Free: (800) 266-8438   Fax: (804) 740-8643
E-mail: vahemophiliaed@verizon.net
Web: www.vahemophilia.org

Summary To provide financial assistance to people from Virginia who have participated in activities of the Virginia Hemophilia Foundation (VHF) and are interested in attending college.

Eligibility This program is open members of the bleeding disorder community and their families who are attending or planning to attend college. Applicants must have a record of prior participation with VHF and be a resident of Virginia or planning to attend college in Virginia. Along with their application, they must submit a brief biographical sketch of themselves that includes their interests, hobbies, vocational and educational goals, volunteer and community involvement, and work or internship experience; a description of their previous participation with VHF and how they plan to contribute to the organization and support other persons with inherited bleeding disorders; a detailed statement of financial need; a 1-page essay on their career goals; another 1-page essay on a topic of their choice; and 3 letters of recommendation.

Financial data The stipend is $2,000.

Duration 1 year.

Number awarded 2 each year.

Deadline May of each year.

[1039]
MAINE VETERANS DEPENDENTS EDUCATIONAL BENEFITS

Bureau of Veterans' Services
117 State House Station
Augusta, ME 04333-0117
(207) 626-4464   Toll Free: (800) 345-0116 (within ME)
Fax: (207) 626-4471   E-mail: mainebvs@maine.gov
Web: www.maine.gov

Summary   To provide financial assistance for undergraduate or graduate education to dependents of disabled and other Maine veterans.

Eligibility   Applicants for these benefits must be children (high school seniors or graduates under 22 years of age), non-divorced spouses, or unremarried widow(er)s of veterans who meet 1 or more of the following requirements: 1) living and determined to have a total permanent disability resulting from a service-connected cause; 2) killed in action; 3) died from a service-connected disability; 4) died while totally and permanently disabled due to a service-connected disability but whose death was not related to the service-connected disability; or 5) a member of the armed forces on active duty who has been listed for more than 90 days as missing in action, captured, forcibly detained, or interned in the line of duty by a foreign government or power. The veteran parent must have been a resident of Maine at the time of entry into service or a resident of Maine for 5 years preceding application for these benefits. Children may be working on an associate or bachelor's degree. Spouses, widows, and widowers may work on an associate, bachelor's, or master's degree.

Financial data   Recipients are entitled to free tuition at institutions of higher education supported by the state of Maine.

Duration   Children may receive up to 8 semesters of support; they have 6 years from the date of first entrance to complete those 8 semesters. Continuation in the program is based on their earning a GPA of 2.0 or higher each semester. Spouses are entitled to receive up to 120 credit hours of educational benefits and have 10 years from the date of first entrance to complete their program.

Additional data   College preparatory schooling and correspondence course are not supported under this program.

Number awarded   Varies each year.

Deadline   Deadline not specified.

[1040]
MANNERS MEMORIAL SCHOLARSHIP

Disabled American Veterans-Department of New Jersey
135 West Hanover Street, Fourth Floor
Trenton, NJ 08618
(609) 396-2885   Fax: (609) 396-9562
Web: www.davnj.org

Summary   To provide financial assistance to the children of members of the Disabled American Veterans in New Jersey who are interested in attending college in any state.

Eligibility   This program is open to graduating high school seniors who are the child of a member of the Disabled American Veterans in New Jersey. Applicants must be planning to attend a college or university in any state. Along with their application, they must submit 1) letters of recommendation; 2) a letter giving the reasons for their choice of vocation; 2) a transcript that includes information on their GPA, SAT scores, and class rank; and 3) a 500-word article on a topic that changes regularly (recently, students were asked to present their opinion on the war in Iraq). Selection is based on character (20%), Americanism and community service (20%), leadership (20%), scholarship (20%), and need (20%).

Financial data   The stipend is $1,000.

Duration   1 year; nonrenewable.

Number awarded   1 each year.

Deadline   March of each year.

[1041]
MARCIA LARICHE SCHOLARSHIP PROGRAM

Cleveland Scholarship Programs, Inc.
Attn: Financial Aid Department
BP Tower, Suite 3820
200 Public Square
Cleveland, OH 44114
(216) 241-5587   Toll Free: (800) NEED-AID
Fax: (216) 241-6184   E-mail: nfocareto@cspohio.org
Web: www.cspohio.org/csp/ManagedFunds.aspx

Summary   To provide financial assistance for college to students whose parent has been diagnosed with Amyotrophic Lateral Sclerosis (ALS).

Eligibility   This program is open to graduating high school seniors, current undergraduates, and students between 18 and 25 years of age who are not currently attending college. Applicants must be dependents of a parent who has ALS. They must have a GPA of 2.0 or higher and be able to demonstrate financial need. Along with their application, they must submit a 500-word essay on their purpose in going to college, career objectives, and future goals. Selection is based on that essay, academic record, community service, SAT and ACT scores, recommendations, and financial need.

Financial data   A stipend is awarded (amount not specified).

Duration   1 year; may be renewed up to 3 additional years, provided the recipient maintains a GPA of 2.0 or higher.

Number awarded   Varies each year.

Deadline   May of each year.

[1042]
MARILYN YETSO MEMORIAL SCHOLARSHIP

Ulman Cancer Fund for Young Adults
Attn: Scholarship Program Coordinator
10440 Little Patuxent Parkway, Suite 1G
Columbia, MD 21044
(410) 964-0202, ext. 106   Toll Free: (888) 393-FUND
E-mail: scholarship@ulmanfund.org
Web: www.ulmanfund.org

Summary To provide financial assistance for college or graduate school to students from Washington, D.C., Maryland, or Virginia who have or have lost a parent to cancer.
Eligibility This program is open to students who have or have lost a parent or guardian to cancer. Applicants must be residents of Washington, D.C., Maryland, or Virginia or attending college there. They must be 35 years of age or younger and attending, or planning to attend, a 2- or 4-year college, university, or vocational program to work on an undergraduate or graduate degree. The parent or guardian must have been first diagnosed with cancer after the applicant was 15 years of age. Along with their application, they must submit an essay of at least 1,000 words on how their parent's cancer experience has impacted their outlook on life and the legacy that they desire to leave behind. Selection is based on demonstrated dedication to community service, commitment to educational and professional goals, use of their cancer experience to impact the lives of other young adults affected by cancer, medical hardship, and financial need.
Financial data The stipend is $2,500. Funds are paid directly to the educational institution.
Duration 1 year.
Additional data These scholarships were first awarded in 2002. Recipients must agree to complete 80 hours of community service.
Number awarded Varies each year; recently, 2 of these scholarships were awarded.
Deadline April of each year.

[1043]
MARK REAMES MEMORIAL SCHOLARSHIPS

Hemophilia Society of Colorado
Attn: Scholarship Committee
P.O. Box 4943
Englewood, CO 80155
(303) 629-6990   Toll Free: (888) 687-CLOT
Fax: (303) 629-7035   E-mail: hsc@cohemo.org
Web: www.cohemo.org

Summary To provide financial assistance for higher education to members of the Hemophilia Society of Colorado (HSC) and to members of their families.
Eligibility This program is open to HSC members who have hemophilia or a related inherited bleeding disorder and their immediate family members. Applicants must be enrolled or planning to enroll at a 2-year or 4-year college or university, vocational/technical school, or graduate school. Along with their application, they must submit an essay on why they think they should receive this scholarship and how it might affect their future goals. Selection is based on the essay, demonstrated scholastic ability and intellectual promise, letters of recommendation, community involvement (especially involvement with the hemophilia community), and financial need.
Financial data The stipend is $1,000. Funds must be used for tuition, room, board, and related educational expenses.
Duration 1 year.

Number awarded 2 each year.
Deadline April of each year.

[1044]
MARY M. GOOLEY HEMOPHILIA SCHOLARSHIP

Mary M. Gooley Hemophilia Center
Attn: Scholarship Selection Committee
1415 Portland Avenue, Suite 500
Rochester, NY 14621
(585) 922-5700   Fax: (585) 922-5775
E-mail: Tricia.oppelt@rochestergeneral.org
Web: www.hemocenter.org/Scholarship%20Info.asp

Summary To provide financial assistance to people with a bleeding disorder and their families who plan to attend college.
Eligibility This program is open to people who are affected directly or indirectly by hemophilia, von Willebrand Disease, hereditary bleeding disorder, or hemochromatosis. Applicants must be enrolled or planning to enroll at an accredited 2- or 4-year college or university, vocational/technical school, or certified training program. Along with their application, they must submit 1) a 1,000-word essay on their goals and aspirations, their biggest challenge and how they met it, and anything else they want the selection committee to know about them; and 2) a 250-word essay on any unusual family or personal circumstances have affected their achievement in school, work, or participation in school and community activities, including how the bleeding disorder of themselves or their family member has affected their life. Selection is based on the essays, academic performance, participation in school and community activities, work or volunteer experience, personal or family circumstances, recommendations, and financial need.
Financial data The maximum stipend is $2,000.
Duration 1 year.
Additional data This program was established in 1996.
Number awarded 1 or 2 each year.
Deadline April of each year.

[1045]
MARYELLEN LOCHER FOUNDATION SCHOLARSHIP

MaryEllen Locher Foundation
Attn: Laurie Richardson
P.O. Box 4032
Chattanooga, TN 37405
(423) 842-3329
Web: www.maryellenlocherfoundation.org

Summary To provide financial assistance for college to students who have a parent who died from or survived breast cancer.
Eligibility This program is open to students who have been accepted as a full-time enrollee at an accredited 2-year or 4-year college or university. Applicants must have lost a parent to breast cancer or complication resulting from breast cancer, or have a mother who has survived breast cancer. Along with their application, they must sub-

mit 3 essays on assigned topics related to the impact of breast cancer on their family. Selection is based on those essays, grades, and financial need.

Financial data Stipends are $3,000 or $1,500.

Duration 1 year; may be renewed up to 3 additional years.

Additional data This program began in 2002 as the Children of Breast Cancer Foundation Scholarship.

Number awarded Varies each year; recently, 34 of these scholarships were awarded.

Deadline February of each year.

[1046]
METHODIST SEPTEMBER 11 MEMORIAL SCHOLARSHIPS

United Methodist Higher Education Foundation
Attn: Scholarships Administrator
1001 19th Avenue South
P.O. Box 340005
Nashville, TN 37203-0005
(615) 340-7385   Toll Free: (800) 811-8110
Fax: (615) 340-7330
E-mail: umhefscholarships@gbhem.org
Web: www.umhef.org

Summary To provide financial assistance to undergraduate and graduate students at Methodist institutions and Methodist students whose parent or guardian was disabled or killed in the terrorist attacks on September 11, 2001.

Eligibility This program is open to 1) students attending a United Methodist-related college or university in the United States, and 2) United Methodist students attending a higher education institution in the United States. Applicants must have lost a parent or guardian or had a parent or guardian disabled as a result of the September 11, 2001 terrorist attacks. They must be enrolled as full-time undergraduate or graduate students. U.S. citizenship or permanent resident status is required.

Financial data The stipend depends on the number of applicants.

Duration 1 year; may be renewed as long as the recipients maintain satisfactory academic progress as defined by their institution.

Number awarded Varies each year; a total of $30,000 is available for this program.

Deadline Applications may be submitted at any time.

[1047]
MICHAEL A. HUNTER MEMORIAL SCHOLARSHIP

Orange County Community Foundation
Attn: Program Associate, Donor Relations and
  Scholarships
30 Corporate Park, Suite 410
Irvine, CA 92606
(949) 553-4202, ext. 46   Fax: (949) 553-4211
E-mail: cmontesano@oc-cf.org
Web: www.oc-cf.org/default.asp?contentID=89

Summary To provide financial assistance for college to leukemia and lymphoma patients and the children of non-surviving leukemia and lymphoma patients.

Eligibility This program is open to graduating high school seniors, community college students, and 4-year university students nationwide. Applicants must be leukemia or lymphoma patients and/or the children of non-surviving leukemia or lymphoma patients who are enrolled or planning to enroll full time. They must have a GPA of 3.0 or higher and be able to document financial need. Along with their application, they must submit an essay (up to 600 words) on how leukemia or lymphoma has affected their life, including the type of leukemia or lymphoma, date of diagnosis, and current status.

Financial data The stipend is $5,000.

Duration 1 year.

Number awarded 2 each year.

Deadline February of each year.

[1048]
MICHIGAN CHILDREN OF VETERANS TUITION GRANTS

Michigan Department of Treasury
Michigan Higher Education Assistance Authority
Attn: Office of Scholarships and Grants
P.O. Box 30462
Lansing, MI 48909-7962
(517) 373-0457   Toll Free: (888) 4-GRANTS
Fax: (517) 335-6851   E-mail: osg@michigan.gov
Web: www.michigan.gov/mistudentaid

Summary To provide financial assistance for college to the children of Michigan veterans who are totally disabled or deceased as a result of service-connected causes.

Eligibility This program is open to children of Michigan veterans who have been totally and permanently disabled as a result of a service-connected illness or injury prior to death and have now died, have died or become totally and permanently disabled as a result of a service-connected illness or injury, have been killed in action or died from another cause while serving in a war or war condition, or are listed as missing in action in a foreign country. Applicants must be between 16 and 26 years of age and must have lived in Michigan at least 12 months prior to the date of application. They must be enrolled or planning to enroll at least half time at a public institution of higher education in Michigan. U.S. citizenship or permanent resident status is required.

Financial data Recipients are exempt from payment of the first $2,800 per year of tuition or any other fee that takes the place of tuition.

Duration 1 year; may be renewed for up to 3 additional years if the recipient maintains full-time enrollment and a GPA of 2.25 or higher.

Additional data This program was formerly known as the Michigan Veterans Trust Fund Tuition Grants, administered by the Michigan Veterans Trust Fund within the Department of Military and Veterans Affairs. It was transforred to the Office of Scholarships and Grants in 2006.

Number awarded Varies each year; recently, 400 of these grants were awarded.
Deadline Deadline not specified.

[1049]
MID-ATLANTIC CHAPTER MS SOCIETY SCHOLARSHIP PROGRAM

National Multiple Sclerosis Society-Mid-Atlantic
 Chapter
9801-I Southern Pine Boulevard
Charlotte, NC 28273
(704) 525-2955   Fax: (704) 986-7981
E-mail: ncp@nmss.org
Web: was.nationalmssociety.org

Summary To provide financial assistance to high school seniors and graduates from South Carolina and western North Carolina who have multiple sclerosis (MS) or have a parent with MS and who are planning to attend college in any state.
Eligibility This program is open to graduating high school seniors, recent graduates, and GED recipients from South Carolina and western North Carolina who have MS or a parent who has MS. Applicants must be planning to enroll as a first-time student at a 2- or 4-year college, university, or vocational/technical school in the United States on at least a half-time basis. Along with their application, they must submit an essay on the impact MS has had on their lives. Selection is based on that essay, academic record, leadership and participation in school or community activities, work experience, goals and aspirations, an outside appraisal, special circumstances, and financial need. U.S. citizenship or permanent resident status is required.
Financial data The stipend is $2,000.
Duration 1 year.
Number awarded Varies each year; recently, 4 of these scholarships were awarded.
Deadline January of each year.

[1050]
MIKE HYLTON AND RON NIEDERMAN SCHOLARSHIPS

Factor Support Network Pharmacy
Attn: Scholarship Committee
900 Avenida Acaso, Suite A
Camarillo, CA 93012-8749
(805) 388-9336   Toll Free: (877) FSN-4-YOU
Fax: (805) 482-6324
E-mail: Scholarships@FactorSupport.com
Web: www.factorsupport.com/scholarships.htm

Summary To provide financial assistance for college to men with hemophilia and their immediate families.
Eligibility This program is open to men with bleeding disorders and their immediate family members. Applicants must be entering or attending a college, university, juniors college, or vocational school. They must submit 3 short essays: 1) their career goals; 2) how hemophilia or von Willebrand Disease has affected their life; and 3) their efforts to be involved in the bleeding disorder community

and what they can do to education their peers and others outside their family about bleeding disorders. Selection is based on academic goals, volunteer work, school activities, other pertinent experience and achievements, and financial need.
Financial data The stipend is $1,000. Funds are paid directly to the recipient.
Duration 1 year.
Additional data This program was established in 1999.
Number awarded 10 each year.
Deadline April of each year.

[1051]
MILLIE BROTHER SCHOLARSHIPS

Children of Deaf Adults Inc.
c/o Jennie E. Pyers, Scholarship Committee
Wellesley College
106 Central Street, SCI480
Wellesley, MA 02842
(781) 283-3736   Fax: (781) 283-3730
E-mail: coda.scholarship@gmail.com
Web: coda-international.org/blog/scholarship

Summary To provide financial assistance for college to the children of deaf parents.
Eligibility This program is open to the hearing children of deaf parents who are high school seniors or graduates attending or planning to attend college. Applicants must submit a 2-page essay on 1) how their experience as the child of deaf parents has shaped their life and goals, and 2) their future career aspirations; essays are judged on organization, content, and creativity. In addition to the essay, selection is based on a high school and/or college transcript and 2 letters of recommendation.
Financial data The stipend is $3,000.
Duration 1 year; recipients may reapply.
Number awarded 2 each year.
Deadline March of each year.

[1052]
MINNESOTA CHAPTER MS SOCIETY SCHOLARSHIP PROGRAM

National Multiple Sclerosis Society-Minnesota Chapter
Attn: Scholarship Program
200 12th Avenue South
Minneapolis, MN 55415
(612) 335-7955   Toll Free: (800) 582-5296
Fax: (612) 335-7997 E-mail: msparks@mssociety.org
Web: was.nationalmssociety.org

Summary To provide financial assistance to high school seniors and graduates from Minnesota who have multiple sclerosis (MS) or have a parent with MS and are planning to attend college in any state.
Eligibility This program is open to graduating high school seniors, recent graduates, and GED recipients from Minnesota who have MS or a parent who has MS. Applicants must be planning to enroll as a first-time student at a 2- or 4-year college, university, or vocational/technical school in the United States on at least a half-time basis. Along with their application, they must submit an essay on

the impact MS has had on their lives. Selection is based on that essay, academic record, leadership and participation in school or community activities, work experience, goals and aspirations, an outside appraisal, special circumstances, and financial need. U.S. citizenship or permanent resident status is required.

Financial data Stipends average approximately $2,000.

Duration 1 year.

Number awarded Varies each year; recently, 52 of these scholarships were awarded.

Deadline January of each year.

[1053]
MINNESOTA G.I. BILL PROGRAM

Minnesota Office of Higher Education
Attn: Manager of State Financial Aid Programs
1450 Energy Park Drive, Suite 350
St. Paul, MN 55108-5227
(651) 642-0567   Toll Free: (800) 657-3866
Fax: (651) 642-0675   TDD: (800) 627-3529
E-mail: Ginny.Dodds@state.mn.us
Web: www.ohe.state.mn.us

Summary To provide financial assistance for college or graduate school in the state to residents of Minnesota who served in the military after September 11, 2001 and the families of deceased or disabled military personnel.

Eligibility This program is open to residents of Minnesota enrolled at colleges and universities in the state as undergraduate or graduate students. Applicants must be 1) a veteran who is serving or has served honorably in a branch of the U.S. armed forces at any time on or after September 11, 2001; 2) a non-veteran who has served honorably for a total of 5 years or more cumulatively as a member of the Minnesota National Guard or other active or Reserve component of the U.S. armed forces, and any part of that service occurred on or after September 11, 2001; or 3) a surviving child or spouse of a person who has served in the military at any time on or after September 11, 2001 and who has died or has a total and permanent disability as a result of that military service. Financial need is also considered in the selection process.

Financial data The stipend is $1,000 per semester for full-time study or $500 per semester for part-time study.

Duration 1 year; may be renewed up to 4 additional years, provided the recipient continues to make satisfactory academic progress.

Additional data This program was established by the Minnesota Legislature in 2007.

Number awarded Varies each year.

Deadline Deadline not specified.

[1054]
MISSISSIPPI LAW ENFORCEMENT OFFICERS AND FIREMEN SCHOLARSHIP PROGRAM

Mississippi Office of Student Financial Aid
3825 Ridgewood Road
Jackson, MS 39211-6453
(601) 432-6997 Toll Free: (800) 327-2980 (within MS)
Fax: (601) 432-6527   E-mail: sfa@ihl.state.ms.us
Web: www.mississippi.edu

Summary To provide financial assistance to the spouses and children of disabled or deceased Mississippi law enforcement officers and fire fighters who are interested in attending college in the state.

Eligibility This program is open to children and spouses of law enforcement officers, full-time fire fighters, and volunteer fire fighters who became permanently and totally disabled or who died in the line of duty and were Mississippi residents at the time of death or injury. Applicants must be high school seniors or graduates interested in attending a state-supported postsecondary institution in Mississippi on a full-time basis. Children may be natural, adopted, or stepchildren up to 23 years of age; spouses may be of any age.

Financial data Students in this program receive full payment of tuition fees, the average cost of campus housing, required fees, and applicable course fees at state-supported colleges and universities in Mississippi. Funds may not be used to pay for books, food, school supplies, materials, dues, or fees for extracurricular activities.

Duration Up to 8 semesters.

Number awarded Varies each year.

Deadline September of each year.

[1055]
MISSOURI PUBLIC SERVICE OFFICER OR EMPLOYEE'S CHILD SURVIVOR GRANT PROGRAM

Missouri Department of Higher Education
Attn: Student Financial Assistance
3515 Amazonas Drive
Jefferson City, MO 65109-5717
(573) 751-2361   Toll Free: (800) 473-6757
Fax: (573) 751-6635   E-mail: info@dhe.mo.gov
Web: www.dhe.mo.gov/publicserviceofficer.shtml

Summary To provide financial assistance for college to 1) disabled and deceased Missouri public employees and public safety officers, and 2) their spouses and children.

Eligibility This program is open to residents of Missouri who are 1) public safety officers who were permanently disabled in the line of duty; 2) spouses of public safety officers who were permanently and totally disabled in the line of duty; or 3) children of Missouri public safety officers or Department of Transportation employees who were killed or permanently disabled while engaged in the construction or maintenance of highways, roads, and bridges. Applicants must be Missouri residents enrolled or accepted for enrollment as a full-time undergraduate student at a participating Missouri college or university; children must be younger than 24 years of age. Students working on a degree or certificate in theology or divinity are not eligible. U.S. citizenship or permanent resident status is required.

Financial data   The maximum annual grant is the lesser of 1) the actual tuition charged at the school where the recipient is enrolled, or 2) the amount of tuition charged to a Missouri undergraduate resident enrolled full time in the same class level and in the same academic major as an applicant at the University of Missouri at Columbia.

Duration   1 year; may be renewed.

Additional data   Public safety officers include fire fighters, police officers, capitol police officers, parole officers, probation officers, state correctional employees, water safety officers, conservation officers, park rangers, and highway patrolmen.

Number awarded   Varies each year; recently, 11 students received $47,045 in support from this program.

Deadline   There is no application deadline, but early submission of the completed application is encouraged.

[1056]
MOUSE HOLE SCHOLARSHIPS

Blind Mice Mart
16810 Pinemoor Way
Houston, TX 77058
(713) 883-7277   E-mail: blindmicemart@att.net
Web: www.blindmicemart.com

Summary   To provide financial assistance for college to blind students and the children of blind parents.

Eligibility   This program is open to visually impaired students and to sighted students who have visually impaired parents. Applicants must be high school seniors or graduates who have never been enrolled in college. Along with their application, they must submit an essay, between 3 and 15 pages in length, on a topic that changes annually; recently, students were asked to speculate on what will be happening to them in the following 10 years. Essays are judged on originality, creativity, grammar, spelling, and the judge's overall impression of the applicant.

Financial data   The maximum stipend is $1,250.

Duration   1 year.

Additional data   These scholarships were first awarded in 2003.

Number awarded   Varies each year; the program attempts to award 2 scholarships at $1,250 and others depending on the availability of funds. Recently, a total of $4,250 in scholarships were awarded.

Deadline   May of each year.

[1057]
NATIONAL AMPUTEE GOLF ASSOCIATION SCHOLARSHIP

National Amputee Golf Association
Attn: Scholarship Grant Program
11 Walnut Hill Road
Amherst, NH 03031
(603) 672-6444   Toll Free: (800) 633-NAGA
Fax: (603) 672-2987   E-mail: info@nagagolf.org
Web: www.nagagolf.org/scholarship1.shtml

Summary   To provide financial assistance for college to members of the National Amputee Golf Association and their dependents.

Eligibility   This program is open to amputee members in good standing in the association and their dependents. Applicants must submit information on their scholastic background (GPA in high school and college, courses of study); type of amputation and cause (if applicable), a cover letter describing their plans for the future; and documentation of financial need. They need not be competitive golfers. Selection is based on academic record, financial need, involvement in extracurricular or community activities, and area of study.

Financial data   The stipend for a 4-year bachelor's degree program is $2,000 per year. The stipend for a 2-year technical or associate degree is $1,000 per year.

Duration   Up to 4 years, provided the recipient maintains at least half-time enrollment and a GPA of 2.0 or higher and continues to demonstrate financial need.

Number awarded   1 or more each year.

Deadline   August of each year.

[1058]
NATIONAL CORNERSTONE HEALTHCARE SERVICES SCHOLARSHIPS

National Cornerstone Healthcare Services Inc
24747 Redlands Boulevard, Suite B
Loma Linda, CA 92354
Toll Free: (877) 616-6247   Fax: (877) 777-5717
E-mail: customerservice@nc-hs.com
Web: www.nc-hs.com

Summary   To provide financial assistance for college to people who have a bleeding disorder and members of their family.

Eligibility   This program is open to graduating high school seniors who are planning to attend an accredited technical school, college, or university. Applicants must have been diagnosed with a bleeding disorder or be the parent, spouse, partner, child, or sibling of a person with such a disorder. They must have a GPA of 2.5 or higher during their entire senior year of high school. Along with their application, they must submit a brief description of their dreams, goals, and objectives for attending postsecondary education. Financial need is not considered in the selection process.

Financial data   Stipends range from $500 to $1,000.

Duration   1 year.

Number awarded   1 or more each year.

Deadline   March of each year.

[1059]
NATIONAL GUARD ASSOCIATION OF INDIANA EDUCATIONAL GRANTS

National Guard Association of Indiana
Attn: Educational Grant Committee
2002 South Holt Road, Building 9
Indianapolis, IN 46241-4839
(317) 247-3196   Toll Free: (800) 219-2173
Fax: (317) 247-3575   E-mail: director@ngai.net
Web: ngai.net/index.php?main_page=page&id=16

Summary To provide financial assistance to members of the National Guard Association of Indiana (NGAI) and their dependents who plan to attend college in any state.

Eligibility This program is open to NGAI members who are currently serving in the Indiana National Guard and their dependents. Children and widow(er)s of former Guard members killed or permanently disabled while on duty with the Indiana National Guard are also eligible. Applicants must be attending or planning to attend a college or university in any state. Along with their application, they must submit 2 letters of recommendation, a copy of high school or college transcripts, SAT or ACT scores (if taken), a letter of acceptance from a college or university (if not currently attending college), and an essay on the educational program they intend to pursue and the goals they wish to attain. Selection is based on academic achievement, commitment and desire to achieve, extracurricular activities, accomplishments, goals, and financial need.

Financial data The stipend is $1,000.

Duration 1 year; recipients may reapply.

Number awarded A limited number are awarded each year.

Deadline February of each year.

[1060]
NATIONAL KIDNEY FOUNDATION SERVING CONNECTICUT SCHOLARSHIPS

National Kidney Foundation Serving Connecticut
2139 Silas Deane Highway, Suite 208
Rocky Hill, CT 06067-2337
(860) 257-3770   Toll Free: (800) 441-1280
Fax: (860) 257-3429   E-mail: nkfct@kidney.org
Web: www.kidneyct.org/site/index.cfm?ch=102

Summary To provide financial assistance to residents of Connecticut who are dialysis patients, kidney recipients or donors, or dependents of patients and interested in attending college in any state.

Eligibility This program is open to residents of Connecticut who are dialysis patients, transplant recipients, dependents of a dialysis or transplant patient, or living kidney donors. Applicants must be attending or planning to attend a 2- or 4-year college, university, or trade/technical school in any state. Along with their application, they must submit a 2-page essay on 1) establishing and working toward their goals; 2) how they stay motivated despite chronic illness; or 3) the transplant experience or the kidney donation experience. Selection is based on the essay, academic merit, extracurricular activities or community service, and financial need. For applicants who have been out of school

for many years, work or life experience may also be considered. U.S. citizenship is required.

Financial data The stipend is $1,000.

Duration 1 year.

Number awarded 3 each year.

Deadline May of each year.

[1061]
NATIONAL KIDNEY FOUNDATION SERVING MAINE SCHOLARSHIPS

National Kidney Foundation Serving Maine
c/o National Kidney Foundation Serving New England
85 Astor Avenue, Suite 2
Norwood, MA 02062-5040
(781) 278-0222   Toll Free: (800) 542-4001
Fax: (781) 278-0333   E-mail: nkfmarinhvt@kidney.org
Web: www.kidney.org/site/patients/index.cfm?ch=103

Summary To provide financial assistance to residents of Maine who are kidney patients or their family members and interested in attending college in any state.

Eligibility This program is open to residents of Maine who are kidney patients (dialysis patients, kidney transplant recipients, or newly diagnosed patients who are in early intervention programs) or immediate family members of patients. Applicants must be attending or planning to attend an accredited college or university in any state. Along with their application, they must submit documentation of financial need and brief essays on their educational goals and how kidney disease has impacted their life. Financial need is considered in the selection process.

Financial data A stipend is awarded (amount not specified).

Duration 1 year.

Number awarded Varies each year; recently, 7 of these scholarships were awarded.

Deadline July of each year.

[1062]
NATIONAL KIDNEY FOUNDATION SERVING NEW ENGLAND ACADEMIC AWARD

National Kidney Foundation Serving New England
Attn: Academic Awards Committee
85 Astor Avenue, Suite 2
Norwood, MA 02062-5040
(781) 278-0222   Toll Free: (800) 542-4001
Fax: (781) 278-0333   E-mail: nkfmarinhvt@kidney.org
Web: www.kidney.org/site/index.cfm?ch=105

Summary To provide financial assistance to high school seniors and graduates from New England who have kidney disease or are related to a person with kidney disease and are interested in attending college in any state.

Eligibility This program is open to high school seniors and graduates from Massachusetts, Rhode Island, New Hampshire, and Vermont who are planning to enroll at a college or university in any state. Applicants must have active and current kidney disease or be immediate relatives (parents, siblings, children, legal guardians) of a person with active and current kidney disease; the disease must have a significant impact on the applicant's life. Along with their application, they must submit a 1-page essay describing how the presence of kidney disease in their family has affected their life and education goals. Selection is based on academic achievement and financial need.

Financial data The stipend is $1,000. Funds are paid directly to the student.

Duration 1 year.

Number awarded 1 each year.

Deadline March of each year.

[1063]
NATIONAL MS SOCIETY SCHOLARSHIP PROGRAM

National Multiple Sclerosis Society
Attn: Scholarship Fund
900 South Broadway, Suite 200
Denver, CO 80209
(303) 698-6100, ext. 15102
E-mail: susan.goldsmith@nmss.org
Web: www.nationalMSsociety.org/scholarship

Summary To provide financial assistance for college to students who have Multiple Sclerosis (MS) or are the children of people with MS.

Eligibility This program is open to 1) high school seniors who have MS and will be attending an accredited postsecondary school for the first time; 2) high school seniors who are the children of people with MS and will be attending an accredited postsecondary school for the first time; 3) high school (or GED) graduates of any age who have MS and will be attending an accredited postsecondary school for the first time; and 4) high school (or GED) graduates of any age who have a parent with MS and will be attending an accredited postgraduate school for the first time. Applicants must be U.S. citizens or permanent residents who plan to enroll in an undergraduate course of study at an accredited 2- or 4-year college, university, or vocational/technical school in the United States to work on a degree, license, or certificate. Along with their application, they must submit a 1-page personal statement on the impact MS has had on their life. Selection is based on that statement, academic record, leadership and participation in school or community activities, work experience, goals and aspirations, an outside appraisal, special circumstances, and financial need. The 2 highest-ranked applicants are designated as the National MS Society Presidential Scholar and the National MS Society Mike Dugan Scholar.

Financial data Stipends range from $1,000 to $3,000 per year.

Duration 1 year; may be renewed.

Additional data This program, which began in 2003, is managed by ACT Scholarship and Recognition Services, 301 ACT Drive, P.O. Box 4030, Iowa City, IA 52243-4030, (877) 789-4228.

Number awarded Varies each year; recently, 510 of these scholarships (332 new awards and 178 renewals) with a value of $1,021,600 were awarded.

Deadline January of each year.

[1064]
NCFOP FOUNDATION SCHOLARSHIPS

North Carolina Fraternal Order of Police
Attn: NCFOB Foundation, Inc.
1500 Walnut Street
Cary, NC 27511-5927
(919) 461-4939   Toll Free: (877) 628-8063
E-mail: ncfop@nc.rr.com
Web: www.ncfop.com/ht/d/sp/i/204/pid/204

Summary To provide financial assistance for college to families of disabled or deceased law enforcement officers in North Carolina.

Eligibility This program is open to North Carolina residents who are enrolled in an appropriate postsecondary institution, including colleges and vocational schools. Applicants must be the child or spouse of a North Carolina law enforcement officer killed or disabled in the line of duty.

Financial data A stipend is awarded (amount not specified).

Duration 1 year.

Number awarded Varies each year; recently, 3 of these scholarships were awarded.

Deadline Deadline not specified.

[1065]
NEBRASKA CHAPTER NHF SCHOLARSHIPS

National Hemophilia Foundation-Nebraska Chapter
Attn: Scholarship Selection Committee
215 Centennial Mall South, Suite 512
Lincoln, NE 68508
(402) 742-5663   Fax: (402) 742-5677
E-mail: office@nebraskanhf.org
Web: www.nebraskanhf.org

Summary To provide financial assistance for attendance at a college in any state to high school seniors in Nebraska who have a bleeding disorder, are relatives of a person with a bleeding disorder, or are a carrier of a defective gene related to a bleeding disorder.

Eligibility This program is open to seniors graduating from high schools in Nebraska who plan to attend a college or university in any state. Applicants must have a bleeding disorder, be an immediately family member of a person with a bleeding disorder, or be the carrier of a defective gene related to a bleeding disorder. Along with their application, they must submit a brief statement on how a bleeding disorder influences their family life and a 250-word essay on their purpose and motivation for pursuing a postsecondary educational degree. Selection is based on that statement and essay, academic promise, and financial need. Preference is given to members of the Nebraska Chapter of the National Hemophilia Foundation (NHF).

Financial data The stipend ranges from $500 to $1,000.

Duration 1 year.

Number awarded 1 or more each year.

Deadline June of each year.

[1066]
NEBRASKA WAIVER OF TUITION FOR VETERANS' DEPENDENTS

Department of Veterans' Affairs
State Office Building
301 Centennial Mall South, Sixth Floor
P.O. Box 95083
Lincoln, NE 68509-5083
(402) 471-2458   Fax: (402) 471-2491
E-mail: john.hilgert@nebraska.gov
Web: www.vets.state.ne.us

Summary To provide financial assistance for college to dependents of deceased and disabled veterans and military personnel in Nebraska.

Eligibility Eligible are spouses, widow(er)s, and children who are residents of Nebraska and whose parent, stepparent, or spouse was a member of the U.S. armed forces and 1) died of a service-connected disability; 2) died subsequent to discharge as a result of injury or illness sustained while in service; 3) is permanently and totally disabled as a result of military service; or 4) is classified as missing in action or as a prisoner of war during armed hostilities after August 4, 1964. Applicants must be attending or planning to attend a branch of the University of Nebraska, a state college, or a community college in Nebraska.

Financial data Tuition is waived at public institutions in Nebraska.

Duration The waiver is valid for 1 degree, diploma, or certificate from a community college and 1 baccalaureate degree.

Additional data Applications may be submitted through 1 of the recognized veterans' organizations or any county service officer.

Number awarded Varies each year; recently, 311 of these grants were awarded.

Deadline Deadline not specified.

[1067]
NEW JERSEY BANKERS EDUCATION FOUNDATION SCHOLARSHIPS

New Jersey Bankers Association
Attn: New Jersey Bankers Education Foundation, Inc.
411 North Avenue East
Cranford, NJ 07016-2436
(908) 272-8500, ext. 614   Fax: (908) 272-6626
E-mail: j.meredith@njbankers.com
Web: www.njbankers.com

Summary To provide financial assistance to dependents of deceased and disabled military personnel who have a connection to New Jersey and are interested in attending college in any state.

Eligibility This program is open to the spouses, children, stepchildren, and grandchildren of members of the armed services who died or became disabled while on active duty; it is not required that the military person died in combat. Applicants must have a high school or equivalency diploma and be attending college in any state. Adult dependents who wish to obtain a high school equivalency

diploma are also eligible. Either the dependent or the servicemember must have a connection to New Jersey; the applicant's permanent address must be in New Jersey or the servicemember's last permanent address or military base must have been in the state. Financial need is considered in the selection process.

Financial data A stipend is awarded (amount not specified).

Duration 1 year; may be renewed if the recipient maintains a "C" average.

Additional data This program was established in 2005.

Number awarded 1 or more each year.

Deadline June of each year.

[1068]
NEW YORK STATE MILITARY SERVICE RECOGNITION SCHOLARSHIPS

New York State Higher Education Services
  Corporation
Attn: Student Information
99 Washington Avenue
Albany, NY 12255
(518) 473-1574   Toll Free: (888) NYS-HESC
Fax: (518) 473-3749   TDD: (800) 445-5234
E-mail: webmail@hesc.com
Web: www.hesc.com

Summary To provide financial assistance to disabled veterans and the family members of deceased or disabled veterans who are residents of New York and interested in attending college in the state.

Eligibility This program is open to New York residents who served in the armed forces of the United States or state organized militia at any time on or after August 2, 1990 and became severely and permanently disabled as a result of injury or illness suffered or incurred in a combat theater or combat zone or during military training operations in preparation for duty in a combat theater or combat zone of operations. Also eligible are the children, spouses, or financial dependents of members of the armed forces of the United States or state organized militia who at any time after August 2, 1990 1) died, became severely and permanently disabled as a result of injury or illness suffered or incurred, or are classified as missing in action in a combat theater or combat zone of operations, 2) died as a result of injuries incurred in those designated areas, or 3) died or became severely and permanently disabled as a result of injury or illness suffered or incurred during military training operations in preparation for duty in a combat theater or combat zone of operations. Applicants must be attending or accepted at an approved program of study as full-time undergraduates at a public college or university or private institution in New York.

Financial data At public colleges and universities, this program provides payment of actual tuition and mandatory educational fees; actual room and board charged to students living on campus or an allowance for room and board for commuter students; and allowances for books, supplies, and transportation. At private institutions, the award is equal to the amount charged at the State University of

New York (SUNY) for 4-year tuition and average mandatory fees (or the student's actual tuition and fees, whichever is less) plus allowances for room, board, books, supplies, and transportation.

Duration This program is available for 4 years of full-time undergraduate study (or 5 years in an approved 5-year bachelor's degree program).

Number awarded Varies each year.

Deadline April of each year.

[1069]
NEW YORK STATE WORLD TRADE CENTER MEMORIAL SCHOLARSHIPS

New York State Higher Education Services
  Corporation
Attn: Student Information
99 Washington Avenue
Albany, NY 12255
(518) 473-1574   Toll Free: (888) NYS-HESC
Fax: (518) 473-3749   TDD: (800) 445-5234
E-mail: webmail@hesc.com
Web: www.hesc.com

Summary To provide financial assistance to undergraduates in New York 1) who were killed or severely and permanently disabled as a result of the terrorist attacks on September 11, 2001 or 2) who are their relatives.

Eligibility This program is open to 1) the children, spouses, and financial dependents of deceased or severely and permanently disabled victims of the September 11, 2001 terrorist attacks or the subsequent rescue and recovery operations; and 2) survivors of the terrorist attacks who are severely and permanently disabled as a result of injuries sustained in the attacks or the subsequent rescue and recovery operations. Applicants must be attending or accepted at an approved program of study as full-time undergraduates at a public college or university or private institution in New York.

Financial data At public colleges and universities, this program provides payment of actual tuition and mandatory educational fees; actual room and board charged to students living on campus or an allowance for room and board for commuter students; and allowances for books, supplies, and transportation. At private institutions, the award is equal to the amount charged at the State University of New York (SUNY) for 4-year tuition and average mandatory fees (or the student's actual tuition and fees, whichever is less) plus allowances for room, board, books, supplies, and transportation.

Duration This program is available for 4 years of full-time undergraduate study (or 5 years in an approved 5-year bachelor's degree program).

Number awarded Varies each year.

Deadline April of each year.

[1070]
NORTH CAROLINA SCHOLARSHIPS FOR CHILDREN OF WAR VETERANS

Division of Veterans Affairs
Albemarle Building
325 North Salisbury Street, Suite 1065
Raleigh, NC 27603-5941
(919) 733-3851   Fax: (919) 733-2834
E-mail: ncdva.aso@ncmail.net
Web: www.doa.state.nc.us

Summary To provide financial assistance to the children of disabled and other classes of North Carolina veterans who plan to attend college in the state.

Eligibility Eligible applicants come from 5 categories: Class I-A: the veteran parent died in wartime service or as a result of a service-connected condition incurred in wartime service; Class I-B: the veteran parent is rated by the U.S. Department of Veterans Affairs (VA) as 100% disabled as a result of wartime service and currently or at the time of death was drawing compensation for such disability; Class II: the veteran parent is rated by the VA as much as 20% but less than 100% disabled due to wartime service, or was awarded a Purple Heart medal for wounds received, and currently or at the time of death drawing compensation for such disability; Class III: the veteran parent is currently or was at the time of death receiving a VA pension for total and permanent disability, or the veteran parent is deceased but does not qualify under any other provisions, or the veteran parent served in a combat zone or waters adjacent to a combat zone and received a campaign badge or medal but does not qualify under any other provisions; Class IV: the veteran parent was a prisoner of war or missing in action. For all classes, applicants must 1) be under 25 years of age and have a veteran parent who was a resident of North Carolina at the time of entrance into the armed forces; or 2) be the natural child, or adopted child prior to age 15, who was born in North Carolina, has been a resident of the state continuously since birth, and is the child of a veteran whose disabilities occurred during a period of war.

Financial data Students in Classes I-A, II, III, and IV receive $4,500 per academic year if they attend a private college or junior college; if attending a public postsecondary institution, they receive free tuition, a room allowance, a board allowance, and exemption from certain mandatory fees. Students in Class I-B receive $1,500 per academic year if they attend a private college or junior college; if attending a public postsecondary institution, they receive free tuition and exemption from certain mandatory fees.

Duration 4 academic years.

Number awarded An unlimited number of awards are made under Classes I-A, I-B, and IV. Classes II and III are limited to 100 awards each year in each class.

Deadline Applications for Classes I-A, I-B, and IV may be submitted at any time; applications for Classes II and III must be submitted by February of each year.

[1071]
NORTH CAROLINA SHERIFFS' ASSOCIATION UNDERGRADUATE CRIMINAL JUSTICE SCHOLARSHIPS

North Carolina State Education Assistance Authority
Attn: Grants, Training, and Outreach Department
10 T.W. Alexander Drive
P.O. Box 13663
Research Triangle Park, NC 27709-3663
(919) 549-8614   Toll Free: (800) 700-1775
Fax: (919) 248-4687 E-mail: information@ncseaa.edu
Web: www.ncseaa.edu/Ncsheriffs.htm

Summary To provide financial assistance to residents of North Carolina, especially children of deceased or disabled law enforcement officers, who are majoring in criminal justice at a college in the state.

Eligibility Eligible for this program are North Carolina residents enrolled full time in a criminal justice program at any of the 10 state institutions offering that major: Appalachian State University, East Carolina University, Elizabeth City State University, Fayetteville State University, North Carolina Central University, North Carolina State University, the University of North Carolina at Charlotte, the University of North Carolina at Pembroke, the University of North Carolina at Wilmington, and Western Carolina University. First priority in selection is given to children of law enforcement officers killed in the line of duty; second priority is given to children of sheriffs or deputy sheriffs who are deceased, retired (regular or disability), or currently active in law enforcement in North Carolina; third priority is given to other resident criminal justice students meeting their institution's academic and financial need criteria.

Financial data The stipend is $2,000 per year.

Duration 1 year; nonrenewable.

Additional data Funding for this program is provided by the North Carolina Sheriffs' Association. Recipients are selected by the financial aid office at the university they plan to attend or are currently attending; after selection, students obtain a letter of endorsement from the sheriff of the county in North Carolina where they reside.

Number awarded Up to 10 each year: 1 at each of the participating universities.

Deadline Deadline not specified.

[1072]
NORTH CAROLINA TROOPERS ASSOCIATION SCHOLARSHIPS

North Carolina Troopers Association
3505 Vernon Woods Drive
Summerfield, NC 27358
Toll Free: (800) 446-7334   Fax: (336) 644-6205
Web: www.nctroopers.org

Summary To provide financial assistance for college to children of members of the North Carolina Troopers Association (NCTA) and of disabled and deceased North Carolina Highway Patrol troopers.

Eligibility This program is open to dependent children between 10 and 23 years of age of active or deceased members of the NCTA. Applicants must be attending or planning to attend a university, college, community college, technical college, or trade school in North Carolina as a full-time student. Along with their application, they must submit an essay on how the scholarship will benefit them. Special applications are accepted from the children of disabled or deceased troopers of the North Carolina State Highway Patrol.

Financial data Stipends are $1,000 for students at 4-year colleges and universities or $500 for students at community, technical, and trade colleges.

Duration 1 year; may be renewed as long as the recipient remains enrolled full time with a grade average of "C" or higher.

Additional data This program includes the Colonel Bob Barefoot Scholarship for a student at a 4-year college or university and the Captain Ivan Stroud Scholarship for a student at a community college.

Number awarded 10 each year: 5 at $1,000 to students at 4-year institutions and 5 at $500 to students at 2-year institutions.

Deadline March of each year.

[1073]
NORTH CENTRAL CHAPTER MS SOCIETY SCHOLARSHIP PROGRAM

National Multiple Sclerosis Society-North Central
  Chapter
2508 South Carolyn Avenue
Sioux Falls, SD 57106
(605) 336-7017   Fax: (605) 336-8088
E-mail: nth@nmss.org
Web: was.nationalmssociety.org

Summary To provide financial assistance to high school seniors and graduates from Iowa, North Dakota, or South Dakota who have multiple sclerosis (MS) or have a parent with MS and are planning to attend college in any state.

Eligibility This program is open to graduating high school seniors, recent graduates, and GED recipients from Iowa, North Dakota, or South Dakota who have MS or a parent who has MS. Applicants must be planning to enroll as a first-time student at a 2- or 4-year college, university, or vocational/technical school in the United States on at least a half-time basis. Along with their application, they must submit an essay on the impact MS has had on their lives. Selection is based on that essay, academic record, leadership and participation in school or community activities, work experience, goals and aspirations, an outside appraisal, special circumstances, and financial need. U.S. citizenship or permanent resident status is required.

Financial data A stipend is awarded (amount not specified).

Duration 1 year.

Number awarded Varies each year; recently, 3 of these scholarships were awarded.

Deadline January of each year.

[1074]
NORTH DAKOTA EDUCATIONAL ASSISTANCE FOR DEPENDENTS OF VETERANS

Department of Veterans Affairs
4201 38th Street S.W., Suite 104
P.O. Box 9003
Fargo, ND 58106-9003
(701) 239-7165   Toll Free: (866) 634-8387
Fax: (701) 239-7166
Web: www.nd.gov/veterans/benefits/waiver.html

Summary To provide financial assistance for college to the spouses, widow(er)s, and children of disabled and other North Dakota veterans and military personnel.

Eligibility This program is open to the spouses, widow(er)s, and dependent children of veterans who are totally disabled as a result of service-connected causes, or who were killed in action, or who have died as a result of wounds or service-connected disabilities, or who were identified as prisoners of war or missing in action. Veteran parents must have been born in and lived in North Dakota until entrance into the armed forces (or must have resided in the state for at least 6 months prior to entrance into military service) and must have served during wartime.

Financial data Eligible dependents receive free tuition and are exempt from fees at any state-supported institution of higher education, technical school, or vocational school in North Dakota.

Duration Up to 45 months or 10 academic semesters.

Number awarded Varies each year.

Deadline Deadline not specified.

[1075]
OHIO WAR ORPHANS SCHOLARSHIP

Ohio Board of Regents
Attn: State Grants and Scholarships
30 East Broad Street, 36th Floor
Columbus, OH 43215-3414
(614) 752-9528   Toll Free: (888) 833-1133
Fax: (614) 466-5866
E-mail: jabdullah-simmons@regents.state.oh.us
Web: regents.ohio.gov/sgs/war_orphans

Summary To provide financial assistance to the children of deceased or disabled Ohio veterans who plan to attend college in the state.

Eligibility This program is open to residents of Ohio who are under 25 years of age and interested in enrolling full time at an eligible college or university in the state. Applicants must be the child of a veteran who 1) was a member of the U.S. armed forces, including the organized Reserves and Ohio National Guard, for a period of 90 days or more (or discharged because of a disability incurred after less than 90 days of service); 2) served during World War I, World War II, the Korean Conflict, the Vietnam era, or the Persian Gulf War; 3) entered service as a resident of Ohio; and 4) as a result of that service, either was killed or became at least 60% service-connected disabled. Also eligible are children of veterans who have a permanent and total non-service connected disability and are receiving disability benefits from the U.S. Department of Veterans

Affairs. If the veteran parent served only in the organized Reserves or Ohio National Guard, the parent must have been killed or became permanently and totally disabled while at a scheduled training assembly, field training period (of any duration or length), or active duty for training, pursuant to bona fide orders issued by a competent authority. Financial need is considered in the selection process.

Financial data At Ohio public colleges and universities, the program provides payment of 80% of tuition and fees. At Ohio private colleges and universities, the stipend is $4,400 per year (or 80% of the average amount paid to students attending public institutions).

Duration 1 year; may be renewed up to 4 additional years, provided the recipient maintains a GPA of 2.0 or higher.

Additional data Eligible institutions are Ohio state-assisted colleges and universities and Ohio institutions approved by the Board of Regents. This program was established in 1957.

Number awarded Varies, depending upon the funds available. If sufficient funds are available, all eligible applicants are given a scholarship. Recently, 861 students received benefits from this program.

Deadline June of each year.

[1076]
OKLAHOMA CHAPTER MS SOCIETY SCHOLARSHIP PROGRAM

National Multiple Sclerosis Society-Oklahoma Chapter
4606 East 67th Street, Building 7, Suite 103
Tulsa, OK 74136
(918) 488-0882   Fax: (918) 488-0913
E-mail: lisa.gray@oke.nmss.org
Web: was.nationalmssociety.org

Summary To provide financial assistance to high school seniors and graduates from Oklahoma who have multiple sclerosis (MS) or have a parent with MS and who are planning to attend college in any state.

Eligibility This program is open to graduating high school seniors, recent graduates, and GED recipients from Oklahoma who have MS or a parent who has MS. Applicants must be planning to enroll as a first-time student at a 2- or 4-year college, university, or vocational/technical school in the United States on at least a half-time basis. Along with their application, they must submit an essay on the impact MS has had on their lives. Selection is based on that essay, academic record, leadership and participation in school or community activities, work experience, goals and aspirations, an outside appraisal, special circumstances, and financial need. U.S. citizenship or permanent resident status is required.

Financial data Stipends range from $1,000 to $3,000.

Duration 1 year.

Additional data This program includes the Linda Chance Memorial Scholarship.

Number awarded Varies each year; recently, 14 of these scholarships were awarded.

Deadline January of each year.

[1077]
OPERATION ENDURING FREEDOM AND OPERATION IRAQI FREEDOM SCHOLARSHIP

Vermont Student Assistance Corporation
Attn: Scholarship Programs
10 East Allen Street
P.O. Box 2000
Winooski, VT 05404-2601
(802) 654-3798   Toll Free: (888) 253-4819
Fax: (802) 654-3765 TDD: (800) 281-3341 (within VT)
E-mail: info@vsac.org
Web: services.vsac.org

Summary To provide financial assistance for college to residents of Vermont whose parent has served or is serving in Operating Enduring Freedom in Afghanistan or Operation Iraqi Freedom.

Eligibility This program is open to residents of Vermont who are children of a member of any branch of the armed forces or National Guard whose residence or home of record is in Vermont. Applicants must plan to enroll full time in a certificate, associate degree, or bachelor's degree program at an accredited postsecondary school. The parent must have served or currently be serving in Operation Enduring Freedom or Operation Iraqi Freedom. Preference is given to applicants whose parent was killed, was wounded, or became permanently disabled as a result of their service. Along with their application, they must submit 1) a 100-word essay on any significant barriers that limit their access to education; and 2) a 250-word essay on their short- and long-term academic, educational, career, vocational, and/or employment goals. Selection is based on those essays, a letter of recommendation, and financial need.

Financial data The stipend ranges from $3,500 to $7,000 per year.

Duration 1 year; may be renewed up to 3 additional years.

Additional data These scholarships were first awarded in 2007.

Number awarded 1 or more each year.

Deadline June of each year.

[1078]
OREGON CHAPTER MS SOCIETY SCHOLARSHIP PROGRAM

National Multiple Sclerosis Society-Oregon Chapter
104 S.W. Clay Street
Portland, OR 97201
(503) 223-9511   Fax: (503) 223-2911
E-mail: info@defeatms.com
Web: was.nationalmssociety.org

Summary To provide financial assistance to high school seniors and graduates from Oregon who have multiple sclerosis (MS) or have a parent with MS and who are planning to attend college in any state.

Eligibility This program is open to graduating high school seniors, recent graduates, and GED recipients from Oregon who have MS or a parent who has MS. Applicants must be planning to enroll as a first-time student at a 2- or 4-year college, university, or vocational/technical school in the United States on at least a half-time basis. Along with their application, they must submit an essay on the impact MS has had on their lives. Selection is based on that essay, academic record, leadership and participation in school or community activities, work experience, goals and aspirations, an outside appraisal, special circumstances, and financial need. U.S. citizenship or permanent resident status is required.

Financial data Stipends range from $1,500 to $3,000.

Duration 1 year.

Number awarded Varies each year; recently, 4 of these scholarships were awarded.

Deadline January of each year.

[1079]
OREGON DECEASED OR DISABLED PUBLIC SAFETY OFFICER GRANT PROGRAM

Oregon Student Assistance Commission
Attn: Grants and Scholarships Division
1500 Valley River Drive, Suite 100
Eugene, OR 97401-2130
(541) 687-7466   Toll Free: (800) 452-8807, ext. 7466
Fax: (541) 687-7414   TDD: (800) 735-2900
E-mail: awardinfo@osac.state.or.us
Web: www.getcollegefunds.org

Summary To provide financial assistance for college or graduate school in the state to the children of disabled or deceased Oregon public safety officers.

Eligibility This program is open to the natural, adopted, or stepchildren of Oregon public safety officers (fire fighters, state fire marshals, chief deputy fire marshals, deputy state fire marshals, police chiefs, police officers, sheriffs, deputy sheriffs, county adult parole and probation officers, correction officers, and investigators of the Criminal Justice Division of the Department of Justice) who, in the line of duty, were killed or disabled. Applicants must be enrolled or planning to enroll as a full-time undergraduate student at a public or private college or university in Oregon. Children of deceased officers are also eligible for graduate study. Financial need must be demonstrated.

Financial data At a public 2- or 4-year college or university, the amount of the award is equal to the cost of tuition and fees. At an eligible private college, the award amount is equal to the cost of tuition and fees at the University of Oregon.

Duration 1 year; may be renewed for up to 3 additional years of undergraduate study, if the student maintains satisfactory academic progress and demonstrates continued financial need. Children of deceased public safety officers may receive support for 12 quarters of graduate study.

Number awarded Varies each year.

Deadline Deadline not specified.

[1080]
OREGON LEGION AUXILIARY DEPARTMENT NURSES SCHOLARSHIP

American Legion Auxiliary
Department of Oregon
30450 S.W. Parkway Avenue
P.O. Box 1730
Wilsonville, OR 97070-1730
(503) 682-3162   Fax: (503) 685-5008
E-mail: alaor@pcez.com

Summary To provide financial assistance to the wives, widows, and children of Oregon veterans who are interested in studying nursing at a school in any state.

Eligibility This program is open to Oregon residents who are the wives or children of veterans with disabilities or the widows of deceased veterans. Applicants must have been accepted by an accredited hospital or university school of nursing in any state. Selection is based on ability, aptitude, character, determination, seriousness of purpose, and financial need.

Financial data The stipend is $1,500.

Duration 1 year; may be renewed.

Number awarded 1 each year.

Deadline May of each year.

[1081]
OREGON LEGION AUXILIARY DEPARTMENT SCHOLARSHIPS

American Legion Auxiliary
Department of Oregon
30450 S.W. Parkway Avenue
P.O. Box 1730
Wilsonville, OR 97070-1730
(503) 682-3162   Fax: (503) 685-5008
E-mail: alaor@pcez.com

Summary To provide financial assistance to the dependents of Oregon veterans who are interested in attending college in any state.

Eligibility This program is open to Oregon residents who are children or wives of disabled veterans or widows of veterans. Applicants must be interested in obtaining education beyond the high school level at a college, university, business school, vocational school, or any other accredited postsecondary school in the state of Oregon. Selection is based on ability, aptitude, character, seriousness of purpose, and financial need.

Financial data The stipend is $1,000.

Duration 1 year; nonrenewable.

Number awarded 3 each year; 1 of these is to be used for vocational or business school.

Deadline March of each year.

[1082]
OREGON OCCUPATIONAL SAFETY AND HEALTH DIVISION WORKERS MEMORIAL SCHOLARSHIPS

Oregon Student Assistance Commission
Attn: Grants and Scholarships Division
1500 Valley River Drive, Suite 100
Eugene, OR 97401-2146
(541) 687-7395   Toll Free: (800) 452-8807, ext. 7395
Fax: (541) 687-7414   TDD: (800) 735-2900
E-mail: awardinfo@osac.state.or.us
Web: www.osac.state.or.us/osac_programs.html

Summary To provide financial assistance to the children and spouses of disabled or deceased workers in Oregon who are interested in attending college or graduate school in any state.

Eligibility This program is open to residents of Oregon who are U.S. citizens or permanent residents. Applicants must be high school seniors or graduates who 1) are dependents or spouses of an Oregon worker who has suffered permanent total disability on the job; or 2) are receiving, or have received, fatality benefits as dependents or spouses of a worker fatally injured in Oregon. They may be attending a college or graduate school in any state. Along with their application, they must submit an essay of up to 500 words on how the injury or death of their parent or spouse has affected or influenced their decision to further their education. Financial need is not required, but it is considered in the selection process.

Financial data Stipend amounts vary; recently, they were at least $4,786.

Duration 1 year.

Number awarded 1 or more each year.

Deadline February of each year.

[1083]
PARALYZED VETERANS OF AMERICA EDUCATIONAL SCHOLARSHIP PROGRAM

Paralyzed Veterans of America
Attn: Education and Training Foundation
801 18th Street, N.W.
Washington, DC 20006-3517
(202) 416-7651   Fax: (202) 416-7641
TDD: (202) 416-7622   E-mail: foundations@pva.org
Web: www.pva.org

Summary To provide financial assistance for college to members of the Paralyzed Veterans of America (PVA) and their families.

Eligibility This program is open to PVA members, spouses of members, and unmarried dependent children of members under 24 years of age. Applicants must be attending or planning to attend an accredited U.S. college or university. They must be U.S. citizens. Along with their application, they must submit a personal statement explaining why they wish to further their education, short- and long-term academic goals, how this will meet their career objectives, and how it will affect the PVA membership. Selection is based on that statement, academic records, letters of recommendation, and extracurricular and community activities.

Financial data Stipends are $1,000 for full-time students or $500 for part-time students.

Duration 1 year.

Additional data This program was established in 1986.

Number awarded Varies each year; recently 14 full-time and 3 part-time students received these scholarships. Since this program was established, it has awarded more than $300,000 in scholarships.

Deadline May of each year.

[1084]
PENNSYLVANIA EDUCATIONAL GRATUITY FOR VETERANS' DEPENDENTS

Office of the Deputy Adjutant General for Veterans
 Affairs
Building S-0-47, FTIG
Annville, PA 17003-5002
(717) 865-8910
Toll Free: (800) 54 PA VET (within PA)
Fax: (717) 861-8589   E-mail: jamebutler@state.pa.us
Web: www.milvet.state.pa.us/DMVA/201.htm

Summary To provide financial assistance for college to the children of disabled or deceased Pennsylvania veterans.

Eligibility This program is open to children (between 16 and 23 years of age) of honorably discharged veterans who are rated totally and permanently disabled as a result of wartime service or who have died of such a disability. Applicants must have lived in Pennsylvania for at least 5 years immediately preceding the date of application, be able to demonstrate financial need, and have been accepted or be currently enrolled in a Pennsylvania state or state-aided secondary or postsecondary educational institution.

Financial data The stipend is $500 per semester ($1,000 per year). The money is paid directly to the recipient's school and is to be applied to the costs of tuition, board, room, books, supplies, and/or matriculation fees.

Duration The allowance is paid for up to 4 academic years or for the duration of the course of study, whichever is less.

Number awarded Varies each year.

Deadline Deadline not specified.

[1085]
PENNSYLVANIA NATIONAL GUARD SCHOLARSHIP FUND

Pennsylvania National Guard Associations
Attn: Executive Director
Biddle Hall
Fort Indiantown Gap
Annville, PA 17003-5002
(717) 865-9631   Toll Free: (800) 997-8885
Fax: (717) 861-5560   E-mail: oswalddean@aol.com
Web: www.pngas.net/member.htm

Summary To provide financial assistance to Pennsylvania National Guard members and the children of disabled or deceased members who are interested in attending college in any state.

Eligibility This program is open to active members of the Pennsylvania Army or Air National Guard. Children of members of the Guard who died or were permanently disabled while on Guard duty are also eligible. Applicants must be entering their first year of higher education as a full-time student or presently attending a college or vocational school in any state as a full-time student. Along with their application, they must submit an essay that outlines their military and civilian plans for the future. Selection is based on that essay, academic achievement, leadership abilities, and contributions to citizenship.

Financial data Stipends are $1,000 or $400.

Duration 1 year.

Additional data The sponsoring organization includes the National Guard Association of Pennsylvania and the Pennsylvania National Guard Enlisted Association. This program began in 1977.

Number awarded 23 each year: 3 at $1,000 and 20 at $400.

Deadline June of each year.

[1086]
PENTAGON ASSISTANCE FUND

Navy-Marine Corps Relief Society
Attn: Education Division
875 North Randolph Street, Suite 225
Arlington, VA 22203-1757
(703) 696-4960   Fax: (703) 696-0144
E-mail: education@hq.nmcrs.org
Web: www.nmcrs.org/goldstar.html

Summary To provide financial assistance for college to the children and spouses of deceased military personnel who died at the Pentagon on September 11, 2001.

Eligibility This program is open to the children and spouses of deceased military personnel who died at the Pentagon as a result of the terrorist attack of September 11, 2001. Applicants must be enrolled or planning to enroll full time (spouses may enroll part time) at a college, university, or vocational/technical school. They must have a GPA of 2.0 or higher and be able to demonstrate financial need. Children must be 23 years of age or younger. Spouses may be eligible if the service member became disabled as a result of the attack.

Financial data Stipends range from $500 to $2,500 per year. Funds are disbursed directly to the financial institution.

Duration 1 year; may be renewed up to 3 additional years.

Number awarded Varies each year.

Deadline Children must apply by February of each year. Spouses must apply at least 2 months prior to the start of their studies.

[1087]
PINKROSE BREAST CANCER SCHOLARSHIP

PinkRose Foundation, Inc.
P.O. Box 4025
Dedham, MA 02027
E-mail: info@pinkrose.org
Web: www.pinkrose.org/scholarship.htm

Summary   To provide financial assistance for college to high school graduates who have lost a parent to breast cancer.

Eligibility   This program is open to legal residents of the United States who are younger than 25 years of age and have lost a parent or legal guardian to breast cancer. Applicants must have a high school diploma or equivalent and be planning to enroll in a postsecondary education or certificate training program. Along with their application, they must submit a 2-page statement that includes 1) autobiographical information describing the significant impact of breast cancer on their life and how it altered their academic motivation and interests, professional and volunteer experience, and career objectives; and 2) their interest in this scholarship, especially how obtaining a postsecondary degree or certificate will benefit their future by helping to fulfill their goals and dreams. Financial need is not considered in the selection process.

Financial data   A stipend is awarded (amount not specified).

Duration   1 year.

Number awarded   Varies each year.

Deadline   August of each year.

[1088]
PINNACOL FOUNDATION SCHOLARSHIP PROGRAM

Pinnacol Foundation
Attn: Elizabeth Starkey
7501 East Lowry Boulevard
Denver, CO 80230
(303) 361-4775   Toll Free: (800) 873-7248, ext. 4775
Fax: (303) 361-5775
E-mail: elizabeth.starkey@pinnacol.com
Web: www.pinnacol.com/foundation

Summary   To provide financial assistance to Colorado residents whose parent was killed or permanently disabled in a work-related accident and who are interested in attending college in any state.

Eligibility   This program is open to the natural, adopted, step, or fully dependent children of workers killed or permanently injured in a compensable work-related accident during the course and scope of employment with a Colorado-based employer and entitled to receive benefits under the Colorado Workers' Compensation Act. Applicants must be between 16 and 25 years of age and attending or planning to attend a college or technical school in any state. Selection is based on academic achievement and aptitude, community service, and financial need.

Financial data   The amount of the stipend depends on the need of the recipient.

Duration   1 year; may be renewed.

Additional data   Pinnacol Assurance, a workers' compensation insurance carrier, established this program in 2001. Students are eligible regardless of the insurance carrier for their parent's accident.

Number awarded   Varies each year; recently, 86 of these scholarships, with a value of $251,250, were awarded.

Deadline   March of each year.

[1089]
REMISSION OF FEES FOR CHILDREN OF INDIANA VETERANS

Indiana Department of Veterans' Affairs
302 West Washington Street, Room E-120
Indianapolis, IN 46204-2738
(317) 232-3910   Toll Free: (800) 400-4520 (within IN)
Fax: (317) 232-7721
Web: www.in.gov/dva/2378.htm

Summary   To enable the children of disabled and other Indiana veterans to attend public colleges and universities in the state without payment of tuition.

Eligibility   This program is open to natural and legally-adopted children of veterans who served on active duty in the U.S. armed forces during a period of wartime and have been residents of Indiana for at least 36 consecutive months during their lifetime. The veteran must 1) have sustained a service-connected disability as verified by the U.S. Department of Veterans Affairs or a military service; 2) have received a Purple Heart Medal; or 3) have been a resident of Indiana at the time of entry into the service and declared a prisoner of war (POW) or missing in action (MIA) after January 1, 1960. Students who were veteran-related pupils at the Indiana Soldiers' and Sailors' Children's Home are also eligible. Applicants must be attending or planning to attend a state-supported postsecondary college or university in Indiana as an undergraduate or graduate student.

Financial data   Qualified students receive remission of 100% of tuition and mandatory fees.

Duration   Fees are remitted for up to 124 semester hours of education.

Number awarded   Varies each year.

Deadline   Requests for assistance may be submitted at any time.

[1090]
RENEE FELDMAN SCHOLARSHIPS

Blinded Veterans Association Auxiliary
c/o Barbara Stocking, Scholarship Chair
3801 Coco Grove Avenue
Miami, FL 33133
(305) 446-8008

Summary   To provide financial assistance for college to spouses and children of blinded veterans.

Eligibility   This program is open to children and spouses of blinded veterans who are attending or planning to attend a college, university, community college, or vocational school. The veteran is not required to be a member of the Blinded Veterans Association. Applicants must submit a

300-word essay on their career goals and aspirations. Selection is based on that essay, academic achievement, and letters of reference.

Financial data Stipends are $2,000 or $1,000. Funds are paid directly to the recipient's school to be applied to tuition, books, and general fees.

Duration 1 year.

Number awarded 5 each year: 3 at $2,000 and 2 at $1,000.

Deadline April of each year.

[1091]
ROBYN KIMBERLY MEREDITH MULTIPLE SCLEROSIS MEMORIAL SCHOLARSHIP

National Multiple Sclerosis Society-Blue Ridge
Chapter
One Morton Drive, Suite 106
Charlottesville, VA 22903
(434) 971-8010   Toll Free: (800) 344-4867
Fax: (434) 979-4475   E-mail: vab@nmss.org
Web: was.nationalmssociety.org

Summary To provide financial assistance to high school seniors and current college students from the area served by the Blue Ridge Chapter of the National Multiple Sclerosis Society whose parent has multiple sclerosis (MS) and who are attending or planning to attend college in any state.

Eligibility This program is open to graduating high school seniors and current college students from 51 counties in western Virginia, eastern Kentucky, and the state or West Virginia who have a parent who has MS. Applicants must be planning to enroll as a first-time student at a 2- or 4-year college or university in the United States. Along with their application, they must submit a 2-page essay on their experiences growing up in a household in which a parent has MS, their goals for the future, what they plan as their major field of study, and any career plans they may have.

Financial data A stipend is awarded (amount not specified).

Duration 1 year.

Number awarded Varies each year.

Deadline Applications may be submitted at any time.

[1092]
SAD SACKS NURSING SCHOLARSHIP

AMVETS-Department of Illinois
2200 South Sixth Street
Springfield, IL 62703
(217) 528-4713 Toll Free: (800) 638-VETS (within IL)
Fax: (217) 528-9896
Web: www.ilamvets.org/prog_scholarships.cfm

Summary To provide financial assistance for nursing education to Illinois residents, especially descendants of disabled or deceased veterans.

Eligibility This program is open to seniors at high schools in Illinois who have been accepted to an approved nursing program and students already enrolled in an approved school of nursing in Illinois. Priority is given to dependents of deceased or disabled veterans. Selection is

based on academic record, character, interest and activity record, and financial need. Preference is given to students in the following order: third-year students, second-year students, and first-year students.

Financial data A stipend is awarded (amount not specified).

Duration 1 year.

Number awarded Varies each year; recently, 3 of these scholarships were awarded.

Deadline February of each year.

[1093]
SCHOLARSHIP PROGRAM OF THE COLORADO CHAPTER MS SOCIETY

National Multiple Sclerosis Society-Colorado Chapter
000 South Broadway, Second Floor
Denver, CO 80209
(303) 698-7400   Toll Free: (800) 344-4867
Fax: (303) 698-7421
E-mail: COCreceptionist@nmss.org
Web: was.nationalmssociety.org

Summary To provide financial assistance to high school seniors and graduates from Colorado who have multiple sclerosis (MS) or have a parent with MS and are planning to attend college in any state.

Eligibility This program is open to graduating high school seniors, recent graduates, and GED recipients from Colorado who have MS or a parent who has MS. Applicants must be planning to enroll as an undergraduate student at a 2- or 4-year college, university, or vocational/technical school in the United States on at least a half-time basis. Along with their application, they must submit an essay on the impact MS has had on their lives. Selection is based on that essay, academic record, leadership and participation in school or community activities, work experience, goals and aspirations, an outside appraisal, special circumstances, and financial need. U.S. citizenship or permanent resident status is required.

Financial data A stipend is awarded (amount not specified).

Duration 1 year.

Number awarded Varies each year; recently, 3 of these scholarships were awarded.

Deadline January of each year.

[1094]
SFM FOUNDATION SCHOLARSHIP

SFM Foundation
P.O. Box 582992
Minneapolis, MN 55458-2992
(952) 838-4200   Fax: (952) 838-2055
E-mail: foundation@sfmic.com
Web: www.sfmic.com

Summary To provide financial assistance to residents of Minnesota and Wisconsin whose parent was injured or killed in a work-related accident and who are interested in attending college, preferably in those state.

Eligibility This program is open to residents of Minnesota and Wisconsin between 16 and 25 years of age who are high school students, GED recipients, or high school graduates. Applicants must be the natural, adopted, or stepchild of a worker injured or killed in a work-related accident during the course and scope of employment with a Minnesota- or Wisconsin-based employer and entitled to receive benefits under the Minnesota Workers' Compensation Act or Worker's Compensation Act of Wisconsin. They must be planning to work on an associate or bachelor's degree or a certificate or license from any accredited school; preference is given to students attending institutions within the Minnesota State Colleges and Universities system or the University of Wisconsin Colleges system. Financial need is considered in the selection process.

Financial data Stipends range from $1,000 to $5,000 per year. Funds are paid directly to the educational institution.

Duration 1 year; may be renewed, provided the recipient maintains a GPA of 2.0 or higher.

Number awarded Varies each year.

Deadline March of each year.

[1095]
SOUTH CAROLINA TUITION PROGRAM FOR CHILDREN OF CERTAIN WAR VETERANS

South Carolina Division of Veterans Affairs
c/o VA Regional Office Building
6437 Garners Ferry Road, Suite 1126
Columbia, SC 29209
(803) 647-2434   Fax: (803) 647-2312
E-mail: va@oepp.sc.gov
Web: www.govoepp.state.sc.us/va/benefits.html

Summary To provide free college tuition to the children of disabled and other South Carolina veterans.

Eligibility This program is open to the children of wartime veterans who were legal residents of South Carolina both at the time of entry into military or naval service and during service, or who have been residents of South Carolina for at least 1 year. Veteran parents must 1) be permanently and totally disabled as determined by the U.S. Department of Veterans Affairs; 2) have been a prisoner of war; 3) have been killed in action; 4) have died from other causes while in service; 5) have died of a disease or disability resulting from service; 6) be currently missing in action; 7) have received the Congressional Medal of Honor; 8) have received the Purple Heart Medal from wounds received in combat; or 9) now be deceased but qualified under categories 1 or 2 above. The veteran's child must be 26 years of age or younger and working on an undergraduate degree.

Financial data Children who qualify are eligible for free tuition at any South Carolina state-supported college, university, or postsecondary technical education institution. The waiver applies to tuition only. The costs of room and board, certain fees, and books are not covered.

Duration Students are eligible to receive this support as long as they are younger than 26 years of age and working on an undergraduate degree.

Number awarded Varies each year.

Deadline Deadline not specified.

[1096]
STEVEN M. PEREZ FOUNDATION SCHOLARSHIPS

Steven M. Perez Foundation
P.O. Box 955
Melville, NY 11747
(631) 367-9016   Fax: (631) 367-3848
E-mail: info@smpfoundation.org
Web: www.smpfoundation.org

Summary To provide financial assistance for college to high school seniors who have survived leukemia or lost a family member to cancer or a related disease.

Eligibility This program is open to graduating high school seniors who have survived leukemia or who have lost a parent or sibling to cancer or a related disease. Applicants must be planning to attend a college or university in any state. Along with their application, they must submit medical certification, a recommendation from a counselor, and an essay that describes their connection to leukemia.

Financial data Stipend amounts vary; recently, they averaged $1,450.

Duration 1 year.

Number awarded Varies each year; recently, 10 of these scholarships were awarded.

Deadline April of each year.

[1097]
SURVIVORS' AND DEPENDENTS' EDUCATIONAL ASSISTANCE PROGRAM

Department of Veterans Affairs
Attn: Veterans Benefits Administration
810 Vermont Avenue, N.W.
Washington, DC 20420
(202) 418-4343   Toll Free: (888) GI-BILL1
Web: www.gibill.va.gov/GI_Bill_Info/benefits.htm

Summary To provide financial assistance for undergraduate or graduate study to children and spouses of deceased and disabled veterans, MIAs, and POWs.

Eligibility Eligible for this assistance are spouses and children of 1) veterans who died or are permanently and totally disabled as the result of active service in the armed forces; 2) veterans who died from any cause while rated permanently and totally disabled from a service-connected disability; 3) servicemembers listed as missing in action or captured in the line of duty by a hostile force; 4) servicemembers listed as forcibly detained or interned by a foreign government or power; and 5) servicemembers who are hospitalized or receiving outpatient treatment for a service-connected permanent and total disability and are likely to be discharged for that disability. Children must be between 18 and 26 years of age, although extensions may be granted. Spouses and children over 14 years of age with physical or mental disabilities are also eligible.

Financial data Monthly stipends from this program for study at an academic institution are $925 for full time, $694 for three-quarter time, or $461 for half-time. For farm cooperative work, the monthly stipends are $745 for full-time, $559 for three-quarter time, or $372 for half-time. For an apprenticeship or on-the-job training, the monthly stipend is $674 for the first 6 months, $505 for the second 6 months, $333 for the third 6 months, and $168 for the remainder of the program. For special restorative training by beneficiaries with a physical or mental disability, the monthly stipend for full-time training is $925.

Duration Up to 45 months (or the equivalent in part-time training). Spouses must complete their training within 10 years of the date they are first found eligible. For spouses of servicemembers who died on active duty, benefits end 20 years from the date of death.

Additional data Benefits may be used to work on associate, bachelor, or graduate degrees at colleges and universities, including independent study, cooperative training, and study abroad programs. Courses leading to a certificate or diploma from business, technical, or vocational schools may also be taken. Other eligible programs include apprenticeships, on-the-job training programs, farm cooperative courses, correspondence courses (for spouses only), secondary school programs (for recipients who are not high school graduates), tutorial assistance, remedial deficiency and refresher training, or work-study (for recipients who are enrolled at least three-quarter time). Eligible children who are handicapped by a physical or mental disability that prevents pursuit of an educational program may receive special restorative training that includes language retraining, lip reading, auditory training, Braille reading and writing, and similar programs. Eligible spouses and children over 14 years of age who are handicapped by a physical or mental disability that prevents pursuit of an educational program may receive specialized vocational training that includes specialized courses, alone or in combination with other courses, leading to a vocational objective that is suitable for the person and required by reason of physical or mental handicap. Ineligible courses include bartending; audited courses; non-accredited independent study courses; any course given by radio; self-improvement courses, such as reading, speaking, woodworking, basic seamanship, and English as a second language; audited courses; any course that is avocational or recreational in character; courses not leading to an educational, professional, or vocational objective; courses taken and successfully completed previously; courses taken by a federal government employee and paid for under the Government Employees' Training Act; and courses taken while in receipt of benefits for the same program from the Office of Workers' Compensation Programs.

Number awarded Varies each year.

Deadline Applications may be submitted at any time.

[1098]
TENNESSEE DEPENDENT CHILDREN SCHOLARSHIP

Tennessee Student Assistance Corporation
Parkway Towers
404 James Robertson Parkway, Suite 1510
Nashville, TN 37243-0820
(615) 741-1346   Toll Free: (800) 342-1663
Fax: (615) 741-6101   E-mail: TSAC.Aidinfo@tn.gov
Web: www.tn.gov

Summary To provide financial assistance to the dependent children of disabled or deceased Tennessee law enforcement officers, fire fighters, or emergency medical service technicians who plan to attend college in the state.

Eligibility This program is open to Tennessee residents who are the dependent children of a Tennessee law enforcement officer, fire fighter, or emergency medical service technician who was killed or totally and permanently disabled in the line of duty. Applicants must be enrolled or accepted for enrollment as a full-time undergraduate student at a college or university in Tennessee.

Financial data The award covers tuition and fees, books, supplies, and room and board, minus any other financial aid for which the student is eligible.

Duration 1 year; may be renewed for up to 3 additional years or until completion of a program of study.

Additional data This program was established in 1990.

Number awarded Varies each year; recently, 19 students received $77,786 in support from this program.

Deadline July of each year.

[1099]
TEXAS CHILDREN OF DISABLED OR DECEASED FIREMEN, PEACE OFFICERS, GAME WARDENS, AND EMPLOYEES OF CORRECTIONAL INSTITUTIONS EXEMPTION PROGRAM

Texas Higher Education Coordinating Board
Attn: Grants and Special Programs
1200 East Anderson Lane
P.O. Box 12788, Capitol Station
Austin, TX 78711-2788
(512) 427-6340   Toll Free: (800) 242-3062
Fax: (512) 427-6127
E-mail: grantinfo@thecb.state.tx.us
Web: www.collegeforalltexans.com

Summary To provide educational assistance to the children of disabled or deceased Texas fire fighters, peace officers, game wardens, and employees of correctional institutions.

Eligibility Eligible are children of Texas paid or volunteer fire fighters; paid municipal, county, or state peace officers; custodial employees of the Department of Corrections; or game wardens. The parent must have suffered an injury in the line of duty, resulting in disability or death. Applicants must be under 21 years of age.

Financial data Eligible students are exempted from the payment of all dues, fees, and tuition charges at publicly-supported colleges and universities in Texas.

Duration Support is provided for up to 120 semester credit hours of undergraduate study or until the recipient reaches 26 years of age, whichever comes first.

Number awarded Varies each year; recently, 140 students received support through this program.

Deadline Deadline not specified.

[1100]
TEXAS MUTUAL SCHOLARSHIP PROGRAM

Texas Mutual Insurance Company
Attn: Office of the President
6210 East Highway 290
Austin, TX 78723-1098
(512) 224-3820   Toll Free: (800) 859-5995, ext. 3820
Fax: (512) 224-3889   TDD: (800) 853-5339
E-mail: information@texasmutual.com
Web: www.texasmutual.com/workers/scholarship.shtm

Summary   To provide financial assistance for college to workers and their families covered by workers' compensation insurance in Texas.

Eligibility   This program is open to 1) employees who qualify for lifetime income benefits as a result of injuries suffered on the job as covered by the Texas Workers' Compensation Act; 2) children and spouses of injured workers; and 3) children and unremarried spouses of employees who died as a result of a work-related injury. Workers must be covered by the Texas Mutual Insurance Company, formerly the Texas Workers' Compensation Insurance Fund. Children must be between 16 and 25 years of age. Surviving spouses must still be eligible for workers' compensation benefits. Financial need is considered in the selection process.

Financial data   Scholarships are intended to cover normal undergraduate, technical, or vocational school tuition and fees, to a maximum of $4,000 per semester. Those funds are paid directly to the college or vocational school. The cost of course-related books and fees are also reimbursed, up to a maximum of $500 per semester. Those funds are paid directly to the student.

Duration   1 year; may be renewed if the recipient maintains a GPA of 2.5 or higher.

Number awarded   Varies each year.

Deadline   Applications may be submitted at any time.

[1101]
THROUGH THE LOOKING GLASS SCHOLARSHIPS

Through the Looking Glass
2198 Sixth Street, Suite 100
Berkeley, CA 94710-2204
(510) 848-1112   Toll Free: (800) 644-2666
Fax: (510) 848-4445   TDD: (510) 848-1005
E-mail: scholarships@lookingglass.org
Web: lookingglass.org/scholarships/index.php

Summary   To provide financial assistance for college to high school seniors who have a parent with a disability.

Eligibility   This program is open to graduating high school seniors and full-time college students who are 21 years of age or younger. Applicant must have at least 1 parent who has a disability. Along with their application, they must submit a 3-page essay describing the experience of growing up with a parent with a disability. Selection is based on that essay, academic performance, community service, and letters of recommendation; financial need is not considered.

Financial data   The stipend is $1,000.

Duration   1 year.

Number awarded   10 each year: 5 to high school seniors and 5 to college students.

Deadline   March of each year.

[1102]
TOBY WRIGHT SCHOLARSHIP FUND

Workers' Compensation Association of New Mexico
Attn: Brock Carter
P.O. Box 35757, Station D
Albuquerque, NM 87176
(505) 881-1112   Toll Free: (800) 640-0724
E-mail: brock@safetycounseling.com
Web: www.wcaofnm.com

Summary   To provide financial assistance for college to residents of New Mexico whose parent was permanently disabled or killed in an employment-related accident.

Eligibility   This program is open to residents of New Mexico between 16 and 25 years of age who attending or planning to attend a college, university, or trade school in the state. Applicants must have a parent who was permanently or catastrophically injured or killed in an employment-related accident that resulted in a New Mexico workers' compensation claim. The parent's death or injury must have resulted in a substantial decline in the family income.

Financial data   A stipend is awarded (amount not specified). Funds may be used for tuition, books, housing, meals, and course fees.

Duration   1 semester or quarter; may be renewed if the recipient maintains a GPA of 2.5 or higher and full-time enrollment.

Number awarded   Varies each year; recently, 8 of these scholarships were awarded.

Deadline   Deadline not specified.

[1103]
TRIO SCHOLARSHIPS

Transplant Recipients International Organization, Inc.
Attn: Scholarship Committee
2100 M Street, N.W., Suite 170-353
Washington, DC 20037-1233
(202) 293-0980   Toll Free: (800) TRIO-386
E-mail: info@trioweb.org
Web: www.trioweb.org

Summary   To provide financial assistance for college to members of the Transplant Recipients International Organization (TRIO) and their families.

Eligibility   This program is open to TRIO members and their immediate family who are organ or tissue candidates, recipients, donors, or their immediate family members. Applicants must be attending or planning to attend an accredited college, university, or trade/technical certificate program. They must have a cumulative GPA of 2.5 or higher and be able to demonstrate financial need. Along with their application, they must submit a 500-word essay on their personal history and educational and career ambitions.

Financial data   The stipend is $1,000.

Duration   1 year; nonrenewable.

Number awarded Several each year. Since the program was established 13 years ago, it has awarded 74 scholarships.

Deadline June of each year.

[1104]
TROY BARBOZA EDUCATIONAL FUND

Hawai'i Community Foundation
Attn: Scholarship Department
1164 Bishop Street, Suite 800
Honolulu, HI 96813
(808) 566-5570   Toll Free: (888) 731-3863
Fax: (808) 521-6286
E-mail: scholarships@hcf-hawaii.org
Web: www.hawaiicommunityfoundation.org

Summary To provide financial assistance for college to disabled public employees in Hawaii or their dependents.

Eligibility This program is open to 1) disabled public employees in Hawaii who were injured in the line of duty; 2) dependents or other immediate family members of public employees in Hawaii who were disabled or killed in the line of duty; and 3) private citizens who have performed a heroic act for the protection and welfare of others. The public employee must work or have worked in a job where lives are risked for the protection and safety of others. The injury must have left the employee incapacitated or incapable or continuing in his or her profession and must have occurred after October 22, 1987. Applicants must submit a short statement describing their course of study, career goals, outstanding attributes, talents, community service, family circumstances, and any other relevant information. Financial need is considered in the selection process.

Financial data The amount awarded varies, depending upon the needs of the recipient and the funds available.

Duration 1 year; scholarships for employees and their dependents may be renewed; scholarships for private citizens who have performed a heroic act are nonrenewable.

Additional data This program was established in 1991.

Number awarded 1 or more each year.

Deadline February of each year.

[1105]
UCB FAMILY EPILEPSY SCHOLARSHIP PROGRAM

UCB, Inc.
Family Scholarship Program
c/o Hudson Medical Communications
200 White Plains Road, Second Floor
Tarrytown, NY 10591
Toll Free: (866) 825-1920
E-mail: questions@hudsonmc.com
Web: www.ucbepilepsyscholarship.com

Summary To provide financial assistance for college or graduate school to epilepsy patients and their family members and caregivers.

Eligibility This program is open to epilepsy patients and their family members and caregivers. Applicants must be working on or planning to work on an undergraduate or graduate degree at an institution of higher education in the United States. They must be able to demonstrate academic achievement, a record of participation in activities outside of school, and service as a role model. Along with their application, they must submit a 1-page essay explaining why they should be selected for the scholarship, how epilepsy has impacted their life either as a patient or as a family member or caregiver, and how they will benefit from the scholarship. U.S. citizenship or permanent resident status is required.

Financial data The stipend is $5,000.

Duration 1 year; nonrenewable.

Additional data This program, previously known as the Keppra Family Epilepsy Scholarship Program, was established in 2004.

Number awarded 40 each year.

Deadline April of each year.

[1106]
UCB FAMILY RA SCHOLARSHIP PROGRAM

UCB, Inc.
8010 Arco Corporate Drive
Raleigh, NC 27617
(919) 567-3384   Fax: (919) 767-2570
Web: www.reachbeyondra.com/scholarship

Summary To provide financial assistance to undergraduate and graduate students who have rheumatoid arthritis (RA) and their families.

Eligibility This program is open to students who are either working on an associate, undergraduate, or graduate degree or are enrolled in a trade school educational program. Applicants must have been diagnosed with RA or be an immediate family member (parent, spouse, child, or sibling) of a person with RA. Along with their application, they must submit an essay of 1 to 2 pages describing how they are living beyond the boundaries of RA to demonstrate academic ambition and personal achievement and how the scholarship would impact their life.

Financial data Stipends range up to $10,000.

Duration 1 year; nonrenewable.

Additional data This program began on a pilot basis in 2008.

Number awarded 31 each year.

Deadline March of each year.

[1107]
UTAH HEMOPHILIA FOUNDATION SCHOLARSHIPS

Utah Hemophilia Foundation
772 East 3300 South, Suite 210
Salt Lake City, UT 84106
(801) 484-0325   Toll Free: (877) INFO-VWD
Fax: (801) 484-4177 E-mail: info@hemophiliautah.org
Web: www.hemophiliautah.org

Summary To provide financial assistance for attendance at a college in any state to residents of Utah who have a bleeding disorder and their families.

Eligibility This program is open to people in Utah with bleeding disorders and to their spouses, children, and parents. Applicants must be members of the bleeding disorders community served by the Utah Hemophilia Foundation and/or the Hemophilia Treatment Center in Salt Lake City. They must be attending or planning to attend a college, university, trade school, or technical program in any state.

Financial data Stipends range from $500 to $1,500.

Duration 1 year.

Number awarded Varies each year.

Deadline May of each year.

[1108]
VERA YIP MEMORIAL SCHOLARSHIP

Ulman Cancer Fund for Young Adults
Attn: Scholarship Committee Coordinator
4725 Dorsey Hall Drive, Suite A
PMB 505
Ellicott City, MD 21042
(410) 964-0202   Toll Free: (888) 393-FUND, ext. 103
E-mail: scholarship@ulmanfund.org
Web: www.ulmanfund.org/Default.aspx?tabid=329

Summary To provide financial assistance for college or graduate school to students from Washington, D.C., Maryland, or Virginia who either have or had cancer or have or have lost a parent to cancer.

Eligibility This program is open to students who either 1) have or had cancer, or 2) have or have lost a parent or guardian to cancer. Applicants must be residents of Washington, D.C., Maryland, or Virginia or attending college there. They must be 35 years of age or younger and attending, or planning to attend, a 2- or 4-year college, university, or vocational program to work on an undergraduate or graduate degree. Either they or their parent or guardian must have been diagnosed (including initial or secondary diagnosis, relapse, or active treatment) with cancer after they were 15 years of age. Along with their application, they must submit an essay of at least 1,000 words on how their cancer experience has shaped, changed, and/or reinforced the principles by which they live their life. Selection is based on demonstrated dedication to community service, commitment to educational and professional goals, use of their cancer experience to impact the lives of other young adults affected by cancer, medical hardship, and financial need.

Financial data The stipend is $2,500. Funds are paid directly to the educational institution.

Duration 1 year; nonrenewable.

Additional data Recipients must agree to complete 80 hours of community service.

Number awarded Varies each year; recently, 2 of these scholarships were awarded.

Deadline April of each year.

[1109]
VIRGIN ISLAND NATIONAL GUARD GRANTS

Virgin Islands Board of Education
Dronningen Gade 60B, 61, and 62
P.O. Box 11900
St. Thomas, VI 00801
(340) 774-4546   Fax: (340) 774-3384
E-mail: stt@myviboe.com
Web: myviboe.com

Summary To provide financial assistance to the children of deceased or disabled members of the Virgin Islands National Guard who wish to attend a college in the territory or on the mainland.

Eligibility This program is open to children under 25 years of age of members of the National Guard of the Virgin Islands who have died or sustained permanent and total disability in the line of official duty while on territorial active military duty, federal active duty, or training duty. Applicants must have a GPA of 2.0 or higher and be attending or accepted for enrollment at an accredited institution of higher learning in the territory or on the mainland. They may be planning to major in any field. Financial need is considered in the selection process.

Financial data The stipend is $2,000 per year.

Duration 1 year; may be renewed up to 3 additional years.

Additional data This program is offered as part of the Special Legislative Grants of the Virgin Islands Board of Education.

Number awarded 1 or more each year.

Deadline April of each year.

[1110]
VIRGINIA MILITARY SURVIVORS AND DEPENDENTS EDUCATION PROGRAM

Virginia Department of Veterans Services
270 Franklin Road, S.W., Room 503
Roanoke, VA 24011-2215
(540) 857-7101   Fax: (540) 857-7573
Web: www.dvs.virginia.gov/statebenefits.htm

Summary To provide educational assistance to the children and spouses of disabled and other Virginia veterans or service personnel.

Eligibility This program is open to residents of Virginia whose parent or spouse served in the U.S. armed forces (including the Reserves, the Virginia National Guard, or the Virginia National Guard Reserves) during any armed conflict subsequent to December 6, 1941, as a result of a terrorist act, during military operations against terrorism, or on a peacekeeping mission. The veterans must be at least 90% disabled due to an injury or disease incurred as a result of such service, has died, or is listed as a prisoner of war or missing in action. Applicants must have been accepted at a public college or university in Virginia as an undergraduate or graduate student. Children must be between 16 and 29 years of age; there are no age restrictions for spouses. The veteran must have been a resident of Virginia at the time of entry into active military service or for at least 5 consecutive years immediately prior to the date of application or death. The surviving spouse must have been a resident of Virginia for at least 5 years prior to marrying the veteran or for at least 5 years immediately prior to the date on which the application was submitted.

Financial data The maximum allowable stipend is $1,500 per year, but current funding is set at a maximum of $1,350, payable at the rate of $675 per term for full-time students, $450 per term for students enrolled at least half time but less than full time, or $225 per term for students enrolled less than half time.

Duration Entitlement extends to a maximum of 48 months.

Additional data Individuals entitled to this benefit may use it to pursue any vocational, technical, undergraduate, or graduate program of instruction. Generally, programs listed in the academic catalogs of state-supported institutions are acceptable, provided they have a clearly-defined educational objective (such as a certificate, diploma, or degree). This program was formerly known as the Virginia War Orphans Education Program.

Number awarded Varies each year; recently, funding allowed for a total of 740 of these awards.

Deadline Deadline not specified.

[1111]
WISCONSIN CHAPTER MS SOCIETY SCHOLARSHIP PROGRAM

National Multiple Sclerosis Society-Wisconsin Chapter
Attn: Scholarship Program
1120 James Drive, Suite A
Hartland, WI 53029
(262) 369-4420   Toll Free: (800) 242-3358 (within WI)
Fax: (262) 369-4410
E-mail: Meghan.schnabl@wisMS.org
Web: was.nationalmssociety.org

Summary To provide financial assistance to high school seniors and graduates from Wisconsin who have multiple sclerosis (MS) or have a parent with MS and are planning to attend college in any state.

Eligibility This program is open to graduating high school seniors, recent graduates, and GED recipients from Wisconsin who have MS or a parent who has MS. Applicants must be planning to enroll as a first-time student at a 2- or 4-year college, university, or vocational/technical school in the United States on at least a half-time basis. Along with their application, they must submit an essay on the impact MS has had on their lives. Selection is based on that essay, academic record, leadership and participation in school or community activities, work experience, goals and aspirations, an outside appraisal, special circumstances, and financial need. U.S. citizenship or permanent resident status is required.

Financial data Stipends average approximately $1,500.

Duration 1 year.

Number awarded Varies each year; recently, 30 of these scholarships were awarded.

Deadline January of each year.

[1112]
WISCONSIN G.I. BILL TUITION REMISSION PROGRAM

Wisconsin Department of Veterans Affairs
30 West Mifflin Street
P.O. Box 7843
Madison, WI 53707-7843
(608) 266-1311   Toll Free: (800) WIS-VETS
Fax: (608) 267-0403
E-mail: WDVAInfo@dva.state.wi.us
Web: www.dva.state.wi.us/Ben_education.asp

Summary To provide financial assistance for college or graduate school to Wisconsin veterans and their dependents.

Eligibility This program is open to current residents of Wisconsin who 1) were residents of the state when they entered or reentered active duty in the U.S. armed forces, or 2) have moved to the state and have been residents for any consecutive 12-month period after entry or reentry into service. Applicants must have served on active duty for at least 2 continuous years or for at least 90 days during specified wartime periods. Also eligible are 1) qualifying children and unremarried surviving spouses of Wisconsin veterans who died in the line of duty or as the direct result of a service-connected disability; and 2) children and spouses of Wisconsin veterans who have a service-connected disability rated by the U.S. Department of Veterans Affairs as 30% or greater. Children must be between 17 and 25 years of age (regardless of the date of the veteran's death or initial disability rating) and be a Wisconsin resident for tuition purposes. Spouses remain eligible for 10 years following the date of the veteran's death or initial disability rating; they must be Wisconsin residents for tuition purposes but they may enroll full or part time. Students may attend any institution, center, or school within the University of Wisconsin (UW) System or the Wisconsin Technical College System (WCTS). There are no income limits, delimiting periods following military service during which the benefit must be used, or limits on the level of study (e.g., vocational, undergraduate, professional, or graduate).

Financial data Veterans who qualify as a Wisconsin resident for tuition purposes are eligible for a remission of 100% of standard academic fees and segregated fees at a UW campus or 100% of program and material fees at a WCTS institution. Veterans who qualify as a Wisconsin veteran for purposes of this program but for other reasons fail to meet the definition of a Wisconsin resident for tuition purposes at the UW system are eligible for a remission of 100% of non-resident fees. Spouses and children of deceased or disabled veterans are entitled to a remission of 100% of tuition and fees at a UW or WCTS institution.

Duration Up to 8 semesters or 128 credits, whichever is greater.

Additional data This program was established in 2005 as a replacement for Wisconsin Tuition and Fee Reimbursement Grants.

Number awarded   Varies each year.

Deadline   Applications must be submitted within 14 days from the office start of the academic term: in October for fall, March for spring, or June for summer.

[1113]
YANCEY SCHOLARSHIP

Disabled American Veterans-Department of New Jersey
135 West Hanover Street, Fourth Floor
Trenton, NJ 08618
(609) 396-2885   Fax: (609) 396-9562
Web: www.davnj.org

Summary   To provide financial assistance to the children and grandchildren of members of the Disabled American Veterans in New Jersey who are interested in attending college in any state.

Eligibility   This program is open to graduating high school seniors who are the child or grandchild of a member of the Disabled American Veterans in New Jersey. Applicants must be planning to attend a college or university in any state. Along with their application, they must submit 1) letters of recommendation; 2) a transcript that includes information on their GPA, SAT scores, and class rank; and 3) a 500-word article on a topic that changes regularly (recently, students were asked to present their opinion on the war in Iraq). Selection is based on character (20%), Americanism and community service (20%), leadership (20%), scholarship (20%), and need (20%).

Financial data   The stipend is $1,000.

Duration   1 year; nonrenewable.

Number awarded   1 each year.

Deadline   March of each year.

Fellowship/Grants

[1114]
ALABAMA G.I. DEPENDENTS' SCHOLARSHIP PROGRAM

Alabama Department of Veterans Affairs
770 Washington Avenue, Suite 530
Montgomery, AL 36102-1509
(334) 242-5077   Fax: (334) 242-5102
E-mail: willie.moore@va.state.al.us
Web: www.va.state.al.us/scholarship.htm

Summary   To provide educational benefits to the dependents of disabled, deceased, and other Alabama veterans.

Eligibility   Eligible are spouses, children, stepchildren, and unremarried widow(er)s of veterans who served honorably for 90 days or more and 1) are currently rated as 20% or more service-connected disabled or were so rated at time of death; 2) were a former prisoner of war; 3) have been declared missing in action; 4) died as the result of a service-connected disability; or 5) died while on active mili-

tary duty in the line of duty. The veteran must have been a permanent civilian resident of Alabama for at least 1 year prior to entering active military service; veterans who were not Alabama residents at the time of entering active military service may also qualify if they have a 100% disability and were permanent residents of Alabama for at least 5 years prior to filing the application for this program or prior to death, if deceased. Children and stepchildren must be under the age of 26, but spouses and unremarried widow(er)s may be of any age.

Financial data   Eligible dependents may attend any state-supported Alabama institution of higher learning or enroll in a prescribed course of study at any Alabama state-supported trade school without payment of any tuition, book fees, or laboratory charges.

Duration   This is an entitlement program for 4 years of full-time undergraduate or graduate study or part-time equivalent. Spouses and unremarried widow(er)s whose veteran spouse is rated between 20% and 90% disabled, or 100% disabled but not permanently so, may attend only 2 standard academic years.

Additional data   Benefits for children, spouses, and unremarried widow(er)s are available in addition to federal government benefits. Assistance is not provided for non-credit courses, placement testing, GED preparation, continuing educational courses, pre-technical courses, or state board examinations.

Number awarded   Varies each year.

Deadline   Applications may be submitted at any time.

[1115]
BARBARA PALO FOSTER MEMORIAL SCHOLARSHIP

Ulman Cancer Fund for Young Adults
Attn: Scholarship Program Coordinator
10440 Little Patuxent Parkway, Suite 1G
Columbia, MD 21044
(410) 964-0202, ext. 106   Toll Free: (888) 393-FUND
E-mail: scholarship@ulmanfund.org
Web: www.ulmanfund.org

Summary   To provide financial assistance to undergraduate and graduate nursing students who have a parent with cancer.

Eligibility   This program is open to nursing students who have or have lost a parent to cancer. Applicants must be younger than 35 years of age and enrolled in, or planning to enroll in, an undergraduate or graduate program in nursing. They must demonstrate an interest in furthering patient education, focusing on persons from medically underserved communities and/or women's health issues. Along with their application, they must submit an essay of at least 1,000 words on they ways in which their experiences as a member of a marginalized group within the cancer community (i.e., young adults affected by cancer) have taught them lessons that inspire them to be of service to other socially, politically, and or economically marginalized people in the healthcare system. Selection is based on demonstrated dedication to community service, commitment to educational and professional goals, use of their cancer experience to impact the lives of other young adults affected by cancer, medical hardship, and financial need.

Financial data The stipend is $2,500. Funds are paid directly to the educational institution.

Duration 1 year; nonrenewable.

Additional data Recipients must agree to complete 50 hours of community service.

Number awarded 1 each year.

Deadline April of each year.

[1116]
BRYON RIESCH SCHOLARSHIPS

Bryon Riesch Paralysis Foundation
P.O. Box 1388
Waukesha, WI 53187-1388
(262) 547-2083   E-mail: info@brpf.org
Web: www.brpf.org/scholarships.htm

Summary To provide financial assistance to 1) undergraduate and graduate students who have a neurological disability or 2) the children of people with such a disability.

Eligibility This program is open to students entering or enrolled at a 2- or 4-year college or university as an undergraduate or graduate student. Applicants must have a neurological disability or be the child of a person with such a disability. They must have a GPA of 2.5 or higher in high school or college. Along with their application, they must submit a 200-word essay on why they deserve the scholarship, a statement of their 5- and 10-year goals, and a list of work experience. Financial need is not considered in the selection process.

Financial data Stipends range from $1,000 to $2,000.

Duration 1 year; may be renewed.

Number awarded 2 to 3 each semester.

Deadline June of each year for fall semester; December of each year for spring semester.

[1117]
DEPARTMENT OF HOMELAND SECURITY SMALL BUSINESS INNOVATION RESEARCH GRANTS

Department of Homeland Security
Homeland Security Advanced Research Projects
  Agency
Attn: SBIR Program Manager
Washington, DC 20528
(202) 254-6768   Toll Free: (800) 754-3043
Fax: (202) 254-7170
E-mail: elissa.sobolewski@dhs.gov
Web: www.dhs.gov

Summary To support small businesses (especially those owned by minorities, disabled veterans, and women) that have the technological expertise to contribute to the research and development mission of the Department of Homeland Security (DHS).

Eligibility For the purposes of this program, a "small business" is defined as a firm that is organized for profit with a location in the United States; is in the legal form of an individual proprietorship, partnership, limited liability company, corporation, joint venture, association, trust, or cooperative; is at least 51% owned and controlled by 1 or more individuals who are citizens or permanent residents of the United States; and has (including its affiliates) fewer than 500 employees. The primary employment of the principal investigator must be with the firm at the time of award and during the conduct of the proposed project. Preference is given to women-owned small business concerns, service-disabled veteran small business concerns, veteran small business concerns, and socially and economically disadvantaged small business concerns. Women-owned small business concerns are those that are at least 51% owned by a woman or women who also control and operate them. Service-disabled veteran small business concerns are those that are at least 51% owned by a service-disabled veteran and controlled by such a veteran or (for veterans with permanent and severe disability) the spouse or permanent caregiver of such a veteran. Veteran small business concerns are those that are at least 51% owned by a veteran or veterans who also control and manage them. Socially and economically disadvantaged small business concerns are at least 51% owned by an Indian tribe, a Native Hawaiian organization, a Community Development Corporation, or 1 or more socially and economically disadvantaged individuals (African Americans, Hispanic Americans, Native Americans, Asian Pacific Americans, or subcontinent Asian Americans). The project must be performed in the United States. Currently, DHS has 7 research priorities: explosives; border and maritime security; command, control, and interoperability; human factors; infrastructure and geophysical; chemical and biological; and domestic nuclear detection. Selection is based on the soundness, technical merit, and innovation of the proposed approach and its incremental progress toward topic or subtopic solution; the qualifications of the proposed principal investigators, supporting staff, and consultants; and the potential for commercial application and the benefits expected to accrue from this commercialization.

Financial data Grants are offered in 2 phases. In phase 1, awards normally range up to $100,000 (or $150,000 for domestic nuclear detection); in phase 2, awards normally range up to $750,000 (or $1,000,000 for domestic nuclear detection).

Duration Phase 1 awards may extend up to 6 months; phase 2 awards may extend up to 2 years.

Number awarded Varies each year. Recently, 61 Phase 1 awards were granted.

Deadline February of each year.

[1118]
EDWARD T. CONROY MEMORIAL SCHOLARSHIP PROGRAM

Maryland Higher Education Commission
Attn: Office of Student Financial Assistance
839 Bestgate Road, Suite 400
Annapolis, MD 21401-3013
(410) 260-4563   Toll Free: (800) 974-1024, ext. 4563
Fax: (410) 260-3200   TDD: (800) 735-2258
E-mail: lasplin@mhec.state.md.us
Web: www.mhec.state.md.us

Summary To provide financial assistance for college or graduate school in Maryland to children and spouses of victims of the September 11, 2001 terrorist attacks and to specified categories of veterans, public safety employees, and their children or spouses.
Eligibility This program is open to entering and continuing undergraduate and graduate students in the following categories: 1) children and surviving spouses of victims of the September 11, 2001 terrorist attacks who died in the World Trade Center in New York City, the Pentagon in Virginia, or United Airlines Flight 93 in Pennsylvania; 2) veterans who have, as a direct result of military service, a disability of 25% or greater and have exhausted or are no longer eligible for federal veterans' educational benefits; 3) children of armed forces members whose death or 100% disability was directly caused by military service; 4) POW/MIA veterans of the Vietnam Conflict and their children; 5) state or local public safety officers or volunteers who became 100% disabled in the line of duty; and 6) children and unremarried surviving spouses of state or local public safety employees or volunteers who died or became 100% disabled in the line of duty. The parent, spouse, veteran, POW, or public safety officer or volunteer must have been a resident of Maryland at the time of death or when declared disabled. Financial need is not considered.
Financial data The amount of the award is equal to tuition and fees at a Maryland postsecondary institution, to a maximum of $19,000 for children and spouses of the September 11 terrorist attacks or $9,000 for all other recipients.
Duration Up to 5 years of full-time study or 8 years of part-time study.
Additional data Recipients must enroll at a 2-year or 4-year Maryland college or university as a full-time or part-time degree-seeking undergraduate or graduate student or attend a private career school.
Number awarded Varies each year.
Deadline July of each year.

[1119]
GEORGE AND LINDA PRICE SCHOLARSHIP

Hemophilia Association of the Capital Area
10560 Main Street, Suite PH-4
Fairfax, VA 22030-7182
(703) 352-7641   Fax: (703) 352-2145
E-mail: info@hacacares.org
Web: www.hacacares.org

Summary To provide financial assistance to individuals with bleeding disorders and their families who are members of the Hemophilia Association of the Capital Area (HACA) and interested in attending college or graduate school in any state.
Eligibility This program is open to residents of northern Virginia, Montgomery and Prince George's County in Maryland, and Washington, D.C. who have a bleeding disorder and their siblings and parents. Applicants must be members of HACA. They must be 1) high school seniors or graduates who have not yet attended college; 2) full-time freshmen, sophomores, or juniors at a college, university, or vocational/technical school in any state; or 3) college seniors planning to attend graduate school and students already enrolled at a graduate school in any state. Along with their application, they must submit a 500-word essay on what they have done to contribute to the bleeding disorders community and how they plan to contribute to that community in the future. Financial need is not considered in the selection process.
Financial data The stipend is $2,500.
Duration 1 year; recipients may reapply.
Number awarded 2 each year.
Deadline April of each year.

[1120]
GEORGIA COUNCIL OF THE BLIND SCHOLARSHIPS

Georgia Council of the Blind
850 Gaines School Road
Athens, GA 30605
Toll Free: (877) 667-6815
E-mail: marshafarrow@alltel.net
Web: www.georgiacounciloftheblind.org

Summary To provide financial assistance students in Georgia who plan to attend college or graduate school in any state and are either legally blind or have legally blind parents.
Eligibility This program is open to residents of Georgia who are either 1) legally blind students, or 2) sighted students financially dependent on legally blind parents. Applicants must be enrolled or accepted for enrollment at a vocational/technical school, a 2-year or 4-year college, or a master's or doctoral program in any state. All fields of study are eligible. Selection is based on academic transcripts, 2 letters of recommendation, a 1-page typed statement of the applicant's educational goals, an audio cassette recording of the applicant reading the goals statement, extracurricular activities, and financial need.
Financial data Stipends up to $1,000 per year are available.
Duration 1 year; recipients may reapply.
Additional data This program began in 1988.
Number awarded 1 or more each year.
Deadline June of each year.

[1121]
ILLINOIS GRANT PROGRAM FOR DEPENDENTS OF POLICE OR FIRE OFFICERS

Illinois Student Assistance Commission
Attn: Scholarship and Grant Services
1755 Lake Cook Road
Deerfield, IL 60015-5209
(847) 948-8550   Toll Free: (800) 899-ISAC
Fax: (847) 831-8549   TDD: (800) 526-0844
E-mail: collegezone@isac.org
Web: www.collegezone.com/studentzone/407_633.htm

Summary To provide financial assistance to the children or spouses of disabled or deceased Illinois police or fire officers who plan to attend college or graduate school in the state.

Eligibility This program is open to the spouses and children of Illinois police and fire officers who were at least 90% disabled or killed in the line of duty. Applicants must be enrolled on at least a half-time basis in either undergraduate or graduate study at an approved Illinois public or private 2-year or 4-year college, university, or hospital school. They need not be Illinois residents at the time of application. U.S. citizenship or eligible non-citizen status is required.

Financial data The grants provide full payment of tuition and mandatory fees at approved public colleges in Illinois or an equivalent amount at private colleges.

Duration Up to 8 academic semesters or 12 academic quarters of study.

Number awarded Varies each year.

Deadline September of each year for the academic year; February of each year for spring semester or winter or spring quarter; June of each year for summer term.

[1122]
INDIANA CHILD OF VETERAN AND PUBLIC SAFETY OFFICER SUPPLEMENTAL GRANT PROGRAM

State Student Assistance Commission of Indiana
Attn: Grant Division
150 West Market Street, Suite 500
Indianapolis, IN 46204-2811
(317) 232-2350   Toll Free: (888) 528-4719 (within IN)
Fax: (317) 232-3260   E-mail: grants@ssaci.state.in.us
Web: www.in.gov/ssaci/2338.htm

Summary To provide financial assistance to residents of Indiana who are the children or spouses of specified categories of deceased or disabled veterans or public safety officers and interested in attending college or graduate school in the state.

Eligibility This program is open to 1) children of disabled Indiana veterans; 2) children and spouses of members of the Indiana National Guard killed while serving on state active duty; and 3) children and spouses of Indiana public safety officers killed in the line of duty. The veterans portion is open to Indiana residents who are the natural or adopted children of veterans who served in the active-duty U.S. armed forces during a period of wartime. Applicants may be of any age; parents must have lived in Indiana for at least 3 years during their lifetime. The veteran parent must also 1) have a service-connected disability as determined by the U.S. Department of Veterans Affairs or the Department of Defense; 2) have received a Purple Heart Medal; or 3) have been a resident of Indiana at the time of entry into the service and declared a POW or MIA after January 1, 1960. Students at the Indiana Soldiers' and Sailors' Children's Home are also eligible. The National Guard portion of this program is open to children and spouses of members of the Indiana National Guard who suffered a service-connected death while serving on state active duty. The public safety officer portion of this program is open to 1) the children and spouses of regular law enforcement officers, regular fire fighters, volunteer fire fighters, county police reserve officers, city police reserve

officers, paramedics, emergency medical technicians, and advanced emergency medical technicians killed in the line of duty, and 2) the children and spouses of Indiana state police troopers permanently and totally disabled in the line of duty. Children must be younger than 23 years of age and enrolled full time in an undergraduate or graduate degree program at a public college or university in Indiana. Spouses must be enrolled in an undergraduate program and must have been married to the covered public safety officer at the time of death or disability.

Financial data Qualified applicants receive a 100% remission of tuition and all mandatory fees for undergraduate or graduate work at state-supported postsecondary schools and universities in Indiana. Support is not provided for such fees as room and board.

Duration Up to 124 semester hours of study.

Additional data The veterans portion of this program is administered by the Indiana Department of Veterans' Affairs, 302 West Washington Street, Room E-120, Indianapolis, IN 46204-2738, (317) 232-3910, (800) 400-4520, Fax: (317) 232-7721, E-mail: jkiser@dva.state.in.us. The National Guard portion of this program is administered by Joint Forces Headquarters, Attn: Education Services Office, 9301 East 59th Street, Lawrence, IN 46216, (317) 964-7023, Fax: (317) 964-7028.

Number awarded Varies each year.

Deadline Applications must be submitted at least 30 days before the start of the college term.

[1123]
JAMES DOYLE CASE MEMORIAL SCHOLARSHIPS

Mississippi Council of the Blind
P.O. Box 31112
Jackson, MS 39286-1112
(601) 371-0616   Toll Free: (888) 346-5622 (within MS)
Web: www.acb.org/mcb

Summary To provide financial assistance to legally blind residents of Mississippi and their children who plan to attend college or graduate school in any state.

Eligibility This program is open to residents of Mississippi who are legally blind or the children of at least 1 legally blind parent. Applicants must be enrolled or accepted for enrollment in an undergraduate or graduate program in any state and carrying or planning to carry at least 12 academic hours. Along with their application, they must submit a 2-page autobiographical sketch, transcripts, standardized test scores (ACT or SAT for undergraduates; GRE, MCAT, LSAT, etc. for graduate students), 2 letters of recommendation, proof of acceptance from a postsecondary school, and verification of blindness of the qualifying person (applicant or parent).

Financial data The stipend is $1,500 per year.

Duration 4 years.

Number awarded 2 each year.

Deadline February of each year.

[1124]
KATHERN F. GRUBER SCHOLARSHIPS

Blinded Veterans Association
477 H Street, N.W.
Washington, DC 20001-2694
(202) 371-8880   Toll Free: (800) 669-7079
Fax: (202) 371-8258   E-mail: bva@bva.org
Web: www.bva.org/services.html

Summary To provide financial assistance for undergraduate or graduate study to spouses and children of blinded veterans.

Eligibility This program is open to dependent children and spouses of blinded veterans of the U.S. armed forces. The veteran need not be a member of the Blinded Veterans Association. The veteran's blindness may be either service connected or nonservice connected, but it must meet the following definition: central visual acuity of 20/200 or less in the better eye with corrective glasses, or central visual acuity of more than 20/200 if there is a field defect in which the peripheral field has contracted to such an extent that the widest diameter of visual field subtends an angular distance no greater than 20 degrees in the better eye. Applicants must have been accepted or be currently enrolled as a full-time student in an undergraduate or graduate program at an accredited institution of higher learning. Along with their application, they must submit a 300-word essay on their career goals and aspirations. Financial need is not considered in the selection process.

Financial data The stipend is $2,000; funds are intended to be used to cover the student's expenses, including tuition, other academic fees, books, dormitory fees, and cafeteria fees. Funds are paid directly to the recipient's school.

Duration 1 year; recipients may reapply.

Additional data Scholarships may be used for only 1 degree (vocational, bachelor's, or graduate) or nongraduate certificate (e.g., nursing, secretarial).

Number awarded 6 each year.

Deadline April of each year.

[1125]
KIDS' CHANCE OF INDIANA SCHOLARSHIP PROGRAM

Kids' Chance of Indiana, Inc.
Attn: Scholarship Committee
721 East Broadway
Fortville, IN 46040
(317) 485-0043, ext. 123   Fax: (317) 485-4299
E-mail: office@kidschancein.org
Web: www.kidschancein.org/scholarship.html

Summary To provide financial assistance to Indiana residents whose parent was killed or permanently disabled in a work-related accident and who are interested in attending college or graduate school in any state.

Eligibility This program is open to Indiana residents between 16 and 25 years of age who are the children of workers fatally or catastrophically injured as a result of a work-related accident or occupational disease. The death or injury must be compensable by the Workers' Compen-

sation Board of the state of Indiana and must have resulted in a substantial decline in the family's income that is likely to impede the student's pursuit of his or her educational objectives. Applicants must be attending or planning to attend a trade/vocational school, junior/community college, 4-year college or university, or graduate school in any state. Financial need is considered in the selection process.

Financial data Stipends range up to $3,000 per year. Funds may be used for tuition and fees, books, room and board, and utilities.

Duration 1 year; may be renewed.

Number awarded Varies each year.

Deadline Deadline not specified.

[1126]
KIDS' CHANCE OF OHIO SCHOLARSHIPS

Kids' Chance of Ohio
Attn: Executive Director
52 East Gay Street
P.O. Box 1008
Columbus, OH 43216-1008
(614) 464-6410   E-mail: raminor@vssp.com
Web: www.kidschanceohio.org/scholarshipprogram.html

Summary To provide financial assistance for undergraduate or graduate study in any state to children of Ohio employees who were killed or disabled as a result of a work-related injury or occupational disease.

Eligibility This program is open to the children between 16 and 25 years of age of employees who have been declared to be permanently and totally disabled or who were fatally injured as a result of a work-related injury or occupational disease. The death, injury, or illness must have occurred as a result of work activities performed for an Ohio employer covered by the Ohio workers' compensation law, although neither the student nor the parent is required to be Ohio residents. The injury or death must have resulted in a decline in the family's income. Applicants must be attending or planning to attend a college, university, community college, trade/vocational school, industrial/commercial training, or graduate school in any state.

Financial data The stipend depends on the need of the recipient, to a maximum of $5,000 per year. Funds may be used for payment of tuition, fees, books, room, and board.

Duration 1 year; recipients may reapply.

Number awarded Varies each year.

Deadline Applications must be submitted at least 1 month prior to the beginning of the semester or quarter.

[1127]
KIDS' CHANCE OF SOUTH CAROLINA SCHOLARSHIPS

Kids' Chance of South Carolina
P.O. Box 11155
Columbia, SC 29211
(803) 356-5862   Fax: (803) 356-0935
E-mail: info@kidschancesc.org
Web: www.kidschancesc.org/scholarship_program.html

Summary To provide financial assistance to South Carolina residents whose parent was killed or permanently disabled in a work-related accident and who are interested in attending college or graduate school in any state.

Eligibility This program is open to South Carolina residents between 16 and 25 years of age who are the children of workers fatally or catastrophically injured as a result of a work-related accident or occupational disease. Applicants must be attending or planning to attend a trade school, vocational school, community or junior college, 4-year college or university, or graduate school in any state. The work-related injury or occupational disease from which their parent suffers or died must be compensable by the Workers' Compensation Board of the state of South Carolina and must have resulted in a substantial decline in the family's income that is likely to interfere with the student's pursuit of his or her educational objectives.

Financial data Stipends range from $500 to $6,000 per year. Funds may be used for tuition and fees, books, room and board, and utilities.

Duration 1 year; may be renewed.

Number awarded Varies each year.

Deadline Applications must be submitted 1 month before the beginning of the semester.

[1128]
MAINE VETERANS DEPENDENTS EDUCATIONAL BENEFITS

Bureau of Veterans' Services
117 State House Station
Augusta, ME 04333-0117
(207) 626-4464   Toll Free: (800) 345-0116 (within ME)
Fax: (207) 626-4471   E-mail: mainebvs@maine.gov
Web: www.maine.gov

Summary To provide financial assistance for undergraduate or graduate education to dependents of disabled and other Maine veterans.

Eligibility Applicants for these benefits must be children (high school seniors or graduates under 22 years of age), non-divorced spouses, or unremarried widow(er)s of veterans who meet 1 or more of the following requirements: 1) living and determined to have a total permanent disability resulting from a service-connected cause; 2) killed in action; 3) died from a service-connected disability; 4) died while totally and permanently disabled due to a service-connected disability but whose death was not related to the service-connected disability; or 5) a member of the armed forces on active duty who has been listed for more than 90 days as missing in action, captured, forcibly detained, or interned in the line of duty by a foreign government or power. The veteran parent must have been a resident of Maine at the time of entry into service or a resident of Maine for 5 years preceding application for these benefits. Children may be working on an associate or bachelor's degree. Spouses, widows, and widowers may work on an associate, bachelor's, or master's degree.

Financial data Recipients are entitled to free tuition at institutions of higher education supported by the state of Maine.

Duration Children may receive up to 8 semesters of support; they have 6 years from the date of first entrance to complete those 8 semesters. Continuation in the program is based on their earning a GPA of 2.0 or higher each semester. Spouses are entitled to receive up to 120 credit hours of educational benefits and have 10 years from the date of first entrance to complete their program.

Additional data College preparatory schooling and correspondence course are not supported under this program.

Number awarded Varies each year.

Deadline Deadline not specified.

[1129]
MARILYN YETSO MEMORIAL SCHOLARSHIP

Ulman Cancer Fund for Young Adults
Attn: Scholarship Program Coordinator
10440 Little Patuxent Parkway, Suite 1G
Columbia, MD 21044
(410) 964-0202, ext. 106   Toll Free: (888) 393-FUND
E-mail: scholarship@ulmanfund.org
Web: www.ulmanfund.org

Summary To provide financial assistance for college or graduate school to students from Washington, D.C., Maryland, or Virginia who have or have lost a parent to cancer.

Eligibility This program is open to students who have or have lost a parent or guardian to cancer. Applicants must be residents of Washington, D.C., Maryland, or Virginia or attending college there. They must be 35 years of age or younger and attending, or planning to attend, a 2- or 4-year college, university, or vocational program to work on an undergraduate or graduate degree. The parent or guardian must have been first diagnosed with cancer after the applicant was 15 years of age. Along with their application, they must submit an essay of at least 1,000 words on how their parent's cancer experience has impacted their outlook on life and the legacy that they desire to leave behind. Selection is based on demonstrated dedication to community service, commitment to educational and professional goals, use of their cancer experience to impact the lives of other young adults affected by cancer, medical hardship, and financial need.

Financial data The stipend is $2,500. Funds are paid directly to the educational institution.

Duration 1 year.

Additional data These scholarships were first awarded in 2002. Recipients must agree to complete 80 hours of community service.

Number awarded Varies each year; recently, 2 of these scholarships were awarded.

Deadline April of each year.

[1130]
MARK REAMES MEMORIAL SCHOLARSHIPS

Hemophilia Society of Colorado
Attn: Scholarship Committee
P.O. Box 4943
Englewood, CO 80155
(303) 629-6990   Toll Free: (888) 687-CLOT
Fax: (303) 629-7035   E-mail: hsc@cohemo.org
Web: www.cohemo.org

Summary To provide financial assistance for higher education to members of the Hemophilia Society of Colorado (HSC) and to members of their families.

Eligibility This program is open to HSC members who have hemophilia or a related inherited bleeding disorder and their immediate family members. Applicants must be enrolled or planning to enroll at a 2-year or 4-year college or university, vocational/technical school, or graduate school. Along with their application, they must submit an essay on why they think they should receive this scholarship and how it might affect their future goals. Selection is based on the essay, demonstrated scholastic ability and intellectual promise, letters of recommendation, community involvement (especially involvement with the hemophilia community), and financial need.

Financial data The stipend is $1,000. Funds must be used for tuition, room, board, and related educational expenses.

Duration 1 year.

Number awarded 2 each year.

Deadline April of each year.

[1131]
METHODIST SEPTEMBER 11 MEMORIAL SCHOLARSHIPS

United Methodist Higher Education Foundation
Attn: Scholarships Administrator
1001 19th Avenue South
P.O. Box 340005
Nashville, TN 37203-0005
(615) 340-7385   Toll Free: (800) 811-8110
Fax: (615) 340-7330
E-mail: umhefscholarships@gbhem.org
Web: www.umhef.org

Summary To provide financial assistance to undergraduate and graduate students at Methodist institutions and Methodist students whose parent or guardian was disabled or killed in the terrorist attacks on September 11, 2001.

Eligibility This program is open to 1) students attending a United Methodist-related college or university in the United States, and 2) United Methodist students attending a higher education institution in the United States. Applicants must have lost a parent or guardian or had a parent or guardian disabled as a result of the September 11, 2001 terrorist attacks. They must be enrolled as full-time undergraduate or graduate students. U.S. citizenship or permanent resident status is required.

Financial data The stipend depends on the number of applicants.

Duration 1 year; may be renewed as long as the recipients maintain satisfactory academic progress as defined by their institution.

Number awarded Varies each year; a total of $30,000 is available for this program.

Deadline Applications may be submitted at any time.

[1132]
MINNESOTA G.I. BILL PROGRAM

Minnesota Office of Higher Education
Attn: Manager of State Financial Aid Programs
1450 Energy Park Drive, Suite 350
St. Paul, MN 55108-5227
(651) 642-0567   Toll Free: (800) 657-3866
Fax: (651) 642-0675   TDD: (800) 627-3529
E-mail: Ginny.Dodds@state.mn.us
Web: www.ohe.state.mn.us

Summary To provide financial assistance for college or graduate school in the state to residents of Minnesota who served in the military after September 11, 2001 and the families of deceased or disabled military personnel.

Eligibility This program is open to residents of Minnesota enrolled at colleges and universities in the state as undergraduate or graduate students. Applicants must be 1) a veteran who is serving or has served honorably in a branch of the U.S. armed forces at any time on or after September 11, 2001; 2) a non-veteran who has served honorably for a total of 5 years or more cumulatively as a member of the Minnesota National Guard or other active or Reserve component of the U.S. armed forces, and any part of that service occurred on or after September 11, 2001; or 3) a surviving child or spouse of a person who has served in the military at any time on or after September 11, 2001 and who has died or has a total and permanent disability as a result of that military service. Financial need is also considered in the selection process.

Financial data The stipend is $1,000 per semester for full-time study or $500 per semester for part-time study.

Duration 1 year; may be renewed up to 4 additional years, provided the recipient continues to make satisfactory academic progress.

Additional data This program was established by the Minnesota Legislature in 2007.

Number awarded Varies each year.

Deadline Deadline not specified.

[1133]
OREGON DECEASED OR DISABLED PUBLIC SAFETY OFFICER GRANT PROGRAM

Oregon Student Assistance Commission
Attn: Grants and Scholarships Division
1500 Valley River Drive, Suite 100
Eugene, OR 97401-2130
(541) 687-7466   Toll Free: (800) 452-8807, ext. 7466
Fax: (541) 687-7414   TDD: (800) 735-2900
E-mail: awardinfo@osac.state.or.us
Web: www.getcollegefunds.org

Summary To provide financial assistance for college or graduate school in the state to the children of disabled or deceased Oregon public safety officers.
Eligibility This program is open to the natural, adopted, or stepchildren of Oregon public safety officers (fire fighters, state fire marshals, chief deputy fire marshals, deputy state fire marshals, police chiefs, police officers, sheriffs, deputy sheriffs, county adult parole and probation officers, correction officers, and investigators of the Criminal Justice Division of the Department of Justice) who, in the line of duty, were killed or disabled. Applicants must be enrolled or planning to enroll as a full-time undergraduate student at a public or private college or university in Oregon. Children of deceased officers are also eligible for graduate study. Financial need must be demonstrated.
Financial data At a public 2- or 4-year college or university, the amount of the award is equal to the cost of tuition and fees. At an eligible private college, the award amount is equal to the cost of tuition and fees at the University of Oregon.
Duration 1 year; may be renewed for up to 3 additional years of undergraduate study, if the student maintains satisfactory academic progress and demonstrates continued financial need. Children of deceased public safety officers may receive support for 12 quarters of graduate study.
Number awarded Varies each year.
Deadline Deadline not specified.

[1134]
OREGON OCCUPATIONAL SAFETY AND HEALTH DIVISION WORKERS MEMORIAL SCHOLARSHIPS

Oregon Student Assistance Commission
Attn: Grants and Scholarships Division
1500 Valley River Drive, Suite 100
Eugene, OR 97401-2146
(541) 687-7395   Toll Free: (800) 452-8807, ext. 7395
Fax: (541) 687-7414   TDD: (800) 735-2900
E-mail: awardinfo@osac.state.or.us
Web: www.osac.state.or.us/osac_programs.html

Summary To provide financial assistance to the children and spouses of disabled or deceased workers in Oregon who are interested in attending college or graduate school in any state.
Eligibility This program is open to residents of Oregon who are U.S. citizens or permanent residents. Applicants must be high school seniors or graduates who 1) are dependents or spouses of an Oregon worker who has suffered permanent total disability on the job; or 2) are receiving, or have received, fatality benefits as dependents or spouses of a worker fatally injured in Oregon. They may be attending a college or graduate school in any state. Along with their application, they must submit an essay of up to 500 words on how the injury or death of their parent or spouse has affected or influenced their decision to further their education. Financial need is not required, but it is considered in the selection process.
Financial data Stipend amounts vary; recently, they were at least $4,786.

Duration 1 year.
Number awarded 1 or more each year.
Deadline February of each year.

[1135]
PARENT PUBLIC POLICY FELLOWSHIP PROGRAM

Joseph P. Kennedy, Jr. Foundation
Attn: Executive Director
1133 19th Street, N.W., 12th Floor
Washington, DC 20035
(202) 393-1240   Fax: (202) 824-0351
E-mail: jpkf@jpkf.org
Web: www.jpkf.org

Summary To provide a public policy fellowship opportunity in Washington, D.C. to the parents of persons with intellectual disabilities.
Eligibility This program is open to the parents of persons with intellectual disabilities who live in the United States. They must be interested in participating in an intensive public policy fellowship in Washington, D.C. Applicants should have experience in state or national-level advocacy for persons with intellectual and developmental disabilities and their families; vocational rehabilitation; education, employment, child care, child welfare, law, employment, community organizing, housing, or development of inclusive community supports and services; health or mental health care for people with mental retardation; or development of family training or family support services. Salaried experience in the field is not a requirement. They should submit a 2- to 4-page letter stating their interests and accomplishments to date and what they hope to do with the knowledge and experience gained from the fellowship, a resume or summary of their involvement in the field, and at least 3 letters of support.
Financial data The program provides a stipend of $75,000 and a relocation allowance.
Duration 1 year, beginning in January.
Additional data This program was established in 1995. During the fellowship year, participants learn how legislation is initiated, developed, and passed by Congress. They work on the staff of a member of Congress, a Congressional committee, or a federal department. The expectation is that fellows will become future leaders in the field of disabilities and return home, after their year in Washington, to make significant contributions to policy and program development in their home state.
Number awarded 1 each year.
Deadline August of each year.

[1136]
REMISSION OF FEES FOR CHILDREN OF INDIANA VETERANS

Indiana Department of Veterans' Affairs
302 West Washington Street, Room E-120
Indianapolis, IN 46204-2738
(317) 232-3910   Toll Free: (800) 400-4520 (within IN)
Fax: (317) 232-7721
Web: www.in.gov/dva/2378.htm

Summary To enable the children of disabled and other Indiana veterans to attend public colleges and universities in the state without payment of tuition.

Eligibility This program is open to natural and legally-adopted children of veterans who served on active duty in the U.S. armed forces during a period of wartime and have been residents of Indiana for at least 36 consecutive months during their lifetime. The veteran must 1) have sustained a service-connected disability as verified by the U.S. Department of Veterans Affairs or a military service; 2) have received a Purple Heart Medal; or 3) have been a resident of Indiana at the time of entry into the service and declared a prisoner of war (POW) or missing in action (MIA) after January 1, 1960. Students who were veteran-related pupils at the Indiana Soldiers' and Sailors' Children's Home are also eligible. Applicants must be attending or planning to attend a state-supported postsecondary college or university in Indiana as an undergraduate or graduate student.

Financial data Qualified students receive remission of 100% of tuition and mandatory fees.

Duration Fees are remitted for up to 124 semester hours of education.

Number awarded Varies each year.

Deadline Requests for assistance may be submitted at any time.

[1137]
SURVIVORS' AND DEPENDENTS' EDUCATIONAL ASSISTANCE PROGRAM

Department of Veterans Affairs
Attn: Veterans Benefits Administration
810 Vermont Avenue, N.W.
Washington, DC 20420
(202) 418-4343   Toll Free: (888) GI-BILL1
Web: www.gibill.va.gov/GI_Bill_Info/benefits.htm

Summary To provide financial assistance for undergraduate or graduate study to children and spouses of deceased and disabled veterans, MIAs, and POWs.

Eligibility Eligible for this assistance are spouses and children of 1) veterans who died or are permanently and totally disabled as the result of active service in the armed forces; 2) veterans who died from any cause while rated permanently and totally disabled from a service-connected disability; 3) servicemembers listed as missing in action or captured in the line of duty by a hostile force; 4) servicemembers listed as forcibly detained or interned by a foreign government or power; and 5) servicemembers who are hospitalized or receiving outpatient treatment for a service-connected permanent and total disability and are likely to be discharged for that disability. Children must be between 18 and 26 years of age, although extensions may be granted. Spouses and children over 14 years of age with physical or mental disabilities are also eligible.

Financial data Monthly stipends from this program for study at an academic institution are $925 for full time, $694 for three-quarter time, or $461 for half-time. For farm cooperative work, the monthly stipends are $745 for full-time, $559 for three-quarter time, or $372 for half-time. For an apprenticeship or on-the-job training, the monthly stipend is $674 for the first 6 months, $505 for the second 6 months, $333 for the third 6 months, and $168 for the remainder of the program. For special restorative training by beneficiaries with a physical or mental disability, the monthly stipend for full-time training is $925.

Duration Up to 45 months (or the equivalent in part-time training). Spouses must complete their training within 10 years of the date they are first found eligible. For spouses of servicemembers who died on active duty, benefits end 20 years from the date of death.

Additional data Benefits may be used to work on associate, bachelor, or graduate degrees at colleges and universities, including independent study, cooperative training, and study abroad programs. Courses leading to a certificate or diploma from business, technical, or vocational schools may also be taken. Other eligible programs include apprenticeships, on-the-job training programs, farm cooperative courses, correspondence courses (for spouses only), secondary school programs (for recipients who are not high school graduates), tutorial assistance, remedial deficiency and refresher training, or work-study (for recipients who are enrolled at least three-quarter time). Eligible children who are handicapped by a physical or mental disability that prevents pursuit of an educational program may receive special restorative training that includes language retraining, lip reading, auditory training, Braille reading and writing, and similar programs. Eligible spouses and children over 14 years of age who are handicapped by a physical or mental disability that prevents pursuit of an educational program may receive specialized vocational training that includes specialized courses, alone or in combination with other courses, leading to a vocational objective that is suitable for the person and required by reason of physical or mental handicap. Ineligible courses include bartending; audited courses; non-accredited independent study courses; any course given by radio; self-improvement courses, such as reading, speaking, woodworking, basic seamanship, and English as a second language; audited courses; any course that is avocational or recreational in character; courses not leading to an educational, professional, or vocational objective; courses taken and successfully completed previously; courses taken by a federal government employee and paid for under the Government Employees' Training Act; and courses taken while in receipt of benefits for the same program from the Office of Workers' Compensation Programs.

Number awarded Varies each year.

Deadline Applications may be submitted at any time.

[1138]
UCB FAMILY EPILEPSY SCHOLARSHIP PROGRAM

UCB, Inc.
Family Scholarship Program
c/o Hudson Medical Communications
200 White Plains Road, Second Floor
Tarrytown, NY 10591
Toll Free: (866) 825-1920
E-mail: questions@hudsonmc.com
Web: www.ucbepilepsyscholarship.com

Summary To provide financial assistance for college or graduate school to epilepsy patients and their family members and caregivers.

Eligibility This program is open to epilepsy patients and their family members and caregivers. Applicants must be working on or planning to work on an undergraduate or graduate degree at an institution of higher education in the United States. They must be able to demonstrate academic achievement, a record of participation in activities outside of school, and service as a role model. Along with their application, they must submit a 1-page essay explaining why they should be selected for the scholarship, how epilepsy has impacted their life either as a patient or as a family member or caregiver, and how they will benefit from the scholarship. U.S. citizenship or permanent resident status is required.

Financial data The stipend is $5,000.

Duration 1 year; nonrenewable.

Additional data This program, previously known as the Keppra Family Epilepsy Scholarship Program, was established in 2004.

Number awarded 40 each year.

Deadline April of each year.

[1139]
UCB FAMILY RA SCHOLARSHIP PROGRAM

UCB, Inc.
8010 Arco Corporate Drive
Raleigh, NC 27617
(919) 567-3384   Fax: (919) 767-2570
Web: www.reachbeyondra.com/scholarship

Summary To provide financial assistance to undergraduate and graduate students who have rheumatoid arthritis (RA) and their families.

Eligibility This program is open to students who are either working on an associate, undergraduate, or graduate degree or are enrolled in a trade school educational program. Applicants must have been diagnosed with RA or be an immediate family member (parent, spouse, child, or sibling) of a person with RA. Along with their application, they must submit an essay of 1 to 2 pages describing how they are living beyond the boundaries of RA to demonstrate academic ambition and personal achievement and how the scholarship would impact their life.

Financial data Stipends range up to $10,000.

Duration 1 year; nonrenewable.

Additional data This program began on a pilot basis in 2008.

Number awarded 31 each year.

Deadline March of each year.

[1140]
VERA YIP MEMORIAL SCHOLARSHIP

Ulman Cancer Fund for Young Adults
Attn: Scholarship Committee Coordinator
4725 Dorsey Hall Drive, Suite A
PMB 505
Ellicott City, MD 21042
(410) 964-0202   Toll Free: (888) 393-FUND, ext. 103
E-mail: scholarship@ulmanfund.org
Web: www.ulmanfund.org/Default.aspx?tabid=329

Summary To provide financial assistance for college or graduate school to students from Washington, D.C., Maryland, or Virginia who either have or had cancer or have or have lost a parent to cancer.

Eligibility This program is open to students who either 1) have or had cancer, or 2) have or have lost a parent or guardian to cancer. Applicants must be residents of Washington, D.C., Maryland, or Virginia or attending college there. They must be 35 years of age or younger and attending, or planning to attend, a 2- or 4-year college, university, or vocational program to work on an undergraduate or graduate degree. Either they or their parent or guardian must have been diagnosed (including initial or secondary diagnosis, relapse, or active treatment) with cancer after they were 15 years of age. Along with their application, they must submit an essay of at least 1,000 words on how their cancer experience has shaped, changed, and/or reinforced the principles by which they live their life. Selection is based on demonstrated dedication to community service, commitment to educational and professional goals, use of their cancer experience to impact the lives of other young adults affected by cancer, medical hardship, and financial need.

Financial data The stipend is $2,500. Funds are paid directly to the educational institution.

Duration 1 year; nonrenewable.

Additional data Recipients must agree to complete 80 hours of community service.

Number awarded Varies each year; recently, 2 of these scholarships were awarded.

Deadline April of each year.

[1141]
VIRGINIA MILITARY SURVIVORS AND DEPENDENTS EDUCATION PROGRAM

Virginia Department of Veterans Services
270 Franklin Road, S.W., Room 503
Roanoke, VA 24011-2215
(540) 857-7101   Fax: (540) 857-7573
Web: www.dvs.virginia.gov/statebenefits.htm

Summary To provide educational assistance to the children and spouses of disabled and other Virginia veterans or service personnel.

Eligibility This program is open to residents of Virginia whose parent or spouse served in the U.S. armed forces (including the Reserves, the Virginia National Guard, or the Virginia National Guard Reserves) during any armed conflict subsequent to December 6, 1941, as a result of a terrorist act, during military operations against terrorism, or on a peacekeeping mission. The veterans must be at least 90% disabled due to an injury or disease incurred as a result of such service, has died, or is listed as a prisoner of war or missing in action. Applicants must have been accepted at a public college or university in Virginia as an undergraduate or graduate student. Children must be between 16 and 29 years of age; there are no age restrictions for spouses. The veteran must have been a resident of Virginia at the time of entry into active military service or for at least 5 consecutive years immediately prior to the date of application or death. The surviving spouse must have been a resident of Virginia for at least 5 years prior to marrying the veteran or for at least 5 years immediately prior to the date on which the application was submitted.

Financial data The maximum allowable stipend is $1,500 per year, but current funding is set at a maximum of $1,350, payable at the rate of $675 per term for full-time students, $450 per term for students enrolled at least half time but less than full time, or $225 per term for students enrolled less than half time.

Duration Entitlement extends to a maximum of 48 months.

Additional data Individuals entitled to this benefit may use it to pursue any vocational, technical, undergraduate, or graduate program of instruction. Generally, programs listed in the academic catalogs of state-supported institutions are acceptable, provided they have a clearly-defined educational objective (such as a certificate, diploma, or degree). This program was formerly known as the Virginia War Orphans Education Program.

Number awarded Varies each year; recently, funding allowed for a total of 740 of these awards.

Deadline Deadline not specified.

[1142]
WISCONSIN G.I. BILL TUITION REMISSION PROGRAM

Wisconsin Department of Veterans Affairs
30 West Mifflin Street
P.O. Box 7843
Madison, WI 53707-7843
(608) 266-1311   Toll Free: (800) WIS-VETS
Fax: (608) 267-0403
E-mail: WDVAInfo@dva.state.wi.us
Web: www.dva.state.wi.us/Ben_education.asp

Summary To provide financial assistance for college or graduate school to Wisconsin veterans and their dependents.

Eligibility This program is open to current residents of Wisconsin who 1) were residents of the state when they entered or reentered active duty in the U.S. armed forces, or 2) have moved to the state and have been residents for any consecutive 12-month period after entry or reentry into service. Applicants must have served on active duty for at least 2 continuous years or for at least 90 days during specified wartime periods. Also eligible are 1) qualifying

children and unremarried surviving spouses of Wisconsin veterans who died in the line of duty or as the direct result of a service-connected disability; and 2) children and spouses of Wisconsin veterans who have a service-connected disability rated by the U.S. Department of Veterans Affairs as 30% or greater. Children must be between 17 and 25 years of age (regardless of the date of the veteran's death or initial disability rating) and be a Wisconsin resident for tuition purposes. Spouses remain eligible for 10 years following the date of the veteran's death or initial disability rating; they must be Wisconsin residents for tuition purposes but they may enroll full or part time. Students may attend any institution, center, or school within the University of Wisconsin (UW) System or the Wisconsin Technical College System (WCTS). There are no income limits, delimiting periods following military service during which the benefit must be used, or limits on the level of study (e.g., vocational, undergraduate, professional, or graduate).

Financial data Veterans who qualify as a Wisconsin resident for tuition purposes are eligible for a remission of 100% of standard academic fees and segregated fees at a UW campus or 100% of program and material fees at a WCTS institution. Veterans who qualify as a Wisconsin veteran for purposes of this program but for other reasons fail to meet the definition of a Wisconsin resident for tuition purposes at the UW system are eligible for a remission of 100% of non-resident fees. Spouses and children of deceased or disabled veterans are entitled to a remission of 100% of tuition and fees at a UW or WCTS institution.

Duration Up to 8 semesters or 128 credits, whichever is greater.

Additional data This program was established in 2005 as a replacement for Wisconsin Tuition and Fee Reimbursement Grants.

Number awarded Varies each year.

Deadline Applications must be submitted within 14 days from the office start of the academic term: in October for fall, March for spring, or June for summer.

Grants-in-Aid

[1143]
ADA FOUNDATION RELIEF GRANT PROGRAM

American Dental Association
Attn: ADA Foundation
211 East Chicago Avenue
Chicago, IL 60611
(312) 440-2547   Fax: (312) 440-3526
E-mail: adaf@ada.org
Web: www.ada.org/ada/adaf/grants/relief.asp

Summary To provide relief grants to dentists and their dependents who, because of accidental injury, a medical condition, or advanced age, are not self-supporting.

Eligibility This program is open to dentists, their spouses, and their children under 18 years of age. Dependents of deceased dentists are also eligible. Membership in the American Dental Association (ADA) is not required and members receive no special consideration in awarding of grants. Applicants must be seeking assistance because an accidental injury, advanced age, physically-debilitating illness, or medically-related condition prevents them from gainful employment and results in an inability to be wholly self-sustaining. They must apply through their component or constituent dental society, which forwards the application to the trustees of this fund.

Financial data The amount of the grant depends on the particular circumstances of each applicant, including financial need, age and physical condition, opportunity for assistance from immediate family members, financial assets, and all other relevant factors.

Duration Initial grants are for 6 months. Renewal grants are for an additional 12 months. Emergency grants are 1-time awards.

Additional data The ADA has been making relief grants to needy dentists since 1906.

Number awarded Varies each year; recently, a total of $209,964 in these grants was awarded.

Deadline Applications may be submitted at any time.

[1144]
AIR FORCE AID SOCIETY RESPITE CARE

Air Force Aid Society
Attn: Financial Assistance Department
241 18th Street South, Suite 202
Arlington, VA 22202-3409
(703) 607-3072, ext. 51   Toll Free: (800) 429-9475
Fax: (703) 607-3022
Web: www.afas.org

Summary To provide financial assistance to Air Force personnel and their families who have a family member with special needs.

Eligibility This program is open to active-duty Air Force members and their families who are responsible for 24 hour a day care for an ill or disabled family member (child, spouse, or parent) living in the household. Applicants must be referred by the Exceptional Family Member Program (EFMP) or the Family Advocacy Office. Selection is based on need, both financial need and the need of the family for respite time.

Financial data Assistance is provided as a grant that depends on the needs of the family.

Number awarded Varies each year.

Deadline Applications may be submitted at any time.

[1145]
ALABAMA AD VALOREM TAX EXEMPTION FOR SPECIALLY ADAPTED HOUSES

Alabama Department of Revenue
Attn: Property Tax Division
Gordon Persons Building
50 North Ripley Street, Room 4126
P.O. Box 327210
Montgomery, AL 36132-7210
(334) 242-1525
Web: www.ador.state.al.us

Summary To provide a property tax exemption to the owners of specially adapted housing (housing adapted for disabled veterans) in Alabama.

Eligibility The home of any veteran which is or was acquired pursuant to the provisions of Public Law 702, 80th Congress (specially adapted housing grants for veterans) as amended (38 USC) will be exempted from ad valorem taxation if the house is owned and occupied by the veteran or the veteran's unremarried widow(er).

Financial data Qualifying houses are exempt from all ad valorem taxation.

Duration This exemption continues as long as the qualifying veteran or the unremarried widow(er) resides in the house.

Number awarded Varies each year.

Deadline Deadline not specified.

[1146]
ALABAMA MILITARY RETIREE INCOME TAX EXEMPTION

Alabama Department of Revenue
Attn: Income Tax Division
Gordon Persons Building
50 North Ripley Street, Room 4212
P.O. Box 327410
Montgomery, AL 36132-7410
(334) 242-1105   Fax: (334) 242-0064
E-mail: erohelpdesk@revenue.state.al.us
Web: www.ador.state.al.us

Summary To exempt a portion of the income of veterans and their survivors from taxation in Alabama.

Eligibility Eligible are Alabama recipients of regular military retired pay or military survivors benefits. Recipients of benefits paid by the U.S. Department of Veterans Affairs (including disability retirement payments) are also eligible for this exemption.

Financial data All income received as military retired pay, veterans' disability payment, or military survivors benefits is exempt from state, county, or municipal income taxation.

Duration The exemption continues as long as the recipient resides in Alabama.

Deadline Deadline not specified.

[1147]
ANDRE SOBEL GRANTS

André Sobel River of Life Foundation
Attn: Awards
8899 Beverly Boulevard, Suite 111
Los Angeles, CA 90048
(310) 276-7111 Fax: (310) 276-0244
E-mail: info@andreriveroflife.org
Web: www.andreriveroflife.org

Summary To provide assistance to single mothers who have a child with a life-threatening illness.

Eligibility This assistance is available to single mothers who are referred by a pre-selected pediatric medical facility. Candidates must have a child experiencing a life-threatening medical crisis. They must have exhausted all other sources of support and need assistance for such purposes as household expenses, groceries, utilities, transportation, medical expenses, housing, or burial expenses.

Financial data Grants depend on the need of the recipient. Recently, single grants ranged up to $2,204 and total assistance ranged up to $14,475 for an individual.

Duration Grants are awarded as needed and may be repeated.

Number awarded Varies each year; recently, 38 mothers were receiving support from this program.

Deadline Applications may be submitted at any time.

[1148]
ARKANSAS DISABLED VETERANS PROPERTY TAX EXEMPTION

Arkansas Assessment Coordination Department
1614 West Third Street
Little Rock, AR 72201-1815
(501) 324-9100 Fax: (501) 324-9242
E-mail: dasbury@acd.state.ar.us
Web: www.arkansas.gov/acd

Summary To exempt from taxation the property owned by blind or disabled veterans, surviving spouses, and minor dependent children in Arkansas.

Eligibility This program is open to disabled veterans in Arkansas who have been awarded special monthly compensation by the U.S. Department of Veterans Affairs and who have 1) the loss of or the loss of use of 1 or more limbs, 2) total blindness in 1 or both eyes, or 3) total and permanent disability. The benefit also extends to veterans' unremarried surviving spouses and their minor children.

Financial data Qualifying veterans (or their unremarried widows or dependent children) are exempt from payment of all state taxes on their homestead and personal property.

Duration This exemption continues as long as the qualifying veteran (or dependent) resides in Arkansas.

Number awarded Varies each year.

Deadline Applications may be submitted at any time.

[1149]
ARKANSAS INCOME TAX CREDIT FOR PHENYLKETONURIA DISORDER

Arkansas Department of Finance and Administration
Attn: Office of Income Tax Administration
Joel Ledbetter Building, Room 110
1800 Seventh Street
P.O. Box 3628
Little Rock, AR 72203-3628
(501) 682-7225 Fax: (501) 682-7692
E-mail: individual.income@rev.state.ar.us
Web: www.arkansas.gov/dfa/income_tax/tax_index.html

Summary To provide a state income tax credit for taxpayers in Arkansas who have a child with phenylketonuria (PKU) disorder or other metabolic disorders.

Eligibility This income tax credit is available to Arkansas individuals and families with a dependent child or children with PKU, galactosemia, organic acidemias, or disorders of amino acid metabolism. Taxpayers must have expenses incurred for the purchase of medically necessary foods and low protein modified food products.

Financial data The maximum state income tax credit is $2,400.

Duration The certificate that qualifies the taxpayer for this credit (AR1113) must be attached to the taxpayer's individual income tax return annually. Any unused credit amount may be carried forward for an additional 2 years.

Additional data The Arkansas legislature established this credit in 1999.

Number awarded Varies each year.

Deadline Deadline not specified.

[1150]
ARKANSAS INCOME TAX EXEMPTIONS FOR RETIREMENT AND DISABILITY PAY

Arkansas Department of Finance and Administration
Attn: Office of Income Tax Administration
Joel Ledbetter Building, Room 110
1800 Seventh Street
P.O. Box 3628
Little Rock, AR 72203-3628
(501) 682-7225 Fax: (501) 682-7692
E-mail: individual.income@rev.state.ar.us
Web: www.arkansas.gov/dfa/income_tax/tax_index.html

Summary To exempt a portion of the income from retirement or disability plans from state income taxes in Arkansas.

Eligibility Eligible are residents of Arkansas receiving income from retirement or disability plans. Surviving spouses also qualify for the exemption.

Financial data Exempt from state income taxation is the first $6,000 in disability pay, retired pay, or survivors benefits. Any resident who receives both military retirement or disability pay and other retirement or disability benefits is entitled to only a single $6,000 deduction. Surviving spouses are also limited to a single $6,000 exemption. Military retirees may adjust their figures if the payment includes survivor's benefit payments; the amount of adjustment must be listed on the income statement, and supporting documentation must be submitted with the return.

Duration The exemption continues as long as the recipient resides in Arkansas.

Deadline Deadline not specified.

[1151]
BEF LUNG TRANSPLANT GRANT PROGRAM

Boomer Esiason Foundation
c/o Jerry Cahill
483 Tenth Avenue, Suite 300
New York, NY 10018
(646) 292-7930   Fax: (646) 292-7945
E-mail: jcahillbef@aol.com
Web: esiason.org

Summary To provide funding for travel and relocation costs during lung transplants to families of patients who have cystic fibrosis (CF).

Eligibility This program is open to families of CF patients who have lung transplants. Applicants must need funds to pay for expenses not covered by their insurance, including, but not limited to, 1) patient and family transportation costs for evaluation, surgery, and post-transplant clinic visits; and 2) housing, food, and living expenses associated with relocation to the transplant site. Along with their application, they must provide a letter from a social worker verifying that the patient has CF and needs assistance and a detailed cost breakdown specifying how the requested funds will be allocated.

Financial data Grants cover qualified expenses.

Duration These are 1-time grants.

Number awarded Varies each year.

Deadline Applications may be submitted at any time.

[1152]
BOBBE AND JERRY MARCUS RESPITE CARE GRANT PROGRAM

ALS Association-DC/Maryland/Virginia Chapter
Attn: Director of Patient Services
7507 Standish Place
Rockville, MD 20855
(301) 978-9855   Toll Free: (866) FITE-ALS
Fax: (301) 978-9854   E-mail: info@ALSinfo.org
Web: www.ALSinfo.org

Summary To provide funding for respite care to Amyotrophic Lateral Sclerosis (ALS) caregivers in Maryland, Virginia, and Washington, D.C.

Eligibility This assistance is available to residents of Maryland, Virginia, and Washington, D.C. who have a confirmed diagnosis of ALS and their family caregivers. Applicants must be registered with the local chapter of the ALS Association. They must be seeking funding to allow the caregiver some regular interval of renewal: for business or social activities, a weekend getaway, or even to sleep on occasion through the night. A professional service will provide needed care.

Financial data Grants provide up to $1,250 per family per year.

Duration 1 year; may be renewed.

Number awarded Varies each year.

Deadline Applications may be submitted at any time.

[1153]
CALIFORNIA DISABLED VETERAN EXEMPTION FROM THE IN LIEU TAX FEE FOR A MANUFACTURED HOME OR MOBILEHOME

Department of Housing and Community Development
Attn: Registration and Titling
1800 Third Street
P.O. Box 2111
Sacramento, CA 95812-2111
(916) 323-9224   Toll Free: (800) 952-8356
Web: www.hcd.ca.gov

Summary To provide a special property tax exemption to blind or disabled California veterans and/or their spouses who own and occupy a mobile home.

Eligibility This program is open to disabled veterans and/or their spouses in California who have a manufactured home or mobile home as their principal place of residence. Veterans must be disabled as a result of injury or disease incurred in military service and have been a resident of California 1) at the time of entry into the service and be blind, or have lost the use of 1 or more limbs, or be totally disabled; 2) on November 7, 1972 and be blind in both eyes, or have lost the use of 2 or more limbs; or 3) on January 1, 1976 and be totally disabled. The spouses and unremarried surviving spouses of those disabled veterans are also eligible.

Financial data The exemption applies to the first $20,000 of the assessed market value of the manufactured home or mobile home. Veterans and/or spouses whose income falls below a specified level are entitled to an additional $10,000 exemption. The amount of the exemption is 100% if the home is owned by a veteran only, a veteran and spouse, or a spouse only; 50% if owned by a veteran and another person other than a spouse or by a spouse and another person other than the veteran; 67% if owned by a veteran, the spouse, and another person; 34% if owned by a veteran and 2 other people other than a spouse or by a spouse and 2 other people; 50% if owned by a veteran, the spouse, and 2 other people; or 25% if owned by a veteran and 3 other people or by a spouse and 3 other people.

Duration The exemption is available annually as long as the applicant meets all requirements.

Number awarded Varies each year.

Deadline Deadline not specified.

[1154]
CALIFORNIA PROPERTY TAX EXEMPTIONS FOR VETERANS

California Department of Veterans Affairs
Attn: Division of Veterans Services
1227 O Street, Room 101
Sacramento, CA 95814
(916) 503-8397
Toll Free: (800) 952-LOAN (within CA)
Fax: (916) 653-2563   TDD: (800) 324-5966
E-mail: ruckergl@cdva.ca.gov
Web: www.cdva.ca.gov/VetService/Overview.aspx

Summary To exempt a portion of the property of blind or disabled veterans in California and their spouses from taxation.

Eligibility This exemption is available to homeowners in California who are wartime veterans in receipt of service-connected disability compensation that is 1) at the totally disabled rate, 2) for loss or loss of use of 2 or more limbs, or 3) for blindness. Unremarried surviving spouses, including registered domestic partners, of veterans who are in receipt of service-connected death benefits are also eligible.

Financial data For veterans and spouses whose total household income from all sources is greater than $49,979 per year, up to $111,296 of the assessed value of a home is exempt from taxation. For veterans and spouses whose total household income from all sources is less than $49,979 per year, up to $166,944 of the assessed value of a home is exempt from taxation.

Duration The exemption is available as long as the veteran or spouse owns a home in California.

Additional data Information is available from the local county assessors office in each California county.

Number awarded Varies each year.

Deadline Applications may be submitted at any time.

[1155]
CLAYTON DABNEY FOUNDATION FOR KIDS WITH CANCER GRANTS

Clayton Dabney Foundation for Kids with Cancer
6500 Greenville Avenue, Suite 342
Dallas, TX 75206
(214) 361-2600   Fax: (214) 217-5199
E-mail: admin@claytondabney.org
Web: www.claytondabney.org

Summary To provide assistance to families whose child is in the terminal stage of cancer.

Eligibility This assistance is available to families who have a child younger than 21 years of age whose cancer has progressed to a terminal stage. The family must demonstrate financial need, although that includes middle-income families where both parents are working though unable to take time off because they are working so hard to cover all of the family expenses and medical bills. Applications must be initiated by a licensed representative (case worker, child life specialist, nurse, or doctor) from a recognized organization or agency (hospital, hospice care, social work, or volunteer group).

Financial data Assistance is generally limited to $2,000 per family.

Number awarded Varies each year.

Deadline Applications may be submitted at any time.

[1156]
COAL MINERS BLACK LUNG BENEFITS

Department of Labor
Employment Standards Administration
Office of Workers' Compensation Programs
Attn: Division of Coal Mine Workers' Compensation
200 Constitution Avenue, N.W., Room C3520
Washington, DC 20210
(202) 693-0046   Toll Free: (800) 638-7072
TDD: (800) 326-2577
Web: www.dol.gov/dol/topic/workcomp/index.htm

Summary To provide monthly benefits to coal miners who are disabled because of pneumoconiosis (black lung disease) and to their surviving dependents.

Eligibility Present and former coal miners (including certain transportation and construction workers who were exposed to coal mine dust) and their surviving dependents, including surviving spouses, orphaned children, and totally dependent parents, brothers, and sisters, may file claims if they are totally disabled.

Financial data Benefit amounts vary; recently; the basic monthly benefit was $599 for a single totally disabled miner or surviving spouse, $898 per month for a claimant with 1 dependent, $1,048 per month for a claimant with 2 dependents, or $1,197 per month for a claimant with 3 or more dependents. Benefit payments are reduced by the amounts received for pneumoconiosis under state workers' compensation awards and by excess earnings.

Duration Benefits are paid as long as the miner is unable to work in the mines or until the miner dies.

Number awarded Varies; recently, 8,654 miners, 23,690 surviving spouses, 1,230 other eligible persons, 6,442 dependents of miners, 777 dependents of surviving spouses, and 132 dependents of other eligible persons received benefits from this program.

Deadline Deadline not specified.

[1157]
COLORADO PROPERTY TAX EXEMPTION FOR DISABLED VETERANS

Division of Veterans Affairs
7465 East First Avenue, Suite C
Denver, CO 80230
(303) 343-1268   Fax: (303) 343-7238
Web: www.dmva.state.co.us/page/va/prop_tax

Summary To provide a partial exemption of taxes on property owned by disabled veterans in Colorado.

Eligibility This exemption is open to veterans who reside in Colorado and have been rated 100% service-connected disabled by the U.S. Department of Veterans Affairs. Applicants must have been honorably discharged and must own property in Colorado which they use as their primary residence. The exemption also applies to members of the National Guard or Reserves who sustained their injury during a period in which they were called to active duty, property owned by a veteran's spouse if both occupy the property as their primary residence, and property owned by a trust or other legal entity if the veteran or spouse is a major of the trust or other legal entity, the property was transferred solely for estate planning purposes, and the veteran or spouse would otherwise be the owner of record.

Financial data For qualifying veterans, 50% of the first $200,000 of actual value of the primary residence is exempted from taxes.

Duration The exemption continues as long as the veteran resides in the property.

Additional data This program was approved by Colorado voters in 2006.

Number awarded Varies each year.

Deadline Applications must be submitted by June of the year for which the exemption is requested.

[1158]
CONNECTICUT REAL ESTATE TAX EXEMPTION FOR DISABLED VETERANS

Office of Policy and Management
Attn: Intergovernmental Policy Division
450 Capitol Avenue
Hartford, CT 06106-1308
(860) 418-6278   Toll Free: (800) 286-2214 (within CT)
Fax: (860) 418-6493   TDD: (860) 418-6456
E-mail: leeann.graham@ct.gov
Web: www.ct.gov

Summary To exempt Connecticut veterans with disabilities and their surviving spouses from the payment of a portion of their local property taxes.

Eligibility There are 2 categories of Connecticut veterans who qualify for exemptions from their dwelling house and the lot on which it is located: 1) those with major service-connected disabilities (paraplegia or osteochondritis resulting in permanent loss of the use of both legs or permanent paralysis of both legs and lower parts of the body; hemiplegia with permanent paralysis of 1 leg and 1 arm or either side of the body resulting from injury to the spinal cord, skeletal structure, or brain, or from disease of the spinal cord not resulting from syphilis; total blindness; amputation of both arms, both legs, both hands or both feet, or the combination of a hand and a foot; sustained through enemy action or resulting from an accident occurring or disease contracted in such active service) and 2) those with less severe disabilities (loss of use of 1 arm or 1 leg because of service-connected injuries). Surviving unremarried spouses of eligible deceased veterans are entitled to the same exemption as would have been granted to the veteran, as long as they continue to be the legal owner/occupier of the exempted residence. An additional exemption is available to veterans and spouses whose total adjusted gross income is less than $30,500 if unmarried or $37,300 if married. If the veteran is rated as 100% disabled by the U.S. Department of Veterans Affairs (VA), the maximum income levels are $10,000 if unmarried or $21,000 if married.

Financial data Veterans in the first category receive an exemption from local property taxation of $10,000 of assessed valuation. Veterans in the second category receive exemptions of $5,000 of assessed valuation. For veterans whose income is less than the specified levels, additional exemptions of $20,000 for the first category or $10,000 for the second category are available from municipalities that choose to participate. For veterans whose income exceeds the specified levels, the additional exemption from participating municipalities is $5,000 for the first category or $2,500 for the second category. Connecticut municipalities may also elect to exempt from taxation specially adapted housing acquired or modified by a veteran under the provisions of Section 801 of Title 38 of the United States Code.

Duration 1 year; exemptions continue as long as the eligible resident (or surviving spouse) owns/occupies the primary residence and lives in Connecticut.

Number awarded Varies each year; recently, a total of 22,944 veterans received property tax exemptions through this and other programs in Connecticut.

Deadline Applications for the additional municipality exemption must be submitted to the assessor's office of the town or residence by September of every other year.

[1159]
CONNECTICUT VETERANS' ADDITIONAL EXEMPTION TAX RELIEF PROGRAM

Office of Policy and Management
Attn: Intergovernmental Policy Division
450 Capitol Avenue
Hartford, CT 06106-1308
(860) 418-6278   Toll Free: (800) 286-2214 (within CT)
Fax: (860) 418-6493   TDD: (860) 418-6456
E-mail: leeann.graham@ct.gov
Web: www.ct.gov

Summary To exempt disabled veterans and their surviving spouses who are residents of Connecticut from a portion of their personal property taxes.

Eligibility Eligible to apply for this exemption are Connecticut veterans who are rated as disabled by the U.S. Department of Veterans Affairs (VA). Unremarried surviving spouses of qualified veterans are also eligible. An additional exemption may be available to veterans and spouses whose total adjusted gross income is less than $30,500 if unmarried or $37,300 if married. If the veteran is rated as 100% disabled by the U.S. Department of Veterans Affairs (VA), the maximum income levels are $18,000 if unmarried or $21,000 if married.

Financial data The amount of the exemption depends on the level of the VA disability rating: for 10% to 25%, it is $1,500; for more than 25% to 50%, $2,000; for more than 50% to 75%, $2,500; for more than 75% and for veterans older than 65 years of age with any level of disability, $3,000. Municipalities may elect to provide an additional exemption, equal to twice the amount provided, to veterans and spouses whose income is less than the qualifying level. For veterans and spouses who do not meet the income requirement, the additional exemption from participating municipalities is equal to 50% of the basic state exemption.

Duration 1 year; exemptions continue as long as the eligible resident lives in Connecticut.

Number awarded Varies each year; recently, a total of 20,117 veterans received property tax exemptions through this and other programs in Connecticut.

Deadline Applications for the additional municipality exemption must be submitted to the assessor's office of the town of residence by September of every other year.

[1160]
DEATH PENSION FOR SURVIVORS OF VETERANS

Department of Veterans Affairs
Attn: Veterans Benefits Administration
810 Vermont Avenue, N.W.
Washington, DC 20420
(202) 418-4343　　Toll Free: (800) 827-1000
Web: www.vba.va.gov/bin/21/pension/spousepen.htm

Summary To provide pensions to disabled and other spouses and children of deceased veterans with wartime service.

Eligibility This program is open to surviving spouses and unmarried children of deceased veterans who were discharged under conditions other than dishonorable and who had at least 90 days of active military service, at least 1 day of which was during a period of war. Veterans who enlisted after September 7, 1980 generally had to have served at least 24 months or the full period for which they were called to active duty. The countable income of spouses and children must be below specified limits.

Financial data The pension program pays the difference, in 12 monthly installments, between countable income and the specified income level. Currently, those limits are the following: surviving spouse without dependent children, $7,933; surviving spouse with 1 dependent child, $10,385; surviving spouse in need of regular aid and attendance without dependent children, $12,681; surviving spouse in need of regular aid and attendance with 1 dependent child, $15,128; surviving spouse permanently housebound without dependent children, $9,696; surviving spouse permanently housebound with 1 dependent child, $12,144; increase for each additional dependent child, $2,020; surviving children who are living alone, $2,020.

Duration For surviving spouse: until remarriage. For surviving unmarried child: until the age of 18, or 23 if attending a VA-approved school. For surviving child with disability: as long as the condition exists or until marriage.

Number awarded Varies each year.

Deadline Applications may be submitted at any time.

[1161]
DORIS LAKNER RESPITE CARE PROGRAM

ALS Association-Rocky Mountain Chapter
Attn: Patient Services Director
7403 Church Ranch Road, Suite 109
Westminster, CO 80021
(303) 832-2322　　Toll Free: (866) ALS-3211
Fax: (303) 832-3365　　E-mail: leslie@alsaco.org
Web: www.alscolorado.org/index.php?s=75

Summary To provide funding for respite care to caregivers of persons with Amyotrophic Lateral Sclerosis (ALS) in Colorado.

Eligibility This assistance is available to caregivers of patients who have a definitive diagnosis of ALS and reside in Colorado. Applicants must be seeking funding for respite care to be delivered either by a licensed home care agency or through an in-patient facility. Funding is not available for services provided by a family member.

Financial data Grants provide up to $1,000 per patient per year.

Duration 1 year; may be renewed.

Number awarded Varies each year.

Deadline Applications may be submitted at any time.

[1162]
FEDERAL INCOME TAX CREDIT FOR ADOPTION EXPENSES

Internal Revenue Service
1111 Constitution Avenue, N.W.
Washington, DC 20224
Toll Free: (800) TAX-FORM
Web: www.irs.gov

Summary To provide a credit against federal income taxes to people who adopt children, especially special needs children.

Eligibility This credit is available to people who, during the preceding year, adopted a U.S. citizen who was either a child under 18 years of age or a disabled person unable to care for himself or herself. Different rules apply for adopting a child classified as having special needs. To qualify as a special needs child, the state in which the adoptee resides must have determined that the child cannot or should not be returned to his or her parents' home and probably will not be adopted unless assistance is provided to the adoptive parents. Factors used by states to make that determination include: 1) the child's ethnic background and age; 2) whether the child is a member of a minority or sibling group; and 3) whether the child has a medical condition or a physical, mental, or emotional handicap. This credit is not available to taxpayers whose modified adjusted gross income is greater than $214,730.

Financial data Taxpayers may utilize qualified adoption expenses as a credit against their federal income taxes, to a maximum of $11,650. Taxpayers who adopt a special needs child are entitled to the full credit of $11,650, regardless of their actual adoption expenses. The amount of the credit is reduced for taxpayers whose modified adjusted gross income is greater than $174,730 but less than $214,730.

Duration This credit is available for each qualifying child who is adopted.

Number awarded Varies each year.

Deadline This credit is taken on the qualifying taxpayers' federal income tax return, which is due in April of each year.

[1163]
FEDERAL INCOME TAX DEDUCTION FOR CHILD AND DEPENDENT CARE EXPENSES

Internal Revenue Service
1111 Constitution Avenue, N.W.
Washington, DC 20224
Toll Free: (800) TAX-FORM
Web: www.irs.gov

Summary To provide a federal income tax credit for a portion of the expenses of caring for a child or disabled dependent.

Eligibility Eligible for this credit are U.S. citizens or residents who have earned income and who live with a qualifying dependent who is either 1) under the age of 13; 2) a spouse who is physically or mentally unable to care for himself or herself; or 3) another dependent who is physically or mentally unable to care for himself or herself and for whom the taxpayer can claim an exemption. Qualifying expenses include amounts paid for household services and care of the dependent while the taxpayer worked or looked for work.

Financial data A percentage of the qualifying expenses in excess of $3,000 for 1 dependent or $6,000 for 2 or more dependents is applied as a credit against taxes; the percentage depends on the adjusted gross income of the taxpayer, ranging from 35% for incomes less than $15,000 to 20% for incomes greater than $43,000. The maximum credit is $5,000 or $2,500 if married filing separately.

Duration 1 year; taxpayers must reapply each year.

Number awarded Varies each year.

Deadline This credit is applied to the qualifying tax filers' federal income tax return, which is due in April of each year.

[1164]
FLORIDA SERVICE-CONNECTED TOTAL AND PERMANENT DISABILITY PROPERTY TAX EXEMPTION

Florida Department of Revenue
Attn: Taxpayer Services
1379 Blountstown Highway
Tallahassee, FL 32304-2716
(850) 488-6800   Toll Free: (800) 352-3671
TDD: (800) 367-8331
Web: www.myflorida.com/dor/property/exemptions.html

Summary To exempt from property taxation real estate owned by disabled veterans and their surviving spouses.

Eligibility This exemption is available to Florida residents who have real estate that they own and use as a homestead. Applicants must be honorably-discharged veterans with a service-connected total and permanent disability. Under certain circumstances, the benefit of this exemption can carry over to a surviving spouse.

Financial data All real estate used and owned as a homestead, less any portion used for commercial purposes, is exempt from taxation.

Duration The exemption applies as long as the taxpayer owns the property in Florida.

Additional data Initial applications should be made in person at the appropriate county property appraiser's office.

Number awarded Varies each year.

Deadline Applications must be submitted by February of the year for which the exemption is sought.

[1165]
GEORGIA HOMESTEAD TAX EXEMPTION FOR DISABLED VETERANS

Georgia Department of Revenue
Attn: Property Tax Division
4245 International Parkway, Suite A
Hapeville, GA 30354-3918
(404) 968-0707   Fax: (404) 968-0778
E-mail: Local.Government.Services@dor.ga.gov
Web: etax.dor.ga.gov

Summary To exempt from property taxation a portion of the value of homesteads owned by disabled veterans in Georgia and their families.

Eligibility This program is open to residents of Georgia who qualify as a 100% disabled veteran under any of several provisions of state law. Surviving spouses and minor children are also eligible. Applicants must actually occupy a homestead and use it as their legal residence for all purposes.

Financial data The first $50,000 of assessed valuation of the homestead owned by disabled veterans or their family members is exempt from property taxes for state, county, municipal, and school purposes.

Duration The exemption remains in effect as long as the veteran or family member owns and resides in the homestead.

Number awarded Varies each year.

Deadline Applications must be filed with local tax officials by February of each year.

[1166]
GRANTS FOR ACCESSIBILITY

Corporation for Independent Living
157 Charter Oak Avenue, Third Floor
Hartford, CT 06106
(860) 563-6011, ext. 221   Fax: (860) 563-2562
E-mail: access@cilhomes.org
Web: www.cilhomes.org/accessolutions.html

Summary To provide grants to low- or moderate-income residents of Connecticut who have physical disabilities (as well as their parents) and need to modify their existing housing.

Eligibility Eligible to participate in this program are Connecticut residents who have a physical disability (including people in wheelchairs, the deaf or hearing impaired, the blind or visually impaired, and people who have multiple sclerosis, cerebral palsy, traumatic brain injury, or any other physical disability), own their homes, and have a total household income at or below 80% of median income. Also eligible are homeowner parents of a child who is physically disabled and tenants who have the landlord's written consent to make accessibility renovations. Applicants must have total household income that is less than 80% of the state median. Grant funds may be used to purchase and install fixtures and improvements required to improve accessibility and/or usability of a residential dwelling in Connecticut.

Financial data Grants range from $5,000 to $50,000. Initially, a full lien is placed against the recipient's home. Total lien amounts are reduced automatically by 10% every year. At the end of 10 years, the grant is forgiven in full and the lien is removed.

Additional data Funding for this program, which began in 1984, is provided by the Connecticut Department of Economic and Community Development.

Number awarded Varies each year. Since the program began, more than 1,500 individuals have received grants.

Deadline Applications may be submitted at any time.

[1167]
HAWAII CHILDREN'S CANCER FOUNDATION FAMILY ASSISTANCE PROGRAM

Hawaii Children's Cancer Foundation
1814 Liliha Street
Honolulu, HI 96817
(808) 528-5161 Toll Free: (866) 443-HCCF (within HI)
Fax: (808) 521-4689 E-mail: hccf@lava.net
Web: www.hccf.org/legacy/family.html

Summary To provide funding to families in Hawaii who have a child with cancer.

Eligibility This program is open to families in Hawaii who need assistance for a child with cancer. Support is available for payment of treatment bills, travel to treatment, medical supplies, prescriptions and medications, or other costs related to cancer.

Financial data Grants up to $4,000 per family are available for the first year of treatment and up to $2,000 per family for subsequent years of treatment. Funds are provided only for costs not covered by health insurance or other assistance programs.

Duration Grants are provided on an annual basis as long as the need continues.

Additional data This foundation was established in 1991.

Number awarded Varies each year; recently, 85 families received approximately $250,000 from this program.

Deadline Deadline not specified.

[1168]
HAWAII PROPERTY TAX EXEMPTIONS FOR DISABLED VETERANS

Office of Veterans Services
Attn: Veterans Services Coordinator
459 Patterson Road
E-Wing, Room 1-A103
Honolulu, HI 96819-1522
(808) 433-0420 Fax: (808) 433-0385
E-mail: ovs@ovs.hawaii.gov
Web: www.dod.state.hi.us/ovs/benefits.html

Summary To exempt the homes of disabled veterans and surviving spouses in Hawaii from real estate taxation.

Eligibility This program is open to totally disabled veterans in Hawaii and their surviving spouses.

Financial data The real property owned and occupied as a home is exempt from taxation.

Duration The exemption applies as long as the disabled veteran or his/her widow(er) resides in Hawaii.

Deadline Deadline not specified.

[1169]
HEMOPHILIA ASSOCIATION OF THE CAPITAL AREA FAMILY ASSISTANCE PROGRAM

Hemophilia Association of the Capital Area
10560 Main Street, Suite PH-4
Fairfax, VA 22030-7182
(703) 352-7641 Fax: (703) 352-2145
E-mail: info@hacacares.org
Web: www.hacacares.org

Summary To provide emergency financial aid to individuals with bleeding disorders and their families in the Washington, D.C. area.

Eligibility This program is open to 1) residents of northern Virginia, Montgomery and Prince George's County in Maryland, and Washington, D.C.; and 2) people who receive treatment for bleeding disorders at Children's National Medical Center or Georgetown University Hospital in Washington, D.C. Also eligible are parents and caregivers of people living in their home who have a bleeding disorder relevant to the mission of the Hemophilia Association of the Capital Area (HACA). Applicants must be able to demonstrate need for assistance for 1) uncovered medical bills associated with the diagnosis and treatment of a bleeding disorder and any complications from that; or 2) basic living expense emergencies.

Financial data The amount of the assistance depends on the need of the grantee.

Duration Assistance is provided only once per calendar year.

Number awarded Varies each year.

Deadline Applications may be submitted at any time.

[1170]
HOMECHOICE MORTGAGE LOAN PROGRAM

Fannie Mae
Attn: Resource Center
13150 Worldgate Drive
Herndon, VA 20170-4376
Toll Free: (800) 7-FANNIE
E-mail: resource_center@fanniemae.com
Web: www.fanniemae.com

Summary   To provide mortgage loans to people with disabilities and their families.

Eligibility   This program is open to people with low to moderate income who have a disability as defined by the Americans with Disabilities Act of 1990 or have family members with disabilities living with them. Applicants must be interested in obtaining a mortgage loan for purchase of owner-occupied single-family detached homes, townhouses, or condominiums. Non-occupant co-borrowers may be considered if they are a family member or legal guardian. Nontraditional credit histories are considered.

Financial data   No loan limits are specified. The program offers flexibility in the areas of loan-to-value ratios, down payment sources, qualifying ratios, and the establishment of credit.

Duration   15- and 30-year fixed-rate mortgages are available.

Additional data   Loans under this program are available through coalitions in 23 states comprised of organizations and agencies working together to create homeownership opportunities for people with disabilities. For further information on those coalitions, contact Fannie Mae.

Number awarded   Varies each year.

Deadline   Applications may be submitted at any time.

[1171]
IDAHO INCOME TAX EXEMPTION FOR MAINTAINING A HOME FOR THE DEVELOPMENTALLY DISABLED

Idaho State Tax Commission
Attn: Public Information Office
800 Park Boulevard, Plaza IV
P.O. Box 36
Boise, ID 83722-0410
(208) 334-7660   Toll Free: (800) 972-7660
TDD: (800) 377-3529
Web: tax.idaho.gov

Summary   To exempt from state taxation a portion of the income of residents of Idaho who maintain a home for a family member, including themselves and their spouses, who is developmentally disabled.

Eligibility   Individuals in Idaho who maintain a household that includes a developmentally disabled person (of any age) are eligible for this program if they provide at least half of the support of the developmentally disabled family member. The taxpayer and spouse may be included as a member of the family. Developmental disability is defined as a chronic disability that 1) is attributable to an impairment such as mental retardation, cerebral palsy, epilepsy, autism, or related condition; 2) results in substantial func-

tional limitation in 3 or more of the following areas of life activity: self-care, receptive and expressive language, learning, mobility, self-direction, capacity for independent living, or economic self-sufficiency; and 3) reflects the need for a combination and sequence of special, interdisciplinary or generic care, treatment, or other services that are of lifelong or extended duration and individually planned and coordinated.

Financial data   The amount of the deduction is $1,000 for each developmentally disabled family member, up to a maximum of $3,000.

Duration   Application for the deduction must be submitted each year.

Additional data   This deduction also applies to taxpayers maintaining a home for a family member who is 65 years of age or older. Taxpayers who do not claim the $1,000 deduction may be able to claim a tax credit of $100 for each member of the family who is developmentally disabled or elderly, to a maximum of 3 members.

Number awarded   Varies each year.

Deadline   April of each year.

[1172]
IDAHO RETIREMENT BENEFITS DEDUCTION

Idaho State Tax Commission
Attn: Public Information Office
800 Park Boulevard, Plaza IV
P.O. Box 36
Boise, ID 83722-0410
(208) 334-7660   Toll Free: (800) 972-7660
TDD: (800) 377-3529
Web: tax.idaho.gov

Summary   To deduct the retirement and disability income of certain residents from state income tax in Idaho.

Eligibility   Eligible for this deduction are full-year residents of Idaho who are age 65 or older, or disabled and age 62 and older, and who are receiving the following annuities and benefits: 1) retirement annuities paid by the United States to a retired civil service employee or the unremarried widow of the employee; 2) retirement benefits paid from the firemen's retirement fund of the state of Idaho to a retired fireman or the unremarried widow of a retired fireman; 3) retirement benefits paid from the policeman's retirement fund of a city within Idaho to a retired policeman or the unremarried widow of a retired policeman; or 4) retirement benefits paid by the United States to a retired member of the U.S. military service or the unremarried widow of those veterans.

Financial data   The amount of retirement or disability benefits may be deducted from taxable state income in Idaho, to a maximum deduction of $39,330 for married couples or $26,220 for single persons.

Duration   1 year; must reapply each year.

Number awarded   Varies each year.

Deadline   April of each year.

[1173]
IDAHO WAR VETERAN'S EMERGENCY GRANT PROGRAM

Idaho Division of Veterans Services
Attn: Office of Veterans Advocacy
444 Fort Street
Boise, ID 83702
(208) 577-2300   Fax: (208) 577-2333
E-mail: info@veterans.idaho.gov
Web: www.veterans.idaho.gov/Veterans_Advocacy.aspx

Summary To provide emergency assistance to disabled veterans, wartime veterans, and their families in Idaho.

Eligibility Eligible for these grants are veterans who had at least 90 days of honorable wartime military service while a resident of Idaho. Veterans with a service-connected disability are eligible with earlier separation. Surviving spouses and dependent children are also eligible. Applicants must be current residents of Idaho in need of assistance because of a major catastrophe (e.g., natural disaster or death of a spouse or child), loss of job because of a disability, or other extreme financial emergency (e.g., cut-off notice from a utility company, eviction notice from a landlord, arrears payment notice from the lien holder of a home).

Financial data The maximum amount available under this program is $1,000, issued in small incremental grants.

Duration The limit of $1,000 applies for the lifetime of each veteran or his/her family.

Additional data This program was established by the Idaho legislature in lieu of granting a wartime bonus to Idaho veterans.

Number awarded Varies each year.

Deadline Deadline not specified.

[1174]
ILLINOIS SPECIALLY ADAPTED HOUSING TAX EXEMPTION

Illinois Department of Veterans' Affairs
833 South Spring Street
P.O. Box 19432
Springfield, IL 62794-9432
(217) 782-6641   Toll Free: (800) 437-9824 (within IL)
Fax: (217) 524-0344   TDD: (217) 524-4645
E-mail: webmail@dva.state.il.us
Web: www.veterans.illinois.gov/benefits/realestate.htm

Summary To provide an exemption on the assessed value of specially adapted housing to Illinois veterans with disabilities and their spouses.

Eligibility Specially adapted housing units for disabled veterans that have been purchased or constructed with federal funds are eligible for this exemption. The exemption is extended to the veteran, the spouse, or the unremarried surviving spouse.

Financial data Under this program, an exemption is allowed on the assessed value of eligible real property, up to a maximum of $70,000 of assessed valuation.

Duration 1 year; renewable as long as the veteran, or spouse, or unremarried surviving spouse resides in the specially adapted housing in Illinois.

Number awarded Varies each year.

Deadline Applications for the exemption may be submitted at any time.

[1175]
ILLINOIS TAX EXEMPTION FOR MOBILE HOMES

Illinois Department of Veterans' Affairs
833 South Spring Street
P.O. Box 19432
Springfield, IL 62794-9432
(217) 782-6641   Toll Free: (800) 437-9824 (within IL)
Fax: (217) 524-0344   TDD: (217) 524-4645
E-mail: webmail@dva.state.il.us
Web: www.veterans.illinois.gov/benefits/realestate.htm

Summary To provide an exemption on the assessed value of mobile homes to Illinois veterans with disabilities and their spouses.

Eligibility This exemption applies to taxes imposed on mobile homes in Illinois. The property must be owned and used exclusively by a disabled veteran, spouse, or unremarried surviving spouse as a home. The veteran must have received authorization of the Specially Adapted Housing Grant by the U.S. Department of Veterans Affairs, whether that benefit was used or not. Disabled veterans who currently live in a mobile home and never received the Specially Adapted Housing Grant are not eligible.

Financial data Qualifying veterans, spouses, and unmarried surviving spouses are exempt from property taxes imposed by the state of Illinois on mobile homes.

Duration 1 year; renewable as long as the veteran, or spouse, or unremarried surviving spouse resides in the mobile home in Illinois.

Number awarded Varies each year.

Deadline Applications for the exemption may be submitted at any time.

[1176]
INDIANA PROPERTY TAX DEDUCTIONS FOR DISABLED VETERANS

Department of Local Government Finance
Indiana Government Center North, Room 1058
100 North Senate Avenue
Indianapolis, IN 46201
(317) 232-3777   Fax: (317) 232-8779
E-mail: PropertyTaxInfo@dlgf.in.gov
Web: www.in.gov/dlgf

Summary To exempt disabled Indiana veterans and their spouses from a portion of their property taxes.

Eligibility This program is open to the following categories of veterans who are residents of Indiana: 1) served honorably at least 90 days and are either totally disabled (the disability does not need to be service-connected) or are at least 62 years of age and have at least a 10% service-connected disability; 2) served honorably during wartime and have at least a 10% service-connected disability; or 3) served honorably during wartime and either have a 100% service-connected disability or are at least 62 years of age and have at least a 10% service connected disability. A statutory disability rating for pulmonary tuberculosis does not qualify. A disability incurred during Initial Active Duty for Training (IADT) with the National Guard or Reserves is eligible only if the disability occurred from an event during the period of active duty and that duty was performed during wartime. Surviving spouses of those 3 categories of veterans are also eligible.

Financial data Property tax exemptions are $12,480 for veterans and spouses in the first category (only if the assessed value of the combined real and personal property owned by the veteran or spouse does not exceed $143,160), $24,960 in the second category, or $37,440 in the third category; there is no limit on the value of the property owned by a surviving spouse).

Duration 1 year; may be renewed as long as the eligible veteran or surviving unremarried spouse owns and occupies the primary residence in Indiana.

Number awarded Varies each year.

Deadline Applications must be submitted no later than May of each year.

[1177]
INJURED MARINE SEMPER FI GRANTS

Injured Marine Semper Fi Fund
c/o Wounded Warrior Center
Building H49
P.O. Box 555193
Camp Pendleton, CA 92055-5193
(760) 725-3680   Fax: (760) 725-3685
E-mail: info@semperfifund.org
Web: www.semperfifund.org

Summary To provide supplemental assistance to Marines injured in combat and training operations and their families.

Eligibility This program is open to Marines injured in combat operations and training accidents and their families. Applicants must need financial assistance to deal with the personal and financial disruption associated with leaving their home, their family, and their job during hospitalization, rehabilitation, and recuperation. Applications are available at military hospitals.

Financial data Funds are available for such expenses as child care, travel expenses for families, and other necessities. Assistance is also available for the purchase of adaptive transportation, home modifications, and specialized equipment such as wheelchairs, audio/visual equipment for the blind, and software for traumatic brain injuries.

Duration Grants are provided as needed.

Additional data This fund was established in 2004 by a small group of Marine Corps spouses.

Number awarded Varies each year. Since this program was established, it has awarded more than 18,300 grants worth more than $37 million.

Deadline Applications may be submitted at any time.

[1178]
IOWA INCOME TAX DEDUCTION OF EXPENSES INCURRED FOR CARE OF A DISABLED RELATIVE

Iowa Department of Revenue
Attn: Taxpayer Services
Hoover State Office Building
1305 East Walnut
P.O. Box 10457
Des Moines, IA 50306-0457
(515) 281-3114   Toll Free: (800) 367-3388 (within IA)
Fax: (515) 242-6487   E-mail: idr@iowa.gov
Web: www.iowa.gov/tax

Summary To deduct the cost of caring for a disabled relative from taxable income of Iowa residents.

Eligibility This deduction applies to the expenses incurred in caring for a disabled relative in the home of an Iowa resident. The expenses must be for the care of a grandchild, child, parent, or grandparent. The disabled person must be unable, by reason of physical or mental disability, to live independently and must be receiving or be eligible to receive medical assistance benefits through Social Security. Only expenses that are not reimbursed can be claimed. An itemized list of expenses must be included with the income tax return.

Financial data Expenses up to $5,000 per year may be deducted from the taxable income of a qualifying resident.

Duration The deduction continues as long as the recipient remains a resident of Iowa for state income tax purposes and incurs expenses to care for a disabled relative.

Number awarded Varies each year.

Deadline Deadline not specified.

[1179]
IOWA PENSION/RETIREMENT INCOME EXCLUSION

Iowa Department of Revenue
Attn: Taxpayer Services
Hoover State Office Building
1305 East Walnut
P.O. Box 10457
Des Moines, IA 50306-0457
(515) 281-3114   Toll Free: (800) 367-3388 (within IA)
Fax: (515) 242-6487   E-mail: idr@iowa.gov
Web: www.iowa.gov/tax

Summary To exempt a portion of the income received by disabled and other retirees in Iowa, as well as their surviving spouses, from state taxation.

Eligibility This exemption applies to the retirement income of residents of Iowa who are 1) 55 years of age or older, 2) disabled, or 3) a surviving spouse or a survivor having an insurable interest in an individual who would have qualified from the exclusion on the basis of age or disability.

Financial data For joint filers, the exclusion is the lesser of $12,000 or the taxable amount of the retirement income; for all other statuses of filers, each eligible taxpayer can claim as an exemption the lesser of $6,000 or the taxable amount of the retirement income.

Duration The exemption continues as long as the recipient remains a resident of Iowa for state income tax purposes.

Number awarded Varies each year.

Deadline Deadline not specified.

[1180]
JACK NORTON FAMILY RESPITE CARE PROGRAM

ALS Association-Minnesota Chapter
Attn: Patient Services Coordinator
333 North Washington Avenue, Suite 105
Minneapolis, MN 55401
(612) 672-0484   Toll Free: (888) 672-0484
Fax: (612) 672-9110   E-mail: anne@alsmn.org
Web: webmn.alsa.org

Summary To provide funding for respite care to residents of Minnesota and North Dakota who are a Person with Amyotrophic Lateral Sclerosis (PALS) or family member.

Eligibility This assistance is available to any PALS or family member living in Minnesota or North Dakota. The family caregiver must be living with and caring for a PALS on a full-time basis.

Financial data The program provides funding to pay for a family caregiver to assist in caring for the PALS.

Duration Funding is provided for 18 hours a month.

Additional data The Minnesota Chapter of the ALS Association arranges with an appropriate licensed home care agency to provide the respite care.

Number awarded Varies each year.

Deadline Applications may be submitted at any time.

[1181]
KANSAS DISABLED ACCESS INCOME TAX CREDIT

Kansas Department of Revenue
Attn: Taxpayer Assistance Center
Robert B. Docking State Office Building
915 S.W. Harrison Street
Topeka, KS 66612-1712
(785) 368-8222   Toll Free: (877) 526-7738
Fax: (785) 291-3614   TDD: (785) 296-6461
Web: www.ksrevenue.org/taxcredits-disabled.htm

Summary To provide an income tax credit to individual and business taxpayers in Kansas who incur certain expenditures to make their property accessible to people with disabilities.

Eligibility This credit is available to state income taxpayers in Kansas who make buildings or facilities accessible and usable by persons with disabilities in conformity with the Americans with Disabilities Act of 1990. The credit applies to the taxpayer's principal dwelling or the principal dwelling of a lineal ascendant or descendant, including construction of a small barrier-free living unit attached to the principal dwelling. The only expenditures that qualify for this credit are those that are specifically intended to 1) make an existing facility accessible to people with disabilities; 2) remove existing architectural barriers; or 3) modify or adapt an existing facility or piece of equipment in order to employ people with disabilities.

Financial data For individuals, the amount of the credit depends on adjusted gross income and the amount of the expenditure, ranging from 100% of the expenditure for incomes less than $25,000, to 50% for incomes greater than $45,000 but less than $55,000; persons with incomes greater than $55,000 do not qualify for the credit; the maximum individual credit is $9,000. For businesses, the credit is 50% of the amount of the expenditure, to a maximum of $10,000.

Duration This is a 1-time credit.

Number awarded Varies each year.

Deadline Claims are filed with the state income tax return, due in April.

[1182]
LONGSHORE AND HARBOR WORKERS' COMPENSATION PROGRAM

Department of Labor
Employment Standards Administration
Office of Workers' Compensation Programs
Attn: Division of Longshore and Harbor Workers'
  Compensation
200 Constitution Avenue, N.W., Room C4315
Washington, DC 20210
(202) 693-0038   Toll Free: (800) 638-7072
Fax: (202) 693-1380   TDD: (800) 326-2577
Web: www.dol.gov/dol/topic/workcomp/index.htm

Summary To provide benefits to maritime workers disabled or killed during the course of employment and to their spouses.

Eligibility This program is open to longshoremen, harbor workers, and other maritime workers who are injured during the course of employment; by extension, various other classes of private industry workers (including workers engaged in the extraction of natural resources on the outer continental shelf, employees of defense contractors overseas, and employees at post exchanges on military bases) are also eligible if they become disabled for work-related causes. In addition, survivor benefits are provided if the work-related injury causes the employee's death.

Financial data The compensation for disability is 66 2/3% of the employee's average weekly wage, with a minimum of 50% of the national average weekly wage (NAWW) and a maximum of 200% of the NAWW. In a recent year, the Department of Labor calculated the NAWW as $612.33, so the minimum weekly disability payment was $306.17 and the maximum was $1,224.66. Death benefits are equivalent to the average weekly wage of the deceased employee, with a minimum equivalent to 100% of the NAWW and a maximum equivalent to 200% of the NAWW.

Duration Benefits are paid as long as the worker remains disabled; death benefits are paid for the life of the qualified survivor.

Additional data This program also provides medical benefits and rehabilitation services to qualifying longshoremen, harbor workers, and other workers.

Number awarded Varies; more than 15,000 maritime workers recently received compensation and medical benefits through this program.

Deadline Deadline not specified.

[1183]
LOUISIANA INCOME TAX CREDIT FOR EMPLOYMENT-RELATED EXPENSES FOR MAINTAINING A HOUSEHOLD FOR CERTAIN DISABLED DEPENDENTS

Louisiana Department of Revenue
Attn: Individual Income Tax
P.O. Box 201
Baton Rouge, LA 70821
(225) 219-0102
Web: www.revenue.louisiana.gov

Summary To provide a state income tax credit to people in Louisiana who maintain a household that includes dependents with disabilities.

Eligibility This credit is available to residents of Louisiana who maintain a household that includes dependents who are physically or mentally disabled. They must have expenses for household services and care of a qualifying individual that are incurred to enable the taxpayer to be gainfully employed.

Financial data Qualifying taxpayers are entitled to a credit of 35% of employment-related expenses; the percentage is reduced by 1 percentage point (but not below 20%) for each $2,000 (or fraction thereof) of a taxpayer's adjusted gross income that exceeds $15,000 in a taxable year.

Duration The benefit continues as long as the recipient meets all program requirements.

Number awarded Varies each year.

Deadline Deadline not specified.

[1184]
MAINE PROPERTY TAX EXEMPTIONS FOR VETERANS

Maine Revenue Services
Attn: Property Tax Division
P.O. Box 9106
Augusta, ME 04332-9106
(207) 287-2011   Fax: (207) 287-6396
E-mail: prop.tax@maine.gov
Web: www.maine.gov

Summary To exempt the estates of disabled Maine veterans and selected family members from property taxation.

Eligibility Eligible for this program are veterans who served in wartime during World War I, World War II, the Korean campaign, the Vietnam war, the Persian Gulf war, or other recognized service periods, are legal residents of Maine, and are either older than 62 years of age or are receiving a pension or compensation from the U.S. government for total disability (whether service connected or not). Vietnam veterans must have served 180 days on active duty unless discharged earlier for a service-connected disability. The exemption also includes 1) property held in joint tenancy with the veterans' spouses, and 2) property of unremarried widow(er)s, minor children, and mothers of deceased veterans, if those dependents are receiving a pension or compensation from the U.S. government.

Financial data Estates of disabled veterans and eligible dependents, including both real and personal property, are exempt up to $6,000 of just valuation. For veterans and dependents who served in wartime prior to World War II, estates up to $7,000 are exempt.

Duration Veterans, spouses, unremarried widow(er)s, and mothers are eligible for this exemption throughout their lifetimes; minor children of veterans are eligible until they reach the age of 18.

Number awarded Varies each year.

Deadline When an eligible person first submits an application, the proof of entitlement must reach the assessors of the local municipality prior to the end of March. Once eligibility has been established, notification need not be repeated in subsequent years.

[1185]
MAINE TAX EXEMPTION FOR SPECIALLY ADAPTED HOUSING UNITS

Maine Revenue Services
Attn: Property Tax Division
P.O. Box 9106
Augusta, ME 04332-9106
(207) 287-2011   Fax: (207) 287-6396
E-mail: prop.tax@maine.gov
Web: www.maine.gov

Summary To exempt the specially adapted housing units of paraplegic veterans or their surviving spouses from taxation in Maine.

Eligibility Veterans who served in the U.S. armed forces during any federally-recognized war period, are legal residents of Maine, are paraplegic veterans within the meaning of U.S. statutes, and have received a grant from the U.S. government for specially adapted housing are eligible. The exemption also applies to property held in joint tenancy with the veteran's spouse and to the specially adapted housing of unremarried widow(er)s of eligible veterans.

Financial data Estates of paraplegic veterans are exempt up to $50,000 of just valuation for a specially adapted housing unit.

Duration The exemption is valid for the lifetime of the paraplegic veteran or unremarried widow(er).

Number awarded Varies each year.

Deadline When an eligible person first submits an application, the proof of entitlement must reach the assessors of the local municipality prior to the end of March. Once eligibility has been established, notification need not be repeated in subsequent years.

[1186]
MARYLAND INCOME TAX ADJUSTMENTS FOR ADOPTING SPECIAL NEEDS CHILDREN

Comptroller of Maryland
Attn: Revenue Administration Division
80 Calvert Street
Annapolis, MD 21411
(410) 260-7980
Toll Free: (800) MD-TAXES (within MD)
Fax: (410) 974-3456   TDD: (410) 260-7157
E-mail: taxhelp@comp.state.md.us
Web: individuals.marylandtaxes.com

Summary   To reduce the reportable taxable income of Maryland residents who adopt special needs (particularly disabled) children.

Eligibility   Residents of Maryland who adopt disabled and other special needs children through a public or non-profit adoption agency are eligible for this program.

Financial data   Eligible parents are permitted to reduce their reportable taxable income to cover the amount expended for filing fees, attorney's fees, and travel costs incurred in connection with the adoption of a qualifying child, up to a maximum of $6,000 (up to $5,000 for parents who adopt a child without special needs).

Duration   This is a 1-time deduction.

Deadline   Deadline not specified.

[1187]
MARYLAND PENSION EXCLUSION FOR DISABLED AND ELDERLY RESIDENTS

Comptroller of Maryland
Attn: Revenue Administration Division
80 Calvert Street
Annapolis, MD 21411
(410) 260-7980
Toll Free: (800) MD-TAXES (within MD)
Fax: (410) 974-3456   TDD: (410) 260-7157
E-mail: taxhelp@comp.state.md.us
Web: individuals.marylandtaxes.com

Summary   To exempt a portion of the income of disabled and elderly residents (and selected spouses) from state income taxation in Maryland.

Eligibility   Eligible are Maryland residents who receive income from a pension, annuity, or endowment from an employee retirement system and who are at least 65 years of age or classified as totally disabled; spouses of disabled persons also qualify. The disability must be a mental or physical impairment that prevents the person from engaging in gainful activity and that is expected to be of long, continuing, or indefinite duration (or to result in death).

Financial data   Persons with disabilities, who have a spouse who is totally disabled, or who are 65 years of age or older may exclude from state taxation up to $24,000 of income received as a pension, annuity, or endowment.

Duration   The exemption continues as long as the recipient resides in Maryland.

Deadline   Deadline not specified.

[1188]
MARYLAND PROPERTY TAX EXEMPTION FOR BLIND PERSONS

Maryland Department of Assessments and Taxation
Attn: Property Taxes
301 West Preston Street
Baltimore, MD 21201-2395
(410) 767-1184   Toll Free: (888) 246-5941
TDD: (800) 735-2258
Web: www.dat.state.md.us/sdatweb/exempt.html

Summary   To exempt the homes of blind people and their surviving spouses from property taxation in Maryland.

Eligibility   This exemption is available to residents of Maryland who have a central visual acuity of 20/200 or less in the better eye. Applicants must own a dwelling house in Maryland. Surviving spouses of deceased blind people are also eligible for the exemption.

Financial data   The dwelling houses of eligible blind people and their surviving spouses is exempt from $15,000 of assessment on their dwelling house for purposes of real property taxes.

Duration   The exemption is available as long as the blind person or surviving spouse owns the dwelling house in Maryland.

Number awarded   Varies each year.

Deadline   Applications may be submitted at any time.

[1189]
MARYLAND PROPERTY TAX EXEMPTION FOR DISABLED VETERANS AND SURVIVING SPOUSES

Maryland Department of Assessments and Taxation
Attn: Property Taxes
301 West Preston Street
Baltimore, MD 21201-2395
(410) 767-1184   Toll Free: (888) 246-5941
TDD: (800) 735-2258
Web: www.dat.state.md.us/sdatweb/exempt.html

Summary   To exempt the homes of disabled veterans and their surviving spouses from property taxation in Maryland.

Eligibility   This exemption is available to armed services veterans with a permanent service-connected disability rated 100% by the U.S. Department of Veterans Affairs who own a dwelling house in Maryland. Unremarried surviving spouses are also eligible.

Financial data   The dwelling houses of eligible veterans and surviving spouses is exempt from real property taxes.

Duration   The exemption is available as long as the veteran or surviving spouse owns the dwelling house in Maryland.

Number awarded   Varies each year.

Deadline   Applications may be submitted at any time.

[1190]
MARYLAND REAL PROPERTY TAX EXEMPTION FOR DISABLED VETERANS

State Department of Assessments and Taxation
Attn: Tax Credit Program
301 West Preston Street, Room 900
Baltimore, MD 21201-2395
(410) 767-1184   Toll Free: (888) 246-5941 (within MD)
TDD: (800) 735-2258
E-mail: taxcredits@dat.state.md.us
Web: www.dat.state.md.us

Summary   To exempt the homes of disabled veterans and their spouses from property taxation in Maryland.

Eligibility   This program is open to Maryland residents who are veterans with a 100% service-connected permanent disability and their surviving spouses.

Financial data   The dwelling houses owned by qualifying disabled veterans and their spouses are exempt from real property taxes in Maryland.

Duration   This exemption continues as long as the qualifying disabled veterans or spouses reside in Maryland and own their home.

Deadline   Deadline not specified.

[1191]
MASSACHUSETTS INCOME TAX DEDUCTION FOR CARE OF ELDERLY DEPENDENTS WITH DISABILITIES

Massachusetts Department of Revenue
Attn: Personal Income Tax
P.O. Box 7010
Boston, MA 02204
(617) 887-MDOR
Toll Free: (800) 392-6089 (within MA)
Fax: (617) 887-1900
Web: www.mass.gov

Summary   To provide a deduction for the care of elderly dependents from state income taxation in Massachusetts.

Eligibility   Eligible for this deduction are residents of Massachusetts who can document expenses for the care of a dependent over 65 years of age who has a disability. The disabled person may not be the resident or the spouse. Married taxpayers filing separately are not eligible for this deduction.

Financial data   Up to $3,600 for the care of 1 person or up to $7,200 for the care of 2 or more persons may be deducted from income for state taxation purposes.

Duration   The benefit continues as long as the taxpayer provides for the care of a dependent with a disability.

Number awarded   Varies each year.

Deadline   Deadline not specified.

[1192]
MASSACHUSETTS INCOME TAX DEDUCTION FOR EMPLOYMENT-RELATED CARE OF FAMILY MEMBERS WITH DISABILITIES

Massachusetts Department of Revenue
Attn: Personal Income Tax
P.O. Box 7010
Boston, MA 02204
(617) 887-MDOR
Toll Free: (800) 392-6089 (within MA)
Fax: (617) 887-1900
Web: www.mass.gov

Summary   To exempt employment-related expenses for the care of disabled children and spouses from state income taxation in Massachusetts.

Eligibility   Eligible for this deduction are residents of Massachusetts who can document employment-related expenses for the care of a child or spouse with a disability. Married taxpayers filing separately are not eligible for this deduction.

Financial data   Up to $4,800 for the care of 1 person or up to $9,600 for the care of 2 or more persons may be deducted from income for state taxation purposes.

Duration   The benefit continues as long as the taxpayer provides for the care of a child or spouse with a disability.

Number awarded   Varies each year.

Deadline   Deadline not specified.

[1193]
MASSACHUSETTS PROPERTY TAX EXEMPTION FOR VETERANS AND THEIR FAMILIES

Massachusetts Department of Revenue
Attn: Division of Local Services
100 Cambridge Street
Boston, MA 02114
(617) 626-2386   Fax: (617) 626-2330
E-mail: juszkiewicz@dor.state.ma.us
Web: www.mass.gov

Summary   To provide a property tax exemption to blind, disabled, and other veterans (and their families) in Massachusetts.

Eligibility   This program is open to veterans who are residents of Massachusetts, were residents for at least 6 months prior to entering the service, have been residents for at least 5 consecutive years, and are occupying property as their domicile. Applicants must have an ownership interest in the domicile that ranges from $2,000 to $10,000, depending on the category of exemption. Veterans must have been discharged under conditions other than dishonorable. Several categories of veterans and their families qualify: 1) veterans who have a service-connected disability rating of 10% or more; veterans who have been awarded the Purple Heart; Gold Star mothers and fathers; and surviving spouses of eligible veterans who do not remarry; 2) veterans who suffered, in the line of duty, the loss or permanent loss of use of 1 foot, 1 hand, or 1 eye; veterans who received the Congressional Medal of Honor, Distinguished Service Cross, Navy Cross, or Air Force

Cross; and their spouses or surviving spouses; 3) veterans who suffered, in the line of duty, the loss or permanent loss of use of both feet, both hands, or both eyes; and their spouses or surviving spouses; 4) veterans who suffered total disability in the line of duty and received assistance in acquiring specially adapted housing, which they own and occupy as their domicile; and their spouses or surviving spouses; 5) unremarried surviving spouses of military personnel who died due to injury or disease from being in a combat zone, or are missing and presumed dead due to combat; 6) veterans who suffered total disability in the line of duty and are incapable of working; and their spouses or surviving spouses; and 7) veterans who are certified by the Veterans Administration as paraplegic and their surviving spouses.

Financial data Qualified veterans and family members are entitled to an annual exemption from their taxes for the different categories: 1, $400; 2, $750; 3, $1,250; 4, $1,500; 5, full, but with a cap of $2,500 after 5 years; 6, $1,000; or 7, total.

Duration The exemptions are provided each year that the veteran or unremarried surviving spouse lives in Massachusetts and owns the property as a domicile.

Additional data Applications are available from local assessor's offices.

Number awarded Varies each year.

Deadline Applications must be filed with the local assessor by December of each year.

[1194]
MICHIGAN HOMESTEAD PROPERTY TAX CREDIT FOR VETERANS AND BLIND PEOPLE

Michigan Department of Treasury
Attn: Homestead Exemption
Treasury Building
430 West Allegan Street
Lansing, MI 48922
(517) 373-3200   Toll Free: (800) 827-4000
TDD: (517) 636-4999
E-mail: treasPtd2@michigan.gov
Web: www.michigan.gov/treasury

Summary To provide a property tax credit to veterans, military personnel, their spouses, blind people, and their surviving spouses in Michigan.

Eligibility Eligible to apply are residents of Michigan who are 1) blind and own their homestead; 2) a veteran with a service-connected disability or his/her surviving spouse; 3) a surviving spouse of a veteran deceased in service; 4) a pensioned veteran, a surviving spouse of those veterans, or an active military member, all of whose household income is less than $7,500; or 5) a surviving spouse of a non-disabled or non-pensioned veteran of the Korean War, World War II, or World War I whose household income is less than $7,500. All applicants must own or rent a home in Michigan, have been a Michigan resident for at least 6 months during the year in which application is made, and fall within qualifying income levels (up to $82,650 in household income).

Financial data The maximum credit is $1,200. The exact amount varies. For homeowners, the credit depends on the state equalized value of the homestead and on an allowance for filing category. For renters, 20% of the rent is considered property tax eligible for credit.

Duration 1 year; eligibility must be established each year.

Number awarded Varies each year.

Deadline December of each year.

[1195]
MICHIGAN INCOME TAX EXEMPTION FOR DISABLED VETERANS

Michigan Department of Treasury
Attn: Income Tax
Treasury Building
430 West Allegan Street
Lansing, MI 48922
(517) 373-3200   Toll Free: (800) 827-4000
TDD: (517) 636-4999
E-mail: treasIndTax@michigan.gov
Web: www.michigan.gov/treasury

Summary To exempt a portion of the income of disabled veterans and their families in Michigan from state income taxation.

Eligibility Residents of Michigan may claim this exemption if 1) the taxpayer or spouse is a qualified disabled veteran; or 2) a dependent of the taxpayer is a qualified disabled veteran. The qualifying individual must be a veteran of the active military, naval, marine, coast guard, or air service who received an honorable or general discharge and has a disability incurred or aggravated in the line of duty. This exemption may be claimed in addition to any other exemption for which the taxpayer is eligible.

Financial data Qualifying veterans with disabilities and their eligible family members receive an exemption of $250 from their adjusted gross income for purposes of state taxation.

Duration The exemption continues as long as the recipient resides in Michigan.

Additional data This exemption was first available for 2008 income.

Deadline Deadline not specified.

[1196]
MICHIGAN VETERANS TRUST FUND EMERGENCY GRANTS

Department of Military and Veterans Affairs
Attn: Michigan Veterans Trust Fund
2500 South Washington Avenue
Lansing, MI 48913-5101
(517) 483-5469   E-mail: paocmn@michigan.gov
Web: www.michigan.gov/dmva

Summary To provide temporary financial assistance to disabled and other Michigan veterans and their families, if they are facing personal emergencies.

Eligibility Eligible for this assistance are veterans and their families residing in Michigan who are temporarily unable to provide the basic necessities of life. Support is not provided for long-term problems or chronic financial difficulties. The qualifying veteran must have been discharged under honorable conditions with at least 180 days of active wartime service or have been separated as a result of a physical or mental disability incurred in the line of duty.

Financial data No statutory limit exists on the amount of assistance that may be provided; a local board in each Michigan county determines if the applicant is genuinely needy and the amount of assistance to be awarded.

Duration This assistance is provided to meet temporary needs only.

Number awarded Varies each year.

Deadline Applications may be submitted at any time.

[1197]
MINNESOTA STATE SOLDIERS ASSISTANCE PROGRAM

Minnesota Department of Veterans Affairs
Veterans Service Building
20 West 12th Street, Room 206C
St. Paul, MN 55155-2006
(651) 757-1556   Toll Free: (888) LINK-VET
Fax: (651) 296-3954
E-mail: kathy.schwartz@state.mn.us
Web: www.mdva.state.mn.us/financialassistance.htm

Summary To provide emergency financial assistance to disabled veterans and their families in Minnesota.

Eligibility This assistance is available to veterans who are unable to work because of a temporary disability (from service-connected or other causes). Their dependents and survivors are also eligible. Applicants must also meet income and asset guidelines and be residents of Minnesota.

Financial data The maximum grant is $1,500. Funds may be used to pay for food and shelter, utility bills, and emergency medical treatment (including optical and dental benefits).

Duration This is a short-term program, with benefits payable up to 6 months only. If the veteran's disability is expected to be long term in nature or permanent, the department may continue to provide assistance while application is made for long-term benefits, such as Social Security disability or retirement benefits.

Number awarded Varies each year. A total of $1.4 million is available for this program annually.

Deadline Applications may be submitted at any time.

[1198]
MISSISSIPPI INCOME TAX EXEMPTION FOR THE BLIND

Mississippi State Tax Commission
Attn: Individual Income Tax Division
P.O. Box 1033
Jackson, MS 39215-1033
(601) 923-7089   Fax: (601) 923-7039
Web: www.mstc.state.ms.us/taxareas/individ/main.htm

Summary To exempt a portion of the income of blind people and their spouses from state income tax liability in Mississippi.

Eligibility Eligible for this exemption are residents of Mississippi who have been declared legally blind and their spouses.

Financial data The exemption is $1,500.

Duration The exemption continues as long as the blind person resides in Mississippi.

Number awarded Varies each year.

Deadline The exemption must be requested on the resident's state income tax return, which is due in April.

[1199]
MISSOURI SENIOR CITIZEN, DISABLED VETERAN, AND DISABLED PERSON PROPERTY TAX CREDIT CLAIM

Missouri Department of Revenue
Attn: Taxation Division
301 West High Street, Room 330
P.O. Box 2800
Jefferson City, MO 65105-2800
(573) 751-3505   Toll Free: (800) 877-6881
TDD: (800) 735-2966
E-mail: PropertyTaxCredit@dor.mo.gov
Web: www.dor.mo.gov/tax/personal

Summary To provide a property tax credit to low-income disabled veterans, senior citizens, and other persons with disabilities or their spouses in Missouri.

Eligibility This program is open to residents of Missouri (or their spouses) whose net household income does not exceed certain limits ($27,500 per year if they rented or did not own and occupy their home for the entire year, $30,000 if they owned and occupied their home for the entire year) and have paid property tax or rent on their homestead during the tax year. Applicants must be 1) 65 years of age or older, 2) classified by the U.S. Department of Veterans Affairs as a 100% service-connected disabled veteran, 3) 60 years of age or older and receiving surviving spouse Society Security benefits, or 4) 100% disabled.

Financial data The tax credit depends on the claimant's income and amount paid in property taxes or rent, up to a maximum of $1,100 per year for property tax or $750 per year for rent.

Duration The tax credit is available annually.

Number awarded Varies each year.

Deadline Eligible veterans, people with disabilities, and senior citizens may claim this credit when they file their state income tax return, in April of each year.

[1200]
MISSOURI SPECIAL NEEDS ADOPTION TAX CREDIT

Missouri Department of Revenue
Attn: Taxation Division
301 West High Street, Room 330
P.O. Box 2200
Jefferson City, MO 65105-2200
(573) 751-3505   Toll Free: (800) 877-6881
TDD: (800) 735-2966   E-mail: taxcredit@dor.mo.gov
Web: www.dor.mo.gov/tax/personal

Summary To provide an income tax credit to residents of Missouri who adopt a child with special needs.

Eligibility This credit is available to residents of Missouri who adopt a child that has special needs, i.e., a child for whom it has been determined by the Department of Social Services, a child-placing agency licensed by the state, or a court of competent jurisdiction to have a specific factor or condition (e.g., ethnic background, age, membership in a minority or sibling group, medical condition, handicap) that makes it difficult to place the child with adoptive parents. Applicants must have incurred nonrecurring adoption expenses, such as reasonable and necessary adoption fees, court costs, attorney fees, and other expenses that are directly related to the adoption of a special needs child and are not in violation of federal, state, or local laws.

Financial data Qualifying taxpayers may claim up to $10,000 per child for nonrecurring adoption expenses. The full credit may be claimed when the adoption is final, or a claim for 50% of the credit may be made when the child is placed in the home and the remaining 50% may be claimed when the adoption is final.

Duration This credit is available for a total of 5 consecutive years, beginning when the credit is first taken or the adoption is final, whichever occurs first.

Number awarded Varies each year.

Deadline The credit must be claimed by April of each year.

[1201]
MONTANA DISABLED AMERICAN VETERAN PROPERTY TAX BENEFIT

Montana Department of Revenue
Attn: Property Tax
125 North Roberts, Third Floor
P.O. Box 5805
Helena, MT 59604-5805
(406) 444-6900   Toll Free: (866) 859-2254
Fax: (406) 444-1505   TDD: (406) 444-2830
Web: mt.gov/revenue

Summary To reduce the property tax rate in Montana for disabled veterans and their surviving spouses.

Eligibility This benefit is available to residents of Montana who own and occupy property in the state. Applicants must have been honorably discharged from active service in the armed forces and be currently rated 100% disabled or compensated at the 100% disabled rate because of a service-connected disability. They must have an adjusted gross income less than $52,899 if married or $45,846 if single. Also eligible are unremarried surviving spouses with an adjusted gross income less than $39,968 whose spouse was a veteran with a 100% service-connected disability or compensation at the 100% disabled rate at the time of death, died while on active duty, or died of a service-connected disability.

Financial data Qualifying veterans and surviving spouses are entitled to a reduction in local property taxes on their residence, 1 attached or detached garage, and up to 1 acre of land. The amount of the reduction depends on the status of the applicant (married, single, or surviving spouse) and adjusted gross income, but ranges from 50% to 100%.

Duration The reduction continues as long as the recipient resides in Montana and owns and occupies property used as a primary residence.

Number awarded Varies each year.

Deadline Applications must be filed with the local Department of Revenue Office by April of each year.

[1202]
MONTANA DISABLED DEPENDENT CHILDREN TAX EXEMPTION

Montana Department of Revenue
Attn: Individual Income Tax
125 North Roberts, Third Floor
P.O. Box 5805
Helena, MT 59604-5805
(406) 444-6900   Toll Free: (866) 859-2254
Fax: (406) 444-6642   TDD: (406) 444-2830
Web: mt.gov/revenue

Summary To provide a state income tax exemption to the parents of disabled children in Montana.

Eligibility Eligible are all persons considered Montana residents for purposes of state income taxation who have a disabled child claimed as a regular dependent. The child must be certified by a physician as at least 50% permanently disabled.

Financial data Parents may claim an additional exemption of $2,140 for each child with a disability reported as a dependent.

Duration The exemption continues as long as the recipient resides in Montana with a dependent child with a disability.

Deadline Deadline not specified.

[1203]
MONTANA INCOME TAX EXEMPTION FOR THE BLIND

Montana Department of Revenue
Attn: Individual Income Tax
125 North Roberts, Third Floor
P.O. Box 5805
Helena, MT 59604-5805
(406) 444-6900   Toll Free: (866) 859-2254
Fax: (406) 444-6642   TDD: (406) 444-2830
Web: mt.gov/revenue

Summary To provide a state income tax exemption to blind residents of Montana and their spouses.

Eligibility Eligible are all persons considered Montana residents for purposes of state income taxation who are blind or whose spouse is blind.

Financial data Blind people and their spouses may claim an additional exemption of $2,140 from their income for state taxation purposes.

Duration The exemption continues as long as the recipient resides in Montana.

Deadline Deadline not specified.

[1204]
MONTANA TAX EXEMPTION FOR CERTAIN DISABLED OR DECEASED VETERANS' RESIDENCES

Montana Veterans' Affairs Division
1900 Williams Street
P.O. Box 5715
Helena, MT 59604
(406) 324-3740   Fax: (406) 324-3745
E-mail: lehall@mt.gov
Web: dma.mt.gov/mvad/functions/state.asp

Summary To exempt from taxation the real property of disabled or deceased veterans and their widow(er)s in Montana.

Eligibility This exemption applies to residential property in Montana that is owned and occupied by an honorably-discharged veteran who is rated as 100% disabled or is being paid at the 100% disabled rate by the U.S. Department of Veterans Affairs (DVA). Also eligible are unremarried spouses of deceased veterans who own and occupy a residence in Montana. Spouses must obtain documentation from the DVA that the veteran was rated as 100% disabled or was being paid at the 100% disabled rate at the time of death, or that the veteran died while on active duty.

Financial data Eligible veterans or spouses are entitled to real property tax relief that depends on their income. Single veterans with an income of $30,000 or less are exempt from all property taxes; if their income is $30,001 to $33,000, they pay 20% of the regular tax; those with income from $33,001 to $36,000 pay 30% of the regular tax; and those with income from $36,001 to $39,000 pay 50% of the regular tax. Married veterans with an income of $36,000 or less are exempt from all property taxes; if their income is $36,001 to $39,000, they pay 20% of the regular tax; those with income from $39,001 to $42,000 pay 30% of the regular tax; and those with income from $42,001 to $45,000 pay 50% of the regular tax. Surviving spouses with an income of $25,000 or less are exempt from all property taxes; if their income is $25,001 to $28,000, they pay 20% of the regular tax; those with income from $28,001 to $31,000 pay 30% of the regular tax; and those with income from $31,001 to $34,000 pay 50% of the regular tax.

Duration The exemption continues as long as the residence in Montana is owned and occupied by the disabled veteran or, if deceased, by the veteran's unremarried spouse.

Number awarded Varies each year.

Deadline Deadline not specified.

[1205]
NATIONAL ASSOCIATION FOR THE TERMINALLY ILL ASSISTANCE

National Association for the Terminally Ill
P.O. Box 368
Shelbyville, KY 40066-0368
Toll Free: (866) 668-1724   Fax: (502) 647-9107
E-mail: info@terminallyill.org
Web: www.terminallyill.org

Summary To provide assistance to the families of children who have cancer or other terminal illness.

Eligibility This assistance is available to families of children who are suffering from cancer or other terminal illness and have a life expectancy of 2 years or less. U.S. citizenship is not required, but applicants must have resided legally for at least 12 months. They must need assistance for telephone bills, home or auto repairs, electric bills, rent or mortgage payments, groceries, or medications.

Financial data Assistance depends on the need of the recipient.

Duration Grants are for 3 months; they may be renewed.

Number awarded Varies each year.

Deadline Applications may be submitted at any time.

[1206]
NATIONAL CHILDREN'S CANCER SOCIETY FINANCIAL ASSISTANCE

National Children's Cancer Society
Attn: Patient and Family Services
One South Memorial Drive, Suite 800
St. Louis, MO 63102
(314) 241-1600   Toll Free: (800) 5-FAMILY
Fax: (314) 241-1996
E-mail: SSchuetz@children-cancer.org
Web: www.nationalchildrenscancersociety.com

Summary To provide financial assistance to children with cancer and their families.

Eligibility This assistance is available to children (under 18 years of age) with cancer and their families. Applicants must be facing medical and non-medical expenses related to treatment, including meals during treatment, health insurance premiums, medical expenses not covered by insurance, lodging during treatment, long distance calling cards, and transportation during treatment. Families with liquid assets in excess of $5,000 may be asked to partially or completely "spend down" those assets prior to receiving this assistance. Children must be U.S. citizens or permanent residents.

Financial data Assistance depends on the need of the recipient.

Duration Assistance may be provided for up to 2 months; if continuing support is still required, a request for renewal may be submitted by a hospital professional.

Number awarded Varies each year.

Deadline Applications may be submitted at any time.

[1207]
NEBRASKA HOMESTEAD EXEMPTION

Nebraska Department of Revenue
301 Centennial Mall South
P.O. Box 94818
Lincoln, NE 68509-4818
(402) 471-5729
Toll Free: (800) 742-7474 (within NE and IA)
Web: www.revenue.state.ne.us/homestead.htm

Summary To exempt the property of Nebraska residents who are elderly, disabled, or veterans and their widow(er)s from a portion of taxation.

Eligibility This exemption is available to 3 categories of Nebraska residents: the elderly, certain people with disabilities, and certain disabled veterans and their widow(er)s. Elderly people are those 65 years of age or older who own a homestead with a value less than $95,000 or 200% of their county's average assessed value of single family residential property, whichever is greater. Disabled people are those who 1) have a permanent physical disability and have lost all mobility such as to preclude locomotion without the regular use of a mechanical aid or prosthesis; 2) have undergone amputation of both arms above the elbow, or 3) have a permanent partial disability of both arms in excess of 75%. They must own a homestead with a value less than $110,000 or 225% of their county's average assessed value of single family residential property, whichever is greater. Veterans are those who served on active duty in the armed forces of the United States (or a government allied with the United States) during specified periods of war and received an honorable discharge. They must 1) be drawing compensation from the U.S. Department of Veterans Affairs (VA) because of a 100% service-connected disability; 2) be totally disabled by a nonservice-connected illness or accident; or 3) own a home that is substantially contributed to by VA. Also eligible are unremarried widow(er)s of veterans who died because of a service-connected disability, whose death while on active duty was service-connected, who died while on active duty during wartime, or who drew compensation from VA because of a 100% service-connected disability The homestead maximum value is $110,000 or 225% of the county's average assessed value of single family residential property, whichever is greater. Elderly people must have a household income less than $31,301 if single or $36,801 if married. Disabled persons, veterans, and widow(er)s (except veterans and widow(er)s who own a home that is substantially contributed to by the VA) must have a household income less than $34,401 if single or $39,701 if married.

Financial data Exemptions depend on the income of the applicant, ranging from 25% to 100% of the value of the homestead. For the elderly, the maximum exemption is the taxable value of the homestead up to $40,000 or 100% of the county's average assessed value of single family residential property, whichever is greater. For disabled people and veterans, the maximum exemption is the taxable value of the homestead up to $50,000 or 120% of the county's average assessed value of single family residential property, whichever is greater. For veterans and widow(er)s whose home was substantially contributed to by the VA,

the homestead is 100% exempt regardless of the value of the homestead or the income of the owner.

Duration The exemption is provided as long as the qualifying homestead owner resides in Nebraska.

Number awarded Varies each year.

Deadline Applications must be filed by June of each year.

[1208]
NEVADA DISABLED VETERAN'S TAX EXEMPTION

Nevada Office of Veterans' Services
Attn: Executive Director
5460 Reno Corporate Drive
Reno, NV 89511
(775) 688-1653   Fax: (775) 688-1656
Web: veterans.nv.gov/NOVS/Veterans%20Benefits.html

Summary To exempt from taxation in Nevada a portion of the property owned by disabled veterans or their surviving spouses.

Eligibility This program is open to veterans who are residents of Nevada and have incurred a service-connected disability of 60% or more. Applicants must have received an honorable separation from military service. The widow(er) of a disabled veteran, who was eligible at the time of death, may also be eligible for this benefit.

Financial data Veterans and widow(er)s are entitled to exempt from taxation a portion of their property's assessed value. The amount depends on the extent of the disability and the year filed; it ranges from $6,250 to $20,000 and doubles over a 4-year period.

Duration Disabled veterans and their widow(er)s are entitled to this exemption as long as they live in Nevada.

Additional data Disabled veterans and widow(er)s are able to split their exemption between vehicle taxes and/or property taxes. Further information is available at local county assessors' offices.

Number awarded Varies each year.

Deadline Deadline not specified.

[1209]
NEW HAMPSHIRE PROPERTY TAX EXEMPTION FOR CERTAIN DISABLED VETERANS

New Hampshire Department of Revenue
  Administration
109 Pleasant Street
Concord, NH 03301
(603) 271-2191   Fax: (603) 271-6121
TDD: (800) 735-2964
Web: revenue.nh.gov

Summary To exempt from taxation certain property owned by New Hampshire disabled veterans or their surviving spouses.

Eligibility Eligible for this exemption are New Hampshire residents who are honorably discharged veterans with a total and permanent service-connected disability that involves double amputation of the upper or lower extremities or any combination thereof, paraplegia, or blindness of both eyes with visual acuity of 5/200 or less. Applicants or their surviving spouses must own a specially adapted homestead that has been acquired with the assistance of the U.S. Department of Veterans Affairs.

Financial data Qualifying disabled veterans and surviving spouses are exempt from all taxation on their specially adapted homestead.

Duration 1 year; once the credit has been approved, it is automatically renewed as long as the qualifying person owns the same residence in New Hampshire.

Number awarded Varies each year.

Deadline The original application for a permanent tax credit must be submitted by April.

[1210]
NEW HAMPSHIRE PROPERTY TAX EXEMPTION FOR IMPROVEMENTS TO ASSIST PERSONS WITH DISABILITIES

New Hampshire Department of Revenue
  Administration
109 Pleasant Street
Concord, NH 03301
(603) 271-2191   Fax: (603) 271-6121
TDD: (800) 735-2964
Web: revenue.nh.gov

Summary To exempt improvements designed to assist disabled New Hampshire residents from state real estate taxes.

Eligibility This program is open to residents of New Hampshire who own residential real estate where they reside and to which they have made improvements to assist a person with a disability who also resides on such real estate.

Financial data The value of such improvements is deducted from the assessed value of the residential real estate.

Duration 1 year; this exemption will be continued as long as the recipient meets the eligibility requirements.

Number awarded Varies each year.

Deadline The original application for a permanent tax credit must be submitted by April.

[1211]
NEW HAMPSHIRE SERVICE-CONNECTED TOTAL AND PERMANENT DISABILITY TAX CREDIT

New Hampshire Department of Revenue
  Administration
109 Pleasant Street
Concord, NH 03301
(603) 271-2191   Fax: (603) 271-6121
TDD: (800) 735-2964
Web: revenue.nh.gov

Summary To provide property tax credits in New Hampshire to disabled veterans or their surviving spouses.

Eligibility Eligible for this tax credit are honorably discharged veterans residing in New Hampshire who 1) have a total and permanent service-connected disability, or 2) are a double amputee or paraplegic because of a service-connected disability. Unremarried surviving spouses of qualified veterans are also eligible.

Financial data Qualifying disabled veterans and surviving spouses receive an annual credit of $700 for property taxes on residential property. In addition, individual towns in New Hampshire may adopt a local option to increase the dollar amount credited to disabled veterans, to a maximum of $2,000.

Duration 1 year; once the credit has been approved, it is automatically renewed for as long as the qualifying person owns the same residence in New Hampshire.

Number awarded Varies each year.

Deadline The original application for a permanent tax credit must be submitted by April.

[1212]
NEW JERSEY PROPERTY TAX EXEMPTION FOR DISABLED VETERANS OR SURVIVING SPOUSES

New Jersey Division of Taxation
Attn: Information and Publications Branch
50 Barrack Street
P.O. Box 281
Trenton, NJ 08695-0281
(609) 292-6400
Toll Free: (800) 323-4400 (within NJ, NY, PA, DE, and
  MD)
TDD: (800) 286-6613 (within NJ, NY, PA, DE, and
MD)   E-mail: taxation@tax.state.nj.us
Web: www.state.nj.us/treasury/taxation/otherptr.shtml

Summary To provide a real estate tax exemption to New Jersey veterans with disabilities and certain surviving widow(er)s.

Eligibility This exemption is available to New Jersey residents who have been honorably discharged with active wartime service in the U.S. armed forces and have been certified by the U.S. Department of Veterans Affairs as totally and permanently disabled as a result of wartime service-connected conditions. Unremarried surviving spouses of eligible disabled veterans or of certain wartime servicepersons who died on active duty are also entitled to this exemption. Applicants must be the full owner of and a permanent resident in the dwelling house for which the exemption is claimed.

Financial data A 100% exemption from locally-levied real estate taxes is provided.

Duration 1 year; the exemption continues as long as the eligible veteran remains a resident of New Jersey.

Additional data This program is administered by the local tax assessor or collector. Veterans who are denied exemptions have the right to appeal the decision to their county and state governments.

Number awarded Varies each year.

Deadline Applications may be submitted at any time.

[1213]
NEW MEXICO DISABLED VETERAN
PROPERTY TAX EXEMPTION

New Mexico Department of Veterans' Services
Attn: Benefits Division
407 Galisteo Street, Room 142
Santa Fe, NM 87504
(505) 827-6374   Toll Free: (866) 433-VETS
Fax: (505) 827-6372
E-mail: alan.martinez@state.nm.us
Web: www.dvs.state.nm.us/benefits.html

Summary To exempt disabled veterans and their spouses from payment of property taxes in New Mexico.

Eligibility This exemption is available to veterans who are rated 100% service-connected disabled by the U.S. Department of Veterans Affairs, are residents of New Mexico, and own a primary residence in the state. Also eligible are qualifying veterans' unremarried surviving spouses, if they are New Mexico residents and continue to own the residence.

Financial data Veterans and surviving spouses are exempt from payment of property taxes in New Mexico.

Duration 1 year; continues until the qualifying veteran or spouse no longer live in the residence.

Number awarded Varies each year.

Deadline Deadline not specified.

[1214]
NEW MEXICO INCOME TAX DEDUCTION FOR
THE ADOPTION OF A SPECIAL NEEDS CHILD

New Mexico Taxation and Revenue Department
Attn: Tax Information and Policy Office
1100 South St. Francis Drive
P.O. Box 630
Santa Fe, NM 87504-0630
(505) 827-2523
Web: www.state.nm.us/tax

Summary To provide income tax exemptions to residents of New Mexico who adopt a special needs child.

Eligibility Residents of New Mexico who have adopted a child defined as "difficult to place" on or after January 1 of the tax year are eligible to claim a deduction for that child (and each special needs adopted child) who is under 18 years of age. The classification of children as "difficult to place" may be based on a physical or mental handicap or emotional disturbance that is at least moderately disabling. A copy of the certification issued by the New Mexico Human Services Department must be attached to the resident's tax form for each child for whom a deduction is claimed.

Financial data The deduction is $500 if the resident is married and filing separately or $1,000 if single, head of household, or married and filing jointly.

Duration The deduction continues as long as the qualifying resident remains in the state.

Number awarded Varies each year.

Deadline The qualifying resident claims the deduction on the New Mexico state income tax return, which is due in April.

[1215]
NEW MEXICO TAX EXEMPTION FOR THE
BLIND AND ELDERLY

New Mexico Taxation and Revenue Department
Attn: Tax Information and Policy Office
1100 South St. Francis Drive
P.O. Box 630
Santa Fe, NM 87504-0630
(505) 827-2523
Web: www.state.nm.us/tax

Summary To exempt a portion of the income of New Mexico residents who are blind or over the age of 65, and their surviving spouses, from state income tax liability.

Eligibility This exemption is available to residents of New Mexico who are 65 years of age or older or who are blind.

Financial data The income exemption ranges from $1,000 to $8,000, depending on filing status and income. The maximum income that still qualifies for an exemption is $25,500 for married individuals filing separate returns, $51,000 for heads of household, surviving spouses, and married individuals filing joint returns, or $28,500 for single individuals.

Duration The exemption continues as long as the qualifying resident remains in the state.

Number awarded Varies each year.

Deadline The qualifying resident claims the exemption on the New Mexico state income tax return, which is due in April.

[1216]
NEW YORK ALTERNATIVE PROPERTY TAX
EXEMPTIONS FOR VETERANS

New York State Division of Veterans' Affairs
5 Empire State Plaza, Suite 2836
Albany, NY 12223-1551
(518) 474-6114
Toll Free: (888) VETS-NYS (within NY)
Fax: (518) 473-0379   E-mail: dvainfo@ogs.state.ny.us
Web: veterans.ny.gov/property_tax_exemption.html

Summary To provide wartime veterans and their spouses who are residents of New York with a partial exemption from property taxes.

Eligibility This program is open to veterans who served during specified periods of wartime. Applicants must have been discharged under honorable conditions; additional benefits are available to those who served in a combat zone and to those who have a service-connected disability. The legal title to the property must be in the name of the veteran or the spouse of the veteran or both, or the unremarried surviving spouse of the veteran. The property must be used exclusively for residential purposes. This program is only available in counties, cities, towns, and villages in New York that have opted to participate.

Financial data This program provides an exemption of 15% of the assessed valuation of the property, to a basic maximum of $12,000 per year; local governments may opt for reduced maximums of $9,000 or $6,000, or for increased maximums of $15,000 to $36,000. For combat-zone veterans, an additional 10% of the assessed valuation is exempt, to a basic maximum of $8,000 per year; local governments may opt for a reduced maximum of $6,000 or $4,000, or for increased maximums of $10,000 to $24,000. For disabled veterans, the exemption is the percentage of assessed value equal to half of the service-connected disability rating, to a basic maximum of $40,000 per year; local governments may opt for a reduced maximum of $30,000 or $20,000, or for increased maximums of $50,000 to $120,000. At its option, New York City and other high appreciation municipalities may use the following increased maximum exemptions: war veteran, $54,000; combat-zone veteran, $36,000; disabled veteran, $180,000.

Duration   This exemption is available annually.

Number awarded   Varies each year.

Deadline   Applications must be filed with the local assessor by "taxable status date;" in most towns, that is the end of February.

[1217]
NEW YORK "ELIGIBLE FUNDS" PROPERTY TAX EXEMPTIONS FOR VETERANS

New York State Division of Veterans' Affairs
5 Empire State Plaza, Suite 2836
Albany, NY 12223-1551
(518) 474-6114
Toll Free: (888) VETS-NYS (within NY)
Fax: (518) 473-0379   E-mail: dvainfo@ogs.state.ny.us
Web: veterans.ny.gov

Summary   To provide a partial exemption from property taxes to veterans and their surviving spouses who are residents of New York.

Eligibility   This program is open to veterans who have purchased properties in New York with pension, bonus, or insurance money (referred to as "eligible funds"). Specially adapted homes of paraplegics, or the homes of their widowed spouses, are also covered.

Financial data   This exemption reduces the property's assessed value to the extent that "eligible funds" were used in the purchase, generally to a maximum of $5,000. It is applicable to general municipal taxes but not to school taxes or special district levies.

Duration   This exemption is available annually.

Number awarded   Varies each year.

Deadline   Applications must be filed with the local assessor by "taxable status date;" in most towns, that is the end of February.

[1218]
NEW YORK STATE BLIND ANNUITY

New York State Division of Veterans' Affairs
5 Empire State Plaza, Suite 2836
Albany, NY 12223-1551
(518) 474-6114
Toll Free: (888) VETS-NYS (within NY)
Fax: (518) 473-0379   E-mail: dvainfo@ogs.state.ny.us
Web: veterans.ny.gov/blind_annuity.html

Summary   To provide an annuity to blind wartime veterans and their surviving spouses in New York.

Eligibility   This benefit is available to veterans who served on active duty during specified periods of war. Applicants must 1) meet the New York State standards of blindness; 2) have received an honorable or general discharge, or a discharge other than for dishonorable service; and 3) be now, and continue to be, residents of and continuously domiciled in New York State. The annuity is also payable to unremarried spouses of deceased veterans who were receiving annuity payments (or were eligible to do so) at the time of their death, and are residents of and continuously domiciled in New York State.

Financial data   The annuity is currently $1,173.84 per year.

Number awarded   Varies each year.

Deadline   Deadline not specified.

[1219]
NORTH DAKOTA INCOME TAX ADJUSTMENTS FOR ADOPTING CHILDREN WITH DISABILITIES

Office of State Tax Commissioner
State Capitol Building
600 East Boulevard Avenue, Department 127
Bismarck, ND 58505-0599
(701) 328-3127   Toll Free: (800) 638-2901
Fax: (701) 328-3700   TDD: (800) 366-6888
E-mail: taxinfo@state.nd.us
Web: www.nd.gov/tax

Summary   To provide an income tax deduction to North Dakota residents who adopt children with disabilities.

Eligibility   For the purposes of this program, disabled children are defined as being under the age of 21 and having irreversible mental retardation, blindness, or other disabilities covered under Title XVI of the U.S. Social Security Act. To qualify, the parent must have adopted a child meeting these requirements and supported the child during the taxable year.

Financial data   The reportable taxable income of eligible North Dakota residents is reduced by $750 for each qualifying adopted child. In addition, on a 1-time basis, eligible parents are permitted to reduce their reportable taxable income up to $1,000 to cover the amount expended for filing fees, attorney's fees, and travel costs incurred in connection with the adoption of a qualifying child.

Duration   The $750 reduction continues until the qualifying child reaches 21 years of age.

Number awarded   Varies each year.

Deadline   The deduction is claimed when filing the state income tax return by April of each year.

[1220]
NORTH DAKOTA PROPERTY TAX CREDIT FOR DISABLED VETERANS

Office of State Tax Commissioner
State Capitol Building
600 East Boulevard Avenue, Department 127
Bismarck, ND 58505-0599
(701) 328-2770　　　　　Toll Free: (800) 638-2901
Fax: (701) 328-3700　　　TDD: (800) 366-6888
E-mail: taxinfo@state.nd.us
Web: www.nd.gov/tax

Summary To provide property tax credits to disabled North Dakota veterans and their surviving spouses.

Eligibility This property tax credit is available to honorably-discharged veterans who have more than a 50% service-connected disability as certified by the U.S. Department of Veterans Affairs. Applicants must own and occupy a homestead according to state law. Unremarried surviving spouses are also eligible. If a disabled veteran co-owns the property with someone other than a spouse, the credit is limited to the disabled veteran's interest in the fixtures, buildings, and improvements of the homestead.

Financial data The credit is applied against the first $120,000 of true and full valuation of the fixtures, buildings, and improvements of the homestead, to a maximum amount calculated by multiplying $120,000 by the percentage of the disabled veteran's disability compensation rating for service-connected disabilities.

Duration 1 year; renewable as long as qualified individuals continue to reside in North Dakota and live in their homes.

Number awarded Varies each year.

Deadline Applications may be submitted to the county auditor at any time.

[1221]
NORTH DAKOTA PROPERTY TAX EXEMPTION FOR DISABLED PERSONS CONFINED TO A WHEELCHAIR

Office of State Tax Commissioner
State Capitol Building
600 East Boulevard Avenue, Department 127
Bismarck, ND 58505-0599
(701) 328-2770　　　　　Toll Free: (800) 638-2901
Fax: (701) 328-3700　　　TDD: (800) 366-6888
E-mail: taxinfo@state.nd.us
Web: www.nd.gov/tax

Summary To provide partial tax exemption in North Dakota to persons permanently confined to the use of a wheelchair and their spouses.

Eligibility Persons permanently confined to the use of a wheelchair are those who cannot walk with the assistance of crutches or any other device and will never be able to do so; this must be certified by a physician selected by a local governing board. The property must be owned and occupied as a homestead according to state law. The homestead may be owned by the spouse or jointly owned by the disabled person and spouse provided both reside on the homestead. Qualified residents and, if deceased, their

unremarried surviving spouses are entitled to this exemption. Income and assets are not considered in determining eligibility for the exemption.

Financial data The maximum benefit may not exceed $3,600 taxable value, because a homestead is limited to $80,000 market value.

Duration The exemption continues as long as the homestead in North Dakota is owned by the disabled person and/or the spouse.

Additional data The exemption does not apply to special assessments levied upon the homestead.

Number awarded Varies each year.

Deadline Deadline not specified.

[1222]
NORTH DAKOTA PROPERTY TAX EXEMPTION FOR THE BLIND

Office of State Tax Commissioner
State Capitol Building
600 East Boulevard Avenue, Department 127
Bismarck, ND 58505-0599
(701) 328-2770　　　　　Toll Free: (800) 638-2901
Fax: (701) 328-3700　　　TDD: (800) 366-6888
E-mail: taxinfo@state.nd.us
Web: www.nd.gov/tax

Summary To provide partial tax exemption in North Dakota to blind persons and their spouses.

Eligibility Blind persons are defined as those who are totally blind, who have visual acuity of not more than 20/200 in the better eye with correction, or whose vision is limited in field so that the widest diameter subtends an angle no greater than 20 degrees. Eligible for this exemption is property that is owned by a blind person, by the spouse of a blind person, or jointly by a blind person and a spouse. The property that is exempt includes the entire building classified as residential, and owned and occupied as a residence by a person who qualifies, as long as the building contains no more than 2 apartments or rental units that are leased.

Financial data The exemption applies to all or any part of fixtures, building, and improvements upon any nonfarm-land up to a taxable valuation of $7,200.

Duration The exemption continues as long as the blind person resides in the home in North Dakota.

Number awarded Varies each year.

Deadline Deadline not specified.

[1223]
NORTH DAKOTA PROPERTY TAX EXEMPTION FOR VETERANS WHO LIVE IN SPECIALLY ADAPTED HOUSING

Office of State Tax Commissioner
State Capitol Building
600 East Boulevard Avenue, Department 127
Bismarck, ND 58505-0599
(701) 328-2770　　　　　Toll Free: (800) 638-2901
Fax: (701) 328-3700　　　TDD: (800) 366-6888
E-mail: taxinfo@state.nd.us
Web: www.nd.gov/tax

Summary To provide property tax exemptions to North Dakota veterans and their surviving spouses who have been awarded specially adapted housing.

Eligibility This exemption is available to paraplegic disabled veterans of the U.S. armed forces or any veteran who has been awarded specially adapted housing by the U.S. Department of Veterans Affairs. The paraplegic disability does not have to be service connected. The unremarried surviving spouses of such deceased veterans are also eligible. Income and assets are not considered in determining eligibility for the exemption.

Financial data The maximum benefit may not exceed $5,400 taxable value, because the exemption is limited to the first $120,000 of true and full value of fixtures, buildings, and improvements.

Duration 1 year; renewable as long as qualified individuals continue to reside In North Dakota and live in their homes.

Number awarded Varies each year.

Deadline Applications may be submitted to the county auditor at any time.

[1224]
OHIO HOMESTEAD EXEMPTION FOR SENIOR CITIZENS, DISABLED PERSONS AND SURVIVING SPOUSES

Ohio Department of Taxation
Attn: Tax Equalization Division
P.O. Box 530
Columbus, OH 43216-0530
(614) 466-5744 Toll Free: (800) 282-1780 (within OH)
Fax: (614) 752-9822
Web: tax.ohio.gov

Summary To exempt a portion of the value of homesteads owned by senior citizens and disabled persons (along with their surviving spouses) from property taxation in Ohio.

Eligibility This exemption is available to residents of Ohio who are 65 years of age or older or who have a total and permanent disability. Applicants must own and occupy their home as their principal place of residence. Surviving spouses of persons who were receiving the exemption at the time of their death are also eligible if they were at least 59 years of age on the date of the decedent's death. There is no income limitation.

Financial data Qualifying homeowners may exempt up to $25,000 from the assessed value of their home for purposes of property taxation.

Duration The exemption is available as long as the recipient resides in Ohio and owns his or her home.

Number awarded Varies each year.

Deadline Applications must be submitted to the county auditor by May of each year.

[1225]
OHIO VETERANS' FINANCIAL ASSISTANCE

Ohio Department of Veterans Services
77 South High Street, 7th Floor
Columbus, OH 43215
(614) 644-0898   Toll Free: (888) DVS-OHIO
Fax: (614) 728-9498   E-mail: ohiovet@dvs.ohio.gov
Web: dvs.ohio.gov

Summary To provide emergency aid to Ohio veterans, military personnel, and their dependents who, because of disability or disaster, are in financial need.

Eligibility This assistance is available to veterans and active-duty members of the U.S. armed forces, as well as their spouses, surviving spouses, dependent parents, minor children, and wards. Applicants must have been residents of the Ohio county in which they are applying for at least 3 months. They must be able to demonstrate need for relief because of sickness, accident, or destitution.

Financial data The amount granted varies, depending on the needs of the recipient.

Duration These are emergency funds only and are not designed to be a recurring source of income.

Additional data These grants are made by the various county veterans services offices in Ohio.

Number awarded Varies each year.

Deadline Applications may be submitted at any time.

[1226]
OKLAHOMA FINANCIAL ASSISTANCE PROGRAM

Oklahoma Department of Veterans Affairs
Veterans Memorial Building
2311 North Central Avenue
P.O. Box 53067
Oklahoma City, OK 73152
(405) 521-3684   Fax: (405) 521-6533
E-mail: scylmer@odva.state.ok.us
Web: www.ok.gov

Summary To provide emergency aid to Oklahoma veterans and their families who, because of disability or disaster, are in financial need.

Eligibility This program is open to veterans with at least 90 days of wartime service and an honorable discharge who are current residents of Oklahoma and have resided in the state for at least 1 year immediately preceding the date of application. Applicants must be seeking assistance because of an interruption or loss of job and income resulting from illness, injury, or disaster (such as loss of home due to fire, floor, or storm). Widow(er)s and minor children may also qualify for the benefit.

Financial data The amount of the grant depends on the need of the recipient.

Duration The grant is available only on a 1-time basis.

Additional data No financial assistance will be granted when regular monetary benefits are being received from other state agencies. The funds cannot be used for old debts, car payments, or medical expenses.

Number awarded Varies each year.

Deadline Applications must be submitted to the local post or chapter of a veterans services organization for initial approval or disapproval. They may be submitted at any time during the year.

[1227]
OKLAHOMA INCOME TAX EXEMPTION FOR THE BLIND

Oklahoma Tax Commission
Attn: Income Tax
2501 North Lincoln Boulevard
Oklahoma City, OK 73194-0009
(405) 521-3160 Toll Free: (800) 522-8165 (within OK)
Fax: (405) 522-0063 E-mail: otcmaster@tax.ok.gov
Web: www.tax.ok.gov/incometax.html

Summary To exempt a portion of the income of blind people and their spouses in Oklahoma from state taxation.

Eligibility This exemption is available to residents of Oklahoma and their spouses who are legally blind.

Financial data Each qualifying resident is entitled to claim an additional exemption of $1,000.

Duration The exemption is available as long as the recipient resides in Oklahoma.

Deadline Deadline not specified.

[1228]
OKLAHOMA PROPERTY TAX EXEMPTION FOR DISABLED VETERANS

Oklahoma Tax Commission
Attn: Property Tax
2501 North Lincoln Boulevard
Oklahoma City, OK 73194-0009
(405) 521-3178 Toll Free: (800) 522-8165 (within OK)
Fax: (405) 522-0063 E-mail: otcmaster@tax.ok.gov
Web: www.tax.ok.gov

Summary To exempt the property of disabled veterans and their surviving spouses from taxation in Oklahoma.

Eligibility This program is available to Oklahoma residents who are veterans honorably discharged from a branch of the armed forces or the Oklahoma National Guard. Applicants must have a 100% permanent disability sustained through military action or accident or resulting from a disease contracted while in active service; the disability must be certified by the U.S. Department of Veterans Affairs. They must own property that qualifies for the Oklahoma homestead exemption. Surviving spouses of qualified veterans are also eligible.

Financial data Qualified veterans and surviving spouses are eligible for exemption of the taxes on the full fair cash value of their homestead.

Duration The exemption is available as long as the veteran or surviving spouse resides in Oklahoma and owns a qualifying homestead.

Additional data This exemption was first available in 2006.

Deadline Deadline not specified.

[1229]
OREGON PROPERTY TAX EXEMPTION FOR VETERANS WITH DISABILITIES AND THEIR SPOUSES

Oregon Department of Revenue
Attn: Property Tax Division
Revenue Building
955 Center Street, N.E.
Salem, OR 97310-2551
(503) 378-4988 Toll Free: (800) 356-4222 (within OR)
TDD: (800) 886-7204 (within OR)
Web: www.oregon.gov/DOR/PTD/IC_310_676.shtml

Summary To exempt disabled Oregon veterans and their spouses from a portion of their property taxes.

Eligibility Qualifying veterans are those who received a discharge or release under honorable conditions after service of either 1) 90 consecutive days during World War I, World War II, or the Korean Conflict; or 2) 210 consecutive days after January 31, 1955. Eligible individuals must meet 1 of these conditions: 1) a war veteran who is officially certified by the U.S. Department of Veterans Affairs (VA) or any branch of the U.S. armed forces as having disabilities of 40% or more; 2) a war veteran who is certified each year by a licensed physician as being 40% or more disabled and has total gross income that is less than 185% of the federal poverty level (currently $18,130 for a family of 1, rising to $62,160 for a family of 8); or 3) a war veteran's surviving spouse who has not remarried, even if the veteran's spouse was not disabled or did not take advantage of the exemption if disabled. Recipients of this exemption must own and live on a property in Oregon.

Financial data The exemption is $15,450 of the homestead property's real market value.

Duration 1 year; may be renewed as long as the eligible veteran or surviving unremarried spouse owns and occupies the primary residence.

Number awarded Varies each year.

Deadline This exemption is not automatic. Applications must be submitted by March of each year.

[1230]
OREGON PROPERTY TAX EXEMPTION FOR VETERANS WITH SERVICE-CONNECTED DISABILITIES AND THEIR SPOUSES

Oregon Department of Revenue
Attn: Property Tax Division
Revenue Building
955 Center Street, N.E.
Salem, OR 97310-2551
(503) 378-4988 Toll Free: (800) 356-4222 (within OR)
TDD: (800) 886-7204 (within OR)
Web: www.oregon.gov/DOR/PTD/IC_310_676.shtml

Summary To exempt Oregon veterans with service-connected disabilities and their spouses from a portion of their property taxes.

Eligibility Qualifying veterans are those who received a discharge or release under honorable conditions after service of either 1) 90 consecutive days during World War I, World War II, or the Korean Conflict; or 2) 210 consecutive days after January 31, 1955. Eligible individuals must meet 1 of these conditions: 1) a war veteran who is certified by the U.S. Department of Veterans Affairs (VA) or any branch of the U.S. armed forces as having service-connected disabilities of 40% or more; or 2) a surviving spouse of a war veteran who died because of service-connected injury or illness or who received at least 1 year of this exemption. Recipients of this exemption must own and live on a property in Oregon.

Financial data The exemption is $18,540 of the homestead property's real market value.

Duration 1 year; may be renewed as long as the eligible veterans or surviving spouse owns and occupies the primary residence.

Number awarded Varies each year.

Deadline This exemption is not automatic. Applications must be submitted by March of each year.

[1231]
PARENT-INFANT FINANCIAL AID PROGRAM

Alexander Graham Bell Association for the Deaf and Hard of Hearing
Attn: Financial Aid Coordinator
3417 Volta Place, N.W.
Washington, DC 20007-2778
(202) 337-5220   Fax: (202) 337-8314
TDD: (202) 337-5221   E-mail: financialaid@agbell.org
Web: nc.agbell.org/NetCommunity/Page.aspx?pid=499

Summary To provide financial aid to the parents of young children with moderate to profound hearing loss who need assistance to cover expenses associated with early intervention services.

Eligibility Applicants must be parents or guardians of children less than 3 years of age who have been diagnosed as having a moderate to profound hearing loss (the child must have an unaided Pure-Tone Average (PTA) of 55dB or more in the better hearing ear in the speech frequencies of 500, 1000, and 2000 Hz). Children with cochlear implants are eligible, but those with unilateral hearing loss are not. Spoken communication must be the child's primary mode of communication. The family must be able to demonstrate financial need. Residents of Canada, the United States, and its territories are eligible.

Financial data The amount awarded depends on the needs of the child; most awards range from $300 to $1,000 per year.

Duration 1 year.

Number awarded Varies each year.

Deadline September of each year.

[1232]
PENNSYLVANIA DISABLED VETERANS REAL ESTATE TAX EXEMPTION

Office of the Deputy Adjutant General for Veterans Affairs
Building S-0-47, FTIG
Annville, PA 17003-5002
(717) 865-8907
Toll Free: (800) 54 PA VET (within PA)
Fax: (717) 861-8589   E-mail: jamebutler@state.pa.us
Web: www.milvet.state.pa.us/DMVA/592.htm

Summary To exempt blind and disabled Pennsylvania veterans and their unremarried surviving spouses from all state real estate taxes.

Eligibility Eligible to apply for this exemption are honorably-discharged veterans who are residents of Pennsylvania and who are blind, paraplegic, or 100% disabled from a service-connected disability sustained during wartime military service. The dwelling must be owned by the veteran solely or jointly with a spouse, and financial need for the exemption must be determined by the State Veterans' Commission. Veterans whose income is less than $79,050 per year are presumed to have financial need; veterans with income greater than $79,050 must document need. Upon the death of the veteran, the tax exemption passes on to the veteran's unremarried surviving spouse.

Financial data This program exempts the principal residence (and the land on which it stands) from all real estate taxes.

Duration The exemption continues as long as the eligible veteran or unremarried widow resides in Pennsylvania.

Number awarded Varies each year.

Deadline Deadline not specified.

[1233]
PENNSYLVANIA VETERANS EMERGENCY ASSISTANCE

Office of the Deputy Adjutant General for Veterans Affairs
Building S-0-47, FTIG
Annville, PA 17003-5002
(717) 865-8905
Toll Free: (800) 54 PA VET (within PA)
Fax: (717) 861-8589   E-mail: jamebutler@state.pa.us
Web: www.milvet.state.pa.us/DMVA/185.htm

Summary To provide financial aid on an emergency and temporary basis to Pennsylvania veterans (or their dependents) who are disabled, sick, or without means.

Eligibility Eligible to apply for this assistance are honorably-discharged veterans who served in the U.S. armed forces during wartime and are now disabled, sick, or in financial need. Widow(er)s or orphan children of recently deceased veterans are also eligible if the veteran would have qualified prior to death. Applicants must have been residents of Pennsylvania for 1 year prior to the date of application.

Financial data Financial aid for the necessities of life (food, shelter, fuel, and clothing) is provided. The amount depends on the number of persons in the household and the Pennsylvania county in which the veteran or dependent lives; recently, monthly grants for 1-person households ranged from $174 to $215, for 2-person households from $279 to $330, for 3-person households from $365 to $431, for 4-person households from $454 to $514, for 5-person households from $543 to $607, and for 6-person households from $614 to $687.

Duration Aid is provided on a temporary basis only, not to exceed 3 months in a 12-month period.

Number awarded Varies each year.

Deadline Applications may be submitted at any time, but the factors that caused the emergency must have occurred within 180 days prior to the application.

[1234]
PRESCHOOL FINANCIAL AID PROGRAM

Alexander Graham Bell Association for the Deaf and
  Hard of Hearing
Attn: Financial Aid Coordinator
3417 Volta Place, N.W.
Washington, DC 20007-2778
(202) 337-5220   Fax: (202) 337-8314
TDD: (202) 337-5221 E-mail: financialaid@agbell.org
Web: nc.agbell.org/NetCommunity/Page.aspx?pid=497

Summary To provide financial aid to the parents of preschool children with moderate to profound hearing loss who need assistance to cover expenses associated with early intervention services.

Eligibility Applicants must be parents or guardians of children between 4 and 6 years of age who have been diagnosed as having a moderate to profound hearing loss (the child must have an unaided Pure-Tone Average (PTA) of 55dB or more in the better hearing ear in the speech frequencies of 500, 1000, and 2000 Hz). Children with cochlear implants are eligible, but those with unilateral hearing loss are not. Spoken communication must be the child's primary mode of communication. The family must be able to demonstrate financial need. Residents of Canada, the United States, and its territories are eligible.

Financial data The amount awarded depends on the needs of the child; most grants range from $300 to $1,000 per year.

Duration 1 year; may be renewed upon reapplication, but preference is given to new applicants who are just enrolling their child in preschool.

Number awarded Varies each year.

Deadline July of each year.

[1235]
RESPITE CARE GRANT PROGRAM OF THE JIM "CATFISH" HUNTER CHAPTER

ALS Association-Jim "Catfish" Hunter Chapter
Attn: Patient and Family Services
120-101 Penmarc Drive
Raleigh, NC 27603
(919) 755-9001   Toll Free: (877) 568-4347
Fax: (919) 755-0910
E-mail: katie@CatfishChapter.org
Web: catfish.prolitical.com/outchapter/programs

Summary To provide funding for respite care to caregivers of patients with Amyotrophic Lateral Sclerosis (ALS) in North Carolina.

Eligibility This assistance is available to caregivers of patients who have a definitive diagnosis of ALS and reside in North Carolina. Applicants must be able to demonstrate financial need for assistance. They may choose to receive direct reimbursement for expenses of respite care by submitting a billing receipt or they may arrange for direct billing to the chapter from the service provider. Selection depends on need, the number of applicants, and availability of funds.

Financial data Each grant is $500. Caregivers may obtain 4 grants per fiscal year, or funding of $2,000 annually.

Duration 1 year.

Additional data The North Carolina Chapter of the ALS Association was formed in 1987. In 2000, it expanded its services to include South Carolina and, in 2002, adopted the name of former professional baseball player Jim "Catfish" Hunter. In 2006, a separate South Carolina chapter was formed, so this chapter again limits its services to North Carolina.

Number awarded Varies each year.

Deadline Applications must be submitted by the 25th day of each month.

[1236]
RUTH BILLOW MEMORIAL PERSONAL AID

Delta Gamma Foundation
Attn: Director, Service for Sight
3250 Riverside Drive
P.O. Box 21397
Columbus, OH 43221-0397
(614) 481-8169   Fax: (614) 481-0133
E-mail: dgfoundation@deltagamma.org
Web: www.deltagamma.org

Summary To provide financial assistance to members of Delta Gamma sorority who are in need because of their visual impairment or that of a family member.

Eligibility This program is open to members of the sorority who require assistance 1) in order to restore or retain their sight; or 2) because of their responsibilities directly related to dependents who are blind or visually impaired. Applicants must be residents of the United States or Canada.

Financial data The amount awarded varies, depending upon individual circumstances.

Duration 1 year or more.

Number awarded Varies each year.

Deadline Applications may be submitted at any time.

[1237]
SOCIAL SECURITY DISABILITY INSURANCE (SSDI) BENEFITS

Social Security Administration
6401 Security Boulevard
Baltimore, MD 21235-0001
(410) 594-1234   Toll Free: (800) 772-1213
TDD: (800) 325-0778
Web: www.ssa.gov

Summary To provide monthly benefits to workers and their families if the worker becomes disabled or blind.

Eligibility This program defines disabled people as those who are unable to do any kind of work for which they are suited and whose disability has lasted or is expected to last for at least a year or to result in death. Blind people qualify if their vision cannot be corrected to better than 20/200 in their better eye or if their visual field is 20 degrees or less, even with corrective lenses. Family members who are eligible include 1) unmarried children, including adopted children and, in some cases, stepchildren and grandchildren who are under 18 years of age (19 if still in high school full time); 2) unmarried children, over 18 years of age, if they have a disability that started before age 22; and 3) spouses who are 62 years of age or older, or of any age if caring for a child of the disabled worker who is under 16 years of age or disabled. For deceased workers, disabled widow(er)s 50 years of age or older are also eligible. Applicants must also have worked long enough and recently enough under Social Security in order to qualify. Workers who become disabled before the age of 24 need 6 credits in the 3-year period ending when the disability begins; workers who become disabled between the ages of 24 and 31 must have credit for having worked half the time between the age of 21 and the date of disability; workers 31 years of age or older at the time of disability must have earned as many total credits as needed for retirement (from 20 credits if disabled at age 31 through 42 to 40 credits if disabled at age 62 or older) and must have earned at least 20 of the credits in the 10 years immediately before becoming disabled. An exception applies to blind workers who need no recent credit but may have earned the required credit any time after 1936.

Financial data The amount of the monthly benefit depends on several factors, including the worker's age at the time of disability, the number of dependents, and the amount of earnings on which Social Security taxes have been paid. Recently, the average monthly benefit was $1,062.10 for disabled workers, $286.90 for spouses of disabled workers, and $316.40 for children of disabled workers.

Duration For a disabled or blind person, whether a worker, widow, widower, surviving divorced spouse, or person over the age of 18 who became disabled before the age of 22, monthly benefits continue until the person is no longer disabled or dies. For a dependent spouse, benefits are paid until the worker is no longer disabled or dies. For a dependent child, the benefits continue until the child marries or reaches the age of 18 (19 if still enrolled as a full-time high school student).

Additional data Disabled workers may test their ability to return to work for a trial work period of up to 9 months, during which time they receive full SSDI benefits. At the end of that period, a decision is made as to whether or not they are able to engage in substantial gainful activity. Persons who find that they cannot continue substantial gainful employment continue to receive SSDI benefits without interruption. Persons who can engage in substantial gainful activity receive benefits for an additional 3 months, after which payments cease. Several factors are considered to determine if the person can engage in substantial gainful employment, but the most important is income; for disabled people the amount is $980 a month gross wages and for blind people the income is $1,640 monthly.

Number awarded Varies; recently, approximately 7,623,000 disabled workers were receiving SSDI monthly benefits, along with 158,000 spouses and 1,681,000 children.

Deadline Deadline not specified.

[1238]
SOUTH CAROLINA DISABLED PERSON PROPERTY TAX EXEMPTION

South Carolina Department of Revenue
Attn: Property Division
301 Gervais Street
P.O. Box 125
Columbia, SC 29214
(803) 898-5480   Fax. (803) 898-5822
Web: www.sctax.org

Summary To exempt the home of disabled residents of South Carolina and their surviving spouses from property taxation.

Eligibility Eligible for this exemption are residents of South Carolina who are defined as paraplegic or hemiplegic and own a dwelling house that is their domicile. The exemption is allowed to the surviving spouse of the person as long as the spouse does not remarry, resides in the dwelling, and obtains the fee or a life estate in the dwelling. Paraplegic or hemiplegic includes a person with Parkinson's Disease, multiple sclerosis, or amyotrophic lateral sclerosis that has caused the same ambulatory difficulties as a person with paraperesis or hemiparesis. Surviving spouses of those persons are not eligible for this exemption.

Financial data The exemption applies to all taxes on 1 house and a lot (not to exceed 1 acre).

Duration The exemption extends as long as the person with a disability resides in the house.

Number awarded Varies each year.

Deadline Applications may be submitted at any time.

[1239]
SOUTH CAROLINA HOMESTEAD EXEMPTION PROGRAM

South Carolina Department of Revenue
301 Gervais Street
P.O. Box 125
Columbia, SC 29214
(803) 898-5680   Toll Free: (800) 763-1295
Fax: (803) 898-5822   E-mail: MillerC@sctax.org
Web: www.sctax.org

Summary   To provide a homestead exemption to South Carolina residents who are elderly, disabled, or blind, and their widow(er)s.

Eligibility   Legal residents of South Carolina who own a house or mobile home are eligible for this exemption if they are 65 years of age or older, totally and permanently disabled, or legally blind. Spouses of deceased persons who were eligible also qualify to receive the exemption if they were at least 50 years of age when their spouse died.

Financial data   The first $50,000 of the fair market value of the qualified applicant's home is exempted from property taxes. The exemption is from county, municipal, school, and special assessment real estate property taxes.

Duration   The exemption continues as long as the homeowners live in their primary residence in South Carolina.

Additional data   This program, established in 1972, is administered by county auditors.

Number awarded   Varies each year.

Deadline   Persons applying for this exemption for the first time must do so prior to July of each year; subsequently, no re-application is necessary unless the title or use of the property changes.

[1240]
SOUTH CAROLINA INCOME TAX EXEMPTION FOR THE ADOPTION OF A SPECIAL NEEDS CHILD

South Carolina Department of Revenue
301 Gervais Street
P.O. Box 125
Columbia, SC 29214
(803) 898-5000   Toll Free: (800) 763-1295
Fax: (803) 898-5822
Web: www.sctax.org

Summary   To provide income tax exemptions to residents of South Carolina who adopt a special needs child.

Eligibility   South Carolina residents who adopt a special needs child and provide the child's chief financial support are eligible for this exemption. For the purposes of the program, "special needs" is defined as a child with disabilities (physical, mental, or emotional), ethnic minority status, sibling group membership, medical condition, or age status that makes unassisted adoption unlikely. The child must be under the age of 21 or be incapable of self-support because of mental or physical disabilities to qualify for the program.

Financial data   Eligible parents receive a $2,000 per year state income tax exemption.

Duration   This exemption continues as long as the dependent is under 21 years of age, unless the child is regularly enrolled in an accredited school or college or is incapable of self-support because of mental or physical disabilities.

Additional data   The entire deduction is allowed for a taxable year, even if the special needs child does not survive for the entire year. The program was started in 1985.

Number awarded   Varies each year.

Deadline   The exemption is filed on the parent's state income tax form each year, due in April.

[1241]
SOUTH CAROLINA PROPERTY TAX EXEMPTION FOR DISABLED VETERANS, LAW ENFORCEMENT OFFICERS, AND FIREFIGHTERS

South Carolina Department of Revenue
Attn: Property Division
301 Gervais Street
P.O. Box 125
Columbia, SC 29214
(803) 898-5480   Fax: (803) 898-5822
Web: www.sctax.org

Summary   To exempt the residence of disabled South Carolina veterans, law enforcement officers, fire fighters, their unremarried widow(er)s, and others from property taxation.

Eligibility   This exemption is available to owners of homes in South Carolina who are veterans of the U.S. armed forces, former law enforcement officers, or former fire fighters (including volunteer fire fighters). Applicants must be permanently and totally disabled from service-connected causes. The exemption is also available to qualified surviving spouses (defined to include unremarried spouses of disabled veterans, law enforcement officers, and fire fighters, as well as surviving spouses of servicemembers killed in the line of duty, law enforcement officers who died in the line of duty, and fire fighters who died in the line of duty).

Financial data   The exemption applies to all taxes on 1 house and a lot (not to exceed 1 acre).

Duration   The exemption extends as long as the veteran, law enforcement officer, or fire fighter resides in the house, or as long as the spouse of a deceased veteran, servicemember, law enforcement officer, or fire fighter remains unremarried and resides in the original house or a single new dwelling.

Number awarded   Varies each year.

Deadline   Applications may be submitted at any time.

[1242]
SOUTH DAKOTA PROPERTY TAX EXEMPTION FOR PARAPLEGIC VETERANS

South Dakota Department of Revenue and Regulation
Attn: Property Tax Division
445 East Capitol Avenue
Pierre, SD 57501-3185
(605) 773-3311　　　　Toll Free: (800) TAX-9188
Fax: (605) 773-6729　　E-mail: PropTaxIn@state.sd.us
Web: www.state.sd.us

Summary To exempt from property taxation the homes of disabled veterans in South Dakota and their widow(er)s.

Eligibility This benefit is available to residents of South Dakota who are 1) paraplegic veterans, 2) veterans with loss or loss of use of both lower extremities, or 3) unremarried widows or widowers of such veterans. Applicants must own and occupy a dwelling (including the house, garage, and up to 1 acre on which the building is located) that is specifically designed for wheelchair use within the structure. The veteran's injury does not have to be service-connected.

Financial data Qualified dwellings are exempt from property taxation in South Dakota.

Duration The exemption applies as long as the dwelling is owned and occupied by the disabled veteran or widow(er).

Number awarded Varies each year.

Deadline Deadline not specified.

[1243]
SOUTH DAKOTA PROPERTY TAX REDUCTION FOR PARAPLEGICS

South Dakota Department of Revenue and Regulation
Attn: Property Tax Division
445 East Capitol Avenue
Pierre, SD 57501-3185
(605) 773-3311　　　　Toll Free: (800) TAX-9188
Fax: (605) 773-6729　　E-mail: PropTaxIn@state.sd.us
Web: www.state.sd.us

Summary To provide a reduction in property taxes on the homes of people with disabilities in South Dakota and their widow(er)s.

Eligibility This benefit is available to residents of South Dakota who are 1) paraplegic individuals, 2) individuals with loss or loss of use of both lower extremities, or 3) unremarried widows or widowers of such individuals. Applicants must own and occupy a dwelling (including the house, garage, and up to 1 acre on which the building is located) that is specifically designed for wheelchair use within the structure. They must have a federal adjusted income of less than $8,000 if they live in a single-member household or less than $12,000 if they live in a multiple-member household.

Financial data The reduction depends on the federal adjusted gross income of the applicant. For single-member households, the reduction is 100% if the income is less than $5,000, 75% if the income is between $5,000 and $6,000, 50% if the income is between $6,000 and $7,000, or 25% if the income is between $7,000 and $8,000. For multiple-member household, the reduction is 100% if the income is less than $9,000, 75% if the income is between $9,000 and $10,000, 50% if the income is between $10,000 and $11,000, or 25% if the income is between $11,000 and $12,000.

Duration The reduction applies as long as the dwelling is owned and occupied by the disabled person or widow(er).

Number awarded Varies each year.

Deadline Deadline not specified.

[1244]
TENNESSEE PROPERTY TAX RELIEF FOR DISABLED VETERANS AND THEIR SPOUSES

Tennessee Comptroller of the Treasury
Attn: Property Tax Relief Program
James K. Polk State Office Building
505 Deaderick Street, Room 1600
Nashville, TN 37243-1402
(615) 747-8871　　　　　　Fax: (615) 532-3866
E-mail: Kim.Darden@state.tn.us
Web: www.comptroller.state.tn.us/pa/patxr.htm

Summary To provide property tax relief to blind and disabled veterans and their spouses in Tennessee.

Eligibility This exemption is offered to veterans or their surviving unremarried spouses who are residents of Tennessee and own and live in their home in the state. The veteran must have served in the U.S. armed forces and 1) have acquired, as a result of such service, a disability from paraplegia, permanent paralysis of both legs and lower part of the body resulting from traumatic injury, disease to the spinal cord or brain, legal blindness, or loss or loss of use of both legs or arms from any service-connected cause; 2) have been rated by the U.S. Department of Veterans Affairs (VA) as 100% permanently disabled as a result of service as a prisoner of war for at least 5 months; or 3) have been rated by the VA as 100% permanently and totally disabled from any other service-connected cause. The relief does not extend to any person who was dishonorably discharged from any of the armed services.

Financial data The amount of the relief depends on the property assessment and the tax rate in the city or county where the beneficiary lives. The maximum market value on which tax relief is calculated is $175,000.

Duration 1 year; may be renewed as long as the eligible veteran or surviving unremarried spouse owns and occupies the primary residence.

Number awarded Varies each year.

Deadline Deadline not specified.

[1245]
TEXAS PROPERTY TAX EXEMPTION FOR DISABLED VETERANS AND THEIR FAMILIES

Texas Veterans Commission
P.O. Box 12277
Austin, TX 78711-2277
(512) 463-5538
Toll Free: (800) 252-VETS (within TX)
Fax: (512) 475-2395   E-mail: info@tvc.state.tx.us
Web: www.tvc.state.tx.us/StateBenefits.html

Summary To extend property tax exemptions on the appraised value of their property to blind, disabled, and other Texas veterans and their surviving family members.

Eligibility Eligible veterans must be Texas residents rated at least 10% service-connected disabled. Surviving spouses and children of eligible veterans are also covered by this program.

Financial data For veterans in Texas whose disability is rated as 10% through 29%, the first $5,000 of the appraised property value is exempt from taxation; veterans rated as 30% through 49% disabled are exempt from the first $7,500 of appraised value; those with a 50% through 69% disability are exempt from the first $10,000 of appraised value; the exemption applies to the first $12,000 of appraised value for veterans with disabilities rated as 70% to 99%; veterans rated as 100% disabled are exempt from 100% of the appraised value of their property. A veteran whose disability is 10% or more and who is 65 years or older is entitled to exemption of the first $12,000 of appraised property value. A veteran whose disability consists of the loss of use of 1 or more limbs, total blindness in 1 or both eyes, or paraplegia is exempt from the first $12,000 of the appraised value. The unremarried surviving spouse of a deceased veteran who died on active duty and who, at the time of death had a compensable disability and was entitled to an exemption, is entitled to the same exemption. The surviving spouse of a person who died on active duty is entitled to exemption of the first $5,000 of appraised value of the spouse's property. Surviving spouses, however, are not eligible for the 100% exemption. A surviving child of a person who dies on active duty is entitled to exemption of the first $5,000 of appraised value of the child's property, as long as the child is unmarried and under 21 years of age.

Duration 1 year; may be renewed as long as the eligible veteran (or unremarried surviving spouse or child) owns and occupies the primary residence in Texas.

Additional data This program is administered at the local level by the various taxing authorities.

Number awarded Varies each year.

Deadline April of each year.

[1246]
THOMARA LATIMER CANCER FOUNDATION GRANTS

Thomara Latimer Cancer Foundation
Attn: Cancer Funding Committee
Franklin Plaza Center
29193 Northeastern Highway, Suite 528
Southfield, MI 48034-1006
(248) 557-2346   Fax: (248) 557-8063
E-mail: funding@thomlatimercares.org
Web: www.thomlatimercares.org

Summary To provide funding to cancer patients and family members who are unable to meet expenses.

Eligibility This program is open to cancer patients and family members who, after a thorough investigation of other resources, are unable to meet expenses that are causing a financial burden. Applicants must be seeking funding for homecare assistance (including child care); medication or treatment not covered by insurance (including alternative care, family lodging for out-of-town treatment); transportation to and from treatment, physician, support facilities; special needs funds for wigs or head coverings for diagnosis or treatment related to hair loss; or assistance with final arrangements.

Financial data Grant amounts depend on the availability of funds.

Duration These are 1-time grants.

Number awarded Varies each year.

Deadline Applications may be submitted at any time.

[1247]
UTAH BLIND PROPERTY TAX EXEMPTION

Utah State Tax Commission
Attn: Property Tax Division
210 North 1950 West
Salt Lake City, UT 84134
(801) 297-3600   Toll Free: (800) 662-4335, ext. 3600
Fax: (801) 297-7699   TDD: (801) 297-2020
Web: www.tax.utah.gov

Summary To exempt from taxation a portion of the real and tangible property of blind people and their families in Utah.

Eligibility This exemption is available to legally blind property owners in Utah, along with their unremarried surviving spouses or minor orphans. First-year applications must be accompanied by a signed statement from an ophthalmologist and, if appropriate, a death certificate.

Financial data The first $11,500 of the taxable value of real and tangible personal property is exempt from taxation.

Duration The exemption is available each year the beneficiary owns property in Utah.

Number awarded Varies each year.

Deadline Applications must be submitted by August of each year.

[1248]
UTAH DISABLED VETERAN PROPERTY TAX ABATEMENT

Utah Division of Veteran's Affairs
Attn: Director
550 Foothill Boulevard, Room 202
Salt Lake City, UT 84108
(801) 326-2372   Toll Free: (800) 894-9497 (within UT)
Fax: (801) 326-2369   E-mail: veterans@utah.gov
Web: veterans.utah.gov

Summary To exempt a portion of the property of disabled veterans and their families in Utah from taxation.

Eligibility This program is available to residents of Utah who are disabled veterans or their unremarried widow(er)s or minor orphans. The disability must be at least 10% and incurred as the result of injuries in the line of duty.

Financial data The exemption is based on the disability rating of the veteran, to a maximum of $219,164 for a 100% disability.

Duration This benefit is available as long as the disabled veteran or family members reside in Utah.

Deadline Tax exemption applications must be filed with the county government of residence by August of the initial year; once eligibility has been established, reapplication is not required.

[1249]
UTAH VETERAN'S PROPERTY TAX EXEMPTION

Utah State Tax Commission
Attn: Property Tax Division
210 North 1950 West
Salt Lake City, UT 84134
(801) 297-3600   Toll Free: (800) 662-4335, ext. 3600
Fax: (801) 297-7699   TDD: (801) 297-2020
Web: www.tax.utah.gov

Summary To exempt from taxation a portion of the real and tangible property of disabled veterans and their families in Utah.

Eligibility This exemption is available to property owners in Utah who are veterans with a disability of at least 10% incurred in the line of duty, along with their unremarried surviving spouses or minor orphans. First year applications must be accompanied by proof of military service and proof of disability or death.

Financial data The exemption depends on the percentage of disability, up to $228,505 of taxable value of a residence.

Duration The exemption is available each year the beneficiary owns property in Utah.

Number awarded Varies each year.

Deadline Applications must be submitted by August of each year.

[1250]
VERMONT PROPERTY TAX EXEMPTION FOR DISABLED VETERANS

Vermont Department of Taxes
Attn: Property Valuation and Review Division
P.O. Box 1577
Montpelier, VT 05601-1577
(802) 828-5860   Fax: (802) 828-2824
Web: www.state.vt.us/tax/pvrmilitary.shtml

Summary To exempt disabled Vermont veterans and their dependents from the payment of at least a portion of the state's property tax.

Eligibility Entitled to a property tax exemption are veterans of any war (or their spouses, widow(er)s, or children) who are receiving wartime disability compensation for at least a 50% disability, wartime death compensation, wartime dependence and indemnity compensation, or pension for disability paid through any military department or the Department of Veterans Affairs. Unremarried widow(er)s of previously qualified veterans are also entitled to the exemption whether or not they are receiving government compensation or a pension.

Financial data Up to $10,000 of the assessed value of real and personal property belonging to eligible veterans or their unremarried widow(er)s is exempt from taxation; individual towns may increase the exemption to as much as $40,000.

Duration 1 year; may be renewed as long as the eligible veteran or widow(er) continues to be the owner/occupant of the residence and lives in Vermont.

Additional data Only 1 exemption may be allowed on a property.

Number awarded Varies each year.

Deadline April of each year.

[1251]
WASHINGTON PROPERTY TAX ASSISTANCE PROGRAM FOR WIDOWS OR WIDOWERS OF VETERANS

Washington State Department of Revenue
Attn: Property Tax Division
P.O. Box 47471
Olympia, WA 98504-7471
(360) 570-5873   Toll Free: (800) 647-7706
Fax: (360) 586-7602   TDD: (800) 451-7985
Web: dor.wa.gov

Summary To exempt from taxation in Washington a portion of the assessed valuation of property owned by senior citizens and people with disabilities who are widows or widowers of veterans.

Eligibility This exemption is available to residents of Washington who are either 62 years of age or older or who have a disability that prevents them from being gainfully employed and is expected to last for at least 12 months. Applicants must be the unmarried widow or widower of a veteran who 1) died as a result of a service-connected disability; 2) was 100% disabled for 10 years prior to his or her death; 3) was a former prisoner of war and rated as 100% disabled for at least 1 year prior to death; or 4) died in active duty or in active training status. They must own property that they use as their principal home for at least 6 months of the year; mobile homes may qualify as a residence even if its owner does not own the land where it is located. Their annual disposable income may not exceed $40,000 per year.

Financial data The exemption is $100,000 of the home's assessed value if disposable income is $30,000 or less, $75,000 if disposable income is $30,001 to $35,000, or $50,000 if disposable income is $35,001 to $40,000.

Duration The exemption is available as long as the widow or widower meets the eligibility requirements.

Additional data This program offered assistance beginning with the 2006 tax year.

Number awarded Varies each year.

Deadline Applications are due 30 days before taxes are due.

[1252]
WASHINGTON PROPERTY TAX EXEMPTIONS FOR SENIOR CITIZENS AND DISABLED PERSONS

Washington State Department of Revenue
Attn: Property Tax Division
P.O. Box 47471
Olympia, WA 98504-7471
(360) 570-5867   Toll Free: (800) 647-7706
Fax: (360) 586-7602   TDD: (800) 451-7985
Web: dor.wa.gov

Summary To exempt a portion of the property owned by senior citizens and people with disabilities, including their surviving spouses, from taxation in Washington.

Eligibility This exemption is available to residents of Washington who are 1) unable to work because of a disability, 2) veterans with a 100% service-connected disability, 3) at least 61 years of age, or 4) a surviving spouse at least 57 years of age of a person who was approved for this exemption. Applicants must own property that they use as their principal home for at least 6 months of the year; mobile homes may qualify as a residence even if its owner does not own the land where it is located. Their annual disposable income may not exceed $35,000 per year.

Financial data Property owners whose annual income is $25,000 or less are exempt from regular property taxes on the first $60,000 or 60% of their home's assessed value, whichever is greater. Property owners whose annual income is between $25,001 and $30,000 are exempt from regular property taxes on $50,000 or 35% of the assessed value, whichever is greater, not to exceed $70,000 or the assessed value. Property owners whose annual income is $35,000 or less are exempt from all levies that have been approved by voters in excess of regular property taxes.

Duration The exemption is available as long as the property owner meets the eligibility requirements.

Number awarded Varies each year.

Deadline Applications for each year are due by December of the preceding year.

[1253]
WEST VIRGINIA SENIOR CITIZEN OR DISABILITY INCOME TAX EXEMPTION

West Virginia State Tax Department
Attn: Taxpayer Services Division
P.O. Box 3784
Charleston, WV 25337-3784
(304) 558-3333 Toll Free: (800) 982-8297 (within WV)
Fax: (304) 558-3269   TDD: (800) 282-9833
Web: www.wva.state.wv.us/wvtax/default.aspx

Summary To provide income tax exemptions for West Virginia residents with disabilities and their surviving spouses.

Eligibility Residents of West Virginia who are totally and permanently disabled (or 65 years of age or older) are eligible for this income tax exemption. Surviving spouses of eligible residents are also entitled to the exemption.

Financial data Qualifying taxpayers may deduct from state income taxation up to $8,000 for a single return or a maximum of $8,000 per person for a joint return.

Duration The exemption continues as long as the eligible resident (or his/her spouse) remains a resident of West Virginia.

Deadline Deadline not specified.

[1254]
WISCONSIN VETERANS AND SURVIVING SPOUSES PROPERTY TAX CREDIT

Wisconsin Department of Revenue
Attn: Customer Service and Education Bureau
2135 Rimrock Road
P.O. Box 8949
Madison, WI 53708-8949
(608) 266-2776   Fax: (608) 267-1030
Web: www.revenue.wi.gov

Summary To provide an income tax credit to disabled Wisconsin veterans and their surviving spouses equal to the amount of property taxes they pay.

Eligibility This credit is available to Wisconsin veterans who served on active duty under honorable conditions in the U.S. armed forces and have resided in Wisconsin for any consecutive 5-year period after entry into active duty. Applicants must have either a service-connected disability rating of 100% or a 100% disability rating based on individual unemployability. Also eligible are unremarried surviving spouses of such disabled veterans and of members of the National Guard or a Reserve component of the U.S. armed forces who were residents of Wisconsin and died in the line of duty while on active or inactive duty for training purposes.

Financial data Eligible veterans and surviving spouses are entitled to an income tax credit equal to the amount of property taxes they pay on their principal residence.

Duration The credit is available as long as the recipient resides in Wisconsin.

Number awarded Varies each year.

Deadline Income tax returns must be filed by April of each year.

[1255]
WYOMING VETERANS PROPERTY TAX EXEMPTION

Wyoming Department of Revenue
Attn: Property Tax Relief Program
122 West 25th Street, Second Floor West
Cheyenne, WY 82002-0110
(307) 777-5235 Fax: (307) 777-7527
E-mail: DirectorOfRevenue@wy.gov
Web: revenue.state.wy.us

Summary To provide a partial tax exemption on the property owned by veterans and their surviving spouses in Wyoming.

Eligibility This program is open to honorably-discharged veterans who were Wyoming residents at the time they entered military service and have resided in Wyoming for 3 years prior to applying for this exemption. Applicants must have served during specified periods of wartime or have received an armed forces expeditionary medal or other authorized service or campaign medal for service in an armed conflict in a foreign country. Surviving spouses of qualified veterans are also eligible. The exemption applies to county fees only, not state fees.

Financial data Veterans and spouses may exempt $3,000 in assessed value of property from taxation per year. Disabled veterans are entitled to additional exemptions that depend on the level of their disability, to a maximum of $2,000 for a 100% disability.

Duration Veterans and spouses are entitled to use these exemptions as long as they reside in Wyoming and own the property as their principal residence.

Number awarded Varies each year.

Deadline Applicants must advise their county assessor of their intent to use the exemption by May of each year.

Awards

[1256]
JAY AND ROSE PHILLIPS CAREGIVER AWARD

Courage Center
Attn: Vocational Services Department
3915 Golden Valley Road
Minneapolis, MN 55422
(763) 520-0263 Toll Free: (888) 8-INTAKE
Fax: (763) 520-0562 TDD: (763) 520-0245
E-mail: information@couragecenter.org
Web: www.couragecenter.org

Summary To recognize and reward residents of designated states who have performed outstanding service as a caregiver for a person with a disability.

Eligibility This program is open to residents of Iowa, Minnesota, North Dakota, South Dakota, and Wisconsin who are professional caregivers or family members who provide key support to a person with a disability. Nominees must provide support that directly influences the person with a disability's ability to live independently and participate fully in the community. In the selection process, attitude, dependability, character, and competence are considered.

Financial data The award is $2,000.

Duration The award is presented annually.

Additional data This program was established in 2008.

Number awarded 1 each year.

Deadline May of each year.

[1257]
VSA ARTS PLAYWRIGHT DISCOVERY AWARD

VSA arts
Attn: Education Office
818 Connecticut Avenue, N.W., Suite 600
Washington, DC 20006
(202) 628-2800 Toll Free: (800) 933-8721
Fax: (202) 429-0868 TDD: (202) 737-0645
E-mail: playwright@vsarts.org
Web: www.vsarts.org/x244.xml

Summary To recognize and reward young playwrights who submit scripts that deal with disabilities.

Eligibility This program is open to U.S. citizens and permanent residents in grades 6-12 who submit an original, unproduced, and unpublished script for a 1-act play (less than 40 pages in length) that addresses the issue of disability. Applicants are not required to have a disability, but their script must examine how disability affects their lives and the lives of others. They may write from their own experience or about an experience in the life of another person or fictional character. Plays are intended for an audience of middle through high school students and adults and must be appropriate in language and subject matter for that age group.

Financial data The winner receives an award of $2,000, a trip to Washington, D.C. to attend the award presentation and see a professional production or staged reading of their play at the John F. Kennedy Center for the Performing Arts, a mentoring luncheon with distinguished members of the selection committee, and press opportunities.

Duration The competition is held annually.

Additional data The sponsor, VSA arts, was formerly known as Very Special Arts.

Number awarded 1 each year.

Deadline April of each year.

Indexes

Program Title Index •

Sponsoring Organization Index •

Residency Index •

Tenability Index •

Subject Index •

Calendar Index •

Program Title Index

If you know the name of a particular funding program and want to find out where it is covered in the directory, use the Program Title Index. Here, program titles are arranged alphabetically, word by word. To assist you in your search, every program is listed by all its known names or abbreviations. In addition, we've used a two-character alphabetical code (within parentheses) to help you determine if the program falls within your scope of interest. The first character (capitalized) in the code identifies availability group: V = Visual Disabilities; H = Hearing Disabilities; O = Orthopedic and Developmental Disabilities; C = Communication and Other Disabilities; D = Disabilities in General; F = Families of the Disabled. The second character (lower cased) identifies funding type: s = scholarships; f = fellowships/grants; g = grants-in-aid; a = awards. Here's how the code works: if a program is followed by (H–f) 271, the program is described in the Hearing Disabilities chapter under fellowships/grants, in entry 271. If the same program title is followed by another entry number—for example, (F–g) 1157—the program is also described in the Families of the Disabled chapter, under grants-in-aid, in entry 1157. Remember: the numbers cited here refer to program entry numbers, not to page numbers in the book.

V—Visual H—Hearing O—Orthopedic/Developmental C—Communication/Other D—Disabilities in General F—Families
s—scholarships f—fellowships/grants g—grants-in-aid a—awards

V—Visual H—Hearing O—Orthopedic/Developmental C—Communication/Other D—Disabilities in General F—Families
s—scholarships t—fellowships/grants g—grants-in-aid a—awards

Craig Memorial Scholarship. *See* Andrew Craig Memorial Scholarship, entry (C—s) 409

Crammatte Fellowship. *See* Alan B., '32, and Florence B., '35, Crammatte Fellowship, entry (H—f) 293

Crashing Through Award for Independent Travel, (V—a) 263

Cremer Scholarship. *See* Hemophilia of Iowa Scholarships, entries (C—s) 466, (F—s) 1003

Cristin Ann Bambino Memorial Scholarship, (C—s) 431

Culpepper Exum Scholarship for People with Kidney Disease, (C—s) 432

Cummings PSYCHE Prize. *See* Nicholas and Dorothy Cummings PSYCHE Prize, entry (D—a) 937

Curtis Pride Scholarship for the Hearing Impaired, (H—s) 271

CVS/All Kids Can Scholars Program, (C—s) 433

Cynthia Ruth Russell Memorial Grants, (O—s) 334, (O—f) 365

Cystic Fibrosis Scholarships, (C—s) 434

D

Dabney Foundation for Kids with Cancer Grants. *See* Clayton Dabney Foundation for Kids with Cancer Grants, entry (F—g) 1155

Dakota Pequeno Memorial Scholarship, (C—s) 435

Dale M. Schoettler Scholarship for Visually Impaired Students, (V—s) 15, (V—f) 129

Dana Walters Scholarships, (C—s) 436, (F—s) 961

DAV Disaster Relief Fund, (D—g) 811

Dave Madeiros Continued Education Scholarships, (C—s) 437, (F—s) 962

Dave Madeiros Creative Arts Scholarship, (C—s) 438, (F—s) 963

David Nelson Jr. Memorial Fund Scholarship, (F—s) 964

David Newmeyer Scholarship, (V—s) 16

David Peikoff, '29 Fellowship. *See* Gallaudet University Alumni Association Graduate Fellowship Fund, entry (H—f) 300

Davidow Memorial Scholarship. *See* Dr. Mae Davidow Memorial Scholarship, entry (V—s) 19

Davis Award. *See* Patient Advocate Foundation Scholarships for Survivors, entries (C—s) 524, (C—f) 584

Davis Graduate Award. *See* Trinka Davis Graduate Award, entry (V—f) 182

Davis Scholarship Fund. *See* Larry Dean Davis Scholarship Fund, entry (C—s) 484

Dawson Memorial Scholarship. *See* Calvin Dawson Memorial Scholarship, entry (C—s) 425

Deaf and Hard of Hearing Section Scholarship Fund, (H—s) 272, (H—f) 296

Death Pension for Survivors of Veterans, (D—g) 812, (F—g) 1160

Debbie Fox Foundation Grants-in-Aid. *See* National Craniofacial Association Client Travel Grants-in-Aid, entry (O—g) 385

Defense Intelligence Agency Undergraduate Training Assistance Program, (D—s) 660

Delaware Chapter MS Society Scholarship Program, (O—s) 335, (F—s) 965

Delaware Income Tax Deduction for Blind and Elderly Persons, (V—g) 199

Delaware Income Tax Exclusion for Disabled and Elderly Persons, (D—g) 813

Delaware Pension Benefits for Paraplegic Veterans, (O—g) 376

Delgadillo Scholarship. *See* Scott Delgadillo Scholarship, entries (C—s) 545, (C—f) 591

Delson Memorial Scholarship. *See* Eric Delson Memorial Scholarship, entries (C—s) 452, (C—f) 572

Delta Gamma Foundation Florence Margaret Harvey Memorial Scholarship. *See* Florence Margaret Harvey Memorial Scholarship, entries (V—s) 28, (V—f) 137

Delta Gamma Foundation Ruth Billow Memorial Education Fund, (V—s) 17, (V—f) 130

Demarest Memorial Scholarship. *See* National Federation of the Blind of Connecticut Scholarships, entries (V—s) 70, (V—f) 161

Dennis R. Kelly Memorial Scholarship. *See* Robert J. and Dennis R. Kelly Memorial Scholarship, entry (C—s) 534

Department of Homeland Security Small Business Innovation Research Grants, (D—f) 738, (F—f) 1117

DesChamps Scholarship Award. *See* EAGA Scholarship Award, entries (O—s) 337, (F—s) 970

DeWitt Scholarship. *See* Hemophilia Health Services Memorial Scholarships, entries (C—s) 465, (C—f) 575

Diane Donnelly Stone Award. *See* Novo Nordisk Donnelly Awards, entry (C—a) 643

DiCaprio Scholarship. *See* Dr. Nicholas S. DiCaprio Scholarship, entry (V—s) 20

DiCarlo Scholarship. *See* Louis DiCarlo Scholarship, entry (H—f) 308

Dick Griffiths Memorial Scholarship, (C—s) 439, (C—f) 570

Dillman Memorial Scholarship. *See* Rudolph Dillman Memorial Scholarship, entries (V—s) 106, (V—f) 177

Dillon Alaska Research Award. *See* Geological Society of America Graduate Student Research Grants, entry (D—f) 750

Director's Award for Distinguished Teaching Scholars, (D—f) 739, (D—a) 932

Disability Pension Program for Veterans, (D—g) 814

Disabled American Veterans Disaster Relief Fund. *See* DAV Disaster Relief Fund, entry (D—g) 811

Disabled War Veterans Scholarships, (D—s) 661

Disabled Workers Committee Scholarship, (F—s) 966

Distinguished Teaching in Psychology Award. *See* Charles L. Brewer Distinguished Teaching of Psychology Award, entry (D—a) 931

District of Columbia Disability Income Tax Exclusion, (D—g) 815

District of Columbia Income Tax Exclusion for the Disabled, (D—g) 816

V—Visual   H—Hearing   O—Orthopedic/Developmental   C—Communication/Other   D—Disabilities in General   F—Families
s—scholarships   f—fellowships/grants   g—grants-in-aid   a—awards

---

GuildScholar Program, (V—s) 36

Guthrie PKU Scholarship. *See* Robert Guthrie PKU Scholarship, entry (C—s) 533

GWOT Assistance Fund, (F—s) 998

H

Haas Scholarship. *See* Hemophilia Health Services Memorial Scholarships, entries (C—s) 465, (C—f) 575

Hank Hofstetter Opportunity Grants, (V—s) 37, (V—f) 143, (V—g) 204

Hank LeBonne Scholarship, (V—s) 38, (V—f) 144

Harbison Scholarship. *See* Anne and Matt Harbison Scholarship, entry (C—s) 411

Harold T. Stearns Fellowship Award. *See* Geological Society of America Graduate Student Research Grants, entry (D—f) 750

Harriett G. Jenkins Predoctoral Fellowship Program, (D—f) 752

Harry and Miriam Levinson Scholarship. *See* APF/COGDOP Graduate Research Scholarships, entry (D—f) 727

Harry G. Starr Award, (V—s) 39

Harry Gregg Foundation Grants, (D—s) 671, (D—g) 826

Harry Ludwig Memorial Scholarship, (V—s) 40, (V—f) 145

Harvey Memorial Scholarship. *See* Florence Margaret Harvey Memorial Scholarship, entries (V—s) 28, (V—f) 137

Hawaii Association of the Blind Scholarship, (V—s) 41

Hawaii Children's Cancer Foundation Family Assistance Program, (F—g) 1167

Hawaii Grants for Special Housing for Disabled Veterans, (D—g) 827

Hawaii Income Tax Exclusion for Patients with Hansen's Disease, (C—g) 611

Hawaii Income Tax Exemption for Disabled Residents, (V—g) 205, (H—g) 319, (D—g) 828

Hawaii Property Tax Exemptions for Disabled Veterans, (D—g) 829, (F—g) 1168

Hayley's Hope and Michaela's Miracle MS Memorial Fund, (O—s) 342, (F—s) 999

Hazel Staley Memorial Scholarship. *See* Robert and Hazel Staley Memorial Scholarship, entry (V—s) 104

Hazel ten Broek Memorial Scholarship, (V—s) 42, (V—f) 146

Hazlewood Exemption for Dependents of Texas Veterans. *See* Exemption for Dependents of Texas Veterans, entry (F—s) 974

HealthWell Foundation Grants, (C—g) 612

Heard Education Scholarship Program. *See* L. Marie Heard Education Scholarship Program, entry (O—s) 344

Hearing Impaired Kids Endowment Fund Grants. *See* HIKE Fund Grants, entry (H—g) 320

Hearne/AAPD Leadership Awards. *See* Paul G. Hearne/AAPD Leadership Awards, entry (D—a) 938

Hécaen Scholarship. *See* Benton-Meier Neuropsychology Scholarships, entry (D—f) 733

Hecker High School Scholarship. *See* Henry C. Hecker High School Scholarship, entry (H—s) 277

Hedner Scholarships. *See* Professor Ulla Hedner Scholarships, entry (C—s) 529

Heisner Scholarship. *See* Hemophilia of Iowa Scholarships, entries (C—s) 466, (F—s) 1003

Hemophilia Association of New Jersey Awards, (C—s) 461

Hemophilia Association of the Capital Area Family Assistance Program, (C—g) 613, (F—g) 1169

Hemophilia Federation of America Artistic Encouragement Grants, (C—f) 574

Hemophilia Federation of America Educational Scholarships, (C—s) 462

Hemophilia Federation of America Parent Continuing Education Scholarships, (F—s) 1000

Hemophilia Federation of America Sibling Continuing Education Scholarships, (F—s) 1001

Hemophilia Foundation of Michigan Academic Scholarships, (C—s) 463, (F—s) 1002

Hemophilia Foundation of Michigan Emergency Financial Assistance Program, (C—g) 614

Hemophilia Foundation of Minnesota/Dakotas Scholarships, (C—s) 464

Hemophilia Health Services Memorial Scholarships, (C—s) 465, (C—f) 575

Hemophilia of Iowa Scholarships, (C—s) 466, (F—s) 1003

Henry C. Hecker High School Scholarship, (H—s) 277

Henry H. Arnold Education Grant Program. *See* General Henry H. Arnold Education Grant Program, entry (F—s) 985

Henry Hécaen Scholarship. *See* Benton-Meier Neuropsychology Scholarships, entry (D—f) 733

Henry Syle Memorial Fellowship for Seminary Studies, (H—f) 303

Herbert P. Feibelman, Jr. Scholarship, (H—s) 278, (H—f) 304

Herchenbach Memorial Scholarships. *See* Peter Herchenbach Memorial Scholarships, entry (C—s) 527

Hermione Grant Calhoun Scholarship, (V—s) 43, (V—f) 147

Hersh Memorial Scholarship. *See* Bob Hersh Memorial Scholarship, entries (C—s) 420, (F—s) 950

Herter Memorial Scholarship. *See* Christian A. Herter Memorial Scholarship, entry (D—s) 656

High Plains Division Cancer Survivor Scholarships, (C—s) 467, (C—f) 576

High Risk Research in Anthropology Grants, (D—f) 753

Higher Education Scholarship Program of the Spina Bifida Association of Alabama, (O—s) 343, (O—f) 367

HIKE Fund Grants, (H—g) 320

Hissey College Scholarships. *See* Walter W. and Thelma C. Hissey College Scholarships, entries (H—s) 291, (H—f) 315

Hiteshew Memorial Scholarships. *See* Doug Hiteshew Memorial Scholarships, entry (C—s) 441

V—Visual   H—Hearing   O—Orthopedic/Developmental   C—Communication/Other   D—Disabilities in General   F—Families
s—scholarships   f—fellowships/grants   g—grants-in-aid   a—awards

---

V—Visual   H—Hearing   O—Orthopedic/Developmental   C—Communication/Other   D—Disabilities in General   F—Families

s—scholarships   f—fellowships/grants   g—grants-in-aid   a—awards

V—Visual	H—Hearing	O—Orthopedic/Developmental	C—Communication/Other	D—Disabilities in General	F—Families
s—scholarships		f—fellowships/grants		g—grants-in-aid	a—awards

---

V—Visual   H—Hearing   O—Orthopedic/Developmental   C—Communication/Other   D—Disabilities in General   F—Families

s—scholarships   f—fellowships/grants   g—grants-in-aid   a—awards

Manfred Meier Scholarship. *See* Benton-Meier Neuropsychology Scholarships, entry (D—f) 733

Manners Memorial Scholarship, (F—s) 1040

ManTech International Corporation Teacher's Scholarship. *See* MG Eugene C. Renzi, USA (Ret.)/ManTech International Corporation Teacher's Scholarship, entries (D—s) 682, (D—f) 758

Marcelino Memorial Scholarship. *See* National Federation of the Blind of California Scholarships, entries (V—s) 68, (V—f) 160

Marcena Lozano Donate Life Scholarship Fund, (C—s) 494

Marchello Scholarships. *See* Stephen T. Marchello Scholarships, entry (C—s) 553

Marcia LaRiche Scholarship Program, (F—s) 1041

Marco Camastra Scholarship Award, (C—s) 495

Marcus Respite Care Grant Program. *See* Bobbe and Jerry Marcus Respite Care Grant Program, entry (F—g) 1152

Marder Scholarship Program. *See* Eric C. Marder Scholarship Program, entry (C—s) 451

Marilyn Yetso Memorial Scholarship, (F—s) 1042, (F—f) 1129

Marine Corps League Scholarships, (D—s) 679

Marine Patient Emergency Assistance Fund. *See* Nancy J. Marine Patient Emergency Assistance Fund, entry (C—g) 620

Marion Bales Scholarship. *See* L. Marie Heard Education Scholarship Program, entry (O—s) 344

Marion Huber Learning through Listening Awards, (C—s) 496

Mark Reames Memorial Scholarships, (C—s) 497, (C—f) 579, (F—s) 1043, (F—f) 1130

Mary Kathryn and Michael Panitch Scholarships. *See* Chicago Lighthouse Scholarships, entries (V—s) 12, (V—f) 127

Mary M. Gooley Hemophilia Scholarship, (C—s) 498, (F—s) 1044

Mary MacDill Napheide Scholarships. *See* National Federation of the Blind of Illinois Scholarships, entries (V—s) 73, (V—f) 162

Mary Main Memorial Scholarship. *See* National Federation of the Blind of Connecticut Scholarships, entries (V—s) 70, (V—f) 161

Mary P. Oenslager Scholastic Achievement Awards, (V—a) 265

Mary Switzer Research Fellowships. *See* Research Fellowships of the National Institute on Disability and Rehabilitation Research, entry (D—f) 771

Mary T. Christian Award. *See* Patient Advocate Foundation Scholarships for Survivors, entries (C—s) 524, (C—f) 584

Mary Zoe Allee Scholarship, (V—s) 59

Maryanne Swaton Memorial Scholarship. *See* NFBNY Scholarships, entries (V—s) 94, (V—f) 169

MaryEllen Locher Foundation Scholarship, (F—s) 1045

Maryland Community Cancer Scholarship, (C—s) 499, (C—f) 580

Maryland Income Tax Adjustments for Adopting Special Needs Children, (F—g) 1186

Maryland Income Tax Exemption for Blind and Elderly Residents, (V—g) 215

Maryland Income Tax Exemption for Readers for Blind Residents, (V—g) 216

Maryland Pension Exclusion for Disabled and Elderly Residents, (D—g) 854, (F—g) 1187

Maryland Property Tax Exemption for Blind Persons, (V—g) 217, (F—g) 1188

Maryland Property Tax Exemption for Disabled Veterans and Surviving Spouses, (D—g) 855, (F—g) 1189

Maryland Real Property Tax Exemption for Disabled Veterans, (D—g) 856, (F—g) 1190

Maryland State Grange Deaf Scholarship, (H—s) 282, (H—f) 311

Mason E. Liftig Endowed Scholarship, (C—s) 500

Massachusetts Income Tax Deduction for Care of Elderly Dependents with Disabilities, (F—g) 1191

Massachusetts Income Tax Deduction for Employment-Related Care of Family Members with Disabilities, (F—g) 1192

Massachusetts Income Tax Exemption for Blind People, (V—g) 218

Massachusetts Property Tax Exemption for Blind People, (V—g) 219

Massachusetts Property Tax Exemption for Veterans and their Families, (V—g) 220, (D—g) 857, (F—g) 1193

Massachusetts Rehabilitation Commission or Commission for the Blind Tuition Waiver Program, (V—s) 60, (D—s) 680

Massachusetts Veterans Annuity Program, (V—g) 221, (O—g) 381, (D—g) 858

Matarazzo Scholarship. *See* APF/COGDOP Graduate Research Scholarships, entry (D—f) 727

Matt Harbison Scholarship. *See* Anne and Matt Harbison Scholarship, entry (C—s) 411

Matt Stauffer Memorial Scholarships, (C—s) 501, (C—f) 581

Matthews and John E. Swift Educational Trust Scholarships. *See* Francis P. Matthews and John E. Swift Educational Trust Scholarships, entry (F—s) 980

Max Edelman Scholarship, (V—s) 61

May Memorial Scholarship. *See* National Federation of the Blind of Connecticut Scholarships, entries (V—s) 70, (V—f) 161, (D—s) 718, (D—f) 784

Mays Mission Scholarships, (D—s) 681

McAdam Scholarship Fund. *See* Bill McAdam Scholarship Fund, entries (C—s) 417, (F—s) 947

McCraw Scholarships. *See* John T. McCraw Scholarships, entry (V—s) 51

McGowan Leadership Scholarship Award. *See* Michael J. McGowan Leadership Scholarship Award, entry (V—s) 63

V—Visual	H—Hearing	O—Orthopedic/Developmental	C—Communication/Other	D—Disabilities in General	F—Families
s—scholarships		f—fellowships/grants	g—grants-in-aid		a—awards

---

V—Visual   H—Hearing   O—Orthopedic/Developmental   C—Communication/Other   D—Disabilities in General   F—Families

s—scholarships   f—fellowships/grants   g—grants-in-aid   a—awards

---

V—Visual   H—Hearing   O—Orthopedic/Developmental   C—Communication/Other   D—Disabilities in General   F—Families
s—scholarships   f—fellowships/grants   g—grants-in-aid   a—awards

V—Visual   **H—Hearing**   **O—Orthopedic/Developmental**   **C—Communication/Other**   **D—Disabilities in General**   **F—Families**

s—scholarships   **f—fellowships/grants**   **g—grants-in-aid**   **a—awards**

Z

Sponsoring Organization Index

The Sponsoring Organization Index makes it easy to identify agencies that offer financial aid to persons with disabilities and members of their families. In this index, sponsoring organizations are listed alphabetically, word by word. In addition, we've used a two–character alphabetical code (within parentheses) to help you identify which programs sponsored by these organizations fall within your scope of interest. The first character (capitalized) in the code identifies availability group: V = Visual Disabilities; H = Hearing Disabilities; O = Orthopedic/Developmental Disabilities; C = Communication and Other Disabilities; D = Disabilities in General; F = Families of the Disabled. The second character (lower cased) identifies funding type: s = scholarships; f = fellowships/grants; g = grants–in–aid; and a = awards. Here's how the code works: if the name of a sponsoring organization is followed by (D–f) 770, a program sponsored by that organization is described in the Disabilities in General chapter, under fellowships/grants, in entry 770. If that sponsoring organization's name is followed by another entry number—for example, (F–a) 1256—the same or a different program sponsored by that organization is described in the Families of the Disabled chapter, under awards, in entry 1256. Remember: the numbers cited here refer to program entry numbers, not to page numbers in the book.

A

Abbott Laboratories, (D—f) 744, 768, 770

Academic Library Association of Ohio, (D—f) 722

ACE INA Foundation, (F—s) 1030

ACT Scholarship and Recognition Services, (O—s) 351, (F—s) 1063

Ad Club Seattle, (F—s) 1018

Adirondack Spintacular, (O—s) 345, (C—s) 487

Advancing Hispanic Excellence in Technology, Engineering, Math, and Science, Inc., (D—s) 686

Air Force Aid Society, (F—s) 985, (F—g) 1144

Air Force Officers' Wives' Club of Washington, D.C., (C—s) 413

Air Force Sergeants Association, (D—s) 655, (F—s) 958

Air Line Pilots Association, (F—s) 940

Airmen Memorial Foundation, (D—s) 655, (F—s) 958

Alabama Council of the Blind, (V—f) 123

Alabama Department of Rehabilitation Services, (F—s) 942

Alabama Department of Revenue, (V—g) 187-189, (H—g) 317, (D—g) 788-792, (F—g) 1145-1146

Alabama Department of Veterans Affairs, (F—s) 941, (F—f) 1114

Alabama Law Foundation, (F—s) 1034

Alabama State Bar. Workers' Compensation Section, (F—s) 1034

Alaska. Office of the State Assessor, (D—g) 793

Alexander Graham Bell Association for the Deaf and Hard of Hearing, (H—s) 267-269, 272-274, 278-279, 281, 285-286, 290-291, (H–f) 294, 296, 298-299, 302, 304, 307-308, 310, 313-315, (H—g) 325-326, (F—g) 1231, 1234

Alpha One, (D—s) 697, (D—f) 769

ALS Association. DC/Maryland/Virginia Chapter, (C—g) 637, (F—g) 1152

ALS Association. Jim "Catfish" Hunter Chapter, (C—g) 609, (F—g) 1235

ALS Association. Minnesota Chapter, (C—g) 617, (F—g) 1180

ALS Association. Rocky Mountain Chapter, (F—g) 1161

Alternatives in Motion, (O—g) 371

American Association of People with Disabilities, (D—a) 938

V—Visual   H—Hearing   O—Orthopedic/Developmental   C—Communication/Other   D—Disabilities in General   F—Families
s—scholarships   f—fellowships/grants   g—grants-in-aid   a—awards

441

V—Visual   H—Hearing   O—Orthopedic/Developmental   C—Communication/Other   D—Disabilities in General   F—Families
s—scholarships   f—fellowships/grants   g—grants-in-aid   a—awards

V—Visual   H—Hearing   O—Orthopedic/Developmental   C—Communication/Other   D—Disabilities in General   F—Families
s—scholarships   f—fellowships/grants   g—grants-in-aid   a—awards

V—Visual   H—Hearing   O—Orthopedic/Developmental   C—Communication/Other   D—Disabilities in General   F—Families
s—scholarships   f—fellowships/grants   g—grants-in-aid   a—awards

---

V—Visual   H—Hearing   O—Orthopedic/Developmental   C—Communication/Other   D—Disabilities in General   F—Families
s—scholarships   f—fellowships/grants   g—grants-in-aid   a—awards

V—Visual   H—Hearing   O—Orthopedic/Developmental   C—Communication/Other   D—Disabilities in General   F—Families
s—scholarships   f—fellowships/grants   g—grants-in-aid   a—awards

Residency Index

Some programs listed in this book are restricted to residents of a particular state or region. Others are open to applicants wherever they may live. The Residency Index will help you pinpoint programs available only to residents in your area as well as programs that have no residency restrictions at all (these are listed under the term "United States"). To use this index, look up the geographic areas that apply to you (always check the listings under "United States"), jot down the entry numbers listed after the availability groups and program types that apply to you, and use those numbers to find the program descriptions in the directory. To help you in your search, we've provided some "see also" references in each index entry. Remember: the numbers cited here refer to program entry numbers, not to page numbers in the book.

Communication and other disabilities: **Scholarships,** 502, 522; **Grants-in-aid,** 626

Disabilities in general: **Scholarships,** 672; **Fellowships/Grants,** 722; **Grants-in-aid,** 892-894

Families of the disabled: **Scholarships,** 1029, 1075; **Fellowships/Grants,** 1126; **Grants-in-aid,** 1224-1225

See also United States

Oklahoma

Visual Disabilities: **Grants-in-aid,** 243

Orthopedic and developmental disabilities: **Scholarships,** 353

Communication and other disabilities: **Scholarships,** 467; **Fellowships/Grants,** 576

Disabilities in general: **Scholarships,** 672; **Grants-in-aid,** 895-897

Families of the disabled: **Scholarships,** 1076; **Grants-in-aid,** 1226-1228

See also United States

Oregon

Visual Disabilities: **Scholarships,** 40, 77, 100; **Fellowships/Grants,** 145, 164; **Grants-in-aid,** 190, 244-245

Orthopedic and developmental disabilities: **Scholarships,** 355

Communication and other disabilities: **Scholarships,** 428, 473

Disabilities in general: **Scholarships,** 672; **Grants-in-aid,** 899-902

Families of the disabled: **Scholarships,** 1078-1082; **Fellowships/Grants,** 1133-1134; **Grants-in-aid,** 1229-1230

See also United States

P

Pennsylvania

Visual Disabilities: **Scholarships,** 19, 39, 52, 56-58, 78, 102, 109, 116; **Fellowships/Grants,** 157, 180-182, 186; **Grants-in-aid,** 246-247

Orthopedic and developmental disabilities: **Scholarships,** 337; **Grants-in-aid,** 393-394

Communication and other disabilities: **Grants-in-aid,** 631

Disabilities in general: **Scholarships,** 695, 703; **Grants-in-aid,** 903-904

Families of the disabled: **Scholarships,** 970, 1030, 1084-1085; **Grants-in-aid,** 1232-1233

See also United States

Pennsylvania, eastern

Communication and other disabilities: **Scholarships,** 476

Families of the disabled: **Scholarships,** 964

See also Pennsylvania

Pennsylvania, southeastern

Disabilities in general: **Grants-in-aid,** 803

See also Pennsylvania

Prince George's County, Maryland

Communication and other disabilities: **Scholarships,** 457; **Fellowships/Grants,** 573; **Grants-in-aid,** 613

Families of the disabled: **Scholarships,** 986; **Fellowships/Grants,** 1119; **Grants-in-aid,** 1169

See also Maryland

Puerto Rico

Communication and other disabilities: **Scholarships,** 414, 465, 546; **Fellowships/Grants,** 566, 575; **Grants-in-aid,** 619

Disabilities in general: **Scholarships,** 686

See also Caribbean; United States

R

Rhode Island

Visual Disabilities: **Scholarships,** 39, 52, 57-58; **Fellowships/Grants,** 182; **Grants-in-aid,** 248

Orthopedic and developmental disabilities: **Scholarships,** 337

Communication and other disabilities: **Scholarships,** 440, 515, 521

Disabilities in general: **Scholarships,** 672, 699

Families of the disabled: **Scholarships,** 967, 970, 1062

See also New England states; United States

S

South Carolina

Visual Disabilities: **Scholarships,** 23, 39, 52, 57-58, 95; **Fellowships/Grants,** 132, 182; **Grants-in-aid,** 251

Orthopedic and developmental disabilities: **Scholarships,** 348; **Grants-in-aid,** 396

Communication and other disabilities: **Grants-in-aid,** 606, 633-635

Disabilities in general: **Scholarships,** 662, 672; **Fellowships/Grants,** 742; **Grants-in-aid,** 908-910

Families of the disabled: **Scholarships,** 1031, 1049, 1095; **Fellowships/Grants,** 1127; **Grants-in-aid,** 1238-1241

See also United States

South Dakota

Visual Disabilities: **Scholarships,** 107; **Fellowships/Grants,** 178

Orthopedic and developmental disabilities: **Scholarships,** 352; **Grants-in-aid,** 397-398; **Awards,** 407

Communication and other disabilities: **Scholarships,** 464, 506

Disabilities in general: **Scholarships,** 701, 703; **Grants-in-aid,** 911; **Awards,** 936

Families of the disabled: **Scholarships,** 981, 1073; **Grants-in-aid,** 1242-1243; **Awards,** 1256

See also United States

T

Tennessee

Visual Disabilities: **Scholarships,** 64; **Grants-in-aid,** 256-257

Orthopedic and developmental disabilities: **Grants-in-aid,** 403-404

Communication and other disabilities: **Scholarships,** 443, 505

Tenability Index

Some programs listed in this book can be used only in specific cities, counties, states, or regions. Others may be used anywhere in the United States (or even abroad). The Tenability Index will help you locate funding that is restricted to a specific area as well as funding that has no tenability restrictions (these are listed under the term "United States"). To use this index, look up the geographic areas where you'd like to go (always check the listings under "United States"), jot down the entry numbers listed after the availability group and program types that relate to you, and use those numbers to find the program descriptions in the directory. To help you in your search, we've provided some "see also" references in each index entry. Remember: the numbers cited here refer to program entry numbers, not to page numbers in the book.

Subject Index

There are more than 150 different subject areas indexed in this directory. Use the Subject Index when you want to identify the subject focus of available funding programs. To help you pinpoint your search, we've also included hundreds of "see" and "see also" references. In addition to looking for terms that represent your specific subject interest, be sure to check the "General programs" entry; hundreds of programs are listed there that can be used to support study, research, or other activities in *any* subject area (although the programs may be restricted in other ways). Remember: the numbers cited in this index refer to program entry numbers, not to page numbers in the book.

A

Accounting
   Disabilities in general: **Scholarships,** 654
   Families of the disabled: **Scholarships,** 957
   See also Finance; General programs

Acquired Immunodeficiency Syndrome. *See* AIDS

Acting. *See* Performing arts

Administration. *See* Business administration; Management; Personnel administration; Public administration

Advertising
   Families of the disabled: **Scholarships,** 1018
   See also Communications; General programs; Marketing; Public relations

Aeronautical engineering. *See* Engineering, aeronautical

Aeronautics
   Disabilities in general: **Fellowships/Grants,** 752
   See also Engineering, aeronautical; General programs; Physical sciences

Aerospace engineering. *See* Engineering, aerospace

Aerospace sciences. *See* Space sciences

African American studies
   Disabilities in general: **Fellowships/Grants,** 723
   See also General programs

Aged and aging
   Disabilities in general: **Fellowships/Grants,** 764, 766
   See also General programs; Social sciences

Agriculture and agricultural sciences
   Disabilities in general: **Scholarships,** 650, 708
   See also Biological sciences; General programs

AIDS
   Communication and other disabilities: **Scholarships,** 473
   See also Disabilities; General programs; Medical sciences

Anthropology
   Disabilities in general: **Fellowships/Grants,** 728, 732, 753, 776
   See also General programs; Social sciences

Applied arts. *See* Arts and crafts

Aquatic sciences. *See* Oceanography

Archaeology
   Disabilities in general: **Fellowships/Grants,** 728, 753, 776
   See also General programs; History; Social sciences

Architecture
   Visual Disabilities: **Scholarships,** 44; **Fellowships/ Grants,** 149
   See also Fine arts; General programs

Architecture, naval. *See* Naval architecture

Arithmetic. *See* Mathematics

Art
   Visual Disabilities: **Scholarships,** 31; **Awards,** 261
   Hearing Disabilities: **Fellowships/Grants,** 297
   Communication and other disabilities: **Scholarships,** 543; **Fellowships/Grants,** 574, 590
   See also Fine arts; General programs; names of specific art forms

Arts and crafts
   Visual Disabilities: **Awards,** 261
   See also Art; General programs; names of specific crafts

Astronomy
   Disabilities in general: **Fellowships/Grants,** 731, 752
   See also General programs; Physical sciences

Astrophysics
    Disabilities in general: **Fellowships/Grants,** 731
    See also Astronomy; General programs
Athletics
    Disabilities in general: **Fellowships/Grants,** 783
    See also General programs; names of specific sports
Atmospheric sciences
    Disabilities in general: **Fellowships/Grants,** 728, 752, 778
    See also General programs; Physical sciences
Attorneys. *See* Law, general
Automation. *See* Computer sciences; Technology

B

Ballet. *See* Dance
Behavioral sciences
    Disabilities in general: **Fellowships/Grants,** 732, 761, 764, 773-774
    See also General programs; Social sciences; names of special behavioral sciences
Biochemistry
    Disabilities in general: **Fellowships/Grants,** 770, 778
    See also Biological sciences; Chemistry; General programs
Biological sciences
    Visual Disabilities: **Scholarships,** 21, 101; **Fellowships/Grants,** 131, 174
    Disabilities in general: **Scholarships,** 660; **Fellowships/Grants,** 728, 738, 752, 761, 774, 778
    Families of the disabled: **Fellowships/Grants,** 1117
    See also General programs; Sciences; names of specific biological sciences
Biomedical engineering. *See* Engineering, biomedical
Biomedical sciences
    Disabilities in general: **Fellowships/Grants,** 764, 773
    See also Biological sciences; General programs; Medical sciences
Black American studies. *See* African American studies
Blindness. *See* Visual impairments
Brain research. *See* Neuroscience
Building trades
    Communication and other disabilities: **Scholarships,** 500
    See also General programs
Business administration
    Visual Disabilities: **Scholarships,** 5, 97, 105; **Fellowships/Grants,** 135, 171, 175
    Hearing Disabilities: **Fellowships/Grants,** 293
    Disabilities in general: **Scholarships,** 654; **Fellowships/Grants,** 755
    Families of the disabled: **Scholarships,** 957, 1018
    See also Entrepreneurship; General programs; Management
Business enterprises. *See* Entrepreneurship
Business law
    Visual Disabilities: **Fellowships/Grants,** 135
    See also General programs; Law, general

C

Cell biology
    Disabilities in general: **Fellowships/Grants,** 778
    See also Biological sciences; General programs
Chemical engineering. *See* Engineering, chemical
Chemistry
    Visual Disabilities: **Scholarships,** 21; **Fellowships/Grants,** 131
    Disabilities in general: **Scholarships,** 660; **Fellowships/Grants,** 738, 752, 761, 778
    Families of the disabled: **Fellowships/Grants,** 1117
    See also Engineering, chemical; General programs; Physical sciences
Choruses. *See* Voice
Church music. *See* Music, church
City and regional planning
    Disabilities in general: **Fellowships/Grants,** 778
    See also General programs
Civil engineering. *See* Engineering, civil
Classical music. *See* Music, classical
Colleges and universities. *See* Education, higher
Commerce. *See* Business administration
Communications
    Visual Disabilities: **Fellowships/Grants,** 135
    Families of the disabled: **Scholarships,** 1018
    See also General programs; Humanities
Community colleges. *See* Education, higher
Computer engineering. *See* Engineering, computer
Computer sciences
    Visual Disabilities: **Scholarships,** 14, 53, 101; **Fellowships/Grants,** 128, 174
    Communication and other disabilities: **Scholarships,** 546
    Disabilities in general: **Scholarships,** 660-661, 670, 683, 696; **Fellowships/Grants,** 751-752, 761
    See also General programs; Mathematics; Technology
Computers. *See* Computer sciences
Conservation. *See* Environmental sciences
Construction. *See* Building trades
Counseling
    Visual Disabilities: **Scholarships,** 98; **Fellowships/Grants,** 172
    See also Behavioral sciences; General programs; Psychology
Counter-intelligence service. *See* Intelligence service
Crafts. *See* Arts and crafts
Creative writing
    Visual Disabilities: **Scholarships,** 31
    Orthopedic and developmental disabilities: **Fellowships/Grants,** 364, 370
    See also Fine arts; General programs; Literature
Criminal justice
    Families of the disabled: **Scholarships,** 1071
    See also General programs; Law, general

D

Dance
Communication and other disabilities: **Scholarships,** 542
See also General programs; Performing arts

Data entry. *See* Computer sciences

Deafness. *See* Hearing impairments

Dentistry
Disabilities in general: **Fellowships/Grants,** 754; **Grants-in-aid,** 787
Families of the disabled: **Grants-in-aid,** 1143
See also General programs; Health and health care; Medical sciences

Disabilities
Visual Disabilities: **Scholarships,** 6, 26; **Fellowships/ Grants,** 122, 134
Orthopedic and developmental disabilities: **Scholarships,** 354
Disabilities in general: **Scholarships,** 647, 694; **Fellowships/Grants,** 725, 771; **Awards,** 939
Families of the disabled: **Awards,** 1257
See also General programs; Rehabilitation; names of specific disabilities

Disabilities, hearing. *See* Hearing impairments

Disabilities, visual. *See* Visual impairments

Disability law
Visual Disabilities: **Scholarships,** 6, 26; **Fellowships/ Grants,** 122, 134
Disabilities in general: **Fellowships/Grants,** 734
See also General programs; Law, general

Divinity. *See* Religion and religious activities

Documentaries. *See* Filmmaking

E

Earth sciences
Disabilities in general: **Fellowships/Grants,** 728, 761
See also General programs; Natural sciences; names of specific earth sciences

Ecology. *See* Environmental sciences

Economic planning. *See* Economics

Economics
Disabilities in general: **Scholarships,** 654; **Fellowships/Grants,** 728, 732, 755, 776, 778
Families of the disabled: **Scholarships,** 957
See also General programs; Social sciences

Education
Visual Disabilities: **Fellowships/Grants,** 158; **Awards,** 262
Communication and other disabilities: **Scholarships,** 420
Disabilities in general: **Fellowships/Grants,** 739; **Grants-in-aid,** 916; **Awards,** 932
Families of the disabled: **Scholarships,** 950
See also General programs; Social sciences; names of specific types and levels of education

Education, elementary
Visual Disabilities: **Scholarships,** 85; **Fellowships/ Grants,** 166
See also Education; General programs

Education, higher
Visual Disabilities: **Scholarships,** 85; **Fellowships/ Grants,** 166
See also Education; General programs

Education, music
Disabilities in general: **Scholarships,** 685; **Fellowships/Grants,** 759
See also Education; General programs; Music

Education, science and mathematics
Disabilities in general: **Scholarships,** 661, 682; **Fellowships/Grants,** 758; **Grants-in-aid,** 916
See also Education; General programs; Sciences

Education, secondary
Visual Disabilities: **Scholarships,** 85; **Fellowships/ Grants,** 166
See also Education; General programs

Education, special
Visual Disabilities: **Scholarships,** 6, 17, 26, 28, 98, 106, 117; **Fellowships/Grants,** 122, 130, 134, 137, 172, 177, 181
Hearing Disabilities: **Scholarships,** 282; **Fellowships/ Grants,** 311
Orthopedic and developmental disabilities: **Scholarships,** 354
Disabilities in general: **Grants-in-aid,** 916
See also Disabilities; Education; General programs

Electrical engineering. *See* Engineering, electrical

Electronic engineering. *See* Engineering, electronic

Elementary education. *See* Education, elementary

Employment
Disabilities in general: **Scholarships,** 716; **Fellowships/Grants,** 782; **Grants-in-aid,** 922
See also General programs; Occupational therapy

Engineering
Visual Disabilities: **Scholarships,** 21, 44, 101; **Fellowships/Grants,** 131, 149, 174
Hearing Disabilities: **Scholarships,** 285; **Fellowships/ Grants,** 313
Disabilities in general: **Scholarships,** 660, 666, 686; **Fellowships/Grants,** 739, 746-748, 752, 762; **Grants-in-aid,** 818, 822; **Awards,** 932
See also General programs; Physical sciences; names of specific types of engineering

Engineering, aeronautical
Disabilities in general: **Fellowships/Grants,** 761
See also Aeronautics; Engineering; General programs

Engineering, aerospace
Disabilities in general: **Scholarships,** 661, 687; **Fellowships/Grants,** 752, 760
See also Engineering; General programs; Space sciences

Engineering, biomedical
Disabilities in general: **Fellowships/Grants,** 752
See also Biomedical sciences; Engineering; General programs

Microcomputers. *See* Computer sciences

Microscopy. *See* Medical technology

Missionary work. *See* Religion and religious activities

Molecular biology
  Disabilities in general: **Fellowships/Grants,** 749, 765, 778
  See also Biological sciences; General programs

Motel industry. *See* Hotel and motel industry

Music
  Visual Disabilities: **Scholarships,** 31, 103
  Communication and other disabilities: **Scholarships,** 542; **Fellowships/Grants,** 574
  Disabilities in general: **Scholarships,** 685; **Fellowships/Grants,** 759; **Grants-in-aid,** 871; **Awards,** 933, 935
  See also Education, music; Fine arts; General programs; Humanities; Performing arts

Music, church
  Visual Disabilities: **Scholarships,** 34; **Fellowships/Grants,** 141
  See also General programs; Music; Performing arts; Religion and religious activities

Music, classical
  Visual Disabilities: **Scholarships,** 34; **Fellowships/Grants,** 141
  Disabilities in general: **Awards,** 933
  See also General programs; Music

Music education. *See* Education, music

Music, jazz
  Disabilities in general: **Awards,** 933
  See also General programs; Music

Music therapy
  Disabilities in general: **Scholarships,** 685; **Fellowships/Grants,** 759
  See also General programs; Music

Musicology
  Disabilities in general: **Scholarships,** 685; **Fellowships/Grants,** 759
  See also General programs; Music

N

National security. *See* Security, national

Natural sciences
  Visual Disabilities: **Scholarships,** 44; **Fellowships/Grants,** 149
  See also General programs; Sciences; names of specific sciences

Naval architecture
  Disabilities in general: **Fellowships/Grants,** 761
  See also Architecture; General programs; Naval science

Naval science
  Disabilities in general: **Fellowships/Grants,** 762
  See also General programs

Neuroscience
  Disabilities in general: **Fellowships/Grants,** 733, 741, 770
  See also General programs; Medical sciences

Neuroscience nurses and nursing. *See* Nurses and nursing, neuroscience

Nurses and nursing, general
  Communication and other disabilities: **Scholarships,** 556
  Families of the disabled: **Scholarships,** 946, 1080, 1092; **Fellowships/Grants,** 1115
  See also General programs; Health and health care; Medical sciences; names of specific nursing specialties

Nurses and nursing, neuroscience
  Disabilities in general: **Fellowships/Grants,** 732, 770
  See also General programs; Neuroscience; Nurses and nursing, general

O

Occupational therapy
  Communication and other disabilities: **Scholarships,** 556
  See also Counseling; Employment; General programs

Ocean engineering. *See* Engineering, ocean

Oceanography
  Disabilities in general: **Fellowships/Grants,** 728, 761, 778
  See also General programs

Opera. *See* Music; Voice

Optics
  Disabilities in general: **Fellowships/Grants,** 761
  See also General programs; Physics

P

Painting
  Visual Disabilities: **Awards,** 261, 264
  Orthopedic and developmental disabilities: **Fellowships/Grants,** 364, 370
  Communication and other disabilities: **Scholarships,** 542-543; **Fellowships/Grants,** 574, 590
  See also Art; General programs

Performing arts
  Visual Disabilities: **Scholarships,** 31
  Hearing Disabilities: **Scholarships,** 268
  Communication and other disabilities: **Scholarships,** 542
  See also Fine arts; General programs; names of specific performing arts

Personnel administration
  Visual Disabilities: **Fellowships/Grants,** 135
  See also General programs; Management

Pharmaceutical sciences
  Disabilities in general: **Scholarships,** 660; **Fellowships/Grants,** 770
  See also General programs; Medical sciences

Philology. *See* Language and linguistics

Photography
  Visual Disabilities: **Awards,** 261, 264
  Orthopedic and developmental disabilities: **Fellowships/Grants,** 364, 370

Calendar Index

Since most financial aid programs have specific deadline dates, some may have already closed by the time you begin to look for funding. You can use the Calendar Index to identify which programs are still open. To do that, check the type of funding sections and recipient categories that apply to you, think about when you'll be able to complete your application forms, go to the appropriate months, jot down the entry numbers listed there, and use those numbers to find the program descriptions in the directory. Keep in mind that the numbers cited here refer to program entry numbers, not to page numbers in the book.

Scholarships

Fellowships/Grants

Grants-in-aid

Awards

Visual disabilities:
February: 263
March: 261
April: 261-262, 264-266

Hearing disabilities:
June: 330
Deadline not specified: 329

Orthopedic and developmental disabilities:
May: 407

Communication and other disabilities:
January: 644
March: 641-642
April: 643
June: 645

Disabilities in general:
February: 935
April: 939
May: 934, 936
September: 932, 938
November: 931, 933, 937

Families of the disabled:
April: 1257
May: 1256